Table of Contents

AutoCAD
A Problem Solving Approach
(Release 13, Windows)

Sham Tickoo

Associate Professor
Department of Manufacturing Engineering Technologies
and Supervision
Purdue University Calumet
Hammond, Indiana

CADCIM Technologies

Schererville, Indiana, U.S.A.

Press

I(T)P An International Thomson Publishing Company

Albany • Bonn • Boston • Cincinnati • Detroit • London • Madrid
Melbourne • Mexico City • New York • Pacific Grove • Paris • San Francisco
Singapore • Tokyo • Toronto • Washington

NOTICE TO THE READER

Trademarks
AutoCAD® and the AutoCAD® logo are registered trademarks of Autodesk, Inc.
Windows is a trademark of the Microsoft Corporation.
All other product names are acknowledged as trademarks of their respective owners.

COPYRIGHT © 1996
By Delmar Publishers
Autodesk Press imprint
an International Thomson Publishing Company

The ITP logo is a trademark under license

Printed in the United States of America

For more information, contact:

Delmar Publishers
3 Columbia Circle , Box 15015
Albany, New York 12212-5015

International Thomson Publishing Europe
Berkshire House 168-173
High Holborn
London, WC1V7AA
England

Thomas Nelson Australia
102 Dodds Street
South Melbourne, 3205
Victoria, Australia

Nelson Canada
1120 Birchmont Road
Scarborough, Ontario
Canada M1K 5G4

International Thomson Editores
Campos Eliseos 385, Piso 7
Col Polanco
11560 Mexico D F Mexico

International Thomson Publishing GmbH
Königswinterer Strasse 418
53227 Bonn
Germany

International Thomson Publishing Asia
221 Henderson Road
#05 -10 Henderson Building
Singapore 0315

International Thomson Publishing - Japan
Hirakawacho Kyowa Building, 3F
2-2-1 Hirakawacho
Chiyoda-ku, Tokyo 102
Japan

1 2 3 4 5 6 7 8 9 10 XXX 01 00 99 98 97 96 95

Library of Congress Cataloging-in-Publication Data

Tickoo, Sham.
    AutoCAD: a problem solving approach, release 13, Windows/Sham Tickoo
        p.   cm.
    Includes index.
    ISBN: 0-8273-7432-1
    1. Computer graphics.   2. AutoCAD for Windows.   I. Title

T385. T5242 1995
620'.0042'02855369–dc20

95-48762
CIP

Chapter 22: Model Space Viewports, Paper Space Viewports, Dynamic Viewing of 3D Objects

Chapter 23: Solid Modeling

Chapter 24: Rendering

Chapter 25: Geometry Calculator

Chapter 26: Prototype Drawings

Chapter 27: Script Files and Slide Shows

Chapter 28: Creating Linetypes and Hatch Patterns

Appendices

Index

Preface

AutoCAD, developed by Autodesk Inc., is the most popular PC-CAD system available in the market. Over one million people in 80 countries around the world use AutoCAD to generate various kinds of drawings. In 1994 the market share of AutoCAD grew to 74 percent, making it the worldwide standard for generating drawings. Also, AutoCAD's open architecture has allowed third-party developers to write application software that has significantly added to its popularity. For example, the author of this book has developed a software package, "SMLayout" for sheet metal products, that generates flat layout of various geometrical shapes such as transitions, intersections, cones, elbows, and tank heads. Several companies in Canada and the United States are using this software package with AutoCAD to design and manufacture various products. AutoCAD has also provided facilities that allow users to customize AutoCAD to make it more efficient and therefore increase their productivity.

This book contains a detailed explanation of AutoCAD Release 13 commands and how to use them in solving drafting and design problems. The book also unravels the customizing power of AutoCAD. Every AutoCAD command and customizing technique is thoroughly explained with examples and illustrations that make it easy to understand their function and application. At the end of each topic, there are examples that illustrate the function of the command and how it can be used in the drawing. When you are done reading this book, you will be able to use AutoCAD commands to make a drawing, create text, make and insert symbols, dimension a drawing, create 3D objects and solid models, write script files, define linetypes and hatch patterns, write your own menus, write shape and text files, define new commands, write programs in the AutoLISP programming languages, create your own dialogue boxes using DCL, customize the status line using DIESEL, and edit the Program Parameter file (ACAD.PGP).

The book also covers basic drafting and design concepts - such as orthographic projections, dimensioning principles, sectioning, auxiliary views, and assembly drawings - that provide you with the essential drafting skills you need to solve drawing problems with AutoCAD. In the process, you will discover some new applications of AutoCAD that are unique and might have a significant effect on your drawings. You will also get a better idea of why AutoCAD has become such a popular software package and an international standard in PC-CAD. Please refer to the following table for conventions used in this text.

Convention	Example
♦ Command names appear capitalized.	the MOVE command
♦ A key icon appears when you should respond by pressing the Enter or Return key.	◄┘
♦ Command sequences are indented. Responses are indicated by boldface. Directions are indicated by italics. Comments are enclosed in parenthesis.	Command: **MOVE** Select object: **G** Enter group name: *Enter a group name* *(the group name is group1)*
♦ The command selection from the screen and pull-down menus are enclosed in parenthesis.	Screen menus: (Select DRAW 1/Ellipse) Pull-down menus: (Select Draw/Ellipse/Center)

DEDICATION

*To teachers, who make it possible to disseminate knowledge
to enlighten the young and curious minds
of our future generations*

*To students, who are dedicated to learning new technologies
and making the world a better place to live*

Thanks

*To the faculty and students of the METS department of Purdue University
Calumet for their cooperation*

*To Bhawani Kaul, Renu Muthoo, Suma, and Santosh Tickoo
of CADSoft Technologies for their
valuable help*

Chapter 1

Getting Started

Learning objectives

After completing this chapter, you will be able to:
- Invoke AutoCAD commands from the pull-down menu, screen menu, digitizer, command line, or tool bar for Windows.
- Draw lines using the LINE command and its options.
- Understand different coordinate systems used in AutoCAD.
- Use the ERASE command to erase objects.
- Create selection sets using Window and Crossing options.
- Save the work using different file-saving commands.
- Open an existing file and start a new drawing.
- Draw circles using different options of the CIRCLE command.
- Use display and ZOOM command options.
- Plot drawings.
- Understand the functioning of dialogue boxes in AutoCAD.

STARTING AUTOCAD

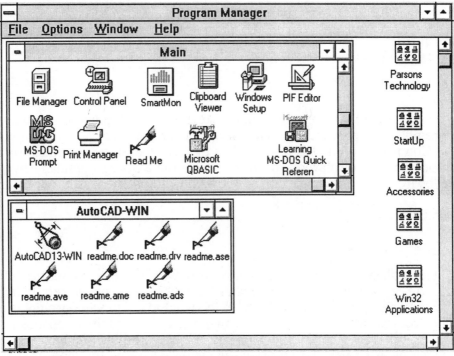

Figure 1-1 AutoCAD for Windows screen with toolbars

When you turn on your computer, the operating system is automatically loaded. For example, if you are using DOS (disk operating system) the DOS software is automatically loaded and the DOS prompt (C:\>) is displayed on the screen. To run Windows, type WIN at the DOS prompt. This will display the Windows screen with different application icons. You can load AutoCAD by double clicking on the AutoCAD13-WIN icon as shown in the Figure 1-1.

If you are using AutoCAD for DOS, AutoCAD can be loaded by entering the name of the batch file that loads AutoCAD. For example, if the name of the batch file is ACADR13, you can start AutoCAD by entering ACADR13 or acadr13 at the DOS prompt:

C:\> ACADR13   *(ACADR13 is the name of the batch file.)*

When you enter the name of the batch file, the statements in the batch file are executed in the same sequence as they appear in the file. For AutoCAD to work properly, you need to let it know where the system files are located so that it can load them when needed. When you run the batch file (ACADR13), it automatically sets the environment variables and the search path. Also, the AutoCAD batch file can be used to load the drivers that you need to run the system (drivers for digitizer, printer, plotter, or graphics display). Similarly, if you start AutoCAD from Windows, the environment variables and the search path are set automatically as defined in the ACAD.INI file.

SELECTING COMMANDS IN AUTOCAD

This chapter assumes that the software is loaded on your system and you are familiar with the hardware that you are using. When you start AutoCAD and you are in the drawing editor, you need to enter or select AutoCAD commands to perform any operation. For example, if you want to draw a line, first you have to enter the **LINE** command, then define the start and end points of the line. Similarly, if you want to erase objects, you must enter the **ERASE** command, then select the objects you want to erase. AutoCAD has provided the following methods to enter or select commands:

Keyboard
Toolbar
Screen menu
Pull-down menu
Digitizing tablet

Keyboard

You can type any AutoCAD command at the keyboard by typing the command name at the **Command:** prompt, then pressing the **Enter** key or the **Spacebar**. Before you enter a command, make sure the Command: prompt is displayed as the last line in the command prompt area. If the Command: prompt is not displayed, you must cancel the existing command by pressing the **Esc** key on the keyboard. The following example shows how to enter the LINE command:

Command: **LINE** ←⎦

Toolbar

In Windows the toolbar is an easy and convenient way to select a particular command. For example, you can invoke the LINE command by picking the upper left button on the **Draw** toolbar. The command prompts are displayed in the windows command prompt area. The different toolbars can be accessed from the **Tools** pull-down menu. Each toolbar contains a group of display icons representing different AutoCAD commands. When you move the cursor over the icons of a toolbar, the name of that particular command is displayed below the icon on which the cursor is resting. The desired command can be invoked by clicking on its icon button. To the right of icons is a small black triangle, which indicates that the icon has a flyout that contains the sub commands or the related commands. For example, in the Circle flyout you have the **CIRCLE** command options, which includes the **DONUT** command. The commands in a flyout can be invoked by holding down the pick button of your pointing device on the main icon, dragging the cursor over the flyout until it is over the desired icon, then releasing the pick button to select that command.

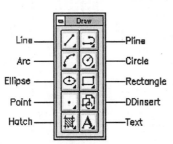

Figure 1-2 Selecting the LINE command from the Draw toolbar

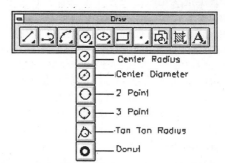

Figure 1-3 Circle flyout in the Draw toolbar

The toolbars can be moved anywhere on the screen by placing the cursor on the title bar area and then dragging it to the desired location. You must hold the pick button down while dragging. You can also change the shape of the toolbars by placing the cursor anywhere on the border of the toolbar and then dragging it in the desired direction. You can also customize toolbars to meet your requirements (See Chapter 32).

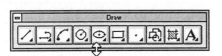

Figure 1-4 Draw toolbar

Figure 1-5 Draw toolbar reshaped

Screen Menu

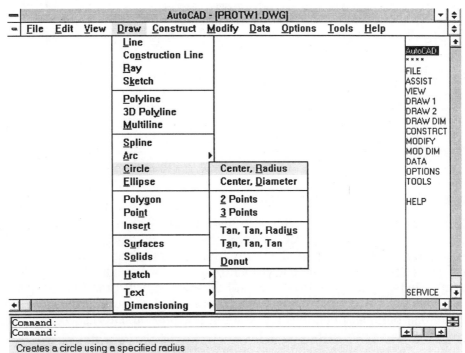

Figure 1-6 AutoCAD screen display with the Draw pull-down menu

The screen menus are displayed on the right side of the computer screen. You can select an item from the screen menu by moving the cursor up or down along the screen menu bar until the item you want to select is highlighted. When the item is highlighted, you can select it by pressing the pick button of your pointing device. When you start AutoCAD, the first screen menu that AutoCAD displays is called the **root menu**. In the screen menus the commands are arranged in different groups. For example, if you want to select the ELLIPSE command, you must first select DRAW 1 from the root menu, then select Ellipse: (Figure 1-7). In this text this selection sequence will be referenced as **(Select DRAW 1, Ellipse:)**. A menu item that consists of all uppercase letters without a colon at the end (DRAW 1) represents a group heading. If you select this item it will automatically load that submenu and display the submenu items in the screen menu area. A menu item that has a colon at the end (Ellipse:) represents an AutoCAD command. If you select this item, AutoCAD will automatically pick that command and also display its options in the screen menu area. You can always return to the root menu by selecting the menu item **AutoCAD**, which is displayed at the top of every screen menu. In Windows the screen menus are not displayed by default. To display the screen menus, select the **Screen Menu** check box in the **Preferences** dialogue box (Figure 1-8). This dialogue box can be accessed from the **Options** pull-down menu.

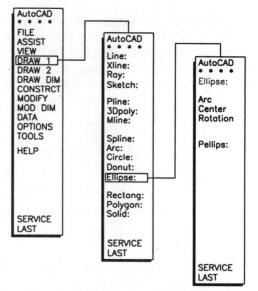

Figure 1-7 Selecting the ELLIPSE command from the screen menu

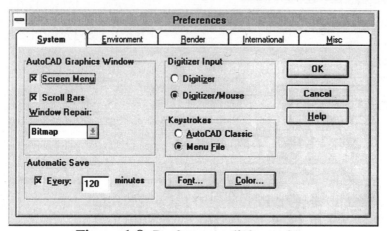

Figure 1-8 Preferences dialogue box

Pull-down Menu

You can also select commands from the pull-down menu. The **menu bar** that displays the menu bar titles is at the top of the screen. As you move the pointing device sideways, different menu bar titles are highlighted. You can choose the desired item by pressing the pick button of your pointing device. Once the item is selected the corresponding pull-down menu is displayed directly under the title. You can select a command from the pull-down menu by pressing the pick button of your pointing device. Some of the menu items in the pull-down menu display an arrow on right side, which indicates that the menu item has a cascading menu. You can display the cascading menu by selecting the menu item or by just moving the arrow pointer to the right of that item. You can then select any item in the cascading menu by highlighting the item or command and pressing the pick button of your pointing device or simply by pressing the stylus (pen) down if you are using a stylus with your digitizer.

For example, if you want to draw an ellipse using the Center option, select **Draw** from the menu bar, select **Ellipse** from the pull-down menu, then select **Center** from the cascading menu (Figure 1-10). In this text this command selection sequence will be referenced as **(Select Draw, Ellipse, Center)**.

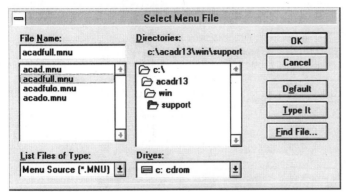

Figure 1-9 Select Menu File dialogue box

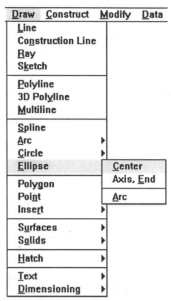

Figure 1-10 Selecting the ELLIPSE command from the pull-down menu

By default all the menu bar titles are not present on the Windows screen. The pull-down menus are defined in the **MNU** files. When you start AutoCAD the ACAD.MNU file (Figure 1-12) is automatically loaded which allows only a few menu bar titles to be displayed on the screen. If you want all pull-down menus to be present, you must load the ACADFULL.MNU file (Figure 1-11). You can load this file from the **Select Menu File** dialogue box (Figure 1-9), which can be invoked by entering **MENU** at the Command: prompt.

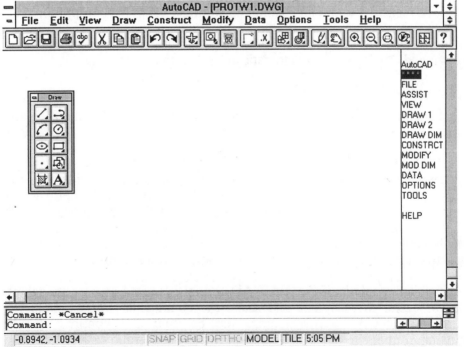

Figure 1-11 AutoCAD for Windows screen with toolbars (Acadfull.mnu)

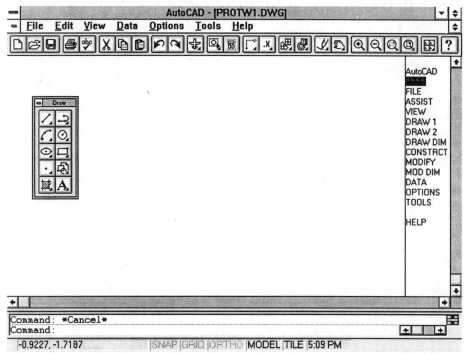

Figure 1-12 AutoCAD for Windows screen with toolbars (Acad.mnu)

Digitizing Tablet

The digitizing tablet provides a powerful alternative for entering commands. In the digitizing tablet, the commands are picked from the template that is secured on the surface of the tablet (Figure 1-13). To use the tablet menu you need a digitizing tablet and a pointing device. You also need a tablet template that contains AutoCAD commands arranged in various groups for easy identification. To select a command from the digitizer, move your pointing device so that the cross-hairs of the pointing device or the tip of the stylus is directly over the block that contains the command that you want to select. Now press the pick button of the pointing device or simply press the stylus down and AutoCAD will automatically select that command.

Advantages of the Tablet Menu

The tablet menu has the following advantages over the screen menu, pull-down menu, or keyboard:

1. In the tablet menu the commands are arranged in such a way so that the most frequently used commands can be accessed directly, which can save considerable time. In the screen menu some of the commands cannot be accessed directly. For example, to draw a horizontal dimension you first select DRAW DIM from the root menu, then Linear:, and then the horizontal dimensioning option. In the tablet menu you can select the horizontal dimensioning command directly from the digitizer. This saves time and eliminates the distraction that takes place as you page through different screens.

2. The graphical symbols of the AutoCAD commands are drawn on the tablet template, which makes it easier to recognize and select the commands. For example, if you are not an expert in AutoCAD dimensioning, the baseline and continue dimensioning can be confusing. But if the command is supported by the graphical symbol of what a command does, your chances of selecting a wrong command are minimized.

3. You can assign any number of commands to the tablet overlay. The number of commands you can assign to a tablet is limited only by the size of the digitizer and the size of the rectangular blocks.

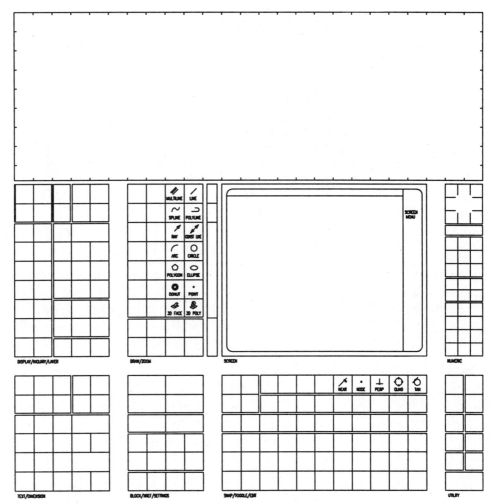

Figure 1-13 Partial AutoCAD Release 13 tablet template

DRAWING LINES IN AUTOCAD

Toolbar:	Draw, Line
Pull-down:	Draw, Line
Screen:	DRAW1, Line:

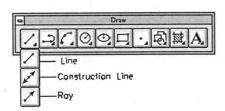

Figure 1-14 Selecting the LINE
command from the Draw toolbar

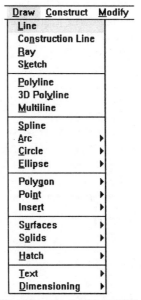

Figure 1-15 Selecting the LINE command
from the pull-down menu

The most fundamental object in a drawing is the line. A line, between any two points, can be drawn by using AutoCAD's LINE command. When you get into the drawing editor, AutoCAD displays the **Command:** prompt at the bottom left corner of the screen. The command name **LINE** is typed at this prompt. In Windows you can also invoke this command from the **Draw** tool-bar (Figure 1-14) by selecting the **Line** icon from the **Line** flyout, or from the screen menu (Select DRAW 1, Line:), or from the pull-down menu (Select Draw, Line) (Figure 1-15). When you invoke the **LINE** command, the next prompt **From point:** requires you to specify the starting point of the line. After the first point is selected, AutoCAD will prompt you to enter the second point at the **To point:** prompt. When you select the second point of the line, AutoCAD will again display the prompt **To point:** on the screen (Figure 1-16). At this point you may continue to select points or terminate the line command by pressing the Enter key or the Space bar. After terminating the line command AutoCAD will again display the **Command:** prompt. The prompt sequence is as follows:

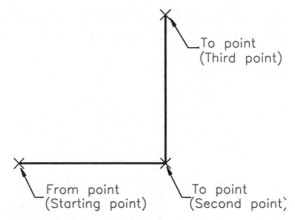

Figure 1-16   Drawing lines using the LINE command

```
Command: LINE ◄─┘
From point: 2,4 ◄─┘          (Specify the first point.)
To point: 6,4 ◄─┘            (Specify the second point.)
To point: 6,8 ◄─┘            (Specify the third point.)
To point: ◄─┘
```

Note

To clear the graphics area (drawing screen) to get space to work out the exercises and the examples, type ERASE at the Command: prompt and press the Enter key. The screen cross-hairs will change into a box called a pick box and AutoCAD will prompt you to select objects. You can select the object by positioning the pick box anywhere on the object and pressing the pick button of the pointing device. Once you have finished selecting the objects, press the Enter key to terminate the ERASE command and the objects that you selected will be erased. If you enter All at the Select objects: prompt, AutoCAD will erase all objects from the screen. (See ERASE command discussed later in this chapter.)

```
Command: ERASE ◄─┘
Select objects: Select objects.      (Select objects using the pick box.)
Select objects: ◄─┘
Command: R ◄─┘                        (Type R for redraw.)
Command: ERASE ◄─┘
Select objects: ALL ◄─┘
Select objects: ◄─┘
```

The LINE command has the following three options:
Continue
Close
Undo

The Continue Option

After exiting from the LINE command you may want to draw another line starting from the point where the previous line ended. In such cases you can use the **Continue** option. This option enables you to grab the end point of the previous line and continue drawing the line from that point (Figure 1-17). The following is the prompt sequence for the Continue option:

Command: **LINE** ◄─┘
From point: **2,2** ◄─┘   *(First point of the line.)*
To point: **6,2** ◄─┘   *(Second point.)*
To point: ◄─┘
Command: **LINE**   *(Or press the Enter key to repeat the command.)*
From point: ◄─┘   *(Press the Enter key or pick Continue from the Line: screen menu.)*
To point: **6,5** ◄─┘   *(Second point of the second line.)*
To point: ◄─┘

You can also type the **@** symbol instead of selecting the **Continue** option from the Line: screen menu. For example:

Command: **LINE** ◄─┘
From point: **2,2** ◄─┘
To point: **6,2** ◄─┘
To point: ◄─┘
Command: **LINE** ◄─┘
From point: **@** ◄─┘   *(Continues drawing line from the last point 6,2.)*
To point: **6,5** ◄─┘
To point: ◄─┘

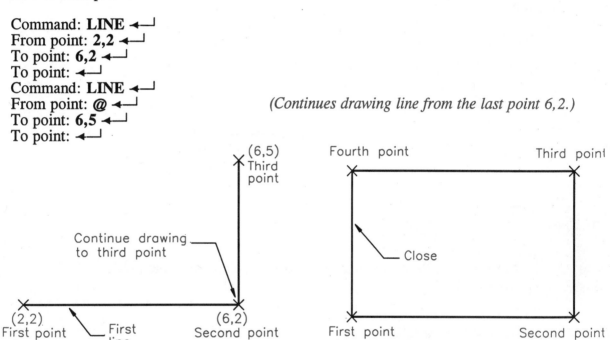

Figure 1-17 Using the Continue option with the LINE command

Figure 1-18 Using the Close option with the LINE command

The Close Option

The **Close** option can be used to join the current point with the initial point of the first line when two or more lines are **drawn in continuation**. For example, this option can be used when an open figure needs one more line to close it and make it a polygon (a polygon is a closed figure with at least three sides; for example, a triangle or a rectangle). The following is the prompt sequence for the Close option (Figure 1-18):

Command: **LINE** ◄─┘
From point: **3,3** ◄─┘   *(First point.)*
To point: **7,3** ◄─┘   *(Second point.)*
To point: **7,6** ◄─┘   *(Third point.)*
To point: **3,6** ◄─┘   *(Fourth point.)*
To point: **C** ◄─┘   *(Joins the fourth point with the first point.)*

Instead of typing Close or C at the **To point:** prompt, you can also pick the **Close** option from the screen menu.

The Undo Option

If you draw a line, then realize that you made an error, you can remove the line using the **Undo** option. If you need to remove more than one line, you can use this option multiple times and go as far back as you want. In this option, you can either type Undo or just U at the **To point:** prompt, or you can select the **Undo** option from the Line: screen menu. The following example illustrates the use of the Undo option (Figure 1-19):

Command: **LINE** ◄─┘
From point: **2,1** ◄─┘   *(First point.)*
To point: **5,1** ◄─┘   *(Second point.)*
To point: **7,3** ◄─┘   *(Third point.)*
To point: **4,3** ◄─┘   *(Fourth point.)*
To point: **Undo** ◄─┘   *(Removes last line from point 3 to point 4.)*
To point: **Undo** ◄─┘   *(Removes next line from point 2 to point 3.)*
To point: ◄─┘

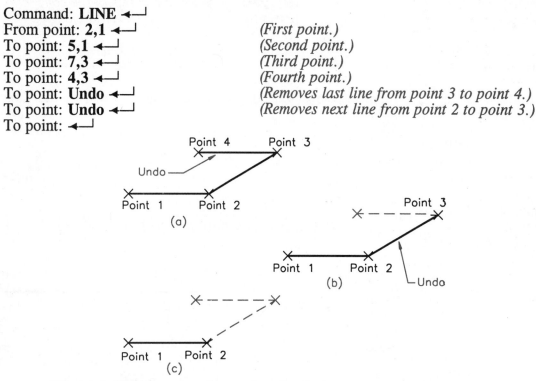

Figure 1-19 Removing lines using the Undo option of the LINE command

COORDINATE SYSTEMS

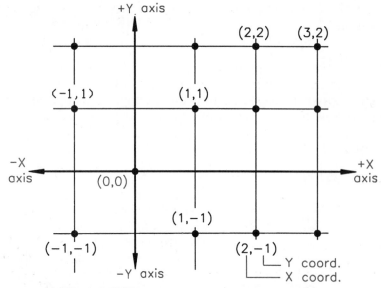

Figure 1-20 Cartesian coordinate system

To specify a point in a plane, we take two mutually perpendicular lines as references. The horizontal line is called the **X axis** and the vertical line is called the **Y axis**. The point of intersection of these two axes is called the **origin**. The X and Y axes divide the X-Y plane into four parts, generally known as quadrants. The X coordinate measures the horizontal distance from the origin (how far left or right) on the X axis. The Y coordinate measures the vertical distance from the origin (how far up or down) on the Y axis. The origin has the coordinate values of X = 0, Y = 0. The origin is taken as the reference for locating any point in the X-Y plane. The X coordinate is positive if measured to the right of the origin and negative if measured to the left of the origin. The Y coordinate is positive if measured above the origin and negative if measured below the origin. This method of specifying points in a plane is called the **Cartesian coordinate system**. When using AutoCAD the default origin is located at the lower left corner of the graphics area of the screen. AutoCAD uses the following coordinate systems, which can be used to locate a point in X-Y plane.

> **Absolute coordinate system**
> **Relative coordinate system**
> **Polar coordinate system**

Absolute Coordinate System

In the absolute coordinate system the points are located with respect to the origin (0,0). For example, a point with X = 4 and Y = 3 is measured four units horizontally (displacement along the X axis) and three units vertically (displacement along the Y axis) from the origin.

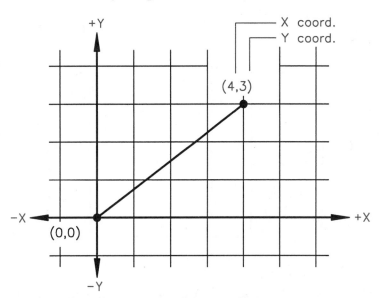

Figure 1-21 Absolute coordinate system

In AutoCAD, the absolute coordinates are specified by entering the X and Y coordinates separated by a comma. The following example illustrates the use of absolute coordinates.

Command: **LINE** ←⏎
From point: **1,1** ←⏎   *(X = 1 and Y = 1.)*
To point: **4,1** ←⏎   *(X = 4 and Y = 1.)*
To point: **4,3** ←⏎
To point: **1,3** ←⏎
To point: **1,1** ←⏎
To point: ←⏎

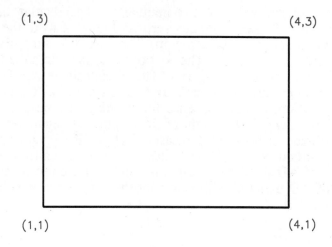

Figure 1-22 Drawing lines using absolute coordinates

Example 1

For the following figure, enter the absolute coordinates of the points in the given table, then draw the figure using absolute coordinates.

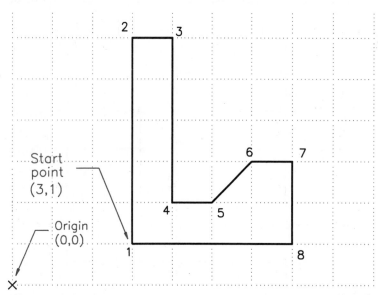

Figure 1-23 Drawing a figure using absolute coordinates

Point	Coordinates		Point	Coordinates
1	3,1		5	5,2
2	3,6		6	6,3
3	4,6		7	7,3
4	4,2		8	7,1

Once the coordinates of the points are known you can draw the figure by using AutoCAD's LINE command. The prompt sequence is:

Command: **LINE** ◄─┘
From point: **3,1** ◄─┘   *(Start point.)*
To point: **3,6** ◄─┘
To point: **4,6** ◄─┘

To point: **4,2** ◄┘
To point: **5,2** ◄┘
To point: **6,3** ◄┘
To point: **7,3** ◄┘
To point: **7,1** ◄┘
To point: **3,1** ◄┘
To point: ◄┘

Exercise 1

For the following figure, enter the absolute coordinates of the points in the given table, then use these coordinates to make the drawing shown in Figure 1-24.

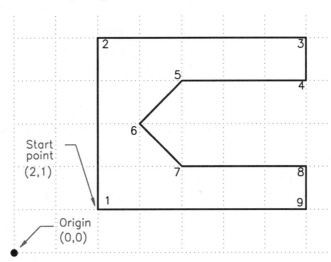

Figure 1-24 Drawing for Exercise 1

Point	Coordinates		Point	Coordinates
1	2, 1		6	_____
2	_____		7	_____
3	_____		8	_____
4	_____		9	_____
5	_____			

Relative Coordinate System

In the relative coordinate system the displacements (DX and DY) along X and Y axes are measured with reference to the previous point rather than the origin. In AutoCAD the relative coordinate system is designated by the symbol @ and should precede any entry. The following prompt sequence illustrates the use of the relative coordinate system to draw a rectangle that has the lower left corner at point (1,1). The length of the rectangle is 4 units and the width is 3 units (Figure 1-25).

Command: **LINE** ◄┘
From point: **1,1** ◄┘   *(Start point.)*
To point: **@4,0** ◄┘   *(Second point DX = 4, DY = 0.)*
To point: **@0,3** ◄┘   *(Third point DX = 0, DY = 3.)*
To point: **@-4,0** ◄┘   *(Fourth point DX = -4, DY = 0.)*
To point: **@0,-3** ◄┘   *(Start point DX = 0, DY = -3.)*
To point: ◄┘

Sign Convention

As mentioned earlier, in the relative coordinate system the displacements along the X and Y axes are measured with respect to the previous point. Imagine a horizontal and a vertical line passing through the previous point so that you get four quadrants. If the new point is located in the first quadrant, the displacements DX and DY are both positive. If the new point is located in the third quadrant, the displacements DX and DY are both negative.

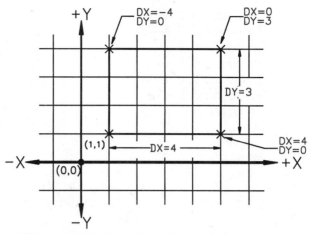

Figure 1-25   Drawing lines using relative coordinates

Example 2

Enter the relative coordinates of the points in the given table for the Figure 1-26, then draw the figure using relative coordinates.

Point	Coordinates		Point	Coordinates
1	3,1		8	@-1,-1
2	@4,0		9	@-1,1
3	@0,1		10	@-1,0
4	@-1,0		11	@0,-2
5	@1,1		12	@1,-1
6	@0,2		13	@-1,0
7	@-1,0		14	@0,-1

Figure 1-26   Using relative coordinates in the LINE command

Once you know the coordinates of the points, you can draw the figure by using AutoCAD's **LINE** command, then enter the coordinates of the points.

```
Command: LINE  ←┘
From point: 3,1  ←┘          (Start point.)
To point: @4,0  ←┘
To point: @0,1  ←┘
To point: @-1,0  ←┘
To point: @1,1  ←┘
To point: @0,2  ←┘
To point: @-1,0  ←┘
To point: @-1,-1  ←┘
To point: @-1,1  ←┘
To point: @-1,0  ←┘
To point: @0,-2  ←┘
To point: @1,-1  ←┘
To point: @-1,0  ←┘
To point: @0,-1  ←┘
To point:  ←┘
```

Exercise 2

For Figure 1-27, enter the relative coordinates of the points in the given table, then use these coordinates to draw the figure.

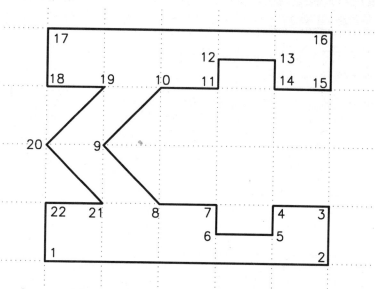

Figure 1-27 Drawing for Exercise 2

Point	Coordinates
1	2, 1
2	_____
3	_____
4	_____
5	_____
6	_____
7	_____
8	_____
9	_____
10	_____
11	_____

Point	Coordinates
12	_____
13	_____
14	_____
15	_____
16	_____
17	_____
18	_____
19	_____
20	_____
21	_____
22	_____

Polar Coordinate System

In the polar coordinate system a point can be located by defining the distance of the point from the current point, and the angle that the line between the two points makes with the positive X axis. The prompt sequence to draw a line from a point at 1,1 to a point at a distance of 5 units from the point (1,1), and at an angle of 30 degrees to the X axis, is:

Command: **LINE** ←⏎
From point: **1,1** ←⏎
To point: **@5<30** ←⏎

Sign Convention

In the polar coordinate system the angle is measured using the horizontal axis. Also, the angle is positive if measured in a counterclockwise direction and negative if measured in a clockwise direction. Here we assume that the default set up of angle measurement has not been changed. For more information about changing default set up, see AutoCAD's **UNITS** command (Chapter 3).

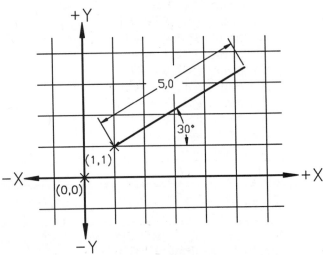

Figure 1-28 Drawing a line using polar coordinates

Example 3

For Figure 1-29, enter the polar coordinates of each point in the given table, then generate the drawing. Use absolute coordinates for the start point (1.5, 1.75). The dimensions are as shown in the drawing.

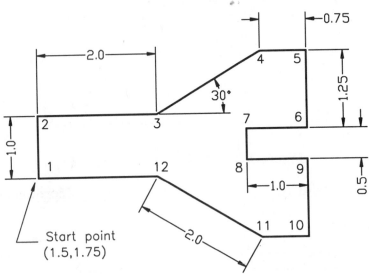

Figure 1-29 Drawing for Example 3

Point	Coordinates	Point	Coordinates
1	1.5,1.75	7	@1.0<180
2	@1.0<90	8	@0.5<270
3	@2.0<0	9	@1.0<0
4	@2.0<30	10	@1.25<270

5	@0.75<0	11	@0.75<180
6	@1.25<-90 *(or <270)*	12	@2.0<150

Once you know the coordinates of the points, you can generate the drawing by using AutoCAD's **LINE** command, then enter the coordinates of the points.

```
Command: LINE ←
From point: 1.5,1.75 ←          (Start point.)
To point: @1<90 ←
To point: @2.0<0 ←
To point: @2<30 ←
To point: @0.75<0 ←
To point: @1.25<-90 ←
To point: @1.0<180 ←
To point: @0.5<270 ←
To point: @1.0<0 ←
To point: @1.25<270 ←
To point: @0.75<180 ←
To point: @2.0<150 ←
To point: C ←                   (Joins the last point with the first point.)
```

Exercise 3

Draw the object shown in Figure 1-30 using the absolute, relative, and polar coordinate systems to locate the points. Do not draw the dimensions. They are for reference only. Assume the missing dimensions.

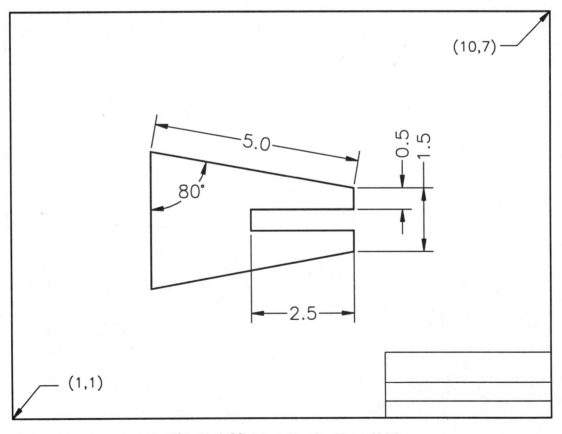

Figure 1-30   Drawing for Exercise 3

ERASING OBJECTS

Toolbar:	Modify, Erase
Pull-down:	Modify, Erase
Screen:	MODIFY, Erase:

Figure 1-31 Selecting the **ERASE** command from the Modify toolbar

After drawing some objects you may want to erase some of them from the screen. To erase the objects you can use AutoCAD's **ERASE** command. This command is used exactly the same way as an eraser in manual drafting to remove unwanted information. You can invoke the ERASE command by entering ERASE at the

Figure 1-32 Selecting the ERASE command from the pull-down menu

Command: prompt. You can also invoke the **ERASE** command from the **Modify** toolbar by selecting the **Erase** icon, from the pull-down menu (Select Modify, Erase), and from the screen menu (Select MODIFY, Erase).

When you select the ERASE command a small box replaces the screen cursor. This box is known as the **pick box**. To erase an object move the pick box so that it touches the object. You can select the object by pressing the pick button of your pointing device. AutoCAD confirms the selection by changing the selected objects into dashed lines and the **Select objects:** prompt returns. You can continue selecting objects or press the Enter key to terminate the object selection process and erase the selected objects. If you are entering the command from the keyboard, you can type E or ERASE. The following is the prompt sequence:

Command: **ERASE** ←┘
Select objects: *Select first object.*
Select objects: *Select second object.*

Select objects: ←┘

If you enter All at **Select objects:** prompt, AutoCAD will erase all objects in the drawing, even if the objects are outside the screen display area.

Command: **ERASE** ←┘
Select objects: **All**

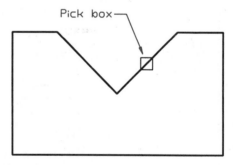

Figure 1-33 Selecting objects by positioning the pick box at the top of the object, then pressing the pick button on the pointing device

OOPS COMMAND

Toolbar:	Miscellaneous, Oops!
Pull-down:	Modify, Oops!
Screen:	MODIFY, Oops:

Figure 1-34 Selecting the OOPS command from the Miscellaneous toolbar

Sometimes you unintentionally erase some object from the screen and when you discover the error, you want to correct it by restoring the erased object. The **OOPS** command is used in such situations. This command can be selected from the Miscellaneous toolbar by selecting the Oops! icon, from the pull-down menu (Select Modify, Oops!), and from screen menu (Select MODIFY, Oops:), or by entering OOPS at the **Command:** prompt. The OOPS command restores objects that have been accidentally erased by the previous ERASE command. Whenever you use the ERASE command, a list of objects erased is saved by AutoCAD. In case another erase is done, the list of objects that were erased by the previous ERASE command is replaced by the list of the objects erased by the latest ERASE command; hence OOPS can only restore the objects erased by the latest ERASE command. The prompt sequence is:

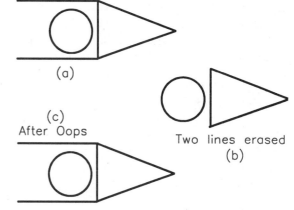

> Command: **ERASE** ◄─┘
> Select objects: *Select the object to be erased.*
> Select objects: ◄─┘
> Command: **OOPS** ◄─┘

In Figure 1-35, two lines were accidentally erased using the ERASE command. Both of these objects were restored using the OOPS command.

Figure 1-35 Use of the OOPS command

CANCELLING A COMMAND

If you are in a command and you want to cancel or get out of that command, press the **Esc** (Escape) key on the keyboard. For DOS press the Ctrl and C keys.

> Command: **ERASE** ◄─┘
> Select objects: *Press the Esc (Escape) key to cancel the command.*

CREATING SELECTION SETS

One of the ways to select objects is to select them individually, which can be time consuming if you have a number of objects to edit. This problem can be solved by creating a selection set that enables you to select several objects at a time. The selection set options can be used with those commands that require object selection, such as MOVE, ERASE, etc. There are many selection options, like ALL, Last, Add, etc., for creating a selection set. At this point we will explore two options: **Window** and **Crossing**. The remaining options are discussed in the next chapter.

The Window Option

This option is used to select an object or group of objects by drawing a box or window around them. The objects to be selected should be completely enclosed within the window; those objects that lie partially inside the boundaries of the window are not selected. You can invoke the **Window** option by selecting the **Window** icon in the **Select Objects** toolbar (Figure 1-36), by

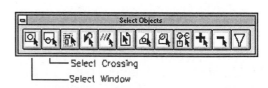

Figure 1-36 Selecting Window and Crossing options from the Select Objects toolbar

typing W at the **Select objects:** prompt, or from the pull-down menu (Select Assist, Select Objects, Window). AutoCAD will prompt you to select the two opposite corners of the window. After selecting the first corner, you can select the other corner by moving the cursor to the desired position and picking the particular point. As you move the cursor, a box or window is displayed that changes in size as you move the cursor. The objects selected by the Window option are displayed as dashed objects (Figure 1-37). The following prompt sequence illustrates the use of Window option with the **ERASE** command:

Command: **ERASE** ◄─┘
Select objects: **W** ◄─┘
First corner: *Select the first corner.*
Other corner: *Select the second corner.*
Select objects: ◄─┘

You can also select the **Window** option by selecting a blank point on the screen at the **Select objects:** prompt. This is automatically taken as the first corner of the window. By dragging the cursor to the right a window is displayed. After getting all the objects to be selected inside this window, you can pick the other corner with your pointing device. The objects that are completely enclosed within the window will be selected and highlighted. The following is the prompt sequence for automatic window selection with the **ERASE** command:

Command: **ERASE** ◄─┘
Select objects: *Select a blank point as the first corner of the window.*
Other corner: *Drag the cursor to the right to select the other corner of the window.*
Select objects: ◄─┘

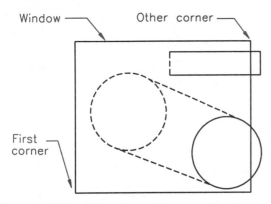

Figure 1-37 Selecting objects using the Window option

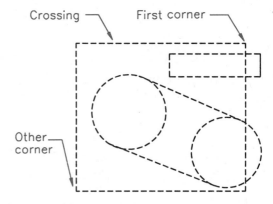

Figure 1-38 Selecting objects using the Crossing option

The Crossing Option

This option is used to select an object or group of objects by creating a box or window around them. The objects to be selected should be touching the window boundaries or completely enclosed within the window. You can invoke the **Crossing** option by selecting the **Crossing** icon in the **Select Objects** toolbar (Figure 1-36), by typing C at the **Select objects:** prompt, or from the pull-down menu (Select Assist, Select Objects, Crossing). After invoking the Crossing option AutoCAD prompts you to select the first corner at the **First corner:** prompt. After selecting the first corner, a box or window made of dashed lines is displayed. By moving the cursor you can change the size of the crossing box, hence putting the objects to be selected within (or touching) the box. Here you can select the other corner. The objects selected by the Crossing option are highlighted by displaying them as dashed objects (Figure 1-38). The following prompt sequence illustrates the use of the Crossing option with the ERASE command:

Command: **ERASE** ◄─┘
Select objects: **C** ◄─┘
First corner: *Select the first corner of the crossing window.*
Other corner: *Select the other corner of the crossing window.*
Select objects: ◄─┘

You can also select the **Crossing** option automatically by selecting a blank point on the screen at the Select objects: prompt and dragging the cursor to the left. The blank point you selected becomes the first corner of the crossing window and AutoCAD will then prompt you to select the other corner. As you move the cursor, a box or window made of dashed lines is displayed. The objects that are touching or completely enclosed within the window will be selected. The objects selected by the Crossing option are highlighted by displaying them as dashed objects. The prompt sequence for automatic crossing selection is:

Command: **ERASE** ←┘
Select objects: *Select a blank point as the first corner of the crossing window.*
Other corner: *Drag the cursor to the left to select the other corner of the crossing window.*
Select objects: ←┘

SAVING YOUR WORK

In AutoCAD or any computer system, you must save your work before you exit from the drawing editor or turn the system off. Also, it is recommended that you save your drawings after regular time intervals. In case there is a power failure, serious editing error, or some other problem, all work saved prior to the problem will be retained. The commands that AutoCAD has provided to save the work can be entered at the **Command:** prompt, or by selecting the appropriate command from the pull-down menu (Select File), Figure 1-39 or the screen menu (Select FILE).

AutoCAD has provided the following commands that let you save your work on the hard disk of the computer or on the floppy diskette:

    SAVE
    SAVEAS
    QSAVE

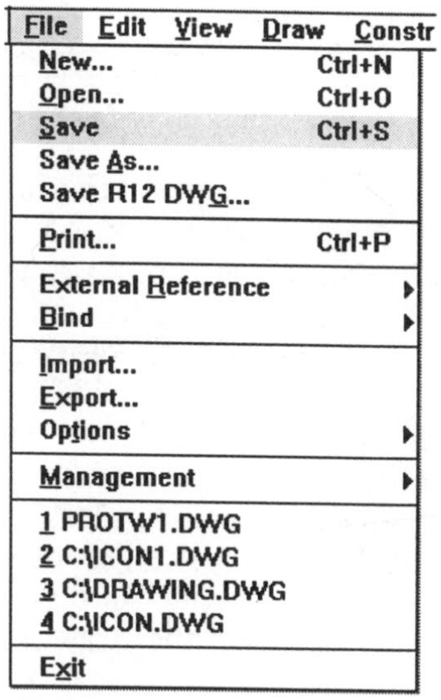

File **Edit** **View** **Draw** **Constr**	
New...	Ctrl+N
Open...	Ctrl+O
Save	Ctrl+S
Save **A**s...	
Save R12 D**W**G...	
Print...	Ctrl+P
External **R**eference	▶
Bind	▶
Import...	
Export...	
Op**t**ions	▶
Management	▶
1 PROTW1.DWG	
2 C:\ICON1.DWG	
3 C:\DRAWING.DWG	
4 C:\ICON.DWG	
E**x**it	

Figure 1-39 Different Save options in the pull-down menu

Note

For saving the drawing automatically after a specified interval of time, you can also use the SAVETIME system variable. You can change the time by entering SAVETIME at AutoCAD Command prompt. The default automatic save time is 120 minutes and the auto-save filename is AUTO.SV$.

SAVE Command

The **SAVE** command allows you to save your drawing by writing it to a permanent storage device, such as a hard drive, or on a diskette in the A or B drive. This command can be invoked by typing SAVE at the **Command:** prompt, then pressing the Enter key. (Save in the pull-down menu, the screen menu, or the Save icon in the Standard toolbar is the QSAVE command discussed on page 1-23). The format for the SAVE command is:

Command: **SAVE** ←┘

Next, AutoCAD displays the dialogue box entitled **Save Drawing As** on the screen (Figure 1-40). Here you are supposed to enter the filename in which the drawing will be saved.

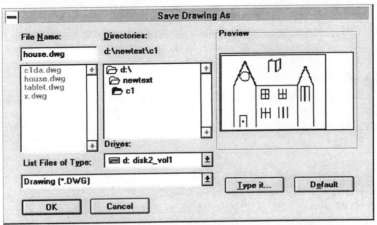

Figure 1-40 Save Drawing As dialogue box

The dialogue box displays the information related to the drawing files on your system. Below the title **File Name:** are an edit box and a list box. To save your work, enter the name of the drawing in the **File Name:** edit box or choose a file from the list box. The drawing extension **.dwg** is not required because AutoCAD automatically assumes the .dwg extension. AutoCAD will save the drawing in the default directory as shown in the dialogue box. For example, in the dialogue box in Figure 1-40 the drawing will be saved in the C1 subdirectory of the NEWTEXT directory under the filename HOUSE. However, you can enter the path information with the filename. For example, if you enter **c:\acad\dwg\proj101**, AutoCAD will save the drawing as proj101.dwg in the **dwg** subdirectory. Similarly, if you want to save the drawing on the A drive, enter **a:proj101** and AutoCAD will write the information to the diskette in the A drive. You can also select a drive from the Save Drawing As dialogue box. If you select a filename from the **File Name:** list box, the bitmap image of the drawing under the particular filename will be displayed in the **Preview** area.

> **Note**
>
> *If want to save a drawing on the A or B drive, make sure the diskette you are using to save the drawings is formatted.*
>
> *Other features of the Save Drawing As dialogue box are described at the end of this chapter.*

Using the Command Line

If you want to save a drawing from the command line (without invoking the standard dialogue boxes), turn the **FILEDIA** system variable off or set its value to zero. If FILEDIA is off, AutoCAD will not display any file-related dialogue box on the screen, including the **Save Drawing As** dialogue box.

    Command: **FILEDIA** ←┘
    New value for FILEDIA <1>: **0** ←┘

Now you can enter the SAVE or SAVEAS command at the **Command:** prompt and type the file name with or without the path information. In the following example, assume that the filename is myproj and the file is to be saved on the default drive.

    Command: **SAVE** ←┘
    Save Drawing As <current name>: **MYPROJ** ←┘

To save the drawing in a different subdirectory, you can define the path with the filename. In the following example the drawing will be saved in the DWG subdirectory of C drive.

Command: **SAVE** ◄┘
Save Drawing As <current name>: **C:\ACAD\DWG\MYPROJ** ◄┘

You can also save the file in the A or B drive by defining the appropriate drive and path information with the file.

Command: **SAVE** ◄┘
Save Drawing As <current name>: **A:MYPROJ** ◄┘

SAVEAS Command

> **Pull-down:** File, Save As
> **Screen:**   FILE, SaveAs:

The SAVEAS command works in the same way as the SAVE command, but in addition to saving the drawing it sets the name of the current drawing to the filename you specify. You can invoke this command from the pull-down menu (Select File, Save As...) (Figure 1-39), or from the screen menu (Select FILE, SaveAs:), or by entering SAVEAS at the **Command:** prompt. When you enter the SAVEAS command, AutoCAD displays the standard file dialogue box entitled **Save Drawing As**. The format of the SAVEAS command is:

Command: **SAVEAS** ◄┘

QSAVE Command

> **Toolbar:**   Standard toolbar, Save
> **Pull-down:** File, Save
> **Screen:**   FILE, Save:

The QSAVE command saves the current named drawing without asking you to enter a filename, thus allowing you to do a quick save. This command can be invoked from the pull-down menu (Select File, Save) (Figure 1-39), from the screen menu (Select FILE, Save:), or by selecting the **Save** icon from the **Standard** toolbar. It can also be invoked by entering QSAVE at the **Command:** prompt. If the current drawing is unnamed, QSAVE acts like SAVEAS and will prompt you to enter the filename in the **Save Drawing As** dialogue box. The command format is:

Command: **QSAVE** ◄┘

OPENING AN EXISTING FILE

> **Toolbar:**   Standard toolbar, Open
> **Pull-down:** File, Open
> **Screen:**   FILE, Open:

To open an existing file in the drawing editor, you can use the **OPEN** command. The OPEN command can be invoked from the **Standard** toolbar by selecting the **Open** icon, from the pull-down menu (Select File, Open...) (Figure 1-39), or the screen menu (Select FILE, Open...), or by entering OPEN at the **Command:** prompt.

Command: **OPEN** ◄┘

When you enter the OPEN command, AutoCAD displays the **Select File** dialogue box (Figure 1-41). You can enter the name of the drawing file you want to open in the **File Name:** edit box, or you can select the name of the drawing from the **Files Name:** list box. If you have been drawing before entering the OPEN command, AutoCAD lets you save that work first by displaying a dialogue box.

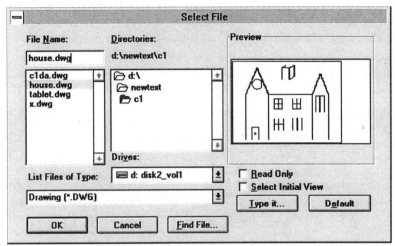

Figure 1-41 Select File dialogue box

Note

Other features of the Open Drawing dialogue box are described at the end of this chapter.

Using the Command Line

If you want to open a drawing from the command line (without invoking the standard dialogue boxes), turn the FILEDIA off or set its value to zero. Then, enter the OPEN command at the **Command:** prompt. The prompt sequence is:

Command: **FILEDIA** ←⏎
New value for FILEDIA <1>: **0** ←⏎
Command: **OPEN** ←⏎
Enter name of drawing: *Enter the drawing name which you want to open.*

STARTING A NEW DRAWING

When you run AutoCAD, it automatically puts you in the drawing editor and the drawing you create is unnamed. You can save the drawing using the SAVE or SAVEAS command. You can also specify the filename first and then begin work. This can be achieved by using the **NEW** command. The NEW command can also be used to create a new unnamed drawing while you are in an editing session.

NEW Command

Toolbar:	Standard toolbar, New
Pull-down:	File, New
Screen:	FILE, New:

The NEW command can be invoked from the **Standard** toolbar by selecting the **New** icon, the pull-down menu (Select File, New...) (Figure 1-39), or the screen menu (Select FILE, New:), or by entering NEW at the **Command:** prompt.

Command: **NEW** ◄─┘

After you enter the NEW command AutoCAD will display the **Create New Drawing** dialogue box (Figure 1-42). Enter the name of the new drawing in the **New Drawing Name:** edit box, then select OK or press the Enter key.

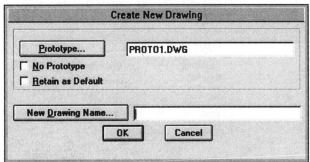

Figure 1-42 Create New Drawing
dialogue box

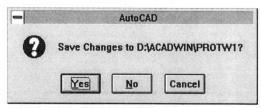

Figure 1-43 AutoCAD dialogue box

If you have been drawing before selecting the NEW command, AutoCAD allows you to save that work first through a dialogue box (Figure 1-43). You can also discard the current drawing.

Note
Other features of the Create New Drawing dialogue box are described at the end of this chapter.

Using the Command Line

A filename for a new drawing can also be specified from the command line if the **FILEDIA** system variable is set to 0. The prompt sequence will be:

Command: **FILEDIA** ◄─┘
New value for FILEDIA < 1 > : **0** ◄─┘
Command: **NEW** ◄─┘
Enter name of drawing: *Enter the name of the new drawing*.

If a drawing exists with the filename you have specified, AutoCAD displays the **AutoCAD Message** dialogue box on the screen that lets you replace the existing drawing.

QUITTING A DRAWING

Pull-down: File, Exit
Screen: FILE, Exit:

You can exit from the drawing editor by using the EXIT, QUIT, or END commands. The EXIT command can be invoked from the pull-down menu (Select File, Exit), screen menu (Select FILE, Exit:) or by entering EXIT, QUIT, or END at AutoCAD's Command: prompt. The END command first saves the drawing and then quits from the drawing editor.

DRAWING CIRCLES

> **Toolbar:**   Draw, Circle
> **Pull-down:** Draw, Circle
> **Screen:**   DRAW1, Circle:

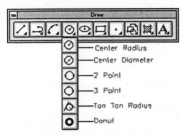

Figure 1-44 Selecting the Circle command from the Draw toolbar

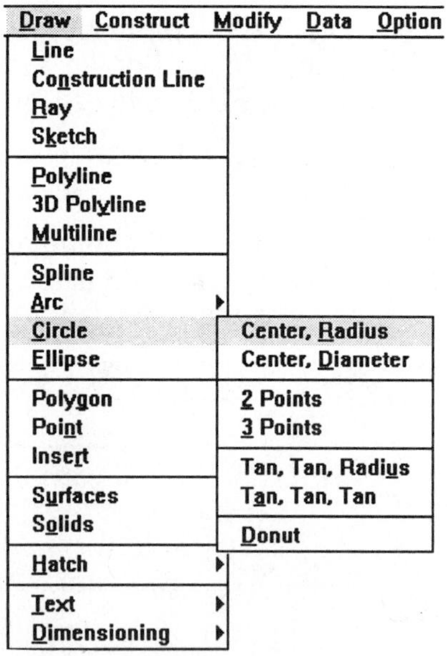

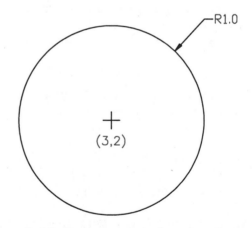

Figure 1-45 Selecting the Circle option from the pull-down menu

To draw a circle you can use AutoCAD's **CIRCLE** command. The CIRCLE command can be invoked by typing CIRCLE or C at the **Command:** prompt, by selecting it from the pull-down menu (Select Draw, Circle) or from the screen menu (Select DRAW 1, Circle:). In Windows this command can also be invoked from the **Draw** toolbar by selecting the desired circle option icon from the **Circle** flyout. The following is the prompt sequence for the CIRCLE command:

Command: **CIRCLE** ←┘
3P/2P/TTR/ < Center point > :

The Center and Radius Option

In this option you can draw a circle by defining the center and the radius of the circle. After entering the CIRCLE command, AutoCAD will prompt you to enter the center of the circle that can be selected by picking a point on the screen or by entering the coordinates of the center point. Next, you will be prompted to enter the radius or diameter of the circle. Here you can accept the default value, enter a new value, or select a point on the circumference of the circle. The following is the prompt sequence for drawing a circle with center at 3,2 and a radius of one unit:

Figure 1-46 Drawing a circle using the Center and Radius option

Command: **CIRCLE** ←┘
3P/2P/TTR/ < Center point > : **3,2** ←┘
Diameter/ < Radius > < current > : **1** (or @1 < 0, or @1,0) ←┘

The Center and Diameter Option

 In this option you can draw a circle by defining the center and diameter of the circle. After entering the CIRCLE command, AutoCAD prompts you to enter the center of the circle, which can be selected by picking a point on the screen or by entering the coordinates of the center point. Next, you will be prompted to enter the radius or diameter of the circle. At this prompt enter **D**. After this you will be prompted to enter the diameter of the circle. For entering the diameter you can accept the default value, enter a new value, or drag the circle to the desired diameter and select a point. The following is the prompt sequence for drawing a circle with the center at 2,3 and a diameter of two units (Figure 1-47):

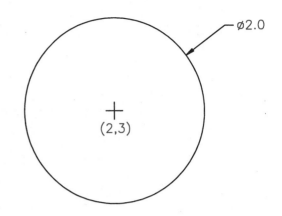

Figure 1-47 Drawing a circle using the Center and Diameter option

    Command: **CIRCLE** ◄─┘
    3P/2P/TTR/<Center point>: **2,3** ◄─┘
    Diameter/<Radius> <current>: **D** ◄─┘
    Diameter <current>: **2** ◄─┘

The Two-Point Option

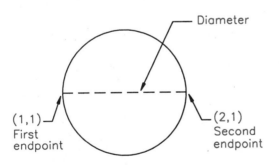 You can also draw a circle using the two-point option. In this option AutoCAD lets you draw the circle by specifying the two end points of the circle's diameter. For example, if you want to draw a circle that passes through the points 1,1 and 2,1, you can use the CIRCLE command with 2P option, as shown in the following example (Figure 1-48):

    Command: **CIRCLE** ◄─┘
    3P/2P/TTR/<Center point>: **2P** ◄─┘
    First point on diameter: **1,1** ◄─┘
    Second point on diameter: **2,1** ◄─┘   *(You can also use polar or relative coordinates)*

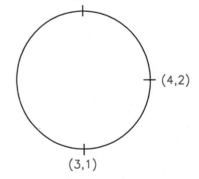

Figure 1-48 Drawing a circle using the Two-Point option

Figure 1-49 Drawing circle using the Three-Point option

The Three-Point Option

For drawing a circle, you can also use the three-point option by defining three points on the circumference of the circle. The three points may be entered in any order. To draw a circle that passes through the points 3,3, 3,1 and 4,2 (Figure 1-49), the prompt sequence is:

```
Command: CIRCLE ←
3P/2P/TTR/<Center point>: 3P ←
First point: 3,3 ←
Second point: 3,1 ←
Third point: 4,2 ←
```

You can also use **relative coordinates** to define the points:

```
Command: CIRCLE ←
3P/2P/TTR/<Center point>: 3P ←
First point: 3,3 ←
Second point: @0,-2 ←
Third point: @1,1 ←
```

The Tangent Tangent Radius Option

A tangent is an object (line, circle, or arc) that contacts the circumference of a circle at only one point. In this option you specify two objects that are to be tangents to the circle, and the radius of the circle. The following is the prompt sequence for drawing a circle using the **TTR** option:

```
Command: CIRCLE ←
3P/2P/TTR/<Center point>: TTR ←
Enter Tangent spec: Select first line, circle, or arc.
Enter second Tangent spec: Select second line, circle, or arc.
Radius<current>: 0.75 ←
```

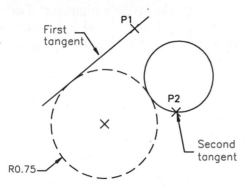

Figure 1-50 Tangent, tangent, radius (TTR) option

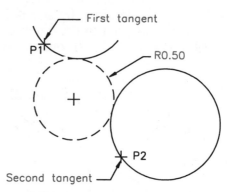

Figure 1-51 Drawing a circle using the tangent, tangent, radius (TTR) option

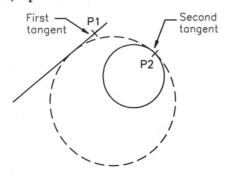

Figure 1-52 Tangent, tangent, radius (TTR) option

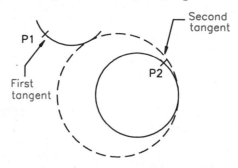

Figure 1-53 Tangent, tangent, radius (TTR) option

In Figures 1-50 through 1-53, the dotted circles represent the circles that are drawn by using the **TTR** option. The circle AutoCAD will draw depends on how you select the objects that are to be tangent to the new circle. The figures show the effect of selecting different points on the objects. The dashed circles represent the circles that are drawn using the TTR option.

The Tangent, Tangent, Tangent Option

You can invoke this option from the pull-down menu or the screen menu. In this option you have to select three objects that are to be the tangents to circle. The following is the prompt sequence for drawing a circle using the **Tan, Tan, Tan** option (Figure 1-54):

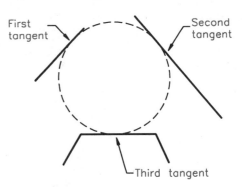

Figure 1-54 Drawing circle using the tan, tan, tan option

Command: **CIRCLE** ←
3P/2P/TTR/ < Center point > : *Pick the Tan, Tan, Tan option from pull-down or screen menu.*
  3P First point: _tan to *Pick the first object.*
  Second point: _tan to *Pick the second object.*
  Third point: _tan to *Pick the third object.*

Exercise 4

Generate the following figure using different options of the LINE and CIRCLE commands. Use absolute, relative, or polar coordinates for drawing the triangle. The vertices of the triangle will be used as the center of the circles. The circles can be drawn using the Center and Radius, Center and Diameter, or TTT option. (The height of the triangle = 2.25 x Sin 60 = 1.949.) Do not draw the dimensions; they are for reference only.

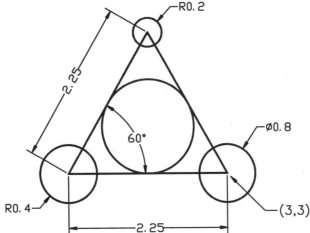

Figure 1-55 Drawing for Exercise 4

BASIC DISPLAY COMMANDS

Drawing in AutoCAD is much simpler than manual drafting in many ways. Sometimes while drawing, it is very difficult to see and alter minute details. In AutoCAD, you can overcome this problem by viewing only a specific portion of the drawing. This is done using the **ZOOM** command, which lets you enlarge or reduce the size of drawing displayed on the screen. We will discuss some of the drawing display commands, like **REDRAW, REGEN, and ZOOM**. (A detailed explanation of these commands and other display options appears in Chapter 5.)

Redraw Command

Toolbar:	Standard toolbar, Redraw View
Pull-down:	View, Redraw View
Screen:	VIEW, Redraw:

This command redraws the screen, thereby removing the cross marks that appear when a point is picked on the screen. These marks are known as blip marks or **blips**. Blip marks indicate the points you have selected (points picked). You can invoke this command from the **Standard** toolbar by selecting the **Redraw** icon, from the pull-down menu (Select View, Redraw View), (Figure 1-56), from the screen menu (Select VIEW, Redraw:), the tablet menu (if you have the tablet facility). You can also invoke this command by entering **R** or **REDRAW** at Command: prompt.
Command: **REDRAW** ◄─┘

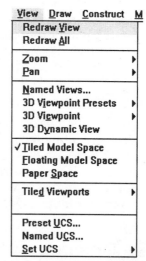

Figure 1-56 Selecting the REDRAW command from the pull-down menu

Regen Command

The REGEN command makes AutoCAD regenerate the entire drawing to update it. The need for regeneration usually occurs when you change certain aspects of the drawing. All the entities in the drawing are recalculated and the current viewport is redrawn. This is a longer process than REDRAW and is seldom needed. One of the advantages of this command is that the drawing is refined by smoothing out the circles and arcs. To use this command, enter **REGEN** at the **Command:** prompt. Command: **REGEN** ◄─┘

Zoom Command

Toolbar:	Standard toolbar, Zoom
Pull-down:	View, Zoom
Screen:	VIEW, Zoom:

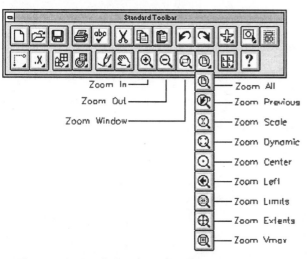

Figure 1-57 Selecting the Zoom command from the Standard toolbar

Figure 1-58 Selecting the Zoom command from the pull-down menu

Creating drawings on the screen would not be of much use if you could not get a magnified view of your drawing to work on minute details. You can zoom in or zoom out by using the **ZOOM** command. In other words, this command enlarges or reduces the size of the drawing on the screen, but it does not affect the actual size of the drawing. The ZOOM command can be invoked by selecting the desired Zoom option icon from the **Standard** toolbar (Figure 1-57), from the pull-down menu (Select View, Zoom) (Figure 1-58), from the screen menu (Select VIEW, Zoom:), or by entering the ZOOM at the **Command:** prompt. After the ZOOM command has been entered, different options can be used to obtain the desired display. The following is the prompt sequence of the **ZOOM** command and some of the ZOOM options:

Command: **ZOOM** ←⏘
All/Center/Dynamic/Extents/Left/Previous/Vmax/Window/ < Scale(X/XP) > :

Window Option

This is the most commonly used option of the ZOOM command. It lets you specify the area you want to zoom in by letting you pick two opposite corners of a rectangular window. The center of the specified window becomes the center of the new display screen. The area inside the window is magnified in size to fill the display as completely as possible. The points can be specified by picking them with the help of the pointing device or by entering their coordinates. The prompt sequence is:

Command: **ZOOM** ←⏘
All/Center/Dynamic/Extents/Left/Previous/Vmax/Window/ < Scale(X/XP) > : **W** ←⏘
First corner: *Pick first point*.
Other corner: *Pick second point*.

Previous Option

While working on a complex drawing, you may need to zoom in to a portion of the drawing to edit some minute details. When you have completed the editing you may want to return to the previous view. This can be done using the **Previous** option of the ZOOM command. The prompt sequence for this option is:

Command: **ZOOM** ←⏘
All/Center/Dynamic/Extents/Left/Previous/Vmax/Window/ < Scale(X/XP) > : **P** ←⏘

Successive **ZOOM P** commands can restore the previous 10 views. The term **view** here refers to the area of the drawing defined by its display extents. If you erase some objects and then issue a ZOOM previous command, the previous display extents are restored but the erased objects are not.

All Option

This option of the ZOOM command displays the drawing limits or extents, whichever is greater. Even if the objects are not within the limits, they are still included in the display. Hence, with the help of the **All** option, you can view the entire drawing in the current viewport (Figure 1-60).

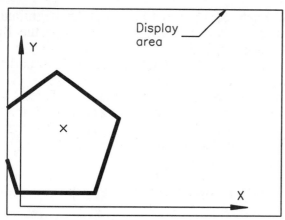

Figure 1-59 Drawing showing limits

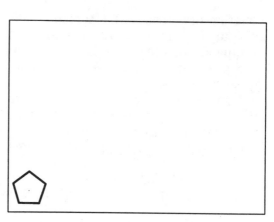

Figure 1-60 Zoom All option

Extents Option

As the name indicates, this option lets you zoom to the extents of the drawing. The extents of the drawing comprise that area that has the drawings in it. The rest of the empty area is neglected. Hence, with the use of this option, all objects in the drawing are magnified to the largest possible display.

PLOTTING DRAWINGS

Toolbar:	Standard toolbar, Print
Pull-down:	File, Print
Screen:	FILE, Print:

Drawings can be plotted by using the **PLOT** command. This command can be invoked by selecting the **Print** icon from the **Standard** toolbar, from the pull-down menu (Select File, Print...) (Figure 1-61), from the screen menu (Select FILE, Print:), or by entering **PLOT** at the Command: prompt. The display of the dialogue box depends on the CMDDIA system variable. If CMDDIA is set to 1, AutoCAD will display the **Plot Configuration** dialogue box (Figure 1-63) when you enter or select PLOT command.

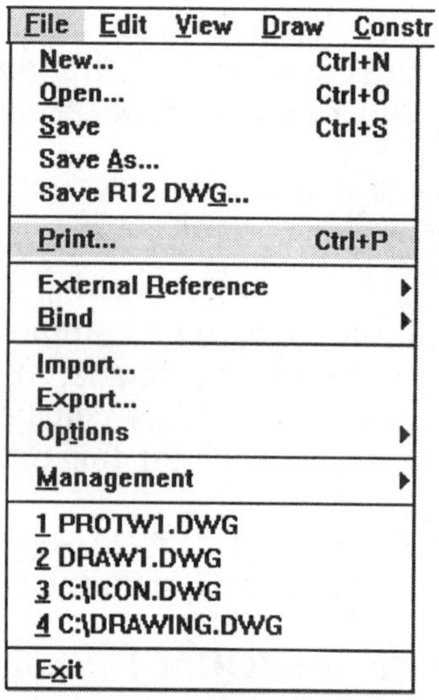

Figure 1-61 Selecting the Print command from the pull-down menu

Command: **PLOT**

The values in this dialogue box are the ones that were set during the configuring of AutoCAD. If the displayed values conform to your requirements, you can start plotting without making any changes. If necessary, you can make changes in the default values according to your plotting requirements.

Basic Plotting

In this section you will learn how to set up the basic plotting parameters. Later in the text you will learn about the advance option which allows you to plot the drawing according to your plot drawing specifications. Basic plotting involves selecting the correct output device (plotter), specifying the area that you want to plot, selecting paper size, specifying the plot origin and plot rotation, and specifying the plot scale. The following example illustrates the process involved in plotting a drawing.

Example 4

In this example you will plot the drawing of Example 3 (page 1-16) using the Window option to select the area you want to plot. Assume that AutoCAD is configured for two output devices, System Printer and HPGL-7475 (these are output device names).

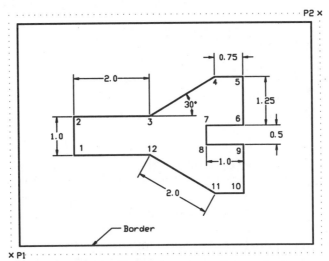

Figure 1-62 Drawing for Example 4

Step 1
Invoke the **Plot Configuration** dialogue box from the **Standard** toolbar, pull-down menu (Select File, Print), or screen menu (Select FILE, Print:), or by entering **PLOT** at the **Command:** prompt.

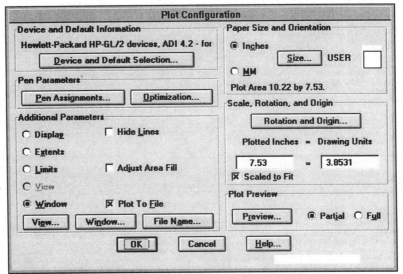

Figure 1-63 Plot Configuration dialogue box

Step 2
Select the **Device and Default Selection** button to display the **Device and Default Selection** dialogue box (Figure 1-64). Information about the current configured device is displayed in this box. For example, if you have configured AutoCAD for two output devices, System Printer and HPGL-7475, AutoCAD will display these names in the **Select Device** list area. If you want to plot the drawing on System Printer, select System Printer (if it is not already selected). Select the OK button to return to the **Plot Configuration** dialogue box.

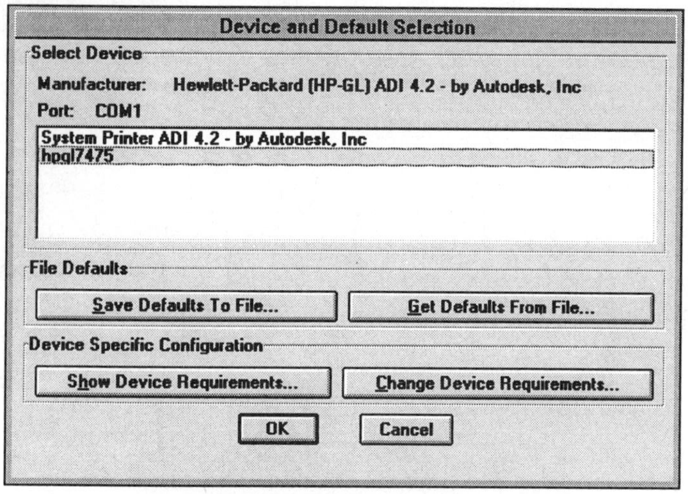

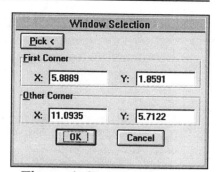

Figure 1-64 Device and Default
Selection dialogue box

Figure 1-65 Window
Selection dialogue box

Step 3

Select the **Window...** box (located between the View and File Name boxes) in the **Plot Configuration** dialogue box to display the **Window Selection** dialogue box (Figure 1-65). You can enter the first and second corner of the area that you want to plot by entering the X and Y coordinates or by using the **Pick** box to pick points on the screen. In this example you will use the **Pick** box, which is located at the upper left corner of the **Window Selection** dialogue box. When you select the **Pick** box, the dialogue boxes will temporarily disappear and the drawing will appear on the screen. Now, select the first and second corners (points P1 and P2), specifying the plot area (the area you want to plot). Once you have defined the two corners, the **Window Selection** dialogue box will reappear. Select the OK button to return to the **Plot Configuration** dialogue box.

Step 4

To set the size for the plot, pick the **Size...** button to display the **Paper Size** dialogue box (Figure 1-66), which lists all the plotting sizes that the present plotter can support. You can select any one of the sizes listed in the dialogue box or specify a size (width and height) of your own in the USER edit boxes. You can define up to five plot sizes. The MAX entry in the list of predefined sizes gives you the maximum size the present plotter can support. Once you select a size, the sections in the **Plot Configuration** dialogue box pertaining to Paper size and Orientation are automatically revised to reflect the new paper size and orientation. In this example you will specify paper size of 8 by 10.5. Enter these values in the Width and Height edit boxes. After entering the values select the OK button.

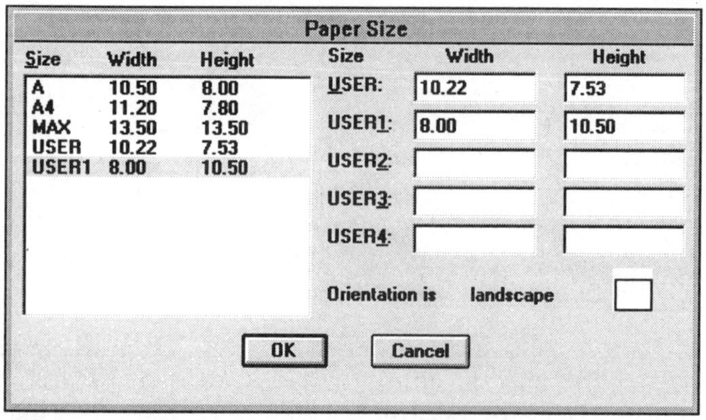

Figure 1-66 Paper Size dialogue box

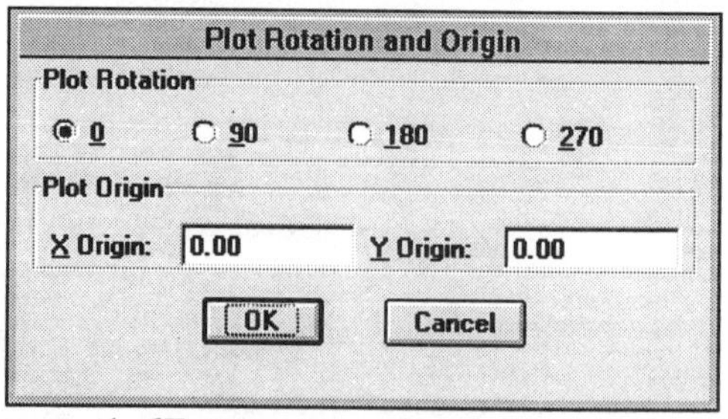

Figure 1-67 Plot Rotation and Origin
dialogue box

Step 5

Pick the **Rotation and Origin** button in the **Plot Configuration** dialogue box to display the **Plot Rotation and Origin** dialogue box on the screen (Figure 1-67). In this dialogue box, you can specify the rotation of the plot in the Plot Rotation area by selecting any one of the four angles. The rotations are performed in a clockwise direction. The location for the origin of the plot can be specified in the Plot Origin area by entering the X and Y coordinates of the origin point. The default plot origin is at (0,0). For this example, select 90 degrees rotation and 0 shift in plot origin (X=0 and Y=0). After specifying the rotation and origin, select the OK button to return to the **Plot Configuration** dialogue box.

Step 6

The default scale for the plot is displayed in the **Plotted Inches = Drawing Units** edit boxes. You can enter the scale factor in this edit box. For example, if your scale factor is of 48, i.e., one unit in the plot is equal to 48 units of the drawing, enter 1 in the **Plotted Inches** edit box and 48 in the **Drawing Units** edit box. If you

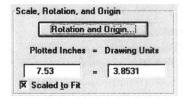

Figure 1-68 Using Scaled to Fit option

want the drawing to be plotted so that it fits on the specified sheet of paper, pick the **Scaled to Fit** check box. When you check this box, AutoCAD will determine the scale factor and display the scale factor in the **Plotted Inches = Drawing Units** edit boxes. If the **Scaled to Fit** check box is disabled, the edit boxes will display the previously set scale, or 1=1 if no previous scale exists. In this example, you will plot the drawing so that it fits on 8 x 10.5 size paper. Therefore pick the Scaled to Fit check box and notice the change in the **Plotted Inches = Drawing Units** edit boxes.

Step 7

You can view the plot on the specified paper size before actually plotting it by picking the **Preview...** button in the **Plot Configuration** dialogue box. This way you can save time and stationery. AutoCAD provides two types of Plot Previews, partial and full. To generate partial preview of a plot, pick the **Partial** radio button, then the **Preview** button. The **Preview Effective Plotting Area** dialogue box is displayed on the screen (Figure 1-70). To display the drawing on the screen just as it would be plotted on the paper, select the **Full** radio button and then the **Preview** button. Full preview takes more time than Partial preview because the drawing is regenerated. Once regeneration is complete, the dialogue boxes on the screen are temporarily removed and the **Plot Preview** dialogue box is displayed on the screen (Figure 1-69). It contains two buttons, Pan and Zoom, and End Preview. To exit the Preview image, select the End Preview box.

Figure 1-69 Full plot preview with Plot Preview dialogue box

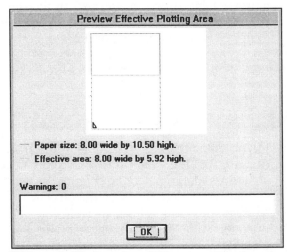

Figure 1-70 Preview Effective Plotting Area dialogue box

Step 8
If the plot preview is satisfactory and you want to plot the drawing, select the **OK** button in the **Plot Configuration** dialogue box. AutoCAD will plot the drawing on the specified plotter.

Note

The following sections describe in detail the New, Save, and Open dialogue boxes. If you are using AutoCAD for the first time, you can skip the remainder of this chapter and come back to it later to get more information about the dialogue boxes.

AUTOCAD DIALOGUE BOXES

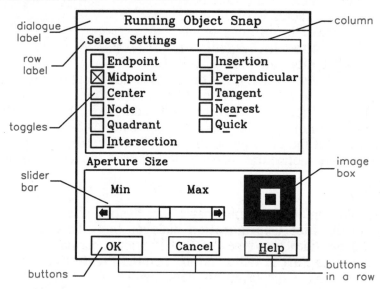

Figure 1-71 Components of a dialogue box

The dialogue boxes defined in AutoCAD are not dependent on the platform; therefore, they can run on any system that supports AutoCAD. However, depending on the **graphical user interface (GUI)** of the platform, the appearance of the dialogue boxes might change from one system to another. The functions defined in the dialogue box will still work without making any changes in the dialogue box or the application program (AutoLISP or ADS) that uses these dialogue boxes. A dialogue box can consist of a dialogue label, toggle buttons, radio buttons, edit boxes, slider bars, image boxes, and a box that encloses these components. These components are also referred to as tiles. Some of the components of a dialogue box are shown in the figure.

NEW DIALOGUE BOX

If you enter the **NEW** command to create a new drawing, AutoCAD will display the **Create New Drawing** dialogue box (Figure 1-72) on the screen, provided the system variable FILEDIA is set to 1. If the system variable FILEDIA is set to 0, the file-related dialogue boxes will not be displayed.

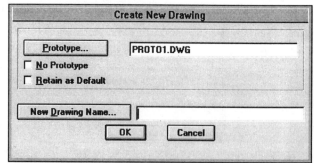

Figure 1-72 Create New Drawing dialogue box

Prototype...

A prototype drawing is a drawing that AutoCAD uses as a pattern to create a new drawing. It defines the initial setup of the new drawing. When you run AutoCAD for the first time, **acad** appears in the **Prototype...** edit box. The drawing file **Acad** (acad.dwg) is the default prototype drawing. You can retain the prototype as acad or enter a different drawing name as a prototype drawing. If you select the **Prototype...** tile, AutoCAD will display the **Prototype Drawing File** dialogue box as shown in Figure 1-73 From this dialogue box you can select a drawing file as a prototype drawing.

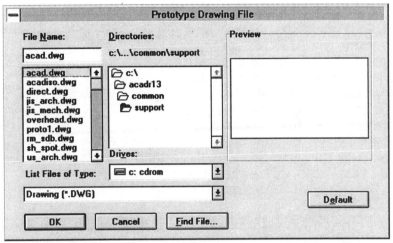

Figure 1-73 Prototype Drawing File dialogue box

No Prototype

If you do not want to use a prototype drawing (set all AutoCAD variables to default values), select the **No Prototype** check box.

Retain as Default

This check box should be picked to retain a drawing that is defined in the **Prototype:** edit box as the default prototype. If you pick both the **No Prototype** and **Retain as Default** check boxes, No Prototype is retained as the default.

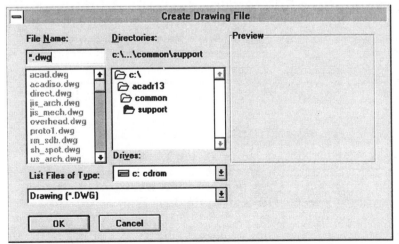

Figure 1-74 Create Drawing File dialogue box

New Drawing Name...

To enter a new drawing name, type the desired name in the **New Drawing Name...** edit box. To save a drawing in a particular directory, the path name for that directory should be entered (C:\ACAD\DWG\MYPROJ). If no path name is specified, the drawing is saved in the current directory. If you want to use one of the existing drawing names for the new drawing name, pick the **New Drawing Name...** tile. When you select this tile, AutoCAD displays the **Create Drawing File** dialogue box (Figure 1-74), which enables you to search and select the drawing you want.

If you enter or select the name of the new drawing and it already exists on the specified drive, AutoCAD warns you that the specified file already exists and lets you replace it (Figure 1-75). If you select the **Yes** button from the **AutoCAD Message** dialogue box, the filename you selected is used for your new drawing. Now, you can select OK from the **Create Drawing File** dialogue box or just press the Enter key to accept the filename and exit the dialogue box. If you want to cancel your selection, select the cancel button from the dialogue box or press Esc.

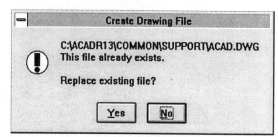

Figure 1-75 AutoCAD Message dialogue box

SAVE DIALOGUE BOX

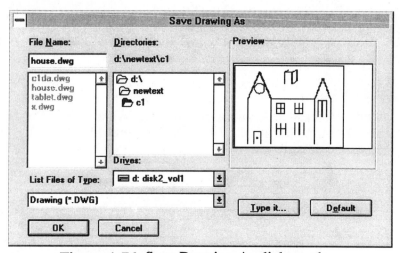

Figure 1-76 Save Drawing As dialogue box

List Files of Type: and Drives: List boxes

The **List Files of Type:** list box (pictured at the right) is used to specify a search pattern for any type of files. For example, you want to list all the files that have the **DWG** extension (drawing files), select *.DWG from the **List Files of Type:** list box and press the Enter key. All the files with the DWG extension in the current directory will be displayed in the **File Name:** (Figure 1-76) list box. The **Drives:** list box lists all the drives available. You can choose the one you want to work in.

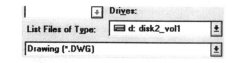

File Name: List and Edit boxes

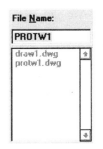

The **File Name:** edit box (picture at the right) is used to enter the name of the file you want to use. This can be done by typing the filename or picking it from the **File Name:** list box. If you pick the filename you want from the **File Name:** list box, the name you select automatically appears in the **File Name:** edit box. If you have already assigned a name to the drawing, the current drawing name is taken as default. If the drawing is unnamed, there is no default name; therefore, no filename will be displayed in the File Name: edit box.

Directories: List box

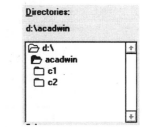

The current drive and path information is listed below the text **Directories:** (Figure 1-77). If you want to change the current drive or directory, you can pick the drive or directory you want from the **Directories:** list box.

Figure 1-77 Directories list box

Default Button

To restore the dialogue box to its original condition (like returning to the original path name), pick the **Default** action button.

Type It Button

If you select the **Type It** button, AutoCAD clears the standard file dialogue box and you can enter the filename in the command prompt area of the screen. The Type It button is grayed out if the option is not available for the current command.

OK and Cancel Buttons

If the existing file name is acceptable to you, pick the **OK** button or press the Enter key. AutoCAD uses the information in the dialogue box to complete the command. If you pick the **Cancel** button or press **Esc** key, AutoCAD cancels any changes you have made in the dialogue box and returns to the **Command:** prompt.

Preview

The Preview area is on the right side of the **Directories:** list box. If you select a filename from the File Name: list box to save your drawing, the bitmap image of that particular file is displayed in the Preview box. If you enter a new filename under which you want to save your drawing, the Preview box remains blank.

OPEN DIALOGUE BOX

When you enter the OPEN command or select Open from the screen or pull-down menu, AutoCAD displays the **Open Drawing** dialogue box (Figure 1-78). This box is identical to the **Save Drawings As** dialogue box (described earlier), except that the **Find File...** button and check boxes for selecting an initial view and for setting read-only mode are included in this dialogue box. The **Select Initial View** option allows you to load a drawing with a specified view and the **Read Only Mode** option enables you to protect a file from being edited. The Find File... displays the Browse/Search dialogue box.

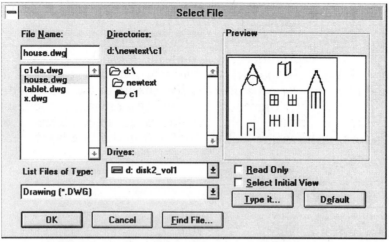

Figure 1-78   Open Drawing dialogue box

Select Initial View

A view is defined as the way you look at an object. The **Select Initial View** option allows you to specify the view you want to load initially when AutoCAD loads the drawing. This option will work if the drawing has saved views. You can save a desired view by using AutoCAD's **VIEW** command (see VIEW Command, Chapter 5). If the drawing does not have any saved views, selecting this option will load the last view. If you select the **Select Initial View** check box, then the **OK** button, AutoCAD will display the **Select Initial View** dialogue box (Figure 1-79). You can select the view name from this dialogue box, and AutoCAD will load the drawing with the selected view displayed on the screen.

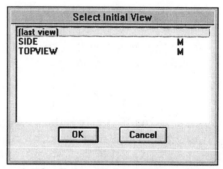

Figure 1-79   Select Initial View dialogue box

Read Only Mode

If you want to view a drawing without altering it, you must select the Read Only check box. In other words, Read Only protects the drawing file from changes. AutoCAD does not prevent you from editing the drawing, but if you try to save the opened drawing to the original filename, AutoCAD warns you that the drawing file is **write protected** (Figure 1-80). However, you can save the edited drawing to a file with a different filename.

Figure 1-80   AutoCAD Alert dialogue box

Find File

Click on this button to display **Browse/Search** dialogue box (Figure 1-81). This allows you to search files in different drives and subdirectories.

Browse

The file name of the drawing that is currently selected is displayed in the **File Name:** edit box. The bitmap images of the drawings in the current directory are displayed in the **File Name:** list box. The drawing display size can be made small, medium, or large by selecting the desired option in the **Size:** list box. The **Drives:** and **Directories:** list boxes display the different drives and directories available.

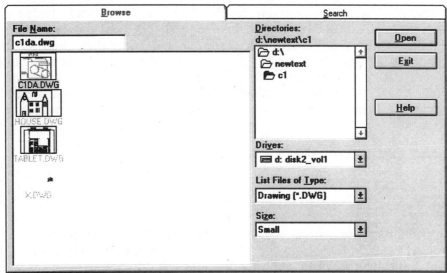

Figure 1-81 Browse/Search dialogue box (Browse)

Search

To activate the Search dialogue box (Figure 1-82), click on the word Search in the upper right portion. To start the searching routine, click on the **Search** button. Searching for files depends on the file type or creation date. As the search continues the searching progress is updated in the **Files** list box. After the search is completed, the bitmap images and the file names of those files that fulfill the search criteria are displayed in the **Files** list box. The total number of these files is also displayed. The **Search Pattern** allows you to search for files having a specific pattern of specified file type. In the **File Types** list box you can select the desired file type for searching. In the **Date Filter** area you can specify a certain time and date so that only those files are searched which have been created before or after the particular time and date. The time and date can be specified in the **Time** and **Date** text boxes in the Date Filter area. In the **Search Location** area you can specify the drives and paths for searching. In the **Drives** list box you can specify the drive for searching. The **All Drives** list box displays all the fixed drives. In the **Path** edit box you can specify the directories to be searched. The **Edit** text box is used to edit a path.

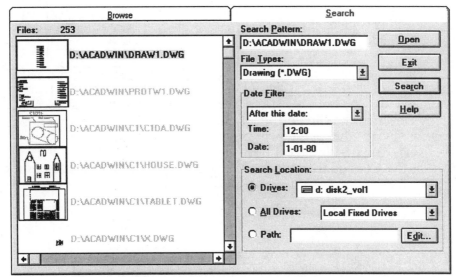

Figure 1-82 Browse/Search dialogue box (Search)

AUTOMATIC TIMED SAVE

AutoCAD allows you to save your work automatically at specific intervals. To change the time intervals you can use the system variable SAVETIME. You can also change the time intervals from the **Preferences** dialogue box, which can be invoked from the **Options** pull-down menu. Depending on the power supply, hardware, and type of drawings, you should decide on an appropriate time and assign that time to this variable. AutoCAD saves the drawing under the filename AUTO.SV$. You can also set the time interval and the filename by configuring AutoCAD (Enter CONFIG command, select Config operating parameters, select Automatic save feature, then enter the name of the auto-save drawing). The extension of auto-save file is .SV$.

Command: **SAVETIME** ←┘
New value for SAVETIME <120>: *Enter time in minutes.*

CREATION OF BACK-UP FILES

If the drawing file already exists and you use SAVE or SAVEAS commands to update the current drawing, AutoCAD creates a back-up file. AutoCAD takes the previous copy of the drawing and changes it from a file type **.dwg** to **.bak** and the updated drawing is saved as a drawing file with the .dwg extension. For example, if the name of the drawing is MYPROJ.DWG, AutoCAD will change it to MYPROJ.BAK and save the current drawing as MYPROJ.DWG.

CREATING TEXT

Toolbar:	Draw, Text, Single-Line Text
Pull-down:	Draw, Text, Single-Line Text

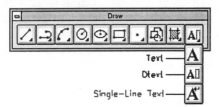

Figure 1-83 Selecting Single - Line Text from the Draw toolbar

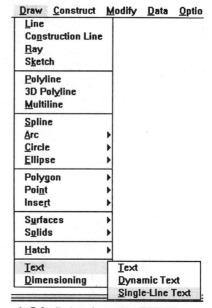

Figure 1-84 Selecting the TEXT command from the pull-down menu

 The TEXT command lets you write text on a drawing. The TEXT command can be invoked from the **Draw** toolbar by selecting the **Single-Line Text** icon in the **Text** flyout, the pull-down menu (Select Draw, Text, Single-Line Text), or by entering **TEXT** at the **Command:** prompt. The text commands are discussed in detail in Chapter 5.

SELF EVALUATION TEST

Answer the following questions and then compare your answers with the correct answers given at the end of this chapter.

1. If you exit the LINE command after drawing a the line and then select LINE command again, the _____ option can be used to draw a line from the end point of the last line.

2. The _____ coordinates of a point are located with reference to the previous point.

3. To draw a line from point (2,2) to another point at a distance of 3 units and an angle of 60 degrees, you will have the prompt sequence:
    Command: _____
    From point: _____
    To point: _____

4. When using the **Window** option in the ERASE command, the objects to be erased must _____ lie within the window.

5. The prompt sequence for drawing a circle with its center at (4,5) and a diameter of 3 units is:
    Command: _____
    3P/2P/TTR/<Center point>: _____
    Diameter/<Radius> <current>: _____
    Diameter<current>: _____

6. The _____ option of the CIRCLE command can be used to draw a circle, if you want the circle to be tangent to two previously drawn objects.

7. You can erase a previously drawn line using the _____ option of the LINE command.

8. A _____ drawing is used as a pattern for creating a new drawing.

9. The _____ system variable can be used to change the time interval for automatic save.

10. When you select the ERASE command, a small box known as the _____ replaces the screen cursor.

11. Display of the Plot dialogue box can be controlled with the help of the _____ system variable.

12. The _____ command is used to plot a drawing.

13. By selecting the _____ radio button in the Plot Configuration dialogue box, you can specify the section of the drawing to be plotted with the help of a _____ .

14. A plot can be rotated at an angle of ___ , ____ , ____ , or _____ degrees.

15. The rotation of a plot is performed in a _____ direction.

REVIEW QUESTIONS

Answer the following questions.

1. The prompt sequence for the LINE command is
    Command: _____

    _____

    _____

2. The _____ option can be used to draw the last side of a polygon.

3. In the two mutually intersecting lines for the X and Y coordinates, the X coordinate value is calculated along the _____ line, and the Y coordinate value is calculated along the _____ line.

4. In the _____ coordinate system the points are located with respect to origin 0,0

5. In the relative coordinate system, if you want a displacement of 6 units along the Y axis and 0 displacement along the X axis, you should enter _____ at the **To point:** prompt.

6. In the polar coordinate system, you need to specify the _____ of the point from the _____ point and the _____ it makes with the positive X axis.

7. The ERASE command can be selected from the _____ screen menu or by entering _____ at the **Command:** prompt.

8. When AutoCAD puts you in the drawing editor, the _____ command is used to create a new drawing that you can name before you start working on the drawing.

9. The NEW command can be selected from the _____ pull-down menu or by entering _____ at the **Command:** prompt.

10. The prompt sequence for drawing a circle with (2,2), (4,5), and (7,1) as three points on its circumference is:
    Command: _____
    3P/2P/TTR/<Center point>: _____
    First point: _____
    Second point: _____
    Third point: _____

11. To open or load an existing file into the drawing editor, you can use the _____ command.

12. A filename for a new drawing can also be specified from the command line if the _____ system variable is set to 0.

13. When you enter the SAVEAS command, AutoCAD displays the standard file dialogue box entitled _____ .

14. What is the difference between the **Window** option and the **Crossing** option?_____

15. Explain the function of various boxes in the **Create New Drawing** dialogue box._____

16. Explain briefly the function of the **Create Drawing File** dialogue box. Which edit boxes are found in the Create Drawing File dialogue box? _____

17. How will you create a new file with the name **Draw** using the command line and not through the dialogue box? _____

18. Explain the differences between the SAVE, SAVEAS, and QSAVE commands._____

19. Explain the functions of various components of the **Save Drawing As** standard file dialogue box._____

20. You can view the plot on the specified paper size before actually plotting it by picking the _____ button in the Plot Configuration dialogue box.

EXERCISES

Exercise 5

Use the following relative and absolute coordinate values in the LINE command to draw the object.

Point	Coordinates	Point	Coordinates
1	3.0, 3.0	5	@3.0,5.0
2	@3,0	6	@3,0
3	@-1.5,3.0	7	@-1.5,-3
4	@-1.5,-3.0	8	@-1.5,3

Exercise 6

For Figure 1-85, enter the relative coordinates of the points in the given table, then use these coordinates to draw the figure.

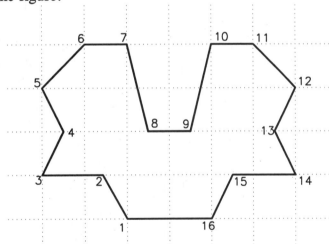

Figure 1-85 Drawing for Exercise 6

Point	Coordinates	Point	Coordinates
1	3.0, 1.0	9	_____
2	_____	10	_____
3	_____	11	_____
4	_____	12	_____
5	_____	13	_____
6	_____	14	_____
7	_____	15	_____
8	_____	16	_____

Exercise 7

For Figure 1-86, enter the polar coordinates of the points in the given table, then use these coordinates to draw the figure. Do not draw the dimensions.

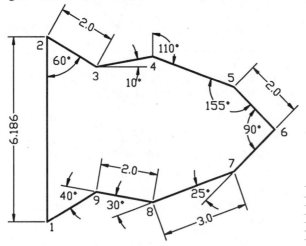

Figure 1-86 Drawing for Exercise 7

Point	Coordinates		Point	Coordinates
1	1.0, 1.0		6	_____
2	_____		7	_____
3	_____		8	_____
4	_____		9	_____
5	_____			

Exercise 8

Generate the drawing in Figure 1-87 using the absolute, relative, or polar coordinate system. Draw as per the dimensions shown in the figure, but do not draw the dimensions.

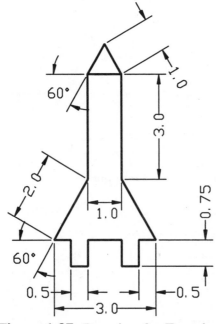

Figure 1-87 Drawing for Exercise 8

Exercise 9

Draw Figure 1-88 using the LINE command and the TTR option of the CIRCLE command.

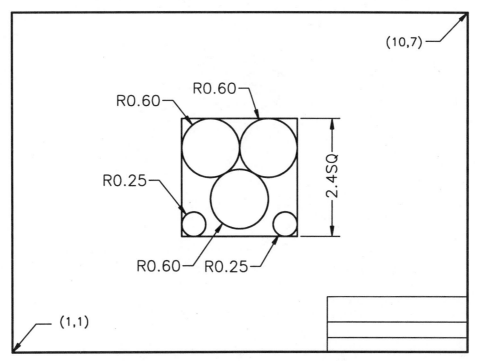

Figure 1-88 Drawing for Exercise 9

Exercise 10

Draw the object shown in Figure 1-89 using the LINE and CIRCLE commands. Do not draw the dimensions.

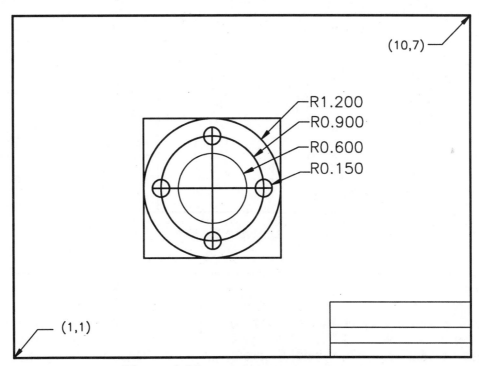

Figure 1-89 Drawing for Exercise 10

Exercise 11

Draft Figure 1-90 using various options of the CIRCLE and LINE commands. The dimensions are given in the figure.

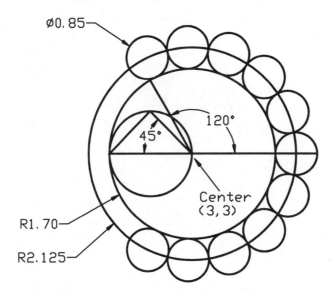

Figure 1-90 Drawing for Exercise 11

Exercise 12

Make the drawing in Figure 1-91 using the pointing device to select points. The drawing you generate should resemble the one shown in the figure.

Figure 1-91 Drawing for Exercise 12

Answers

The following are the correct answers to the questions in the self evaluation test.
1 - Continue, 2 - relative, 3 - LINE / 2,2 / @3 < 60, 4 - completely, 5 - CIRCLE / 4,5 / D / 3,
6 - Tangent Tangent Radius, 7 - Undo, 8 - prototype, 9 - SAVETIME, 10 - pick box, 11 -
CMDDIA, 12 - PLOT, 13 - window, window, 14 - 0, 90, 180, 270, 15 - clockwise

Chapter 2

Draw Commands

(ARC, RECTANGLE, ELLIPSE, POLYGON, TRACE, POLYLINE, DOUGHNUT, POINT)

Learning objectives

After completing this chapter, you will be able to:
- ◆ Draw arcs using different options.
- ◆ Draw rectangles, ellipses, and elliptical arcs.
- ◆ Draw polygons like hexagons, pentagons, etc.
- ◆ Draw traces, polylines, and doughnuts.
- ◆ Draw points and change point style and point size.

DRAWING ARCS

Toolbar:	Draw, Arc
Pull-down:	Draw, Arc
Screen:	DRAW1, Arc:

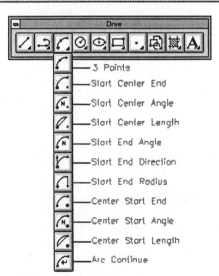

Figure 2-1 Selecting the Arc command from the Draw toolbar

Figure 2-2 Selecting the Arc option from the pull-down menu

An arc is defined as a part of circle; it can be drawn using the **ARC** command. This command can be invoked from the **Draw** toolbar by selecting the desirable **Arc** icon in the **Arc** flyout (Figure 2-1), or the pull-down menu (Select Draw, Arc), the screen menu (Select **DRAW1**, Arc), or by typing ARC or A at the **Command:** prompt. An arc can be drawn in 11 distinct ways using the options listed under the ARC command. The default method for drawing an arc is the **three-point** option. Other options can be invoked by entering the appropriate letter to select an option. If you have set the **DRAGMODE** variable to Auto, the last parameter to be specified in any arc generation is automatically dragged into relevant location.

Three-Point Option

When you enter ARC at the **Command:** prompt, you automatically get into the **three-point** option. The three-point option requires the start point, second point, and end point of the arc. The arc can be drawn in a clockwise or counterclockwise direction by dragging the arc with the cursor. The following is the prompt sequence to draw an arc with a start point at (2,2), second point at (3,3), and end point at (3,4). (You can also specify the points by moving the cursor and then picking points on the screen.)

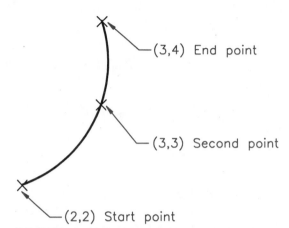

Figure 2-3 Drawing an arc using the three-point option

Command: **ARC** ◄┘
Center/ < Start point > : **2,2** ◄┘
Center/End/ < Second point > : **3,3** ◄┘
End point: **3,4** ◄┘

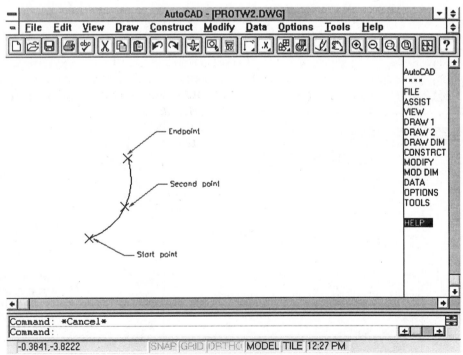

Figure 2-4 Drawing an arc using the three-point option

Exercise 1

Draw several arcs using three-point option. The points can be selected by entering coordinates or specifying points on the screen. Also, try to create a circle by drawing two separate arcs and by drawing a single arc. Notice the limitations of the ARC command.

The Start, Center, End (St,C,End) Option

This option is slightly different from the three-point option. In this option, instead of entering the second point, you enter the center of the arc. Choose this option when you know the start point, end point, and center point of the arc. The arc is drawn in a counterclockwise direction from the start point to the end point around the specified center. The end point specified need not be on the arc and is used only to calculate the angle at which the arc ends. The radius of the arc is determined by the distance between the center point and the start point. The prompt sequence for drawing an arc with a start point of (3,2), center point of (2,2), and end point of (2,3.5) is as follows:

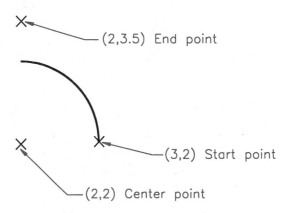

Figure 2-5 Drawing an arc using the Start, Center, End option

Command: **ARC** ↵
Center/<Start point>: **3,2** ↵
Center/End/<Second point>: **C** ↵
Center: **2,2** ↵
Angle/Length of chord/<End point>: **2,3.5** ↵

The Start, Center, Angle (St,C,Ang) Option

This option is the best choice if you know the included angle of the arc. The **included angle** is the angle formed by the start point and the end point of the arc with the center. This option draws an arc in a counterclockwise direction with the specified center and start point spanning the indicated angle. If the specified angle is negative, the arc is drawn in a clockwise direction.

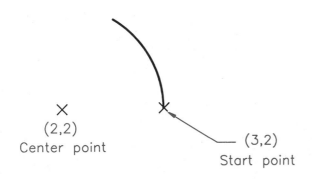

Figure 2-6 Drawing arc using Start, Center, Angle option

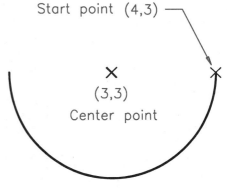

Figure 2-7 Drawing an arc using the negative angle value in the Start, Center, Angle option

The prompt sequence for drawing an arc with the center at (2,2), start point of (3,2), and the included angle of 60 degrees (Figure 2-6) is:

    Command: **ARC** ←
    Center/ < Start point > : **3,2** ←
    Center/End/ < Second point > : **C** ←
    Center: **2,2** ←
    Angle/Length of chord/ < End point > : **A** ←
    Included angle: **60** ←

You can draw arcs with negative angle values in the start, center, included angle (St,C,Ang) option by entering "**-**" (negative sign) followed by the angle values of your requirement at the **Included angle:** prompt (Figure 2-7). This is illustrated by the following prompt sequence:

    Command: **ARC** ←
    Center/ < Start point > : **4,3** ←
    Center/End/ < Second point > : **C** ←
    Center: **3,3** ←
    Angle/Length of chord/ < End point > : **A** ←
    Included angle: **-180** ←

Exercise 2

a. Draw an arc using the **St,C,Ang** option. The start point is (6,3), the center point is (3,3), and the angle is 240 degrees.

b. Make the drawing shown in Figure 2-8. The distance between the dotted lines is 0.5 units. Create the radii by using the arc command options as indicated in the drawing.

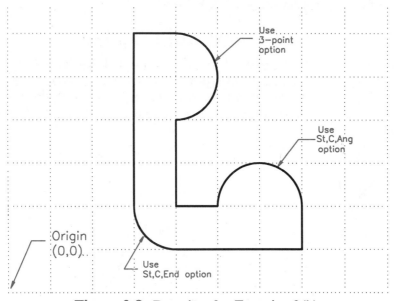

Figure 2-8   Drawing for Exercise 2(b)

The Start, Center, Length of Chord (St,C,Len) Option

In this option you are required to specify the start point, center point, and length of the chord. A **chord** is defined as the straight line connecting the start point and the end point of an arc. The chord length needs to be specified so that AutoCAD can calculate the ending angle. Identical start, center, and chord length specification can be used to define four different arcs. AutoCAD settles this problem by always drawing this type of arc counterclockwise from the start point. Therefore, a positive chord length gives the smallest possible arc with that length. This is known as the **minor arc**. The minor arc is less than 180 degrees. A negative value for chord length results in the largest possible arc, also known as the **major arc**. The chord length can be determined by using the standard chord length tables or using the mathematical relation (L = 2*Sqrt [h(2r-h)]). For example, an arc of radius 1 unit, with an included angle of 30 degrees, has a chord length of **0.51764** units. The prompt sequence for drawing an arc (Figure 2-9) that has a start point of (3,1), center of (2,2) and the chord length of (2) is:

    Command: **ARC** ◄─┘
    Center/< Start point > : **3,1** ◄─┘
    Center/End/< Second point > : **C** ◄─┘
    Center: **2,2** ◄─┘
    Angle/Length of chord/< End point > : **L** ◄─┘
    Length of chord: **2** ◄─┘

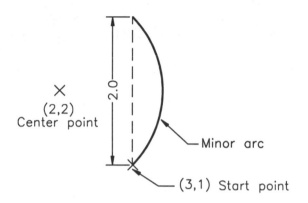

Figure 2-9 Drawing an arc using the Start, Center, Length of chord option

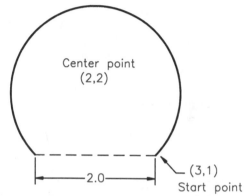

Figure 2-10 Drawing an arc using the negative chord length value in St,C,Len option

You can draw the major arc by defining the length of the chord as negative (Figure 2-10). In this case the arc with a start point of (3,1), center point of (2,2), and a negative chord length of (-2) is drawn with the following prompt sequence:

    Command: **ARC** ◄─┘
    Center/< Start point > : **3,1** ◄─┘
    Center/End/< Second point > : **C** ◄─┘
    Center: **2,2** ◄─┘
    Angle/Length of chord/< End point > : **L** ◄─┘
    Length of chord: **-2** ◄─┘

Exercise 3

Draw a minor arc with the center point at (3,4), start point at (4,2), and chord length of 4 units.

The Start, End, Angle (St,E,Ang) Option

With this option you can draw an arc by specifying the start point of the arc, the end point, and the included angle. A positive included angle value draws an arc in a counterclockwise direction from the start point to the end point spanning the included angle; a negative included angle value draws the arc in a clockwise direction.

The prompt sequence for drawing an arc with a start point of (3,2), end point of (2,4), and an included angle of 120 degrees is:

Command: **ARC** ↵
Center/ < Start point > : **3,2** ↵
Center/End/ < Second point > : **E** ↵
End point: **2,4** ↵
Angle/Direction/Radius/ < Center point > : **A** ↵
Included angle: **120** ↵

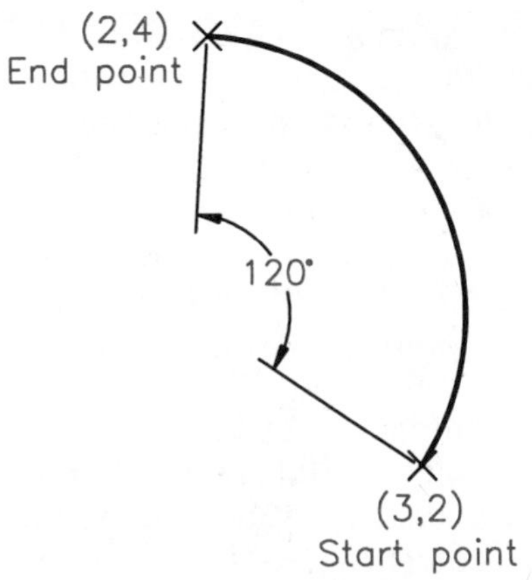

The Start, End, Starting Direction (St,E,Dir) Option

In this option you can draw an arc by specifying the start point, end point, and the starting direction of the arc in degrees. In other words, the arc starts in the direction you specify (the start of the arc is established **tangent to the direction you specify**). This option can be used to draw a major or minor arc, in a clockwise or counterclockwise direction. The size and position of the arc are determined by the distance between the start point and end point and the direction specified. To illustrate the positive direction option (Figure 2-12), the prompt sequence for an arc having a start point of (4,3), end point of (3,5), and the direction of 90 degrees is:

Figure 2-11 Drawing an arc using the Start, End, Angle option

Command: **ARC** ↵
Center/ < Start point > : **4,3** ↵
Center/End/ < Second point > : **E** ↵
End point: **3,5** ↵
Angle/Direction/Radius/ < Center point > : **D** ↵
Direction from start point: **90** ↵

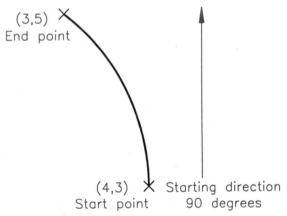

Figure 2-12 Drawing an arc using the Start, End, Direction option

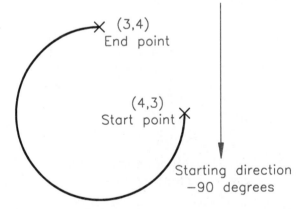

Figure 2-13 Drawing an arc using a negative direction in the Start, End, Direction option

To illustrate the option using a negative direction degree specification (Figure 2-13), the prompt sequence for an arc having a start point of (4,3), end point of (3,4), and direction of -90 degrees is:

Command: **ARC** ↵
Center/ < Start point > : **4,3** ↵
Center/End/ < Second point > : **E** ↵
End point: **3,4** ↵
Angle/Direction/Radius/ < Center point > : **D** ↵
Direction from start point: **-90** ↵

Exercise 4

a. Specify the directions and the coordinates of two arcs in such a way that they form a circular figure.

b. Make the drawing shown in Figure 2-14. Create the radii by using the arc command options indicated in the drawing. (Use the @ symbol to snap to the previous point. Example: Center/ < Start point > :@)

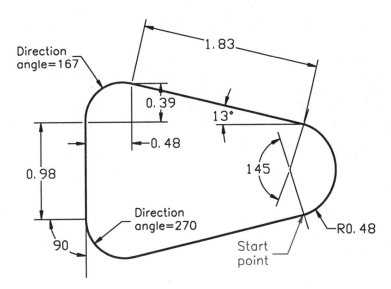

Figure 2-14 Drawing for Exercise 4(b)

The Start, End, Radius (St,E,Rad) Option

This option is used when you know the start point, end point, and radius of the arc. The same values for the three variables (start point, end point, and radius) can result in four different arcs. AutoCAD resolves this by always drawing this type of arc in a counterclockwise direction from the start point. Hence, a positive radius value results in a **minor arc** (smallest arc between start and end point), while a negative radius value results in a **major arc** (largest arc between two end points). The prompt sequence to draw a major arc having a start point of (3,3), end point of (2,5), and radius of -2 is:

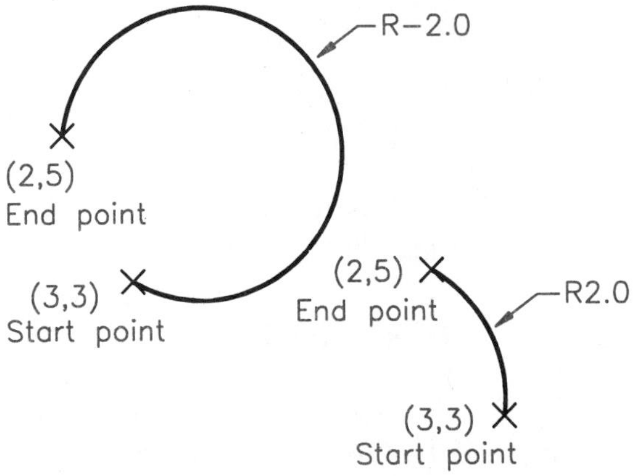

Figure 2-15 Drawing an arc using the Start, End, Radius option

    Command: **ARC** ←┘
    Center/ < Start point > : **3,3** ←┘
    Center/End/ < Second point > : **E** ←┘
    End point: **2,5** ←┘
    Angle/Direction/Radius/ < Center point > : **R** ←┘
    Radius: **-2** ←┘

The prompt sequence to draw a minor arc having its start point at (3,3), end point at (2,5), and radius as 2 is:

Command: **ARC** ↵
Center/<Start point>: **3,3** ↵
Center/End/<Second point>: **E** ↵
End point: **2,5** ↵
Angle/Direction/Radius/<Center point>: **R** ↵
Radius: **2** ↵

The Center, Start, End (Ce,S,End) Option

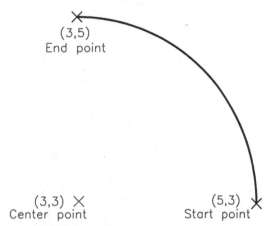

The **Center, Start, End** option is a modification of the Start, Center, End option. You should use this option whenever it is easier to start drawing an arc by establishing the center first. Here the arc is always drawn in a counterclockwise direction from the start point to the end point around the specified center. The prompt sequence for drawing an arc (Figure 2-16) that has a center point at (3,3), start point at (5,3), and end point at (3,5) is:

Command: **ARC** ↵
Center/<Start point>: **C** ↵
Center: **3,3** ↵
Start point: **5,3** ↵
Angle/Length of chord/<End point>: **3,5** ↵

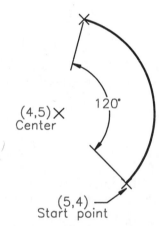

Figure 2-16 Drawing an arc using the Center, Start, End option

Figure 2-17 Drawing an arc using the Center, Start, Angle option

The Center, Start, Angle (Ce,S,Ang) Option

The **Center, Start, Angle** option is a variation of the Start, Center, Angle option. You should use this option whenever it is easier to draw an arc by establishing the center first. The prompt sequence for drawing an arc (Figure 2-17) that has a center point at (4,5), start point at (5,4), and included angle of 120 degrees is:

Command: **ARC** ↵
Center/<Start point>: **C** ↵
Center: **4,5** ↵
Start point: **5,4** ↵
Angle/Length of chord/<End point>: **A** ↵
Included angle: **120** ↵

The Center, Start, Length of Chord (Ce,S,Len) Option

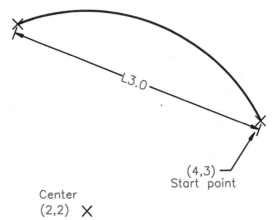

The **Center, Start, Length of Chord** option is a modification of the Start, Center, Length of Chord option. This option is used whenever it is easier to start drawing an arc by establishing the center first. The prompt sequence for drawing an arc which has a center point at (2,2), start point at (4,3), and the length of chord at 3 is:

```
Command: ARC ←┘
Center/<Start point>: C ←┘
Center: 2,2 ←┘
Start point: 4,3 ←┘
Angle/Length of chord/<End point>: L ←┘
Length of chord: 3 ←┘
```

Figure 2-18 Drawing an arc using the Center, Start, Length of Chord option

Continue (ArcCont:) Option

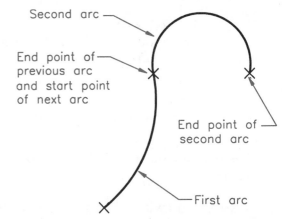

With the help of this option you can continue drawing an arc from a previously drawn arc or line. This option resembles the **Start, End, Starting Direction** option in that if you do not specify a start point but just press the Enter key, or pick the **Continue** option (pull-down menu) or the **ArcCont:** option (screen menu). The start point and direction of the arc will be taken from the **end point and ending direction** of the previous line or arc drawn on the current screen. When this option is used to draw arcs, each successive arc is tangent to the previous one. Most often this option is used to draw arcs tangent to a previously drawn line.

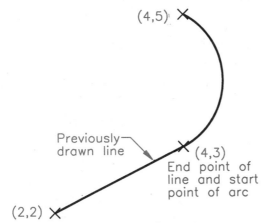

Figure 2-19 Drawing an arc using the ArcCont: option

Figure 2-20 Drawing an arc using the ArcCont: option

The prompt sequence to draw an arc using the ArcCont: option (Figure 2-19), tangent to an earlier drawn line is:

```
Command: LINE ←┘
From point: 2,2 ←┘
To point: 4,3 ←┘
To point: ←┘
Command: ARC ←┘
Center/<Start point>: Pick the ArcCont: option.
End point: 4,5 ←┘
```

The following illustration demonstrates the case of an arc continued from a previously drawn arc (Figure 2-20):

> Command: **ARC** ←⏎
> Center/ <Start point> : **2,2** ←⏎
> Center/End/ <Second point> : **E** ←⏎
> End point: **3,4** ←⏎
> Angle/Direction/Radius/ <Center point> : **R** ←⏎
> Radius: **2** ←⏎
> Command: **ARC** ←⏎
> Center/ <Start point> : ←⏎
> End point: **5,4** ←⏎

Continue (LineCont:) Option

With the help of this option you can continue drawing a line from the end point of the previously drawn arc. This option is available only in the Arc: screen menu. When you select this option the start point and direction of the line will be taken from the **end point and ending direction** of the previous arc. In other words, the line will be tangent to the arc drawn on the current screen. The prompt sequence to draw a line using the LineCont: option, tangent to an earlier drawn arc, is as follows:

> Command: **ARC** ←⏎
> Center/ <Start point> : **4,3:**
> Center/End/ <Second point> : **E** ←⏎
> End point: **3.37,3.92** ←-
> Command: **ARC** ←⏎
> Center/ <Start point> : *Pick the **LineCont** option from ARC screen menu.*
> Length of line: **1.5**

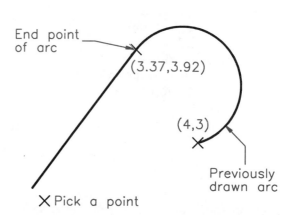

Figure 2-21 Drawing an arc using the LineCont: option

Exercise 5

a. Use the **Center, Start, Angle** and the **Continue** options to draw the figures shown in Figure 2-22.

b. Make the drawing shown in Figure 2-23. The distance between the dotted lines is 1.0 units. Create the radii as indicated in the drawing by using arc command options.

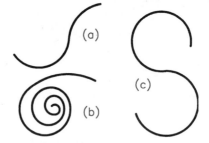

Figure 2-22 Drawing for Exercise 5(a)

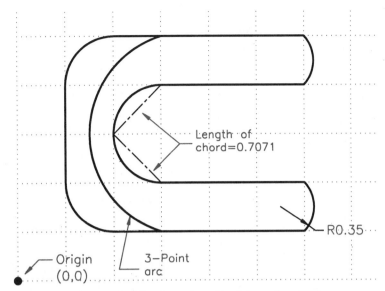

Figure 2-23 Drawing for Exercise 5(b)

DRAWING RECTANGLES

Toolbar: Draw, Rectangle
Pull-down: Draw, Polygon, Rectangle
Screen: DRAW1, Rectang:

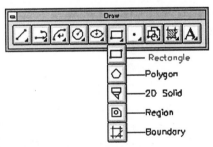

Figure 2-24 Selecting the Rectangle command from the Draw toolbar

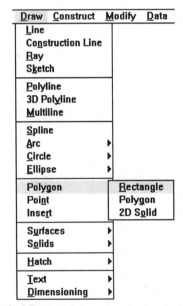

Figure 2-25 Selecting the Rectangle command from the pull-down menu

A rectangle can be drawn using the **RECTANGLE** command. This command also can be invoked from the **Draw** toolbar by selecting the **Rectangle** icon in the **Rectangle** flyout (Figure 2-24), from the pull-down menu (Select Draw, Polygon, Rectangle, Figure 2-25), or from the screen menu (Select DRAW 1, Rectangle:). This command can also be invoked by entering RECTANGLE at the **Command:** prompt. After invoking the RECTANGLE command, you are prompted to specify the first corner of the rectangle at the **First Corner:** prompt. Here you can enter the coordinates of the first corner or pick the desired point with the pointing device. The first corner can be any one of the four corners. Then you are prompted to enter the coordinates or pick the other corner at the **Other Corner:** prompt. This corner is taken as the corner diagonally opposite to the first corner. The prompt sequence for drawing a rectangle with (3,3) as its lower left corner coordinate and (6,5) as its upper right corner (Figure 2-26) is:

Command: **RECTANGLE** ↵
First Corner: **3,3** ↵   *(Lower left corner location.)*
Other Corner: **6,5** ↵   *(Upper right corner location.)*

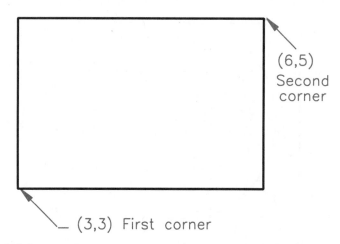

Figure 2-26 Drawing a rectangle using the RECTANGLE command

You can also specify the first corner and drag the cursor to specify the other corner.

Note
The rectangle generated on the screen is treated as a single object. Hence, the individual sides can be edited only after the rectangle has been exploded using the EXPLODE command.

Exercise 6

Draw a rectangle 4 units long, 3 units high, and with its first corner at (1,1). Inside the first rectangle draw another rectangle whose sides are 0.5 units.

DRAWING ELLIPSES

If a circle is observed from an angle, the shape seen is called an **ellipse**. An ellipse can be created using various options listed within the **ELLIPSE** command. Up to Release 12, ellipses were based on polylines. They were made of multiple polyarcs; as a result, it was difficult to edit an ellipse. For example, if you select an ellipse, the grips will be displayed at the end points of each polyarc. If you move a vertex point, you get the shape shown in Figure 2-27(b). Also, you cannot snap to the center or the quadrant points of a polyline-based ellipse. In AutoCAD Release 13, you can still draw the polyline-based ellipse by setting the value of **PELLIPSE system variable to 1**. If the PELLIPSE is set to 0 (default), AutoCAD creates a true ellipse also known as NURBS-based (Non-Uniform Rational Basis Spline)

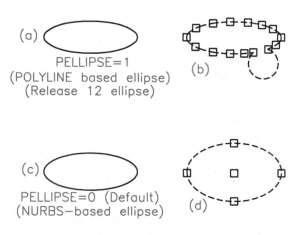

Figure 2-27 Drawing polyline and NURBS-based ellipses

ellipse. The true ellipse has a center and quadrant points. If you select it, the grips will be displayed at the center and the quadrant points of the ellipse. If you move one of the grips located on the perimeter of the ellipse, the major or minor axis will change, which results in the ellipse changing size as shown in Figure 2-27(d).

The **ELLIPSE** command can be invoked from the **Draw** toolbar by selecting the desired **Ellipse** icon in the **Ellipse** flyout (Figure 2-28), pull-down menu (Select Draw, Ellipse Figure 2-29), screen menu (Select DRAW 1, Ellipse:), or by entering ELLIPSE at the **Command:** prompt. Once you invoke the ELLIPSE command by any of these methods, AutoCAD will acknowledge with the prompt **Arc/ Center/ Isocircle/ <Axis endpoint 1>:**. The response to this prompt depends on the option you want to choose. The different options are explained below.

Toolbar:	Draw, Ellipse
Pull-down:	Draw, Ellipse
Screen:	DRAW1, Ellipse:

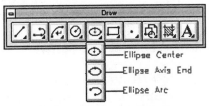

Figure 2-28 Selecting the Ellipse command from the Draw toolbar

Drawing an Ellipse Using the Axis and Eccentricity Option

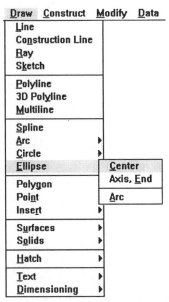

Figure 2-29 Selecting the Ellipse command from the pull-down menu

In this option you can draw an ellipse by specifying one of its axes and its eccentricity. To use this option, acknowledge the **Arc/Center/<Axis endpoint 1>:** prompt by specifying a point either by picking a point using a pointing device, or by entering its coordinates. This is the first end point of one axis of the ellipse. AutoCAD will then respond with the prompt **Axis end point 2:**. Here, specify the other end point of the axis. The angle at which the ellipse is drawn depends on the angle made by these two axis end points. Your response to the next prompt determines whether the axis is the **major axis** or the **minor axis**. The next prompt is **<Other axis distance>/Rotation:**. If you specify a distance, it is presumed as half the length of the second axis. You can also specify a point. The distance from this point to the midpoint of the first axis is again taken as half the length of this axis. The ellipse will pass through the selected point only if it is perpendicular to the midpoint of the first axis. To visually analyze the distance between the selected point and the midpoint of the first axis, AutoCAD appends an elastic line to the cross-hairs with one end fixed at the midpoint of the first axis. You can also drag the point, dynamically specifying half of the other axis distance. This helps you to visualize the ellipse. The prompt sequence for drawing an ellipse whose one axis end point is located at (3,3), the other at (6,3), and the distance of the other axis one (1) (Figure 2-30) is:

    Command: **ELLIPSE** ↵
    Arc/Center/<Axis endpoint 1>: **3,3** ↵
    Axis endpoint 2: **6,3** ↵
    <Other axis distance>/Rotation: **1** ↵

Another example for drawing an ellipse (Figure 2-31) using the **Axis and Eccentricity** option is illustrated by the following prompt sequence:

    Command: **ELLIPSE** ↵
    Arc/Center/<Axis endpoint 1>: **3,3** ↵
    Axis endpoint 2: **4,2** ↵
    <Other axis distance>/Rotation: **2** ↵

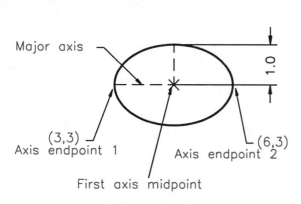

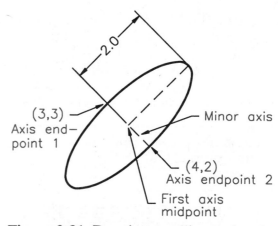

Figure 2-30 Drawing an ellipse using the Axis and Eccentricity option

Figure 2-31 Drawing an ellipse using the Axis and Eccentricity option

If you enter Rotation or R at the: **<Other axis distance>/Rotation:** prompt, the first axis specified is automatically taken as the major axis of the ellipse. The next prompt is **Rotation around major axis:**. The **major axis** is taken as the diameter line of the circle and the rotation takes place around this diameter line into the third dimension. The ellipse is formed when AutoCAD projects this rotated circle into the drawing plane. You can enter the rotation angle value between the range of **0** to **89.4** degrees only, because an angle value greater than 89.4 degrees changes the circle into a line. Instead of entering a definite angle value at the Rotation around major axis: prompt, you can specify a point relative to the midpoint of the major axis. This point can be dragged to specify the ellipse dynamically. The following is the prompt sequence for a rotation of 0 degrees around the major axis (Figure 2-32(a)).

Command: **ELLIPSE** ←⏎
Arc/Center/<Axis endpoint 1>: *Select point P1.*
Axis endpoint 2: *Select another point P2.*
<Other axis distance>/Rotation: **R** ←⏎
Rotation around major axis: **0** ←⏎

Figure 2-32 shows rotations of 45 degrees, 60 degrees, and 89.4 degrees.

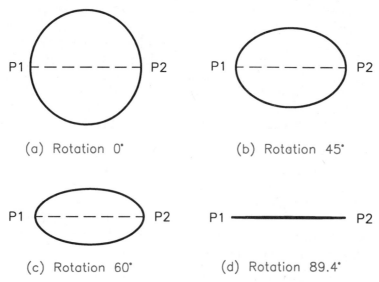

(a) Rotation 0°

(b) Rotation 45°

(c) Rotation 60°

(d) Rotation 89.4°

Figure 2-32 Rotation about the major axis

Note

The Isocircle option is not available if the Isometric suboption in the Style option of the SNAP command is set to Off. In this section the SNAP mode Isometric option is not being used.

The Arc option is not available if you have set the PELLIPSE system variable to 1.

Exercise 7

Draw an ellipse whose major axis is four units and whose rotation around this axis is 60 degrees. Draw another ellipse whose rotation around the major axis is 15 degrees.

Drawing Ellipse Using the Center and Two Axes Option

In this option you can construct an ellipse by specifying its center point, end point of one axis, and length of the other axis. The only difference between this method and the ellipse by axis and eccentricity method is that instead of the second end point of the first axis, the center of the ellipse is specified. The center of an ellipse is defined as the point of intersection of major and minor axes. In this option the first axis need not be the major axis. For example, to draw an ellipse with the center at (4,4), axis end point at (6,4) and length of the other axis as 2 units (Figure 2-33), the command sequence is:

Command: **ELLIPSE** ◄─┘
Arc/Center/<Axis endpoint 1>: **C** ◄─┘
Center of ellipse: **4,4** ◄─┘
Axis endpoint: **6,4** ◄─┘
<Other axis distance>/Rotation: **1** ◄─┘

Instead of entering distance you can enter Rotation or R at the **<Other axis distance>/ Rotation:** prompt. This takes the first axis specified as the major axis. The next prompt, **Rotation around major axis:**, prompts you to enter the rotation angle value. The rotation takes place around the major axis, which is taken as the diameter line of the circle. The rotation angle values should range from 0 to 89.4 degrees.

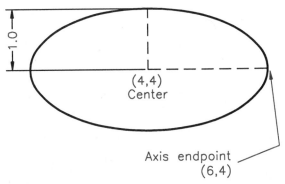

Figure 2-33 Drawing an ellipse using the Center and Two Axes option

Drawing Elliptical Arcs

You can use the Arc option of the NURBS-based ELLIPSE command (PELLIPSE=0) to draw an elliptical arc. When you enter the ELLIPSE command and select the Arc option, AutoCAD will prompt you to enter information about the geometry of the ellipse and the arc limits. You can define the arc limits by using the following options:

1. Start and End angle of the arc;
2. Start and Included angle of the arc;
3. Specifying Start and End parameters.

The angles are measured with the positive X axis and in a counterclockwise direction if AutoCAD's default set up has not been changed. The following example illustrates the use of these three options.

Example 1

Draw the following elliptical arcs:

        a. Start angle = -45   End angle = 135

        b. Start angle = -45   Included angle = 225

        c. Start parameter = @1,0   End parameter = @1<225

Specifying Start and End Angle of the Arc (Figure 2-34(a))

Command: **ELLIPSE**
Arc/Center/<Axis endpoint 1>: **A**
Arc/Center/<Axis endpoint 1>: *Select the first end point.*
Axis endpoint 2: *Select the second end point.*
<Other axis distance>/Rotation: *Select a point or enter a distance.*
Parameter/Include/<start angle>: **-45**
Parameter/Include/<end angle>: **135** *(Angle where arc ends.)*

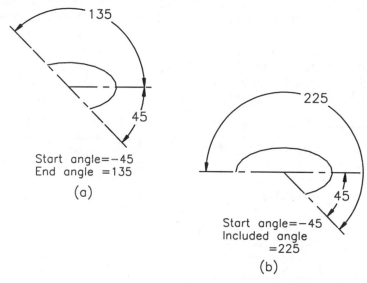

Start angle=−45
End angle =135
(a)

225
45
Start angle=−45
Included angle
=225
(b)

Figure 2-34 Drawing NURBS-based ellipses

Specifying Start and Included Angle of the Arc (Figure 2-34(b))

Command: **ELLIPSE**
Arc/Center/<Axis endpoint 1>: **A**
Arc/Center/<Axis endpoint 1>: *Select the first end point.*
Axis endpoint 2: *Select the second end point.*
<Other axis distance>/Rotation: *Select a point or enter distance.*
Parameter/Include/<start angle>: **-45**
Parameter/Include/<end angle>: **225** *(Included angle.)*

Specifying Start and End Parameters (Figure 2-35)

Command: **ELLIPSE**
Arc/Center/<Axis endpoint 1>: **A**
Arc/Center/<Axis endpoint 1>: *Select the first end point.*
Axis endpoint 2: *Select the second end point.*
<Other axis distance>/Rotation: *Select a point or enter distance.*
Parameter/Include/<start angle>: **A**
Angle/<start parameter>: **@1,0**
Angle/Include/<end parameter>: **@1<225**

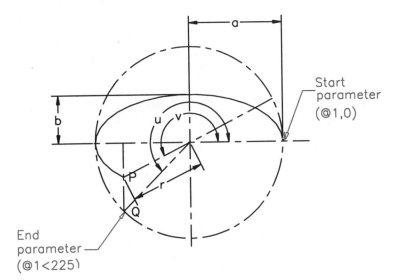

Figure 2-35 Drawing an elliptical arc by specifying the start and end parameters

Calculating Parameters for an Elliptical Arc

The start and end parameters of an elliptical arc are determined by specifying a point on the circle whose diameter is equal to the major diameter of the ellipse as shown in Figure 2-35. In this drawing, the major axis of the ellipse is 2.0 and the minor axis is 1.0. The diameter of the circle is 2.0. To determine the start and end parameters of the elliptical arc, you must specify the points on the circle. In the example, the start parameter is @1,0 and the end parameter is @1<225. Once you specify the points on the circle, AutoCAD will project these points on the major axis and determine the end point of the elliptical arc. In the figure, Q is the end parameter of the elliptical arc. AutoCAD projects point Q on the major axis and locates intersection point P, which is the end point of the elliptical arc. The coordinates of point P can be calculated by using the following equations:

The equation of an ellipse with center as origin is
$$x^2/a^2 + y^2/b^2 = 1$$

In parametric form
$$x = a * cos(u)$$
$$y = b * sin(u)$$

For the example
$$a = 1$$
$$b = 0.5$$

Therefore
$$x = 1 * cos(225) = -0.707$$
$$y = 0.5 * sin(225) = -0.353$$

The coordinates of point P are (-0.707, -0.353) with respect to the center of the ellipse.

Note:
$$v = atan(b/a*tan(u)) = end\ angle$$
$$v = atan(0.5/1*tan(225)) = 206.56°$$

Also
$$e = 1-b^2/a^2)^.5 = eccentricity$$
$$e = 1-.5^2/1^2)^.5 = .866$$
$$r = x^2 + y^2)^.5$$
$$r = .707^2 + .353^2)^.5 = 0.790$$

or using the polar equation
$$r = b/(1 - e^2 * cos(v)^2)^.5$$
$$r = .5/(1 - .866^2 * cos(206.56)^2)^.5$$
$$r = 0.790$$

Exercise 8

a. Construct an ellipse with its center at (2,3), axis end point at (4,6), and the other axis end point a distance of 0.75 units from the midpoint of the first axis.

b. Make the drawing as shown in Figure 2-36. The distance between the dotted lines is 1.0 units. Create the elliptical arcs using ELLIPSE command options.

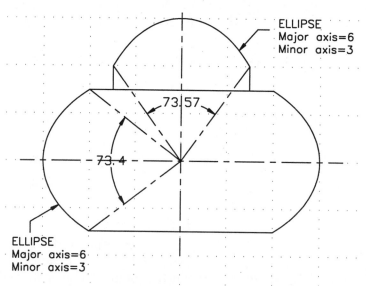

Figure 2-36 Drawing for Exercise 8(b)

DRAWING REGULAR POLYGONS

Toolbar: Draw, Rectangle, Polygon
Pull-down: Draw, Polygon, Polygon
Screen: DRAW1, Polygon:

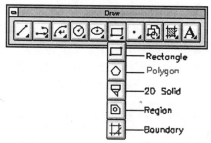

Figure 2-37 Selecting the POLYGON command from the Draw toolbar

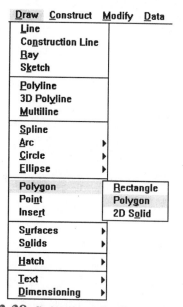

Figure 2-38 Selecting the Polygon command from the pull-down menu

A **Regular Polygon** is a closed geometric figure with equal sides and equal angles. The number of sides varies from **3** to **1024**. For example, a triangle is a three-sided polygon and a pentagon is a five-sided polygon. In AutoCAD, the **POLYGON** command is used to draw regular two-dimensional polygons. The characteristics of a polygon drawn in AutoCAD are those of a closed polyline having 0 width. You can change the width of the polyline forming the polygon. This command can be invoked from the **Draw** toolbar by selecting the **Polygon** icon in the **Rectangle** flyout (Figure 2-37), the pull-down menu (Select Draw, Polygon, Polygon, Figure 2-38), or the screen menu (Select DRAW1, Polygon:), or by typing POLYGON at the **Command:** prompt. The prompt sequence is:

Command: **POLYGON** ◄┘
Number of sides <4>:

Once you invoke the POLYGON command, it prompts you to enter the number of sides. The number of sides determines the type of polygon (for example, six sides defines a hexagon). The default value for the number of sides is four. You can change the number of sides to your requirement (in the range of 3 to 1024) and then the new value becomes the default. You can also have a different default value for the number of sides by using the **POLYSIDES** system variable. For example, if you want the default for the number of sides to be three, the prompt sequence is:

Command: **POLYSIDES** ◄┘
New value for POLYSIDES <4>: **3** ◄┘

After entering the number of sides, the next prompt displayed is **Edge/<Center of polygon>:**.

The Center of Polygon Option

The default option prompts you to select a point that is taken as the center point of the polygon. The next prompt is **Inscribed in circle/Circumscribed about circle (I/C) <I>:**. A polygon is said to be **inscribed** when it is drawn inside an imaginary circle and its vertices (corners) touch the circle (Figure 2-39). Likewise, a polygon is **circumscribed** when it is drawn outside the imaginary circle and the sides of the polygon are tangent to the circle (midpoint of each side of the polygon will lie on the circle) (Figure 2-40). If you want to have an inscribed polygon, enter INSCRIBED or I at the above-mentioned prompt. The next prompt issued is **Radius of circle:**. Here you are required to specify the radius of the circle on which all the vertices of the polygon will lie. Once you specify the radius, a polygon will be generated. If you want to select the circumscribed option, enter CIRCUMSCRIBED or C at the prompt **Inscribed in circle/Circumscribed about circle (I/C) <I>:**. After this you will be prompted to enter the radius of the circle as in the inscribed option. The inscribed or circumscribed circle is not drawn on the screen. The radius of the circle can be dynamically dragged instead of entering a numerical value. The prompt sequence for drawing an inscribed octagon, with the center at (4,4), and a radius of 1.5 units (Figure 2-39), is:

Command: **POLYGON** ◄┘
Number of sides <4>: **8** ◄┘
Edge/<Center of polygon>: **4,4** ◄┘
Inscribed in circle/Circumscribed about circle (I/C) <I>: **I** ◄┘
Radius of circle: **1.5** ◄┘

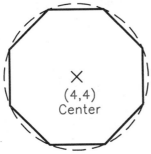

Inscribed octagon

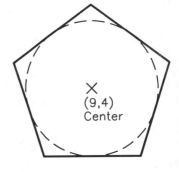

Circumscribed pentagon

Figure 2-39 Drawing an inscribed polygon using the Center of Polygon option

Figure 2-40 Drawing a circumscribed polygon using the Center of Polygon option

The prompt sequence for drawing a circumscribed pentagon (polygon having five sides), with the center at (9,4), and a radius of 1.5 units (Figure 2-40), is:

Command: **POLYGON** ←┘
Number of sides <4>: **5** ←┘
Edge/ <Center of polygon>: **9,4** ←┘
Inscribed in circle/circumscribed about circle (I/C) <I>: **C** ←┘
Radius of circle: **1.5** ←┘

Note

If you pick a point to specify the radius of an inscribed polygon, one of the vertices is positioned on the selected point. In the case of circumscribed polygons, the midpoint of an edge is placed on the point you have specified. In this manner you can specify size and rotation of the polygon.

In case of numerical specification of the radius, the bottom edge of the polygon is rotated by the prevalent snap rotation angle.

Exercise 9

Draw a circumscribed polygon of eight sides. The polygon should be drawn with the Center of Polygon method.

The Edge Option

The other method to draw a polygon is by selecting the **Edge** option. This can be done by entering EDGE or E at the **Edge/ <Center of polygon>:** prompt. The next two prompts issued are **First endpoint of edge:** and **Second endpoint of edge:**. Here you need to specify the two end points of an edge of the polygon. The polygon is drawn in a counterclockwise direction, with the two points entered defining its first edge. To draw a hexagon (six-sided polygon) using the Edge option, with the first end point of the edge at (2,4), and the second end point of the edge at (2,2.5) (Figure 2-41), the following will be the prompt sequence:

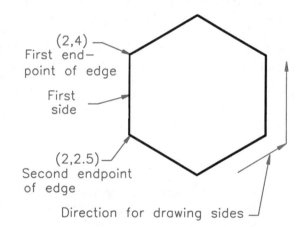

Figure 2-41 Drawing a polygon (hexagon) using the Edge option

Command: **POLYGON** ←┘
Number of sides <4>: **6** ←┘
Edge/ <Center of polygon>: **E** ←┘
First endpoint of edge: **2,4** ←┘
Second endpoint of edge: **2,2.5** ←┘

Exercise 10

Draw a polygon with 10 sides using the **Edge** option. Let the first end point of the edge be at (7,1) and the second end point at (8,2).

DRAWING TRACES

Toolbar:	Miscellaneous, Trace
Screen:	DRAW2, Trace:

Figure 2-42 Selecting the Trace command from the Miscellaneous toolbar

Traces are lines that have a thickness (specified as its width). Traces are solid-filled if the FILL mode is on. If the FILL mode is off, only the trace outline is drawn. The fill option can be accessed through the **FILL** command or the **FILLMODE** system variable. The **TRACE** command is used to draw traces and can be invoked from the **Miscellaneous** toolbar by selecting the **Trace** icon, the screen menu (Select DRAW2, Trace:), or by entering TRACE at the **Command:** prompt.

The specifications of a trace are entered just like those of a line. The difference between the LINE command and the TRACE command is that in the latter the width of the trace is entered before entering the rest of the specifications. To specify the width of the trace, you can enter the distance or select two points. AutoCAD automatically measures the distance between those two points and assumes it as the width of the trace. All of the trace segments drawn by a single TRACE command will have the same width. The default value for the width of the trace is the width of the previous trace drawn. This value is stored in the **TRACEWID** system variable; hence you can change the default setting for the width of the trace through the **TRACEWID** variable. The end points of the trace lie on the center of the trace width. The start and end of traces are always cut square and are made of TRACE segments. The drawing of each segment is suspended until you specify the next segment or you end the trace by pressing the Enter key. This is because trace ends are shaped to fit the start of the next segment. For example, to draw a solid-filled trace (Figure 2-43) with a width of 0.25 units, starting from (1,3), to point (3,3), to point (2,1), the prompt sequence is:

Command: **FILLMODE** ↵
New value for Fillmode <1>: **1** ↵
Command: **TRACE** ↵
Trace width <0.0500>: **0.25** ↵
From point: **1,3** ↵
To point: **3,3** ↵
To point: **2,1** ↵
To point: ↵

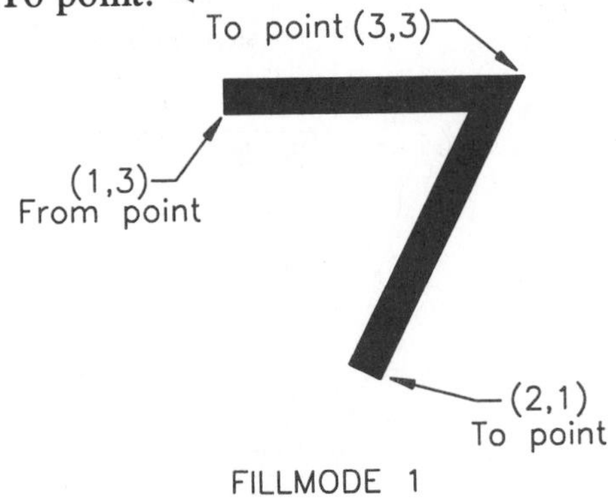

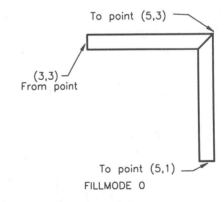

Figure 2-43 Drawing a solid trace using the TRACE command

Figure 2-44 Drawing a nonsolid trace using the TRACE command

The prompt sequence to draw a nonsolid trace (Figure 2-44) with a width of 0.25 units, starting from point (3,3), to point (5,3), to point (5,1) is:

Command: **FILLMODE** ↵
New value for FILLMODE <1>: **0** ↵

Command: **TRACE** ◄⏎
Trace width <0.2500>: **0.25** ◄⏎
From point: **3,3** ◄⏎
To point: **5,3** ◄⏎
To point: **5,1** ◄⏎
To point: ◄⏎

Note

You should always set the FILL mode off if there are many traces to be drawn because regeneration takes less time for nonsolid traces. You can turn the FILL mode on when the drawing has taken final shape, then use the REGEN command to fill the traces in the drawing.

Exercise 11

Using the Trace command, draw "Au" on the screen (both as a solid-filled trace and nonsolid trace) as shown in Figure 2-45. Assume the width of the trace = 0.20 units.

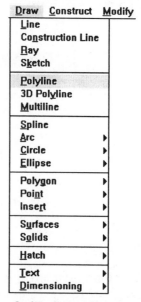

Figure 2-45 Drawing for Exercise 11

DRAWING POLYLINES

A **polyline** is defined as a line that can have different characteristics. The term polyline can be broken into two parts: poly and line. Poly is synonymous with many. This signifies that a polyline can have many features. Some of the features of polyline are:

1. Polylines, like traces, are thick lines having a desired width.
2. Polylines are very flexible and can be used to draw any shape, such as a filled circle or a doughnut.
3. Polylines can be used to draw objects in any linetype (e.g., hidden linetype).
4. Advanced editing commands can be used to edit polylines (e.g., PEDIT command).
5. A single polyline object can be formed by joining polylines and polyarcs of different thicknesses.
6. It is easy to determine the area or perimeter of a polyline feature. Also, it is easy to offset when drawing walls.

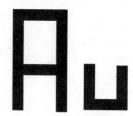

Toolbar:	Draw, Polyline
Pull-down:	Draw, Polyline
Screen:	DRAW1, Pline:

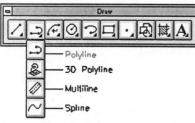

Figure 2-46 Selecting the Polyline command from the Draw toolbar

Figure 2-47 Selecting the Polyline command from the pull-down menu

The command to draw a polyline is **PLINE**. You can invoke this command from the **Draw** toolbar by selecting the **Polyline** icon in the **Polyline** flyout (Figure 2-46), the pull-down menu (Select Draw, Polyline), the screen menu (Select DRAW1, Pline:), or by entering PLINE or PL at the **Command:** prompt. A **PLINE** command fundamentally functions like the LINE command except that additional options are provided and all the segments of the polyline form a single object. After invoking the PLINE command, the next prompt is:

From point: *Pick the starting point or enter its coordinates.*
Current line width is nn.n.

Current line width is nn.n is displayed automatically, which indicates that the polyline drawn will have nn.n width. If you want the polyline to have a different width, invoke the **Width** option at the next prompt and then set the polyline width. The next prompt is:

Arc/Close/Halfwidth/Length/Undo/Width/<Endpoint of line>:

The options that can be invoked at the above prompt, depending on your requirement, are:

End Point of Line
This option is maintained as the default, and is used to specify the end point of the current polyline segment. If additional polyline segments are added to the first polyline, AutoCAD automatically makes the end point of the first polyline segment the starting point of the next polyline segment. The prompt sequence is:

Command: **PLINE** ◄─┘
From point: *Specify the starting point of the polyline.*
Current line width is 0.0000.
Arc/Close/Halfwidth/Length/Undo/Width/<Endpoint of line>: *Specify the end point of first polyline segment.*
Arc/Close/Halfwidth/Length/Undo/Width/<Endpoint of line>: *Specify the end point of the second polyline segment or give a null response to exit the command.*

Width
If the current polyline width needs to be changed, you can do this by entering W (width option) at the last prompt.

Arc/Close/Halfwidth/Length/Undo/Width/<Endpoint of line>: **W** ◄─┘

Once the Width option is selected, you are prompted for the starting width and the ending width of the polyline. You can get a tapered polyline by entering two different values at the starting width and the ending width prompts.

Starting width <0.0000>: *Specify the starting width.*
Ending width <starting width>: *Specify the ending width.*

The starting width value is taken as the default value for the ending width. Hence, to have a uniform polyline you need to give a null response (press Enter key) at the **Ending width <starting width>:** prompt. Just as in the case of traces, the start and end points of the polyline are located at the center of the line width. To draw a uniform polyline (Figure 2-48) with a width of 0.25 units, a start point at (4,5), an end point at (5,5), and the next end point at (3,3), the following will be the prompt sequence:

Command: **PLINE** ◄─┘
From point: **4,5** ◄─┘
Current line-width is 0.0000

Arc/Close/Halfwidth/Length/Undo/Width/ < Endpoint of line > : **W** ◄┘
Starting width < 0.0000 > : **0.25** ◄┘
Ending width < 0.25 > : ◄┘
Arc/Close/Halfwidth/Length/Undo/Width/ < Endpoint of line > : **5,5** ◄┘
Arc/Close/Halfwidth/Length/Undo/Width/ < Endpoint of line > : **3,3** ◄┘
Arc/Close/Halfwidth/Length/Undo/Width/ < Endpoint of line > : ◄┘

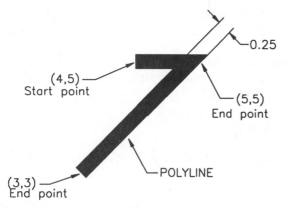

Figure 2-48 Drawing a uniform polyline using the PLINE command

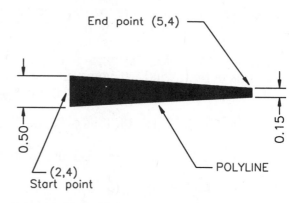

Figure 2-49 Drawing a tapered polyline using the PLINE command

To draw a tapered polyline (Figure 2-49) with a starting width of 0.5 units and an ending width of 0.15 units, the start point at (2,4), and the end point at (5,4), the prompt sequence is:

Command: **PLINE** ◄┘
From point: **2,4** ◄┘
Current line-width is 0.0000
Arc/Close/Halfwidth/Length/Undo/Width/ < Endpoint of line > : **W** ◄┘
Starting width < 0.0000 > : **0.50** ◄┘
Ending width < 0.50 > : **0.15** ◄┘
Arc/Close/Halfwidth/Length/Undo/Width/ < Endpoint of line > : **5,4** ◄┘
Arc/Close/Halfwidth/Length/Undo/Width/ < Endpoint of line > : ◄┘

Close

This option closes the polyline by drawing a polyline segment from the most recent end point to the initial start point, and on doing so exits from the PLINE command. This option can be invoked by entering Close or C at the following prompt:

Arc/Close/Halfwidth/Length/Undo/Width/ < Endpoint of line > : **C** ◄┘

The width of the closing segment can be changed by using the Width/Halfwidth option before invoking the Close option.

Halfwidth

With this option you can specify the starting and ending halfwidth of a polyline. This halfwidth distance is equal to half of the actual width of the polyline. This option can be invoked by entering Halfwidth or H at the following prompt:

Arc/Close/Halfwidth/Length/Undo/Width/ < Endpoint of line > : **H** ◄┘
Starting halfwidth < 0.0000 > : **0.12** ◄┘ *(Specify desired starting halfwidth.)*
Ending halfwidth < 0.1200 > : **0.05** ◄┘ *(Specify desired ending halfwidth.)*

Length

This option prompts you to enter the length of a new polyline segment. The new polyline segment will be the length you have entered. It will be drawn at the same angle as the last polyline segment or tangent to the previous polyarc segment. This option can be invoked by entering Length or L at the following prompt:

Arc/Close/Halfwidth/Length/Undo/Width/<Endpoint of line>: **L** ↵
Length of line: *Specify the desired length of the Pline.*

Undo

This option erases the most recently drawn polyline segment. This option can be invoked by entering Undo or U at the following prompt:

Arc/Close/Halfwidth/Length/Undo/Width/<Endpoint of line>: **U** ↵

You can use this option repeatedly until you reach the starting point of the first polyline segment. Further use of **Undo** option evokes this message:

All segments already undone

Arc

This option is used to switch from drawing polylines to drawing polyarcs, and provides you the options associated with drawing polyarcs. The **Arc** option can be invoked by entering Arc or A at the following prompt:

Arc/Close/Halfwidth/Length/Undo/Width/<Endpoint of line>: **A** ↵

The next prompt generated is:

Angle/CEnter/CLose/Direction/Halfwidth/Line/Radius/Second pt/Undo/Width/
<Endpoint of arc>:

By default the arc segment is drawn tangent to the previous segment of the polyline. The direction of the previous line, arc, or polyline segment is default for polyarc. The above prompt contains options associated with the PLINE Arc. The detailed explanation of each of these options is as follows:

Angle

This option prompts you to enter the **included angle** for the arc. If you enter a positive angle, the arc is drawn in a counterclockwise direction from the start point to the end point. If the angle specified is negative, the arc is drawn in a clockwise direction. The prompt issued for this option is:

Included angle: *Specify the included angle.*

The next prompt issued is:

Center/Radius/<Endpoint>:

Center refers to the center of the arc segment, Radius refers to the radius of the arc, and Endpoint draws the arc.

CEnter

This option prompts you to specify the center of the arc to be drawn. As mentioned before, usually the arc segment is drawn so that it is tangent to the previous polyline segment; in such cases AutoCAD determines the center of the arc automatically. Hence, the **CEnter** option provides you the freedom to choose the center of the arc segment. The CEnter option can be invoked by entering CE at the **Angle/ CEnter/ CLose/ Direction / Halfwidth / Line / Radius / Second pt / Undo / Width / <Endpoint of arc>:** prompt. Once you specify the center point, AutoCAD issues the prompt:

Angle/Length/<Endpoint>:

Angle refers to the included angle, Length refers to the length of the chord, and End point refers to the end point of the arc.

CLose
This option closes the polyline by drawing a polyarc segment from the previous end point to the initial start point, and on doing so exits from the PLINE command. The **CLose** option can be invoked by entering CL.

Direction
Usually the arc drawn with the PLINE command is tangent to the previous polyline segment. In other words, the starting direction of the arc is the ending direction of the previous segment. The **Direction** option allows you to specify **tangent direction** of your choice for the arc segment to be drawn. The next prompt is:

Direction from start point:

You can also specify the direction by specifying a point. AutoCAD takes it as a direction from the starting point. Once the direction is specified, AutoCAD prompts:

End point: *Specify the end point of arc.*

Halfwidth
This option is the same as for the Line option and prompts you to specify the starting and ending halfwidth of the arc segment.

Line
This option takes you back to the **Line mode**. You can draw polylines only in Line mode.

Radius
This option prompts you to specify the **radius** of the arc segment. The prompt sequence is:

Radius: *Specify the radius of the arc segment.*
Angle/<Endpoint>:

If you specify a point, the arc segment is drawn. If you enter Angle, you will have to specify the angle and the direction of the chord at the **Included angle:** and **Direction of chord <current>:** prompts, respectively.

Second pt
This option selects the second point of an arc in the three-point arc option. The prompt sequence is:

Second point: *Specify the second point on the arc.*
Endpoint: *Specify the third point on the arc.*

Undo
This option reverses the changes made in the previously drawn segment.

Width

This option prompts you to enter the width of the arc segment. To draw a tapered arc segment you can enter different values for the starting width and the ending width prompts. The prompt sequence is identical to that of the polyline.

Endpoint of arc

This option is maintained as the default and prompts you to specify the end point of the current arc segment. The following is the prompt sequence for drawing an arc with the start point at (3,3), the end point at (3,5), the starting width of 0.50 units, and the ending width of 0.15 units (Figure 2-50):

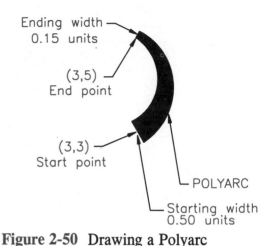

Figure 2-50 Drawing a Polyarc

Command: **PLINE** ←⏎
From point: **3,3** ←⏎
Current line-width is 0.0000
Arc/Close/Halfwidth/Length/Undo/Width/ < Endpoint of line > : **A** ←⏎
Angle/CEnter/CLose/Direction/Halfwidth/Line/Radius/Second pt/Undo/Width/
                    < Endpoint of arc > : **W** ←⏎
Starting width < current > : **0.50** ←⏎
Ending width < 0.50 > : **0.15** ←⏎
Angle/CEnter/CLose/Direction/Halfwidth/Line/Radius/Second pt/Undo/Width/
                    < Endpoint of arc > : **3,5** ←⏎
Angle/CEnter/CLose/Direction/Halfwidth/Line/Radius/Second pt/Undo/Width/
                    < Endpoint of arc > : ←⏎

Exercise 12

Draw the objects shown in Figure 2-51. Approximate the width of different polylines.

Figure 2-51 Drawing for Exercise 12

DRAWING DOUGHNUTS

Toolbar: Draw, Circle, Donut
Pull-down: Draw, Circle, Donut
Screen: DRAW1, Donut:

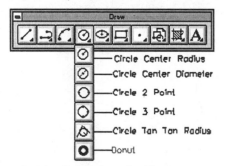

Figure 2-52 Selecting the Donut command from the Draw toolbar

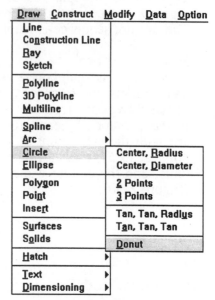

Figure 2-53 Selecting the Donut command from the pull-down menu

In AutoCAD the **DOUGHNUT** or **DONUT** command is issued to draw an object that looks like a filled circle ring called a doughnut. Actually AutoCAD's doughnuts are made of two semi-circular polyarcs having a certain width. Hence the DONUT command allows you to draw a thick circle. The doughnuts can have any inside and outside diameter. If the FILLMODE is off, the doughnuts look like circles (if the inside diameter is zero), or concentric circles (if the inside diameter is not zero). You can also select a point for the center of the doughnut anywhere on the screen with the help of a pointing device. The DOUGHNUT command can be invoked from the **Draw** toolbar by selecting the **Donut** icon in the **Circle** flyout (Figure 2-52), from the pull-down menu (Select Draw, Circle, Donut, Figure 2-53), from the screen menu (Select DRAW1, Donut:), or by entering DONUT at the **Command:** prompt. The prompt sequence for drawing doughnuts is:

> Command: **DOUGHNUT** or **DONUT** ←┘
> Inside diameter <current>: *Specify the inner diameter of the donut.*
> Outside diameter <current>: *Specify the outer diameter of the donut.*
> Center of doughnut: *Specify the center of the donut.*
> Center of doughnut: *Specify the center of the donut to draw more donuts of previous*
> *specifications or give a null response to exit.*

The defaults for inside and outside diameters are the respective diameters of the most recent doughnut drawn. The values for the inside diameter and outside diameter are saved in the **DONUTID** and **DONUTOD** system variables. You can specify a new diameter of your choice by entering a numeric value or specifying two points to indicate the diameter. A solid-filled circle is drawn by specifying the inside diameter as zero (FILLMODE is on). Once the diameter specification is completed, the doughnuts are formed at the cross-hairs and can be placed anywhere on the screen. The location at which you want the doughnuts to be drawn has to be specified at the **Center of doughnut:** prompt. You can enter the coordinates of the point at that prompt or specify the point by dragging the center point. Once you have specified the center of the doughnut, AutoCAD repeats the **Center of doughnut:** prompt. As you go on specifying the locations for the center point, doughnuts with the specified diameters at specified locations are drawn. To end the DONUT command, you should give a null response to this prompt by pressing the Enter key. Since doughnuts are circular polylines, the doughnut can be edited with the **PEDIT** command or any other editing command that can be used to edit polylines.

Example 2

If you want to draw a doughnut that is not filled (Figure 2-54), with an inside diameter of 0.75 units, an outside diameter of 2.0 units, and centered at (2,2), the following is the prompt sequence:

Command: **FILLMODE** ◄┘
New value for FILLMODE <1>: **0** ◄┘
Command: **DONUT** ◄┘
Inside diameter <0.5000>: **0.75** ◄┘
Outside diameter <1.000>: **2** ◄┘
Center of doughnut: **2,2** ◄┘
Center of doughnut: ◄┘

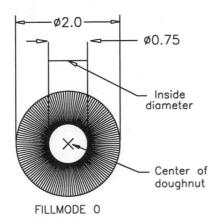

FILLMODE 0

Figure 2-54 Drawing a non-filled doughnut using the DONUT command

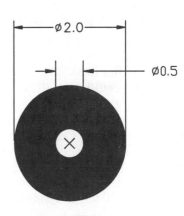

FILLMODE 1

Figure 2-55 Drawing a filled doughnut using the DONUT command

The following is the prompt sequence for drawing a filled doughnut (Figure 2-55) with inside diameter of 0.5 units, outside diameter of 2.0 units, centered at a specified point.

Command: **FILLMODE** ◄┘
New value for FILLMODE <1>: **1** ◄┘
Command: **DONUT** ◄┘
Inside diameter <0.7500>: **0.50** ◄┘
Outside diameter <2.000>: **2** ◄┘
Center of doughnut: *Specify a point.*
Center of doughnut: ◄┘

To draw a solid-filled doughnut with an outside diameter of 2.0 units (Figure 2-56), the following is the prompt sequence:

Command: **DOUGHNUT** ◄┘
Inside diameter <0.5000>: **0** ◄┘
Outside diameter <2.000>: **2** ◄┘
Center of doughnut: *Pick a point.*
Center of doughnut: ◄┘

Doughnut with inside diameter zero

Figure 2-56 Solid-filled doughnut

DRAWING POINTS

Toolbar: Draw, Point
Pull-down: Draw, Point
Screen: DRAW1, Point:

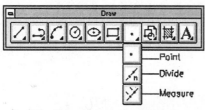

Figure 2-57 Selecting the Point command from the Draw toolbar

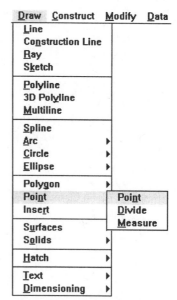

Figure 2-58 Selecting the Point command from the pull-down menu

The **point** is the basic drawing object. Points are invaluable in building a drawing file. To draw a point anywhere on the screen, AutoCAD provides you with the **POINT** command. The POINT command can be invoked from the **Draw** toolbar by selecting the **Point** icon in the **Point** flyout (Figure 2-57), from the pull-down menu (Select Draw, Point, Point, Figure 2-58), or from the screen menu (Select DRAW2, Point:). You can also invoke the POINT command by entering POINT at the **Command:** prompt.

Command: **POINT** ←┘
Point: *Specify the location where you want to plot the point.*

When a point is drawn a mark appears on the screen. This mark is known as a **blip** and is the construction marker for the point. The blip mark is cleared once the screen is redrawn with the **REDRAW** command and a point of the specified point type is left on the screen. If you invoke the **POINT** command by entering POINT at the **Command:** prompt, you can draw only one point in a single point command. On the other hand, if you invoke the POINT command from the toolbar, the pull-down menu or the screen menu, you can draw as many points as you desire in a single command. In this case you can exit from the POINT command by pressing the Esc key.

Changing the Point Type

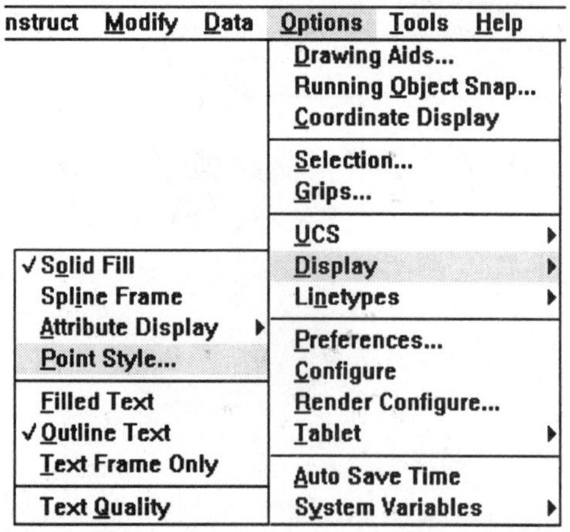

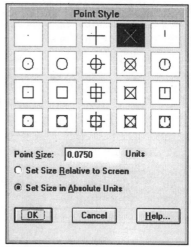

Figure 2-59 Selecting Point Style from the pull-down menu

Figure 2-60 Point Style dialogue box

The type of point drawn is controlled by the **PDMODE** (Point Display MODE) system variable. The point type can be set either from the **Point Style** dialogue box or by entering PDMODE at the **Command**: prompt. There are 20 combinations of point types. The **Point Style** dialogue box can be accessed from the pull-down menu (Select Options, Display, Point Style...) or the screen menu (Select DRAW2, Point:, DDptype). You can select a point style in this dialogue box by clicking your pointing device on the point style of your choice. A box is formed around that particular point style to acknowledge the selection made. Next, click on the OK button. Now all the points will be drawn in the selected style until you change it to a new style.

You can also invoke **PDMODE** from the screen menu (Select DRAW2, Point:, Pdmode), or by entering PDMODE at the **Command:** prompt and changing its value to that of required point type.

Command: **PDMODE** ◄─┘
New value for PDMODE <current>: *Enter the new value*.
Command: **POINT** ◄─┘
Point: *Select a point*.

The PDMODE values for different point types are:

1. A value of **0** is the default for the PDMODE variable and results in generation of a dot at the specified point.

2. A value of **1** for the PDMODE variable results in no generation at the specified point.

3. A value of **2** for the PDMODE variable results in generation of a plus mark (+) through the specified point.

4. A value of **3** for the PDMODE variable results in generation of a cross mark (X) through the specified point.

5. A value of **4** for the PDMODE variable results in generation of a vertical line in the upward direction from the specified point.

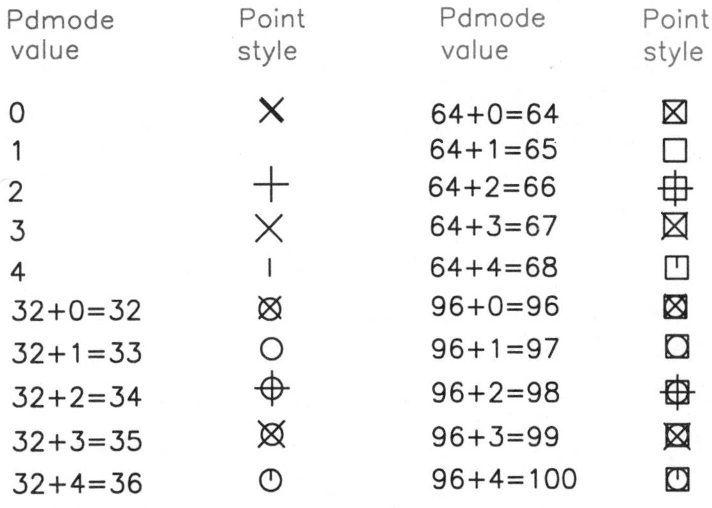

Pdmode value	Point style	Pdmode value	Point style
0	X	64+0=64	⊠
1		64+1=65	□
2	+	64+2=66	⊞
3	X	64+3=67	⊠
4	l	64+4=68	⊓
32+0=32	⊗	96+0=96	⊠
32+1=33	O	96+1=97	⊡
32+2=34	⊕	96+2=98	⊞
32+3=35	⊗	96+3=99	⊠
32+4=36	⊙	96+4=100	⊡

Figure 2-61 Different point types

6. When you add **32** to the PDMODE values of 0 to 4, a circle is generated around the symbol obtained by the original PDMODE value. For example, to draw a point having a cross mark and a circle around it, the value of the PDMODE variable will be $3+32 = 35$. Similarly, you can have a square around the symbol generated by the PDMODE of value 0 to 4 by adding **64**

to the original PDMODE value. For example, to draw a point having a plus mark and a square around it, the value of the PDMODE variable will be **2+64 = 66**. You can also have a square and a circle around the symbol generated by the PDMODE of value 0 to 4 by adding **96** to the original PDMODE value. For example, to draw a point having a dot mark and a circle and a square around it, the value of the PDMODE variable will be **0+96 = 96**

When the value of the PDMODE is changed or a new point type is selected from the dialogue box, all of the previously drawn points retain their styles until the drawing is regenerated. After REGEN, all of the points on the drawing are drawn in the shape designated by the current value of the PDMODE variable. The REGEN command does the calculations for all the objects on the screen and draws them according to the new values obtained upon calculation.

Exercise 13

Check what types of points are drawn for each values of PDMODE variable. Use the REGEN command to regenerate the drawing and notice the change in the previously drawn points.

Changing the Point Size

The system variable, **PDSIZE** (Point Display SIZE) governs the size of the point (except for the PDMODE values of **0** and **1**). The size of a point can be set from the **Point Style** dialogue box (Figure 2-60), by entering the desired point size in the **Point Size** edit box. The point size can also be set by invoking Pdsize from the screen menu (Select DRAW2, Point:, Pdsize) or by entering PDSIZE at the **Command:** prompt and then changing its value to a new one. A value of 0 for the PDSIZE variable generates the point at 5 percent of the graphics area height. A positive value for PDSIZE defines an absolute size for the point. This can also be specified by

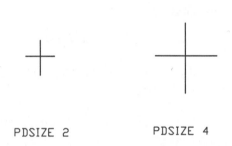

PDSIZE 2   PDSIZE 4

Figure 2-62 Changing point size using the PDSIZE variable

picking the **Set Size in Absolute Units** radio button in the Point Style dialogue box. If the PDSIZE is negative or if the **Set Size Relative to Screen** radio button is picked in the dialogue box, the size is taken as percentage of the viewport size and as such the appearance (size) of the point is not altered by the use of the ZOOM command (the ZOOM command should perform regeneration). For example, a setting of 5 makes the point five units high; a setting of -5 makes the point 5 percent of the current drawing area. The prompt sequence for changing the size of the point is:

Command: **PDSIZE** ↵
New value for PDSIZE <0.000>: **1** ↵
Command: **POINT** ↵
Point: *Select a point*.

PDMODE and PDSIZE values can also be changed through the SETVAR command.

Exercise 14

a. Try out various combinations of the PDMODE and PDSIZE variables.

b. Check the difference between the points generated from negative values of PDSIZE and points generated from positive values of PDSIZE. Use the ZOOM command to zoom in, if needed.

SELF EVALUATION TEST

Answer the following questions and then compare your answers with the correct answers given at the end of this chapter.

1. Different options for drawing arcs can be invoked by entering the ARC command and then selecting an appropriate letter. (T/F)

2. A negative value for chord length in the **St,C,Len** option results in the largest possible arc, also known as the major arc. (T/F)

3. If you do not specify a start point but just press the Enter key or pick the **Continue** option, the start point and direction of the arc will be taken from the end point and ending direction of the previous line or arc drawn on the current screen. (T/F)

4. If you pick a point to specify the radius of a circumscribed polygon, one of the vertices is positioned on the selected point. In the case of inscribed polygons, the midpoint of an edge is placed on the point you have specified. (T/F)

5. When the value of PDMODE is changed, all the previously drawn points also change to the type designated by the PDMODE variable when the drawing is regenerated. (T/F)

6. Fill in the Command, entries, and operations required to draw an arc whose start point is at (3,3), center at (2,3), and which has an included angle of 80 degrees:
   Command: _____
   Center/<Start point>: _____
   Center/End/<Second point>: _____
   Center: _____
   Angle/Length of chord/<End point>: _____
   Included angle: _____

7. Fill in the Command, entries, and operations required to draw an ellipse whose first and second axis end points are at (4,5) and (7,5), respectively, and the distance of the other axis is 1 unit:
   Command: _____
   <Axis endpoint 1>/Center: _____
   Axis endpoint 2: _____
   <Other axis distance>/Rotation: _____

8. Fill in the Command entries and operations needed to erase the most recently drawn object in a figure comprising many objects:
   Command: _____
   Select objects: _____
   1 found
   Select objects: _____

9. The system variable _____ governs the size of the point.

10. The maximum number of sides a polygon can have in AutoCAD is _____ .

11. The Fill option can be accessed through the _____ command or the _____ system variable.

12. The values for the inside and outside diameter of a doughnut are saved in the _____ and _____ system variables.

13. Summarize the various ways of drawing an ellipse._____

14. What is the function of the FILLMODE system variable? _____
_____

15. Define inscribed and circumscribed polygons._____
_____

REVIEW QUESTIONS

Answer the following questions.

1. The default method of drawing an arc is the three-point option. (T/F)

2. An arc can be drawn only in a counterclockwise direction. (T/F)

3. In the **St,C,Ang** option, if the specified angle is negative, the arc is drawn in a counterclockwise direction. (T/F)

4. In the **St,C,Len** option, the arc is drawn in a counterclockwise fashion from the start point.(T/F)

5. In the **St,C,Len** option, positive chord length gives the largest possible arc (known as the major arc) with that length. (T/F)

6. A unit radius arc with an included angle of 45 degrees has a chord length of 0.765 units. (T/F)

7. In the **St,E,Rad** option a positive radius value results in a major arc, while a negative radius value results in a minor arc. (T/F)

8. In the **St,E,Dir** option, the start of the arc is established tangent to the specified direction. (T/F)

9. Using the **RECTANGLE** command, the rectangle generated on the screen is treated as a combination of different objects, hence individual sides can be edited immediately. (T/F)

10. The **ELLIPSE** command draws an ellipse as a composition of small arc segments forming a polyline. (T/F)

11. The characteristics of a polygon drawn in AutoCAD are those of a closed polyline having zero width and no tangent specification. (T/F)

12. If the FILL mode is off, only the trace outlines are drawn. (T/F)

13. Regeneration or redrawing takes the same amount of time for both non-solid filled traces and solid-filled traces. (T/F)

14. Polylines can be used with any type of line. (T/F)

15. Doughnuts in AutoCAD are circular polylines. (T/F)

16. After regeneration, all the points on the drawing are drawn in the shape designated by the current value of the PDMODE variable. (T/F)

17. The system variable PDSIZE controls the size of the point except for the PDMODE values of 0 and 1. (T/F)

18. While a selection set is being formed using the **Last** option, only one object is selected, even if you use the Last option a number of times. (T/F)

19. Fill in the Command, entries, and operations required to draw an arc tangent to the end point of a previously drawn arc:
Command: _____
Center/ < Start point > : _____
End point: _____

20. Fill in the Command, entries, and operations required to draw an ellipse whose first and second axis end points are at (2,3) and (5,3) respectively with a rotation of 45 degrees around the major axis:
Command: _____
Arc/Center/ < Axis endpoint 1 > : _____
Axis endpoint 2: _____
< Other axis distance > /Rotation: _____
Rotation around major axis: _____

21. Give the Command, entries, and operations required to draw an ellipse by the center and two axes method. The center of the ellipse is located at (5,6), axis end point at (6,6) and the width of the other axis is 2 units:
Command: _____
Arc/Center/ < Axis endpoint > : _____
Center of ellipse: _____
Axis endpoint: _____
< Other axis distance > /Rotation: _____

22. Fill in the Command, entries, and operations needed to draw a pentagon with the edge option, where the first and second end points of the edge are at (4,2) and (3,3), respectively.
Command: _____
Number of sides <4> : _____
Edge/ < Center of polygon > : _____
First endpoint of edge: _____
Second endpoint of edge: _____

23. Traces are solid filled if _____ is on.

24. To save time, you can turn on the Fill mode when the drawing has taken the final shape and then use the _____ command to fill the traces in the drawing.

25. The _____ option of the **PLINE** command closes the polyline by drawing a polyline segment from the most recent end point to the initial start point.

26. The _____ option of the **PLINE** command is used to switch from drawing polylines to drawing polyarcs, and provides you the options associated with the drawing of polyarcs.

27. The type of point drawn is controlled by the _____ system variable.

28. You can have _____ combinations of point types.

29. A value of zero for the PDSIZE variable generates the point at _____ of the graphics area height.

30. A positive value for PDSIZE defines an _____ size for the point.

EXERCISES

Exercise 15

Make the drawing shown in Figure 2-63. The distance between the dotted lines is 1.0 units. Create the radii by using appropriate ARC command options.

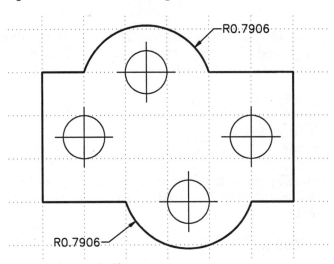

Figure 2-63 Drawing for Exercise 15

Exercise 16

Make the drawing shown in Figure 2-64. The distance between the dotted lines is 1.0 units. Create the radii using appropriate ARC command options.

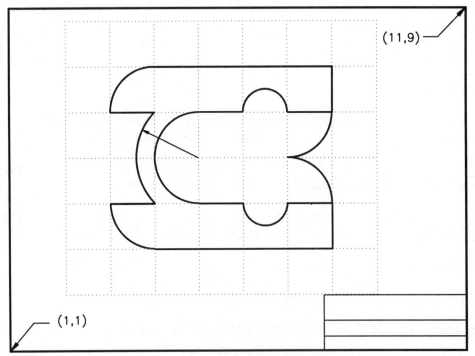

Figure 2-64 Drawing for Exercise 16

Exercise 17

Make the drawing shown in Figure 2-65. Create the radii using appropriate ARC command options.

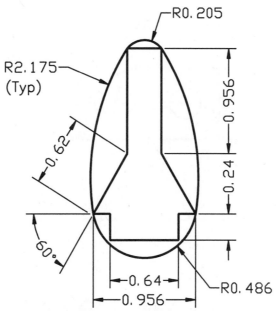

Figure 2-65 Drawing for Exercise 17

Exercise 18

Make the drawing shown in Figure 2-66. The distance between the dotted lines is 0.5 units. Create the ellipses using ELLIPSE command.

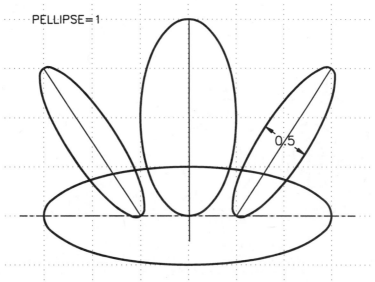

Figure 2-66 Drawing for Exercise 18

Exercise 19

Use the appropriate options of the CIRCLE, LINE, and ARC commands to generate the drawing in Figure 2-67. The dimensions are as shown in the figure. Use the POINT command to draw the center points of the circles.

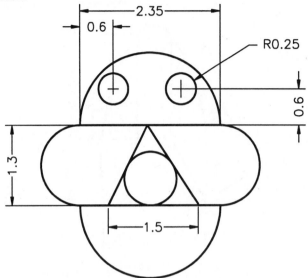

Figure 2-67 Drawing for Exercise 19

Exercise 20

Make the drawing shown in Figure 2-68. You must use only the LINE, CIRCLE, and ARC command options. Use the POINT command to draw the center points of the circles and arcs.

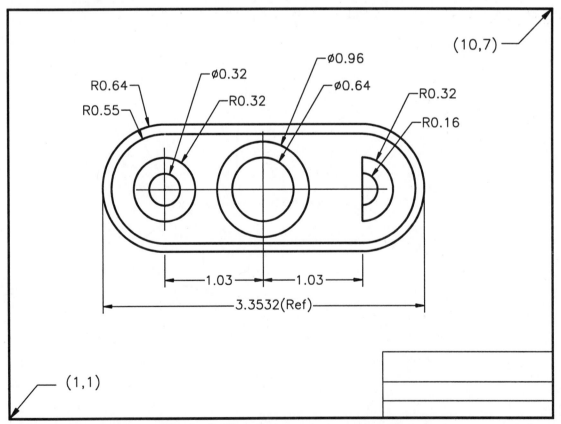

Figure 2-68 Drawing for Exercise 20

Exercise 21

Draw Figure 2-69 using the POLYGON and CIRCLE commands. The drawing must be drawn according to the given dimensions. Use the POINT command to draw the center lines going through the circles.

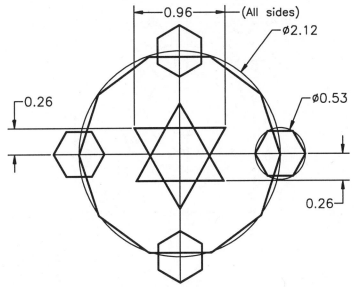

Figure 2-69 Drawing for Exercise 21

Exercise 22

Generate the drawing in Figure 2-70 using only the RECTANGLE command.

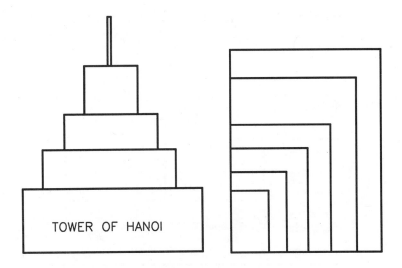

Figure 2-70 Drawing for Exercise 22

Exercise 23

Draw Figure 2-71 using only the LINE, CIRCLE, and ARC commands or their options.

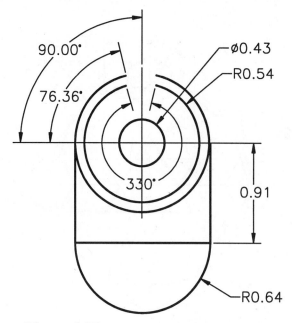

Figure 2-71 Drawing for Exercise 23

Exercise 24

Use relevant commands to draw Figure 2-72. The figure you draw should resemble the given figure as much as possible.

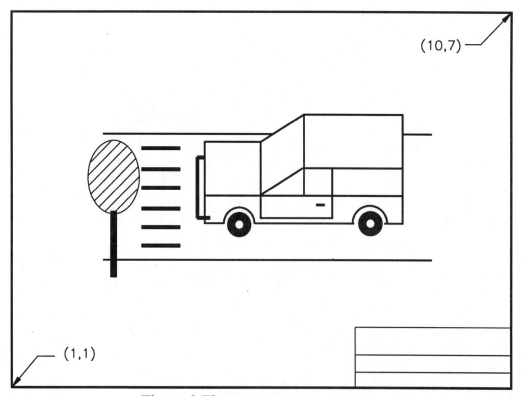

Figure 2-72 Drawing for Exercise 24

Exercise 25

Draw Figure 2-73 using the PLINE command and its options.

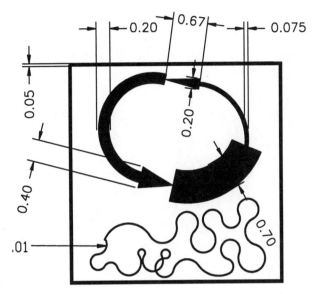

Figure 2-73   Drawing for Exercise 25

Answers:

The following are the correct answers to the questions in the self evaluation test.
1 - T, **2** - T, **3** - T, **4** - F, **5** - T, **6** - ARC, 3,3 / C, 2,3 / A / 80, **7** - ELLIPSE / 4,5 / 7,5
/ 1, **8** - ERASE / LAST, ⏎ , **9** - PDSIZE, **10** - 1024, **11** - FILL / FILLMODE, **12** -
DONUTID / DONUTOD, **13** - NURBS Ellipse, Defining two axis end points of ellipse,
Defining center and axis end point of ellipse, **14** - Turns the fill on, **15** - An inscribed polygon
is drawn inside the circle and a circumscribed polygon is drawn outside the circle

Chapter **3**

Drawing Aids

Learning objectives

After completing this chapter, you will be able to:
- Set up units using the Units Control dialogue box and the UNITS command.
- Set up and determine limits for a given drawing.
- Determine limits for engineering, architectural, and metric drawings.
- Set up layers and assign colors and linetypes to them.
- Set up grid, snap, and ortho modes based on the drawing requirements.
- Use object snaps and understand their applications.
- Combine object snap modes and set up running object snap modes.

In this chapter you will learn about the drawing setup. This involves several factors that can affect the quality and accuracy of your drawing. This chapter contains a detailed description of how to set up units, limits, and layers. You will also learn about some of the drawing aids like grid, snap, and ortho. These aids will help you to draw accurately and quickly.

SETTING UNITS

Using the Units Control Dialogue Box

Pull-down:	Data, Units
Screen:	DATA, Units:

The **UNITS** command is used to choose a format for the units of distance and angle measurement. You can use the **Units Control** dialogue box to set the units. This dialogue box can be invoked from the pull-down menu (Select Data, Units..., Figure 3-1), from the screen menu (Select DATA, Units:), or by entering **DDUNITS** at the **Command:** prompt. From the **Units Control** dialogue box (Figure 3-2) you can select a desired format of units or angles by selecting the button to the left of the item. You can also select the precision of units and angles by selecting the arrow in the **Precision:** edit box (Figure 3-3).

Data	Options	Tools	Help
Object Creation...			
Layers...			
Color			
Linetype...			
Multiline Style...			
Text Style			
Dimension Style...			
Shape File...			
Units...			
Drawing Limits			
Time			
Status			
Rename...			
Purge		▶	

Figure 3-1 Selecting Units from the pull-down menu

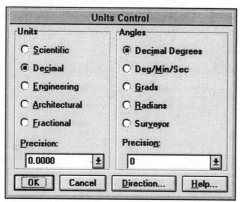

Figure 3-2 Units Control dialogue box

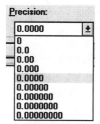

Figure 3-3 Selecting Precision from the
Units Control dialogue box

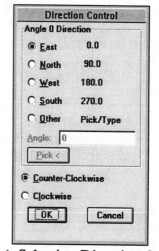

Figure 3-4 Selecting Direction from the
Units Control dialogue box

Specifying Units Format

You can use the **Units Control** dialogue box
to specify the units that you want to use in
the drawing. You can choose one of the
following five formats:

1. **Scientific**
2. **Decimal**
3. **Engineering**
4. **Architectural**
5. **Fractional**

If you select the Scientific, Decimal, or Fractional format, you can enter the distances or
coordinates in any of these formats; i.e., scientific, decimal, or fractional. You cannot enter
distances or coordinates in engineering or architectural units. In the following example, the
units are set as decimal, scientific, fractional, and decimal and fractional units to enter the
coordinates of different points.:

```
Command: LINE ←
From point: 1.75,0.75 ←          (Decimal.)
To point: 1.75E+1,3.5E+0 ←       (Scientific.)
To point: 10-3/8,8-3/4 ←         (Fractional.)
To point: 0.5,17/4 ←             (Decimal and fractional.)
```

If you choose the Engineering or Architectural format, you can enter the distances or
coordinates in any formats; i.e., scientific, decimal, engineering, architectural, or fractional.
In the following example the units are set as architectural, hence different formats are used to
enter the coordinates of points:

```
Command: LINE ←
From point: 1-3/4,3/4 ←          (Fractional.)
To point: 1'1-3/4",3-1/4 ←       (Architectural.)
```

To point: **0'10.375,0'8.75** ◄┘   *(Engineering.)*
To point: **0.5,4-1/4"** ◄┘   *(Decimal and engineering.)*

Note

The inch symbol (") is optional. For example, 1'1-3/4" is same as 1'1-3/4 or 3/4" is same as 3/4.

You cannot use the feet (') or inch (") symbols if you have selected Scientific, Decimal, or Fractional unit formats.

Specifying Angle Format

You can choose one of the following five angle measuring systems:

1. **Decimal degrees**
2. **Degrees/minutes/seconds**
3. **Grads**
4. **Radians**
5. **Surveyor's units**

You can enter the angle in the Decimal, Degrees/minutes/seconds, Grads, or Radians system, but you cannot enter the angle in Surveyor's units. However, if you select Surveyor's units, you can enter the angles in any of the five systems. In the following example the system of angle measure is Surveyor's units and different systems of angle measure are used to define the angle of the line:

Command: **LINE** ◄┘
From point: **3,3** ◄┘
To point: **@3<45.5** ◄┘   *(Decimal degrees.)*
To point: **@3<90d30'45"** ◄┘   *(Degrees/min/sec.)*
To point: **@3<75g** ◄┘   *(Grads.)*
To point: **@3<N45d30'E** ◄┘   *(Surveyor's units.)*

In **Surveying units** you must specify the bearing angle that the line makes with the north-south direction (Figure 3-4). For example, if you want to define an angle of 60 degrees with North, in the surveying units the angle will be specified as N60dE. Similarly you can specify angles like S50dE, S50dW, N75dW, as shown in Figure 3-5. You cannot specify an angle that exceeds 90 degrees (N120E). The angles can also be specified in **radians** or **grads**. 180 degrees is equal to **PI** (3.14159) radians. You can convert degrees into radians or radians into degrees using the following relations:

Radians = Degrees x 3.14159 / 180
Degrees = Radians x 180 / 3.14159

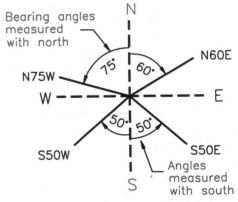

Figure 3-5 Specifying angles in surveying units

Grads are generally used in land surveying. There are 400 grads or 360 degrees in a circle. A 90-degree angle is equal to 100 grads.

In AutoCAD, by default, the angles are positive if measured in counterclockwise direction. The angles are negative if measured clockwise. If you want the angles measured positive in clockwise direction, pick the **Clockwise** button. Now the positive angles will be measured in clockwise direction and the negative angles measured in counterclockwise direction.

Using UNITS Command

You can also set up units by entering **UNITS** at the **Command:** prompt. The prompt sequence is:

Command: **UNITS** ◄──┘

The next screen shows five formats and their examples. They are:

Report formats:	(Examples)
1. Scientific	1.55E+01
2. Decimal	15.50
3. Engineering	1'-3.50"
4. Architectural	1'-3 1/2"
5. Fractional	15 1/2

With the exception of the Engineering and Architectural formats, these formats can be used with any basic units of measurement. For example, Decimal mode is perfect for metric units as well as decimal English units.

Enter choice, 1 to 5 <default>:

AutoCAD is now waiting for you to choose a format of your choice. After the selection is made, AutoCAD will prompt you to select the precision required depending on the chosen format. For choice 1, 2, or 3 the next prompt says:

Number of digits to the right of decimal point (0 to 8) <default>:

If the default value is acceptable to you, press the Enter key; otherwise, enter your choice. For example, the number 2.1250 has four digits to the right of decimal point; therefore, you will enter 4 at this prompt. For choices 4 and 5 the prompt says:

Denominator of smallest fraction to display
(1, 2, 4, 8, 16, 32, 64, 128 or 256) <default>:

You can now enter your choice or choose default by hitting the Enter key. For example, if you want the distances or coordinates measured up to 1/64 (2-1/64), enter 64. After entering the format and precision for distances and coordinates, the UNITS command proceeds to angles and allows you to select any one of the five listed systems of angle measurement.

Systems of angle measure:	(Examples)
1. Decimal degrees	45.0000
2. Degrees/minutes/seconds	45d0'0"
3. Grads	50.0000g
4. Radians	0.7854r
5. Surveyor's units	N 45d0'0" E

Enter choice, 1 to 5 <default>:
Number of fractional places for display of angles (0 to 8) <default>:

After you select the system of angle measure and precision to display angles, you must choose a direction for angle measurement. The prompt says:

```
Direction for angle 0:
        East        3 o'clock       = 0
        North       12 o'clock      = 90
        West        9 o'clock       = 180
        South       6 o'clock       = 270
Enter direction for angle 0 <current>:
```

You can now choose any starting direction to measure angles. In the default mode, angle measurement always starts from 0 degrees corresponding to east. You can enter a new direction or press the Enter key to select 0 degrees. The next prompt says:

Do you want angles measured clockwise? <current>:

In AutoCAD the default is angles measured in a counterclockwise direction. To choose this default enter **N**. If you want angles measured clockwise enter **Y**. If you enter N, then a positive angle is measured in a counterclockwise direction and a negative angle is measured clockwise. However, if you enter Y, a positive angle is measured clockwise and a negative angle is measured counterclockwise. This is the last prompt for setting the units and is followed by the **Command:** prompt.

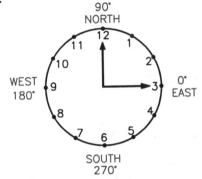

Figure 3-6 N, S, E, W directions

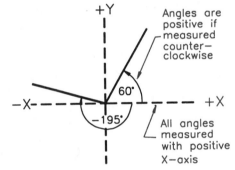

Figure 3-7 Measuring angles counterclockwise with positive X-axis (default)

Example 1

In this example we will set the units for a drawing according to the following specifications:

1. Set **UNITS** to fractional with the denominator of the smallest fraction equal to 32.
2. Set the angular measurement to surveyor's units with the number of fractional places for display of angles equal to zero.
3. Set the direction to 90 degrees (north) and the direction of measurement of angles to clockwise (angles measured positive in clockwise direction).

Command: **UNITS** ◄┘

Report formats: (Examples)

```
        1. Scientific          1.55E+01
        2. Decimal             15.50
        3. Engineering         1'-3.50"
        4. Architectural       1'-3 1/2"
        5. Fractional          15 1/2
```

With the exception of Engineering and Architectural formats, these formats can be used with any basic units of measurement. For example, Decimal mode is perfect for metric units as well as decimal English units.

Enter choice, 1 to 5 <default>: **5** ◄⏎
Denominator of smallest fraction to display.
(1,2,4,8,16,32, 64, 128 or 256) <default>: **32** ◄⏎

Systems of angle measure: (Examples)

    1. Decimal degrees   45.0000
    2. Degrees/minutes/seconds   45d0'0"
    3. Grads   50.0000g
    4. Radians   0.7854r
    5. Surveyor's units   N 45d0'0" E

Enter choice, 1 to 5 <default>: **5** ◄⏎
Number of fractional places for display of angles (0 to 8) <default>: **0** ◄⏎

Direction for angle E:
    East   3 o'clock   = E
    North   12 o'clock   = N
    West   9 o'clock   = W
    South   6 o'clock   = S

Enter direction for angle E <current>: **N** ◄⏎
Do you want angles measured clockwise? <current>: **Y** ◄⏎

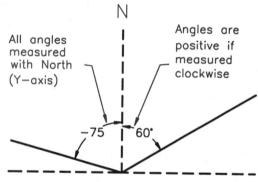

Figure 3-8 Angles measured with North (Y-axis)

With the units set, you will draw Figure 3-9 using polar coordinates. Here the units are fractional and the **angles are measured with north** (90-degree axis). Also, the angles are measured **positive** in a clockwise direction and **negative** in a counterclockwise direction.

Command: **LINE** ◄⏎
From point: **2,2** ◄⏎
To point: **@2.0<0** ◄⏎
To point: **@2.0<60** ◄⏎
To point: **@1<180** ◄⏎
To point: **@1<90** ◄⏎
To point: **@1<180** ◄⏎
To point: **@2.0<60** ◄⏎
To point: **@0.5<90** ◄⏎
To point: **@2.0<180** ◄⏎
To point: **C** ◄⏎

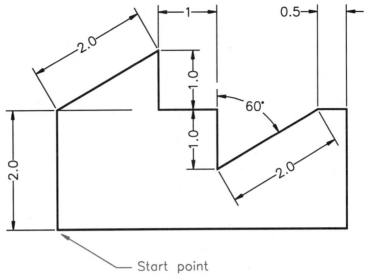

Figure 3-9 Drawing for Example 1

Forcing Default Angles

When you define the direction by specifying the angle, the output of the angle depends on the following (Figure 3-10):

Angular unit
Angle direction
Angle base

For example, if you are using AutoCAD's default setting, <70 represents an angle of 70 in decimal degrees with the positive X-axis measured counterclockwise. The decimal degrees represent **angular unit**, X-axis represents the **angle base**, and counterclockwise represents the **angle direction**. If you have changed the default settings for measuring

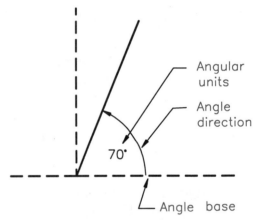

Figure 3-10 Angular units, direction, and base

angles, it might be confusing to enter the angles. AutoCAD lets you bypass the current settings by entering < < or < < < before the angle. If you enter < < before the angle, AutoCAD will bypass the current angle settings and use the angle as decimal degrees with the default angle base and default angle direction (angles are referenced with positive X-axis and are positive if measured counterclockwise). If you enter < < < in front of the angle, AutoCAD will use current angular units, but it will bypass the current settings of angle base and angle direction and use the default angle setting (angles are referenced with positive X-axis and are positive if measured counterclockwise).

In Example 1, you have changed the current settings and made the system of angle measure radians, angle base north, and the direction clockwise. Now if you enter <1.04r, all the current settings will be taken into consideration and you will get an angle of 1.04 radians, measured in a clockwise direction from the positive Y-axis (Figure 3-11a). If you enter < <60. AutoCAD will bypass the current settings and reference the angle with positive X-axis, measuring 60 degrees in a counterclockwise direction (Figure 3-11b). If you enter < < <1.04r, AutoCAD will use the current angular units but will bypass the current angle base and angle direction. Hence, the angle will be referenced with positive X-axis, measuring 1.04 radians in a counterclockwise direction (Figure 3-11c).

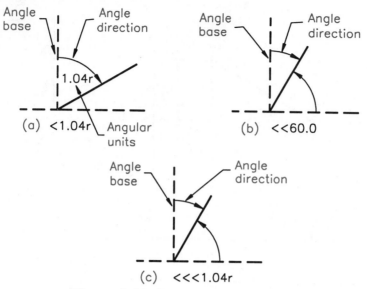

Figure 3-11 Forcing default angles

The effect of using the above-mentioned left angle brackets is summarized in the following table.

Angle prefix	Angular units	Angle direction	Angle base	Example
<	current	current	current	<1.04r
<<	degrees	default	default	<<60.0
<<<	current	default	default	<<<1.04r

LIMITS COMMAND

> **Pull-down:** Data, Drawing Limits
> **Screen:** DATA, Limits:

When you start AutoCAD, the default limits are 12.00,9.00. You can use the **LIMITS** command to set up new limits. This command can be invoked by entering LIMITS at the **Command:** prompt. You can also select the LIMITS command from the pull-down menu (Select Data, Drawing Limits, Figure 3-12) or from the screen menu (Select DATA, Limits:). The following is the prompt sequence of the **LIMITS** command for setting the limits of 24,18:

Data	Options	Tools	Help
Object Creation...			
Layers...			
Color			
Linetype...			
Multiline Style...			
Text Style			
Dimension Style...			
Shape File...			
Units...			
Drawing Limits			
Time			
Status			
Rename...			
Purge			

Figure 3-12 Selecting Drawing Limits from the pull-down menu

Command: **LIMITS** ←┘
ON/OFF/<Lower left corner> <current>: **0,0** ←┘
Upper right corner <current>: **24,18** ←┘

At the above two prompts you are required to specify the lower left corner and the upper right corner of the sheet. Normally you choose (0,0) as the lower left corner, but you can enter any other point. If the sheet size is 24x18, enter 24,18 as the coordinates of the upper right corner.

SETTING LIMITS

Limits are needed to size up a drawing area. The limits of the drawing area are usually determined by the following factors:

1. The actual size of the drawing.
2. Space needed for putting down the dimensions, notes, bill of materials, and other necessary details.
3. Space between different views so that the drawing does not look cluttered.
4. Space for the border and a title block, if any.

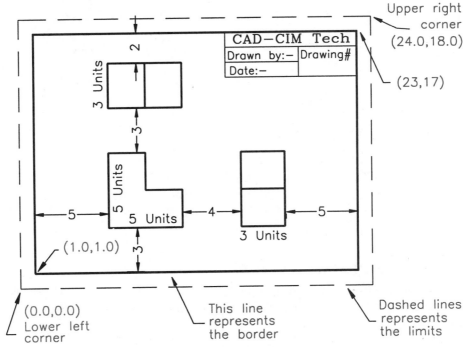

Figure 3-13 Setting limits in a drawing

To get a good idea of how to set up limits, it is always better to draw a rough sketch of the drawing to help calculate the area needed. For example, if an object has a front view size 5 x 5, side view size 3 x 5, and top view size 5 x 3, the limits should be set so that it can accommodate the drawing and everything associated with it. In Figure 3-13, the space between the front and side view is 4 units and the front and top view is 3 units. Also, the space between the border and drawing is 5 units on the left, 5 units on the right, 3 units at the bottom, and 2 units at the top. (The space between the views and the space between the border line and the drawing depends on the drawing.) After you know the size of different views and you have determined the space required between views, the space between the border and the drawing, and the space between the border line and the edges of the paper, you can calculate the limits as follows:

Length (X-limit) = 1 + 5 + 5 + 4 + 3 + 5 + 1 = 24
Width (Y-limit) = 1 + 3 + 5 + 3 + 3 + 2 + 1 = 18

Therefore, the limits for the drawing are 24 x 18.

Standard Sheet Sizes

When you make a drawing, you might want to plot the drawing to get a hard copy. Several standard sheet sizes are available to plot your drawing. Although in AutoCAD you can select any work area, it is recommended that you select the work area based on the sheet size that you will be using to plot the drawing. The sheet size is the deciding factor for determining the limits (work area), text size (TEXTSIZE), dimensioning scale factor (DIMSCALE), linetype scale factor (LTSCALE) and other drawing-related parameters. The following tables list standard sheet sizes and the corresponding drawing limits for different scale factors (1:1, 1:4, 1/4"=1', and 1:1, 1:20 for metric size):

English System

Letter size	Sheet size	Limits (1:1)	Limits (1:4)	Limits (1/4"=1')
A	12 x 9	12,9	48,36	48',36'
B	18 x 12	18,12	72,48	72',48'
C	24 x 18	24,18	96,72	96',72'
D	36 x 24	36,24	144,96	144',96'
E	48 x 36	48,36	192,144	192',144'

Metric System

Letter size	Sheet size	Limits (1:1)	Limits (1:20)
A4	210 x 297	210,297	4200,5940
A3	297 x 420	297,420	5940,8400
A2	420 x 594	420,597	8400,11940
A1	595 x 841	595,841	11940,16820
A0	841 x 1189	841,1189	16820,23780

Limits for Architectural Drawings

Most architectural drawings are drawn at a scale of 1/4" = 1', 1/8" = 1', or 1/16" = 1'. You must convert the limits accordingly. The following example illustrates how to calculate the limits in architectural drawings:

Given
Sheet size = 24 x 18
Scale = 1/4" = 1'

Calculate limits
Scale is 1/4" = 1'
     or 1/4" = 12"
       or 1" = 48"
X-limit = 24 x 48
        = 1152" or 1152 Units
        = 96'
Y-limit = 18 x 48
        = 864" or 864 Units
        = 72'

Therefore, the scale factor is 48 and the limits are 1152",864" or 96',72'.

Example 2

In this example you will calculate limits and determine an appropriate drawing scale factor for Figure 3-14. The drawing is to be plotted on a 12" x 9" sheet.

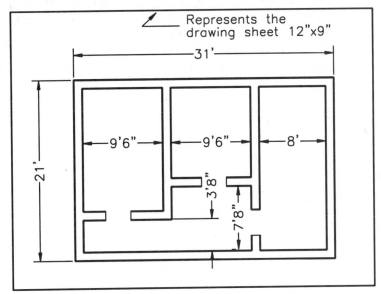

Figure 3-14 Drawing for Example 2

The scale factor can be calculated as follows:

Given or known
Overall length of the drawing = 31'
Length of the sheet = 12"
Approximate space between the drawing and the edges of the paper = 2"

Calculate scale factor
To calculate the scale factor, you have to try different scales until you find one that satisfies the given conditions. After some experience you will find this fairly easy to do. For this example, assume a scale factor of 1/4" = 1'

$$\text{Scale factor } 1/4" = 1'$$
$$\text{or} \quad 1" = 4'$$

Therefore, a line 31' long will be = 31'/4' = 7.75" on paper. Similarly, a line 21' long = 21'/4' = 5.25".

Approximate space between the drawing and the edges of paper = 2"
Therefore, total length of the sheet = 7.75 + 2 + 2 = 11.75"
Similarly, total width of the sheet = 5.25 + 2 + 2 = 9.25"

Because you selected the scale 1/4" = 1', the drawing will definitely fit on the given sheet of paper (12" x 9"). Therefore the scale for this drawing is 1/4" = 1'.

Calculate limits
Scale factor = 1" = 48" or 1" = 4'
The length of the sheet is 12"
Therefore, X-limit = 12 x 4' = 48'
Also, Y-limit = 9 x 4' = 36'

Limits for Metric Drawings

When the drawing units are metric, you must use **standard metric size sheets** or calculate the limits in millimeters (mm). For example, if the sheet size you decide to use is 24 x 18, the limits after conversion to the metric system will be 609.6,457.2 (multiply length and width by 25.4). You can round these numbers to the nearest whole numbers 610,457. Note that the metric drawings do not require any special setup, except for the limits. Metric drawings are like any other drawings that use decimal units. Like architectural drawings, you can draw metric drawings to a scale. For example, if the scale is 1:20 you must calculate the limits accordingly. The following example illustrates how to calculate the limits for the metric drawings.

    Given
    Sheet size = 24" x 18"
    Scale = 1 : 20

    Calculate limits
    Scale is 1 : 20
    Therefore, scale factor = 20
    X-limit = 24 x 25.4 x 20 = 12192 Units
    Y-limits = 18 x 25.4 x 20 = 9144 Units
Therefore limits are 12192 and 9144

Exercise 1

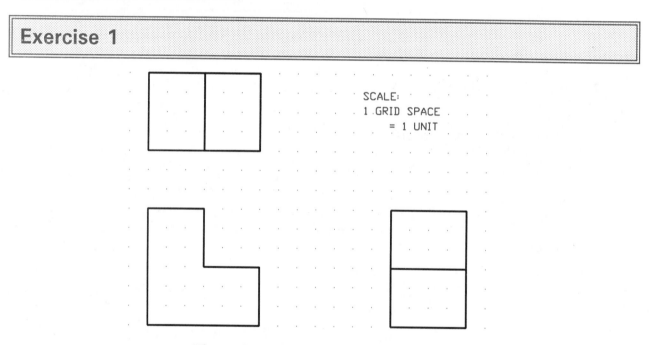

SCALE:
1 GRID SPACE
= 1 UNIT

Figure 3-15 Drawing for Exercise 1

Set the units of the drawing according to the following specifications and then make the drawing in Figure 3-15

1. Set **UNITS** to decimal units with two digits to the right of the decimal point.
2. Set the angular measurement to decimal degrees with the number of fractional places for display of angles equal to 1.
3. Set the direction to 0 degrees (east) and the direction of measurement of angles to counterclockwise (angles measured positive in counterclockwise direction).

Now determine and set the limits of the drawing. Also set an appropriate value for grid and snap. Leave a space of 3 to 5 units around the drawing for dimensioning and title block.

LAYERS

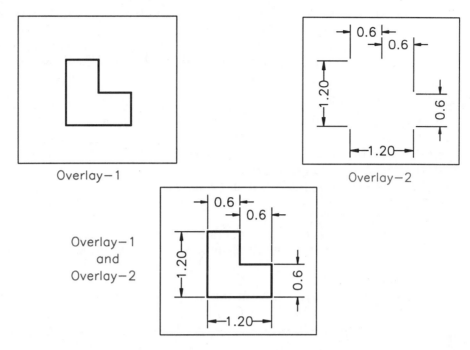

Figure 3-16 Drawing lines and dimensions in different overlays

The concept of layers can be best explained by using the concept of overlays in manual drafting. In manual drafting, different details of the drawing can be drawn on different sheets of paper, or overlays. Each overlay is perfectly aligned with the others and when all of them are placed on top of each other you can reproduce the entire drawing. As shown in Figure 3-16, the object lines have been drawn in the first overlay and the dimensions in the second overlay. You can place these overlays on top of each other and get a combined look at the drawing.

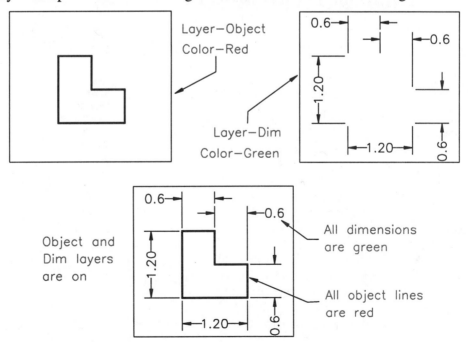

Figure 3-17 Drawing lines and dimensions in different layers

In AutoCAD, instead of using overlays you use layers. Each layer is assigned a name. You can also assign a color and linetype to these layers. For example, in Figure 3-17 the object lines have been drawn in the OBJECT layer and the dimensions have been drawn in the DIM layer. The object lines will be red because the red color has been assigned to the OBJECT layer. Similarly, the dimension lines will be green because the DIM layer has been assigned the green color. You can display all of the layers or you can display the layers individually or in any combination.

Advantages of Layers

1. Each layer can be assigned a different color. Assigning a particular color to a group of objects is very important for plotting. For example, if all object lines are red, at the time of plotting you can assign red color to a slot (pen) that has the desired tip width (e.g.,medium). Similarly, if the dimensions are green, you can assign the green color to another slot (pen) that has a thin tip. By assigning different colors to different layers you can control the width of the lines when the drawing is plotted.

2. The layers are useful for some editing operations. For example, if you want to erase all dimensions in a drawing, you can freeze all layers except the dimension layer and then erase all dimensions by using the **Crossing** option to select objects.

3. You can turn a layer off or freeze a layer that you do not want to be displayed or plotted.

4. You can lock a layer, which will prevent the user from accidently editing the objects in that layer.

5. The colors also help you to distinguish different groups of objects. For example, in architectural drafting the plans for foundation, floors, plumbing, electrical, and heating systems may all be made in different layers. In electronics drafting and in PCB (printed circuit board), design of each level of a multilevel circuit board can be drawn on separate layers.

LAYER CONTROL DIALOGUE BOX

Toolbar:	Object Properties, Layers
Pull-down:	Data, Layer
Screen:	DATA, DDlmode:

You can use the **Layer Control** dialogue box to perform the functions associated with the **LAYER** command. For example, you can create new layers, assign colors, assign linetypes, or perform any operation that is shown in the dialogue box. Using this dialogue box for layers is efficient and provides a convenient way to use various options. You can invoke the Layer Control dialogue box from the pull-down menu (Select Data, Layer...,Figure 3-18), from the screen menu (Select DATA, DDlmode:), or by typing **DDLMODES** at the **Command:** prompt. You can also invoke the Layer Control dialogue box and the other subdialogue boxes directly from the **Object properties** toolbar (Figure 3-19). From this toolbar you can also perform the different layer functions directly. If you have already created some layers they will be listed, with their current status, in the dialogue box as shown in Figure 3-20.

Figure 3-18 Selecting the Layer Control dialogue box from the pull-down menu

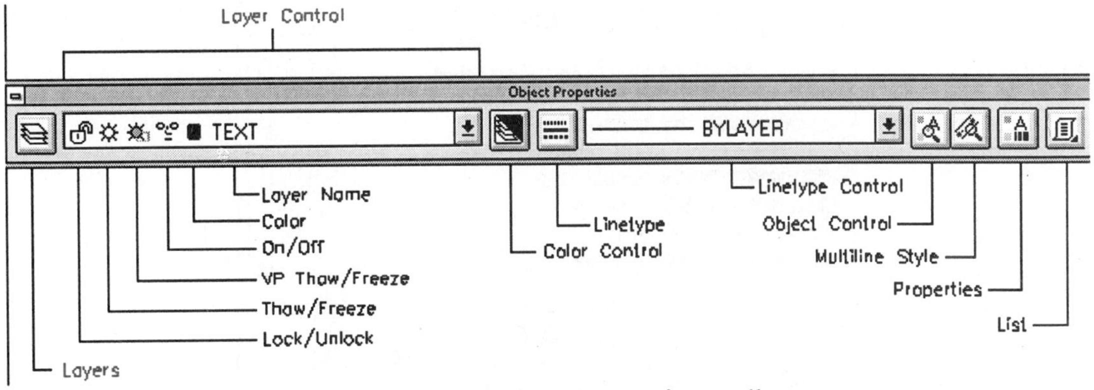

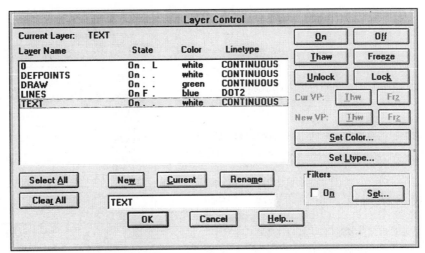

Figure 3-19 Object Properties toolbar

Figure 3-20 Layer Control dialogue box

Creating New Layers

The rectangular box just below the New, Current, Rename buttons is called the **Layer** edit box. If you want to create new layers, enter the names of the layers separated by a comma, then pick the **New** button. The layer names will be displayed in the **Layer Name** list box. This option creates new layers without affecting the status of the current layer.

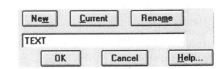

Layer Names

1. A layer name can be up to 31 characters long including letters, numbers, and special characters but no spaces.
2. The layers should be named to help the user identify the contents of the layer. For example, if the layer name is HATCH, a user can easily recognize the layer and its contents. On the other hand, if the layer name is X261, it is hard to identify the contents of the layer.
3. Layer names should be short, but should also convey the meaning.

Assigning a Linetype or a Color to a Layer

To assign a linetype or a color to a layer, you must first select the layer or layers that you want to assign a linetype or color. The layer can be selected by moving the arrow near the layer, then clicking the pointing device. You can **deselect a layer** by clicking on the selected layer or picking the **Clear All** button.

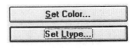

Figure 3-21 Select Linetype sub-dialogue box

Once you have selected one or more layers, pick the **Set Ltype** button from the dialogue box. AutoCAD will display the **Select Linetype** sub-dialogue box (Figure 3-21) that displays the linetypes that are defined and loaded on your system. You can also invoke this subdialogue box from the Object Properties toolbar by selecting the Linetype icon, or by selecting Linetype from the Data pull-down menu, or by selecting DDltype: from the DATA screen menu. To select a linetype, click on the desired linetype, then pick the OK button. The linetype you select will be assigned to the layer or layers you selected initially. The layers are by default assigned continuous linetype and white color. If the linetypes have not been loaded on your system, click on the **Load** button in the **Select**

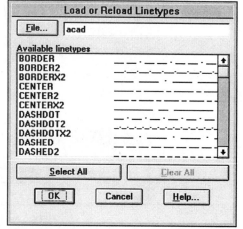

Figure 3-22 Load or Reload Linetypes dialogue box

Linetype sub-dialogue box. This displays the **Load or Reload Linetypes** dialogue box (Figure 3-22) that displays all the linetypes in the ACAD.LIN file. In this dialogue box you can select all the linetypes or individual linetypes for loading. You can also use AutoCAD's **LINETYPE** command to load the linetypes.

```
Command: Linetype ◄─┘
?/Create/Load/Set: L ◄─┘
Linetype(s) to load: * ◄─┘          (Loads all linetypes from the ACAD.LIN file.)
File to search <default>: acad ◄─┘
```

To assign a color, select the layer and then pick the **Set Color** button from the dialogue box. AutoCAD will display a **Color** sub-dialogue box on the screen. You can select a desired color, then pick the OK button. The color you selected will be assigned to the layer or layers you selected earlier. The number of colors is determined by your graphics card and monitor. Some color systems may support eight or more colors. If your system allows it, you may choose a color number between 0 and 255 (256 colors). The following are the first seven standard colors:

Color number	Color name	Color number	Color name
1	Red	5	Blue
2	Yellow	6	Magenta
3	Green	7	White
4	Cyan		

Making a Layer Current

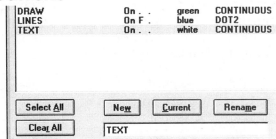

Figure 3-23 Making a layer current

To make a layer current, click on the desired layer and then pick the **Current** button (Figure 3-23). AutoCAD will display the current layer at the top of the dialogue box. After you select OK to exit the Layer Control dialogue box, the current layer will also be displayed in the status line at the top of the screen. Only one layer can be made current at any time. If the layer you select is off, it turns the layer on and makes it the current layer. Nevertheless, the layer you want to set must already exist.

Controlling Display of Layers

You can control display of the layers by selecting the layers and then picking the On, Off, Thaw, Freeze, Unlock, or Lock button.

With the **ON** and **OFF** options you can turn the layers on or off. The layers that are turned on are displayed on the screen and can be plotted. The layers that are turned off are not displayed on the screen and cannot be plotted. If you turn the current layer off, AutoCAD will display a warning at the bottom of the dialogue box informing you that the current drawing layer has been turned off.

While working on a drawing, if you do not want to see certain layers you can use the **Freeze** option to freeze the layers. For example, while editing a drawing, you may not want the dimensions displayed on the screen. To avoid this, you can freeze the DIM layer. The frozen layers are invisible and cannot be plotted. The difference between the **OFF** option and the **Freeze** option is that the frozen layers are not calculated by the computer while regenerating the drawing. This saves time. The current layer cannot be frozen. The **Thaw** option negates the effect of the **Freeze** option, and the frozen layers are restored to normal.

While working on a drawing, if you do not want to accidentally edit some objects on a particular layer but you still need to have them visible, you can use the **LOck** option to lock the layers. When a layer is locked you can still use the objects in the locked layer for object snaps. You can also make the locked layer as the current layer and draw objects on it. The locked layers are plotted. The **Unlock** option negates the **LOck** option and allows you to edit objects on the layers previously locked.

Selecting and Clearing Layers

You can select all layers by picking the **Select All** button in the Layer Control dialogue box. If you want to clear the selected layers, pick the **Clear All** button. You can also clear or deselect a layer by clicking on a different layer you wish to select.

Using Filters for Selective Display of Layers

If you have a limited number of layers it is easy to scan through them. However, if you have many layers it is sometimes difficult to search through them. To solve this problem you can use **Filters** to selectively display the layers. To define the filter specification, pick the **Set** button under Filters in the Layer Control dialogue box. When loaded initially, this dialogue box contains the default specifications. The **Set Layer Filters** sub-dialogue box (Figure 3-24) will be displayed on the screen. You can also use the **Reset** button to force display of the default values. To define the filter specification, select the edit box next to the item, then enter the value.

For example, if you want to list all layers that start with D, enter D* in the **Layer Names**: edit box, then pick the OK button to exit this sub-dialogue box. When you are in the Layer Control dialogue box, turn the filters on by selecting the **On** toggle box in the Filters section. AutoCAD will display the layers that start with D in the Layer Name list box. If you deselect the **On** toggle box, all layers will be displayed. You can also filter layers based on their linetype, color, or layer name, or whether they are on or off, frozen or thawed, locked or unlocked, or frozen in the current viewport or in the new viewport.

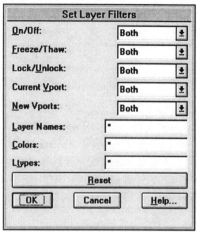

Figure 3-24   Set Layer Filters sub-dialogue box

Freezing Layers in Viewports

When the tilemode is turned off, you can freeze or thaw the selected layers in the current model space viewport or paper space by picking **Curr VP Frz** or **Curr VP Thw**. If the layers are frozen in the current

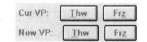

viewport, AutoCAD will display the letter "C" next to the layer name in the **State** column of the layer list box. It will display a period (**.**) if the layer is thawed. The frozen layers will still be visible in other viewports. If you want to freeze some layers in the new viewports, select the layers that you want to freeze, then pick the **New VP Frz** button. AutoCAD will freeze the layers in the new viewports without affecting the viewports that already exist. When you freeze a layer using the **New VP Frz** option, the letter "N" will be displayed next to the selected layer name in the **State** column of the dialogue box. Paper space is discussed later in chapter 22. Also, check the VPLAYER command for selectively freezing the layers in viewports.

Note

You can access the above options from the Object Properties toolbar (Figure 3-19) by selecting the appropriate icon.

LAYER Command

You can also set layers by using the **LAYER** command. You can invoke the LAYER command by entering LAYER at the **Command:** prompt. The LAYER command helps you to select a variety of options for working with the layers. The prompt sequence is:

Command: **LAYER** ⏎
?/Make/Set/New/ON/OFF/Color/Ltype/Freeze/Thaw/LOck/Unlock:

You can perform any function on the layer by entering the appropriate option at the above prompt. For example, if you want to create two new layers, DIM and CEN, the prompt sequence is:

Command: **LAYER** ⏎
?/Make/Set/New/ON/OFF/Color/Ltype/Freeze/Thaw/LOck/Unlock: **N** ⏎
New layer name(s): **DIM,CEN** ⏎

Similarly if your current layer is VIEW and you want to create a new layer, OBJECT, and also make it the current layer, the prompt sequence is:

Command: **LAYER** ⏎
?/Make/Set/New/ON/OFF/Color/Ltype/Freeze/Thaw/LOck/Unlock: **M** ⏎
New current layer <VIEW>: **OBJECT** ⏎

Example 3

Set up four layers with the following linetypes and colors, then make the drawing (without dimensions) as shown in Figure 3-25.

Layer name	Color	Linetype
Obj	Red	Continuous
Hid	Yellow	Hidden
Cen	Green	Center
Dim	Blue	Continuous

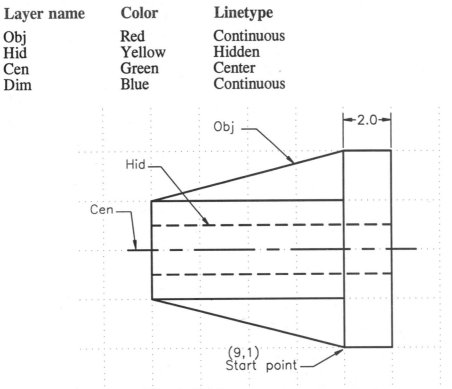

Figure 3-25 Drawing for Example 3

In this example assume that the limits and units are already set. Before drawing the lines you need to create layers and assign colors and linetypes to these layers. Also, depending on the objects that you want to draw, you need to set that layer current. The following is the command prompt sequence for making the drawing in Figure 3-25.

Command: **LAYER** ⏎
?/Make/Set/New/ON/OFF/Color/Ltype/Freeze/Thaw/LOck/Unlock: **N** ⏎
New layer name(s): **Obj,Hid,Cen,Dim** ⏎
?/Make/Set/New/ON/OFF/Color/Ltype/Freeze/Thaw/LOck/Unlock: **C** ⏎
Color: **Red** ⏎
Layer name(s) for color 1 (red) <0>: **Obj** ⏎
?/Make/Set/New/ON/OFF/Color/Ltype/Freeze/Thaw/LOck/Unlock: **C** ⏎
Color: **Yellow** ⏎
Layer name(s) for color 2 (yellow) <0>: **Hid** ⏎
?/Make/Set/New/ON/OFF/Color/Ltype/Freeze/Thaw/LOck/Unlock: **C** ⏎
Color: **Green** ⏎
Layer name(s) for color 3 (green) <0>: **Cen** ⏎
?/Make/Set/New/ON/OFF/Color/Ltype/Freeze/Thaw/LOck/Unlock: **C** ⏎

Color: **Blue** ←┘
Layer name(s) for color 5 (blue) <0>: **Dim** ←┘
?/Make/Set/New/ON/OFF/Color/Ltype/Freeze/Thaw/LOck/Unlock: **L** ←┘
Linetype (or ?) <CONTINUOUS>: **Hidden** ←┘
Layer name(s) for linetype HIDDEN <0>: **Hid** ←┘
?/Make/Set/New/ON/OFF/Color/Ltype/Freeze/Thaw/LOck/Unlock: **L** ←┘
Linetype (or ?) <CONTINUOUS>: **Center** ←┘
Layer name(s) for linetype CENTER <0>: **Cen** ←┘
?/Make/Set/New/ON/OFF/Color/Ltype/Freeze/Thaw/LOck/Unlock: **S** ←┘
New current layer <0>: **Obj** ←┘
?/Make/Set/New/ON/OFF/Color/Ltype/Freeze/Thaw/LOck/Unlock: ←┘

Command: **LINE** ←┘
Line From point: **9,1** ←┘
To point: **9,9** ←┘
To point: **11,9** ←┘
To point: **11,1** ←┘
To point: **9,1** ←┘
To point: **1,3** ←┘
To point: **1,7** ←┘
To point: **9,9** ←┘
To point: ←┘

Command: **LINE** ←┘
Line From point: **1,3** ←┘
To point: **9,3** ←┘
To point: ←┘

Command: **LINE** ←┘
Line From point: **1,7** ←┘
To point: **9,7** ←┘
To point: ←┘

Command: **LAYER** ←┘
?/Make/Set/New/ON/OFF/Color/Ltype/Freeze/Thaw/LOck/Unlock: **S** ←┘

New current layer <OBJ>: **Hid** ←┘
?/Make/Set/New/ON/OFF/Color/Ltype/Freeze/Thaw/LOck/Unlock: ←┘

Command: **LINE** ←┘
Line From point: **1,4** ←┘
To point: **11,4** ←┘
To point: ←┘

Command: **LINE** ←┘
Line From point: **1,6** ←┘
To point: **11,6** ←┘
To point: ←┘

Command: **LAYER** ←┘
?/Make/Set/New/ON/OFF/Color/Ltype/Freeze/Thaw/LOck/Unlock: **S** ←┘

New current layer <HID>: **Cen** ←┘
?/Make/Set/New/ON/OFF/Color/Ltype/Freeze/Thaw/LOck/Unlock: ←┘

Command: **LINE** ←┘
Line From point: **0,5** ←┘

To point: **12,5** ←┘
To point: ←┘

Exercise 2

Set up layers with the following linetypes and colors, then make the drawing (without dimensions) as shown in Figure 3-26.

Layer name	Color	Linetype
Object	Red	Continuous
Hidden	Yellow	Hidden
Center	Green	Center
Dimension	Blue	Continuous

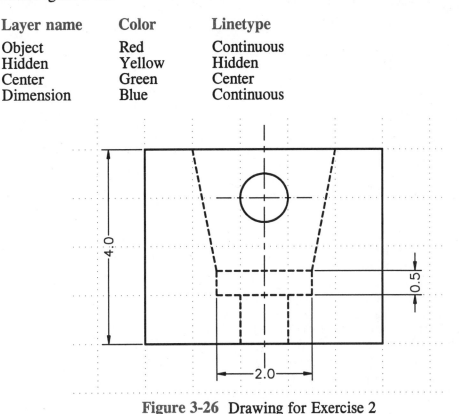

Figure 3-26 Drawing for Exercise 2

DRAWING AIDS DIALOGUE BOX

Pull-down: Options, Drawing Aids
Screen: OPTIONS, DDrmode:

You can use the **Drawing Aids** dialogue box to set grid, snap, and drawing modes such as ortho, solid fill, blips, etc. This dialogue box can be invoked from the pull-down menu (Select Options, Drawing Aids..., Figure 3-27), from the screen menu (Select OPTIONS, DDrmode:), or by entering DDRMODES at the **Command:** prompt. The grid can be turned on or off by clicking on the **On** check box. You can set the grid spacing by entering either the same or different values in the **X Spacing** and **Y Spacing** edit boxes.

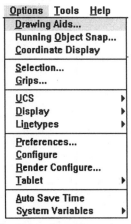

Figure 3-27 Selecting Drawing Aids from the pull-down menu

Figure 3-28 Drawing Aids dialogue box

GRID COMMAND

Status Line:	GRID
Pull-down:	Edit, Grid

The GRID command can be used to display dotted lines on the screen at predefined spacing (Figure 3-30). These dotted lines act as a graph that can be used as reference lines in a drawing. You can change the distance between the grid lines according to your requirement. The grid pattern appears within the drawing limits, which helps to define the working area. The grid lines also give you a sense of the size of the drawing objects. You can turn the grid on or off by pressing the **F7** key, by double-clicking on GRID in the Status Line at the bottom of the screen (Figure 3-31), or from the Edit pull-down menu (Figure 3-29). You can also turn the grid on/off and change the grid spacing in the **Drawing Aids** dialogue box, or by entering GRID at the **Command:** prompt and then using its different options.

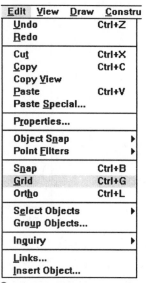

Figure 3-29 Selecting the GRID command from the pull-down menu

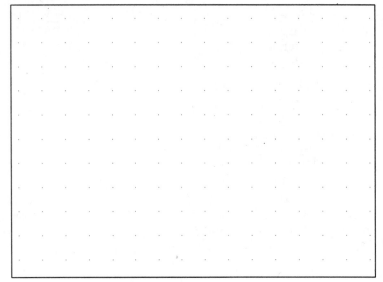

Figure 3-30 Grid lines

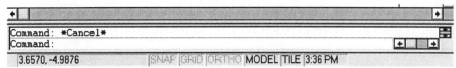

Figure 3-31 Selecting the GRID command from the Status Line

The following is the prompt sequence for the GRID command:

Command: **GRID** ←⏎
Grid spacing(X) or ON/OFF/Snap/Aspect <current>:

Spacing(X)-Defining Grid Spacing

The spacing option is used to define a desired grid spacing. For example, to set the grid spacing to 0.5 units, enter 0.5 in response to the **Grid spacing(X):** prompt. To accept the default value, just press the Enter key at the next prompt (Figure 3-32).

Command: **GRID** ←⏎
Grid spacing(X) or ON/OFF/Snap/Aspect <0>: **0.5** ←⏎

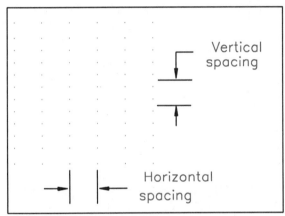

Figure 3-32 Controlling grid spacing

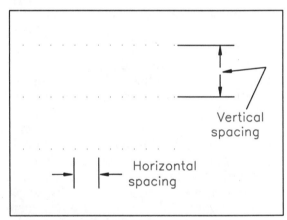

Figure 3-33 Using the Aspect option to create unequal grid spacing

Aspect-Assigning Different Grid Spacing

This option allows you to enter different values for horizontal and vertical grid spacing (Figure 3-33). The prompt sequence to set the vertical spacing of 1.0 and the horizontal spacing of 0.5 is:

Command: **GRID** ←⏎
Grid spacing(X) or ON/OFF/Snap/Aspect<0.5>: **A** ←⏎
Horizontal spacing(X) <0.5>: ←⏎
Vertical spacing(X) <0.5>: 1.0 ←⏎

In this example, the horizontal spacing is retained as 0.5, but the vertical spacing is changed to 1.

ON/OFF-Turning the Grid On or Off

The **ON** and **OFF** option can be used to turn the grid on or off. When a grid is turned on after having been off, the grid is set to the previous grid spacing.

Snap-Setting the Grid at Snap Value

The grid and the snap grid (discussed in the next section) are independent of each other. However, you can display the grid lines at the same resolution as that of the snap grid by using the **Snap** option. When you use this option, AutoCAD will automatically change the grid spacing to zero and display the grid lines at the same resolution as set for snap.

Note
In the Grid command, to specify the grid spacing as a multiple of the snap spacing, enter X after the value (2X). If the grid spacing is specified as zero it automatically adjusts to the snap resolution.

SNAP COMMAND

Status Line:	SNAP
Pull-down:	Edit, Snap

The snap is used to set increments for cursor movement. While moving the cursor it is sometimes difficult to position a point accurately. The SNAP command allows you to set up an invisible grid (Figure 3-34) that allows the cursor to move in fixed increments from one snap point to another. The snap points are the points where the invisible snap lines intersect. The snap spacing is independent of the grid spacing, so the two can have equal or different values. You can turn the snap on or off by using the function key **F9**, by pressing **Ctrl + B** keys, by double-clicking on SNAP in the Status Line at the bottom of the screen, or by selecting the Snap option in the Edit pull-down menu. You can turn the snap on/off and set the snap spacing

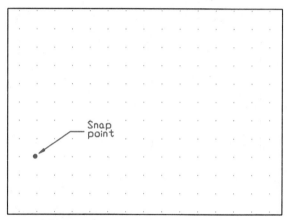

Figure 3-34 Invisible snap grid

from the **Drawing Aids** dialogue box or by entering SNAP at the **Command:** prompt. The format of the **SNAP** command is:

Command: **Snap** ◄┘
Snap spacing or ON/OFF/Aspect/Rotate/Style <current>: **0.5** ◄┘

ON/OFF-Turning the Snap On or Off

As in the case of Grid, the **ON/OFF** selection turns the invisible snap grid on or off and moves the cursor by increments. If the SNAP is off, the cursor will not move by increments. It will move freely as you move the pointing device. When you turn the snap off, AutoCAD remembers the value of the snap and this value is restored when you turn the snap on.

Aspect-Assigning Different Increments

This option is used to assign a different value to the horizontal and vertical snap increment. If the values are different and the snap is on, the cursor increment will change accordingly. The following is the prompt sequence for setting the aspect ratio:

Command: **SNAP** ◄┘
Snap spacing or ON/OFF/Aspect/Rotate/Style <current>: **A** ◄┘
Horizontal spacing <current>: **0.5** ◄┘
Vertical spacing <current>: **1** ◄┘

Rotate-Rotating the Snap Grid

The **Rotate** option is used to rotate the snap grid through an angle. Normally, the snap grid has horizontal and vertical lines, but sometimes you need the snap grid at an angle. For example, when you are drawing an auxiliary view (a drawing view that is at an angle to other views of the drawing), it is more useful to have the snap grid at an angle. If you know the angle, you can use the Rotate option to rotate the snap grid through an angle. After selecting this option you will be prompted to select a new base point and the angle of rotation. The base point is the pivot point around which the snap grid is rotated. If the rotation angle is positive the grid rotates in a counterclockwise direction and if the rotation angle is negative, it rotates in a clockwise direction. The following example illustrates the use of **Rotate** option:

Figure 3-35 Snap grid rotated 30 degrees

Command: **SNAP** ←⎤
Snap spacing or ON/OFF/Aspect/Rotate/Style <current>: **R** ←⎤
Base point <0,0>: **2,2** ←⎤   *(New base point.)*
Rotation angle <0>: **30** ←⎤

Example 4

Draw the auxiliary view of the object whose front view is shown in Figure 3-36. The thickness of the plate is 4 units; the length of the incline's face is 12 units. The following are the three different ways to draw the auxiliary view:

Rotating the Snap Grid

Command: **SNAP** ←⎤
Snap spacing or ON/OFF/Aspect/Rotate/Style <current>: **R** ←⎤
Base point <current>: *Select point P0.*   *(Use object snap.)*
Rotation angle <current>: **30** ←⎤
Command: **LINE** ←⎤
From point: *Select point (P1).*
To point: *Move the cursor 4 units right and select point (P2).*
To point: *Move the cursor 10 units up and select point (P3).*
To point: *Move the cursor 4 units left and select point (P4).*
To point: **C** ←⎤

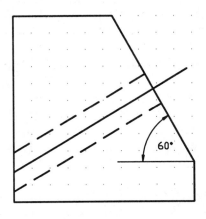

Figure 3-36 Front view of the plate for Example 4

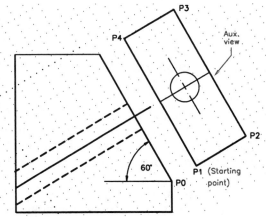

Figure 3-37 Auxiliary view using rotated snap grid

Using Polar Coordinates

Command: **LINE** ←⎯
From point: *Select the starting point P1.*
To point: **@4<30** ←⎯
To point: **@10<120** ←⎯
To point: **@4<210** ←⎯
To point: **C** ←⎯

Note that the angle measurements do not change even though you have rotated the snap. The angle is still measured with reference to the positive X-axis.

Rotating UCS Icon

When you rotate the UCS by 30 degrees, the X-axis and Y-axis also rotate through the same angle and the UCSICON will automatically align with the rotated snap grid. (See the UCS command for a detailed explanation.)

Command: **UCS** ←⎯
Origin/ZAxis/3point/Object/View/X/Y/Z/Prev/Restore/Save/Del/?/<World>: **Z** ←⎯
Rotation angle about Z axis <0>: **30** ←⎯

Command: **LINE** ←⎯
From point: *Select the starting point P1.*
To point: **@4<0** ←⎯
To point: **@10<90** ←⎯
To point: **@4<180** ←⎯
To point: **C** ←⎯

Style-Setting the Snap Style

You can use the **Style** option to set the snap grid to a standard or isometric pattern. The default is standard. The isometric pattern is used to make isometric drawings. In the isometric drawings the isometric axes are at angles of 30, 90, and 150 degrees. The Style option enables you to display the grid lines along these axes. When you use this option, AutoCAD will also let you change the vertical spacing between the grid lines as shown in the following example:

Command: **SNAP** ←⎯
Snap spacing or ON/OFF/Aspect/
    Rotate/Style <current>: **S** ←⎯
Standard/Isometric <current>: **I** ←⎯
Vertical spacing <current>: **1.5** ←⎯

Figure 3-38 Isometric snap grid

Once you set the isometric snap, AutoCAD automatically changes the cursor to align with the isometric axis. You can adjust the cursor orientation when you are working on the left, top, or right plane of the drawing by holding down the **Ctrl** key and then pressing the **E** key. By using this key combination you can cycle the cursor through different isometric planes (left, right, top).

You can also use the **Drawing Aids** dialogue box to set the above options in the snap. You can turn the snap on or off by clicking on the **On** check/toggle box and the spacing can be set by entering the desired values in the **X Spacing** and **Y Spacing** edit boxes. You can rotate the snap grid by entering the desired angle in the **Angle** edit box.

ORTHO COMMAND

Status Line:	ORTHO
Pull-down:	Edit, Ortho

The ORTHO command allows you to draw lines at right angles only. Whenever you are using the pointing device to specify the next point, the movement of the rubberband line connected to the cursor is either horizontal (parallel to the X-axis) or vertical (parallel to the Y-axis). If you want to draw a line in the ortho mode, specify the starting point at the **From point:** prompt. To specifying the second point, move the cursor with the pointing device and pick a desired point. The line drawn will be either vertical or horizontal depending on the direction in which you moved the cursor. You can turn the ortho mode on or off by pressing the **F8** key, by clicking on the **Ortho** check box in the **Drawing Aids** dialogue box, by selecting Ortho in the **Edit** pull-down menu, or by double-clicking on ORTHO in the Status Line at the bottom of the screen. You can also invoke this command by entering ORTHO at the **Command:** prompt. The prompt sequence is:

Command: **ORTHO** ←⏎
ON/OFF <current>:

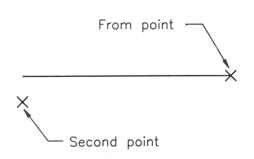

Figure 3-39 Drawing horizontal line using the Ortho mode

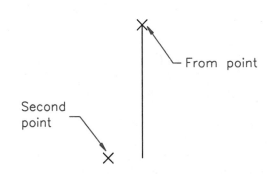

Figure 3-40 Drawing vertical line using the Ortho mode

OBJECT SNAPS

Object snaps is one of the most useful features of AutoCAD. It improves your performance and the accuracy of your drawing and makes drafting much simpler than it normally would be. The term object snap refers to the cursor's ability to snap exactly to a point on an object.

You can select these snaps from the **Object Snap** toolbar (Figure 3-41), from the **Standard** toolbar by selecting the desired icon from the **Object Snap** flyout, or from the cursor menu (Figure 3-42), which can be accessed by holding down the Shift key on the keyboard, then pressing the Enter button on your pointing device. You can also select object snaps from the pull-down menu (Select Edit, Object Snap, Figure 3-43), from the screen menu by selecting **** from any screen menu, or by entering the object snap mode name at the prompt.

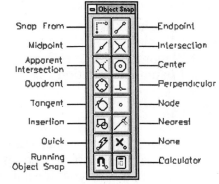

Figure 3-41 Object Snap toolbar

Toolbar:	Standard toolbar, or Object Snap, Object Snap
Pull-down:	Edit, Object Snap
Screen:	****

From

Endpoint
Midpoint
Intersection
Apparent Intersection
Center
Quadrant
Perpendicular
Tangent
Node
Insertion
Nearest
Quick,

None

.X
.Y
.Z
.XZ
.YZ
.XY

Figure 3-42 Selecting object snap modes from the cursor menu

| Edit | View | Draw | Construct | Modify | Data | Opti |

Undo   Ctrl+Z
Redo

Cut   Ctrl+X
Copy   Ctrl+C
Copy View
Paste   Ctrl+V
Paste Special...

Properties...

Object Snap
Point Filters

Snap   Ctrl+B
Grid   Ctrl+G
Ortho   Ctrl+L

Select Objects
Group Objects...

Inquiry

Links...
Insert Object...

1:

ɔ a temporary reference point

From

Endpoint
Midpoint
Intersection
Apparent Intersection
Center
Quadrant
Perpendicular
Tangent
Node
Insertion
Nearest
Quick,

None

Figure 3-43 Selecting object snap modes from the pull-down menu

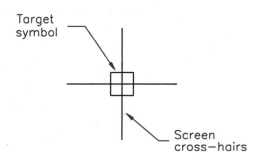

Figure 3-44 Target symbol

The advantage of using object snaps is that you do not have to pick an exact point. For example, if you want to place a point at the midpoint of a line, you may not be able to pick the exact point. Using the MIDpoint object snap, all you do is pick a point somewhere on the object and AutoCAD automatically snaps to the middle point. Whenever you use object snaps a target symbol is attached to the screen cross-hairs (Figure 3-44). The target is used to pick the desired point by positioning it over the object. For more information on target, see the APERTURE command, chapter 3. The object snaps only recognize the objects that are visible on the screen, which includes the objects in the locked layers. The objects on layers that are turned off or frozen are not visible so they cannot be used for object snaps. The following are the object snap modes available in AutoCAD:

NEArest	CENter	QUIck	TANgent
ENDpoint	QUAdrant	NONE	PERpendicular
MIDpoint	INTersect	INSert	NODe
APParent Intersection			

NEArest

The **NEArest** object snap mode selects a point on an object (line, arc, circle) that is visually closest to the graphics cursor (cross-hairs). To use this mode, enter the command; if you are not in the command mode, then select the NEArest object snap. Now move the cross-hairs so that the intended point on the object is within the target box and then select the object. AutoCAD will grab a point on the line that is nearest to the cursor. The following is the prompt sequence for drawing a line from a point on a line (Figure 3-46):

Command: **LINE** ◄─┘
From point: **NEA** ◄─┘   *(NEArest object snap.)*
to *Select a point near an existing object.*
To point: *Select end point of the line.*

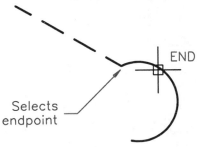

Figure 3-45 ENDpoint object snap mode

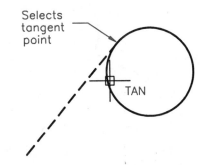

Figure 3-46 NEArest object snap mode

ENDpoint

The **ENDpoint** object snap mode snaps to the closest end point of a line or an arc. To use this object snap mode, select or enter the ENDpoint and move the target anywhere close to the endpoint of the object and then pick that point. AutoCAD will grab the end point of the object. If there are several objects within the target box, AutoCAD will grab the end point of the object that is closest to the graphics cursor. The following is the prompt sequence for drawing a line from the end point of a line (Figure 3-45):

Command: **LINE** ◄─┘
From point: **END** ◄─┘   *(ENDpoint object snap.)*
of *Move the target box and select the line.*
To point: *Select the end point of the line.*

MIDpoint

The **MIDpoint** object snap mode snaps to the midpoint of a line or an arc. To use this object snap mode, select or enter MIDpoint and pick the object anywhere. AutoCAD will grab the midpoint of the object. The following is the prompt sequence for drawing a line to the midpoint of a line (Figure 3-47):

Command: **LINE** ◄─┘
From point: *Select the starting point of the line.*
To point: **MID** ◄─┘   *(MIDpoint object snap.)*
of *Move the target box and select the original line.*

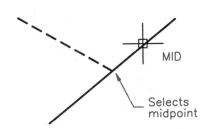

Figure 3-47 MIDpoint object snap mode

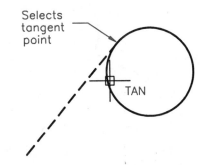

Figure 3-48 TANgent object snap mode

TANgent

The TANgent object snap allows you to draw a tangent to or from an existing circle or arc. To use this object snap, the target box should be placed on the circumference of the circle or arc to select it. The following is the prompt sequence for drawing a line tangent to a circle (Figure 3-48):

Command: **LINE** ◄─┘
From point: *Select the starting point of the line.*
To point: **TAN** ◄─┘ *(TANgent object snap).*
to *Move the target box and select the circle.*

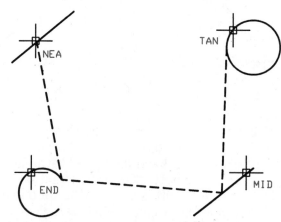

Figure 3-49 Using NEArest, ENDpoint, MIDpoint, and TANgent object snap modes

CENter

The **CENter** object snap mode allows you to snap to the center point of a circle or an arc. After selecting this option you must point to the visible part of the circumference of a circle or arc. The following is the prompt sequence for drawing a line from the center of a circle (Figure 3-50):

Command: **LINE** ◄─┘
From point: **CEN** ◄─┘ *(CENter object snap.)*
of *Move the target box and select the circle.*
To point: *Select the end point of the line.*

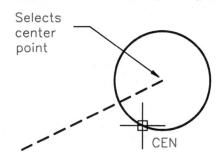

Figure 3-50 CENter object snap mode

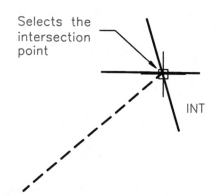

Figure 3-51 INTersect object snap mode

INTersection

The INTersection object snap mode is used if you need to snap to a point where two or more lines or arcs intersect. To use this object snap, move the target box close to the desired intersection so that the intersection is within the target box and then pick that point. The following is the prompt sequence for drawing a line from an intersection (Figure 3-51):

Command: **LINE** ◄─┘
From point: **INT** ◄─┘   *(INTersection object snap.)*
of *Position the target box near the intersection and select it.*
To point: *Select the end point of the line.*

QUAdrant

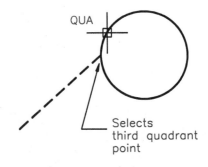

Figure 3-52 QUAdrant object snap mode

This option is used when you need to snap to a quadrant point of an arc or circle. A circle has four quadrants and each quadrant subtends an angle of 90 degrees. The quadrant points are located at 0, 90, 180, 270-degree positions. If the circle is inserted as a block that is rotated, the quadrant points are also rotated by the same amount. To use this object snap, position the target box on the circle or arc closest to the desired quadrant. The prompt sequence for drawing a line from the third quadrant of a circle (Figure 3-52,-53,-54) is:

Command: **LINE** ◄─┘
From point: **QUA** ◄─┘   *(QUAdrant object snap.)*
of *Move the target box close to third quadrant of the circle and select it.*
To point: *Select the end point of the line.*

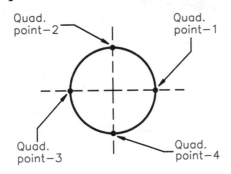

Figure 3-53 Four quadrants of a circle

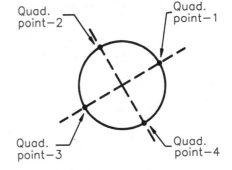

Figure 3-54 Quadrant points are rotated when the block is rotated

PERpendicular

The **PER**pendicular object snap mode is used to draw a perpendicular on a line. When you use this mode and select an object, AutoCAD calculates the point on the selected object so that the previously selected point is perpendicular to the line. The object can be selected by positioning the target box anywhere on the line. The following is the prompt sequence for drawing a line that is perpendicular to a given line (Figure 3-55):

Command: **LINE** ◄─┘
From point: *Select the starting point of the line.*
To point: **PER** ◄─┘   *(PERpendicular object snap.)*
to *Select the line on which you want to draw perpendicular.*

When you select the line first, the rubberband feature of the line is disabled. The line will appear only after the second point is selected. The prompt sequence for drawing a line perpendicular from a given line (Figure 3-56) is:

Command: **LINE** ←⏎
From point: **PER** ←⏎   *(PERpendicular object snap.)*
to   *Select the line on which you want to draw perpendicular.*
To point: *Select the endpoint of the line.*

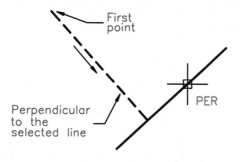

Figure 3-55 Selecting the start point, then the perpendicular snap

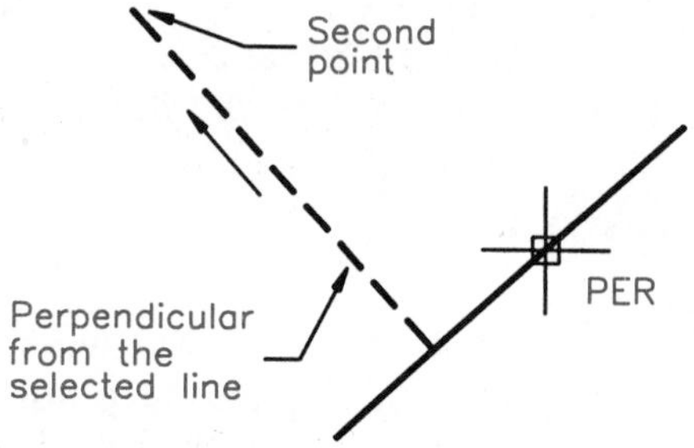

Figure 3-56 Selecting the perpendicular snap first

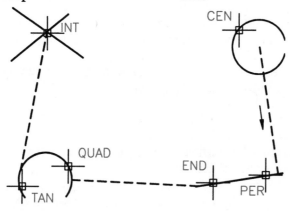

Figure 3-57 Using CENter, INTersect, QUAdrant, and PERpendicular object snap modes

Exercise 3

In Figure 3-58, P1 and P2 are the center points of the top and bottom arc. The space between the dotted lines is one unit.

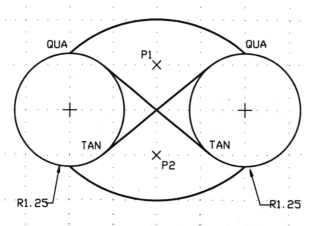

Figure 3-58 Drawing for Exercise 3

QUIck

If you are using an object snap when several objects cross the target box, AutoCAD normally searches all objects for the specified object snap mode and selects the closest point. Depending on your hardware setup, this will cause a delay in searching the specified point. The **QUIck** option stops searching as soon as AutoCAD finds a point on the object with the specified object snap. You can use the **QUIck** option with any object snap mode. The following is the prompt sequence for using the **QUIck** and MIDpoint object snap mode:

Command: **LINE** ←⎤
From point: *Select the starting point of the line.*
To point: **QUI, MID** ←⎤   *(QUIck and MIDpoint object snaps.)*
of *Select the line.*

NODe

The NODe object snap can be used to snap to a point object. In Figure 3-59, three points have been drawn using AutoCAD's POINT command. You can snap to these points by using NODe snap mode as shown on the following example:

Command: **LINE** ←⎤
From point: **NOD** ←⎤
of *Select point P1.*
To point: **NOD** ←⎤   *(NODe object snap.)*
of *Select point P2.*
To point: **NOD** ←⎤
of *Select point P3.*

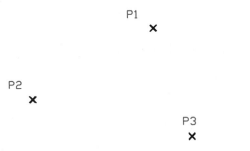

Figure 3-59 Point objects

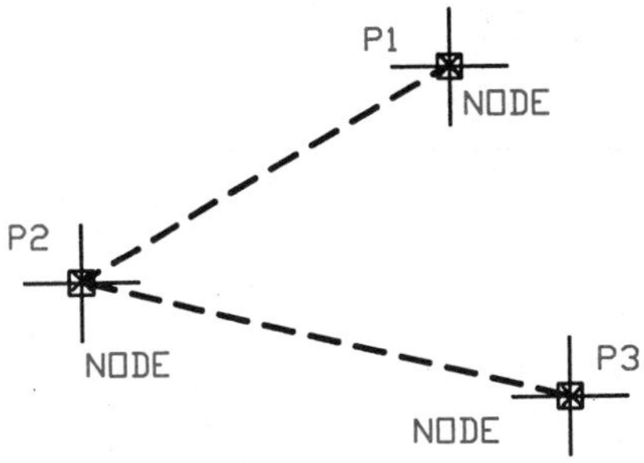

Figure 3-60 Using NODe object snap

INSert

The **INSert** object snap mode is used to snap to the insertion point of a text, shape, block, attribute, or attribute definition. In the following figure, the text, **WELCOME**, is left justified and the text, **AutoCAD**, is center justified. The point with respect to which the text is justified is the insertion point of that text string. If you want to snap to these insertion points or the insertion point of a block, you must use the INSert snap mode as shown in the following prompt sequence:

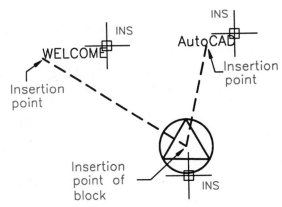

Figure 3-61 INSert object snap mode

Command: **LINE** ←⅃
From point: **INS** ←⅃   *(INSert object snap.)*
of *Select WELCOME text.*
To point: **INS** ←⅃
of *Select the block.*
To point: **INS** ←⅃
of *Select AutoCAD text.*

NONE

The **NONE** object snap mode turns off any object snap and returns to the normal command prompt. The following example illustrates the use of this object snap mode:

Command: **LINE** ←⅃
From point: **MID** ←⅃   *(MIDpoint object snap.)*
to **NONE** ←⅃   *(NONE object snap.)*
Invalid point.
From point: *(Returns to the normal command prompt.)*

APParent Intersection

The **APParent Intersection** object snap mode is similar to the INTersection snap mode, except that this mode selects the visual intersections. The visual intersections are those intersections that are not present on the screen but are imaginary ones that can be formed if any two objects are extended. Sometimes two objects appear to intersect each other in the current view but in the 3D space the two objects do not actually intersect. The APParent INTersection snap mode also selects such intersections. The prompt sequence is:

Command: **LINE** ←⅃
From point: **APP**   *(APParent Intersection object snap.)*
of *Select first object.*
and *Select second object.*
To point: *Select the endpoint of the line.*

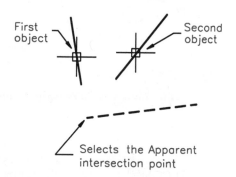

Figure 3-62 Using the Apparent Intersection snap mode

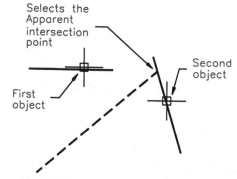

Figure 3-63 Using the Apparent Intersection snap mode

Combining Object Snap Modes

You can also combine the snaps by separating the snap modes with a comma. AutoCAD will search for the specified modes and grab the point on the object that is closest to the point where the object is selected. The prompt sequence for the use of MIDpoint and ENDpoint object snaps.

Command: **LINE** ←⅃
From point: **MID,END** ←⅃   *(MIDpoint or ENDpoint object snap.)*
to *Select the object.*

In this example, you have defined two object snap modes, MIDpoint and ENDpoint. The point that it will grab depends on where you pick the line. If you select the line at a point that is closer to the midpoint of the line, AutoCAD will snap to the midpoint. If you pick the line closer to the end point of the line, the line will snap to the end point of the selected line.

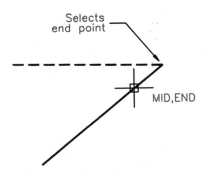

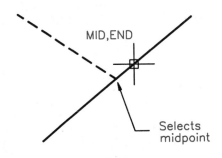

Figure 3-64 Using MIDpoint, ENDpoint snaps (Picking end point)

Figure 3-65 Using MIDpoint, ENDpoint snaps (Picking midpoint)

Exercise 4

Make the drawing in Figure 3-66. The space between the dotted lines is 1 unit.

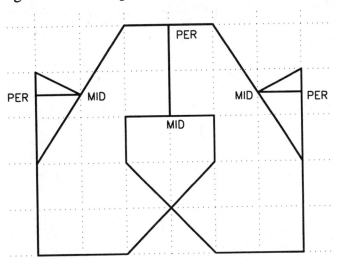

Figure 3-66 Drawing for Exercise 4

RUNNING OBJECT SNAP MODE

In the previous sections you have learned how to use the object snaps to snap to different points of an object. One of the drawbacks of these object snaps is that you have to select them every time you use them, even if it is the same snap mode. This problem can be solved by using **running object snaps**. You can set running object snaps by using AutoCAD's **OSNAP** command. You can invoke this command from the screen menu (Select ****, Osnap:), or by entering OSNAP at the **Command:** prompt. After you enter the command AutoCAD will prompt you to enter the object snap modes. You can now type the first three letters of the mode that you want to use. Once you set the running object snap mode, you are automatically in that mode and the target box is displayed with the cross-hairs. For example, if you want to set **ENDpoint** as the running object snap mode, the prompt sequence is:

Command: **OSNAP** ←┘
Object snap modes: **END** ←┘

You can also define several object snap modes as running object snap, in which case the object snap modes have to be separated with a comma. If you had selected a combination of modes, AutoCAD selects the mode that is closest to the screen cross-hairs. The prompt sequence for setting ENDpoint, TANgent, and CENter as the running object snap modes is:

Command: **OSNAP** ←┘
Object snap modes: **END,TAN,CEN** ←┘

Overriding the Running Snap

When you select the running object snaps, all other object snap modes are ignored unless you pick another object snap mode. Once you pick a different object snap mode, the running OSNAP mode is temporarily overruled. After the operation has been performed, the running OSNAP mode goes into effect again. If you want to discontinue the current running object snap modes totally, enter NONE or OFF or press the Enter key at the **Object snap modes:** prompt.

Command: **OSNAP** ←┘
Object snap modes: **NONE** ←┘

If you are overriding the running OSNAP modes for a point selection and no point is found to satisfy the override object snap mode, AutoCAD displays a message to this effect. For example, if you specify an override object snap mode of CENter and no circle or arc is found at that location, AutoCAD will display the following message:

No center found for specified point.

Using the Running Object Snap Dialogue Box

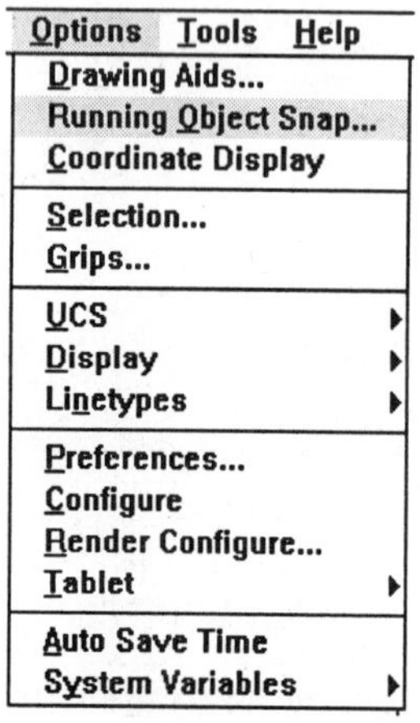

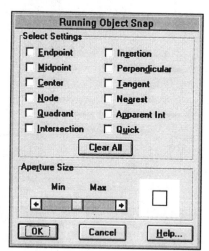

Figure 3-67 Selecting Running Object Snap from the pull-down menu

Figure 3-68 Running Object Snap dialogue box

You can also use the **Running Object Snap** dialogue box (Figure 3-68) to set the running object snap modes. You can invoke the dialogue box from the screen menu (Select ****, DDosnap), from the pull-down menu (Select Options, Running Object Snap..., Figure 3-67), or by entering DDOSNAP at the **Command:** prompt. You can also invoke this dialogue box from the **Object Snap** toolbar by selecting the **Running Object Snap** icon, or from the **Standard** toolbar by selecting the **Running Object Snap** icon in the **Object Snap** flyout. In the dialogue box, you can set the running object snap modes by selecting the rectangular boxes next to the snap modes. For example, if you want to select the ENDpoint and TANGENT snaps, select the toggle boxes next to them, then pick the OK button. The major advantage of using the dialogue box is that it displays the running object snap modes that you have set and you can toggle the values by picking the boxes.

Aperture

As discussed earlier, a target box is added to the screen cross-hairs as soon as the APERTURE command is activated. This is known as the aperture, and only objects residing within or touching the aperture are selected. The size of the aperture is measured in pixels, short for picture elements. Picture elements are dots that make up the screen picture. The aperture size can be changed using the APERTURE command. You can change the aperture in the **Running Object Snap** dialogue box or by typing APERTURE at the **Command:** prompt. In AutoCAD the default value for the aperture size is six pixels. The prompt sequence for changing the aperture size is as follows:

Command: **APERTURE** ←⏎
Object snap target height (1-50 pixels) <current>: *Enter the required number of pixels.*

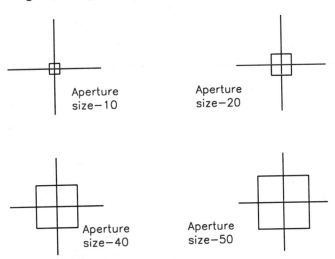

Figure 3-69   Relative aperture sizes

The values of the aperture size range from 1 to 50. Choose a value that suits you best. AutoCAD remembers the value until it is changed. In the **Running Object Snap** dialogue box there is an Aperture Size box with a slider bar, which you can use to adjust the size. If you select the left arrow, the target size decreases by

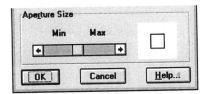

Figure 3-70   Aperture Size box

about one pixel; if you select the right arrow the target size increases by about one pixel. You can also change the target size by dragging the indicator box. On most systems, you can use the slider bar to set the aperture size from 1 to 20. Once you have adjusted the aperture size, select the **OK** button to return to drawing editor.

FUNCTION KEYS

The following is a list of function keys.

F1	Graphics Screen/Text Screen	F8	Ortho On/Off
F5	Iso Top/Iso Right/Iso Left	F9	Snap On/Off
F6	Coordinate dial On/Off	F10	Tablet On/Off
F7	Grid On/Off		

SELF EVALUATION TEST

Answer the following questions and then compare your answers with the correct answers given at the end of this chapter.

1. In the default mode the measurement of angles always starts from 90 degrees corresponding to north. (T/F)

2. The layers that are turned on are displayed on the screen and cannot be plotted. (T/F)

3. The TANgent object snap mode allows you to draw a tangent to or from an existing line. (T/F)

4. You can also combine the snaps by separating the snap modes with a comma. (T/F)

5. The INSert object snap mode is used to snap to the insertion point of a block only. (T/F)

6. In the Surveyors units you are required to specify the bearing angle that the line makes with the _____.

7. The layers are by default assigned _____ linetype and white color.

8. You can display the grid lines at the same resolution as that of the snap grid by using the _____.

9. The _____ object snap can be used to snap to a point object.

10. You can also load and display the **Layer Control** dialogue box by typing _____ at the **Command:** prompt.

REVIEW QUESTIONS

Answer the following questions.

1. You can use decimal unit mode for metric units as well as decimal English units. (T/F)

2. You cannot use the feet (') or inch (") symbols if you have selected the Scientific, Decimal, or Fractional unit format. (T/F)

3. If you select Decimal, Degrees/minutes/seconds, Grads, or Radians, you can enter an angle in any of the five measuring systems. (T/F)

4. Assigning a color to a group of objects is very important for plotting. (T/F)

5. You can lock a layer, which will prevent the user from accidently editing the objects in that layer. (T/F)

6. The **Set** option of the LAYER command allows you to create a new layer and simultaneously make it the current layer. (T/F)

7. When a layer is locked you cannot use the objects in the locked layer for object snaps. (T/F)

8. When the tilemode is turned off, you can freeze the selected layers in the current model space viewport or the paper space by picking **Curr VP Frz**. (T/F)

9. To specify the grid spacing as a multiple of the snap spacing in the GRID command, enter X after the value (2x). (T/F)

10. If the grid spacing is specified as 1 it automatically adjusts to the snap resolution. (T/F)

11. When you are drawing an auxiliary view (a drawing view that is at an angle to other views of the drawing) it is useful to have the snap grid at an angle. (T/F)

12. The **CENter** object snap mode allows you to snap to the center point of a circle or an arc. (T/F)

13. To use the **QUAdrant** object snap, position the target box anywhere on the circle or arc. (T/F)

14. In AutoCAD the default is: angles measured in the _____ direction are positive.

15. If you enter _____ before the angle, AutoCAD will bypass the current angle settings and use the angle as decimal degrees with the default angle base and default angle direction

16. If you enter _____ in front of the angle, AutoCAD will use current angular units, but it will bypass the current settings of angle base and angle direction and use the default angle setting.

17. You can also load the **Unit Control** dialogue box by typing _____ at AutoCAD's Command: prompt.

18. A layer name can be up to _____ characters long, including letters, numbers, and special characters.

19. The difference between the **OFF** option and the **Freeze** option is that the frozen layers are not _____ by the computer while regenerating the drawing.

20. You can use the _____ option of the **Layer Control** dialogue box to selectively display the layers.

21. You can use the **Style** option to set the snap grid to a standard or _____ .

22. The _____ object snap option stops searching as soon as AutoCAD finds a point on the object with the specified object snap.

23. The size of the aperture is measured in _____ , short for picture elements.

EXERCISES

Exercise 5

Set the units for a drawing according to the following specifications:

1. Set the **UNITS** to architectural with the denominator of the smallest faction equal to 16.
2. Set the angular measurement to degrees/minutes/seconds with the number of fractional places for display of angles equal to 2.
3. Set the direction to 0 degrees (east) and the direction of measurement of angles to counterclockwise (angles measured positive in a counterclockwise direction).

Based on the drawing in Figure 3-71, determine and set the limits of the drawing. Also, set an appropriate value for grid and snap. The scale for this drawing is 1/4" = 1'. Leave enough space around the drawing for dimensioning and title block. (Hint: Scale factor = 48; sheet size required 12 x 9; therefore, limits are 12 x 48, 9 x 48 = 576, 432)

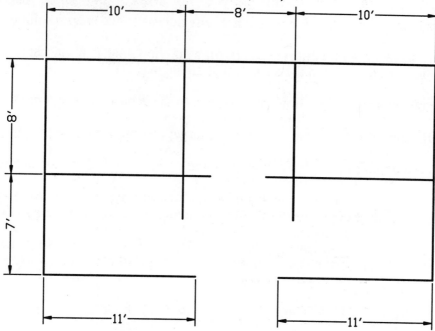

Figure 3-71   Drawing for Exercise 5

Exercise 6

Based on the drawing in Figure 3-72, determine and set the limits and units of the drawing. Also, set an appropriate value for grid and snap. The scale for this drawing is 1 : 10. Leave enough space around the drawing for dimensioning and title block. (Hint: Scale factor = 10; sheet size required 600 x 450; therefore, limits 600 x 10, 450 x 10 = 6,000, 4,500. Also, change the LTSCALE to 500 so that the hidden lines are displayed as hidden lines on screen).

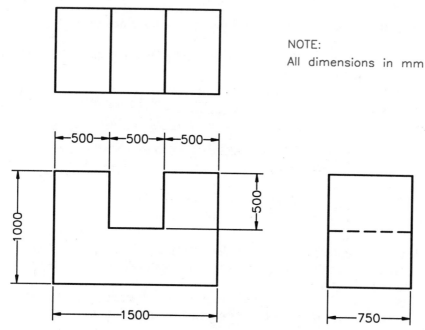

Figure 3-72   Drawing for Exercise 6

Exercise 7

Set up four layers with the following linetypes and colors, then make the drawing (without dimensions) as shown in Figure 3-73.

Layer name	Color	Linetype
Object	Red	Continuous
Hidden	Yellow	Hidden
Center	Green	Center

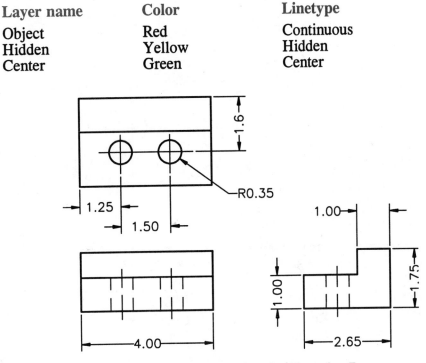

Figure 3-73 Drawing for Exercise 7

Exercise 8

Set up a drawing with the following layers, linetypes, and colors, then make the drawing as shown in Figure 3-74. The distance between the dotted lines is 1 unit.

Layer name	Color	Linetype
Object	Red	Continuous
Hidden	Yellow	Hidden

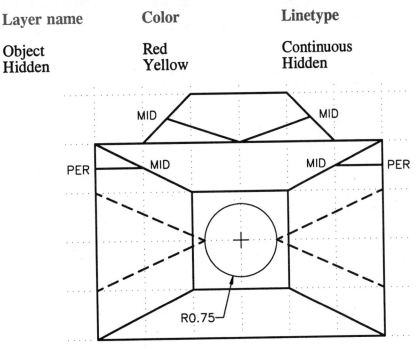

Figure 3-74 Drawing for Exercise 8

Exercise 9

Set up a drawing with the following layers, linetypes, and colors, then make the drawing (without dimensions) as shown in Figure 3-75.

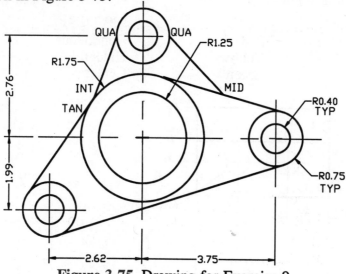

Figure 3-75 Drawing for Exercise 9

Layer name	Color	Linetype
Object	Red	Continuous
Center	Green	Center

Chapter 4

Editing Commands

Learning objectives

After completing this chapter, you will be able to:
◆ Create selection sets using various object selection options.
◆ Use the MOVE command to move objects.
◆ Make copies of existing objects using the COPY command.
◆ Use the OFFSET and BREAK commands.
◆ Fillet and chamfer objects using the FILLET and CHAMFER commands.
◆ Cut and extend objects using the TRIM and EXTEND commands.
◆ Stretch objects using the STRETCH command.
◆ Use the DIVIDE and MEASURE commands.
◆ Create polar and rectangular arrays using the ARRAY command.
◆ Use the ROTATE and MIRROR commands.
◆ Scale objects using the SCALE command.

CREATING A SELECTION SET

Toolbar: Select Objects Toolbar
          Standard, Select Objects
Pull-down: Edit, Select Objects
Screen: SERVICE

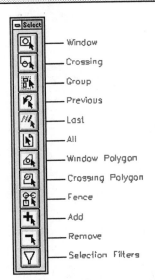

Edit	View	Draw	Construct	Modify	Data
Undo	Ctrl+Z			Window	
Redo				Crossing	
Cut	Ctrl+X			Group	
Copy	Ctrl+C			Previous	
Copy View				Last	
Paste	Ctrl+V			All	
Paste Special...				Window Polygon	
Properties...				Crossing Polygon	
				Fence	
Object Snap				Add	
Point Filters				Remove	
Snap	Ctrl+B			Selection Filters...	
Grid	Ctrl+G			√ Group Selection	
Ortho	Ctrl+L			Hatch Selection	
Select Objects	▶				
Group Objects...					
Inquiry	▶				
Links...					
Insert Object...					

Figure 4-1 Selecting Selection Set options from the Select Objects toolbar

Figure 4-2 Selecting Selection Set options from the pull-down menu

In Chapter 1, we discussed two options (**Window, Crossing**) of the selection set. In this chapter you will learn additional selection set options that you can use to select objects. The selection set options can be accessed from the **Select Objects** toolbar (Figure 4-1) by selecting the desirable icon, from the pull-down menu (Select Edit, Select Objects, Figure 4-2), from the screen menu (Select SERVICE), or by entering the name of the option at the **Select objects:** prompt. The following options are explained here.

Last	**CPolygon**	**Add**	**Undo**
Previous	**Fence**	**Box**	**Single**
All	**Group**	**AUto**	
WPolygon	**Remove**	**Multiple**	

Last

This is the most convenient option if you want to select the most recently drawn object that is visible on the screen. While a selection set is being formed using the **Last** option, only one object is selected even if you use the Last option a number of times. You can use the Last selection option with any command that requires selection of objects (e.g., COPY, MOVE, ERASE). After entering the particular command at the Command: prompt, enter LAST or L at the **Select objects:** prompt or select the **Last** option from the pull-down or the screen menu. The most recently drawn object on the screen will be selected and highlighted. For example, if you use the Last option after drawing Figure 4-3(a), you would get figures (b), (c), and (d) upon each use of the Last option in the **ERASE** command. The prompt sequence is:

Command: **ERASE** ◄┘
Select objects: **LAST** ◄┘
1 found
Select objects: ◄┘   *(Figure b obtained.)*

Command: **ERASE** ◄┘
Select objects: **LAST** ◄┘
1 found
Select objects: ◄┘   *(Figure c obtained.)*

Command: **ERASE** ◄┘
Select objects: **LAST** ◄┘
1 found
Select objects: ◄┘   *(Figure d obtained.)*

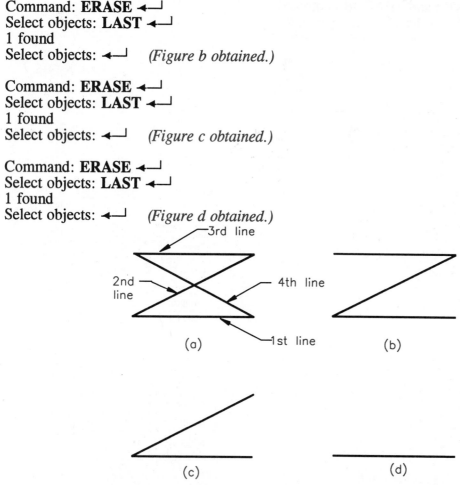

Figure 4-3 Erasing objects using the Last selection option

Exercise 1

Using the LINE command, draw a polygon with eight sides. Then use the **Last** option with the ERASE command to erase the four most recently drawn sides.

Previous

The **Previous** selection option automatically selects the objects in the most recently created selection set. To invoke this option you can enter Previous or P at the **Select objects:** prompt. AutoCAD saves the previous selection set and lets you select it again by using the Previous option. In other words, with the help of the Previous option you can edit the previous set without reselecting its objects individually. Another advantage of the Previous selection option is that you need not remember the objects if more than one editing operation has to be carried out on the same set of objects. For example, if you want to copy a number of objects and then you want to move them, you can use the **Previous** option to select the same group of objects with the MOVE command. The prompt sequence will be as follows:

Command: **COPY** ←┘
Select objects: *Select the objects.*
Select objects: ←┘
<Base point or displacement>/Multiple: *Select the base point.*
Second point of displacement: *Select the point for displacement.*
Command: **MOVE** ←┘
Select objects: **PREVIOUS** ←┘
found

The previous option does not work with some editing commands, like **STRETCH**. A previous selection set is cleared by the various deletion operations and the commands associated with them, like **UNDO**. You cannot select the objects in model space and then use same selection set in paper space or vice versa, because AutoCAD notes the space (paper space or model space) in which the individual selection set is obtained.

All

AutoCAD provides the **ALL** selection option to select all the objects on the drawing screen. Objects that are on the frozen or locked layers are not selected with the ALL selection option. You can use this selection option to erase or move or use any other command that requires object selections. After invoking this particular command, the ALL option can be entered at the **Select objects:** prompt. Once you select the **All** selection option, all the objects drawn on the screen will be highlighted (dotted). For example, if there are four objects on the drawing screen and you want to erase all of them, the prompt sequence will be as follows:

Command: **ERASE** ←┘
Select objects: **ALL** ←┘
4 found
Select objects: ←┘

You can use this option in combination with other selection options. To illustrate this concept, consider there are five objects on the drawing screen and you want to erase three of them. After invoking the ERASE command you can enter ALL at the **Select objects:** prompt, then enter R (R is to remove an object from the selection set) at the next **Select objects:** prompt, followed by CP (CPolygon) at the **Remove objects:** prompt to remove the two particular objects from the selection set. Hence, the remaining three objects are erased.

WPolygon

 This option is similar to the **Window** option, except that in this option you can define a window that consists of an irregular polygon. You can specify the selection area by picking points around the object you want to select (Figure 4-4). In other words, the objects to be selected should be completely enclosed within the polygon. The polygon is formed as you specify the points and can take any shape except the one in which it intersects itself. The last segment of the polygon is automatically drawn to close the polygon. The polygon can be created by specifying the coordinates of the points or by picking the points with the help of a pointing device. With the **Undo** option, the most recently specified

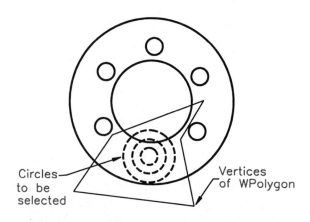

Figure 4-4 Selecting objects using the WPolygon option

WPolygon point can be undone. To use the **WPolygon** option with object selection commands (like ERASE, MOVE, COPY), first enter the particular command at the Command: prompt, then enter WP at the **Select objects:** prompt. The prompt sequence for the WPolygon option is:

Select objects: **WP** ←┘
First polygon point: *Pick the first point.*
Undo < Endpoint of line > : *Pick the second point.*
Undo < Endpoint of line > : *Pick the third point.*
Undo < Endpoint of line > : *Pick the fourth point.*
Undo < Endpoint of line > : ←┘   *(Press the Enter key after picking the last point of the*
polygon.)

Exercise 2

Draw a number of objects on the screen, then erase some of them using the WPolygon to select the objects you want to erase.

CPolygon

 This method of selection is similar to the WPolygon method except that CPolygon also selects those objects that are not completely enclosed within the polygon but are touching the polygon boundaries. In other words, if a portion of an object is lying inside the polygon, the particular object is also selected in addition to those objects that are completely enclosed within the polygon (Figure 4-5). CPolygon is formed as you specify the points. The points can be specified at the Command line or by picking points with a pointing device. Just as in the WPolygon option, the crossing polygon can take any shape except one in which it intersects itself. Also, the last segment is automatically drawn, so that the CPolygon is closed at all times. The prompt sequence for **CPolygon** option is:

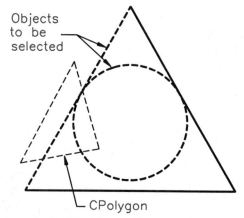

Figure 4-5 Selecting objects using the CPolygon option

Select objects: **CP** ◄┘
First polygon point: *Pick the first point.*
Undo < Endpoint of line > : *Pick the second point.*
Undo < Endpoint of line > : *Pick the third point.*
Undo < Endpoint of line > : ◄┘ *(When finished picking the last point of the polygon.)*

Fence

In this method, a selection set is created by drawing an open polyline fence through the objects to be selected. Any object touched by the fence polyline is selected (Figure 4-6). This mode of selection is just like the **CPolygon** option except that in the fence option the last line of the selection polygon is not closed. The selection fence can be created by entering the coordinate specification at the Command line or by picking the points with the pointing device. More flexibility for selection is provided because the fence can intersect itself. The Undo option can be used to undo the most recently selected fence point. Like the other selection set options, the **Fence** option is also used with commands that need object selection. The prompt sequence is:

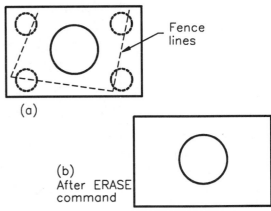

Figure 4-6 Erasing objects using the Fence option

Select objects: **FENCE** ◄┘
First fence point: *Pick the first point.*
Undo < Endpoint of line > : *Pick the second point.*
Undo < Endpoint of line > : *Pick the third point.*
Undo < Endpoint of line > : *Pick the fourth point.*
Undo < Endpoint of line > : ◄┘ *(Press the Enter key.)*

Group

The **Group** option enables you to select a group of objects by their group name. You can create a group and assign a name to it with the help of the **GROUP** command. Once a group has been created, you can select the group using the Group option for editing purposes. This makes the object selection process easier and faster, as a set of objects is selected by entering just the group name. The prompt sequence is:

Command: **MOVE** ◄┘
Select objects: **GROUP** ◄┘
Enter group name: *Enter the name of the predefined group you want to select*
4 found
Select objects: ◄┘

Remove

This option is used to remove an object from the selection set (not from the drawing). Selection of the objects takes place in the **Add mode** (any newly selected objects are added to the selection set). The **R** (Remove) option is used to shift from the Add mode to the **Remove mode**. The Select objects: prompt changes to the **Remove objects:** prompt. You can now select the objects to be removed from the selection set. The Remove option can be used with different commands that require object selection (like ERASE, MOVE, COPY). The following is the prompt sequence illustrating the use of Remove option in the ERASE command:

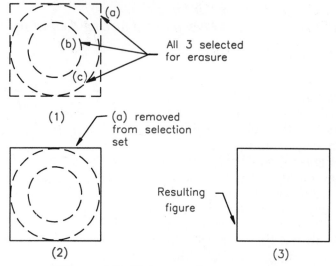

Figure 4-7 Using the Remove option

Command: **ERASE** ←⟋
Select objects: *Select objects "a", "b", and "c".*

If you do not want to erase say object "a", you could continue the prompt sequence as follows:

Select objects: **R** ←⟋
Remove objects: *Select object "a".*
Remove objects: ←⟋

Exercise 3

Draw 6 circles and select all of them to erase using the ERASE command with the **All** option. Now change the selection set contents by removing alternate circles from the selection set using the **Remove** option so that alternate circles are erased.

Add

The **Add** option can be used to return to the **Add mode** from the Remove mode. In the Add mode you can add objects to the selection set. When you begin creating a selection set, you are in the Add mode. You can get into the Add mode by entering ADD or A at the Remove objects: prompt.

Select objects: *Select object.*
Select objects: **R** ←⟋   *(Enter R to get into Remove mode.)*
Remove objects: *Select object to be removed from selection set.*
Remove objects: **A** ←⟋   *(Enter A to get into Add mode.)*
Select objects: *Select object to be included in the selection set.*

Box

The **Box** selection option is used to select objects inside a rectangle. After you enter BOX at the **Select objects:** prompt, you are required to specify the two corners of a rectangle at the **First corner:** and the **Other corner:** prompts. If you specify the first corner on the right and the second corner on the left, the BOX is equivalent to the Crossing selection option, hence it also selects those objects that are touching the rectangle boundaries in addition to those that are completely enclosed within the rectangle. If you specify the first corner on the left and the second corner on the right, this option is equivalent to the Window option and selects only those objects that are completely enclosed within the rectangle. The prompt sequence is:

Select objects: **BOX** ◄─┘
First corner: *Specify a point.*
Other corner: *Specify another point.*

AUto

The **AUto** option is used to establish automatic selection. You can select a single object by picking that object as well as select a number of objects by creating a window or a crossing. If you pick a single object, it is selected, and if you pick a point in the blank area you are automatically in the BOX selection option and the point you have picked becomes the first corner of the box.

Multiple

When you enter M or Multiple at the **Select objects:** prompt you can pick objects at successive Select objects: prompts without the objects being highlighted, hence making the process of selection faster. Once you give a null response to the Select objects: prompt, all the selected objects are highlighted together.

Undo

This option removes the most recently selected object from the selection set.

SIngle

When you enter Single or SI at the **Select objects:** prompt, the selection takes place in the single selection mode. The **Select objects:** prompt repeats until you do the selection. Once you select an object or a number of objects using a Window or Crossing option, the Select objects: prompt is not repeated and AutoCAD proceeds with the command for which the selection is made. You can also create a selection set with the help of SELECT command. The prompt sequence is as follows:

Command: **SELECT** ◄─┘
Select objects: *Use any selection method.*

EDITING COMMANDS

To use AutoCAD effectively, you need to know the editing commands and how to use them to edit the drawing. In this section you will learn about AutoCAD's editing commands. The editing commands can be selected from the toolbar, screen menu, pull-down menu, or they can be entered at AutoCAD's Command: prompt. The MEASURE and DIVIDE commands cannot be accessed from Modify or the Construct pull-down menus. In this section we are going to discuss the following editing commands. (The ERASE and OOPS commands have been discussed in Chapter 1):

MOVE	SCALE	EXTEND	MIRROR
COPY	FILLET	STRETCH	BREAK
OFFSET	CHAMFER	LENGTHEN	MEASURE
ROTATE	TRIM	ARRAY	DIVIDE

MOVE COMMAND

Toolbar: Modify, Move
Pull-down: Modify, Move
Screen: MODIFY, Move:

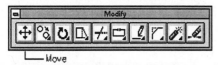

Figure 4-8 Selecting the MOVE command from the Modify toolbar

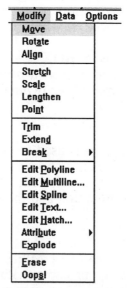

Figure 4-9 Selecting the MOVE command from the pull-down menu

Sometimes the objects may not be located where they should be. In such situations you can use the **MOVE** command. The MOVE command can be invoked from the **Modify** toolbar by selecting the **Move** icon (Figure 4-8), from the pull-down menu (Select, Modify, Move), Figure 4-9), from the screen menu (Select MODIFY, Move:), or by entering MOVE at the **Command:** prompt. This command lets you move the object (or objects) from their present location to a new one. This shifting does not change the size or orientation of the objects. After you enter this command, AutoCAD will prompt you to select the objects to be moved. You can pick the objects individually or use any selection techniques discussed earlier (Window, Crossing, etc.). Next AutoCAD prompts you for the base point. This is any point on or next to the object. It is better to select a point on the object, a corner (if the object has one), or the center of a circle. The next prompt asks you for a second point of displacement. This is the location where you want to move the object. The selected objects are moved from the specified base point to the second point of displacement.

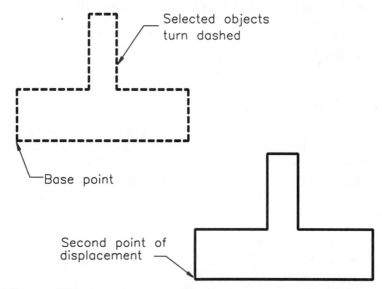

Figure 4-10 Moving an object using the MOVE command

The prompt sequence is as follows:

    Command: **MOVE** ↵
    Select objects: *Choose objects individually or use the selection set.*

Select objects: ◄─┘
Base point or displacement: *Specify any point on or near the object.*
Second point of displacement: *Select the new location by specifying a point on the screen.*

Exercise 4

Draw two concentric circles and move both of them to a different location without changing their relative position with respect to each other.

COPY COMMAND

Toolbar: Modify, Copy Object
Pull-down: Construct, Copy
Screen: CONSTRCT, Copy:

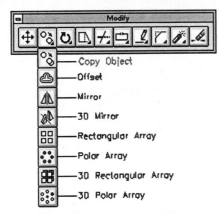

Figure 4-11 Selecting the COPY
command from the Modify toolbar

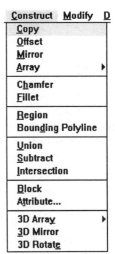

Figure 4-12 Selecting the COPY command
from pull-down menu

This command is used to copy an existing object. This command is similar to the MOVE command in the sense that it makes copies of the selected object and places them at specified locations, but the originals are left intact. In this command, you also need to select the objects and then specify the base point. Now you are required to specify the second point where you want the objects to be copied. The **COPY** command can be invoked from the **Modify** toolbar by selecting the **Copy Object** icon (Figure 4-11), from the pull-down menu (Select Construct, Copy, Figure 4-12), from the screen menu (Select CONSTRCT, Copy:), or by entering COPY at the **Command:** prompt. The prompt sequence is:

Command: **COPY** ◄─┘
Select objects: *Pick the objects to copy.*
Select objects: ◄─┘
<Base point or displacement>/Multiple: *Pick the base point.*
Second point of displacement: *Specify a new position on the screen.*

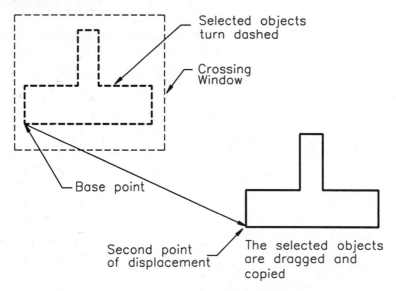

Figure 4-13 Using the COPY command

Multiple Copies

This option of the **COPY** command is used to make multiple copies of the same object. To use this option, select the **Multiple** option or enter M at the **<Base point or displacement>/Multiple:** prompt. You can also pick Multiple from the screen menu. Next, AutoCAD prompts you to enter the second point. When you select a point a copy is placed at that point and the prompt is automatically repeated until you press the Enter key to terminate the COPY command. The prompt sequence for the COPY command with the Multiple option is:

Command: **COPY** ←⏎
<Base point or displacement>/Multiple: **M** ←⏎
Base point: *Specify the base point.*
Second point of displacement: *Specify a point for placement.*
Second point of displacement: *Specify another point for placement.*
Second point of displacement: *Specify another point for placement.*
Second point of displacement: ←⏎

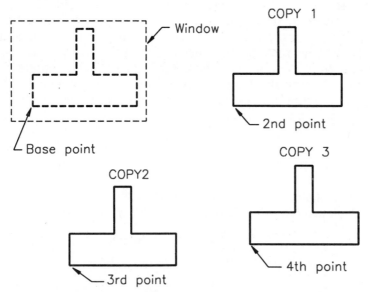

Figure 4-14 Making multiple copies using the COPY command

Exercise 5

a. Draw a circle and use the COPY command to make a single copy of the circle or any other figure you have drawn.
b. Make four copies of the figure drawn in (a) using the Multiple (M) option.

OFFSET COMMAND

Toolbar:	Modify, Copy Object, Offset
Pull-down:	Construct, Offset
Screen:	CONSTRCT, Offset:

If you want to draw parallel lines, polylines, concentric circles, arcs, curves, etc., you can use the **OFFSET** command. This command creates another object that is similar to the selected one. When offsetting an object you need to specify the offset distance and the side to offset. You can also specify a point through which you want to offset the selected object. Depending on the side to offset, you can create smaller or larger circles, ellipses, and arcs. If the offset side is toward the inner side of the perimeter, the arc, ellipse, or circle will be smaller than the original. This command can be invoked from the **Modify** toolbar by selecting the **Offset** icon in the **Copy** flyout, from the pull-down menu (Select Construct, Offset), from the screen menu (Select CONSTRCT, Offset:), or by entering OFFSET at the **Command:** prompt. The prompt sequence is:

Command: **OFFSET** ↵
Offset distance or Through <current>:

At the above prompt you can either enter the **Offset distance** or the **Through** option. The offset distance can be specified by entering a value or by picking two points with the pointing device. AutoCAD will measure the distance between these two points and use it as the offset distance. The prompt sequence for the **Offset distance** option is:

Offset distance or Through <current>: *Pick two points or enter a value.*
Select object to offset: *Pick the object to offset.*
Side to offset? *Specify the side for offsetting.*
Select object to offset: *Pick another object or press the Enter key to complete the command.*

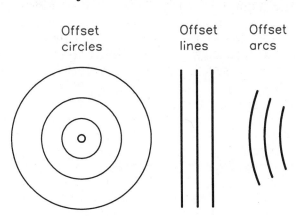

Figure 4-15 Using the OFFSET command

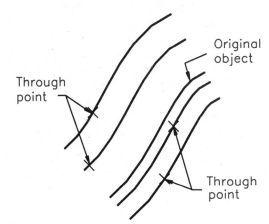

Figure 4-16 Using the Through option in the OFFSET command

In case of **Through** option, you don't have to specify a distance; simply specify an offset point. The offset object is created at the specified point. The prompt sequence is:

Offset distance or Through <current>: **T** ◄─┘
Select object to offset: *Pick the object.*
Through point: *Specify the offset point.*

The offset distance is stored in the **OFFSETDIST** system variable. You can offset lines, arcs, 2D polylines, xlines, circles, ellipses, rays, and planar splines. If you try to offset objects other than these, a message, **Cannot offset that object**, is displayed. The extrusion direction of the selected object does not have to be parallel to the Z axis of the user coordinate system (UCS).

Exercise 6

1. Draw five concentric circles using the OFFSET command.
2. Use the OFFSET edit command to draw Figure 4-17.

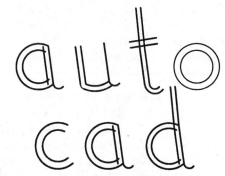

Figure 4-17 Drawing for Exercise 6

ROTATE COMMAND

Toolbar:	Modify, Rotate
Pull-down:	Modify, Rotate
Screen:	MODIFY, Rotate:

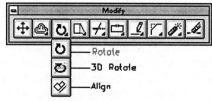

Figure 4-18 Selecting the ROTATE command from the Modify toolbar

Sometimes when making drawings you may need to rotate an object or a group of objects. You can accomplish this by using **ROTATE** command. When you invoke this command, AutoCAD will prompt you to select the objects and the base point about which the selected object will be rotated. You should be careful when selecting the base point, because it is easy to get confused if the rotation base point is not located on a known objects. After you specify the base point you are required to enter a rotation angle. Positive angles produce a counterclockwise rotation; negative angles produce a clockwise rotation. You can invoke this command from the **Modify** toolbar by selecting the **Rotate** icon from the **Rotate** flyout (Figure 4-18), from the pull-down menu (Select Modify, Rotate), from the screen menu (Select MODIFY, Rotate:), or by entering ROTATE at the **Command:** prompt. The prompt sequence is:

Command: **ROTATE** ◄─┘
Select objects: *Pick the objects for rotation.*
Base point: *Specify a base point on or near the object.*
<Rotation angle>/Reference: *Enter a positive or negative rotation angle, or pick a point.*

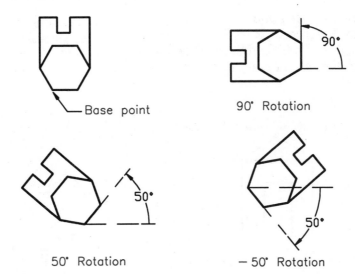

Figure 4-19 Rotation of objects with different rotation angles

If you need to rotate a previously rotated object again with respect to the previous position, you can do this in two different ways using the **Reference** option. The first way is by specifying the angle between the actual position and the current position of the object as a reference angle followed by the proposed angle. The prompt sequence is :

Command: **ROTATE** ◄─┘
Select objects: *Pick the objects for rotation.*
Base point: *Specify the base point.*
<Rotation angle>/Reference : **R** ◄─┘
Reference angle <0>: **135** ◄─┘
New angle: **45** ◄─┘

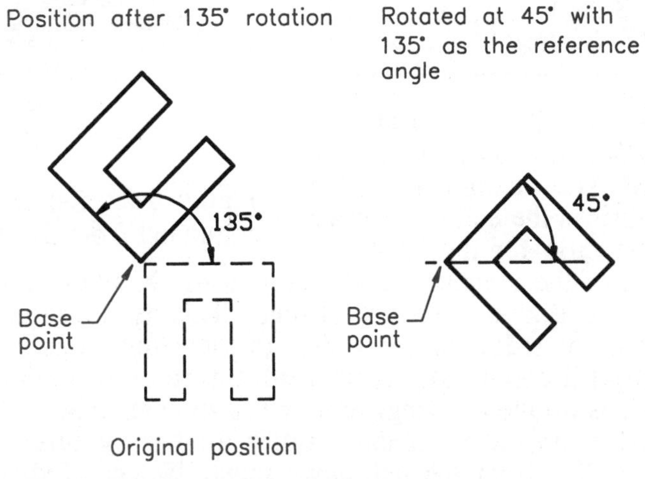

Figure 4-20 Rotation using the Reference Angle option

Here the object is rotated by the new angle from the original position. The original position refers to the position of the object before it was rotated by the particular reference angle. The other method is to pick a reference line on the object and rotate the object with respect to this line. In other words, the reference line of the object is rotated with respect to the X axis. The prompt sequence is:

Command: **ROTATE** ◄─┘
Select objects: *Pick the object for rotation.*

Base point: *Specify the base point.*
<Rotation angle>/Reference: **R** ◂⎯⎦
Reference angle <0>: *Pick the first point on the reference line.*
Second point: *Pick the second point on the reference line.*
New angle: **45** ◂⎯⎦

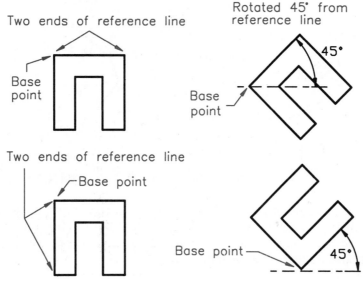

Figure 4-21 Rotation using the Reference Line option

SCALE COMMAND

Toolbar: Modify, Stretch, Scale
Pull-down: Modify, Scale
Screen: MODIFY, Scale:

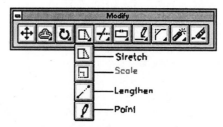

Figure 4-22 Selecting the SCALE command from the Modify toolbar

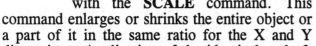

Many times you will need to change the size of a drawing. You can do this with the **SCALE** command. This command enlarges or shrinks the entire object or a part of it in the same ratio for the X and Y dimensions. Application of the identical scale factor to the X and Y dimensions ensures that the shape of the object being scaled does not change. This is a useful and time-saving editing command because instead of redrawing an object to the required size, you can scale the entire object with a single SCALE command. Another advantage of this command is that if you have already put the dimensions on the drawing, they will also change according to the new size. You can invoke the **SCALE** command from the **Modify** toolbar by selecting the **Scale** icon in the **Stretch** flyout (Figure 4-22), from the pull-down menu (Select Modify, Scale), from the screen menu (Select MODIFY, Scale:), or by entering SCALE at the **Command:** prompt. The prompt sequence is:

Command: **SCALE** ◂⎯⎦
Select objects: *Select objects to be scaled.*
Select objects: ◂⎯⎦
Base point: *Specify the base point, preferably a known point.*
<Scale factor>/Reference: **0.75** ◂⎯⎦

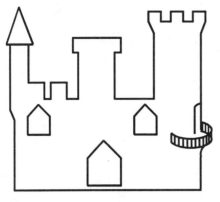
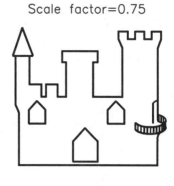

Scale factor=0.75

Original object   Scaled object

Figure 4-23 Using the Scale factor option in the SCALE command

When a drawing is rescaled, a scale factor is used to change the size of selected objects around a chosen base point. The chosen base point remains fixed, whereas everything around it may increase or reduce in size according to the scale factor. For example:

Scale factor	Resulting size
0.25	1/4 of the actual size
0.50	1/2 of the actual size
0.75	3/4 of the actual size
1	No change
2	2 times larger
5	5 times larger

In short, to reduce the size of an object, the scale factor should range from 0 to less than 1; to increase the size of an object, the scale factor should be greater than 1. You can enter a scale factor as given above or pick two points to specify a distance as a factor.

Sometimes it is time-consuming to calculate the relative scale factor. In such cases you can scale the object by specifying a desired size in relation to the existing size (dimension). In other words, instead of using scale factor you can use a **reference length**. To do this, type **R** at the **<Scale factor>/Reference:** prompt. After this you either pick two points to specify the length or enter a length. At the next prompt, enter the desired length. In this option, the scale base point remains a constant. You should try to use object snaps wherever possible. For example, a line is **2.5** units long and you want the length of the line to be **1.00** units. Instead of calculating the relative scale factor, you will use the **Reference** option of the SCALE command. This is illustrated as follows:

Command: **SCALE** ←┘
Select objects: *Select the object.*
Select objects: ←┘
Base point: *Pick the base point.*
<Scale factor>/Reference: **R** ←┘
Reference length: **2.5** ←┘
New length: **1.0** ←┘

If you haven't used the required drawing units for a drawing, the Reference option of the **SCALE** command can be used to correct the error. Select the entire drawing with the help of the **ALL** selection option. Specify the **Reference** option, then pick the end points of the object whose desired length you know. Specify the desired length, and all objects in the drawing will be rescaled automatically to the desired size.

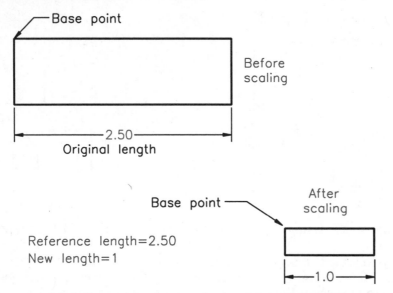

Figure 4-24 Using the Reference option in the SCALE command

FILLET COMMAND

Toolbar:	Modify, Chamfer, Fillet
Pull-down:	Construct, Fillet
Screen:	CONSTRCT, Fillet:

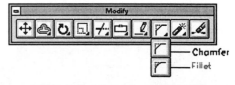

Figure 4-25 Selecting the FILLET command from the Modify toolbar

 This command is used to create smooth round arcs to connect two objects. In mechanical drafting, inside rounded corners are known as fillets and outside ones are known as rounds, but in AutoCAD all rounded corners are referred to as fillets. The **FILLET** command helps you form round corners between any two lines by asking you to identify the two lines. This can be done by picking them with the cursor. This command can be invoked from the **Modify** toolbar by selecting the **Fillet** icon in the **Chamfer** flyout (Figure 4-25), from the pull-down menu (Select Construct, Fillet), from the screen menu (Select CONSTRCT, Fillet:), or by entering FILLET at the **Command:** prompt. A fillet can be drawn between two intersecting parallel lines as well as non-intersecting and non-parallel lines, arcs, polylines, xlines, rays, splines, circles, and true ellipses. The radius of the arc to create the fillet has to be specified. The prompt sequence is:

Command: **FILLET** ↵
Polyline/Radius/Trim/<Select first object>:

Select First Object Option

This is the default method to fillet two objects. As the name implies, it prompts for the first object required for filleting. The prompt sequence is:

Command: **FILLET** ↵
Polyline/Radius/Trim/<Select first object>:R
Enter fillet radius <current>: *Enter a fillet radius.*

Command: **FILLET** ↵
Polyline/Radius/Trim/<Select first object>: *Specify first object.*
Select second object: *Select second object.*

You can select lines with the Window, Crossing, or Last option, but it is safer to select by picking objects individually. Also, selection by picking objects is necessary in the case of arcs and circles that have the possibility of more than one fillet. They are filleted closest to the pick points (Figure 4-26).

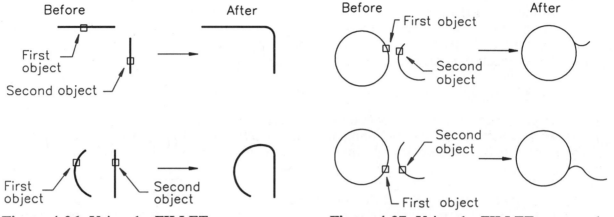

Figure 4-26 Using the FILLET command

Figure 4-27 Using the FILLET command on circles and arcs

You also can fillet a 3D solid (see the Chapter 4 for details). Here you have to pick different edges to fillet, but the edges should be picked individually. The prompt sequence is:

Enter radius <current>: *Specify a radius.*
Chain/Radius <Select edge>:

Select edge
You can go on picking individual edges. Press the Enter key to come out of this option.

Chain
Here you can select a single edge or chain. If you select Chain, all the tangential edges to the selected single edge are automatically chosen. The prompt sequence is:

Chain/Radius <Select edge>: **C** ↵
Edge/Radius/<Select edge chain>: *Select edge chain, or enter E to shift to single edge mode, or R to specify a radius.*

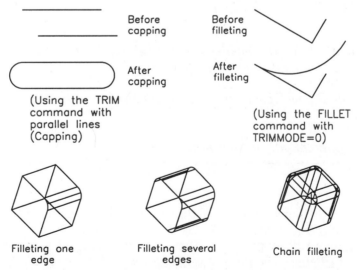

Figure 4-28 Capping parallel lines with the FILLET command, filleting without cutting the geometry, filleting polylines.

The **FILLET** command can also be used to **cap** the ends of two parallel lines. The cap is a semicircle whose radius is equal to half the distance between the two parallel lines. The cap distance, radius of the semicircle, is automatically calculated when you select the two parallel lines for filleting.

> Command: **FILLET**
> (Trim mode) Current fillet radius = 0.0000
> Polyline/Radius/Trim <Select first object>: *Select the first parallel line.*
> Select second object: *Select the second parallel line.*

Radius Option

The fillet you create depends on the radius you specify. The default radius is zero. The new radius you enter becomes the default and remains in effect until changed. Fillet with zero radius creates sharp corners and is used to clean up lines at corners (in case they overlap). The prompt sequence is:

> Polyline/Radius/Trim/<Select first object>: **R** ←┘
> Enter fillet radius <current>: *Enter a fillet radius or press* ←┘ *to accept current value.*

Trim Option

Depending on this option, the selected objects are either trimmed to the fillet arc end points or left intact. The prompt sequence is:

> Polyline/Radius/ Trim/<Select first object>: **T** ←┘
> Trim/No Trim <current>: *Enter T to trim the edges, N to leave them intact.*

Setting TRIMMODE

TRIMMODE is a system variable that eliminates any size restriction on the **FILLET** command. By setting Trimmode to 0, you can create a fillet of any size without actually cutting the existing geometry. Also, there is no restriction on the fillet radius; the fillet radius can be larger than one or both objects that are being filleted. The value of the Trimmode system variable can also be set by entering **TRIMMODE** at AutoCAD's Command: prompt:

> Command: **TRIMMODE**
> New value for TRIMMODE <1>: **0**

Note

TRIMMODE = 0   *Fillet or chamfer without cutting the existing geometry*
TRIMMODE = 1   *Extend or trim the geometry*

When you enter the FILLET command, AutoCAD displays the current Trimmode and the current fillet radius.

You cannot trim different polylines or polyline arcs.

Polyline Option

Using this option you can fillet polylines. If the polyline is selected with the Window, Crossing, or Last options the most recent vertex is filleted. If you select the **P** option AutoCAD prompts you to select a polyline, then all its vertices are filleted. If the selected polyline is not closed then the beginning corner is not filleted. The prompt sequence is:

> Command: **FILLET** ←┘

Polyline/Radius/ Trim/ <Select first object> : **P** ◄─┘
Select 2D polyline: *Pick the polyline.*

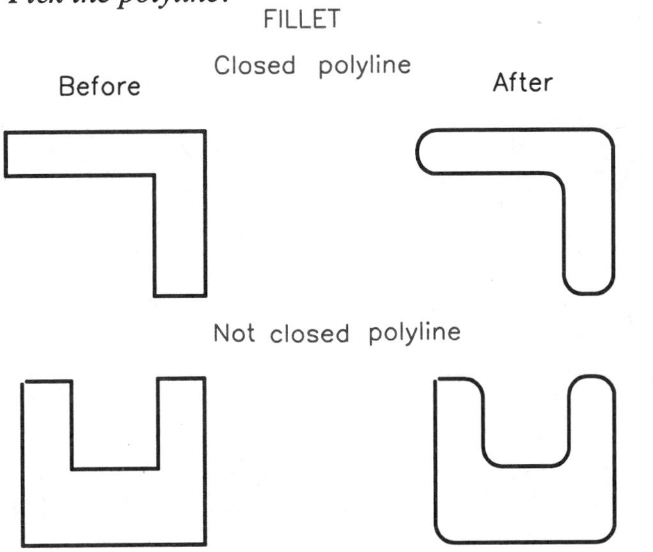

FILLET
Closed polyline

Before   After

Not closed polyline

Figure 4-29 Using the FILLET command on polylines

Filleting Objects with Different UCS

The fillet command will also fillet the objects that are not in the current UCS plane. To create a fillet for such objects, AutoCAD will automatically change the UCS transparently so that it can generate a fillet between the selected objects.

CHAMFER COMMAND

Toolbar:	Modify, Chamfer
Pull-down:	Construct, Chamfer
Screen:	CONSTRCT, Chamfer:

In drafting, the chamfer is defined as the taper provided on a surface. Sometimes the chamfer is used to avoid a sharp corner. In AutoCAD a chamfer is any angled corner of a drawing. A beveled line connects two separate objects to create a chamfer. The size of a chamfer depends on its distance from the corner. If a chamfer is equidistant from the corner in both directions, it is a 45-degree chamfer. A chamfer can be drawn between two lines that may or may not intersect. This command also works on a single polyline. You can invoke this command from the **Modify** toolbar by selecting the **Chamfer** icon in the **Chamfer** flyout, from the pull-down menu (Select Construct, Chamfer), from the screen menu (Select CONSTRCT, Chamfer:), or by entering CHAMFER at the **Command:** prompt. The prompt sequence is:

Command: **CHAMFER** ◄─┘
Polyline/Distances/Angle/Trim/Method/ <Select first line> :

The next prompts displayed are dependent on the option you choose at the above prompt. The different options are as follows:

Select First Line Option

In this option you need to select two non-parallel objects so that they are joined with a beveled line. The prompt sequence is:

Command: **CHAMFER** ◄─┘
Polyline/Distances/Angle/Trim/Method/<Select first line>:**D**
Enter first chamfer distance <current>: *Specify a distance.*
Enter second chamfer distance <current>: *Specify a distance.*

Command: **CHAMFER** ◄─┘
Polyline/Distances/Angle/Trim/Method/<Select first line>: *Specify the first line.*
Select second line: *Select the second line.*

You can also chamfer a 3D solid using this command (Chapter 22 for details). Here AutoCAD prompts you to specify the base surface, which can be either of the two edges that are adjacent to the selected edge. The prompt sequence for a 3D solid is:

Select base surface:
Next/<OK>:

At the **Next/<OK>:** prompt, enter OK if the selected surface itself is the base surface. If you enter N, AutoCAD selects one of the adjacent surfaces to the selected edge as the base surface. The next prompts are:

Enter base surface distance <current>: *Enter distance.*
Enter adjacent surface distance <current>: *Enter distance.*
Loop/<Select edge>:

The default is the **Select edge** option where you can select a single edge to chamfer. If you enter **L**, you are in the **Loop** option and you need to select a loop edge at the **Edge/<Select edge loop>:** prompt. This chamfers all the edges on the loop surface.

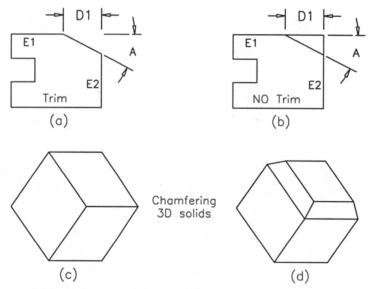

Figure 4-30 Using the CHAMFER command to create a chamfer

Distances Option

Under this option you can enter the chamfer distance. To do this, type **D** at the **Polyline / Distances / Angle / Trim / Method / <Select first line>:** prompt. Next, enter the first and the second chamfer distances. The default value for the chamfer distance is zero. This creates a sharp corner. The new chamfer distances remain in effect until you change them. Instead of entering the two distance values you may simply pick two points on the lines. The prompt sequence is:

Polyline/Distances/Angle/Trim/Method/<Select first line>: **D** ◄─┘

Enter first chamfer distance <current>: *Specify a distance.*
Enter second chamfer distance <current>: *Specify a distance.*

The first and second chamfer distances are stored in the **CHAMFERA** and **CHAMFERB** system variables.

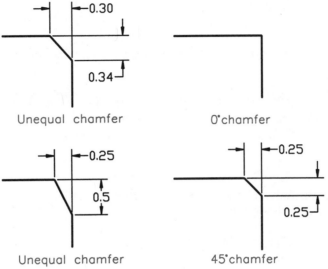

Figure 4-31 Different types of chamfers

Polyline Option

You can use the **CHAMFER** command to chamfer each corner of a closed or open polyline. To do this, select the **Polyline** option after entering the command. Next select the polyline. In case of a closed polyline all the corners of the polyline are chamfered to the set distance values. Sometimes the polyline may appear closed, but if the Close option was not used, it may not be. In this case the beginning corner is not chamfered.

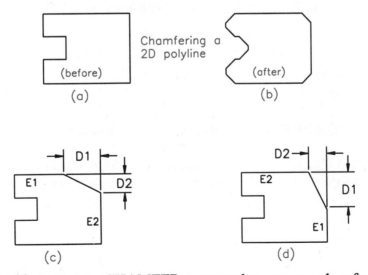

Figure 4-32 Using the CHAMFER command to create a chamfer between two lines or polyline segments

The prompt sequence is:

> Command: **CHAMFER** ◄⏎
> Polyline/Distance/Angle/Trim/Method? <Select first line>: **P** ◄⏎
> Select 2D polyline: *Pick the polyline.*

Angle Option

The Angle option is used to set the chamfer distance by specifying an angle and a distance. The prompt sequence is:

> Polyline/Distance/Angle/Trim/Method? <Select first line>: **A** ◄⏎
> Enter first chamfer distance <current>: *Specify a distance.*
> Enter angle from the first line <current>: *Specify an angle.*

Trim Option

Depending on this option, the selected objects are either trimmed to the end points of the chamfer line or left intact. The prompt sequence is:

> Polyline/Distance/Angle/Trim/Method? <Select first line>: **T** ◄⏎
> Trim/No Trim <current>:

Method Option

By using this option you can choose between the **Distance** option or the **Angle** option. The prompt sequence is:

> Distance/Angle <current>: *Enter D for distance option, A for Angle option.*

Note

If you set the TRIMMODE system variable to 1, the objects will be trimmed after they are chamfered and filleted. If TRIMMODE is set to zero, the objects are left untrimmed.

Setting the CHAMFER System Variable

The chamfer modes, distances, length and angle can also be set by using the following system variables:

CHAMMODE = 0	Distance/Distance (default)
CHAMMODE = 1	Length/Angle
CHAMFERA	Sets the first chamfer distance on the first selected line (default = 0)
CHAMFERB	Sets the second chamfer distance on the second selected line (default = 0)
CHAMFERC	Sets the chamfer length (default = 0)
CHAMFERD	Sets the chamfer angle from the first line (default = 0)

Exercise 7

Draw the top illustration in Figure 4-33, then use the FILLET, CHAMFER, and TRIM commands to obtain the figure as shown in the bottom of Figure 4-33. (Set the SNAP=0.05; assume the missing dimensions.)

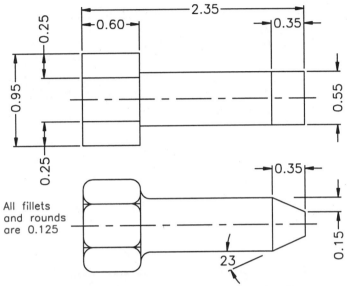

Figure 4-33 Drawing for Exercise 7

TRIM COMMAND

Toolbar:	Modify, Trim
Pull-down:	Modify, Trim
Screen:	MODIFY, Trim:

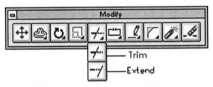

Figure 4-34 Selecting the TRIM command from the Modify toolbar

You may need to trim existing objects of a drawing. Breaking individual objects takes time if you are working on a complex drawing with a large number of objects. The **TRIM** command trims objects that extend beyond a required point of intersection. With this command you must select the cutting edge or boundary first. There can be more than one cutting edge. After the cutting edge or edges are selected you must select the object to be trimmed. If you want to break a single object into two by deleting a portion, you can select two cutting edges on the same object, then select the object to trim between those two cutting edges. You can trim lines, circles, arcs, polylines, splines, and rays. This command can be invoked from the **Modify** toolbar by selecting the **Trim** icon from the **Trim** flyout (Figure 4-34), from the pull-down menu (Select Modify, Trim), from the screen menu (Select MODIFY, Trim:), or by entering TRIM at the **Command:** prompt. The prompt sequence is:

Command: **TRIM** ◄─┘
Select cutting edges: (Projmode = UCS, Edgemode = No extend)
Select objects: *Pick the first cutting edge.*
Select objects: *Pick the second cutting edge.*
Select objects: ◄─┘
<Select object to trim>/Project/Edge/Undo:

Select Object to Trim Option

Here you have to specify the objects you want to trim. This prompt is repeated until you press the Enter key. This way you can select several objects with a single TRIM command. The prompt sequence is:

Command: **TRIM** ◄─┘
Select cutting edges: (Projmode = UCS, Edgemode = No extend)
Select objects: *Pick the first cutting edge.*
Select objects: *Pick the second cutting edge.*
Select objects: ◄─┘
<Select object to trim>/Project/Edge/Undo: *Pick the first object to trim.*
<Select object to trim>/Project/Edge/Undo: *Pick the second object to trim.*
<Select object to trim>/Project/Edge/Undo: ◄─┘

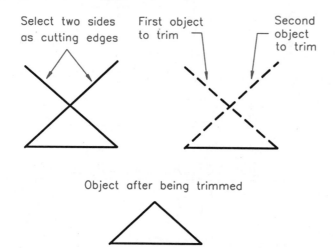

Figure 4-35 Using the TRIM command

Edge Option

This option is used whenever you want to trim those objects that do not intersect the cutting edges but would intersect if the cutting edges are extended. The prompt sequence is:

<Select object to trim>/Project/Edge/Undo: **E** ◄─┘
Extend/No extend <current>:

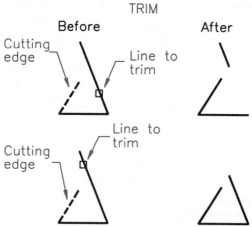

Figure 4-36 Trimming an object using the Edge option (Extend)

Project Option

In this option you can use the projection mode while trimming objects. The prompt sequence is:

<Select object to trim>/Project/Edge/Undo: **P** ◄─┘
None/UCS/View <current>:

The **None** option is used whenever the objects to trim intersect the cutting edges in the 3D space. If you want to trim those objects that do not intersect the cutting edges in the 3D space, use the **UCS** option. In the **View** option, the view is specified along the current view direction.

Undo Option

If you want to remove the previous change created by the TRIM command, enter **U** at the <**Select object to trim**> / **Project** / **Edge** / **Undo:** prompt.

EXTEND COMMAND

Toolbar:	Modify, Trim, Extend
Pull-down:	Modify, Extend
Screen:	MODIFY, Extend:

This command may be considered the opposite of the **TRIM** command. In the **TRIM** command you trim objects; in the **EXTEND** command you can lengthen or extend lines or arcs to meet other lines, arcs, polylines, circles, and rays. This command does not work on closed lines or polylines. The command format is similar to that of the **TRIM** command. You are required to select the boundary edges first. The boundary edges are those objects that the selected lines or arcs extend to meet. These edges can be lines, polylines, circles, arcs, ellipses, rays, splines, text or even viewports. If a polyline is selected as the boundary edge, the line extends to the polylines center. The **EXTEND** command can be invoked from the **Modify** toolbar by selecting the **Extend** icon in the **Trim** flyout, from the pull-down menu (Select Modify, Extend), from the screen menu (Select MODIFY, Extend:), or by entering EXTEND at the **Command:** prompt. The following is the prompt sequence:

Command: **EXTEND** ◄─┘
Select boundary edges: (Projmode = UCS, Edgemode = No extend)
Select objects: *Pick the boundary edge.*
Select objects: ◄─┘
<Select object to extend>/Project/Edge/Undo:

Project Option

In this option you can use the projection mode while trimming objects. The prompt sequence is:

Command: **EXTEND** ◄─┘
Select boundary edges: (Projmode = UCS, Edgemode = No extend)
Select objects: *Pick the boundary edge.*
Select objects: ◄─┘
<Select object to extend>/Project/Edge/Undo: **P** ◄─┘
None/UCS/View <current>:

The **None** option is used whenever the objects to be extended intersect with the boundary edge in the 3D space. If you want to extend those objects that do not intersect the boundary edge in the 3D space, use the **UCS** option. In the **View** option, the view is specified along the current view direction.

Select Object to Extend Option

Here you have to specify the object you want to extend to the particular boundary (Figure 4-37). This prompt is repeated until you press the Enter key. This way you can select a number of objects in a single **EXTEND** command.

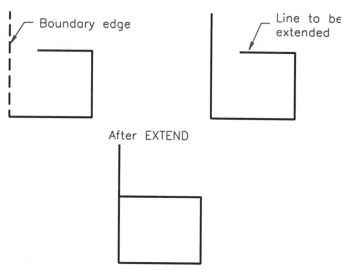

Figure 4-37 Using the EXTEND command

Edge Option

You can use this option whenever you want to extend objects that do not actually intersect the boundary edge in 3D space, but would intersect its implied edge (Figure 4-38). If you enter E at the prompt, the selected object is extended to the implied boundary edge. If you enter N at the prompt, those objects that actually intersect the boundary edge are extended. The prompt sequence is:

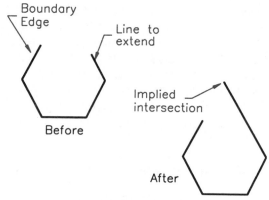

Figure 4-38 Extending an object using the Edge option

    Command: **EXTEND** ◄─┘
    Select boundary edges: (Projmode = UCS,
     Edgemode = No extend)
    Select objects: *Pick the boundary edge.*
    Select objects: ◄─┘
    <Select object to extend>/Project/Edge/Undo: **E** ◄─┘
    Extend/No extend <current>: **E** ◄─┘
    <Select object to extend>/Project/Edge/Undo: *Select the line to extend.*

Undo Option

If you want to remove the previous change created by the EXTEND command, enter **U** at the **<Select object to extend>/ Project/ Edge/ Undo:** prompt.

Trimming and Extending with Text, Region, or Spline

The **TRIM** and **EXTEND** commands can be used with text, region, or spline as edges (Figure 4-39). This makes the TRIM and EXTEND commands two of the most useful editing commands in AutoCAD. The TRIM and EXTEND commands can also be used with splines, ellipses, 3D Pline, Ray, and Xline.

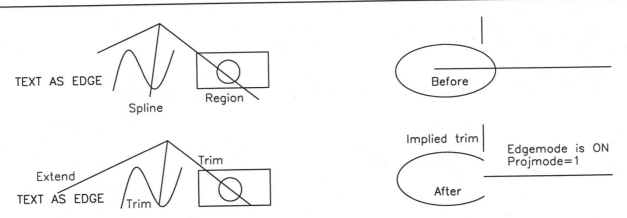

Figure 4-39 Using the TRIM and EXTEND commands with text, spline, and region

Figure 4-40 Using implied trim without a declared edge

The system variables **PROJMODE** and **EDGEMODE** determine how the TRIM and EXTEND commands are executed. The PROJMODE variable is saved with the drawing file; the EXTEDGE variable is not. The following is the list of the values that can be assigned to these variables:

Value	PROJMODE	EDGEMODE
0	True 3D mode	Use regular edge without extension (default)
1	Project to current UCS XY plane (default)	Extend the edge to natural boundary
2	Project to current view plane	

STRETCH COMMAND

Toolbar:	Modify, Stretch
Pull-down:	Modify, Stretch
Screen:	MODIFY, Stretch:

This command can be used to stretch objects. The term stretching an object means changing only one of its dimensions; i.e., changing its length, or width, or height. With this command you may lengthen objects, shorten them, and alter their shapes. If you use this command, you can select the objects individually or use the selection set (Window or Crossing). This command can be invoked from the **Modify** toolbar by selecting the **Stretch** icon in the **Stretch** flyout, from the pull-down menu (Select Modify, Stretch), from the screen menu (Select MODIFY, Stretch:), or by entering STRETCH at the **Command:** prompt. The prompt sequence is:

Command: **STRETCH** ←⏎
Select objects to stretch by crossing -window or -polygon...
Select objects: *Pick the objects using crossing window or polygon.*
Select objects: ←⏎

After selecting the objects you have to specify the point of displacement. You should select only that portion of the object that needs stretching. If the entire object is selected the **STRETCH** command works like the MOVE command.

Base point or displacement: *Pick the base point.*
Second point of displacement: *Specify the displacement point.*

The objects that cross the window or polygon are stretched to the new point. The objects that are inside the crossing window or polygon are moved to the point of displacement.

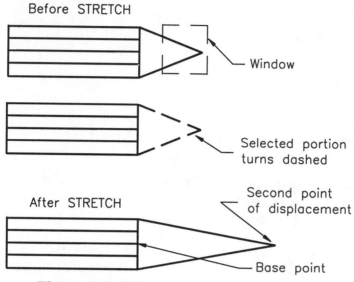

Figure 4-41 Using the STRETCH command

LENGTHEN COMMAND

Toolbar:	Modify, Stretch, Lengthen
Pull-down:	Modify, Lengthen
Screen:	MODIFY, Lengthn:

Like the TRIM and EXTEND commands, the **LENGTHEN** command can be used to extend or shorten lines. The LENGTHEN command has several options that allow you to change the length of objects by dynamically dragging the object end point, entering the delta value, entering percentage value, or entering total length of the object. The **LENGTHEN** command also allows repeated selection of objects for editing. The LENGTHEN command does not have any effect on closed objects, like circles. This command can be invoked from the **Modify** toolbar by selecting the **Lengthen** icon in the **Stretch** flyout, from the pull-down menu (Select Modify, Lengthen), from the screen menu (Select MODIFY, Lengthn:), or by entering LENGTHEN at the **Command:** prompt. The prompt sequence is:

Command: **LENGTHEN**
DElta/Percent/Total/DYnamic/ < Select object > :

< Select object >
This is the default option that returns the length or angle of the selected object. If the object is a line, AutoCAD only returns length. However, if the selected object is an arc, AutoCAD returns the length and angle.

DElta
The **DElta** option is used to increase or decrease the length or angle of an object by defining the delta distance or delta angle. The delta value can be entered by entering a numerical value or by picking two points. A positive value will increase (Extend) the length of the selected

object and a negative value will decrease the length (Trim). The following is the command prompt sequence for decreasing the angle of an arc by 30 degrees (Figure 4-42):

> Command: **LENGTHEN**
> DElta/Percent/Total/DYnamic/<Select object>: **DE**
> Angle/<Enter delta length (default)>: **A**
> Enter delta angle <default>: **-30**
> <Select object to change>/Undo: *Select object.*
> <Select object to change>/Undo: ⏎

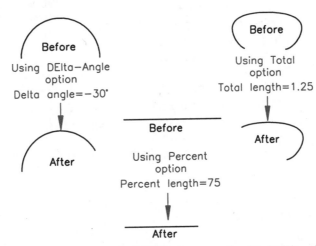

Figure 4-42 Using the LENGTHEN command with DElta, Percent, and Total options

Percent
The **Percent** option is used to extend or trim an object by defining the change as a percentage of the original length of the angle. For example, a positive number of 150 will increase the length by 50 percent and a positive number of 75 will decrease the length by 25 percent of the original value. (Negative values are not allowed).

Total
The **Total** option is used to extend or trim an object by defining the new total length or angle. For example, if you enter a total length of 1.25, AutoCAD will automatically increase or decrease the length of the object so that the new length of the object is 1.25. The value can be entered by entering a numerical value or by picking two points. The object is shortened or lengthened with respect to the end point that is closest to the selection point. The selection point is determined by where the object was selected.

DYnamic
The **DYnamic** option allows you to dynamically change the length or angle of an object by picking one of the end points and dragging it to a new location. The other end of the object stays fixed and is not affected by dragging.

ARRAY COMMAND

Toolbar:	Modify, Copy Object, Array
Pull-down:	Construct, Array
Screen:	CONSTRCT, Array:

In some drawings you may need to specify an object multiple times in rectangular or circular arrangement. For example, suppose you have to draw six chairs around a table. This job can be accomplished by drawing each chair separately, or using the COPY command to make multiple copies of the chair. You could also draw one chair and then with the help of the ARRAY command, create the other five. This method is more efficient and less time-consuming. The ARRAY command allows you to make copies of selected objects in a **rectangular** or **polar** fashion. Each resulting element of the array can be controlled separately. This command can be invoked from the **Modify** toolbar by selecting the desired **Array** icon in the **Copy Object** flyout, from the pull-down menu (Select Construct, Array, Figure 4-43), from the screen menu (Select CONSTRCT, Array:), or by entering ARRAY at the **Command:** prompt. The prompt sequence is:

Figure 4-43 Selecting the ARRAY command from the pull down menu

```
Command: ARRAY ◄─┘
Select objects: Pick objects to copy.
Select objects: ◄─┘
Rectangular or Polar array (R/P) <current>:
```

In the above prompt, **<current>** is the default method to generate the array. The function and results obtained by using the ARRAY command varies depending on which type of array you want to generate: rectangular or polar.

Rectangular Array

A rectangular array is formed by making copies of the selected object along the X and Y axes (along rows and columns). The command allows you to choose the number of rows and columns. The row and column counts must be whole numbers. The default value for both these numbers is 1. The prompt sequence is:

```
Rectangular or Polar array (R/P): R ◄─┘
Number of rows(---) <1>: 3 ◄─┘
Number of columns(|||) <1>: 3 ◄─┘
```

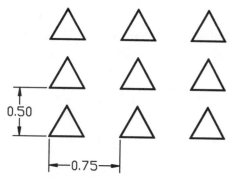

Distance between rows = 0.50
Distance between columns = 0.75

Figure 4-44 Rectangular array with row and column distance

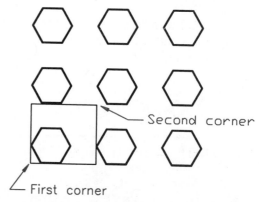

Second corner

First corner

Figure 4-45 Rectangular array selecting unit cell distance

The direction is shown in the parentheses: (---) for horizontal and (|||) for vertical. Next, you are prompted to enter the distances between the rows and the columns. You can simply enter the distance between the rows and the distance between the columns (Figure 4-44):

Unit cell or distance between rows (---): **0.5** ◄┘
Distance between columns(|||): **0.75** ◄┘

Another way to designate the unit cell or distance is by selecting two opposite corners of the rectangle to specify the row and the column spacing. In both cases the height of the original object is included in the distance between rows and the width is included in the distance between columns.

If both the distances between rows and columns are positive, the array is generated above and to the right of the cornerstone element. If the row distance is negative, rows are added downward. Similarly, a negative column distance causes columns to be added to the left. The prompt sequence for **-R,-C** is as follows:

Number of rows (---): **2** ◄┘
Number of columns (|||): **2** ◄┘
Unit cell or distance between rows (---): **-0.40** ◄┘
Distance between columns (|||): **-0.40** ◄┘

As with any command, the process can be terminated before completion by pressing **Esc**.

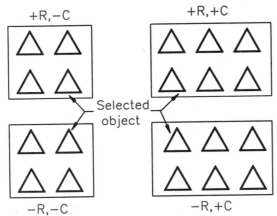

Figure 4-46 Specification of the direction of arrays

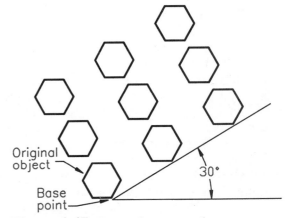

Figure 4-47 Rotated rectangular array

Rotated Rectangular Array

Normally, the **Snap rotation angle** is 0 degrees and AutoCAD builds the array along a baseline defined by this angle. Because of this, rectangular arrays are normally orthogonal. You can change this and create a rotated array by first changing the Snap rotation angle. If you now create an array, it is constructed along a baseline defined by the current Snap rotation angle. In the following example the array is constructed with the Snap rotation angle at **30 degrees**. The prompt sequence is:

Command: **SNAP** ◄┘
Snap spacing or ON/OFF/Aspect/Rotate/Style <0.2500>: **R** ◄┘
Base point <0.0000,0.0000>: *Specify base point.*
Rotation angle <0>: **30** ◄┘

Command: **ARRAY** ◄┘
Select objects: *Pick object to be arrayed.*
Select objects: ◄┘

Rectangular or Polar array (R/P) <current>: **R** ◄┘
Number of rows (---) <1>: **3** ◄┘
Number of columns (|||) <1>: **3** ◄┘
Unit cell or distance between rows (---): **0.5** ◄┘
Distance between columns (|||): **0.75** ◄┘

Polar Array

A polar array is an arrangement of objects around a point in a circular pattern. You can use the **Polar** option of the ARRAY command to draw this kind of array (Figure 4-48). The prompt sequence is:

Command: **ARRAY** ◄┘
Select objects: *Pick object to be arrayed.*
Select objects: ◄┘
Rectangular or Polar array (R/P): **P** ◄┘

The next prompt is:

Center point of array:

Here enter the point around which you want the array to be constructed. In the next three prompts, AutoCAD asks you to enter three parameters:

The number of items in the array.
The angle to fill.
The angle between the items in the array.

You have the option of specifying any two of the three parameters. For the first prompt, **Number of items:**, enter the total number of items in the array, including the original item. If you give a null response to the above written prompt you will have to specify angle to fill as well as the angle between the items. The next prompt sequence is **Angle to fill (+=CCW,-=CW) <360>:**. The letters in the parentheses stand for the counterclockwise and clockwise directions. As is clear from the prompt, a positive angle generates an array in a counterclockwise direction, and a negative angle generates it in a clockwise direction. The array is completely defined if you specify the number of items and the angle to fill. If you supply only one of the two parameters, AutoCAD prompts you for the angle between the items in the array at the prompt **Angle between items (+=CCW,-=CW):**. You should specify the direction of the array at this prompt. If you have not previously specified the number of items, AutoCAD will calculate them automatically. To construct the array, AutoCAD calculates the distance from the array's center point to a point of reference on the last object selected. The reference point applied depends on the object. For example:

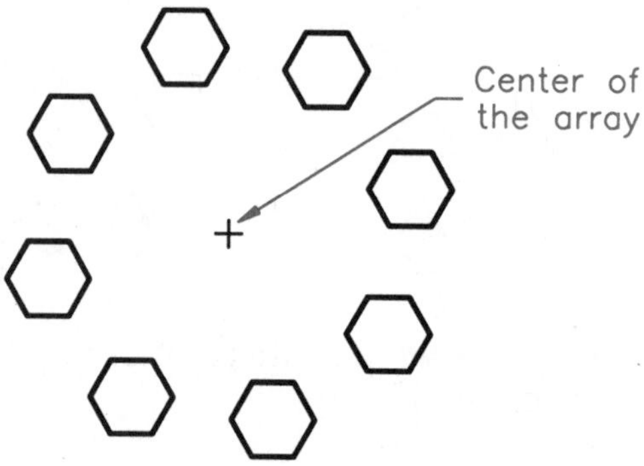

Figure 4-48 Using the Polar option to create a circular array

Point	Insertion point
Circle, Arc	Center point
Block, Shape	Insertion base point
Text	Starting point
Line, Trace, Cone	End point

If you select a group of objects, the entire selection is considered an array item. The copied object is placed at the calculated distance from the array's center point. The next prompt is:

Rotate objects as they are copied? < Y > :

If you respond to this prompt with **N**, the objects are not rotated as they are copied. This means that the replicated objects remain in the same orientation as the original object. You can have the objects rotated as they are copied around a pivot point by entering **Y** at this prompt. Here, the same face of each object points toward the pivot point. The prompt sequence for objects not rotated (Figure 4-49) is:

Command: **ARRAY** ◄─┘
Select objects: *Pick the object to be arrayed.*
Select objects: ◄─┘
Rectangular or Polar array (R/P): **P** ◄─┘
Center point of array: *Pick the center point.*
Number of items: **6** ◄─┘
Angle to fill (+ =ccw, -=cw) < 360 > : ◄─┘
Rotate objects as they are copied? < Y > : **N** ◄─┘

To rotate the objects (Figure 4-50), enter Y or simply press the Enter key at the last prompt.

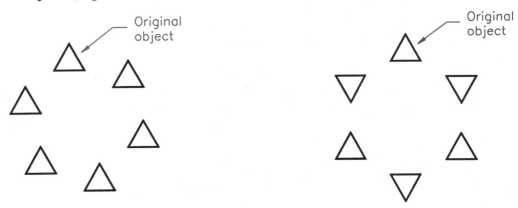

Figure 4-49 Objects not rotated as they are arrayed

Figure 4-50 Objects rotated as they are arrayed

MIRROR COMMAND

Toolbar:	Modify, Copy Object, Mirror
Pull-down:	Construct, Mirror
Screen:	CONSTRCT, Mirror:

The **MIRROR** command creates a mirror copy of the selected objects; the objects can be mirrored at any angle. This command is helpful in drawing symmetrical figures. When you invoke this command, AutoCAD will prompt you to select the objects and then the mirror line. The MIRROR command can be invoked from the **Modify** toolbar by selecting the **Mirror** icon in the **Copy Object** flyout, from the pull-down menu (Select Construct, Mirror), from the screen menu (Select CONSTRCT, Mirror:), or by entering MIRROR at the **Command:** prompt.

After you select the objects to be mirrored, AutoCAD prompts you to enter the beginning and end point of a **mirror line**. The imaginary line about which objects are reflected is called the **mirror**

line. You can specify the end points of the mirror line by picking the points, or by entering their coordinates. The mirror line can be specified at any angle. After the first end point has been selected, AutoCAD displays the selected objects as they would appear on a mirror. Next you need to specify the second end point of the mirror line. Once this is accomplished, AutoCAD prompts you to specify whether you want to retain the original figure (Figure 4-51) or delete it and just keep the mirror image of the figure (Figure 4-52). The prompt sequence is:

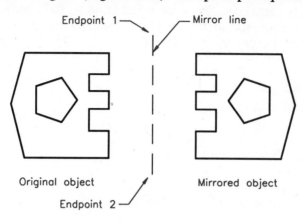

Figure 4-51   Reflecting an object using the MIRROR command

Command: **MIRROR** ◄──┘
Select objects: *Pick the objects to be mirrored.*
Select objects: ◄──┘
First point of mirror line: *Specify the first end point.*
Second point: *Specify the second end point.*
Delete old objects ? < N > : *Enter Y for deletion,* ◄──┘ *or N for retaining the previous objects.*

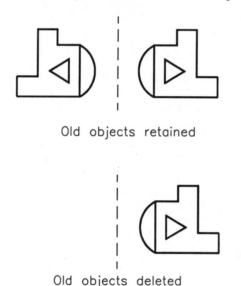

Figure 4-52   Retaining and deleting old objects using the MIRROR command

Text Mirroring

By default, the MIRROR command reverses all the objects, including texts and dimensions. But you may not want the text reversed (written backward). In such a situation, you should use the system variable **MIRRTEXT**.

The MIRRTEXT variable has the following two values (Figure 4-53):

1 = Text is reversed in relation to the original object. This is the default value.

0 = Inhibits the text from being reversed with respect to the original object.

Hence, if you want the existing object to be mirrored but at the same time you want the text be readable and not reversed, set the MIRRTEXT variable to **0**, then use the MIRROR command.

Command: **MIRRTEXT** ←⏎
New value for MIRRTEXT <1>: **0** ←⏎
Command: **MIRROR** ←⏎
Select objects: *Select the objects.*
Select objects: ←⏎
First point of mirror line: *Specify the first point of the mirror line.*
Second point: *Specify the second point.*
Delete old objects? <N>: *Enter Y to delete, N to retain the original objects.*

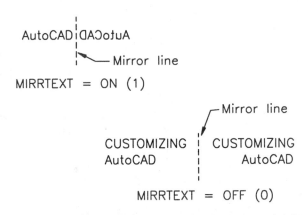

Figure 4-53 Using the MIRRTEXT variable to mirror the text

BREAK COMMAND

Toolbar:	Modify, 1 Point (Break)
Pull-down:	Modify, Break
Screen:	MODIFY, Break:

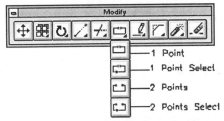

Figure 4-54 Selecting the BREAK command from the Modify toolbar

This command cuts existing objects into two or erases portions of the object. In other words, this command can be used to remove a part of the selected object or break objects like line, arc, circle, ellipse, xline, ray, spline, or polyline.

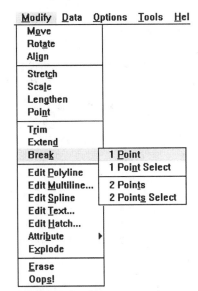

Figure 4-55 Selecting the BREAK command from the pull-down menu

You can select this command from the **Modify** toolbar by selecting the desired **Break** icon from the **1 Point (Break)** flyout (Figure 4-54), from the pull-down menu (Select Modify, Break, Figure 4-55), from the screen menu (Select MODIFY, Break:), or by entering BREAK at the **Command:** prompt. After entering this command, AutoCAD prompts you to select the object to be broken and then the break points. There are four different options for using the break command:

1 Point Option

Using this option, you can break the object into two parts. Here the selection point is taken as the break point and the object is broken there. The prompt sequence is:

Command: **BREAK** ◄─┘
Select object: *Pick the object to be broken.*
Enter second point (or F for first point): **@** ◄─┘

If you select this option from the toolbar, the pull-down menu, or the screen menu, then **@** is automatically entered at the last prompt and the object is broken at the point of selection.

1 Point Select Option

Using the 1 Point Select option you can break the object into two parts, but you are allowed to pick a different break point. In other words, the selection point does not affect the break point. The prompt sequence is:

Command: **BREAK** ◄─┘
Select object: *Pick the object to be broken.*
Enter second point (or F for first point): **F** ◄─┘
Enter first point: *Pick a new break point*
Enter second point: **@** ◄─┘

If you select this option from the toolbar, the pull-down menu, or the screen menu, then **F** and **@** are automatically entered at their respective prompts.

2 Points Option

Here you are allowed to break an object between two selected points. The prompt sequence is:

Command: **BREAK** ◄─┘
Select object: *Pick the object to be broken.*

The pick point becomes your first break point. You are then prompted to enter the second break point. The prompt is:

Enter second point (or F for first point): *Pick the second break point*

Hence the object is broken between those two points and the in-between portion of the object is removed.

2 Points Select Option

This option is similar to the 2 Point option; the only difference is that instead of making the selection point as the first break point, you are allowed to pick a new first point. The prompt sequence is:

Command: **BREAK** ◄─┘
Select object: *Pick the object to be broken.*
Enter second point (or F for first point): **F** ◄─┘
Enter first point: *Pick a new first break point.*
Enter second point: *Pick the second break point.*

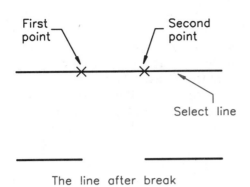

Figure 4-56 Using the BREAK command on a line

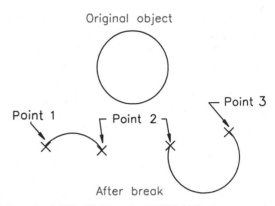

Figure 4-57 Using the BREAK command on arcs and circles

If you need to work on arcs or circles, make sure that you work in a counterclockwise direction or you may end up cutting the wrong part. In this case the second point should be selected in a counterclockwise direction with respect to the first one. You can use the 2 Points and 2 Points Select options to break an object into two without removing a portion in between. This can be achieved by specifying the same point on the object as the first and second break point. If you specify the first break point on the line and the second break point beyond the end of the line, one complete end starting from the first break point will be removed. The extrusion direction of the selected object need not be parallel to the Z axis of the UCS.

Exercise 8

Break a line at five different points, then erase the alternate segments. Next, draw a circle and break it into four equal parts.

MEASURE COMMAND

Toolbar:	Draw, Point, Measure
Pull-down:	Draw, Point, Measure
Screen:	DRAW2, Measure:

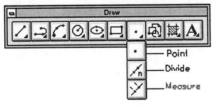

Figure 4-58 Selecting the MEASURE command from the Draw toolbar

 While drawing, you may need to segment an object at fixed distances without actually dividing it. You can use the **MEASURE** command to do so. This command places marks on the given object at a specified distance. The MEASURE command

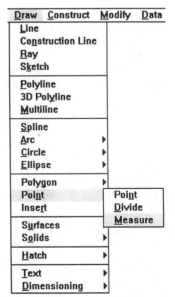

Figure 4-59 Selecting the MEASURE command from the pull-down menu

starts measuring the object from the end point closest to where the object is picked. When a circle is to be measured, an angle from the center is formed that is equal to the Snap rotation angle. This angle becomes the starting point of measurement, and the markers are placed at equal intervals in a counterclockwise direction. This command goes on placing markers at equal intervals of the specified distance without considering whether the last segment is the same distance or not. Instead of entering a value, you can also pick two points that will be taken as the distance. The **MEASURE** command is invoked from the **Draw** toolbar by selecting the **Measure** icon from the **Point** flyout (Figure 4-58), from the pull-down menu (Select Draw, Point, Measure, Figure 4-59), from the screen menu (Select DRAW2, Measure:), or by entering MEASURE at the **Command:** prompt. In the following example a line and a circle is measured at .40 unit distance. The Snap rotation angle is zero degrees.

The prompt sequence is (PDMODE is set to 3):

Command: **MEASURE** ◄┘
Select object to measure: *Pick the object to be measured.*
< Segment length >/Block: **.40** ◄┘

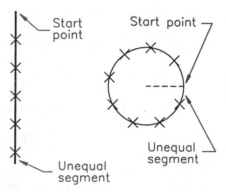

Figure 4-60 Using the MEASURE command

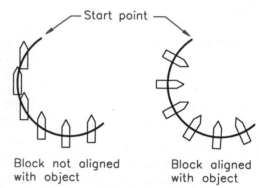

Figure 4-61 Using blocks with the MEASURE command

You can also place blocks as markers, but the block should be defined within the drawing. You can align these blocks with the object to be measured. The prompt sequence is:

Command: **MEASURE** ◄┘
Select object to measure: *Pick the object to be measured.*
< Segment length >/Block: **B** ◄┘
Block name to insert: *Enter the name of the block.*
Align block with object? <Y>: *Enter Y to align, N to not align.*
Segment length: *Enter the distance.*

DIVIDE COMMAND

Toolbar:	Draw, Point, Divide
Pull-down:	Draw, Point, Divide
Screen:	DRAW2, Divide:

This command is used to divide an object into a number of segments of equal length without actually breaking it. This command is similar to the MEASURE command except that here you don't have to specify the distance. The **DIVIDE** command calculates the full length of the object and places markers at equal intervals. This makes the last interval equal to the rest of the intervals. This command can be invoked from the **Draw** toolbar by selecting the **Divide** icon from the **Point** flyout, from the pull-down menu (Select Draw, Point, Divide), from the screen menu (Select DRAW2, Divide:), or by entering DIVIDE at the **Command:** prompt. If you want a line to be divided, first enter the DIVIDE command and select the object to be divided. After this you enter the number of divisions or segments. The number of divisions entered can range from 2 to 32,767.

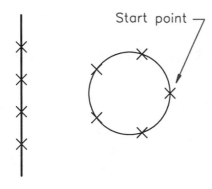

Start point

Divided into five equal parts

Figure 4-62 Using the DIVIDE command

Blocks not aligned with object

Blocks aligned with object

Figure 4-63 Using block with the DIVIDE command

The prompt sequence for dividing a line and circle into five equal parts is:

Command: **DIVIDE** ◄──┘
Select object to divide: *Pick the object you want to divide.*
<Number of segments>/Block: **5** ◄──┘

You can also place blocks as markers, but the block should be defined within the drawing. You can align these blocks with the object to be measured. The prompt sequence is:

Command: **DIVIDE** ◄──┘
Select object to measure: *Pick the object to be measured.*
<Number of segments>/Block: **B** ◄──┘
Block name to insert: *Enter the name of the block.*
Align block with object? <Y>: *Enter Y to align, N to not align.*

Note

The size and shape of points placed by the DIVIDE and MEASURE commands are controlled by the PDSIZE and PDMODE system variables.

Exercise 9

a. Use the MEASURE command to divide a circle into parts with a of length 0.75" and divide a line into 10 equal segments (set PDMODE to 3).

b. Draw the Figure 4-64. Use the DIVIDE command to divide the circle and use the NODE object snap to pick the points.

Figure 4-64 Drawing for Exercise 9

SELF EVALUATION TEST

Answer the following questions and then compare your answers with the correct answers given at the end of this chapter.

1. When you shift a group of objects using the MOVE command, the size and orientation of those objects is changed. (T/F)

2. The COPY command makes copies of the selected object, leaving the original object intact. (T/F)

3. Depending on the side to offset, you can create smaller or larger circles, ellipses, and arcs in the OFFSET command. (T/F)

4. In the BREAK command, when you select an object, the selection pick point becomes the first break point. (T/F)

5. A fillet cannot be created between two parallel and non-intersecting lines. (T/F)

6. A chamfer is equidistant from the corner in both directions only if it is a 45-degree chamfer (T/F)

7. The MEASURE command starts measuring the object from the point where you picked the object. (T/F)

8. The _____ command prunes objects that extend beyond a required point of intersection.

9. The offset distance is stored in the _____ system variable.

10. The _____ command calculates the full length of the object and then places markers at equal intervals.

11. Instead of specifying the scale factor, you can use the **Reference** option to scale an object. (T/F)

12. If the MIRRTEXT system variable is set to a value of 1, the mirrored text is not reversed with respect to the original object. (T/F)

13. A rectangular array can be rotated. (T/F)

14. There are two types of arrays: _____ and _____ .

15. The _____ option of the _____ command is used to draw an array in which the objects of the array are placed in a circular pattern around a point.

REVIEW QUESTIONS

Answer the following questions.

1. In case of the **Through** option of the OFFSET command, you don't have to specify a distance, you simply have to specify an offset point. (T/F)

2. In the BREAK command you cannot break an object in two without removing a portion in between. (T/F)

3. In the FILLET command, the extrusion direction of the selected object must be parallel to the Z axis of the UCS. (T/F)

4. In the FILLET command there can be more than one fillet in the case of arcs and circles. (T/F)

5. The _____ command helps you form round corners between any two lines by asking you to identify the two lines.

6. The _____ command does not work on closed lines or polylines.

7. If the entire object is selected, the _____ command works like the MOVE command.

8. The _____ option of the EXTEND command is used to extend objects to the implied boundary.

9. The term stretching of an object means changing only one of its _____ .

10. If you select the _____ option in the FILLET command, all the tangential edges to the selected single edge are automatically chosen.

11. When a circle is to be measured using the MEASURE command, an angle from the center is formed that is equal to the _____ . This angle becomes the starting point of measurement.

12. The size and shape of points placed by the DIVIDE and MEASURE commands is controlled by the _____ and _____ system variables.

13. In the FILLET command, if the selected polyline is not closed the _____ corner is not filleted.

14. When the chamfer distance is zero, the chamfer created is in the form of a _____ .

15. In the MEASURE command the markers to be placed on the objects are either _____ or _____ .

16. Compare the commands EXTEND and STRETCH._____

17. Describe the commands FILLET and CHAMFER._____

18. Explain how you can move an object from one position to other. _____

19. AutoCAD saves the previous selection set and lets you select it again by using the _____ selection option.

20. The R (Remove) option is used to shift from Add mode to _____ mode.

21. The _____ command restores objects that have been erased by the previous ERASE command.

22. With the help of the **Previous** selection option, you can edit the previous set by reselecting its objects individually. (T/F)

23. Objects on the frozen or locked layers are selected by the **ALL** selection option. (T/F)

24   The **Remove** selection option removes the selected object from the drawing. (T/F)

25.   When you use the **SIngle** selection option with the ERASE command, you can select either a single object or multiple objects. (T/F)

26.   The _____ selection option is used to select objects by touching the objects to be selected with the selection line.

27.   The _____ variable is used to set the default for the number of sides in a polygon

28.   In the case of numerical specification of the radius, the bottom edge of the polygon is rotated by the prevalent _____ angle.

29.   The _____ selection option is used if you want to select the most recently drawn object on the screen.

30.   The _____ selection option enables you to select all the objects on the drawing screen.

31.   In the ARRAY command, if you specify _____ column distance, the columns are added to the left.

32.   You can use the _____ option of the _____ command to rotate an object that has been rotated previously with respect to its original position.

33.   What is the purpose of the ARRAY command? _____
    _____

34.   Explain the difference between a polar and a rectangular array. _____
    _____

35.   Before creating a rectangular array, what values should you know? _____
    _____

36.   Define a unit cell. _____
    _____

37.   Suppose an object is 2 inches wide and you want a rectangular array with 1-inch spacing between objects. What should the column distance be? _____
    _____

38.   Explain how you can create a rotated rectangular array. _____
    _____

39.   In a polar array suppose you enter a value for "Number of items" prompt. From the following options, pick the one you are not required to give:

    A. Angle to fill.
    B. Angle between items
    C. Center point.
    D. Rotate objects as they are copied.

40.   The _____ can be used to increase the length of a line by 25 percent.

EXERCISES

Exercise 10

Draw the object shown in Figure 4-65 and save the drawing. Assume the missing dimensions.

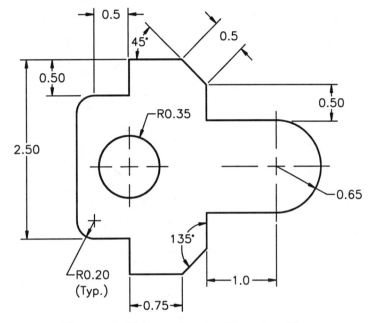

Figure 4-65 Drawing for Exercise 10

Exercise 11

Make the drawing shown in Figure 4-66 and save the drawing. You can use the ARRAY command to make copies of the bolt hole details.

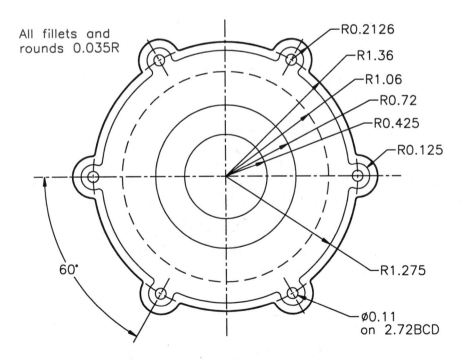

Figure 4-66 Drawing for Exercise 11

Exercise 12

Make the drawing shown in Figure 4-67 and save the drawing.

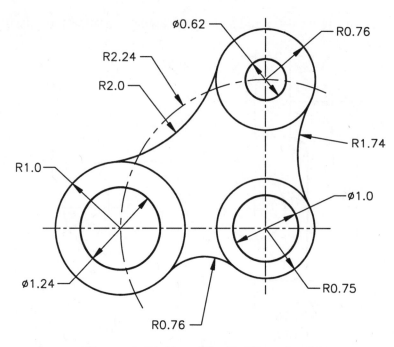

Figure 4-67 Drawing for Exercise 12

Exercise 13

Make the drawing shown in Figure 4-68 and save the drawing. Assume the missing dimensions.

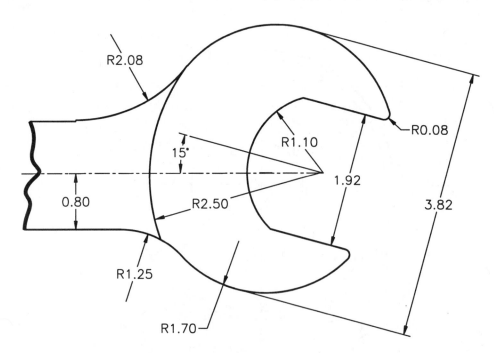

Figure 4-68 Drawing for Exercise 13

Exercise 14

Make the drawing shown in Figure 4-69 using draw and edit commands and save the file. Assume the missing dimensions.

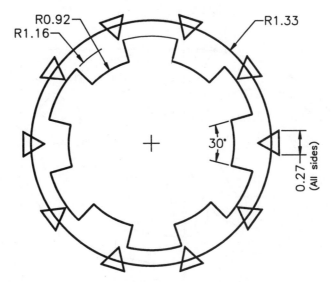

Figure 4-69 Drawing for Exercise 14

Exercise 15

Draw Figure 4-70 using draw and edit commands. Save the file. Assume the missing dimensions.

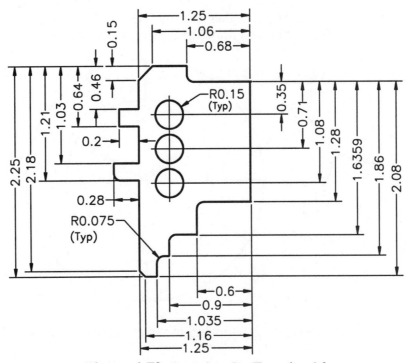

Figure 4-70 Drawing for Exercise 16

Exercise 16
Make the drawing shown in Figure 4-71 and save the drawing.

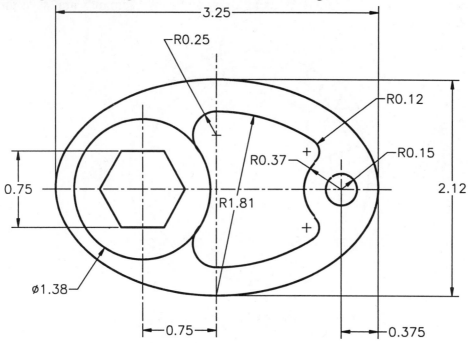

Figure 4-71 Drawing for Exercise 18

Exercise 17
Make the drawing shown in part (a), and then use the ARRAY command to obtain the drawing shown in part (b) of Figure 4-72. You can draw the figure to any size.

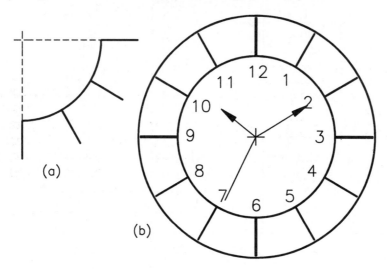

Figure 4-72 Drawing for Exercise 19

Answers

Following are the correct answers to the questions of the self evaluation test.
1 - F, 2 - T, 3 - T, 4 - T, 5 - F, 6 - T, 7 - F, 8 - TRIM, 9 - OFFSETDIST, 10 - DIVIDE, 11 - T, 12 - F, 13 - T, 14 - Rectangular, Polar, 15 - Polar, ARRAY

Chapter 5

Controlling Drawing Display
Creating Text

Learning objectives

After completing this chapter, you will be able to:
♦ Use the REDRAW and REGEN commands.
♦ Use the ZOOM command and its options.
♦ Understand the PAN and VIEW commands.
♦ Use AutoCAD's text commands such as TEXT and DTEXT.
♦ Draw special characters in AutoCAD.
♦ Determine text height for drawings with different scales.
♦ Create text styles using the STYLE command.
♦ Edit text using the DDEDIT command.
♦ Create paragraph text for DOS and Windows.
♦ Edit paragraph text using the DDEDIT and DDMODIFY commands.

BASIC DISPLAY OPTIONS

Drawing in AutoCAD is much simpler than manual drafting in many ways. Sometimes while drawing, it is very difficult to see and alter minute details. In AutoCAD, you can overcome this problem by viewing only a specific portion of the drawing. For example, if you want to display a part of the drawing on a larger area you can use **ZOOM** command. This command lets you enlarge or reduce the size of the drawing displayed on the screen. Similarly, you can use REGEN command to regenerate the drawing and REDRAW to refresh the screen. In this chapter you will learn some of the drawing display commands, like **REDRAW, REGEN, PAN, ZOOM** and **VIEW**.

REDRAW COMMAND

This command redraws the screen, thereby removing the small cross marks that appear when a point is picked on the screen. These marks are known as blip marks or **blips**. Blip marks indicate the points you have selected (points picked). The blip mark is not treated as an element of the drawing. In AutoCAD several commands redraw the screen automatically (for example, when a grid is turned off), but it is sometimes useful to explicitly redraw the screen. Redrawing is used to remove blips and fill empty spaces left on the screen after objects have been deleted from the drawing. It also redraws the objects that do not display on the screen as a result of editing some other object. In AutoCAD the **REDRAW** command can also be used in the **transparent** mode. Transparent commands are commands that can be used while another command is in progress. ZOOM, PAN, and VIEW are some other transparent commands. Once you have completed the process involved with a transparent command, AutoCAD automatically returns you to the command with which you were working before you invoked the transparent command.

Toolbar: Standard toolbar, Redraw
             View
Pull-down: View, Redraw View
Screen: VIEW, Redraw:

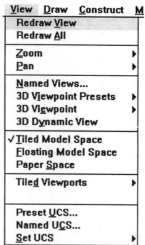

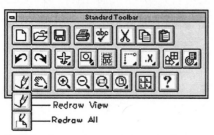

Figure 5-1 Selecting Redraw View from the toolbar

Figure 5-2 Selecting the REDRAW command from the pull-down menu

Use of the **REDRAW** command does not involve a prompt sequence; instead, the redrawing process takes place without prompting you for any kind of information. You can invoke this command by entering **R** or **REDRAW** at the **Command:** prompt, from the **Standard** toolbar by selecting the **Redraw View** icon (Figure 5-1), from the pull-down menu (Select View, Redraw View, Figure 5-2), from the screen menu (Select VIEW, Redraw:) or from the tablet menu if you have the tablet facility. The prompt sequence is:

Command: **REDRAW** ◄┘

If the command is to be entered while you are working inside another command, type an apostrophe in front of the command. The apostrophe appended to a command indicates that the command is to be used as a transparent command (Command: **'REDRAW** ◄┘).

As with any other command, pressing **Esc** stops the command from taking effect and takes you back to the **Command:** prompt. The REDRAW command affects only the current viewport. If you have more than one viewport you can use the **REDRAWALL** command to redraw all the viewports. This command is also present in the **VIEW** screen menu and the **View** pull-down menu.

While working on complex drawings it may be better to set the blipmode off instead of using REDRAW command to clear blips. This can be done by using the **BLIPMODE** command. The prompt sequence is:

Command: **BLIPMODE** ◄┘
ON/OFF <current>: **OFF** ◄┘

Now the blips will not be displayed when you pick a point on the screen. You can turn the BLIPMODE on to get the blips. The blips can also be turned **off/on** in the **Drawing Aids** dialogue box. This dialogue box can be invoked from the pull-down menu (Select Options, Drawing Aids...,Figure 5-3) or by entering

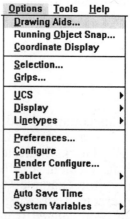

Figure 5-3 Selecting the Drawing Aids from the pull-down menu

DDRMODES at the **Command:** prompt. The **Drawing Aids** dialogue box (Figure 5-4) is displayed with a number of options, one of which is **Blips**. You can switch the blips on/off by picking the toggle button next to it.

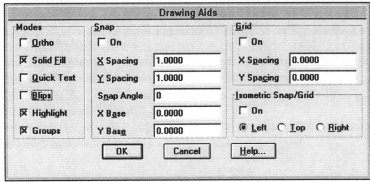

Figure 5-4 Drawing Aids dialogue box

REGEN COMMAND

The **REGEN** command makes AutoCAD regenerate the entire drawing to update it. The need for regeneration usually occurs when you change certain aspects of the drawing. All the objects in the drawing are recalculated and the current viewport is redrawn. This is a longer process than REDRAW and is seldom needed. One of the advantages of this command is that the drawing is refined by smoothing out circles and arcs. To use this command, enter **REGEN** at the **Command:** prompt:

Command: **REGEN** ←⏎

AutoCAD displays the message **Regenerating drawing** while it regenerates the drawing. The REGEN command affects only the current viewport. If you have more than one viewport you can use the **REGENALL** command to regenerate all the viewports. Like the REDRAW command, the REGEN command can also be aborted by pressing the **Esc** key. This saves time if you're going to use another command that causes automatic regeneration. As mentioned above, the REGEN command can also be used as a transparent command. In such a case, the REGEN command is entered in the following manner:

Command: **'REGEN** ←⏎

Note

Under certain conditions, the ZOOM, PAN, and VIEW commands automatically regenerate the drawing. Some other commands also perform regenerations under certain conditions.

AUTOCAD'S VIRTUAL SCREEN

You can understand the ZOOM command better if you understand the relationship between REDRAW, REGEN, and the virtual screen. First, it should be understood that different features (such as coordinate values, angle, diameter, radii, etc.) associated with drawn objects are saved in the AutoCAD database as **floating point numbers**. The floating point format is used to achieve a high degree of accuracy, but these calculations take longer time than calculations done with integers. If you load a new drawing or use the REGEN command, AutoCAD converts the floating point values stored in the database to **integer screen pixel coordinates**. A considerable amount of time is spent in the conversion process, which AutoCAD avoids whenever feasible. AutoCAD upholds a screen between the drawing and each active viewport. AutoCAD recalculates the points as if the display were a 32,000 x 32,000-pixel screen. This is known as the virtual screen, and it contains the last recalculation (or regeneration) of the graphic database. When regeneration takes place, the floating point database is converted into the integer coordinates of the virtual screen. Next, a redraw is performed that translates the virtual screen coordinates to the physical screen coordinates (much more quickly), resulting in a drawing of the figure. AutoCAD translates the calculated image into a drawing on your current viewport.

Note

AutoCAD can perform a redraw several times faster than a regeneration, so you should use REDRAW to refresh the screen. Use REGEN (REGENERATE) only when you want to re-calculate the drawing vectors.

ZOOM COMMAND

Toolbar:	Standard toolbar, Zoom
Pull-down:	View, Zoom
Screen:	VIEW, Zoom:

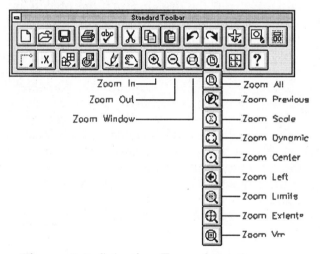

Figure 5-5 Selecting Zoom from the toolbar

Figure 5-6 Selecting the ZOOM command from the pull-down menu

Creating drawings on the screen would not be of much use if you could not magnify the drawing view to work on minute details. Getting close to or away from the drawing is the function of the ZOOM command. In other words, this command enlarges or reduces the size of the drawing on the screen, but it does not affect the actual size. In this way the **ZOOM** command functions like the zoom lens on a camera. When you magnify the apparent size of a section of the drawing, you see that area in greater detail. On the other hand, if you reduce the apparent size of the drawing, you see a larger area. The ability to zoom in or magnify has been helpful in creating the miniscule circuits used in the electronics and the computer industries. This command is one of the most frequently used. Also, this command can be used transparently, which means that it can be used while working in other commands. This command has 10 options and can be used in a number of ways. The **ZOOM** command can be invoked from the **Standard** toolbar by selecting the desired **Zoom** icon (Figure 5-5), from the pull-down menu (Select View, Zoom, Figure 5-6), from the screen menu (Select VIEW, Zoom:), or by entering ZOOM at the **Command:** prompt. After the ZOOM command has been entered, different options are listed:

Command: **ZOOM** ↵
All/Center/Dynamic/Extents/Left/Previous/Vmax/Window/ < Scale(X/XP) > :

ALL Option

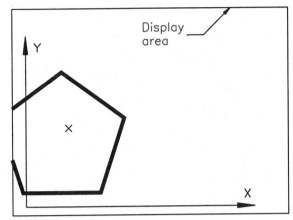

This option of the **ZOOM** command displays the drawing limits (Figure 5-7) or extents, whichever is greater. Even if the objects are not within the limits, they are still included in the display. Hence, with the help of the **ALL** option, you can view the entire drawing in the current viewport (Figure 5-8).

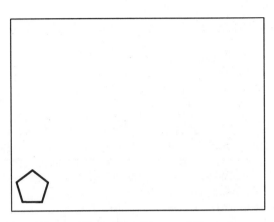

Figure 5-7 Drawing showing Limits

Figure 5-8 The Zoom All option

Center Option

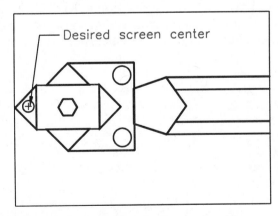

This option lets you define a new display window by specifying its center point. Here, you are required to enter the **center** and the **height** of the subsequent screen display. Instead of entering a height you can enter the **magnification factor** by typing a number. If the height you enter is the same as the current height, magnification does not take place. For example, if the current height is 2.7645 and you enter 2.7645 at the **Magnification or Height <2.7645>:** prompt, magnification will not take place. The smaller the value the greater the enlargement of the image. You can also enter a number followed by **X**. This indicates the change in magnification, not as an absolute value but as a value relative to the current screen.

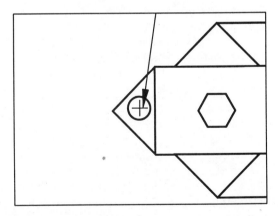

Figure 5-9 Drawing before using the Zoom Center option

Figure 5-10 Drawing after using the Zoom Center option

The following is the prompt sequence:

Command: **ZOOM** ◄┘
All/Center/Dynamic/Extents/Left/Previous/Vmax/Window/ < Scale(X/XP) > : **C** ◄┘
Center point: *Pick a center point*.
Magnification or Height <current> : **5X** ◄┘

In Figure 5-10 the current magnification height is 5, and the new one is 2. Because we have specified a lesser value than the current one, the image size has been increased.

The prompt sequence is:

Command: **ZOOM** ←⏎
All/Center/Dynamic/Extents/Left/Previous/Vmax/Window/ < Scale(X/XP) > : **C** ←⏎
Center point: *Select a point.*
Magnification or Height < 5.0 > : **2** ←⏎

Extents Option

 As the name indicates, this option lets you zoom to the extents of the drawing. The extents of the drawing comprises the area that has the drawings in it. The rest of the empty area is neglected. With this option, all the objects in the drawing are magnified to the largest possible display.

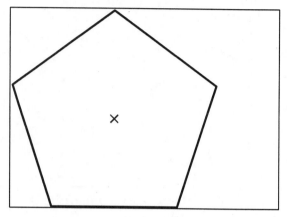

Figure 5-11 The Zoom Extents Option

Dynamic Option

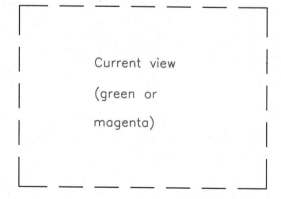 This option displays the portion of the drawing that you have already specified. The prompt sequence for using this option of the ZOOM command is:

Command: **ZOOM** ←⏎
All/Center/Dynamic/Extents/Left/Previous/Vmax/Window/ < Scale(X/XP) > : **D** ←⏎

You can now specify the area you want to be displayed by constructing a view box representing your viewport. This option lets you enlarge or shrink the view box and move it around. When you have the view box in the proper position and size, the current viewport is cleared by AutoCAD and a special view selection screen is displayed. This special screen comprises information regarding the current as well as available views. In a color display the different viewing windows are very easy to distinguish because of their different colors, but in a monochrome monitor they can be distinguished by their shape.

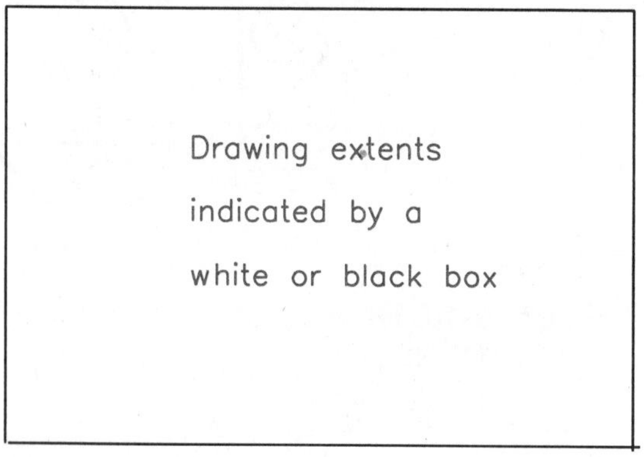

Drawing extents
indicated by a
white or black box

Current view
(green or
magenta)

Figure 5-12 Box representing drawing extents

Figure 5-13 Representation of the current view

White Box Representing Drawing Extents
Drawing extents are represented by a white or a black box (Figure 5-12), which constitutes the larger of the drawing limits or the actual area occupied by the drawing.

Green or Magenta Box Representing the Current View
A green or magenta dashed box is formed to represent the area that the current viewport comprises when the **Dynamic** option of the ZOOM command is invoked (Figure 5-13).

Generated Area Represented by Four Red Corners:
Four red corners indicate the portion of the drawing generated by AutoCAD to be viewed at high speed (Figure 5-14). Although moving outside this area is valid, it forces PAN or ZOOM to proceed at the speed of REGEN rather than at REDRAW's faster speed.

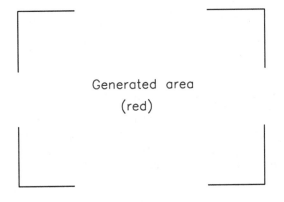

Figure 5-14 The generated area

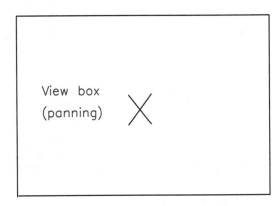

Figure 5-15 The panning view box

Panning View Box (X in the center)
A view box initially of the same size as the current view box (the green or magenta box) is displayed with an X in the center (Figure 5-15). You can move this box with the help of your pointing device. This box is known as the **panning view box** and it helps you to find the center point of the zoomed display you want. When you have found the center, press the pick button to make the zooming view box appear.

Zooming View Box (arrow on the right side)
After you press the pick button in the center of the panning view box, the X in the center of the view box is replaced by an arrow pointing to the right edge of the box. This is the **zooming view box** and indicates the ZOOM mode. You can now increase or decrease the area of this box according to the area you want to zoom into. To shrink the box, move the pointer to the left; to increase it, move the pointer to the right. You can move the box up or down and then increase or decrease, it but the box cannot be moved to the left. When you have the zooming view box in the exact position for your zoom display, press the Enter key to complete the

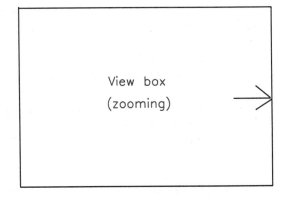

Figure 5-16 The zooming view box

command and zoom into the desired area of the drawing. Before pressing the Enter key, if you want to change the position of the zooming view box, click the pick button of your pointing device to make the panning view box reappear. After repositioning it press the Enter key.

Speed Considerations in the ZOOM Dynamic Command

The ZOOM dynamic command causes AutoCAD to draw the currently generated image within the image box (the red corners box). This drawing takes place in the background and while it is being performed, you can perform the panning and zooming operations. These two operations are fast. If an area outside the red corners is selected or if the area to zoom into is very small, AutoCAD has to regenerate the drawing. This takes a long time. To indicate and warn the user of this condition an hourglass is displayed in the lower left corner of the screen (Figure 5-17). This indicates that the current view box requires a regeneration.

Figure 5-17 The hourglass shape

Left Option

This option lets you pick the **lower left corner** of screen display. Then it prompts you for the **height** or **magnification**. Just as in the **Center** option, you can enter a number followed by an X. This indicates the change in magnification, not as an absolute value, but as a value relative to the current screen. Hence this option is identical to the Center option, except that instead of entering the center you enter the lower left corner. For example:

Command: **ZOOM** ↵
All/Center/Dynamic/Extents/Left/Previous/Vmax/Window/ < Scale(X/XP) > : **L** ↵
Lower left corner: *Pick a point*.
Magnification or Height < current > : **5X** ↵

Previous Option

While working on a complex drawing, you may need to zoom in to a portion of the drawing to edit some minute details. Once the editing is over you may want to return to the previous view. This can be done using the **Previous** option of the ZOOM command. Without this option it would be very tedious to zoom back to previous views. AutoCAD saves the current viewport whenever it is being altered by any of the ZOOM options or by the PAN, VIEW Restore, DVIEW, or PLAN commands (which are discussed later). Up to 10 views are saved for each viewport. The prompt sequence for this option is:

Command: **ZOOM** ↵
All/Center/Dynamic/Extents/Left/Previous/Vmax/Window/ < Scale(X/XP) > : **P** ↵

Successive ZOOM P commands can restore the previous 10 views. The term **view** here refers to the area of the drawing defined by its display extents. If you erase some objects and then issue a ZOOM Previous command, the previous display extents are restored but the erased objects are not.

Vmax Option

As discussed earlier, there is a **virtual screen** with approximately four billion pixels in the X and Y axes. The **Vmax** option lets you zoom out as far as possible on the current viewport's virtual screen without forcing a complete regeneration of your drawing. The prompt sequence is:

Command: **ZOOM** ←⏎
All/Center/Dynamic/Extents/Left/Previous/Vmax/Window/ < Scale(X/XP) > : **Vmax** ←⏎

Window Option

This is the most commonly used option of the ZOOM command. It lets you specify the area you want to zoom in, by letting you pick two opposite corners of a rectangular window. The center of the specified window becomes the center of the new display screen. The area inside the window is magnified or reduced in size to fill the display as completely as possible. The points can be specified either by picking them with the help of the pointing device or by entering their coordinates. The prompt sequence is:

Command: **ZOOM** ←⏎
All/Center/Dynamic/Extents/Left/Previous/Vmax/Window/ < Scale(X/XP) > : *Pick a point.*
Other corner: *Pick another point.*

Whenever the **ZOOM** command is invoked, the window method is one of the default options. This is illustrated by the previous prompt sequence, where you can specify the two corner points of the window without invoking any option of the ZOOM command. The **Window** option can also be used by entering **W**. In this case the prompt sequence is:

Command: **ZOOM** ←⏎
All/Center/Dynamic/Extents/Left/Previous/Vmax/Window/ < Scale(X/XP) > : **W** ←⏎
First corner: *Pick a point.*
Other corner: *Pick another point.*

Scale Option

The **Scale** option is the default option of the ZOOM command. This particular option can be used in a number of ways:

Scale-Relative to Full View

This option of the ZOOM command lets you magnify or reduce the size of a drawing according to a scale factor. A scale factor equal to 1 displays the entire drawing, which is defined by the established limits. To get a magnification relative to the full view you can enter any other number. For example, you can type **4** if you want the displayed image to be enlarged four times. If you want to decrease the magnification relative to the full view, you need to enter a number that is less than 1.

Figure 5-18 Drawing before Zoom Scale option

Figure 5-19 Drawing after Zoom Scale option

In Figure 5-18 and 5-19, the image size decreased because the scale factor is less than 1. In other words, the image size is half of the full view because the scale factor is 0.5. The prompt sequence is:

Command: **ZOOM** ◄─┘
All/Center/Dynamic/Extents/Left/Previous/Vmax/Window/<Scale(X/XP)>: **0.5** ◄─┘

Scale-Relative to Current View

The second way to scale is with respect to the current view. In this case, instead of entering only a number, enter a number followed by an **X**. The scale is calculated with reference to the current view. For example, if you enter **0.25X**, each object in the drawing will be displayed at one fourth (1/4) of its current size. The following example increases the display magnification by a factor of two relative to its current value (Figure 5-20 and 5-21):

Command: **ZOOM** ◄─┘
All/Center/Dynamic/Extents/Left/Previous/Vmax/Window/<Scale(X/XP)>: **2X** ◄─┘

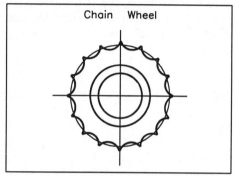

Figure 5-20 Drawing before Zoom Scale(X) option

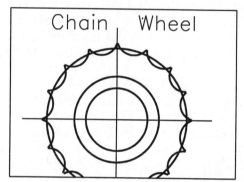

Figure 5-21 Drawing after Zoom Scale(X) option

Scale-Relative to Paper Space Units

The third method of scaling is with respect to paper space. You can use paper space in a variety of ways and for various reasons. For example, you can array and plot various views of your model in paper space. To scale each view relative to paper space units you can use the **ZOOM XP** option. Each view can have an individual scale. The drawing view can be at any scale of your choice in a model space viewport. For example, to display a model space at one fourth (1/4) the size of the paper space units, the prompt sequence is:

Command: **ZOOM** ◄─┘
All/Center/Dynamic/Extents/Left/Previous/Vmax/Window/<Scale(X/XP)>: **1/4XP** ◄─┘

Note
For a better understanding of this topic, refer to Model Space and Paper Space in Chapter 22.

Zoom In and Out

 You can also zoom into the drawing using the **In** option, which doubles the image size.

 Similarly you can use the **Out** option to decrease the size of the image by half. To invoke these options from the command line, enter **ZOOM 2X** for the **In** option or **ZOOM .5X** for the **Out** option at the **Command:** prompt.

PAN COMMAND

Toolbar:	Standard toolbar, Pan
Pull-down:	View, Pan
Screen:	VIEW, Pan:

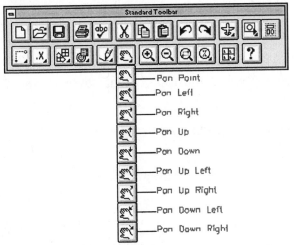

Figure 5-22 Selecting the Pan command from the Standard toolbar

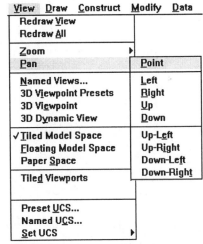

Figure 5-23 Selecting the PAN command from the pull-down menu

You may want to draw on a particular area outside the current viewport. You can do this using the **PAN** command, which can be invoked from the **Standard** toolbar by selecting the desired **Pan** icon from the **Pan** flyout (Figure 5-22), from the pull-down menu (Select View, Pan, Point, Figure 5-23), from the screen menu (Select VIEW, Pan:), or by entering PAN at the **Command:** prompt. If done manually, this would be like holding one corner of the drawing and dragging it across the screen. The PAN command allows you to bring into view portions of the drawing that were lying outside the current viewport. This is done without changing the magnification of the drawing. The effect of this command can also be illustrated by imagining that you are looking at a big drawing through a window known as the **display window** that allows you to slide the drawing right, left, up, and down to bring the part you want to view under this display window. You must supply the command with a displacement. To do this you need to specify in what direction to move the drawing and by what distance. You can give the displacement either by entering the coordinates of the points or by specifying the coordinates by using a pointing device.

The coordinates can be entered in two ways. One way is to specify a single coordinate pair. In this case AutoCAD takes it as a relative displacement of the drawing with respect to the screen. For example, in the following case the **PAN** command would shift the displayed portion of the drawing two units to the right and two units up.

    Command: **PAN** ←┘
    Displacement: **2,2** ←┘
    Second point: ←┘

In the second case you can specify two coordinate pairs. AutoCAD computes the displacement from the first point to the second. Here displacement is calculated between point (3,3) and point (5,5).

    Command: **PAN** ←┘
    Displacement: **3,3** ←┘   *(Or pick a point.)*
    Second point: **5,5** ←┘   *(Or pick a point.)*

There are different options under the **PAN** command which can be used to pan a small portion of the screen in a particular direction or a combination of two directions. The different options are:

 Left - This option brings into view a fraction of the left hand portion of the screen.

Right - This option of the PAN command brings into view a small portion of the right hand side of the screen.

 Up - This option moves the drawing toward the bottom so that some of the top portion of the screen is brought into view.

 Down - This option moves the drawing toward the top so that some of the bottom portion of the screen is brought into view.

Up Left - This option moves the drawing toward the bottom right side.

Up Right - This option moves the drawing toward the bottom left side.

Down Left - This option slides the drawing in the upper right side by a small distance.

Down Right - This option slides the drawing toward the top left corner by a small distance.

VIEW COMMAND

While working on a drawing, you may be working frequently with the ZOOM and PAN commands and you may need to work on a particular drawing view (some portion of the drawing) more often than others. Instead of wasting time by recalling your zooms and pans and picking up the same area from the screen over and over again, you can store the view under a name and restore the view using the name you have given it. The VIEW command is used to save the current viewport under a name so that you can restore (display) it later. This command can be invoked by entering VIEW at the **Command:** prompt. The prompt sequence is:

Command: **VIEW** ◄─┘
?/Delete/Restore/Save/Window:

The following are the different options in the View command:

? Option

This option is used to display a list of the named views in the drawing. If you want a list of all the named views in the drawing, press Enter at the **View(s) to list <*>:** prompt; otherwise enter the names separated by commas. Wild cards (e.g., ??Viewname, #Viewname) can also be used to specify a set of named views. The list appears with the names of all specified views and also the space in which each was defined, indicating M for Model space or P for Paper space (both will be discussed in Chapter 22). The prompt sequence for this option is:

Command: **VIEW** ◄─┘
?/Delete/Restore/Save/Window: **?** ◄─┘
View(s) to list <*>: *Press Enter key or enter the names.*

Delete Option

If you need to remove any views from the list of saved views you can use this option. You can enter the name of any view to be deleted, or a list of view names separated by commas. You may use wild cards to specify a set of named views to delete. The prompt sequence is:

Command: **VIEW** ◄─┘
?/Delete/Restore/Save/Window: **D** ◄─┘
View name(s) to delete: *Enter the names*.

Restore Option

With the help of the **Restore** option, the display in the current viewport is replaced by the view you specify. AutoCAD uses the center point and magnification of each saved view and executes a **ZOOM Center** with this information when a view is restored. The prompt sequence is:

Command: VIEW ◄─┘
?/Delete/Restore/Save/Window: **R** ◄─┘
View name to restore: *Enter the name*.

If you try to restore a Model space while working in Paper space, AutoCAD automatically switches to Paper space and vice versa. In this case AutoCAD will further prompt you as follows:

Restoring model space view
Select viewport for view:

You can select the viewport you want by picking its border. That particular viewport must be on and active. The restored viewport also becomes the current one.

Note
Refer to Chapter 22. Also, if TILEMODE is on you cannot restore a Paper space view.

Save Option

Use this option to save the display in the current viewport by giving it a name. It is saved as a drawing file and if there is an existing view with the same name, it is replaced by the display in the current viewport.

Window Option

This option lets you save a rectangular portion of the current drawing as a view (without first zooming in on that area). You are asked to specify two points to describe the window. The prompt sequence is:

Command: VIEW ◄─┘
?/Delete/Restore/Save/Window: **W** ◄─┘
View name(s) to save: *Enter the name*.
First corner: *Specify a point*.
Other corner: *Specify another point*.

View Control Dialogue Box

Toolbar:	View, Named Views
Pull-down:	View, Named Views
Screen:	VIEW, DDview

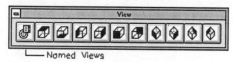

Figure 5-24 Selecting Named Views from the View toolbar

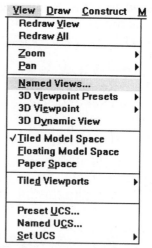

Figure 5-25 Selecting Named Views from the pull-down menu

You can also save, delete, and restore the views from the **View Control** dialogue box. You can invoke this dialogue box from the **View** toolbar by selecting the **Named Views** icon (Figure 5-24), from the pull-down menu (Select View, Named view...,Figure 5-25), from the screen menu (Select VIEW, DDview), or by entering DDVIEW at the **Command:** prompt. This dialogue box (Figure 5-26) is very useful when you are saving and restoring many view names. Using this dialogue box you can name the current view or restore some other view. The list box shows all the existing named views. This dialogue box can be used to restore a named view, create a new view, or delete an existing one. You can also see a description of the general parameters of any view.

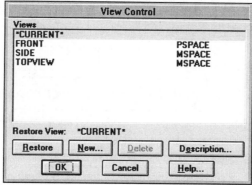

Figure 5-26 View Control dialogue box

CREATING TEXT

In manual drafting, lettering is accomplished by hand using a lettering device, pen, or pencil. This is a very time-consuming and tedious job. Computer-aided drafting has made this process extremely simple. In engineering drawings there are certain standards to be followed in connection with the placement of a text on a drawing. In this section you will learn how text can be added in a drawing by using TEXT, DTEXT, and MTEXT commands. The following is a list of some of the functions associated with **TEXT**, **DTEXT**, and **MTEXT** commands that are described in this section:

1. Using the TEXT, DTEXT and MTEXT commands to create text.
2. Changing the text styles using the **STYLE** command.
3. Drawing special symbols using the proper control characteristics.
4. Using the **QTEXT** command for the quick text mode.
5. Creating paragraph text using the MTEXT command
6. Editing paragraph text.

TEXT COMMAND

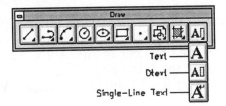

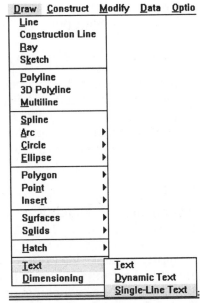

Figure 5-27 Selecting Single-Line Text from the Draw toolbar

 The TEXT command lets you write text on a drawing. AutoCAD provides a number of different character patterns, known as **fonts**, and the text can be drawn in any of them. By applying a **style** to the font, you may stretch, compress, or mirror the text. In this way you can make the text oblique or draw it in a vertical column. A text string may be rotated and justified to suit your requirement. Text string is defined as the combination of characters and is treated as a single object. The text height may be changed according to need, keeping in view the scale factor. The TEXT command can be invoked from the **Draw** toolbar by selecting the **Single-Line Text** icon in the **Text** flyout (Figure 5-27), from the pull-down menu (Select Draw, Text, Single-Line Text Figure 5-28), or by entering **TEXT** at the **Command:** prompt.

Figure 5-28 Selecting the TEXT command from the pull-down menu

Text Alignment

AutoCAD offers different options to align the text. Alignment refers to the layout of the text. The main text alignment modes are **left, center**, and **right**. You can align a text using a combination of modes; e.g., top/middle/baseline/bottom and left/center/right. Top refers to the line along which the top points of the capital letters lie; baseline refers to the line along which their bases lie. Letters with descenders (such as p, g, y) dip below the baseline to the bottom.

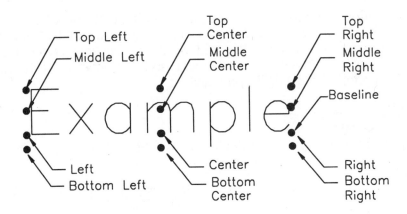

Figure 5-29 Text alignment positions

The TEXT command prompt sequence is as follows:

Command: **TEXT** ←⏎
Justify/Style/ < Start point > :

Start Point Option

This is the default and the most commonly used option in the TEXT command. By specifying a start point, the text is left-justified along its baseline starting from the location of the starting point. Specifying a start point does let you **left justify** your text, but before AutoCAD draws the text it needs some more parameters. AutoCAD must know the text height, the rotation angle for the baseline, and the text string to be drawn. It prompts you for all this information. The prompt sequence is:

Height < default > :
Rotation angle < default > :
Text:

The **Height:** prompt determines the distance by which the text extends above the baseline, measured by the capital letters. This distance is specified in drawing units. You can specify the text height by picking two points or entering a value. In case of a null response, the default height, i.e., the height used for the previous text drawn in the same style, will be used.

Next comes the **Rotation angle:** prompt. It determines the angle at which the text line will be drawn. The default value of the rotation angle is **0 degrees** (3 o'clock or east) and in this case the text is drawn horizontally from the specified start point. The rotation angle is measured in a counterclockwise direction. The last angle specified becomes the current rotation angle and if you give a null response, the last angle specified will be used as default. You can also specify the rotation angle by picking a point. The text is drawn upside-down if a point is picked at a location left of the start point.

As a response to the **Text:** prompt enter the text string. Spaces are allowed between words. After entering the text, press the Enter key. The following example illustrates these prompts:

Command: **TEXT** ←⏎
Justify/Style/ < Start point > : **1,1** ←⏎
Height < 0.25 > :.**0.15** ←⏎
Rotation angle < 0 > : ←⏎
Text: *Enter the text string.*

Justify Option

When the **Justify** option is invoked, the user can place text in one of the 14 various alignment types by selecting the desired alignment option. The orientation of the text style determines the command interaction for Text Justify. We will be discussing text styles and fonts later in this chapter, page 27. For now assume that the text style orientation is horizontal. The prompt sequence using this option of the TEXT command is:

Command: **TEXT** ←⏎
Justify/Style/ < Start point > : **J** ←⏎
Align/Fit/Center/Middle/Right/TL/TC/TR/ML/MC/MR/BL/BC/ BR: *Select any of these*
options.

If the text style is vertically oriented (refer to the STYLE command, page 5-24), the prompt sequence is as follows:

Command: **TEXT** ◄┘
Justify/Style/‹Start point›: **J** ◄┘
Align/Center/Middle/Right:

The alignment and the corresponding abbreviations of text justification options are as follows:

Alignment	Abbreviation	Orientation
Align	A	Horizontal/Vertical
Fit	F	Horizontal
Center	C	Horizontal/Vertical
Middle	M	Horizontal/Vertical
Right	R	Horizontal/Vertical
Top/left	TL or Tleft	Horizontal
Top/center	TC or Tcenter	Horizontal
Top/right	TR or Tright	Horizontal
Middle/left	ML or Mleft	Horizontal
Middle/center	MC or Mcenter	Horizontal
Middle/right	MR or Mright	Horizontal
Bottom/left	BL or Bleft	Horizontal
Bottom/center	BC or Bcenter	Horizontal
Bottom/right	BR or Bright	Horizontal

Align Option

This option is invoked under the **Justify** option. Here enter **Align** or **A** at the **Align/Fit/-Center/Middle/Right/TL/TC/TR/ML/MC/MR/BL/BC/BR:** prompt. In this option the text string is written between two points. You must specify the two points that act as the end points of the baseline. The two points may be picked horizontally or at an angle. AutoCAD adjusts the text width (compresses or expands it) so that it fits between those two points. The text height is also changed depending on the distance between the points and the number of letters. The prompt is:

Command: **TEXT** ◄┘
Justify/Style/‹Start point›: **J** ◄┘
Align/Fit/Center/Middle/Right/TL/TC/TR/ML/MC/MR/BL/BC/BR: **A** ◄┘
First text line point: *Pick a point.*
Second text line point: *Pick a point.*
Text: *Enter the text string.*

Fit Option

This option is very similar to the previous one. The only difference is that in this case you select the text height and it does not vary according to the distance between the two points. AutoCAD adjusts the letter width to fit the text between the two given points, but the height remains constant. The **Fit** option is not accessible for vertically oriented text. If you try the Fit option on the vertical text style, you will notice that the text string does not appear in the prompt. The prompt sequence is:

Command: **TEXT** ◄┘
Justify/Style/‹Start point›: **J** ◄┘
Align/Fit/Center/Middle/Right/TL/TC/TR/ML/MC/MR/BL/BC/BR: **F** ◄┘
First text line point: *Pick the starting point.*
Second text line point: *Pick the ending point.*
Height‹current›: *Enter the height.*
Text: *Enter the text.*

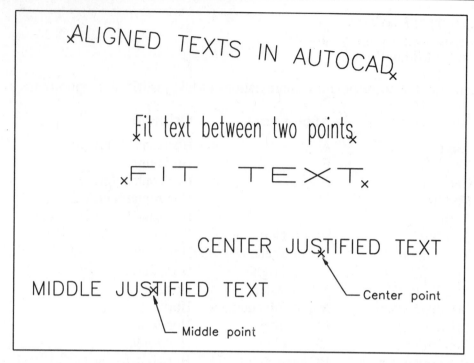

Figure 5-30 Writing the text using Align, Fit, Center, and Middle options

Center Option

You can use this option to select the midpoint of the baseline for the text. This option can be invoked by entering **Justify** and then **Center** or **C**. After you select or pick the center point, you must enter the letter height and the rotation angle (Figure 5-30). The prompt sequence is:

Command: **TEXT** ◄┘
Justify/Style/<Start point>: **J** ◄┘
Align/Fit/Center/Middle/Right/TL/TC/TR/ML/MC/MR/BL/BC/BR: **C** ◄┘
Center point: *Pick a point.*
Height<current>: **0.15** ◄┘
Rotation angle<0>: ◄┘
Text: **CENTER JUSTIFIED TEXT** ◄┘

Middle Option

Using this option you can center a text not only horizontally, as in the previous case, but also vertically. In other words, you can specify the middle point of the text string (Figure 5-30). You can alter the text height and the angle of rotation to your requirement. The prompt sequence is:

Command: **TEXT** ◄┘
Justify/Style/<Start point>: **J** ◄┘
Align/Fit/Center/Middle/Right/TL/TC/TR/ML/MC/MR/BL/BC/BR: **M** ◄┘
Middle point: *Pick a point.*
Height<current>: **0.15** ◄┘
Rotation angle <0>: ◄┘
Text: **MIDDLE JUSTIFIED TEXT** ◄┘

Right Option

This option is similar to the Start point option. The only difference is that the text string is aligned with the lower right corner (the end point you specify); i.e., the text is **right-justified** (Figure 5-31). The prompt sequence is :

Command: **TEXT** ←┘
Justify/Style/<Start point>: **J** ←┘
Align/Fit/Center/Middle/Right/TL/TC/TR/ML/MC/MR/BL/BC/ BR: **R** ←┘
Height<current>: **0.15** ←┘
End point: *Pick a point.*
Rotation angle <0>: ←┘
Text: **RIGHT JUSTIFIED TEXT** ←┘

TL Option

The full form of this abbreviation has already been written. From that you can deduce that in this option the text string is justified from the **top left**. The command prompt sequence is:

Command: **TEXT** ←┘
Justify/Style/<Start point>: **J** ←┘
Align/Fit/Center/Middle/Right/TL/TC/TR/ML/MC/MR/BL/BC/ BR: **TL** ←┘
Top/left: *Pick a point.*
Height<current>: **0.15** ←┘
Rotation angle <0>: ←┘
Text: **TOP/LEFT JUSTIFIED TEXT** ←┘

TC Option

Using this option you can justify the text at the **top center** as illustrated by Figure 5-31. The prompt sequence is :

Command: **TEXT** ←┘
Justify/Style/<Start point>: **J** ←┘
Align/Fit/Center/Middle/Right/TL/TC/TR/ML/MC/MR/BL/BC/ BR: **TC** ←┘
Top/center: *Pick a point.*
Height<current>: **0.13** ←┘
Rotation angle <0>: ←┘
Text: **TOP/CENTER JUSTIFIED TEXT** ←┘

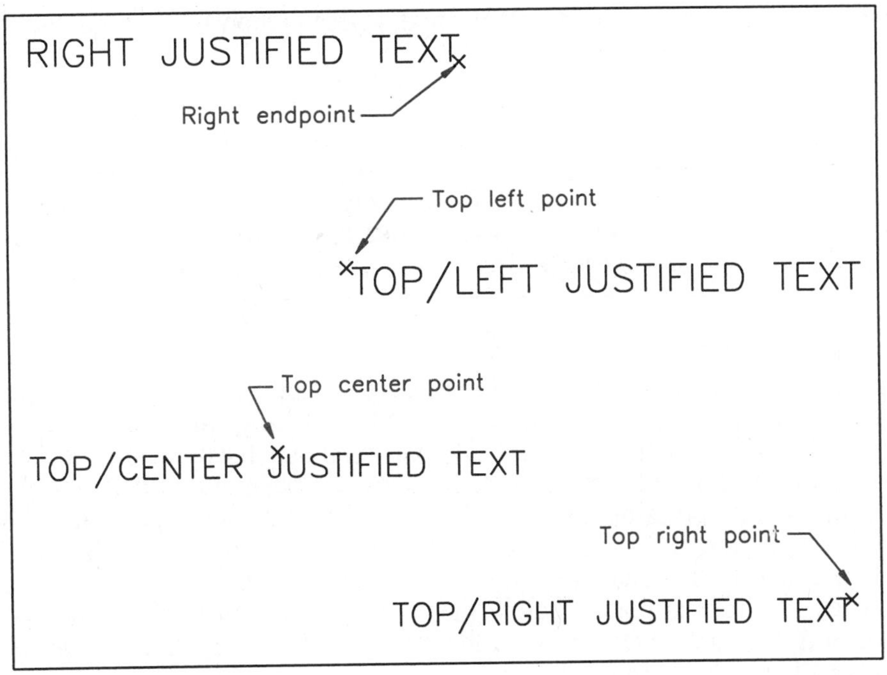

Figure 5-31 Writing text using the Right, Top-Left, Top-Center, and Top-Right options

TR Option

This option allows you to justify the text at the **top right** as in Figure 5-31. The prompt sequence is :

Command: **TEXT** ←⏎
Justify/Style/ < Start point > : **J** ←⏎
Align/Fit/Center/Middle/Right/TL/TC/TR/ML/MC/MR/BL/BC/ BR: **TC** ←⏎
Top/center: *Pick a point*.
Height < current > : **0.13** ←⏎
Rotation angle < 0 > : ←⏎
Text: **TOP/CENTER JUSTIFIED TEXT** ←⏎

The rest of the text alignment options are similar to those discussed above and you can try them on your own. The prompt sequence is almost the same as those given for the previous examples.

Style Option

With this option you can load another text style from already existing ones. Different text styles have different text fonts, heights, obliquing angles, and other features. This option can be invoked by entering **TEXT** and then **S** at the next prompt. The prompt sequence is:

Command: **TEXT** ←⏎
Justify/Style/ < Start point > : **S** ←⏎
Style name (or ?) < current > :

If you want to work in the previous text style just press the Enter key at the last prompt. If you want to activate another text style, enter the name of the style at the last prompt. You can also choose from a list of available text styles, which can be displayed by entering **?**. After you enter **?** the next prompt is:

Text style(s) to list < * > :

Press the Enter key to display the available text styles. Choose one and then make it current. Return to the screen by pressing the F1 key.

> **Note**
>
> *With the help of the Style option of the TEXT command you can select a text style from an existing list. If you want to create a new style, make use of the STYLE command, which is explained later in this chapter on page 24.*

Multiple Line Text

Text comprising multiple lines can be automatically spaced (one below the other) in AutoCAD. Thus each string will have the same **angle**, **height**, and **alignment**. The multiple lines can be entered using the TEXT command (or DTEXT commands, discussed in the next section). When you press the Enter key after the first line of the text has been entered, AutoCAD brings back the **Command:** prompt. By pressing the Enter key again you can repeat the previous command, which in this case is the TEXT command. The next prompt is **TEXT Justify/Style/ < Start point > :** and by pressing the Enter key you automatically justify the next line below the first. As mentioned earlier, the text is placed below the previous line, with the same style, color, height, and orientation, on the same layer and with the same justification. To enter more lines, continue in the same manner. The prompt sequence is:

Command: **TEXT** ←⏎
Justify/Style/ < Start point > : *Pick the start point*.

Height<current>: **0.15** ←┘
Rotation angle<0>: ←┘
Text: **The purpose of this** ←┘   *(First line of the text.)*
Command: ←┘
TEXT Justify/Style/<Start point>: ←┘
Text: **topic is to make the** ←┘   *(Second line of the text.)*

Enter the rest of the lines similarly.

DTEXT COMMAND

Toolbar:	Draw, Text, Dtext
Pull-down:	Draw, Text, Dynamic
Screen:	DRAW2, Dtext:

DTEXT stands for dynamic text. This command performs all the functions that the TEXT command does, and in addition, you can see the text on the screen as you type it. This command also allows you to delete what has been typed by using the backspace key. It also lets you enter multiple lines in one command. The command **DTEXT** can be invoked from the **Draw** toolbar by selecting the **Dtext** icon in the **Text** flyout, from the pull-down menu (Select Draw, Text, Dynamic), from the screen menu (Select DRAW2, DText:), or by entering DTEXT at the **Command:** prompt. The sequence of prompts in the DTEXT command is the same as for the TEXT command; the only difference is that here the **Text:** prompt is issued repeatedly. The DTEXT command displays a box after you enter the start point and the height. This box identifies the start point and the size of the text height entered. The characters appear on the screen as you enter them. When you press the Enter key after typing a line, the cursor automatically places itself at the start of the next line and repeats the prompt **Text:**. You can end the command by giving a null response to the **Text:** prompt. This command can be cancelled by pressing **Esc**. If you do this the entire text entered during this particular command sequence is erased.

The screen cross-hairs can be moved irrespective of the cursor box for the text. If you pick a point, this command will complete the current line of the text and move the cursor box to the point you selected. This cursor box can be moved and placed anywhere on the screen, hence multiple lines of text can be entered at any desired locations on the screen with a single DTEXT command. By pressing the backspace key you can delete one character to the left of the current position of the cursor box. Even if you have entered several lines of the text, you can use backspace and go on deleting until you reach the start point of the first line entered. Upon deletion of an entire line, DTEXT displays a ***deleted*** message in the command prompt area.

This command can be used with most of the text alignment modes, although it is most useful in case of left-justified texts. In case of aligned texts, this command assigns a height appropriate for the width of the first line to every line of the text. Irrespective of the **Justify** option chosen, the text is first left-aligned at the selected point. After the DTEXT command ends, the text is momentarily erased from the screen and regenerated with the requested alignment. For example, if you use the **middle** option, the text will first appear on the screen as left-justified, starting at the point you designated as the middle point. After you end the command and press the Enter key, it is regenerated with the proper alignment.

Determining Text Height

The actual text height is equal to the product of the **scale factor** and the **plotted text height**. Hence scale factors are important numbers for plotting the text at the correct height. This factor is a reciprocal of the drawing scale. For example, if you plot a drawing at a scale of 1/4 = 1, calculate the scale factor for text height as follows:

1/4" = 1"   (i.e. the scale factor is 4)

The scale factor for an architectural drawing that is to be plotted at a scale of 1/4" = 1'0" is calculated as:

1/4" = 1'0", or 1/4" = 12", or 1 = 48

Therefore, in this case, the scale factor is 48.

For a civil engineering drawing with a scale 1" = 50', the scale factor is as follows:

1" = 50', or 1" = 50*12", or 1 = 600

Therefore, the scale factor is 600.

Next, calculate the height of the AutoCAD text. If it is a full-scale (1=1) drawing and the text is to be plotted at 1/8" (0.125), it should be drawn at that height. However, in a civil engineering drawing a text drawn 1/8" high will look like a dot. This is because the scale for a civil engineering drawing is 1" = 50', which means that the drawing you are working on is 600 times larger. To draw a normal text height, multiply the text height by 600. Now the height will be:

0.125"x600 = 750

Similarly, in an architectural drawing, which has a scale factor of 48, a text that is to be 1/8" high on paper must be drawn 6 units, as shown in the following calculation:

0.125x48 = 6.0

It is very important to evaluate scale factors and text heights before you begin a drawing. It would be even better to include the text height in your prototype drawing by assigning the value to the **TEXTSIZE** system variable.

EDITING TEXT (DDEDIT Command)

You can use the **DDEDIT** command to edit the text. This command can be selected from the pull-down menu (Select Modify, Edit Text), from the screen menu (Select MODIFY, DDedit:), or by entering DDEDIT at the **Command:** prompt. When you enter the DDEDIT command, you are required to select the text for editing. Then AutoCAD displays the **Edit Text** dialogue box (Figure 5-32), where the selected text is displayed in the **Text:** edit box.

Command: **DDEDIT**
< Select a TEXT or ATTDEF object > Undo: *Select a text object.*

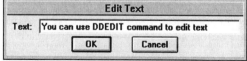

Figure 5-32 Using the Edit Text dialogue box to edit text (DDEDIT)

DRAWING SPECIAL CHARACTERS

In almost all drafting applications, you need to draw special characters (symbols) in the normal text and the dimension text. For example, you may want to draw the degree symbol (°) or the diameter symbol (ϕ), or you may want to underscore or overscore some text. In AutoCAD this can be achieved with the appropriate sequence of control characters (control code). For each symbol the control sequence starts with a percent sign written twice (**%%**). The character immediately following the double percent sign depicts the symbol. The control sequences for some of the symbols are:

Control sequence	Special character
%%c	**Diameter symbol (ϕ)**
%%d	**Degree symbol (°)**
%%p	**Plus/minus tolerance symbol (±)**
%%o	**Toggle for overscore mode on/off**
%%u	**Toggle for underscore mode on/off**
%%%	**Single percent sign (%)**

For example, if you want to draw **25°Celsius**, you need to enter **25%%dCelsius**. If you enter **43.0%%c**, you get **43.0ϕ** on the drawing screen. To underscore (underline) text, use the **%%u** control sequence followed by the text to be underscored. For example, to underscore the text: **UNDERSCORED TEXT IN AUTOCAD**, enter **%%uUNDERSCORED TEXT IN AUTOCAD** at the prompt asking for text to be entered. To underscore and overscore a text string, include **%%u%%o** at the start of the text string.

None of these codes will be translated in the DTEXT command until this command is complete. For example, to draw the degree symbol you can enter **%%d**. As you are entering these symbols, they will appear as %%d on the screen. After you have completed the command and pressed the Enter key, the code %%d will be replaced by the degree symbol (°).

You may be wondering why a percent sign should have a control sequence when a percent symbol can be easily entered at the keyboard by pressing the percent (%) key. The reason is that sometimes a percent symbol is immediately followed (without a space) by a control sequence. In this case, the **%%%** control sequence is needed to draw a single percent symbol. To make the concept clear, assume you want to draw 67%±3.5. Try drawing this text string by entering **67%%p3.5**. The result will be **67%p3.5**, which is wrong. Now enter **67%%%%p3.5** and notice the result on the screen. Here you obtain the correct text string on the screen; i.e., **67%±3.5**. If there were a space between the 67% and ±3.5, you could enter 67% %%p3.5 and the result would be **67% ±3.5**. Figure 5-33 illustrates some special characters.

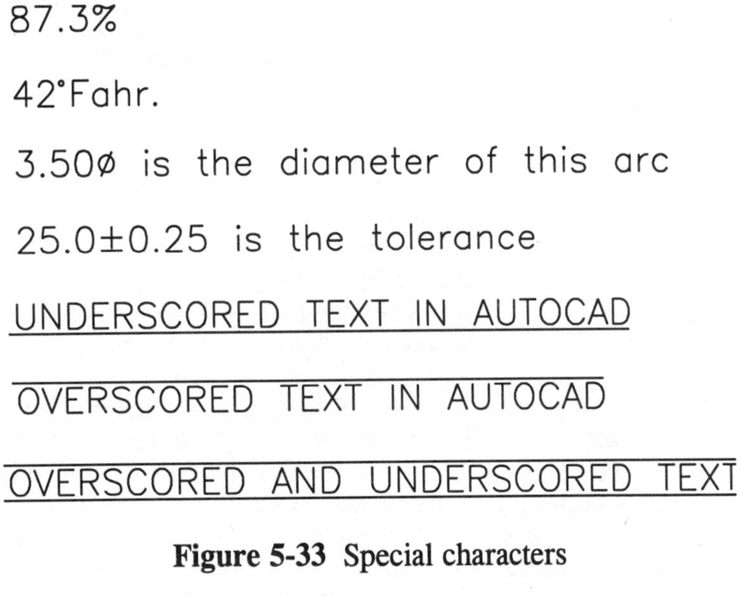

87.3%

42°Fahr.

3.50ϕ is the diameter of this arc

25.0±0.25 is the tolerance

<u>UNDERSCORED TEXT IN AUTOCAD</u>

OVERSCORED TEXT IN AUTOCAD

OVERSCORED AND UNDERSCORED TEXT

Figure 5-33 Special characters

In addition to the control sequences shown above, you can use the **%%nnn** control sequence to draw special characters. The nnn can take a value in the range of 1 to 126. For example, to draw the **&** symbol, enter the text string **%%038**.

STYLE COMMAND

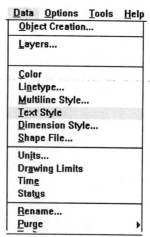

Pull-down:	Data, Text Style
Screen:	DRAW2, Style:

You can change the text styles in the TEXT command using the **Style** option, but to create new text styles and modify the existing style you need the STYLE command. This command can be invoked from the pull-down menu (Select Data, Text Style, Figure 5-34), from the screen menu (Select DRAW2, Style:), or by entering **STYLE** at the **Command:** prompt. The prompt sequence is:

Command: **STYLE** ◄─┘
Text style name (or ?) <current>:

Figure 5-34 Selecting the STYLE command from the pull-down menu

At the above prompt you can enter a new style name that you want to create, or the name of an existing one for modification. Here the **Select Font File** dialogue box (Figure 5-35) is displayed. This box has different text fonts, such as .shx, .pfb, .pfa, and .ttf. You can select any one. If this style already exists, the message **Existing style** is displayed on the command line. For a new style, the message **New style** is displayed.

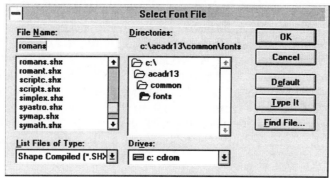

Figure 5-35 Select Font File dialogue box

The next prompts are as follows:

Height <default>: *Enter the desired character height.*
Width factor <default>: *Enter the desired width.*
Obliquing angle <default>: *Enter the slant angle.*
Backwards <N>: *Enter Y for backward text,* ◄─┘ *for normal text.*
Upside-down? <N>: *Enter Y for upside-down text,* ◄─┘ *for normal. text.*
Vertical? <N>: *Enter Y for vertical text,* ◄─┘ *for normal text.*

At the **Height <default>:** prompt you can enter 0 or the text height. If you specify the height of the text at this prompt, AutoCAD will not prompt you to enter the text height when using the TEXT or DTEXT command. If you specify the text height as 0, you will be prompted to enter text height. For the **Width factor**, 1 is the default. If you want the letters expanded, give a width factor greater than 1; for compressed letters, give a width factor less than 1. Similarly, for the **Obliquing angle**, 0 is the default and it writes the letters vertically. If you want the slant of the letters toward the right, the value should be greater than 0; to slant the letters toward the left, the value should be less than 0. Hence, a new style with the above properties will be created.

If you want to see the features of any of the text style you can enter **?** at the **Text style name (or ?) <current>:** prompt. The next prompt is:

> Text style(s) to list <*>:

You can enter the name of an existing style at this prompt. The name, font file, height, width factor, obliquing angle, and generation of that particular style will be displayed. If you want the features of all the existing styles to be displayed, enter * or press the Enter key at the **Text style(s) to list <*>:** prompt.

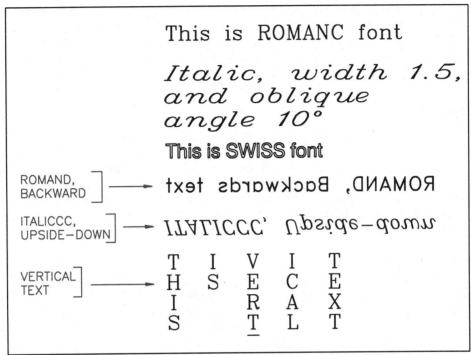

Figure 5-36 Specifying different features to text style files

CREATING PARAGRAPH TEXT
(MTEXT Command)

Toolbar:	Draw, Text
Pull-down:	Draw, Text, Text
Screen:	DRAW2, Mtext:

You can use the **MTEXT** command to write a paragraph text whose width can be specified by defining two corners of the text boundary, or by entering the width of the paragraph. The text created by the **MTEXT** command is a single object regardless of the number of lines it contains. The text boundary is not plotted, although it is a part of the MTEXT object. The MTEXT command can be invoked from the **Draw** toolbar by selecting the **Text** icon in the **Text** flyout, from the pull-down menu (Select Draw, Text, Text), from the screen menu (Select DRAW2, Mtext:), or by entering **MTEXT** at the **Command:** prompt. The following is the prompt sequence of MTEXT command:

Command: **MTEXT**
Attach/Rotation/Style/Height/Direction/<Insertion Point>: *Select text insertion point.*

Attach/Rotation/Style/Height/Direction/Width/2Points/ < Other corner > : *Select an option or select a point to specify other corner.*

Once you have defined the width of the paragraph text, AutoCAD will display the **Edit MText** dialogue box (explained later). In this dialogue box you can enter the paragraph text.

The **MTEXT** command has the following options:

Insertion Point

The Insertion Point determines the point where the text is inserted. For example, if the text justification is top-right (TR), the text paragraph is to the left and bottom of the insertion point. Similarly, if the text justification is middle-center (MC), the text paragraph is centered around the insertion point, regardless of how you define the width of the paragraph. The insertion point also indicates the first corner of the text boundary.

Other Corner

The point you enter or select at this prompt specifies the other corner of the text boundary. When you define the text boundary, it does not mean that the text paragraph will fit within the defined boundary. AutoCAD only uses the width of the defined boundary as the width of the text paragraph. The height of the text boundary has no effect on the text paragraph. Once you select the other corner, AutoCAD displays the text editor (on DOS system), and automatically assigns a filename like AC000512, ACA00512, etc. You can enter the text and once you are done entering the text, save the file. The text will be inserted automatically at the specified insertion point.

Command: **MTEXT**
Attach/Rotation/Style/Height/Direction/ < Insertion Point > : *Select text insertion point.*
Attach/Rotation/Style/Height/Direction/Width/2Points/ < Other corner > : **@1.25,0**
(Select an option or select a point to specify other corner.)

Attach

The **Attach** option is used to control the justification of text paragraph. For example, if the text justification is bottom-right (BR), the text paragraph will spill to the left and above the insertion point, regardless of how you define the width of the paragraph.

Command: **MTEXT**
Attach/Rotation/Style/Height/Direction/ < Insertion Point > : **A**
TL/TC/TR/ML/MC/MR/BL/BC/BR: *Select an option.*

Figure 5-37 shows different text justifications for MTEXT.

Rotation

The rotation option specifies the rotation of the text. For example, if the rotation angle is 10 degrees, the text will be rotated 10 degrees in a counterclockwise direction.

Style

The **Style** option specifies the text style. The text style that you want to use must be predefined.

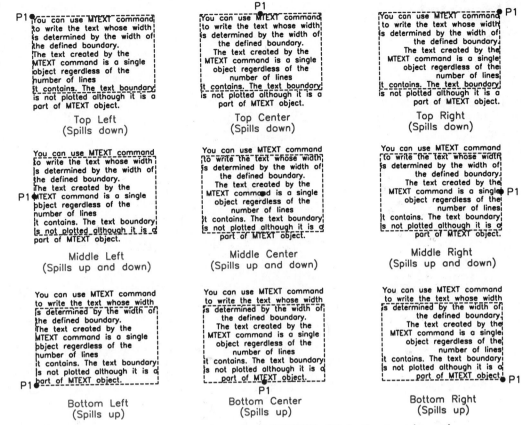

Figure 5-37 Text justifications for MTEXT. P1 is the text insertion point

Height

The **Height** option specifies the height of the text. Once you specify the height, AutoCAD retains that value unless you change it. The **MTEXT** height does not affect the size (TEXTSIZE system variable) specified for TEXT or DTEXT commands.

Direction

The Direction option specifies the direction of the text paragraph. It has two options, H for horizontal and V for vertical. In English the text is read horizontally, therefore entering H or V will not have any effect. However, in some languages, like Chinese and Japanese, the text is read vertically.

Width

The **Width** option specifies the width of the text paragraph. The width can be entered by specifying a value or entering a point. The distance between the insertion point and the second point determines the width of the paragraph.

Command: **MTEXT**
Attach/Rotation/Style/Height/Direction/<Insertion Point>: *Select text insertion point.*
Attach/Rotation/Style/Height/Direction/Width/2Points/<Other corner>: **W**
Object width: **1.25**   *(Enter the paragraph width or specify the second point (@1.25,0).)*

Two Points

The **two points** option can be used to specify the width of the text paragraph by specifying any two points, regardless of the text insertion point.

Command: **MTEXT**
Attach/Rotation/Style/Height/Direction/<Insertion Point>: *Select text insertion point.*
Attach/Rotation/Style/Height/Direction/Width/2Points/<Other corner>: **2P**
First point: **5,0**   *(Specify first point (5,0).)*
Second point: **@1.25,0**   *(Specify the second point (@1.25,0).)*

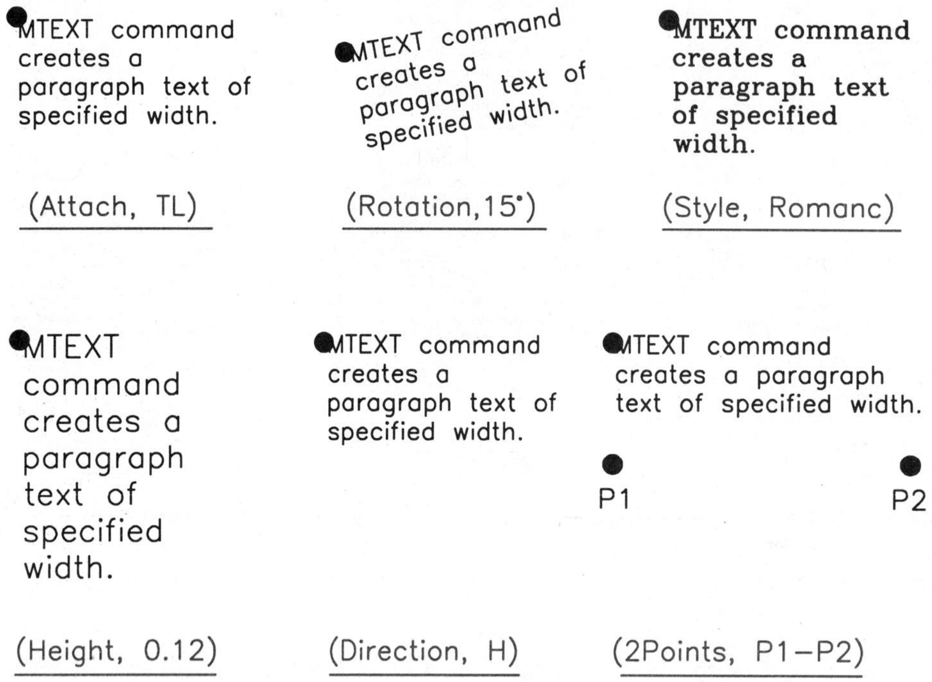

Figure 5-38 Attach options for text generated by the MTEXT command

CHANGING MTEXT PROPERTIES (MTPROP Command)

Using the MText Properties Dialogue Box

You can invoke the **MText Properties** dialogue box by entering the **MTPROP** command at the **Command:** prompt. When you enter the command, AutoCAD will prompt you to select the text. Once the text is selected, the **MText Properties** dialogue box (Figure 5-39) will be displayed on the screen. The dialogue box allows you to change the text style, text height, text direction, text attachment, text width, and text rotation. To change the text style, select the text or the arrow. AutoCAD will display a pop-up list of all defined text styles. You can select a text style by clicking on the text style name in the pop-up list. Similarly, the direction and attachment can be changed by selecting the text or the arrow and clicking on the desired direction or text justification. The other values, like text height, text width, and text rotation, can be changed by entering a value in the corresponding edit box. Once you have entered the new MText properties, select the OK button to exit the dialogue box. AutoCAD will update the properties of the selected MText object.

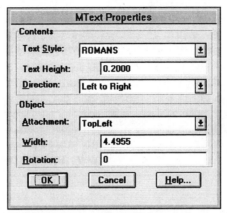

Figure 5-39 Using MText Properties dialogue box to change properties
of MText

FORMATTING PARAGRAPH TEXT IN A TEXT EDITOR

The text can be formatted by entering formatting codes in the text. To enter a paragraph text, you can use the text editor for DOS or the text editor in Windows. With the formatting codes you can underline or overline a text string, create stacked text, or insert nonbreaking space between two words. You can also use the formatting codes to change the color, font, text height, oblique angle, or width of the text. Figure 5-40 lists the formatting codes for paragraph text.

\O...\o	Turns overline on and off	Turns \Ooverline\o on and off	Turns overline on and off
\L...\l	Turns underline on and off	Turns \Lunderline\l on and off	Turns underline on and off
\~	Inserts a nonbreaking space	Keeps the\~words together	Keeps the words together
\\	Inserts a backslash	Inserts \\ a backslash	Inserts \ a backslash
\{...\}	Inserts an opening and closing brace	This is \{bracketed\} word	The {bracketed} word
\Cvalue;	Changes to the specified color	Change \C1; the color	Change the color
\File name;	Changes to the specified font file	Change \Fromanc; this word	Change **this word**
\Hvalue;	Changes to the specified text height	Change \H0.15; this word	Change this word
\S...^...	Stacks the subsequent text at the \ or ^ symbol	2.005\S+0.001^−0.001	+0.001 2.005−0.001
\Tvalue;	Adjusts the space between characters from .75 to 4 times	\T2;TRACKING	T R A C K I N G
\Qangle;	Changes obliquing angle	\Q15;OBLIQUE TEXT	*OBLIQUE TEXT*
\Wvalue;	Changes width factor to produce wide text	\W2;WIDE LETTERS	WIDE LETTERS
\P	Ends paragraph	First paragraph\PSecond paragraph	First paragraph Second paragraph

Figure 5-40 Formatting codes for paragraph text

Example
To obtain the paragraph text shown in Figure 5-41, use the following formatting codes:

{\H0.15{\FROMANC;{\LNOTE\l}}}
{\FROMANC;Hardness} unless
otherwise specified
{\FROMANC;60RC}\S+3.0^-2.0

NOTE
Hardness unless
otherwise specified
+3.0
60RC−2.0

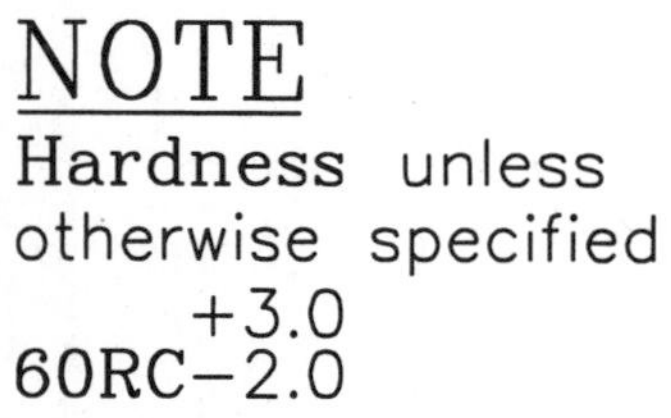

Figure 5-41 Using format codes for paragraph text

Note

Use the curly braces if you want to apply the format codes only to the text within the braces.

The curly braces can be nested up to eight levels deep.

TrueType Text Support

AutoCAD supports TrueType fonts. You can use your own TrueType fonts by adding them to the **Fonts** directory. You can also keep your fonts in a separate directory in which case you must specify the location of your fonts directory in AutoCAD's search path.

The resolution and text fill of the TrueType font text is controlled by the TEXTFILL and TEXTQLTY system variables. If the TEXTFILL is set to 1, the text will be filled. If the value is set to 0, the text will not be filled. The TEXTQLTY variable controls the quality of the TrueType font text. The value of this variable can range from 0 to 100. The default value is 50, which gives a resolution of 300 DPI (dots per inch). If the value is set to 100, the text will be drawn at 600 DPI. The higher the resolution, the more time it takes to regenerate or plot the drawing.

Example
The paragraph text in Figure 5-42 uses the TrueType font SWISS.TTF.

{\H0.15{\FSWISS;{\LNOTE\l}}}
{\FSWISS;Hardness} unless
otherwise specified
{\FSWISS;60RC}\S+3.0^-2.0

NOTE
Hardness unless
otherwise specified
+3.0
60RC−2.0

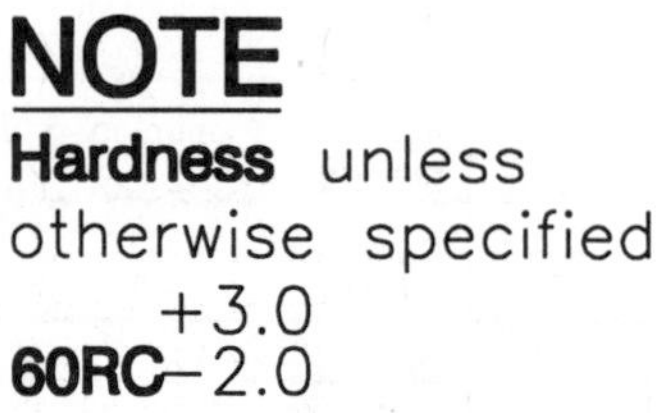

Figure 5-42 Using TrueType font to format paragraph text

EDITING MTEXT

The contents of an MText object (Paragraph text) can be edited by using the DDMODIFY and DDEDIT commands. You can also use AutoCAD's editing commands, like MOVE, ERASE, ROTATE, COPY, MIRROR, and GRIPS to edit MText.

Editing MText Using DDMODIFY Command

When you enter the DDMODIFY command and select the text, AutoCAD displays the **Modify MText** dialogue box (Figure 5-43). The text object that you select for editing is displayed in the **Contents** display box. If you select the **Edit Contents...** button, AutoCAD automatically switches to the **Edit MText** dialogue box, where you can make changes to the paragraph text. If you select the **Edit Properties...** button, AutoCAD displays the **MText Properties** dialogue box. You can use this dialogue box to change the properties of the paragraph text as discussed earlier.

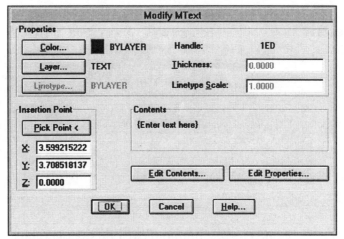

Figure 5-43 Modify MText dialogue box

Editing MText Using the DDEDIT Command

The paragraph text (MTEXT) can also be edited using DDEDIT command. When you enter this command and select the paragraph text (MText) you want to edit, AutoCAD will automatically switch to the **Edit MText** dialogue box, where you can edit the paragraph text.

EDIT MTEXT DIALOGUE BOX

You can create the paragraph text using the MTEXT command. This will display the **Edit MText** dialogue box (Figure 5-44). The following is a description of different options available in **Edit MText** dialogue box.

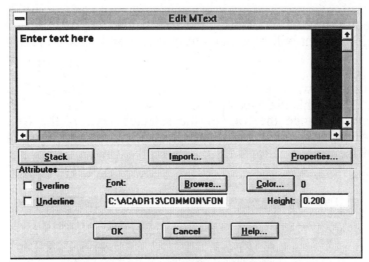

Figure 5-44 Edit MText dialogue box

Text Box
The **Text Box** area displays the text you enter. The width of the active text area is determined by the specified width of paragraph text.

Stack
The **Stack** option stacks the selected text. The text or fractions are stacked vertically.

Import
When you select this option, AutoCAD displays the **Import Text File** dialogue box (Figure 5-45). In this dialogue box you can select any file you want to import in the **Edit MTEXT**

dialogue box. The imported text is displayed in the text area. Note that only ASCII files are interpreted properly.

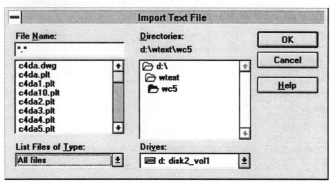

Figure 5-45 Import Text File dialogue box

Properties

When you select this option, AutoCAD displays the **MText Properties** dialogue box. You can use this dialogue box to change the text style, text height, direction, width, rotation, and attachment. For details, see "MTEXT Properties Dialogue Box" later in this section.

Attributes

Overline
This button overlines the new or the selected text.

Underline
This button underlines the new or the selected text.

Font
You can specify the font by entering the font name (and path information) in the **Font** edit box. The selected font will be applied to new text and selected text.

Browse
If you select the Browse option, AutoCAD displays the **Change Font** dialogue box (Figure 5-46). You can use this dialogue box to browse through the font files and specify a font for the new text or change the font of the selected text. If the font is not recognized by Windows, AutoCAD will display the **Select Font** dialogue box (Figure 5-47). You can select one of the supported fonts from the list.

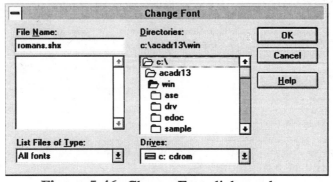

Figure 5-46 Change Font dialogue box

Color
If you select the **Color** button, AutoCAD displays the **Select Color** dialogue box. You can use this dialogue box to specify a color for new text or change the color of selected text.

Height

In the **Height** edit box, you can specify the text height of new text or change the height of selected text.

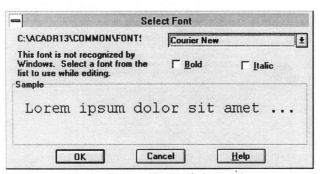

Figure 5-47 Select Font dialogue box

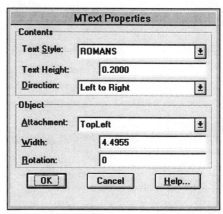

Figure 5-48 MText Properties dialogue box

MText Properties Dialogue Box

You can change the MTEXT properties with the **MText Properties** dialogue box (Figure 5-48). You can invoke this box by selecting the Properties button in the Edit MTEXT dialogue box or by entering MTPROP at the **Command:** prompt.

Contents Area

Text Style

In the **Text Style** edit box you can specify the text style you want to use for new paragraph text.

Text Height

Use the **Text Height** edit box to specify the text height for all text. The text height specified here becomes the default height for text, unless you override it by specifying a different height for the selected text.

Direction

The **Direction** option can be used to specify the direction in which the text must be read. Some languages, like Chinese and Japanese, are read from top to bottom, whereas English is read from left to right.

Object Area

Attachment

Use the **Attachment** option to specify the text justification and text spill in relation to the text boundary.

Width

Use the **Width** edit box to specify the horizontal width of the text boundary.

Rotation

Use the **Rotation** edit box to specify the rotation angle of the text boundary.

Checking Spelling

Toolbar:	Standard Toolbar, Spelling
Pull-down:	Tools, Spelling
Screen:	TOOLS, Spell:

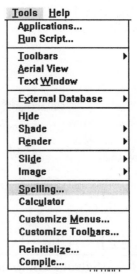

You can check the spelling of text (text generated by the TEXT, DTEXT, or MTEXT commands) by using the **SPELL** command. You can invoke this command from the **Standard** toolbar by selecting the **Spelling** icon, from the pull-down menu (Select Tools, Spelling, Figure 5-49), from the screen menu (Select TOOLS, Spell:), or by entering SPELL at the **Command:** prompt. The prompt sequence is:

Command: **SPELL**
Select object: *Select the text that you want to spell check.*

Figure 5-49 Selecting Spelling from pull-down menu

If the spelling is not correct for any word in the selected text, AutoCAD displays the **Check Spelling** dialogue box (Figure 5-50). The misspelled word is displayed in the current word box and correctly spelled alternate words are listed in the **Suggestions:** box. You may select a word from the list, ignore the correction and continue with the spell check, or accept the change.

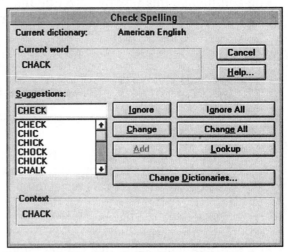

Figure 5-50 Check Spelling dialogue box

SELF EVALUATION TEST

Answer the following questions and then compare your answers with the answers given at the end of this chapter

1.   Transparent commands cannot be used while another command is in progress. (T/F)

2.   The virtual screen contains the last regeneration of the graphics database. (T/F)

3.   An absolute magnification value is specified by a value followed by X. (T/F)

4.   The DTEXT command does not allow you to enter multiple lines of text with a single DTEXT command. (T/F)

5.   The DTEXT command does not allow you to delete typed text with the backspace key. (T/F)

6.   Regeneration does not involve redrawing action. (T/F)

7.   The TEXT command does not allow you to enter multiple lines of text with a single TEXT command. (T/F)

8.   Give the prompt sequence to create a view named VIEW1 on the current screen display
Command: _____
?Delete/Restore/Save/Window: _____
View name to save: _____

9.   The scale factor is a reciprocal of the _____.

10.   The four main text alignment modes are_____ , _____ , _____ , and _____ .

11.   To scale a view relative to paper space units, the ZOOM _____ option is used.

12.   While using the ZOOM **Previous** option, you can go back up to _____ views for a viewport.

13.   You can use _____ to write a paragraph text whose width can be specified by defining _____ of the text boundary, or by entering the _____ of the paragraph

14   The **Attach** option is used to control the _____ of text paragraph

15.   AutoCAD supports TrueType fonts. (T/F)

REVIEW QUESTIONS

Answer the following questions.

1.   Blip marks are a part of the drawing. (T/F)

2.   The REDRAW command can be used as a transparent command. (T/F)

3.   After completion of a transparent command, AutoCAD returns you to the **Command:** prompt. (T/F)

4.   If the BLIPMODE variable is set to On, blip marks do not appear on the screen. (T/F)

5.   Drawn objects are recalculated after a REGEN command. (T/F)

6.   Drawn objects are recalculated after a REDRAW command. (T/F)

7.   In the regeneration process, the floating point database is converted into integer coordinates of the virtual screen. (T/F)

8.   With the ZOOM command the actual size of the object changes. (T/F)

9.   You can use the ZOOM command an indefinite number of times on a drawing. (T/F)

10.   A relative magnification value is specified by a value followed by X. (T/F)

11   The DTEXT command allows you to see the text on the screen as you type it. (T/F)

12.   The TEXT command does not allow you to see the text on the screen as you type it.(T/F)

13. In DTEXT command the screen cross-hairs can be moved to specify a new location of the cursor box for the text. (T/F)

14. Give the prompt sequence to zoom in on the center of a drawing with the magnification of two times.
    Command: _____
    All/ Center/ Dynamic/ Extents/ Left/ Previous/ Vmax/ Window/ <Scale(X/XP)>: _____
    Magnification or Height<current>: _____

15. By specifying the start point you need, your text is _____ justified along its _____.

16. The _____ of a text determines how far above the baseline the capital letters can extend.

17. The _____ determines the orientation of the text baseline with respect to the start point.

18. You can view the entire drawing (even if it is beyond limits) with the help of the _____ option.

19. With the _____ option, you can specify lower left corner and the magnification factor.

20. In the ZOOM **Window** option, the area inside the window is _____ to completely _____ the display.

21. Explain the difference between the REDRAW and REGEN commands. _____

22. What are blips and what commands make them disappear from the screen? _____

23. Name the command that allows you to change the display of blips. _____

24. Explain the difference between the **Extents** and the **All** options of the ZOOM command. _____

25. When, during the drawing process, should you use the ZOOM command? _____

26. Name the view boxes that are displayed during the ZOOM Dynamic command and explain the significance of each one. _____

27. What is a virtual screen? _____

28. What is the PAN command and how does it work? _____

29. Give the letter you must enter at the prompt after entering the Justify option for the TEXT command for

    a. Top/left justified text.
    b. Right justified text.

30. What command do you use to see the text on the screen as it is typed?

31. Calculate the AutoCAD text height for a text to be plotted 1/8" using a half scale; i.e., 1" = 2" Scale.

32 Find the AutoCAD text height for a text to be plotted 1/8" high using a scale of 1/16" = 1'-0".

33. What is the function of the REGENALL and REDRAWALL commands? _____
_____

34. The text created by the MTEXT command is a single object regardless of the number of lines it contains. (T/F)

35. The text boundary of paragraph text is also plotted when you plot the drawing. (T/F).

36. The insertion point also indicates the _____ of the text boundary.

37. The Direction option specifies the direction of the text paragraph. It has two options, _____ and _____ .

38. The **MText Properties** dialogue box can be invoked by entering the _____ command at **Command:** prompt.

39. With the formatting codes you can underline or overline a text string, create stacked text, or insert nonbreaking space between two words. (T/F)

40. The resolution and text fill of the TrueType font text are controlled by the _____ and the _____ system variables.

41. The contents of an MText objects (paragraph text) can be edited by using the _____ and the _____ commands.

EXERCISES

Exercise 1

Draw the text on the screen as shown in Figure 5-51. Use the text justification that will produce the text as shown in the drawing. Assume a value for text height.

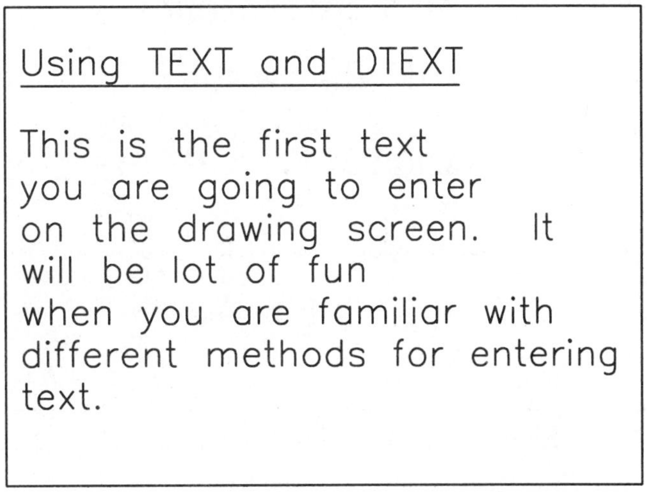

Using TEXT and DTEXT

This is the first text
you are going to enter
on the drawing screen. It
will be lot of fun
when you are familiar with
different methods for entering
text.

Figure 5-51 Drawing for Exercise 1

Exercise 2

Draw the text on the screen as shown in Figure 5-52. Use the text justification options shown in the drawing. The text height is 0.25 units.

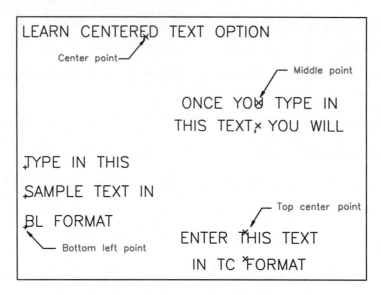

Figure 5-52 Drawing for Exercise 2

Exercise 3

Draw the text on the screen shown in Figure 5-53. You must first define text style files with the attributes as shown in the drawing. The text height is 0.25 units. Do not dimension the drawing.

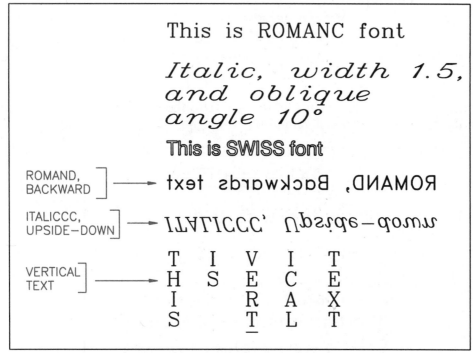

Figure 5-53 Drawing for Exercise 3

Exercise 4

Draw Figure 5-54 using the **MIRROR** command to duplicate the features that are symmetrical. Also, use display commands to facilitate the drawing process. Do not dimension the drawing.

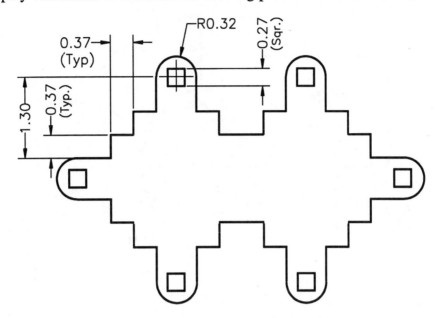

Figure 5-54 Drawing for Exercise 4

Exercise 5

Draw Figure 5-55 making use of the draw, edit, and display commands.

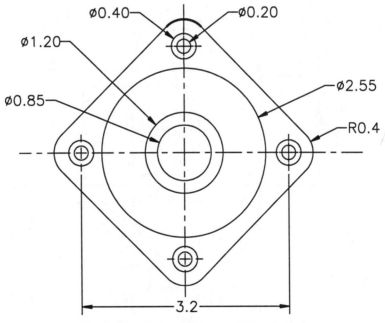

Figure 5-55 Drawing for Exercise 5

Exercise 6

Draw Figure 5-56 making use of the commands studied in this chapter to the maximum advantage. Do not dimension the drawing.

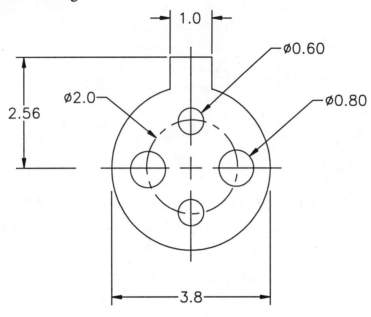

Figure 5-56 Drawing for Exercise 6

Exercise 7

Draw Figure 5-57 according to the given dimensions. Do not dimension the drawing.

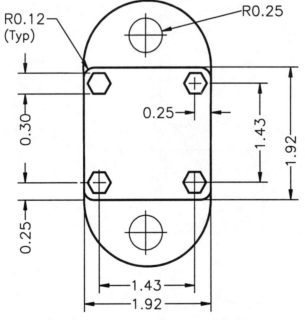

Figure 5-57 Drawing for Exercise 7

Exercise 8

Draw the text on the screen as shown in Figure 5-58. Use the text justification that will produce the text as shown in the drawing. Assume a value for text height.

Figure 5-58 Drawing for Exercise 8

Exercise 9

Make the drawing shown in Figure 5-59. Assume the distance between the dotted lines.

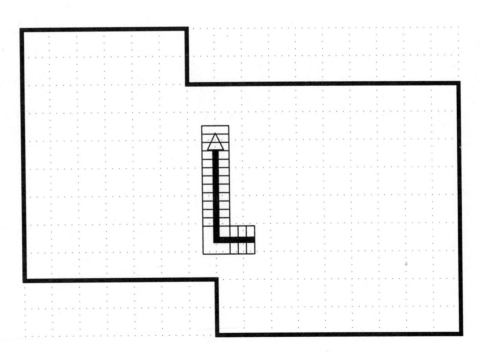

Figure 5-59 Drawing for Exercise 9

Exercise 10

Make the drawing shown in Figure 5-60. Assume the distance between the dotted lines.

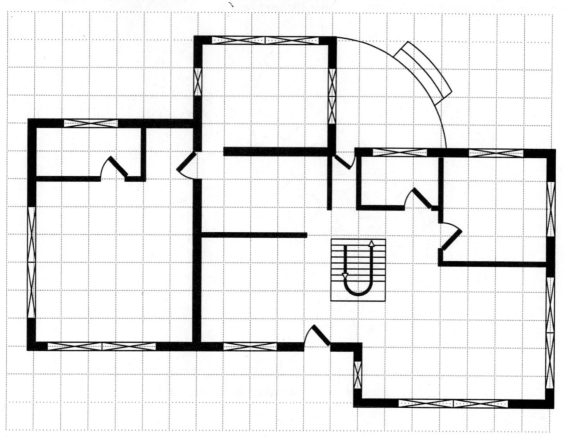

Figure 5-60 Drawing for Exercise 10

Answers

The following are the correct answers to the questions in the self evaluation test
1 - F, **2** - T, **3** - F, **4** - F, **5** - F, **6** - F, **7** - T, **8** - View / Save / VIEW1, **9** - drawing scale, **10** - Align / Center / Middle / Right, **11** - XP, **12** - 10, **13** - MTEXT, two Corners, width, **14** - Justification, **15** - T

Chapter 6

Basic Dimensioning
Changing Dimension Settings

Learning objectives

After completing this chapter, you will be able to:
- Understand the need for dimensioning in drawings.
- Understand the fundamental dimensioning terms.
- Select dimensioning commands in AutoCAD.
- Understand associative dimensioning.
- Create linear, aligned, rotated, baseline, and continue dimensions.
- Create angular, radial, diameter, and ordinate dimensions.
- Use the LEADER command to attach annotation to an object.
- Change dimension settings.

NEED FOR DIMENSIONING

To make designs more informative and practical, the drawing must convey **more than** just the graphic picture of the product. To manufacture an object, the drawing must contain size descriptions such as the length, width, height, angle, radius, diameter, and location of features. All of this information is added to the drawing with the help of **dimensioning**. Some drawings also require information about tolerances with the size of features. All of this information conveyed through dimensioning is vital and often just as important as the drawing itself. With the advances in computer-aided design/drafting and computer-aided manufacturing, it has become mandatory to draw the part to actual size so that the dimensions reflect the actual size of the features. At times it may not be necessary to draw the object the same size as the actual object would be when manufactured, but it is absolutely essential that the dimensions be accurate. Incorrect dimensions will lead to manufacturing errors.

By dimensioning, you are not only giving the size of a part, you are also giving a series of instructions to a machinist, engineer, or architect. The way the part is positioned in a machine, the sequence of machining operations, and the location of different features of the part depend on how you dimension the part. For example, the number of decimal places in a dimension (2.000) determines the type of machine that will be used to do that machining operation. The machining cost of such an operation is significantly higher than for a dimension that has only one digit after the decimal (2.0). Similarly, if a part is to be forged or cast, the radii of the edges and the tolerance you provide to these dimensions determines the cost of the product, the number of defective parts, and the number of parts you get from a single die.

DIMENSIONING IN AUTOCAD

The objects that can be dimensioned in AutoCAD range from straight lines to arcs. The dimensioning commands provided by AutoCAD can be classified into four categories. They are:

Dimension Drawing Commands
Dimension Style Commands
Dimension Editing Commands
Dimension Utility Commands

While dimensioning an object, AutoCAD automatically calculates the length of the object or the distance between two specified points. Also, settings like gap between the dimension text and the dimension line, space between two consecutive dimension lines, arrow size, text size, etc., are maintained and used when the dimensions are being generated for a particular drawing. The generation of arrows, lines (dimension lines, extension lines), and other objects that form a dimension are automatically performed by AutoCAD to save the user's time. This also results in uniform drawings. However, you can override the default measurements computed by AutoCAD and change the settings of various standard values. The modification of dimensioning standards can be achieved through the dimension variables.

The dimensioning functions offered by AutoCAD provide you with extreme flexibility in dimensioning by letting you dimension various objects in a variety of ways. This is of great help because different industries, like architectural, mechanical, civil, electrical, etc., have different standards for the placement of dimensions.

FUNDAMENTAL DIMENSIONING TERMS

Before studying AutoCAD's dimensioning commands, it is important to know and understand various dimensioning terms that are common to linear, angular, radial, diameter, and ordinate dimensioning. The following drawing shows some dimensioning objects.

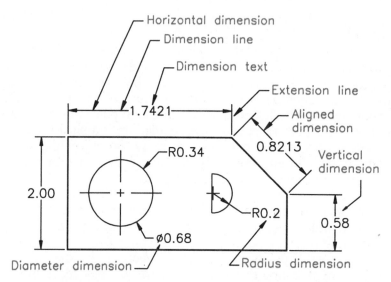

Figure 6-1 AutoCAD's dimensioning terms

Dimension Line

The dimension line indicates which distance or angle is being measured. Usually this line has arrows at both ends and the dimension text is placed along the dimension line. By default the dimension line is drawn between the extension lines. If the dimension line does not fit inside, two short lines with arrows pointing inward are drawn outside the extension lines. The dimension line for angular dimensions (which are used to dimension angles) is an arc. You can control the positioning and various other features of the dimension lines by setting the dimensioning system variables. (The dimensioning system variables are discussed in Chapter 8.)

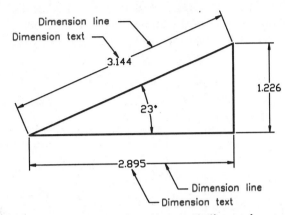

Figure 6-2 Dimension line and dimension text

Dimension Text

Dimension Text is a text string that reflects the actual measurement (dimension value) between the selected points as calculated by AutoCAD. You can accept the value that AutoCAD returns or enter your own value. In case you use the default text, AutoCAD can be supplied with instructions to append the tolerances to it. Also, you can attach prefixes or suffixes of your choice to the dimension text. The format of the default dimension text is determined by the **DIMUNIT** settings. The dimension text style can be controlled by using **DIMTXSTY** dimension variable.

Arrows

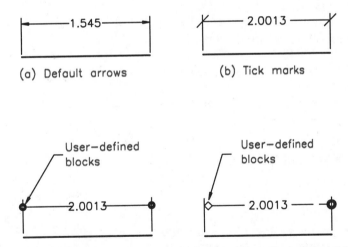

Figure 6-3 Using arrows, tick marks, and user-defined blocks

An arrow is a symbol used at the end of a dimension line (where dimension lines meet the extension lines). Arrows are also called terminators because they signify the end of the dimension line. Since the drafting standards differ from company to company, AutoCAD allows you to draw arrows, tick marks, closed arrows, open arrows, dots, right angle arrows, or user-defined blocks. The user-defined blocks at the two ends of the dimension line can be customized to your requirements. The size of the arrows, tick marks, user blocks, etc., can be regulated by using the dimension variables.

Extension Lines

Extension Lines are drawn from the object measured to the dimension line. These lines are also called witness lines. Extension lines are used in linear and angular dimensioning. Generally extension lines are drawn perpendicular to the dimension line. However, you can make extension lines incline at an angle by using the **OBLIQUE** command. AutoCAD also allows you to suppress either one or both extension lines in a dimension. Other aspects of the extension line can be controlled by using the dimension variables (these variables are discussed in Chapter 8).

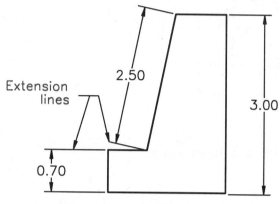

Figure 6-4   Extension lines

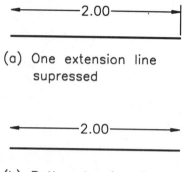

(a) One extension line supressed

(b) Both extension lines supressed

Figure 6-5   Extension line suppression

Leader

A leader is a line that stretches from the dimension text to the object being dimensioned. Sometimes the text for dimensioning and other annotations do not adjust properly near the object. In such cases you can use a leader and place the text at the end of the leader line. For example, the circle shown in Figure 6-6 has a keyway slot that is too small to be dimensioned. In a situation like this, a leader can be drawn from the text to the keyway feature. Also, a leader can be used to attach annotations to an object like part numbers, notes, and instructions.

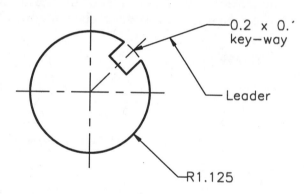

Figure 6-6   Leader used to attach annotation

Center Mark and Center Lines

The center mark is defined as a cross mark that identifies the center point of a circle or an arc. Center lines are mutually perpendicular lines passing through the center of the circle/arc and intersecting the circumference of the circle/arc. A center mark or center lines are automatically drawn when you dimension a circle or arc. The length of the center mark and the extension of the center line beyond the circumference of the circle is determined by the value assigned to the **DIMCEN** dimension variable.

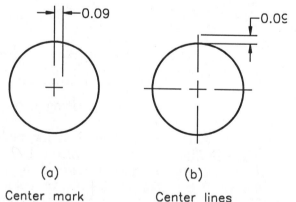

(a)
Center mark

(b)
Center lines

Figure 6-7   Center mark and center lines

Alternate units

With the help of alternate units you can generate dimensions for two systems of measurement at the same time. For example, if the dimensions are in inches, you can use the alternate units dimensioning facility to append metric dimensions to the dimensions (controlling the alternate units through the dimension variables are discusses in Chapter 8).

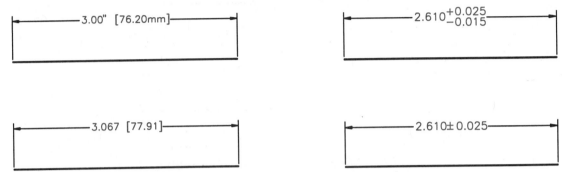

Figure 6-8 Using alternate units dimensioning

Figure 6-9 Using tolerances with dimensions

Tolerances

Tolerance is defined as the amount by which the actual dimension can vary. AutoCAD can attach the plus/minus tolerances to the dimension text (actual measurement computed by AutoCAD). This is also known as variance-style tolerance. The plus and minus tolerance that you specify can be the same or different. In case the plus and minus amounts are equal, AutoCAD draws them with a $\pm$ symbol. Otherwise the tolerances are drawn in two lines. You can use the dimension variables to control the tolerance feature (these variables are discussed in Chapter 8).

Limits

Instead of appending the tolerances to the dimension text, you can apply the tolerances to the measurement itself. Once you define the tolerances, AutoCAD will automatically calculate the upper and lower limits of the dimension. These values are then displayed as a dimension text.

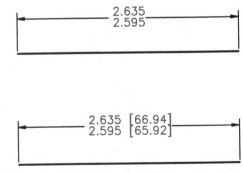

For example, if the actual dimension as computed by AutoCAD is 2.610 units and the tolerance values are +0.025 and -0.015, the upper and lower limits are 2.635 and 2.595. After calculating the limits, AutoCAD will display them as dimension text as shown in Figure 6-10. The dimension variables that control the limits are discussed in Chapter 8.

Figure 6-10 Using limits dimensioning

ASSOCIATIVE DIMENSIONS

Associative dimensioning is defined as a method of dimensioning in which the dimension is associated with the object that is dimensioned. In other words, the dimension is influenced by the changes in the size of the object. In Associative dimensioning, the items constituting a dimension (like dimension lines, arrows, leaders, extension lines, and dimension text) are drawn as a single object. If the associative dimension is disabled, the dimension lines, arrows, leaders, extension lines, and the dimension text are drawn as separate objects. In that case you can edit the dimension lines, extension lines, text, arrowheads as individual objects. You can also use the **EXPLODE** command to split an associative dimension into individual items (just as in the case when associative dimensions is disabled).

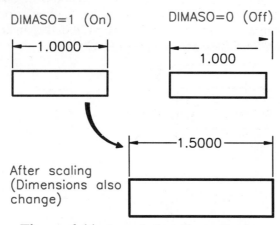

Figure 6-11 Associative dimensioning

The dimensioning variable **DIMASO** controls associativity of dimensions. Its default setting is on. When DIMASO is set on and you edit the object (e.g., trimming or stretching), the dimensions associated with that object also change. Also, the appearance of associative dimensions can be preserved when they are edited by commands such as **STRETCH** or **TEDIT**. For example, a vertical associative dimension is retained as a vertical dimension even after an editing operation. The associative dimension is always generated with the same dimension variable settings as defined in the dimension style.

SELECTING DIMENSIONING COMMANDS IN AUTOCAD

Using Toolbar, Pull-down and Screen Menus

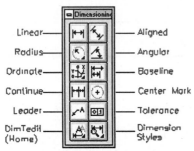

Figure 6-12 Selecting dimension commands from the Dimensioning toolbar

You can select the dimension commands from the **Dimensioning** toolbar by selecting the desired dimension icons, or from the pull-down menu (Select Draw, Dimensioning), or from the screen menu (Select DRAW DIM). When you use the toolbar, pull-down menu, or screen menu to invoke the dimensioning command, only one dimensioning operation can be performed at a time. After you perform a

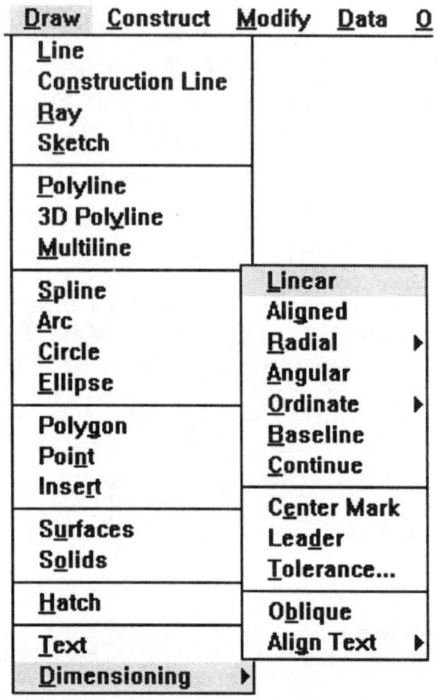

Figure 6-13 Selecting dimensions from the pull-down menu

dimensioning operation, AutoCAD automatically exits from the dimensioning mode. If you select the DRAW DIM option from the root menu, AutoCAD will display the dimensioning menu in the screen menu area. From this menu you can select any dimensioning command.

Using the Command Line

Using Dimensioning Commands

You can use the dimensioning commands at The **Command:** prompt without using the DIM Command. For example, if you want to draw the linear dimension, the **DIMLINEAR** (or **DIMLIN**) command can be entered directly at the Command: prompt:

Command: **DIMLINEAR or DIMLIN**
First extension line origin or RETURN to select: *Select a point or press the Enter key.*
Second extension line origin: *Select second point.*
Dimension line location (Text/Angle/Horizontal/Vertical/Rotates): *Select a point to locate the position of the dimension.*
Command: *(After you have finished dimensioning, AutoCAD returns to the Command: prompt.)*

DIM and DIM1 Commands

Since dimensioning has several options, it also has its own command mode and prompt. The **DIM** command keeps you in the dimension mode and the **Dim:** prompt is repeated after each dimensioning command, until you exit from the dimensioning mode to return to the normal AutoCAD's **Command:** prompt. To exit from the dimension mode, enter **Exit** (or just **E**) at **Dim:** prompt. You can also exit by pressing the **Esc** key, or by pressing the third button of the digitizer puck. The previous command will be repeated if you press the space bar or the **Enter** key at the Dim: prompt. In the dimension mode, it is not possible to execute the normal set of AutoCAD commands except function keys, object snap overrides, control-key combinations, transparent commands, dialogue boxes, and menus.

Command: **DIM**
Dim: **Hor**
First extension line origin or RETURN to select: *Select a point or press the Enter key.*
Second extension line origin: *Select the second point.*
Dimension line location (Text/Angle): *Select a point to locate the position of the dimension.*
Dimension text < default >: *Press the Enter key to accept the default dimension.*
Dim: *(After you have finished dimensioning, AutoCAD returns to the Dim: prompt.)*

The **DIM1** command lets you execute a single dimension command, then automatically takes you back to the normal Command: prompt.

Command: **DIM1**
Dim: **Hor**
First extension line origin or RETURN to select: *Select a point or press the Enter key.*
Second extension line origin: *Select the second point.*
Dimension line location (Text/Angle/Horizontal/Vertical/Rotates): *Select a point to locate the position of the dimension.*
Dimension text < default >: *Press the Enter key to accept the default dimension.*
Command: *(After you are done dimensioning, AutoCAD returns Command: prompt.)*

AutoCAD has provided the following five fundamental dimensioning types:

Linear dimensioning   **Diameter dimensioning**
Angular dimensioning   **Ordinate dimensioning**
Radius dimensioning

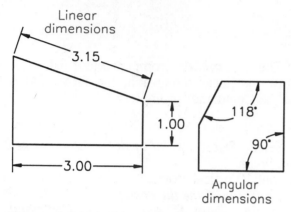

Figure 6-14(a) Linear and angular dimensions

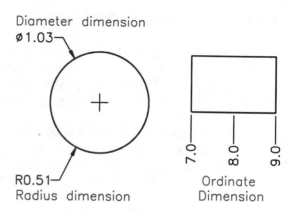

Figure 6-14(b) Radius, diameter, and ordinate dimensions

LINEAR DIMENSIONING

Toolbar:	Dimensioning, Linear
Pull-down:	Draw, Dimensioning, Linear
Screen:	DRAW DIM, Linear:

Linear dimensioning applies to those dimensioning commands that measure the distance between two points. The points can be any two points in the space, the end points of an arc or line, or any set of points that can be identified. To achieve a greater degree of accuracy, **selecting points must be done with the help of object snaps**. Linear dimensions include **Horizontal** and **Vertical** dimensioning. When you select a dimensioning command, AutoCAD will prompt you to enter information about the dimension. The dimension is not drawn until you respond to all of the dimensioning prompts.

Horizontal and Vertical Dimensioning

The horizontal and vertical dimensions can be created by invoking the **Linear** dimensioning option from the **Dimensioning** toolbar, from the pull-down menu (Select Draw, Dimensioning, Linear), or from the screen menu (Select DRAW DIM, Linear:). Linear dimensioning can be also created by entering DIMLINEAR or DIM command at The **Command:** prompt.

Using DIMLINEAR Command

Command: **DIMLINEAR** or **DIMLIN**
First extension line origin or RETURN to select: ◄─┘ *(Press the Enter key)*.
Select the object to dimension: *Select the object.*
Dimension line location (Text/Angle/Horizontal/Vertical/Rotates): *Select a point to locate the position of the dimension.*

Instead of selecting the object, you can also select the two end points of the line (Figure 6-15) that you want to dimension. The prompt sequence is as follows:

Command: **DIMLINEAR**
First extension line origin or RETURN to select: *Select a point or press the Enter key.*
Second extension line origin: *Select second point.*
Dimension line location (Text/Angle/Horizontal/Vertical/Rotates): *Select a point to locate the position of the dimension.*

When using the **DIMLINEAR** command, you can obtain the horizontal or vertical dimension by simply defining the dimension location point. If you select a point above or below the dimension, AutoCAD creates a horizontal dimension. If you select a point that is on the left or right of the dimension, AutoCAD creates a vertical dimension through that point.

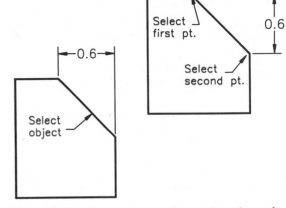

DIMLINEAR Options

Text Option
The **Text** option allows you to override the default dimension. However, If you override the default dimensions, the

Figure 6-15 Drawing horizontal and vertical dimension

dimensional associativity of the **dimension text** is lost and AutoCAD will not recalculate the dimension when the object is scaled.

Command: **DIMLINEAR**
First extension line origin or RETURN to select: *Select a point or press the Enter key.*
Second extension line origin: *Select second point.*
Dimension line location (Text/Angle/Horizontal/Vertical/Rotated): **T** *(Enter T to override the default text. Enter dimension text in the Edit MText dialogue box.)*
Dimension line location (Text/Angle/Horizontal/Vertical/Rotated): *Select a point to locate the position of the dimension.*

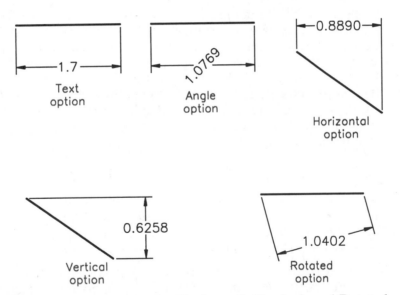

Figure 6-16 Using Text, Angle, Horizontal, Vertical, and Rotated options

Angle Option
The **Angle** option lets you change the angle of the dimension text.

Horizontal Option
The **Horizontal** option lets you create a horizontal dimension regardless of where you specify the dimension location.

Vertical Option

The **Vertical** option lets you create a vertical dimension regardless of where you specify the dimension location.

Rotated Option

The **Rotated** option lets you create a dimension that is rotated at a specified angle.

Using the DIM Command

Command: **DIM**
Dim: **Hor** or **Vert**
First extension line origin or RETURN to select: ◄─┘ *Press the Enter key.*
Select the object to dimension: *Select the object.*
Dimension line location (Text/Angle): *Select a point to locate the position of the dimension.*
Dimension text <default>: *Press the Enter key to accept the default dimension.*

Instead of selecting the object, you can also select the two end points of the line that you want to dimension as follows:

Command: **DIM1**
Dim: **Hor** or **Vert**
First extension line origin or RETURN to select: *Select a point.*
Second extension line origin: *Select second point.*
Dimension line location (Text/Angle): *Select a point to locate the position of the dimension.*
Dimension text <default>: *Press the Enter key to accept the default dimension.*

After you have selected the DIM command and the dimensioning type, select the points on the object to be dimensioned. Usually the points on the object are selected by using the **object snaps** (end points, intersection, center, etc). Once you have selected the points, AutoCAD will automatically measure the object and prompt you to pick a location for the dimension line. AutoCAD will compute the distance and display it as the default in the next prompt. You can retain AutoCAD's measurements as the dimension text or enter the text of your specification at the **Dimension text < value obtained by AutoCAD >:** prompt. It is very important to have an accurate drawing to have accurate dimensioning because AutoCAD calculates the dimensions on the basis of the specified points on the drawing.

Note

If you override the default dimensions, the dimensional associativity of the dimension text is lost and AutoCAD will not recalculate the dimension when the object is scaled.

The working of the **Horizontal** and **Vertical** commands is identical except that the **Horizontal** command dimensions horizontal objects (measures horizontal distances) and the **Vertical** command dimensions vertical objects (measures vertical distances). In other words, the angle of the dimension line in Horizontal dimensioning is 0 whereas for Vertical dimensioning it is 90 degrees.

Example 1

In this example you will use the DIMLINEAR command to dimension a line by selecting the object and by specifying the first and second extension line origins (Figure 6-18). The following is the command prompt sequence for DIM command:

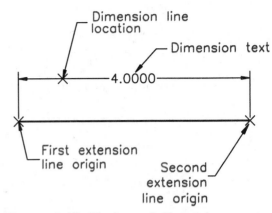

Figure 6-17 Horizontal dimension

Selecting the Object

1. Enter the DIMLINEAR command at The **Command:** prompt. You can also select this command from the pull-down menu (Select Draw, Dimensioning, Linear) or from the screen menu (Select DRAW, DIM, Linear).

   Command: **DIMLINEAR** or **DIMLIN**

2. At the next prompt press the Enter key to select the line. The end points of the line are taken as the origins for the extension line

   First extension line origin or RETURN to select: ◄─┘
   Select object to dimension: *Select the line.*

3. At the next prompt pick the location for the dimension line. This information is used by AutoCAD to set the location to place the dimension line. With the Text option, you can override the default dimension text.

   Dimension line location (Text/Angle/Horizontal/Vertical/Rotated): **T**

4. When you select the Text option AutoCAD displays the Edit MText dialogue box on the screen. Enter the dimension text in the dialogue box and select the OK button to exit the dialogue box.

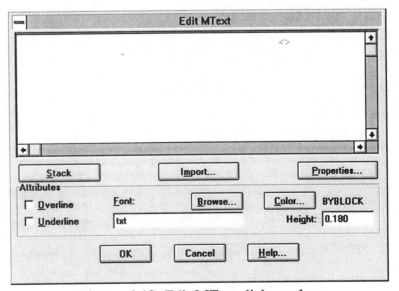

Figure 6-18 Edit MText dialogue box

Dimension line location (Text/Angle/Horizontal/Vertical/Rotated): *Select a point.*

Specifying Extension Line Origins

1. In case you want to specify the two end points (extension line origin) on the line, the command prompt sequence is as follows:

Command: **DIMLINEAR**
First extension line origin or RETURN to select: *Pick the first end point of the line using the Endpoint object snap.*
Second extension line origin: *Pick the second end point of the line using the Endpoint object snap.*
Dimension line location (Text/Angle/Horizontal/Vertical/Rotated): *Enter the location for the dimension line.*

ALIGNED DIMENSIONING

Toolbar:	Dimensioning, Aligned, Dimension
Pull-down:	Draw, Dimensioning, Aligned
Screen:	DRAW DIM, Aligned:

You may want to dimension an object that is inclined at an angle, not parallel to the X axis or Y axis. In such a situation you can use aligned dimensioning. With the help of aligned dimensioning, you can measure the true distance between the two points. In horizontal or vertical dimensioning, you can only measure the distance from the first extension line origin to the second extension line origin along the horizontal or vertical axis respectively. The working of the **ALIGNED** command is similar to the other linear dimensioning commands. The dimension created with the **ALIGNED** command is

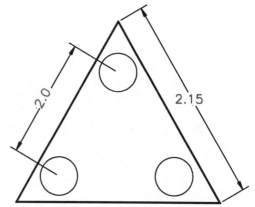

Figure 6-19   Aligned dimensioning

parallel to the object being dimensioned. This command can be invoked from the **Dimensioning** toolbar by selecting the **Aligned dimension** icon, the screen menu (Select DRAW DIM, Aligned:), the pull-down menu (Select Draw, Dimensioning, Aligned). You can also invoke the ALIGNED dimensioning command by entering DIMALIGNED at the **Command:** prompt or Align (or Al) at the **Dim:** prompt.

Command: **DIMALIGNED**
or
Command: **DIM**
Dim: **Aligned** or **Al**

Figure 6-19 illustrates aligned dimensioning. The prompt sequence for aligned dimensioning is the same as that for other linear dimensions. The only difference is that you have to select the Aligned dimension option (enter Aligned at the Dim: prompt). The following is the prompt sequence for the Aligned dimensioning command:

Command: **DIM**
Dim: **ALIGNED**
First extension line origin or RETURN to select: *Pick the first extension line origin.*
Second extension line origin: *Pick the second extension line origin.*

Dimension line location (Text/Angle): *Select the dimension line location.*
Dimension text <measured>: *Enter new text to override the distance computed by AutoCAD or press the Enter key to retain the default dimension text.*

You can also respond to the First extension line origin or RETURN to select: prompt by pressing the Enter (Return) key. AutoCAD will prompt you to select the object to dimension. Once you select the object, AutoCAD will automatically align the dimension with the selected object.

Exercise 1

Draw the following figure and then use the DIMLINEAR and DIMALIGNED commands to dimension the part. The distance between the dotted lines is 0.5 units.

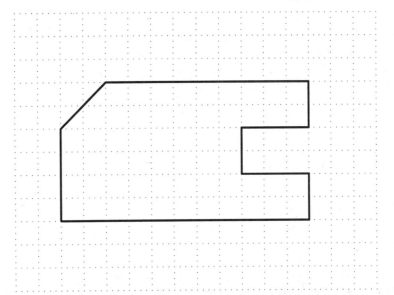

Figure 6-20 Using the DIMLINEAR and DIMALIGNED commands to dimension the part

ROTATED DIMENSIONING

Rotated dimensioning is used when you want to place the dimension line at an angle (if you do not want to align the dimension line with the extension line origins selected). The **Rotated** dimension command will prompt you to specify the dimension line angle. You can invoke this command by using DIMLINEAR (Rotate option) or by entering Rotated (or Rot) at the Dim: command prompt. The following is the command prompt sequence for drawing the Rotated dimension:

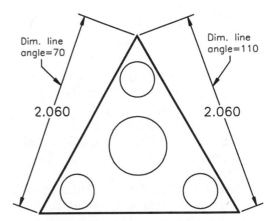

Figure 6-21 Rotated Dimensioning

Dim: **ROTATED** or **ROT**
Dimension line angle <0>: **110**
First extension line origin or RETURN to select: *Select the lower right corner of the triangle.*
Second extension line origin: *Select the top corner.*
Dimension line location (Text/Angle): *Select the location for the dimension line.*
Dimension text <2.060>: ↵

Note
You can draw horizontal and vertical dimensioning by specifying the rotation angle of 0 degrees for horizontal dimensioning and 90 degrees for vertical dimensioning.

BASELINE DIMENSIONING

Toolbar:	Dimensioning, Baseline
Pull-down:	Draw, Dimensioning, Baseline
Screen:	DRAW DIM, Baselin:

Sometimes in manufacturing you may want to locate different points and features of a part with reference to a fixed point (base point or reference point). This can be accomplished by using **Baseline** dimensioning. With this command you can continue a linear dimension from the first extension line origin of the first dimension. The new dimension line is automatically offset by a fixed amount to avoid drawing a dimension line and dimension text on top of the previous dimension. **There must already be a Linear, Ordinate, or Angular associative dimension to use the Baseline or Continue dimensions**.

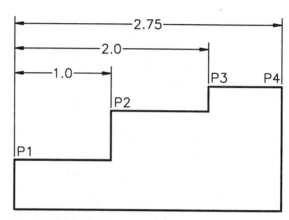

Figure 6-22 Baseline dimensioning

The **Baseline** command can be invoked from the **Dimensioning** toolbar by selecting the **Baseline Dimension** icon, from the pull-down menu (Select Draw, Dimensioning, Baseline), from the screen menu (Select DRAW DIM, Baselin:). You can also use **DIMBASELINE** (or DIMBASE) at the **Command:** prompt or enter **BAS** at the **Dim:** prompt. The following example illustrates the working of the Baseline dimension:

Command: **DIM**
Dim: **HORIZONTAL**
First extension line origin or RETURN to select: *Pick left corner (P1). (Use endpoint object snap.)*
Second extension line origin: *Pick the origin of the second extension line (P2).*
Dimension line location (Text/Angle): *Pick the location of the first dimension line.*
Dimension text <1.0000>: **1.0**
Dim: **BASELINE** or **BAS**
Second extension line origin or RETURN to select: *Pick the origin of next extension line (P3).*
Dimension text <2.0000>: **2.0**
Dim: **BASE**
Second extension line origin or RETURN to select: *Pick the origin of next extension line (P4).*
Dimension text <3.000>: **2.75**

If you press the Enter key at the prompt **Second extension line origin or RETURN to select:**, the next prompt is **Select base dimension:**. AutoCAD uses the extension line origin nearest to the selection point as the origin for the first extension line. The next dimension line is automatically spaced and drawn by AutoCAD.

CONTINUE DIMENSIONING

Toolbar:	Dimensioning, Continue
Pull-down:	Draw, Dimensioning, Continue
Screen:	DRAW DIM, Continu:

With the **CONTINUE** command you can continue a linear dimension from the second extension line of the previous dimension. This is also referred to as chained or incremental dimensioning. The **CONTINUE** and **BASELINE** commands are used in a similar manner. The **CONTINUE** command can be invoked from the **Dimensioning** toolbar by selecting the **Continue Dimension** icon, from the pull-down menu (Select Draw, Dimensioning, Continue), or from the screen menu (Select DRAW DIM, Continu:). You can also use the **DIMCONTINUE** (or DIMCONT) at the **Command:** prompt or enter **CONTINUE** (or CONT) at the **DIM:** prompt.

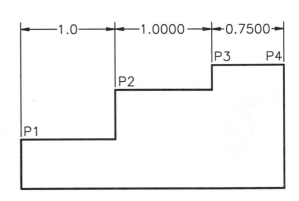

Figure 6-23   Continue dimensioning

Command: **DIMLINEAR**
First extension line origin or RETURN to select: *Pick left corner (P1). (Use the end point object snap).*
Second extension line origin: *Pick second point with the end point object snap (P2).*
Dimension line location (Text/Angle/Horizontal/Vertical/Rotated): *Pick the location of the first dimension line.*

Command: **DIMCONTINUE** or **DIMCONT**
Second extension line origin or RETURN to select: *Pick the origin of next extension line (P3).*
Second extension line origin or RETURN to select: *Pick the origin of next extension line (P4).*

The default base (first extension line) for the dimensions created with the **CONTINUE** command is the previous dimension's second extension line. You can override the default by pressing the Enter key (RETURN option) at the **Second extension line origin or RETURN to select:** prompt, then specifying the other dimension. AutoCAD uses the extension line origin nearest to the selection point as the origin for the first extension line.

Note

When you use the DIMCONTINUE command, AutoCAD does not let you change the default dimension text. Use the DIM command if you want to override the default dimension text.

If you have not drawn any dimension in the current drawing session and you use Continue or Baseline Dimensioning commands, AutoCAD will prompt you to select a dimension for Continue or Baseline Dimensioning.

Command: DIMCONTINUE
Select continued dimension.

Exercise 2

Make the following drawing, then use the DIMBASELINE command to dimension the top half and DIMCONTINUE to dimension the bottom half. The distance between the dotted lines is 0.5 unit.

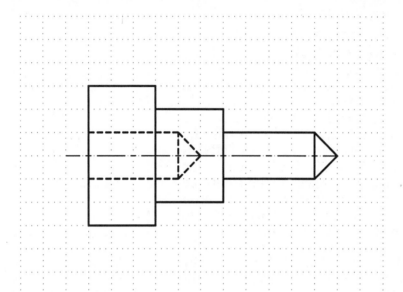

Figure 6-24 Using the DIMBASELINE and DIMCONTINUE commands to dimension the part

ANGULAR DIMENSIONING

Toolbar:	Dimensioning, Angular
Pull-down:	Draw, Dimensioning, Angular
Screen:	DRAW DIM, Angular:

Angular dimensioning is used when you want to dimension an angle. This command generates a dimension arc (dimension line in the shape of an arc with arrowheads at both ends) to indicate the angle between two non-parallel lines. This command can also be used to dimension the vertex and two other points, a circle with another point, or the angle of an arc. For every set of points there exists one acute angle and one obtuse angle (inner and outer angle). If you pick the dimension arc location between the two points, you will get the acute angle; if you pick it outside the two points, you will get the obtuse angle. Figure 6-25 shows the four ways to dimension two non-parallel lines.

The **Angular** dimensioning command can be invoked by from the **Dimensioning** toolbar by selecting the **Angular Dimension** icon, from the pull-down menu (Select Draw, Dimensioning, Angular), or from the screen menu (Select DRAW DIM, Angular). You can also invoke the command by using **DIMANGULAR** (or DIMANG) at the **Command:** prompt or entering **ANGULAR** (or ANG) at the **Dim:** prompt.

Command: **DIMANGULAR** or **DIMANG**

Dim: **ANGULAR** or **ANG**
Select arc, circle, line, or RETURN:

Dimensioning the Angle Between Two Nonparallel Lines

The angle between two non-parallel lines or straight line segments of a polyline can be dimensioned with the **Angular** dimensioning command. The vertex of the angle is taken as the point of intersection of the two lines. The location of the extension lines and dimension arc is determined by how you pick the dimension arc location. The following example illustrates the dimensioning of two non-parallel lines using the **ANGULAR** command:

Command: **DIMANG**
Select arc, circle, line, or RETURN: *Pick the first line.*
Second line: *Pick the second line.*
Dimension arc line location (Text/Angle): **T**   *(Enter the new value in the Edit MText dialogue box.)*
Dimension arc line location (Text/Angle): *Pick the dimension arc location.*

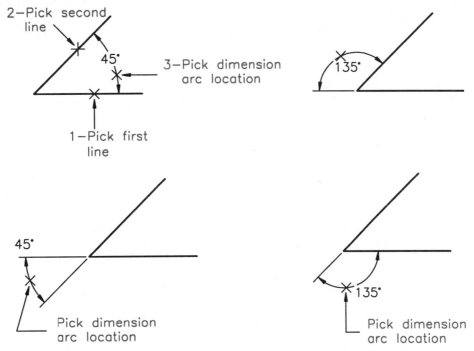

Figure 6-25 Angular dimensioning between two nonparallel lines

Dimensioning the Angle of an Arc

Angular dimensioning can also be used to dimension the angle of an arc. In this case, the center point of the arc is taken as the vertex and the two end points of the arc are used as the extension line origin points for the extension lines. The following example illustrates the dimensioning of an arc using the **ANGULAR** command. The prompt sequence is as follows:

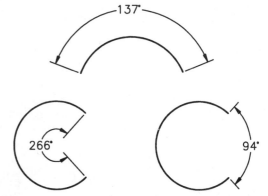

Figure 6-26 Angular dimensioning of arcs

Command: **DIM**
Dim: **ANGULAR**
Select arc, circle, line, or RETURN: *Select the arc.*
Dimension arc line location (Text/Angle): *Select the location for the dimension line.*
Dimension text <current value>: *Press Enter key or enter a new value.*
Enter text location (or RETURN): *Pick a location for the dimension text.*

Angular Dimensioning of Circles

The angular feature associated with the circle can be dimensioned by selecting a circle object at the **Select arc, circle, line, or RETURN:** prompt. The center of the selected circle is used as the vertex of the angle. The first point picked (when the circle is selected for angular dimensioning) is used as the origin of the first extension line. In a similar manner, the second point picked is taken as the origin of the second extension line. The following is the command prompt sequence for dimensioning a circle:

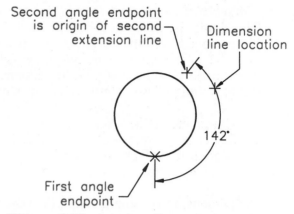

Figure 6-27 Angular dimensioning of circles

Command: **DIMANGULAR**
Select arc, circle, line, or RETURN: *Select the circle at the point where you want the first extension line.*
Second angle end point: *Pick the second point on or away from the circle.*
Dimension arc line location (Text/Angle): **T** *(Enter the new value in the Edit MText dialogue box.)*
Dimension arc line location (Text/Angle): *Select the location for the dimension line.*

Angular Dimensioning Based on Three Points

If you press the Return key at the **Select arc, circle, line, or RETURN:** prompt, AutoCAD allows you to select three points to create an angular dimension. The first point is used as the vertex point, and the other two points are used as the first and second angle end points of the angle. The coordinate specification of the first angle end point and the second angle end point must not be identical. However, the angle vertex and one of the angle end point coordinates can be identical. The following example illustrates angular dimensioning by defining three points:

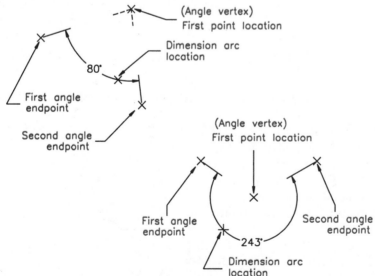

Figure 6-28 Angular dimensioning for three points

Command: **DIM**
Dim: **ANGULAR**
Select arc, circle, line, or RETURN: *Press the Enter key.*
Angle vertex: *Specify the first point, vertex.*
First angle end point: *Specify the second point.*
Second angle end point: *Specify the third point.*

Dimension arc line location (Text/Angle): *Select the location for the dimension line.*
Dimension text <current value>: *Press the Enter key or enter a value.*
Enter text location (or RETURN): *Pick a location for the dimension text.*

Note

If you use the DIMANGULAR command, you cannot specify the text location. In the DIMANGULAR command, AutoCAD automatically positions the dimensioning text. If you want to position the dimension text, you should use the DIM, Angular command.

Exercise 3

Make the following drawing and then use the DIMANGULAR command to dimension all angles of the part. The distance between the dotted lines is 0.5 unit.

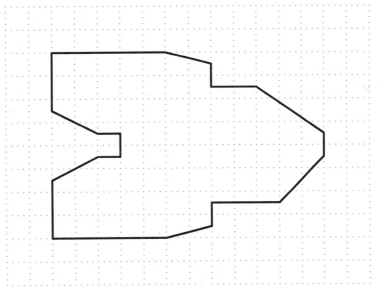

Figure 6-29 Drawing for Exercise 3

RADIAL DIMENSIONING

Diameter Dimensioning

Toolbar:	Dimensioning, Radial, Diameter
Pull-down:	Draw, Dimensioning, Radial, Diameter
Screen:	DRAW DIM, Diametr:

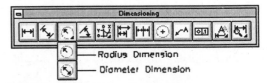

Figure 6-30 Selecting the Diameter option from the Dimensioning toolbar

Diameter dimensioning is used to dimension a circle: you can also use it to dimension an arc. In the Diameter option the measurement is done between two diametrically opposite points on the circumference of the circle or arc. The dimension text generated by AutoCAD commences with the letter ϕ to indicate a diameter dimension. The **Diameter** dimensioning command can be invoked from the **Dimensioning** toolbar by selecting the **Diameter** icon in the **Radius** flyout, from the pull-down menu (Select Draw, Dimensioning, Radial, Diameter), or from the screen menu (Select DRAW DIM, Diametr:). This command can also be invoked by entering **DIMDIAMETER** (or **DIMDIA**) at the **Command:** prompt or entering **DIAMETER** (or **DIA**) at the **Dim:** prompt. The following is the prompt sequence for dimensioning a circle:

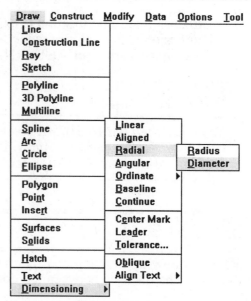

Figure 6-31 Selecting Diameter option from the pull down menu

Command: **DIMDIAMETER** or **DIMDIA**
Select arc or circle: *Select an arc or circle by picking anywhere on its circumference.*
Dimension line location (Text/Angle): *Pick a point to position the dimension.*

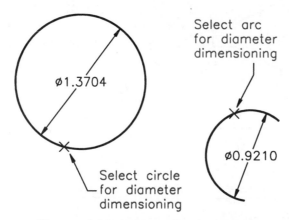

Figure 6-32 Diameter dimensioning

If you want to override the default value of the dimension text , use the Text option as follows:

Command: **DIMDIAMETER** or **DIMDIA**
Select arc or circle: *Select an arc or circle.*
Dimension line location (Text/Angle): **T**   *(Enter the new value, %%C2.5, in the Edit MText dialogue box.)*
Dimension line location (Text/Angle): *Move the cursor and pick a point.*

The control sequence **%%C** is used to obtain the diameter ϕ symbol. It is followed by the dimension text that you want to appear in the diameter dimension. You can also suppress the entire text by entering blank spaces in the Edit MText dialogue box.

Note

*The control sequence **%%d** can be used to generate the degree symbol* ° *(45°).*

Radius Dimensioning

Toolbar:	Dimensioning, Radius
Pull-down:	Draw, Dimensioning, Radial, Radius
Screen:	DRAW DIM, Radius:

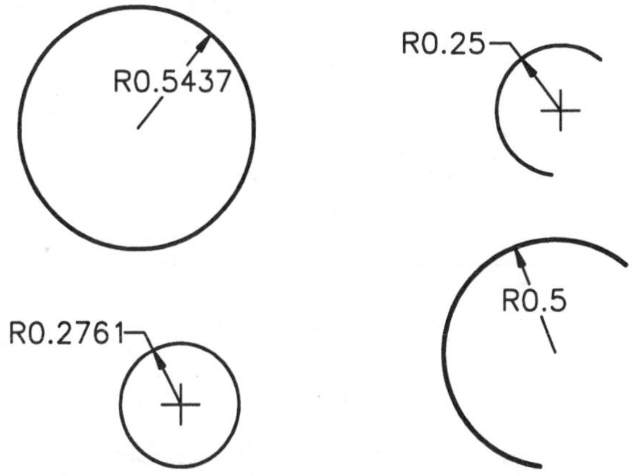

Radius dimensioning is used to dimension an arc: you can also use it to dimension a circle. The **Radius** dimensioning command can be invoked from the **Dimensioning** toolbar by selecting the **Radius** icon in the **Radius** flyout, from the pull-down menu (Select Draw, Dimensioning, Radial, Radius), or from the screen menu (Select DRAW DIM, Radius:). This command can also be invoked by entering **DIMDRADIUS** (or DIMRAD) at the **Command:** prompt or entering **RADIUS** (or RAD) at the **Dim:** prompt.

Figure 6-33 Radius dimensioning

With the **RADIUS** command you can dimension the radius of a circle or an arc. Radius and Diameter dimensioning are similar; the only difference is that instead of the diameter line a radius line is drawn (half of the diameter line). The dimension text generated by AutoCAD is preceded by the letter **R** to indicate a Radius dimension. If you want to use the default dimension text (dimension text generated automatically by AutoCAD), simply pick a point to position the dimension at the **Dimension line location (Text/Angle):** prompt. You can also enter a new value or specify a prefix or suffix, or suppress the entire text by entering a blank space following the **Dimension text <current>:** prompt. A center mark for the circle/arc is automatically drawn, provided the center mark value (DIMCEN) is not 0.

> Command: **DIMRADIUS** or **DIMRAD**
> Select arc or circle: *Select the object you want to dimension.*
> Dimension line location (Text/Angle): *Move the cursor and pick a point.*

If you want to override the default value of the dimension text, use the Text option as follows:

> Command: **DIMRADIUS** or **DIMRAD**
> Select arc or circle: *Select an arc or circle.*
> Dimension line location (Text/Angle): **T**   *(Enter the new value, R0.25, in the Edit MText dialogue box.)*
> Dimension line location (Text/Angle): *Move the cursor and pick a point.*

GENERATING CENTER MARKS AND CENTER LINES

Toolbar:	Dimensioning, Center Mark
Pull-down:	Draw, Dimensioning, Center Mark
Screen:	DRAW DIM, Center:

When circles or arcs are dimensioned with the **RADIUS** or **DIAMETER** command, a small mark may be drawn in the center of the circle/arc. This mark is known as the center mark. Sometimes you may want to mark the center of a circle or an arc without using the **RADIUS** or **DIAMETER** dimensioning commands. This can be achieved by entering **DIMCENTER** at the **Command:** prompt or **CENTER** (or CEN) at the **Dim:** prompt. The

CENTER dimensioning command can be invoked from the **Dimensioning** toolbar by selecting the **Center Mark** icon, from the pull-down menu (Select Draw, Dimensioning, Center Mark), or from the screen menu (Select DRAW DIM, Center:).

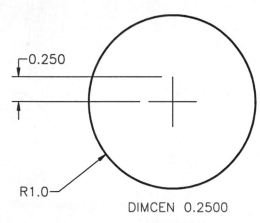

Figure 6-34 Using the DIMCEN variable to control the size of the center mark

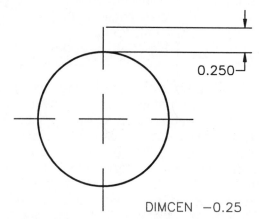

Figure 6-35 Using a negative value for DIMCEN

The **DIMCEN** variable is used to control the size of the center mark of a circle or arc. The value assigned to the DIMCEN variable determines the length of the lines that constitute the center mark. For example, if the DIMCEN variable is set to 0, center marks and center lines will not be generated. If the value of the DIMCEN variable is greater than 0, the center marks are drawn and their size is governed by the value of the DIMCEN. For example, a value of 0.250 displays center dashes that are 0.5 (0.25 x 2 = 0.5) unit long. The prompt sequence for setting the DIMCEN variable and the DIMCENTER command is:

Command: **DIMCEN**
New value for DIMCEN <current value>: **0.25**
Command: **DIMCENTER**
Select arc or circle: *Select arc or circle.*

When the value of the DIMCEN variable is **less than 0** (negative value), the center lines and the center marks are drawn. The size of the center mark and the extension of the center lines beyond the circle is determined by the absolute value of the DIMCEN variable. For example, a value of -0.25 for the DIMCEN variable will draw a center dash 0.5 (0.25 x 2) unit long and the center lines will extend beyond the circle/arc by a distance of 0.25 unit.

Exercise 4

Make the following drawing, then use the DIMRADIUS and DIMDIAMETER commands to dimension the part. Use the DIMCENTER command to draw the center lines through the circles. The distance between the dotted lines is 0.5 unit.

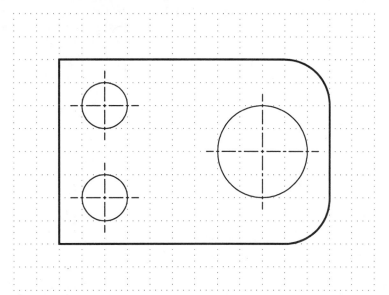

Figure 6-36 Using the DIMRADIUS and DIMDIAMETER commands to dimension the part

ORDINATE DIMENSIONING

Toolbar:	Dimensioning, Ordinate
Pull-down:	Draw, Dimensioning, Ordinate
Screen:	DRAW DIM, Ordinat:

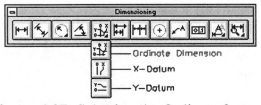

Figure 6-37 Selecting the Ordinate from the Dimensioning toolbar

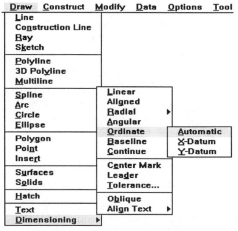

Figure 6-38 Selecting the Ordinate option from the Draw pull-down menu

Ordinate dimensioning is also known as arrowless dimensioning because no arrowheads are drawn in this type of dimensioning. Ordinate dimensioning is also called Datum dimensioning, because all dimensions are related to a common base point. The current UCS (user coordinate system) origin becomes the reference or the base point for Ordinate dimensioning. With ordinate dimensioning you can determine the X or Y displacement of a selected point from the current UCS origin. To locate the **UCS**, you can use the UCS command. The **Ordinate** dimensioning command can be invoked from the **Dimensioning** toolbar by selecting the **Ordinate** icon from the **Ordinate** flyout, from the pull-down menu (Select Draw, Dimensioning, Ordinate), or from the screen menu (Select DRAW DIM, Ordinat:). You can also invoke this command by entering **DIMORDINATE** (or DIMORD) at the **Command:** prompt or **ORDINATE** (or ORD) at the **Dim:** prompt.

In Ordinate dimensioning, AutoCAD automatically places the dimension text (X or Y coordinate value) and the leader line along the X or Y axis. Since the ordinate dimensioning pertains to either the X coordinate or the Y coordinate, you should keep ORTHO on. When ORTHO is off, the leader line is automatically given a bend when you pick the second leader line point that is offset from the first point. In ordinate dimensioning, only one extension line (leader line) is drawn.

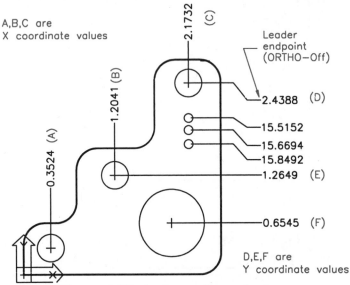

Figure 6-39 Ordinate dimensioning

The leader line for an X coordinate value will be drawn perpendicular to the X axis and the leader line for a Y coordinate value will be drawn perpendicular to the Y axis. By default, the leader line drawn perpendicular to the X axis will have the dimension text aligned with the leader line. The dimension text is the X datum of the selected point. The leader line drawn perpendicular to the Y axis will have the dimension text, which is the Y datum of the selected point, aligned with the leader line. Any other alignment specification for the dimension text is nullified. Hence changes in the values of DIMTIH and DIMTOH variables have no effect on the alignment of dimension text. You can specify the coordinate value you want to dimension at the **Leader end point (Xdatum/Ydatum/Text):** prompt.

For example, if you enter Y at the above prompt, AutoCAD will dimension the Y coordinate of the selected feature. Similarly, if you enter X, AutoCAD will dimension the X coordinate of the selected point. However, if you select or enter a point instead of an option, AutoCAD checks the difference between the feature location and the leader end point. If the difference in the X coordinates is greater, the dimension measures the Y coordinate; otherwise, the X coordinate is measured. In this manner AutoCAD determines whether it is an X or Y type of ordinate dimension. The following is the command prompt sequence for ordinate dimensioning:

Command: **DIMORDINATE** or **DIMORD**
Select feature: *Pick a point.*
Leader end point (Xdatum/Ydatum/Text): **T**   *(Enter the new value in the Edit MText dialogue box.)*
Leader end point (Xdatum/Ydatum/Text): *Pick the end point of the leader line.*

Exercise 5

Make the following drawing, then use the DIMORDINATE command to dimension the part. The distance between the dotted lines is 0.5 unit.

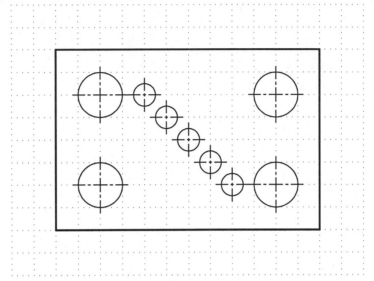

Figure 6-40   Using the DIMORDINATE command to
dimension the part

LEADER

Toolbar:	Dimensioning, Leader
Pull-down:	Draw, Dimensioning, Leader
Screen:	DRAW DIM, Leader:

The **LEADER** command draws a line that extends from the object being dimensioned to the dimension text. The leader line is used to attach annotations to an object or when the user wants to show a dimension without using another dimensioning command. Sometimes leaders for the circles or arcs are so complicated that you need to construct a leader of your own rather than using the leader generated by the **DIAMETER** or **RADIUS** commands. The **Leader** dimensioning command can be invoked from the **Dimensioning** toolbar by selecting the **Leader** icon, from the pull-down menu (Select Draw, Dimensioning, Leader), or from the screen menu (Select DRAW DIM, Leader). You can also invoke this command by entering LEADER at the **Command:** prompt or **LEADER** (or L) at the **Dim:** prompt.

Using the Dim Command to Draw the Leader

Once you select enter the DIM command and specify the first point, the prompt sequence of the **LEADER** command is similar to that of the LINE command as both of these commands prompt you to specify the points to draw line segments. Also, as in the LINE command, you can use **U** (Undo) to undo the last leader segment drawn. The start point of the leader should be specified at the point closest to the object being dimensioned. Once you have drawn the leader, you can enter the dimension text by giving a null response or pressing the Enter key at **To Point:** prompt.

Command: **DIM**
Dim: **Leader** or **L**
Leader start: *Specify the starting point of the leader.*

To point: *Specify the end point of the leader.*
To point: *Specify next point or press the Enter key.*
Dimension text <default>: *Enter dimension text.*

The value between the angle brackets is the default value that is the measurement of the most recently dimensioned object. If you want to retain the default text, press the Enter key at the **Dimension text <measurement>:** prompt. You can enter text of your choice, specify a prefix/suffix, or suppress the text. The text can be suppressed by pressing the space bar, then pressing the Enter key at the **Dimension text <measurement>:** prompt. An arrow is drawn at the start point of the leader segment if the length of the segment is greater than two arrows length. If the length of the line segment is less than or equal to two arrow lengths, only a line is drawn.

Note
Since the leader is not an associative dimension object, AutoCAD does not update the leader text if the dimensioned object is altered by an editing operation.

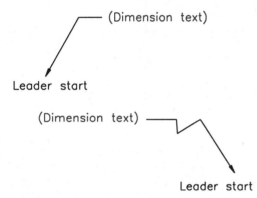

Figure 6-41 Using the Leader option of the DIM command to draw leaders

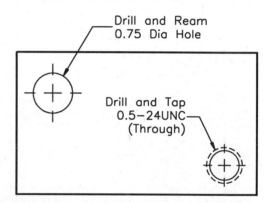

Figure 6-42 Using the LEADER command to draw leaders

Using the LEADER Command to Draw a Leader

A leader can also be drawn by using the LEADER command. A leader drawn by using the LEADER command is an associative dimension, whereas a leader drawn by using the Leader option of the DIM command is not an associative dimension. The following is the command prompt sequence of the LEADER command:

Command: **Leader**
Leader start: *Specify the starting point of the leader.*
To point: *Specify the end point of the leader.*
To point (Format/Annotation/Undo)<Annotation>: *Specify next point or press the Enter key.*
Annotation (or RETURN for options): *Enter annotation text (for example, Drill and Tap).*
Mtext: *Enter next line of annotation text (for example, 0.75 Dia Hole).*
Mtext: *Press Enter key when done entering text.*

Exercise 6

Make the following drawing, then use LEADER commands to dimension the part as shown. The distance between the dotted lines is 0.5 unit.

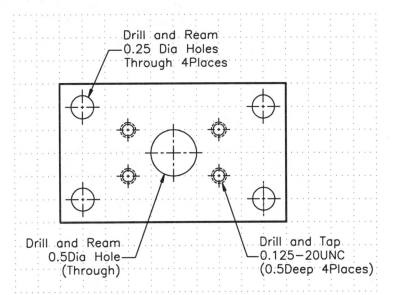

Figure 6-43 Using the LEADER command to dimension the part

CHANGING DIMENSION SETTINGS

You will now learn how to use some of the dimensioning variables to change the appearance of dimensions. A detailed description about the application of other dimension variables and how to create dimensioning styles is described in Chapter 8. You can set the dimension variables by entering the name of the dimension variable at The **Command:** prompt or **Dim:** prompt. You can also use the **Dimension Styles** dialogue box to set the values. This dialogue box (Figure 6-44) can be invoked from the **Dimensioning** toolbar by selecting the **Dimension Styles** icon, from the pull-down menu (Select Data, Dimension Styles), or from the screen menu (Select DRAW DIM, DDim:).

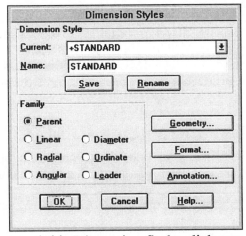

Figure 6-44 Dimension Styles dialogue box

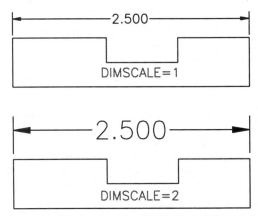

Figure 6-45 Using the DIMSCALE variable

Changing Dimension Scale Factor (DIMSCALE)

The **DIMSCALE** (Dimension scale factor) variable affects all size-related dimension variables like center mark size, text size, arrow size, etc. The default value for this variable is 1.0, in which case the dimensioning variables assume their preset values. If the drawing is to be plotted at half the size, the scale factor is the reciprocal of the drawing size. Hence, the scale factor or the DIMSCALE value will be the reciprocal of 1/2, which is 2. If the DIMSCALE is changed to 2, all of the dimensioning variable values are doubled (Figure 6-45). You can set the value of the DIMSCALE variable by entering DIMSCALE at the **Command:** or **Dim:** prompt.

> Command: **DIM**
> Dim: **DIMSCALE**
> Current value <1.0000> New value: **2**

You can also set the DIMSCALE values by entering the new value in the Overall Scale edit box of the **Geometry** dialogue box (Figure 6-46). You can invoke the Geometry dialogue box from the **Dimension Styles** dialogue box by selecting the **Geometry...** button.

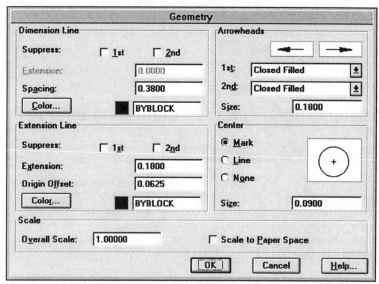

Figure 6-46   Geometry dialogue box

If you are in the middle of the dimensioning process and you change the DIMSCALE value, only those dimensions that are drawn after you change the DIMSCALE variable will be affected. To update the dimensions that were drawn before changing DIMSCALET, use the Update option of DIM command (see Chapter 7 for details). You can also use the DIMOVERRIDE, DDMODIFY, and DIMSTYLE commands to update the dimensions. DIMSCALE does not affect the measured lengths, coordinates, angles, or tolerances.

Positioning Dimension Text Above Dimension Line (DIMTAD)

You may want to place the dimension text above the dimension line. This can be accomplished with the help of the **DIMTAD** variable (Figure 6-47). If DIMTAD is on, the dimension text is placed above the dimension line. If DIMTAD is off, DIMTVP variable controls the text vertical placement. You can set the value of DIMTAD variable by entering DIMTAD at the **Command:** or **Dim:** prompt.

> Command: **DIMTAD**
> New value for DIMTAD <0>: **1**

You can also use the **Format** dialogue box (Figure 6-48) to set the vertical justification. This dialogue box can be invoked from the **Dimension Styles** dialogue box by selecting the Format button. In the Format dialogue box select down arrow in Vertical Justification and then select Above. To set **DIMTIH** and **DIMTOH** to off, select the **Inside Horizontal** and **Outside Horizontal** toggle boxes in the **Format** dialogue box.

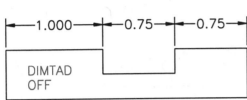

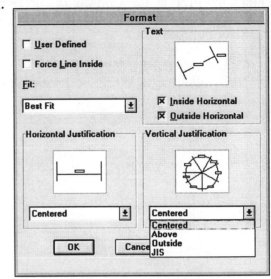

Figure 6-47 Using DIMTAD variable to place dimensions above dimension line

Figure 6-48 Format dialogue box

Aligning Dimension Text between Extension Lines (DIMTIH, DIMTOH)

The **DIMTIH** dimension variable controls the alignment of the dimension text for linear, radius, and diameter dimensioning. If DIMTIH is on (Default setting), it forces the dimension text inside the extension lines to be placed horizontally. If DIMTIH is off, the dimension text is aligned with the dimension line. Similarly, the **DIMTOH** variable controls the dimension text outside the extension lines. If DIMTOH is off, the dimension text outside the extension lines is placed horizontally. To set DIMTIH and DIMTOH off, use the Inside Horizontal and Outside Horizontal toggle boxes in the **Format** dialogue box (Figure 6-48).

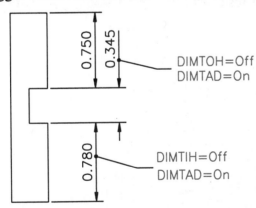

Figure 6-49 Using DIMTAD, DIMTOH, and DIMTIH for vertical dimensioning

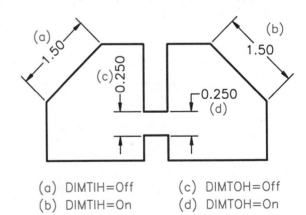

(a) DIMTIH=Off   (c) DIMTOH=Off
(b) DIMTIH=On   (d) DIMTOH=On

Figure 6-50 Using the DIMTIH and DIMTOH dimension variables

Changing the Arrowhead Size (DIMASZ)

When dimensioning in AutoCAD, arrowheads are drawn at the ends of the dimension lines and the leader lines. Sometimes you will need to change the size of the arrows. The **DIMASZ** (dimension arrowhead size) variable can be used to specify the size of these arrows. The default size for the arrowheads is **0.18 unit**. The actual size of the arrowhead that you get when dimensioning is the product of DIMASZ and DIMSCALE (actual arrow size = DIMSCALE x DIMASZ). For example, if the arrow size (DIMASZ) is 0.125 and the dimensioning scale factor (DIMSCALE) is 2, the actual arrow size is 0.25 (0.125 x 2 = 0.25). To assign a value to the DIMASZ variable, enter DIMASZ at the **Command:** or **Dim:** prompt, then enter the desired arrow size. You can also use the **Geometry** dialogue box to set the arrowhead size by entering the arrowhead size in the **Size:** edit box.

Command: **DIMASZ**
New value for DIMASZ <0.1800>: **0.125**

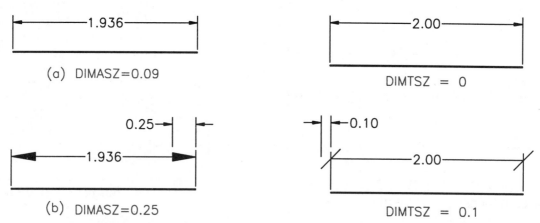

Figure 6-51 Changing the arrowhead size by using the DIMASZ variable

Figure 6-52 Using tick marks by assigning a value to the DIMTSZ variable

Using Tick Marks Instead of Arrowheads

In some drafting applications like architectural drafting, tick marks are drawn at the ends of the dimension line instead of arrowheads. You can specify the size of the ticks with the DIMTSZ (dimension tick size) variable. **If the DIMTSZ value is 0, arrows are drawn. If the DIMTSZ value is not 0, ticks are drawn**. The size of the ticks is computed as DIMTSZ x DIMSCALE. Therefore, if the DIMSCALE factor is 1, the size of the tick is equal to the DIMTSZ value. For example, if you want to use tick marks of 0.20 unit instead of the arrowheads, you can use the DIMTSZ variable as follows:

Command: **DIMTSZ**
New value for DIMASZ <0.0000>: **0.20**

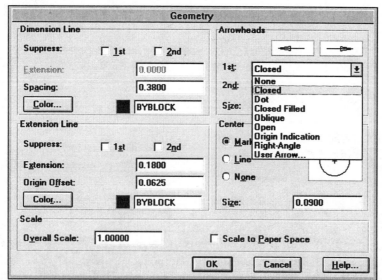

Figure 6-53 Selecting tick marks from the Geometry dialogue box

You can also set the tick marks (dimension line terminators) by using the **Geometry** dialogue box (Figure 6-53). Under Arrowheads, select the down arrow in the **1st:** edit box and then select Oblique (Figure 6-53).

Controlling the Height of the Dimension Text (DIMTXT)

The dimension text height is controlled by the DIMTXT dimension variable. The default text height is 0.1800. The actual height of the text is the product of DIMSCALE and DIMTXT. The prompt sequence for controlling the height of text is as follows:

Command: **DIMTXT**
Current value <0.1800> New value: *Enter new text height or press the Enter key to accept the current text height.*

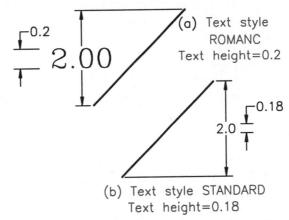

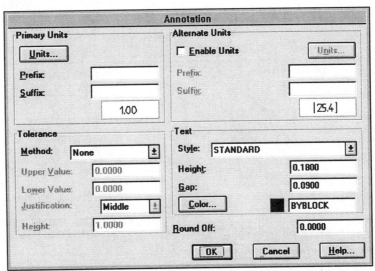

Figure 6-54 Changing dimension style and dimension text height

You can also specify the size of the dimension text by using the **Annotation** dialogue box (Figure 6-55). This dialogue box can be invoked from the **Dimension Styles** dialogue box by selecting the Annotation... button. Under Text enter the dimension text height in the **Annotation** dialogue box in the **Height:** edit box.

Figure 6-55 Specifying text height in the Annotation dialogue box

Changing Dimension Text Style (DIMTXSTY)

While dimensioning, the dimension text is drawn in the current dimension text style. For example, if the current dimension text style is STANDARD and the text height is 0.1800, all dimension text will be drawn in STANDARD style with a height of 0.1800. The dimension text height is controlled by the DIMTXT variable and the default dimension text height in AutoCAD is 0.1800. As mentioned before, the text height can be changed by using DIMTXT variable. The text style can be changed by using **DIMTXSTY** dimension variable. When the text style is changed, the previous dimension text is not affected. The following is the command prompt sequence for changing the text style by using the **DIMTXSTY** command:

Command: **DIMTXSTY**
New text style <Current>: *Enter a new text style name or press the Enter key to accept the current style.*

You must define the text style before changing the text style of the dimensioning text. To create a new style, you can use the STYLE command at The **Command:** prompt. You can also specify various aspects of text like height, width factor, oblique angle, backward, upside down, vertical, etc. (See the **STYLE** command for details.) You can also specify dimension text style by using the **Annotation** dialogue box (Enter DDIM, Select Annotation... button: Under Text select the dimension text style in the Style: list box).

Setting DIMDEC, DIMUPT, DIMFIT Variables

The **DIMDEC** variable sets the number of decimal places for the value of primary dimension. For example, if DIMDEC is set to 3, AutoCAD will display the decimal dimension up to three decimal places (2.037).

The **DIMUPT** variable controls the positioning of dimension text. For example, if DIMUPT is set to 0, the cursor controls the dimension line location. If DIMUPT is set to 1, the cursor position controls the dimension text as well as the dimension line location.

The **DIMFIT** variable controls the placement of arrowheads and dimension text inside or outside the extension lines based on the space available between the extension lines.

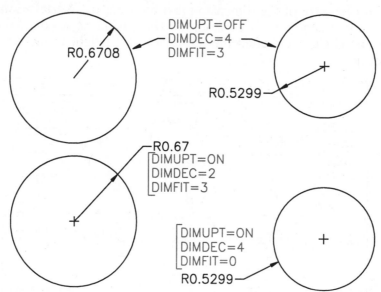

Figure 6-56 Using the DIMDEC, DIMUPT, and DIMFIT dimensioning variables

Note

For a detailed description of these variables, see Chapter 8.

Answer the following questions and then compare your answers with the answers given at the end of this chapter.

1. With the **DIM1** command, more than one dimensioning operation can be performed at a time. (T/F)

2. You can exit from the dimensioning mode by entering E at the **Dim:** prompt. (T/F)

3. By default the dimension line is aligned with the object being dimensioned. (T/F)

4. Only arrow marks can be generated at the two ends of the dimension line. (T/F)

5. You can specify dimension text of your own or accept the measured value computed by AutoCAD. (T/F)

6. Appending suffixes to dimension text is not possible. (T/F)

7. Appending prefixes to dimension text is not possible. (T/F)

8. The size of the dimension arrows can be regulated. (T/F)

9. With alternate units dimensioning, the dimension text generated is for a single system of measurement. (T/F)

10. When using tolerances in dimensioning, if the tolerance values are equal, the tolerances are drawn one over the other. (T/F)

11. Limits are appended to the dimension text. (T/F)

12. Dimension variables control all aspects of a dimension. (T/F)

13. The dimension variables can be set using the **SETVAR** command, then entering the name of the dimension variable. (T/F)

14. A dimension variable can be set by entering the variable name at the **Command:** prompt. (T/F)

15. The _____ command is used to invoke Dimension Style dialogue box.

REVIEW QUESTIONS

Answer the following questions.

1. Fill in the command and entries required to dimension an inclined line of length 3.95 units. You must change the dimension text from 3.9500 to 4.0. The dimension line must be aligned with the line being dimensioned.

    Command: _____
    Dim: _____
    First extension line origin or RETURN to select: _____
    Second extension line origin: _____
    Dimension line location (Text/Angle): _____

Dimension text <3.9500>: _____

2.   Fill in the relevant information to dimension an arc. The dimension text should be R0.750. The radius of the arc is 0.75 units. After completing the dimensioning return to the Command mode.

Command: _____
Select arc or circle: _____
Dimension line location (Text/Angle): _____

3.   Fill in the relevant information to dimension the diameter of a circle. The radius of the circle is 2.0 units. The dimension text should have a ϕ symbol.

Command: _____
Select arc or circle: _____
Dimension line location (Text/Angle): _____

4.   Fill in the blanks with the command and entries required to dimension the angle between three points.

Command: _____
Dim: _____
Select arc, circle, line, or RETURN: _____
Angle vertex: _____
First angle end point: _____
Second angle end point: _____
Dimension arc line location (Text/Angle): _____
Dimension text <measured angle>: _____
Enter text location (or RETURN): _____

5.   Give the command and entries required to dimension the angle of an arc.

Command: _____
Dim: _____
Select arc, circle, line, or RETURN: _____
Dimension arc line location (Text/Angle): _____
Dimension text <current value>: _____
Enter text location (or RETURN): _____

6.   Fill in the command and other entries required to draw the center mark for the existing circles/arcs. The size of the center mark should be 0.25 unit.

Command: _____
Current value <0.0900> New value: _____
Command: _____
Select arc or circle: _____

7.   Give the command and entries needed to change the dimensioning style from the current style to Gothicg.

Command: _____
Dim: _____
New text style <Current>: _____

8.   Give the command and entries needed to change the dimension text height from default text height to 0.1500.

Command: _____

Current value <0.1800> New value: _____

9.   The dimension variable DIMTAD is used to _____.

10.   The dimension variable DIMASZ is used to control the _____.

11.   The dimension variable DIMTSZ is used to control the _____.

12.   The dimension variable DIMTIH is used to determine whether the _____.

13.   The dimension variable DIMTXT controls the _____.

14.   The dimension variable DIMTCEN controls the _____.

15.   Why is dimensioning needed? _____
_____

16.   Specify three ways to return to the **Command:** prompt from the **Dim:** prompt (dimensioning mode). _____
_____

17.   What are the differences between the DIM and DIM1 commands? _____
_____

18.   Explain briefly the five fundamental dimensioning types provided by AutoCAD. List the different dimensioning options available in each of them. _____
_____

19.   Explain briefly Dimension line, Dimension text, and Dimension arrows. _____
_____

20.   Describe Extension lines and Leader. _____
_____

21.   Explain the term Associative dimensioning. _____
_____

22.   What two commands in the Dimension mode support dimensioning for angled surfaces? Explain the difference between them. _____
_____

23.   Which dimensioning type generates the coordinate value of X or Y of a location in the drawing? _____
_____

24.   How can you change the current text style to some other text style? _____
_____

25.   In associative dimensioning, the dimensioning objects are drawn as individual items. (T/F)

26.   Changes in the size of an object, dimensioned with Associative dimensioning, change the dimensions also. (T/F)

27.   In Aligned dimensioning, the dimension text by default is aligned with the object being dimensioned. (T/F)

28.   Only inner angles (acute angles) can be dimensioned with Angular dimensioning. (T/F)

29. In addition to the most recently drawn dimension (the default base dimension), you can use any other linear dimension as the base dimension. (T/F)

30. In Continued dimensions, the base for successive Continued dimensions is the base dimension's first extension line. (T/F)

31. Horizontal dimension measures displacement along the Y axis. (T/F)

32. Vertical dimension measures displacement along the X axis. (T/F)

33. When you change the text style, the previous dimension text is also affected. (T/F)

34. In Rotated dimensioning, the dimension line is always aligned with the object being dimensioned. (T/F)

35. The Rotated dimension can be specified to get the effect of Horizontal or Vertical dimension. (T/F)

36. The center point of arc/circle is taken as the angle vertex in the Angular dimensioning of the arc/circle. (T/F)

37. The ϕ symbol can be generated by entering %%C at the dimension text prompt. (T/F)

38. The ORDINATE command is used to dimension the X coordinate of an object only. (T/F)

39. Describe how you can change arrows to ticks by using dialogue boxes. _____

40. How can you calculate the DIMSCALE for a drawing? Explain. _____

EXERCISES

Exercise 7

Draw the object shown in Figure 6-57, then dimension it. Save the figure drawn in the DIMEXR7 drawing file.

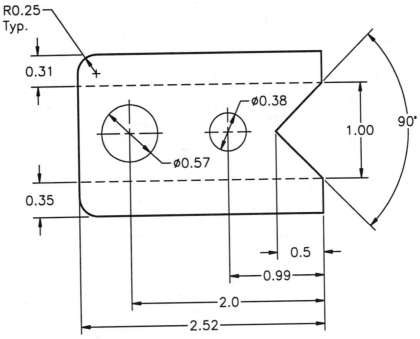

Figure 6-57 Drawing for Exercise 7

Exercise 8

Draw and dimension the object shown in Figure 6-58. The UCS origin is the lower left corner of the object. Save the drawing as DIMEXR8.

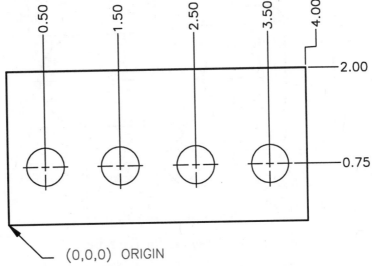

Figure 6-58 Drawing for Exercise 8

Exercise 9

Draw the object shown in Figure 6-59, then dimension it. Save the drawing as DIMEXR9.

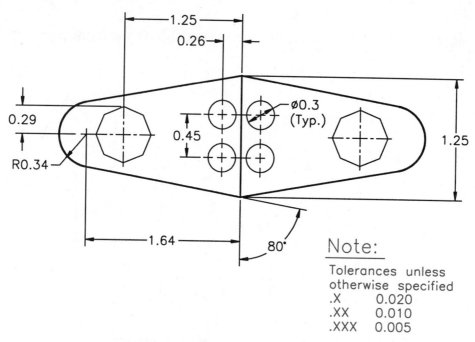

Figure 6-59 Drawing for Exercise 9

Exercise 10

Draw the object shown in Figure 6-60, then dimension it. Save the drawing as DIMEXR10.

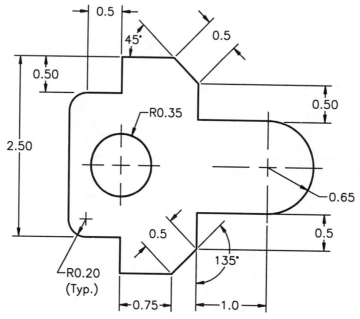

Figure 6-60 Drawing for Exercise 10

Exercise 11

Draw and dimension the object shown in Figure 6-61 and save it as DIMEXR11. You can use the ARRAY command to facilitate drawing the figure.

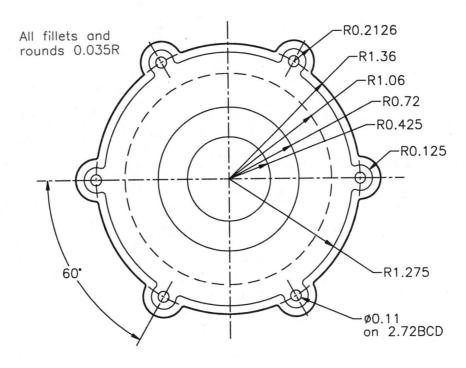

Figure 6-61 Drawing for Exercise 11

Exercise 12

Draw and dimension Figure 6-62 and save it as DIMEXR12.

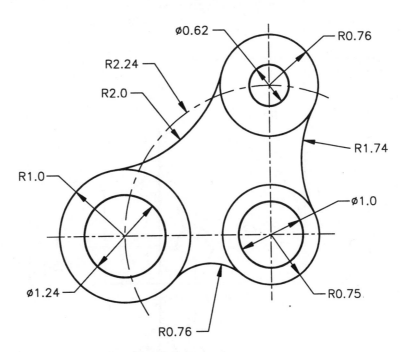

Figure 6-62 Drawing for Exercise 12

Exercise 13

Draw and dimension Figure 6-63, then save it as DIMEXR13.

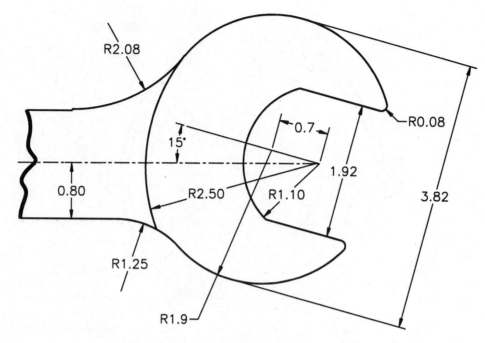

Figure 6-63 Drawing for Exercise 13

Exercise 14

Draw Figure 6-64 and dimension it. Save the drawing as DIMEXR14.

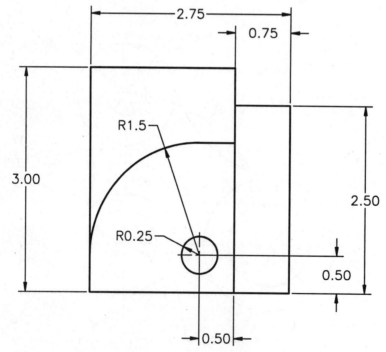

Figure 6-64 Drawing for Exercise 14

Exercise 15

Draw Figure 6-65 and dimension it. After you have drawn one of the doughnuts, use the **ARRAY** command to obtain other doughnuts. Save the drawing as DIMEXR15.

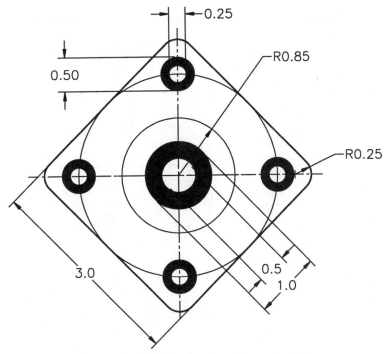

Figure 6-65 Drawing for Exercise 15

Exercise 16

Draw Figure 6-66 and dimension it. The FILLET command should be used where needed. Save the figure as DIMEXR16.

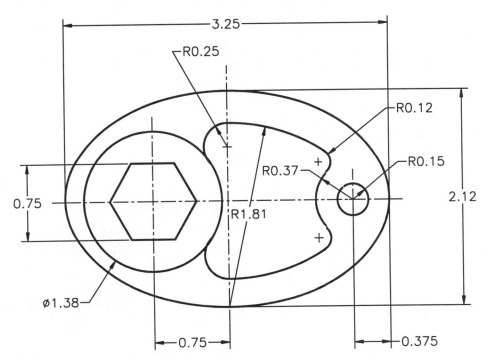

Figure 6-66 Drawing for Exercise 16

Exercise 17

Draw Figure 6-67 and dimension it exactly as shown in the figure. Set the DIMDLI variable to 0.40. Save the figure as DIMEXR17.

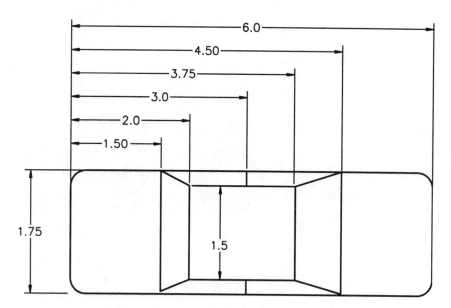

Figure 6-67 Drawing for Exercise 17

Exercise 18

Draw and dimension Figure 6-68 and save it as DIMEXR18.

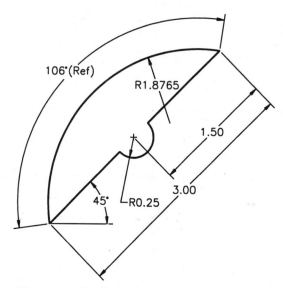

Figure 6-68 Drawing for Exercise 18

Chapter 7

Editing Dimensions

Learning objectives

After completing this chapter, you will be able to:
◆ Understand Associative dimensioning.
◆ Edit dimensions.
◆ Stretch, extend, and trim dimensions.
◆ Use the DIMEDIT and DIMTEDIT command options to edit dimensions.
◆ Update dimensions using the DIM, Update and DIMSTYLE, Apply commands.
◆ Use GRIPS to edit dimensions.
◆ Use the DDMODIFY command to edit dimensions.
◆ Dimension in Model space and Paper space.

ASSOCIATIVE DIMENSIONS

Before learning to edit dimensions, it is important to understand how AutoCAD handles the dimensioning objects. One of the features that determines the effect of editing commands is the associativity of dimensions. Associative dimensioning is defined as a method of dimensioning in which the dimension is influenced by the changes in the size of the object. For example, editing operations like **stretching**, **extending**, or **trimming** an object result in modifications of the dimensions related to that object. In Associative dimensioning the items constituting a dimension (such as dimension line, arrows, leaders, extension lines, and the dimension text) are drawn as a **single object**. For example, you can scale a dimension object, rotate the dimension text, or erase the entire dimension by picking any point on the dimension. Any selection method can be used to select the Associative dimension objects you want to edit. Any other objects contained in the selection set are neglected by the dimensioning command. This way you can use the dimensioning commands to make a general change to all the dimension objects in the Model space or Paper space. You can use the window selection to cover the entire drawing. If Associative dimensioning is disabled, the dimension lines, arrows, leaders, extension lines, and the dimension text are drawn as **independent** (unrelated) objects. In this case you can edit a dimension by editing the individual object that constitutes a dimension. An Associative dimension can be broken into individual items (just as they are when the associative dimensioning is disabled) by using the **EXPLODE** command. The DIMASO dimensioning variable governs associative dimensioning; its default setting is on. When DIMASO is set to on, editing commands like trimming or stretching alter the dimensions associated with that object. The prompt sequence for this variable is:

Command: **DIMASO**
New value for DIMASO < on >:

Another advantage of associative dimensioning is that you can edit dimension objects as single objects with various commands. The dimensioning commands that are affected by Associative dimensioning are the **Horizontal**, **Vertical**, **Aligned**, **Rotated**, **Radius**, **Diameter**, and **Angular** commands. Only the **Center** and **Leader** commands are not affected by associative dimensioning. The associative dimension is always generated with the same dimension variable settings as defined in the creation of the dimension style. The present linetype and the text style is used for the drawing of text.

Updating Associative Dimensions

As mentioned above, an associative dimension is one in which all the dimension objects are generated as a single object. As such all dimensioning objects forming a single associative dimension are revised automatically as you edit associated objects in the drawing. For this automatic revision of the associative dimension objects, the **definition points of the dimension object must be contained in the selection set** formed for the editing. Therefore, you should be familiar with the definition points of different types of dimensions as it will make it easier to edit the dimension.

DEFINITION POINTS

Definition points are defined as the points drawn at the positions used to generate an associative dimension object. The definition points are used by the associative dimensions to control their updating and re-scaling. AutoCAD draws these points on a special layer called **DEFPOINTS**. These points are not plotted on the plotter, but they are visible. This is true even if the DEFPOINTS layer is off. AutoCAD does not plot any object on the DEFPOINTS layer. To plot the objects on the DEFPOINTS layer, the layer needs to be renamed. If you rename the DEFPOINTS layer, a new DEFPOINTS layer is created by AutoCAD for any further definition points in your drawing. If you explode an associative dimension (which is as good as turning DIMASO off), the definition points are converted to point objects on the DEFPOINTS layer. In Figure 7-1, the small circles indicate the definition points for different objects.

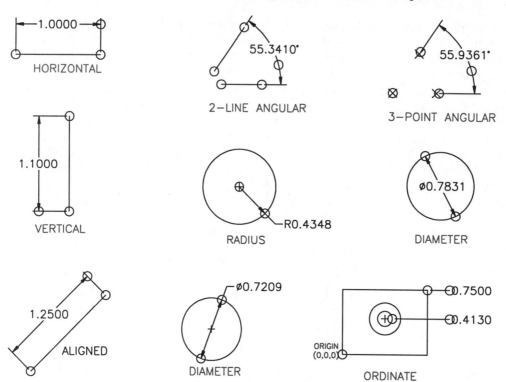

Figure 7-1 Definition points of linear, angular, and ordinate dimensions

The definition points for Linear associative dimensions are the points used to specify the extension lines and the point of intersection of the first extension line and the dimension line. The definition points for the Angular dimension are the end points of the lines used to specify the dimension and the point used to specify the dimension line arc. For example, for three-point angular dimension the definition points are the extension line end points, the angle vertex, and the point used to specify the dimension line arc.

The definition points for the Radius dimension are the center point of the circle or arc and the point where the arrow touches the object. The definition points for the Diameter dimension are the points where the arrows touch the circle. The definition points for the Ordinate dimension are the UCS origin, the feature location, and the leader end point.

Note

In addition to the definition points mentioned above, the middle point of the dimension text serves as a definition point for all types of dimensions.

EDITING DIMENSIONS

For editing dimensions, AutoCAD has provided some special editing commands that work with dimensions. These editing commands can be used to define new dimension text, return to home text, create oblique dimensions, and rotate and update the dimension text. You can also use the TRIM, STRETCH, and EXTEND commands to edit the dimensions.

Stretching Dimensions

To stretch a dimension object, appropriate definition points must be included in the selection crossing box of the **STRETCH** command. As the middle point of the dimension text is a definition point for all types of dimensions, you can use the **STRETCH** command to move the dimension text to any location you want. If you stretch the dimension text but do not want the dimension line broken, the gap in the dimension line gets filled automatically. The dimension type remains the same after stretching. When editing, the definition points of the dimension being edited must be included in the selection crossing box. The aligned dimension adjusts itself so that it is aligned with the object being dimensioned; the dimension is automatically calculated as well. The Vertical dimension maintains itself as a Vertical dimension and measures the vertical distance between the base and the top of the triangle even though the line it dimensions may no longer be a vertical line. The following example illustrates the use of the STRETCH command in stretching a dimension.

Example 1

In the following example you will stretch the objects and the dimension to a new location. The drawing shown in Figure 7-2(a) should already be drawn on the screen.

1. At AutoCAD's Command: prompt, enter the STRETCH command. At the next prompt, use the crossing option to select the objets and dimensions that you want to stretch.

   Command: **STRETCH**
   Select objects to stretch by window polygon...
   Select objects: **C**
   First corner: *Select the first corner of the crossing box.*
   Other corner: *Select the second corner of the crossing box.*
   Select objects: ⏎

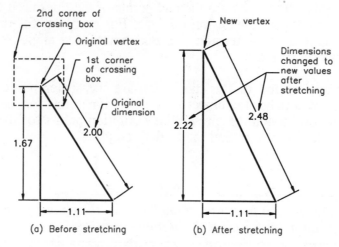

Figure 7-2 Using the STRETCH command to stretch the dimension

2. Next, AutoCAD will prompt you to enter the base point and the second point of displacement. When you enter this information, the objects and the dimensions will be stretched as shown in Figure 7-2(b).

Base point of displacement: *Specify the base point.*
Second point of displacement: *Specify the point where you want to stretch the objects.*

Exercise 1

In the following drawing the two dimensions in Figure 7-3(a) are too close. You are required to fix the drawing by stretching the dimension as shown in Figure 7-3(b).

1. Stretch the outer dimension to the right so that there is some distance between the two dimensions.
2. Stretch the dimension text of the outer dimension so that the dimension text is staggered (lower than the first dimension).

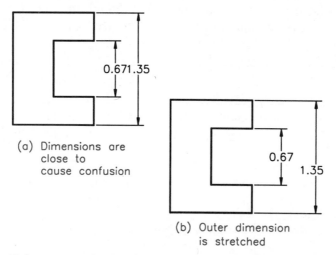

Figure 7-3 Drawing for Exercise 1, stretching dimensions

Trimming and Extending Dimensions

Trimming and extending operations can be carried out with all types of linear (Horizontal, Vertical, Aligned, Rotated) dimensions and the Ordinate dimension. AutoCAD trims or extends a

Linear dimension between the extension line definition points and the object used as a boundary or trimming edge. To extend or trim an Ordinate dimension, AutoCAD moves the feature location (location of the dimensioned coordinate) to the boundary edge. To retain the original ordinate value, the boundary edge to where the feature location point is moved is orthogonal to the measured ordinate. In both cases, the imaginary line drawn between the two extension line definition points is trimmed or extended by AutoCAD and the dimension is adjusted automatically.

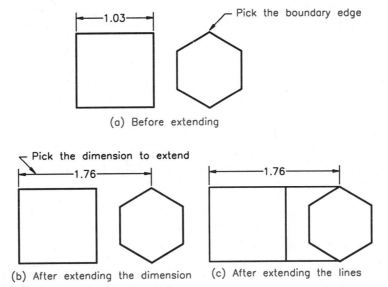

Figure 7-4 Using the EXTEND command to extend dimensions

Exercise 2

In the following drawing use the TRIM command to trim the dimension at the top as shown in Figure 7-5(b).
1. Make the drawing and dimension it as shown in Figure 7-5(a). Assume the dimensions where necessary.
2. Stretch the dimension as shown in Figure 7-5(b). You can also trim the dimension by setting the EDGEMODE to 1, then using the TRIM command. In this case you do not need to draw a line to trim.

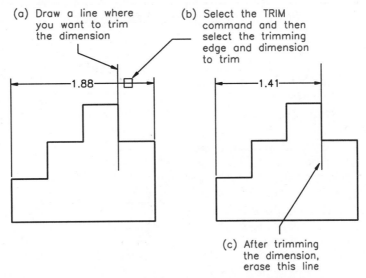

Figure 7-5 Drawing for Exercise 2

EDITING DIMENSIONS (DIMEDIT Command)

The dimension text can be edited by using the **DIMEDIT** command. This command has four options: Home, New, Rotate, and Oblique. The DIMEDIT command can be invoked from the screen menu (Select MOD DIM/ DimEdit). You can also invoke this command by entering **DIMEDIT** at the **Command:** prompt.

Command: **DIMEDIT**
Dimension Edit (Home/New/Rotate/Oblique) <Home>: *Enter an option.*

New

You can use the New option to replace the existing dimension text with a new text string. This command can also be invoked by entering NEWTEXT at the **Dim:** prompt.

Command: **DIMEDIT**
Dimension Edit (Home/New/Rotate/Oblique) <Home>: **N**
Dimension text <default>: *Enter new text in the Edit MText dialogue box.*
Select objects: *Select the dimensions and press Enter key.*

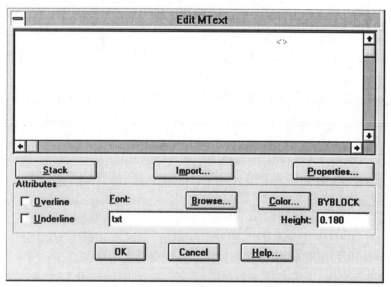

Figure 7-6 Edit MText dialogue box

Command: **DIM**
Dim: **NEWTEXT**
Dimension text <default>: *Enter new text.*
Select objects: *Select the dimensions and press the Enter key.*

In case a null response is given at the **Dimension text:** prompt, the actual dimension text is taken as the text. The < > prefix or suffix facility can also be used when you enter the new text string. In this case the prefix/suffix is appended before or after the dimension measurement that is placed instead of the < > characters.

If information about the dimension style is available on the selected dimension, AutoCAD uses it to redraw the dimension, or the prevailing dimension variable settings are used for the redrawing process.

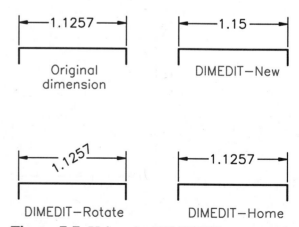

Figure 7-7 Using the DIMEDIT command to edit dimensions

Rotate

Using the Rotate option, you can position the dimension text at the angle you specify. The angle can be specified by entering its value at the **Text angle:** prompt, or by specifying two points at the required angle. You will notice that the text rotates around its middle point. When the dimension text alignment is set to Orient Text Horizontally, the dimension text is aligned with the dimension line. If the information about the dimension style is available on the selected dimension, AutoCAD uses it to redraw the dimension, or the prevailing dimension variable settings are used for the redrawing process. With this command you can alter the orientation (angle) of the dimension text of any number of associative dimensions. You can also invoke this option by entering TROTATE at the **Dim:** prompt.

> Command: **DIMEDIT**
> Dimension Edit (Home/New/Rotate/Oblique) <Home>: **R**
> Enter text angle: *Enter text angle.*
> Select objects: *Select the dimensions and press the Enter key.*
>
> Dim: **TROTATE**
> Enter text angle: *Enter text angle.*
> Select Objects: *Select the dimensions and press the Enter key.*

The angle of rotation can be entered at the **Enter new text angle:** prompt or it can be specified by selecting two points. An angle value of zero places the text in its default orientation. If the dimension text alignment is set to Orient Text Horizontally, the dimension text is aligned with the dimension line.

Home

The **Hometext** command restores the text of an associative dimension to its original (home/default) location if the position of the text has been changed using the STRETCH or DIMEDIT command. You can also invoke this command by using HOMETEXT at the **Dim:** prompt.

> Command: **DIMEDIT**
> Dimension Edit (Home/New/Rotate/Oblique) <Home>: **H**
> Select objects: *Select the dimension and press the Enter key.*
>
> Dim: **HOMETEXT**
> Select objects: *Select the dimension objects.*

Oblique

In the linear dimensions, extension lines are drawn perpendicular to the dimension line. The **OBLIQUE** command bends the linear associative dimensions. It draws extension lines at an oblique angle. This command is particularly important when creating isometric dimensions and can be used to resolve conflicting situations due to the overlapping of extension lines with other objects. Making an existing dimension oblique by specifying an oblique angle to it does not affect the generation of new linear dimensions. The oblique angle is maintained even after performing several editing operations. (See Chapter 19 for details about how to use this command.)

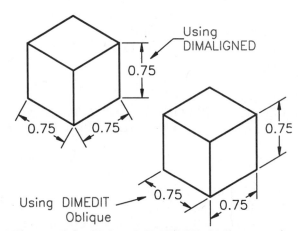

Figure 7-8 Using DIMEDIT-Oblique option to edit dimensions

Command: **DIMEDIT**
Dimension Edit (Home/New/Rotate/Oblique) <Home>: **O**
Select objects: *Select the dimensions and press Enter key.*
Enter Obliquing angle (RETURN for none): *Enter obliquing angle.*

Dim: **OBLIQUE**
Select objects: *Select the dimensions and press Enter key.*
Enter Obliquing angle (RETURN for none): *Enter obliquing angle.*

EDITING DIMENSION TEXT (DIMTEDIT Command)

Toolbar:	Dimensioning, Align Dimension Text (Home)
Pull-down:	Draw, Dimensioning, Align Text
Screen:	MOD DIM, DimTedt:

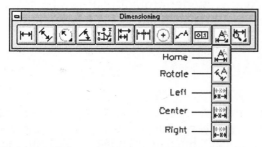

Figure 7-9 Selecting the Editing commands from the Align Dimension Text (Home) toolbar

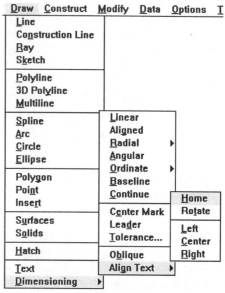

Figure 7-10 Selecting the editing commands from the pull-down menu

The dimension text can also be edited by using the DIMTEDIT command. This command is used to edit the placement and orientation of a single existing Associative dimension. The practical application of this command can be, for example, in cases where dimension text of two or more dimensions is too close, resulting in confusion. In such cases the **DIMTEDIT** command is invoked to move the dimension text to some other location so that there is no confusion. This command has four options: Left, Right, Home, and Angle. The **DIMTEDIT** command can be invoked from the **Dimensioning** toolbar (Figure 7-9) by selecting the desired icon in the **Align Dimension Text (Home)** flyout, from the pull-down menu (Select Draw, Dimensioning, Align Text) (Figure 7-10), or from the screen menu (Select MOD DIM, DimTedt:). You can also invoke this command by entering DIMTEDIT at the **Command:** prompt.

Command: **DIMTEDIT**
Select dimension: *Select a dimension.*
Enter text location (Left/Right/Home/Angle): *Enter an option or select a point.*

The dimension text can also be edited by entering TEDIT at the **Dim:** prompt:

Command: **DIM**
Dim: **TEDIT**
Select dimension: *Select a dimension.*
Enter text location (Left/Right/Home/Angle): *Enter an option.*

If the **DIMSHO** variable is on, you will notice that as you move the cursor, the dimension text of the selected associative dimension is dragged with the cursor. In this manner you can see where to place the dimension text while you are dynamically dragging the text. Another advantage of having DIMSHO on is that the dimension updates dynamically as you drag it. If DIMSHO is off, the dimension text and the extension lines are not dragged with the cursor, hence, it is difficult to see the position of the text as you move the cursor. The splits in the dimension line are calculated keeping in mind the new location of the dimension text. Another method of moving text (automatically) is by using any of the Left, Right, Home, or Angle options provided in the **Enter text location (Left/Right/Home/Angle):** prompt. The effect of these options is as follows:

Left

With this option you can left-justify the dimension text along the dimension line. The vertical placement setting determines the position of the dimension text. The horizontally aligned text is moved to the left and the vertically aligned text is moved down. This option can be used only with the Linear, Diameter, and Radius dimensions.

Right

With this option you can right-justify the dimension text along the dimension line. As in the case of the Left option, the vertical placement setting determines the position of the dimension text. The horizontally aligned text is moved to the right and the vertically aligned text is moved up. This option can be used only with the Linear, Diameter, and Radius dimensions.

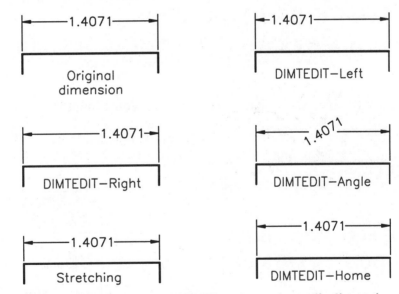

Figure 7-11 Using the DIMTEDIT command to edit dimension text

Home

This option works similarly to the **HOMETEXT** command. With the use of the **Home** option, the dimension text of an associative dimension is restored (moved) to its original (home/default) location if the position of the text has been changed.

Angle

With the Angle option you can position the dimension text at the angle you specify. This option works similarly to the **TROTATE** command. The angle can be specified by entering its value at the **Text angle:** prompt, or by specifying two points at the required angle. You will notice that the text rotates around its middle point. If the dimension text alignment is set to Orient Text Horizontally, the dimension text is aligned with the dimension line. If information about the dimension style is available on the selected dimension, AutoCAD uses it to redraw the dimension, or the prevailing dimension variable settings are used for the redrawing process.

UPDATING DIMENSIONS

The **Update** option of the DIM command regenerates (updates) prevailing associative dimension objects (like arrows, text height, etc.) using current settings of the dimension variables, dimension style, text style, and units settings.

Command: **DIM**
Dim: **UPDATE**
Select Objects: *Select the dimension objects.*

The dimensions can also be updated by using the **Apply** option of the **DIMSTYLE** command. (For details, see Chapter 8.)

Command: **DIMSTYLE**
Dimension Style Edit (Save/Restore/STatus/Variables/Apply/?) < Restore >: **A**
Select Objects: *Select the dimension objects.*

EDITING DIMENSIONS WITH GRIPS

You can also edit the dimensions by using GRIP editing modes. Grip editing is the easiest way to edit dimension. You can perform the following operations with GRIPS. (See Chapter 10 for details.)

1. Position the text anywhere along the dimension line. You cannot move the text and position it above or below the dimension line.
2. Stretch a dimension to change the spacing between the dimension line and the object line.
3. Stretch the dimension along the length. When you stretch a dimension, the dimension text automatically changes.
4. Move, rotate, copy, or mirror the dimensions.

EDITING DIMENSIONS USING THE DDMODIFY COMMAND

Toolbar:	Object Properties, Properties
Pull-down:	Edit, Properties...
Screen:	MODIFY, Modify:

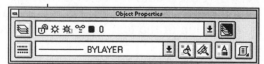

Figure 7-12 Selecting Properties from the Object Properties toolbar

Edit	View	Draw	Constru
<u>U</u>ndo		Ctrl+Z	
<u>R</u>edo			
Cu<u>t</u>		Ctrl+X	
<u>C</u>opy		Ctrl+C	
Copy <u>V</u>iew			
<u>P</u>aste		Ctrl+V	
Paste <u>S</u>pecial...			
Pr<u>o</u>perties...			
<u>O</u>bject Snap		▶	
Point <u>F</u>ilters		▶	
S<u>n</u>ap		Ctrl+B	
<u>G</u>rid		Ctrl+G	
Ort<u>h</u>o		Ctrl+L	
S<u>e</u>lect Objects		▶	
Gro<u>u</u>p Objects...			
<u>I</u>nquiry		▶	
<u>L</u>inks...			
<u>I</u>nsert Object...			

Figure 7-13 Selecting Properties option from the pull-down menu

You can also modify a dimension or leader created with the LEADER command by using the DDMODIFY command. You can select the DDMODIFY command from the **Object Properties** toolbar by selecting the **Properties** icon (Figure 7-12), from the pull-down menu (Select Edit, Properties...) (Figure 7-13), from the screen menu (Select MODIFY, Modify:), or enter **DDMODIFY** at the **Command:** prompt. When you select this command, AutoCAD will prompt you to select the object that you want to modify. If you select a dimension, the **Modify Dimension** dialogue box is displayed on the screen (Figure 7-14). Similarly, if you select a leader the **Modify Leader** dialogue box is displayed.

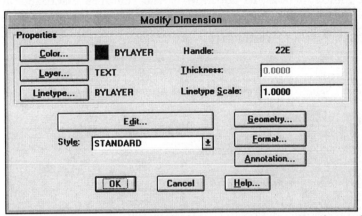

Figure 7-14 Using the DIMTEDIT command to edit dimension text (Modify Dimension dialogue box)

Modify Dimension Dialogue Box

You can use the **Modify Dimension** dialogue box to change the properties of a dimension, change the dimension text style, or change geometry, format, and annotation-related features of the selected dimension.

Changing Color, Layer, and Linetype
When you select the Color button, the **Select Color** dialogue box is displayed on the screen. You can use this dialogue box to specify a color for the selected dimension. Similarly the Layer and Linetype buttons invoke the Select Layer and Select Linetype dialogue boxes that can be used to change the layer or linetype of the selected dimension.

Changing Handle and Linetype Scale
The number that is displayed next to **Handle:** is the handle of the selected object and cannot be changed. The linetype scale can be changed by entering the value in the corresponding edit box.

Editing the Dimension Text and Dimension Style
If you select the **Edit...** button, AutoCAD switches to the **Edit Mtext** dialogue box where you can edit or enter a text string. The text string can be a single line or multiple lines. After you exit the dialogue box, the dimension text is replaced with the new text. The dimension text is treated as paragraph text (MTEXT).

You can change the dimension style of the selected dimension by selecting a predefined dimension style from the style pop-up list. The defined dimension styles can be displayed by picking the arrow button in the **Style:** list box.

Editing Geometry, Format, and Annotation
The Geometry, Format, and Annotation buttons can be used to edit the features and values specified in the corresponding dialogue boxes. For example, if you select the Geometry button, AutoCAD will display the **Geometry** dialogue box that you can use to edit dimension

lines, extension lines, arrowheads, and center marks. The next example illustrates the use of DDMODIFY command to edit dimensions.

Modify Leader Dialogue Box

The **Modify Leader** dialogue box is invoked when you select a leader that was created by using the LEADER command. If you select the text that is attached to the leader, then the **Modify Mtext** dialogue box is displayed. The **Modify Leader** dialogue box (Figure 7-15) is similar to **Modify Dimension** dialogue box. In addition to the features discussed above, you can use the **Modify Leader** dialogue box to change the leader type (spline or straight) or disable the arrows at the end of the leader. The following example illustrates the application of this dialogue box:

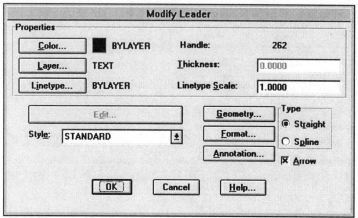

Figure 7-15 Using DIMTEDIT command to edit dimension text
(Modify Leader dialogue box)

Example 2

In this example, use the DDMODIFY command to modify the dimensions in Figure 7-16 so that it matches Figure 7-17.

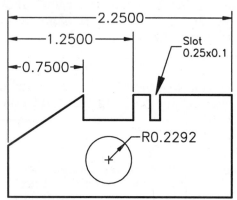

Figure 7-16 Drawing for Example 2

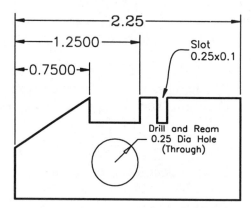

Figure 7-17 Drawing after editing the dimensions

1. Enter the **DDMODIFY** command at **Command:** prompt or select it from the pull-down or screen menu. Select the dimension (2.2500) that you want to modify. When you select the dimension, AutoCAD displays the Modify Dimension dialogue box.

2. To change the text style and the number of decimal places, select the Annotations button to invoke the **Annotation** dialogue box. Use this dialogue box to change the units precision to two places of decimal and select ROMANC text style. It is assumed that ROMANC is a

predefined text style. Select the OK button to exit the Annotation and Modify Dimension dialogue boxes.

3. To edit the leader, enter the **DDMODIFY** command and select the leader. AutoCAD will display the **Modify Leader** dialogue box. Select the Geometry button and change the arrowhead size to 0.09 in the **Geometry** dialogue box. Select the OK button to exit to the **Modify Leader** dialogue box. To change the leader to a spline, select the **Spline** radio button and then select the OK button to exit the dialogue box.

4. To edit the radius text, enter the **DDMODIFY** command again and select the radius text (R0.2292). From the **Modify Dimension** dialogue box select the EDIT... button. AutoCAD will automatically display the **Edit MText** dialogue box. Enter the new text as shown in the drawing and then pick the OK button in the Edit MText dialogue box. Select the OK button to exit the Modify Dimension dialogue box.

MODEL SPACE AND PAPER SPACE DIMENSIONING

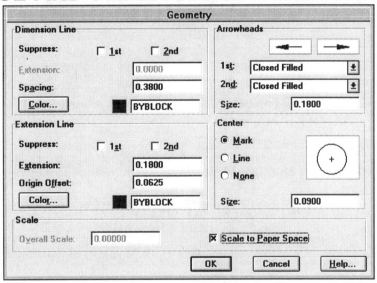

Figure 7-18   Selecting Paper space scaling in the Geometry dialogue box

Dimensioning objects can be drawn in Model space or Paper space. If the drawings are in Model space, Associative dimensions should also be created in Model space. If the drawing is in Model space and the Associative dimension in paper space, the dimensions will not change when you perform such editing operations as stretching, trimming, or extending, or such display operations as zoom or pan in the Model space viewport. The definition points of a dimension are located in the space where the drawing is drawn. You can check the Paper Space Scaling check box in any one of the sub-dialogue boxes accessible through the Dimension Styles and Variables dialogue box so that AutoCAD calculates a scale factor that is compatible between the Model space and the Paper space viewports. The drawing shown in Figure 7-19 uses Paper space scaling. The main drawing and detail drawings are located in different Paper space viewports. The zoom scale factor for these viewports is different, 0.75XP, 1.0XP, and 1.5XP, respectively. When you use Paper scaling or set DIMSCALE to 0, AutoCAD automatically calculates the scale factor for dimensioning so that the dimensions are uniform in all Model space viewports. When the dimensions describing something in Model space are generated in Paper space, the Viewport option in the DIMLFAC variable should be set for the Paper space as follows:

Command: **DIM**
Dim: **DIMLFAC**
Current value <current> New value (Viewport): **V**
Select viewport to set scale: *Pick the desired viewport.*

The DIMLFAC variable is automatically adjusted to the zoom scale factor of the Model space viewport. This method does not work with Ordinate dimensions.

Note

The option to select the viewport option can be accessed only from Paper space (TILEMODE=0).

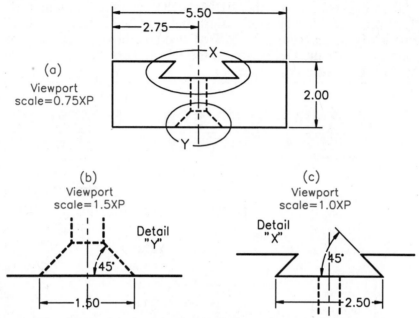

Figure 7-19 Dimensioning in Paper Model space viewports using Paper space scaling or setting DIMSCALE to 0

SELF EVALUATION TEST

Answer the following questions and then compare your answers with the correct answers given at the end of this chapter.

1.   What is Associative dimensioning? _____

2.   Explain the use and working of the STRETCH command. _____
     _____

3.   Explain the use and working of the TRIM command. _____
     _____

4.   In Associative dimensioning the items constituting a dimension (such as dimension lines, arrows, leaders, extension lines, and the dimension text) are drawn as a **single object**. (T/F)

5.   If Associative dimensioning is disabled, the dimension lines, arrows, leaders, extension lines, and the dimension text are drawn as **independent** objects. (T/F)

6.   The DIMASO dimensioning variable governs Associative dimensioning. (T/F)

7.   In Associative dimensioning you cannot edit the dimension objects as a single object with various commands. (T/F)

8.   The **Horizontal**, **Vertical**, **Aligned**, and **Rotated** dimensions cannot be Associative dimensions. (T/F)

9.   Only the **CENTER** and **LEADER** commands are affected by Associative dimensioning (T/F)

10. The _____ command can be used to break an Associative dimension into individual items. (T/F)

REVIEW QUESTIONS

Answer the following questions.

1.   To automatically revise Associative dimension objects, the **definition points** of the dimension object must be contained in the selection set formed for the editing. (T/F)

2.   Definition points are defined as the points drawn at the positions used to generate an Associative dimension object. (T/F)

3.   AutoCAD draws the definition points on a special layer called _____.

4.   In AutoCAD no object is plotted on the _____ layer, so to plot the definition points the _____ layer needs to be renamed.

5.   To stretch a dimension object, appropriate definition points must be included in the _____ of the **STRETCH** command.

6.   Trimming and extending operations can be carried out with all types of Linear (Horizontal, Vertical, Aligned, Rotated) dimensions and with the Ordinate dimension. (T/F)

7.   To extend or trim an Ordinate dimension, AutoCAD moves the feature location (location of the dimensioned coordinate) to the boundary edge. (T/F)

8.   With the _____ command you can edit the dimension text of Associative dimensions.

9.   The _____ command is particularly important for creating isometric dimensions and is applicable in resolving conflicting situations due to overlapping of extension lines with other objects.

10.   The _____ command is used to edit the placement and orientation of a single existing Associative dimension.

11.   The _____ command restores the text of an Associative dimension to its original (home/default) location if the position of the text has been changed by the STRETCH, TEDIT, or TROTATE commands.

12.   The _____ command regenerates (updates) prevailing Associative dimension objects (like arrows, text height, etc.) using the current settings of the dimension variables, dimension style, text style, and Units settings.

13.   If the drawings are in Model space, you should create Associative dimensions in _____.

14.   The _____ variable is automatically adjusted to the zoom scale factor of the Model space viewport.

15.   Explain the function of **EXPLODE** command in dimensioning. _____
_____

16.   Explain the term Definition points. _____
_____

17.   Explain when to use the EXTEND command and how it works. _____
_____

18.   Explain the use and working of the DDMODIFY command for editing dimensions. _____

EXERCISES

Exercise 3

In this exercise you will perform the following tasks:
1. Make the drawing as shown in Figure 7-20. Assume the dimensions where necessary.
2. Dimension the drawing as shown in Figure 7-20
3. Edit the dimensions as shown in Figure 7-21 using the STRETCH, EXTEND, and TRIM commands.
4. Edit the dimensions as shown in Figure 7-21 using GRIPS.

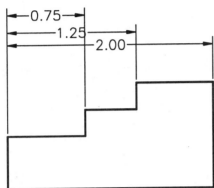

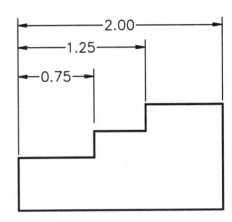

Figure 7-20 Drawing for Exercise 3, before editing dimensions

Figure 7-21 Drawing for Exercise 3, after editing dimensions

Exercise 4

In this exercise you will perform the following tasks:
1. Make the drawing as shown in Figure 7-22 (a). Assume the dimensions where necessary.
2. Dimension the drawing as shown in Figure 7-22(a).
3. Edit the dimensions as shown in Figure 7-22(b) using GRIPS.

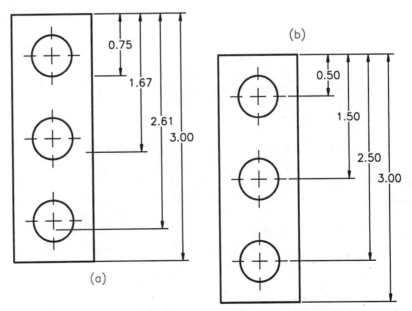

Figure 7-22 Drawing for Exercise 4, showing dimensions before and after editing

Exercise 5

In this exercise you will perform the following tasks:
1. Make the drawing as shown in Figure 7-23. Assume the dimensions where necessary.
2. Dimension and then edit the dimensions as shown.

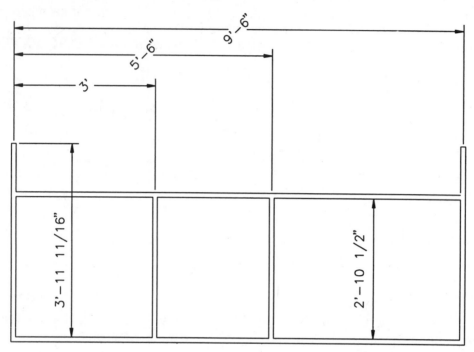

Figure 7-23 Drawing for Exercise 5, editing dimensions

Answers

The following are the correct answers to the questions in the self evaluation test.
1 - Associative dimensioning is defined as a method of dimensioning in which the dimension is influenced by the changes in the size of the object. For example, editing operations like **stretching**, **extending**, or **trimming** an object result in modification of the dimensions related to that object. In Associative dimensioning the items constituting a dimension (such as dimension line, arrows, leaders, extension lines, and the dimension text) are drawn as a **single object**. **2** - The STRETCH command can be used to stretch the Associative dimension. For stretching a dimension object, appropriate definition points must be included in the selection crossing box of the **STRETCH** command. **3** - The trimming operations can be carried out with all types of linear (Horizontal, Vertical, Aligned, Rotated) dimensions and the Ordinate dimension. AutoCAD trims a Linear dimension between the extension line definition points and the object used as trimming edge. For extending or trimming an Ordinate dimension, AutoCAD moves the feature location (location of the dimensioned coordinate) to the boundary edge. **4** - T, **5** - T, **6** - T, **7** - F, **8** - F, **9** - F, **10** - T

Chapter 8

Dimension Styles and Dimensioning System Variables

Learning objectives

After completing this chapter, you will be able to:
- Use styles and variables to control dimensions.
- Create dimensioning styles using dialogue boxes and the command line.
- Set dimension variables using the Geometry dialogue box and command line.
- Set dimension variables using the Format dialogue box and command line.
- Set dimension variables using the Annotation dialogue box and command line.
- Set other dimension variables that are not in dialogue boxes.
- Understand dimension style families and how to apply them in dimensioning.
- Use dimension style overrides.
- Compare and list dimension styles.
- Use externally referenced dimension styles.

USING STYLES AND VARIABLES TO CONTROL DIMENSIONS

In AutoCAD the appearance of dimensions on the drawing screen and the manner in which they are saved in the drawing database is controlled by a set of dimension variables. The dimensioning commands use these variables as arguments. The variables that control the appearance of the dimensions can be managed with dimension styles. You can use the **Dimension Style** dialogue box to control dimension styles and dimension variables through a set of dialogue boxes. You can also do it by entering relevant commands at the **Command:** or **Dim:** prompt. The **Dimension Style** dialogue box can be invoked from the **Dimensioning** toolbar by selecting the **Dimension Styles** icon in the **Dimension Styles** flyout (Figure 8-1), from the pull-down menu (Select Data, Dimension Style..., Figure 8-2), or from the screen menu (Select DATA, DDim:). It can also be invoked by entering **DDIM** at AutoCAD's **Command:** prompt.

Toolbar:	Dimensioning, Dimension Styles
Pull-down:	Data, Dimension Style
Screen:	DATA, DDim:

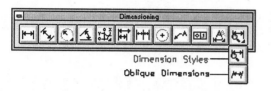

Figure 8-1   Selecting dimension style from the Dimensioning toolbar

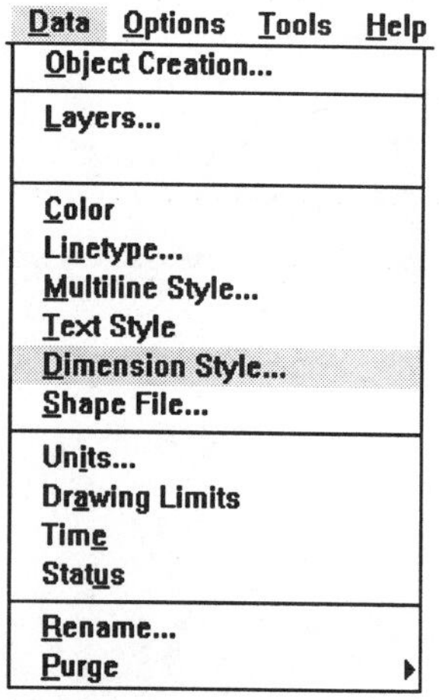

Figure 8-2   Selecting dimension style from the pull-down menu

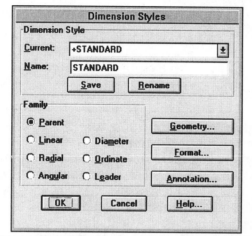

Figure 8-3   Dimension Styles dialogue box

CREATING AND RESTORING DIMENSION STYLES

Using the Dialogue Box

Dimension style controls the appearance and positioning of dimensions. If the default dimensioning style (STANDARD) does not meet your requirements, you can select another dimensioning style or create one that does. The default dimension style filename is **STANDARD**. Parent dimension styles can be created by entering the dimension style name in the **Name:** edit box (in the **Dimension Styles** dialogue box, Figure 8-3) and then selecting the save button. The current dimension style name is listed in the **Current:** dimension styles list box. A style can be made current (restored) by picking the name of the dimension style that you want to make current from the list of defined dimension styles. The list of dimension styles can be displayed by picking the arrow in the **Current:** dimension styles list box (pop-up list). The dimension style name must not exceed 29 characters and the name should not end with a family member suffix code. (See Using Dimension Style Families later in this chapter.)

Using the Command Line

You can also create dimension styles from the command line by entering DIMSTYLE at the **Command:** prompt or by entering SAVE at **Dim:** prompt:

Command: **DIMSTYLE**
Dimension Style Edit (Save/Restore/STatus/Variables/Apply/?) <Restore>: **SAVE**
?/Name for new dimension style: *Enter the name of the dimension style.*

Command: **DIM**
Dim: **SAVE**
?/Name for new dimension style: *Enter the name of the dimension style.*

You can also restore the dimensions from the command line by entering DIMSTYLE at **Command:** prompt or by entering RESTORE at **Dim:** prompt.

Command: **DIMSTYLE**
Dimension Style Edit (Save/Restore/STatus/Variables/Apply/?) <Restore>: **RESTORE**
?/Enter dimension style name or RETURN to select dimension: *Enter the dimension style name.*

Command: **DIM**
DIM: **RESTORE**
Dimension style: *AutoCAD displays the current style name.*
?/Enter dimension style name or RETURN to select dimension: *Enter the dimension style name.*

You can also select a dimension style by picking a dimension on a drawing. This can be accomplished by pressing the Enter key (null response) at the prompt **?/Enter dimension style name or RETURN to select dimension:**. This way you can select the dimension style without knowing the name of the dimension style. With the help of dimension styles, you can easily create and save groups of settings for as many types of dimensions as you require. Styles can be created to support almost any standards, including ANSI, DIN, and ARCH.

GEOMETRY DIALOGUE BOX

The Geometry dialogue box (Figure 8-4) can be used to specify the dimensioning attributes (variables) that affect the geometry of the dimensions. This dialogue box can be invoked by selecting the **Geometry** button in the **Dimension Styles** dialogue box. If the settings of the dimension variables have not been altered in the current editing session, the settings displayed in the dialogue box are the default settings.

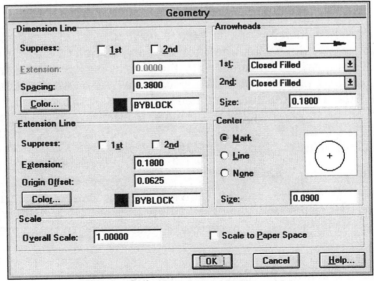

Figure 8-4 Geometry dialogue box

Dimension Line

Suppress

The **Suppress:** check boxes control the drawing of the first and second dimension line. By default, both dimension lines will be drawn. You can suppress one or both dimension lines by selecting their corresponding check boxes. The values of these check boxes are stored in the DIMSD1 and DIMSD2 variables.

DIMSD1, DIMSD2 (Using Command Line)

Command: **DIM**
Dim: **DIMSD1**
Current value <off> New value : **on**

> **Note**
>
> *The first and second dimension lines are determined by how you select the extension line origins. If the first extension line origin is on the right, the first dimension line is also on right. The initial value of DIMSD1 and DIMSD2 if off.*

Extension

The **Extension** (Oblique tick extension) edit box is used to specify the distance by which the dimension line will extend beyond the extension line. The **Extension** edit box can be used only when you have selected the oblique arrowhead in the Arrowhead pop-up list. The extension value entered in the Extension edit box gets stored in the DIMDLE variable. By default this edit box is disabled because the oblique arrowhead is not selected.

DIMDLE (Using the Command Line)

DIMDLE is used only when DIMTSZ variable is other than 0 (when the DIMTSZ variable is other than 0, oblique arrowheads are drawn instead of arrows). The dimension line will extend past the extension line by the value of DIMDLE. The default value for this variable is 0.0. The prompt sequence to extend the dimension line by 0.25 units past the extension lines is:

Command: **DIMDLE**
New value for DIMDLE <0.0000>: **0.25**

Spacing

The **Spacing** (Baseline Increment) edit box is used to control the dimension line increment (gap between successive dimension lines) for the continuation of a linear dimension drawn with the **BASELINE** command. You can specify the dimension line increment to your requirement by entering the desired value in the **Spacing:** edit box. Also, when you are creating Continued dimensions with the **DIMContinue** command, the contents of **Spacing:** edit box specify the offset distance for the successive dimension lines, if needed to avoid drawing over the previous dimension line. The default value displayed in the **Spacing:** edit box is 0.38 unit. The spacing (baseline increment) value is stored in the DIMDLI variable.

DIMDLI (Using Command Line)

This variable governs the spacing between the successive dimension lines when linear dimensioning is created with the BASELINE commands. Successive dimension lines are offset by the DIMDLI value, if needed, to avoid drawing over the previous dimension.

Command: **DIMDLI**
Current value for DIMDLI <0.3800>: *Enter new value.*

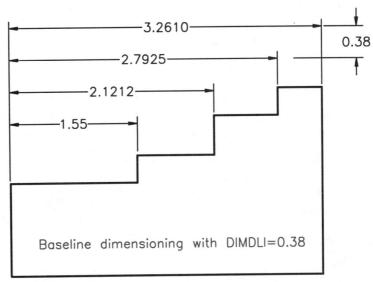

Figure 8-5 DIMDLI, baseline increment

Dimension Line Color

Dimension arrows have the same color as the dimension line because arrows constitute a part of the dimension line. You can establish a color for the dimension line and the dimension arrows. The color number or the special color label is stored in the **DIMCLRD** variable. The default color label for the dimension line is BYBLOCK. You can specify the color of the dimension line by selecting the **Color...** button or the color swatch box. When you select these boxes, AutoCAD displays the **Select Color** dialogue box, which you can use to specify a color. You can also enter the color name or color number in the Color edit box.

DIMCLRD (Using the Command Line)

This dimension variable is used to assign colors to dimension lines, arrowheads, and dimension line leaders. This variable can take any permissible color number, color name (such as Red, Yellow, Blue, etc.), or the special color label BYBLOCK or BYLAYER as its value. If you are using the **Dim:** prompt, you can assign color values by specifying a color number or entering any of the standard color names (such as Red, Yellow, Green, etc.), or the special names such as BYBLOCK, BYLAYER, etc. For example, if you want the Dimension line color to be cyan, the following prompt sequence is required:

Command: **DIM**
Dim: **DIMCLRD**
Current value <BYBLOCK> New value: **CYAN**
Dim: **DIMCLRD**
Current value <4(cyan)> New value:

In the above prompt notice that the color number (4) of the color (cyan) is also displayed. If you are using the SETVAR command you must specify the integer color number, not the color name. For example:

Command: **SETVAR**
Variable name or? <DIMASO>: **DIMCLRD**
New value for DIMCLRD <4>: *Specify a relevant color number.*

If you are editing the DIMCLRD variable from the Command prompt, you need to specify the integer color number. You cannot specify a color name. For example:

Command: **DIMCLRD**
New value for DIMCLRD <4>: **Red**

Requires an integer between 0 and 256
New value for DIMCLRD <4>:

Extension Line

Suppress

Suppress: check boxes control the display of the extension lines. By default, both extension lines will be drawn. You can suppress one or both extension lines by selecting the corresponding check boxes. The values of these check boxes are stored in the DIMSE1 and DIMSE2 variables.

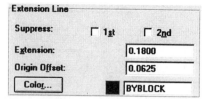

Figure 8-6 Extension Line area of the Geometry dialogue box

DIMSE1, DIMSE2 (Using Command Line)

Command: **DIM**
Dim: **DIMSE1**
Current value <off> New value : **on**

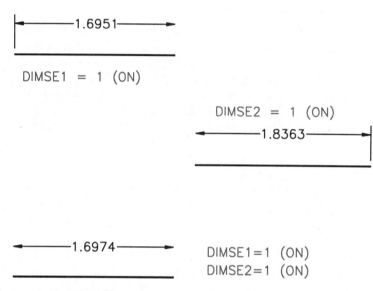

Figure 8-7 Visibility of extension lines DIMSE1 and DIMSE2

Note

The first and second extension lines are determined by how you select the extension line origins. If the first extension line origin is on the right, the first extension line is also on right. The initial value of DIMSE1 and DIMSE2 is off.

Extension

Extension is the distance the extension line should extend past the dimension line. You can change the extension line offset by entering the desired distance value in the **Extension:** edit box. The value of this box is stored in the **DIMEXE** variable. The default value for extension distance is 0.1800 unit.

DIMEXE (Using the Command Line)

The extension of the extension line past the dimension line is governed by the DIMEXE (Dimension Extension line Extension) variable. The default value for the DIMEXE variable is 0.18 unit. You can control this distance to meet your requirement. For example if you want to change the distance of extension lines beyond the dimension lines from 0.18 unit to 0.36 unit, you will have the following prompt sequence:

Command: **DIMEXE**
Current value <0.1800> New value: **0.36**

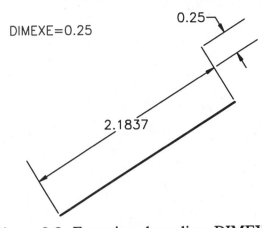

Figure 8-8 Extension above line, DIMEXE

Origin Offset

This edit box displays the distance value the extension lines are offset from the extension line origins you specify. You may have noticed a small space exists between the origin points you specify and the start of the extension lines. This space is due to specified offset. You can specify an offset distance of your choice by entering it in this box. AutoCAD stores this value in the **DIMEXO** variable. The default value for this distance is 0.0625.

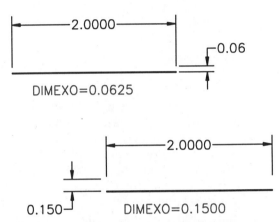

Figure 8-9 Origin offset, DIMEXO

DIMEXO (Using the Command Line)

Command: **DIMEXO**
New value for DIMEXO <0.0625>:

Extension Line Color

In this box you can examine the existing extension lines color. The default extension lines color is BYBLOCK. You can change the color by assigning a new color to the extension lines. For example, if you want the extension lines color to be yellow, pick the **Color...** button or the color swatch box and select the desired color from the **Select Color** dialogue box. You can also specify the color by entering the color name or number in the Color edit box. The color number or the color label is saved in the DIMCLRE variable.

DIMCLRE (Using the Command Line)

The DIMCLRE variable is used to assign color to the dimension extension lines. If you are using the **Dim:** prompt you can assign the color values by specifying a color number or entering any of the standard color names such as Red, Yellow, Green, etc., or the special names such as BYBLOCK, BYLAYER, etc. For example, if you want to set the color of the extension lines to yellow, the command prompt sequence is as follows:

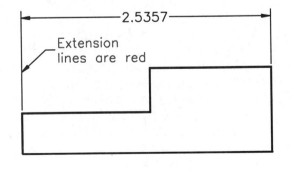

Figure 8-10 Changing extension line color, DIMCLRE

Command: **DIM**
Dim: **DIMCLRE**
Current value <BYBLOCK> New value: **Yellow**

If you are using the Setvar command then you must specify the integer color number and not a color name. For example:

Command: **SETVAR**
Variable name or? <DIMASO>: **DIMCLRE**
New value for DIMCLRE <4>: *Specify the color number.*

If you are editing the DIMCLRE variable from the **Command:** prompt, you need to specify the integer color number. You cannot specify a color name. For example:

Command: **DIMCLRE**
New value for DIMCLRE <4>: **Red**
Requires an integer between 0 and 256
New value for DIMCLRE <4>:

Arrowheads

1st: and 2nd: pop-up boxes

When you create a dimension, AutoCAD draws the terminator symbols at the two ends of the dimension line. These terminator symbols, generally referred to as arrowhead types, represent the beginning and end of a dimension. AutoCAD has provided seven standard termination symbols that you can apply at each end of the dimension line. In addition to these, you can create your own arrows or terminator symbols. By default, the same arrowhead type is applied at both ends of the dimension line. If you select the first arrowhead, it is automatically applied to the second by default. However, if you want to specify a different arrowhead at the second dimension line end point, you must select the desired arrowhead type or user-defined block from the second arrowhead list box.

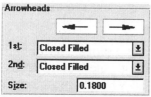

Figure 8-11 The Arrowheads area of the Geometry dialogue box

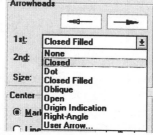

Figure 8-12 The Arrowheads pop-up list

The first end point of the dimension line is the intersection point of the first extension line and the dimension line. The first extension line is determined by the first extension line origin. However, in angular dimensioning the second end point is located in a counterclockwise direction from the first point, regardless of how the points were selected when creating the angular dimension. The specified arrowhead types are displayed in the arrowhead image box. The first arrowhead types is saved in the **DIMBLK1** system variable and the second arrowhead type is saved in the **DIMBLK2** system variable. As mentioned earlier, by default arrows are drawn at the two end points of the dimension line. If you specify a different block from the arrowhead, the name of the block is stored in the DIMBLK system variable.

User Arrow

If you want to specify that instead of the standard arrows a user-defined block is drawn at the ends of the dimension line, select the **User Arrow...** from the first or second arrowheads pop-up list to display the User Arrow dialogue box. Enter the name of the pre-defined block name, then select the OK button. The size of the block is determined by the value stored in the Arrow Size edit box. If there is no existing block by the name you specify, the message **Can't find the arrow block** is displayed in the lower left-hand corner of the dialogue box. The name of the block you select is stored in the DIMBLK1 or DIMBLK2 variable.

DIMBLK, DIMBLK1, and DIMBLK2 (Using the Command Line)

If no value is set for DIMBLK1 and DIMBLK2, AutoCAD by default uses the arrows as terminator symbols. Arrows are drawn if DIMTSZ variable is set to 0. If the DIMTSZ has a value other than 0 AutoCAD draws oblique tick marks instead of arrows, regardless of the values set for DIMBLK1 and DIMBLK2 variables. If you want AutoCAD to draw a different arrowhead type, the value must be assigned to DIMBLK system variable. For example, if you want DOT symbols to be used instead of arrows, assign DOT to DIMBLK variable as follows.

Command: **DIMBLK**
New value for DIMBLK, or . for none < . > : **DOT**

Similarly, you can assign a value to DIMBLK1 and DIMBLK2

Command: **DIMBLK1**
New value for DIMBLK1, or . for none < . > : **OPEN**

Command: **DIMBLK2**
New value for DIMBLK2, or . for none < . > : **CLOSED**

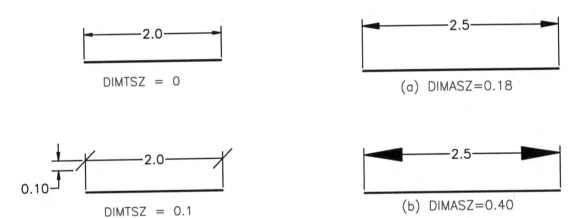

Figure 8-13 Tick marks are drawn if DIMTSZ is not 0

Figure 8-14 Controlling arrow size, DIMASZ

Size

Arrowheads and terminator symbols are drawn according to the size specified in the **Size:** edit box. The default value is 0.18 unit. This value is stored in the **DIMASZ** system variable. The arrowhead size value is stored in the DIMASZ variable. By default DIMTSZ is set to 0 and DIMASZ is 0.18. The size of the ticks or arrowhead blocks is computed as DIMTSZ x DIMSCALE for ticks or DIMASZ x DIMSCALE for arrowhead blocks. Hence, if the DIMSCALE factor is 1, the size of the tick is equal to the DIMTSZ value.

DIMASZ (Using the Command Line)

Command: **DIMASZ**
New value for DIMASZ < 0.1800 > : *Enter new value.*

Creating Custom Arrowheads

As mentioned earlier, a value assigned to the DIMBLK variable replaces the default arrowheads at the end of the dimension lines with a user-defined block. The default for DIMBLK is no block. To discard an existing block name, set its value to a single period (.). Figure 8-15 shows a block comprising a custom arrow. You can use this arrow to define a block and then assign it to the DIMBLK (DIMBLK1 or DIMBLK2) variable. When you create a dimension, the custom arrow will automatically appear at the end point of the dimension line, replacing the standard arrow.

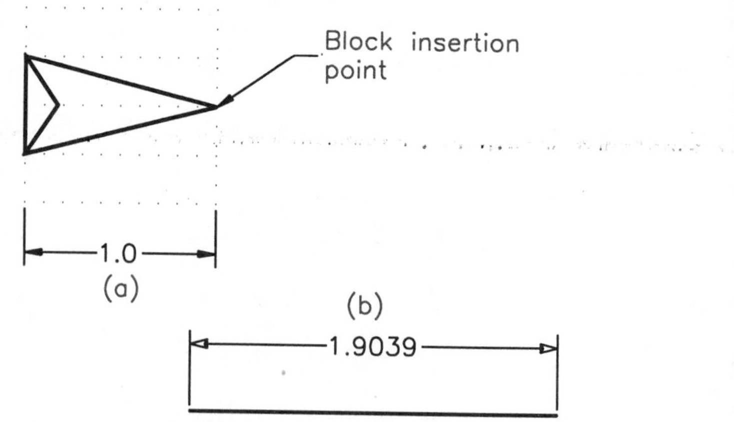

Figure 8-15 Using arrows, tick marks, and user-defined blocks

Considerations for Creating an Arrowhead Block

1. When you create a block for arrowhead, the arrowhead block must be created in a 1 by 1 box. AutoCAD automatically scales the block to the size as set in the DIMASZ system variable. For example, if DIMASZ is set to 0.25, the length of the arrow will be 0.25. Also, if the length of the arrow is not 1 unit, it will leave a gap between the dimension line and the arrowhead block.
2. The arrowhead must be drawn as it would appear on the right-hand side of the dimension line.
3. The insertion point of the arrowhead block must be the point that will coincide with the extension line.

The following is the prompt sequence for creating a block and then assigning the block name to DMBLK system variable:

Command: **BLOCK**
Block name (or?): *Give a name; e.g., MYARROW.*
Insertion base point: *Select the end point as shown in the figure.*
Select objects: *Select the arrow.*
Select objects: *Press the Enter key.*

Command: **DIMBLK**
New value for DIMBLK, or . for none <.>: **MYARROW**

If you dimension a line, the standard dimension arrows will be replaced by the arrowhead block (MYARROW). The user-defined arrowhead blocks at the end of dimension line are controlled by the DIMSAH variable. If it is off, normal arrowheads or the user-defined arrowheads are used as set by DIMBLK. If the DIMSAH variable is on, the user-defined arrowhead blocks are used.

Scale

Overall Scale

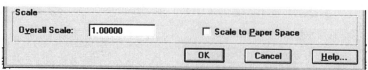

Figure 8-16 Scale area of the Geometry dialogue box

The current general scaling factor that pertains to all of the size-related dimension variables, like text size, center mark size, arrow size, etc., is displayed in the **Overall Scale:** edit box. You can alter the scaling factor to your requirement by entering the scaling factor of your choice in this box. Altering the contents of this box alters the value of the **DIMSCALE** variable since the current scaling factor is stored in it. DIMSCALE is not applied to the measured lengths, coordinates, angles, or tolerance. The default value for this variable is 1.0; and in this case the dimensioning variables assume their preset values and the drawing is plotted at full scale. If the drawing is to be plotted at half size, the scale factor is the reciprocal of the drawing size. Hence the scale factor or the DIMSCALE value will be the reciprocal of 1/2 which is 2/1 = 2.

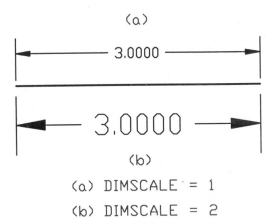

Figure 8-17 Using overall scaling to scale dimensions, DIMSCALE

DIMSCALE (Using the Command Line)
As mentioned before, the DIMSCALE dimensioning variable controls all of the size-related dimension variables, like text size, center mark size, arrow size, etc.

Command: **DIM**
Dim: **DIMSCALE**
Current value < 1.0000 > New value: *Enter new value.*

> **Note**
>
> *If you are in the middle of the dimensioning process and you change the DIMSCALE value, only dimensions that are drawn after the change has been made to the DIMSCALE variable will be affected.*

Scale to Paper Space
If you select the **Scale to Paper Space** check box, the scale factor between the current model space viewport and Paper space is automatically computed. Also, by selecting this check box the **Overall Scale:** edit box is disabled (it is grayed out in the dialogue box) and DIMSCALE is set to 0. When DIMSCALE is assigned a value of 0.0, AutoCAD calculates an acceptable default value based on the scaling between the current Model space viewport and Paper space. If you are in Paper space, or are not using the paper space feature, AutoCAD sets DIMSCALE to 1.0; otherwise AutoCAD calculates a scale factor that makes it possible to plot text sizes, arrow sizes, and other scaled distances at the values in which they have been previously set. (For further details, see "Model and Paper Space Dimensioning" in Chapter 7.)

Center

Mark
The **Size:** edit box in the Center area of the **Geometry** dialogue box displays the current size of the center marks. The center marks are created by using the **Center, Diameter,** and **Radius** dimensioning commands. The center marks are also created if you use the **DIMCENTER** command. In the case of

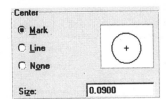

Figure 8-18 The Center area of the Geometry dialogue box

Radius and Diameter dimensioning, the center mark is drawn only if the dimension line is located outside the circle or arc. You can specify the size of the center mark by entering the required value in the **Size:** edit box. If you do not want a center mark, enter 0 in the edit box or better select the **None** radio button. This value is stored in the DIMCEN variable. The default value in for DIMCEN is 0.09.

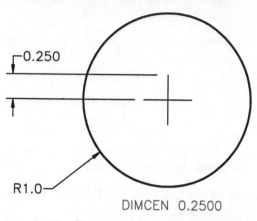

Figure 8-19 Center mark size, DIMCEN

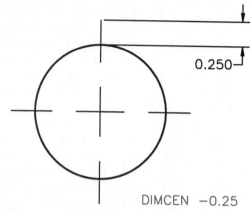

Figure 8-20 Mark with center lines, (negative DIMCEN)

Line

If you want to draw center lines for a circle or arc, pick the **Line:** button. The value in the **Size:** edit box determines the size of the center lines, as shown in Figure 8-20. The value you enter in the **Size:** edit box is stored as a negative value in the **DIMCEN** variable. In case of Radius and Diameter dimensioning, center lines are drawn only when the dimension line is located outside the circle or arc. The default setting is off (not checked), resulting in the generation of dimensions without center lines.

None

If you select the **None** radio button, the center marks are not drawn and AutoCAD automatically disables the **Size:** edit box

DIMCEN (Using the Command Line)

Command: **DIMCEN**
New value for DIMCEN <0.0900>: *Enter new value.*

A positive value will create a center mark and a negative value will create a center line. If the value is 0, AutoCAD does not create center marks or center lines.

Note

*Unlike specifying a negative value for the DIMCEN variable, you cannot enter a negative value in the **Center Mark Size** box. Picking the **Line** radio button automatically treats the value in the Size edit box as the size for the center lines.*

Exercise 1

Draw the following figure and then set the values in the Geometry dialogue box to dimension the drawing as shown in the figure. (Dimension line spacing = 0.25, Extension line extension = 0.10, Origin offset = 0.05, Arrowhead size = 0.09.) Assume the missing dimensions.

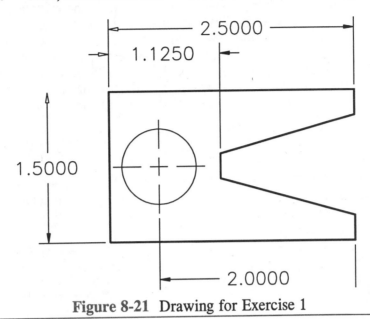

Figure 8-21 Drawing for Exercise 1

CONTROLLING DIMENSION FORMAT

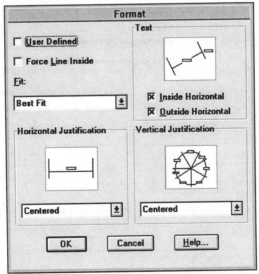

Figure 8-22 The Format dialogue box

You can control the dimension format through the **Format** dialogue box (Figure 8-22) or by assigning appropriate values to dimension variables. In the dimension format you can control the placement, horizontal justification, and vertical justification of dimension text. For example, you can force AutoCAD to align the dimension text along the dimension line. You can also force the dimension text to be displayed at the top of the dimension line. Some settings are interdependent. For example, if you select the User Defined option for text placement, the horizontal justification is automatically disabled. You can save the settings in a dimension style file for future use. The

Format dialogue box has image tiles that update dynamically to display the text placement as the settings are changed. Individual items of the Format dialogue box and the related dimension variables are described in the next section.

User Defined

When you dimension, AutoCAD places the dimension text in the middle of the dimension line (if there is enough space). If you pick the **User Defined** check box, you can position the dimension text anywhere along the dimension line. You will also notice that when you select this check box, the Horizontal Justification list box is automatically disabled. This setting is saved in the **DIMUPT** system variable. The default value of this variable is **off**. If you set the DIMUPT variable **on**, AutoCAD will place the dimension text at the point that you have specified as the dimension line location. This enables you to position the dimension text anywhere along the dimension line.

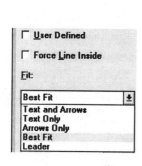

Figure 8-23 Fit area of the Format dialogue box

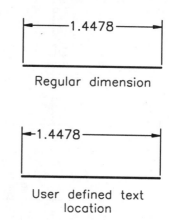

Figure 8-24 User-defined dimension text position

Force Lines Inside

If the dimension text and the dimension lines are outside the extension lines and you want the dimension lines to be placed between the extension lines, pick the **Force Lines Inside** check box. When you pick this box in the Radius and Diameter dimensions (when Default text placement is horizontal), the dimension line and arrows are drawn inside the circle or arc, while the text and leader are drawn outside. When you select the **Force Line Inside** check box, the **DIMTOFL** variable is set to **on** by AutoCAD. The default setting is off (not checked), resulting in generation of the dimension line outside the extension lines when the dimension text is located outside the extension lines.

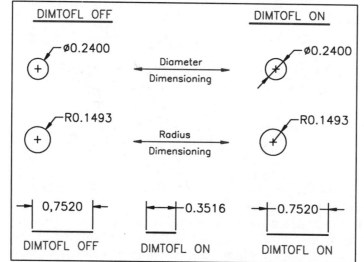

Figure 8-25 Force lines inside, DIMTOFL

Fit

When you select the down arrow in the **Fit:** pop-up list, AutoCAD displays the available options for fitting the arrows and dimension text between the extension lines. The value of the **Fit** option is stored in **DIMFIT** system variable. The **Fit** options are:

Text and Arrows

If you select this option, AutoCAD will place the arrows and dimension text between the extension lines if there is enough space available to fit both. Otherwise, both text and arrowheads are placed outside the extension lines. In this setting, **DIMFIT = 0**.

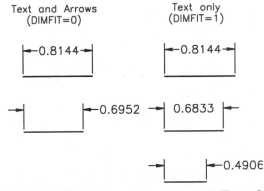

Figure 8-26 Text and Arrows and Text Only options

Text Only

When you select this option, AutoCAD places the text and arrowheads inside the extension lines if there is enough space to fit both. If space is not available for both arrows and text, the text is placed inside the extension lines and the arrows are placed outside the extension lines. If there is not enough space for text, both text and arrowheads are placed outside the extension lines. In this setting, **DIMFIT = 1**.

Arrows Only

When you select this option, AutoCAD places the text and arrowheads inside the extension lines if there is enough space to fit both. If there is enough space to fit the arrows, the arrows will be placed inside the extension lines and the dimension text outside the extension lines. If the there is not enough space for either text or arrowheads, both are placed outside the extension lines. In this setting, **DIMFIT = 2**.

Best Fit

This is the default option. In this option, AutoCAD places the dimension where it fits best between the extension lines. In this setting, **DIMFIT = 3**.

Leader

In this option, AutoCAD creates leader lines if there is not enough space available to fit the dimension text between the extension lines. The horizontal justification determines whether the text is placed to the right or the left of the leader. In this setting, **DIMFIT = 4**.

Horizontal Justification

Horizontal Justification controls the placement of the dimension text. To display the available options, select the down arrow in the pop-up list located just below the Horizontal Justification image tile. The selected setting is stored in **DIMJUST** system variable. The default option is Centered. The following is the list of the available options with DIMJUST values:

Options	Description	DIMJUST
Centered	Places text between extension lines	0
1st Extension Line	Places text next to first extension line	1
2nd Extension Line	Places text next to second extension line	2
Over 1st Extension	Places text aligned with and above the first extension line	3
Over 2nd Extension	Places text aligned with and above the second extension line	4

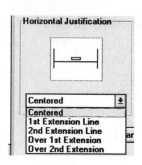

Figure 8-27   Horizontal Justification area of the Format dialogue box

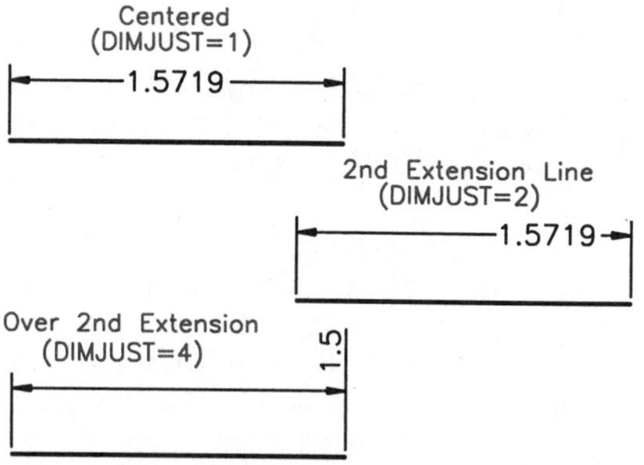

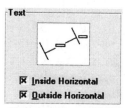

Figure 8-28   Using Horizontal Justification options to position text

Text

You can use the **Text** option to specify the alignment of the dimension text with the dimension line. These options can be used to control alignment of the dimension text for linear, radius, and diameter dimensions. By default the inside and outside dimension text is drawn horizontally.

Figure 8-29   Text area of Format dialogue box

Inside Horizontal

By default the dimension text is drawn horizontally with respect to the UCS (user coordinate system). Therefore, the **Inside Horizontal** check box is **on**. The alignment of the dimension line does not affect the text alignment. In this case the **DIMTIH** variable is turned on. If you turn this check box off, the dimension text is aligned with the dimension line only when the dimension text is between the extension lines. Picking this option turns the **DIMTIH** system variable **off**.

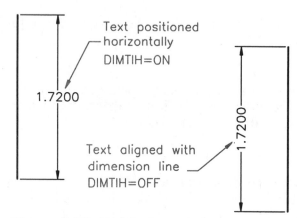

Figure 8-30   Dimension text inside horizontal, DIMTIH

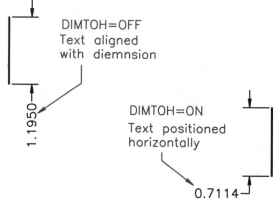

Figure 8-31   Dimension text outside horizontal, DIMTOH

Outside Horizontal

By default the dimension text is drawn horizontally with respect to the UCS (user coordinate system). Therefore, the **Outside Horizontal** check box is **on**. The alignment of the dimension line does not affect the text alignment. If you turn this check box off, the dimension text is aligned with the dimension line only when the dimension text is outside the extension lines. Picking this option turns the system variable **DIMTOH off**.

Vertical Justification

Just as the Horizontal pop-up list controls the horizontal placement of the dimension text, the **Vertical** pop-up list controls the vertical placement of the dimension text. The current setting will be highlighted. Controlling the vertical placement of dimension text is possible only when the dimension text is drawn in its normal (default) location. This setting is stored in the **DIMTAD** system variable. Following are the vertical text placement settings:

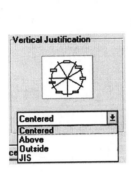

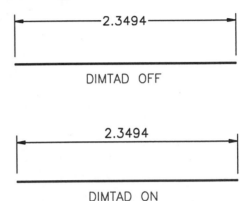

Figure 8-32 Controlling vertical justification

Figure 8-33 Using Centered justification to place text above dimension line, DIMTAD

Centered

If this option is picked, the dimension text gets centered on the dimension line in such a way that the dimension line is split to allow for placement of the text. Picking this option turns DIMTAD off. In this setting **DIMTAD = 0**.

Above

If this option is picked, the dimension text is placed above the dimension line, except when the dimension line is not horizontal and the dimension text inside the extension lines is horizontal (DIMTIH=1). The distance of the dimension text from the dimension line is controlled by the DIMTGAP value. This results in an unbroken solid dimension line drawn under the dimension text. In this setting **DIMTAD = 1**.

Outside

This option places the dimension text on the side of the dimension line. In this setting **DIMTAD = 2**.

JIS

This option lets you place the dimension text to conform to JIS representation. In this setting **DIMTAD = 3**.

Exercise 2

Draw the following figure, then set the values in the Geometry and Format dialogue boxes to dimension the drawing as shown in the figure. (Dimension line spacing = 0.25, Extension line extension = 0.10, Origin offset = 0.05, Arrowhead size = 0.09.) Assume the missing dimensions and set DIMTXT = 0.09.

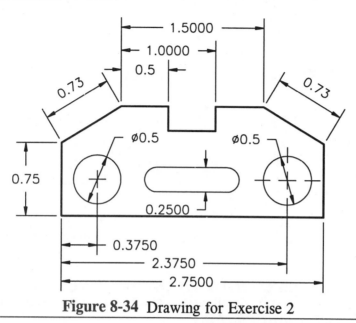

Figure 8-34 Drawing for Exercise 2

ANNOTATION DIALOGUE BOX

You can use the **Annotation** dialogue box to control the dimension text format. AutoCAD lets you attach a user-defined prefix or suffix to the dimension text. For example, you can define the diameter symbol as a prefix by entering %%C in the **Prefix** edit box; AutoCAD will automatically attach the diameter symbol in front of the dimension text. Similarly, you can define a unit type, such as **mm**, as a suffix. By defining this as a suffix, AutoCAD will attach **mm** at the end of every dimension text. This dialogue box also enables you to define tolerances, alternate units, zero suppression, and dimension text format.

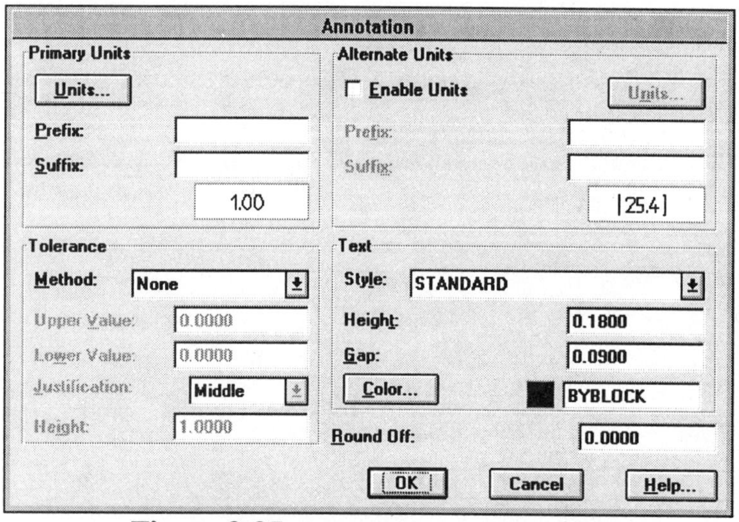

Figure 8-35 Annotation dialogue box

Primary Units

The Primary Units area of the **Annotation** dialogue box consists of Units, Prefix, and Suffix. It also has an image tile that displays the current dimension text format. If you pick this image tile, AutoCAD cycles the displayed value through different tolerance methods. The following is a description of Units, Prefix, and Suffix options:

Units

When you select the **Units...** button, AutoCAD displays the **Primary Units** dialogue box (Figure 8-36). You can use this dialogue box to control Units, Dimension Precision, and Zero Suppression for dimension measurements. If you select the down arrow in the **Units** pop-up list, AutoCAD displays unit formats such as Decimal, Scientific, Architectural, etc. You can select one of the listed units to use when dimensioning. Notice that by selecting a dimension unit format, the drawing units (that you might have selected by using the DDUNITS or UNITS command) are not affected. You can also control unit precision by using the Precision: pop-up list. The units setting for linear dimensions is stored in DIMUNIT system variable, unit setting for angular dimensions in DIMAUNIT, setting of precision (number of decimal places) in DIMDEC, and setting of precision for tolerance (number of decimal places for tolerance) in DIMTDEC.

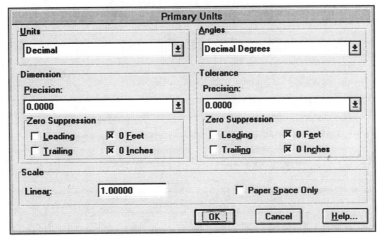

Figure 8-36 Primary Units dialogue box for dimensioning

Zero Suppression

If you want to suppress the feet portion of a feet-and-inches dimension when the distance is less than 1 foot (when there is a 0 in the feet portion of the text), pick the **0 Feet** check box. For example, if you pick the 0 Feet check box, the dimension text 0'-8 3/4" becomes 8 3/4". By default 0 Feet and 0 Inches value is suppressed. If you want to suppress the inches part of a feet-and-inches dimension when the distance in the feet portion is an integer number and the inches portion is zero, pick the **0 Inches** check box. For example, if you pick the 0 Inches check box, the dimension text 3'-0" becomes 3".

If you want to suppress the leading zeros in all of the distances measured in decimals, check the **Leading** check box. For example, by picking this box, 0.0750 becomes .0750. If you want to suppress the trailing zeros in all the distances measured in decimals, check the **Trailing** check box. For example, by picking this box, 0.0750 becomes 0.075. Trailing zeros are of significance to the tolerance, so keep in mind the degree of accuracy required in the dimension tolerance. AutoCAD stores zero suppression as an integer value in the **DIMZIN** variable in the following manner:

If you pick the 0 Feet check box, an integer value 3 is stored in DIMZIN variable by AutoCAD. If you pick the 0 Inches check box, an integer value 2 is stored in DIMZIN variable by AutoCAD. If you pick the Leading check box, an integer value 4 is stored in DIMZIN variable by AutoCAD. If you pick the Trailing check box, an integer value 9 is stored in DIMZIN variable by AutoCAD. A combination of not picking the 0 Feet and 0 Inches check boxes results in display of the 0 feet as well as the 0 inches of a measurement. For this combination, the value stored in DIMZIN is 1.

Remember that by default, **the 0 Feet and 0 Inches check boxes are active** (selected, picked). This is displayed by a cross mark in these two check boxes. The table below shows the result of selecting one of the DIMZIN values:

DIMZIN Value	Meaning
0 (default)	Suppress zero feet and exactly zero inches
1	Include zero feet and exactly zero inches
2	Include zero feet, suppress zero inches
3	Include zero inches, suppress zero feet

The following table illustrates the above results with examples.

DIMZIN Value	Examples			
0	2'-0 2/3"	8"	2'	4/5"
1	2'-0 2/3"	0'-8"	2'-0"	0'-0 4/5"
2	2'-0 2/3"	0'-8"	2'	0'-0.4/5"
3	2'-0 2/3"	8"	2'-0"	4/5"

If the dimension has feet and a fractional inch part, the number of inches is included even if it is 0. This is independent of the DIMZIN setting. For example, a dimension such as 1'-2/3" never exists. It will be in the form 1'-0 2/3".

The integer values 0-3 of the DIMZIN variable control the feet-and-inch dimension only. If you set DIMZIN to 4 (0+4 = 4), the leading zeroes will be omitted in all decimal dimensions; for example, 0.2600 becomes .2600. If you set DIMZIN to 8 (4+4 = 8), the trailing zeroes are omitted; for example, 4.9600 becomes 4.96. If you set DIMZIN to 12 (4+8 = 12), the leading and the trailing zeroes are omitted; for example, 0.2300 becomes .23. The same thing applies to zero suppression for tolerance values. The setting of Zero Suppression for tolerance is stored in DIMZIN system variable.

Scale

You can specify a global scale factor for linear dimension measurements by entering the desired scale factor in the **Linear** edit box. All the linear distances measured by dimensions, which includes radii, diameters, and coordinates, are multiplied by the existing value in the Linear scaling edit box. The angular dimensions are not affected. In this manner the value of the Linear scaling factor affects the content of the default (original) dimension text. Default value for Linear scaling is 1. With the default value the dimension text generated is the actual measurement of the object being dimensioned. The Linear scaling value is saved in the **DIMLFAC** variable.

Note

The linear scaling value is not exercised on rounding value or plus or minus tolerance values. Therefore, changing the linear scaling factor will not affect the tolerance values.

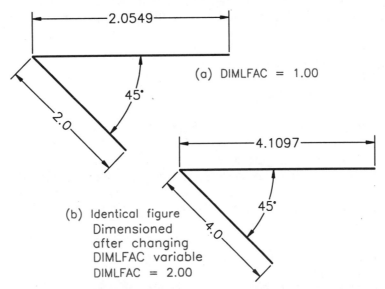

Figure 8-37 Changing dimension length scaling factor, DIMLFAC

Prefix

You can append a prefix to the dimension measurement by entering the desired prefix in the **Prefix:** edit box. The dimension text is converted into the **Prefix < dimension measurement >** format. For example, if you enter the text "Ht" in the Prefix edit box, "Ht" will be placed in front of the dimension text. The prefix string is saved in the **DIMPOST** system variable.

Note

Once you specify a prefix, default prefixes such as R in radius dimensioning and φ in diameter dimensioning are canceled.

Suffix

Just like appending a prefix, you can append a suffix to the dimension measurement by entering the desired suffix in the **Suffix** edit box. For example, if you enter the text cm in the Text Suffix edit box, the dimension text will have < dimension measurement > cm format. When tolerances are enabled (DIMTOL is on), the specified suffix is appended to the main dimension as well as to the upper and lower tolerances values. AutoCAD stores the suffix string in the **DIMPOST** variable.

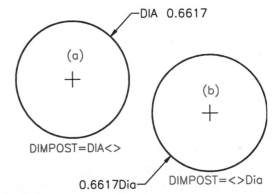

Figure 8-38 Using text prefix and text suffix in dimensioning, DIMPOST

DIMPOST (Using Command Line)

The **DIMPOST** variable is used to define a prefix or suffix to the dimension text. DIMPOST takes a string value as its argument. For example, if you want to have a suffix for centimeters, set DIMPOST to cm. The prompt sequence is as follows:

Command: **DIMPOST**
Current value for DIMPOST, or . for none < "" >: **< >cm**

A distance of 4.0 unit will be displayed as 4.0cm. When tolerances are enabled, the suffix you have defined is applied to the tolerances as well as to the main dimension. To establish a prefix to a dimension text, type the prefix text string and then "< >". For example, if you want R as the prefix for the radius dimension, you can achieve this as follows:

Command: **DIMPOST**
Current value for DIMPOST, or . for none < "" >: **R< >**
Command: **DIMRAD**
Select arc or circle: *Select the circle.*

When you define a prefix with the DIMPOST variable, this prefix nullifies any default prefixes like R in Radius dimensions. For angular dimensions, the < > mechanism is used. To define a prefix or suffix or to prefix the dimension text in DIMPOST, the < > mechanism is used. In this way AutoCAD treats the DIMPOST values like text entered at the **Dimension text:** prompt. For example, if you want to have the prefix **Radius** and the suffix **cm** with the default text, you can set the DIMPOST in the following manner:

Command: **DIMPOST**
Current value < > New value: **Radius < > cm**
Command: **DIMRAD**
Select arc or circle: *Pick the circle and press the Enter key.*

If you want to add the user-defined text above or below the dimension line, use the separator symbol \X. The text that precedes the \X is aligned with the dimension line and positioned above the lines. The text that follows the \X is positioned below the dimension line and aligned with the line. If you want to add more lines, use the symbol \P. (For a detailed description of these symbols, see the MTEXT command in Chapter 5.) The following example illustrates the use of these symbols:

Command: **DIMPOST**
Current value < > New value: **Radius < >\X[In centimeters]**

DIMPOST value	You enter	Value	Type	Dimension text
Default (nil)	*null response*	*1*	*Linear*	*3.00*
Len < >	*null response*	*1*	*Linear*	*Len 3.00*
Default (nil)	*null response*	*3*	*Radial*	*R3.00*
< > R	*null response*	*3*	*Radial*	*3.00 R*
< > R	*< >adius in cm*	*3*	*Radial*	*3.00 Radius in cm*
nil	*Radius < >*	*3*	*Radial*	*Radius 3.00*
mm	*null response*	*1*	*Linear*	*3.00mm*

Tolerance

The **Tolerance** area (Figure 8-39) of the **Annotation** dialogue box lets you specify the tolerance method, tolerance value, justification of tolerance text, and the height of the tolerance text. For example, if you do not want a dimension to deviate more than plus 0.01 and minus 0.02, you can specify that by selecting **Deviation** from the **Method:** pop-up list, then specifying the plus and minus deviation in the **Upper Value:** and the **Lower Value:** edit boxes.

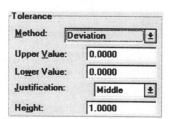

Figure 8-39 Tolerance area of Annotation dialogue box

When you dimension, AutoCAD will automatically append the tolerance to the dimension. Different settings and their effect on relevant dimension variables are explained in the following sections:

Method

The **Method:** pop-up list lets you select the tolerance method. The tolerance methods supported by AutoCAD are Symmetrical, Limits, Deviation, and Basic. The following is the description of these tolerance methods:

Symmetrical

If you select **Symmetrical**, the Lower Value: edit box is disabled and the value specified in the Upper Value: edit box is applied to both plus and minus tolerance. For example, if the value specified in the Upper Value edit box is 0.05, the tolerance appended to the dimension text is ± 0.05.

Deviation

If you select the **Deviation** tolerance method, the values in the **Upper Value** and **Lower Value** edit boxes will be displayed as plus and minus dimension tolerances. If the Upper Value: and the Lower Value: edit boxes contain identical values (both plus and minus tolerances are same), AutoCAD draws a ± symbol followed by the tolerance value when the dimension is drawn. For example, if you enter 0.50 in both the edit boxes the resulting dimension text generated will have the format <dimension measurement> ±0.50.

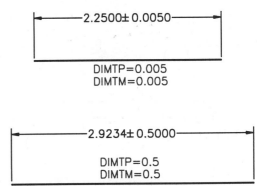

Figure 8-40 Dimensioning with deviation tolerance (when upper value = lower value)

If you do not enter identical values for the plus and minus tolerances, AutoCAD appends a plus sign (+) to the positive values of the tolerance and a negative sign (-) to the negative values of tolerance. For example, if the upper value of the tolerance is 0.005 and the lower value of the tolerance is 0.002, the resulting dimension text generated will have a positive tolerance of 0.005 and a negative tolerance of 0.002:

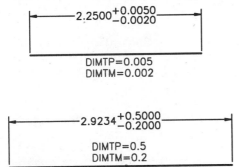

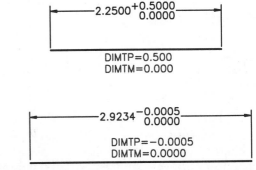

Figure 8-41 Dimensioning with deviation tolerance (when upper value is not equal to lower value)

Figure 8-42 Dimensioning with deviation tolerance

If one of the tolerance values is 0, no sign is appended to it. On picking the deviation tolerance, AutoCAD turns the **DIMTOL** variable on and the **DIMLIM** variable off. The values in the Upper Value and Lower Value edit boxes are saved in the **DIMTP** and **DIMTM** system variables, respectively.

Limits

If you pick the **Limits** tolerance method from the Method: pop-up list, AutoCAD adds the upper value (contents of **Upper Value** edit box) to the dimension text (actual measurement) and subtracts the lower value (contents of the **Lower Value** edit box) from the dimension text. The resulting values are drawn with the dimension text. Selecting **Limits** tolerance method results in turning the **DIMLIM** variable on and the **DIMTOL** variable off. The numeral values in the Upper Value and Lower Value edit boxes are saved in the **DIMTP** and **DIMTM** system variables respectively.

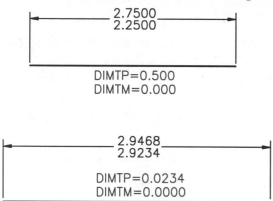

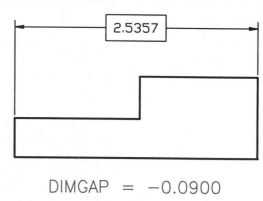

Figure 8-43 Dimensioning with limits tolerance

Figure 8-44 Basic dimension (DIMGAP assigned a negative value)

Basic

A basic dimension text is dimension text with a box drawn around it. Reference dimensions are used primarily in geometric dimensioning and tolerance. The Basic dimension can be realized by picking the basic tolerance method. The Basic dimension is also called a Reference dimension. The distance provided around the dimension text (distance between dimension text and the rectangular box) is stored as a negative value in the **DIMGAP** variable. The negative value signifies basic dimension. The default setting is off (not checked), resulting in generation of dimensions without the box around the dimension text.

None

If you select None in the Method: pop-up list, AutoCAD disables the **Tolerance** area of the Annotation dialogue box. If you do so, no tolerances are appended to dimensions.

Justification

Justification lets you justify the dimension tolerance text. Three justifications are possible: Bottom, Middle, and Top. If you select the Limits tolerance method, the Justification pop-up list is automatically disabled. The settings are saved in the **DIMTOLJ** system variable (Bottom = 0, Middle = 1, and Top = 2).

Height

The **Height** edit box lets you specify the height of the dimension tolerance text relative to the dimension text height. The default value is 1; the height of tolerance text is the same as the dimension text height. If you want the tolerance text to be 75 percent of dimension height text, enter 0.75 in the Height edit box. The ratio of the tolerance height to the dimension text height is calculated by AutoCAD and then stored in the DIMTFAC variable. **DIMTFAC = Tolerance Height/Text Height**

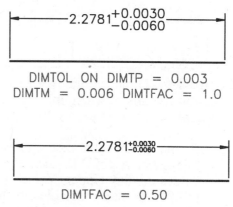

Figure 8-45 Tolerance height, DIMTFAC

Alternate Units

By default, the Alternate Units area is disabled and the value of **DIMALT** variable is turned off. If you want to perform alternate units dimensioning, pick the **Enable Units** check box. By doing so, AutoCAD activates the Units..., Prefix, and Suffix edit boxes. If you select the **Units...** box, AutoCAD displays the **Alternate Units** dialogue box (Figure 8-46) that is identical to **Primary Units** dialogue box discussed

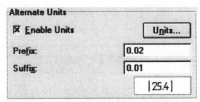

Figure 8-46 Alternate Units area of Annotation dialogue box

earlier. In this dialogue box you can specify the values that will be applied only to alternate dimensions. To generate a value in the alternate system of measurement, you need a factor with which all the linear dimensions will be multiplied. The value for this factor can be entered in the Linear: edit box located in the Scale area of the Alternate Units dialogue box.

Suffixes can be appended to all types of dimensions except angular dimensions. Figure 8-47 shown illustrates the result of entering information in the Alternate Units area. The decimal places get saved in the DIMALTD variable, the scaling value (contents of Linear edit box) in the DIMALTF variable, the angle format for angular dimensions in DIMAUNIT, and the suffix string (contents of the Suffix edit box) in the DIMAPOST variable. Similarly, the number of decimal places for the tolerance value of an alternate dimension is stored in DIMALTTD, suppression of zeros for tolerance values in DIMALTTZ, units format for alternate units in DIMALTU, and suppression of zeros for alternate unit decimal values in DIMALTZ.

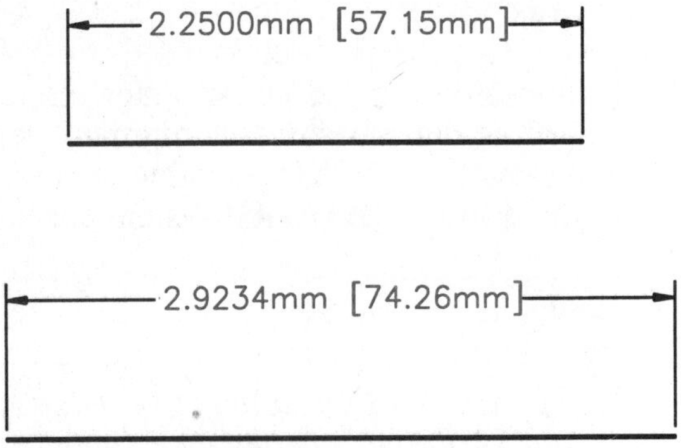

2.2500mm [57.15mm]

2.9234mm [74.26mm]

Figure 8-47 Dimensioning with alternate units

Text

The **Text** area of the **Annotation** dialogue box lets you specify the text style, text height, text gap, and the color of the dimension text. The following is the description of these options:

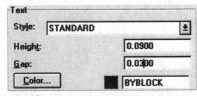

Figure 8-48 Text area of the Annotation dialogue box

Style

If you pick the down arrow in the **Style:** pop-up list, AutoCAD displays the names of the pre-defined text styles. From this list you can pick the style name that you want to use for dimensioning. You must define the text style before you can use it in dimensioning (see the STYLE command). The value of this setting is stored in **DIMTXSTY** system variable. The change in dimension text style does not affect the text style that you are using to draw the text.

Text Height

You can customize the height of the dimension text by entering the required text height in the **Height:** edit box. You can change the dimension text height only when the current text style does not have a fixed height. In other words, the text height specified in the **STYLE** command should be zero because a predefined (specified in the **STYLE** command) text height overrides any other setting for the dimension text height. The value in the Height edit box is stored in the **DIMTXT** variable. The default text height is 0.1800 unit.

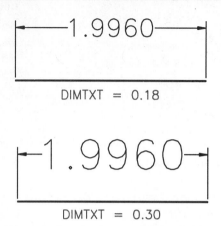

Figure 8-49   Dimension text height, DIMTXT

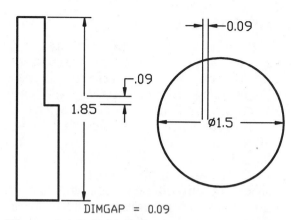

Figure 8-50   Dimension text gap, DIMGAP

Text Gap

The **Gap:** edit box is used to specify the distance between the dimension line and the dimension text. You can enter the text gap you need in this edit box. Text Gap value is also used as the measure of minimum length for the segments of the dimension line and in basic tolerance. The default value specified in this box is 0.09 unit. The value of this setting is stored in the **DIMGAP** system variable.

Note

*You cannot enter a negative value in the **Text Gap** box. Once the **Basic dimension** check box is picked, the negative value is stored in the DIMGAP variable.*

Dimension Text Color

A color can be assigned to the dimension text by specifying it in the **Color:** edit box. The color number or special color label is held in the **DIMCLRT** variable. The default color label is BYBLOCK. Selection of colors has been described in detail earlier in this chapter (see Dimension line, Color in Geometry dialogue box).

Round Off

If you want to round off the dimension distances to a particular value, you can do it by entering the value in the **Round Off:** edit box. For example, if you want to round off all distances to the nearest 0.25 unit, enter 0.25 in the Round Off edit box. The default value for Round Off is 0; rounding does not take place with this value. The round off value does not affect the angular dimensions. The rounding value is saved in the **DIMRND** variable.

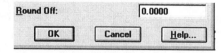

Figure 8-51   Round off area

Note

*The precision value set by the **DIMDEC** command governs the number of digits that lie to the right of the decimal point. DIMRND is independent of the precision value set for the drawing.*

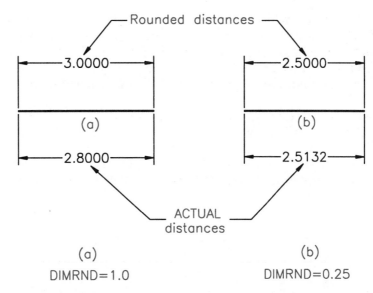

Figure 8-52 Rounding dimension measurements, DIMRND

Exercise 3

Draw the following figure, then set the values in the Geometry, Format, and Annotation dialogue boxes to dimension it as shown. (Dimension line spacing = 0.25, Extension line extension = 0.10, Origin offset = 0.05, Arrowhead size = 0.09, Dimension text height = 0.09). Assume the missing dimensions.

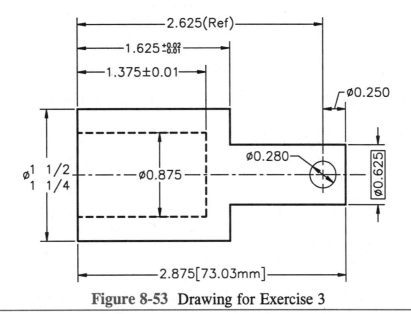

Figure 8-53 Drawing for Exercise 3

OTHER DIMENSIONING VARIABLES

Positioning Dimension Text (DIMTVP)

You can position the dimension text with respect to dimension line by using the **DIMTVP** system variable. In certain cases DIMTVP is used as **DIMTAD** to control the vertical position of the dimension text. DIMTVP value holds only when DIMTAD is off. To select the vertical position of the dimension text to meet your requirement (over or under the dimension line), you must first calculate the numerical value by which you want to offset the text from the dimension line. The vertical placing of the text is done by offsetting the dimension text. The magnitude of the offset of dimension text is a product of text height and DIMTVP value. If the value of DIMTVP is 1.0, DIMTVP acts as DIMTAD. For example, if you want to position the text 0.25 unit (Relative Position) from the dimension line, the value of DIMTVP is calculated as follows:

DIMTVP = Relative Position value/Text Height value.
DIMTVP = 0.25/0.09 = 2.7778

The value 2.7778 is stored in the dimension variable DIMTVP. If the absolute value is less than 0.70, the dimension line is broken to accommodate the dimension text. Relative positioning is not effective on angular dimensions.

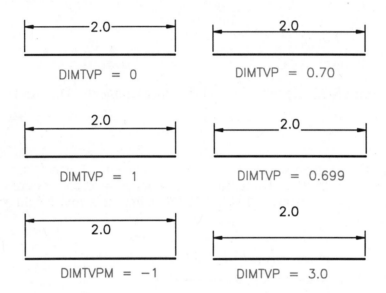

Figure 8-54 DIMTVP, Dimension text vertical position

Horizontal Placement of Text (DIMTIX and DIMSOXD)

DIMTIX System Variable

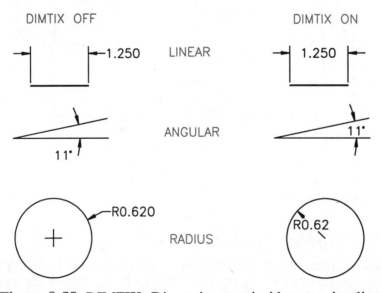

Figure 8-55 DIMTIX, Dimension text inside extension lines

With the help of the DIMTIX (Dimension Text Inside Extension lines) variable, the dimension text can be placed between the extension lines even if it would normally be placed outside the lines. This can be achieved when DIMTIX is on (1). If DIMTIX is off (the default setting), the placement of the dimension text depends on the type of dimension. For example, if the dimensions are Linear or Angular, the text will be placed inside the extension lines by AutoCAD, if there is enough space available. For the Radius and Diameter dimensions, the text is placed outside the object being dimensioned.

Dim: **DIMTIX**
Current value <off> New value:

DIMSOXD System Variable

If you want to place a numeral inside the extension lines, you will have to turn the DIMTIX variable on. And if you want to suppress the dimension lines and the arrowheads you will have to turn the DIMDSOXD (Dimension Suppress Outside Extension Dimension lines) variable on. DIMSOXD suppresses the drawing of dimension lines and the arrowheads when they are placed outside the extension lines. If DIMTIX is on and DIMSOXD is off and there is not enough space inside the extension lines to draw the dimension lines, the lines will be drawn outside the extension lines. In such a situation, if both DIMTIX and DIMSOXD are on, the dimension line will be totally suppressed. DIMSOXD works only when DIMTIX is on. The default value for DIMSOXD and DIMTIX is off.

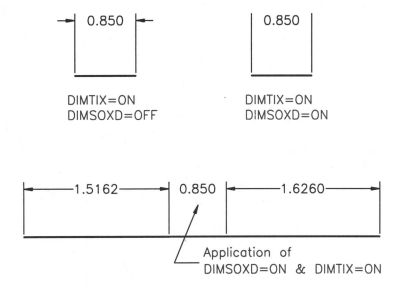

Figure 8-56 DIMSOXD and DIMTIX suppress outside extension lines
and Dimension text inside extension lines

REDEFINITION OF DIMENSION (DIMSHO)

The associative dimension computes dynamically as the dimension is dragged. This feature is controlled by the DIMSHO system variable. By default it is **on**, which means that the dimension will be redefined as it is dragged. Although it is a good feature, sometimes dynamic dragging can be very slow. In that case you can turn it off by setting DIMSHO to **Off**. When you dimension a circle or an arc, the DIMSHO setting is ignored.

DIMENSION STYLE FAMILIES

The dimension style feature of AutoCAD lets the user define a dimension style with values that are common to all dimensions. For example, the arrow size, dimension text height, or color of dimension line are generally the same in all types of dimensioning, like linear, radial, diameter, angular, etc. These dimensioning types belong to same family because they have some characteristics in common. In AutoCAD this is called a **Dimension Style Family**, and the values assigned to the family are called **Dimension Style Family Values**.

After you have defined the Dimension Style Family Values, you can specify variations on it for other types of dimension like radial, diameter, etc. For example, in radial dimensioning if you want to limit the number of decimal places to two, you can specify that value for radial dimensioning. The other values will stay the same as the family values to which this dimension type belongs. When you use the radial dimension, AutoCAD automatically uses the style that was defined for radial dimensioning; otherwise it creates a radial dimension with the values as defined for the family. After you have created and saved a Dimension Family Style, any changes in the parent style are not applied to family members. Special suffix codes are appended to the Family Dimension style name that correspond to different dimension types. For example, if the family dimension style name is MYSTYLE and you define a diameter type of dimension, AutoCAD will append $4 at the end of the Family Dimension style name. The name of the diameter type of dimension will be MYSTYLE$4. The following are the suffix codes for different types of dimensioning:

Suffix Code	Dimension Type	Suffix Code	Dimension Type
0	Linear	2	Angular
3	Radius	4	Diameter
6	Ordinate	7	Leader

The following example illustrates the concepts of Family Style dimensioning:

Example 1

In this example you will perform the following tasks:

1. Specify the values for Dimension Style Family.
2. Specify the values for linear type dimension.
3. Specify the values for diameter type dimension.
4. After saving the dimension style, you will use it to dimension the given drawing.

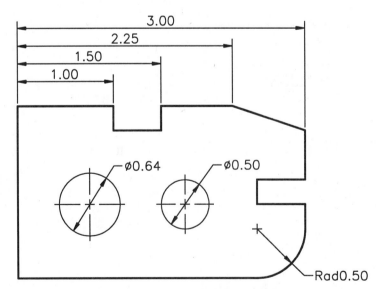

Figure 8-57 Dimensioning using Dimension Style Families

Step 1

Invoke the **Dimension Styles** dialogue box by entering **DDIM** command at AutoCAD Command: prompt. You can also invoke it from the **Dimensioning** toolbar by selecting the **Dimension Styles** icon, the pull-down menu (Select Data, Dimension Style), or the screen menu (Select DRAW DIM, DDim:). If you have not defined any dimension style, AutoCAD will display STANDARD in the Current: edit box. If it does not, select the STANDARD style from the pop-up list.

Step 2

Select the parent button (if it is not already selected), then select the Geometry button to invoke the **Geometry** dialogue box. In this dialogue box change the following values.

Spacing	0.15	**Extension**	0.07	**Origin Offset**	0.03
Arrow Size	0.09	**Center Size**	0.05		

Select the OK button to exit the Geometry dialogue box, then select Annotation button to invoke the **Annotation** dialogue box. In this dialogue box change the following values:

Text Height	0.09	**Text Gap**	0.03

After entering the values, select the OK button to return to the **Dimension Styles** dialogue box. In the **Name:** edit box enter MYSTYLE (the name of the dimension style). Select the Save button to save the dimension style file (MYSTYLE). This dimension style file contains the values that are common to all dimensions types.

Step 3

From the Dimension Styles dialogue box select the Linear radio button, then select the Format button. In the **Format** dialogue box set the following values:

1. Turn off the Inside Horizontal and Outside Horizontal check boxes.
2. In Vertical Justification, select **Above**.

Select the OK button to return to the Dimension Styles dialogue box. From this box select the Annotation button to display the **Annotation** dialogue box. In this dialogue box change the following values:

1. Decimal units.
2. Dimension precision to 2 places of decimal.
3. Tolerance precision to 2 places of decimal.

Select the OK button to return to the Annotation dialogue box. Select the OK button again to return to the Dimension Styles dialogue box. Select the Save button to save the changes.

Step 4

In the **Dimension Styles** dialogue box select the Diameter radio button, then select the Format button. In the **Format** dialogue box select the User Defined check box. Select the OK button to return to the Dimension Styles dialogue box. In this dialogue box select the Annotation button. In the **Annotation** dialogue box select the Units button and set the precision to two places of decimal. Return to the Dimension Styles dialogue box. Select the Save button to save the changes. Select the OK button to exit from the Dimension Styles dialogue box.

Step 5

Use the **DIMLIN** and **DIMBASE** commands to draw the linear dimensions as shown in Figure 8-57. Notice that when you enter any linear dimensioning command, AutoCAD automatically uses the values that were defined for the Linear type of dimensioning.

Step 6
Use the DIMDIA command to dimension the circles as shown in Figure 8-57. Again notice that the dimensions are drawn according to the values specified for Diameter type of dimensioning.

Step 7
Now define the values for the Radial type of dimensioning, then dimension the arc as shown in Figure 8-57. Good luck!

USING DIMENSION STYLE OVERRIDES

Most of the dimension characteristics are common in a production drawing. The values that are common to different dimensioning types can be defined in the dimension style family. However, at times you might have different dimensions. For example, you may need two types of linear dimensioning; one with tolerance and one without. One way to draw these dimensions is to create two dimensioning styles. You can also use the dimension variable overrides to override the existing values. For example, you can define a dimension style (MYSTYLE) that draws dimensions without tolerance. Now, to draw a dimension with tolerance or update an existing dimension, you can override the previously defined value. You can override the values through the Dimension Styles dialogue box or by setting the variable values at Command prompt. The following example illustrates how to use the dimension style overrides:

Example 2

In this example you will update the overall dimension (3.00) so that the tolerance is displayed with the dimension. You will also add two linear dimensions as shown in Figure 8-58.

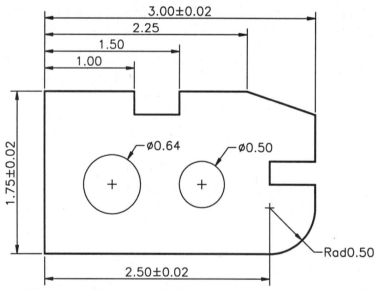

Figure 8-58   Overriding the dimension style values

Using Dimension Styles

Step 1
Invoke the **Dimension Styles** dialogue box and select the **Annotation** button to display the Annotation dialogue box. In this dialogue box specify the tolerance, symmetrical with upper value 0.02. Select the OK button to exit the dialogue box. Notice that the current style has changed to +MYSTYLE, indicating that override exists for MYSTYLE dimension style. If you override another value or any number of values, they will be saved in +MYSTYLE. AutoCAD does not create additional files to store other overridden values.

Step 2
Use the DIMSTYLE command to apply the change to the existing dimensions.

> Command: **DIMSTYLE**
> Dimension Style Edit (Save/Restore/STatus/Variables/Apply/?) <Restore>: **A**
> Select objects: *Select the dimensions that you want to update.*

After you select the dimension, AutoCAD will update the dimension and the tolerance will be appended to the selected dimension. If you create a new dimension, the tolerance value will be automatically displayed with the dimension, unless you make DIMSTYLE (Dimension style) current. This is not possible if you override a dimension style value using other commands, like DDMODIFY or DIMOVERRIDE.

Using DDMODIFY Command

Step 1
You can also use the **DDMODIFY** command to modify a dimension. Enter DDMODIFY at Command prompt and select the dimension you want to modify.

> Command: **DDMODIFY**
> Select object to modify: *Select the dimension.*

Step 2
After you select the dimension, AutoCAD will display the **Modify Dimension** dialogue box. From this dialogue box select the Annotation button to display the **Annotation** dialogue box. Specify the tolerance for linear dimension: Symmetrical with Upper Value 0.02. Select the OK button to exit the Annotation and Modify Dimension dialogue boxes. The dimension will be updated to new specifications. (See Chapter 7, "Editing Dimensions", for details.)

Using DIMOVERRIDE Command

Step 1
You can also use the **DIMOVERRIDE** command to override a dimension value. If you want to have tolerance displayed with the dimension, make sure the tolerances are specified. Use the following command to specify the tolerance:

> Command: **DIMTP**
> The value for DIMTP <0.0000>:): 0.02

> Command: **DIMTM**
> The value for DIMTM <0.0000>:): 0.02

Step 2
Use the DIMOVERRIDE command to override the selected dimension.

> Command: **DIMOVERRIDE**
> Dimension variable to override (or Clear to remove overrides): **DIMTOL**
> Current value <off> New value: **ON**
> Dimension variable to override: ←⏎
> Select objects: *Select the object that you want to update.*

You can also update a dimension by entering **Update** at **Dim:** prompt. For details, see Chapter 7, "Editing Dimensions."

COMPARING AND LISTING DIMENSION STYLES (DIMSTYLE COMMAND)

The Save, Restore, and Apply options of the **DIMSTYLE** command have been discussed earlier in this chapter. You can also use this command to ascertain the status of a dimension style or compare a dimension style with the current style.

Comparing Dimension Styles

You can compare the current dimension style with another style by appending the tilde (~) symbol in front of the dimension style name.

> Command: **DIMSTYLE**
> Dimension Style Edit (Save/Restore/STatus/Variables/Apply/?) <Restore>: **R**
> ?/Enter dimension style name or RETURN to select dimension: **~Standard**

AutoCAD will display a listing of dimension variable names and their values for the standard dimension style and the current dimension style. Only those variables that have different values in the current and the named styles are listed.

Listing Dimension Styles

The **STatus** option of **DIMSTYLE** command displays the **current** dimensioning status. You can also use the question mark (**?**) to display the named dimension styles in the current drawing.

> Command: **DIMSTYLE**
> Dimension Style Edit (Save/Restore/STatus/Variables/Apply/?) <Restore>: **ST** or **?**

If you select the **Variables** option, AutoCAD will display the dimension status of the named dimension style or the dimension style that is associated with the selected dimension.

> Command: **DIMSTYLE**
> Dimension Style Edit (Save/Restore/STatus/Variables/Apply/?) <Restore>: **V**
> ?/Enter dimension style name or RETURN to select dimension: **MYSTYLE**

USING EXTERNALLY REFERENCED DIMENSION STYLES

The externally referenced dimensions cannot be used directly in the current drawing. When you XREF a drawing, the drawing name is appended to the style name and the two are separated by the vertical bar (|) symbol. It uses the same syntax as other externally dependent symbols. For example, if the drawing (FLOOR) has a dimension style called DECIMAL and you Xref this drawing in the current drawing, AutoCAD will rename the dimension style to FLOOR|DECIMAL. You cannot make this dimension style current, nor can you modify it. However, you can use it as a template to create a new style. To accomplish this, invoke the **Dimension Styles** dialogue box and make the FLOOR|DECIMAL style current. In the **Name:** edit box enter the name of the dimension style and save it. AutoCAD will create a new dimension style with the same values as those of the externally referenced dimension style (FLOOR|DECIMAL).

LIST OF DIMENSIONING VARIABLES

VARIABLE NAME	DEFAULT SETTING	DESCRIPTION
DIMALT	0	Alternate units
DIMALTD	2	Decimal places
DIMALTF	25.4000	Alternate Units Scale Factor
DIMALTTD	2	Decimal places for tolerance value of alternate units
DIMALTTZ	0	Suppression of zeros for tolerance value
DIMALTU	2	Units format for alternate units
DIMALTZ	0	Suppression of zeros for alternate units
DIMAPOST	25.4000	Alternate Units Text Suffix
DIMASO	1	Associative Dimensioning
DIMASZ	0.1800	Arrow Size
DIMAUNIT	0	Angle format
DIMBLK	0.1800	Arrow Block
DIMBLK1	0.1800	Separate Arrow Block 1
DIMBLK2	0.1800	Separate Arrow Block 2
DIMCEN	0.0900	Center Mark Size
DIMCLRD	0	Dimension Line Color
DIMCLRE	0	Extension Line Color
DIMCLRT	0	Dimension Text Color
DIMDEC	4	Decimal places for dimension units
DIMDLE	0.0000	Dimension Line Extension
DIMDLI	0.3800	Dimension Line Increment
DIMEXE	0.1800	Extension Line Extension
DIMEXO	0.0625	Extension Line Offset
DIMFIT	3	Extension Line Offset
DIMGAP	0.0900	Dimension Line Gap and Reference Dimensioning

VARIABLE NAME	DEFAULT SETTING	DESCRIPTION
DIMJUST	0	Horizontal dim. text position
DIMLFAC	1.0000	Length Factor
DIMLIM	0	Dimensioning of Limits
DIMPOST	0	Dimension Text Prefix, Suffix, or both
DIMRND	0.0000	Rounding a Value
DIMSAH	0	Separate Arrow Blocks
DIMSCALE	1.0000	Dimension Feature Scale Factor
DIMSD1	Off	Suppress first dimension line
DIMSD2	off	Suppress second dimension line
DIMSE1	0	Suppress Extension Line 1
DIMSE2	0	Suppress Extension Line 2
DIMSHO	0	Show Dragged Dimension
DIMSOXD	0	Suppress Outside Dimension Lines
DIMSTYLE		Current Dimension Style Name
DIMTAD	0	Text Above Dimension Line
DIMTDEC	4	Decimal places for tolerance value
DIMTFAC	1.0000	Tolerance Text Scale Factor
DIMTIH	1	Text Inside Horizontal
DIMTIX	0	Text Inside Extension Lines
DIMTM	0.0000	Minus Tolerance Value
DIMTOFL	0	Text Outside, Force Line Inside
DIMTOH	1	Text Outside Horizontal
DIMTOL	Off	Tolerance Dimensioning
DIMTOLJ	Off	Vertical justification for tolerance Dimensioning
DIMTP	0.0000	Plus Tolerance Value
DIMTSZ	0.0000	Tick Size

VARIABLE NAME	DEFAULT SETTING	DESCRIPTION
DIMTVP	0.0000	Text Vertical Position
DIMTXSTY	Standard	Dimension Text Style
DIMTXT	0.1800	Text Size
DIMTZIN	0	Suppress zeros for tolerance value
DIMUNIT	2	Unit format for dimension style
DIMUPT	Off	Cursor functionality
DIMZIN	0	Zero Suppression

SELF EVALUATION TEST

Answer the following questions and then compare your answers with the correct answers given at the end of this chapter

1. What is the function of the DDIM command? _____
    _____

2. How can you create a dimension style of your requirement? _____
    _____

3. Fill in the command and entries required to scale the dimensioning variables that reflect sizes, distances, or offsets (such as arrow size, text size, etc.) by a value of 2.0.
    Command: _____
    DIM: _____
    Current value <1.0000> New value: _____

4. Fill in the command and entries required to specify suffix inches to an alternate dimensioning measurement.
    Command: _____
    DIM: _____
    Current value < > New value: _____

5. Fill in the command and entries required to place the dimension text above the dimension line by a magnitude of 1 unit. Let the value of DIMTXT be 0.1800.
    Command: _____
    DIM: _____
    Current value <0.0000> New value: _____

6. The **DIMALT** variable controls the alternate units dimensioning. (T/F)

7. The size of the center mark is governed by the **DIMCEN** variable. (T/F)

8. The **DIMEXE** variable governs the distance the extension lines are offset from the origin points of the extension lines that you have specified. (T/F)

9. All the dimensioning variables specifying sizes, offsets, or distances are scaled by the contents of the **DIMLFAC** variable. (T/F)

10. With the **DIMPOST** variable, you can only define a suffix to the dimension text. (T/F)

11. Setting the value of the **DIMZIN** variable to 0 results in the suppression of 0 feet and exactly 0 inches. (T/F)

12. A negative value (greater than -.7) for the **DIMTVP** variable results in generation of dimension text below the dimension line. (T/F)

13. If the **DIMTIH** variable is on, the dimension text inside the extension lines is always drawn horizontally. (T/F)

14. A value of 0.50 for the **DIMTFAC** variable results in a text height for the tolerance values of half of the main dimension text height. (T/F)

15. The **DIMCLRD** variable is used to assign color to the arrowheads. (T/F)

REVIEW QUESTIONS

Answer the following questions

1. Fill in the command and entries required to change the color of the dimension line to red.
    Command: _____
    DIM: _____
    Current value <BYBLOCK> New value: _____

2. Fill in the command and entries required to extend the dimension line past the extension lines (when tick marks are used instead of the regular arrow marks) by a distance of 0.0250 unit.
    Command: _____
    New value for _____ <0.0000>: _____

3. Fill in the command and entries required to change the offset distance for the extension lines (distance between the dimension line and start of the extension line) to 0.1000.
    Command: _____
    DIM: _____
    Current value <0.0625> New value: _____

4. Fill in the command and entries required to multiply all linear distances such as radii, diameters, and coordinates by a factor of 2.0.
    Command: _____
    New value for _____ <1.0000>: _____

5. Fill in the command and entries required to specify prefix Depth and suffix cm to the dimension measurement.
    Command: _____
    DIM: _____
    Current value < > New value: _____

6. Fill in the command and entries required to specify suffix feet to the dimension measurement as well as the tolerances.
    Command: _____
    DIM: _____
    Current value < > New value: _____

7. Fill in the command and entries required to generate an alternate dimensioning measurement in centimeters considering that the main dimension is showing distance in inches.
   Command: _____
   DIM: _____
   Current value <off> New value: _____
   DIM: _____
   Current value <25.4000> New value: _____

8. The **DIMALT** variable governs the factor by which all linear dimensions will be multiplied to generate a value in alternate units. (T/F)

9. The character string specified in the **DIMAPOST** variable is appended at the end of the main dimension text. (T/F)

10. By default the **DIMASO** variable is off, therefore associative dimensioning is disabled. (T/F)

11 The **DIMBLK** variable stores the name of the block that is to be drawn at the two ends of the dimension line instead of the regular arrows. (T/F)

12. If **DIMASH** is on and you only define one arrow block (say **DIMBLK1**), the arrow at the other end will be the arrow block defined by **DIMBLK**; otherwise a default arrow is drawn. (T/F)

13. If the value in the **DIMCEN** variable is greater than zero, center lines are drawn. (T/F)

14. The **DIMCLRE** variable is used to specify the color of the dimension text. (T/F)

15. The **DIMGAP** variable controls the distance between the beginning of the extension lines and the origin points of the extension lines. (T/F)

16. If you specify a negative value for the **DIMGAP** variable, a box is drawn around the dimension text. (T/F)

17. The **DIMSCALE** variable acts as a general scale factor for linear dimension measurements, hence all linear distances are multiplied by the contents of **DIMSCALE** variable before being output as the dimension text. (T/F)

18. If the **DIMSE1** variable is on, the first extension line is suppressed. (T/F)

19. Setting the value of the **DIMZIN** variable to 2 results in the inclusion of zero feet and suppresses zero inches. (T/F)

20. Setting the value of the **DIMZIN** variable to 1 results in the inclusion of zero feet and exactly zero inches. (T/F)

21. You can control the text style with the help of the **DIMTXT** variable. (T/F)

22. If the absolute value of the **DIMTVP** variable is less than 0.7, the dimension line does not split to accommodate the dimension text. (T/F)

23. If the **DIMTOH** variable is on, the dimension text outside the extension lines is always aligned with the dimension line. (T/F)

24. What is the dimension style family and how does it help in dimensioning? _____

25. What are the different ways to access the Dimension Styles dialogue box?

26. Explain various methods that can be used to change the value of a dimension variable._____
_____

27. How can you use the dimension style that has been defined in the Xref drawing? Explain. _____
_____

28. Explain dimension overrides. _____
_____

29. What are the different ways to override an existing dimensions? _____
_____

30. How can you compare a named dimension style with the current style? _____
_____

31. The dimension variable DIMEXO controls the _____.

32. The dimension variable DIMTVP controls the _____.

33. The dimension variable DIMSE1 controls the _____.

34. The dimension variable DIMSE2 controls the _____.

35. The dimension variable DIMDLI controls the _____.

36. The dimension variable DIMDLI controls the _____.

37. Explain the use of the DIMOVERRIDE command and how it works. _____
_____

38. How can you compare the settings of the dimension variables of the current dimension style with those of another dimension style? _____
_____

39. Which dimensioning command is used to display the list of all dimension variables and their current settings? _____
_____

40. In oblique dimensioning, the extension lines are always drawn perpendicular to the dimension line. (T/F)

41. A group of dimension variables with some setting is termed a dimension style. (T/F)

42. Dimension style cannot have a name. (T/F)

43. The dimension style used to create a particular dimension can be revoked later by picking that dimension. (T/F)

44. When the DIMTVP variable has a negative value, the dimension text is placed below the dimension line. (T/F)

45. The named dimension style associated with the dimension being updated with the **Override** command is not updated. (T/F)

46. You can restore an existing dimension style as the current style with the **Restore** Command. (T/F)

EXERCISES

Exercises 4 - 9

Make the drawings as shown in Figure 8-59 through Figure 8-64. You must create dimension style files and specify values for different dimension types like linear, radial, diameter, and ordinate. Assume the missing dimensions.

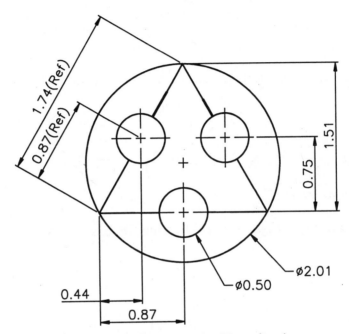

Figure 8-59 Drawing for Exercise 4

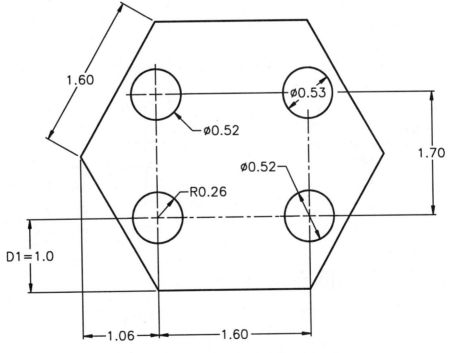

Figure 8-60 Drawing for Exercise 5

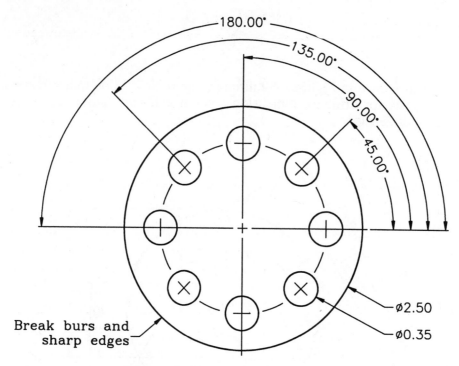

Figure 8-61 Drawing for Exercise 6

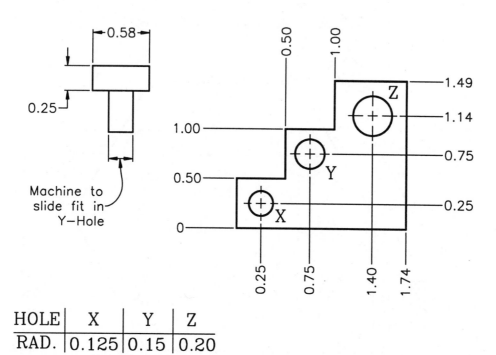

HOLE	X	Y	Z
RAD.	0.125	0.15	0.20

Figure 8-62 Drawing for Exercise 7

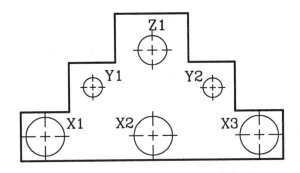

HOLE	X1	X2	X3	Y1	Y2	Z1
DIM.	R0.2	R0.2	R0.2	R0.1	R0.1	R0.15
QTY.	1	1	1	1	1	1
X	0.25	1.375	2.50	0.75	2.0	1.375
Y	0.25	0.25	0.25	0.75	0.75	1.125
Z	THRU	THRU	THRU	1.0	1.0	THRU

Figure 8-63 Drawing for Exercise 8

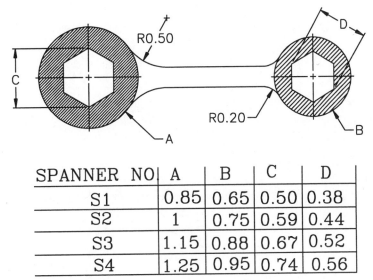

SPANNER NO	A	B	C	D
S1	0.85	0.65	0.50	0.38
S2	1	0.75	0.59	0.44
S3	1.15	0.88	0.67	0.52
S4	1.25	0.95	0.74	0.56

Figure 8-64 Drawing for Exercise 9

Answers

The following are the correct answers to the questions in the self evaluation test.
1 - Invokes Dimension Styles dialogue box. **2** - By using the Dimension Styles dialogue box or by assigning values to dimensioning variables, **3** - DIM/DIMSCALE/2, **4** - DIM/DIMPOST/inches. **5** - DIM/DIMTVP/5.555, **6** - T, **7** - T, **8** - F, **9** - F, **10** - F, **11** - T, **12** - T, **13** - T, **14** - T, **15** - T

Chapter 9

Geometric Dimensioning and Tolerancing

Learning objectives

After completing this chapter, you will be able to:
- Use geometric tolerance components to specify tolerances.
- Use feature control frames and geometric characteristics symbols.
- Use tolerance values and material condition modifier.
- Use complex feature control frames.
- Combine geometric characteristics and create composite position tolerancing.
- Use projected tolerance zones.
- Use feature control frames with leader.

GEOMETRIC DIMENSIONING AND TOLERANCING

One of the most important parts of the design process is giving the dimensions and tolerances, since every part is manufactured from the dimensions given in the drawing. Therefore, every designer must understand and have a thorough knowledge of the standard practices used in industry to make sure that the information given on the drawing is correct and can be understood by other people. Tolerancing is equally important, especially in the assembled parts. Tolerances and fits determine how the parts will fit. Incorrect tolerances may result in a product that is not usable.

In addition to dimensioning and tolerancing, the function and the relationship that exists between the mating parts is important if the part is to perform the way it was designed. This aspect of the design process is addressed by **Geometric Dimensioning and Tolerancing**, generally known as GDT. Geometric dimensioning and tolerancing is a means to design and manufacture parts with respect to actual function and the relationship that exists between different features of the same part or the features of the mating parts. Therefore, a good design is not achieved by just giving dimensions and tolerances. The designer has to go beyond dimensioning and think of the intended function of the part and how the features of the part are going to affect its function. For example, Figure 9-1 shows a part that has the required dimensions and tolerances. However, in this drawing there is no mention of the relationship that exists between the pin and the plate. Is the pin perpendicular to the plate? If it is, to what degree should it be perpendicular? Also, it does not mention on which surface the perpendicularity of the pin is to be measured. A design like this is open to individual interpretation based on intuition and experience. This is where geometric dimensioning and tolerancing plays an important part in the product design process.

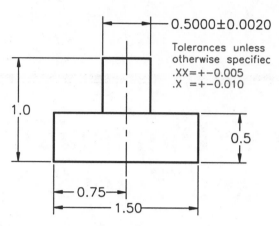

Figure 9-1 Using traditional dimensioning and tolerancing technique

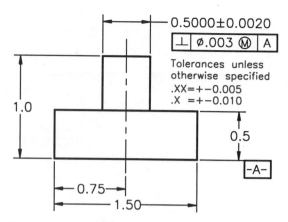

Figure 9-2 Using geometric dimensioning and tolerancing

Figure 9-2 has been dimensioned using geometric dimensioning and tolerancing. The feature symbols define the datum (reference plane) and the permissible deviation in the perpendicularity of the pin with respect to the bottom surface. In a drawing like this, the chances of making a mistake are minimized. Before discussing the application of AutoCAD commands in geometric dimensioning and tolerancing, you need to understand the following feature symbols and tolerancing components:

GEOMETRIC CHARACTERISTICS AND SYMBOLS

Figure 9-3 shows the geometric characteristics and symbols used in geometric dimensioning and tolerancing. These symbols are the building blocks of geometric dimensioning and tolerancing.

KIND OF FEATURE	TYPE OF FEATURE	CHARACTERISTICS	
INDIVIDUAL	FORM	Straightness	—
		Flatness	▱
		Circularity	○
INDIVIDUAL or RELATED	PROFILE	Cylindricity	⌀
		Profile of a line	⌒
		Profile of a surface	⌓
RELATED	ORIENTATION	Angularity	∠
		Perpendicularity	⊥
		Parallelism	//
	LOCATION	Position	⊕
		Concentricity	◎
		Symmetry	=
	RUNOUT	Cicular runout	∕
		Total runout	⌰

Figure 9-3 Geometric characteristics and symbols used in geometric dimensioning and tolerancing

GEOMETRIC TOLERANCE COMPONENTS

The following is the list of the geometric tolerance components; Figure 9-4 shows their placement in the tolerance frame.

Feature control frame
Geometric characteristics symbol
Tolerance value
Tolerance zone descriptor
Material condition modifier
Datum reference

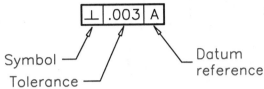

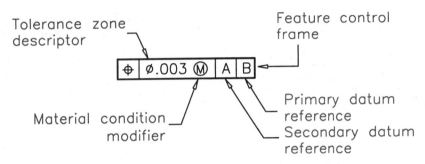

Figure 9-4 Components of geometric tolerance

Feature Control Frame

The feature control frame is a rectangular box that contains the geometric characteristics symbols and tolerance definition. The box is automatically drawn to standard specifications; you do not need to specify its size.

Geometric Characteristics Symbol

Toolbar:	Dimensioning, Tolerance
Pull-down:	Draw, Dimensioning, Tolerance...
Screen:	DRAW DIM, Toleran:

Figure 9-5 Selecting Tolerance from the Dimensioning toolbar

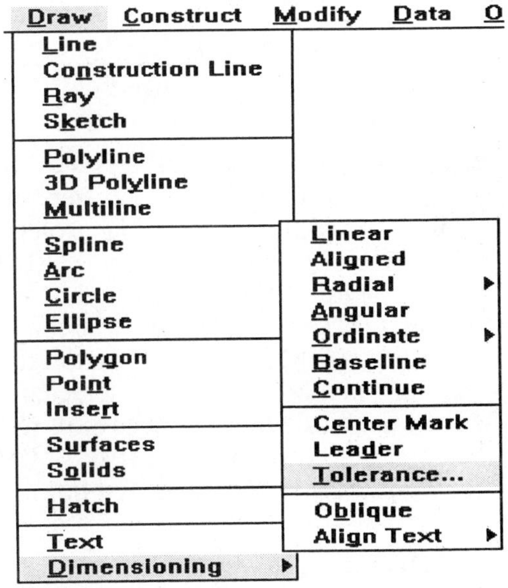

Figure 9-6 Selecting Tolerance from the pull-down menu

The Geometric Characteristics Symbol indicates the characteristics of the feature. For example, straightness, flatness or perpendicularity describe the characteristics of a feature. These symbols can be picked from the **Symbol** dialogue box (Figure 9-7). This dialogue box can be invoked from the **Dimensioning** toolbar (Figure 9-5) by selecting the **Tolerance** icon, from the pull-down menu (Select Draw, Dimensioning, Tolerance..., Figure 9-6), from the screen menu

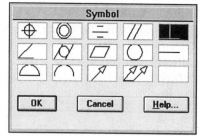

Figure 9-7 The Symbol dialogue box

(Select DRAW DIM, Toleran:), or by entering **TOL** at the **Command:** prompt. You can also access this dialogue box by selecting the **Sym** box in the Geometric Tolerance dialogue box.

Tolerance Value and Tolerance Zone Descriptor

The Tolerance Value specifies the tolerance on the feature as indicated by the tolerance zone descriptor. For example, if the value is .003, that indicates that the feature must be within 0.003 tolerance zone. Similarly, ϕ.003 indicates that this feature must be located at true position within 0.003 diameter. The tolerance value can be entered in the **Value** edit box of Geometric Tolerance dialogue box. The Tolerance Zone Descriptor can be selected by picking the box labeled Dia. The **Geometric Tolerance** dialogue box (Figure 9-8) can be invoked by selecting the **OK** button in the **Symbol** dialogue box after selecting the desired symbol.

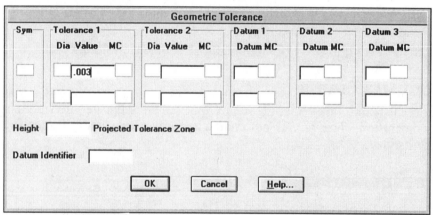

Figure 9-8 The Geometric Tolerance dialogue box

Material Condition Modifier

The Material Condition Modifier specifies the material condition when the tolerance value takes effect. For example, ϕ.003(M) indicates that this feature must be located at true position within 0.003 diameter at maximum material condition (MMC). The material condition modifier symbol can be selected from the **Material Condition** dialogue box (Figure 9-9).

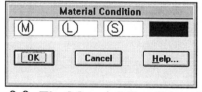

Figure 9-9 The Material Condition dialogue box

This dialogue box can be invoked by selecting the **MC** button located just below Datum MC in the **Geometric Tolerance** dialogue box.

Datum

The Datum is the origin, surface, or feature from which the measurements are made. The datum is also used to establish the geometric characteristics of a feature. The Datum feature symbol consists of a reference character enclosed in a feature control frame. You can create the datum feature symbol by entering characters (**-A-**) in the **Datum Identifier** edit box in the **Geometric Tolerance** dialogue box and then selecting a point where you want to establish that datum.

You can also combine datum references with geometric characteristics. AutoCAD automatically positions the datum references on the right end of the feature control frame.

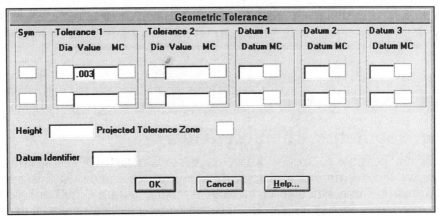

Figure 9-10 The Geometric Tolerance dialogue box

Example 1

In the following example you will create a feature control frame to require a perpendicularity specification.

Step 1
Use the TOLERANCE command to display the **Symbol** dialogue box. Select the perpendicularity symbol in the dialogue box and then select the **OK** button to display the **Geometric Tolerance** dialogue box.

Step 2
The perpendicularity symbol will be displayed in the **Sym** edit box on the first row of the **Geometric Tolerance** dialogue box. Select the **Dia** edit box in the Tolerance 1 area on the first row. A diameter symbol will appear to denote a cylindrical tolerance zone.

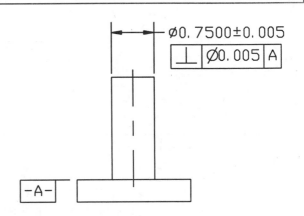

Figure 9-11 Drawing for Example 1

Step 3
Select the **Value** edit box in the Tolerance 1 area on the first row and enter 0.005.

Step 4
Select the **Datum** edit box in the Datum 1 area on the first row and enter A.

Step 5
Select the OK button to accept the changes made in the **Geometric Tolerance** dialogue box. The **Enter tolerance location:** prompt is displayed in the Command line area. Here select a point to insert the frame. This point will be the middle left point of the frame.

Step 6

To place the datum symbol, use the **TOLERANCE** command to display the **Symbol** dialogue box. Select the OK button to display the **Geometric Tolerance** dialogue box. Select the **Datum Identifier** edit box and enter -A-.

Step 7

Select the OK button to accept the changes to the **Geometric Tolerance** dialogue box and then select a point to insert the frame. This point will be the upper left point of the frame.

COMPLEX FEATURE CONTROL FRAMES

Combining Geometric Characteristics

Sometimes it is not possible to specify all geometric characteristics in one frame. For example, Figure 9-12 shows the drawing of a plate with a hole in the center. In this part it is determined that surface C must be perpendicular to surfaces A and B within 0.002 and 0.004, respectively. Therefore, we need two frames to specify the geometric characteristics of surface C. The first frame specifies the allowable deviation in perpendicularity of surface C with respect to surface A. The second frame specifies the allowable deviation in perpendicularity of surface C with respect to surface B. In addition to these two frames, we need a third frame that identifies datum surface C.

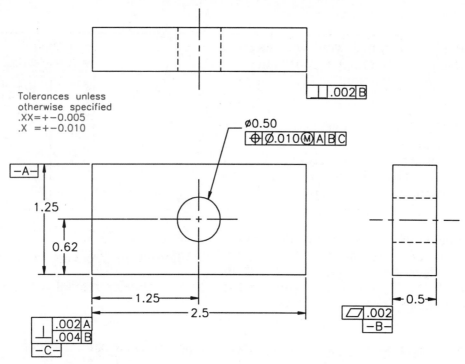

Figure 9-12 Combining feature control frames with different geometric characteristics

To create these three feature control frames, each frame has to be defined separately. These three frames can be created as follows:

1. To create the first frame, enter the **TOL** command to invoke the **Symbol** dialogue box. Select the perpendicular symbol, then select the OK button. AutoCAD will display the **Geometric Tolerance** dialogue box.

2. Enter the geometric characteristics and the datum reference in the Geometric Tolerance dialogue box. Select the OK button.

3. Select the point where you want to insert the frame.

4. To create the second and third frames, repeat the above steps (1 through 3) and specify the values that must appear in this frame. In the **Datum Identifier** edit box enter -C-, then select the OK button to exit the dialogue box.

The third frame can be created as follows:

1. To create the third frame, select the OK button in the **Symbol** dialogue box. AutoCAD will display the **Geometric Tolerance** dialogue box.

2. In this dialogue box, enter the letter C with dashes (-C-) in the Datum 1 column. Select the OK button and position the frame just below the second frame. You can also create the second and third frames by making a copy of the first frame and using the DDEDIT command to edit the values. When you select the frame to be edited, AutoCAD displays the Geometric Tolerance dialogue box on the screen. You can enter the new values, then select the OK button to update the selected feature control frame.

Composite Position Tolerancing

Sometimes the accuracy required within a pattern is more important than the location of the pattern with the datum surfaces. To specify such a condition, composite position tolerancing may be used. For example, Figure 9-13 shows four holes (pattern) of diameter 0.15. The design allows a maximum tolerance of 0.025 with respect to datums A, B, and C at the Maximum Material Condition (holes are smallest). The designer wants to maintain a closer positional tolerance (0.010 at MMC) between the holes within the pattern. To specify this requirement, the designer must insert the second frame to specify this requirement. This is generally known as Composite Position Tolerancing. AutoCAD provides the facility to create the two composite position tolerance frames by using the Geometric Tolerance dialogue box. The composite tolerance frames can be created as follows:

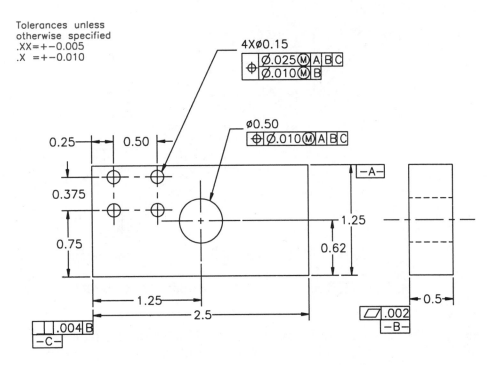

Figure 9-13 Using composite position tolerancing

1. Enter the TOL command to invoke the **Symbol** dialogue box. Select the position symbol, then select the OK button from this dialogue box. AutoCAD will display the **Geometric Tolerance** dialogue box.

2. In the first row of the Geometric Tolerance dialogue box, enter the geometric characteristics and the datum references required for the first position tolerance frame.

3. In the second row of the **Geometric Tolerance** dialogue box, enter the geometric characteristics and the datum references required for the second position tolerance frame.

4. When you have finished entering the values, select the OK button in the Geometric Tolerance dialogue box, then select the point where you want to insert the frames. AutoCAD will create the two frames and automatically align them with common position symbol as shown in Figure 9-13.

Projected Tolerance Zone

Figure 9-14 shows two parts that are joined with a bolt. The lower part is threaded and the top part has a drilled hole. When these two parts are joined, the bolt that is threaded in the lower part will have the orientation error that exists in the threaded hole. In other words, the error in the threaded hole will extend beyond the part thickness, which might cause interference and the parts may not assemble.

To avoid this problem, projected tolerance is used. The projected tolerance establishes a tolerance zone that extends above the surface. In Figure 9-14, the position tolerance for the threaded hole is 0.010, which extends 0.25 above the surface (datum A). By using the projected tolerance, you can ensure that the bolt is within the tolerance zone up to the specified distance.

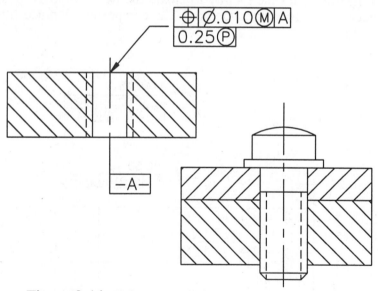

Figure 9-14 Using composite position tolerancing

You can use AutoCAD's GDT feature to create feature control frames for the projected tolerance zone as follows:

1. Enter the **TOL** command to invoke the **Symbol** dialogue box. Select the position symbol, then select the OK button from this dialogue box. AutoCAD will display the **Geometric Tolerance** dialogue box.

2. In the first row of the **Geometric Tolerance** dialogue box, enter the geometric characteristics and the datum references required for the first position tolerance frame (See Figure 9-15).

3. In the **Height** edit box, enter the height of the tolerance zone (0.25 for the given drawing) and pick the edit box to the right of **Projected tolerance zone**. The projected tolerance zone symbol will be displayed in the box.

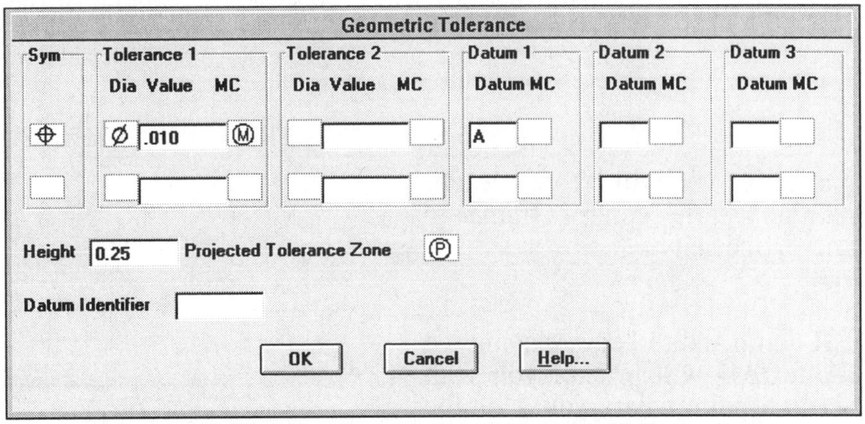

Figure 9-15 The Geometric Tolerance dialogue box

4. Once you are done entering the values, select the OK button in the **Geometric Tolerance** dialogue box, then select the point where you want to insert the frames. AutoCAD will create the two frames and automatically align them as shown in Figure 9-15.

USING FEATURE CONTROL FRAMES WITH THE LEADER COMMAND

The LEADER command has the Tolerance option, which allows you to create the Feature Control Frame and attach it to the end of the leader extension line. The following is the command prompt sequence for using the LEADER command with the Tolerance option:

Command: **LEADER**
From point: Select a point where you want the arrow (P1)
To point (Format/Annotatio/Undo)<Annotation>: *Select a point (P2).*
To point (Format/Annotatio/Undo)<Annotation>: *Select a point (P3).*
To point (Format/Annotatio/Undo)<Annotation>: ←⟍
Annotation (or RETURN for options): ←⟍
Tolerance/Copy/Block/None/<Mtext>: **T**

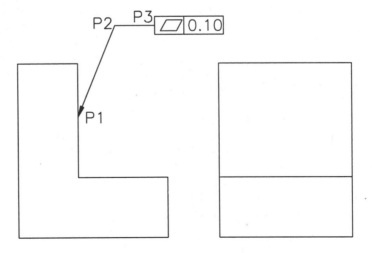

Figure 9-16 Using feature control frame with the leader

When you select the Tolerance (T) option, AutoCAD will display the **Symbol** dialogue box. Select the desired symbol, then pick the OK button to invoke the **Geometric Tolerance** dialogue box. Enter the required values and select the OK button to exit the dialogue box. The feature control frame with the defined geometric characteristics will be inserted at the end of the extension line as shown in Figure 9-16.

Example 2

In the following example you will create a leader with a combination feature control frame to control runout and cylindricity.

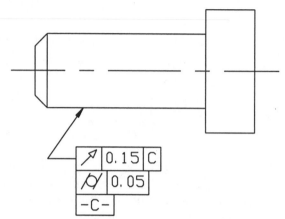

Figure 9-17 Drawing for Example 2

Step 1
Use the **LEADER** command to begin placing the control frame. AutoCAD will prompt you with **From point:**. Select a point where you want the tip of the arrow to be placed. AutoCAD will prompt you with **To point:**. Select a point where the first bend in the leader line will be placed. Then AutoCAD will prompt you with **To point:**. Select a point where the middle left side of the control frame will be placed.

Step 2
AutoCAD will again prompt you with **To point:**. Here press RETURN to select the default option **Annotation**. Press RETURN again to display the Annotation options. Enter **T** to display the **Symbol** dialogue box.

Step 3
Select the runout symbol in the dialogue box and then select the OK button to display the **Geometric Tolerance** dialogue box.

Step 4
The runout symbol will be displayed in the Symbol edit box on the first row of the Geometric Tolerance dialogue box. Select the **Value** edit box in the Tolerance 1 area on the first row and enter 0.15.

Step 5
Select the **Datum** edit box in the Datum 1 area on the first row and enter C.

Step 6
Select the **Sym** edit box on the second row of the **Geometric Tolerance** dialogue box to display the **Symbol** dialogue box. Select the cylindricity symbol in the dialogue box and then select the OK button to display the Geometric Tolerance dialogue box.

Step 7
The cylindricity symbol will be displayed in the **Sym** edit box on the second row of the Geometric Tolerance dialogue box. Select the **Value** edit box in the Tolerance 1 area on the second row and enter 0.05.

Step 8
Select the **Datum Identifier** edit box and enter -C-.

Step 9
Select the **OK** button to accept the changes to the **Geometric Tolerance** dialogue box and the control frames will be drawn in place.

SELF EVALUATION TEST

Answer the following questions and then compare your answers with the correct answers given at the end of the chapter.

1. What is the advantage of showing tolerance and fits in a drawing? _____

2. Geometric dimensioning and tolerancing is generally known as _____.

3. List the components of geometric tolerance. _____

4. Give three examples of geometric characteristics that indicate the characteristics of a feature. ___
   _____

5. Give an example of a Material Condition Modifier that specifies the material condition when the tolerance value takes effect. _____

6. To create three feature control frames, each frame has to be defined separately. (T/F)

7. What is projected tolerance zone? Explain. _____

8. The LEADER command has the Tolerance option, which allows you to create the Feature Control Frame and attach it to the end of the leader extension line. (T/F)

9. Name two characteristics of the Location Feature. _____

10. Explain Maximum Material Condition. _____

REVIEW QUESTIONS

Answer the following questions.

1. One of the most important parts of the design process is to give the dimensions and tolerances. Why? _____

2. Geometric dimensioning and tolerancing is a means to design and manufacture parts with respect to actual function and the relationship that exists between different features. (T/F)

3. _____ symbols are the building blocks of geometric dimensioning and tolerancing.

4. The feature control frame is a circular shape that contains geometric characteristics symbols and tolerance definition. (T/F)

5. Give an example of Tolerance Value that specifies the tolerance on the feature as indicated by the tolerance zone descriptor._____
   _____

6. The datum is the _____, _____, or feature from which the measurements are made.

7. Sometimes the accuracy required within a pattern is more important than the location of the pattern with the datum surfaces. To specify such a condition, composite position tolerancing may be used. (T/F)

8.   You cannot use AutoCAD's GDT feature to create Feature Control Frames for projected tolerance zone. (T/F)

9.   Draw a picture of Feature Control Frame and explain its features._____
_____

10.   Name three characteristics of the Form Feature._____

EXERCISES

Exercise 1

Draw the following figure, then use the TOL and LEADER commands to draw the geometric tolerances as shown.

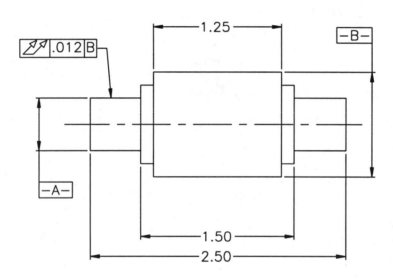

Figure 9-18   Drawing for Exercise 1

Answers

The following are the correct answers to the questions in the self evaluation test.
1 - Tolerances and fits determine how the parts will fit. Incorrect tolerances may result in a product that is not functional. **2** - GDT, **3** - Feature control frame, Geometric characteristics symbol, Tolerance value, Tolerance zone descriptor, Material condition modifier, Datums. **4** - straightness, flatness, perpendicularity. **5** - Example: ϕ.003(M) indicates that this feature must be located at true position within 0.003 diameter at maximum material condition (MMC). **6** - T, **7** - The projected tolerance establishes a tolerance zone that extends above the surface. **8** - T, **9** - Position, Concentricity, Symmetry. **10** - When the part has maximum material; for example, if the part has a hole, the material will be maximum when the hole diameter is minimum.

Chapter 10

Editing with GRIPS

Learning objectives

After completing this chapter, you will be able to:
- ◆ Edit objects with GRIPS.
- ◆ Adjust GRIPS settings.
- ◆ Select objects with GRIPS.
- ◆ Move, rotate, scale, and mirror objects with GRIPS.
- ◆ Use GRIPS system variables.

EDITING WITH GRIPS

Grips provide a convenient and quick means of editing objects. With grips you can stretch, move, rotate, scale, and mirror objects. Grips are small squares that are displayed on an object at its defining points when the object is selected. The number of grips depends on the selected object. For example, a line has three grip points, a polyline has two, and an arc has three. Similarly, a circle has five grip points and a dimension (Vertical) has five. When you enable grips, AutoCAD displays a small square at the intersection of the cross-hairs.

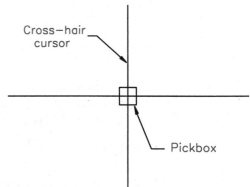

Figure 10-1 Pickbox at the intersection of cross-hair cursor

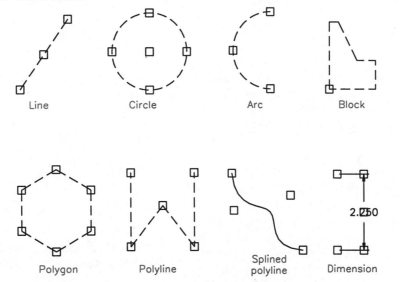

Figure 10-2 Grip location of various objects

Note

AutoCAD also displays a small square at the intersection of cross-hairs when the PICKFIRST (Noun/Verb selection) system variable is set to 1 (On).

ADJUSTING GRIPS SETTINGS

Pull-down: Options, Grips...
Screen: OPTIONS, DDgrips:

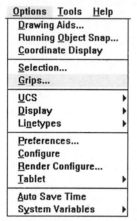

Figure 10-3 Selecting Grips from the pull-down menu

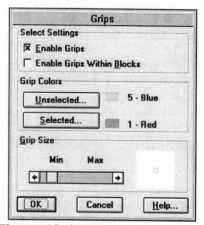

Figure 10-4 Grips dialogue box

Grip settings can be adjusted through the **Grips** dialogue box (Figure 10-4). The dialogue box is activated from the pull-down menu (Select Options, Grips...), from the screen menu (Select OPTIONS, DDgrips:), or by entering DDGRIPS at the **Command:** prompt.

   Command: **DDGRIPS**

   The **Grips** dialogue box has the following areas:
   1. Select Settings
   2. Grip Colors
   3. Grip Size

Select Settings

The **Select Settings** area has two check boxes: **Enable Grips** and **Enable Grips Within Blocks**. The grips can be enabled by picking Enable Grips check box. They can also be enabled by setting the **GRIPS** system variable to 1.

   Command: **GRIPS**
   New value for GRIPS <0>: **1**

The second check box, **Enable Grips Within Blocks**, enables the grips within a block. If you check this box, AutoCAD will display grips for every object in the block. If you disable the display of grips within a block, the block will have only one grip at its insertion point. You can

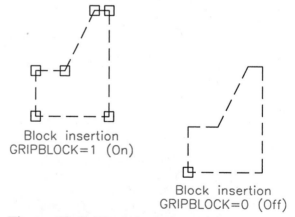

Block insertion
GRIPBLOCK=1 (On)

Block insertion
GRIPBLOCK=0 (Off)

Figure 10-5 Block insertion with GRIPBLOCK set to 1 and 0

also enable the grips within a block by setting the system variable **GRIPBLOCK** to 1 (On). If GRIPBLOCK is set to 0 (Off), AutoCAD will display only one grip for a block at its insertion point.

> **Note**
>
> *If the block has a large number of objects, and if GRIPBLOCK is set to 1 (On), AutoCAD will display grips for every object in the block. Therefore, it is recommended that you set the system variable GRIPBLOCK to 0 or disable the* **Enable Grips Within Blocks** *check box in the Grips dialogue box.*

Grip Colors

The **Grip Colors** area of the dialogue box has two buttons, Unselected... and Selected.... These two buttons let you select the color for unselected and selected grips. When you select any of these buttons, AutoCAD displays the standard **Select Color** dialogue box from which you can select the desired color. By default, the unselected grips have blue color and the selected grips have red color (filled red square). The color of the unselected grips can also be changed by using the **GRIPCOLOR** system variable. Similarly, the color of the selected grips can also be changed by using the **GRIPHOT** system variable.

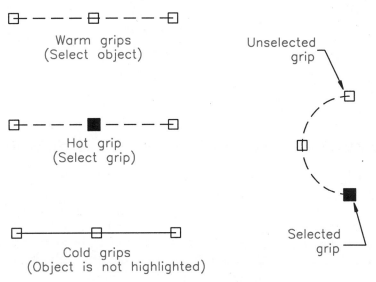

Figure 10-6 Hot, warm, cold, selected, and unselected grips

Grip Types

Grips can be classified into three types: hot grips, warm grips, and cold grips. When you select an object, the grips are displayed at the defining points of the object and the object is highlighted by displaying it as a dotted line. These grips are called **warm grips** (blue). Now, if you select a grip on this object, the grip becomes a **hot grip** (filled red square). Once the grip is hot, the object can be edited. To cancel the grip, press the **Esc** key. If you press the Ctrl-C key twice, the hot grip changes to **cold grip**. When the grip is cold, the object is not highlighted, as shown in Figure 10-6.

Grip Size

The **Grip Size** area of the **Grips** dialogue box consists of a slider bar and a rectangular box that displays the size of the grip. To adjust the size of the grip, move the slider box left or right. The size of the grip can also be adjusted by using the system variable **GRIPSIZE**. GRIPSIZE is defined in pixels and its value can range from 1 to 255 pixels.

STRETCHING OBJECTS WITH GRIPS (STRETCH MODE)

If you select an object, AutoCAD displays grips (warm grips) at the defining points of the object. When you select a grip for editing, you are automatically in the **STRETCH** mode. The STRETCH mode has the same function as the STRETCH command. In the STRETCH mode, you can select several grips and stretch them simultaneously. You can also make copies of the selected objects or define a new base point. The following example illustrates the use of STRETCH mode:

1. Use the PLINE command to draw a W-shaped figure as shown in Figure 10-7(a). If you use the LINE command, AutoCAD will display three grips for each object.

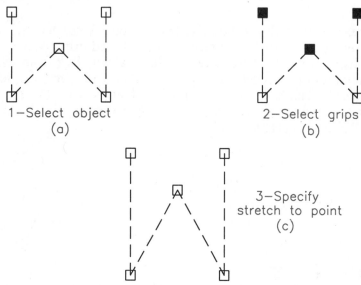

Figure 10-7 Using the STRETCH mode to stretch the lines

2. Select the object that you want to stretch (Figure 10-7(a)). When you select the object, grips will be displayed at the end points of each object. A polyline has two grip points; a line has three.

3. Hold the **Shift** key down and select the grips that you want to stretch (Figure 10-7(b)). The selected grips will become hot grips and the color of the grip will change from blue to red.

> **Note**
>
> *By holding down the Shift key, you can select several grips. If you do not hold down the Shift key, only one grip can be selected.*

4. Choose one of the selected (hot grip) grips and specify a point where you want to stretch the line (Figure 10-7(c)). When you select a grip, the following prompt is displayed in the command prompt area:

   STRETCH
   <Stretch to point>/Base point/Copy/Undo/eXit:
   The **STRETCH** mode has several options: Base point, Copy, Undo, and eXit. You can use the Base point option to define the base point and the Copy option to make copies.

5. Select the grip where the two lines intersect as shown in Figure 10-8(a). Enter **C** for copy, then select the points as shown in Figure 10-8(b). Each time you select a point, AutoCAD will make a copy.

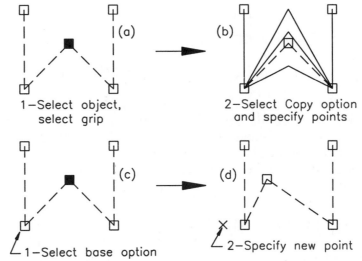

Figure 10-8 Using the STRETCH mode's copy and base point options

6. Make a copy of the drawing as shown in Figure 10-8(c). Select the object, then select the grip where the two lines intersect. When AutoCAD displays the **STRETCH** prompt, select the base point option by entering **B**. Select the bottom left grip as the base point and then give the displacement point as shown in Figure 10-8(d).

MOVING OBJECTS WITH GRIPS (MOVE MODE)

The **MOVE** mode lets you move the selected objects to a new location. When you move objects, the size of the objects and their angle do not change. You can also use this mode to make copies of the selected objects or redefine the base point. The following example illustrates the use of **MOVE** mode:

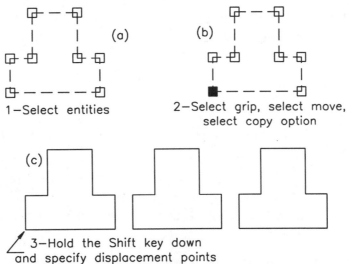

Figure 10-9 Using the MOVE mode to move and make copies of the selected objects

1. Use the **PLINE** command to draw the shape as shown in Figure 10-9(a). When you select the objects, grips will be displayed at the defining points and the object will be highlighted.

2. Select the grip located at the lower left corner, then enter **MOVE** or **MO** at the keyboard or give a null response by pressing the space bar. AutoCAD will display the following prompt in the command prompt area:

MOVE
<Move to point>/Base point/Copy/Undo/eXit:

At this prompt, select the copy option by entering COPY or C.

3. Hold down the **Shift** key, then enter the first displacement point. The distance between the first and the second object defines the snap offset for subsequent copies. While holding down the **Shift** key, move the screen cross-hair to next snap point and pick the point. AutoCAD will make a copy of the object at that location. If you release the **Shift** key, you can specify any point where you want to place a copy of the object. You can also enter coordinates to specify the displacement.

ROTATING OBJECTS WITH GRIPS
(ROTATE MODE)

The **ROTATE** mode allows you to rotate objects around the base point without changing their size. The options of ROTATE mode can be used to redefine the base point, specify a reference angle, or make multiple copies that are rotated about the specified base point. You can access the ROTATE mode by selecting the grip and then entering **ROTATE** or **RO** at the keyboard or giving a null response twice by pressing the space bar. The following example illustrates the use of ROTATE mode:

1. Use the PLINE command to draw the shape as shown in Figure 10-10(a). When you select the objects, grips will be displayed at the defining points and the object will be highlighted.

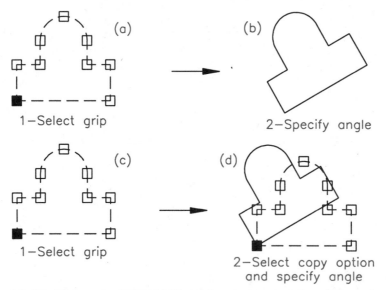

Figure 10-10 Using the ROTATE mode to rotate and make copies of the selected objects

2. Select the grip located at the lower left corner and then enter ROTATE or give null response twice by pressing the space bar. AutoCAD will display the following prompt in the command prompt area:

ROTATE
<Rotation angle>/Base point/Copy/Undo/Reference/eXit:

3. At this prompt, enter the rotation angle. AutoCAD will rotate the selected objects by the specified angle (Figure 10-10(b)).

4. Make a copy of the original drawing as shown in Figure 10-10(c). Select the objects, then select the grip located at the lower left corner of the object. Enter ROTATE or give null response twice to access ROTATE mode. At the following prompt enter C (Copy), then enter the rotation angle. AutoCAD will rotate a copy of the object through the specified angle (Figure 10-10(d)).

   ROTATE
   <Rotation angle>/Base point/Copy/Undo/Reference/eXit: **C**

5. Make another copy of the object as shown in Figure 10-11(a). Select the object, then select the grip at point P0. Access the ROTATION mode and copy option as described earlier and enter R (Reference) at the following prompt:

   ROTATE
   <Rotation angle>/Base point/Copy/Undo/Reference/eXit: **R**
   Reference angle <0>: *Select the grip at P1.*
   Second point: *Select the grip at P2.*

   In response to **Reference angle <0>:** prompt, select the grips at points P1 and P2 to define the reference angle. If you enter the new angle, AutoCAD will now rotate and insert a copy at the specified angle (Figure 10-11(c)). For example, if the new angle is 45 degrees, the selected objects will be rotated about the base point (P0) so that the line P1, P2 makes 45 degrees with positive X axis.

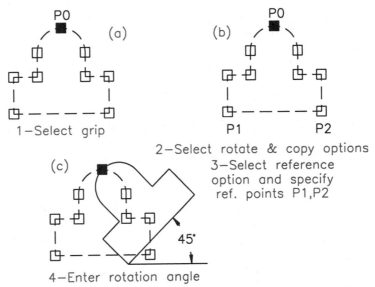

Figure 10-11 Using the ROTATE mode to rotate by giving a reference angle

SCALING OBJECTS WITH GRIPS (SCALE MODE)

The **SCALE** mode allows you to scale objects with respect to the base point without changing their orientation. The options of SCALE mode can be used to redefine the base point, specify a reference length, or make multiple copies that are scaled with respect to the specified base point. You can access the SCALE mode by selecting the grip and then entering SCALE or SC on the keyboard or giving a null response three times by pressing the space bar. The following example illustrates the use of SCALE mode:

1. Use the **PLINE** command to draw the shape as shown in Figure 10-12(a). When you select the objects, grips will be displayed at the defining points and the object will be highlighted.

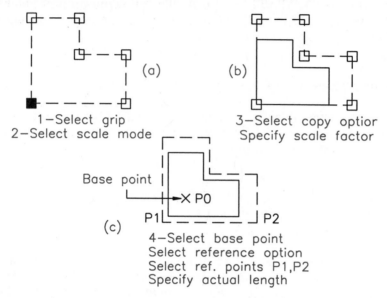

Figure 10-12 Using the SCALE mode to scale and make copies of selected objects

2. Select the grip located at the lower left corner, then enter **SCALE** or **SC** at the keyboard or give null response three times by pressing the space bar. AutoCAD will display the following prompt in the command prompt area:

   SCALE
   <Scale factor>/Base point/Copy/Undo/Reference/eXit:

3. At this prompt enter the scale factor; AutoCAD will scale the selected objects by the specified scale factor (Figure 10-12(b)). If the scale factor is less than 1 (<1), the objects will be scaled down by the specified factor. Similarly, if the scale factor is greater than 1, the objects will be scaled up.

4. Make a copy of the original drawing as shown in Figure 10-12(c). Select the objects, then select the grip located at the lower left corner of the object. Enter SCALE or give null response three times to access SCALE mode. At the following prompt, enter C (Copy), then enter B for base point.

   SCALE
   <Scale factor>/Base point/Copy/Undo/Reference/eXit: **B**

5. Select the point P0 as the new base point and then enter R at the following prompt.

   SCALE
   <Scale factor>/Base point/Copy/Undo/Reference/eXit: **R**
   Reference length <1.000>: Select grips at P1 and P2.

   After specifying the reference length, enter the actual length of the line. AutoCAD will scale the objects so that the length of the bottom edge is equal to the specified value (Figure 10-12(c)).

MIRRORING OBJECTS WITH GRIPS (MIRROR MODE)

The **MIRROR** mode allows you to mirror the objects across the mirror axis without changing the size of the objects. The mirror axis is defined by specifying two points. The first point is the base point and the second point is the point that you pick when AutoCAD prompts for the second point. The options of the MIRROR mode can be used to redefine the base point and make a mirror copy of the objects. You can access the MIRROR mode by selecting a grip and then entering MIRROR or MI at the keyboard or giving a null response four times by pressing the space bar four times. The following example illustrates the use of MIRROR mode:

1. Use the **PLINE** command to draw the shape as shown in Figure 10-13(a). When you select the objects, grips will be displayed at the defining points and the objects will be highlighted.

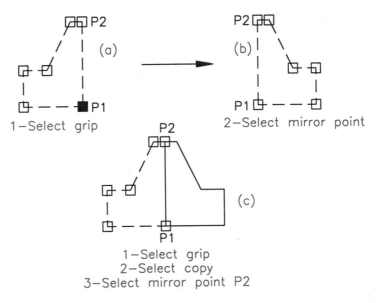

Figure 10-13 Using the **MIRROR** mode to create a mirror image of selected objects

2. Select the grip located at the lower right corner (P1) and then enter MIRROR or MI at the keyboard or give null response four times by pressing the space bar. AutoCAD will display the following prompt in the command prompt area:

    MIRROR
    < Second point > /Base point/Copy/Undo/eXit:

3. At this prompt enter the second point (P2). AutoCAD will mirror the selected objects with line P1, P2 as the mirror axis, Figure 10-13(b).

4. Make a copy of the original figure as shown in Figure 10-13(c). Select the objects, then select the grip located at the lower right corner (P1) of the object. Enter MIRROR or give null response four times to access the MIRROR mode. At the prompt, enter C (Copy) to make a mirror image while retaining the original object:

    MIRROR
    < Second point > /Base point/Copy/Undo/eXit: **C**

5. Select point P2 in response to the prompt **<Second point>**. AutoCAD will create a mirror image and the original object will be retained. If you hold down the **Shift** key, you can make several mirror copies by specifying the second point.

Note

You can use some editing commands, like ERASE, MOVE, ROTATE, SCALE, MIRROR, and COPY, on an object with warm grips (Selected object), provided the system variable PICKFIRST is set to 1 (On).

You cannot select an object once you select a grip (when the grip is hot)

GRIPS SYSTEM VARIABLES

System variable	Default	Setting	Function
GRIPS	1	1=On, 0=Off	Enables or disables Grip mode
GRIPBLOCK	0	1=On, 0=Off	Controls the display of grips in a block
GRIPCOLOR	5	1 - 255	Specifies the color of unselected grips
GRIPHOT	1	1-255	Specifies the color of selected grips
GRIPSIZE	3	1-255	Specifies the size of the grip box in pixels

---

SELF EVALUATION TEST

Answer the following questions and then compare your answers with the correct answers given at the end of this chapter.

1.   What editing functions can you perform with GRIPS? _____
     _____

2.   A grip is a small square that is displayed on an object at its _____ points.

3.   The number of grips depends on the selected object. (T/F)

4.   A line has _____ grip points and a polyline has _____ .

5.   The grip settings can be adjusted with the **GRIPS** command. (T/F)

6.   The **Grips** dialogue box is activated by entering _____ at the **Command:** prompt

7.   You can enable grips within a block by setting the system variable _____ to 1 (On).

8.   The color of the unselected grips can also be changed by using the _____ system variable.

9.   You can access the MIRROR mode by selecting a grip and then entering _____ or _____ from the keyboard or giving a null response four times by pressing the space bar four times.

REVIEW QUESTIONS

Answer the following questions.

1. If you select a grip of an object, the grip becomes a cold grip. (T/F)

2. To cancel the grip, press the **Shift** and **C** keys. (T/F)

3. The GRIPSIZE is defined in pixels and its value can range from _____ to _____ pixels.

4. The size of the grip can also be adjusted by using the system variable _____.

5. When you select a grip for editing, you are automatically in the _____ _____ mode.

6. The _____ mode lets you move the selected objects to a new location.

7. What happens if you hold down the **Shift** key and then enter the first displacement point?_____

8. The **ROTATE** mode allows you to rotate objects around the base point without changing their size. (T/F)

9. The _____ mode allows you to scale the objects with respect to the base point without changing their orientation.

10. The **MIRROR** mode allows you to mirror the objects across the _____ without changing the size of the objects.

EXERCISES

Exercise 1

1. Use the PLINE or LINE command to make the drawing as shown in Figure 10-14(a).
2. Dimension the drawing and place the dimensions as shown in Figure 10-14(a).
3. Use the Grips to correct the dimensions and place them as shown in Figure 10-14(b)

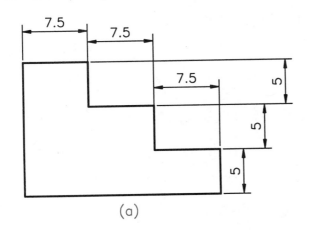
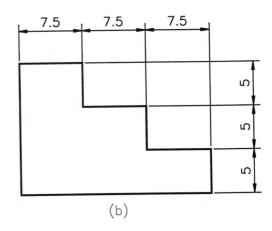

Figure 10-14 Drawings for Exercise 1

Exercise 2

1. Use the PLINE command to draw the shape as shown in Figure 10-15(a).
2. Use the Grips (STRETCH mode) to get the shape as shown in Figure 10-15(b).
3. Use the ROTATE and STRETCH modes to get the copies as shown in Figure 10-15(c)

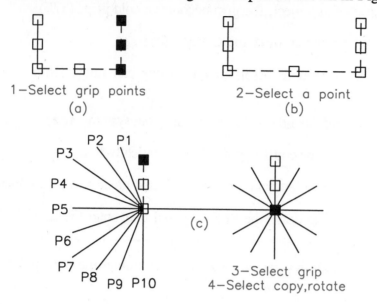

Figure 10-15 Drawing for Exercise 2

Exercise 3

1. Use the PLINE or LINE command to draw a line, a circle, an arc, and a triangle, labeled "given" in Figure 10-16.
2. Use the Grips (STRETCH mode) to get the shapes as shown in Figures 10-16(a), (b), (c).
3. Use the ROTATE mode to get the copies as shown in Figure 10-16(d)

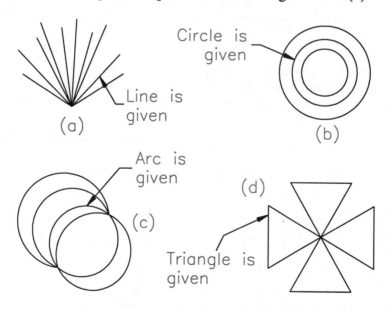

Figure 10-16 Drawing for Exercise 3

Exercise 4

1. Use the PLINE or LINE command to make the drawing as shown in Figure 10-17(a).
2. Use the Grips to get the shapes as shown in Figure 10-17(b). (Do not use any AutoCAD command except GRIPS. Points P1, P2, and P3 are midpoints).

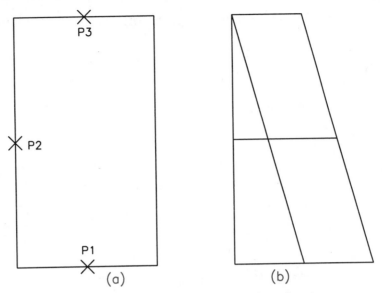

Figure 10-17   Drawing for Exercise 4

Exercise 5

1. Use the PLINE or LINE command to draw a triangle and a rectangle as shown in Figure 10-18(a).
2. Use the DIST command to find the height (X) of the rectangle. You can also use the DIM command to dimension the height of the rectangle as shown in Figure 10-18(b).
3. Use the Grips (SCALE Mode) to scale the copy of the triangle so that the height of the triangle is the same as the height of rectangle.

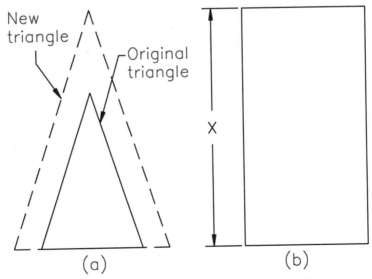

Figure 10-18   Drawing for Exercise 5

Exercise 6

1. Use the PLINE or LINE command to make the drawing as shown in Figure 10-19(a).

2. Dimension the drawing and place the dimension as shown in Figure 10-19(a).

3. Use the Grips to correct the dimensions and place them as shown in Figure 10-19(b)

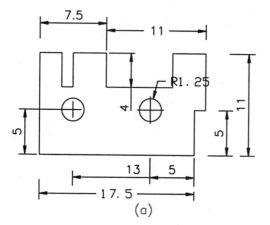
(a)

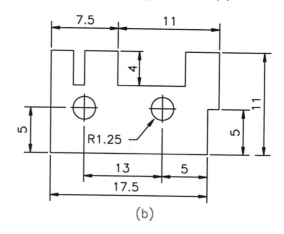
(b)

Figure 10-19 Drawings for Exercise 6

Answers:

The following are the correct answers to the questions in the self evaluation test.
1 - With GRIPS you can stretch, move, rotate, scale, and mirror objects, **2** - defining, **3** - T
, **4** - three, two, **5** - F, (Grips dialogue box), **6** - DDGRIPS, **7** - GRIPBLOCK, **8** -
GRIPCOLOR, **9** - MIRROR, MI.

Chapter 11

Hatching

Learning objectives

After completing this chapter, you will be able to:
♦ Use the BHATCH command to hatch an area.
♦ Use boundary hatch options and predefined as well as user-defined hatch patterns.
♦ Specify pattern properties.
♦ Preview and apply hatching.
♦ Use advanced hatching options.
♦ Edit associative hatch and hatch boundary.
♦ Hatch inserted blocks.
♦ Align hatch lines in adjacent hatch areas.
♦ Hatch by using the HATCH command at the Command: prompt.

HATCHING

In many drawings (such as sections of solids or sections of objects), the area must be filled with some pattern. Different filling patterns make it possible to distinguish between different parts or components of an object. Also, the material the object is made of can be indicated by the filling pattern. Filling the objects with a pattern is known as hatching. This hatching process can be accomplished by using the **HATCH** or **BHATCH** command.

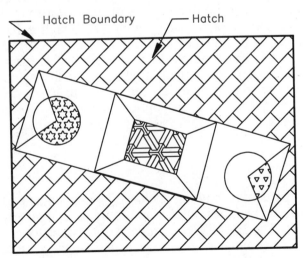

Figure 11-1 Illustration of hatching

Before using the BHATCH and HATCH commands, you need to understand some terms that are used when hatching. Following is the description of some of the terms:

Hatch Patterns

Figure 11-2 Some hatch patterns

AutoCAD supports a variety of hatch patterns. Every hatch pattern is comprised of one or more hatch lines. These lines are placed at specified angles and spacing. You can change the angle and the spacing between the hatch lines. These lines may be broken into dots and dashes or may be continuous, as required. The hatch pattern is trimmed or repeated, as required, to exactly fill the specified area. The lines comprising the hatch are drawn in the current drawing plane. The basic mechanism behind hatching is that the line objects of the pattern you have specified are generated and incorporated in the desired area in the drawing. Although a hatch can contain many lines, AutoCAD normally groups them together into an internally generated block and treats them as such for all practical purposes. For example, if you want to perform an editing operation, such as erasing the hatch, all you need to do is pick any point on the hatch. The block created for the hatch lines gets deleted automatically when all references to it are deleted. Also the hatch blocks created are not listed when you use the list option of the INSERT command to list the defined blocks. If you want to break a pattern into individual lines to edit an individual line, you can use AutoCAD's **EXPLODE** command.

Hatch Boundary

Hatching can be used on parts of a drawing enclosed by a boundary. This boundary may be Line, Circle, Arc, Plines, 3D face, or other objects and must be completely displayed on the screen or within the active viewport. The **BHATCH** command automatically defines the boundary, whereas in the case of the **HATCH** command, you have to define the boundary by selecting the objects that form the boundary of the hatch area.

THE BHATCH COMMAND

Toolbar:	Draw, Hatch
Pull-down:	Draw, Hatch, Hatch...
Screen:	CONSTRCT, Bhatch:

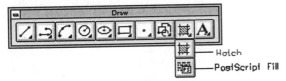

Figure 11-3 Selecting the HATCH icon
from the Hatch flyout in the Draw toolbar

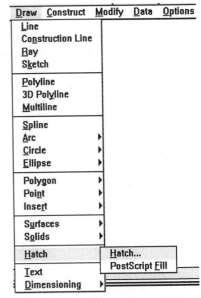

Figure 11-4 Selecting BHATCH command
from Draw pull-down menu

The **BHATCH** or the boundary hatch command allows you to hatch a region enclosed within a boundary (closed area) by picking a point inside the boundary or by selecting the object to be hatched. This command automatically designates a boundary and ignores any other objects (whole or partial) that may not be a part of this boundary. One of the advantages of this command is that you don't have to select each object comprising the boundary of the area you want to hatch as in the case of the HATCH command (discussed later). This is because this command defines a boundary by creating a polyline from all the objects comprising the boundary. By default this polyline gets deleted; however, if you want to retain it, you can specify that. This command also allows you to preview the hatch before actually applying it. Another advantage of this command is that hatching of nested objects in the desired manner is made easy by just picking the objects you want to hatch. The **Boundary Hatch** dialogue box can be invoked from the hatch flyout in the **Draw** toolbar (Select Hatch icon, Figure 11-4) from the pull-down menu (Select Draw, Hatch, Hatch..., Figure 11-5), or from the screen menu (Select CONSTRCT, Bhatch:). It can also be invoked by entering **BHATCH** at AutoCAD Command: prompt.

Command: **BHATCH** ←⏎

Figure 11-5 Boundary Hatch dialogue box.

Example 1

In this example you will hatch a circle using the default hatch settings. Later in the chapter you will learn how to change the settings to get a desired hatch pattern.

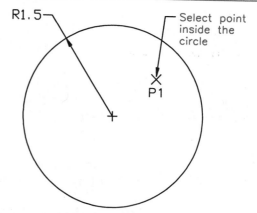

1. Invoke the Boundary Hatch dialogue box (Figure 11-5) by entering **BHATCH** at AutoCAD's Command: prompt.

2. Select the Pick Points button from the Boundary Hatch dialogue box. (This button is located in the Boundary area of the dialogue box.)

3. Pick a point inside the circle (P1).

Figure 11-6 Using the BHATCH command to hatch an object

4. Select the Preview Hatch button; AutoCAD will display the hatched circle. To exit, select the continue in the dialogue box.

5. Select the Apply button to apply the hatch to the selected object.

BOUNDARY HATCH OPTIONS

The **Boundary Hatch** dialogue box has several options that let you control various aspects of hatching, like pattern type, scale, angle, boundary parameters, and associativity. The following is a description of these options. The options have been grouped by the area in which they are found in the Boundary Hatch dialogue box.

Pattern Type

This area lets you choose the type of hatch pattern you want. You can choose a predefined hatch pattern to develop a new hatch pattern of your specifications. The default hatch pattern is predefined. If you select the down arrow, AutoCAD displays a list of the available options, like User-Defined, Custom, and Predefined.

Predefined

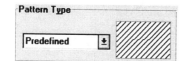

Figure 11-7 Pattern type area

The Predefined pattern type is the default. For predefined hatch patterns the graphic image of the hatch pattern is displayed in the image box. You can cycle through the predefined hatch patterns by clicking on the image box. The corresponding hatch pattern name is displayed in the Pattern edit box. If

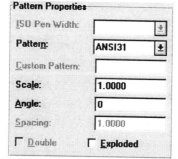

Figure 11-8 Pattern Type area of the Boundary Hatch dialogue box

you have not specified a hatch pattern, the default hatch pattern name is ANSI31. In the current drawing session the default values are taken from the last BHATCH/HATCH operation.

User-Defined Hatch Pattern

If you want to define a simple pattern, you can pick the User-Defined pattern type in the pattern type list box. You will notice that the Pattern: and Scale: edit boxes in the Pattern Properties area are disabled. Two other boxes are enabled: the Spacing: edit box and the Double Hatch check box.

Angle

You can specify an angle by entering a value in the Angle: edit box. This value is considered with respect to the X axis of the current UCS. This value is stored in the **HPANG** system variable.

Spacing

This edit box lets you specify the space between the hatch lines. The entered spacing value is stored in the **HPSPACE** system variable.

Double

This option makes AutoCAD draw a second set of lines at right angles to the original lines. If the Double Hatch box is selected, AutoCAD sets the **HPDOUBLE** system variable to 1.

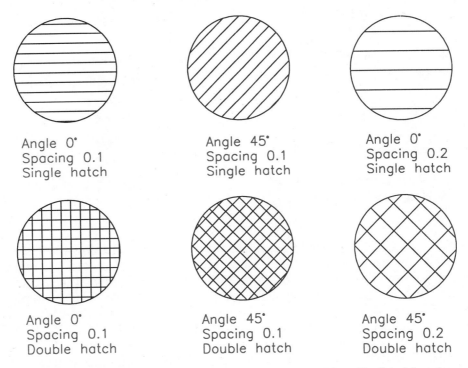

Figure 11-9 Specifying angle and spacing for User-Defined hatch

Custom

The description of the Custom pattern type is given under Custom Pattern in the next section.

Pattern Properties

The options in the Pattern Properties area of the Boundary Hatch dialogue box let you control various aspects of hatching, like pattern type, scale, and angle. The following is the description of these options:

ISO Pen Width

The ISO Pen Width option is only valid for ISO hatch patterns. The pen width can be selected by picking the desired value from the ISO Pen Width pop-up list. The value selected specifies ISO-related pattern scaling.

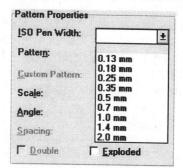

Figure 11-10 Selecting ISO Pen Width

Pattern

There are two ways to specify a hatch pattern from the group of stored hatch patterns. The first is by picking the down arrow in the Pattern edit box. When you select the down arrow, AutoCAD displays the stored Hatch Pattern. You can select a hatch pattern by clicking on the desired hatch pattern name. The graphic image of the selected hatch pattern type is displayed in the image box located in the Pattern Type area. You will also notice that when you are using the predefined hatch patterns, AutoCAD grays out (disables) the **Spacing:** edit box and **Double** check box. This is because the hatch patterns provided by AutoCAD are predefined, hence you cannot change the spacing between the lines forming the hatch pattern and you cannot use the double hatching option on these patterns.

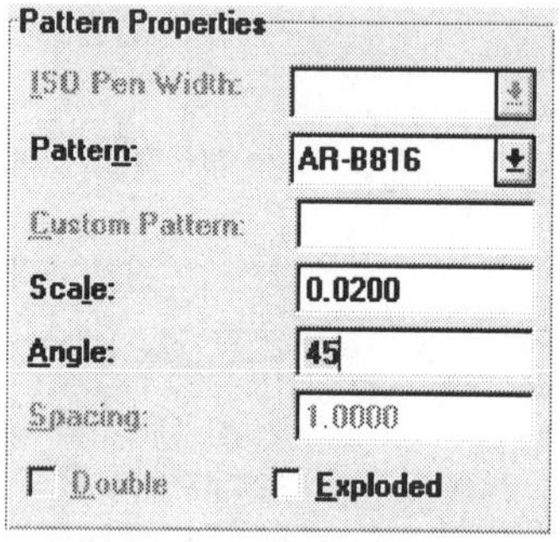

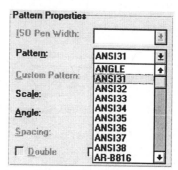

Figure 11-11 Pattern Properties area of the Boundary Hatch dialogue box

Figure 11-12 Pattern type list box

Custom Pattern

The second way to select a predefined hatch pattern is by selecting the Custom pattern type, then entering the name of the stored hatch pattern in the **Custom Pattern:** edit box. The Custom pattern type can be selected by choosing the down arrow in the Pattern Type list box. You can do this if you know the name of the hatch pattern. For example, you can enter BRASS or STEEL as a hatch pattern. The name is held in the **HPNAME** system variable. In AutoCAD all hatch patterns are stored in the file named **ACAD.PAT**. If AutoCAD doesn't locate the entered pattern in the ACAD.PAT file, it searches for it in a file with the same name as the pattern. Therefore, if the entered name is PLASTIC and the pattern is not located in the file ACAD.PAT, AutoCAD searches for it in a file named PLASTIC.pat.

Scale

This option lets you expand or contract the pattern; i.e., scale the hatch pattern. All patterns are assigned an initial scale of 1. You can enter the scale factor of your choice in the edit box next to the Scale: option. This value is stored in the **HPSCALE** system variable. If you enter a value of 1, it does not mean that the distance between the hatch lines is 1 unit. The distance between the hatch lines and other parameters of a hatch pattern is governed by the values specified in the hatch definition. For example, in the ANSI31 hatch pattern definition, the specified distance between the hatch lines is 0.125. If you select a scale factor of 1, the distance between the lines will be 0.125. If you enter a scale factor of 0.5, the distance between the hatch lines will be 0.5 x 0.125 = 0.0625.

Angle

This option lets you rotate the hatch pattern with respect to the X axis of the current UCS. All patterns are assigned an initial angle rotation of 0°. You can enter the angle of rotation value of your choice in the edit box next to the Angle: option. This value is stored in the **HPANG** system variable. The angle of hatch lines of a hatch pattern are governed by the values specified in the hatch definition. For example, in the ANSI31 hatch pattern definition, the specified angle of hatch lines is 45 degrees. If you select an angle of 0, the angle of hatch lines will be 45. If you enter an angle of 45 degrees, the angle of the hatch lines will be 90 degrees.

Exploded Hatch

While hatching, AutoCAD normally groups all the hatch lines into one block. For the purpose of convenience during editing, you may want all the hatch lines to be separate objects. You can pick the Exploded Hatch check box to make the hatch lines separate (individual) objects. The **EXPLODE** command can also be used for this purpose.

Exercise 1

In this exercise you will hatch the given drawing using the hatch pattern for steel. The hatch scale may be obtained from the drawing shown in Figure 11-13.

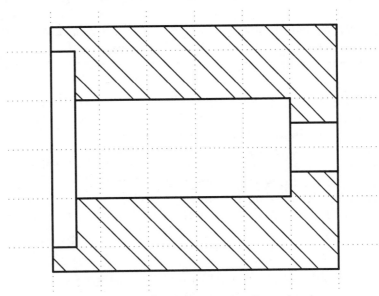

Figure 11-13 Drawing for Exercise 1

Boundary Area

The options available in the Boundary area of the Boundary Hatch dialogue box allow you to define the hatch boundary by picking a point inside the area or by selecting the objects. The other options are for removing islands, viewing the selection, and setting advanced options.

Pick Points<

This option makes AutoCAD automatically construct a boundary. To select this option, choose the Pick Points< button in the Boundary Hatch Dialogue box. The following prompts appear:

Select internal point: *Pick a point inside the object.*
Selecting everything ...
Selecting everything visible...
Analyzing the selected data.
Select internal point: *Pick a point or press the Enter key to end selection.*

In case you want to hatch an object and leave another object contained in it alone, pick a point inside the object you want to hatch, then pick another point inside the object you do not want hatched. By selecting multiple internal points, you can create multiple boundaries. In Figure 11-14, the Pick Points< button has been used to hatch the square but not the triangle.

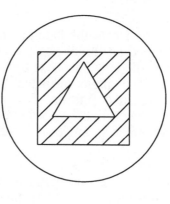

1. Click on Pick Points button.
2. Pick a point inside the square close to its boundary.
3. Pick a point inside the triangle and press the Enter key
4. Pick Apply or Preview Hatch.

Figure 11-14 Defining multiple hatch boundaries by picking points inside the nested objects

---

Note

The user must exercise caution in selecting the Pick Points because by default, BHATCH finds the boundary for the hatch "nearest" to the point picked

---

Boundary Definition Errors

A **Boundary Definition Error** dialogue box is displayed if AutoCAD finds that the selected point isn't inside the boundary or that the boundary isn't closed. If you want to know the reason for the error, pick the Look At It button. What is displayed depends on the error.

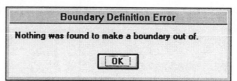

Figure 11-15 Boundary Definition Error dialogue box

For instance, if the boundary of the area to be hatched isn't closed, a line is displayed in that direction.

Select objects<

This option in the Boundary Hatch Dialogue box lets you select objects that form the boundary for hatching. When you select this option, AutoCAD will prompt you to select objects. You can select the objects individually or use other object selection methods. This option can also be used after a boundary has been defined. This way you can select any object that may be present within the boundary so that it is not hatched. Figure 11-16 illustrates this:

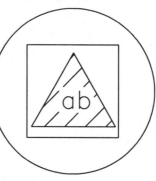

1. Click on Pick Points button.
2. Pick a point inside the triangle and press the Enter key
3. Pick the button Select objects.
4. Select the text and press Enter
5. Choose "Preview Hatch" or "Apply" option.

Figure 11-16 Using the Select Objects option to specify the hatching boundary

Remove Islands

This option is used to remove any islands from the hatching area. For example, if you have a rectangle and a circle as shown Figure 11-17 and you use the Pick Points option to pick a point inside the rectangle, AutoCAD will select both the circle and rectangle. To remove the circle (island) you can use the Remove Islands option. When you select this option, AutoCAD will prompt you to select the islands to remove.

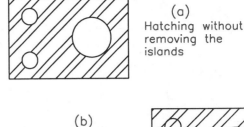

(a)
Hatching without removing the islands

(b)
Using the Remove Islands option to remove the islands

View Selections

This option lets you view the selected boundary.

Figure 11-17 Using the Remove Islands option to remove islands from the hatch area

Advanced

The advanced options and their application are described later in this chapter.

Preview Hatch <

You can use this option after you have selected the area to be hatched to see the hatching before it is actually applied. When you pick the Preview Hatch button, the dialogue box is cleared from the screen and the object picked for hatching is temporarily filled with the specified hatch pattern. Pressing the Enter key redisplays the Boundary Hatch dialogue box so that the hatching operation can be completed and modifications made if required. Since this option is applicable only after you have selected the area to be hatched, this button is disabled (grayed out) until the boundary selection has been made.

Inherit Properties <

If you want to have the same hatching pattern and style as that of an existing hatch on the screen, pick the Inherit Properties button. The dialogue box is cleared from the screen and the following prompts appear:

Select hatch object: *Select a hatch pattern.*
Select hatch object: ←⏎

When you press the Enter key, the Boundary Hatch dialogue box reappears on the screen with the name of the copied hatch pattern in the Pattern: edit box. The inherited hatch pattern is also displayed in the hatch image box. The selected pattern now becomes the current hatch pattern.

Associative

The **Associative** button controls the associativity of hatch with the hatch boundary. By default the hatch associativity is on. One of the major advantages with the associative hatch feature is that you can edit the hatch pattern or edit the geometry that is hatched. After editing, AutoCAD will automatically regenerate the hatch and the hatch geometry to reflect the changes. The hatch pattern can be edited by using the HATCHEDIT command and the hatch geometry can be edited by using GRIPS or some AutoCAD editing commands.

Apply

By choosing the Apply button you can apply hatching in the area specified by the hatch boundary. This option works whether or not you have previewed your hatch. This button is disabled if the hatch boundary is not defined.

Exercise 2

In this exercise you will hatch the drawing in Figure 11-18 using the hatch pattern for brass.

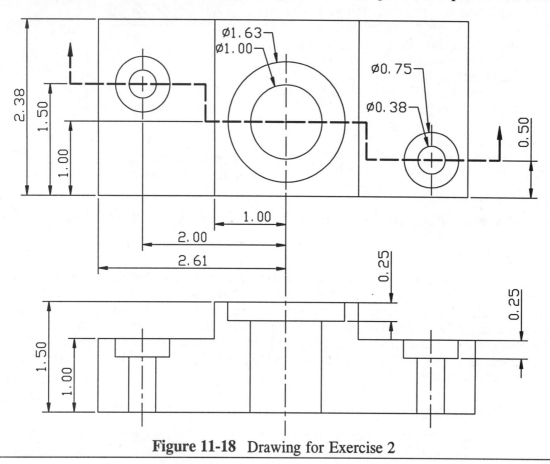

Figure 11-18 Drawing for Exercise 2

ADVANCED OPTIONS

Defining a boundary by specifying an internal point is quite simple in the case of small and less-complicated drawings. It may take more time in the case of large, complicated drawings because AutoCAD examines everything that is visible in the current viewport, so the larger and more complicated the drawing, the more time it takes to locate the boundary edges. In such cases you can improve the hatching speed by setting parameters in the Advanced Options dialogue box. When you select the Advanced button the **Advanced Options** dialogue box (Figure 11-19) is displayed on the screen.

Object Type

The **Object Type** option controls the type of object AutoCAD will create when you define a boundary. It has two options: Polyline and Region. You can choose the desired option by selecting one of these options from the pop-up list.

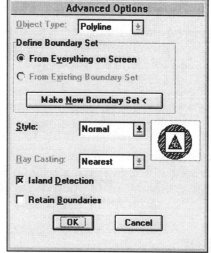

Figure 11-19 Advanced Options dialogue box

Define Boundary Set

You can specify the boundary set by using the Advanced Options dialogue box. The boundary set comprises the objects that the BHATCH command uses when constructing the boundary. The default boundary set comprises everything that is visible in the current viewport. A boundary can be produced faster by specifying a boundary set because in this case AutoCAD does not have to examine everything on screen. If there is no existing boundary set, the button **From Existing Boundary Set** is disabled.

Make New Boundary Set

This option is used to create a new boundary set. All the dialogue boxes are cleared from the screen to allow selection of objects to be included in the new boundary set. While constructing the boundary set, AutoCAD uses only those objects that you select and are hatchable. If a boundary set already exists, it is eliminated for the new one. If you don't select any hatchable objects, no new boundary set is created and AutoCAD retains the current set if there is any. Once you have formed a boundary set, you will notice that the From Existing Boundary Set radio button turns on. When you invoke the BHATCH command and you have not formed a boundary set, the **From Existing Boundary Set** radio button is grayed out and the **From Everything on Screen** radio button is active (selected). The Advanced Options dialogue box reappears after you have picked the Make New Boundary Set button and selected objects to create a selection set. The benefit of creating a selection set is that when you pick a point or select the objects to define the hatch boundary, AutoCAD will only search for the objects that are in the selection set. By confining the search to the objects in the selection set, the hatching process is faster. If you select an object that is not a part of the selection set, AutoCAD displays this message on the screen: **Nothing was found to make a boundary out of**. When a boundary set is formed, it becomes the default for hatching until you exit the BHATCH command or select the **From Everything on Screen** button.

Style

The hatching style can be specified by selecting a style from the Style list box (figure 11-20). The styles are displayed by selecting the down arrow in the Style edit box. There are three styles from which you can choose: Normal, Outer, and Ignore. The image box reflects the effect when you select a hatch style from the style list box. These hatching styles are discussed below.

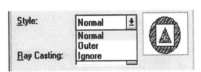

Figure 11-20 Hatching styles

Normal

This style hatches inward starting at the area boundary (outermost area), at each end of the hatch line. If it encounters an internal intersection, it turns off the hatching at each end of this hatch line. An internal intersection causes the hatching to turn off until another intersection is encountered. In this manner alternate areas of the selected object are hatched starting with the outermost area. Thus, areas separated from the outside of the hatched area by an odd number of intersections are hatched, while those separated by an even number of intersections are not.

Outer

This particular option also lets you hatch inward from an area boundary but the hatching is turned off if an internal intersection is encountered. Unlike the previous case, it does not turn the hatching on again. The hatching process in this case starts from both ends of each hatch line, so only the outermost level of the structure is hatched, hence the name **Outer**.

Ignore

In this option all areas bounded by the outermost boundary are hatched, ignoring any hatch boundaries that are within the outer boundary.

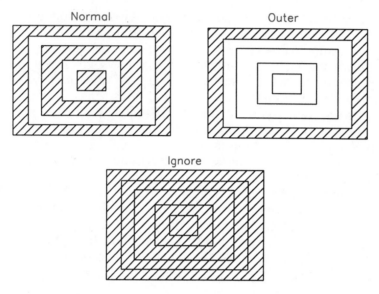

Figure 11-21 Using hatching styles

Ray Casting

You can use the Ray Casting technique to define a hatch boundary. Ray casting is enabled only when Island Detection is turned off. In ray casting, AutoCAD casts an imaginary ray in all directions and locates the object that is nearest to the point you have selected. After locating the object, it takes a left turn to trace the boundary.

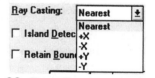

Figure 11-22 Ray Casting pop-up list

This mechanism is known as **ray casting**. If the first ray is intercepted by an internal area or internal text, it results in a boundary definition error. To avoid boundary definition errors, or to force the ray casting in a particular directions, you can use the ray casting options. These options are listed in the Ray Casting pop-up list. You can use these options to control the way AutoCAD casts the ray to form a hatch boundary. The available options are **Nearest, +X, -X, +Y,** and **-Y**.

Nearest

The Nearest option is selected by default. When this option is used, AutoCAD sends an imaginary line to the nearest hatchable object, then takes a turn to the left and continues the tracing process in an effort to form a boundary around the internal point. To make this process work properly, the point you select inside the boundary should be closer to the boundary than any other object that is visible on the screen. This may be difficult when the space between two boundaries is very narrow. In such cases it is better to use one of the other four options. Figure 11-23 shows you some of the conditions in which these options can be used.

+X, -X, +Y, and -Y Options

These options can be better explained by studying Figure 11-23. Figure 11-23(a) shows that the points that can be selected are those that are nearest to the right-hand edge of the circumference of the circle, because the ray casting takes place in the direction of the positive X.

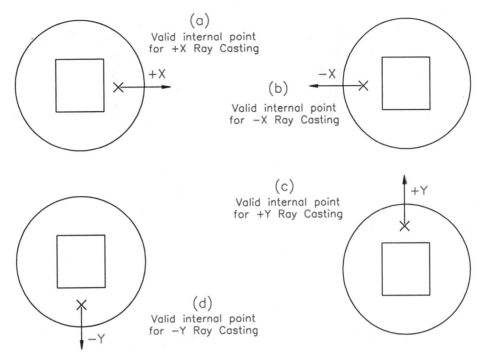

Figure 11-23 Valid points for casting a ray in different directions to select the circle as boundary

Figure 11-23(b) shows that the points that can be used for selection are those that are nearest to the left-hand edge of the circle, because the ray casting takes place in the negative X direction.

In Figure 11-23(c) the ray casting takes place in the positive Y direction so the points that can be used for selection are the ones closest to the upper edge of the circle.

In Figure 11-23(d) the ray casting takes place in the negative Y direction so the internal points that can be selected are the ones closest to the lower edge of the circle.

The effect of hatching for the above-mentioned ray casting options is shown in the following figures:

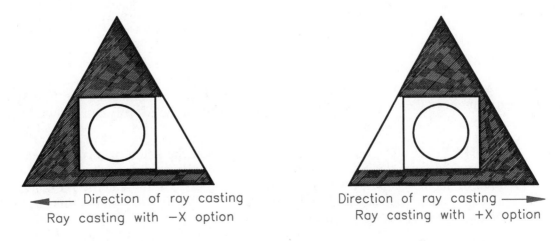

Figure 11-24(a) Effect of hatching for ray casting

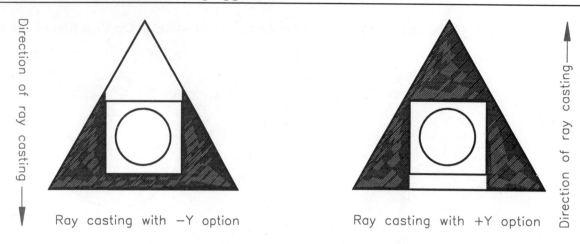

Figure 11-24(b) Effect of hatching for ray casting

Retain Boundaries

Retain Boundaries can be used to retain the defined boundary. If the hatching was successful and you want to leave the boundary as a polyline or region to use it again, you can pick the Retain Boundaries check box.

EDITING ASSOCIATIVE HATCH PATTERNS (HATCHEDIT COMMAND)

Toolbar:	Modify, Edit Polyline, Edit Hatch
Pull-down:	Modify, Edit Hatch...
Screen:	MODIFY, HatchEd:

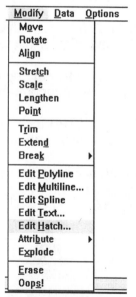

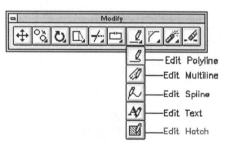

Figure 11-25 The Edit Hatch icon in the Special Edit flyout in the Modify toolbar

Figure 11-26 Selecting the Edit Hatch... option in the Modify pull-down menu

The **HATCHEDIT** command can be used to edit the hatch pattern. This command can be invoked from the Edit Polyline flyout in **Modify** toolbar (Select Edit Hatch, Figure 11-25), from the pull-down menu (Select Modify, Edit Hatch..., Figure 11-26), or from the screen menu (Select MODIFY, HatchEd:). When you enter this command, the **Hatchedit** dialogue box is displayed on the screen.

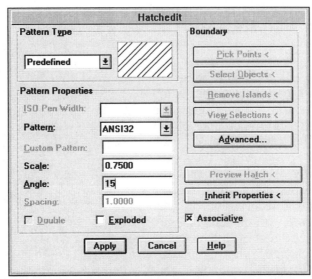

Figure 11-27 Using Hatchedit dialogue box to edit the hatch pattern

You can redefine the hatch pattern by entering the new hatch pattern name in the Pattern edit box. You can also change the scale or angle by entering the new value in the Scale and Angle edit boxes. If you select the Explode button, AutoCAD will remove the associativity of hatch. You can also define the hatch style by picking the Advanced... button and then selecting Normal, Outer, or Ignore styles. If you want to copy the properties from an existing hatch pattern, select the Inherit Properties button, then select the hatch. Figures 11-28 and 11-29 show hatch patterns before and after editing.

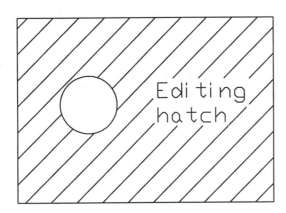

Figure 11-28 ANSI31 hatch pattern

Figure 11-29 Using the HATCHEDIT command to edit the hatch pattern

You can also edit the hatch pattern from the Command: prompt line by preceding the **HATCHEDIT** command with a dash (-). The following is the command prompt sequence for the **-HATCHEDIT** command:

Command: **-HATCHEDIT**
Select hatch object: *Select the hatch pattern*
Disassociate/<Properties>: **P**
Pattern (? or name/U, style) <ANSI31>: *Enter the pattern name.*
Scale for pattern <1.00>: *Enter scale.*
Angle for crosshatch lines <0>: *Enter angle.*

You can also use the **DDMODIFY** command to edit the hatch pattern. When you select a hatch pattern for editing, AutoCAD will display the **Modify Associative Hatch** dialogue box on the screen. You can change the hatch pattern properties by selecting the Hatch Edit... button.

EDITING HATCH BOUNDARY
Using GRIPS

One of the ways you can edit the hatch boundary is by using grips. You can select the hatch pattern or the hatch boundaries. If you select the hatch pattern, the hatch highlights and object grips are displayed at the vertex point of each object that defines the boundary of the hatch pattern. If there are any islands or text, the object grips will be displayed at their vertex points. However, if you select an object that defines the hatch boundary, the object grips are displayed at the vertex points of the selected object. Once you change the boundary definition, AutoCAD will re-evaluate the hatch boundary and then hatch the area. When you

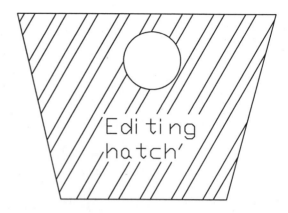

Figure 11-30 Using Object Grips to edit the hatch boundary

edit the hatch boundary, make sure that there are no open spaces in the hatch boundary. AutoCAD **will not** create a hatch if the outer boundary is not closed. Figure 11-30 shows the hatch after moving the circle and text and shortening the bottom edge of the hatch boundary. The objects were edited by using grips.

Using AutoCAD's Editing Commands

When you use the editing commands, like MOVE, COPY, SCALE, STRETCH, or MIRROR, associativity is maintained provided all objects that define the boundary are selected for editing. If any object is missing, the associativity will be lost and AutoCAD will display the message **Associativity was removed from (n) hatch block(s)**. When you rotate or scale an associative hatch, the new rotation angle and the scale factor are saved with the hatch block's extended object data. This data is then used to update the hatch. If you explode an associative hatch pattern, the associativity between the hatch pattern and the defining boundary is removed. Also, the hatch block is exploded and each line in the hatch pattern becomes a separate object.

HATCHING BLOCKS

The hatching procedure in AutoCAD works on inserted blocks. The internal structure of a block is treated by the HATCH and BHATCH commands as if the block were composed of independent objects. If you are using the BHATCH command you can use the Pick Points button to generate the desired hatch in a block. If you want to hatch a block using the BHATCH command, the objects inside blocks should be parallel to the current UCS. If the block is comprised of objects such as arcs, circles, pline arc segments, they **need not** be uniformly scaled for hatching.

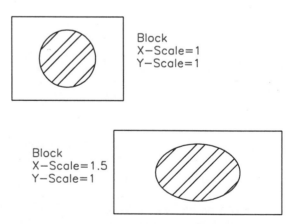

Figure 11-31 Hatching inserted blocks

You can also create a hatch pattern from the Command: prompt line by preceding the **BHATCH** command with a dash (-). The following is the command prompt sequence for the -**BHATCH** command:

    Command: **-BHATCH**
    Properties/Select/Remove islands/Advanced/ < internal point > : **P**

Pattern (? or name/U, style): *Enter the pattern name.*
Angle for crosshatch lines <0>: *Enter angle.*
Spacing between lines <1.00>: *Enter scale.*
Double hatch area? <N>: *Enter Y or N.*
Properties/Select/Remove islands/Advanced/<internal point>:

PATTERN ALIGNMENT DURING HATCHING

(SNAPBASE Variable)

Pattern alignment is an important feature of hatching since on many occasions you need to hatch adjacent areas with similar or sometimes identical hatch patterns while keeping the adjacent hatch patterns properly aligned. Proper alignment of hatch patterns is taken care of automatically by generating all lines of every hatch pattern from the same reference point. The reference point is normally at the origin point (0,0). In Figure 11-32 there are two adjacent hatch areas. If you hatch these areas, the hatch lines may not be aligned, as shown in Figure 11-32(a). To align them you can use the **SNAPBASE** variable so that the hatch lines are aligned, as shown in Figure 11-32(b). The reference point for hatching can be changed using the system variable SNAPBASE. The command prompt sequence is:

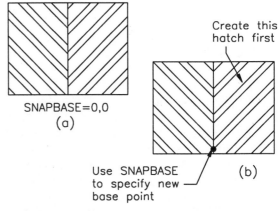

Figure 11-32 Aligning hatch patterns using the SNAPBASE variable

Command: **SNAPBASE**
New value for SNAPBASE(0.00,0.00): *Enter the new reference point.*

Exercise 3

In this exercise you will hatch the given drawing using the hatch pattern for steel. Use the **SNAPBASE** variable to align the hatch lines shown in the drawing.

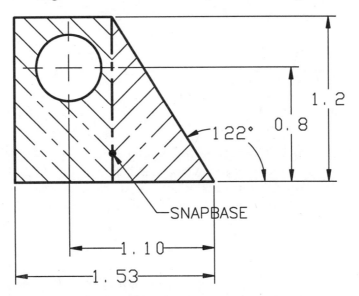

Figure 11-33 Drawing for Exercise 3

THE BOUNDARY COMMAND

Toolbar: Draw, Rectangle, Boundary
Pull-down: Construct, Bounding Polyline
Screen: CONSTRCT, Boundar:

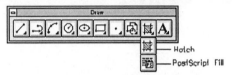

Figure 11-34 Selecting the Boundary icon from Draw the toolbar

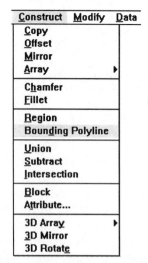

Figure 11-35 Selecting the BOUNDARY command from the Construct pull-down menu

This command is used to create a polyline or a region by defining a hatch boundary. You can invoke this command from the **Draw** toolbar by selecting the **Boundary** icon in the Rectangle flyout (Figure 11-34), from the pull-down menu (Select Construct, Bounding Polyline, Figure 11-35), or from the screen menu (Select CONSTRCT, Boundar:). When this command is entered, AutoCAD displays the **Boundary Creation** dialogue box shown in Figure 11-36:

Command: **BOUNDARY**

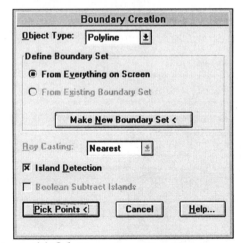

Figure 11-36 Boundary Creation dialogue box

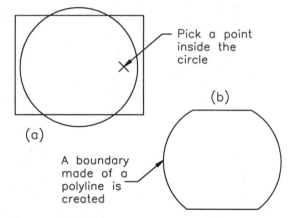

Figure 11-37 Using BOUNDARY command to create a polyline or region hatch boundary

The options shown in the **Boundary Creation** dialogue box are identical to the options in the Advanced Options dialogue box discussed earlier, except for the Pick Points option. The Pick Points option in the Boundary Creation dialogue box is used to create a boundary by picking a point inside the objects. When you pick this option, the dialogue box is cleared from the screen and the following prompt is displayed:

Select internal point:

Once you select an internal point, a polyline or a region is formed around the boundary. To end this process, press the Enter key at the **Select internal point:** prompt. The polyline or region is determined by the **Object Type** you have specified in the Boundary Creation dialogue box.

Exercise 4

Make the drawing as shown in Figure 11-39, then use the BOUNDARY command to create a hatch boundary. Copy the boundary as shown in Figure 11-38, then hatch.

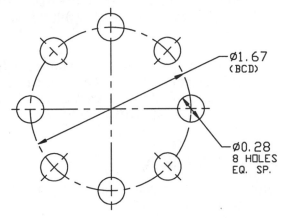

Figure 11-38 First drawing for Exercise 4

Figure 11-39 Second drawing for Exercise 4

HATCHING BY USING THE HATCH COMMAND

Hatches can also be created with the help of the **HATCH** command. However, such hatches are non-associative. You can invoke this command by entering **HATCH** at AutoCAD's Command: prompt. When you enter the **HATCH** command, it does not display a dialogue boxes as in the case of BHATCH command. The command prompt sequence is:

Command: **HATCH**
Pattern(? or name/U, style) <default>: *Enter a pattern name.*

If you know the name of the pattern, enter it. You can also use the following options in response to this prompt:

?
If you enter **?** as the response to the Pattern (**? or name/U, style):** prompt, the following prompt is displayed:

Pattern(s) to list < * >:

If you give a null response to the above prompt, the names and descriptions of all defined hatch patterns are displayed on the screen. If you are not sure about the name of the pattern you want to use you can select this option before entering a name. You can also list a particular pattern by specifying it at the above prompt.

U
This option is used for creating a user-defined array or double-hatched grid of straight lines. To invoke this option enter U at the **Pattern (? or name/U, style):** prompt. After you enter **U**, the following prompts are displayed on the screen.

Angle for crosshatch lines <0>:
Spacing between lines < 1.0000 >:
Double hatch area? <N>

At the **Angle for crosshatch lines <0>:** prompt, you need to specify the angle at which you want the hatch to be drawn. This angle is measured with respect to the X axis of the current UCS. You can also specify the angle by picking two points on the screen. This value is stored in the **HPANG** system variable.

At the second prompt, **Spacing between lines<1.0000>:**, you can specify the space between the hatch lines. The default value for spacing is 1.00. The specified spacing value is stored in the **HPSPACE** system variable.

At the third prompt, **Double hatch area?<N>**, you can specify whether you want double hatching. The default is no (N) and in this case double hatching is disabled. You can enter **Y** (YES) if you want double hatching and in this case AutoCAD draws a second set of lines at right angles to the original lines. If the Double Hatch is active AutoCAD sets the **HPDOUBLE** system variable to 1.

Hatching by Specifying the Pattern and Style Name

When you enter the HATCH command, you can also specify the hatch style and the name of the hatch pattern at the pattern prompt. The format is as follows:

Command: **HATCH**
Pattern(? or name/U, style)<default>: **Stars,I** *(Enter a pattern and style name.)*

Stars,I
By specifying Stars,I you are specifying the hatch pattern as stars and the hatch style as inner. The other styles you can use are: **Normal**, **Outer**, and **Ignore**.

These three options have been discussed in detail under BHATCH command. The following is a short description of these styles:

Normal
This is the default option and hatches inward starting from the area boundary at each end of every hatch line.

Outer
This option hatches the area between the outermost boundary and the next inner boundary.

Ignore
This option ignores all the inner boundaries and hatches everything inside the outer boundary.

Specifying the Scale and Angle for hatching
After you enter the name of a stored pattern (not U), the following two prompts will be displayed:

> Scale for pattern<default>:
> Angle for pattern<default>:

All the stored hatch patterns are assigned an initial scale (size), and a rotation of 0 degrees with respect to the positive X axis. You can expand or contract according to your needs. You can scale the pattern by specifying a scale factor. You can also rotate the pattern with respect to the positive direction of the current UCS by entering a desired angle in response to the Angle prompt. You can even specify the angle manually by picking or entering two points. The default values for both these prompts are the scale and angle values specified for the previous HATCH/BHATCH command. For example, Figure 11-40 illustrates the hatch pattern ANSI31 with different scales and angles. The scale and angle are shown with the figures.

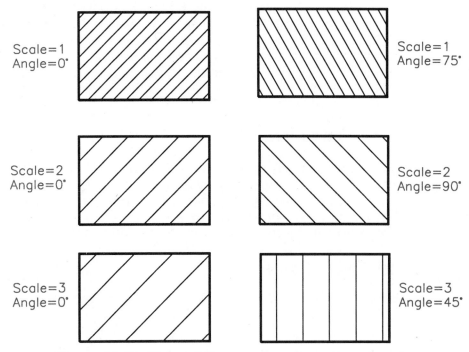

Figure 11-40 Using different values for scale and angle

Selecting Objects for Hatching

Once you are finished specifying the pattern and the style for the hatch, AutoCAD prompts you to select objects for hatching.

Select objects:

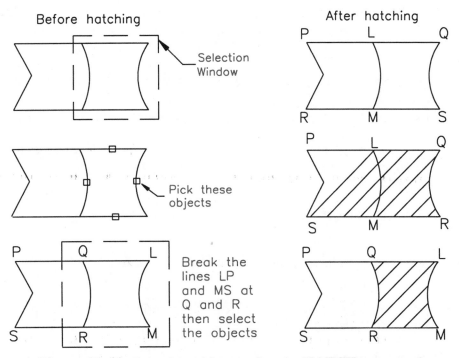

Figure 11-41 Selecting objects using the HATCH command

Defining the boundaries in the HATCH command is a bit tedious compared with defining them with the BHATCH command. In the BHATCH command the boundaries are automatically defined, whereas with the HATCH command you need to define the boundaries by selecting the objects. The objects that form the boundary must intersect at their end points and the objects you select must completely define the boundary. You can use any object selection method to select the objects that define the boundary of the area to be hatched and the objects that you want to exclude from hatching. For example, in the first illustration in Figure 11-41, no hatching takes place because only two lines lie completely within the window and the boundary is not closed. In such a case AutoCAD displays the message:

Hatching did not intersect the figure.

In the second illustration the boundary is selected by picking objects. In this illustration the lines LQ and MR extend beyond the hatch boundary, which results in the hatch going outside the intended hatch area. You must break the top and bottom line at points Q and R so that lines LQ, QR, RM, and ML define the hatch boundary. Now, if you select the objects, AutoCAD will hatch the area bound by the four selected objects as shown in the third illustration.

Hatching around Text, Traces, Attributes, Shapes, and Solids

The hatch lines do not pass through the text, attributes, or shapes present in an object being hatched because AutoCAD places an imaginary box around these objects, which does not allow the hatch lines to pass through it. You must select the text/ attribute/ shape when defining the hatch boundary. Figure 11-42 shows you the selection of boundaries for hatching using the window selection method.

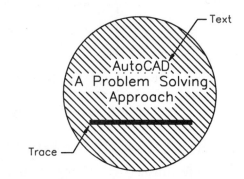

Figure 11-42 Hatching around text and trace

Answer the following questions and then compare your answers with the correct answers given at the end of this chapter.

1.   The material the object is made of can be indicated by the hatch pattern. (T/F)

2.   The _____ command automatically defines the boundary, whereas in the case of the _____ command you have to define the boundary by selecting the objects that form the boundary of the hatch area.

3.   The Boundary Hatch dialogue box can be invoked by entering _____ at the Command: prompt.

4.   You can define a simple pattern by picking the User-Defined pattern type in the pattern type list box. (T/F)

5.   One of the ways to specify a hatch pattern from the group of stored hatch patterns is by picking the down arrow in the Pattern edit box. (T/F)

6.   If AutoCAD doesn't locate the entered pattern in the _____ file, it searches for it in a file with the same name as the pattern.

7. The _____ option lets you rotate the hatch pattern with respect to the X axis of the current UCS. All patterns are assigned an initial angle rotation of _____.

8. The _____ option in the Boundary Hatch Dialogue box lets you select objects that form the boundary for hatching.

9. You can use the _____ option after you have selected the area to be hatched to see the hatching before it is actually applied.

10. By picking the _____ button you can apply hatching in the area specified by the hatch boundary.

11. When a boundary set is formed it does not becomes the default for hatching. (T/F)

12. The selection of Normal hatch style carries meaning only if the objects to be hatched are _____.

13. In ray casting, AutoCAD casts an imaginary ray in all directions and locates the object that is _____ to the point that you have selected

14. You can edit the hatch boundary by using GRIPS. (T/F)

15. Different filling patterns make it possible to distinguish between different parts or components of an object. (T/F)

REVIEW QUESTIONS

Answer the following questions.

1. The hatching process can be accomplished by using the _____ or _____ commands.

2. The hatch boundary may be comprised of Line, Circle, Arc, Plines, 3D face, or other objects and must be completely displayed on the screen or within the active viewport. (T/F)

3. The BHATCH command does not allows you to hatch a region enclosed within a boundary (closed area) by picking a point inside the boundary. (T/F)

4. One of the advantages of the _____ command is that you don't have to select each object comprising the boundary of the area you want to hatch, as in the case of the _____ command.

5. You can cycle through the predefined hatch patterns by clicking on the image box. (T/F)

6. If the Double Hatch box is selected, AutoCAD sets the _____ system variable to 1.

7. The Iso Pen Width option is only valid for _____.

8. One way to select a predefined hatch pattern is to select the Custom pattern type and then enter the name of the stored hatch pattern in the **Custom Pattern:** edit box. (T/F)

9. If AutoCAD doesn't locate the entered pattern in the ACAD.PAT file, it does not load any hatch pattern file. (T/F)

10. The _____ option lets you scale the hatch pattern. All patterns are assigned an initial scale of _____.

11. A Boundary Definition Error dialogue box is displayed if AutoCAD finds that the selected point is inside the boundary or that the boundary isn't closed. (T/F)

12. The _____ option is used to remove the islands from the hatching area.

13. The _____ option lets you view the selected boundary.

14. If you want to have the same hatching pattern and style as that of an existing hatch on the screen, pick the _____ button.

15. The **Associative** button controls the _____ of hatch with the hatch boundary.

16. You can improve the speed of hatching by setting parameters in the Advanced Options dialogue box. (T/F)

17. The **Object Type** option in Advanced Options dialogue box controls the type of object AutoCAD will create when you define a boundary. It has two options: _____ and _____.

18. The hatching style cannot be specified by selecting a style from the style list box. (T/F)

19. There are three hatching styles from which you can choose: _____, _____, and _____.

20. If you select the ignore style, all areas bounded by the outermost boundary are hatched, ignoring any hatch boundaries that are within the outer boundary. (T/F)

21. Ray casting is enabled only when Island Detection is turned on. (T/F)

22. You can use ray casting options to control the way AutoCAD casts the ray to form a hatch boundary. The available options are _____, _____, _____, _____, and _____.

23. The **HATCHEDIT** command can be used to edit the hatch pattern. (T/F)

24. You can also edit the hatch pattern from the Command: prompt line by preceding the BHATCH command with a dash (-). (T/F)

25. When you use the editing commands like MOVE, COPY, SCALE, STRETCH, or MIRROR, associativity is lost. (T/F)

26. If you explode an associative hatch pattern, the associativity between the hatch pattern and the defining boundary is not affected. (T/F)

27. The Hatching procedure in AutoCAD does not work on inserted blocks. (T/F)

28. If the block comprises objects such as arcs, circles or pline arc segments, it must be exploded before hatching. (T/F)

29. To align the hatches in adjacent hatch areas you can use the _____ variable.

30. The BOUNDARY command creates a polyline or a region by defining a hatch boundary. (T/F)

31. The specified hatch spacing value is stored in the _____ system variable.

32. Defining the boundaries in the HATCH command is a bit tedious compared with defining the boundaries with the BHATCH command. (T/F)

EXERCISES

Exercise 5

In this exercise you will hatch the given drawings using the hatch pattern for steel.

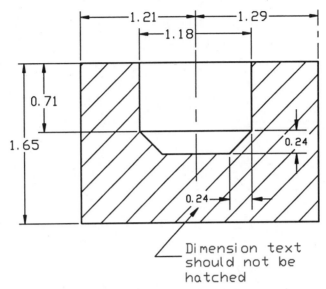

Figure 11-43 Drawing for Exercise 5

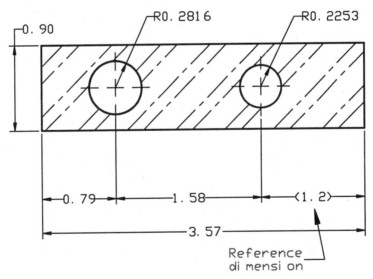

Figure 11-44 Drawing for Exercise 5

Exercise 6

In this exercise you will hatch the given drawing using the hatch pattern for steel. Use the SNAPBASE variable to align the hatch lines as shown in the drawing.

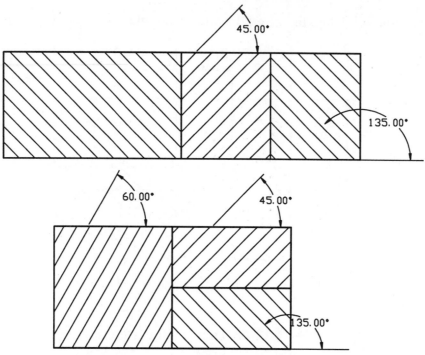

Figure 11-45 Drawing for Exercise 6

Exercise 7

Figure 11-46 shows the top and front views of an object. It also shows the cutting plane line. Based on the cutting plane line, hatch the front views in section. Use the hatch pattern of your choice.

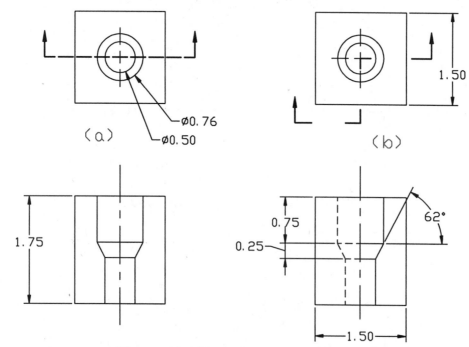

Figure 11-46 Drawing for Exercise 7

Exercise 8

Figure 11-47 shows the top and front views of an object. Hatch the front view in full section. Use the hatch pattern of your choice.

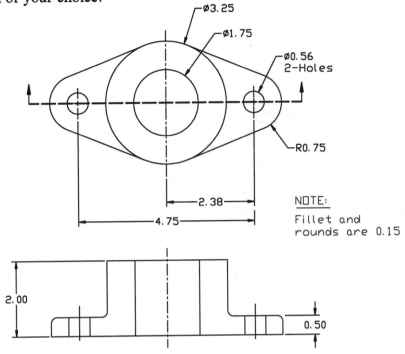

Figure 11-47 Drawing for Exercise 8

Exercise 9

Figure 11-48 shows the front and side views of an object. Hatch the left-hand side view in half section. Use the hatch pattern of your choice.

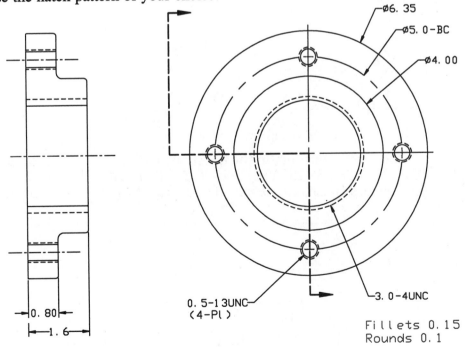

Figure 11-48 Drawing for Exercise 9

Exercise 10

Figure 11-49 shows the front and side views of an object. Hatch the left-hand aligned section view. Use the hatch pattern of your choice.

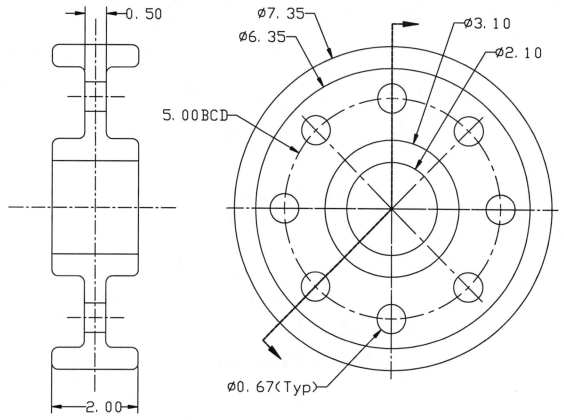

Figure 11-49 Drawing for Exercise 10

Chapter 12

Blocks

Learning objectives

After completing this chapter, you will be able to:
♦ Create blocks with the BLOCK command.
♦ Insert blocks with the INSERT command.
♦ Perform editing operations on blocks.
♦ Create write blocks using the WBLOCK command.
♦ Split a block into individual objects using the EXPLODE command.

THE CONCEPT OF BLOCKS

The ability to store parts of a drawing, or the entire drawing, so that they need not be redrawn when needed again in the same drawing or another drawing, is extremely beneficial to the user. These parts of a drawing, entire drawings, or symbols (also known as blocks) can be placed (inserted) in a drawing at the location of your choice, in the desired orientation, with the desired scale factor. The block is given a name (block name) and the block is referenced (inserted) by its name. All the objects within a block are treated as a single object. You can MOVE, ERASE, or LIST the block as a single object; i.e., you can select the entire block simply by selecting a point on it. As far as the EDIT and INQUIRY commands are concerned, the internal structure of a block is immaterial since a block is treated as a primitive object, like a polygon. If a block definition is changed, all references to the block in the drawing are updated to incorporate the changes made to the block. Two types of blocks are supported by AutoCAD. They are:

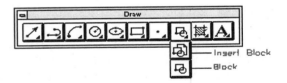

Figure 12-1 Block flyout in Draw toolbar

1. **BLOCK**   2. **WBLOCK**

The **BLOCK** command is used to create Blocks and the **WBLOCK** command is used to create WBlocks. The main difference between the two is that a WBlock can be inserted in any drawing file, but a block can be inserted only in the drawing file in which it was created.

Another feature of AutoCAD is that instead of inserting a symbol as a block or wblock (which results in adding the content of the referenced drawing to the drawing in which it is inserted), you can reference drawings. This means that the contents of the referenced drawing are not added to the current drawing file although they become part of that drawing on the screen. This is explained in detail in Chapter 14, External References. Named objects, referenced drawings, and blocks are referred to as dependent symbols. Whenever a dependent symbol is edited, all the drawings it is referenced to are automatically updated when those drawings are loaded.

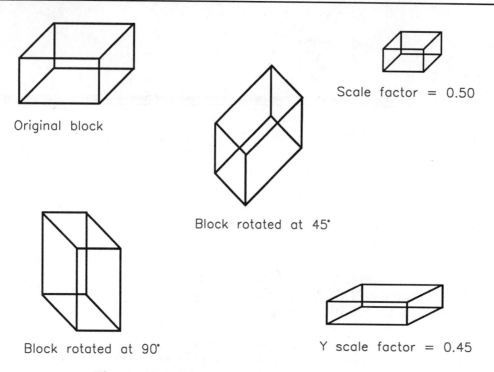

Figure 12-2 Block with different specifications

Advantages of Using Blocks

Blocks offer many advantages; some of them are as follows:

1. Drawings often have some repetitive feature. Instead of drawing the same feature again and again, you can create a block of that feature and insert it wherever required. This style of working helps you to reduce drawing time and better organize your work.

2. Another advantage of using blocks is that they can be drawn and stored for future use. You can thus create a custom library of objects required for different applications. For example, if your drawings are concerned with gears, you could create blocks of gears and then integrate these blocks with custom menus (see the customizing section). In this manner you could create an application environment of your own in AutoCAD.

3. The size of a drawing file increases as you add objects to it. AutoCAD keeps track of information about the size and position of each object in the drawing; i.e., the points, scale factors, radii, etc. If you combine several objects into a single object by forming a block out of them with the **BLOCK** command, there will be a single scale factor, rotation angle, position, etc., for all objects in the block, hence saving storage space.

4. If the specification for an object changes, the drawing needs to be modified. This is a very tedious task if you need to detect each location where the change is to be made and edit it individually. But if this object has been defined as a block, you can redefine it and everywhere the object appears it is revised automatically.

5. Attributes (textual information) can be appended to blocks. Different attributes can be appended to each insertion of a block.

6. You can create symbols and then store them as blocks with the **BLOCK** command. Later on, with the **INSERT** command, you can insert the blocks in the drawing in which they were defined. There is no limit to the number of times you can insert a block in a drawing.

FORMATION OF BLOCKS

Drawing Objects for Blocks

The first step in creating blocks is to draw the object(s) to be converted into a block. You can consider any symbol, shape, or view, that may be used more than once for conversion into a block. Even a drawing that is to be used more than once can be converted into a block. If you do not have the object to be converted into block, use the relevant AutoCAD commands to draw it.

Checking Layers

You should be particularly careful about the layers on which the objects to be converted into a block are drawn. The objects must be drawn on layer 0 if you want the block to inherit the linetype and color of the layer on which it is inserted. If you want the block to inherit the linetype and color of the layer on which it was drawn, draw the objects defining the block on that layer. For example, if you want the block to have the linetype and color of layer OBJ, draw the objects comprising the block on layer OBJ. Now, even if you insert the block on any layer, the linetype and color of the block will be those of layer OBJ. To change the layer associated with an object, use the **LAyer** option of the **CHPROP** command or any other relevant command.

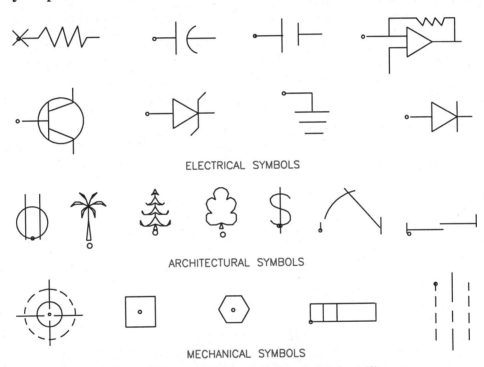

ELECTRICAL SYMBOLS

ARCHITECTURAL SYMBOLS

MECHANICAL SYMBOLS

Figure 12-3 Symbols created to store in a library

Converting the Objects into a Block (BLOCK Command)

Toolbar:	Draw, Insert Block, Block
Pull-down:	Construct, Block

The next step is to create a block from the desired objects. You can use the **BLOCK** command to save any object as a block. This command can be invoked from the Insert Block flyout in **Draw** toolbar (Select Block icon, Figure 12-1), from the pull-down menu (Select Construct, Block, Figure 12-4) or by entering BLOCK at the Command: prompt.

Command: **BLOCK** ←┘

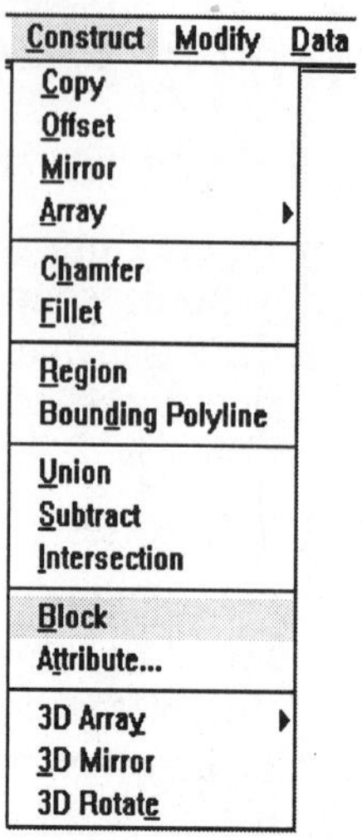

The next prompt asks you for the block name. The block name cannot be longer than 31 characters. The name can contain letters and digits, as well as special characters: the $ (dollar sign), - (hyphen), and _ (underscore).

> Block name(or ?): *Specify the block name.*

If a block already exists with the block name that you have specified at the **Block name (or ?):** prompt, AutoCAD displays the message **Block<name> already exists**. The next prompt AutoCAD issues is:

> Redefine it? <N>:

Figure 12-4 Selecting the BLOCK command from the pull-down menu

At this prompt you are provided the option of redefining the existing block or coming out of the **BLOCK** command without changing it. If you enter **N** or give a null response, the BLOCK command terminates without changing the existing block. If you enter **Y**, the existing block can be redefined by specifying a new insertion point and the objects that will form the redefined block. Checking the list of blocks defined in the drawing is discussed later in this section. After you have specified a block name, you are prompted for the insertion base point. This point is used as a reference point to insert the block. Usually either the center of the block or the lower left corner of the block is defined as the insertion base point. Later on, when you insert the block, you will notice that the block appears at the insertion point and you can insert the block with reference to this point. The point you specify as the insertion base point is taken as the origin point of the block's coordinate system. The block's coordinate system is the same as the UCS that existed when the **BLOCK** command was invoked.

> Insertion Base point: *Pick a point.*

Finally, you need to select the objects on the screen that will constitute the block. The object(s) can be selected by any selection method.

> Select objects: *Select all the objects comprising the block.*
> Select objects: *Press the Enter key when selection is complete.*

Once you have selected the objects defining the block, AutoCAD acknowledges creation of the block by removing the objects defining the block from the screen. However, you can get back the objects at the same position by entering **OOPS**. The following prompt sequence saves a symbol as a block named **SYMBOLX**.

> Command: **BLOCK** ↵
> Block name(or ?): **SYMBOLX** ↵
> Insertion Base point: *Pick a point.*
> Select objects: *Select all the objects comprising the block.*
> Select objects: *Press the Enter key when selection is complete.*

Listing Blocks

Within the **BLOCK** command, you can list all the blocks defined in that drawing. You can also enter a block name(s) to list or use wild cards. AutoCAD then lists the block names and their number. You can verify whether the block you have defined has been saved in the following manner:

Command: **BLOCK** ◄─┘
Block name (or ?): **?** ◄─┘
Block(s) to list < * >: ◄─┘

Information similar to the following is displayed on the screen:

Defined blocks
SQUARE
CIRCLE
A1
B1

User Blocks	*External References*	*Dependent Blocks*	*Unnamed Blocks*
n	*n*	*n*	*n*

Here **n** denotes a numeric value.

Defined blocks: The names of all the blocks defined in the drawing.

User blocks: The number of blocks created by the user.

External references: The number of external references. These are the drawings that are referenced with the **XREF** command.

Dependent blocks: The number of externally dependent blocks. These are the blocks that are present in a referenced drawing.

Unnamed blocks: The number of unnamed blocks in the drawing. These are objects, like associative dimensions and hatch patterns.

Exercise 1

Draw a unit radius circle and use the **BLOCK** command to create a block. Name the block CIRCLE. Pick the center as the insertion point. Select the BLOCK command again and use the **?** option to see if the block CIRCLE was saved. The circle can also be selected by picking any point on the circumference of the circle. Figure 12-5 shows the steps involved in creating a block. You may use the figure to help you in completing this exercise.

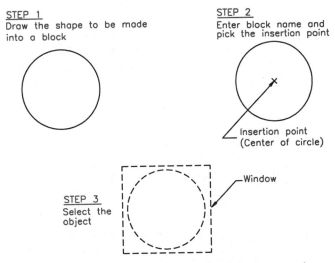

Figure 12-5 Using the BLOCK command

INSERTING BLOCKS

Insertion of a pre-defined block is possible with the **INSERT** or **DDINSERT** command. In case of INSERT command, you can insert a block by entering this command at the Command line. With the DDINSERT command, insertion is carried out using the **Insert** dialogue box. You should determine the layer on which you want to insert the block, the location where you want to insert it, its size, and the angle by which you want the block to be rotated. If the layer on which you want to insert the block is not current, you can use the **Set** option of the **LAYER** command to make it current.

INSERT Command

Toolbar:	Draw, Insert Block
Pull-down:	Draw, Insert, Block...
Screen:	DRAW2, Insert

As mentioned before, predefined blocks can be inserted in a drawing with the **INSERT** command. This command can be invoked from the **Draw** toolbar (Select Insert Block icon), from the pull-down menu (Select Draw, Insert, Block..., Figure 12-6), or from screen menu (Select DRAW2, Insert:). If you use the pull-down menu or the toolbar icon to invoke this command, AutoCAD will display the Insert dialogue box, which has been discussed under the DDINSERT command topic. The following is the prompt sequence for the INSERT command:

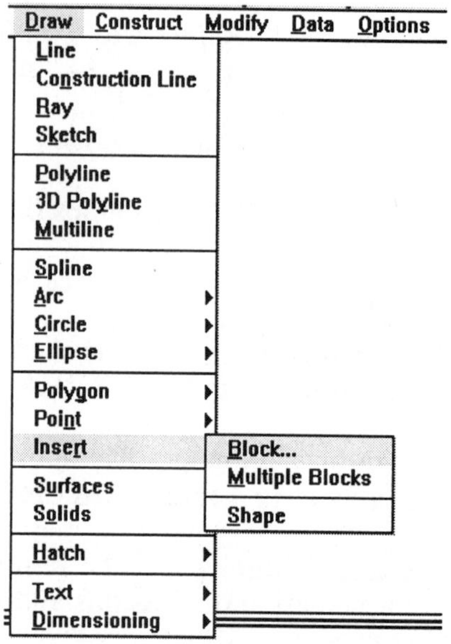

Figure 12-6 Selecting INSERT command from the pull-down menu (Select Draw, Insert, Block...)

Command: **INSERT** ◄─┘
Block name (or ?): *Enter the name of the block to be inserted.*

If you have forgotten the name of the block, enter **?** at the **Block name (or ?):** prompt. The next prompt issued is:

Block(s) to list < * >: ◄─┘

By pressing the Enter key at this prompt, AutoCAD displays the list of blocks available in the current drawing. If you want to insert a drawing file as a block, enter the filename at the **Block name (or ?):** prompt. For example, if you want to insert a drawing file named FIRST into the current drawing, the prompt sequence is:

Command: **INSERT** ◄─┘
Block name (or ?): **FIRST** ◄─┘

To create a block with a different name from the drawing file, enter the block name=filename at the **Block name (or ?):** prompt. For example, if you want to create a block, FIRSTBLK, from a file named FIRST, the prompt sequence is:

Command: **INSERT** ◄─┘
Block name (or ?): **FIRSTBLK=FIRST** ◄─┘   *(Enter block or drawing filename)*

By entering ˜ (tilde character) at the **Block name (or ?):** prompt, the **Select Drawing File** dialogue box is displayed on the screen. If you enter an * (asterisk) before entering the block name, the block is automatically exploded upon insertion. This feature is explained in detail later in this chapter.

The next prompt asks you to specify the insertion point. When a block is inserted, the coordinate system of the block is aligned parallel to the current UCS. The insertion point can be selected accurately by picking or by using OSNAPs. You can also enter the coordinate values of the insertion point.

> Insertion point: *Pick the point where you want the insertion base point for the block [(defined in the BLOCK command) to be located].*

Next two prompts ask you to specify X and Y scale factors.

> X scale factor <1>/Corner/XYZ: *Pick a point, enter a number, or press the Enter key.*
> Y scale factor (default=X): *Pick a point, enter a number, or press the Enter key.*

These scale factors allow you to stretch or compress a block along the X and Y axes, respectively, according to your needs. The scaling of a block becomes easy if you know its exact dimensions. This is why it is advisable to create unit blocks that fit in 1-unit by 1-unit space. For example, if at the time you insert the block CIRCLE (a circle of unit radius) you decide that you want a block that is 3 units long and 2.5 units high you will proceed as follows:

> X scale factor <1>/Corner/XYZ: **3** ←⏎
> Y scale factor(default=X): **2.5** ←⏎

By default, the Y scale factor is equal to the X scale factor. Hence you can maintain identical scale factors by pressing the Enter key at the **Y scale factor(default=X):** prompt.

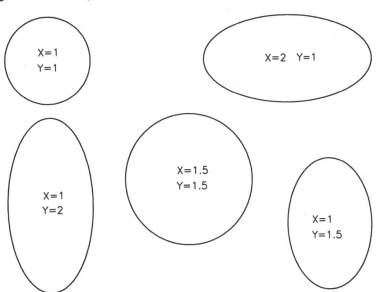

Figure 12-7 Block inserted with different scale factors

At the next prompt, you can specify the angle of rotation for the block to be inserted.

> Rotation angle <0>: *Pick a point or enter an angle.*

The insertion point is taken as the location about which rotation takes place. You can enter the numeral value of the rotation angle at the **Rotation angle <0>:** prompt. You can also pick a point to specify the angle. In this case AutoCAD measures the angle of an imaginary line made by joining the insertion point and the point you have picked. The block is rotated by this angle. Figure 12-7 shows variations of the X and Y scale factors for the block, CIRCLE, during insertion.

Example 1

The following is the prompt sequence to insert a block SQUARE into a drawing. The X scale factor is 4 units, Y scale factor is 4 units, and the angle of rotation is 35 degrees. It is assumed that the block SQUARE is already defined.

Command: **INSERT** ←┘
Block name(or ?): **SQUARE** ←┘
Insertion point: *Specify the insertion point.*
X scale factor<1>/Corner/XYZ: **4** ←┘
Y scale factor (default=X): ←┘
Rotation angle<0>: **35** ←┘

Inserting the Mirror Image of a Block

Scaling of the block being inserted takes place by multiplying the X and Y dimensions of the block by the X and Y scale factors (specified in the **X scale factor<1>/Corner/XYZ:** and **Y scale factor(default=X):** prompts, respectively). If a negative value is specified for the X and Y scale factors, you can get a mirror image of a block. For instance, a scale factor of -1 for X and -1 for Y will mirror the block in the opposite quadrant of the coordinate system. There will be no change in the block size since the magnitude of the scale factor for X and Y variables is 1. For example, we have a block named RECTANGLE. The effect of negative scale factor on the block can be marked by a change in position of insertion point marked by a dot for the following prompt sequence:

Command: **INSERT** ←┘
Block name(or ?): **RECTANGLE** ←┘
Insertion point: *Pick a point.*
X scale factor<1>/Corner/XYZ: **-1** ←┘
Y scale factor(default=X): **-1** ←┘
Rotation angle <0>: ←┘

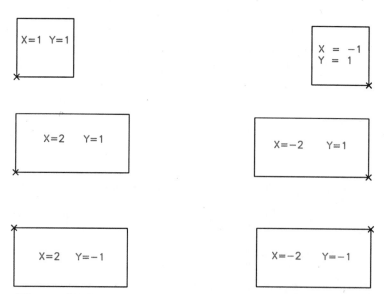

Figure 12-8 Block inserted using negative scale factors

Using the Corner Option

With the **Corner** option you can specify both X and Y scale factors at the same time. When you invoke this option, and the **DRAGMODE** is off, you are prompted to specify the other corner (the first corner of the box is the insertion point). You can also enter a coordinate value instead of moving the cursor. The length and breadth of the box are taken as the X and Y scale factors for the block. For example, if the X and Y dimensions (length and width) of the box are the same as that of the block, the block will be drawn without any change. Points should be picked above and to the right of the insertion block, if you want to insert the block as it was in Figure 12-8. Mirror images will be produced if points are picked below or to the left of the insertion point. The prompt sequence is:

Command: **INSERT** ◄─┘
Block name(or ?): **SQUARE** ◄─┘
Insertion point: *Pick a point.*
X scale factor<1>/Corner/XYZ: **C** ◄─┘
Other corner: *Pick a point as the corner.*

The Corner option also allows you to use a dynamic scaling technique when DRAGMODE is on. In this case after selecting the Corner option as a response to the **X scale factor...** prompt, AutoCAD prompts you for the other corner (the first corner of the box is the insertion point). You can now move the cursor to change the block size dynamically and when the size meets your requirements, pick a point.

> **Note**
>
> *You should try to avoid using the Corner option if you want to have identical X and Y scale factors, because it is difficult to pick a point whose X distance = Y distance, unless the SNAP mode is on. If you use the corner option it is better to specify the X and Y scale factors explicitly or pick the corner by entering coordinates.*

> **Exercise 2**

a. Insert the block CIRCLE created in Exercise 1. Use different X and Y scale factors to get different shapes after inserting this block.
b. Insert the block CIRCLE created in Exercise 1. Use the **Corner** option to specify the scale factor.

XYZ Option

You can insert 3D objects into a drawing with the **XYZ** option. The only difference between this option and the other options is that in 3D you also need to specify the third scale factor (since 3D objects have three dimensions): the Z scale factor. This option works similar to other options. The prompt sequence for inserting 3D blocks is:

Command: **INSERT** ◄─┘
Block name(or ?): *Enter the name of the 3D block.*
Insertion point: *Pick insertion point.*
X scale factor<1>/Corner/XYZ: **XYZ** ◄─┘
X scale factor<1>/Corner: *Enter X scale factor.*
Y scale factor<default=X>: *Enter Y scale factor.*
Z scale factor<default=X>: *Enter Z scale factor.*
Rotation angle <0>: *Specify the angle of rotation.*

PRESETTING THE ROTATION, ANGLE, AND SCALE FACTORS

The scale factor and the rotation of a block can be preset before specifying the block's position of insertion. This option is ideal if you want the block being dragged to assume some values before actually being inserted into the drawing. Once you preset any or both scale factors and angles of rotation, the effect of these values is reflected in the image of the block. For the options with P as a prefix, the preset values can be negated if desired before inserting the block. To realize the presetting function, enter one of the following responses to the **Insertion point:** prompt:

Scale	Xscale	Yscale	PRotate
Zscale	Rotate	PScale	
PXscale	PYscale	PZscale	

Scale

If you enter **Scale** at the **Insertion point:** prompt, you are asked to enter the scale factor. After entering the scale factor, the block assumes the specified scale factor and AutoCAD lets you drag the block until you locate the insertion point on the screen. The X, Y, and Z axes are uniformly scaled by the specified scale factor. Once the insertion point is specified, you are not prompted for the scale factors so you cannot change the scale factor and the block is drawn with the previously specified (preset) scale factor. The prompt sequence when you use the **Scale** option is:

Command: **INSERT** ◄─┘
Block name (or ?): *Enter the block name.*
Insertion point: **SCALE** ◄─┘
Scale factor: *Enter a value to preset general scale factor.*
Insertion point: *Pick the insertion point.*
Rotation angle <0>: *Specify angle of rotation.*

Xscale

With Xscale as the response to the **Insertion point:** prompt, you can specify the X scale factor before specifying the insertion point. This option works similarly to the Scale option. In this option the Y and Z scale factors cannot be specified, hence no scaling can take place along the Y or Z axes. The prompt sequence when you use the Scale option is:

Command: **INSERT** ◄─┘
Block name (or ?): *Enter the block name.*
Insertion point: **XSCALE** ◄─┘
X scale factor: *Enter a value to preset X scale factor.*
Insertion point: *Pick the insertion point.*
Rotation angle <0>: *Specify angle of rotation.*

Yscale

With Yscale as the response to the **Insertion point:** prompt, you can specify the Y scale factor before specifying the insertion point. This option works similarly to the Scale option. In this option the X and Z scale factors cannot be specified, hence no scaling can take place along the X or Z axes.

Zscale

If you enter **Zscale** at the **Insertion point:** prompt, you are asked to specify the Z scale factor before specifying the insertion point. This option works similarly to the Scale option. In this option the X or Y scale factors cannot be specified, hence no scaling can take place along the X and Y axes.

Rotate

If you enter **Rotate** at the **Insertion point:** prompt, you are asked to specify the rotation angle. You can specify the angle by specifying two points. Dragging is resumed only when you specify the angle and the block assumes the specified rotation angle. Once the insertion point is specified, you cannot change the rotation angle, and the block is drawn with the previously specified (preset) rotation angle. The prompt sequence for this option is:

Command: **INSERT** ←⎤
Block name (or ?): *Enter the block name.*
Insertion point: **ROTATE** ←⎤
Rotation angle: *Enter a value to preset rotation angle.*
Insertion point: *Pick the insertion point.*
X scale factor<1>/Corner/XYZ: *Specify the X scale factor.*
Y scale factor(default=X): *Specify the Y scale factor.*

PScale

The **PScale** option is similar to the Scale option. The difference lies in the fact that in case of PScale option the scale factor specified reflects only in the display of the block while it is dragged to a desired position. After you have specified the insertion point for the block, you are again prompted for a scale factor. If you do not enter the scale factor, the block is drawn exactly as it was when created. The prompt sequence for this option is:

Command: **INSERT** ←⎤
Block name (or ?): *Enter the block name.*
Insertion point: **PSCALE** ←⎤
Scale factor: *Enter a value to preset general scale factor.*
Insertion point: *Specify the insertion point for the block.*
X scale factor<1>/Corner/XYZ: *Specify the X scale factor.*
Y scale factor(default=X): *Specify the Y scale factor.*
Rotation angle <0>: *Specify angle of rotation.*

PXscale

This option is similar to the PScale option. The only difference lies in the fact that the X scale factor specified is reflected only in the display of the block while it is dragged to a desired position. After you have specified the insertion point for the block, you are again prompted for the X scale factor and the Y scale factor. If you do not enter the scale factor, the block is drawn exactly as it was when created.

Command: **INSERT** ←⎤
Block name (or ?): *Enter the block name.*
Insertion point: **PXSCALE** ←⎤
X scale factor: *Enter a value to preset X scale factor.*
Insertion point: *Specify the insertion point for the block.*
X scale factor<1>/Corner/XYZ: *Specify the X scale factor.*
Y scale factor(default=X): *Specify the Y scale factor.*
Rotation angle <0>: *Specify angle of rotation.*

PYscale

This option is similar to the PXscale option. The only difference is that in the PYscale option, you can only preset the Y scale factor.

PZscale

This option is similar to the PXscale option. The only difference is that in the PZscale option, you can only preset the Z scale factor.

PRotate

The **PRotate** option is similar to the Rotate option. The difference lies in the fact that the rotation angle specified reflects only in the display of the block while it is dragged to a desired position. After you have specified the insertion point for the block, you are again prompted for an angle of rotation. If you do not enter the rotation angle, the block is drawn exactly as it was when created (with the same angle of rotation as specified on creation of the block). The prompt sequence is:

Command: **INSERT** ◄─┘
Block name (or ?) <current>: *Enter the block name.*
Insertion point: **PROTATE** ◄─┘
Rotation angle: *Specify the preset value for rotation.*
Insertion point: *Specify the insertion point for the block.*
X scale factor <1>/Corner/XYZ: *Specify the X scale factor.*
Y scale factor < default = x>: *Specify the Y scale factor.*
Rotation angle <0>: *Specify angle of rotation.*

Exercise 3

a.   Construct a triangle and form a block of it. Name the block TRIANGLE. Now preset the Y scale factor so that on insertion, the Y scale factor of the inserted block is 2.
b.   Insert the block TRIANGLE with preset rotation of 45 degrees. After defining the insertion point enter X and Y scale factor of 2.

INSERTING BLOCKS USING THE INSERT DIALOGUE BOX (DDINSERT COMMAND)

Toolbar:	Draw, Insert Block
Pull-down:	Draw, Insert, Block...
Screen:	DRAW2, DDinsert

Another method of inserting blocks is by specifying the different parameters of the block to be inserted in the **Insert** dialogue box (Figure 12-9), which can be invoked from the Insert Block flyout in **Draw** toolbar (Select Insert Block icon), from the pull-down menu (Select Draw, Insert, Block...), from the screen menu (Select DRAW2, DDinsert), or by entering the **DDINSERT** command at the **Command:** prompt. Using dialogue boxes is comparatively easier. All the functions of the **INSERT** command can be accessed from the Insert

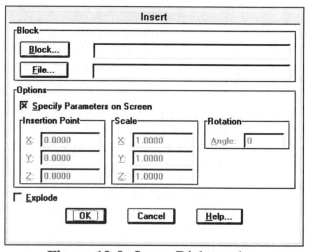

Figure 12-9   Insert Dialogue box

dialogue box. In this dialogue box, the **Select Block Name** area is used to specify the name of the block or drawing file you want to insert. You can specify the position of the block to be inserted in a drawing by picking the **Specify Parameters on Screen** check box. This activates the **Insertion Point**, **Scale**, and **Rotation** areas. Next is the **Explode** check box. This check box has the same function as the **EXPLODE** command. Now we will discuss the various edit boxes and check boxes individually.

Block... Edit Box

This edit box is used to specify the name of the block to be inserted. You can pick the **Block...** button to generate the **Defined Blocks** dialogue box (Figure 12-10). The blocks in the current drawing of the pattern in the **Pattern** edit box are displayed. You can pick the desired block or, if the desired block is a different pattern, specify the pattern in the Pattern edit box. Whichever block name you select, it is displayed in the **Selection** edit box. For example, to insert a block named BLK1, select this block name from the list of block names and then pick the OK button.

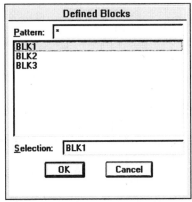

Figure 12-10 Defined Blocks dialogue box

File... Edit Box

If you want to insert a drawing file as a block, enter the filename in the **File...** edit box. When you pick the File... button, the **Select Drawing File** dialogue box (Figure 12-11) is displayed.

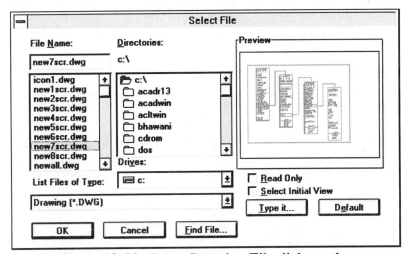

Figure 12-11 Select Drawing File dialogue box

You can pick the drawing file from the listed drawing files existing in the current directory. You can change the directory by selecting the desired directory in the **Directories** list box. Once you select the drawing file in this dialogue box and pick the **OK** button, the drawing filename is displayed in the **File...** edit box. This name is also displayed in the **Block...** edit box so that you can create a block with a different name based on the selected drawing file. Suppose you have selected a drawing file named NEW7SCR.dwg. This name is displayed in both the **File...** and **Block...** edit boxes. If you want to change the block name, just change the name in the Block... edit box. In this manner the drawing NEW7SCR.dwg can be inserted with a different block name.

Specify Parameters on Screen

By default the **Specify Parameters on Screen** check box is selected, hence you can specify the insertion point, scale, and angle of rotation with a pointing device or at the command line. After entering the relevant information in the dialogue box, pick the **OK** button. Once you do so, the **Insert** dialogue box is removed from the screen and you can specify the insertion point, scale, and angle of rotation with a pointing device or at the command line. If you want to specify the above-mentioned features in the Insert dialogue box, deactivate the **Specify Parameters on Screen** check box (the cross mark in the check box is removed). Doing so activates the **Insertion Point**, **Scale**, and **Rotation** areas in the dialogue box. Now you can enter the above-mentioned parameters in the respective edit boxes.

Insertion Point
In this area you can specify the X, Y, and Z coordinate locations of the insertion point of the block.

Scale
In this area you can specify the X, Y, and Z scale factors of the block to be inserted. By default the X scale factor value is assumed by the Y and Z scale factors; however, you can edit the Y and Z scale factor edit boxes to your requirement. All the dimensions in the block are multiplied by the X, Y, and Z scale factors you specify. As discussed before, by specifying negative scale factors for X and Y, you can obtain a mirror image of the block.

Rotation
You can enter the angle of rotation for the block to be inserted in the **Angle:** edit box.

Explode Check Box
By picking this check box, the inserted block is broken and inserted as a collection of individual objects. The function of the **Explode** check box is identical to that of the EXPLODE command. Once a block is exploded, the X, Y, and Z scale factors are identical. Hence, you are provided access to only one scale factor edit box (X scale factor). This scale factor is assigned to the Y and Z scale factors. You must enter a positive scale factor value.

LAYERS, COLORS, AND LINETYPES FOR BLOCKS

A block possesses the properties of the layer on which it is drawn. The block may comprise objects drawn on several different layers, with different colors and linetypes. All this information is preserved in the block. At the time of insertion, each object in the block is drawn on its original layer with the original linetype and color, irrespective of the current drawing layer, object color, and object linetype. You may want all instances of a block to have identical layer, linetype properties, and color. This can be achieved by allocating all the properties explicitly to the objects forming the block. On the other hand, if you want the linetype and color of each instance of a block to be set according to the linetype and color of the layer on which it is inserted, draw all the objects forming the block on layer 0 and set the color and linetype to BYLAYER. If you want the linetype and color of each instance of a block to be set according to the current explicit linetype and color, set the color and linetype to BYBLOCK. You can use the **CHPROP** or **CHANGE** command to change some of the characteristics (such as color, layer, linetype, ltscale) associated with a block. For a further description refer to the **CHPROP** command or the **Properties** option of the **CHANGE** command (Refer to Chapter 16).

Note
The block is inserted on the layer that is current, but the objects comprising the block are drawn on the layers on which they were drawn when the block was being defined.

For example, assume block B1 includes a square and a triangle that were originally drawn on layer X and layer Y, respectively. Let the color assigned to layer X be red and to layer Y, green. Also let the linetype assigned to layer X be continuous and for layer Y be hidden. Now, if we insert B1 on layer L1 with color yellow and linetype dot, the block B1 will be on layer L1, but the square will be drawn on layer X with color red and linetype continuous and the triangle will be drawn on layer Y with color green and linetype hidden.

The **BYLAYER** option instructs AutoCAD to give the block the color and linetype of the layer on which it was created. There are three exceptions:

1. If objects are drawn on a special layer (layer 0), they are drawn on the current layer. These objects assume the characteristics of the current layer (the layer on which the block is inserted) at the time of insertion.

2. Objects created with the special color BYBLOCK are generated with the color that is current at the time of insertion of the block. This color may be explicit or BYLAYER. You are thus allowed to construct blocks that assume the current object color.

3. Objects created with a special linetype, BYBLOCK, are generated with the linetype that is prevalent at the time the block is inserted. Blocks are thus constructed with the current object linetype, which may be BYLAYER or explicit.

Note

If a block is inserted on a frozen layer, the block is not shown on the screen. This is true even when portions of the block lie on non-frozen (thawed) layers.

NESTING OF BLOCKS

The concept of having one block within another block is known as the nesting of blocks. For example, you can insert blocks into the screen (view) and then save the entire view as a block. There is no limit to the degree of nesting. The only limitation in nesting of blocks is that blocks that reference themselves cannot be inserted. The nested blocks must have different block names. Nesting of blocks affects layers, colors, and linetypes. The general rule is:

If an inner block has objects on layer 0, or objects with linetype or color BYBLOCK, these objects may be said to behave like fluids. They "float up" through the nested block structure until they find an outer block with fixed color, layer, or linetype. Now these objects assume the characteristics of the fixed layer. If a fixed layer is not found in the outer blocks, then the objects with color or linetype BYBLOCK are formed; i.e., they assume the color white and the linetype CONTINUOUS.

Example 2

To make the concept of nested blocks clear, consider the following example:

1. Draw a rectangle on layer 0 and form a block of it named X.
2. Change the current layer to OBJ, and set its color to red and linetype to hidden.
3. Draw a circle on OBJ layer.
4. Insert the block X in the OBJ layer.
5. Combine the circle with the block X (Rectangle) to form a block Y.
6. Now insert block Y in any layer (say layer CEN) with color green and linetype continuous.

You will notice that block Y is generated in color red and linetype hidden. Normally, block X, which is nested in block Y and created on layer 0, should have been generated in the color (green) and linetype (continuous) of the layer CEN. The reason for this is that the object (rectangle) on layer 0 floated up through the nested block structure and assumed the color and linetype of the first outer block (Y) with a fixed color (red), layer (OBJ), and linetype (hidden). If both the blocks (X and Y) were on layer 0, the objects in block Y would assume color and linetype of the layer on which the block was inserted.

Exercise 4

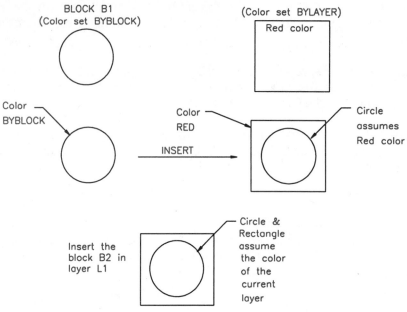

Figure 12-12 Blocks vs. layers and colors

1. Change the color of layer 0 to red.
2. Draw a circle and form a block, B1, of it, with color BYBLOCK. It appears white since color is set to BYBLOCK.
3. Set the color to BYLAYER and draw a rectangle. The color of the rectangle is red.
4. Insert the block B1. Notice that the block B1 (circle) assumes red color.
5. Create another block B2 consisting of Block B1 (circle) and rectangle.
6. Create a layer L1 with green color and hidden linetype. Insert the block B2 in layer L1.
7. Explode the block B2. Notice the change.
8. Explode the block B1, circle. You will notice that the circle changes to white because it was drawn with color set to BYBLOCK.

Exercise 5

Part A
1. Draw a unit square on layer 0 and make it a block named B1.
2. Make a circle with radius 0.5 and change it into block B2.
3. Insert block B1 into a drawing with an X scale factor of 3 and a Y scale factor of 4.
4. Now, insert the block B2 in the drawing and position it at the top of B1.
5. Make a block of the entire drawing and name it PLATE.
6. Insert the block Plate in the current layer.
7. Create different layer with different colors and linetypes and insert the blocks B1, B2, and Plate.

Keep in mind the layers on which the individual blocks were made and that of the inserted block.

Part B
Try nesting the blocks drawn on different layers and with different linetypes.

Part C
Change the layers and colors of the different blocks you have drawn so far.

INSERTING MULTIPLE BLOCKS (MINSERT Command)

Toolbar:	Miscellaneous, Insert Multiple Blocks
Pull-down:	Draw, Insert, Multiple Blocks
Screen:	DRAW2, Minsert:

The **MINSERT** (multiple insert) command is used for multiple insertion of a block. This command comprises features of the INSERT and ARRAY commands. This command can be entered at the command line, or accessed through the Miscellaneous toolbar (Select Insert Multiple Blocks icon), from the pull-down menu (Select Draw, Insert, Multiple Blocks), or from the screen menu (Select DRAW2, Minsert:). Minsert is similar to the INSERT command because it is used to insert blocks at the command level. The difference between these two commands lies in the fact that the **MINSERT** command inserts more than one copy of the block in a rectangular fashion similar to the command ARRAY. With the MINSERT command, only one block reference is created in the drawing. But in addition to the standard features of a block definition (insert point, X/Y scaling, rotation angle and others), this block has repeated row and column counts. In this manner using of this command saves time and disk space. The prompt sequence is very similar to that of the **INSERT** and the **ARRAY** commands. For example, if you want to create an array with a block named BENCH with the following specifications:

Number of rows = 4, Number of columns = 3, Unit cell distance between rows = 0.50, Unit cell distance between columns = 2.0

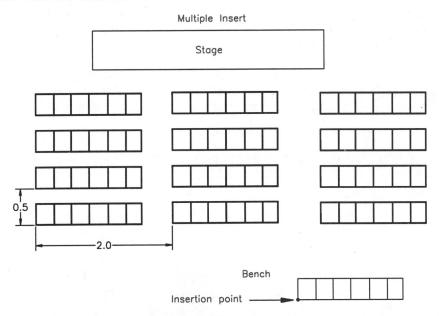

Figure 12-13 Arrangement of benches in an auditorium

The prompt sequence for creating this arrangement of benches in an auditorium is:

Command: **MINSERT** ←
Block name (or ?): **BENCH** ←
Insertion point: *Specify the insertion point.*
X scale factor<1>/Corner/XYZ: ←
X scale factor<default=X>: ←
Rotation angle<0>: ←
Number of rows(---)<1>: **4** ←

Number of columns(|||)<1>: **3** ◄┘
Unit cell distance between rows(---): **0.50** ◄┘
Unit cell distance between columns(|||): **2.0** ◄┘

The responses to these prompts will be clear after you use the INSERT and ARRAY commands. The prompts pertaining to the number of rows and the number of columns requires a positive non-zero integer. For the number of rows exceeding 1 you are prompted to specify the distance between the rows, and if the number of columns exceeds 1, you need to specify the distance between columns. The distance between rows and columns can be a positive or negative value. While inserting a block, if you specify block rotation, each copy of the inserted block is rotated. If you specify rotation angle in the **MINSERT** command, the whole MINSERT block (array) is rotated by the specified rotation angle. If both the block and the MINSERT block (array) are rotated, the block does not seem rotated in the MINSERT pattern. This is same as inserting an array with the rotation angle equal to 0 degrees. If you want to rotate individual blocks within the array, you should first generate a rotated block and then MINSERT it. The **?** option of **Block name (or ?):** prompt lists the names of the blocks.

Note

In the array of blocks generated with the use of MINSERT command you cannot alter the number of rows/columns or the spacing between them. The whole MINSERT pattern is considered one object that cannot be exploded.

EXERCISE 6

1. Create a triangle with each side equal to 3 units.
2. Generate a block of the triangle.
3. Use the **MINSERT** command to insert the block to create a 3 by 3 array. The distance between the rows is 1 unit and the distance between columns is 2 units.
4. Again, use the **MINSERT** command to insert the block to create a 3 by 3 array. The distance between the rows is 2 units, distance between columns is 3 units, and the array is rotated 15 degrees.

CREATING WRITE BLOCKS (WBLOCK Command)

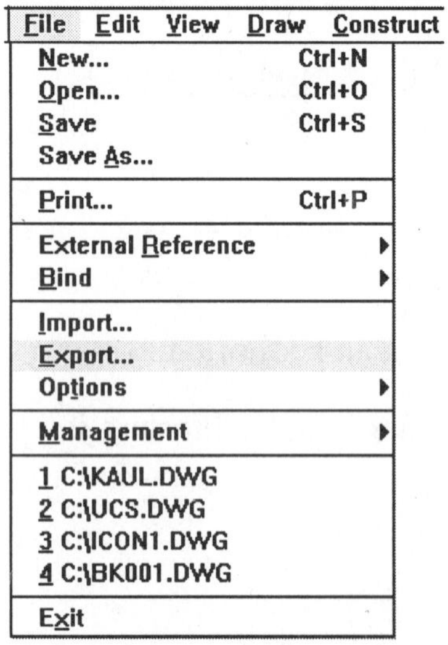

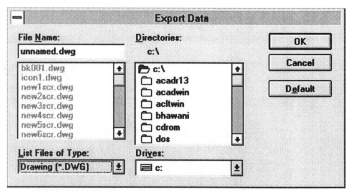

Figure 12-14 Selecting Export command in File pull-down menu

Figure 12-15 Export Data dialogue box

This command is used to create symbols that can be inserted in any drawing. The blocks or symbols created by the BLOCK command can only be used in the drawing in which they were created. This is a shortcoming because you may need to use a particular block in different drawings. With the **WBLOCK** command you can formulate a drawing file (.DWG extension) of a specified blocks or selected objects in the current drawing, or the entire drawing. All the used named objects (linetypes, layers, styles, system variables) of the current drawing are taken by the new drawing created with the WBLOCK command. This block can then be inserted in any drawing. There are a number of ways to make a WBlock. The **WBLOCK** command can be accessed, from the pull-down menu (Select File, Export..., Figure 12-14), from the screen menu (Select FILE, EXPORT, Wblock:), or by entering WBLOCK, at the Command: prompt. If you use the Export... option of the File pull-down menu, AutoCAD displays the **Export Data** dialogue box (Figure 12-15). In this dialogue box you can specify information about the drawing file to be created. Select the *.DWG format from the List Files of Type pop-up list and enter the name of the drawing file in the File name edit box. The dialogue box is cleared from the screen and AutoCAD issues the prompt:

Block name: *Enter the name of a predefined block.*
Insertion base point: *Specify the insertion point.*

In case you want to convert some entities in the current drawing into a WBlock, press the Enter key at the Block name: prompt

Select objects: *Select the objects to be incorporated in the WBlock.*
Select objects: *Press the Enter key when finished selecting.*

When the WBLOCK command is invoked through the screen menu or the Command: prompt, AutoCAD displays the **Create Drawing File** dialogue box (Figure 12-16) except when the system variable **FILEDIA** is set to 0.

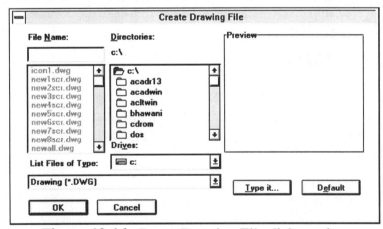

Figure 12-16 Create Drawing File dialogue box

This dialogue box displays a list of all the drawing files in the current directory. You are required to move the pointer to the File edit box, activate it, and specify the name of the output drawing file. Later on you can insert the WBlock with the filename. If the filename you specify is identical to some other file in the same directory path, AutoCAD displays the message:

Warning! Drawing (name) already exists. Do you want to replace it with the new drawing? <N>:

After the new file has been created, the next prompt asks you for the name of an existing block that you want to convert into a permanent symbol.

Block name: *Enter the block name.*

The = Sign

If you want to assign identical names to the output file and the block, enter an = (equal to) sign as a response to the **Block name:** prompt.

    Command: **WBLOCK** ◄─┘
    File name: **SQUARE** ◄─┘
    Block name: = ◄─┘

If a block by the name you have already assigned to the output file does not exist in the current drawing, AutoCAD gives an appropriate message that no block by that name exists in the current drawing and the **Block name:** prompt is repeated.

Creating a New WBlock

If you have not yet created a block, but want to create a WBlock of the objects in the current drawing, enter the **WBLOCK** command and press the Enter key instead of specifying a block name at the **Block name:** prompt. You are then required to pick an insertion point and select the objects to be incorporated in the WBlock. The prompt sequence in this case is:

    Command: **WBLOCK** ◄─┘
    File name: *Enter the name of the output file.*
    Block name: ◄─┘
    Insertion base point: *Pick the insertion point.*
    Select objects: *Select the objects to be incorporated in the WBlock.*
    Select objects: *Press the Enter key when finished selecting.*

The above sequence is similar to that of the BLOCK command. The drawing is saved to the disk, so be sure to specify a path before the filename if you do not want the drawing to be saved in the current directory. For example, if you want to save the drawing named MODEL in the BOOK directory of the C drive, the format is:

    File name: **C:\PROJECTS\MODEL**

Storing an Entire Drawing as a WBlock

You can also store an entire drawing as a WBlock. In other words, the current file is copied into a new one specified in the **Filename:** prompt. To do so, respond to the prompt Block name with an asterisk (*). The prompt sequence is:

    Command: **WBLOCK** ◄─┘
    File name: *Enter the filename.*
    Block name: * ◄─┘

Here, the entire drawing is saved in the file in the directory you have specified. The effect is identical to the **SAVE** command. The lone difference is that if you use the * response in the **WBLOCK** command, all unused named objects are automatically purged. In this manner the size of a drawing containing a number of unused blocks is reduced by a considerable amount. For example, if you want to save the current drawing as a WBlock file named SCREENX, the prompt sequence is:

    Command: **WBLOCK** ◄─┘
    File name: **SCREENX** ◄─┘
    Block name: * ◄─┘

If you want the filename and the block name to be different, specify the block name at the **Block name:** prompt. For example, if the block name is BLOCKPLAN and you want to write these objects to a drawing file PLAN.DWG, the prompt sequence is:

Command: **WBLOCK** ←⏎
File name: **PLAN** ←⏎
Block name: **BLOCKPLAN** ←⏎

DEFINING THE INSERTION BASE POINT (BASE COMMAND)

The **BASE** command lets you set the insertion base point for a drawing just as you set the base insertion point in the prompt sequence of the BLOCK command. This base point is defined so that when you insert the drawing into some other drawing, the specified base point is placed on the specified insertion point. By default, the base point is at the origin (0,0,0). The prompt sequence for setting the base point is:

Command: **BASE** ←⏎
Base point <current>: *Specify the base point.*

Exercise 7

a. Create a WBlock named CHAIR. Get a listing of your .DWG files and make sure that CHAIR.DWG is listed. QUIT the drawing editor.
b. Begin a new drawing and insert the WBlock into the drawing. Save the drawing.

EDITING BLOCKS

Breaking Up a Block

A block may be comprised of different basic objects such as lines, arcs, polylines, and circles. All these objects are grouped together in the block and are treated as a single object. To edit any particular object of a block, the block needs to be "exploded" or split into independent parts. This command is especially useful when an entire view or drawing has been inserted and a small detail needs to be corrected. Regeneration of the drawing takes longer if the block is large. This can be done in two ways.

1. Entering * as the Prefix of Block Name

As we discussed, individual objects within a block cannot be edited unless the block is broken up (exploded). To insert a block as a collection of individual objects you need to type an asterisk before its name. The prompt sequence is:

Command: **INSERT** ←⏎
Block name(or ?): *BLOCK NAME
Insertion point: *Pick the insertion point.*
Scale factor<1>: ←⏎
Rotation angle<0>: ←⏎

The inserted object will no longer be treated as a block. The figure consists of various objects that can be edited separately.

2. Using the EXPLODE Command

As we mentioned before, the other method to break a block into individual objects is by using the **EXPLODE** or **XPLODE** commands. The prompt sequence of **EXPLODE** command is:

Command: **EXPLODE** ↵
Select block reference, polyline, or dimension: *Pick the block to be exploded.*

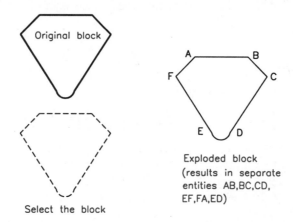

Figure 12-17 Using the EXPLODE command

When a block is exploded there is no visible change in the drawing. The drawing is identical except that the color and linetype may have changed because of floating layers, colors, or linetypes. The exploded block is now a group of objects that may be edited individually. To check whether the breaking of the block has taken place, pick any object that was formerly a part of the block. Only that particular object should be highlighted.

RENAMING BLOCKS

Blocks can be renamed with the **RENAME** command. For example, if you want to rename a block named FIRST to SECOND, the prompt sequence is:

Command: **RENAME**
Block/Dimstyle/LAyer/LType/Style/Ucs/View/VPort: **BLOCK**
Old block name: **FIRST**
New block name: **SECOND**

DELETING UNUSED BLOCKS

Unused blocks can be deleted with the **PURGE** command. For example, if you want to delete an unused block named SECOND, the prompt sequence is:

Command: **PURGE**
Purge unused Blocks/Dimstyles/LAyers/LTypes/SHapes/STyles/APpids/Mlinestyles/ All: **B**
Purge block SECOND? <N>: **Y**

SELF EVALUATION TEST

Answer the following questions and then compare your answers with the correct answers given at the end of this chapter.

1. Individual objects forming a block can be erased. (T/F)

2. A block can be mirrored by providing a scale factor of -1 for X and -1 for Y. (T/F)

3. WBlocks and blocks can be used in any drawing. (T/F)

4. An existing block cannot be redefined. (T/F)

5. At the time of insertion, each object that makes up a block is drawn on the current layer with the current linetype and color. (T/F)

6. If a block is inserted on a frozen layer, the block is generated only if portions of the block lie on non-frozen (thawed) layers. (T/F)

7. The **WBLOCK** command lets you formulate a drawing file (.DWG extension) of a block defined in the current drawing. (T/F)

8. The **RENAME** command can be used to change the name of a Wblock. (T/F)

9. The _____ command is used to place a previously created block in a drawing.

10. You can delete unreferenced blocks with the _____ command.

REVIEW QUESTIONS

Answer the following questions.

1. Only blocks can be scaled. (T/F)

2. Blocks can be scaled or rotated upon insertion. (T/F)

3. WBlocks can be used in any drawing. (T/F)

4. When a block is edited, all the drawings it is referenced to are automatically updated when those particular drawings are loaded. (T/F)

5. An entire drawing can be converted into a block. (T/F)

6. Invoking the **DDINSERT** command causes generation of the **Insert** dialogue box. (T/F)

7. A block possesses the properties, such as color, linetype, etc., of the layer on which it is drawn. (T/F)

8. If the objects forming the block were drawn on layer 0, then at the time of insertion, each object that makes up a block is drawn on the current layer with the current linetype and color. (T/F)

9. Objects created with the special color BYBLOCK are generated with the color that is current at the time the block was inserted. (T/F)

10. Objects created with a special linetype BYBLOCK are generated with the linetype that is current at the time the block was inserted. (T/F)

11. The color, linetype, and layer on which a block is drawn can be changed with the **Properties** option of the **CHANGE** command. (T/F)

12. Suppose Block1 has color BYBLOCK. If you insert Block1 into Block2, which has green color, Block1 also assumes the green color. (T/F)

13. Suppose Block1 has color BYLAYER. If you insert Block1 into Block2, which has red color, it will assume the color of Block2 and not the current layer. (T/F)

14. You can create a rectangular array of a block with a single **MINSERT** command. (T/F)

15. In the array generated with the **MINSERT** command there is no way to change the number of rows/columns or the spacing between them. The whole MINSERT pattern is considered one object that cannot be exploded. (T/F)

16. The **WBLOCK** command allows you to convert an existing block into a permanent symbol. (T/F)

17. You cannot specify different names for the file and the WBlock. (T/F)

18. If a block was inserted with non-uniform scales (unequal X and Y), it can be exploded. (T/F)

19. After exploding an object, the object remains identical except that the color and linetype may change because of floating layers, colors, or linetypes. (T/F)

20. WBLOCK-asterisk method has the same effect as the **PURGE** command. The only difference is that with the PURGE command, deletion takes place automatically. (T/F)

21. The **RENAME** command can be used to change the name of a block. (T/F)

22. The _____ command is used to save any object as a block.

23. The _____ command is used to place a previously created block in a drawing.

24. The _____ option of the **INSERT** command allows you to specify the scale factor dynamically by dragging.

25. The X-scale factor of a block can be preset before specifying its position of insertion by entering _____ at the **Insertion point:** prompt.

26. The X, Y, and Z scale factors of a block can be preset to a uniform value before specifying its position of insertion by entering _____ at the **Insertion point:** prompt.

27. The _____ option lets you redefine the preset Y scale factor even after you have specified the insertion point for the block.

28. The concept of smaller blocks within bigger blocks is known as the _____ .

29. The _____ command is used for multiple insertion of a specified block.

30. This **MINSERT** command comprises the features of _____ and _____ commands.

EXERCISES

Exercise 8

Draw part (a) of Figure 12-18 and define it as a block named A. Then using the block insert command insert the block in the plate as shown.

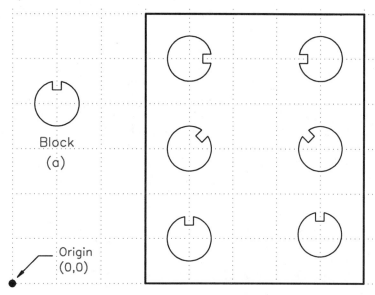

Figure 12-18 Drawing for Exercise 8

Exercise 9

Draw part (a) of Figure 12-19 and define it as a block named B. Then using the relevant insertion method, generate the pattern as shown. Note that the pattern is rotated at 30 degrees.

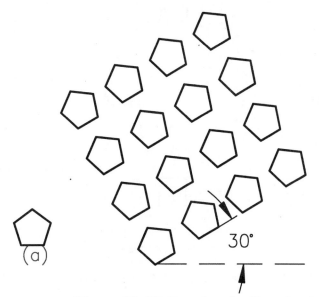

Figure 12-19 Drawing for Exercise 8

Exercise 10

Draw the diagrams in Figures 12-20, 12-21, 12-22, and 12-23 using blocks.
a. Create a block for each different shape.
b. Label the drawings as shown.
c. Use a thick polyline for the flow lines.

Part (a)

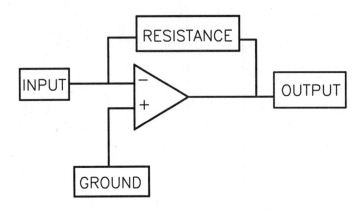

BLOCK DIAGRAM OF INVERTER USING OPAMP

Figure 12-20 Drawing for Exercise 10, part (a)

Part (b)

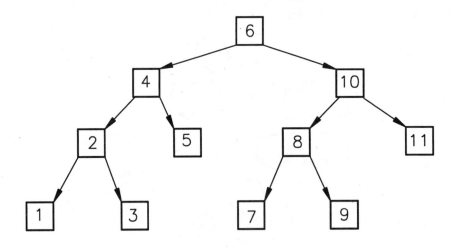

BINARY TREE TRAVERSAL

Figure 12-21 Drawing for Exercise 10, part (b)

Part (c)

The architecture of a typical computer

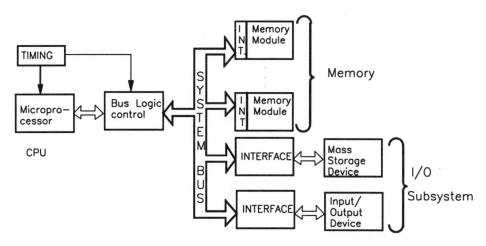

CPU—Central Processing
           Unit
INT—Interface

Figure 12-22 Drawing for Exercise 10, part (c)

Part (d)

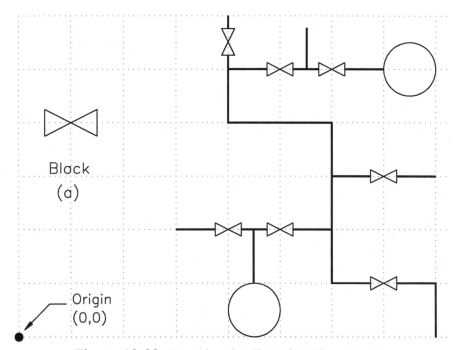

Figure 12-23 Drawing for Exercise 10, part (d)

Answers

The following are the correct answers to the questions in the self evaluation test.
1 - F, **2** - T, **3** - F, **4** - F, **5** - F, **6** - F, **7** - T, **8** - F, **9** - INSERT, **10** - PURGE

Chapter 13

Defining Block Attributes

Learning objectives

After completing this chapter, you will be able to:
- Understand what attributes are and how to define attributes with a block.
- Edit attribute tag names.
- Insert blocks with attributes and assign values to attributes.
- Extract attribute values from the inserted blocks.
- Control attribute visibility.
- Perform global and individual editing of attributes.
- Insert a text file in the drawing to create bill of material.

ATTRIBUTES

AutoCAD has provided a facility that allows the user to attach information with the blocks. This information can then be retrieved and processed by other programs for various purposes. For example, you can use this information to create a bill of material, find the total number of computers in a building, or determine the location of each block in a drawing. The information associated with a block is known as **attribute value,** or simply **attribute.** AutoCAD references the attributes with a block through tag names.

Before you can assign attributes to a block, you must create an attribute definition by using the **DDATTDEF** or **ATTDEF** command. The attribute definition, called the **attribute tag**, describes the characteristics of the attribute. You can define several attribute definitions (tags) and include them in the block definition. Each time you insert the block, AutoCAD will prompt you to enter the value of the attribute. The attribute value automatically replaces the attribute tag name. The information (attribute values) assigned to a block can be extracted and written to a file by using AutoCAD's **DDATTEXT** or **ATTEXT** command. This file can then be inserted in the drawing or processed by other programs to analyze the data. The attribute values can be edited by using the **DDATTE** or **ATTEDIT** command. The display of attributes can be controlled with **ATTDISP** command.

DEFINING ATTRIBUTES

(DDATTDEF COMMAND)

Toolbar:	Attribute, Define Attribute
Pull-down:	Construct, Attribute...
Screen:	CONSTRCT, DDatDef:

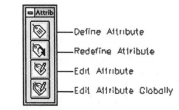

Figure 13-1 Attribute toolbar

You can define the block attributes by entering the **ATTDEF** command at the AutoCAD command prompt. However, the most convenient way to define the block attributes is by using the **Attribute Definition** dialogue box, which can be invoked by entering **DDATTDEF** at the AutoCAD command prompt. You can also invoke this dialogue box from the **Attribute** toolbar by selecting the Define Attribute icon (Figure 13-1), from the pull-down menu (Select Construct, Attribute..., Figure 13-2), or from the screen menu (Select CONSTRCT, DDatDef:).

When you create an attribute definition, you must define the mode, attributes, insertion point, and text information for each attribute as shown in the Attribute Definition dialogue box (Figure 13-3). Following is a description of each area of this dialogue box.

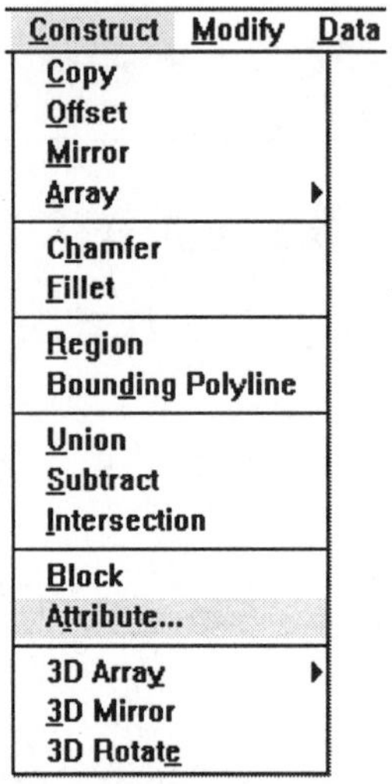

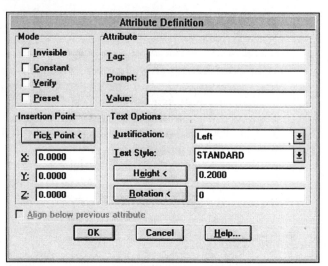

Figure 13-2 Selecting the ATTDEF command from the Draw pull-down menu

Figure 13-3 Attribute Definition dialogue box

Mode

The **Mode** area (Figure 13-4) of the dialogue box has four options: Invisible, Constant, Verify, and Preset. These options determine the display and edit features of the block attributes. For example, if an attribute is invisible, the attribute is not displayed on the screen. Similarly, if an attribute is constant, its value

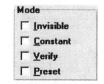

Figure 13-4 Mode area of the Attribute Definition dialogue box

cannot be changed. Following is a detailed description of these options:

Invisible
The **Invisible** option lets you create an attribute that is not visible on the screen. This mode is useful when you do not want the attribute values to be displayed on the screen to avoid cluttering the drawing. Also, if the attributes are invisible it takes less time to regenerate the drawing. If you want to make the invisible attribute visible, use the **ATTDISP** command discussed later in this chapter.

Constant
The **Constant** option lets you create an attribute that has a fixed value and cannot be changed later. When you select this mode the Prompt edit box and the Verify and Preset check boxes are disabled.

Verify
The **Verify** option allows you to verify the attribute value that you have entered when inserting a block. If the value is incorrect you can correct it by entering the new value.

Preset

The **Preset** option allows you to create an attribute that is automatically set to default value. The attribute value is not requested when you use this option to define a block attribute. Unlike a constant attribute, the preset attribute can be edited.

Attribute

The **Attribute** area (Figure 13-5) of the Attribute Definition dialogue box has three edit boxes: Tag, Prompt, and Value. To enter a value you must first select the corresponding edit box and then enter the value. You can enter up to 256 characters in these edit boxes.

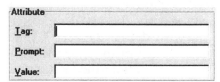

Figure 13-5 Attribute area of the Attribute Definition dialogue box

Tag

The **Tag** is like a label that is used to identify an attribute. For example, the tag name COMPUTER can be used to identify an item. The tag names can be uppercase, lowercase, or both. Any lowercase letters are automatically converted into uppercase. The tag name cannot be null. Also, the tag name must not contain any blank spaces. You should select the tag names that reflects the contents of the item that is being tagged. For example, the tag name COMP or COMPUTER is an appropriate name for labeling computers.

Prompt

The text that you enter in the **Prompt:** edit box is used as a prompt when you insert a block that contains the defined attribute. If you have selected the constant option in the Mode area, the **Prompt:** edit box is disabled because no prompt is required if the attribute is constant. If you do not enter anything in the **Prompt:** edit box, the entry made in the Tag: edit box is used as prompt.

Value

The entry in the **Value:** edit box defines the default value of the specified attribute, that is, if you do not enter a value, it is used as the value for the attribute. The entry of value is optional.

Insertion Point

The **Insertion Point** area (Figure 13-6) of the Attribute Definition dialogue box lets you define the insertion point of block attribute text. You can define the insertion point by entering the values in the X, Y, and Z edit boxes or by selecting Pick Point < button. If you select this button, the dialogue box clears and you can enter the X, Y, and Z values of the insertion point at the command line or specify the point by selecting a point on the screen. When you are done specifying the insertion point, the Attribute definition dialogue box reappears.

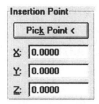

Figure 13-6 Insertion Point area of the Attribute Definition dialogue box

Just under the Insertion Point area of the dialogue box is a button labeled **Align below previous attribute**. You can use this button to automatically place the subsequent attribute text just below the previously defined attribute. This check box is disabled if no attribute has been defined. When you select this check box, the Insertion Point area and the Text Options areas are disabled because AutoCAD assumes previously defined values for text like text height, text style, text justification, and text rotation. Also, the text is automatically placed on the following line. After insertion the attribute text is responsive to the setting of **MIRRTEXT** system variable.

Text Options

The **Text Options** area of the Attribute Definition dialogue box lets you define the justification, text style, height, and rotation of the attribute text. To set the text justification, enter the justification in the **Justification:** edit box. You can also set the justification by selecting the arrow that invokes the pop-up list and then selecting the desired text justification. Similarly, you can use the **Text Style:** edit box to define the text style. The text style can also be set from the pop-up list. You can specify the text height and text rotation in the **Height** < and **Rotation** < edit boxes. You can also define the text height by selecting the Height < button. If you select this button, AutoCAD temporarily exits the dialogue box and lets you enter the value from the command line. Similarly, you can define the text rotation by selecting the Rotation < button.

Note

The text style must be defined before it can be used to specify the text style.

If you select a style that has the height predefined, AutoCAD automatically disables the Height < edit box.

If you have selected the Align option for the text justification, the Height < and Rotation < buttons are disabled.

If you have selected the Fit option for the text justification, the Rotation < button is disabled.

DEFINING ATTRIBUTES (ATTDEF COMMAND)

As mentioned earlier you can define the block attributes by entering the **ATTDEF** command at the Command: prompt.

Command: **ATTDEF**
Attribute modes - Invisible:N   Constant:N   Verify:N   Preset:N
Enter (ICVP) to change, RETURN when done:

The default value of all attribute modes is N (No). To reverse the default mode, enter I, C, V or P. For example, if you enter I, AutoCAD will change the invisible mode from N to Y (Yes). This will make the attribute visible. After setting the modes, press the Enter key to go to the next prompt.

Attribute tag:

The tag is like a label that is used to identify an attribute. The tag names can be uppercase, lowercase, or both. Any lowercase letters are automatically converted into uppercase. The tag name cannot be null. Also, the tag name must not contain any blank spaces. After entering the Attribute tag name press the Enter key to go to next prompt.

Attribute prompt:

The text that you enter at this prompt is used as a prompt when you insert a block that contains the defined attribute. If you have selected the Constant mode, AutoCAD does not display this prompt since no prompt is required for a constant attribute. If you do not enter anything at this prompt, the attribute tag name is used as prompt. The next prompt is:

Default attribute value:

The entry at this prompt defines the default value of the specified attribute; that is, if you do not enter a value, it is used as the value for the attribute. The entry of value is optional. If you have selected the Constant mode, AutoCAD displays the following prompt:

Attribute value:

Next, AutoCAD will display the following text prompts:

Justify/Style/ < Start point > :
Height < 0.200 > :
Rotation angle < 0 > :

After responding to these prompts the attribute text will be placed at the specified location. If you press the Enter key at Justify/Style/ < Start point > :, AutoCAD will automatically place the subsequent attribute text just below the previously defined attribute and it assumes previously defined values for text like text height, text style, text justification, and text rotation. Also, the text is automatically placed on the following line.

Example 1

In this example you will define the following attributes for a computer and then create a block using the BLOCK command. The name of the block is COMP.

Mode	Tag name	Prompt	Default value
Constant	ITEM		Computer
Preset, Verify	MAKE	Enter make:	CAD-CIM
Verify	PROCESSOR	Enter processor type:	Unknown
Verify	HD	Enter Hard-Drive size:	100MB
Invisible, Verify	RAM	Enter RAM:	4MB

1. Draw the computer as shown in Figure 13-7. Assume the dimensions or measure the dimensions of the computer that you are using for AutoCAD.

2. Invoke the **DDATTDEF** command. The Attribute Definition dialogue box is displayed.

3. Define the first attribute as shown in the table of Example 1. Select **Constant** in the **Mode area** because the mode of the first attribute is constant. In the **Tag:** edit box enter the tag name, ITEM. Similarly, enter Computer in the **Value:** edit box. The **Prompt:** edit box is disabled because the variable is constant.

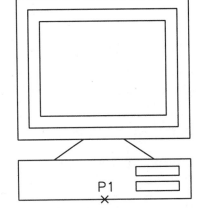

Figure 13-7 Drawing for Example 1

4. In the **Insertion Point** area select Pick Point button to define the text insertion point. Select a point where you want to insert the attribute text.

5. In the **Text Options** area select justification, style, height, and rotation of the text.

6. Select the **OK** button when you are done entering information in the Attribute Definition dialogue box.

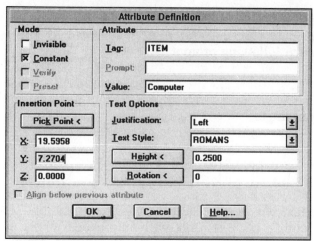

Figure 13-8 Enter information in the Attribute Definition dialogue box

ITEM
MAKE
PROCESSOR
HD
RAM

Figure 13-9 Define attributes below the computer drawing

7. Enter **DDATTDEF** at the Command: prompt to invoke the Attribute Definition dialogue box. Enter the Mode and Attribute information for the second attribute as shown in the table of Example 1. You do not need to define Insertion Point and Text Options. Select the **Align below previous attribute** button that is located just below the Pick Point area. When you select this button the Insertion Point and Text Justification areas are disabled. AutoCAD places the attribute text just below the previous attribute text.

8. Define the remaining attributes.

9. Use the **BLOCK** command to create a block. The name of the block is COMP and the insertion point of the block is P1, midpoint of the base. When you select the objects for the block make sure that you also select the attributes. For detailed information about the BLOCK command refer to BLOCK command discussed in Chapter 12.

EDITING ATTRIBUTE TAGS

Using the DDEDIT Command

Toolbar:	Modify, Edit Polyline, Edit Text
Pull-down:	Modify, Edit Text
Screen:	MODIFY, DDedit:

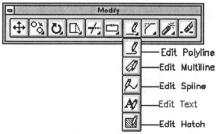

Figure 13-10 Edit Text icon in the Modify toolbar

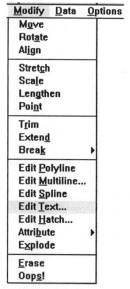

Figure 13-11 Selecting the Edit Text option from the Modify pull-down menu

The **DDEDIT** command lets you edit text and attribute definitions. This command can be invoked from the **Modify** toolbar by selecting the Edit Text icon from the Edit Polyline flyout (Figure 13-10), from the pull-down menu (Select Modify, Edit Text, Figure 13-11), from the screen menu (Select MODIFY, DDedit:), or by entering **DDEDIT** at the Command: prompt. After invoking this command, AutoCAD will prompt you to select a text or attribute definition object. If you select an attribute definition, the Edit Attribute Definition dialogue box, listing the tag name, prompt, and the default value of the attribute, is displayed on the screen. You can click in the edit box and enter the changes. Once you are done making the required change, select the OK button in the dialogue box. After you exit the dialogue box, AutoCAD will prompt you to select text or attribute object (Attribute tag). If you are done editing the attributes, press the Enter key to return to command prompt.

Command: **DDEDIT**
<Select an annotation object object>/Undo: *Select the attribute tag.*

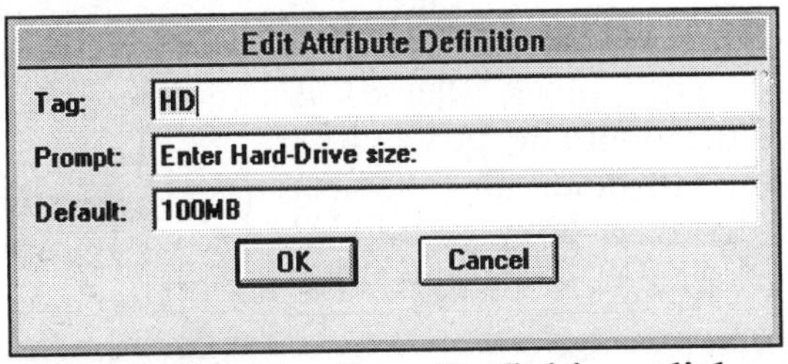

Edit Attribute Definition

Tag: HD

Prompt: Enter Hard-Drive size:

Default: 100MB

OK   Cancel

Figure 13-12 Edit Attribute Definitions dialogue box

Using the CHANGE Command

You can also use the **CHANGE** command to edit text or attribute objects. The following is the command prompt sequence for the CHANGE command:

Command: **CHANGE**
Select Objects: *Select objects.*
Select objects: ⏎
Properties/<Change point>: ⏎
Enter text insertion point: ⏎
Text style: ⏎
New style or RETURN for no change:
New height <current>: ⏎
New rotation angle <0>: ⏎
New tag <current>: *Enter new tag name or* ⏎.
New prompt <current>: *Enter new prompt or* ⏎.
New default value <current>: *Enter new default or* ⏎.
Select objects: ⏎

INSERTING BLOCKS WITH ATTRIBUTES

Using the Dialogue Box

The value of the block attributes can be specified in the Edit Attribute dialogue box. The Edit Attribute dialogue box is invoked by using the INSERT or DDINSERT command with the system variable ATTDIA set to 1. The default value of ATTDIA variable is 0, which disables the dialogue box.

Command: **ATTDIA**
New value for ATTDIA<0>: **1**

Command: **INSERT**
Block name (or ?): *Enter block name.*
Insertion point: *Specify the insertion point.*
X scale factor < 1 >/Corner/XYZ: *Enter X scale factor.*
Y scale factor (default)=X): *Enter Y scale factor.*
Rotation angle < 0 >: *Enter rotation angle.*

After you respond to the above-mentioned prompts, AutoCAD will display the Enter Attributed dialogue box (Figure 13-13) on the screen. The dialogue box will display up to 10 block attribute prompts and the default value of each attribute. If there are more than 10 attributes, they can be accessed by using the **Next** or **Previous** buttons. You can enter the attribute values in the edit box located next to the attribute prompt. The block name is displayed at the top of the dialogue box. Once you are done entering the attribute values, select the OK button in the dialogue box; AutoCAD will place these attribute values at the specified location.

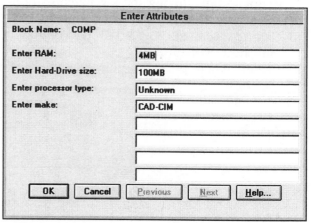

Figure 13-13 Enter attribute values in the Enter Attribute dialogue box

---

Note

If you use the dialogue box to define the attribute values, the Verify mode is ignored because the Enter Attribute dialogue box allows the user to examine and edit the attribute values.

Using the Command Line

You can also define attributes from the command line by setting the system variable ATTDIA equal to 0 (default value). When you use the INSERT command with ATTDIA set to 0, AutoCAD does not display the Enter Attribute dialogue box on the screen. Instead AutoCAD will prompt you to enter the attribute values for various attributes that have been defined in the block. To define the attributes from the command line, enter the INSERT command at the Command: prompt. After defining the insertion point, scale, and rotation, AutoCAD will display the following prompt:

Enter attribute values

It will be followed by the prompts that have been defined with the block using the ATTDEF command. For example:

Enter processor type < Unknown >:
Enter hard drive size < 100MB >:

Example 2

In this exercise you will use the INSERT command to insert the block (COMP) that was defined in Exercise 1. The following is the list of the attribute values for computers.

ITEM	MAKE	PROCESSOR	HD	RAM
Computer	Gateway	486-60	150MB	16MB
Computer	Zenith	486-30	100MB	32MB

Computer	IBM	386-30	80MB	8MB
Computer	Del	586-60	450MB	64MB
Computer	CAD-CIM	Pentium-90	100 Min	32MB
Computer	CAD-CIM	Unknown	600MB	Standard

1. Make the floor plan drawing as shown in Figure 13-14 (assume the dimensions).

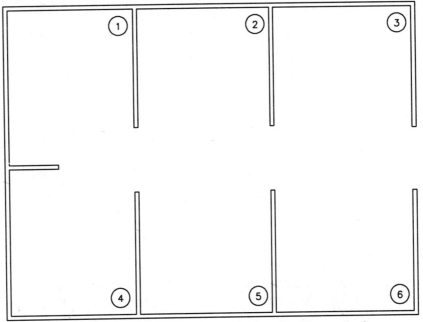

Figure 13-14 Floor plan drawing for Example 2

2. Set the system variable **ATTDIA** to 1. Use the **INSERT** command to insert the blocks and define the attribute values in the Enter Attributes dialogue box (Figure 13-15).

Command: **ATTDIA**
New value for ATTDIA<0>: **1**

Command: **INSERT**
Block name (or ?): **COMP**
Insertion point: *Specify the insertion point.*
X scale factor<1>/Corner/XYZ: ←┘
Y scale factor (default)=X): ←┘
Rotation angle<0>: ←┘

Enter Attributes
Block Name: COMP
Enter RAM: 64MB
Enter Hard-Drive size: 450MB
Enter processor type: 586-60
Enter make: DEL
OK   Cancel   Previous   Next   Help...

Figure 13-15 Enter the attribute values in the Enter Attributes dialogue box

3. Repeat the **INSERT** command to insert other blocks and define their attribute values as shown in Figure 13-16.

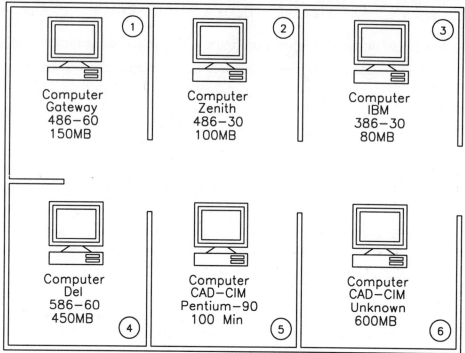

Figure 13-16 The floor plan after inserting blocks and defining their attribute value

EXTRACTING ATTRIBUTES

(DDATTEXT AND ATTEXT COMMANDS)

Using Dialogue Box (DDATTEXT)

Screen:	FILE, EXPORT, DDattEx:

To use the dialogue box for extracting the attributes, enter **DDATTEXT** at the Command: prompt. This command can also be invoked from the screen menu (Select FILE, EXPORT, DDattEx:). The information about the File Format, Template File, and Output File must be entered in the dialogue box to extract the defined attribute. Also, you must select the blocks whose attribute values you want to extract.

Figure 13-17 Attribute Extraction dialogue box

File Format

The File Format areas of the dialogue box let you select the file format of the extracted data. You can select Comma Delimited, Space Delimited, or Drawing Interchange Files. The format selection is determined by the application that you plan to use to process the data.

Comma Delimited File (CDF)

In CDF format, each character field is enclosed in single quotes and each records is separated by a delimiter (comma by default). CDF file is a text file with the extension **.TXT**.

Space Delimited File (SDF)

In SDF format, the records are of fixed width as specified in the Template File. The records are not separated by a comma and the character fields are not enclosed in single quotes. The SDF file is a text file with the extension **.TXT**.

Drawing Interchange File (DXF)

If you select the Drawing Interchange File format, the Template File name and the Template File edit box in the Attribute Extraction dialogue box is automatically disabled. The file created by this option contains only block references, attribute values, and end of sequence objects. The extension of these files is **.DXX**.

Template File

The **Template File** allows you to specify the attribute values that you want to extract and the information you want to retrieve about the block. It also lets you format the display of the extracted data. The file can be created by using any text editor like Edit or Edlin. You can also use a word processor or a database program to write the file. The template file must be saved as an **ASCII** file and the extension of the file must be **.TXT**. The following are the fields that you can specify in a template file (the comments given on the right are for explanation only; they must not be entered with the field description):

BL:LEVEL	Nwww000	*(Block nesting level)*
BL:NMAE	Cwww000	*(Block name)*
BL:X	Nwwwddd	*(X coordinate of block insertion point)*
BL:Y	Nwwwddd	*(Y coordinate of block insertion point)*
BL:X	Nwwwddd	*(Z coordinate of block insertion point)*
BL:NUMBER	Nwww000	*(Block counter)*
BL:HANDLE	Cwww000	*(Block's handle)*
BL:LAYER	Cwww000	*(Block insertion layer name)*
BL:ORIENT	Nwwwddd	*(Block rotation angle)*
BL:XSCALE	Nwwwddd	*(X scale factor of block)*
BL:YSCALE	Nwwwddd	*(Y scale factor of block)*
BL:ZSCALE	Nwwwddd	*(Z scale factor of block)*
BL:XEXTRUDE	Nwwwddd	*(X component of block's extrusion direction)*
BL:YEXTRUDE	Nwwwddd	*(Y component of block's extrusion direction)*
BL:ZEXTRUDE	Nwwwddd	*(Z component of block's extrusion direction)*
Attribute tag		*(The tag name of the block attribute)*

The extract file may contain several fields. For example, the first field might be item name and the second field might be the price of the item. Each line in the template files specifies one field in the extract file. Any line in a template file consists of the name of the field, the width of the field in characters, and its numerical precision (if applicable). For example:

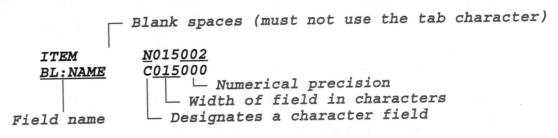

BL:NAME or **ITEM**

These are the field names. The field name can be of any length.

C C designates a character field, that is, the field contains characters or it starts with characters. If the file contains numbers or starts with numbers then C will be replaced by **N**. For example, **N015002**.

015 It designates a field that is 15 characters long.

002 It designates the numerical precision. In this example the numerical precision is 2, two places after decimal. The decimal point and the two digits after decimal are **included in the field width**. In the second example (000), the numerical precision is not applicable because the field does not have any numerical value (the field contains letters only).

Note

You can put any number of spaces between the field name and the character C or N (ITEM N015002). However, you must not use the tab characters. Any alignment in the fields must be done by inserting spaces after the field name.

In the template file a field name must not appear more than once.

The template file name and the output file name must be different.

The template file must contain at least one field with an attribute tag name because the tag names determine which attribute values are to be extracted and from what blocks. If several blocks have different block names but the same attribute tag, AutoCAD will extract attribute values from all selected blocks. For example, assume there are two blocks in the drawing with the attribute tag PRICE. When you extract the attribute values, AutoCAD will extract the value from both blocks (if both blocks were selected). To extract the value of an attribute, the tag name must match the field name specified in the template file. AutoCAD automatically converts the tag names and the field names to uppercase letters before making a comparison.

Example 3

In this example you will write a template file for extracting the attribute values as defined in Example 2. These attribute values must be written to a file COMPLST1.TXT and the values arranged as shown in the following table:

Field width in characters					
< 10 >	< 12 >	< 10 >	< 12 >	< 10 >	< 10 >
COMP	Computer	Gateway	486-60	150MB	16MB
COMP	Computer	Zenith	486-30	100MB	32MB
COMP	Computer	IBM	386-30	80MB	8MB
COMP	Computer	Del	586-60	450MB	64MB
COMP	Computer	CAD-CIM	Pentium-90	100 Min	32MB
COMP	Computer	CAD-CIM	Unknown	600MB	Standard

1. Load the drawing you saved in Example 2.

2. Use the **SHELL** command to shell out from the drawing editor and use the Edit function of DOS to write the following template file. You can use any text editor or word processor to write the file. After writing the file save it as an ASCII file under the file name TEMP1.TXT.

BL:NAME	C010000	*(Block name, 10 spaces)*
Item	C012000	*(ITEM, 12 spaces)*
Make	C010000	*(Computer make, 10 spaces)*
Processor	C012000	*(Processor type, 12 spaces)*
HD	C010000	*(Hard drive size, 10 spaces)*
RAM	C010000	*(RAM size, 10 spaces)*

3. Use the **DDATTEXT** command to invoke the Attribute Extraction dialogue box (Figure 13-18) and select the Space Delimited File (SDF) radio button.

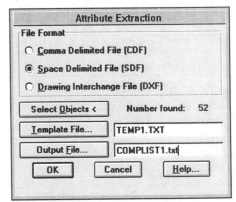

4. Select the objects (blocks). You can also select the objects by using the window or crossing option.

5. In the Template File edit box, enter the name of the template file, TEMP1.TXT.

6. In the Output File edit box, enter the name of the output file, COMPTLST1.TXT.

Figure 13-18 Enter information in the Attribute Extraction dialogue box

7. Select the OK button in the Attribute Extraction dialogue box.

8. Use the SHELL command to shell out from the drawing file and use a text editor or the EDIT function of DOS to list the output file, COMPLST1.TXT. The output file will be similar to the file shown at the beginning of Example 3.

Using the Command Line (ATTEXT)

You can also extract the attributes from the command line by entering the **ATTEXT** command at the Command: prompt. When you enter this command, AutoCAD will first prompt you to enter the type of output file. You could select CDF, SDF, DXF, or Objects. If you select the Objects option, AutoCAD will prompt you to select the objects whose attributes you want to extract. After selecting the objects, AutoCAD will return the prompt, this time without the Objects option. The following is the command prompt sequence for this command.

```
Command: ATTEXT
CDF, SDF, or DXF Attribute extract (or Objects)? <C>: E
Select objects: Select objects.
Select objects:◄─┘
CDF, SDF, or DXF Attribute extract? <C>: C or S
```

If you enter C or S (CDF or SDF), AutoCAD will prompt you to enter the name of the template file. The template files were discussed earlier in this chapter (refer to Template File).

Template file <default>: *Enter the name of the template file.*

After entering the template file name, AutoCAD will prompt you to enter the name of the extract file. The extract file is the output file where you want to write the attribute values. This prompt will be displayed for all attribute extract formats (CDF, SDF, or DXF).

Extract file name <drawing name>: *Enter the name of the output file.*

If you do not enter a file name, AutoCAD assumes that the name of the extract file is the same as the drawing file name with the file extension .TXT or .DXX, depending on the attribute extract format. If you enter the file name and you have selected CDF or SDF file extraction format, the file extension must be .TXT. If you have selected .DXF format the file extension must be .DXX. After entering the file name, AutoCAD will extract the attribute values from the blocks and write the data to the output file.

CONTROLLING ATTRIBUTE VISIBILITY

(ATTDISP COMMAND)

Pull-down:	Options, Display, Attribute Display
Screen:	OPTIONS, DISPLAY, AttDisp:

The **ATTDISP** command allows you to change the visibility of all attribute values. This command can be invoked from the pull-down menu (Select Options, Display, Attribute Display, Figure 13-19), from the screen menu (Select OPTIONS, DISPLAY, AttDisp:), or by entering **ATTDISP** at the Command: prompt. Normally, the attributes are visible unless they are defined invisible by using the invisible mode. The invisible attributes are not displayed on the screen, although they are a part of the block definition. The command prompt of ATTDISP is as follows:

Figure 13-19 Attribute Display option in the Options pull-down menu

Command: **ATTDISP**
Normal/ON/OFF/ <current> :

If you enter ON and press the Enter key, all attribute values will be displayed on the screen, including the attributes that are defined with invisible mode.

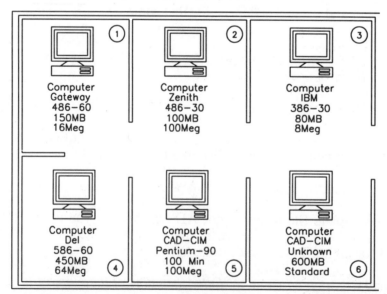

Figure 13-20 Using the ATTDISP command to make RAM attribute values visible

If you select OFF, all attribute values will become invisible. Similarly, if you enter N (Normal), AutoCAD will display the attribute values the way they are defined; that is, the attributes that were defined invisible will stay invisible and the attributes that were defined visible will become visible. In Example 2, the RAM attribute was defined with invisible mode; therefore, the RAM values are not displayed with the block. If you want to make the RAM attribute values visible, enter the ATTDISP command and press the Enter key.

EDITING ATTRIBUTES (DDATTE COMMAND)

Toolbar:	Attribute, Edit Attribute
Pull-down:	Modify, Attribute, Edit...
Screen:	MODIFY, AttEd:

The **DDATTE** command allows you to edit the block attribute values through the Edit Attributes dialogue box. This command can be invoked from the **Attribute** toolbar by selecting the Edit Attribute icon, from the pull-down menu (Select Modify, Attribute, Edit...), from the screen menu (Select MODIFY, AttEd:), or by entering **DDATTE** at the Command: prompt. When you enter this command, AutoCAD prompts you to select the block whose values you want to edit. After selecting the block, the Edit Attribute dialogue is displayed on the screen. The dialogue box shows the prompts and the attribute values of the selected block. If an attribute has been defined with Constant mode, it is not displayed in the dialogue box because a constant attribute value cannot be edited. To make any changes, click in the edit box and enter the new value. After you select the OK button, the attribute values are updated in the selected block.

    Command: **DDATTE**
    Select block: *Select a block with attributes.*

If the selected block has no attributes, AutoCAD will display the alert message, **Block has no attributes**. Similarly, if the selected object is not a block, AutoCAD again displays the alert message, **Object is not a block**.

Note

You cannot use the DDATTE command to do global editing of attribute values.

You cannot use the DDATTE command to modify the position, height, or style of the attribute value.

Example 4

In this example you will use the DDATTE command to change the attribute of the first computer, which is located in Room-1.

1. Load the drawing that was created in Example 2. The drawing has six blocks with attributes. The name of the block is COMP and it has six defined attributes, one of them invisible. Zoom in so that the first computer is displayed on the screen.

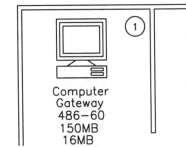

Figure 13-21 Zoomed view of the first computer

2. At AutoCAD command prompt, enter the DDATTE command. AutoCAD will prompt you to select a block. Select the block, first computer located in Room-1.

> Command: **DDATTE**
> Select block: *Select a block.*

AutoCAD will display the Edit Attributes dialogue box (Figure 13-22) on the screen that shows the attribute prompts and the attribute values.

3. Edit the values and select the OK button in the dialogue box. When you exit the dialogue box the attribute values are updated.

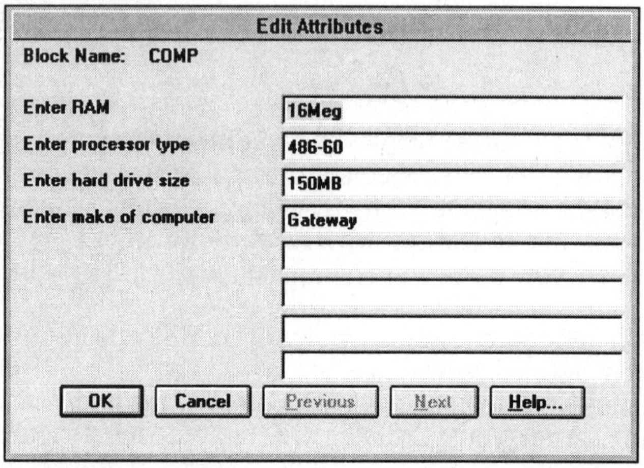

Figure 13-22 Editing attribute values using Edit Attributes dialogue box

EDITING ATTRIBUTES (ATTEDIT COMMAND)

Toolbar:	Attribute, Edit Attribute Globally
Pull-down:	Modify, Attribute, Edit Globally

The ATTEDIT command allows you to edit the attribute values independent of the blocks that contain the attribute reference. For example, if there are two blocks, COMPUTER and TABLE, with the attribute value PRICE, you can globally edit this value (PRICE) independent of the block that references these values. You can also edit the attribute values one at a time. For example, you can edit the attribute value (PRICE) of the block (TABLE) without affecting the value of the other block (COMPUTER). This command can be invoked from the **Attribute** toolbar by selecting the Edit Attribute Globally icon, the pull-down menu (Select Modify, Attribute, Edit Globally), or by entering **ATTEDIT** at the Command: prompt.

Global Editing of Attributes

When you enter ATTEDIT command, AutoCAD displays the following prompt:

> Command: **ATTEDIT**
> Edit attributes one at a time? <Y>: **N**
> Global edit of attribute values

If you enter N at this prompt, it means that you want to do the global editing of the attributes. However, you can restrict the editing of attributes by block names, tag names, attribute values, and visibility of attributes on the screen.

Editing Visible Attributes Only

After you select global editing, AutoCAD will display the following prompt:

Edit only attributes visible on screen? <Y>: **Y**

If you enter Y at this prompt, AutoCAD will edit only those attributes that are visible and displayed on the screen. The attributes might have been defined with visible mode, but if they are not displayed on the screen they are not visible for editing. For example, if you ZOOM in, some of the attributes may not be displayed on the screen. Since the attributes are not displayed on the screen, they are invisible and cannot be selected for editing.

Editing All Attribute

If you enter N at the above-mentioned prompt, AutoCAD flips from graphics to text screen and displays the following message on the screen:

Drawing must be regenerated afterwards

Now AutoCAD will edit all attributes even if they are not visible or displayed on the screen. Also, changes that you make in the attribute values are not reflected immediately. Instead, the attribute values are updated and the drawing regenerated after you are done with the command.

Editing Specific Blocks

Although you have selected global editing, you can confine editing of attributes to specific blocks by entering the block name at the following prompt:

Block name specification<*>: **COMP**

By entering the name of the block, AutoCAD will edit the attributes that have the given block (COMP) reference. You can also use the wild card characters to specify the block names. If you want to edit attributes in all blocks that have attribute defined, press the Enter key.

Editing Attributes with Specific Attribute Tag Names

Like blocks, you can confine attribute editing to those attribute values that have the specified tag name. For example, if you want to edit the attribute values that have the tag name MAKE, enter the tag name at the following AutoCAD prompt:

Attribute value specification<*>: **MAKE**

By specifying the tag name, AutoCAD will not edit attributes that have a different tag name, even if the values being edited are the same. You can also use the wild card characters to specify the tag names. If you want to edit attributes with any tag name, press the Enter key.

Editing Attributes with Specific Attribute Value

Like blocks and attribute tag names, you can confine attribute editing to a specified attribute value. For example, if you want to edit the attribute values that have the value 100MB, enter the value at the following AutoCAD prompt:

Attribute value specification<*>: **100MB**

By specifying the attribute value, AutoCAD will not edit attributes that have a different value, even if the tag name and block specification are the same. You can also use the wild card characters to specify the attribute value. If you want to edit attributes with any value, press the Enter key.

Sometimes the value of an attribute is null and these values are not visible. If you want to select the null values for editing, make sure you have not restricted the global editing to visible attributes. To edit the null attributes, enter \ at the following prompt:

> Attribute value specification < * >: \

After entering the above-mentioned information, AutoCAD will prompt you to select the attributes. You can select the attributes by picking individual attributes or by using one of the object selection options (window, crossing, etc).

> Select attributes: *Select the attribute values.*

After selecting the attributes, AutoCAD will prompt you to enter the string that you want to change and the new string. AutoCAD will retrieve the attribute information, edit it and then update the attribute values.

> String to change:
> New string:

The following is the complete command prompt sequence of **ATTEDIT** command. It is assumed that the editing is global and for visible attributes only.

> Command: **ATTEDIT**
> Edit attributes one at a time? < Y >: **N**
> Global edit of attribute values.
> Edit only attributes visible on screen? < Y >: **Y**
> Block name specification < * >:
> Attribute value specification < * >:
> Attribute value specification < * >:
> String to change:
> New string:

Example 5

In this example you will use the drawing from Example 2 to edit the attribute values that are highlighted in the following table. The tag names are given at the top of the table (ITEM, MAKE, PROCESSOR, HD, RAM). The RAM values are invisible in the drawing.

	ITEM	MAKE	PROCESSOR	HD	RAM
COMP	Computer	Gateway	486-60	150MB	**16MB**
COMP	Computer	Zenith	486-30	100MB	**32MB**
COMP	Computer	IBM	386-30	80MB	**8MB**
COMP	Computer	Del	586-60	450MB	**64MB**
COMP	Computer	**CAD-CIM**	Pentium-90	100 Min	**32MB**
COMP	Computer	**CAD-CIM**	**Unknown**	600MB	Standard

Make the following changes in the highlighted attribute values.

1. Change Unknown to Pentium.
2. Change CAD-CIM to Compaq.

3. Change MB to Meg for all attribute values that have the tag name RAM. (No changes should be made to the values that have the tag name HD.)

The following is the command prompt sequence to change the attribute value **Unknown** to **Pentium**.

1. Enter **ATTEDIT** command at AutoCAD command prompt. At the next prompt enter N (No).

   Command: **ATTEDIT**
   Edit attributes one at a time? < Y >: N
   Global edit of attribute values

2. We want to edit only those attributes that are visible on the screen, so press the Enter key at the following prompt:

   Edit only attributes visible on the screen? < Y >: ◄─┘

3. As shown in the table, the attributes belong to a single block, COMP. In a drawing there could be more blocks. To confine the attribute editing to COMP block only, enter the name of the block (COMP) at the next prompt.

   Block name specification < * >: COMP

4. At the next two prompts enter the attribute tag name and the attribute value specification. By entering these two values, only those attributes that have the specified tag name and attribute value will be edited.

   Attribute tag specification < * >: **Processor**
   Attribute value specification < * >: **Unknown**

5. Next, AutoCAD will prompt you to select attributes. Use the crossing option to select all blocks. AutoCAD will search for the attributes that satisfy the given criteria (attributes belong to the block COMP, the attributes have the tag name Processor, and attribute value is Unknown). Once AutoCAD locates such attributes, they will be highlighted.

   Select Attributes:

6. In the next two prompts enter the string that you want to change, then enter the new string.

   String to change: **Unknown**
   New string: **Pentium**

7. The following is the command prompt sequence to change the make of the computers from **CAD-CIM** to **Compaq**.

   Command: **ATTEDIT**
   Edit attributes one at a time? < Y >: N
   Global edit of attribute values
   Edit only attributes visible on the screen? < Y >: ◄─┘
   Block name specification < * >: **COMP**
   Attribute tag specification < * >: **MAKE**
   Attribute value specification < * >:
   Select Attributes:
   String to change: **CAD-CIM**
   New string: **Compaq**

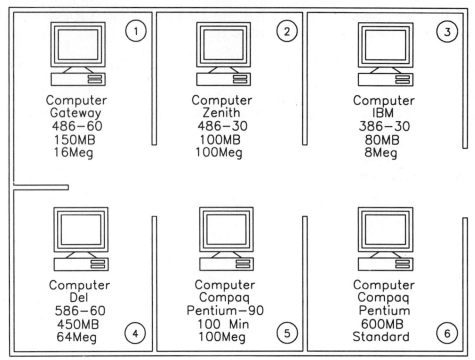

Figure 13-23 Using ATTEDIT to change the attribute values

8. The following is the command prompt sequence to change **MB** to **Meg**.

> Command: **ATTEDIT**
> Edit attributes one at a time? < Y > : **N**
> Global edit of attribute values

At the next prompt, you must enter N because the attributes (Tag name, RAM) that you want to edit are not visible on the screen.

> Edit only attributes visible on the screen? < Y > : **N**
> Drawing must be regenerated afterwards
> Block name specification < * > : **COMP**

In next prompt, about the tag specification, you must specify the tag name because the text string MB also appears in the hard drive size (Tag name, HD). If you do not enter the tag name, AutoCAD will change all MB attribute values to Meg.

> Attribute tag specification < * > : **RAM**
> Attribute value specification < * > :
> Select Attributes:
> String to change: **MB**
> New string: **Meg**

9. Use the **ATTDISP** command to display the invisible attributes on the screen.

> Command: **ATTDISP**
> Normal/ON/OFF/ < current > : **ON**

Individual Editing of Attributes

The **ATTEDIT** command can also be used to edit the attribute values individually. When you enter this command, AutoCAD will prompt **Edit attributes one at a time? < Y > :**. At this prompt press the Enter key to accept the default or enter Y. The next three prompts are about block specification, attribute tag specification, and attribute value specification, which have been discussed in the previous section. These options let you limit the attributes for editing. For example, if you specify a block name, AutoCAD will limit the editing to those attributes that belong to the specified block. Similarly, if you also specify the tag name, AutoCAD will limit the editing to the attributes in the specified block and with the specified tag name.

> Command: **ATTEDIT**
> Edit attributes one at a time? < Y > : ◄┘
> Block name specification < * > : ◄┘
> Attribute tag specification < * > : ◄┘
> Attribute value specification < * > : ◄┘

The next prompt is:

> Select Attributes:

At this prompt, select the objects by clicking on the objects or using an object selection option like window, crossing, wpolygon, cpolygon, or box. By using these options you can further limit the attribute values selected for editing. After selecting the objects, AutoCAD will mark the first attribute it can find with the mark X. The next prompt is:

> Value/Position/Height/Angle/Style/Layer/Color/Next < N > :

Value

The Value option lets you change the value of an attribute. To change the value, enter V at this prompt. AutoCAD will display the following prompt:

> Change or Replace? < R >

The change option allows you to change a few characters in the attribute value. To select the Change option, enter Change or C at the above prompt. AutoCAD will display the next prompt:

> String to change:
> New string:

At **String to change:** prompt, enter the characters that you want to change and press the Enter key. At the next prompt, **New string:** enter the new string.

Note

*You can use ? and * in the string value. When these characters are used in string values, AutoCAD does not interpret them as wild card characters.*

To use the Replace option, enter R or press the Enter key at the **Change to Replace? < R > :** prompt. AutoCAD will display the following prompt:

> New Attribute value:

At this prompt, enter the new attribute value and press the Enter key. AutoCAD will replace the string bearing the X mark with the new string. If the new attribute is null, the attribute will be assigned null value.

Position, Height, Angle

You can change the position, height, or angle of an attribute value by entering P, H, or A at the following prompt:

Value/Position/Height/Angle/Style/Layer/Color/Next < N > :

The position option lets you define the new position of the attribute value. AutoCAD will prompt you to enter the new starting, center, or end point of the string. If the string is aligned, AutoCAD will prompt for two points. You can also define the new height and angle of the text string by entering H or A at the above prompt.

Layer and Color
The Layer and Color option allows you to change the layer or color of the attribute. For color change, you can enter the new color by entering a color number (1 through 255), color name (red, green, etc.), Bylayer, or Byblock.

Example 6

In this example you will use the drawing in Example 2 to edit the attributes individually. Make the following changes in the attribute values.

a. Change the attribute value 100 Min to 100MB.
b. Change the height of all attributes with the tag name RAM to 0.075 units.

1. Load the drawing in Example 2 or load the drawing from the accompanying disk. The drawing file name is _____.

2. At AutoCAD command prompt, enter the **ATTEDIT** command. The following is the command prompt sequence to change the value of 100 Min to 100MB.

> Command: **ATTEDIT**
> Edit attributes one at a time? < Y > : ◄⏎
> Block name specification < * > : **COMP**
> Attribute tag specification < * > : ◄⏎
> Attribute value specification < * > : ◄⏎
> Select Attributes: Select the attribute
> Value/Position/Height/Angle/Style/Layer/Color/Next < N > : **V**
> Change or Replace? < R > : **C**
> String to change: \ **Min**
> New string: **100MB**

When AutoCAD prompts **String to change:**, enter the characters you want to change. In this example, the characters **Min** are preceded by a space. If you enter a space, AutoCAD displays the next prompt, **New string:**. If you need a leading blank space, the character string must start with a backslash (\), followed by the desired number of blank spaces.

3. To change the height of the attribute text, enter the ATTEDIT command as shown above. When AutoCAD displays the following prompt, enter H for height

> Value/Position/Height/Angle/Style/Layer/Color/Next < N > : **H**
> New Height: 0.075

After you enter the new height and press the Enter key, AutoCAD will change the height of the text string that has the X mark. AutoCAD will then repeat the above prompt. Use the **Next** option to move the X mark to the next attribute. To change the height of other attribute values, repeat the above steps.

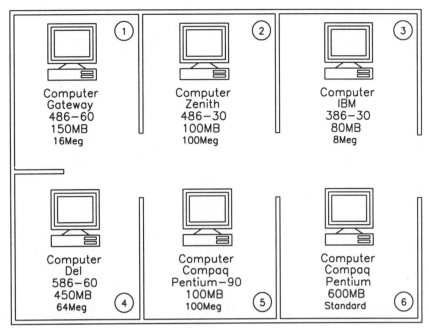

Figure 13-24 Using ATTEDIT to change the attribute values individually

INSERTING TEXT IN THE DRAWING

Using MTEXT Command

Toolbar: Draw, Text, Text
Pull-down: Draw, Text, Text
Screen: DRAW2, Mtext:

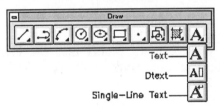

Figure 13-25 The Text icon in the Draw toolbar

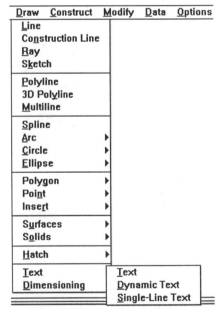

Figure 13-26 The Text option in the Draw pull-down menu

When you are using Windows, you can insert a text file by selecting the **Import** option in the **Edit Mtext** dialogue box. You can invoke this dialogue box by selecting the Text icon from the Text flyout in **Draw** toolbar (Figure 13-25), from the pull-down menu (Select Draw, Text, Text, Figure 13-26), from the screen menu (Select DRAW2, Mtext:), or by entering **MTEXT** at the Command: prompt. Next, AutoCAD will prompt you to enter the insertion point and other corner of the paragraph text box. After entering these points, the **Edit MText** dialogue box (Figure 13-27) appears on the screen.

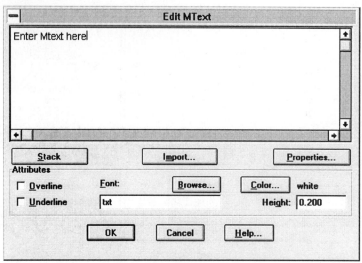

Figure 13-27 Edit MText dialogue box

The following is a brief description of some of the options of Edit Mtext dialogue box:

Import
When you select this option, AutoCAD displays the **Import Text File** dialogue box (Figure 13-28).

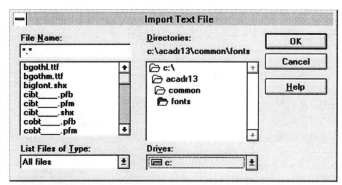

Figure 13-28 Import Text File dialogue box

In this dialogue box you can select any file that you want to import into the Edit MTEXT dialogue box. The imported text is displayed in the text area. Note that only ASCII files are properly interpreted.

Properties
When you select this option, AutoCAD displays the **MText Properties** dialogue box. You can use this dialogue box to change the text style, text height, direction, width, rotation, and attachment.

Attributes

Overline
If you click the overline button, it overlines the new or the selected text.

Underline
This button underlines the new or the selected text.

Font
You can specify the font by entering the font name (and path information) in the **Font** edit box. The selected font will be applied to the new text and the selected text.

Browse

If you select the Browse option, AutoCAD displays the **Change Font** dialogue box. You can use this dialogue box to browse through the font files and specify a font for the new text or change the font of the selected text. If the font is not recognized by Windows, AutoCAD will display the **Select Font** dialogue box. You can select one of the supported fonts from the list.

Color

If you select the **Color** button, AutoCAD displays the **Select Color** dialogue box. You can use this dialogue box to specify a color for the new text or change the color of the selected text.

Height

In the **Height** edit box, you can specify the text height of the new text or change the height of the selected text.

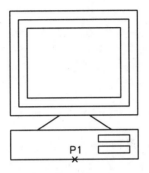

COMP	Computer	Del	586-60	450MB	64ME
COMP	Computer	Gateway	486-60	150MB	16ME
COMP	Computer	CAD-CIM	Unknown	600MB	Standarc
COMP	Computer	CAD-CIM	Pentium-90	100 Min	32ME
COMP	Computer	Zenith	486-30	100MB	32MB
COMP	Computer	IBM	386-30	80MB	8MB

Figure 13-29 Using ATTEDIT to change the attribute values individually

Using MTEXT Command for DOS

If you are using AutoCAD for DOS, you can insert a text file by using MTEXT command. When you enter MTEXT command AutoCAD will prompt you to enter two corners that define the width of the paragraph. After selecting the two points AutoCAD will switch to DOS editor and automatically assign a file name like AC000512. Use the open command to open the output file that contains the extracted attribute data (For example, COMPLST1.TXT). Use the **Save As** command to save this file under the same name as initially assigned to the file (For example AC000512.). Do not forget the period at the end of the file name. Now, exit the DOS editor. The file is inserted in the drawing.

Using ASCTEXT of AutoCAD Release 12

When you extract the attribute values from the blocks, AutoCAD writes the extracted values to a text file, as discussed earlier in this chapter (see Extracting Attributes). You can insert the text file in the drawing by using the **ASCTEXT.LSP** program that came with **AutoCAD Release 12**. You will find this AutoLISP program in the support directory and you can load it by entering the following command:

Command: **(Load "C:/ACAD12/SUPPORT/ASCTEXT")**
Command: **ASCTEXT**
File to read: *Enter filename.*

If the system variable FILEDIA is set to 1, AutoCAD will display the **File to Read** dialogue box on the screen. You can select or enter the filename in the dialogue box and then press the Enter key to exit from the dialogue box. To illustrate the function of this command, insert the text file (COMPLST1.TXT) that was created in Example 2. Once you enter the filename (COMPLST1.TXT), AutoCAD will request the following information:

Start point or Center/Middle/Right/?: *Select a point.*　　*(When you select a point, the text is automatically left justified. If you want to change the justification, select C, M, or R.)*

Height < default > : **0.095**
Rotation angle < default > : **0**
Change text options? < N > : **Y**
Distance between lines/ < Auto > : **0.25** *(The lines will be spaced vertically at the specified (0.25) distance.)*

First line to read/ < 1 > : ◄─┘
Number of lines to read/ < All > : ◄─┘　*(These two lines define the number of lines that you want AutoCAD to read from the text file. For example, if you enter 3 at the first prompt, AutoCAD will skip the first two lines.)*

Underscore each line? < N > : **Y**
Overscore each line? < N > : ◄─┘　　　*(If you enter Y at the above two prompts, AutoCAD will draw a line below and above the text.)*

Change text case? Upper/Lower/ < N > : ◄─┘
Set up columns? < N > : ◄─┘

If you press the Enter key, AutoCAD will insert the text file in the drawing. The drawing in Figure 13-30 shows the picture of the computer (drawing) and below that is the inserted text.

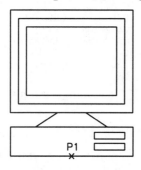

COMP	Computer	Del	586-60	450MB	64MB
COMP	Computer	Gateway	486-60	150MB	16MB
COMP	Computer	CAD-CIM	Unknown	600MB	Standard
COMP	Computer	CAD-CIM	Pentium-90	100 Min	32MB
COMP	Computer	Zenith	486-30	100MB	32MB
COMP	Computer	IBM	386-30	80MB	8MB

Figure 13-30 Using ATTEDIT to change the attribute values individually

If you enter Y at the above prompt, AutoCAD will request the following information about the columns:

Distance between columns:
Number of lines per column:

For example, if the distance between the columns is 6 and the number of lines per column is 3, AutoCAD will create two columns with three lines in each column (since there are six lines in the file).

SELF EVALUATION TEST

Answer the following questions and then compare your answers with the correct answers given at the end of this chapter.

1. The **Verify** option allows you to verify the attribute value that you have entered when inserting a block. (T/F)

2. Unlike a constant attribute, the **Preset** attribute cannot be edited. (T/F)

3. For tag names, any lowercase letters are automatically converted into uppercase. (T/F)

4. The entry in the **Value:** edit box of Enter Attribute dialogue box defines the _____ of the specified attribute.

5. If you have selected the **Align** option for the text justification, the Height < and Rotation < buttons are _____ .

6. You can also use the _____ command to edit text or attribute objects

7. The default value of **ATTDIA** variable is _____ , which disables the dialogue box.

8. In the **Space Delimited** file the records are of fixed width as specified in the _____ file.

9. In the _____ file the records are not separated by a comma and the character fields are not enclosed in single quotes.

10. You must not use the _____ characters. Any alignment in the fields must be done by inserting spaces after the field name. (T/F)

11. You cannot use the **DDATTE** command to modify the position, height, and style of the attribute value. (T/F)

12. The _____ command allows you to edit the attribute values independent of the blocks that contain the attribute reference.

13. The **ATTEDIT** command can also be used to edit the attribute values individually. (T/F)

14. You can use ? and * in the string value. When these characters are used in string values, AutoCAD does not interpret them as wild card characters. (T/F)

15. You can insert the text file in the drawing by entering the _____ command at AutoCAD's command prompt.

REVIEW QUESTIONS

Answer the following questions.

1. Give two major uses of defining block attributes._____

2. The attribute definition, called **Attribute Tag**, describes the characteristics of the attribute. (T/F)

3. The information associated with a block is known as _____ or _____ .

4.   You can define the block attributes by entering _____ at the **Command:** prompt.

5.   The most convenient way to define the block attributes is by using the **Attribute Definition** dialogue box, which can be invoked by entering _____ .

6.   What are the options in the **Mode area** of the **Attribute Definition** dialogue box?_____

7.   The **Constant** option lets you create an attribute that has a fixed value and cannot be changed later. (T/F)

8.   What is the function of the **Preset** option? _____

9.   The attribute value is requested when you use the Preset option to define a block attribute. (T/F)

10.   Name the three edit boxes in the **Attribute area** of the Attribute Definition dialogue box. _____ .

11.   The **Tag** is like a label that is used to identify an attribute. (T/F)

12.   The tag names can only be uppercase (T/F)

13.   The tag name cannot be null. (T/F)

14.   The tag name can contain a blank space. (T/F)

15.   If you select the Constant option in the Mode area of the Enter Attribute dialogue box, the Prompt: edit box is _____ because no prompt is required if the attribute is _____ .

16.   If you do not enter anything in the Prompt: edit box, the entry made in the Tag: edit box is used as prompt. (T/F)

17.   What option/button should you select in the Enter Attribute dialogue box to automatically place the subsequent attribute text just below the previously defined attribute? _____

18.   The text style must be defined before it can be used to specify the text style. (T/F)

19.   If you select a style that has the height predefined, AutoCAD automatically disables the Height < edit box in the Enter Attribute dialogue box. (T/F)

20.   If you have selected the Fit option for the text justification, the _____ button is disabled.

21.   What is the difference between the **ATTDEF** and the **DDATTDEF** commands? _____ _____

22.   The _____ command lets you edit both text and attribute definitions.

23.   The value of the block attributes can be specified in the Edit Attribute dialogue box. (T/F)

24.   The Edit Attribute dialogue box is invoked by using the _____ or _____ command with the system variable _____ set to 1.

25.   If you use the dialogue box to define the attribute values, the Verify mode is _____ because the Enter Attribute dialogue box allows the user to examine and edit the attribute values.

26. You can also define attributes from the command line by setting the system variable _____ equal to 0.

27. To use the dialogue box for extracting the attributes, enter _____ at the Command: prompt.

28. You can select Comma Delimited, Space Delimited, or Drawing Interchange Files. The format selection is determined by the text editor you use. (T/F)

29. In the comma delimited file, each character field is enclosed in _____ and each record is separated by a _____ .

30. If you select the _____ file format, AutoCAD does not request the Template Filename and the Template File edit box in the Attribute Extraction dialogue box is automatically disabled.

EXERCISES

Exercise 1

In this exercise you will define the following attributes for a resistor and then create a block using the BLOCK command. The name of the block is RESIS.

Mode	Tag name	Prompt	Default value
Verify	RNAME	Enter name	RX
Verify	RVALUE	Enter resistance	XX
Verify, Invisible	RPRICE	Enter price	00

1. Draw the resistor as shown in Figure 13-31.

2. Enter **DDATTDEF** at AutoCAD command prompt to invoke the Attribute Definition dialogue box.

3. Define the attributes as shown in the table of Exercise 1 and position the attribute text as shown in Figure 13-31.

4. Use the **BLOCK** command to create a block. The name of the block is RESIS and the insertion point of the block is at the left end of the resistor. When you select the objects for the block, make sure that you also select the attributes.

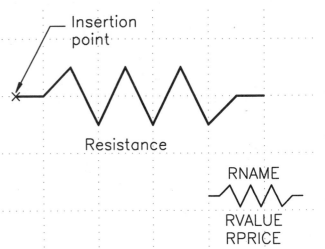

Figure 13-31 Drawing of resistor for Exercise 1

Exercise 2

In this exercise you will use the INSERT command to insert the block (RESIS) that was defined in Exercise 1. The following is the list of the attribute values for the resistances in the electric circuit.

RNAME	RVALUE	RPRICE
R1	35	0.32
R2	27	0.25
R3	52	0.40
R4	8	0.21
RX	10	0.21

1. Draw the electric circuit diagram as shown in Figure 13-32 (assume the dimensions).

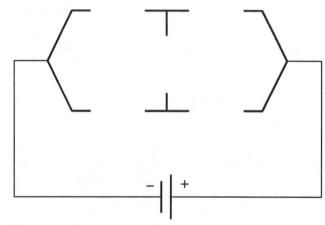

Figure 13-32 Drawing of the electric circuit diagram without resistors for Exercise 2

2. Set the system variable **ATTDIA** to 1. Use the **INSERT** command to insert the blocks and define the attribute values in the **Enter Attributes** dialogue box.

3. Repeat the **INSERT** command to insert other blocks and define their attribute values as given in the table. Save the drawing as ATTEXR2.DWG.

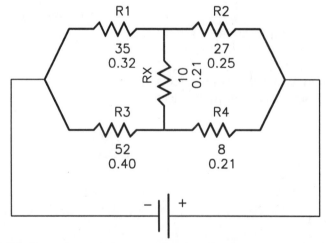

Figure 13-33 Drawing of the electric circuit diagram with resistors for Exercise 2

Exercise 3

In this example you will write a template file for extracting the attribute values as defined in Exercise 2. These attribute values must be written to a file RESISLST.TXT and the values arranged as shown in the following table.

Field width in characters			
< 10 >	< 10 >	< 10 >	< 10 >
RESIS	R1	35	0.32
RESIS	R2	27	0.25
RESIS	R3	52	0.40
RESIS	R4	8	0.21
RESIS	RX	10	0.21

1. Load the drawing ATTEXR2 that you saved in Exercise 2.

2. Use the **SHELL** command to shell out from the drawing editor and use any text editor to write the template file. After writing the file, save it as ASCII file under the file name TEMP2.TXT.

3. Use the **DDATTDEF** command to invoke the Attribute Extraction dialogue box and select the Space Delimited File (SDF) radio button.

4. Select the objects (blocks). You can also select the objects by using the window or crossing option.

5. In the Template File edit box, enter the name of the template file, TEMP2.TXT.

6. In the Output File edit box, enter the name of the output file, RESISLST.TXT.

7. Select the OK button in the Attribute Extraction dialogue box.

8. Use the SHELL command to shell out from the Drawing Editor and use a Text Editor to list the output file, RESISLST.TXT. The output file should be similar to the file shown in the beginning of Exercise 3.

Exercise 4

In this exercise you will use the DDATTE or ATTEDIT command to change the attributes of the resistances that are highlighted in the following table. You will also extract the attribute values and insert the text file in the drawing.

1. Load the drawing ATTEXR2 that was created in Exercise 2. The drawing has five resistances with attributes. The name of the block is RESIS and it has three defined attributes, one of them invisible.

2. Use AutoCAD's DDATTE or ATTEDIT command to edit the values that are highlighted in the following table.

RESIS	R1	**40**	0.32
RESIS	R2	**29**	0.25
RESIS	R3	52	**0.45**
RESIS	R4	8	**0.25**
RESIS	**R5**	10	0.21

3. Extract the attribute values and write the values to a text file.

4. Use the MTEXT command to insert the text file in the drawing.

Exercise 5

Use the information given in Exercise 3 to extract the attribute values and write the data to the output file. The data in the output file should be comma delimited CDF. Use the DDATTEXT and ATTEXT commands to extract the attribute values.

Answers

The following are the correct answers to the questions in the self evaluation test.
1 - T, **2** - F, **3** - T, **4** - default value, **5** - disabled, **6** - change, **7** - 0, **8** - template, **9** - space delimited, **10** - tab, **11** - T, **12** - ATTEDIT, **13** - T, **14** - T, **15** - MTEXT command

Chapter 14

External References

Learning objectives

After completing this chapter, you will be able to:
♦ Understand external references and their application.
♦ Understand dependent symbols.
♦ Use the XREF command and its options.
♦ Use the ATTACH, RELOAD, DETACH, and BIND commands.
♦ Change the path of a drawing.
♦ Use the XBIND command to add dependent symbols.

EXTERNAL REFERENCES

The **external reference** feature lets you reference an external drawing without making that drawing a permanent part of the existing drawing. For example, assume that we have an assembly drawing ASSEM1 that consists of two parts, SHAFT and BEARING. The SHAFT and BEARING are separate drawings drawn by two CAD operators or provided by two different vendors. We want to create an assembly drawing from these two parts. One way to create an assembly drawing is to insert these two drawings as blocks by using the **INSERT** command. Now assume that the design of BEARING has changed due to customer or product requirements. To update the assembly drawing we have to make sure that we insert the BEARING drawing after the changes have been made. If we forget to update the assembly drawing, then the assembly drawing will not reflect the changes made in the piece part drawing. In a production environment this could have serious consequences.

You can solve this problem by using the **external reference** facility, which lets you link the piece part drawings with the assembly drawing. If the external referenced drawings (piece part) get updated, the changes are automatically reflected in the assembly drawing. This way the assembly drawing stays updated no matter when the changes were made in the piece part drawings. There is no limit to the number of drawings that you can reference. You can also have **nested references**. For example, the piece part drawing BEARING could be referenced in the SHAFT drawing, then the SHAFT drawing could be referenced in the assembly drawing ASSEM1. When you open or plot the assembly drawing, AutoCAD automatically loads the referenced drawing SHAFT and the nested drawing BEARING.

If you use the **INSERT** command to insert the piece parts, the piece parts become a permanent part of the drawing and, therefore, the drawing has a certain size. However, if you use external reference feature to link the drawings, the piece part drawings are not saved with the assembly drawing. AutoCAD only saves the reference information with the assembly drawing; therefore, the size of the drawing is minimized. Like blocks, the external referenced drawings can be positioned at any desired location, scaled, or rotated.

DEPENDENT SYMBOLS

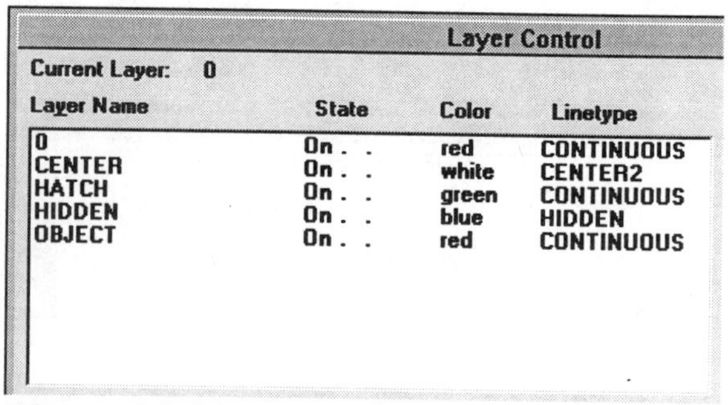

If you insert a drawing, the information about the named objects is lost. The **named objects** are entries like blocks, layers, text styles, layers, etc. For example, if the assembly drawing has a layer HIDDEN with green color and HIDDEN linetype and the piece part BEARING has a layer HIDDEN with blue color and HIDDEN2 linetype, when you insert the BEARING drawing in the assembly drawing, the values set in the assembly drawing will override the values of the inserted drawing. Therefore, in the assembly drawing the layer HIDDEN will retain green color and HIDDEN linetype, ignoring the layer settings of the inserted drawing. Only those layers that have the same names are affected. Remaining layers that have different layer names are added to the current drawing.

Figure 14-1 Layer settings of the current drawing override the layers of the inserted drawing

In the external referenced drawings the information regarding dependent symbols is not lost because AutoCAD will create additional layers with specified layer settings as shown in Figure 14-2. For external referenced drawings, the **dependent symbols** are features like layers, linetypes, object color, text style, etc.

The layer HIDDEN of the Xref drawing (BEARING) is appended with the name of the Xref drawing BEARING and the two are separated by the vertical bar symbol (|). The layer name HIDDEN changes to BEARING|HIDDEN. Similarly, CENTER is renamed BEARING|CENTER and OBJECT is renamed BEARING|OBJECT. The information added to the current drawing is not permanent. It is added only when the Xref drawing is loaded. If you detach the Xref drawing the dependent symbols are automatically erased from the current drawing.

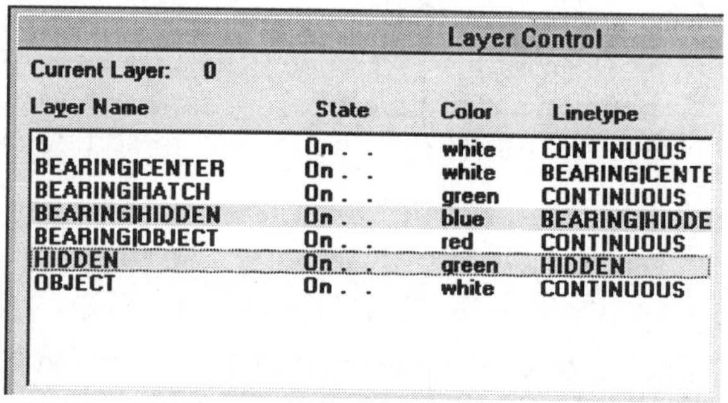

Figure 14-2 Xref creates additional layers

When you Xref a drawing, AutoCAD does not let you reference the symbols directly. For example, you cannot make the dependent layer, BEARING|HIDDEN, current. Therefore, you cannot add any objects to that layer. However, you can change the color, linetype, or visibility (on/off, freeze/thaw) of the layer. If the system variable **VISRETAIN** is set to 0 (default), the settings are retained for the current drawing session. When you save the drawing the changes are discarded and the layer settings return to their default status. If the VISRETAIN variable is set to 1, the layer settings like color, linetype, on/off, freeze/thaw are retained. The settings are saved with the drawing and are used when you Xref the drawing next time.

XREF OPTIONS

Attaching an Xref Drawing (XREF Attach)

Toolbar:	External Reference, Attach
Pull-down:	File, External Reference, Attach
Screen:	FILE, Xref:, Attach

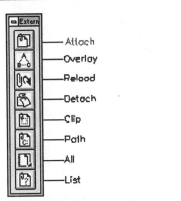

Figure 14-3 External Reference toolbar

Figure 14-4 Selecting External Reference options from the File pull-down menu

The **Attach** option of the **XREF** command can be used to attach an Xref drawing to the current drawing. This option can be invoked from the **External Reference** toolbar by selecting the Attach icon (Figure 14-3), from the pull-down menu (Select File, External Reference, Attach, Figure 14-4), or from the screen menu (Select FILE, Xref:, Attach). The following examples illustrate the process of attaching an Xref to the current drawing. In this example it is assumed that there are two drawings, SHAFT and BEARING. The SHAFT is the current drawing that is loaded on the screen; the BEARING drawing is saved on the disk. We want to Xref the BEARING drawing in the SHAFT drawing.

1. The first step is to make sure that the SHAFT drawing is loaded on the screen. You can copy the drawing from the accompanying disk or create a drawing with assumed dimensions. (One of the drawings does not need to be on the screen. You could attach both drawings, BEARING and SHAFT, to an existing drawing, even if it is a blank drawing.)

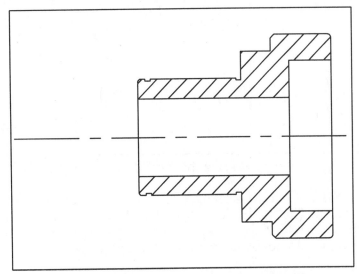

Figure 14-5 Current drawing, SHAFT

2. Use the XREF command to attach the drawing BEARING. After attaching the BEARING drawing save the drawing with the filename SHAFT.

Command: **XREF**
?/Bind/Detach/Path/Reload/Overlay/ < Attach > : ◄⎤
Xref to Attach: **Bearing**
Insertion point: Select a point

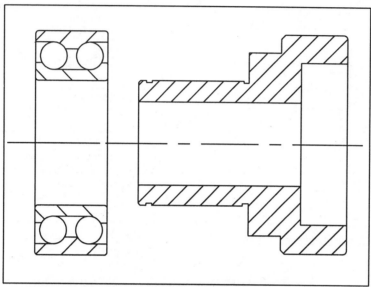

Figure 14-6 Attaching Xref drawing, BEARING

3. Load the drawing BEARING and make the following changes in it. Now, save the drawing with the filename BEARING.

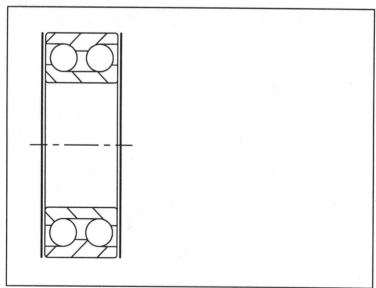

Figure 14-7 Modifying the Xref drawing, BEARING

4. Load the drawing SHAFT on the screen. You will notice that the Xref drawing **BEARING** is automatically updated. This is the most useful feature of XREF command. You could also have inserted the BEARING drawing as a block, but if you updated the BEARING drawing, the inserted drawing would not be updated automatically.

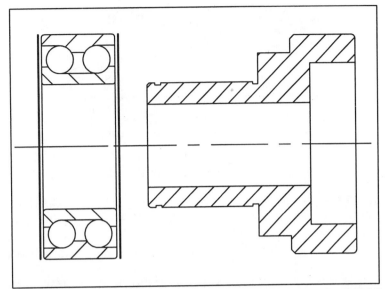

Figure 14-8 After loading the drawing SHAFT, BEARING is automatically updated

When you attach an Xref drawing, AutoCAD remembers the name of the attached drawing. The next time you attach the Xref drawing the previous Xref drawing name becomes the default name. The Xref drawing name is automatically converted to uppercase letters. If the Xref drawing has already been attached, AutoCAD displays a message to that effect as shown below:

Command: **XREF**
?/Bind/Detach/Path/Reload/Overlay/ <Attach> : ◄─┘
Xref to Attach <BEARING> : ◄─┘
Xref BEARING has already been loaded.
Use Xref Reload to update its definition.
Insertion point: *Indicate where to place Xref.*

> **Note**
>
> *If the Xref drawing you want to attach is currently being edited, AutoCAD will attach the drawing that has been saved earlier through the SAVE, WBLOCK, or END command.*

Points to Remember

1. When you enter the name of the Xref drawing, AutoCAD checks for block names and Xref names. If a block exits with the same name as the name of the Xref drawing, the Xref command is terminated and an error message is displayed on the screen.

2. When AutoCAD prompts for the name of the Xref drawing you want to attach, you can enter ~ (tilde) at the **Xref to Attach:** prompt. The tilde sign displays the **Select File to Attach** dialogue box on the screen, even if the FILEDIA system variable is turned off.

3. When you Xref a drawing, the objects that are in the Model space are attached. Any objects that are in the Paper space are not attached to the current drawing.

4. The layer 0 and DEFPOINTS and the linetype CONTINUOUS are treated differently. The layer 0 and DEFPOINTS and the linetype CONTINUOUS will override the layers and linetypes of the Xref drawing. For example, if the layer 0 of the current drawing is white and the layer 0 of the Xref drawing is red, the white color will override the red.

Layer Control			
Current Layer: OBJECT			
Layer Name	State	Color	Linetype
0	On . .	white	CONTINUOUS
BEARING|CENTER	On . .	white	BEARING|CENTE
BEARING|HATCH	On . .	green	CONTINUOUS
BEARING|HIDDEN	On . .	blue	BEARING|HIDDE
BEARING|OBJECT	On . .	red	CONTINUOUS
CENTER	On . .	64	CENTER2
DEFPOINTS	On . .	white	CONTINUOUS
HATCH	On . .	204	CONTINUOUS
OBJECT	On . .	24	CONTINUOUS

Figure 14-9   Layer Control dialogue box

5. The Xref drawings can be nested. For example, if the BEARING drawing contains the reference INRACE and you Xref the BEARING drawing to the current drawing, the INRACE drawing is automatically attached to the current drawing. If you detach the BEARING drawing, the INRACE drawing gets detached automatically.

6. When you attach an Xref drawing, you can assign it a different name. For example, if the name of the Xref drawing is BEARING and you want to assign it the name OBEARING, the command sequence is as follows:

Command: **XREF**
?/Bind/Detach/Path/Reload/Overlay/ < Attach > : ◄─┘
Xref to Attach: **OBEARING=BEARING**
Insertion point: Select a point

If you detach the Xref drawing **BEARING** it will have no effect on the Xref drawing **OBEARING**.

7. When you Xref a drawing, AutoCAD stores the name and path of the drawing. If the name of the Xref drawing or the path where the drawing was originally stored has changed, AutoCAD cannot load the drawing, plot it, or use the reload option of the Xref command. AutoCAD will display the Xref drawing name where it has been referenced (Xref Bearing). AutoCAD will also display an error message as shown in Figure 14-10.

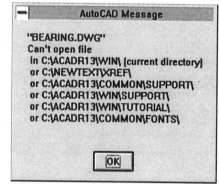

AutoCAD Message
"BEARING.DWG"
Can't open file
in C:\ACADR13\WIN\ [current directory]
or C:\NEWTEXT\XREF\
or C:\ACADR13\COMMON\SUPPORT\
or C:\ACADR13\WIN\SUPPORT\
or C:\ACADR13\WIN\TUTORIAL\
or C:\ACADR13\COMMON\FONTS\
[OK]

Figure 14-10 AutoCAD Alert dialogue box

Updating an Xref Drawing (XREF Reload)

Toolbar:	External Reference, Reload
Pull-down:	File, External Reference, Reload
Screen:	FILE, Xref:, Reload

When you load a drawing, AutoCAD automatically loads the referenced drawings. The **Reload** option of the **XREF** command lets you update the Xref drawings and nested Xref drawings any time. This option can be invoked from the **External Reference** toolbar by selecting the Reload icon, from the pull-down menu (Select File, External Reference, Reload), or from the screen menu (Select FILE, Xref:, Reload). You do not need to exit the Drawing Editor and then reload the drawing. When you enter the Xref command and select reload option, AutoCAD will prompt you to enter the name of the Xref drawing. You could enter the name of one Xref drawing or several drawings separated by comma. AutoCAD will scan for the referenced drawings and the nested Xref drawings. If you enter * (asterisk), AutoCAD will reload all Xref and nested Xref drawings.

Command: **XREF**
?/Bind/Detach/Path/Reload/Overlay/ < Attach > : **R**
Xref(s) to reload: Enter names of Xref drawings

This option is generally used when the Xref drawings are currently being edited and you want to load the updated drawing. The Xref drawings are updated based on what is saved on the disk. Therefore, before reloading an Xref drawing you should make sure that the Xref drawings that are being edited have been saved. If AutoCAD encounters an error while loading the referenced drawings, the XREF command is terminated and the entire reload operation is cancelled.

Detaching an Xref Drawing (Xref Detach)

Toolbar:	External Reference, Detach
Pull-down:	File, External Reference, Detach
Screen:	FILE, Xref:, Detach

The **Detach** option can be used to detach the Xref drawings. This option can be invoked from the **External Reference** toolbar by selecting the Detach icon, from the pull-down menu (Select File, External Reference, Detach), or from the screen menu (Select FILE, Xref:, Detach). If there are any **nested Xref drawings** defined with the Xref drawings, they are also detached. Once a drawing is detached, it is erased from the screen.

Command: **XREF**
?/Bind/Detach/Path/Reload/Overlay/ < Attach > : **D**
Xref(s) to detach: Enter names of Xref drawings

When AutoCAD prompts for Xref to detach, you can enter the name of one Xref drawing or several drawings separated by comma. You can also enter * (asterisk), in which case all referenced drawings, including the nested drawings, will be detached.

Adding an Xref Drawing (XREF Bind)

Toolbar:	External Reference, All
Screen:	FILE, Xref:, Bind

The **Bind** option lets you add the Xref drawings to the current drawing. This option can be invoked from the toolbar by selecting the ALL icon, or from the screen menu (Select FILE, Xref:, Bind). The Xref drawings, including the nested Xref drawings, become a permanent part of the current drawing and the bound drawing cannot be detached or reloaded.

Command: **XREF**
?/Bind/Detach/Path/Reload/Overlay/ < Attach > : **B**
Xref(s) to bind: Enter names of Xref drawings

When AutoCAD prompts for Xref to bind, you can enter the name of one Xref drawing or several drawings separated by comma. You can also enter * (asterisk), in which case all referenced drawings, including the nested drawings, will be added to the current drawing. You can use this option when you want to send a copy of your drawing to your customer for review. Since all the Xref drawing are a part of the existing drawing, you do not need to include the Xref drawings or the path information. You can also use this option to safeguard the master drawing from accidental editing of the piece parts.

Editing an XREF's Path (XREF Path)

Toolbar:	External Reference, Path
Pull-down:	File, External Reference, Path
Screen:	FILE, Xref:, Path

You can use the **Path** option to edit the path where the drawing is located. For example, if the drawing was originally in the C:\CAD\Proj1 subdirectory and the drawing has been moved to A:\Parts directory, the path must be edited so that AutoCAD can load the Xref drawings. In the following example the path of the BEARING Xref drawing has been changed from C:\CAD\Proj1 to A:\parts.

Command: **XREF**
?/Bind/Detach/Path/Reload/Overlay/ < Attach > : **P**
Edit path for which Xref(s): **BEARING**
Old path: C:\CAD\Proj1\Bearing
New path: A:\Parts\Bearing

When AutoCAD prompts **Edit path for which Xref(s)**, you can enter the name of one Xref drawing or several drawings separated by comma. You can also enter * (asterisk), in which case AutoCAD will prompt you for the path name of each Xref drawing.

The path name stays unchanged if you press the Enter key when AutoCAD prompts for new path name. When you enter the path name, AutoCAD will try to locate the file in the specified directory. If AutoCAD cannot locate the specified file, it will display an error message and disregard the new filename. AutoCAD will again prompt for the new path. Once you are done defining the filenames and path information, AutoCAD will reload the Xref drawings automatically. If it encounters any error, the entire path change information is ignored.

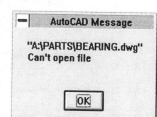

ADDING DEPENDENT SYMBOLS TO DRAWING

(XBIND COMMAND)

Toolbar:	External Reference, Block
Pull-down:	File, Bind
Screen:	FILE, Xbind:

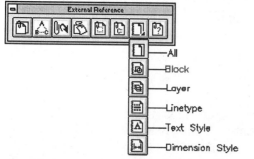

Figure 14-11 All flyout in the External Reference toolbar

Figure 14-12 Selecting Bind options from the File pull-down menu

You can use the **XBIND** command to add the selected dependent symbols of the Xref drawing to the current drawing. Once you XBIND the dependent symbols, AutoCAD does not delete them when you detach the Xref drawing or end the drawing session. This option can be invoked from the **External Reference** toolbar by selecting the desired icon from the All flyout (Figure 14-11), from the pull-down menu (Select File, Bind, Figure 14-12), from the screen menu (Select FILE, Xbind), or by entering **XBIND** at the Command: prompt. The following example describes how to use the XBIND command:

1. Load the drawing BEARING that was created earlier when discussing the Xref attach command. Make sure the drawing has the following layer setup; otherwise, create the following layers.

Layer Name	Color	Linetype
0	White	Continuous
Object	Red	Continuous
Hidden	Blue	Hidden2
Center	White	Center2
Hatch	Green	Continuous

2. Draw a circle and use the **BLOCK** command to create a block. The name of the block is **SIDE**. Save the drawing as BEARING.

3. Start a new drawing with the following layer setup.

Layer Name	Color	Linetype
0	White	Continuous
Object	Red	Continuous
Hidden	Green	Hidden

4. Use the **XREF** command to attach the BEARING drawing to the current drawing. When you Xref the drawing, the layers will be added to the current drawing as discussed earlier in this chapter.

5. Use the **XBIND** command to bind the dependent symbols with the current drawing. The dependent symbol is the block (SIDE) that was created in the BEARING drawing.

   Command: **XBIND**
   Block/Dimstyle/LAyer/LType/Style: **B**
   Dependent Block name(s): **BEARING|SIDE**
   1 Block(s) bound.

   AutoCAD will bind the block with the current drawing and the name of the block will change to BEARING0SIDE. If you want to insert the block, you must enter the new block name (BEARING0SIDE).

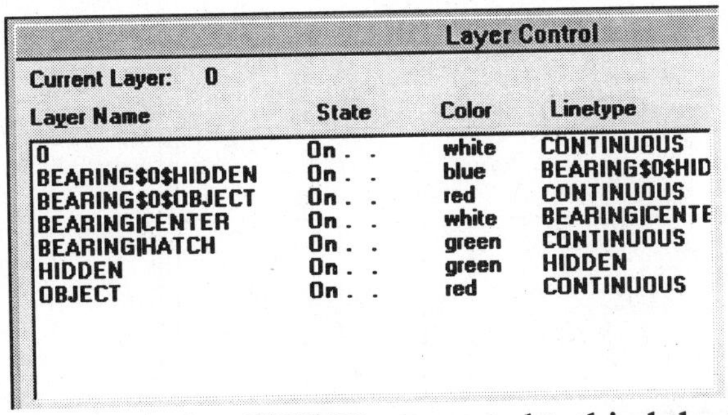

Figure 14-13 Using XBIND command to bind the layers

6. Again, use the **XBIND** command to bind the dependent symbols, HIDDEN and OBJECT layers of the Xref drawing.

Command: **XBIND**
Block/Dimstyle/LAyer/LType/Style: **B**
Dependent Layer name(s): **BEARING|HIDDEN,BEARING|OBJECT**
2 Layer(s) bound.

The layer names will change to BEARING0HIDDEN and BEARING&0$OBJECT. If the layer name BEARING0HIDDEN was already there, the layer will be named BEARING1HIDDEN. These two layers become a permanent part of the current drawing. If the Xref drawing is detached or the current drawing is saved, the layers are not discarded. The other way of adding the dependent symbols to the current drawing is by using the **Bind** option of **XREF** command. The bind option makes the Xref drawing and the dependent symbols a permanent part of the drawing.

THE OVERLAY OPTION

Toolbar:	External Reference, Overlay
Pull-down:	File, External Reference, Overlay
Screen:	FILE, Xref:, Overlay

One of the problems with the XREF Attach option is that you cannot have circular reference. For example, assume that you are designing the plan layout of a manufacturing unit. One person is working on the floor plan and the second person is working on the furniture layout in the offices. The names

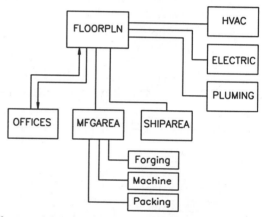

Figure 14-14 Drawing files hierarchy

of the drawings are FLOORPLN and OFFICES respectively. The person who is working on the office layout uses the XREF Attach option to insert the FLOORPLN drawing so that he or she has the latest floor plan drawing. The person who is working on the floor plan wants to XREF the OFFICES drawing. Now, if you use the XREF Attach option to reference the drawing, AutoCAD displays an error message because by inserting the OFFICES drawing you are creating a circular reference. To overcome this problem, you can use the Overlay option to overlay the OFFICES drawing. This is a very useful option, because the Overlay option lets different operators share the drawing data without effecting your drawing. This option can be invoked just any other XREF command option.

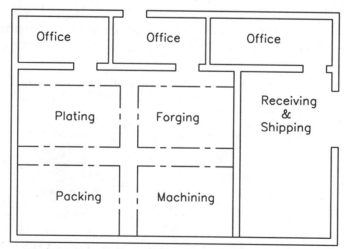

Figure 14-15 Sample plant layout drawing

Searching for External References

When you Xref a drawing, the path information is saved with the drawing. When you reload the drawing using XREF's Reload option or open the drawing, AutoCAD automatically loads the referenced drawing from the directory specified in the path. If the referenced drawing is not found in the specified path, AutoCAD will automatically search the directories specified in the ACAD environment variable. The ACAD environment variable can be set by entering the following line at the system prompt or in the batch file that loads AutoCAD:

Set ACAD=C;\;C:\ACADR13\Support\;D:\Drawings\Proj1

In this environment variable definition it is assumed that the drawings are in Proj1 directory on D drive. If the referenced drawing is not found in the directory as specified in the path, AutoCAD will search the file in the C drive root directory, ACADR13, Support, D drive root directory, Drawings, and Proj1 directories as defined in the environment variable.

Example

In this example you will use the XREF-Attach and XREF-Overlay to attach and reference the drawings. Two drawings, PLAN and PLANFORG are given. The PLAN drawing consists of the floor plan layout and the PLANFORG drawing has the details of the forging section only. The CAD operator who is working on the PLANFORG drawing wants to XREF the PLAN drawing for reference. Also, the CAD operator working on the PLAN drawing should be able to XREF the PLANFORG drawing to complete the project. The following steps illustrate how to accomplish the defined task without creating a circular reference.

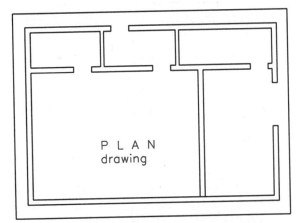

Figure 14-16 PLAN drawing

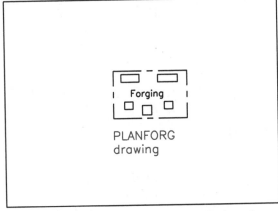

Figure 14-17 PLANFORG drawing

How circular reference is caused:

1. Load the drawing PLANFORG and use the XREF command to attach the PLAN drawing. Now, the drawing consists of PLANFORG and PLAN. Save the drawing.

2. Open the drawing file PLAN and use the XREF command to attach the PLAN drawing. AutoCAD will prevent you from attaching the drawing because it causes circular reference.

One possible solution is that the operator working on PLANFORG drawing detaches the PLAN drawing and then purges the block before saving it. This way the PLANFORG drawing does not contain any reference to the PLAN drawing and would not cause any circular reference. The other solution is to use XREF's Overlay option as follows.

How to prevent circular reference:

3. Open the drawing PLANFORG and use the Overlay option of XREF command to overlay the PLAN drawing. The PLAN drawing is overlaid on the PLANFORG drawing.

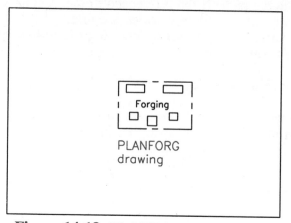

Figure 14-18 PLANFORG drawing

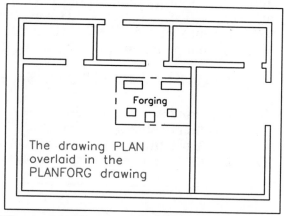

Figure 14-19 PLANFORG drawing after overlaying the PLAN drawing

4. Open the drawing file PLAN and use the Attach option of XREF command to attach the PLANFORG drawing. You will notice that only the PLANFORG drawing is attached. The drawing (PLAN) that was overlaid in the PLANFORG drawing does not appear in the current drawing.

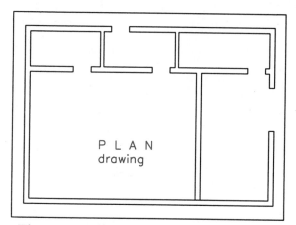

Figure 14-20 PLAN drawing

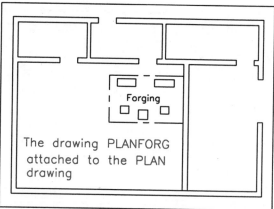

Figure 14-21 PLAN drawing after attaching the PLANFORG drawing

This way the CAD operator working on the PLANFORG drawing can overlay the PLAN drawing and the CAD operator working on the PLAN drawing can attach the PLANFORG drawing without causing a circular reference.

Self Evaluation Test

Answer the following questions and then compare your answers with the correct answers given at the end of this chapter

1. If the assembly drawing has been created by inserting a drawing, the drawing will be updated automatically if a change is made in the drawing that was inserted. (T/F)

2. The external reference facility helps you to keep the drawing updated no matter when the changes were made in the piece part drawings. (T/F)

3. AutoCAD only saves the reference information with the assembly drawing, and therefore the size of the drawing is minimized. (T/F)

4. The _____ are entries like blocks, layers, text styles, layers, etc.

5. What are dependent symbols?_____
_____

6. Can you add objects to a dependent layer? (Y/N)

7. If the VISRETAIN variable is set to _____, the layer settings like color, linetype, on/off, freeze/thaw are retained. The settings are saved with the drawing and are used when you Xref the drawing next time.

8. If a block exists with the same name as the name of the Xref drawing, the Xref command is terminated and an error message is displayed on the screen. (T/F)

9. When you enter ˜ (tilde) in response to **Xref to Attach:** prompt, AutoCAD displays the **Select File to Attach** dialogue box on the screen, even if the FILEDIA system variable is tuned off. (T/F)

10. If you insert a drawing using INSERT command, the information about the named objects is not lost. (T/F)

Review Questions

1. The **external reference** feature lets you reference an external drawing without making that drawing a permanent part of the existing drawing. (T/F)

2. If the assembly drawing has been created by inserting a drawing, what needs to be done to update the drawing if a change has been made in the drawing that was inserted? Explain. _____
_____

3. The **external reference** facility lets you link the piece part drawings with the assembly drawing. (T/F)

4. If the external referenced drawings get updated, the changes are not automatically reflected in the assembly drawing when you open the assembly drawing. (T/F)

5. There is a limit to the number of drawings that you can reference. (T/F)

6. Is is not possible to have nested references. (T/F)

7. If you use external reference feature to link the drawings, the piece parts are saved with the assembly drawing. (T/F)

8. Like blocks, the external referenced drawings can be positioned at any desired location, scaled, or rotated. (T/F)

9. What are the named objects? Explain. _____

10. What happens to the information related to named objects when you insert a drawing?_____

11. In the _____ drawings the information regarding dependent symbols is not lost.

12. For external referenced drawings the _____ are features like layers, linetypes, object color, text style, etc.

13. The information added to the current drawing is not permanent. It is added only when the Xref drawing is loaded. (T/F)

14. If you detach the Xref drawing the dependent symbols are not automatically erased from the current drawing. (T/F)

15. When you Xref a drawing, AutoCAD does not let you reference the symbols directly. For example, you cannot make the dependent layer, BEARING|HIDDEN, current. (T/F)

16. You can change the color, linetype, or visibility (on/off, freeze/thaw) of the dependent layer. (T/F)

17. If the system variable _____ is set to 0 (default), the settings are retained for the current drawing session. When you save the drawing the changes are discarded and the layer settings return to their default status.

18. The _____ option of the **XREF** command can be used to attach an XRef drawing to the current drawing.

19. When you attach an Xref drawing, AutoCAD remembers the name of the attached drawing. Next time you attach the Xref drawing the previous Xref drawing name becomes the default name. (T/F)

20. If the Xref drawing that you want to attach is currently being edited, AutoCAD will not attach the drawing. (T/F)

Exercises

Exercise 1

In this exercise you will start a new drawing and Xref the drawings Part-1 and Part-2. You will also edit one of the piece parts to correct the size and use the XBIND command to bind some of the dependent symbols to the current drawing. Following are detailed instructions for completing this exercise.

1. Start a new drawing, Part-1, and set up the following layers.

Layer Name	Color	Linetype
0	White	Continuous
Object	Red	Continuous
Hidden	Blue	Hidden2
Center	White	Center2
Dim-Part1	Green	Continuous

2. Draw Part-1 with dimensions as shown in the Figure 14-22. Save the drawing as Part-1.

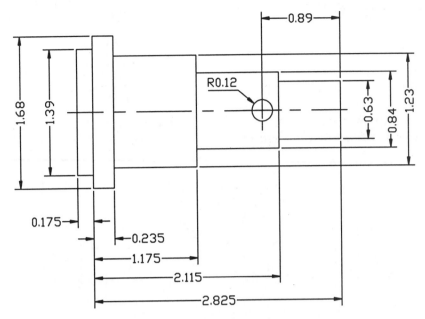

Figure 14-22 Part-1, Drawing for Exercise 1

3. Start a new drawing, Part-2, and set up the following layers.

Layer Name	Color	Linetype
0	White	Continuous
Object	Red	Continuous
Hidden	Blue	Hidden
Center	White	Center
Dim-Part2	Green	Continuous
Hatch	Magenta	Continuous

4. Draw Part-2 with dimensions as shown in the Figure 14-23. Save the drawing as Part-2.

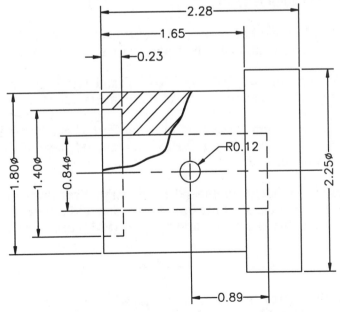

Figure 14-23 Part-2, Drawing for Exercise 1

5. Start a new drawing ASSEM1 and set up the following layers.

Layer Name	Color	Linetype
0	White	Continuous
Object	Blue	Continuous
Hidden	Yellow	Hidden

6. Xref the two drawings Part-1 and Part-2 so that the centers of the two drilled holes coincide. Notice the overlap as shown in Figure 14-24. Save the assembly drawing as ASSEM1.

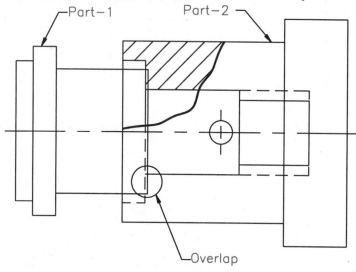

Figure 14-24 Assembly drawing after attaching Part-1 and Part-2

7. Open the drawing Part-1 and correct the mistake so that there is no overlap. You can do it by editing the line (1.175 dimension) so that the dimension is 1.160.

8. Open the assembly drawing ASSEM1 and notice the change in the overlap. The assembly drawing gets updated automatically.

9. Study the layers and notice how AutoCAD renames the layers and linetypes assigned to each layer. Check to see if you can make the layers belonging to Part-1 or Part-2 current.

10. Use the XBIND command to bind the OBJECT and HIDDEN layer that belong to drawing Part-1. Check again if you can make one of these layers current.

11. Use the detach option to detach the Xref drawing Part-1. Study the layer again and notice that the layers that were edited with the XBIND command have not been erased. Other layers belonging to Part-1 are erased.

12. Use the Bind option of XREF command to bind the Xref drawing Part-2 with the assembly drawing ASSEM1. Open the Xref drawing Part-1 and add a border or make any changes in the drawing. Now, open the assembly drawing ASSEM1 and check to see if the drawing is updated.

Answers
The following are the correct answers in the questions on the self evaluation test.
1 - F, **2** - T, **3** - T, **4** - Named objects, **5** - For external referenced drawings, the dependent symbols are features like layers, linetypes, object color, text style, etc., **6** - N, **7** - 1, **8** - T, **9** - T, **10** - F

Chapter 15

Plotting Drawings
Draw Commands

PLOTTING DRAWINGS IN AUTOCAD

When you are done with a drawing you can store it on the computer storage device like hard drive or diskettes. However, to get a hard copy of the drawing you should plot the drawing on a sheet of paper using a plotter or printer. With the help of pen plotters you can obtain a high-resolution drawing. The display of dialogue boxes concerning the PLOT command can be controlled with the **CMDDIA** system variable. If you set the CMDDIA variable to 1 (On), AutoCAD displays the **Plot Configuration** dialogue box on the screen and you can set the plot specifications through the dialogue box. If assigned a value 0 (Off), the dialogue box is not displayed.

PLOT Command

Toolbar:	Standard, Print
Pull-down:	File, Print...
Screen:	FILE, Print:

The PLOT command is used to plot a drawing. This command can be invoked from the Standard toolbar (Select Print icon), from the pull-down menu (Select File, Print..., Figure 15-1), from the screen menu

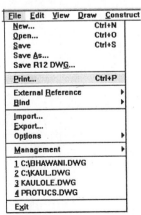

Figure 15-1 Selecting the Print... option from the File pull-down menu

(Select FILE, Print:), or by entering **PLOT** at the Command: prompt. As mentioned before, display of the dialogue boxes depends on the CMDDIA system variable. If the CMDDIA variable is set to 1, after invoking the PLOT command, the **Plot Configuration** dialogue box (Figure 15-2) is displayed on the screen.

Command: **PLOT**

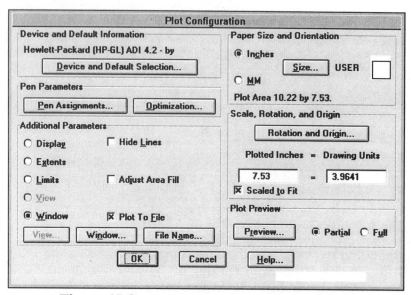

Figure 15-2 Plot Configuration dialogue box

Some values in this dialogue box are set when AutoCAD was first configured. You can examine these values, and if they conform to your requirements, you can start plotting. If you want to alter the plot specifications, you can do so through the options provided in the plot dialogue boxes. The following is the description of the available plot options:

Device and Default Information Area

In this area, information about the current configured device is displayed. If you want to check the information about the configured printers and plotters, pick the Device and Default Selection... button. When you select this button, **Device and Default Selection** dialogue box (Figure 15-3) is displayed on the screen. This dialogue box includes the following:

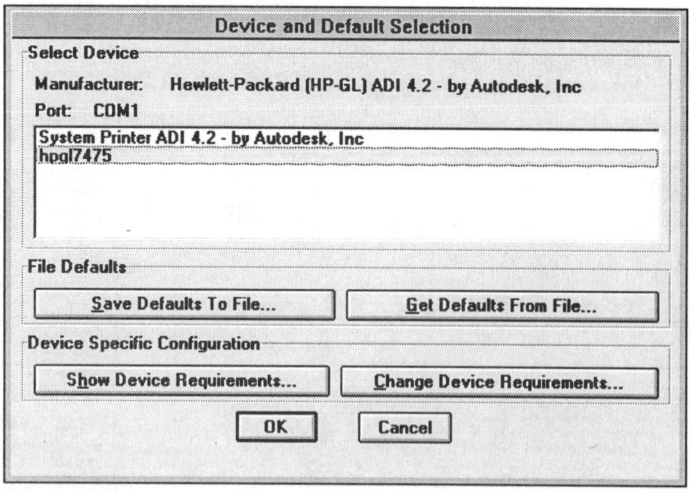

Figure 15-3 Device and Default Selection dialogue box

Select Device area

In this area, you can select a device from the list of devices to make it the current device.

File Defaults area

This area is comprised of the Save Defaults To File... button and Get Defaults From File... button.

Save Defaults To File... button

Pressing this button displays the **Save To File** dialogue box (Figure 15-4) on the screen.

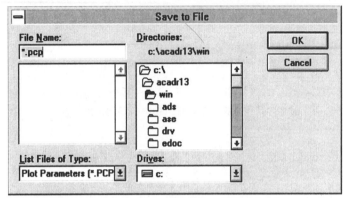

Figure 15-4 Save to File dialogue box

In the File edit box you can specify the name of the PCP file (Plot Configuration Parameters) in which you want to save the current setting of all parameters in the **Plot Configuration** dialogue box.

Get Defaults From File... button

Pressing this button displays the **Obtain from File** dialogue box on the screen. In the File edit box you can specify the name of the PCP file that you want to retrieve. All the plotting parameters are automatically set to their respective values in the specified PCP file. Hence, you can start plotting without having to change the setting of all parameters in the **Plot Configuration** dialogue box. If the PCP file you specify is working properly, AutoCAD acknowledges it with the message **Plot configuration updated without error**. If the PCP file specified is not working properly, AutoCAD acknowledges by displaying the **Error Information On File Defaults** dialogue box. In this dialogue box, all the errors in the selected PCP file are listed. If you want to generate an error file that contains all the errors listed in the Error Information On File Defaults dialogue box, pick the Create Error File button. These files have the same filenames as those of the selected PCP files and have the **.err** extension.

Device Specific Configuration

Sometimes a plotter or printer may have some additional configuration requirement that is not needed by other plotters ar printers. These configurations can be displayed and changed with the **Show Device Requirements** dialogue box and the **Change Device Requirements** dialogue box, respectively.

Show Device Requirements... button

Selecting the Show Device Requirements... button, displays the **Show Device Requirements** dialogue box (Figure 15-5).

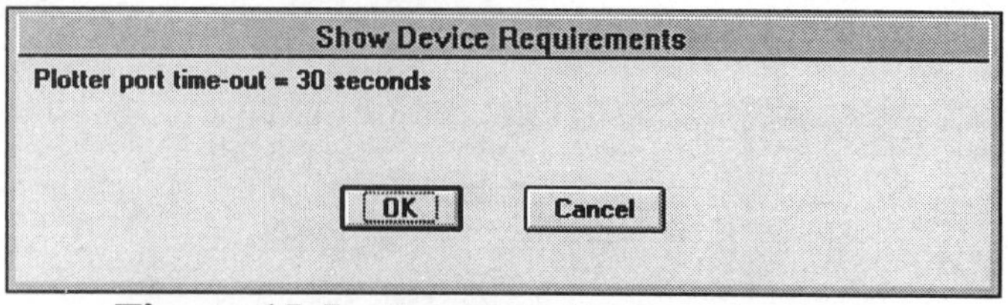

Figure 15-5 Show Device Requirements

As mentioned before, this dialogue box displays any extra configuration requirement of the current plotter or printer. For example, for an HPGL 7470 device, you can have plotter port time-out value as the extra configuration requirement.

Change Device Requirements... button

If you want to modify the additional configuration requirements of the current plotter or printer, select the Change Device Requirements... button. The **Change Device Requirements** dialogue box (Figure 15-6) is displayed. For example, for an HPGL 7470 device, you can change the wait time in this dialogue box. The following message may be displayed in the dialogue box:

How many seconds should we wait for the plotter
port to time-out (0 means wait forever), 30

The current wait time is 30 seconds. You can change it to your requirement.

Figure 15-6 Change Device Requirements dialogue box

Pen Parameters area

Pen Assignments... button

An important feature offered by AutoCAD is that different objects in the same drawing can be plotted in different colors, with different linetypes and line widths using layers. This can also be achieved by using the Pen Assignment dialogue box (Figure 15-7), which is displayed by picking the Pen Assignments... button.

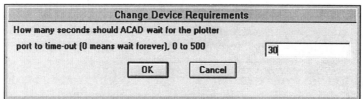

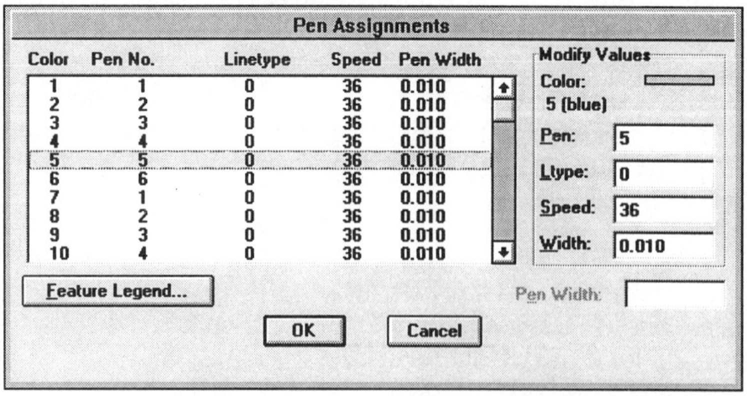

Figure 15-7 Pen Assignments dialogue box

Selecting Values in the Pen Assignments dialogue box

If you want to change the parameters assigned to a color or pen, select the color or pen in the Pen Assignment dialogue box. All parameters for that pen are displayed in the Modify Values area. You can enter the desired parameters such as pen, linetype, speed, and pen width in the corresponding edit boxes in the Modify Values area. For example, if an object is drawn red and with continuous linetype, you can change its linetype by assigning linetype 2 to red color in the Pen Assignment dialogue box. The line will be plotted according to specifications of linetype 2 (depending on the plotter, it may be hidden or dotted linetype). Similarly, you can specify the value for pen width. If you are using a pen that has a tip width of 0.03 inch, you may specify the pen width of 0.03. This way less number of strokes are needed to fill a solid line like trace and polyline. However, if you are using a raster output device like a laser printer, the pen width determines the width of the plotted line. For example, if you assign the red color a pen width of 0.05, all red lines will be plotted 0.05 inch wide.

If multiple pen facility or some parameters are not supported by the current plotter, the edit boxes and list box are grayed out and you cannot access them. AutoCAD also displays the message, **Not available for this device.** For example, if the current plotter does not support multiple colors and speed, all the entries concerning these parameters are grayed out and are inaccessible. If you want to see the linetype, select the Feature Legend button in the **Pen Assignment** dialogue box. AutoCAD displays the **Feature Legend** dialogue box (Figure 15-8).

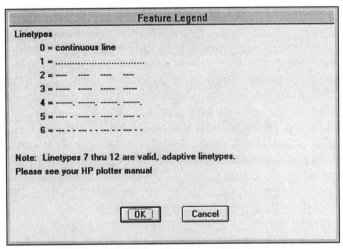

Figure 15-8 Feature Legend dialogue box

Optimization... button

The other button in the Pen Parameters area of the **Plot Configuration** dialogue box is the Optimization... button. When you select this button, the **Optimizing Pen Motion** dialogue box (Figure 15-9) appears on the screen.

Optimizing Pen Motion Dialogue Box

In this dialogue box, various checks boxes are displayed. These check boxes allow you to manipulate the efficiency with which pen movement takes place. By default all the check boxes except the first one and the last two are checked. The optimizations effect is cumulative in such a way that if you pick the fifth entry in the list of check boxes, all the check boxes up to the fifth one (except the first one) are also selected.

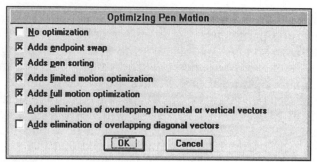

Figure 15-9 Optimizing Pen Motion dialogue box

Additional Parameters area

In this area of the **Plot Configuration** dialogue box, you can specify the area of the current drawing to be plotted. You can also control the way the plotting will be carried out. Various options in this area are:

Display radio button

If you select this radio button while you are in Model space, the whole current viewport is plotted. If you are in Paper space, the whole current view is plotted.

Extents radio button

By selecting this option, the section of drawing that currently holds objects is plotted. In this way this option resembles ZOOM Extents option. If you add objects to the drawing, they too are included in the plot because the extents of the drawing may also be altered. If you reduce the drawing extents by erasing, moving, or scaling objects, you must use the ZOOM Extents or ZOOM All option. Only after this does the Extents option understand the extent of the drawing to be plotted. If you are in Model space, the plot is created in relation to the Model space extents; if you are in Paper space, the plot is created in relation to the Paper space extents. If you invoke the Extents option when the perspective view is on and the position of camera is not outside the drawing extents, the following message is displayed **PLOT Extents incalculable, using display**. In this case, the plot is created as it would be created with the Display option. This option is disabled if the current drawing does not have extents.

Limits radio button

If you select the Limits radio button, the whole area defined by the drawing limits is plotted. The exception is if the current view is not the top view. In this case, the Limits options works exactly as the Extents options by scaling all the objects in the drawing to fit into plotting area.

View radio button

Selecting the View radio button enables you to plot a view that was created with the VIEW command. The view should have been defined in the current drawing. If no view has been created, the View radio button and the View... button are grayed out (disabled). These two options can be activated by creating a view in the current drawing. To select a view for plotting, pick the View... button. AutoCAD displays the **View Name** dialogue box (Figure 15-10). This dialogue box contains a list of all the views created in

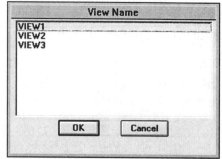

Figure 15-10 View Name dialogue box

the current drawing. Select the view you want to plot and then pick the OK button. In this case the specifications of the plot depends on the specifications of the named view.

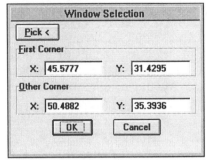

Window radio button
With this option, you can specify the section of the drawing to be plotted. The section of the drawing to be plotted is defined by a lower-left corner and an upper-right corner of the section. A window can be defined by picking the Window... button. The **Window Selection** dialogue box is displayed (Figure 15-11). The lower-left corner and an upper-right corner of the window can be specified by entering the coordinate values in the X and Y edit boxes in the dialogue box. This method is generally used when the window area is greater than the current screen display. Another way is by selecting the Pick button and then specifying the two corners of the window at the First corner and Other Corner prompts, with the help of pointing device, or by entering the coordinate values.

Figure 15-11 Window Selection dialogue box

Hide Lines check box
If you do not want the hidden lines of the objects created in Paper space to be plotted, select the Hide Lines check box.

Adjust Area Fill check box
The pen width for plotting solid-filled traces, polylines with a width, and solids can be controlled with the help of the Adjust Area Fill check box. Selecting this check box will pull the boundaries of the filled region inwards by a distance equal to half a pen width.

Plot To File check box
If you want to store the plot in a file and not have it printed directly on a plotter, select the Plot To File check box. Doing so activates the File Name... button.

File Name... button
The File Name... button displays the **Create Plot File** dialogue box (Figure 15-12) on the screen.

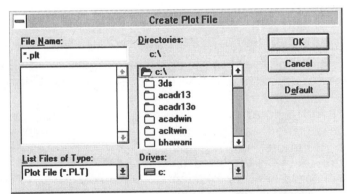

Figure 15-12 Create Plot File dialogue box

The filename for the plot file is to be specified in the File Name edit box. By default the filename is the same as the drawing name. However, you can enter a filename of your choice. The plot files have the **.plt** extension. If a plot file with the name you have specified for the current plot file already exists, AutoCAD gives you a message that the plot file already exists and asks you whether you want to change the previous plot file.

Paper Size and Orientation area

In this area, you can specify the paper size of the plot and the units for the plot size. You have the choice of selecting Inches or MM (millimeters). For example, if you want to make inches the unit for the plot size, select the Inches radio button. The paper orientation of the current plotter is reflected by the orientation icon. Two types of orientation icons are supported by AutoCAD: landscape icon and portrait icon.

Size... button

To set a size for the plot, pick the Size... button. AutoCAD displays the **Paper Size** dialogue box (Figure 15-13).

Setting the Paper Size for the Plot

In this dialogue box, all the plotting sizes that the current plotter can handle are listed. You can select any one of the sizes listed or specify a size (width and height) of your own in the USER edit boxes. You can define five sizes of your own.

Paper Size					
Size	**Width**	**Height**	**Size**	**Width**	**Height**
A	10.50	8.00	USER:	10.22	7.53
A4	11.20	7.80	USER1:		
MAX	15.64	9.96	USER2:		
USER	10.22	7.53	USER3:		
			USER4:		

Orientation is   landscape

OK   Cancel

Figure 15-13 Paper Size dialogue box

The MAX entry in the list of predefined sizes gives you the maximum size the plotter can support. Once you select a size, the sections in the Plot Configuration dialogue box pertaining to paper size and orientation are automatically revised to reflect the new paper size and orientation.

Scale, Rotation, and Origin area

The plot scale, rotation of the plot, and origin of the plot can be specified by picking the Rotation and Origin button in the Scale, Rotation, and Origin area of the **Plot Configuration** dialogue box.

Rotation and Origin... button

Once you pick the Rotation and Origin... button, the **Plot Rotation and Origin** dialogue box (Figure 15-14) is displayed on the screen. In this dialogue box, the rotation of the plot can be specified in the Plot Rotation area by selecting any one of the four angles. If you do not want to specify any angle, pick the radio button labeled 0. The rotations are performed in a clockwise direction. The location for the origin of the plot can be specified in the Plot Origin area by entering the X and Y coordinates of the origin point. The default plot origin is at (0,0).

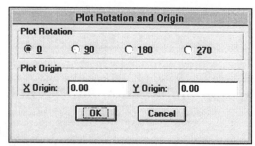

Figure 15-14 Plot Rotation and Origin dialogue box

Scale

The scale for the plot is displayed in the Plotted Inches = Drawing Units edit boxes. For example, if you have a scale factor of 25; i.e., 1 unit in the plot is equal to 25 units of the drawing, enter 1 in the Plotted Inches edit box and 25 in the Drawing Units edit box. If you want the drawing to be arranged automatically so that it fits on the paper, select the Scaled to Fit check box. In this case the edit boxes display the true size of the plot to fit. If this check box is disabled, the edit boxes display the previously set scale, or 1=1 if no previous scale exists. For detailed description read "Customizing Drawings According to Plot Size and Drawing Scale", Chapter 26 and "LTSCALE Factor for Plotting" Chapter 28.

Plot Preview area

You can view the plot on the specified paper size before actually plotting it by picking the Preview... button in the Plot Preview area of the **Plot Configuration** dialogue box. This way you can save time and stationery. AutoCAD provides two types of Plot Previews: partial and full.

Partial radio button

To generate a partial preview of a plot, pick the Partial radio button and then the Preview button. The **Preview Effective Plotting Area** dialogue box (Figure 15-15) is displayed on the screen.

Partial Preview

The paper size is graphically represented by the red rectangle. The paper size is also given numerically. The blue rectangle is the section in the paper that is used by the image. This area is also known as the effective area. The size of the effective area is also given numerically. If the paper boundary and the effective area boundary overlap (are same), it is graphically represented by red and blue dashed line. If you define the origin of the plot so that the effective area is not accommodated in the graphic area of the dialogue box, a green line is displayed along the clipped side and the following message is displayed: **Effective area clipped to display image**. Hence, with the help of a partial preview, you can

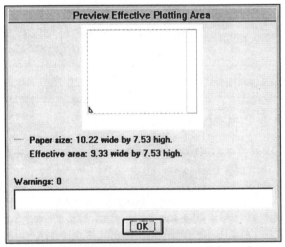

Figure 15-15 Partial preview of the plot

accurately see how the plot will look on the paper. If there is something wrong with the specifications of the plot, AutoCAD provides a warning message so that corrections can be made before actual plotting takes place.

Full radio button

Selecting the Full radio button and then the Preview button displays the drawing on the screen just as it would be plotted on the paper. Full preview takes more time than the Partial preview because regeneration of the drawing takes place. Once regeneration is performed, the dialogue boxes on the screen are removed temporarily and an outline of the paper size is shown. The **Plot Preview** dialogue box (Figure 15-16) is displayed. It contains Pan and Zoom and End Preview buttons.

Pan and Zoom button

This facility helps to zoom into a particular area in the plot preview displayed on the screen and move around it with the pan option. This option is useful in complicated drawings where you need to check minor details of the plot. After picking the Pan and Zoom button, a view box with an X inside it is displayed on the screen. The view box represents your viewport. This option is similar to the ZOOM Dynamic. You can move the pan view box anywhere on the screen. After placing it, press the pick button. This changes the pan view box to the zoom view box. The X mark is replaced with an arrow pointing towards the right side of the box. If you move the

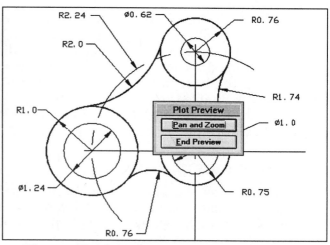

Figure 15-16 Full preview of the plot

pointer toward the right side, the zoom view box increases in size; if you move the pointer toward the left side, the zoom view box decreases in size. You can change the vertical position of the box without changing the size of the box. After specifying the right size and position for the pan and zoom box, press the Enter key. At the pan location, the drawing is displayed again with the selected zoom scale. You will notice that the **Plot Preview** dialogue box has changed. It now contains Zoom Preview and End Preview buttons. If you want to display the full preview on the screen, pick the Zoom Preview button. To end the previewing and switch back to the **Plot Configuration** dialogue box, pick the End Preview button.

Exercise 1

Make the given drawing and plot it according to the following specifications. It is assumed that the plotter supports 6 pens.

1. The object lines must be plotted with Pen-1.
2. The dimension lines and center lines must be plotted with Pen-2.
3. The border and title block must be plotted with Pen-6.

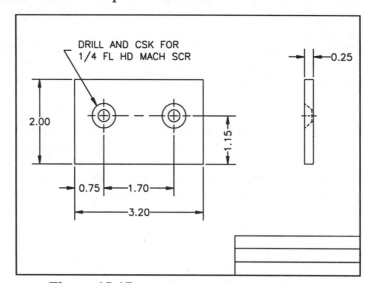

Figure 15-17 Drawing for Exercise 1

CREATING MULTILINES

AutoCAD's Multiline feature allows you to draw composite lines that consist of multiple parallel lines. You can draw these lines with the **MLINE** command. Before drawing multilines, you need to set the multiline style. This can be accomplished using the **MLSTYLE** command. Also, editing of the multilines is made possible by **MLEDIT** command.

DEFINING MULTILINE STYLE (MLSTYLE COMMAND)

Toolbar:	Object Properties, Multiline Style
Pull-down:	Data, Multiline Style...
Screen:	DATA, MLstyle:

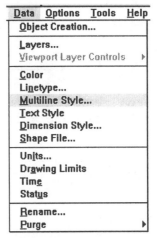

Figure 15-18 Multiline Style... option in Data pull-down menu

The **MLSTYLE** command allows you to set the style of multilines. You can specify the number of elements in the multiline and the properties of each element. The style also controls the end caps, end lines, and the background color of multilines. This command can be invoked from the Object Properties toolbar (Select Multiline Style icon), from the pull-down menu (Select Data, Multiline Style..., Figure 15-18), from the screen menu (Select DATA, MLstyle:), or by entering **MLSTYLE** at the Command: prompt.

When you enter this command, AutoCAD displays the **Multiline Styles** dialogue box (Figure 15-19) on the screen. With this dialogue box, you can set the spacing between the parallel lines, linetype pattern, colors, solid background fill, and capping arrangements. By default, the multiline style (STANDARD) has two lines that are offset at 0.5 and -0.5.

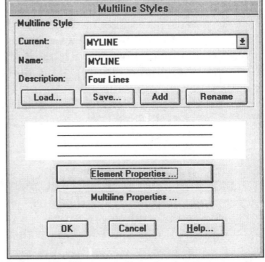

Figure 15-19 Multiline Style dialogue box

The Multiline Style dialogue box has the following options:

Current
The **Current** edit box displays and sets the current multiline style. If several styles have been defined, the name of the current style is displayed in the current edit box. You can use the arrow button to pop up the list predefined styles and make any style current. The list of multiline styles can include the multiline styles that have been defined in an externally referenced drawing (Xref drawings).

Name
The **Name** edit box lets you enter the name of the multiline style that you are defining. You can also use it to rename a style.

Description
The **Description** edit box allows you to enter the description of the multiline style. The length of the description can be up to 255 characters, including spaces.

Load...

The **Load...** button allows you to load a multiline style from an external multiline library file (acad.mln). When you select this button, AutoCAD displays the **Load Multiline Style dialogue box**. With this dialogue box you can select the style that you want to make current. You can also use this dialogue box to load a pre-defined multiline file (.mln file) by selecting the **File...** button and then selecting the file that you want to load. Once the file is loaded, you can select a style that is defined in the **.mln** file.

Save...

The **Save...** button lets you save or copy the current multiline style to an external file (.mln file). When you select this button, AutoCAD displays the **Save Multiline Styles** dialogue box listing the names of the pre-defined multiline style (.mln) files. From the file listing, select the file or enter the name of the file where you want to save the current multiline style.

Add

The **Add** button allows you to add the multiline style name (the Style name displayed in the Name edit box) to the current multiline file (.mln file).

Rename

The **Rename** button allows you to rename the current multiline style. It will rename the multiline style that is displayed in the Current: edit box with the name that is displayed in the Name: edit box. You cannot rename the **Standard** multiline style.

Line Display Panel

The **Multiline Styles** dialogue box also displays the multiline configuration in the display panel. The panel will display the color, linetype, and the relative spacing of the lines.

Element Properties

If you select the Element Properties... button from the **Multiline Styles** dialogue box AutoCAD will display the **Element Properties** dialogue box (Figure 15-20). This dialogue box gives you the following options for setting the properties of the individual lines (elements) that constitute the multiline.

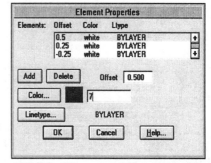

Figure 15-20 Element Properties dialogue box

Elements

The **Elements** box displays the offset, color, and linetype of each line that constitutes the current multiline style. The lines are always listed in descending order based on the offset distance. For example, a line with 0.5 offset will be listed first and a line with 0.25 offset will be listed next.

Add

The Add button lets you add new lines to the current line style. The maximum number of lines that you can add is 16. When you select the Add button, AutoCAD inserts a line with the offset distance of 0.00. After the line is added, you can change its offset distance, color, or linetype by selecting, the Offset, Color..., or Linetype... buttons.

Delete

The **Delete** button allows you to delete the line that is highlighted in the Elements list box.

Offset

The **Offset** button allows you to change the offset distance of the selected line in the Elements list box. The offset distance is defined with respect to the origin 0,0. The offset distance can be a positive or a negative value, which enables you to center the lines.

Color...

The **Color...** button allows you to assign a color to the selected line. When you select this button, AutoCAD displays the standard color dialogue box (Select Color dialogue box). You can select a color from the dialogue box or enter a color number or name in the edit box located to the right of the color swatch box in the Element Properties dialogue box.

Linetype...

The **Linetype...** button allows you to assign a linetype to the selected line. When you select this button, AutoCAD displays the standard linetype dialogue box (Select Linetypes dialogue box). After selecting the linetype, pick the OK button to exit the dialogue box.

> **Note**
>
> *When you change the element properties or the multiline properties, the current multiline style may not be updated. To resolve such problems, add the multiline style to the current multiline style (.mln) file. This can be accomplished by entering the new style name in the Name: edit box of the Multiline Styles dialogue box and then selecting the Add button.*

Multiline Properties

If you select the Multiline Line properties button from the Multiline Style dialogue box, AutoCAD will display the **Multiline Properties** dialogue box (Figure 15-21). You can use this dialogue box to define Multiline properties like display joints, end caps, and background fill. The dialogue box provides the following options:

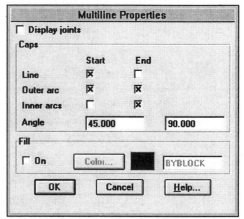

Figure 15-21 Multiline Properties dialogue box

Display Joints

If you select the Display joints check box, AutoCAD will display a **miter** line across all elements of the multiline at the point where two multilines meet. If you draw only one multiline segment, no miter line is drawn because there is no intersection point.

Line

The **Line** option draws a line cap at the start and end of each multiline. It has two check boxes that control the start and end caps.

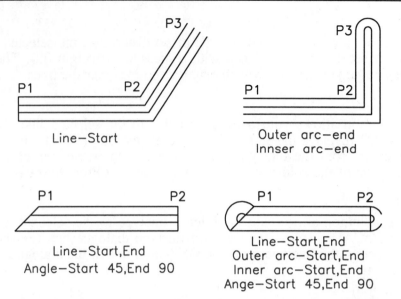

Figure 15-22 Drawing multilines with different end cap specifications

Outer Arc

The **Outer arc** option draws an arc (semicircle) between the end points of the outermost lines.

Inner Arc

The **Inner arc** option controls the inner arcs at the start and end of a multiline. The arc is drawn between the even-numbered inner lines. For example, if there are two inner lines, an arc will be drawn at the ends of these lines. However, if there are three inner lines, the middle line is not capped with an arc.

Angle

The **Angle** option controls the cap angle at the start and end of a multiline. The value of this angle can be from 10 degrees to 170 degrees.

Fill

The **Fill** option toggles the background fill on and off. If the fill is On, you can select the color of the background fill by selecting the color button. When you select this button, AutoCAD will display the standard color dialogue box. You can also set the color by entering the color name or color number in the edit box located to the right of color swatch box.

DRAWING MULTILINES (MLINE COMMAND)

Toolbar:	Draw, Polyline, Multiline
Pull-down:	Draw, Multiline
Screen:	DRAW1, Mline:

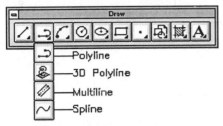

Figure 15-23 Selecting the Multiline icon from the Polyline flyout in Draw toolbar

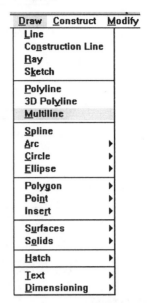

Figure 15-24 Selecting the Multiline option from the Draw pull-down menu

 The **MLINE** command can be used to draw multilines. It can be invoked from the toolbar by selecting the Multiline icon from the Polyline flyout in the **Draw** toolbar (Figure 15-23), from the pull-down menu (Select Draw, Multiline, Figure 15-24), from the screen menu (Select DRAW1, Mline:) or by entering **MLINE** at the Command: prompt. The following is the command prompt sequence of **MLINE** command:

Command: **MLINE**
Justification=Top, Scale=1.00, Style=Mystyle1
Justification/Scale/STyle/<From point>: *Select a point.*
To point: *Select the second point.*
Undo/<To point>: *Select next point or enter U for undo.*
Close/Undo/<To point>: *Select next point, enter U, or C for close.*

When you enter the **MLINE** command, it always displays the status of the multiline justification, scale, and style name. The command provides the following options:

Justification Option
The justification determines how a multiline is drawn between the specified points. Three justifications are available for MLINE command: Top, Zero, and Bottom.

Top
The **Top** justification produces a multiline so that the top line coincides with the selected points. Since the line offsets in a multiline are arranged in descending order, the line with the largest positive offset will coincide with the selected points.

Zero
This option will produce a multiline so that the zero offset position of the multiline coincides with selected points. Multilines will be centered if positive and negative offsets are equal.

Bottom
The **Bottom** option will produce a multiline in which the bottom line (the line with the least offset distance) coincides with the selected point when the line is drawn from left to right.

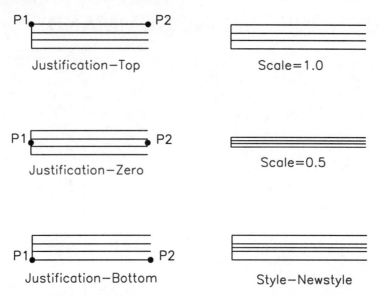

Figure 15-25 Drawing multilines with different justifications

Scale Option

The **Scale** option allows you to change the scale of the multiline. For example, if the scale factor is 0.5, the distance between the lines (offset distance) will be reduced to half. Therefore, the width of the multiline will be half of what was defined in the multiline style. A negative scale factor will flip the order of the offset lines. Multilines are drawn so that the line with the maximum offset distance is at the top and the line with the least offset distance is at the bottom. If you enter a scale factor of -0.5, the order in which the lines are drawn will be flipped and the offset distances will be reduced by half. (The line with the least offset will be drawn at the top.). Here it is assumed that the lines are drawn from left to right. If the lines are drawn from right to left, the offsets are reversed. Also, if the scale factor is 0, AutoCAD forces the multiline into a single line. The line still possesses the properties of a multiline. The scale does not affect the linetype scale (LTSCALE).

STyle Option

The **STyle** option allows you to change the current multiline style. The style must be defined before using the STyle option to change the style.

EDITING MULTILINES (USING GRIPS)

Multilines can be edited using GRIPS. When you select a multiline, the grips appear at the end points based on the justification used when drawing multilines. For example, if the multilines are top-justified, the grips will be displayed at the end point of the first (top) line segment. Similarly, for zero and bottom-justified multilines, the grips are displayed on the center and bottom line, respectively.

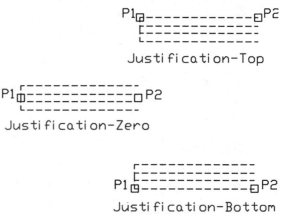

Figure 15-26 Using GRIPS to edit multilines

> **Note**
>
> *Multilines do not support some editing commands, such as BREAK, CHAMFER, FILLET, TRIM or EXTEND. However, commands like COPY, MOVE, MIRROR, STRETCH, EXPLODE and some Object Snap modes can be used with multilines. You must use the MLEDIT command to edit multilines. The MLEDIT command has several options that makes it easier to edit these lines.*

EDITING MULTILINES (USING THE MLEDIT COMMAND)

Toolbar:	Modify, Edit Polyline, Edit Multiline
Pull-down:	Modify, Mledit...
Screen:	MODIFY, Mledit:

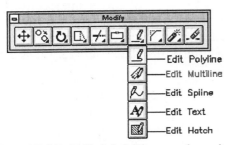

Figure 15-27 Edit Multilines... icon in the Modify toolbar

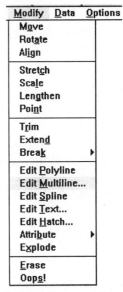

Figure 15-28 Mledit... option in the Modify pull-down menu

The **MLEDIT** command can be invoked toolbar by selecting the Edit Multiline icon from the Edit Polyline flyout in the **Modify** toolbar (Figure 15-27), from the pull-down menu (Select Modify, Mledit..., Figure 15-28), from the screen menu (Select MODIFY, Mledit:), or by entering **MLEDIT** at the Command: prompt. When you enter this command, AutoCAD will display the **Multiline Edit Tools** dialogue box (Figure 15-29) on the screen. The dialogue box contains five basic editing tools. To edit a multiline, first select the editing operation that you want to perform by double clicking on the image tile or by picking the image tile and then picking the OK button. Once you have selected the editing option, AutoCAD will prompt you to select the object or the points, depending on the option you have selected. After you are done editing, if you press the Enter key the dialogue box will return and you can continue editing. The following is the list of options for editing multilines:

Cross Intersection
   Closed Cross
   Open Cross
   Merged Cross
Tee Intersection
   Closed Tee
   Open Tee
   Merged Tee
Corner Joint
Adding and Deleting Vertices
   Add Vertex
   Delete Vertex
Cutting and Welding Multilines
   Cut Single
   Cut All
   Weld All

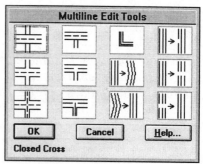

Figure 15-29 Multiline Edit Tools dialogue box

Cross Intersections

With the **MLEDIT** command options you can create three types of cross intersections: Closed, Open, and Merged. You must be careful how you select the objects because the order in which you select them determines the edited shape of a multiline (Figure 15-31). The multilines can belong to the same multiline or two completely different multilines. The following is the command prompt sequence for creating Cross Intersection.

Command: **MLEDIT**
Select first mline: *Select the first multiline.*
Select second mline: *Select the second multiline.*
Select first mline (or Undo):

If you select Undo, AutoCAD undoes the operation and prompts you to select the first multiline. However, if you select another multiline, AutoCAD will prompt you to select the second multiline. If you press the Enter key twice, the Multiline Edit Tools dialogue box is returned.

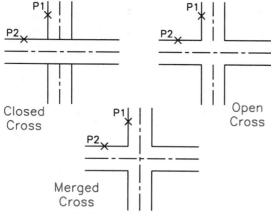

Figure 15-30 Using MLEDIT to edit multilines (Cross Intersection)

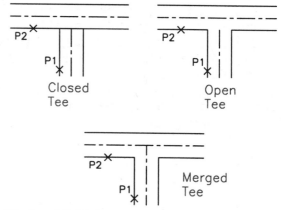

Figure 15-31 Using MLEDIT to edit multilines (Tee Intersection)

Tee Intersection

With the **MLEDIT** command options you can create three types of tee-shaped intersections: Closed, Open, and Merged. As with Cross Intersection, you must be careful how you select the objects, because the order in which you select them determines the edited shape of a multiline (Figure 15-31). The prompt sequence for Tee Intersection is same as for Cross Intersection.

Command: **MLEDIT**
Select first mline: *Select the first multiline.*
Select second mline: *Select the intersecting multiline.*
Select first mline (or Undo): *Select another multiline, enter Undo, or press the Enter key.*

Corner Joint

The **Corner Joint** option creates a corner joint between the two selected multilines. The multilines must be two separate objects (multilines). When you specify the two multilines, AutoCAD trims or extends the first multiline to intersect with the second one. The following is the command prompt sequence for creating a corner joint:

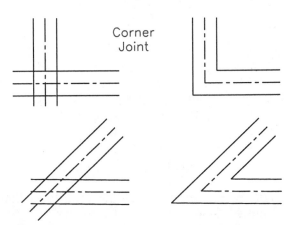

Figure 15-32 Using MLEDIT to edit multilines (Corner Joint)

Command: **MLEDIT**
Select first mline: *Select the multiline to trim or extend.*
Select second mline: *Select the intersecting multiline.*
Select first mline (or Undo): *Select another multiline, enter Undo, or press the Enter key.*

Adding and Deleting Vertices

You can use the **MLEDIT** command to add or delete the vertices of a multiline (Figure 15-33). When you select a multiline for adding a vertex, AutoCAD inserts a vertex point at the point where the object was selected. If you want to move the vertex, use GRIPS. Similarly, you can use the **MLEDIT** command to delete the vertices by selecting the object whose vertex point you want to delete. AutoCAD removes the vertex that is in the positive direction of the selected multiline segment.

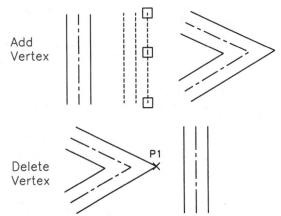

Figure 15-33 Using MLEDIT to edit multilines (Adding and deleting vertices)

Command: **MLEDIT**
Select mline: *Select the multiline for adding vertex.*
Select mline (or Undo): *Select another multiline, enter undo, or press the Enter key.*

Cutting and Welding Multilines

You can use the **MLEDIT** command to cut or weld the lines. When you cut a multiline it does not create two separate multilines. They are still a part of the same object (multiline). Also, the points selected for cutting the multiline do not have to be on the same element of the multiline (Figure 15-34).

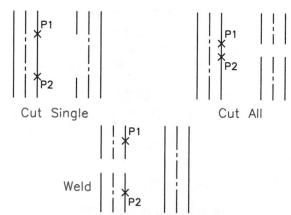

Figure 15-34 Using MLEDIT to edit multilines (Cutting and Welding Multilines)

Command: **MLEDIT**
Select mline: *Select the multiline* (*The point where you select the multiline specifies the first cut point*).
Select second point: *Select the second cut point*.
Select mline (or Undo): *Select another multiline, enter Undo, or press the Enter key*.

The Weld option welds the multilines that have been cut by using MLEDIT command options, Figure 15-34.

Command: **MLEDIT**
Select mline: *Select the multiline*.
Select second point: *Select the second multiline*.
Select mline (or Undo): *Select another multiline, enter Undo, or press the Enter key*.

COMMAND LINE INTERFACE FOR THE MLEDIT COMMAND

You can also edit the multilines without using the Multiline Edit Tools dialogue box. To accomplish this, enter **-MLEDIT** at the Command: prompt.

Command: **-MLEDIT**
Mline editing options AV/DV/CC/OC/MC/CT/OT/MT/CJ/CS/CA/WA:

After selecting an option, AutoCAD will prompt you to select the multilines or specify the points. The prompt sequence will depend on the option you select as discussed earlier under the MLEDIT command. The following are the command line options:

AV	Add Vertex		OT	Open Tee
DV	Delete Vertex		MT	Merged Tee
CC	Closed Cross		CJ	Corner Joint
OC	Open Cross		CS	Cut Single
MC	Merged Cross		CA	Cut All
CT	Closed Tee		WA	Weld All

SYSTEM VARIABLES FOR MLINE

CMLJUST	Store the justification of the current multiline (0-Top, 1-Middle, 2-Bottom)
CMLSCALE	Stores the scale of the current multiline
CMLSTYLE	Stores the name of the current multiline style

Example 1

In the following example you will create a multiline style that represents a wood-frame wall system. The wall system consists of 1/2" wallboard, 3 1/2" 2x4" wood stud, and 1/2" wallboard.

Step 1
Use the **MLSTYLE** command to display the Multiline Styles dialogue box. The current style, STANDARD, will be edited to create the new multiline style.

Step 2
Select the **Name** edit box and replace the word **STANDARD** with **2x4_Wood**.

Step 3
Select the **Description** edit box and enter **Wallboard Wood Framed 2x4 Partition**.

Step 4
Select the **Element Properties...** button to display the Element Properties dialogue box. The element properties of the STANDARD multiline style remain.

Step 5
Select the **0.5** line definition in the **Elements** display box. Select the **Offset** edit box and replace **0.500** with **1.75**. This redefines the first line as being 1.75" above the center line of the wall.

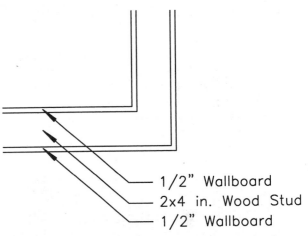

Figure 15-35 Creating a multiline style for wood frame wall system

Step 6
Select the **-0.5** line definition in the **Elements** display box. Select the **Offset** edit box and replace **0.500** with **-1.75**. This redefines the second line as being 1.75" below the center line of the wall.

Step 7
Select the **Add** button to add a new line to the current line style.

Step 8
Select the new **0.0** line definition in the **Elements** display box. Select the **Offset** edit box and replace **0.000** with **2.25**.

Step 9
Select the **Color** edit box and replace **BYLAYER** with **YELLOW**.

Step 10
Repeat steps 7 through 9 this time using the value -2.25 in step 8 to add another line to the current line style.

Step 11
Select the **OK** button to accept the changes to the **Element Properties** and return to the **Multiline Styles** dialogue box. The new multiline style will be displayed.

Step 12
Select the **Add** button to add the new style to the current multiline file.

Step 13
Select the **Save...** button to save the current multiline style to an external file for use in later drawing sessions. From the file listing, select the file or enter the name of the file where you want to save the current multiline style.

Step 14
Select the **OK** button to return to the Drawing Editor. To test the new multiline style use the **MLINE** command and draw a series of lines.

DRAWING CONSTRUCTION LINES

(XLINE AND RAY COMMANDS)

Toolbar:	Draw, Line, Construction Line
Pull-down:	Draw, Construction Line
Screen:	DRAW1, Xline:

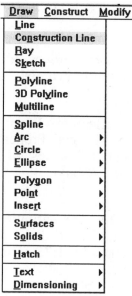

Figure 15-37 Construction Line (XLINE) option in the Draw pull-down menu

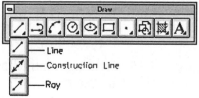

Figure 15-36 Xline icon in the Line flyout of Draw toolbar

The XLINE and RAY commands can be used to draw construction or projection lines. XLINE is a 3D line that extends to infinity on both ends. Since the line is infinite in length, it does not have any end points. A RAY is a 3D line that extends to infinity only on one end. The other end of the ray has a finite end point. Xlines and Rays have zero extents. This means that the extents of the drawing will not change if you use the commands, like ZOOM command with All option, that change the drawing extents. Most of the object snap modes work with both Xlines and Rays with some limitations. You cannot use the end point object snap with the Xline because by definition an Xline does not have any end points. However, for Rays you can use the endpoint snap on one end only. Also, Xlines and Rays take the properties of the layer in which they are drawn. The linetype will be continuous even if the linetype assigned to the layer is not continuous. The XLINE command can be invoked from the **Draw** toolbar by selecting the Construction Line icon from the Line flyout (Figure 15-36), from the pull-down menu (Select Draw, Construction Line, Figure 15-37), from the screen menu (Select DRAW1, Xline:), or by entering **XLINE** at the Command: prompt. The RAY command can be invoked from the **Draw** toolbar by selecting the Ray icon from the Line flyout, from the pull-down menu (Select Draw,

Ray), from the screen menu (Select DRAW1, Ray:), or by entering **RAY** at the Command: prompt.

XLINE Options

<From Point>

If you select the default option, AutoCAD will prompt you to select two point, From point: and Through point:. After you select the first point, AutoCAD will dynamically rotate the Xline with the cursor. When you select the second point, an Xline will be created that passes through the first point and the second point.

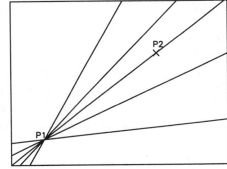

Figure 15-38 Using the Angular option to draw Xlines

> Command: **XLINE**
> Hor/Ver/Ang/Bisect/Offset/<From point>: *Specify a point.*
> Through point: *Specify the second point.*

Horizontal

The **Horizontal** option will create horizontal Xlines of infinite length that will pass through the selected points. The Xlines will be parallel to the X axis of the current UCS.

Vertical

The **Vertical** option will create vertical Xlines of infinite length that will pass through the selected points. The Xlines will be parallel to the Y axis of the current UCS.

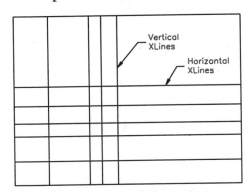

Figure 15-39 Using the Horizontal and Vertical options to draw Xlines

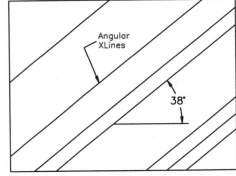

Figure 15-40 Using the Angular option to draw Xlines

Angular

The **Angular** option will create Xlines of infinite length that will pass through the selected point at a specified angle. The angle can be specified by entering a value at the keyboard or using the reference option to select an object and then referencing the angle with the selected line. The following is the command prompt sequence for the Angular option:

> Command: **XLINE**
> Hor/Ver/Ang/Bisect/Offset/<From Point>: **Ang**
> Reference/<Enter angle (0.0000)>: **R**
> Select a line object: Select a line
> Enter angle<0.0000>: Enter angle

(The angle will be measured with respect to the selected line. If the angle is 0, the Xlines will be parallel to the selected line).

Bisect

The **Bisect** option will create an Xline that passes through the angle vertex and bisects an angle. Specify the angle by selecting two points. The Xline created using this option will lie in the plane defined by the selected points. You can use the object snaps to pick the points on the existing objects. The following is the command prompt sequence for this option:

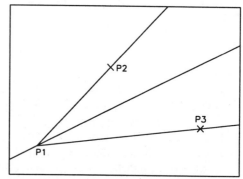

Figure 15-41 Using the Bisect option to draw Xlines

Command: **XLINE**
Hor/Ver/Ang/Bisect/Offset/ < From Point > : **B**
Angle vertex point: *Enter the vertex point.*
Angle start point: *Enter a point.*
Angle end point: *Enter a point*   *(You can use object snaps to select a point).*
Angle end point: ◄┘

Offset

The **Offset** option creates Xlines that are parallel to the selected line/Xline at the specified offset distance. You can specify the offset distance by entering a numerical value or picking two points on the screen. If you select the through option, the offset line will pass through the selected point. (This option works like the OFFSET editing command.)

CREATING NURBS SPLINES

Toolbar:	Draw, Polyline, Spline
Pull-down:	Draw, Spline
Screen:	DRAW1, Spline:

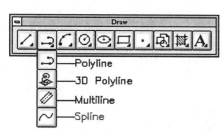

Figure 15-42 SPLINE icon in the Polyline flyout in the Draw toolbar

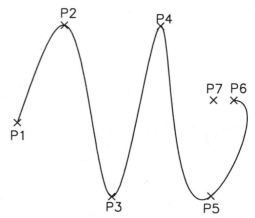

Figure 15-43 Using the SPLINE command to draw splines

NURBS splines can be created using **SPLINE** command. NURBS is an acronym for Nonuniform Rational Bezier-Spline. The spline created with the SPLINE command is different from the spline created using PEDIT command. The Non-Uniform aspect of the spline enables the spline to have sharp corners because the spacing between the spline elements that constitute a spline can be irregular. Rational means that irregular geometry, like arcs, circles, and ellipses can be combined with free form curves. The Bezier-Spline (B-Spline) is the core that enables accurate fitting of curves to input data with Bezier's curve-fitting interface. The SPLINE command can be invoked from the **Draw** toolbar by selecting the Spline icon from the Polyline flyout (Figure 15-42), from the pull-down menu (Select Draw, Spline), from the screen menu (Select DRAW1, Spline:), or by entering **SPLINE** at the Command: prompt. The following is the command prompt sequence for creating the spline shown in Figure 15-43:

Command: **SPLINE**
Object/ < Enter first point > : *Select point, P1.*
Enter point: *Select the second point, P2.*
Close/Fit Tolerance/ < Enter point > : *Select point, P3.*
Close/Fit Tolerance/ < Enter point > : *Select point, P4.*
Close/Fit Tolerance/ < Enter point > : *Select point, P5.*
Close/Fit Tolerance/ < Enter point > : *Select point, P6.*
Close/Fit Tolerance/ < Enter point > : ◄─┘
Enter start tangent: ◄─┘ *(Press Enter key for default).*
Enter end tangent: *Select point, P7.*

SPLINE Command Options

Object
The Object option allows you to change a 2D or 3D splined polyline into a NURBS spline. The original splined polyline is deleted if the variable system DELOB is set to 0. To change a polyline into splined polyline, use the PEDIT command.

Command: **SPLINE**
Object/ < Enter first point > : **O**
Select object: *Select 2D or 3D splined polyline.*

Close
The Close option allows you to close the NURBS spline. When you use this option, AutoCAD will automatically join the end point with the start point of the spline and you will be prompted to define the start tangent only.

Fit Tolerance
The Fit Tolerance option allows you to control the fit of the spline between specified points. If you enter a smaller value, the spline will pass through the defined points as close as possible (Figure 15-44). If the fit tolerance value is 0, the spline passes through the fit points.

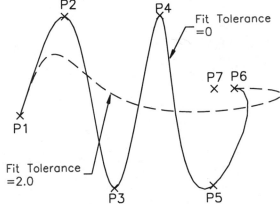

Figure 15-44 Creating a spline with a Fit Tolerance of 2

Command: **SPLINE**
Object/ < Enter first point > : *Select first point.*
Enter point: *Select second point.*
Close/Fit Tolerance/ < Enter point > : **F**
Enter Fit Tolerance < current > : *Enter a value.*
Close/Fit Tolerance/ < Enter point > : *Select third point.*

Start and End Tangents
The Start and End tangents allow you to control the tangency of the spline at the start and end points of the spline. If you press the Enter key at these prompts, AutoCAD will use the default value. By default, the tangency is determined by the slope of the spline at the specified point.

EDITING SPLINES (SPLINEDIT COMMAND)

Toolbar: Modify, Edit Polyline, Edit Spline
Pull-down: Modify, Edit Spline
Screen: MODIFY, SplinEd:

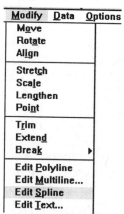

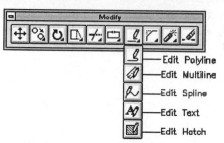

Figure 15-45 Selecting the Edit Spline icon from the Modify toolbar menu

Figure 15-46 Selecting the Edit Spline command from the Modify pull-down menu

The NURBS splines can be edited using the **SPLINEDIT** command. With this command you can fit data in the selected spline, close or open the spline, move vertex points, refine, or reverse a spline. The SPLINEDIT command can be invoked from the Modify toolbar by selecting the Edit Spline icon from the Edit Polyline flyout (Figure 15-45), from the pull-down menu (Select Modify, Edit Spline, Figure 15-46), from the screen menu (Select MODIFY, SplinEd:), or by entering **SPLINEDIT** at the Command: prompt. The following is the prompt sequence of SPLINEDIT command:

Command: **SPLINEDIT**
Select spline:
Fit Data/Close/Move Vertex/Refine/rEverse/Undo/eXit<X>:

Fit Data

When you draw a spline, the spline is fit to the specified points (data points). The **Fit Data** option allows you to edit these points (fit data points). For example, if you want to redefine the start and end tangents of a spline, select the Fit Data option, then select the Tangents option as follows:

Command: **SPLINEDIT**
Select spline:
Fit Data/Close/Move Vertex/Refine/rEverse/Undo/eXit<X>: **F**
Add/Close/Delete/Move/Purge/Tangents/toLerance/eXit<X>: **T**
System Default/<Enter start tangent>: *Select a point (P0).*
System Default/<Enter end tangent>: *Select a point (P7).*

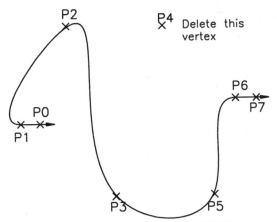

Figure 15-47 Using the SPLINEDIT command to fit data points

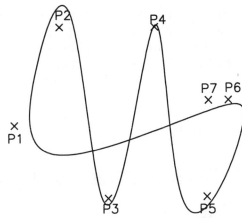

Figure 15-48 Using the SPLINEDIT command to close a spline

Close

The **Close** option allows you to close or open a spline. When you select the Close option, AutoCAD lets you open, move the vertex, refine, or reverse the spline. The following is the command prompt sequence for closing a polyline (Figure 15-48):

Fit Data/Close/Move Vertex/Refine/rEverse/Undo/eXit<X>: **C**
Open/Move Vertex/Refine/rEverse/Undo/eXit<X>: **X**

Move Vertex

When you draw a spline, it is associated with Bezier Control Frame. The **Move Vertex** option allows you to move the vertices of the control frame. To display the frame with the spline, set the value of SPLFRAME system variable to 1. The following is the command prompt sequence for moving one of the vertex points (Figure 15-49):

Fit Data/Close/Move Vertex/Refine/rEverse/Undo/eXit<X>: **M**
Next/Previous/Select Point/eXit/<Enter new location>: S
Select point: *Select a point (P1).*
Next/Previous/Select Point/eXit/<Enter new location>: *Enter new location (P0).*
Next/Previous/Select Point/eXit/<Enter new location>: **X**

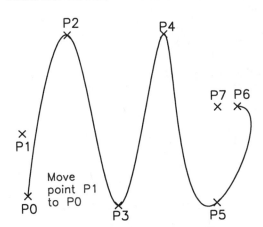

Figure 15-49 Using SPLINEDIT command to move vertex points

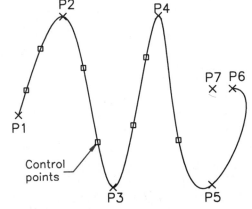

Figure 15-50 Using SPLINEDIT command to refine a spline

Refine

The **Refine** option allows you to refine a spline by adding more control points in the spline, elevating the order, or adding weight to vertex points. For example, if you want to add more control points to a spline, the command prompt sequence is as follows (Figure 15-51):

Fit Data/Close/Move Vertex/Refine/rEverse/Undo/eXit<X>: **R**
Add control points/Elevate Order/Weight/eXit<X>: **A**
Select a point on the spline: *Select a point.*
Select a point on the spline: ◄─┘
Add control points/Elevate Order/Weight/eXit<X>: **X**

Reverse

The **Reverse** option allows you to reverse the spline direction.

Undo

The **Undo** option undoes the previous option.

Exit

The **eXit** option exits the command prompt.

Exercise 2

Draw the illustration as shown at the top of Figure 15-51. Then use the SPLINE, SPLINEDIT, and GRIPS commands to obtain the illustration shown at the bottom. (Assume the missing dimensions.)

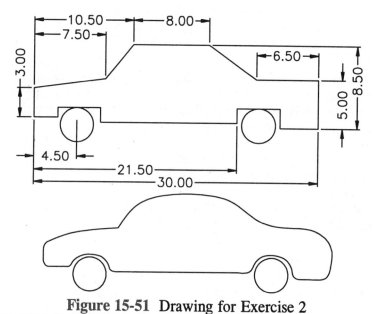

Figure 15-51 Drawing for Exercise 2

SKETCHING FACILITY IN AUTOCAD (SKETCH COMMAND)

Toolbar:	Miscellaneous, Sketch
Pull-down:	Draw, Sketch
Screen:	DRAW1, Sketch:

Sometimes you will need to draw objects that cannot be drawn with the LINE or other commands. For example, if you want to draw the map of a country, topographic maps, freehand designs, signatures etc., you can use AutoCAD's SKETCH command. The **SKETCH** command lets you perform freehand sketching. To sketch, you need to have a pointing device such as a light pen, mouse, or digitizer. Since you want the freehand sketch to be as smooth as possible you should switch SNAP and ORTHO off. The SKETCH command can be accessed from the **Miscellaneous** toolbar by selecting the Sketch icon, from the pull-down menu (Select Draw, Sketch), from the screen menu (Select DRAW1, Sketch:) or by entering **SKETCH** at the Command: prompt.

Command: **SKETCH**

After invoking this command, AutoCAD prompts for the length of the sketch line segment that constitutes the basic building block for sketches. This is also known as the record increment. You can specify the length of the sketch line segment at the prompt:

Record increment < 0.1000 > :

The default size for a single sketch segment is 0.1000 units. If you want to increase the smoothness (accuracy) of the sketch and have more flexibility in drawing sketches, reduce the record increment value. The tradeoff is the computer storage area; i.e., as the individual segment length decreases, the storage area required increases. After specifying the record increment, AutoCAD prompts:

Sketch. Pen eXit Quit Record Erase Connect.

These options are explained as follows:

Pen
With this command, you can start and stop sketching. When you enter P at the Sketch. Pen eXit Quit Record Erase Connect. prompt, AutoCAD responds with <Pen down>. Now you can start sketching by moving the cursor. If you press P again, AutoCAD displays <Pen up>, and sketching is discontinued.

. (Period)
This option is used to draw a straight line between the end point of the most recently sketched line and a specified point. First move the cursor to the desired location and then enter .; AutoCAD automatically draws a line between the point and the end point of the most recently sketched line.

Connect
While sketching, many times you will need to "pen up" to access the menu or to stall sketching. After accessing the menu, or when you are ready to start sketching again, you can start sketching from the last point on the sketch with the Connect option. If you erase a section of the sketch, the Connect option allows you to resume sketching from the last point of the remaining sketch. To invoke this option, enter C.

Sketch. Pen eXit Quit Record Erase Connect . **C**
Connect: *Move to end point of line.*

Place the cursor on the last point on the sketch. Once the cursor touches the sketch line within a distance of one record increment from the end point of the sketch line, AutoCAD performs a "pen down" and you can start sketching again. If there is no sketch line on the screen and you invoke this option, the following message is displayed:

No last point known.

If you invoke the Connect option when the pen is down, you will get the following message:

Connect command meaningless when pen down.

Record
The Record option converts all temporary sketch lines into permanent lines.

Erase
You may make an error while sketching. The Erase option lets you erase the sketch from the end point to a desired point on the sketch. You can use this option when the pen is down and when the pen is up. If the pen is down, AutoCAD automatically performs a pen up.

> Sketch. Pen eXit Quit Record Erase Connect . **E**
> Erase: Select end of delete. <Pen up>

Place the cursor at the point up to the end of the sketch line you want to erase. If you do not want to perform the erasure, enter E or some other command. The following message is displayed:

Erase aborted

If you want to go forward with the erase operation, after specifying the section to be erased, enter P or press the pick button of the pointer to erase the specified portion of the sketch.

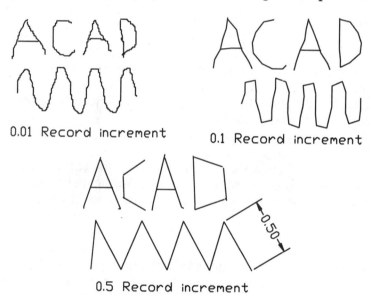

Figure 15-52 Sketches with different record increments

eXit
With this option you can record all the temporary sketch lines and return to the Command: prompt. Instead of selecting the eXit option, you can press the Enter key or spacebar (both have the same effect as the eXit option). AutoCAD displays a message stating the number of lines recorded.

Quit
You can use the Quit option to exit the SKETCH command without recording any temporary lines sketched since the last recording of temporary lines.

DIGITIZING DRAWINGS

In digitizing, the information in the drawing is transferred to a CAD system by locating the points on the drawing that is placed on the top surface of the digitizing tablet. Sometimes it is easier to digitize an existing drawing than to create the drawing again on a CAD system. The digitizing of drawings is an important application in industry. The advantages of a drawing based on a CAD system have prompted companies to digitize drawings.

If you want to digitize a drawing, you should have a digitizer as large as the size of the largest drawing to be digitized so that you do not have to realign the drawing sheet. But situations often arise in which the digitizer is not as large as the drawing to be digitized. In such cases, after digitizing a part of the drawing (as large as the digitizer can accommodate), digitize the other parts until the entire drawing is digitized. Digitizing can be carried out in the tablet mode. In the tablet mode, AutoCAD uses the digitizing tablet as a digitizer, not as a screen pointing device. In this mode, the coordinate system of the paper drawings can be mapped directly into AutoCAD. The tablet mode can be turned on and off with the **TABLET** command or by pressing function key F10.

    Command: **TABLET**
    Option (ON/OFF/CAL/CFG): **ON**

TABLET command

> **Pull-down:** Options, Tablet
> **Screen:** OPTIONS, Tablet:

The first step in digitizing a drawing is to configure the tablet so that the maximum possible area on the tablet can be used. You can do this with the **TABLET** command. This command can be invoked from the pull-down menu (Select Options, Tablet), from the screen menu (Select OPTIONS, Tablet:), or by entering **TABLET** at the Command: prompt.

    Command: **TABLET**

At the next prompt, enter CFG (Configuration option) to configure the tablet.

    Option (ON/OFF/CAL/CFG): **CFG**

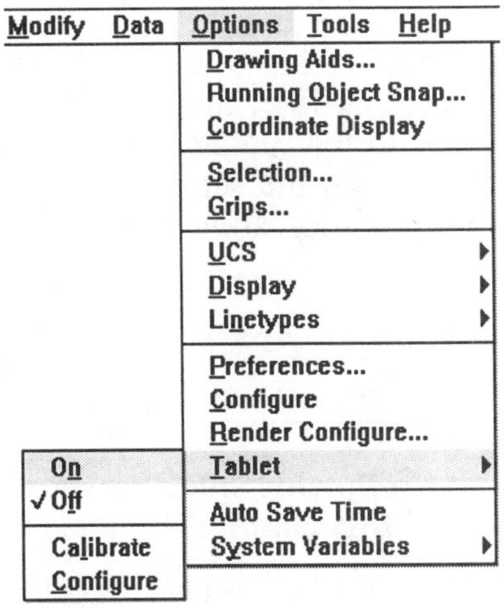

Figure 15-53 Tablet options in Options pull-down menu

After this you are prompted to specify the number of tablet menus you wanted. When digitizing drawings, the whole tablet area is used for digitizing the drawing and hence there are no tablet menus.

    Enter the number of tablet menus desired (0-4)< >: **0**

At the next prompt, enter **Y**, so that reconfiguration of the tablet is possible:

    Do you want to respecify the Fixed Screen Pointing area? <N>**Y**
    Digitize lower left corner of Fixed Screen pointing area: *Specify the lower left corner of the pointing area.*
    Digitize upper right corner of Fixed Screen pointing area: *Specify the upper right corner of the pointing area.*

You may enter N for other prompts like Floating Screen pointing area. The next step in digitizing a drawing is to calibrate the tablet. For this, position the drawing to be digitized to the tablet with the help of adhesive tape. Calibration is possible in Model space and Paper space.

Command: **TABLET**
Option (ON/OFF/CAL/CFG): **CAL**

After you select or enter CAL, the tablet mode is turned on and the screen cross-hairs cursor disappears. The process of calibration involves digitizing two or more points on the drawing and then entering their coordinate values. The points to be picked can be anywhere on the drawing. Once you have specified the position of the points and the coordinate values of those positions, AutoCAD automatically calibrates the digitizing area.

Digitize point #1: *Pick the first point.*
Enter coordinates point #1: *Enter the coordinates of the first point picked.*
Digitize point #2: *Pick the second point.*
Enter coordinates point #2: *Enter the coordinates of the second point picked.*

Digitize point #3 (or RETURN to end): *Pick the third point.*
Enter coordinates point #3: *Enter the coordinates of the second point picked.*

Digitize point #4 (or RETURN to end): *Press Enter to end.*

You can enter any number of point. The more number of points you enter, the more accurate is the digitizing. If you have entered only two points, AutoCAD will automatically compute orthogonal transformation. If you have entered three or more point, AutoCAD will compute orthogonal, Affine, and Projective transformations and determine which best fits the configuration of the selected points. After configuring and calibrating the tablet, the crosshair cursor is redisplayed on the screen. Now, you can use AutoCAD commands to digitize the drawing. For more information about tablet refer to Chapter 31.

SELF EVALUATION TEST

Answer the following questions and then compare your answers with the correct answers given at the end of this chapter.

1. The settings for all plot parameters are saved in the _____ file.

2. If you want to store the plot in a file and not have it printed directly on a plotter, select the _____ check box in the Plot Configuration dialogue box.

3. The scale for the plot can be specified in the _____ edit boxes in the Plot Configuration dialogue box.

4. In partial preview, the _____ size is graphically represented by the red rectangle. The blue rectangle is the section in the paper that is used by the _____ .

5. The **Zero** option will produce a multiline so that the zero offset position of the multiline coincides with the selected points. (T/F)

6. Multilines cannot be edited using grips. (T/F)

7. You can also edit the multilines without using the Multiline Edit Tools dialogue box. To accomplish this, enter _____ at the Command: prompt.

8. The Object option in the SPLINEDIT command allows you to change a 2D or 3D splined polyline into a _____ .

9. The _____ the record increment value, the greater the storage space occupied by the sketch.

10. Quitting the SKETCH command after recording the temporary sketch lines can be accomplished with the _____ option.

11. The size of the plot can be specified by picking the _____ button in the Plot Configuration dialogue box, and then selecting the desired size in the _____ dialogue box.

12. Different objects in the same drawing can be plotted in different colors, with different linetypes and linewidths. (T/F)

13. Full preview takes _____ time than Partial preview.

14. _____ can be used to edit multilines. This command only edits multilines.

15. If you select the _____ radio button in the Plot Configuration dialogue box, the section of drawing that currently holds objects is plotted.

REVIEW QUESTIONS

Answer the following questions.

Plot

1. The display of dialogue boxes concerning the PLOT command can be controlled with the help of the _____ system variable.

2. The _____ command is used to plot a drawing.

3. By selecting the View radio button in the Plot Configuration dialogue box, you can plot a _____ that was created with the _____ command in the current drawing.

4. If you do not want the hidden lines of the objects created in paper space to be plotted, select the _____ check box in the Plot Configuration dialogue box.

5. The pen width for plotting solid-filled traces, polylines with a width, and solids can be controlled with the _____ check box in the Plot Configuration dialogue box.

6. A plot can be rotated at an angle of ___ , ____ , ____ , or _____ degrees.

7. Rotation of a plot is performed in a _____ direction.

8. You can view the plot on the specified paper size before actually plotting it by picking the _____ in the Plot Configuration dialogue box.

9. In a partial preview, if the _____ boundary and the _____ boundary overlap, this is graphically represented by red and blue dashed line.

10. By selecting the _____ radio button and then the Preview _____ in the Plot Configuration dialogue box, the drawing is displayed on the screen just as it would be plotted on the paper.

Mline and Mledit

11. You can draw multilines by using the _____ command.

12. The _____ command allows you to set the style of multilines.

13. The **Description** edit box allows you to enter the description of the _____.

14. The **Save...** button lets you save or copy the current multiline style to an external file (.mln file). (T/F)

15. The justification does not determine how a multiline is drawn between the specified points. (T/F)

16 The _____ option allows you to change the scale of the multiline.

17. The style must be _____ before using the STyle option to change the style.

18. Using the _____ command options you can create three types of cross intersections: Closed, Open, and Merged.

Line, Ray, and Spline

19. The XLINE and RAY commands can be used to draw _____ or _____ lines.

20. XLINE is a 3D line that extends to _____ on both ends.

21. **NURBS** splines can be created using _____ command. NURBS is an acronym for _____.

22. NURBS splines can be edited using the _____ command.

Sketch Command and Digitizing

23. The _____ command can be used to draw a free hand drawing in AutoCAD.

24. Sketching can be performed when the pen is _____.

25. The _____ option of the SKETCH command is used to generate a straight line from the end point of the previous sketch line to the specified point

26. Exiting from the SKETCH command without recording temporary sketch lines can be accomplished with the _____ option.

27. Use the SKETCH command to write your name in freehand.

28. The tablet mode can be turned on and off with the help of the _____ command.

29. The process of calibration involves digitizing _____ on the drawing and then entering their _____.

30. The digitizing process can be used to convert a drawing on paper to a CAD system. (T/F)

EXERCISES

Exercise 3

Make the given drawing and plot it according to the following specifications. It is assumed that the plotter supports 6 pens.

1. The drawing is to be plotted on 10 x 8 inch paper.
2. The border lines (polylines) must be 0.01 inch wide when plotted.
3. Change the DIMSCALE and text size so that the dimension text and text height is 0.125 inch when the drawing is plotted.
4. The object lines must be plotted with Pen-1.
5. The dimension lines and center lines must be plotted with Pen-2.
6. The border and title block must be plotted with Pen-3.

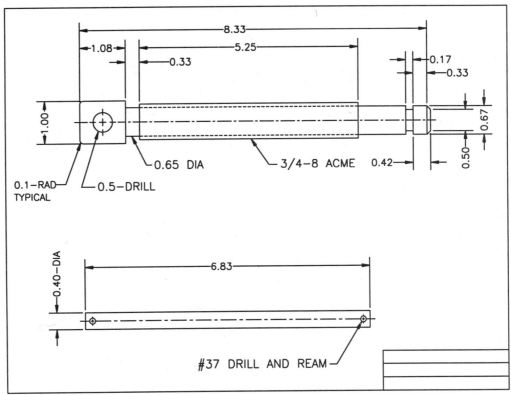

Figure 15-54 Drawing for Exercise 3

Answers:

The following are the correct answers to the questions in the self evaluation test

1 - PCP, **2** - Plot to File, **3** - Plotted Inches = Drawing Units, **4** - paper, image, **5** - T, **6** - F **7** - MLEDIT, **8** - NURBS Spline, **9** - lower, **10** - Exit, **11** - Size, Paper Size, **12** - T, **13** - more, **14** - MLEDIT, **15** - Extents.

Chapter **16**

Object Grouping
Editing Commands

Learning objectives

After completing this chapter, you will be able to:
- Use the GROUP command to group objects.
- Select and cycle through defined groups.
- Change properties and points of objects using the CHANGE command.
- Perform editing operations on polylines using the PEDIT command.
- Explode compound objects using the EXPLODE command.
- Undo previous commands using the UNDO command.
- Rename named objects using the RENAME command.
- Rename drawing files.
- Remove unused named objects using the PURGE command.

OBJECT GROUPING (GROUP COMMAND)

Toolbar:	Standard, Object Group
Pull-down:	Edit, Group Objects...
Screen:	ASSIST, Group:

Figure 16-1 Selecting Object Group from Standard toolbar

You can use the **GROUP** command to group AutoCAD objects and assign a name to the group. Once you have created groups, you can select the objects by group name. The individual characteristics of an object are not affected by forming groups. Groups are simply a mechanism that enables you to form groups and edit objects by groups. It makes the object selection process easier and faster. Objects can be members of several groups.

Edit	View	Draw	Construct
Undo			Ctrl+Z
Redo			
Cut			Ctrl+X
Copy			Ctrl+C
Copy View			
Paste			Ctrl+V
Paste Special...			
Properties...			
Object Snap			▶
Point Filters			▶
Snap			Ctrl+B
Grid			Ctrl+G
Ortho			Ctrl+L
Select Objects			▶
Group Objects...			
Inquiry			▶
Links...			
Insert Object...			

Figure 16-2 Group Objects... option in the Edit pull-down menu

Although an object belongs to a group, you can still select an object as if it did not belong to any group. Groups can be selected by entering the group name or by selecting an object that belongs to the group. You can also highlight the objects in a group or sequentially highlight the groups an object belongs to. You can invoke the **Object Grouping** dialogue box from the **Standard** toolbar by selecting the Object Group icon (Figure 16-1), from the pull-down menu (Select Edit, Group Objects..., Figure 16-2), from the screen menu (Select ASSIST, Group:), or by entering **-GROUP** at the Command: prompt.

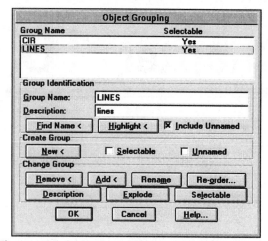

Figure 16-3 Object Grouping dialogue box

Command: **-GROUP**
?/Order/Add/Remove/Explode/REName/Selectable < Make > :

The Object Grouping dialogue box (Figure 16-3) provides the following options:

Group Name

The Group Name area of the Object Grouping dialogue box displays the names of the existing groups.

Group Identification

Group Name
The **Group Name:** edit box displays the name of the existing or selected group. You can also use **Group Name:** edit box to enter the name of the new group. You can enter any name, but it is recommended to use the names that reflect the type of objects in the group. For example, the group name LINES can include all lines and a group name Attributes can include all attribute definitions. The group names can be up to 31 characters long and can include special characters ($, _, and -). The group names can have spaces.

Description
The **Description:** edit box displays the description of the existing or the selected group. It can be used to enter the description of the group. The length of the description text can be up to 64 characters, including spaces.

Find Name
The **Find Name:** button is used to find the group name/names associated with an object. When you select this button, AutoCAD will prompt you to select the object. Once you select the object, the dialogue box will appear on the screen displaying the group names that the selected object belongs to.

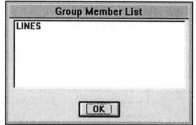

Figure 16-4 Group Member List dialogue box

Highlight
The **Highlight:** button is used to highlight the objects that are in the selected group name. You can select the group name by picking the group name in the Group Names list box at the top of the dialogue box.

Include Unnamed

The **Include Unnamed** button is used to display the names of the unnamed objects in the **Object Grouping** dialogue box. The unnamed groups are created when you copy a named object. AutoCAD automatically assigns a name to the copied objects. The format of the name is Ax (For example *A1, *A2, *A3, ...). If you select the Include Unnamed button, the unnamed object names (*A1, *A2, *A3, ...) will be displayed in the dialogue box. The unnamed groups can also be created by not assigning a name to the group (see **unnamed** in the Create Group section.)

Create Group

New

The **New** button is used to define a new group, after you have entered the group name in the Group Name: edit box. Once you select the **New** button, the dialogue box will temporarily disappear and AutoCAD will prompt you to select objects. After selecting the objects, the dialogue box will reappear on the screen.

Selectable

The **Selectable** button allows you to define a group that is selectable. By doing so, you can select the entire group when one object in the group is selected. The following example illustrates the use of this option.

```
Command: ERASE
Select objects: CTRL+A            (Press the CTRL and A keys.)
<Groups on>: Select an object that belongs to a group.    (If the group has been
                                      defined as selectable, all objects belonging to that
                                      group will be selected.)
```

The group selection can also be turned on or off from the pull-down menu (Select Edit, Select Objects, Group Selection). Group Selection is on if a check mark is displayed in front of the Group Selection item in the pull-down menu. If the group is not defined as selectable, you cannot select all objects in the group, even if you turn the group on by pressing the **Ctrl** and **A** keys.

Note

The combination of Ctrl and A keys is used as a toggle key to turn the group selection on or off. If the group selection is off (< Groups off >), the group selection is disabled.

Unnamed

When you create a group, you can assign it a name or leave it unnamed. If you select Unnamed, AutoCAD will automatically assign a group name to the selected objects. The format of the name is Ax (*A1, *A2, *A3, ...), where x is incremented with each new unnamed group.

Change Group

Remove

The **Remove** button is used to remove objects from the selected group. Once you select the group name from the Group Names list box and select the Remove button, the dialogue box will temporarily disappear and AutoCAD will display the following prompt on the screen:

```
Select objects to remove:
Remove objects: Select objects.        (Select objects that you want to remove from the
                                        selected group.)
```

If you remove all objects from the group, the group name still exists, unless you use the Explode option to remove the group definition (see the Explode in Change Group section).

Add

The **Add** button is used to add objects to the selected group. When you select this option, AutoCAD will prompt you to select the objects that you want to add to the selected group. The prompt sequence is similar to the Remove option.

Rename

The **Rename** button is used to rename the selected group. To rename a group, first you select the group name from the Group Names list box and then enter the name in the Group Name: edit box. Now, select the Rename button and AutoCAD will rename the specified group.

Re-order

The **Re-order** option lets you change the order of the objects in the selected group. The objects are numbered in the order in which you pick them when selecting objects for the group. Sometimes when creating a tool path, you may want to change the order of these objects to get a continuous tool motion. You can do this using the Re-order option. When you select the Re-order button, AutoCAD displays the **Order Group** dialogue box (Figure 16-5). The following example illustrates use of this dialogue box:

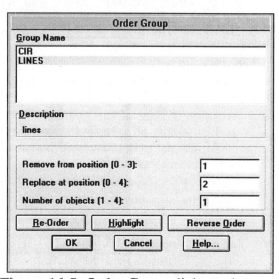

Figure 16-5 Order Group dialogue box

Example 1

Figure 16-6 shows four objects that are in group G1. Determine the order of these objects and then re-order them in a clockwise direction.

1. Invoke the **Object Grouping** dialogue box and make the group (G1) current by selecting it from the Group Name list box.

2. Pick the Re-order button from the dialogue box; the **Order Group** dialogue box is displayed on the screen. Select the group G1, if not already selected.

3. Use the Highlight button to highlight the individual objects in the selected group. You can use the Next and Previous buttons to cycle through the group objects. Figure 16-6(a) shows the order of the objects in group G1. To create a tool path so that the tool moves in a clockwise direction, you need to re-order the objects as shown in Figure 16-6(b).

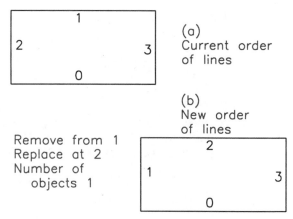

Figure 16-6 Changing the order of group objects

4. To get a clockwise tool path, you must switch object numbers 1 and 2. You can do this by entering the necessary information in the **Order Group** dialogue box. Enter 1 in the

Remove from position edit box and 2 in the **Replace at position** edit box. Enter 1 in the **Number of objects** edit box, since there is only one object to be replaced.

5. After entering the information, select the Re-Order button to re-order the objects. You can confirm the change by selecting the Highlight button again and cycling through the objects.

6. If you want to reverse the order of the objects in the group, select the Reverse Order button.

Description
The **Description** button lets you change the description of the selected group. To change the description of a group, first select the group name from the Group Names list box and then enter the new description in the Description: edit box. Now, select the Description button and AutoCAD will update the description of the specified group. The description cannot exceed 64 characters, including spaces.

Explode
The **Explode** option deletes group definition of the selected group. The objects that were in the group become regular objects without a group reference.

Selectable
The **Selectable** button changes the selectable status of the selected group. To change the selectable status of the group, first select the group name from the Group Names list box, then pick the Selectable button. If the selectable status is "yes," you can select the entire group when one object in the group is selected. If the selectable status is "no," you cannot select the entire group by selecting one object in the group.

SELECTING GROUPS

Pull-down: Edit, Select objects, Group

You can select a group by selecting the Group option from the pull-down menu (Select Edit, Select objects, Group, Figure 16-7) or by entering **G** at the **Select Objects:** prompt.

Example
Command: **MOVE**
Select objects: **G**
Enter group name: *Enter group name.*
4 found
Select objects: ⏎

In the Edit pull-down menu, selecting Group Objects invokes the Object Grouping dialogue box. Also, if you select Group Selection, group selection is turned on or off. A check mark designates that the Group Selection is on; otherwise it is off.

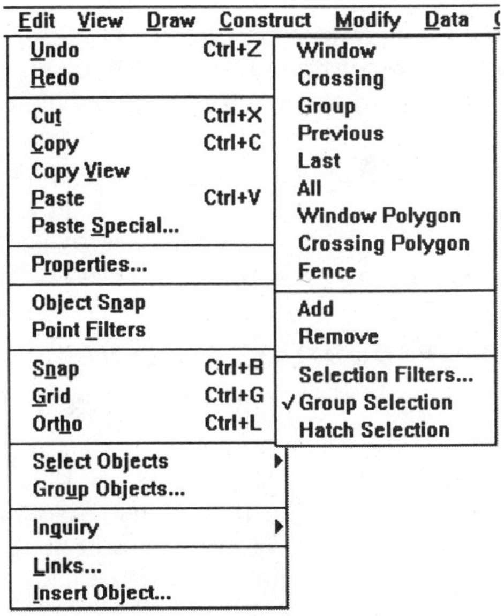

Figure 16-7 Selecting the Group option from the pull-down menu

CYCLING THROUGH GROUPS

When you use the GROUP command to form object groups, AutoCAD lets you sequentially highlight the groups of which the selected object is a member. For example, let us assume that an object belongs to two different groups and you want to highlight the objects in those groups. To accomplish this, press the CTRL key at the **Select objects:** prompt and select the object that belongs to different groups. AutoCAD will highlight the objects in one of the groups and press the pick button of your pointing device to cycle through the groups. The following example illustrates this process:

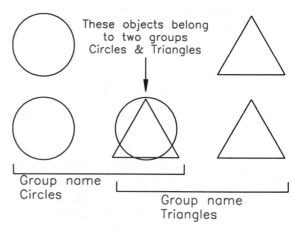

Figure 16-8 Object selection cycling

Command: **ERASE**
Select objects: *Press and hold down the CTRL key.*
< Cycle on>: *Select the object that belongs to different groups. (Press the pick button on your pointing device to cycle through the groups.)*

Select objects: ◄─┘

CHANGING PROPERTIES AND POINTS OF AN OBJECT (CHANGE COMMAND)

Toolbar:	Modify, Stretch, Point
Screen:	MODIFY, Change:

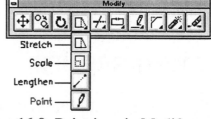

Figure 16-9 Point icon in Modify toolbar

With the help of the **CHANGE** command, you can change some of the characteristics associated with an object such as color, layer, linetype. You can select the CHANGE command from the **Modify** toolbar by selecting the Point icon from the Stretch flyout (Figure 16-9), from the screen menu (Select MODIFY, Change:) or by entering CHANGE at the Command: prompt. The CHANGE command has two options, **Properties** and **Change Point**.

The Properties Option

The **Properties** option can be used to change the characteristics associated with an object.

Changing the Layer of an Object

If you want to change the layer on which you some object exists, you can use the **LAyer** option of the Properties option to change its layer and other characteristics associated with layers. The prompt sequence is:

Command: **CHANGE** ◄─┘
Select objects: *Pick the object whose layer you want to change.*
Select objects: *If you have finished selection, press the Enter key.*
Properties/ < Change point>: **P** ◄─┘
Change what property (Color/Elev/LAyer/Ltype/ltScale/Thickness)? **LA**
New layer< 0>: *Enter a new layer name.*
Change what property (Color/Elev/LAyer/LType/ltScale/Thickness)? ◄─┘
The selected object is now placed on the desired layer.

Changing the Color of an Object

You can change the color of the selected object with the **Color** option of the CHANGE command. If you want to change the color and linetype to match the layer, you can use the **Properties** option of the CHANGE command and then change the color or linetype by entering BYLAYER as follows:

    Command: **CHANGE** ◄─┘
    Select objects: *Pick the block to change.*
    Select objects: *If you have finished selection press the Enter key.*
    Properties/ < Change point > : **P** ◄─┘
    Change what property (Color/Elev/LAyer/Ltype/ltScale/Thickness)? **C**
    New Color < 1(red) > : **BYLAYER** *(Or enter the color name.)*
    Change what property (Color/Elev/LAyer/Ltype/ltScale/Thickness)? ◄─┘

Blocks originally created on layer 0 assume the color of the new layer; otherwise (if it was not created on layer 0) it will retain the color of the layer on which it was created.

Changing the Thickness of an Object

You can change the thickness of an the selected object in the following manner:

    Command: **CHANGE** ◄─┘
    Select objects: *Pick the object whose thickness you want to change.*
    Select objects: ◄─┘
    Properties/ < Change point > : **P** ◄─┘
    Change what property (Color/Elev/LAyer/Ltype/ltScale/Thickness)? **T**
    New thickness < current thickness > : *Specify the new thickness.*

You can see the effect of changing the thickness of an object in 3D view (viewpoint 1,-1,1). Similarly you can change the **elevation**, **linetype**, and **linetype scale** of the selected objects.

Changing Properties
(Using the CHPROP and DDCHPROP Command)

> **Screen:**   MODIFY, Ddchpro:

Instead of using the CHANGE command and then the Properties option, you can use the **CHPROP** (Change Properties) command to change the properties of an object. This command can be selected from the screen menu (Select MODIFY, Ddchpro:) or by entering **DDCHPROP** at the Command: prompt.

    Command: **CHPROP** ◄─┘
    Select objects: *Pick the object whose property you want to change.*
    Select objects: ◄─┘
    Change what property (Color/LAyer/Ltype/ltScale/Thickness)? *Specify property to be changed.*

If the **FILEDIA** variable is set to 1 (on) and you use the **DDCHPROP** command, then after selecting the object, the **Change Property** dialogue box is displayed on the screen.

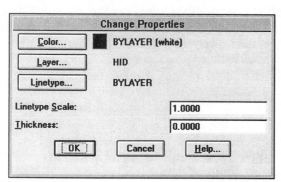

Figure 16-10 Change Properties dialogue box

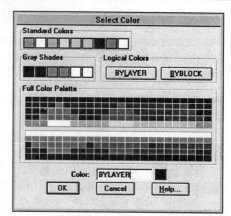

Figure 16-11 Select Color dialogue box

Color... button

By picking this button, **Select Color** dialogue box is displayed on the screen. You can select the new color you want to assign to the selected object by picking the desired color in this dialogue box and then picking the OK button.

Layer... button

Picking this button displays the **Select Layer** dialogue box on the screen. You can select the new layer you want to assign to the selected object from the list of layers in this dialogue box and then pick the OK button.

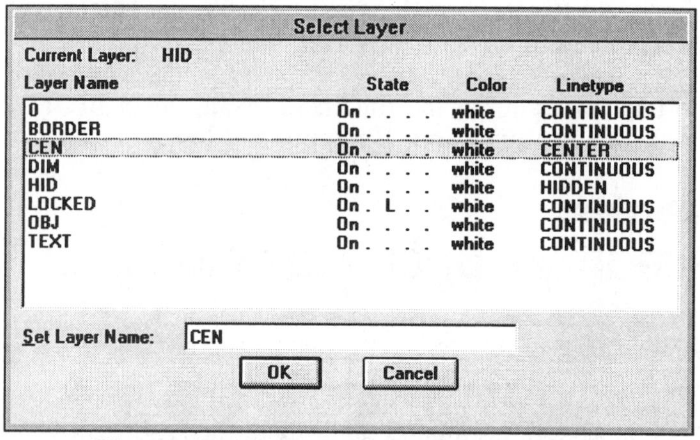

Figure 16-12 Select Layer dialogue box

Linetype... button

Picking the Linetype... button displays the **Select Linetype** dialogue box on the screen. You can select the new linetype you want to assign to the selected object from the list of linetypes in this dialogue box.

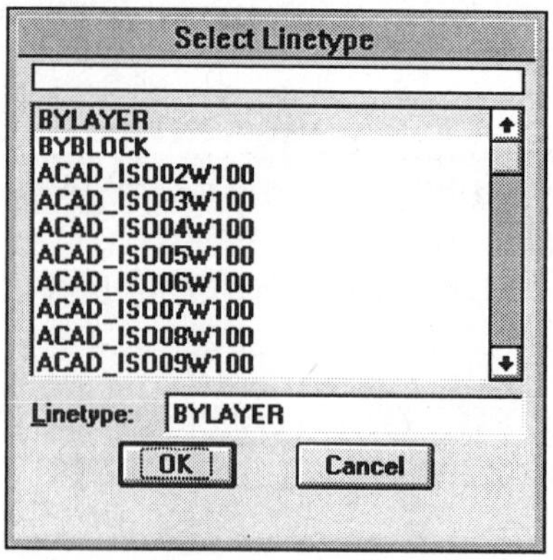

Linetype Scale... edit box

You can enter the new linetype scale factor of the selected object in the Linetype Scale... edit box.

Thickness... edit box

You can enter the new thickness of the

Figure 16-13 Select Linetype dialogue box

selected object in the Thickness... edit box. Once you have made the changes, pick the OK button to change the selected objects.

Exercise 1

Draw a hexagon on layer OBJ in red color. Let the linetype be hidden. Now use the CHPROP command to change the layer to some other existing layer, color to yellow, and linetype to continuous. Use the LIST command to verify that the changes have taken place.

Change Point Option

You can change various features and the location of an object with the **Change point** option of the CHANGE command. For example, to change various **features associated with the text**, the prompt sequence is:

Command: **CHANGE** ◄─┘
Select objects: *Select the text.*
Properties/ < Change point > : ◄─┘
Enter text insertion point: *Specify the new text insertion point (location of text).*
Text style: < current >
New style or RETURN for no change: *Enter the name of the new text style.*

The next prompt is available only for text styles that do not have a fixed height.

New height < current > : *Specify the new text height.*
New rotation angle < current > : *Specify the new rotation angle.*
New text < current > : *Enter the new text.*

The properties of an attribute definition text can be changed just as you change the text. The prompt sequence for changing the properties of an **attribute definition text** is as follows:

Command: **CHANGE**
Select objects: *Select the attribute definition text.*
Properties/ < Change point > : ◄─┘
Enter text insertion point: *Specify the new attribute definition text insertion point (location).*
Text style: < current >
New style or RETURN for no change: *Enter the name of the new text style.*

The next prompt is available only for text styles that do not have a fixed height.

New height < current > : *Specify the new attribute definition text height.*
New rotation angle < current > : *Specify the new rotation angle.*
New text < current > : *Enter the new attribute definition text.*
New tag < current > : *Enter the tag.*
New prompt < current > : *Enter the new prompt.*
New default value < current > : *Enter the new default value.*

You can also change the **position of an existing block** and specify a new rotation angle. The prompt sequence is as follows:

Command: **CHANGE**
Select objects: *Select the block.*
Properties/ < Change point > : ◄─┘
Enter block insertion point: *Specify the new block insertion point.*
New rotation angle < current > : *Specify the new rotation angle for the block.*

The **radius of a circle or end point of a line** can be changed with the Change point option of the CHANGE command. Just specify the new end point in the case of a line or the new radius in the case of the circle. To change the end point of a line, the prompt sequence is:

Command: **CHANGE**
Select objects: *Select the line.*
Properties/<Change point>: *Specify the new point of the end point.*

To change the radius of a circle, the prompt sequence is:

Command: **CHANGE**
Select objects: *Select the circle.*
Properties/<Change point>: *Pick a point to specify the radius of the circle.*

EXPLODE COMMAND

Toolbar:	Modify, Explode
Pull-down:	Modify, Explode
Screen:	MODIFY, Explode:

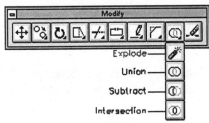

Figure 16-14 Selecting the Explode icon
from the Modify toolbar

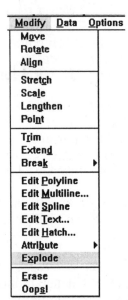

Figure 16-15 Selecting the Explode option
from the pull-down menu

 The **EXPLODE** command is used to split compound objects such as blocks, polylines, regions, polyface meshes, polygon meshes, groups, multilines, 3D solids, 3D meshes, bodies, or dimensions into the objects that make them up. For example, if you explode a polyline, or a 3D polyline, the result will be ordinary lines or arcs (tangent specification and width are not considered). When a 3D polygon mesh is exploded, the result is 3D faces. Polyface meshes are turned into 3D faces, points, and lines. Upon exploding 3D solids, the planar surfaces of the 3D solid turn into regions, and nonplanar surfaces turn into bodies. Multilines are changed to lines. Regions turn into lines, ellipses, splines, or arcs. 2D polylines lose their width and tangent specifications. 3D polylines explode into lines. When a body is exploded, it changes into single-surface bodies, curves, or regions. This command is especially useful when you have inserted an entire view or drawing and you need to alter a small detail. Regeneration of the drawing takes longer if the block is large. This command can be selected from the Modify toolbar by selecting the Explode icon from the Explode flyout (Figure 16-14), from the pull-down menu (Select Modify, Explode, Figure 16-15), from the screen menu (Select MODIFY, Explode:), or by entering **EXPLODE** at the **Command:** prompt.

Command: **EXPLODE** ←⏎
Select block reference, polyline, or dimension: *Pick the block.*

When a block or dimension is exploded, there is no visible change in the drawing. The drawing remains the same except that the color and linetype may have changed because of floating layers, colors, or linetypes. The exploded block is turned into a group of objects that may be modified separately. To check whether the explosion of the block has taken place, pick any object which was a part of the block. If the block has been exploded, only that particular object will be highlighted. With the EXPLODE command only one grouping level is removed at a time. Hence, if there is a nested block or a polyline in a block and you explode it, the inner block or the polyline will not be exploded. Attribute values (if any) are deleted when a block is exploded and the attribute definitions are redisplayed.

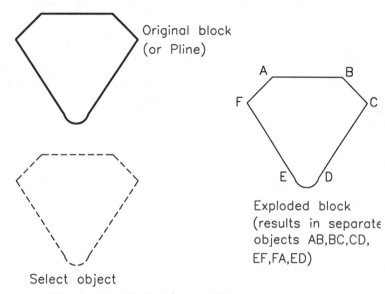

Figure 16-16 Using the EXPLODE command

Note

A block inserted using MINSERT cannot be exploded.

*While inserting a block using the **Insert** dialogue box, you can explode the block you want to insert by picking the Explode button in the dialogue box.*

POLYLINE EDITING (USING THE PEDIT COMMAND)

A polyline can assume various characteristics such as width, linetype, joined polyline, closed polyline, etc. You can edit polylines, polygons, or rectangles to attain the desired characteristics using the PEDIT command. In this chapter we will be discussing how to edit simple 2D polylines. The following are the editing operations that can be performed on a polyline using the PEDIT command. These editing options are discussed in detail later in the chapter. The following are some of the editing operations that can be carried out on the existing polylines:

1. A polyline of varying widths can be converted to a polyline of uniform width.
2. An open polyline can be closed and a closed one can be opened.
3. All bends and curved segments between two vertices can be removed to make a straight polyline.
4. A polyline can be split up into two.
5. Individual polylines, polyarcs connected to each other can be joined into a single polyline.
6. The appearance of the polyline can be changed by moving and adding vertices.
7. Curves of arcs and B-spline curves can be fit to all vertices in the polyline with the specification of the tangent of each vertex being optional.
8. The linetype generation around the vertices of the polyline can be controlled.

PEDIT Command

> **Toolbar:** Modify, Edit Polyline, Edit
> **Pull-down:** Modify, Edit Polyline
> **Screen:** MODIFY, Pedit:

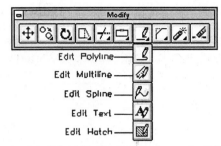

Figure 16-17 Edit Polyline icon in Modify toolbar

You can use the **PEDIT** command to edit any type of polyline. This command can be invoked from the Modify toolbar by picking the Edit Polyline icon from the Edit Polyline flyout (Figure 16-17), from the pull-down menu (Select Modify, Edit Polyline), from the screen menu (Select MODIFY, Pedit:), or by entering **PEDIT** at the Command: prompt. The prompt sequence is:

Command: **PEDIT** ◄─┘
Select polyline: *Pick the polyline to be edited using any selection method.*

If the selected line is an arc or line (not a polyline), AutoCAD issues the following prompt:

Object selected is not a polyline.
Do you want it to turn into one? < Y >

If you want to turn the line or arc into a polyline respond by entering a Y and pressing the Enter key or just pressing the Enter key (null response). Otherwise, you can enter N and exit to the **Command:** prompt. The subsequent prompts and editing options depend on which type of polyline has been selected. In the case of a simple 2D polyline, the next prompt displayed is:

Close/Join/Width/Edit vertex/Fit/Spline/Decurve/Ltype gen/Undo/eXit < X >:

All these options are described in detail as follows:

C (Close) Option
This option is used to close an open polyline. Close creates the segment that connects the last segment of the polyline to the first. You will get this option only if the polyline is not closed. Figure 16-18 illustrates this option.

O (Open) option
If the selected polyline is closed, the **Close** option is replaced by the **Open** option. Entering O for open removes the closing segment. The Open option will only work on a polyline in which the closing segment was created by the Close option. If the last (closing) segment of the polyline was drawn as a polyline and not with the Close option, Open option will not be effective.

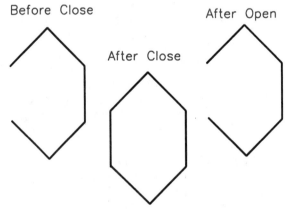

Figure 16-18 The Close option

J (Join) Option
This option appends lines, polylines or arcs that touch a selected polyline at any of its end points and adds (joins) them to it. This option can be used only if a polyline is open. After this option has been selected AutoCAD asks you to select objects. You may also select the polyline

itself. Once you have chosen the objects to be joined to the original polyline, AutoCAD examines them to determine whether any of them has a common end point with the current polyline and joins such an object with the original polyline. The search is then repeated using new end points. AutoCAD will not join if the end point of the object does not meet the polyline. The line touching a polyline at its end point to form a T will not be joined. If two lines meet a polyline in a Y shape, only one of them will be selected and this selection is at random. To verify which lines have been added to the polyline, use the LIST command or select a part of the object. All the segments that are joined to the polyline will be highlighted. Figure 16-20 illustrates the conditions that are required to join polylines.

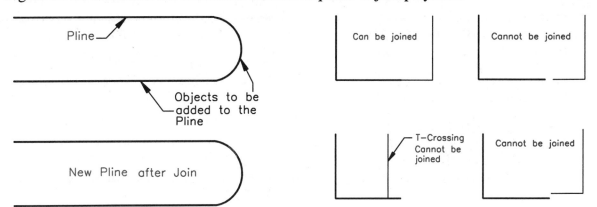

Figure 16-19 Using the Join option

Figure 16-20 Conditions for using the Join option

Width (W) Option

W option allows you to define a new unvarying width for all segments of a polyline. It changes the width of a polyline with a constant or varying width. The desired new width can be specified either by entering the width at the keyboard or by specifying the width as the distance between two specified points. Once the width has been specified, the polyline assumes it. The following prompt sequence will change the width of the given figure from 0.02 to 0.05:

Command: **PEDIT** ◄─┘
Select polyline: *Pick the polyline.*
Close/Join/Width/Edit vertex/Fit/Spline/Decurve/Ltype gen/Undo/eXit <X>: **W** ◄─┘
Enter new width for all segments: **0.05**

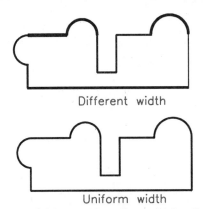

Figure 16-21 Making the width of a polyline uniform

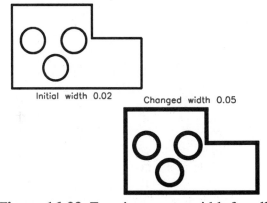

Figure 16-22 Entering a new width for all segments

Note

Circles drawn using the CIRCLE command cannot be changed to polylines. Polycircles can be drawn using the Pline Arc option (by drawing two semicircular polyarcs) or using the DONUT command.

Edit Vertex (E) Option

The **Edit vertex** option lets you select a vertex of a polyline and perform different editing operations on the vertex and the segments following it. A polyline segment has two vertices. The first one is at the start point of the polyline segment, the other one is at end point of the segment. When you invoke this option, an X marker appears on the screen at the first vertex of the selected polyline. If a tangent direction has been specified for this particular vertex, an arrow is generated in that direction. After this option has been selected, the next prompt appears with a list of options of this prompt. The prompt sequence is:

Command: **PEDIT** ◄—┘
Select polyline: *Pick the polyline to be edited.*
Close/Join/Width/Edit vertex/Fit/Spline/Decurve/Ltype gen/Undo/eXit <X>: **E** ◄—┘
Next/Previous/Break/Insert/Move/Regen/Straighten/Tangent/Width/eXit <N>: *Choose an option and press the Enter key.*

The available options of the **Edit vertex** option are discussed as follows:

Next and Previous Options

These options move the X marker to the next or the previous vertex of polyline. The default value in the Edit vertex is one of these two options. The option that is selected as default is the one that you chose last. In this manner the **Next** and **Previous** options help you to move the X marker to any vertex of the polyline by selecting one of these two options and then pressing the Enter key to reach the desired vertex. You cannot reach a vertex twice by only using one of these two options. In other words, you cannot move from vertex n to vertex n even when you have a closed polyline by using either of these two options.

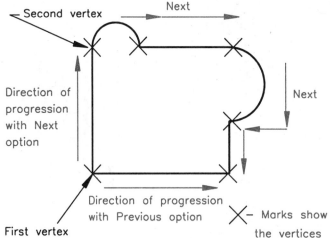

Figure 16-23 The Next and Previous options

The prompt sequence is:

Command: **PEDIT** ◄—┘
Select polyline: *Pick the polyline to be edited.*
Close/Join/Width/Edit vertex/Fit/Spline/Decurve/Ltype gen/Undo/eXit <X>: **E** ◄—┘

Next/Previous/Break/Insert/Move/Regen/Straighten/Tangent/Width/eXit <N>: *Choose N or P and press the Enter key.*

Break Option

With the **Break** option, you can divide a polyline into two parts. The division of polyline can be specified at one vertex or two different vertices. By specifying two different vertices, all the polyline segments and vertices between the specified vertices are erased. If one of the selected vertices is at the end point of the polyline, the Break operation will erase all the segments between the first vertex and the end point of the polyline. The exception to the above statement is that AutoCAD does not erase the entire polyline if you specify the first vertex at the start point (first vertex) of the polyline and the second vertex at the end point (last vertex) of the polyline. If both vertices are at the end point of the polyline or only one vertex is specified and its location is at the end point of the polyline, no change is made to the polyline. The last two selections of vertices are treated as invalid by AutoCAD, which acknowledges this by displaying the message ***Invalid***.

To use the **Break** option, first you need to move the marker to the first vertex where you want the split to start. Placement of the marker can be achieved with the help of the **Next** and **Previous** options. Once you have selected the first vertex to be used in the Break operation, invoke the **Break** option by entering B. AutoCAD takes the vertex where the marker (X) is placed as the first point of breakup. The next prompt asks you to specify the position of the next vertex for breakup. You can enter GO if you want to split the polyline at one vertex only, or use the Next or Previous option to specify the position of next vertex. The prompt sequence is:

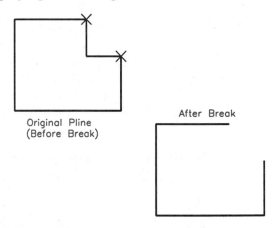

Figure 16-24 Using the Break option

Command: **PEDIT** ←┘
Select polyline: *Pick the polyline to be edited.*
Close/Join/Width/Edit vertex/Fit/Spline/Decurve/Ltype gen/Undo/eXit <X>: **E** ←┘
Next/Previous/Break/Insert/Move/Regen/Straighten/Tangent/Width/eXit <N>: *Enter N or P to locate the first vertex for Break option.*
Next/Previous/Break/Insert/Move/Regen/Straighten/Tangent/Width/eXit <N>: **B** ←┘

Once you invoke the **Break** option, AutoCAD treats the vertex where the marker (X) is displayed as the first point for splitting the polyline. The next prompt issued is:

Next/Previous/Go/eXit <N>: *Move the X marker to the specify the position of next vertex for breakup.*

Enter GO if you want to split the polyline at one vertex only, or use the **Next** or **Previous** option to specify the position of the next vertex for the breakup.

Insert Option

The **Insert** option allows you to define a new vertex to the polyline. You can invoke this option by entering I for Insert. You should invoke it only after moving the marker (X) to the vertex that is located immediately before the new vertex. This is because the new vertex is inserted immediately after the vertex with the X mark.

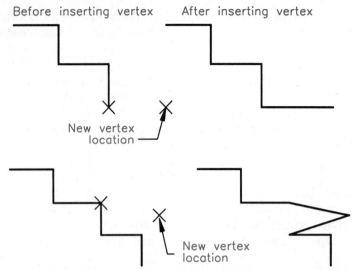

Figure 16-25 Using the Insert option to define new vertex points

Command: **PEDIT** ◄┘
Select polyline: *Pick the polyline to be edited.*
Close/Join/Width/Edit vertex/Fit/Spline/Decurve/Ltype gen/Undo/eXit <X>: **E** ◄┘
Next/Previous/Break/Insert/Move/Regen/Straighten/Tangent/Width/eXit <N>: *Move the marker to the vertex next to which the new vertex is to be inserted.*
Next/Previous/Break/Insert/Move/Regen/Straighten/Tangent/Width/eXit <N>: **I** ◄┘
Enter location of a new vertex: *Move the cursor to specify the location of the new vertex.*

Move Option
This Option lets you move the X-marked vertex to a new position. Before invoking the **Move** option you must move the X marker to the vertex you want to relocate by selecting the **Next** or **Previous** option.

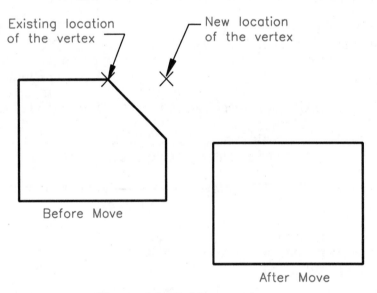

Figure 16-26 Move option

The prompt sequence is:

Command: **PEDIT** ◄┘
Select polyline: *Pick the polyline to be edited.*

Close/Join/Width/Edit vertex/Fit/Spline/Decurve/Ltype gen/Undo/eXit <X>: **E** ↵
Next/Previous/Break/Insert/Move/Regen/Straighten/Tangent/Width/eXit <N>: *Enter N or P to move the X marker to the vertex you want to relocate.*
Next/Previous/Break/Insert/Move/Regen/Straighten/Tangent/Width/eXit <N>: **I** ↵
Enter new location: *Specify the new location for the selected vertex by picking the new location or entering its coordinate values.*

If the marker is at the desired position, you can choose the **Move** option.

Regen Option

The **Regen** option regenerates the polyline. It is used most often with the **Width** option.

Straighten Option

The **Straighten** option can be used to straighten polyline segments or arcs between specified vertices. It deletes the arcs, line segments, or vertices between the two specified vertices and substitutes them with one polyline segment. The prompt sequence is:

Command: **PEDIT** ↵
Select polyline: *Pick the polyline to be edited.*
Close/Join/Width/Edit vertex/Fit/Spline/Decurve/Ltype gen/Undo/eXit <X>: **E** ↵
Next/Previous/Break/Insert/Move/Regen/Straighten/Tangent/Width/eXit <N>: *Move the marker to the desired vertex with the Next or Previous option.*
Next/Previous/Break/Insert/Move/Regen/Straighten/Tangent/Width/eXit <N>: **S**
Next/Previous/Break/Insert/Move/Regen/Straighten/Tangent/Width/eXit <N>: *Move the marker to the next desired vertex.*
Next/Previous/Go/eXit <N>: **G** ↵

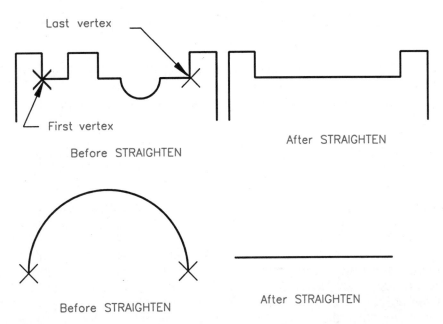

Figure 16-27 Using the Straighten option to straighten polylines

Tangent Option

The **Tangent** option is used to associate a tangent direction to the current vertex (marked by X). The tangent direction is used in curve fitting. This option has been discussed in detail in curve fitting. The prompt is:
Direction of tangent:

You can specify the direction by entering an angle at the **Direction of tangent:** prompt or by picking a point to express the direction with respect to the current vertex.

Width Option

The **Width** option lets you change the starting and the ending widths of a polyline segment that follows the current vertex. By default the ending width is equal to the starting width, hence you can get a polyline segment of uniform width by accepting the default value at the **Enter ending width <starting width>:** prompt. You can specify different starting and ending widths to get a varying width polyline. The prompt sequence is:

Close/Join/Width/Edit vertex/Fit/Spline/Decurve/Ltype gen/Undo/eXit <X>: **E** ◄┘
Next/Previous/Break/Insert/Move/Regen/Straighten/Tangent/Width/eXit <N>: *Move the*
marker to the starting vertex of the segment whose
width is to be altered.
Next/Previous/Break/Insert/Move/Regen/Straighten/Tangent/Width/eXit <N>: **W** ◄┘
Enter starting width <current>: *Enter the revised starting width.*
Enter ending width <revised starting width>: *Enter the revised ending width.*

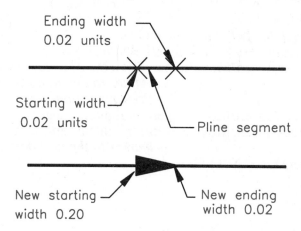

Figure 16-28 Using the Width option to change the width of a polyline

The segment with the revised widths is redrawn only after invoking the **Regen** option.

eXit Option

This option lets you exit from the vertex editing and return to the main PEDIT prompt.

Fit Option

The **Fit** or **Fit curve** option generates a curve that passes through all the corners (vertices) of the polyline, using the tangent directions of the vertices. The curve is composed of series of arcs passing through the corners (vertices) of the polyline. This option is used when you draw a polyline with sharp corners and need to convert it into a series of smooth curves. An example of this is a graph. In a graph we need to show a curve by joining a series of plotted points. The process involved is called curve fitting, hence the name of this option. These vertices of the polyline are also known as the control points. The closer together these control points are, the smoother the curve. Hence, if the **Fit** options does not give optimum results, insert more vertices into the polyline or edit the tangent directions of vertices and then use the Fit option on the polyline. Before using this option you may give each vertex a tangent direction. The curve is then constructed keeping in mind the tangent directions that you have specified. The following prompt sequence illustrates the **Fit** option:

Command: **PEDIT** ◄┘
Select polyline: *Pick the polyline to be edited.*
Close/Join/Width/Edit vertex/Fit/Spline/Decurve/Ltype gen/Undo/eXit <X>: **F** ◄┘

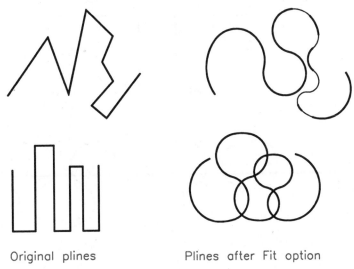

Original plines   Plines after Fit option

Figure 16-29 The Fit curve option

If the tangent directions need to be edited use the **Edit vertex** option of the PEDIT command. Move the mark X to each of the vertices that need to be changed. Now you can invoke the tangent option and either enter the tangent direction in degrees or pick points. The chosen direction is expressed by an arrow placed at the vertex. The prompt sequence is:

Command: **PEDIT** ◄─┘
Select polyline: *Pick the polyline to be edited.*
Close/Join/Width/Edit vertex/Fit/Spline/Decurve/Ltype gen/Undo/eXit <X>: **E** ◄─┘
Next/Previous/Break/Insert/Move/Regen/Straighten/Tangent/Width/eXit <N>: **T** ◄─┘
Direction of tangent: *Specify a direction in + or - degrees or pick a point in the desired direction and press the Enter key.*

Once the tangent directions are specified, use the **eXit** option to return to the previous prompt and use its **Fit curve** option.

Spline Option

The **Spline** option also smooths the corners of a straight segment polyline as does the **Fit** option, but the curve passes only through the first and the last control points (vertices) except in the case of a closed polyline. The spline curve is stretched toward the other control points (vertices) but does not pass through them, as in the case of the Fit option. The greater the number of control points, the greater the force with which the curve is stretched toward them. The prompt sequence is as follows:

Command: **PEDIT** ◄─┘
Select polyline: *Pick the polyline.*
Close/Join/Width/Edit vertex/Fit/Spline/Decurve/Ltype gen/Undo/eXit <X>: **S** ◄─┘

The generated curve is a B-spline curve. The **frame** is the original polyline without any curves in it. If the original polyline has arc segments, these segments are straightened when the spline's frame is formed. A frame that has width produces a spline curve that tapers smoothly from the width of the first vertex to that of the last. Any other width specification between the first width specification and the last is neglected. When a spline is formed from a polyline, the frame is displayed as a polyline with zero width and continuous linetype. Also, AutoCAD saves its frame so that it may be restored to its original form. Tangent specifications on control point vertices do not affect spline construction. By default, the spline frames are not shown on the screen, but you may want them displayed for reference. In such a case, system variable **SPLFRAME** needs to be manipulated. The default value for this variable is zero. If you want to see the spline frame as well, set it to 1. The prompt sequence is:

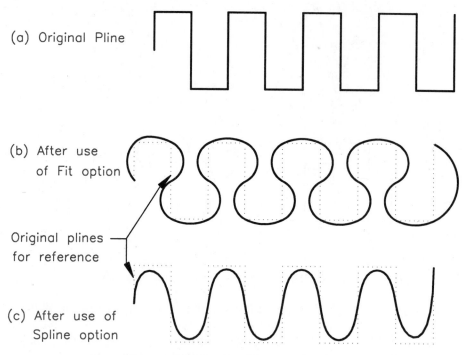

Figure 16-30 The Spline option

Command: **SPLFRAME** ◄─┘
New value for SPLFRAME <0>: **1** ◄─┘

Now whenever the **Spline** option is used on a polyline the frame will also be displayed. There are two types of Spline curves:

1. **Quadratic B-spline**
2. **Cubic B-spline**

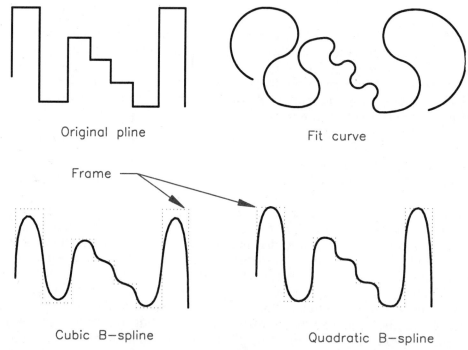

Figure 16-31 Comparison of Fit curve, Quad, and Cubic B-splines

Both of them pass through the first and the last control points, which is characteristic of the Spline curve. The cubic curves are very smooth. The cubic curve passes through the first and last control points and the curve is closer to the other control points. The Quadratic curves are not as smooth as the Cubic ones, but they are smoother than the curves produced by the **Fit curve** option. The quadratic curve passes through the first and last control points and the rest of the curve is tangent to the polyline segments between the remaining control points.

Generation of Different Types of Spline Curves

If you want to edit a polyline into a B-spline curve you are first required to enter a relevant value in the **SPLINETYPE** system variable. A value of **5** produces the **Quadratic** curve, whereas **6** produces a **Cubic** curve. To generate a Quadratic curve and Bezier Fit Mesh the prompt sequence is:

Command: **SPLINETYPE** ◄─┘
New value for SPLINETYPE <6>: **5** ◄─┘

Command: **SURFTYPE** ◄─┘
New value for SPLINETYPE <6>: **8** ◄─┘

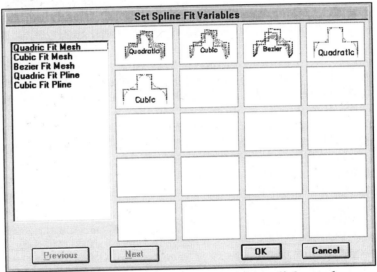

Figure 16-32 Set Spline Fit Variables dialogue box

You can also get different types of splines by selecting the **PolyVars** option in the Pedit screen menu. On doing so, the **Set Spline Fit Variables** dialogue box (Figure 16-32) is displayed on the screen. You can select any type from the list available. The SPLINETYPE variable is automatically set to the value of the type you have chosen from the dialogue box. For example, if you pick the Bezier Fit Mesh type from the dialogue box, the SURFTYPE variable is set to a value of 8.

SPLINESEGS

The system variable **SPLINESEGS** governs the number of line segments used to construct the spline curves so you can use this variable to control the smoothness of the curve. The default value for this variable is 8. With this value a reasonably smooth curve is generated that does not need a much regeneration time. The greater the value of this variable, the smoother the curve, the greater the regeneration time, and the more space occupied by the drawing file.

The prompt sequence for setting the value of SPLINESEGS variable to a value of 500 is:

Command: **SPLINESEGS** ◄─┘
New value for SPLINESEGS <8>: **500**

The following figure shows cubic curves with different value for SPLINESEGS parameter.

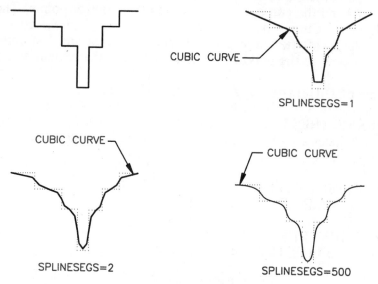

Figure 16-33 Using the SPLINESEGS variable

Decurve Option

The **Decurve** option straightens the curves generated after using the **Fit** or **Spline** options on a polyline to their original shape. Polyline segments are straightened using the Decurve option. The vertices inserted after using the Fit or Spline options are also removed. Information entered for tangent reference is retained for use in future Fit curve operations. You can also use this command to straighten out any curve drawn with the help of the **Arc** option of the PLINE command. The prompt sequence is:

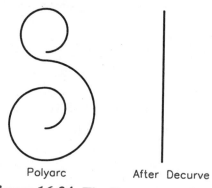

Figure 16-34 The Decurve option

Command: **PEDIT** ◄─┘
Select polyline: *Pick the polyline to be edited.*
Close/Join/Width/Edit vertex/Fit/Spline/Decurve/Ltype gen/Undo/eXit <X>: **D** ◄─┘

Ltype gen Option

You can use this option to control the linetype pattern generation for linetypes other than Continuous with respect to the vertices of the polyline. This option has two modes: **ON** and **OFF**. If turned on, this option generates the linetype in a continuous pattern with respect to the vertices of the polyline. If you turn this option off, it generates the linetype with a dash at each vertex. This option is not applicable on polylines with tapered segments. The linetype generation for new polylines can be controlled with the help of **PLINEGEN** system variable, which acts as a toggle.

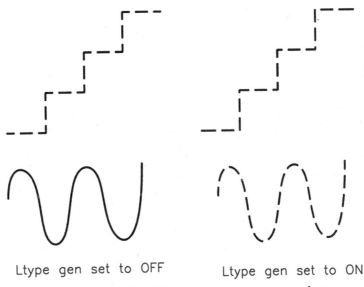

Figure 16-35 Using the Ltype-gen option

U (UNDO) Option

The **Undo** option negates the effect of the most recent PEDIT operation. You can go back as far as you need to in the current PEDIT session by using UNDO option repeatedly until you get the desired screen. If you started editing by converting an object into a polyline, and you want to change the polyline back to the object from which it was created, the Undo option of the PEDIT command will not. In this case you will have to exit to the Command: prompt and use the UNDO command to undo the operation.

eXit Option

The **eXit** option helps you come out of (exit) the PEDIT command and return to the Command: prompt. This option is the default for the PEDIT command.

Breaking a Polyline into Independent Line and Arc Segments

EXPLODE COMMAND

A polyline may be composed of line and arc segments, but when drawn with a single PLINE command it is a single object. The **EXPLODE** command breaks up a polyline into the different line or arc segments of which it is composed. When a polyline is exploded, the resulting objects are drawn along the center line of the original polyline. The prompt sequence is:

Command: **EXPLODE** ←⏎
Select block reference, polyline or dimensions: *Pick the polyline to be exploded.*

The **EXPLODE** command deletes all width characteristics and the tangent information of a polyline. AutoCAD issues the following warning to the user:

Exploding this polyline has lost (width/tangent) information. The UNDO command will restore it.

In this manner, the UNDO command can restore the polyline if you decide that you did not want the polyline to be exploded.

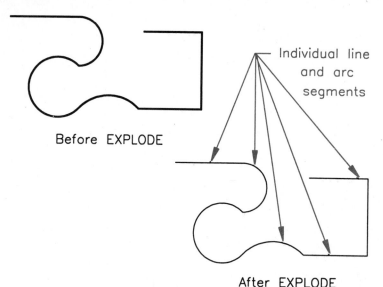

Figure 16-36 Using **EXPLODE** command with polylines

Exercise 2

a. Draw a line from point (0,0) to point (6,6). Convert the line into a polyline with starting width 0.30 and ending width 0.00. Then convert the polyline back into the original line.

b. Draw a polyline of varying width segments and use the Join option to join all the segments into one polyline. Before joining the different segments, make the widths of all the segments uniform.

Exercise 3

a. Draw a staircase-shaped polyline, then use different options of the PEDIT command to generate a Fit curve, Quadratic B-spline, and Cubic B-spline. Then convert the curves back into the original polyline.

b. Draw square wave-shaped polylines and use different options of the Edit vertex option to navigate around the polyline, split the polyline into two at the third vertex, insert more vertices at different locations in the original polyline, and convert the square wave shaped polyline into a straight line polyline.

UNDOING COMMANDS (UNDO COMMAND)

Screen:	ASSIST, Undo:

The LINE and PLINE commands have the Undo option, which can be used to undo (nullify) changes made within these commands. The **UNDO** command can be used to undo a previous command, or undo more than one command at one time. This command can be selected from the screen menu (Select ASSIST, Undo:), or by entering **UNDO** at the Command: prompt. The Undo option is also available in the Assist pull-down menu, but in this case the Undo option can only undo the previous command and only one command at a time. The prompt sequence for the UNDO command is:

Command: **UNDO** ◄─┘
Auto/Control/BEgin/End/Mark/Back/ < Number > :

The various options of this command are discussed below:

Number (N) Option

This is the default option. This number represents the number of previous command sequences to be deleted. For example, if the number entered is 1, the previous command is undone; if the number entered is 4 the previous four commands are undone; and so on. This is identical to invoking the U command four times except that only one regeneration takes place. AutoCAD lets you know which commands were undone by displaying a message after you press the Enter key. The prompt sequence is:

Command: **UNDO** ◄─┘
Auto/Control/BEgin/End/Mark/Back/ < Number > : **3** ◄─┘
PLINE LINE CIRCLE
Command:

Auto (A) Option

Enter A to invoke this option. The following prompt is displayed:

ON/OFF < current > : *Select ON or OFF.*

If Auto is on, any group of commands that was used to insert an object is undone together. If a command contains some other commands, all of them are considered to be a single group and are undone as a single command. If the **Auto** option is off, each command in the group is treated separately.

Back (B) Option

Using the **Back** option allows you to undo everything in the drawing. After invoking this option, AutoCAD issues the following prompt:

This will undo everything:OK? < Y > :

If you want to undo the effect of all the commands, press the Enter key or enter N.

Control (C) Option

This option lets you determine how many of the options are active in the UNDO command. You can disable the options you do not need. With this option you can even disable the UNDO command. To access this option type C. You will get the following prompt:

ALL/None/One < All > :

The options of the control options are discussed below.

All (A)

The All option activates all the features (options) of the UNDO command

None (N)

This option turns off UNDO and the U command. If you have used the BEgin End options or Mark Back options to create UNDO information, all of that information is undone.

Command: **UNDO**
Auto/Control/BEgin/End/Mark/Back/ < Number > : **C**
ALL/None/One < All > : **NONE**

The prompt sequence for the UNDO command after issuing the **None** option is:

Command: **UNDO**
All/None/One < All > :

To enable the UNDO options again you must enter the **ALL** or **ONE** (one mode) option. If you try to use the U command while the UNDO command has been disabled, AutoCAD gives you the following message:

Command: **U** ◄─┘

U command disabled: Use UNDO command to turn it on

One (O)
This option restraints U and UNDO commands to a single operation. All UNDO information saved earlier during editing is scrapped.

Auto/Control/BEgin/End/Mark/Back/ < Number > : **C**
All/None/One < All > : **O** ◄─┘

If you then enter the UNDO or U command, you will get the following prompt:

Command: **UNDO** ◄─┘
Control/ < 1 > :

In response to the above-mentioned prompt you can now either press Enter key to undo only the previous command, or go into the **Control** options by entering C. AutoCAD acknowledges undoing the previous command with messages like:

Command: **UNDO** ◄─┘
Control/ < 1 > : ◄─┘
CIRCLE
Everything has been undone
Command:

BEgin (BE) and End (E) Options
A group of commands is treated as one command for the U and UNDO commands by embedding the commands between the **BEgin** and **End** options of the UNDO command. If you expect to remove a group of successive commands, you can use this option. Since all of the commands after the BEgin option and before the End option are treated as a single command by the U command, they can be undone by a single U command. For example, the following sequence illustrates the possibility of removal of two commands:

Command: **UNDO** ◄─┘
Auto/Control/BEgin/End/Mark/Back/ < Number > : **BE** ◄─┘
Command: **CIRCLE** ◄─┘
CIRCLE 3P/2P/TTR/ < Center point > : *Specify the center.*
Diameter/ < Radius > : *Specify the radius of the circle.*
Command: **PLINE** ◄─┘
From point: *Pick first end point.*
To point: *Pick the other end point.*
Command: **UNDO** ◄─┘
Auto/Control/BEgin/End/Mark/Back/ < Number > : **E** ◄─┘
Command: **U** ◄─┘

To start the next group once you are finished specifying the current group, use the **End** option to end this group. Another method is to enter the **BEgin** option to start the next group while the current group is active. This is equivalent to issuing the End option followed by the BEgin option. The group is complete only when the End option is invoked to match a BEgin option. If U or the Undo command is issued after the BEgin option has been invoked and before the End option has been issued, only one command is undone at a time until it reaches the juncture where the BEgin option has been entered. If you want to undo the commands issued before the BEgin option was invoked, you must enter the End option so that the group is complete. This is demonstrated by Example 2.

Note

The Group option in the Undo screen menu is the same as the BEgin option.

The first U command will undo the TRACE command. If you repeat the U command, the PLINE command will be undone. Any further invoking of the U command will not undo any previously drawn object (POLYGON and CIRCLE in this case) because after the PLINE is undone, you have an UNDO BEgin. Only after you enter UNDO End can you undo the POLYGON and the CIRCLE. In the above example, the second U command will undo the DTEXT command, the third U command will undo the DONUT and PLINE commands (these are enclosed in the group), the fourth U command will undo the POLYGON command, and the fifth U command will undo the CIRCLE command. When the commands in a group are undone, the name of each command/operation is not displayed as it is undone, only the name, GROUP, is displayed.

Note

You can use the BEgin option only when the UNDO Control is set to All.

Mark (M) and Back Options

This option installs a marker in the Undo file. The Back option lets you undo all the operations until the **mark**. In other words the **Back** option returns the drawing to the point where the previous mark was inserted. For example, if you have completed a portion of your drawing and you do not want anything up to this point to be deleted, you insert a marker and then proceed. Now even if you use the UNDO Back option, it will work only until the marker. You can insert multiple markers and with the help of Back option you can return to the successive mark points. The following prompt sequence illustrates this:

    Command: **UNDO** ←┘
    Auto/Control/BEgin/End/Mark/Back/ < Number > : **M** ←┘

After proceeding further with your work if you want to use the UNDO Back option:

    Command: **UNDO** ←┘
    Auto/Control/BEgin/End/Mark/Back/ < Number > : **B** ←┘

Once all the marks have been exhausted with the successive Back options, any further invoking of the Back option displays the message: **This will undo everything. OK? < Y >**.

If you enter Y (Yes) at this prompt, all the operations carried out since you entered the current drawing session will be undone. If you enter N (No) at this prompt, the Back command will be disregarded. You cannot undo certain commands, for example, DIST, LIST, END, DELAY, NEW, OPEN, QUIT, SAVE, and many more. Actually these commands have no effect that can be undone. Commands that change operating modes (GRID, UNITS, SNAP, ORTHO) can be undone though the effect may not be apparent at first. This is the reason why AutoCAD displays the command names as they are undone.

Example 2

Enter the commands in the same sequence as given below and notice the changes that take place on the screen.

```
CIRCLE
POLYGON
UNDO BEgin
PLINE
TRACE
U
DONUT
UNDO End
DTEXT
U
U
U
U
```

REDO COMMAND

> **Pull-down:** Edit, Redo
> **Screen:** ASSIST, Redo:

The **REDO** command brings back the objects that you removed previously using the U and UNDO commands. This command undoes the UNDO command, but it should be entered immediately after the UNDO. You can invoke this command from the pull-down menu (Select Edit, Redo), from the screen menu (Select ASSIST, Redo:), or by entering **REDO** at the Command: prompt.

   Command: **REDO** ←⏎

The objects previously undone reappear on the screen.

RENAMING NAMED OBJECTS (RENAME COMMAND)

> **Pull-down:** Data, Rename...
> **Screen:** DATA, Rename:

You can edit the names of named objects such as blocks, dimension styles, layers, linetypes, styles, UCS, views, and viewports with the help of the **RENAME** command. This command can be entered at the Command: prompt, or selected from the pull-down menu (Select Data, Rename...) or from the screen menu (Select DATA, Rename:). When you pick the RENAME command from the pull-down menu, screen menu, or by entering the **DDRENAME**

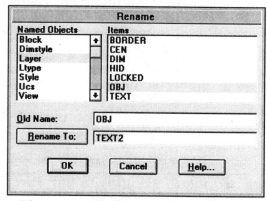

Figure 16-37 Rename dialogue box

command at the Command: prompt, AutoCAD displays the **Rename** dialogue box (Figure 16-37). You can select the type of named object from the list provided in the Named Objects area of the dialogue box. Corresponding names of all the objects of the specified type that can be renamed are displayed in the Items area. For example, if you want to rename the layer named OBJ to TEXT2, the process involved will be:

1. Pick the **Layer** option from the list in the **Named Objects** area. All the layer names that can be renamed are displayed in the Items area.
2. Pick OBJ from the list in the Items area. When you pick OBJ from the list, OBJ is displayed in the Old Name: edit box.
3. Enter TEXT2 in the Rename To: edit box and pick the OK button.

Now the layer named OBJ is renamed to TEXT2. You can rename blocks, dimension styles, linetypes, styles, UCS, views, and viewports in the same way. The prompt sequence for changing the name of the block SQUARE to PLATE1 is:

Command: **RENAME** ◄─┘
Block/Dimstyle/LAyer/LType/Style/Ucs/VIew/VPort: **B** ◄─┘
Old block name: **SQUARE** ◄─┘
New block name: **PLATE1** ◄─┘

Note

This RENAME command cannot be used to rename WBlocks. You can change the name of a WBlock by using the DOS command, RENAME, or the File Utilities dialogue box.

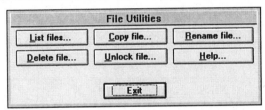

Figure 16-38   File Utilities dialogue box

For example, if you want to change the name of a WBlock from BHAWANI.DWG to KAUL.DWG, you need to perform the following steps:

1. Pick the **Utilities...** option from the pull-down menu (Select File, Management, Utilities...). The **File Utilities** dialogue box is displayed.
2. Pick the **Rename File...** button from this dialogue box. The **Old File Name** dialogue box is displayed.

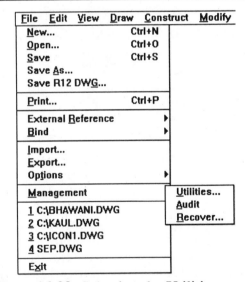

Figure 16-39 Selecting the Utilities... option from the File pull-down menu

3. Enter BHAWANI.DWG in the **File:** edit box and pick the **OK** button. Make sure that this file exists in the current directory.
4. The **New File Name** dialogue box is displayed. Notice that by default, the **File:** edit box contains the name of the file you have specified in the File edit box of the Old File Name dialogue box. Change the default filename to KAUL.DWG and pick the OK button. The WBlock name is changed from C7D14.DWG to C7DA14.DWG.

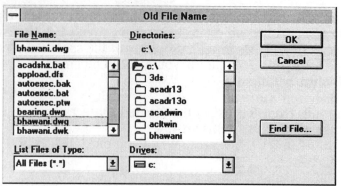

Figure 16-40 Old File Name dialogue box

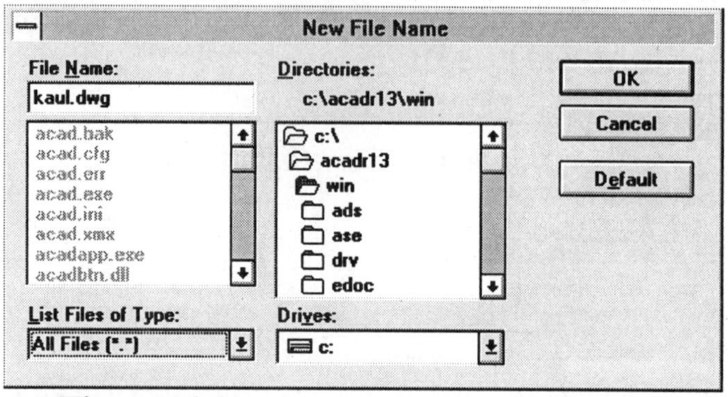

Figure 16-41 New File Name dialogue box

REMOVING UNUSED NAMED OBJECTS (PURGE COMMAND)

Pull-down:	Data, Purge
Screen:	DATA, Purge:

Another editing operation is deletion. You can delete unused named objects such as blocks, layers, dimension styles, linetypes, text styles, and shapes with the help of the **PURGE** command. You can invoke the PURGE command, from the pull-down menu (Select Data, Purge, Figure 16-42), from the screen menu (Select DATA, Purge:), or by entering **PURGE** at the Command: prompt. When you create a new drawing, or open an existing one, AutoCAD records the named objects in that drawing and notes other drawings referencing the named objects. Usually only a few of the named objects (such as layers, linetypes, blocks, etc.) in the drawing are used. For example when you create a new drawing, the prototype drawing settings may contain various text styles, blocks, and layers that you do not want to use. Also,

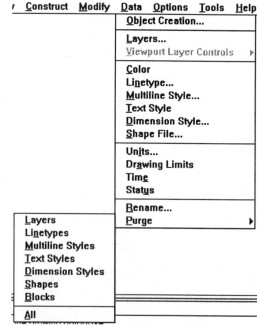

Figure 16-42 Selecting the PURGE option from the pull-down menu

you may want to delete particular unused named objects such as unused blocks in an existing drawing. Deleting inactive named objects is important and useful because doing so reduces the space occupied by the drawing. With the PURGE command, you can select the named objects you want to delete. You can use this command any time in the drawing session. The prompt sequence for the PURGE command is:

Command: **PURGE**
Purge unused Blocks/Dimstyles/LAyers/LTypes/SHapes/STyles/APpids/Mlinestyles/All:
                    Specify the option you want to delete.

If you want to purge a block named SQUARE from a drawing file, the prompt sequence is:

Command: **PURGE**
Purge unused Blocks/Dimstyles/LAyers/LTypes/SHapes/STyles/APpids/Mlinestyles/All: **B**
Purge block SQUARE? <N> **Y**

Once this is done, the PURGE command separately lists all the unused blocks and gives you the option (Y or N) of keeping or deleting them. The **WBLOCK-asterisk** method has the same effect as the PURGE command. The only difference is that in the case of the WBLOCK-asterisk method, unused named objects are removed automatically.

> **Note**
>
> *Standard objects (such as Layer 0, STANDARD text style, and linetype CONTINUOUS) created by AutoCAD cannot be removed by the PURGE command even if these objects are not used.*

OBJECT SELECTION MODES

> **Pull-down:** Options, Selection...
> **Screen:**   OPTIONS, DDselect:

When you select a number of objects, the selected objects are known as a selection set. Selection of the objects is controlled by the **DDSELECT** command. This command can be selected from the pull-down menu (Select Options, Selection..., Figure 16-43), from the screen menu (Select OPTIONS, DDselect:), or by entering **DDSELECT** at the Command: prompt.

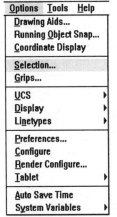

Figure 16-43 Selecting the Selection option from the Options pull-down menu

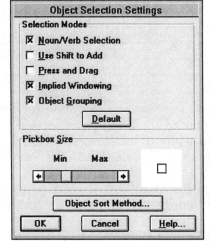

Figure 16-44 Object Selection Setting dialogue box

The **Object Selection Setting** dialogue box (Figure 16-44) is displayed when you invoke the DDSELECT command. Five selection modes are provided in this dialogue box. You can select any one of these modes or a combination of various modes.

Noun/Verb Selection

By selecting the Noun/Verb Selection check box, you can select the objects (noun) first and then specify the operation (verb) (command) to be performed on the selection set. If this selection mode is chosen, a small pickbox is displayed at the intersection of the graphic cursor (cross-hairs). This mode is active by default. For example, if you want to move some objects and Noun/Verb Selection is enabled, first select the objects to be moved, then invoke the MOVE command. The objects selected are highlighted automatically when the MOVE command is invoked and AutoCAD does not issue any Select objects: prompt. The following commands can be used on the selected objects when Noun/Verb Selection mode is active:

ARRAY	BLOCK	CHANGE	CHPROP
COPY	DDCHPROP	DVIEW	ERASE
HATCH	LIST	MIRROR	MOVE
ROTATE	SCALE	STRETCH	WBLOCK
EXPLODE			

The following are some of the commands that are not affected by the Noun/Verb Selection mode. You are required to specify the objects (noun) on which an operation (command/verb) is to be performed, after specifying the command (verb):

BREAK	CHAMFER	DIVIDE	EDGESURF
EXTEND	FILLET	MEASURE	OFFSET
PEDIT	REVSURF	RULESURF	TABSURF
TRIM			

When the Noun/Verb Selection mode is active, the **PICKFIRST** system variable is set to 1 (on). In other words, you can activate Noun/Verb Selection mode by setting the PICKFIRST variable to on.

Command: **PICKFIRST**
New value for PICKFIRST <0>: **1**

Use Shift to Add

The next option in the Selection Modes area of the **Object Selection Setting** dialogue box is Use Shift to Add. Selecting this option establishes additive selection mode. In this mode you have to hold down the SHIFT key when you want to add objects to the selection set. For example, suppose X, Y, and Z are three objects on the screen. Select object X. It is highlighted and put in the selection set. After selecting X, while selecting object Y, if you do not hold down the SHIFT key, object Y is only highlighted and it replaces object X in the selection set. On the other hand, if you hold down the SHIFT key while selecting Y, it is added to the selection set (which contains X) and the resulting selection set contains both X and Y. Also, both X and Y are highlighted. To summarize the concept, objects are added to the selection set only when the SHIFT key is held down while objects are selected. Objects can be discarded from the selection set by selecting the these objects while the SHIFT key is held down.

When the Use Shift to Add mode is active, the **PICKADD** system variable is set to 1 (on). In other words, you can activate Use Shift to Add mode by setting the PICKADD variable to on.

Command: **PICKADD**
New value for PICKADD <0>: **1**

Press and Drag

This selection mode is used to govern the way you can define a selection window or crossing window. When this option is selected, the window can be created by picking one corner of the window and then holding down the pick button of the pointing device and dragging the cursor to define the other diagonal point of the window. When you have the window you want, release the pick button of the pointing device. If the Press and Drag mode is not active, you have to pick twice to specify the two diagonal corners of the window to be defined.

When the Press and Drag mode is active, the **PICKDRAG** system variable is set to 1 (on). In other words, you can activate Press and Drag mode by setting the PICKDRAG variable to on.

> Command: **PICKDRAG**
> New value for PICKDRAG <0>: **1**

Implied Windowing

By selecting this option, you can automatically create a window when the Select objects: prompt is issued. The selection window or crossing window in this case is created in the following manner:

At the Select objects: prompt, pick a point in empty space on the screen. This becomes the first corner point of the selection window. After this, AutoCAD asks you to specify the other corner point of the selection window. If the first corner point is to the right of the second corner point, a Crossing selection is defined; if the first corner point is to the left of the second corner point, a Window selection is defined. If this option is not active, you need to specify Window or Crossing at the Select objects: prompt, depending on your requirement.

When the Implied Windowing mode is active, the **PICKAUTO** system variable is set to 1 (on). In other words, you can activate Implied Windowing mode by setting the PICKAUTO variable to on.

> Command: **PICKAUTO**
> New value for PICKAUTO <0>: **1**

SELF EVALUATION TEST

Answer the following questions and then compare your answers with the answers given at the end of this chapter.

1. Only the CHANGE command can be used to change the properties associated with a object. (T/F)

2. The PURGE command can be used only when you enter the Drawing Editor and before the drawing database has been change by operations involving addition or deletion of objects in the drawing file. (T/F)

3. The One option of the UNDO command restrains U and UNDO commands to a single operation. (T/F)

4. If the last (closing) segment of the polyline was drawn as a polyline and not using the Close option, the Open option will still be effective. (T/F)

5. The Control option lets you determine how many of the UNDO options you want active. (T/F)

6. The Width option of the PEDIT command can be used to change the width of a polyline with a constant and unvarying width. (T/F)

7.   You can move from vertex n to vertex n even in a closed polyline by using either the Next option or the Previous option only. (T/F)

8.   The system variable _____ controls the number of line segments used to construct the Spline curves.

9.   If you want to edit a polyline into a B-spline curve you have to set the system variable _____. A value equal to _____ produces the _____ curve, whereas a value equal to _____ produces a _____ curve.

10.   The group names can be up to _____ characters long and can include special characters ($, _, and -).

11.   The length of the description text can be up to _____ characters, including spaces.

12.   The **Include Unnamed** button is used to display the names of the unnamed objects in the Object Grouping dialogue box. (T/F)

13.   The **Selectable** button allows you to define a group that is selectable. (T/F)

14.   The Join option of the PEDIT command can be used only if a polyline is open. (T/F)

15.   The Width option of the PEDIT command can be used to change the starting and ending widths of a polyline separately to a desired value. (T/F)

REVIEW QUESTIONS

Answer the following questions.

1.   You can use the _____ command to group AutoCAD objects and assign a name to the group.

2.   You can also use the GROUP command from the Command line by entering _____ at the Command: prompt.

3.   The _____ option in the GROUP command lets you change the order of the objects in the selected group.

4.   A group can be selected by selecting the Group option from the pull-down menu or by entering _____ at the AutoCAD **Select Objects:** prompt.

5.   When you use the GROUP command to form object groups, AutoCAD lets you sequentially highlight the groups of which the selected object is a member. (T/F)

6.   The color, linetype, and layer on which a block is drawn can be changed with the help of the CHANGE command. (T/F)

7.   After exploding an object, the object remains identical except that the color and linetype may change because of floating layers, colors, or linetypes. (T/F)

8.   The PURGE command has the same effect as the WBLOCK-asterisk method. The only difference is that with the PURGE command, deletion takes place automatically. (T/F)

9.   The RENAME command can be used to change the name of a WBlock. (T/F)

10. The RENAME command can be used to change the name of a Block. (T/F)

11. If the Auto option of the UNDO command is off, any group of commands that is used to insert an object is undone together. (T/F)

12. If the selected polyline is closed, the Close option is replaced by the Open option. (T/F)

13. Circles drawn using the CIRCLE command can be changed to polylines. (T/F)

14. When you enter the Edit vertex option of the PEDIT command, an X marker appears on the screen at the second vertex of the polyline. (T/F)

15. If a tangent direction has been specified for the vertex selected with the Edit vertex option, an arrow is generated in that direction. (T/F)

16. With the Break option of the PEDIT Command, if there are any polyline segments or vertices between the vertices you have specified, they will be erased. (T/F)

17. The Break operation is valid if both the specified vertices are located at the end point of the polyline or only one vertex is specified and its location is at the end point of the polyline. (T/F)

18. The Move option lets you move the X marked vertex to a new position. (T/F)

19. The Straighten option of the PEDIT command deletes the arcs, line segments, or vertices between the desired two vertices and substitutes them with a single line segment. (T/F)

20. The Width option of the Edit vertex option of the PEDIT command allows you to change the starting and ending width of an existing polyline. (T/F)

21. The spline curve passes through only the first and last vertices and pulls toward the other vertices but does not pass through them, unlike the Fit option. (T/F)

22. The fit curve passes only through the first and last vertices of the polyline. (T/F)

23. The Decurve option removes the vertices inserted after using the Fit or the Spline options. (T/F)

24. The Decurve option cannot be used to straighten out any curve drawn with the help of the Arc option of the PLINE command. (T/F)

25. Quadratic curves are extremely smooth. The Quadratic curve passes through the first and last control points and the curve is closer to the other control points. (T/F)

26. The _____ command can be used to undo any previous command, or undo several commands at once.

27. If you enter 6 at the **Auto/Back/Control/End/Group/Mark/ <Number>:** prompt, _____ previous commands will be undone.

28. The _____ option of the UNDO command disables the UNDO and U command entirely.

29. To activate the UNDO options if they are disabled, you must enter either _____ or _____ (one mode) options.

30. A group of commands is caused to be treated as a single command for the U and UNDO commands by the combined work of the _____ and _____ UNDO options.

EXERCISES

Exercise 4

Draw part (a) shown in Figure 16-45; then using the CHANGE and relevant PEDIT options, convert it into (b), (c), and (d). The linetype used in (d) is HIDDEN.

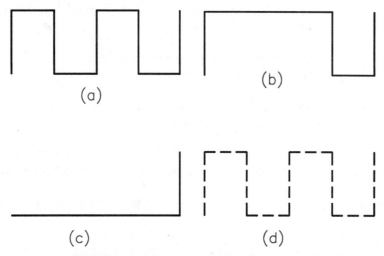

Figure 16-45 Drawing for Exercise 4

Exercise 5

Draw the object in Figure 16-46 using the LINE command. Then change the object to a polyline with a width of 0.01.

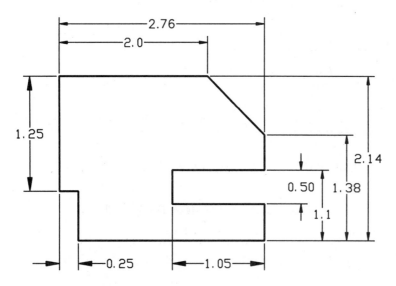

Figure 16-46 Drawing for Exercise 5

Exercise 6

Draw part (a) shown in Figure 16-47; then using the relevant PEDIT options, convert it into drawing (b).

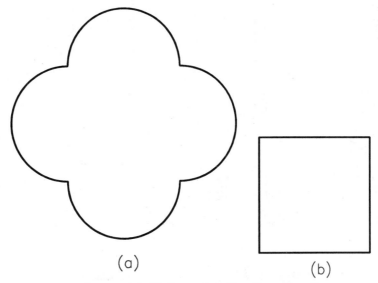

(a)   (b)

Figure 16-47 Drawing for Exercise 6

Exercise 7

Draw part (a) shown in Figure 16-48; then using the relevant PEDIT options, convert it into (b), (c), and (d). Identify the types of curves.

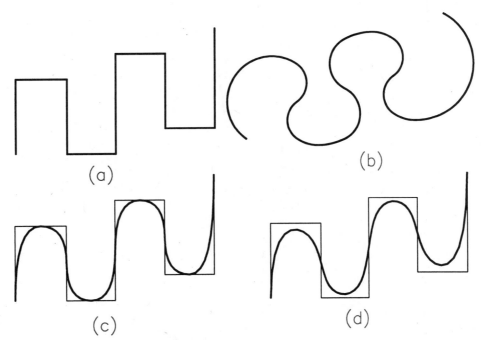

(a)   (b)

(c)   (d)

Figure 16-48 Drawing for Exercise 7

Exercise 8

Draw part (a) shown in Figure 16-49; then using the relevant PEDIT options, convert it into (b).

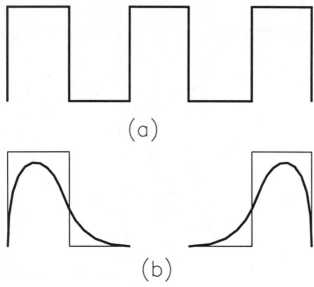

Figure 16-49   Drawing for Exercise 8

Exercise 9

Draw part(a) shown in Figure 16-50; then using the relevant PEDIT options, convert it into (b).

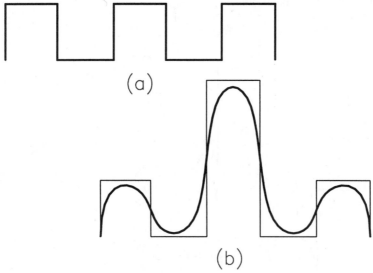

Figure 16-50   Drawing for Exercise 9

Answers

The following are the correct answers to the questions in the self evaluation test.
1 - F, 2 - T, 3 - T, 4 - F, 5 - T, 6 - F, 7 - T, 8 - SPLINESEGS, 9 - SPLINETYPE, 5, Quadratic, 6, Cubic, 10 - 31, 11 - 64, 12 - T, 13 - T, 14 - T, 15 - F

Chapter 17

Inquiry Commands
Data Exchange
Object Linking and Embedding

Learning objectives

After completing this chapter, you will be able to:
◆ Make inquiries about drawings and objects.
◆ Calculate area using the AREA command.
◆ Calculate distances using the DIST command.
◆ Identify a position on the screen using the ID command.
◆ List information about drawings and objects using the DBLIST and LIST commands.
◆ List drawing-related information using the STATUS command.
◆ Import and export files using the DXFOUT and DXFIN commands.
◆ Convert scanned drawings into the Drawing Editor using the DXB command.
◆ Export raster files using the SAVEIMG command.
◆ Use PostScript fonts to create text.
◆ Understand the embedding and the linking functions of the OLE feature of Windows.

MAKING INQUIRIES ABOUT A DRAWING

(INQUIRY COMMANDS)

When you create a drawing or examine an existing one, you often need some information about the drawing. In manual drafting you inquire about the drawing by performing measurements and calculations manually. Similarly, when drawing in an AutoCAD environment, you will need to make inquiries about data pertaining to your drawing. The inquiries can be about the distance from one location on the drawing to another, the area of an object like a polygon or circle, coordinates of a location on the drawing, etc. AutoCAD keeps track of all the details pertaining to a drawing. Since inquiry commands are used to obtain information about the selected objects, these commands do not affect the drawings in any way.

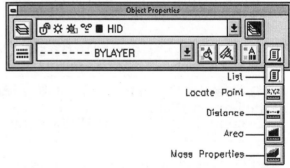

Figure 17-1 Selecting Inquiry commands from the List flyout in the Object Properties toolbar

The following is the list of Inquiry commands:

AREA   DIST   ID   LIST   DBLIST   MASSPROP

All of these commands, except DBLIST, are located in the List flyout in the Object Properties toolbar (Figure 17-1), in the INQUIRY screen menu, or under the Inquiry option in the Edit pull-down menu (Figure 17-2).

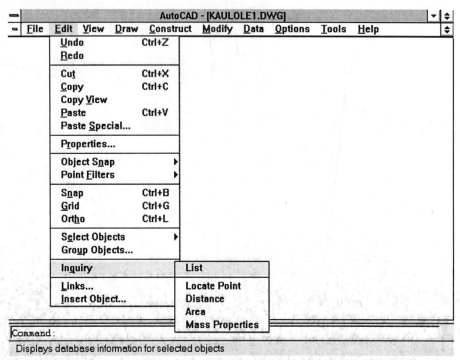

Figure 17-2 Selecting Inquiry commands from the Edit pull-down menu

For most of the Inquiry commands, you are prompted to select objects and once the selection is complete, AutoCAD switches from **graphics mode** to **text mode** and all the relevant information about the selected objects is displayed in the **AutoCAD Text Window**. The display of the text screen can be tailored to your requirement with the help of a pointing device, hence by moving the text screen on one side, you can view the drawing screen and the text screen simultaneously. If you pick the minimize button located at the upper-right corner of the text window, or double click on the button on the upper-left corner of the text window, you will return to the graphics screen. You can also return to the graphics screen by entering **GRAPHSCR** command at the Command: prompt. Similarly, you can return to the AutoCAD Text Window by entering **TEXTSCR** at the Command: prompt.

Calculating the Area of an Object (AREA Command)

Toolbar:	Object Properties, List, Area
Pull-down:	Edit, Inquiry, Area
Screen:	ASSIST, INQUIRY, Area:

Finding the area of a shape or an object manually is time-consuming. In AutoCAD the **AREA** command is used to automatically calculate the area of an object in square units. This command saves time calculating the area of shapes, especially when the shapes are complicated. You can invoke the AREA command by selecting the Area icon from the List flyout in the **Object Properties** toolbar, from the pull-down menu (Select Edit, Inquiry, Area), from the screen menu (Select ASSIST, INQUIRY, Area:). entering **AREA** at the Command: prompt.

You can use the default option of the AREA command to calculate the area and perimeter/circumference of the space enclosed by the sequence of specified points. For example, you may have created an object with the help of the LINE command (Figure 17-3). To find the area of such an object (which is not formed of a single object), you need to pick all the vertices of that object. By picking the points, you define the shape of the object whose area is to be found. This is the default method for determining the area of an object. The only restriction is that all the points you specify must be in a plane parallel to the X-Y plane of the prevailing UCS. You can make the best possible use of object snaps such as ENDpoint,

You can also invoke this command by

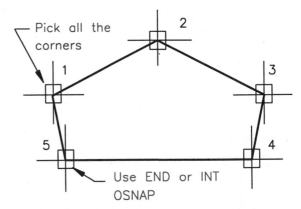

Figure 17-3 Using the AREA command

INTersect, or TANgent, or even use running OSNAPs, to help you pick the vertices quickly and accurately. For AutoCAD to find the area of a shape, the shapes need not have been drawn with polylines, nor do the lines need to be closed. In such cases AutoCAD computes the area by assuming that the first point and the last point are joined. The prompt sequence in this case is:

> Command: **AREA**↵
> < First point >/Object/Add/Subtract: *Pick the first point.*
> Next point: *Pick the second point.*
> Next point: *Continue picking until all the points enclosing the area have been picked and all the objects selected.*
>
> Next point:↵
> Area = (X), Perimeter = (Y)

Here **X** represents the numerical value of the area and **Y** represents the circumference/perimeter. It is not possible to accurately determine the area of a curved object such as an arc with the default (Point) option. However, the approximate area under an arc can be calculated by picking several points on the given arc. If the object whose area you want to find is not closed (formed of independent segments), and has curved lines, you should follow the steps below to determine the area of such an object.

1. Convert all the segments in that object into polylines using the **PEDIT** command.

2. Join all the individual polylines into a single polyline. Once you have performed these operations, the object becomes closed and then you can use the **Object** option of the **AREA** command to determine the area.

If you pick two points on the screen, the AREA command will display the value of the area as 0.00, while the Perimeter value is the distance between the two points.

Object option

You can use the **Object** option of the AREA command to find the area of objects such as polygons, circles, closed polylines, regions, solids, and splines. If the selected object is a closed polyline or polygon, AutoCAD displays the area and perimeter of the polyline. If the selected object is a circle, ellipse, or a planar closed spline curve, AutoCAD will provide you information about its area and circumference. For a solid, the surface area is displayed. For a 3D polyline all vertices must lie in a plane parallel to the XY plane of the prevailing UCS. The extrusion direction of a 2D polyline whose area you want to determine should be parallel to the

Z axis of the prevailing UCS. If any of these conditions is violated, an error message is displayed on the screen. The prompt sequence is:

Command: **AREA**◄─┘
<First point>/Object/Add/Subtract: **O**◄─┘
Select objects : *Pick an object*◄─┘
Area = (X), Circumference = (Y)

The **X** represents numerical values of the area and **Y** represents the circumference/perimeter.

Add option

Sometimes you will want to add areas of different objects to determine a total area. For example, in a plan of a house, you need to add areas of all the rooms to get the total floor area. In such cases you can use the **Add** option. Once you invoke this option, AutoCAD activates the **ADD mode**. Now when you pick an object, the area of the selected object is displayed on the screen. At this time the total area is equal to the area of the selected object. When you select another object, AutoCAD displays the area of the selected object as well as the combined area (Total area) of the previous object and the currently selected object. In this manner you can add areas of different objects. Until the Add mode is active, the string **ADD mode** is displayed along with all subsequent object selection prompts to remind you that the ADD mode is active. When the AREA command is invoked, the total area is initialized to zero.

Subtract option

The action of the **Subtract** option is the reverse of the Add option. Once you invoke this option, AutoCAD activates the **SUBTRACT mode**. Now when you pick an object, the area of the selected object is displayed on the screen. At this time the total area is equal to the area of the selected object. When you select another object, AutoCAD displays the area of the selected object as well as the area obtained by subtracting the area of the currently selected object from the area of the previous object. In this manner you can subtract areas of objects from the total area. Until the SUBTRACT mode is active, the string **SUBTRACT mode** is displayed along with

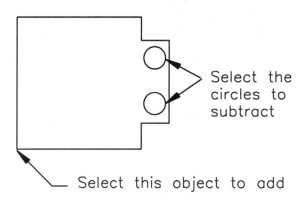

Figure 17-4 Using the ADD and SUBTRACT options

all subsequent object selection prompts to remind you that the SUBTRACT mode is active. To exit from the AREA command, press the Enter key (null response) at the **<First point>/Object/Add/Subtract:** prompt. The prompt sequence for these two modes for Figure 17-4 is:

Command: **AREA** ◄─┘
<First point>/Object/Add/Subtract: **A** ◄─┘
<First point>/Object/Subtract: **O** ◄─┘
(ADD mode) Select objects: *Pick the polyline.*
Area = 2.4438, Perimeter = 6.4999
Total area = 2.4438
(ADD mode) Select objects: ◄─┘
<First point>/Object/Subtract: **S** ◄─┘
<First point>/Object/Add: **O** ◄─┘
(SUBTRACT mode) Select object: *Pick the circle.*
Area = 0.0495, Circumference = 0.7890

Total area = 2.3943
(SUBTRACT mode) Select objects: *Pick the second circle.*
Area = 0.0495, Circumference = 0.7890
Total area = 2.3448
(SUBTRACT mode) Select object:◄─┘
<First point>/Object/Add:◄─┘

The **AREA** and **PERIMETER** system variables hold the area and perimeter (or circumference in the case of circles) of the previously selected polyline (or circle). Whenever you use the AREA command, the AREA variable is reset to zero.

Calculating the Distance Between Two Points (DIST Command)

The **DIST** command is used to measure the distance between two selected points. The angles that the selected points make with the X axis and the X-Y plane are also displayed. The measurements are displayed in current units. Delta X (horizontal displacement), delta Y (vertical displacement), and delta Z are also displayed. The distance computed by the DIST command is saved in the **DISTANCE** system variable. You can invoke this command by selecting the Distance icon from the List flyout in the **Object Properties** toolbar, from the pull-down menu (Select Edit, Inquiry, Distance), from the screen menu (Select ASSIST, INQUIRY, Dist:), or by entering **DISTANCE** at the Command: prompt.

Command: **DIST** ◄─┘
First point: *Pick a point.*
Second point: *Pick a point.*

AutoCAD returns the following information:

Distance = *Calculated distance between the two points.*
Angle in XY plane = *Angle between the two points in XY plane.*
Angle from XY plane = *Angle the specified points make with XY plane.*
Delta X = *Change in X*, Delta Y = *Change in Y*, Delta Z = *Change in Z*

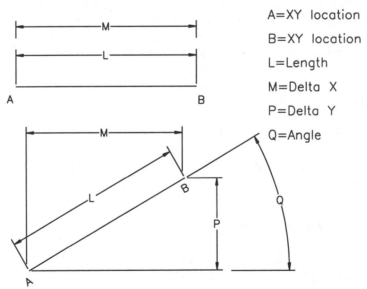

A=XY location
B=XY location
L=Length
M=Delta X
P=Delta Y
Q=Angle

Figure 17-5 Using the DIST command

Note

The Z coordinate is used in 3D distances. If you do not specify the Z coordinates of the two points between which you want to know the distance, AutoCAD takes the current elevation as the Z coordinate value.

Identifying a Position on the Screen (ID Command)

Toolbar:	Draw, List, Locate Point
Pull-down:	Edit, Inquiry, Locate Point
Screen:	ASSIST, INQUIRY, ID:

This command identifies the position of a point you specify and tells you its coordinates. You can invoke this command by selecting the Locate Point icon from the List flyout in the **Object Properties** toolbar, from the pull-down menu (Select Edit, Inquiry, Locate Point), from the screen menu (Select ASSIST, INQUIRY, ID:) or by entering **ID** at the Command: prompt.

Command: **ID** ◄─┘
Point: *Pick the point to be identified.*
X = <X coordinate> Y = <Y coordinate> Z = <Z coordinate>

AutoCAD takes the current elevation as the Z coordinate value. If an OSNAP mode is used to snap to a 3D object in response to the **Point:** prompt, the Z coordinate displayed will be that of the selected feature of the 3D object. You can also use the **ID** command to identify the location on the screen. This can be realized by entering the coordinate values you want to locate on the screen. AutoCAD identifies the point by drawing a blip mark at that location. For example, say you want to find the position on the screen where X = 2.345, Y = 3.674, and Z = 1.0000 is located. This can be achieved with the following prompt sequence:

Command: **ID** ◄─┘
Point: **2.345,3.674,1.00** ◄─┘
X = 2.345 Y = 3.674 Z = 1.0000

You can also use the **X/Y/Z point filters** to specify points on the screen. You can respond to the **Point:** prompt with any desired combination of .X, .Y, .Z, .XY, .XZ, .YZ. The 2D or 3D point is specified by specifying individual (intermediate) points and forming the desired point from the selected X, Y, and Z coordinates of the intermediate points. More simply, you can specify a 2D or 3D point by supplying separate information for the X, Y and Z coordinates. For example, say you want to identify a point whose X, Y, and Z coordinates are marked on the screen separately. This can be achieved in the following manner:

Command: **ID** ◄─┘
Point: **.X** ◄─┘
of   *Pick the location whose X coordinate is the X coordinate of the final desired point to be identified.*
of (need Y): Y of   *Pick the location whose Y coordinate is the Y coordinate of the final desired point to be identified.*
(need Z):   *Pick the location whose Z coordinate is the Z coordinate of the final desired point to be identified.*
X = <X coordinate> Y = <Y coordinate> Z = <Z coordinate>

A blip mark is formed at the point of intersection of the specified X, Y, and Z coordinates. This blip mark identifies the desired point.

Listing Information about Objects (LIST Command)

The **LIST** command displays all the data pertaining to the selected objects. You can invoke this command by selecting the List icon from the List flyout in the Object Properties toolbar, from the pull-down menu (Select Edit, Inquiry, List), from the screen menu (Select ASSIST, INQUIRY, List:), or by entering **LIST** at the Command: prompt.

Command: **LIST** ←⎤
Select objects: *Select objects whose database you want to list.*
Select objects: ←⎤

Once you select the objects to be listed, AutoCAD shifts you from the graphics screen to the AutoCAD Text Window. The information displayed (listed) varies from object to object. Information on object's type, its coordinate position with respect to the current UCS (user coordinate system), name of the layer on which it is drawn, and whether the object is in Model space or Paper space is listed for all types of objects. If the color and the linetype are not BYLAYER, they are also listed. Also if the value of thickness of the object is greater than 0, that is also displayed. The elevation value is displayed in the form of a Z coordinate (in the case of 3D objects). If an object has an extrusion direction different from the Z axis of the current UCS, the object's extrusion direction is also provided. More information based on the objects in the drawing is also provided. For example, for a line the following information is be displayed:

1. The coordinates of the end points of the line.
2. Its length (in 3D)
3. The angle made by the line with respect to the X axis of the current UCS.
4. The angle made by the line with respect to the XY plane of the current UCS.
5. Delta X, delta Y, delta Z: this is the change in each of the three coordinates from the start point to the end point.
6. Line weight.
7. The name of any dimension style; if it is unnamed, AutoCAD lists the dimension style as UNNAMED.

The center point, radius, true area, and the circumference of circles is displayed. For polylines this command displays the coordinates and the tangent direction for each vertex. In addition, for a closed polyline, its true area and perimeter is also given. If the polyline is open, AutoCAD lists its length and also calculates the area by assuming a segment connecting the start and end points of the polyline. In the case of wide polylines all computation is done based on the center lines of the wide segments. For a selected viewport, the LIST command displays whether the viewport is on and active, on and inactive, or off. Information is also displayed about the status of Hideplot and the scale relative to paper space. If you use the LIST command on a polygon mesh, the size of the mesh (in terms of M X N), the coordinate values of all the vertices in the mesh, and whether the mesh is closed or open in M and N directions are all displayed. As mentioned before, if all the information does not fit on a single screen, AutoCAD pauses to allow you to press the RETURN (Enter) key to continue the listing.

Listing Information about All Objects in a Drawing
(DBLIST Command)

The **DBLIST** command displays information pertaining to all the objects in the drawing. Once you invoke this command, information is displayed in AutoCAD Text Window. If the information does not fit on a single screen, AutoCAD pauses to allow you to press the RETURN (Enter) key to continue the listing. To terminate the command, press the **Escape** key. To return to graphics screen close the AutoCAD Text Window. This command can be invoked by entering **DBLIST** at the Command: prompt.

Exercise 1

Draw Figure 17-6 and save it as EX1. Using inquiry commands, determine the following values:

(a) Area of the hexagon.
(b) Perimeter of the hexagon.
(c) Perimeter of the inner rectangle.
(d) Circumference of each circle.
(e) Area of the hexagon minus the inner rectangle.
(f) Use the DBLIST command to get database listing.

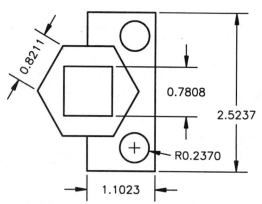

Figure 17-6 Drawing for Exercise 1

Listing Information about Solids and Regions (MASSPROP Command)

Toolbar:	Draw, List, Mass Properties
Pull-down:	Edit, Inquiry, Mass Properties
Screen:	ASSIST, INQUIRY, MassPro:

With the **MASSPROP** command, you can determine volumetric information such as principle axes, center of gravity, and moment of inertia of 2D or 3D objects. You can invoke this command by selecting the Mass Properties icon from the List flyout in the Object Properties toolbar, from the pull-down menu (Select Edit, Inquiry, Mass Properties), from the screen menu (Select ASSIST, INQUIRY, MassPro:), or by entering **MASSPROP** at the Command: prompt.

Command: **MASSPROP** ↵
Select objects: *Pick an object (solid object).*

For a solid sphere, information similar to following will be displayed:

```
--------------------- SOLIDS ------------------------
Mass:                    23.6520
Volume:                  23.6520
Bounding box:            X: 4.8318 -- 8.3932
                         Y: 2.6140 -- 6.1754
                         Z: -1.7807 -- 1.7807
Centroid:                X: 6.6125
                         Y: 4.3947
                         Z: 0.0000
Moments of inertia:      X: 486.8062
                         Y: 1064.1910
                         Z: 1520.9977
Products of inertia:     XY: 687.3322
                         YZ: 0.0000
                         ZX: 0.0000
Radii of gyration:       X: 4.5367
```

Y: 6.7077
Z: 8.0192

Principal moments and X-Y-Z directions about centroid:

I: 29.9995 along [1.0000 0.0000 0.0000]
J: 29.9995 along [0.0000 1.0000 0.0000]
K: 29.9995 along [0.0000 0.0000 1.0000]

Write to a file ? <N>: Y

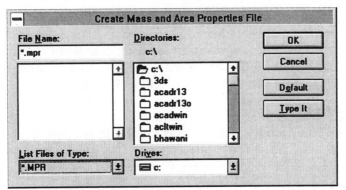

Figure 17-7 Create Mass and Area Properties File dialogue box

If you enter Y (Yes) at the above prompt, the **Create Mass and Area Properties File** dialogue box (Figure 17-7) is displayed on the screen. All the file names of the .MPR type are listed. You can enter the name of the file in the File edit box. The file is automatically given the .MPR extension.

The explanation of various terms displayed on the screen as a result of invoking MASSPROP command is as follows:

For Solids
The information displayed for solids is similar to following:

Mass
This property provides the measure of mass of a solid.

Volume
This tells you the measure of the space occupied by the solid. Since AutoCAD assigns a density of one to the solids, the mass and volume of a solid are equal.

Bounding Box
If the solid were to be enclosed in a 3D box, the coordinates of the diagonally opposite corners are provided by this property.

Centroid
This provides the coordinates of the center of mass for the selected solid. The density of a solid is assumed to be unvarying.

Moments of Inertia
This property provides the mass moments of inertia of a solid about the three axes. The equation used to calculate this value is:

$$\text{mass\_moments\_of\_inertia} = \text{object\_mass} * (\text{radius of axis})^2$$

The radius of axis is nothing but the radius of gyration. The values obtained are used to calculate the force required to rotate an object about the three axes.

Products of Inertia
The value obtained with this property helps to determine the force resulting in the motion of the object. The equation used to calculate this value is:

product _of_inertia YX,XZ = mass * dist centroid_to_YZ * dist centroid_to_XZ

Radii of Gyration
The equation used to calculate this value is:
$$\text{gyration\_radii} = (\text{moments\_of\_inertia/body\_mass})^{1/2}$$

Principal Moments and X-Y-Z Directions about Centroid
This property provides you with the highest, lowest, and middle value for the moment of inertia about an axis passing through the centroid of the object.

For Coplanar and Noncoplanar Regions
The information displayed for coplanar regions is similar to following:

```
---------------------- REGIONS ----------------------------

Area:                      13.6480
Perimeter:                 21.2475
Boundary box:              X: 3.3610 -- 8.5063
                           Y: 4.1330 -- 6.4829
Centroid:                  X: 5.9337
                           Y: 5.3127
Moments of inertia:        X: 390.8867
                           Y: 512.2000
Product of inertia:        XY: 430.2535
Radii of gyration:         X: 5.3516
                           Y: 6.1260
Principal moments & X-Y directions about centroid
                           I: 5.6626 along [1.0000 0.0000]
                           J: 31.6536 along [0.0000 1.0000]
```

Write to a file ?<N>:

CHECKING TIME-RELATED INFORMATION (TIME COMMAND)

Pull-down:	Data, Time
Screen:	DATA, Time:

The time and date maintained by your system is used by AutoCAD to provide information about several time factors related to the drawings. Hence, you should be careful about setting the current date and time in your computer. The **TIME** command can be used to display information pertaining to time related to a drawing and the drawing session. To invoke the TIME command, enter **TIME** at the Command: prompt, or select it from the pull-down menu (Select Data, Time, Figure 17-8), or from the

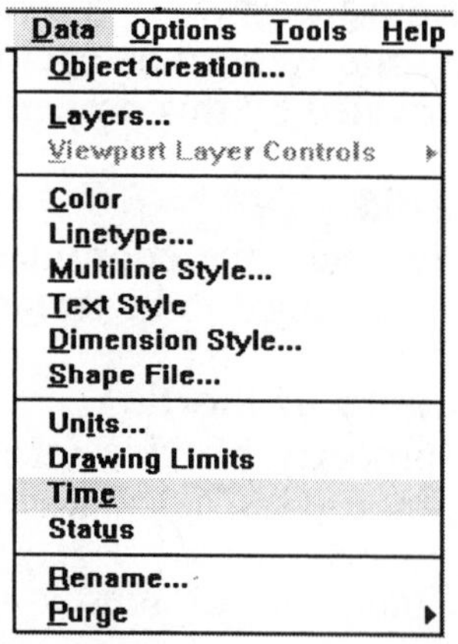

Figure 17-8 TIME option in Data pull-down menu

screen menu (Select DATA, Time:). The display obtained by invoking the TIME command is similar to:

Command: **TIME**
Current time: 13 Apr 1995 at 11:22:35.069
Times for this drawing:
Created: 22 Nov 1993 at 09:34:42.157
Last updated: 07 Jan 1994 at 14:54:25.700
Total editing time: 0 days 07:52:16.205
Elapsed timer (on)   0 days 00:43:07.304
Next automatic save in: 0 days 00:54:27:153

Display/ON/OFF/Reset:

From this display you can obtain information on following features:

Current Time

Provides today's date and the current time.

Drawing Creation Time

Provides date and time current drawing was created. The draw creation time for a drawing is set to the system time when the **NEW, WBLOCK,** or **SAVE** command was used to create that drawing file.

Last Updated Time

Provides the most recent date and time you saved the current drawing. In the beginning, it is set to the drawing creation time and is modified each time you use the **END** or **SAVE** command to save the drawing.

Total Editing Time

This tells you the total time spent on editing the current drawing since it was created. If you terminate the editing session without saving the drawing, the time you have spent on that editing session is not added to the total time spent on editing the drawing. Also, the last update time is not revised.

Elapsed Timer

This timer operates while you are in AutoCAD. You can stop this timer by entering OFF at the **Display/ON/OFF/Reset:** prompt. To activate the timer, enter ON. If you want to know how much time you have spent on the current drawing or part of the drawing in the current editing session, use the **Reset** option as soon as you start working on the drawing or part of the drawing. This resets the user-elapsed timer to zero. By default this timer is ON. If you turn this timer OFF, time accumulated in this timer up to the time you turned it OFF will be displayed.

Next Automatic Save In Time

This tells you when the next automatic save will be performed. The automatic save time interval can be set while configuring AutoCAD or with the SAVETIME system variable. If the time interval has been set to zero, the **TIME** command displays the following message:

Next automatic time save in: < disabled >

If the time interval is not set to zero, and no editing has taken place since the previous save, the TIME command displays the following message:

Next automatic time save in: < no modification yet >

If the time interval is not set to zero, and editing has taken place since the previous save, the TIME command displays the following message:

Next automatic time save in: 0 days hh:mm:ss.msec

hh stands for hours
mm stands for minutes
ss stands for seconds
msec stands for milliseconds

At the end of the display of the TIME command, AutoCAD prompts:

Display/ON/OFF/Reset:

The information displayed by the TIME command is static, i.e., the information is not updated dynamically on the screen. If you respond to the above prompt with Display (or D), the display obtained by invoking the TIME command is repeated. This display contains updated time values.

With the ON response, the user-elapsed timer is started if it were off. As mentioned above, when you enter the drawing editor, by default the timer is on. The OFF response is just the opposite of the ON response and stops the user-elapsed time if it is on. With the **Reset** option, you can set the user-elapsed time to zero.

OBTAINING DRAWING STATUS INFORMATION (STATUS COMMAND)

Pull-down:	Data, Status
Screen:	DATA, Status:

The **STATUS** command displays information about the prevalent settings of various drawing parameters like Snap spacing, Grid spacing, limits, current space, current layer, current color, various memory parameters, etc. The STATUS command can be invoked from the pull-down menu (select Data, Status), from the screen menu (select DATA, Status:), or by entering **STATUS** at the Command: prompt.

Command: **STATUS**

Once you enter this command, AutoCAD displays information similar to:

106 objects in UNNAMED

Model space limits are	X: 0.0000	Y: 0.0000(On)	
	X: 6.0000	Y: 4.4000	
Model space uses	X:0.6335	Y:-0.2459	**Over
	X:8.0497	Y: 4.9710	**Over
Display shows	X: 0.0000	Y:-0.2459	
	X: 8.0088	Y: 5.5266	
Insertion base is	X: 0.0000	Y: 0.0000	Z: 0.0000
Snap resolution is	X: 0.2500	Y: 0.2500	
Grid spacing is	X: 0.2500	Y: 0.2500	

Current space:	Model space
Current layer:	OBJ

Current color:	BYLAYER .... 7 (white)
Current linetype:	BYLAYER .... CONTINUOUS
Current elevation:	0.0000 thickness: 0.0000

Fill on Grid on Ortho off Qtext off Snap off Tablet on
Object snap modes: None
Free disk: 12068864 bytes
Free physical memory: 15.0 Mbytes
Free swap file space: 92.5 Mbytes
Virtual address space: 31.4 Mbytes

All the values (coordinates and distances) on this screen are given in the format declared in the UNITS command. On the right side of the **LIMITS** section in the display you will notice the **Off** option. This means that the limit checking is presently switched off (you can draw outside limits). You will also notice ****Over** in the **Model space uses** or **Paper space uses** line. This signifies that the drawing is not confined within the drawing limits. The amount of memory available on the disk is given in the **Free disk:** line. For example in the above display, the amount of free memory on the disk is 12068864 bytes. Information on the name of the current layer, current color, current space, current linetype, current elevation, snap spacing (snap resolution), grid spacing, and various tools that are on or off (such as Ortho, Snap, Fill, Tablet, Qtext), and which Object snap modes are active is also provided by the display obtained by invoking the STATUS command.

Exercise 2

Use the **STATUS** command to check the disk space available on the hard drive. Also, draw a solid sphere and use the MASSPROP command to list the properties of sphere.

DATA EXCHANGE IN AUTOCAD

Different companies have developed different software for applications such as CAD, desktop publishing, rendering, etc. This non-standardization of software has led to the development of various data exchange formats that enable transfer (translation) of data from one data processing software to another. In this chapter we will discuss various data exchange formats provided in AutoCAD. AutoCAD uses the **DWG** format to store drawing files. This format is not recognized by most other CAD software, such as Intergraph, CADKEY, and MicroStation. To solve this problem so that the files created in AutoCAD may be transferred to other CAD software for further use, AutoCAD provides various data exchange formats such as **DXF (Data Interchange File)** and **DXB (Binary Drawing Interchange)**.

DXF FILE FORMAT (DATA INTERCHANGE FILE)

The DXF file format generates a text file in ASCII code from the original drawing. This allows any computer system to manipulate (read/write) data in a DXF file. Usually DXF format is used for CAD packages based on microcomputers. For example, packages like SmartCAM use DXF files. Some desktop publishing packages, such as, Pagemaker and Ventura Publisher also use DXF files.

Creating a Data Interchange File (DXFOUT Command)

Pull-down:	File, Export, DXF format
Screen:	FILE, EXPORT, DXFout:

The **DXFOUT** command is used to create an ASCII file with a **.DXF** extension from an AutoCAD drawing file. You can create a DXF file using the pull-down menu (Select File, Export, (select *.DXF format in the Export Data dialogue box, Figure 17-10)), from the screen menu (Select FILE, EXPORT, DXFout:), or by entering **DXFOUT** at the Command: prompt.

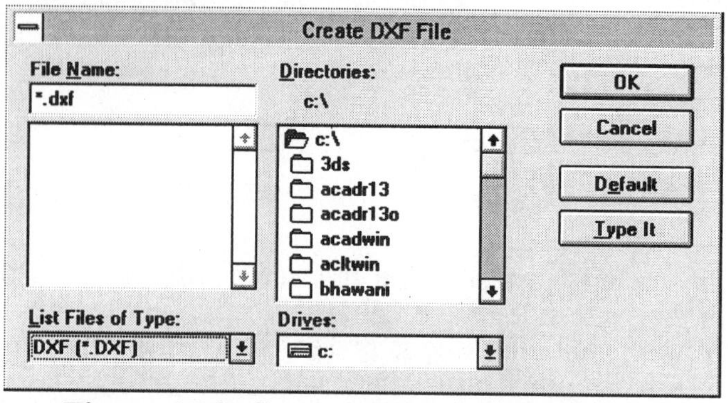

Figure 17-9 Create DXF File dialogue box

Once you invoke the DXFOUT command, the **Create DXF File** dialogue box (Figure 17-9) is displayed on the screen. By default the DXF file to be created assumes the name of the drawing file from which it will be created. However, you can specify a filename of your choice for the DXF file by typing the desired filename in the File edit box. AutoCAD automatically sets the extension of DXF files as **.DXF**. This can be observed in the Pattern edit box. After you have specified a file name, AutoCAD prompts you to enter the degree of accuracy for the numeric values. The default value for the degree of accuracy is six decimal places. You can enter a value between 0 and 16 decimal places.

> Enter decimal places of accuracy (0 to 16)/ Objects/Binary <6>: *Enter the degree of accuracy.*

In the above prompt there is an Objects option, which you can use to specify objects you want to include in the DXF file. In this case information on the drawing setup is not included in the DXF file.

> Enter decimal places of accuracy (0 to 16)/ Objects/Binary <6>: **E**
> Select objects: *Pick the objects to be included in the DXF file.*
> Enter decimal places of accuracy (0 to 16)/Binary <6>: *Enter the degree of accuracy.*

Now an ASCII file with a **.DXF** extension has been created, and this file can be accessed by other CAD systems. This file contains data on the objects specified in the DXFOUT command. By default, with the DXFOUT command files are created in ASCII format. However you can also create binary format files with the Binary option of this command. Binary DXF files are more efficient and occupy only 75 percent of the ASCII DXF file. You can access a file in binary format more quickly than the file in ASCII format.

> Enter decimal places of accuracy (0 to 16)/ Objects/Binary <6>: **B**

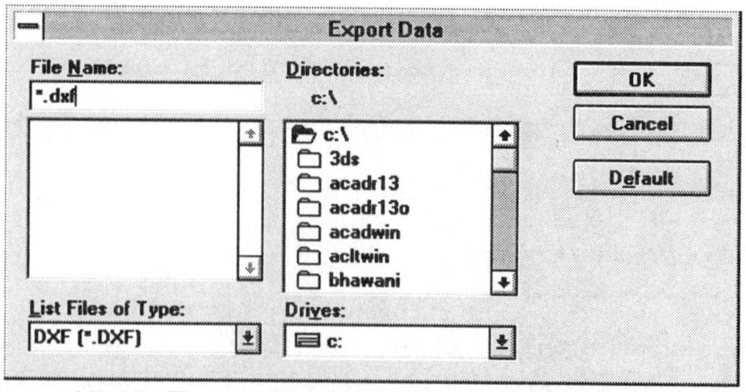

Figure 17-10 Export Data dialogue box with DXF format

Information in a DXF File

The DXF file contains data on the objects specified in the DXFOUT command. You can change the data in this file to your requirement. To examine the data in this file, use the DOS Editor, use DOS command TYPE, or load the ASCII file in a word processing software. A DXF file is a composed of four parts.

Header

In this part of the drawing database, all the variables in the drawing and their values are displayed.

Tables

All the named objects such as linetypes, layers, blocks, text styles, dimension styles, views are listed in this part.

Blocks

The objects that define blocks and their respective values are displayed in this part.

Objects

Objects in the drawing are listed in this part.

Converting DXF Files into a Drawing File (DXFIN Command)

Pull-down:	File, Import, DXF format
Screen:	FILE, IMPORT, DXFin:

You can convert a DXF file into an AutoCAD drawing file with the **DXFIN** command. A DXF file can be imported into AutoCAD using the pull-down menu (Select File, Import, (select *.DXF format in the Import File dialogue box, Figure 17-11)), or from the screen menu (Select FILE, IMPORT, DXFin:), or by entering **DXFIN** at the Command: prompt.

Command: **DXFIN**

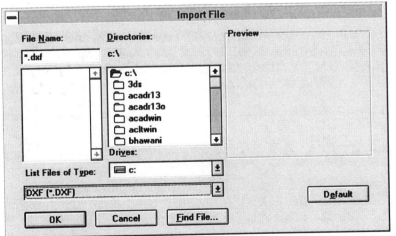

Figure 17-11 Import File dialogue box with file format set to DXF

After you invoke the DXFIN command, the **Select DXF File** dialogue box (Figure 17-12) is displayed. In the File edit box enter the name of the file you want to import into AutoCAD. Pick the OK button. Once this is done, the specified DXF file is converted into a standard DWG file, regeneration is carried out, and the file is inserted into the current drawing. Now you can perform different operations on this file just as with other drawing files.

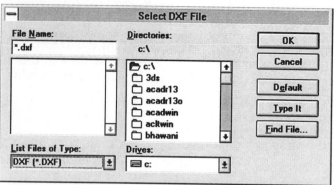

Figure 17-12 Select DXF File dialogue box

Importing Scanned Files into the Drawing Editor
DXB FILE FORMAT

Screen:	FILE, IMPORT, DXBin:

AutoCAD offers another file format for data interchange: DXB. This format is much more compressed than the binary DXF format and is used when you want to translate large amounts of data from one CAD system to another. For example, when a drawing is scanned, a DXB file is created. This file has huge amounts of data in it. The **DXBIN** command is used to create drawing files out of DXB format files. The **DXBIN** command can be accessed from the screen menu (Select FILE, IMPORT, DXBin:), or by entering **DXBIN** at the Command: prompt.

Command: **DXBIN**

After you invoke the DXBIN command, the **Select DXB File** dialogue box is displayed on the screen. In the File edit box enter the name of the file (in DXB format) you want to import into AutoCAD. Pick the OK button. Once this is done, the specified DXB file is converted into a standard DWG file and is inserted into the current drawing.

Note

Before importing a DXF or DXB file, you must create a new drawing file. No editing or drawing setup (limits, units, etc.) can be performed in this file. This is because if you import a DFX or DXB file into an old drawing, the settings (definitions) of layers, blocks, etc., of the file being imported are overruled by the settings of the file into which you are importing the DXF or DXB file.

DATA INTERCHANGE THROUGH RASTER FILES

Until now we have discussed importing/exporting files in the DXF file format. To uphold the accuracy of the drawing, the DXF file includes almost all the information about the original drawing file. The accuracy is maintained at the expense of DXF file size and degree of complexity of these files. There are many applications in which accuracy is not very important, like desktop publishing. In such applications you are primarily concerned with image presentation. A very simple and effective way of storing an image for import/export is in the form of raster files. In a raster file, information is stored in the form of dot pattern on the screen. This bit pattern is also known as a bit map. For example, in a raster file a picture is stored in the form of information about the position and color of the screen pixels. We will be discussing three types of raster files: TIFF files, GIF files, and PCX files. These formats make it possible to transfer a file from AutoCAD to other software.

TIFF (tagged image file format)
This file format has been developed by Aldus and Microsoft.

GIF (graphics interchange format)
This file format has been provided by CompuServe.

PCX (personal computer eXchange)
This file format has been developed by Z-Soft Corporation

Exporting the Raster Files (Using SAVEIMG Command)

Pull-down:	Tools, Image, Save...
Screen:	TOOLS, SaveImg:

If there is a picture on the screen that you want to save as a raster file, use the SAVEIMG command. With this command you can create TIFF, GIF, TGA, or RND types of raster files out of the current drawing. These raster files can be used by most softwares. Sometime the raster files need to be converted into some other format before they can be used by certain software. This operation is performed with file conversion programs such as Hijaak or Pizazz Plus. The SAVEIMG command can be invoked from the pull-down menu (Select Tools, Image, Save..., Figure 17-13), or from the screen menu (Select TOOLS, SaveImg:), or by entering **SAVEIMG** at the Command: prompt.

Command: **SAVEIMG**

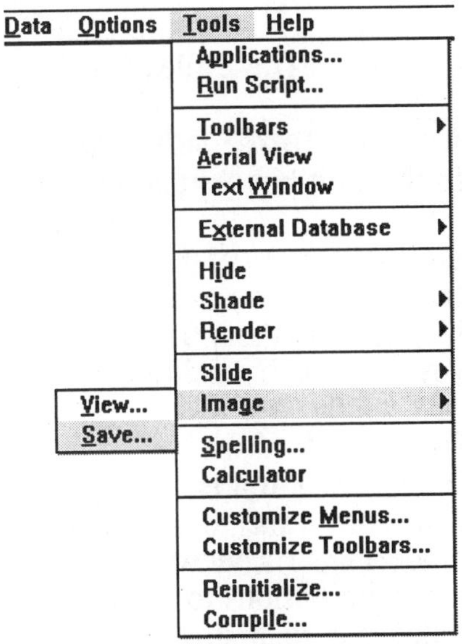

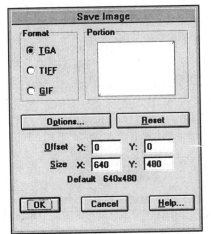

Figure 17-13 Selecting the IMAGE command from the Tools pull-down menu

Figure 17-14 Save Image dialogue box with image tile

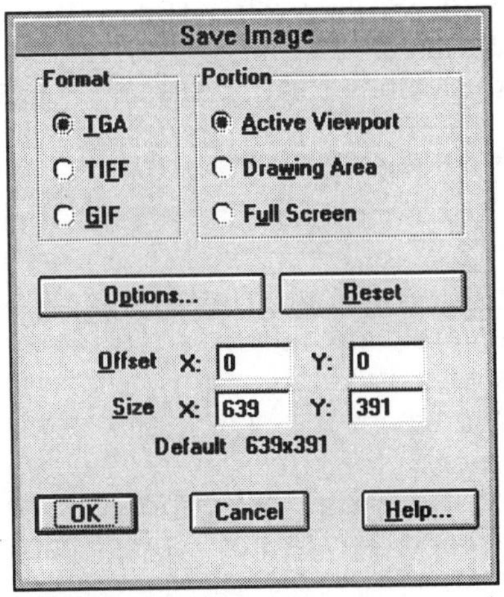

Figure 17-15 Save Image dialogue box without image tile

Once you invoke this command, the **Save Image** dialogue box is displayed on the screen. Depending on the Destination option you have selected in the Render Preferences dialogue box, you will get one of the shown Save Image dialogue boxes (Figures 17-14 and 17-15). The only difference lies in the Position area of the dialogue boxes.

Format

In this area of the **Save Image** dialogue box, you are provided three raster formats: TGA, TIFF, and GIF. You can select any one of the formats by selecting the radio button next to the desired format. A brief description of each format follows.

TGA (default format). With this format you can create compressed or uncompressed 32-bit RGBA Truevision v2.0 format files. These files have the extension **.tga**.

TIFF (tagged image file format). This file format has been developed by Aldus and Microsoft. With this format you can create compressed or uncompressed 32-bit RGBA Tagged Image File Format. These files have the extension **.tif**.

GIF (graphics interchange format). This file format has been provided by CompuServe. These files have the extension **.gif**.

Image Name edit box

In this edit box you specify the name of the image file you want to create.

Directory edit box

In this box, you can specify the directory in which you want to store the raster file. By default it is the directory in which the drawing file to be converted into a raster file lies. However, you can specify a directory of your choice.

Portion

In the Portion area of the **Save Image** dialogue box you can specify the portion of the screen that you want to save in the specified file format. In case AutoCAD is configured for rendering to a viewport (in the Render Preferences dialogue box), the Position area provides you with options to save the active viewport, or the drawing area, or the full screen. If you are rendering to a different window, the portion area contains an image tile. This image tile graphically represents the section of the screen to be saved. You will notice that by default the entire screen is selected for saving. If you want to save only a section of the screen, you need to specify the desired section. This can be achieved by picking two diagonally opposite points on the image tile. Pick the lower left corner of the desired section first, then pick the upper right corner. After specifying the two corner points, AutoCAD creates a box whose lower left corner point and upper right corner point coincide with the respective points you picked. Also, the values for the X and Y Offsets and Size are automatically updated.

Offset and Size

This comprises the X and Y edit boxes. The value you enter in these edit boxes is treated as the X and Y offset. The start point (lower left corner) of the area to be saved as a raster file can be specified by X and Y offset values. The default value for the offset is 0,0. The values entered are taken as the pixel values. The offset values should be specified within the screen size value. If you are rendering to a different window, when you change the offset values, the change in the start point of the image selection area is reflected by a margin formed by two intersecting lines in the image tile. The point of intersection of these two lines is the start point of the image selection area. A value of X and Y offsets greater than the screen size is not accepted by AutoCAD. If you have selected the RND format, the Offset area is not available.

Size

With the Offset option you can specify the lower left corner of the area to be selected for conversion into a raster file format. To specify the area completely, specify the upper right corner of this area. This can be achieved with the Size option. In case of the Offset option the values entered in the X and Y edit boxes are the pixel values. The default for the Size option is the upper right corner of the display area. If you are rendering to a different window, the change in location of upper right corner of the image selection area is reflected by two intersecting lines. If you have selected the RND format, the Offset area is not available.

Options

The display provided by selecting this option varies from one file format to another. If image file compression is not supported by some file format, then the Options button is grayed out.

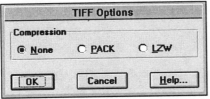

Figure 17-16 TIFF Options dialogue box

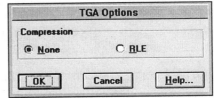

Figure 17-17 TGA Options dialogue box

None

This is the default option. If this option is selected, compression does not take place.

RLE

This option works only for TGA format files. By selecting this option, Run-length encoded image compression can be realized.

PACK

With this option, Run-length encoded image compression can be realized only for TIFF files.

LZW

This option works only for TIFF format files. Selecting this option, Lempel-Ziv and Welch type image compression is carried out.

Reset

By selecting this option, the Offset values and the Size values are set to their default values.

Example 1

In this example you will load a drawing or draw a figure and then use the SAVEIMG command to save the image.

To create an image using the SAVEIMG command involves the following steps. Assume that the drawing is already loaded or drawn on the screen.

1. Invoke the SAVEIMG command by any one of the methods explained.
2. Enter the name you want to give the image file to be created.
3. Specify the file type in the Format area by picking the radio button with the desired file type format.
4. Specify the area you want to save in the image file to be created by selecting the desired offsets and size.
5. Pick the OK button.

After this, AutoCAD starts saving the area selected to the file whose name you have specified in the **Image Name** edit box. The saving operation is acknowledged by the message Writing (filename) file. For example, if the filename is ABC, AutoCAD will display the message Writing ABC file.

Importing Raster Files into AutoCAD

It is possible to import raster files of different formats into AutoCAD. AutoCAD provides a set of three commands to import (read) different types of raster files. These commands are **GIFIN**,

TIFFIN, and **PCXIN.** These commands are somewhat similar to the BLOCK command that is used to import blocks. Since the process involved to read a raster file is almost same for all three of these commands, we will only address importing .GIF files.

```
Pull-down: File, Import, GIF
Screen:    FILE, IMPORT, GIFin:
```

The GIFIN command can be invoked from the pull-down menu (Select File, Import, (select *.GIF format in the Import File dialogue box)), from the screen menu (Select FILE, IMPORT, GIFin:), or by entering **GIFIN** at the Command: prompt. You can import PCX and TIFF format raster images in the same manner.

Command: **GIFIN**
GIF file name: **ABC**

Once you enter the filename, a rectangular box in which the path and filename of the .GIF file is written is displayed on the screen. You can move this rectangular box anywhere on the screen. In the above case you will see a rectangular box with C:\ABC written in it. The next prompt asks you for the insertion point for the rectangular box.

Insertion point <0,0,0>: *Specify the location for the insertion point.*
Scale factor: *Specify the scale factor.*

The scale factor can also be specified by dynamically dragging the box. After specifying the scale factor, whatever is in the specified GIF file is inserted into the AutoCAD screen. From the prompts associated with the GIFIN command, it is obvious that the image is inserted into the AutoCAD drawing file as a block.

Variables Controlling Display of Imported Raster Images

You can change the appearance of an imported raster file with the help of six variables. Basically these variables are ADS functions that work as system variables. All six have a prefix, RI, which stands for Raster In. A brief description of them follows:

RIASPECT

With this variable you can manipulate the aspect ratio of the imported raster file. Aspect ratio is the ratio of width to height or X to Y ratio. Hence, if you increase the value of the RIASPECT variable, the width of the imported raster file increases. If you decrease the value of RIASPECT variable, the height of the imported objects increases.

Command: **RIASPECT**
Raster input pixel aspect ratio <0>:

RIBACKG

You can control the background color of the image with this variable. For example, a value of 0 produces a black background, and a value of 7 produces a white background.

Command: **RIBACKG**
Raster input screen background color <0>:

RIEDGE

With this variable you can control the display of edges of an image. If you set this variable to 0, the edges of the imported image are displayed. The greater the number assigned to this variable, the more outstanding an edge must be to be displayed.

Command: **RIEDGE**
Raster input edge detection <0>:

RIGAMUT

With this variable, you can specify the number (range) of colors used to display the image. The default value for this variable is 256. If you want to reduce the file size, set the RIGAMUT variable to the number of colors your display device supports.

Command: **RIGAMUT**
Raster input color gamut size <256>:

RIGREY

You can convert imported images into grayscale images by setting the RIGREY variable to 1. The file size of such files is very low because AutoCAD does not have many gray shades.

Command: **RIGREY**
Raster input grey scale mode <0>:

RITHRESH

This variable sets a threshold for filtering objects that have a brightness value less than the RITHRESH setting. Hence, objects that have a brightness value greater than the RITHRESH setting are only displayed on the screen.

Command: **RITHRESH**
Raster input threshold <0>:

PostScript Files and Fonts

PostScript is a page description language developed by Adobe Systems. It is mostly used in DTP (desktop publishing) applications. AutoCAD allows you to work with PostScript files. You can create and export PostScript files as well as convert PostScript files into regular AutoCAD drawing files (import). PostScript images have higher resolution than raster images. **.EPS** (Encapsulated PostScript) is the extension for these files.

PSOUT Command

> **Pull-down:** File, Export, EPS
> **Screen:**   FILE, EXPORT, PSOUT:

As mentioned before, any AutoCAD drawing file can be converted into a PostScript file. This can be accomplished with the PSOUT command. You can create a PostScript file from the pull-down menu (Select File, Export, (Select EPS format in Export Data dialogue box)), from the screen menu (Select FILE, EXPORT, PSout), or by entering **PSOUT** at the Command: prompt.

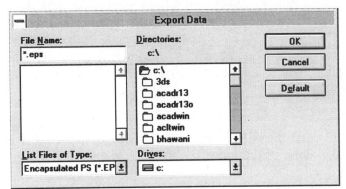

Figure 17-18 Creating a PostScript file using the Export Data dialogue box

Once the PSOUT command is invoked, AutoCAD displays the **Create PostScript file** dialogue box (Figure 17-18).

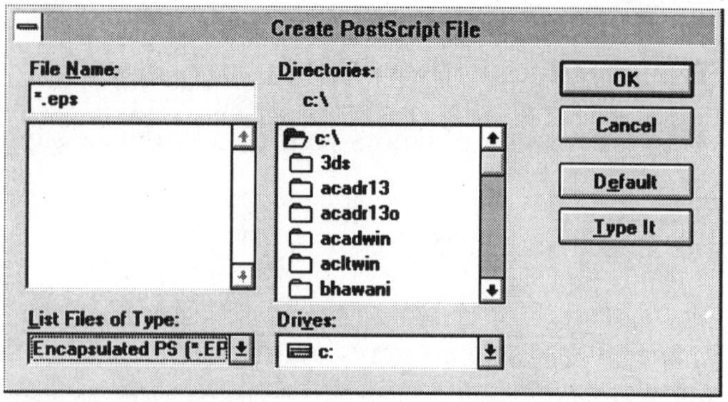

Figure 17-19 Create PostScript file dialogue box

In the File Name edit box, enter the name of the PostScript (EPS) file you want to create. Then pick the OK button. AutoCAD displays the following prompt:

What to plot - Display, Extents, Limits, View or Window <D>:

The options in this prompt are discussed as follows:

Display
If you specify this option when you are in Model space, the image in the current viewport is saved in the specified EPS file. Similarly, if you are in Paper space, the current view is saved in the specified EPS file.

Extents
If you use this option, the PostScript file created will contain the section of the AutoCAD drawing that currently hold objects. In this way this option resembles the ZOOM Extents option. If you add objects to the drawing, they too are included in the PostScript file to be created because the extents of the drawing are also altered. If you reduce the drawing extents by erasing, moving, or scaling objects, then you must use the ZOOM Extents or ZOOM All option. Only then does the Extents option of the PSOUT command understand the extents of the drawing to be exported. If you are in Model space, the PostScript file is created in relation to the Model space extents; if you are in Paper space, the PostScript file is created in relation to the Paper space extents. If you invoke the PSOUT command's Extents option when Perspective view is on and the position of Camera is not out of the drawing extents, the following message is displayed:

PLOT Extents incalculable, using display

In such cases, the EPS file is created as it would be created with the Display option.

Limits
With this option you can export the whole area specified by the drawing limits. If the current view is not the plan view (view point (0,0,1)), the Limits option exports the area just as the Extents option would.

View
Any view created with the VIEW command can be exported with this option. AutoCAD prompts you for the name of the view:

View name:

Window

In this option you need to specify the area to be exported with the help of a window. The window can be specified by defining the lower left corner and the upper right corner of the area to be exported. AutoCAD prompts for the two corners of the window:

First corner:
Second corner:

After you have given a response to the What to plot - Display, Extents, Limits, View or Window <D>: prompt, the next prompt issued is:

Include a screen preview image in the file? (None/EPSI/TIFF) <None>:

You can include a screen preview with the PostScript file. Two types of formats for preview images are supported: EPSI and TIFF. If you want a preview image of TIFF format, enter TIFF at the above prompt. If you select TIFF or EPSI, you are prompted to enter the pixel resolution of the screen preview.

Screen preview image size (128x128 is standard)? (128/256/512) <128>:

At the next prompt, you can specify the size units. The prompt is:

Size units (Inches or Millimeters) <current>:

After specifying the size units, AutoCAD prompts you to specify a scale factor for the EPS output:

Specify scale by entering:
Output units=Drawing units or Fit or ? <default>:

If your response is Fit, the EPS output will be scaled so that the view to be exported is made as large as possible for the specified paper size. You can also set a scale by entering the number of output units and the number of drawing units, with an equal (=) sign between the two values.

In the next prompt, all output sizes are listed.

Standard values for output size

Size	Width	Height
A	8.0	10.50
B	10.0	16.00
User	7.5	10.50

Enter the Size or Width, Height (in Inches) <USER>:

Any one of the listed sizes or a user-defined size can be entered. After specifying the size, the following message is displayed on the screen:

Effective plotting area: xx by yy high

The xx and yy are measurements in the plotting area in current size units. With the completion of this process, a PostScript file is created as per your specifications and you are returned to the Command: prompt.

PSIN Command

Pull-down:	File, Import, EPS
Screen:	FILE, IMPORT, PSin

AutoCAD allows you to import PostScript files. The PSIN (PostScript IN) command can be used to import a PostScript file. You will find similarity between this command and the GIFIN or INSERT commands. The PostScript file is imported into an AutoCAD drawing as a block. You can import a PostScript file using the pull-down menu (Select File, Import, (Select EPS format in Import File dialogue box)), from the screen menu (Select FILE, IMPORT, PSin:), or by entering **PSIN** at the Command: prompt.

Command: **PSIN**

Once you invoke the PSIN command, the **Select PostScript File** dialogue box (Figure 17-20) is displayed on the screen.

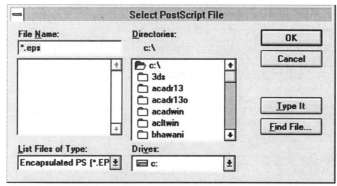

Figure 17-20 Select PostScript File dialogue box

In this dialogue box all the EPS files in the current directory are listed. Select the file you want to import into AutoCAD and then pick OK button. The dialogue box is cleared from the screen and a rectangular box in which the path and filename of the EPS file is written is displayed on the screen. You can move this rectangular box anywhere on the screen. The next prompts asks you for the insertion point and the scale factor for the rectangular box (imported image), respectively:

Insertion point <0,0,0>: *Specify the location for the insertion point.*
Scale factor: *Specify the scale factor.*

The scale factor can also be specified by dynamically dragging the box. After you specify the scale factor, whatever is in the specified EPS file is inserted into the AutoCAD screen. From the prompts associated with PSIN command, it is obvious that the image is inserted into the AutoCAD drawing file as a block. By default a box appears on the screen when you import an EPS file. This box contains the imported image, which you are unable to see until you specify the insertion point and the scale factor. If you want the image immediately instead of the box, set the **PSDRAG** variable to 1. By default the value of this variable is 0; that is why by default you get the box. The quality of the rendering of the imported PostScript file depends on the value of **PSQUALITY** system variable.

Command: **PSQUALITY**
New value for PSQUALITY <current>:

Different settings for PSQUALITY and their effects are as follows:

PSQUALITY = 0

When inserting an EPS file, the rectangular box representing the imported image is displayed. The filename of the imported EPS file is displayed in this rectangular box, and the size of this box corresponds to the size of the imported file.

PSQUALITY = a positive value

In this case the imported image is displayed with the PSQUALITY value number of pixels per AutoCAD drawing unit. In other words, this is the resolution of the imported image. By default the value of PSQUALITY variable is 75. Hence the imported image is displayed with 75 pixels per AutoCAD drawing unit. PostScript objects are filled.

PSQUALITY = a negative value

In such situations the absolute value of the PSQUALITY variable controls the resolution of the imported image. The difference lies in the fact that the PostScript objects are not filled, but are displayed as outlines.

PostScript Fill Patterns (PSFILL Command)

Toolbar: Draw, Hatch, PostScript Fill
Pull-down: Draw, Hatch, PostScript Fill
Screen: ASSIST, INQUIRY, Area:

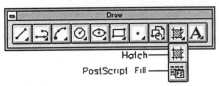

Figure 17-21 PostScript Fill icon in the Hatch flyout in the Draw toolbar

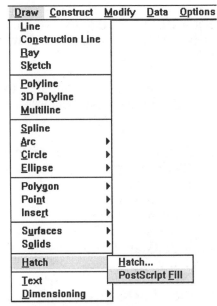

Figure 17-22 PostScript Fill option in the Draw pull-down menu

The **PSFILL** command can be selected from the **Draw** toolbar (Select PostScript Fill icon from Hatch flyout, Figure 17-21), from the pull-down menu (Select Draw, Hatch, PostScript Fill, Figure 17-22), from the screen menu (Select ASSIST, INQUIRY, Area:), or by entering **PSFILL** at the Command: prompt. With the PSFILL command, you can fill closed 2D polylines with PostScript fill patterns. These fill patterns are declared in the ACAD.PSF file. The declarations for a PostScript fill pattern are various parameters and arguments needed to influence the definition of a fill pattern on screen. Some of the PostScript fill patterns are:

GRAYSCALE   LINEARGRAY   RADIALGRAY   SQUARE
WAFFLE   BRICK   ZIGZAG   STARS
AILOGO   SPECKS   RGBCOLOR

You can also define your own fill patterns in the **ACAD.PSF** file with the PostScript procedures. When you assign a fill pattern to a closed polyline, the pattern is not displayed on the screen. However, the fill pattern is recognized by the **PSOUT** command. If you import the PostScript file with a fill pattern using the **PSIN** command, the fill pattern is displayed on the screen as determined by the setting of PSQUALITY, PSDRAG and FILL mode. Also, if you print such a file on a PostScript device, the fill pattern is printed. Depending on the fill pattern you specify, AutoCAD issues prompts concerning various parameters and arguments needed by the fill pattern. For example, if you want to use the STARS fill pattern, the prompt sequence is:

Command: **PSFILL**
Select polyline: *Select the polyline to be filled.*
PostScript fill pattern (. = none) < . >/?: **STARS**
Scale <1.0000>: *Specify the scale factor for the fill pattern.*
LineWidth <1>: *Specify the linewidth for the fill pattern.*
ForegroundGray <0>: *Press the Enter key.*
BackgroundGray <100>:*Press the Enter key.*

Example 2

Draw a rectangle and use the **PSFILL** command to assign waffle pattern to rectangle (Figure 17-23a). Convert the rectangle to PostScript file using **PSOUT** command and then import the PostScript file using **PSIN** command (Figure 17-23b).

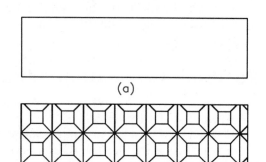

(a)

(b)

Figure 17-23 Assigning waffle Pattern to a polyline

1. Set **PLINEWID** to 0 and use the **RECTANG** command to draw a rectangle (Figure 17-23a).

2. Use the **PSFILL** command to assign the waffle pattern to the rectangle.

Command: **PSFILL**
Select polyline: *Select the rectangle.*
PostScript fill pattern (. = none) < . >/?: **Waffle**
Scale <1.0000>:◄┘
Proportion <30>: ◄┘
LineWidth <1>:◄┘
UpLeftGray <100>: ◄┘
BotRightGray <50>: ◄┘
TopGray <0>: ◄┘

3. Use the **PSOUT** command to convert the drawing into a PostScript file. Once the **PSOUT** command is invoked, AutoCAD displays the **Create PostScript file** dialogue box. In the File Name edit box, enter the name of the PostScript (EPS) file you want to create. Then pick the OK button. AutoCAD displays the following prompt:

What to plot - Display, Extents, Limits, View or Window <D>: **W**
    First corner: *Pick a point.*
    Second corner: *Pick a point.*
Include a screen preview image in the file? (None/EPSI/TIFF) <None>: **E**
Screen preview image size (128x128 is standard)? (128/256/512) <128>:◄┘
Size units (Inches or Millimeters) <current>:◄┘
Specify scale by entering:
Output units=Drawing units or Fit or ? <default>: **F**
Standard values for output size

Size	Width	Height
A	8.0	10.50
B	10.0	16.00
User	7.5	10.50

Enter the Size or Width, Height (in Inches) <USER>: **User**
Effective plotting area: xx by yy high

4. Set **PSQUALITY** to -75 and **PSDRAG** to 0. Use the **PSIN** command to import and insert the PostScript file.

Command: **PSIN**   *(Select the file from the dialogue box)*
Insertion point <0,0,0>: *Specify the location for the insertion point.*
Scale factor: *Specify the scale factor.*

PostScript and TrueType Fonts

AutoCAD provides a number of Adobe Type 1 (PostScript) fonts and TrueType fonts. You can locate these fonts in the ACAD13\COMMON\FONTS subdirectory. These files have the **.PFB** and **.TTF** extension respectively (for example, COBT____.PFB, SWISS.TTF). These fonts can be used by assigning them to a text file. The following example illustrates how to assign the PostScript font to a text file:

Example 3

Use the **STYLE** command to create a new text style file (Mytext) and assign ROMB.PFB PostScript font to the file. Draw some text on the screen to verify the assigned text font.

1. Invoke the **STYLE** command by entering **STYLE** at the Command: prompt.

2. Enter the style name (Mytext) you want to create in which you want the PostScript font to appear.

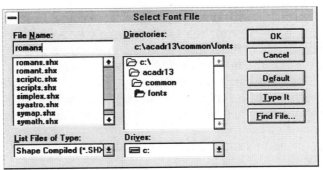

Figure 17-24 Using a PostScript font

Text style name (or?) <current>:   *(Enter a style name)*

3. **The Select Font File** dialogue box (figure 17-25) is displayed.

Figure 17-25 Select Font File dialogue box

4. Pick the desired font file (ROMB.PFB), then pick the OK button to exit the dialogue box. AutoCAD issues the following prompts:

Height <0.0000>:
Width factor <1.0000>:
Obliquing angle <0>:
Backwards ? <N>:
Upside-down ? <N>:

After entering the responses, AutoCAD acknowledges that specified style is the current style.

5. Use the **TEXT** or **DTEXT** command to draw text. If you print this text on a PostScript device the text will be filled.

OBJECT LINKING AND EMBEDDING

With Windows it is possible to work with different Windows-based applications by transferring information between them. You can edit and modify the information in the original Windows application and then update this information in other applications. This is made possible by creating links between the different applications and then updating those links which in turn updates or modifies the information in the corresponding applications. This linking is a function of the OLE feature of Microsoft Windows. The OLE feature can also join together separate pieces of information from different applications into a single document. AutoCAD and other Windows-based applications such as Microsoft Word, Cardfile, and Windows Write support the Windows OLE feature.

For the OLE feature, you should have a **source document** where the actual object is created in the form of a drawing or a document. This document is created in an application called a **server application**. AutoCAD for Windows and Paintbrush can be used as server applications. Now this source document is to be linked to (or embedded in) **destination document**, which is created in a different application known as the **client application**. AutoCAD for Windows, Microsoft Word, and Windows Write can be used as client applications.

Clipboard

The transfer of a drawing from one Windows application to another is performed by copying the drawing or the document from the server application to the Clipboard. Then the drawing or document is pasted in the client application from the Clipboard. Hence a Clipboard is used as a medium for storing the documents while transferring them from one Windows application to another. The drawing or the document in the Clipboard stays there until you copy a new drawing, which overwrites the previous one, or until you exit from Windows. You can save the information present in the Clipboard with the .CLP extension. You can access the Clipboard from the **Main** group of the **Program Manager**.

Object Embedding

You can use the embedding function of the OLE feature when you want to insure that there is no effect on the source document even if the destination document has been changed through the server application. Once a document is embedded, it has no connection with the source. Although editing is always done in the server application but the source document remains unchanged. Embedding can be performed by following the steps given below. In this example AutoCAD for Windows is the server application and Windows Write is the client application.

1. Create a drawing in the server application (AutoCAD).

2. Open the Windows Write (client application) from the **Accessories** group in the Program Manager (Figure 17-26).

3. You have to keep both the client and the server windows active at the same time. It would be preferable if you arrange them on the screen so that both are visible.

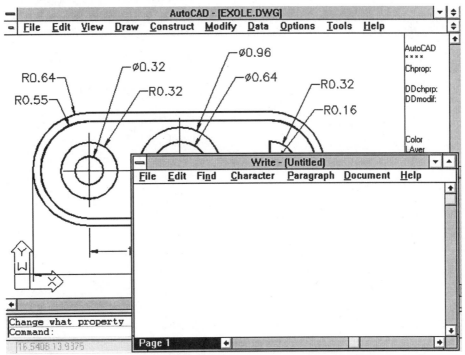

Figure 17-26   AutoCAD graphics screen with the Write window

4.   In the AutoCAD graphic screen use the **COPYCLIP** command. This command can be used in AutoCAD for embedding the drawings. The COPYCLIP command can be invoked from the Standard toolbar by selecting the Copy icon, from the pull-down menu (Select Edit, Copy, Figure 17-27), or by entering **COPYCLIP** at the Command: prompt. The prompt sequence is:

Command: **COPYCLIP**

The next prompt, **Select Objects:**, allows you to pick the entities you want to transfer. You can either select the full drawing by entering **ALL** or you can select some of the entities by picking them. You can use any of the selection set options for selecting the objects. With this command the selected objects are automatically copied to the Windows Clipboard.

Edit	View	Draw	Constru
Undo			Ctrl+Z
Redo			
Cut			Ctrl+X
Copy			Ctrl+C
Copy View			
Paste			Ctrl+V
Paste Special...			
Properties...			
Object Snap			▶
Point Filters			▶
Snap			Ctrl+B
Grid			Ctrl+G
Ortho			Ctrl+L
Select Objects			▶
Group Objects...			
Inquiry			▶
Links...			
Insert Object...			

Figure 17-27   Selecting COPYCLIP from the pull-down menu

5.   After the objects are copied to the Clipboard, make the Write window active. To get the drawing from the Clipboard to the Write application (client), select the **Paste** command in the Write application. Invoke Paste from the **Edit** pull-down menu in the Windows Write. You can also use **Paste Special** from the Edit pull-down menu, which will display a dialogue box (Figure 17-29). In this dialogue box select the Paste button for embedding and the Paste Link button for linking. The drawing is now embedded in the write window.

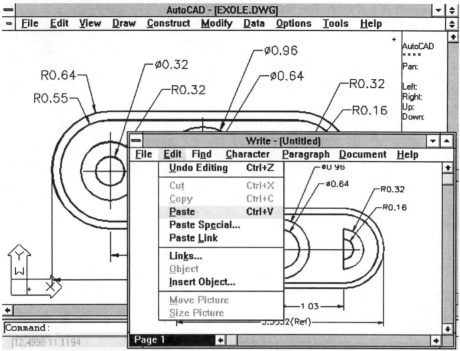

Figure 17-28   Pasting a drawing to the Write application by selecting Paste from the pull-down menu

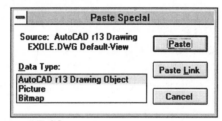

Figure 17-29   Paste Special dialogue box

6. Your drawing is now displayed in the Write window, but it may not be displayed at the proper position. You can get the drawing in the current viewport by moving the scroll button up or down in the Write window. You can also use the **Move Picture** and the **Size Picture** commands to move and size your drawing in the Write application. Both commands can be invoked from the **Edit** pull-down menu. You can also save your embedded drawing by selecting Save from the File pull-down menu. It displays a **Save As** dialogue box where you can enter a filename having a .WRI extension.

7. You can now edit your embedded drawing. Editing is performed in the server application, which in this case is AutoCAD for Windows. You can get the embedded drawing into the server application (AutoCAD) directly from the client application (Write) by double-clicking on the drawing in Write. The other method is by clicking on the drawing once to highlight it and then selecting **Edit AutoCAD Drawing Object** in the Edit pull-down menu. (This menu item has replaced **Object**, which is present before pasting the drawing.)

8. Now you are in AutoCAD with your embedded drawing being displayed on the screen but as a temporary file with a filename such as ASC3C15.DWG. Here you can edit the drawing by changing the color and linetype or by adding and deleting text, entities, etc. In Figure 17-30 the semicircle on the right with the radius R0.32 and the innermost circle on the left with the diameter 0.32 has been erased.

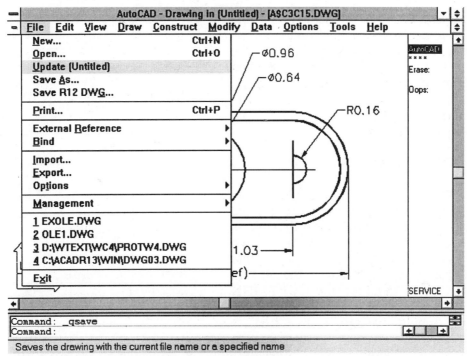

Figure 17-30   Selecting Update (Untitled) from the pull-down menu and screen with embedded temporary file (ASC3C15)

9. After you have finished modifying your drawing, select **Update (Untitled)** from the File pull-down menu in the server (AutoCAD). This menu item has replaced the previous Save menu item. By selecting **Update**, AutoCAD automatically updates the drawing in Write (client application). Now you can exit AutoCAD, which will automatically delete the temporary file of the embedded drawing.

10. This completes the embedding function so you can exit from the Write application. While exiting, a dialogue box is displayed which asks you whether or not to update the embedded objects.

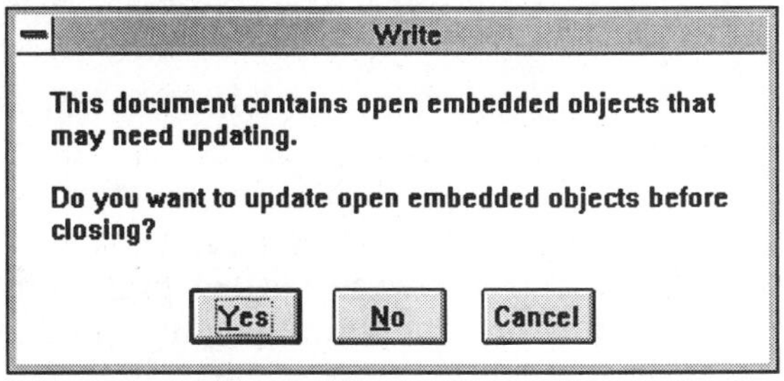

Linking Objects

The Linking function of OLE is similar to the embedding function. The only difference is that here a link is created between the source document and the destination document. If you edit the source you can simply update the link, which automatically updates the client. This allows you to place the same document in number of applications and if you make a change in the source document, the clients will also change by simply updating the corresponding links. Consider AutoCAD for Windows to be the server application and Windows Write to be the client application. Linking can be performed by following these steps:

Figure 17-31   Dialogue box for updating the embedded file

1. Open a drawing in the server application (AutoCAD). If you have created a new drawing then you must save the drawing before you can link it with client application.

2. Open Windows Write (the client application) from Accessories in the Program Manager.

3. You have to keep both the client and the server windows active at the same time. It would be preferable if you arrange them on the screen so that both are visible.

4. In the AutoCAD graphic screen use the **COPYLINK** command. This command can be used in AutoCAD for linking the drawing. This command can be invoked from the pull-down menu (Select Edit, Copy View, Figure 17-32), or by entering **COPYLINK** at the Command: prompt. The prompt sequence is:

Command: **COPYLINK**

The COPYLINK directly copies the whole drawing in the current viewport to the Clipboard. Here you cannot select the objects for linking. If you want only a portion of the drawing to be linked, you can zoom into that view so that it is displayed in the current viewport prior to invoking the COPYLINK command. This command also creates a new view of the drawing having a name OLE1.

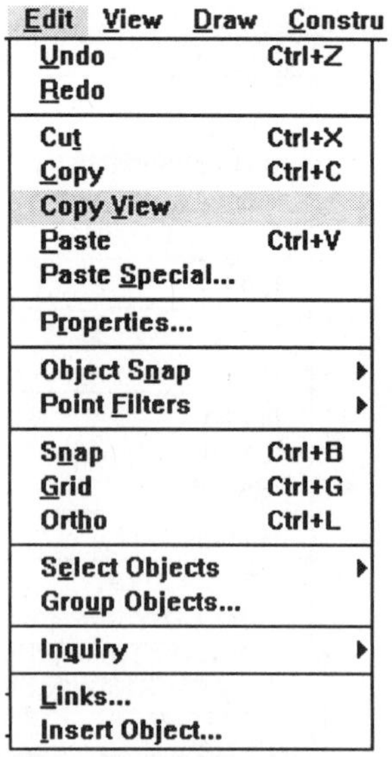

Figure 17-32 Selecting Copy View from the pull-down menu

5. Make the Write window active. To get the drawing from the Clipboard to the Write (client) application, select the **Paste Link** command in the Write application. Invoke Paste Link from the **Edit** pull-down menu in the Windows Write application. You can also use **Paste Special** from the Edit pull-down menu, which will display a dialogue box. In this dialogue box select the Paste Link button for linking.The drawing is now linked to the write window.

6. Your drawing is now displayed in the write window. You can also save your linked drawing by selecting Save from the File pull-down menu. It displays a **Save As** dialogue box where you can enter a filename having a .WRI extension.

7. You can now edit your linked drawing. Editing can be performed in the server application, which in this case is AutoCAD for Windows. You can get the linked drawing in the server (AutoCAD) directly from the client (Write) by double-clicking on the drawing in Write. The other method is by clicking on the drawing once to highlight it and then selecting **Edit AutoCAD Drawing Object** in the Edit pull-down menu. (This menu item has replaced **Object** which is present before pasting the drawing.)

8. Now you are in AutoCAD with your linked drawing being displayed on the screen. You can edit the drawing by changing the color and linetype or by adding and deleting text, entities, etc. Then save your drawing in AutoCAD by using the SAVE command. You can now exit from AutoCAD.

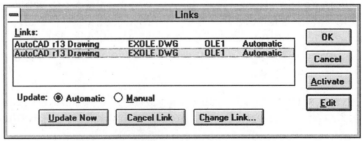

Figure 17-33 Links dialogue box

9. In the Write window select Links... from the Edit pull-down menu. This displays the **Links** dialogue box (Figure 17-33) on the screen. Click on the **Update Now** button and then select

OK. This will update the drawing in the client application and display the updated drawing on the Write screen.

10. Exit from the Write application after saving the updated the file.

SELF EVALUATION TEST

Answer the following questions and then compare your answers with the answers given at the end of this chapter.

1.   The object whose area you want to find with the help of the AREA command must be a closed object.(T/F)

2.   If you QUIT the editing session without saving the drawing, the time you spent on that editing session is added to the total time spent on editing the drawing. Also the last update time is revised. (T/F)

3.   The angle between two points can be measured with the help of the _____ command.

4.   The _____ command displays all the information pertaining the selected objects.

5.   _____ time provides the most recent date and time you edited the current drawing.

6.   You can set the automatic save time interval while configuring AutoCAD or with the _____ system variable.

7.   You can convert a DXF file into an AutoCAD drawing file with the _____ command.

8.   The _____ command is used to create drawing files out of DXB format files.

9.   If you import a DFX or DXB file into an old drawing, the settings of layers, blocks, etc., of the file being imported are _____ by the settings of the file into which you are importing the DXF or DXB file.

10.   A block can be imported into a drawing file only if block definition exist in the _____ drawing file.

11.   The _____ system variable holds the value of distance computed.

12.   The _____ command is used to identify the coordinate values of a point on the screen.

13.   If you import a PostScript file with a fill pattern using the PSIN command, the fill pattern is not displayed on the screen. (T/F)

14.   The _____ command displays all the information pertaining to all the objects in the drawing.

15.   The _____ is used as a medium for storing the documents while transferring them from one Windows application to another.

16.   The _____ command can be used in AutoCAD for embedding drawings.

17.   You can edit your embedded drawing in the _____ application

18. You can get the embedded drawing into the server application directly from the client application by _____ _____ on the drawing

19. The _____ command can be used in AutoCAD for linking the drawing.

20. The COPYLINK command copies the drawing in the _____ to the Clipboard.

REVIEW QUESTIONS

Answer the following questions.

Inquiry

1. Inquiry commands are used to obtain information about the drawn figures. (T/F)

2. The default method of specifying the object whose area you want to find is by picking all the vertices of the object. (T/F)

3. The AREA and PERIMETER system variables are reset to zero whenever you invoke the AREA command.(T/F)

4. To find the circumference/perimeter of an object you can use the _____ command.

5. You can use the _____ option to add subsequent measured areas to the running total.

6. You can use the _____ option to subtract subsequent measured areas to the running total.

7. The distance between two points can be measured with the _____ command.

8. The _____ command can be used to display the data pertaining to time related to a drawing and the drawing session.

9. Drawing _____ provides the date and time the current drawing was created.

10. The drawing creation time for a drawing is set to the system time when the _____ command, or the _____ command, or the _____ command was used to create that drawing file.

Data Exchange

11. The _____ command is used to create an ASCII format file with the .DXF extension from AutoCAD drawing files.

12. With the Binary option of the DXFOUT command you can also create binary format files. Binary DXF files are _____ efficient and occupy only 75 percent of the ASCII DXF file. File access for files in binary format is _____ than the file in ASCII format.

13. When importing DXF files, you should import the DXF file into a _____ file so that valuable information is not lost.

14. In a _____ file, information is stored in the form of a dot pattern on the screen. This bit pattern is also known as _____ .

15. If there is a picture on the screen that you want to save as a raster file, use the _____ command.

16. With the SAVEIMG command you can create _____, _____, _____, or _____ type of raster files from the current drawing.

17. The section of screen to be saved can be specified by picking _____ on the image tile.

18. If you are rendering to a viewport, and you select the _____ option; whatever is in the current viewport is saved to the raster file of the selected format.

19. If you are rendering to a viewport, and you select the _____ option, the entire screen, including the pull-down menu area, screen menu area, and command line area, is saved to the raster file.

20. It is possible to import .TIFF raster files with the ____ command.

21. The _____ variable is used to manipulate the aspect ratio (width to height) of the imported raster file.

22. If you increase the value of the RIASPECT variable, the width of the imported raster file _____.

23. The _____ variable is used to manipulate the background color of the image.

24. The _____ variable is used to control the display of edges of an image.

25. The _____ variable is used to specify the number (range) of colors to be used in displaying the image.

26. You can convert imported images into grayscale images by setting the _____ variable to 1.

27. The _____ variable is used to set a threshold for filtering objects that have a brightness value less than the RITHRESH setting.

EXERCISES

Exercise 3

Draw Figure 17-34 without dimensions and determine the indicated parameters using the required commands. Select the DBLIST command. Select TIME and note the time in the drawing editor. Save the drawing.

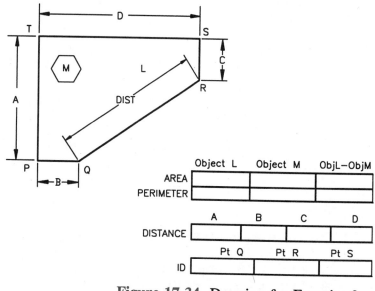

Figure 17-34 Drawing for Exercise 3

Exercise 4

Draw two rectangles and use the **PSFILL** command to assign stars and brick pattern to these rectangles. Convert the rectangles to PostScript file using **PSOUT** command and then import the PostScript file using **PSIN** command.

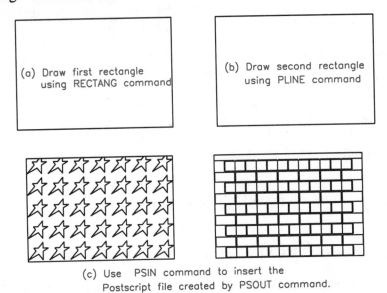

(a) Draw first rectangle using RECTANG command

(b) Draw second rectangle using PLINE command

(c) Use PSIN command to insert the Postscript file created by PSOUT command.

Figure 17-35 PostScript Fill option in Draw pull-down menu

Exercise 5

Use the **STYLE** command to create a new text style files (pscript and tfont). Assign ROMB.PFB PostScript font to pscript file and monosb.ttf to tfont file. Draw the following text on the screen to verify the assigned text fonts.

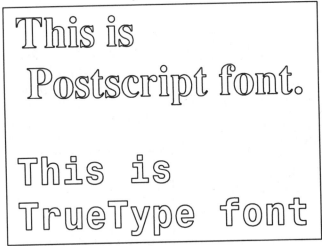

Figure 17-36 Using PostScript font for text

Chapter 18

Technical Drawing
with AutoCAD

Learning objectives

After completing this chapter, you will be able to:
♦ Understand the concepts of multi-view drawings.
♦ Understand X, Y, Z axes; XY, YZ, XZ planes; and parallel planes.
♦ Draw orthographic projections and position the views.
♦ Dimension a drawing.
♦ Understand the basic dimensioning rules.
♦ Draw sectional views using different types of sections.
♦ Hatch sectioned surfaces.
♦ Understand how to use auxiliary views and how to draw them.
♦ Draw assembly and detail drawings.

MULTI-VIEW DRAWINGS

When designers design products, they visualize the shape of the product in their minds. To represent that shape on paper or to communicate the idea to other people, they must draw a picture of the product or its orthographic views. Pictorial drawings, like isometric drawings, convey the shape of the object, but it is difficult to show all of its features and dimensions in an isometric drawing. Therefore, in industry, multi-view drawings are the accepted standard for representing products. Multi-view drawings are also known as **orthographic projection drawings**. To draw different views of an object, it is very important to visualize the shape of the product. The same is true when you are looking at different views of an object to determine its shape. To facilitate visualizing the shapes, you must picture the object in 3D space with reference to the X, Y, and Z axes. These reference axes can then be used to project the image in different planes. This process of visualizing objects with reference to different axes is, to some extent, natural in human beings. You might have noticed that sometimes when looking at objects that are at an angle, people tilt their heads. This is a natural reaction, an effort to position the object with respect to an imaginary reference frame (X, Y, Z axes).

UNDERSTANDING X, Y, Z AXES

To understand the X, Y, Z axes, imagine a flat sheet of paper on the table. The horizontal edge represents the positive X axis and the other edge, the edge along the width of the sheet, represents the positive Y axis. The point where these two axes intersect is the origin. Now, if you draw a line perpendicular to the sheet passing through the origin, the line defines the positive Z axis (Figure 18-1). If you produce the X, Y, and Z axes in the opposite direction beyond the origin, you will get the negative X, Y, and Z axes (Figure 18-2).

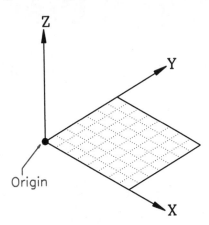

Figure 18-1   X, Y, Z axis

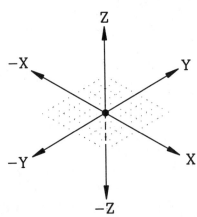

Figure 18-2   Positive and negative axis

The space between the X and Y axes is called the X-Y plane. Similarly, the space between the Y and Z axes is called the Y-Z plane and the space between the X and Z axes is called the X-Z plane (Figure 18-3). A plane that is parallel to these planes is called a parallel plane (Figure 18-4).

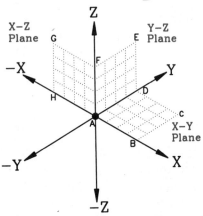

Figure 18-3   X-Y, Y-Z, and X-Z planes

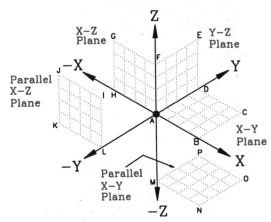

Figure 18-4   Parallel planes

ORTHOGRAPHIC PROJECTIONS

The first step in drawing the orthographic projection is to position the object along the imaginary X, Y, and Z axes. For example, if you want to draw the orthographic projections of the step block as shown in Figure 18-5, position the block so that the far left corner coincides with the origin, then align the block with the X, Y, and Z axes.

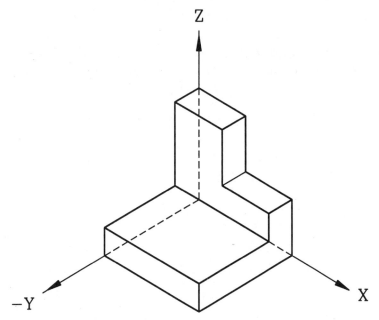

Figure 18-5   Aligning object with X, Y, and Z axis

Now you can look at the object from different directions. If you look at the object along the negative Y axis toward the origin, that is called the front view. Similarly, if you look at the object from the positive X direction, that is called the right-hand side view. To get the top view, you must look at the object from the positive Z axis.

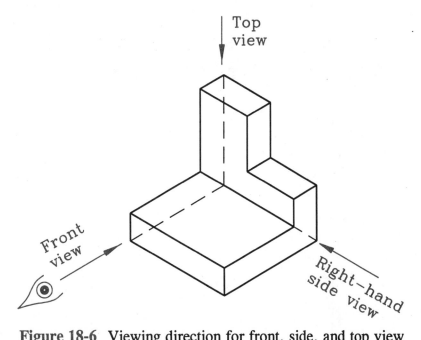

Figure 18-6   Viewing direction for front, side, and top view

To draw the front, side, and top views, project the points on the parallel planes. For example, if you want to draw the front view of the step block, imagine a plane parallel to the X-Z plane located at a certain distance in front of the object. Now, project the points from the object on the parallel plane (Figure 18-7) and join the points to complete the front view.

Note

You can construct a 3D model of this object by using the layout given at the end of this chapter. Cut the layout along the solid lines, then fold along the hidden lines.

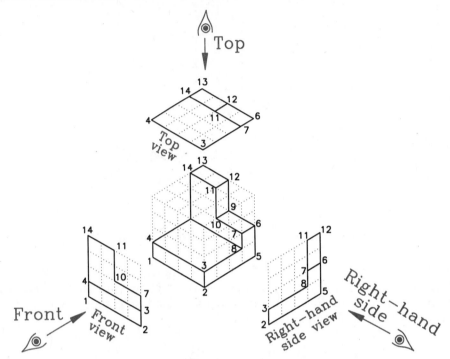

Figure 18-7 Projecting points on parallel planes

Repeat the same process for the side and top views. To represent these views on paper, position the views as shown Figure 18-8.

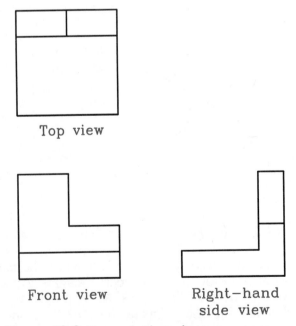

Figure 18-8 Representing views on paper

Another way of visualizing different views is to imagine the object enclosed in a glass box (Figure 18-9).

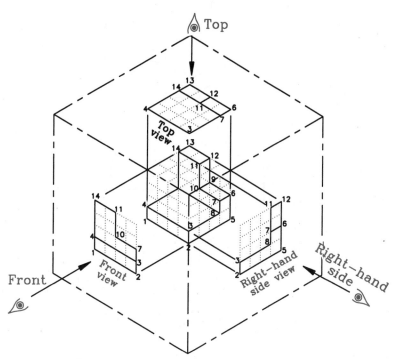

Figure 18-9 Object inside a glass box

Now, look at the object along the negative Y axis and draw the front view on the front glass panel. Repeat the process by looking along the positive X and Z axes and draw the views on the right-hand side and the top panel of the box (Figure 18-10).

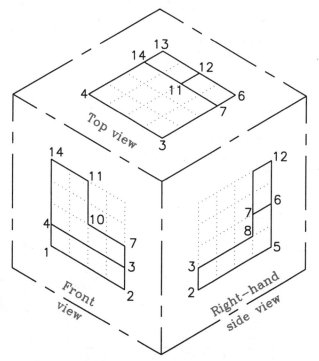

Figure 18-10 Front, top, and side views

To represent the front, side, and top views on paper, open the side and the top panel of the glass box (Figure 18-11). The front panel is assumed to be stationary.

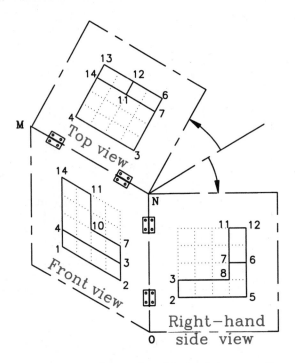

Figure 18-11 Open the side and top panel

After opening the panels through 90 degrees, the orthographic views will appear as shown in Figure 18-12.

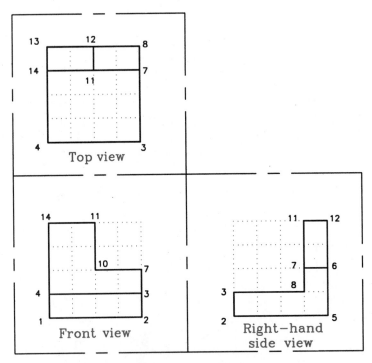

Figure 18-12 Views after opening the box

POSITIONING ORTHOGRAPHIC VIEWS

The orthographic views **must** be positioned as shown in Figure 18-13.

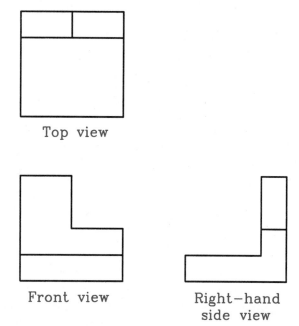

Figure 18-13 Positioning orthographic views

The right-hand side view must be positioned directly on the right side of the front view. Similarly, the top view must be directly above the front view. If the object requires additional views, they must be positioned as shown in Figure 18-14.

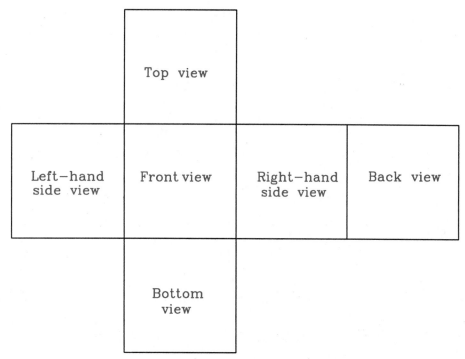

Figure 18-14 Standard placement of orthographic views

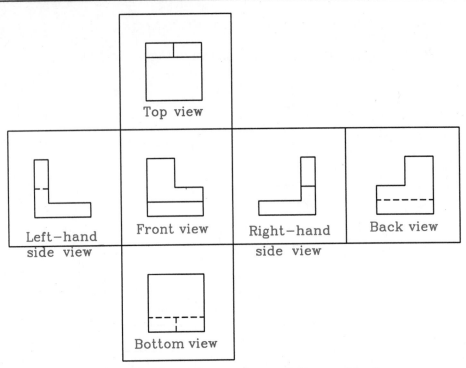

Figure 18-15 Different views of the step block

Example 1

In this example you will draw the required orthographic views of the following object (Figure 18-16).

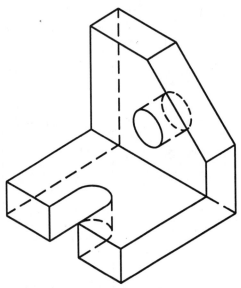

Figure 18-16 Step block with hole and slot

Drawing the orthographic views of an object involves the following steps:

Step 1
Look at the object and determine the number of views required to show all features of the object. For example, the object shown in Figure 18-16 will require three views only (front, side, and top).

Step 2

Based on the shape of the object, select the side you want to show as the front view. Generally the front view is one that shows the maximum number of features or gives a better idea about the shape of the object. Sometimes the front view is determined by how the part is assembled in an assembly.

Step 3

Picture the object in your mind and align it along the imaginary X, Y, Z axes.

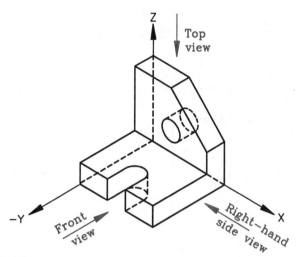

Figure 18-17 Align the object with the imaginary X, Y, Z axes

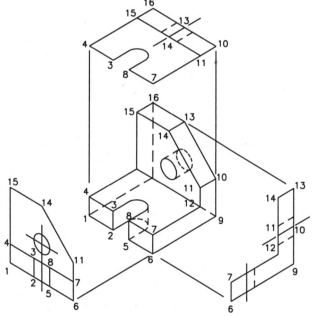

Figure 18-18 Project the image on the parallel planes

Step 4

Look at the object along the negative Y axis and project the image on the imaginary XZ parallel plane, Figure 18-18.

Step 5

Draw the front view of the object according to given dimensions. If there are any hidden features, they must be drawn with hidden lines. The holes and slots must be shown with the center lines.

Step 6
To draw the right-hand side view, look at the object along the positive X axis and project the image on the imaginary YZ parallel plane.

Step 7
Draw the right-hand side view of the object according to given dimensions. If there are any hidden features, they must be drawn with hidden lines. The holes and slots, when shown in side view, must have one center line.

Step 8
Similarly, draw the top view and complete the drawing. Figure 18-19 shows different views of the given object.

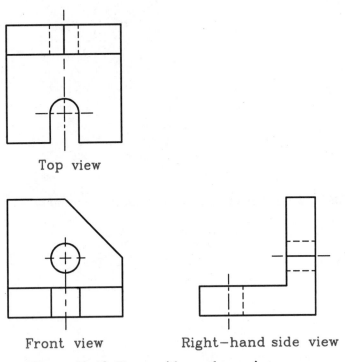

Top view

Front view   Right-hand side view

Figure 18-19 Front, side, and top views

Exercises 1 through 4

Draw the required orthographic views of the following objects. The distance between the dotted lines is 0.5 units.

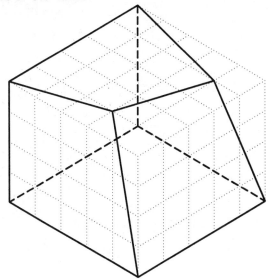

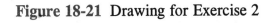

Figure 18-20 Drawing for Exercise 1

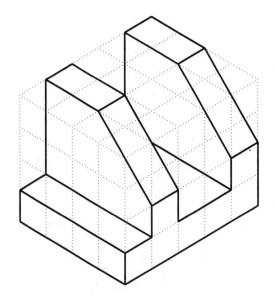

Figure 18-21 Drawing for Exercise 2

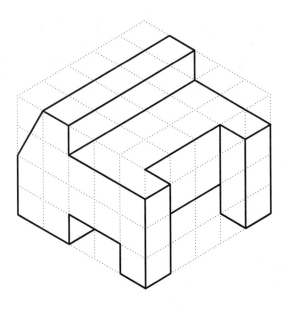

Figure 18-22 Drawing for Exercise 3

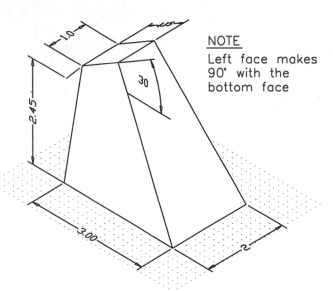

NOTE
Left face makes
90° with the
bottom face

Figure 18-23 Drawing for Exercise 4 (the object is shown as a surfaced wire frame model)

DIMENSIONING

Dimensioning is one of the most important things in a drawing. When you dimension, you not only give the size of a part, you give a series of instructions to a machinist, engineer, or architect. The way the part is positioned in a machine, the sequence of machining operation, and the location of different features of the part depend on how you dimension it. For example, the number of decimal places in a dimension (2.000) determines the type of machine that will be used to do that machining operation. The machining cost of such an operation is significantly higher than a dimension that has only one digit after the decimal (2.0). If you are using a CNC machine, locating a feature may not be a problem, but the number of pieces you can machine without changing the tool depends on the tolerance assigned to a dimension. A closer tolerance (+.0001 - .0005) will definitely increase the tooling cost and ultimately the cost of the product. Similarly, if a part is to be forged or cast, the radius of the edges and the tolerance you provide to these dimensions determines the cost of the product, the number of defective parts, and the number of parts you get from the die.

When dimensioning, you must consider the manufacturing process involved in making a part and the relationships that exists among different parts in an assembly. If you are not familiar with any operation, get help. You must not assume things when dimensioning or making a piece part drawing. The success of a product, to a large extent, depends on the way you dimension a part. Therefore, never underestimate the importance of dimensioning in a drawing.

Dimensioning Components

A dimension consists of the following components:

Extension line
Arrows or tick marks
Dimension line
Leader lines
Dimension text

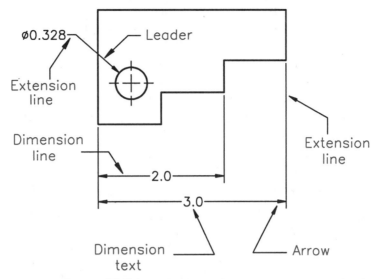

Figure 18-24 Dimensioning components

The **extension lines** are drawn to extend the points that are dimensioned. The length of the extension lines is determined by the number of dimensions and the placement of the dimension lines. These lines are generally drawn perpendicular to the surface. The **dimension lines** are drawn between the extension lines at a specified distance from the object lines. The **dimension text** is a numerical value that represents the distance between the points. The dimension text can also consist of a variable (A,B,X,Y,Z12.....), in which case the value assigned to the variable is defined in a separate table. The dimension text can be centered around the dimension line or at the top of the dimension line. **Arrows** or **tick marks** are drawn at the end of the dimension line that indicates the start and end of the dimension. **Leader lines** are used when dimensioning a circle, arc, or any non-linear element of a drawing. They are also used to attach a note to a feature or give the part numbers in an assembly drawing.

Basic Dimensioning Rules

1. You should make the dimensions in a separate layer/layers. This makes it easy to edit or control the display of dimensions (freeze, thaw, lock, unlock). Also, the dimension layer/layers should be assigned a unique color so that at the time of plotting you can assign the desired pen to plot the dimensions. This helps to control the line width and contrast of dimensions at the time of plotting.

2. The distance of the first dimension line should at least 0.375 unit (10 units for metric drawing) from the object line. In CAD drawing, this distance may be 0.75 to 1.0 unit (19 to 25 units for metric drawings). Once you decide on the spacing, it should be maintained throughout the drawing.

3. The distance between the first dimension line and the second dimension line must at least 0.25 unit. In CAD drawings, this distance may be 0.25 to 0.5 unit (6 to 12 units for metric drawings). If there are more dimension lines (parallel dimensions), the distances between them must be same (0.25 to 0.5 unit). Once you decide on the spacing (0.25 to 0.5), the same spacing should be maintained throughout the drawing. If you are using baseline dimensioning, you can use AutoCAD's **DIMDLI** variable to set the spacing. You must give the dimensions so that they are not crowded, especially when there is not enough space.

4. For parallel dimension lines, the dimension text can be staggered if there is not enough room between the dimension lines to place the dimension text. You can use AutoCAD's Object Grips feature to stagger the dimension text.

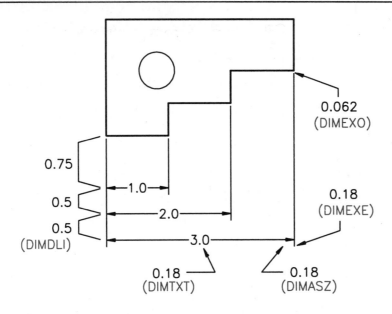

Figure 18-25 Arrow size, text height, and spacing between dimension lines

Note

You can change grid, snap origin, and snap increment to make it easier to place the dimensions. You can also add the following lines to AutoCAD's menu file.

SNAP;R;\0;SNAP;0.25;GRID;0.25
SNAP;R;0,0;0;SNAP;0.25;GRID;0.5

The first line sets the snap to 0.25 unit and allows the user to define the new origin of snap and grid display.

The second line sets the grid to 0.5 and snap to 0.25 unit. It also sets the origin for grid and snap to 0,0.

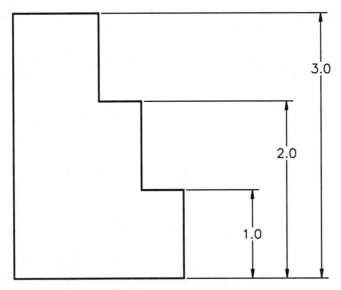

Figure 18-26 Staggered dimensions

5. All dimensions should be given outside the view. However, the dimensions can be shown inside the view if they can be easily understood there and cause no confusion with other dimensions.

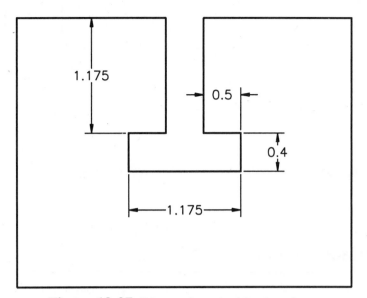

Figure 18-27 Dimensions inside the view

6. The dimension lines should not cross the extension lines. You can accomplish this by giving the smallest dimension first, then the next largest dimension.

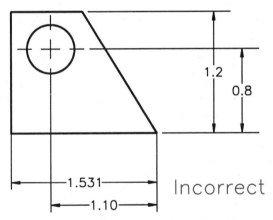

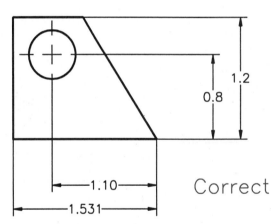

Figure 18-28 Dimension lines should not cross

Figure 18-29 Smallest dimension must be given first

7. If you decide to have the dimension text aligned with the dimension line, then all dimension text in the drawing must be aligned. Similarly, if you decide to have the dimension text horizontal, or above the dimension line, then all dimension text must be horizontal or above the dimension line to maintain uniformity in the drawing.

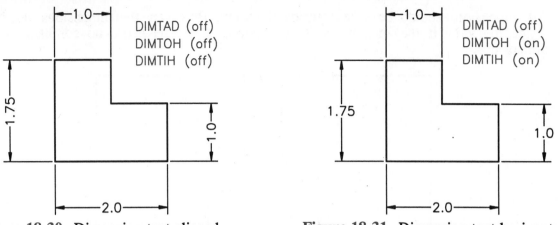

Figure 18-30   Dimension text aligned

Figure 18-31   Dimension text horizontal

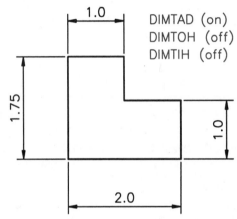

Figure 18-32   Dimension text above dimension line

8. If you have a series of continuous dimensions, they should be placed in a continuous line. Sometimes you may not be able to give the dimensions in a continuous line even after adjusting the dimension variables. In that case, give dimensions that are parallel.

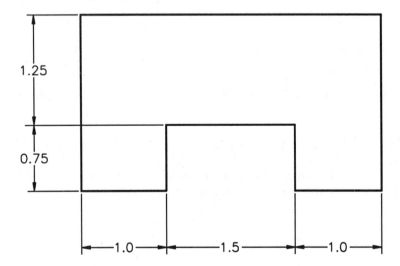

Figure 18-33   Dimension should be continuous

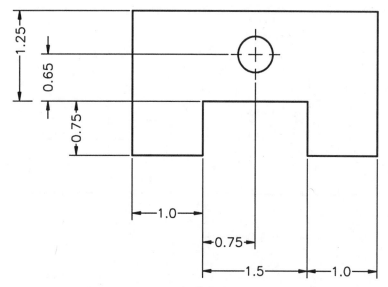

Figure 18-34 Parallel dimensions

9. You should not dimension with hidden lines. The dimension must be given where the feature is visible. However, in some complicated drawings you might be justified to dimension a detail with a hidden line.

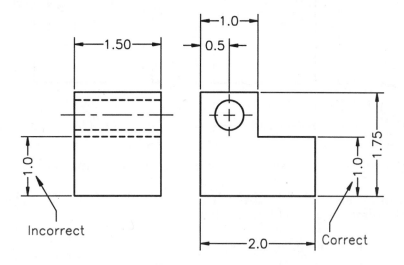

Figure 18-35 Do not dimension with hidden lines

10. The dimensions must be given where the feature that you are dimensioning is obvious and shows the contour of the feature.

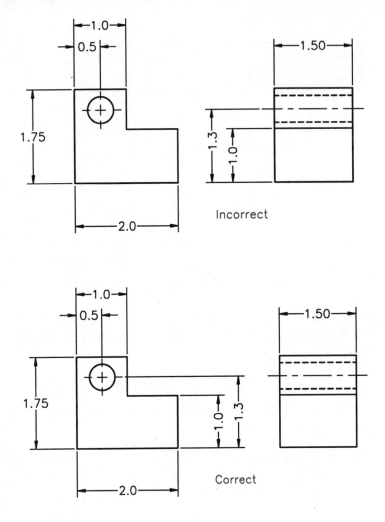

Figure 18-36 Dimensions should be given where they are obvious

11. The dimensions must not be repeated; it makes it difficult to update a dimension and sometimes the dimensions might get confusing.

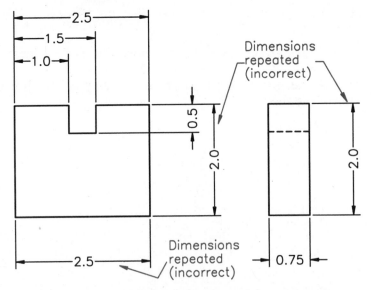

Figure 18-37 Dimension must not be repeated

12. The dimensions must be given depending on how the part is machined and the relationship that exists between different features of the part.

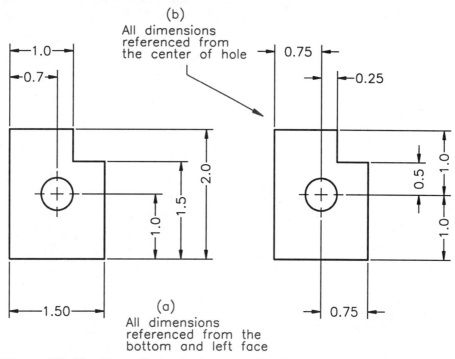

Figure 18-38 When dimensioning consider the machining processes involved

13. When a dimension is not required but you want to give it for reference, it must be a reference dimension. The reference dimension must be enclosed in parentheses.

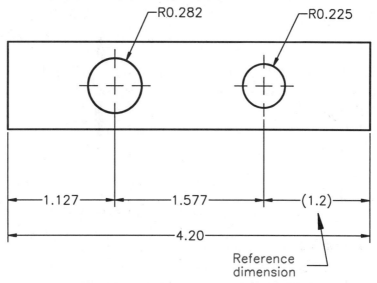

Figure 18-39 Reference dimensions

14. If you give continuous (incremental) dimensioning for dimensioning various features of a part, the overall dimension must be omitted or given as a reference dimension. Similarly, if you give the overall dimension, one of the continuous (incremental) dimensions must be omitted or given as a reference dimension. Otherwise there will be a conflict in tolerances. For example, the total positive tolerance on the three incremental dimensions as shown in Figure 18-40 is 0.06. Therefore, the maximum size based on the incremental dimensions is 3.06 [(1+0.02) +

(1+0.02) + (1+0.02)]. Also, the positive tolerance on the overall dimension 3.0 is 0.02. Based on this dimension the overall size of the part must not exceed 3.02. This causes a conflict in tolerances. When using incremental dimensions the total tolerance is 0.06, and when using the overall dimension the total tolerance is only 0.02.

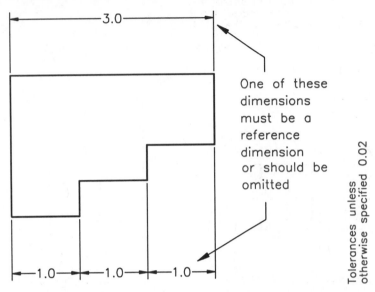

Figure 18-40 Referencing or omitting a dimension

15. If the dimension of a feature appears in a section view, you must not hatch the dimension text. You can accomplish this by first dimensioning the feature with **DIMASO** off and then hatching the area after excluding the dimension text from the hatch boundary. (You can also use the EXPLODE command to explode the dimension and then exclude the dimension text from hatching.)

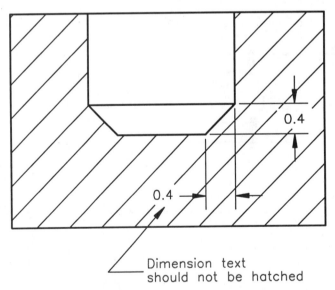

Figure 18-41 Dimension text should not be hatched

16. When dimensioning a circle, the diameter should be preceded by the diameter symbol. AutoCAD automatically puts the diameter symbol in front of the diameter value. However, if you override the default diameter value, you can use **%%c** followed by the value of the diameter (%%c1.25) to put the diameter symbol in front of the diameter dimension.

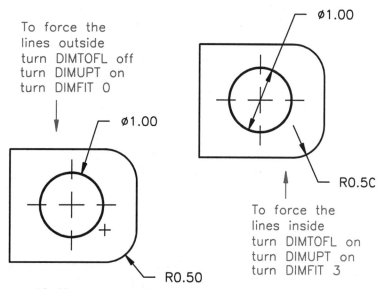

Figure 18-42 Diameter should be preceded by diameter symbol

17. The circle must be dimensioned as diameter, never as radius. The dimension of an arc must be preceded by the abbreviation R (R1.25) and the center of the arc should be indicated by drawing a small cross. You can use AutoCAD's **DIMCEN** variable to control the size of the cross. If the value of this variable is 0, AutoCAD does not draw the cross in the center when you dimension an arc or a circle. You can also use the **DIMCENTER** command or the **CENTER** option of the **DIM** command to draw a cross at the center of the arc or circle.

18. When dimensioning an arc or a circle, the dimension line (leader) must be radial. Also, you should place the dimension text horizontally.

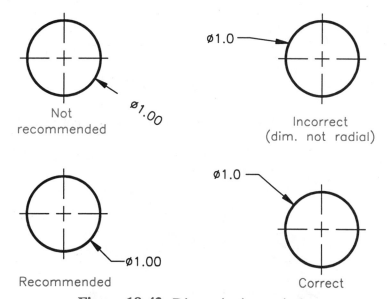

Figure 18-43 Dimensioning a circle

19. A chamfer can be dimensioned by specifying the chamfer angle and the distance of the chamfer, from the edge. A chamfer can also be dimensioned by specifying the distances as shown in Figure 18-44.

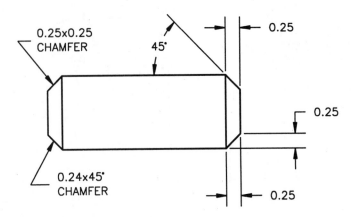

Figure 18-44 Different ways of specifying chamfer

20. A dimension that is not to scale should be indicated by drawing a straight line under the dimension text.

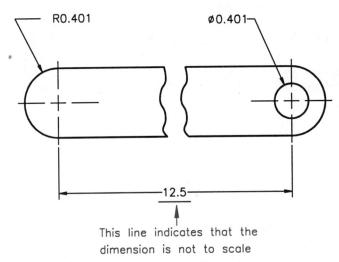

Figure 18-45 Specifying dimensions that are not to scale

21. A bolt circle should be dimensioned by specifying the diameter of the bolt circle, diameter of the holes, and the number of holes in the bolt circle.

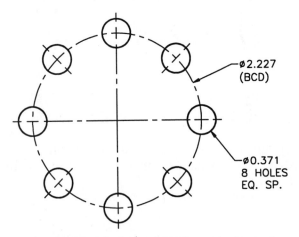

Figure 18-46 Dimensioning a bolt circle

Exercises 5 through 10

Draw the required orthographic views of the following objects and then give the dimensions. The distance between the grid lines is 0.5 unit.

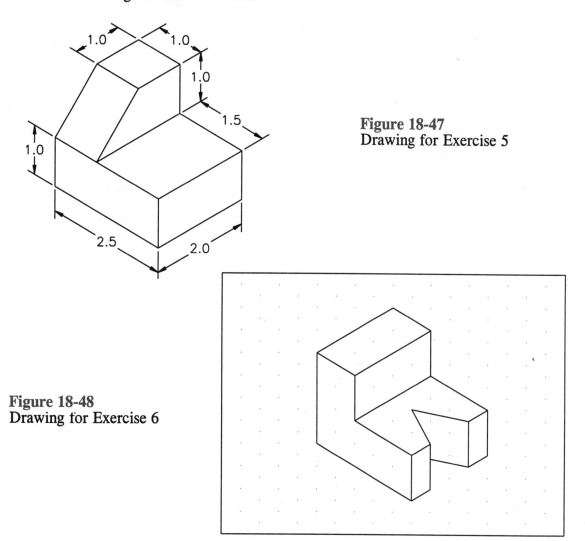

Figure 18-47
Drawing for Exercise 5

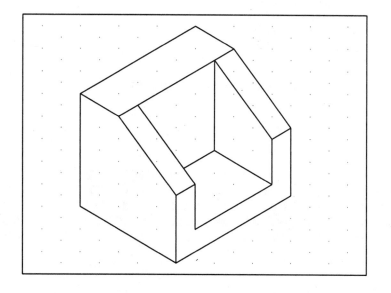

Figure 18-48
Drawing for Exercise 6

Figure 18-49
Drawing for Exercise 7

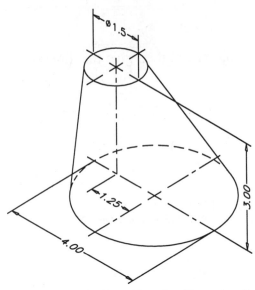

Figure 18-50 Drawing for Exercise 8

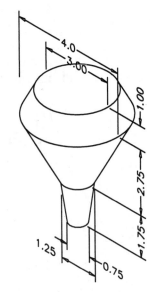

Figure 18-51 Drawing for Exercise 9

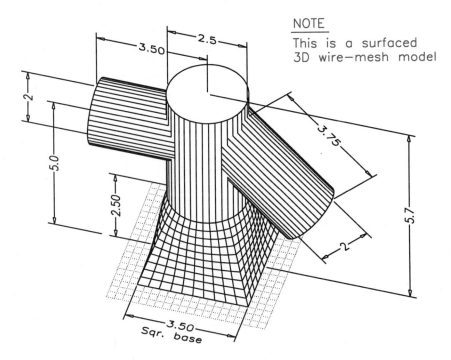

NOTE
This is a surfaced
3D wire—mesh model

Figure 18-52 Drawing for Exercise 10 (Assume the missing dimensions)

SECTIONAL VIEWS

In the principal orthographic views, the hidden features are generally shown by hidden lines. In some objects the hidden lines may not be sufficient to represent the actual shape of the hidden feature. In such situations, sectional views can be used to show the features of the object that are not visible from outside. The location of the section and the direction of sight depend on the shape of the object and the features that need to be shown. There are several ways to cut a section in the object:

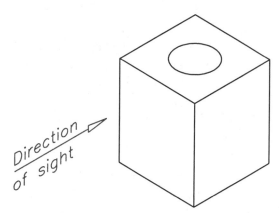

Figure 18-53 Rectangular object with hole

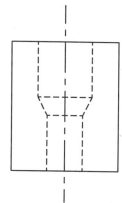

Figure 18-54 Front view without section

Full Section

Figure 18-53 shows an object that has a drilled hole, a counterbore, and a taper. In the orthographic views these features will be shown by hidden lines. To better represent the hidden features, the object must be cut so that the hidden features are visible. In the full section the object is cut along the entire length of the object. To get a better idea of a full section, imagine that the object is cut into two halves along the center line as shown in Figure 18-55. Now remove the left half of the object and look at the right half in the direction that is perpendicular to the sectioned surface.

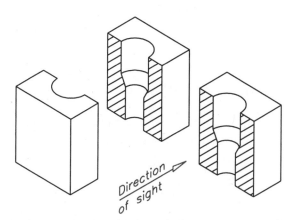

Figure 18-55 One half of the object removed

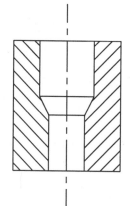

Figure 18-56 Front view in full section

The view you get after cutting the section is called a full section view. In this section view the features that would be hidden in a normal orthographic view are visible. Also, the part of the object where the material is actually cut is indicated by drawing section lines. If the material is not cut, the section lines are not drawn. For example, if there is a hole, no material is cut when the part is sectioned. Therefore the section lines must not be drawn through that area of the section view.

Half Section

If the object is symmetrical, it is not necessary to draw a full section view. For example, in Figure 18-58 the object is symmetrical with respect to the center line of the hole. Therefore a full section is not required. Also, in some objects it may help to understand and visualize the shape of the hidden details better by drawing the view in half section. In half section, one quarter of the object is cut, as shown in Figure 18-57. To draw the view in half section, imagine one quarter of the object removed, then look in the direction that is perpendicular to the sectioned surface.

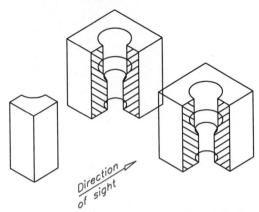

Figure 18-57 One quarter of the object removed

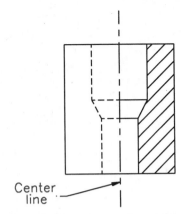

Figure 18-58 Front view in half section

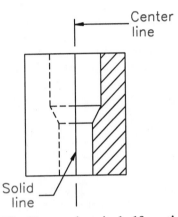

Figure 18-59 Front view in half section

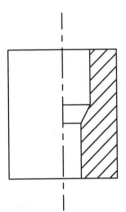

Figure 18-60 Front view in half section

You can also show the front view with a solid line in the middle as shown in Figure 18-59. Sometimes the hidden lines representing the remaining part of the hidden feature are not drawn, as shown in Figure 18-60.

Broken Section

In the broken section only a small portion of the object is cut to expose the features that need to be drawn in section. The broken section is designated by drawing a thick zigzag line in the section view.

Revolved Section

The revolved section is used to show the true shape of the object at the point where the section is cut. The revolved section is used when it is not possible to clearly show the features in any principal view. For example, for the object in Figure 18-62, it is not possible to show the

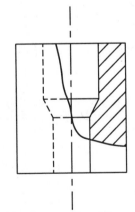

Figure 18-61 Front view in with broken section

actual shape of the middle section in the front, side, or top views. Therefore, a revolved section is required to show the shape of the middle section.

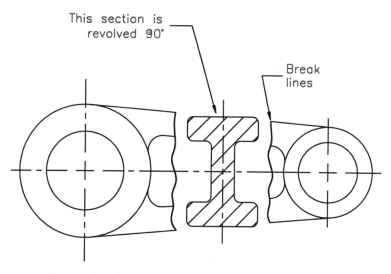

Figure 18-62 Front view with revolved section

The revolved section involves cutting an imaginary section through the object and then looking at the sectioned surface in a direction that is perpendicular to it. To represent the shape, the view is revolved 90 degrees and drawn in the plane of the paper, as shown Figure 18-62. Depending on the shape of the object and for clarity it is recommended to provide a break in the object so that the object lines may not interfere with the revolved section.

Removed Section

The removed section is similar to the revolved section, except that it is shown outside the object. The removed section is recommended when there is not enough space in the view to show the revolved section or if the scale of the section is different from the parent object.

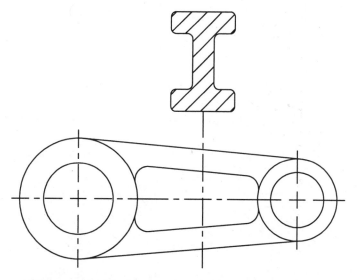

Figure 18-63 Front view with removed section

The removed section can be shown by drawing a line through the object at the point where the revolved section is desired and then drawing the shape of the section, as shown in Figure 18-63.

The other way of showing a removed section is by drawing a cutting plane line through the object where you want to cut the section. The arrows should point in the direction in which you are looking at the sectioned surface. The section can then be drawn at a convenient place in the drawing. The removed section must be labeled as shown in Figure 18-64. If the scale has been changed, it must be mentioned with the view description.

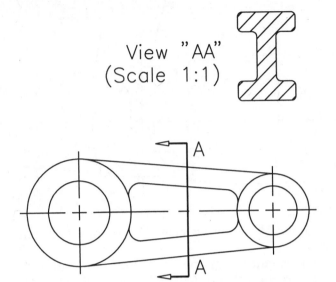

Figure 18-64 Front view with removed section

Offset Section

The offset section is used when the features of the object that you want to section are not in one plane. The offset section is designated by drawing a cutting plane line that is offset through the center of the features that need to be shown in section. The arrows indicate the direction in which the section is viewed.

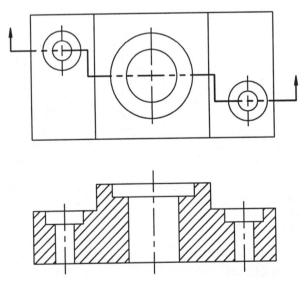

Figure 18-65 Front view with offset section

Aligned Section

In some objects cutting a straight section might cause confusion in visualizing the shape of the section. Therefore, the aligned section is used to represent the shape along the cutting plane (Figure 18-66). Such sections are widely used in circular objects that have spokes, ribs, or holes.

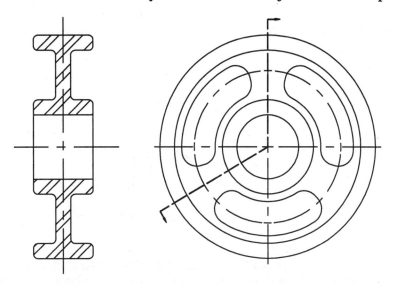

Figure 18-66 Side view in section (aligned section)

Cutting Plane Lines

Cutting plane lines are thicker than object lines. You can use the **PLINE** command to draw the polylines of desired width, generally 0.005 to 0.01. However, for drawings that need to be plotted, you should assign a unique color to the cutting plane lines and then assign that color to the slot of the plotter that carries a pen of the required tip width. (For details read Chapter 15 "Plotting Drawings, Draw Commands.")

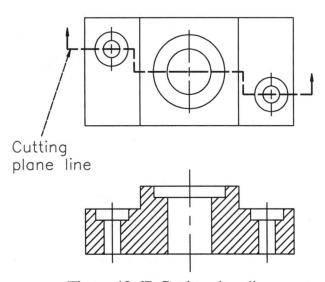

Figure 18-67 Cutting plane line

In industry, generally three types of lines are used to show the cutting plane for sectioning. The first line consists of a series of dashes 0.25 unit long. The second type consists of a series of long dashes separated by two short dashes (Figure 18-68). The length of the long dash can vary from 0.75 to 1.5 units and the short dashes are about 0.12 unit long. The space between the dashes should be about 0.03 unit.

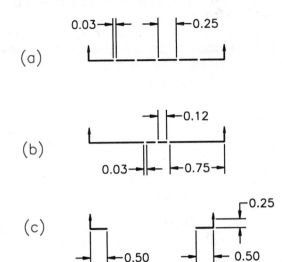

Figure 18-68   Cutting plane lines

Sometimes the cutting plane lines may clutter the drawing or cause confusion with other lines in the drawing. To avoid this problem you can show the cutting plane by drawing a short line at the end of the section (Figures 18-68 and 18-69). The line should be about 0.5 unit long.

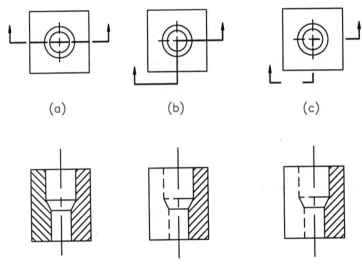

Figure 18-69   Application of cutting plane lines

Note

In AutoCAD you can define a new linetype that you can use to draw the cutting plane lines. Add the following lines to the ACAD.LIN file, then load the linetypes before assigning it to an object or a layer:

```
*CPLANE1,___ __ __ __
A,0.25,-0.03
*CPLANE2,_____
A,1.0,-0.03,0.12,-0.03,0.12,-0.03
```

Spacing for Hatch Lines

The spacing between the hatch (section) lines is determined by the space that is being hatched. If the hatch area is small, the spacing between the hatch lines should be smaller compared with large hatch area.

In AutoCAD you can control the spacing between the hatch lines by specifying the **scale factor** at the time of hatching. If the scale factor is one, the spacing between the hatch lines is the same as defined in the hatch pattern file for that particular hatch. For example, in the following hatch pattern definition the distance between the lines is 0.125:

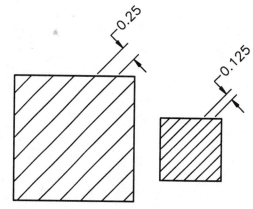

Figure 18-70 Hatch line spacing

> ***ANSI31, ANSI Iron, Brick, Stone masonry
> 45, 0, 0, 0, .125**

When the hatch scale factor is 1, the line spacing will be 0.125. If the scale factor is 2, the spacing between the lines will be 0.25 (0.125 x 2).

Direction of Hatch Lines

The angle for the hatch lines should be 45 degrees. However, if there are two or more hatch areas next to each other representing different parts, the hatch angle must be changed so that the hatched areas look different.

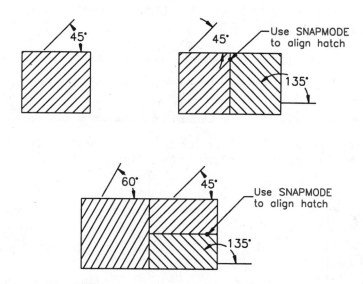

Figure 18-71 Hatch angle for adjacent parts

Also, if the hatch lines fall parallel to any edge of the hatch area, the hatch angle should be changed so that the lines are not parallel to any object line.

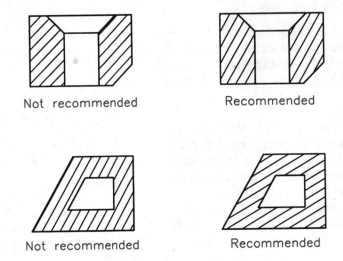

Not recommended   Recommended

Not recommended   Recommended

Figure 18-72   Hatch angle

Points to Remember

1. Some parts like bolts, nuts, shafts, ball bearings, fasteners, ribs, spokes, keys, and other similar items that do not show any important feature, if sectioned, should not be shown in section.

2. Hidden details should not be shown in the section view unless the hidden lines represent an important detail or help the viewer to understand the shape of the object.

3. The section lines (hatch lines) must be thinner than the object lines. You can accomplish this by assigning a unique color to hatch lines and then assigning the color to that slot on the plotter that carries a pen with thin tip.

4. The section lines must be drawn on a separate layer for display and editing purposes.

Exercises 11 and 12

In the following drawings the views have been drawn without a section. Draw these views in section as indicated by the cutting plane lines in each object.

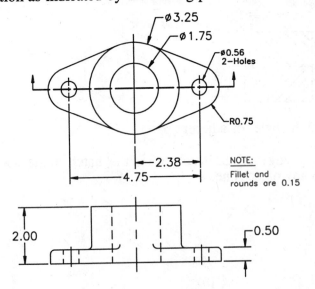

Figure 18-73   Drawing for Exercise 11: draw the front view in section

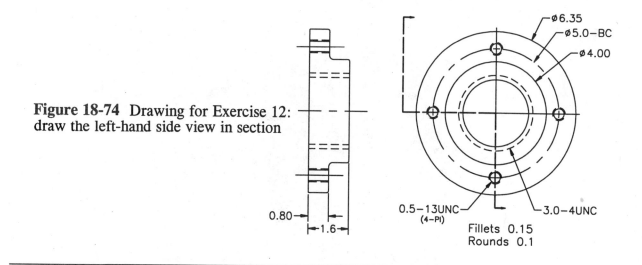

Figure 18-74 Drawing for Exercise 12: draw the left-hand side view in section

Exercises 13 and 14

Draw the required orthographic views for the following objects. Show the front view in section when the object is cut so that the cutting plane passes through the holes. Also draw the cutting plane lines in the top view.

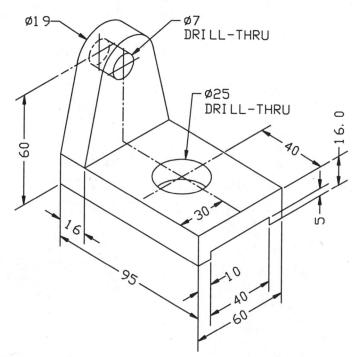

Figure 18-75 Drawing for Exercise 13: draw the front view in full section

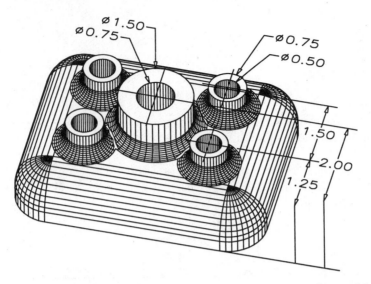

Figure 18-76 Drawing for Exercise 14: draw the front view with offset section

Exercise 15

Draw the required orthographic views for the objects in Figures 18-77, 78 with the front view in section. Also draw the cutting plane lines in the top view to show the cutting plane. The material thickness is 0.25 units. (The object has been drawn as a surfaced 3D wire mesh model.)

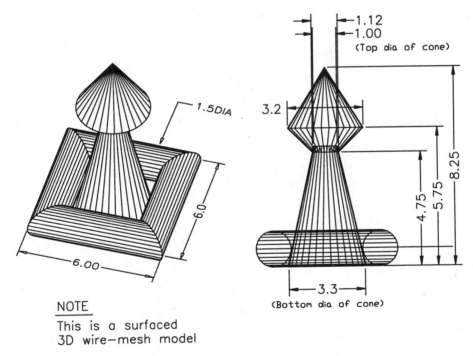

NOTE
This is a surfaced
3D wire—mesh model

Figure 18-77 Draw the front view in half section

Figure 18-78 Draw the front view in half section

AUXILIARY VIEWS

As discussed earlier, most objects generally require three principal views (front view, side view, and top view) to show all features of the object. Round objects may require just two views. Some objects have inclined surfaces. It may not be possible to show the actual shape of the inclined surface in one of the principal views. To get the true view of the inclined surface, you must look at the surface in a direction that is perpendicular to the inclined surface. Now you can project the points on the imaginary auxiliary plane that is parallel to the inclined surface. The view you get after projecting the points is called the **auxiliary view,** as shown in Figures 18-79 and 18-80.

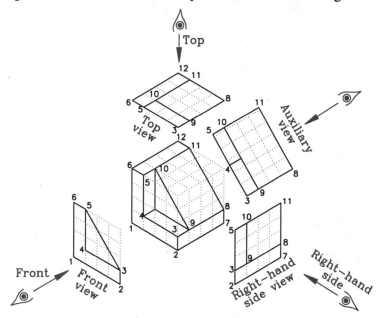

Figure 18-79 Project points on the auxiliary plane

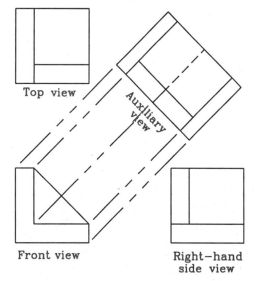

Figure 18-80 Auxiliary, front, side, and top view

In this figure (Figure 18-80) the auxiliary view shows all features of the object as seen from the auxiliary view direction. For example, the bottom left edge is shown as a hidden line. Similarly, the lower right and upper left edges are shown as continuous lines. Although these lines are technically correct, the purpose of the auxiliary view is to show the features of the inclined surface. Therefore, in the auxiliary plane you should only draw those features that are on the inclined face, as shown in Figure 18-81. Other details that will help to understand the shape of the object may also be included in the auxiliary view. The remaining lines should be ignored because they tend to cause confusion in visualizing the shape of the object.

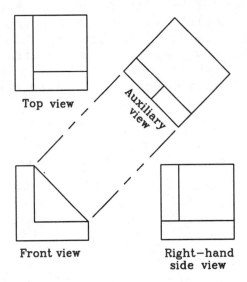

Figure 18-81 Auxiliary, front, side, and top views

How to Draw Auxiliary Views

The following example illustrates how to use AutoCAD to generate an auxiliary view.

Example 2

Draw the required views of the hollow triangular block with a hole in the inclined face as shown in Figure 18-82. (The block has been drawn as a solid model.)

The following steps are involved in drawing different views of this object.

Step 1
Draw the required orthographic views like the front view, side view, and the top view as shown in Figure 18-83(a). The circles on the inclined surface appear like ellipses in the front and top views. These ellipses may not be shown in the orthographic views because they tend to clutter the views (Figure 18-83(b)).

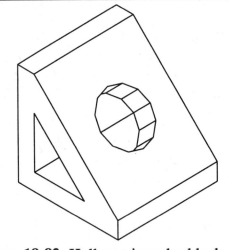

Figure 18-82 Hollow triangular block

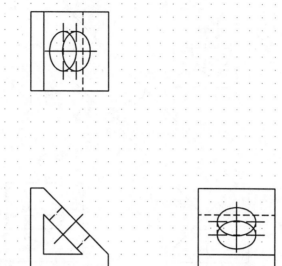

Figure 18-83(a) Front, side, and top view

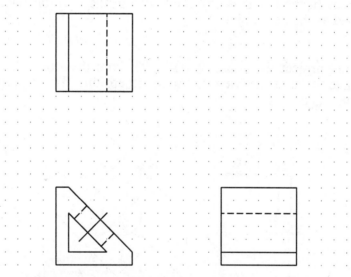

Figure 18-83(b) The ellipses may not be shown in the orthographic views

Step 2
Determine the angle of the inclined surface. In this example, the angle is 45 degrees. Use the **SNAP** command to rotate the snap by 45 degrees.

Command: **SNAP**
Snap spacing or ON/OFF/Aspect/Rotate/Style<0.5>: **R**
Base point<0,0>: **Select P1**
Rotation angle<0>: **45**

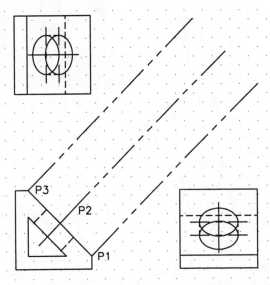

Figure 18-84 Grid lines at 45 degrees

Using the rotate option, the snap will be rotated by 45 degrees and the grid lines also will be displayed at 45 degrees (if the GRID is on). Also, one of the grid lines will pass through point P1, because it was defined as the base point.

Step 3
Turn **ORTHO** on and project the points P1, P2, P3 from the front view in the auxiliary plane. Now you can complete the auxiliary view and give dimensions. The projection lines may be erased after the auxiliary view is drawn.

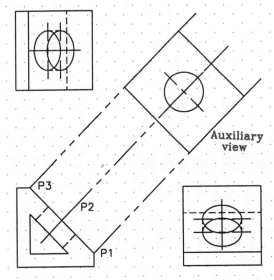

Figure 18-85 Auxiliary view, front, side, and top views

Exercise 16

Draw the required orthographic and auxiliary views for the following object. The object is drawn as a surfaced 3D wire mesh model.

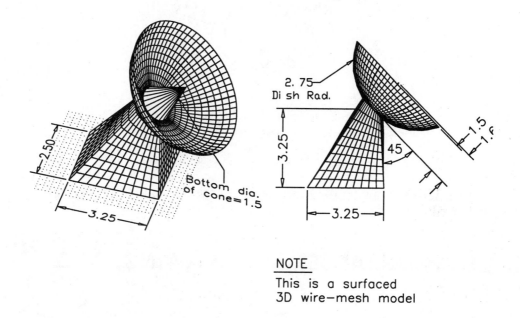

NOTE

This is a surfaced
3D wire-mesh model

Figure 18-86 Drawing for Exercise 16: draw the required orthographic and auxiliary views

Exercises 17 and 18

Draw the required orthographic and auxiliary views for the following objects. The objects are drawn as 3D solid models and are shown at different angles (viewpoints are different).

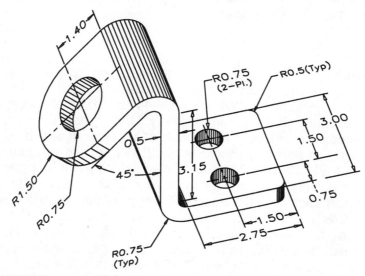

Figure 18-87 Drawing for Exercise 17: draw the required orthographic and auxiliary views

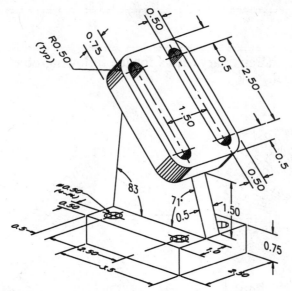

Figure 18-88 Drawing for Exercise 18: draw the required orthographic and auxiliary views

DETAIL DRAWING, ASSEMBLY DRAWING, AND BILL OF MATERIALS

Detail Drawing

A detail drawing is the drawing of an individual component that is a part of the assembled product. Detail drawings are also called piece part drawings. Each detail drawing must be drawn and dimensioned to completely describe the size and shape of the part. It should also contain information that might be needed in manufacturing the part. The finished surfaces should be indicated by using symbols or notes and all necessary operations on the drawing. The material of which the part is made and the number of parts that are required for production of the assembled product must be given in the title block. Detail drawings should also contain part numbers. This information is used in the bill of material and the assembly drawing. The part numbers make it easier to locate the drawing of a part. You should make a detail drawing of each part, regardless of its size, on a separate drawing. When required, these detail drawings can be inserted in the assembly drawing by using **XREF** command.

Assembly Drawing

The assembly drawing is used to show the parts and their relative positions in an assembled product or a machine unit. The assembly drawing should be drawn so that all parts can be shown in one drawing. This is generally called the main view. The main view may be drawn in full section so that the assembly drawing shows nearly all the individual parts and their locations. Additional views should be drawn only when some of the parts cannot be shown in the main view. The hidden lines, as far as possible, should be omitted from the assembly drawing because they clutter the drawing and might cause confusion. However, a hidden line may be drawn if it helps to understand the product. Only assembly dimensions should be shown in the assembly drawing. Each part should be identified on the assembly drawing by the number used in the detail drawing and in the bill of materials. The part numbers should be given as shown in Figure 18-89. It consists of a text string for the detail number, circle (balloon), leader line, and an arrow or dot. The text should be made at least 0.2 inch (5 mm) high and enclosed in a 0.4 inch (10 mm) circle (balloon). The center of the circle must be located not less than 0.8 inch (20 mm) from the nearest line on the drawing. Also, the leader line should be radial with respect to the circle (balloon). The assembly drawing may also contain an exploded isometric or isometric view of the assembled unit.

Bill of Materials

A bill of materials is the list of parts placed on the assembly drawing just above the title block. The bill of materials contains the part number, part description, material, quantity required, and the drawing numbers of the detail drawings. If the bill of materials is placed above the title block, the parts should be listed in ascending order so that the first part is at the bottom of the table. The bill of materials may also be placed at the top of the drawing. In that case, the parts must be listed in descending order with the first part at the top of the table. This structure allows room for any additional items that may be added to the list.

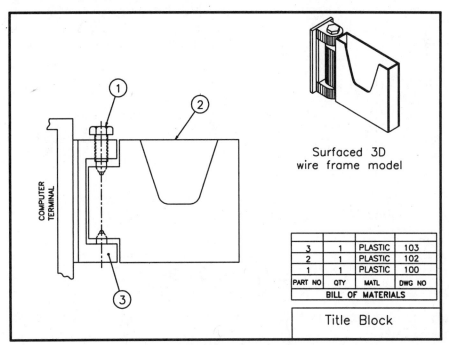

Figure 18-89 Assembly drawing with title block, bill of materials, and surfaced 3D wire frame model

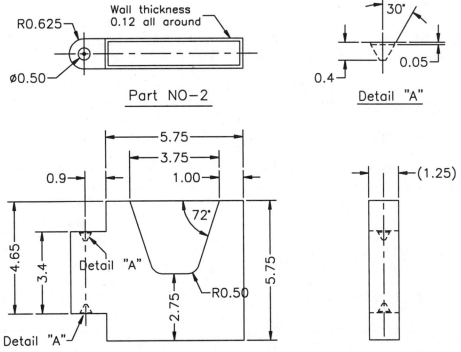

Figure 18-90 Detail drawing (piece part drawing) of part number 2

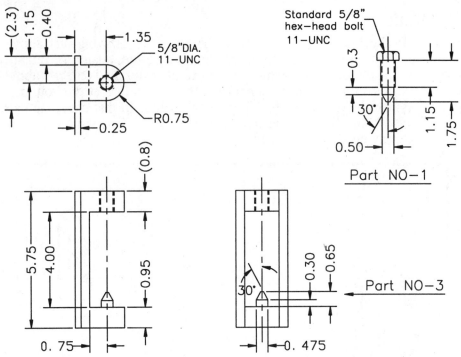

Figure 18-91 Detail drawings of part numbers 1 and 3

SELF EVALUATION TEST

Answer the following questions and then compare your answers with the correct answers given at the end of this chapter.

1.   If you draw a line perpendicular to the X and Y axes, this line defines the _____ axis.

2.   The front view shows the maximum number of features or gives a better idea about the shape of the object. (T/F)

3.   The number of decimal places in a dimension (e.g., 2.000) determines the type of machine that will be used to do that machining operation. (T/F)

4.   The dimension layer/layers should be assigned a unique color so that at the time of plotting you can assign a desired pen to plot the dimensions. (T/F)

5.   All dimensions should be given inside the view. (T/F)

6.   The dimensions can be shown inside the view if the dimensions can be easily understood there and cause no confusion with other object lines. (T/F)

7.   The circle must be dimensioned as _____, never as radius.

8.   If you give continuous dimensioning for dimensioning various features of a part, the overall dimension must be omitted or given as a(n) _____ dimension.

9.   If the object is symmetrical, it is not necessary to draw a full section view. (T/F)

10. The removed section is similar to the _____ section, except that it is shown outside the object.

11. In AutoCAD you can control the spacing between the hatch lines by specifying the _____ at the time of hatching.

12. When dimensioning, you must consider the manufacturing process involved in making a part and the relationship that exists between different parts in an assembly. (T/F)

13. The distance between the first dimension line and the second dimension line must be _____ or _____ unit.

14. The reference dimension must be enclosed in _____.

15. The dimension must be given where the feature is visible. However, in some complicated drawings you might be justified to dimension a detail with a hidden line. (T/F)

REVIEW QUESTIONS

Answer the following questions.

1. Multi-view drawings are also known as _____ drawings.

2. The space between the X and Y axes is called the X-Y plane. (T/F)

3. A plane that is parallel to the XY plane is called a parallel plane. (T/F)

4. If you look at the object along the negative Y axis toward the origin, you will get the side view. (T/F)

5. The top view must be directly below the front view. (T/F)

6. Before drawing orthographic views, you must look at the object and determine the number of views required to show all features of the object. (T/F)

7. By dimensioning, you are not only giving the size of a part, you are giving a series of instructions to a machinist, engineer, or architect. (T/F)

8. What are the components of a dimension? _____
   _____

9. Why should you make the dimensions in a separate layer/layers? _____
   _____

10. The distance of the first dimension line should be _____ or _____ unit from the object line.

11. You can change grid, snap origin, and snap increment to make it easier to place the dimensions. (T/F)

12. For parallel dimension lines, the dimension text can be _____ if there is not enough room between the dimension lines to place the dimension text.

13. You should not dimension with hidden lines. (T/F)

14. A dimension that is not to scale should be indicated by drawing a straight line under the dimension text. (T/F)

15. The dimensions must be given where the feature that you are dimensioning is obvious and shows the contour of the feature. (T/F)

16. When dimensioning a circle, the diameter should be preceded by the _____ .

17. When dimensioning an arc or a circle, the dimension line (leader) must be _____ .

18. In radial dimensioning, you should place the dimension text vertically. (T/F)

19. If the dimension of a feature appears in a section view, you must hatch the dimension text. (T/F)

20. The dimensions must not be repeated; it makes it difficult to update a dimension and the dimensions might get confusing. (T/F)

21. A bolt circle should be dimensioned by specifying the _____ of the bolt circle, the _____ of the holes, and the _____ of the holes in the bolt circle.

22. In the _____ section the object is cut along the entire length of the object.

23. The part of the object where the material is actually cut is indicated by drawing _____ lines.

24. The _____ section is used to show the true shape of the object at the point where the section is cut.

25. The _____ section is used when the features of the object that you want to section are not in one plane.

26. The cutting plane lines are thinner than the object lines. You can use AutoCAD's **PLINE** command to draw the polylines of desired width. (T/F)

27. The spacing between the hatch (section) lines is determined by the space being hatched. (T/F)

28. The angle for the hatch lines should be 45 degrees. However, if there are two are more hatch areas next to each other representing different parts, the hatch angle must be changed so that the hatched areas look different. (T/F)

29. Some parts, like bolts, nuts, shafts, ball bearings, fasteners, ribs, spokes, keys, and other similar items that do not show any important feature, if sectioned, must be shown in section. (T/F)

30. The section lines (hatch lines) must be thicker than the object lines. You can accomplish this by assigning a unique color to hatch lines and then assigning the color to that slot on the plotter carrying a pen with a thick tip. (T/F)

31. The section lines must be drawn on a separate layer for _____ and _____ purposes.

32. In a broken section, only a _____ of the object is cut to _____ the features that need to be drawn in section.

33. The assembly drawing is used to show the _____ and their _____ in an assembled product or a machine unit.

34. In an assembly drawing, additional views should be drawn only when some of the parts cannot be shown in the main view. (T/F)

35. Why shouldn't the hidden lines be shown in the assembly drawing? _____
_____

36. When should the hidden lines be shown in the assembly drawing? _____
_____

37. Only _____ dimensions should be shown in the assembly drawing.

EXERCISES

Exercises 19 through 24

Draw the required orthographic views of the following objects (the isometric view of the objects is given). The dimensions can be determined by counting the number of grid lines. The distance between the isometric grid lines is assumed to be 0.5 unit. Also dimension the drawings.

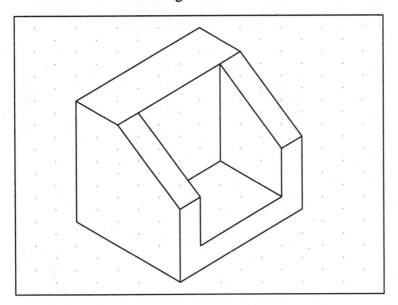

Figure 18-92
Drawing for Exercise 19

Figure 18-93
Drawing for Exercise 20

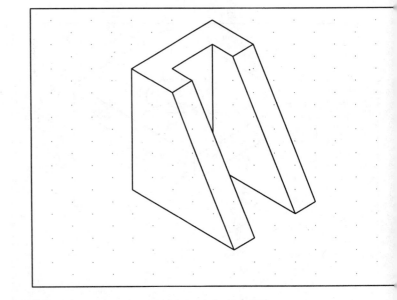

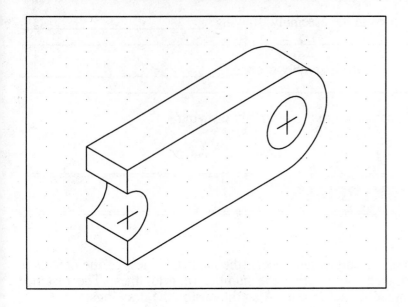

Figure 18-94
Drawing for Exercise 21

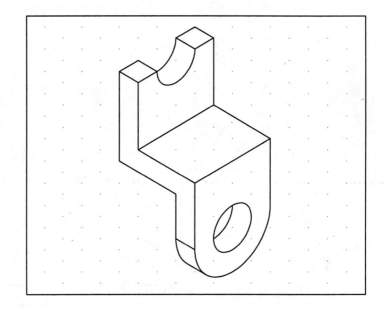

Figure 18-95
Drawing for Exercise 22

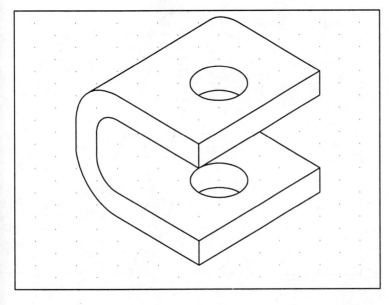

Figure 18-96
Drawing for Exercise 23

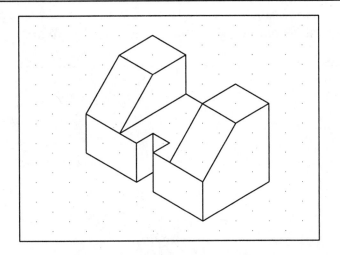

Figure 18-97
Drawing for Exercise 24

Exercises 25 through 26

Draw the required orthographic views of the following objects and give the dimensions. (The objects are drawn as wire frame models.)

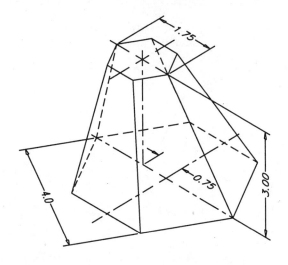

Figure 18-98 Drawing for Exercise 25

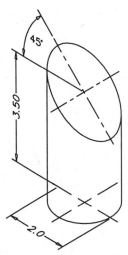

Figure 18-99 Drawing for Exercise 26

Exercise 27

Draw detail drawings of all parts of the model shown in Exercise 15. Also, make the assembly drawing with a bill of materials and a 3D or isometric drawing of the model.

Exercise 28

Draw detail drawings of all parts of the model shown in Exercise 16. Also, make the assembly drawing with a bill of materials and a 3D or isometric drawing of the model.

You can construct a 3D model by cutting the layout along the solid lines and then folding the paper along the hidden lines.

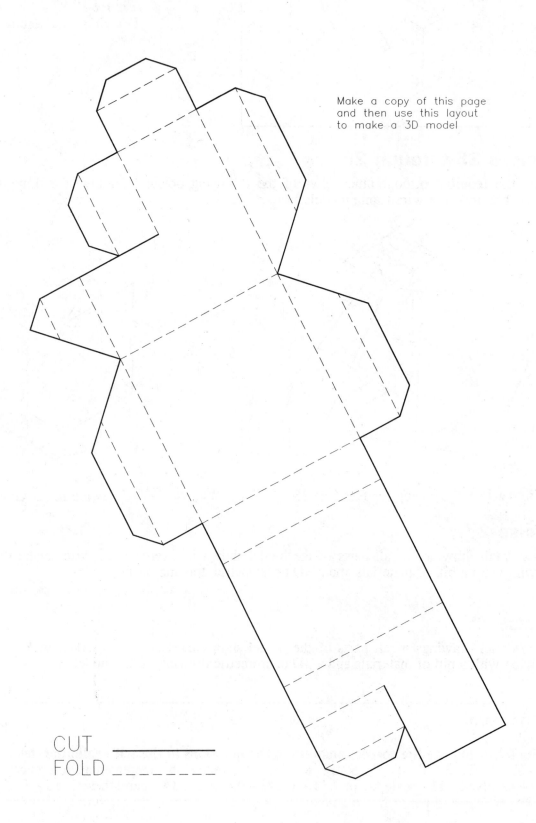

Make a copy of this page
and then use this layout
to make a 3D model

CUT _____
FOLD _ _ _ _ _ _

Chapter 19

Isometric Drawing

Learning objectives

After completing this chapter, you will be able to:
- Understand isometric drawings, isometric axes, and isometric planes.
- Set isometric grid and snap.
- Draw isometrics circles in different isoplanes.
- Dimension isometric objects.
- Place text in an isometric drawing.

ISOMETRIC DRAWINGS

Isometric drawings are generally used to help in visualizing the shape of an object. For example, if you are given the orthographic views of an object (Figure 19-1) it takes time to put the information together to visualize the shape. However, if an isometric drawing is also given with the drawing (Figure 19-2) it is much easier to conceive the shape of the object. Therefore, the isometric drawings are widely used in industry to aid in understanding products and their features.

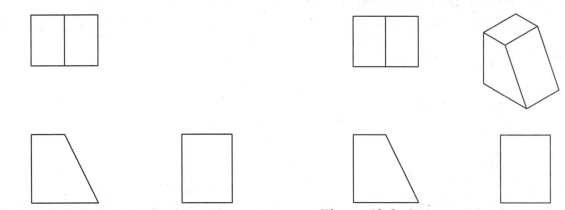

Figure 19-1 Orthographic views of an object

Figure 19-2 Orthographic views with isometric drawing

An isometric drawing should not be confused with a three-dimensional (3D) drawing. An isometric drawing is a two-dimensional (2D) drawing that is drawn in the two-dimensional plane. A 3D drawing is a true three-dimensional model of the object. The model can be rotated and viewed from any direction. A 3D model can be a wireframe model, surface model, or solid model.

ISOMETRIC PROJECTIONS

The word **isometric** means **equal measure** because the three angles between the three principal axes of an isometric drawing are each 120 degrees. An isometric view is obtained by rotating the object by 45 degrees around the imaginary vertical axis, then tilting the object forward through 35° 16' angle. If you project the points and the edges on the frontal plane, the projected length of the edges will be 81 percent (Isometric length/Actual length=9/11) shorter than the actual length of the edges. However, isometric drawings are always drawn to full scale because their purpose is to help the user visualize the shape of the object. Isometric drawings are not meant to describe the actual size of the object. The actual dimensions, tolerances, or feature symbols must be shown in the orthographic views. Also, you should avoid showing any hidden lines in the isometric drawings, unless they show an important feature of the object or help in understanding the shape of the object.

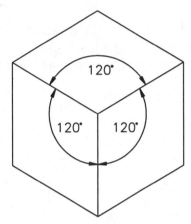

Figure 19-3 Principal axes of an isometric drawing

ISOMETRIC AXES AND PLANES

Isometric drawings have three axes: **right horizontal axis** (P0,P1), **vertical axis** (P0,P2), and **left horizontal axis** (P0,P3). The two horizontal axes are inclined at 30 degrees with the horizontal or X axis (X1,X2). The vertical axis is at 90 degrees.

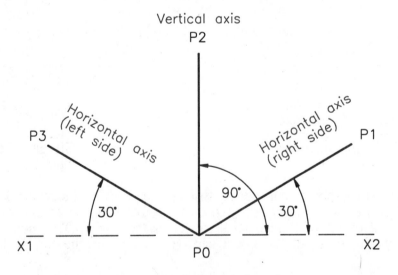

Figure 19-4 Isometric axis

When you draw an isometric drawing the horizontal object lines are drawn along or parallel to the horizontal axis. Similarly, the vertical lines are drawn along or parallel to the vertical axis. For example, if you want to make an isometric drawing of a rectangular block, the vertical edges of the block are drawn parallel to the vertical axis. The horizontal edges on the right-hand side of the block are drawn parallel to the right horizontal axis (P0,P1) and the horizontal edges on the left side of the block are drawn parallel to the left horizontal axis (P0,P3). It is important to remember that the **angles do not appear true** in isometric drawings. Therefore, the edges or surfaces that are at an angle are drawn by locating the end points of the edges. The lines that are parallel to the isometric axis are called **isometric lines**. The lines that are not parallel to the isometric axes are called **non-isometric lines**. Similarly, the planes can be isometric planes or non-isometric planes.

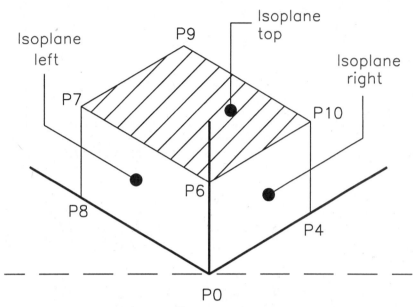

Figure 19-5 Isometric planes

Isometric drawings have three principal planes, **isoplane right**, **isoplane top**, and **isoplane left**, as shown in Figure 19-5. The isoplane right (P0,P4,P10,P6) is the plane as defined by the vertical axis and the right horizontal axis. The isoplane top (P6,P10,P9,P7) is the plane as defined by the right and left horizontal axis. Similarly, the isoplane left (P0,P6,P7,P8) is defined by the vertical axis and the left horizontal axis.

SETTING THE ISOMETRIC GRID AND SNAP

You can use the **SNAP** command to set the isometric grid and snap. The isometric grid lines are displayed at 30 degrees with respect to the horizontal axis. Also the distance between the grid lines is determined by the vertical spacing, which can be specified by using the GRID or SNAP command. The grid lines coincide with the three isometric axes, which makes it easier to make isometric drawings. The following command sequence illustrates the use of the SNAP command to set the isometric grid and snap of 0.5 units.

Command: **SNAP**
Snap spacing or ON/OFF/Aspect/Rotate/Style <0.25>: **S**
Standard/Isometric: **I**
Vertical spacing <0.25>: **0.5**

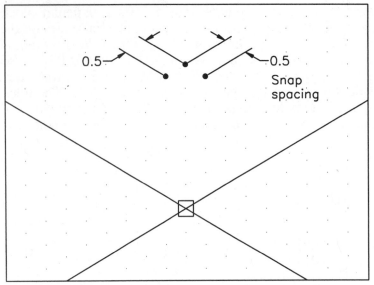

Figure 19-6 Setting isometric grid and snap

When you use the SNAP command to set the isometric grid, the grid lines may not be displayed on the screen. To display the grid lines, turn the grid on using the GRID command or press function key F7.

You cannot set the aspect ratio for the isometric grid. Therefore, the spacing between the isometric grid lines will be same.

You can also set the isometric grid and snap by using the Drawing Aids dialogue box (Figure 19-7), which can be invoked by entering **DDRMODES** at the **Command:** prompt. You can also access this dialogue box by selecting Drawing Aids from the Settings pull-down menu.

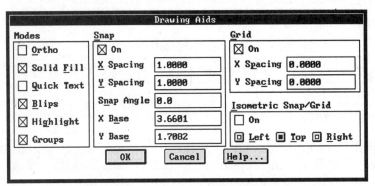

Figure 19-7 Drawing Aids dialogue box

The isometric snap and grid can be turned on or off by clicking the **On** box that is located in the Isometric Snap/Grid box of the Drawing Aids dialogue box. The Isometric Snap/Grid box also contains the radio buttons **Left**, **Top**, and **Right**. These buttons can be use to set the isoplane. To display the grid on the screen, make sure the grid is turned on.

When you set the isometric grid, the display of the cross-hairs also changes. The cross-hairs are displayed at isometric angle and their orientation depends on the current isoplane. You can toggle among isoplane right, isoplane left, and isoplane top by pressing the **Ctrl** and **E** keys simultaneously. You can also toggle among different isoplanes by using the Drawing Aids dialogue box or by entering ISOPLANE command at the **Command:** prompt.

Command: **ISOPLANE**
Left/Top/Right/<Toggle>: **T**
Current Isometric plane is: **Top**

Example 1

In this example you will draw the isometric drawing in Figure 19-8.

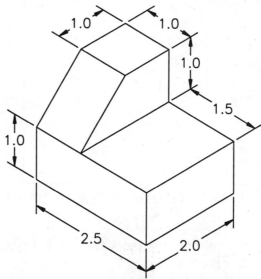

Figure 19-8 Drawing for Example 1

1. Use the **SNAP** command to set the isometric grid and snap. The snap value is 0.5 units.
   Command: **SNAP**
   Snap spacing or ON/OFF/Aspect/Rotate/Style <0.25>: **S**
   Standard/Isometric: **I**
   Vertical spacing <0.25>: **0.5**

2. Change the isoplane to left by pressing the Ctrl and E keys. Enter the LINE command and draw lines between points P1, P2, P3, P4, and P1 as shown in Figure 19-9.

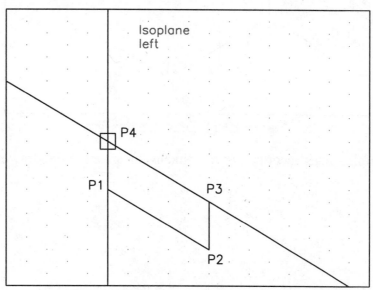

Figure 19-9 Draw the bottom left face

3. Change the isoplane to right by pressing the **Ctrl** and **E** keys. Enter the LINE command and draw the lines as shown in Figure 19-10.

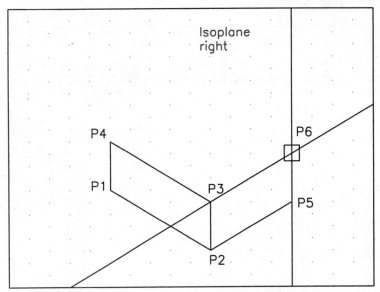

Figure 19-10 Draw the bottom right face

4. Change the isoplane to top by pressing the **Ctrl** and **E** keys. Enter the LINE command and draw the lines as shown in Figure 19-11.

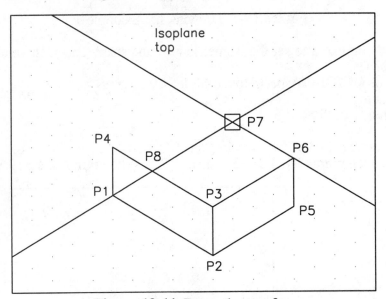

Figure 19-11 Draw the top face

5. Draw the remaining lines according to the dimensions given in the drawing.

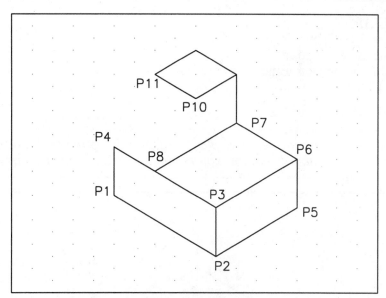

Figure 19-12 Draw the remaining lines

6. The front left end of the object is tapered at an angle. In isometric drawings the oblique surfaces (surfaces that are at an angle with respect to the isometric axis) cannot be drawn like other lines. You must first locate the end points of the lines that define the oblique surface and then draw lines between those points. To complete the drawing of Example 1, draw a line from P10 to P8 and P11 to P4.

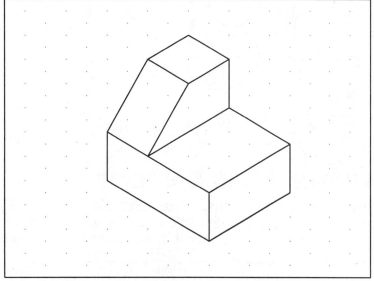

Figure 19-13 Drawing the tapered face

DRAWING ISOMETRIC CIRCLES

Isometric circles are drawn by using the **ELLIPSE** command and then selecting the **Isocircle** option. Before you enter the radius or diameter of the isometric circle you must make sure that you are in the required isoplane. For example, if you want to draw a circle in the right isoplane, you must toggle through the isoplanes until the required isoplane (right isoplane) is displayed. You can also set the required isoplane current before entering the ELLIPSE command. The cross-hairs and the shape of the isometric circle will automatically change as you toggle through different isoplanes. After you enter the radius or diameter of the circle, AutoCAD will draw the isometric circle in the correct plane.

Command: **ELLIPSE**
<Axis endpoint 1>/Center/Isocircle: **I**
Center of circle: Select a point.
<Circle radius>/Diameter: Enter circle radius

You must have the isometric snap on to display the Isocircle option with the ELLIPSE command. If the isometric snap is not on, you cannot draw an isometric circle.

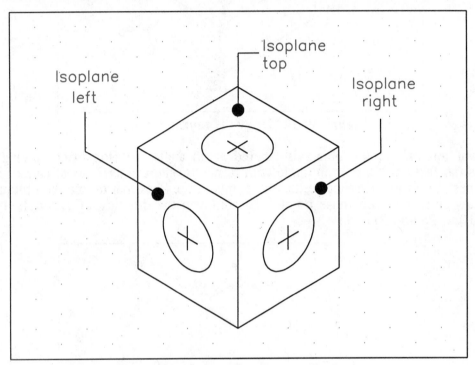

Figure 19-14 Drawing isometric circles

DIMENSIONING ISOMETRIC OBJECTS

Isometric dimensioning involves two steps: first, dimension the drawing using the standard dimensioning commands. Next, edit the dimensions to change them to oblique dimensions. The following example illustrates the process involved in dimensioning an isometric drawing.

Example 2

In this example you will dimension the isometric drawing that you created in Example 1.

1. Dimension the drawing as shown in Figure 19-15. You can use the aligned or vertical dimensioning command to give the dimensions. When you select the points you must use the intersection or end point object snap to grab the end points of the object that you are dimensioning. AutoCAD automatically leaves a gap between the object line and the extension line as specified by the DIMGAP variable.

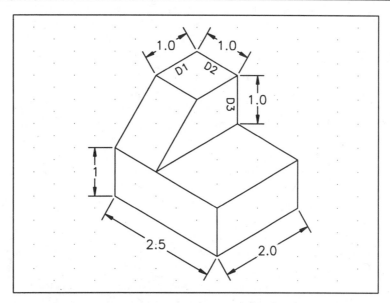

Figure 19-15 Dimensioning an isometric drawing

2. The next step is to edit the dimensions. The dimensions can be edited by first entering the **DIM** command, then entering **OBLIQUE** at the Dim: prompt. After you select the dimension you want to edit, AutoCAD will prompt you to enter the oblique angle. The oblique angle is determined by the angle that the extension line of the isometric dimension makes with the positive X axis.

> Command: **DIM**
> Dim: **OBLIQUE**
> Select object: Select the dimension (D1).
> Enter oblique angle (RETURN for none): **30**

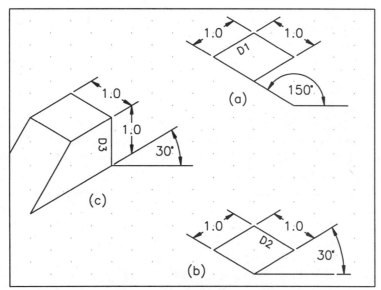

Figure 19-16 Determining the oblique angle

For example, the extension line of the dimension labeled D1 makes a 150-degree angle with the positive X axis; therefore, the oblique angle is 150 degrees. Similarly, the extension lines of the dimension labeled D2 makes a 30-degree angle with the positive X axis; therefore, the oblique angle is 30 degrees. After you edit all dimensions the drawing should appear as shown in Figure 19-17.

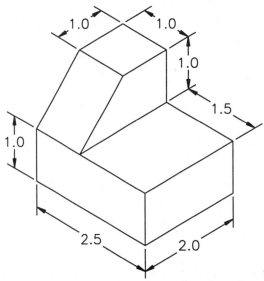

Figure 19-17   Object with isometric dimensions

ISOMETRIC TEXT

You cannot use the regular text when placing text in an isometric drawing because the text in an isometric drawing is obliqued at positive or negative 30 degrees. Therefore you must create two text styles with oblique angles of 30 degrees and negative 30 degrees. You can use the STYLE command to create a new text style as described below. (For details about how to create a new text style refer to "STYLE Command" in Chapter 5.)

Command: **STYLE**
Text Style name (or ?): **ISOTEXT1**
Font file: **ROMANS**
Height: **0.075**
Width factor < 1.00 >: ◄─┘
Oblique angle < current >: **30**
Backwards? < Y/N >: **N**
Upside-down? < Y/N >: **N**
Vertical? < Y/N >: **N**

Similarly, you can create another text style, **ISOTEXT2**, with a negative 30-degree oblique angle. When you place the text in an isometric drawing you must also specify the rotation angle for the text. The text style you use and the text rotation angle depend on the placement of the text in the isometric drawing as shown in Figure 19-18.

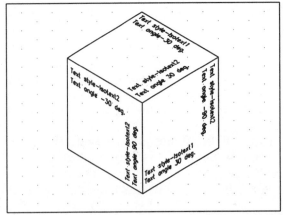

Figure 19-18   Text style and rotation angle for isometric text

SELF EVALUATION TEST

Answer the following questions and then compare your answers with the correct answers given at the end of this chapter.

1. The word **isometric** means _____ because the three angles between the three principal axes of an isometric drawing are each _____ degrees.

2. What is the ratio of isometric length to actual length in an isometric drawing? _____

3. What is the angle between the right isometric horizontal axis and the X axis? _____ degrees

4. Isometric drawings have three principal planes: **isoplane right**, **isoplane top**, and _____.

5. What keys can you use to toggle among isoplane right, isoplane left, and isoplane top? _____

6. You can only use the aligned dimension option to dimension an isometric drawing. (T/F)

7. Should the isometric snap be On to display the Isocircle option with the ELLIPSE command? (Y/N)

8. Do you need to specify the rotation angle when placing text in an isometric drawing? (Y/N) If yes, what are the possible angles? _____

9. The lines that are not parallel to the isometric axes are called _____

10. You should avoid showing any hidden lines in isometric drawings. (T/F)

REVIEW QUESTIONS

Answer the following questions.

1. Isometric drawings are generally used to help in _____ the shape of an object.

2. An isometric view is obtained by rotating the object by _____ degrees around the imaginary vertical axis, then tilting the object forward through _____ angle.

3. If you project the points and the edges on the frontal plane, the projected length of the edges will be _____ percent shorter than the actual length of the edges.

4. When should hidden lines be shown in an isometric drawing?_____

5. Isometric drawings have three axes: **right horizontal axis**, **vertical axis**, and _____

6. The **angles do not appear true** in isometric drawings. (T/F)

7. What are the lines called that are parallel to the isometric axis? _____

8. What command can you use to set the isometric grid and snap? _____

9.   Isometric grid lines are displayed at _____ degrees with respect to the horizontal axis.

10. It is possible to set the aspect ratio for isometric grid. (T/F)

11. You can also set the isometric grid and snap by using the Drawing Aids dialogue box which can be invoked by entering _____ at the **Command:** prompt.

12. Isometric circles are drawn by using the **ELLIPSE** command and then selecting the _____
_____ option.

13. Can you draw an isometric circle without turning the isometric snap on? (Y/N)

14. Only aligned dimensions can be edited to change them to oblique dimensions. (T/F)

15. To place the text in an isometric drawing you must create two text styles with oblique angles of _____ degrees and negative _____ degrees.

EXERCISES

Exercise 1

Draw the following isometric drawings. The dimensions can be determined by counting the number of grid lines. The distance between the isometric grid lines is assumed to be 0.5 unit. Dimension the odd-numbered drawings.

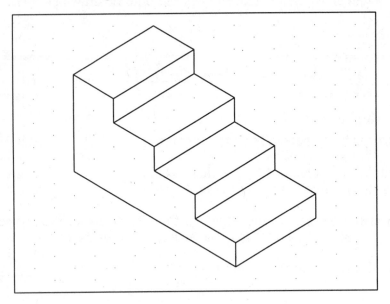

Figure 19-19

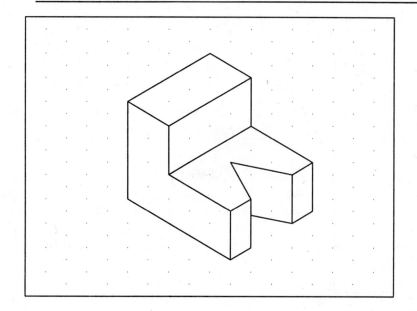

Figure 19-20

Figure 19-21

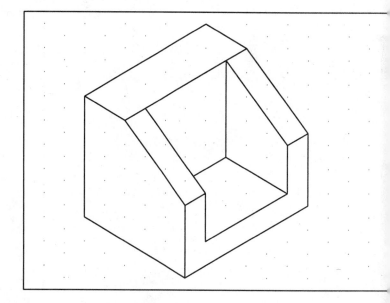

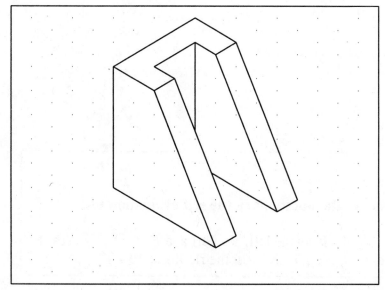

Figure 19-22

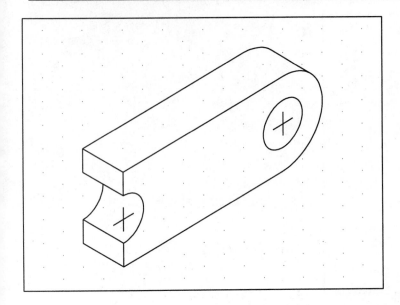

Figure 19-23

Figure 19-24

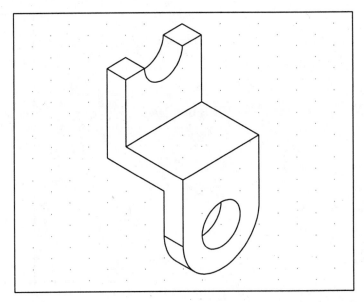

Answers

The following are the correct answers to the questions in the self evaluation test.

1 - Equal measure, 120, **2** - 9/11, **3** - 30, **4** - Isoplane left, **5** - Ctrl and E, **6** - F, **7** - Yes, **8** - Yes, 30 degrees, -30 degrees, 90 degrees, etc., **9** - Non-isometric lines, **10** - T

Chapter 20

User Coordinate System

Learning objectives

After completing this chapter, you will be able to:
♦ Use and understand the user coordinate system and the world coordinate system.
♦ Position the UCS icon using different options of the UCSICON command.
♦ Use coordinate system UCS to create a 3D drawing.
♦ Use different options to redefine the UCS using the UCS command.
♦ Set the UCS to preset orientation.

THE WORLD COORDINATE SYSTEM (WCS)

When you get into AutoCAD's Drawing Editor, by default the WCS (world coordinate system) is established. In the WCS the X, Y, and Z coordinates of any point are measured with reference to the fixed origin (0,0,0). This origin is located at the lower left corner of the screen; therefore, the objects you have drawn up to now use the WCS. This coordinate system is fixed and cannot be moved. The WCS is mostly used in 2D drawings. The world coordinate system and the user coordinate system (UCS) were introduced in AutoCAD Release 10. Earlier releases used the lower left corner of the screen as origin (0,0,0).

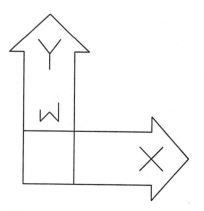

Figure 20-1 World coordinate system (WCS) icon

UCSICON COMMAND

Pull-down:	Options, UCS, Icon
Screen:	OPTIONS, UCSICON:

The orientation of the origin of the current UCS is represented by the UCS icon. This icon is a graphic reminder of the direction of the UCS axes and the location of the origin. This icon also tells you what the viewing direction is, relative to the UCS XY plane. The default location of this symbol is a little to the right and a little above the lower left corner of the viewport. The + sign on the icon reflects that the UCS icon is placed at the origin of the current UCS. Absence of the W on the Y axis indicates that the current coordinate system is not WCS. If there is a box at the icon's base, it means that you are viewing the UCS from above; absence of the box indicates that you are viewing the UCS from below. The UCSICON command controls display of this symbol.

This command can be invoked from the pull-down menu (Select Options, UCS, Icon, Figure 20-3) from the screen menu (Select OPTIONS, UCSICON:), or by entering **UCSICON** at the Command: prompt. The command prompt sequence is:

Command: **UCSICON** ◄─┘
ON/OFF/All/NOorigin/ORigin <ON>: **OFF** ◄─┘

The icon is not displayed on the screen until the program is turned on again.

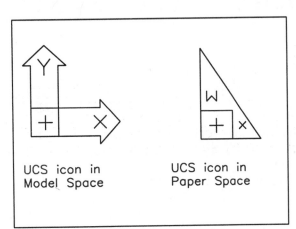

Figure 20-2 Model space and Paper space icons

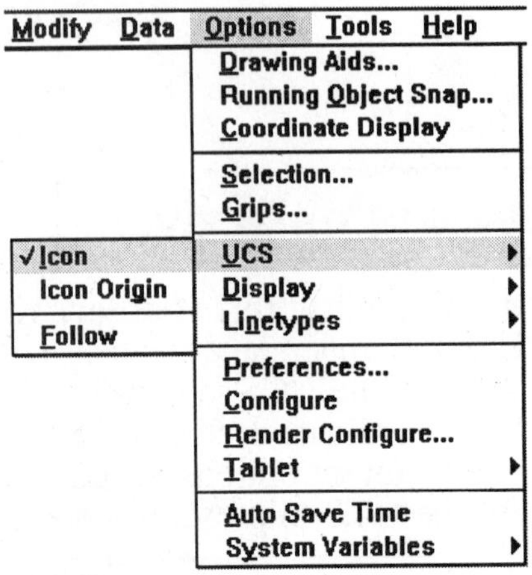

Figure 20-3 Selecting UCSICON option from the Options pull-down menu

Options of the UCSICON command

The UCSICON command has several options that let you control the display and origin of the UCS icon:

ON Option

This option displays the UCS icon in the current viewport.

ON/OFF/All/NOorigin/ORigin<ON>: **ON** ◄─┘

OFF Option

This option disables the UCS icon in the current viewport, causing it not to be displayed.

ON/OFF/All/NOorigin/ORigin<ON>: **OFF** ◄─┘

All Option

This option is used to change the UCS icons in all active viewports. Normally changes are made only to the icon in the current viewport. For example, to turn on UCS icons in all the viewports, the prompt sequence will be:

ON/OFF/All/NOorigin/ORigin<default>: **ALL**
ON/OFF/All/NOorigin/ORigin: **ON**

NO (NOorigin) Option

Makes AutoCAD display the icon, if enabled, at the lower left corner of screen, whatever the position of the current UCS origin may be. This is the default setting.

ON/OFF/All/NOorigin/ORigin<default>: **NO**

OR (ORigin) Option

This option makes AutoCAD display the UCS icon (if enabled) at the origin (0,0,0) of the current coordinate system. If the current origin is off screen or it is not possible to position the icon at the origin without being clipped at the viewport edges, it is displayed at the lower left corner of the screen. Sometimes your view direction may be along the edge of the current UCS (or within one degree of edge direction). In such cases the UCS icon is replaced by a broken pencil icon as to indicate that the pointing locations are meaningless.

ON/OFF/All/NOorigin/ORigin<default>: **OR**

THE USER COORDINATE SYSTEM (UCS)

The user coordinate system (UCS) helps you to establish your own coordinate system. Changing the placement of the base point of your drawing is accomplished by changing the position/ orientation of the coordinate system. As already mentioned, the WCS is fixed, while the UCS can be moved and rotated to any desired position to conform to the shape of the object being drawn. Alterations in the UCS are manifested in the position and orientation of the UCS icon symbol, which is originally located in the lower left corner of the screen. The UCS is mostly used in 3D drawings where you may need to specify points that vary from each other along the X, Y, and Z axes.

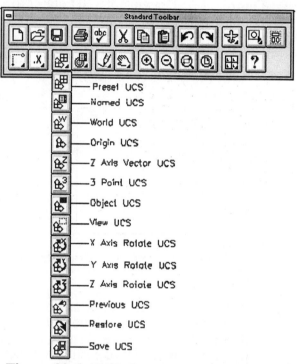

Figure 20-4 UCS flyout in Standard toolbar

Example 1

To illustrate the use of the UCS, draw a tapered rectangular block and a circle on its inclined side. The location of the center of the circle is at a given distance from the lower left corner of the tapered side. This problem can be broken into the following steps:

1. Draw the bottom side of the tapered block.
2. Draw the top side.
3. Draw the other sides.
4. Finally, draw the circle on the inclined side of the block.

To make it easier to visualize and draw the object, the 3D object is shown in Figure 20-5. Follow the above-mentioned steps to draw an identical figure.

1. Start the drawing process by drawing the bottom rectangle. Enter the **LINE** command and pick a point on the screen to draw the first line. Continue drawing lines to complete the rectangle as shown in Figure 20-5. Following is the command sequence:

        Command: **LINE** ↵
        From point: **1,1**
        To point: **@2.20,0** ↵
        To point: **@0,1.30** ↵
        To point: **@-2.20,0** ↵
        To point: **C** ↵

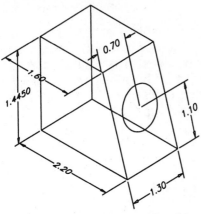

Figure 20-5 Drawing of a 3D object to be drawn

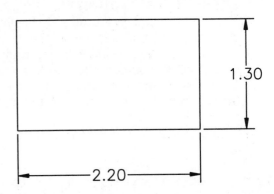

Figure 20-6 First step, draw the bottom rectangle

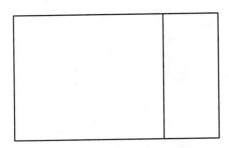

Figure 20-7 Second step, draw the top rectangle

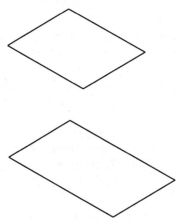

Figure 20-8 Third step, change Vpoint to 1,-1,1

2. The corner of the top rectangle of the tapered block can be established with the WCS, but it could cause some confusion in locating the points since each point must be referenced with the origin. If you use the relative coordinates, you must keep track of the Z coordinate. This problem can be solved easily with the UCS by moving the origin of the coordinate system to a plane 1.4450 units above and parallel to the bottom plane. This can be accomplished by using the UCS command. This command is described in detail later. After you establish the new origin, it is much easier to draw the top side since the drawing plane is 1.4450 units above the plane on which the bottom side was drawn (distance between the bottom side and the top side is 1.4450 units). The prompt sequence is as follows:

> Command: **UCS** ←┘
> Origin/ZAxis/3point/OBject/View/X/Y/Z/Prev/Restore/Save/ Del/?/ <World>: **O** ←┘
> Origin point<0,0,0>: **0,0,1.4450** ←┘

After changing the UCS, the prompt sequence to draw the top side is:
> Command: **LINE** ←┘
> From point: **1,1**
> To point: **@1.60,0** ←┘
> To point: **@0,1.30** ←┘
> To point: **@-1.6,0** ←┘
> To point: **C** ←┘

3. Since you are looking at the object from the top side, the three edges of the top side will overlap the corresponding bottom edges, hence you will not be able to see these three sides.

Once the object is drawn, you can see the 3D shape of the object using the VPOINT command. (The VPOINT command is discussed in detail in the next chapter.)

Command: **VPOINT** ◄─┘
Rotate/ < View point > < current > : **1,-1,1** ◄─┘

Join the corners of the top rectangle with the corresponding corners of the bottom rectangle. You can use the LINE command to draw the edges. Use the ENDpoint or INTersect snap mode to grab the corners.

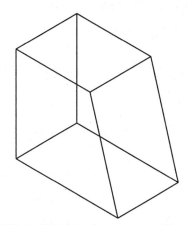

Figure 20-9   Join the corresponding corners

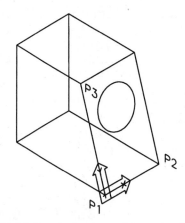

Figure 20-10 Last step, position the UCS icon and draw a circle

4. The last step is to draw the circle on the inclined surface of the object. To draw the circle so that it lies on the inclined surface, you need to make the inclined side (surface) the current drawing plane. Again, this can be accomplished with the 3point option of the UCS command. (This option is discussed later in this chapter.) The prompt sequence is:

Command: **UCS** ◄─┘
Origin/ZAxis/3point/OBject/View/X/Y/Z/Prev/Restore/Save/Del/?/ < World > : **3** ◄─┘
Origin point < 0,0,0 > : *Specify the lower left corner of the inclined side as the origin point (P1)*
Point on positive portion of X axis < default value > : *Pick end point of bottom edge of the inclined surface (P2)*
Point on positive portion of Y axis < default value > : *Pick end point of left edge of the inclined surface (P3)*

To display the UCS icon at the new location specified in the UCS command, you can use the UCSICON command. You don't have to move the UCS icon to the new UCS position, but you can do so to see the current working plane. To shift the UCS icon to the new UCS position, the prompt sequence is:

Command: **UCSICON** ◄─┘
ON/OFF/All/NOorigin/ORigin < ON > : **OR** ◄─┘

Now that you have changed the location of the origin and aligned the current drawing plane with the inclined surface, you can draw the circle. We know the X and Y axes displacements are between the lower corner of the inclined surface and the center of the circle. Use these X and Y displacements to specify the center of the circle and then draw the circle. The command sequence is:

Command: **CIRCLE** ◄─┘
3P/2P/TTR/ < Center point > : **0.7,1.10** ◄─┘

Diameter/ <Radius> <current>: *Specify the desired radius.*

Using the user coordinate system, the circle can be drawn in the plane on which the inclined surface lies and the center of the circle can be easily specified just by entering the displacements about the X and Y axes of the current UCS.

UCS COMMAND

Toolbar:	Standard, UCS flyout
Pull-down:	View, Set UCS
Screen:	VIEW, UCS:

As has already been discussed, the WCS is fixed whereas the UCS enables you to set your own coordinate system. For certain views of the drawing it is better to have the origin of measurements from the corner of the view. This makes locating the features and dimensioning the view easier. The origin and orientation of a coordinate system can be redefined using the UCS command. The UCS command can be invoked from the **Standard** toolbar (Select UCS flyout, Figure 20-4), from the pull-down menu (Select View, Set UCS, Figure 20-11), from the screen menu (Select VIEW, UCS:), or by entering **UCS** at the Command: prompt. The command prompt sequence is:

Figure 20-11 Selecting UCS options from the View pull-down menu

Command: **UCS** ◂┘
Origin/ZAxis/3point/OBject/View/X/Y/Z/Prev/Restore/Save/Del/?/ <World>: Select an
option ◂┘

W (World) Option

Using this option you can set the current UCS to be identical to the world coordinate system. To invoke this option, pick the **World UCS** icon from the UCS flyout in the **Standard** toolbar, or enter **World** (or **W**) at the following prompt:

Command: **UCS** ◂┘
Origin/ZAxis/3point/OBject/View/X/Y/Z/Prev/Restore/Save/Del/?/ <World>: ◂┘

O (Origin) Option

With this option you can define a new UCS by changing the origin of the current UCS. The directions of the X, Y, and Z axes remain unaltered. To invoke this option pick the **Origin UCS** icon from the UCS flyout in the **Standard** toolbar, or enter **Origin** (or **O**) at the following prompt:

Command: **UCS** ◂┘
Origin/ZAxis/3point/OBject/View/X/Y/Z/Prev/Restore/Save/Del/?/ <World>: **O** ◂┘
Origin point <0,0,0>: *Select point P4 using endpoint snap.*

At the **Origin point** **<0,0,0>:** prompt you need to specify any point relative to the current UCS. This point acts as the new origin point. For example, if you want to specify the new origin point at (2,1,0) with respect to the current UCS, enter **2,1,0** at the **Origin point <0,0,0>:** prompt.

You can also pick a point with a pointing device to specify the location of the new origin. **Repeat the command and pick point P3 as new origin.**

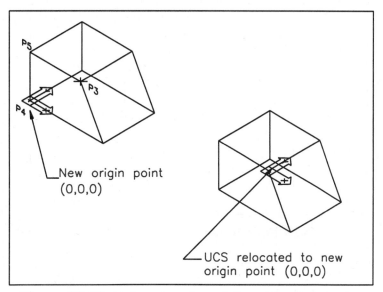

Figure 20-12 Relocating the origin with origin option

Note

If you do not provide a Z coordinate for the origin, the Z coordinate is assigned the current elevation value.

ZA (ZAxis) Option

With this option of the UCS command, you can change the coordinate system by selecting the origin point of the coordinate system and a point on the positive Z axis. After specifying a point on the Z axis, AutoCAD determines the X and Y axes of the new coordinate system accordingly. This option can be invoked by picking the **Z Axis Vector UCS** icon from the UCS flyout in the **Standard** toolbar, or by entering **ZAxis** (or **ZA**) at the following prompt:

Command: **UCS** ⟵
Origin/ZAxis/3point/OBject/View/X/Y/Z/Prev/Restore/Save/Del/?/ < World > : **ZA** ⟵
Origin point < 0,0,0 > : *Specify the origin point* (P4)
Point on positive portion of Z-axis < default value > : *Specify a point on the positive Z axis*
(P6)

If you give a null response for the **Point on the positive portion of Z axis:** prompt, the Z-axis of the new coordinate system will be parallel (in the same direction) to the Z axis of the previous coordinate system. Null responses to the origin point and point on the positive Z axis establishes a new coordinate system in which the direction of the Z axis is identical to that of the previous coordinate system; however, the X and Y axes have been rotated around the Z axis. The positive Z axis direction is also known as the **extrusion direction**. In Figure 20-13, the UCS has been relocated by specifying the origin point and point on positive portion of the Z-axis.

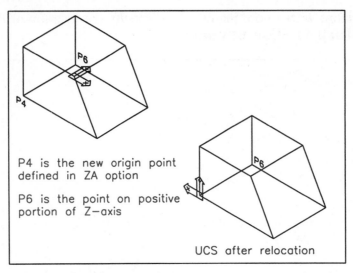

Figure 20-13 Relocating the UCS using the ZA option

3 (3point) Option

In this option you can establish a new coordinate system by specifying the new origin point, a point on the positive X axis, and a point on the positive Y axis. The direction of the Z axis is determined by applying the right–hand rule. In the right-hand rule: Align your thumb with the positive X axis and your index finger with the positive Y axis. Now bend your middle finger so that it is perpendicular to the thumb and the index finger. The direction of the middle finger is the direction of the positive Z axis. The 3point option of the UCS command changes the orientation of the UCS to any angled surface. This option can be invoked by picking the **3 Point UCS** icon from the UCS flyout in the **Standard** toolbar, or by entering **3point** (or **3**) at the following prompt:

Command: **UCS** ◄─┘
Origin/ZAxis/3point/OBject/View/X/Y/Z/Prev/Restore/Save/Del/?/<World>: **3** ◄─┘
Origin point<0,0,0>: *Specify the origin point.*
Point on positive portion of X-axis<default value>: *Specify a point on the positive X axis.*
Point on positive portion of Y-axis<default value>: *Specify a point on the positive Y axis.*

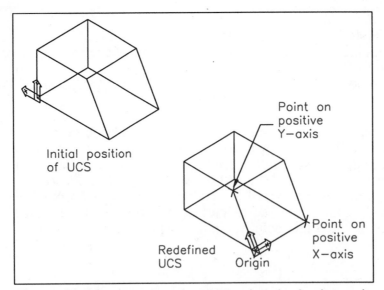

Figure 20-14 Relocating the UCS using the 3point option

A null response to the **Origin point:** prompt will lead to a coordinate system in which the origin of the new UCS is identical to that of the previous UCS. Similarly, null responses to the point on X-or Y-axes prompts will lead to a coordinate system in which the X or Y axes of the new UCS is parallel to that of the previous UCS. In Figure 20-14, the UCS has been relocated by specifying three points (origin point, point on positive portion of X-axis, and point on positive portion of Y-axis).

OB (OBject) Option

With the OB (OBject) option of the UCS command, you can establish a new coordinate system by pointing to any object in an AutoCAD drawing except a 3D polyline, 3D solid, 3D mesh, Viewport object, mtext, xline, ray, leader, ellipse, region, or spline. The positive Z axis of the new UCS is in the same direction as the positive Z axis of the object selected. If the X and Z axes are given, the new Y axis is determined by the right-hand rule. This option can be invoked by picking the **Object UCS** icon from the UCS flyout in the **Standard** toolbar, or by entering **OBject** (or **OB)** at the following prompt:

Command: **UCS** ◄─┘
Origin/ZAxis/3point/OBject/View/X/Y/Z/Prev/Restore/Save/Del/?/ < World > : **OB**

The origin and the X axis of the new UCS are determined by the following rules:

ARC
When you pick an arc, the center of the arc becomes the origin for the new UCS. The X axis passes through the end point of the arc that is closest to the point picked on the object.

CIRCLE
The center of the circle becomes the origin for the new UCS and the X axis passes through the point picked on the object.

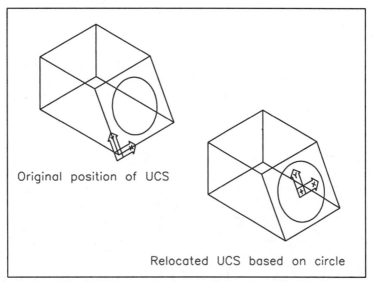

Figure 20-15 Relocating the UCS using the OBject option

LINE
The new UCS origin is the end point of the line that is nearest to the point picked on the line. The X axis is defined so that the line lies in the XY plane of the new UCS. In the new UCS, therefore, the Y coordinate of the second end point of the line is 0.

TRACE
The origin of the new UCS is the "from" point of the Trace. The new X axis lies along the center line of the Trace.

DIMENSION
The middle point of the dimension text becomes the new origin. The X axis direction is identical to the direction of the X axis of the UCS that existed when the dimension was drawn.

POINT
The position of the point is the new origin.

SOLID
The origin of the new UCS is the first point of the solid. The X axis of the new UCS lies along the line between the first and second points of the solid.

2D POLYLINE
The start point of the polyline or polyarc is treated as the new UCS origin. The X axis extends from the start point to the next vertex.

3D FACE
The first point of the 3D face determines the new UCS origin. The X axis is determined from the first two points, and the positive side of the Y axis from the first and fourth points. The Z axis is determined by applying the right-hand rule.

Shape/Text/Insert/Attribute/Attribute Definition
The insertion point of the object becomes the new UCS origin. The new X axis is defined by the rotation of the object around its positive Z axis. Hence, the object you pick will have a rotation angle of zero in the new UCS. In Figure 20-15, the UCS is relocated using the OBject option. The UCS has been aligned to the circle.

Note

Except for 3D faces, the XY plane of the new UCS will be parallel to the XY plane existing when the object was drawn; however, X and Y axes are rotated.

V (View) Option

The V (View) option of the UCS command lets you define a new UCS whose XY plane is perpendicular to your current viewing direction. In other words, the new XY plane is parallel to the screen. The origin of the UCS defined in this option remains unaltered. This option is mostly used to view your drawing from an oblique viewing direction. This option can be invoked by picking the **View UCS** icon from the UCS flyout in the **Standard** toolbar, or by entering **View** (or **V**) at the following prompt:

Command: **UCS** ◄┘
Origin/ZAxis/3point/OBject/View/X/Y/Z/Prev/Restore/Save/Del/?/ < World > : **V** ◄┘

X/Y/Z Options

With these option you can rotate the current UCS around a desired axis.

Command: **UCS** ◄┘
Origin/ZAxis/3point/OBject/View/X/Y/Z/Prev/Restore/Save/Del/?/ < World > : *Specify the axis around which you want to rotate the UCS.*

Rotation angle about **n** axis < 0.0 > : *Specify the angle of rotation.*

You can specify the angle by entering the angle value at the **Rotation angle about the specified axis < 0.0 >:** prompt or by picking two points on the screen with the help of a pointing device. You can specify a positive or a negative angle. The new angle is taken relative to the X axis of the existing UCS. The right-hand rule is used to determine the positive direction of rotation around an axis. The right-hand rule states that if you visualize gripping the axis about which you want the rotation with your right hand, your thumb pointing in the positive direction of that axis, the direction in which your fingers close will determine the positive rotation angle. For example, to rotate the current UCS about the Z axis by an angle of 45 degrees, enter the following prompt:

Command: **UCS** ◄──┘
Origin/ZAxis/3point/OBject/View/X/Y/Z/Prev/Restore/Save/Del/?/ < World > : **Z**
Rotation angle about **n** axis < 0.0 > : **45**

In Figure 20-16, the UCS is relocated using the X option by specifying an angle about the X axis. The upper left part of the figure shows the UCS setting before the UCS was relocated with X option. Enter the following prompt:

Command: **UCS** ◄──┘
Origin/ZAxis/3point/OBject/View/X/Y/Z/Prev/Restore/Save/Del/?/ < World > : **X**
Rotation angle about X axis < 0.0 > : **90**

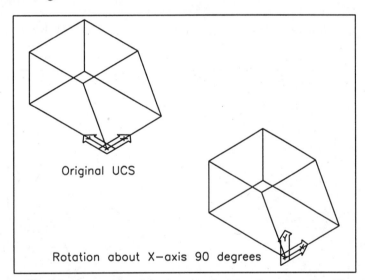

Figure 20-16 Rotating UCS about the X axis using the X option

In Figure 20-17, the UCS is relocated using the Y option by specifying an angle about the Y axis. The upper left part of the figure shows the UCS setting before the UCS was relocated with Y option. Enter the following prompt:

Command: **UCS** ◄──┘
Origin/ZAxis/3point/OBject/View/X/Y/Z/Prev/Restore/Save/Del/?/ < World > : **Y**
Rotation angle about Y axis < 0.0 > : **90**

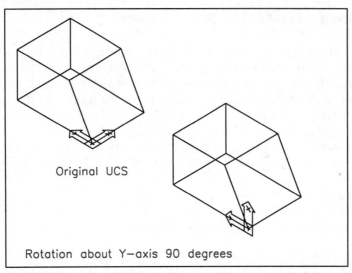

Figure 20-17 Rotating UCS about the Y axis using the Y option

In Figure 20-18, the UCS is relocated using the Z option by specifying an angle about the Z axis. The upper left part of the figure shows the UCS setting before the UCS was relocated with Z option. Enter the following prompt:

Command: **UCS** ◄─┘
Origin/ZAxis/3point/OBject/View/X/Y/Z/Prev/Restore/Save/Del/?/ < World > : **Z**
Rotation angle about Z axis < 0.0 > : **90**

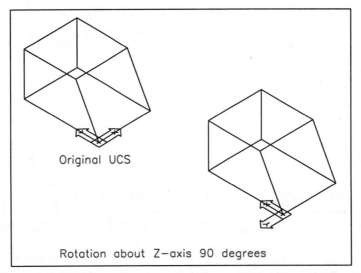

Figure 20-18 Rotating UCS about the Z axis using the Z option

P (Previous) Option

The P (Previous option) restores the previous UCS. The last 10 user coordinate systems settings are saved by AutoCAD. You can go back to the previous 10 UCS settings using the Previous option. If TILEMODE is off, the last 10 coordinate systems in Paper space and Model space are saved. This option can be invoked by picking the **Previous UCS** icon from the UCS flyout in the **Standard** toolbar, or by entering **Previous** (or **P**) at the following prompt:

Command: **UCS** ◄─┘
Origin/ZAxis/3point/OBject/View/X/Y/Z/Prev/Restore/Save/Del/?/ < World > : **P** ◄─┘

R (Restore) Option

 With this option of the UCS command you can restore a previously saved UCS. Once a saved UCS is restored, it becomes the current UCS. The viewing direction of the saved UCS is not restored. This option can be invoked by picking the **Restore UCS** icon from the UCS flyout in the **Standard** toolbar, or by entering **Restore** (or **R**) at the following prompt:

Command: **UCS** ◄┘
Origin/ZAxis/3point/OBject/View/X/Y/Z/Prev/Restore/Save/Del/?/ < World > : **R** ◄┘

After this AutoCAD issues the prompt:

?/Name of UCS to restore: *Enter the name of the UCS you want to restore.*

You can list the UCS names by entering **?** at the above prompt. Next AutoCAD prompts:

UCS name(s) to list < * > :

If you want to list all the UCS names give a null response.

S (Save) Option

 With this option you can name and save the current UCS. When you are naming the UCS, the following should be kept in mind:

1. The name can be up to 31 characters long.
2. The name can contain letters, digits, and the special characters $ (dollar), - (hyphen), and _ (underscore).
3. UCS names are converted to uppercase.

To invoke this option pick the **Save UCS** icon from the UCS flyout in the **Standard** toolbar, or enter **Save** (or **S**) at the following prompt:

Command: **UCS** ◄┘
Origin/ZAxis/3point/OBject/View/X/Y/Z/Prev/Restore/Save/Del/?/ < World > : **S** ◄┘

At the next prompt enter a valid name for the UCS. AutoCAD saves it as a UCS.

?/Desired UCS name:

Just as in the case of the Restore option, you can list the UCS names by entering **?** at the above prompt. Next, AutoCAD prompts:

UCS name(s) to list < * > :

If you want to list all the UCS names give a null response.

D (Delete) Option

The D (Delete) option is used to delete the selected UCS from the list of saved coordinate systems. To invoke this option enter **Delete** (or **D**) at the following prompt:

Command: **UCS** ◄┘
Origin/ZAxis/3point/OBject/View/X/Y/Z/Prev/Restore/Save/Del/?/ < World > : **D** ◄┘
UCS name(s) to delete < none > :

The UCS name you enter at the above prompt is deleted. You can delete more than one UCS by separating the UCS names with commas or by using wild cards.

? Option

By invoking this option, you can list the name of the specified UCS. This option gives you the name, origin, and XYZ axes of all of the coordinate systems relative to the existing UCS. If the current UCS has no name, it is listed as *WORLD* or *NO NAME*. The choice between these two names depends on whether the current UCS is the same as the WCS. This option can be invoked by entering ? at the following prompt:

Command: **UCS** ◄┘
Origin/ZAxis/3point/OBject/View/X/Y/Z/Prev/Restore/Save/Del/?/ < World > : **?** ◄┘
UCS name(s) to list < * > : ◄┘

CONTROLLING UCS AND UCS ORIENTATION THROUGH DIALOGUE BOXES

Toolbar:	Standard, UCS, Named UCS
Pull-down:	View, Named UCS...
Screen:	VIEW, DDUCS:

As with many utilities of AutoCAD, the UCS can also be created, altered, named, renamed, listed, and selected with the help of dialogue boxes. The DDUCS (Dynamic Dialogue UCS) command displays the **UCS Control** dialogue box (Figure 20-20). To activate this dialogue box, enter **DDUCS** at the Command: prompt. (Command: **DDUCS** ◄┘)

You can also activate display of the UCS Control dialogue box through the UCS flyout in the **Standard** toolbar (Select Named UCS icon in the UCS flyout), from the pull-down menu (Select View, Named UCS..., Figure 20-19), or from the screen menu (Select VIEW, DDUCS:).

UCS Control Dialogue Box

The list of all the coordinate systems defined (saved) on your system is displayed in the **UCS Names** area of the dialogue box. You can scroll through this list. The first entry in this list is always *WORLD* coordinate system. The next entry is *PREVIOUS* if you have defined any other coordinate systems in the current editing session. Selecting the *PREVIOUS* entry and then picking the **OK** button repeatedly enables you to go backward through the coordinate systems defined in the current editing session. *NO NAME* is the next entry in the list if you have not named the current coordinate system. The current coordinate system is indicated by the

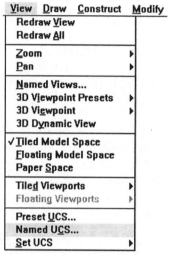

Figure 20-19 Different options concerning UCS in the View pull-down menu

Figure 20-20 UCS Control dialogue box

entry **Current** next to the name of the coordinate system. If you want to make some other coordinate system current, pick the name of that coordinate system in the **UCS Names** area, then pick the **Current** button located just below the UCS Names area. To delete a coordinate system, pick the name of that coordinate system, then pick the **Delete** button. To rename a coordinate system, pick the name of that coordinate system and then enter the desired new name in the **Rename To:** edit box.

Note

All the changes and updating of the UCS information in the drawing is carried out only after you pick the OK button.

If you want to check the current coordinate system's origin and X, Y, and Z axis values, pick the **List...** button. On doing so, the **UCS** sub-dialogue box (Figure 20-21) is displayed containing that information in it.

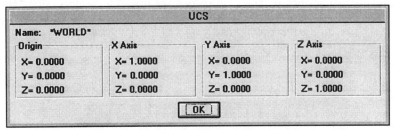

Figure 20-21 UCS sub-dialogue box

SETTING UCS TO PRESET ORIENTATION USING THE DIALOGUE BOX

Toolbar:	Standard, UCS, Preset UCS
Pull-down:	View, Preset UCS...
Screen:	VIEW, DDUCSP:

 You can set the orientation of the UCS with the **UCS Orientation** dialogue box (Figure 20-22). This dialogue box can be invoked from the **Standard** toolbar (Select Preset UCS icon in the UCS flyout), from the pull-down menu (Select View, Preset UCS...), or from the screen menu (Select VIEW, DDucsp:). You can also activate this dialogue box by entering **DDUCSP** at the Command: prompt. Command: **DDUCSP** ◄⎯

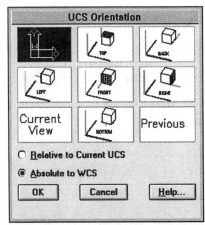

Figure 20-22 UCS Orientation Dialogue box

You can set the UCS to any one of the icon settings in the dialogue box. The icon at the top left of the dialogue box takes you back to the world coordinate system (you may have noticed that this is the WCS icon). Picking the **TOP** icon results in creation of the UCS icon in the top view, also known as the plan view. By picking the **Previous** icon in the dialogue box, the previous UCS is established. If you pick the **Current View** icon, a UCS that is perpendicular to the current view is established. In this dialogue box you are given the choice of establishing a new UCS relative to the current UCS or absolute to the WCS. This choice is offered in the form of two radio buttons: **Relative to Current UCS** and **Absolute to WCS**.

If the WCS is current, the **Absolute to WCS** button is on. In this case the UCS you establish by picking a UCS icon in the dialogue box is based on the WCS. On the other hand, if a UCS is current, the **Relative to Current UCS** button is on and picking an icon from the dialogue box results in creation of a new UCS by rotating the previous UCS by 90 degrees. The axis about which the rotation takes place depends on the icon you pick.

SYSTEM VARIABLES

The coordinate value of the origin of the current UCS is held in the **UCSORG** system variable. The X and Y axes directions of the current UCS are held in **UCSXDIR** and **UCSYDIR** system variables, respectively. The name of the current UCS is held in the **UCSNAME** variable. All the above-mentioned variables are read-only. If the current UCS is identical to the WCS, the **WORLDUCS** system variable is set to 1; otherwise it holds the value 0. The current UCS icon setting can be examined and manipulated with the help of the **UCSICON** system variable. This variable holds the UCS icon setting of the current viewport. If more than one viewport is active, each one can have a different value for the UCSICON variable. If you are in Paper space, the UCSICON variable will contain the setting for the UCS icon of the Paper space. The **UCSFOLLOW** system variable controls the automatic display of a plan view when you switch from one UCS to another. If UCSFOLLOW is set to 1, a plan view is automatically displayed when you switch from one UCS to another.

SELF EVALUATION TEST

Answer the following questions and then compare your answers with the correct answers given at the end of this chapter.

1.   When you get into the AutoCAD environment (i.e., AutoCAD Drawing Editor), by default the _____ is established.

2.   The _____ coordinate system can be moved and rotated to any desired position.

3.   The _____ command controls display of the icon symbol.

4.   The UCS icon is a graphic reminder only of the direction of the UCS origin. (T/F)

5.   The _____ option of the UCSICON command enables (displays) the UCS icon in the current viewport.

6.   With the _____ option of the UCSICON command, changes can be made to the UCS icons in all active viewports.

7.   The ORigin option of the UCSICON command makes AutoCAD display the icon, if enabled, at the lower left corner of the screen, whatever the position of the current UCS origin may be. (T/F)

8.   When using the ORigin option of the UCSICON command, if the current origin is off screen or it is not possible to position the icon at the origin without being clipped at the viewport edges, it is displayed at the lower left corner of the screen. (T/F)

9.   The origin and orientation of a coordinate system can be redefined using the _____ command.

10.   When changing the UCS with the Origin option of the UCS command, the directions of the X, Y, and Z axes can be altered. (T/F)

11.   If you give a null response to the **Point on the positive portion of Z axis:** prompt of the ZAxis option of the UCS command, the Z axis of the new coordinate system will be _____ to the Z axis of the previous coordinate system.

12.   With the OBject option of the UCS command, you can establish a new coordinate system by pointing to any object in an AutoCAD drawing, including a 3D polyline, 3D solid, 3D mesh, viewport object, mtext, xline, ray, leader, ellipse, region, or spline. (T/F)

13.   The View option of the UCS command lets you define a new UCS whose XY plane is parallel to your current viewing direction. (T/F)

14.   If TILEMODE is off, the last 10 coordinate systems in both Paper space and Model space are saved. (T/F)

15.   Once a saved UCS is restored, it becomes the _____ UCS. The viewing direction of the saved UCS is not restored.

REVIEW QUESTIONS

Answer the following questions.

1.   The user coordinate system (UCS) helps you to establish your own coordinate system. (T/F)

2.   To generate the UCS icon to the new location specified in the UCS command, you can use the UCSICON command. (T/F)

3.   The orientation and the origin of the current UCS is graphically represented by the _____.

4.   The + sign on the icon reflects that the UCS icon is placed at the _____ of the current UCS.

5.   Absence of the _____ on the Y axis indicates that the current coordinate system is not WCS.

6.   The _____ option of the UCSICON command disables the UCS icon in the current viewport.

7.   The NOorigin option makes AutoCAD display the UCS icon (if enabled) at origin (0,0,0) of the current coordinate system. (T/F)

8.   Sometimes the user's view direction may be edge-on to the current UCS (or within 1 degree of edge-on). In such cases the UCS icon is replaced by a _____ icon as an indication to the user that the pointing locations are meaningless.

9.   The Origin option of the UCS command lets you define a new UCS by changing the _____ of the current UCS.

10.   Using the _____ option of the UCS command allows you to change the coordinate system by establishing the origin point and a point on the positive Z axis.

11.   The positive X axis direction is also known as the **extrusion direction**. (T/F)

12.   With the _____ option of the UCS command, you can establish a new coordinate system by specifying the new origin point, a point on the positive X axis, and a point on the positive Y axis.

13.   If you have changed the coordinate system with the OBject option of the UCS command, the positive Z axis of the new UCS is in the same direction as the positive Z axis of the object selected. (T/F)

14.   With the _____ option of the UCS command, you can rotate the current the UCS around the Z axis by specifying the angle value at the **Rotation angle about Z axis <0.0>:** prompt.

15.   The _____ option restores the previous UCS.

16.   With the Restore option of the UCS command, you can restore a previously saved UCS. (T/F)

17.   The name of a UCS can be up to 21 characters long. (T/F)

18.   The (Delete) option of the UCS command is used to delete the selected UCS from the list of _____ coordinate systems.

19.   By invoking the _____ option of the UCS command, you can list the name of the specified UCS.

20.   The _____ option of the UCS command gives you the name, origin, and XYZ axes of all coordinate systems relative to the existing UCS.

21.   If you pick the **Current View** icon in the **UCS Orientation** dialogue box, a UCS that is _____ to the current view is established.

22.   In the **UCS Orientation** dialogue box, you are given the choice of establishing a new UCS relative to the current UCS or _____ to the WCS.

23.   The X and Y axes directions of the current UCS are held in the _____ and _____ system variables, respectively.

24.   The name of the current UCS is held in the _____ variable.

25.   If the current UCS is identical to the WCS, the **WORLDUCS** system variable is set to 0; otherwise it holds the value 1. (T/F)

26.   The _____ system variable holds the UCS icon setting of the current viewport.

27.   The _____ system variable controls the automatic display of a plan view when you switch from one UCS to another.

28.   If UCSFOLLOW is set to 0, a plan view is automatically displayed when you switch from one UCS to another. (T/F)

29.   With the _____ option of the UCS command, you can name and save the current UCS.

30.   With the _____ option of the UCS command, you can set the current UCS to be identical to the world coordinate system.

31.   You can set the orientation of the UCS to any one of the icons settings in the **UCS Orientation** dialogue box with the help of the _____ command.

32.   The coordinate value of the origin of the current UCS is held in the _____ system variable.

33.   The _____ dialogue box lists all the coordinate systems.

EXERCISES

Exercises 1 through 4

Draw the given figures using the UCS command and its options to position the Ucsicon so that you can draw the lines on different faces. The dimensions can be determined by counting the number of grid lines. The distance between the isometric grid lines can be assumed to be 0.5 or 1.0 unit. The following drawings do not show the hidden edges. Your drawings should show all lines. You could use 3D Face command to hide the hidden edges, discussed later in the text.

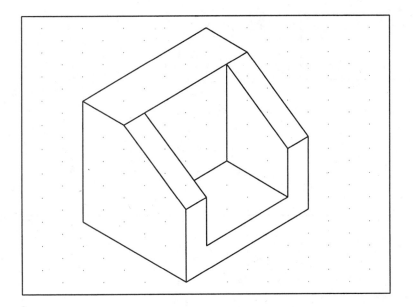

Figure 20-23
Drawing for Exercise 1

Figure 20-24
Drawing for Exercise 2

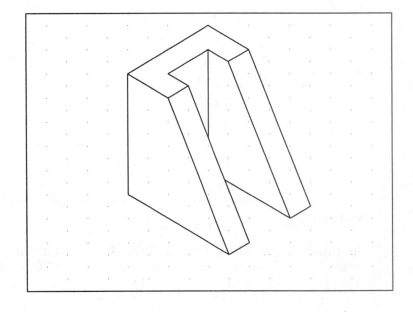

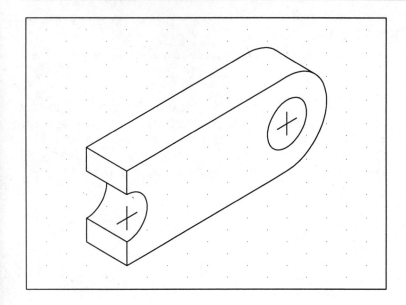

Figure 20-25
Drawing for Exercise 3

Figure 20-26
Drawing for Exercise 4

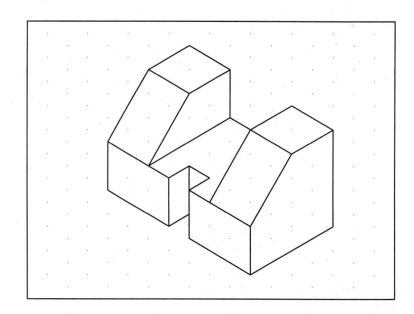

Answers

The following are the correct answers to the questions in the self evaluation test.
1 - world coordinate system, **2** - user, **3** - UCSICON, **4** - F, **5** - ON, **6** - All, **7** - F, **8** - T, **9** - UCS, **10** - F, **11** - parallel, **12** - F, **13** - F, **14** - T, **15** - current

Chapter 21

Drawing Pre-defined 3D Objects
Viewing and Editing 3D Objects
Drawing 3D Surfaces

Learning objectives

After completing this chapter, you will be able to:
- Create pre-defined 3D-surfaced objects: sphere, cone, dome, dish, torus, pyramid, wedge, box, and mesh.
- Set up viewpoints with the VPOINT and PLAN commands.
- Create 3D arrays using the 3DARRAY command.
- Edit 3D objects using the MIRROR3D, ROTATE3D, and ALIGN commands.
- Create 3D surfaces using Rulesurf, Revsurf, Tabsurf, Edgesurf.
- Create 3D surfaces using the 3DMESH, PFACE, and 3DFACE commands.

3D DRAWINGS

Until the preceding chapter, all the drawings you have seen or drawn have been two-dimensional. These drawings were generated in the XY plane. You also viewed these drawings from the Z axis and the picture you see in this manner is also known as the **plan view**. Once you start working with 3D objects, often you will need to view the drawing from different angles. For example, you may require the **3D view**, the **top view**, or the **front view** of the object in space. In AutoCAD it is possible to view an object from any position in the model space. The point from which you view the drawing is known as the **viewpoint**. A viewpoint can be defined for the current viewport with the help of the **VPOINT** command.

DRAWING PRE-DEFINED 3D OBJECTS

In this chapter, you will learn first how to create some pre-defined 3D objects provided by AutoCAD. Later on, you will use these 3D objects to try out various editing operations that can be performed on them. AutoCAD supports a library of 3D objects. To draw these pre-defined objects, you simply specify the values of various parameters pertaining to the selected 3D object. Once you are done entering the information, the object is automatically drawn on the screen. In this manner you can create a number of 3D objects with very little effort. You can create **surfaced wireframe** and **solid primitive** (see Chapter 23, Solid Modeling) types of pre-defined 3D shapes.

Surfaced Wireframes

Toolbar:	Surfaces
Pull-down:	Draw, Surfaces,
	3D Objects...
Screen:	DRAW2, SURFACES,
	object name

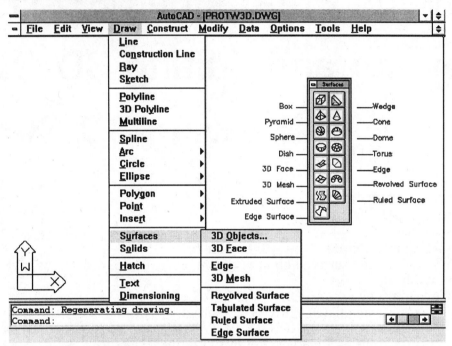

Figure 21-1 Selecting surfaced 3D objects from the Draw pull-down menu and the Surfaces toolbar

Surfaced wireframe models define the edges and the surfaces of a 3D object. In the surfaced wireframes category you can create a box, cone, dome, sphere, torus, dish, wedge, pyramid, or mesh. All these objects are formed as polygon meshes. Once you create surface models on the screen, you will notice that the models resemble wireframes. Only after using the SHADE, HIDE, or RENDER command will these objects appear as surfaced objects. You can create 3D surfaced wireframes from the **Surfaces** toolbar (Figure 21-1), by picking the image tile having the desired shape from the **3D Objects** dialogue box that can be invoked from pull-down menu (select Draw, Surfaces, 3D Objects...,Figure 21-1) or from the screen menu (select DRAW2, SURFACES, object name).

Figure 21-2 3D Objects icon menu

Another way to create a 3D surfaced wireframe object is by entering **3D** at the Command: prompt and then entering the relevant option at the next prompt, or appending **AI_** as a prefix to the name of the 3D object you want to draw. For example, if you want to draw a sphere using this method, enter **AI_Sphere** at the Command: prompt. The **AI** at the start of this command is the abbreviation for the Autodesk Incorporated AutoLISP command definition found in the 3D.LSP file. The specified object will be created as per the specifications user has entered.

Solid Primitives

In the solid primitives category you can create a box, cone, sphere, torus, wedge, or cylinder. Just as with surface models, solid models resemble wireframes when created and only after using the SHADE, HIDE, or RENDER command do these objects appear as solid objects. The solid model can be converted into a surfaced wireframe object by exploding it (solid sphere is an exception since it cannot be exploded). You can create 3D solid primitives by entering the name of the solid at the Command: prompt, from the Solids toolbar, from the pull-down menu (select Draw, Solids), or from the screen menu (select DRAW2, SOLIDS). Construction of solid primitives is discussed in Chapter 23, Solid Modeling.

Constructing a Surfaced Wireframe Sphere

Toolbar:	Surfaces, Sphere
Pull-down:	Draw, Surfaces, 3D
	Objects..., Sphere
Screen:	DRAW2, SURFACES,
	Sphere

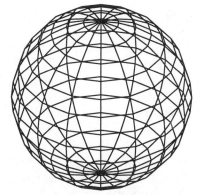

The surfaced wireframe sphere can be created from the **Surfaces** toolbar (select Sphere icon), by picking the sphere shape from the **3D objects** icon menu, which can be invoked from the pull-down menu (select Draw, Surfaces, 3D objects...), or from the screen menu (Select DRAW 2, SURFACES, Sphere:). The central axis of the sphere is parallel to the Z axis, and the latitudinal lines are parallel to the XY plane of the current UCS. You can also append **AI_** as a prefix to sphere and use it as a command, or use the **3D** command and the enter the **Sphere** option at the next prompt. The prompt sequence is as follows:

Figure 21-3 Surfaced wireframe sphere

Command: **3D** ↵
Box/Cone/Dish/DOme/mesh/Pyramid/Sphere/Torus/Wedge: **S** ↵
Center of sphere: *Specify the location of center point.*
Diameter/<radius>: *Specify the diameter/radius of the sphere.*
Number of longitudinal segments <16>: *Specify the number of longitudinal (vertical)*
segments for the sphere.
Number of latitudinal segments <16>: *Specify the number of latitudinal (horizontal)*
segments for the sphere.

Note

Since you cannot see a 3D object properly from plan view (0,0,1), side views, etc., you should change the vpoint (view point) to (1,-1,1) at the end of all the 3D constructions so that you are able to view the objects three dimensionally.

Constructing a Surfaced Wireframe Box

You can create a surfaced wireframe model of a box (Figure 21-4) by using any one of the methods for drawing surfaced wireframe models. The following example illustrates how to draw a box having a length of 3 units, a width of 4 units, a height of 1.50 units, and a 0 degree rotation .

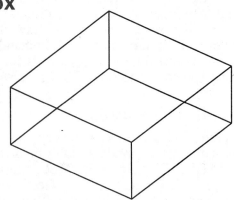

Figure 21-4 Surfaced wireframe box

Command: **3D** ◄⎯⎯

Box/Cone/Dish/DOme/mesh/Pyramid/Sphere/Torus/Wedge: **B** ◄⎯⎯

Corner of box: *Pick the location of the corner of the box.*

Length: **3** ◄⎯⎯

Cube/<Width>: **4** ◄⎯⎯

Height: **1.50** ◄⎯⎯

Rotation angle about Z axis: *Specify the rotation of the box about the Z axis.*

The rotation is carried out about the first corner of the box. The base of the box is parallel to the XY plane of the current UCS. To draw a cube with the length of the sides equal to the length you have specified at the **Length:** prompt, enter C at the **Cube/<Width>:** prompt. For example, to draw a cube with the length of sides equal to 5 units and no rotation about the Z axis, use the following prompt sequence:

Command: **3D** ◄⎯⎯

Box/Cone/Dish/DOme/mesh/Pyramid/Sphere/Torus/Wedge: **B** ◄⎯⎯

Corner of box: *Pick the location of the corner of the box.*

Length: **5** ◄⎯⎯

Cube/<Width>: **C** ◄⎯⎯

Rotation angle about Z axis: **0** ◄⎯⎯

Constructing a Surfaced Wireframe Pyramid

You can create a surfaced wireframe model of a pyramid by using any one of the methods for drawing surfaced wireframe models.

Command: **AI_PYRAMID** ◄⎯⎯

First base point: *Specify the location of the first base point.*

Second base point: *Specify the location of the second base point.*

Third base point: *Specify the location of the third base point.*

Once you have located the three base points on the screen, the next prompt issued is: **Tetrahedron/<Fourth base point>:**. At this prompt you are given the choice of specifying the fourth base point of the pyramid or constructing a tetrahedron. A tetrahedron is defined as a shape that has four sides; all surfaces of the tetrahedron are triangular. On the other hand, a pyramid is defined as a shape that has five sides; four of the five sides are triangular. Both tetrahedrons and pyramids can have an apex or a flattened top. First we will construct a pyramid by responding to the above prompt by specifying the fourth point.

Tetrahedron/<Fourth base point>: *Specify the location of the fourth base point.*

The next prompt issued is:

Ridge/Top/ < Apex point > :

At this prompt you can select any one of the following options:

Pyramid with an Apex -- Apex Point Option

The default option is the Apex point. With this option you can specify the location of the apex of the pyramid. You must enter the XYZ coordinates to specify the location of the apex or use the XYZ filters. If you simply pick a point on the screen, the X and Y coordinates of the apex will assume the X and Y coordinates of the point picked, while the elevation or the Z coordinate will be the same as the Z coordinate of the base points. Hence, the apex of the pyramid will have the same elevation as the base of the pyramid. Only if you are in 3D space (e.g.; your view point is 1,-1,1) can you specify the apex by picking a point on the screen.

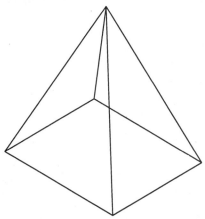

Figure 21-5 Surfaced pyramid with an apex

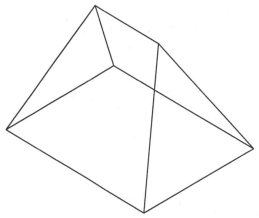

Figure 21-6 Surfaced pyramid with a ridge

Pyramid with a Ridge - Ridge Option

This option can be invoked by entering R at the **Ridge/Top/ < Apex point > :** prompt. When you enter this option, the most recently drawn line of the is base highlighted. This indicates that the first point on the ridge will be perpendicular to the highlighted line. The next prompts displayed are:

First ridge point: *Specify a point inside the highlighted line.*
Second ridge point: *Specify a point inside the second highlighted line.*

Pyramid with a Top -- Top Option

You can invoke this option by entering **T** at the **Ridge/Top/ < Apex point > :** prompt. When you invoke this option, a rubber band line is attached to the first corner of the base. The rubberband line stretches from the corner point to the cross-hairs. This allows you to pick the first top point with respect to the first corner, second top point with respect to the second corner, third top point with respect to the third corner, and fourth top point with respect to the fourth corner. You should use filters to locate the points. If you specify the same location (coordinates) for all four top points, the result is a regular pyramid with its apex at the location where all the four top points are located.

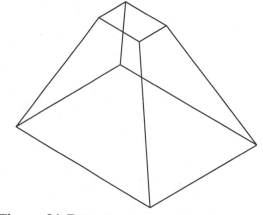

Figure 21-7 Surfaced pyramid with a top

First top point: *Specify the location of the first top point.*
Second top point: *Specify the location of the second top point.*
Third top point: *Specify the location of the third top point.*
Fourth top point: *Specify the location of the fourth top point.*

Tetrahedron

In the previous discussion, we defined tetrahedron. Now, you will learn how to use the Tetrahedron option to draw a tetrahedron. You are going to construct two types of tetrahedrons:. The first has four triangular sides and an apex, second has a flat top. You will first draw the tetrahedron with an apex and then a flat-topped tetrahedron.

Tetrahedron with an Apex -- Apex Option

As mentioned before, with this option you can draw a tetrahedron that has four triangular sides and an apex. The following is the prompt sequence to draw a tetrahedron with an apex:

Command: **AI_PYRAMID** ←⏎
First base point: *Specify the location of the first base point.*
Second base point: *Specify the location of the second base point.*
Third base point: *Specify the location of the third base point.*
Tetrahedron/<Fourth base point>: **T** ←⏎
Top/<Apex point>: *Specify the apex point.*

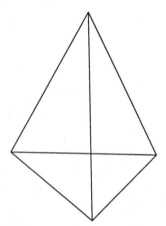

Figure 21-8 Tetrahedron with an apex

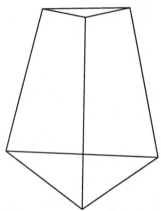

Figure 21-9 Tetrahedron with a top

Flat-Topped Tetrahedron -- Top Option

With this option you can draw a tetrahedron that has a flat top. This option can be invoked by entering T at the **Tetrahedron/<Fourth base point>:** prompt. The next prompts displayed are:

Top/<Apex point>: **T** ←⏎
First top point: *Specify the location of the first top point.*
Second top point: *Specify the location of the second top point.*
Third top point: *Specify the location of the third top point.*

Note

Specify the apex point and all the top points with the XYZ filters or enter the exact coordinate values.

Constructing a Surfaced Wireframe Cone

Toolbar:	Surfaces, Cone
Pull-down:	Draw, Surfaces, 3D Objects..., Cone
Screen:	DRAW2, SURFACES, Cone

You can create a surfaced wireframe model of a cone by using any one of the methods for creating surfaced wireframe models. If you use the **3D** command, the prompt sequence will be:

Command: **3D** ◄─┘
Box/Cone/Dish/DOme/mesh/Pyramid/Sphere/Torus/Wedge: **CONE** ◄─┘

Figure 21-10 Surfaced pointed cone

You can draw a truncated cone or a pointed cone.

Pointed Cone
Three parameters are required to draw a pointed cone.
1. Center point of the base of the cone.
2. Diameter/radius of the base of the cone.
3. Height of the cone.

The prompt sequence for drawing a pointed cone is:

Command: **AI_CONE** ◄─┘
Base center point: *Specify the center of base.*
Diameter/<radius> of base: *Specify the radius of the base.*

The next prompt asks you for the diameter/radius of the top. The default is zero (0) which results in a pointed cone.

Diameter/<radius> of top <0>: *Give a null response.*
Height: *Specify the height of the cone.*
Number of segments <16>: *Specify the number of segments for the cone.*

Truncated Cone

A truncated cone is a cone whose top side (pointed side) has been truncated. To draw a truncated cone you require four parameters.
1. Center point of the base of the cone.
2. Diameter/radius of the base of the cone.
3. Diameter/radius of the top of the cone.
4. Height of the cone.

The prompt sequence for drawing a truncated cone is:

Figure 21-11 Surfaced truncated cone

Command: **AI_CONE** ◄─┘
Base center point: *Specify the center of base.*
Diameter/<radius> of base: *Specify the radius of the base.*
Diameter/<radius> of top <0>: *Specify the radius of the top.*
Height: *Specify the height of the cone.*

Number of segments <16>: *Specify the number of segments for the cone.*

Constructing a Surfaced Wireframe Torus

 A torus is like a thick hollow ring. You can create a surfaced wireframe model of a torus. You can create a surfaced wireframe model of a torus by using any one of the methods for drawing surfaced wireframe models.

Command: **3D** ←⏎
Box/Cone/Dish/DOme/mesh/Pyramid/Sphere/Torus/Wedge: **TORUS** ←⏎
Box/Cone/Dish/DOme/mesh/Pyramid/Sphere/Torus/Wedge: **T** ←⏎
Center of torus: *Specify the center of the torus.*
Diameter/<radius> of torus: *Specify the diameter of torus.*
Diameter/<radius> of tube: *Specify the diameter of tube.*
Segment around tube circumference <16>: *Specify the number of segments for the cone.*
Segment around torus circumference <16>: *Specify the number of segments for the torus.*

The XY plane of the current UCS is parallel to the torus. If the center point of the torus has zero Z coordinate value (the center point of the torus lies in the present construction plane), then the XY plane bisects it.

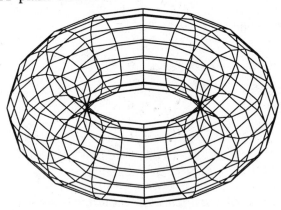

Figure 21-12 Surfaced torus

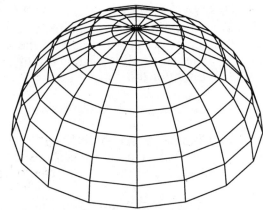

Figure 21-13 Surfaced dome

Constructing a Surfaced Wireframe Dome

 A dome is a hemisphere with the convex surface facing up (toward the top). You can create a surfaced wireframe model of a dome by using any one of the methods for drawing surfaced wireframe models.

Command: **3D** ←⏎
Box/Cone/Dish/DOme/mesh/Pyramid/Sphere/Torus/Wedge: **DO** ←⏎
Center of dome: *Specify the location of the center of the dome.*
Diameter/<radius>: *Specify the diameter of the dome.*
Number of longitudinal segments <16>: *Specify the number of longitudinal (vertical) segments for the dome.*
Number of latitudinal segments <8>: *Specify the number of latitudinal (horizontal) segments for the dome.*

Constructing a Surfaced Wireframe Dish

 A dish is a hemisphere with the convex surface facing toward the bottom. Just as in the case of the dome, you can use any one of the methods described previously for drawing surfaced wireframe models to construct a dish.

Command: **3D** ◄┘
Box/Cone/Dish/DOme/mesh/Pyramid/Sphere/Torus/Wedge: **D** ◄┘
Center of dish: *Specify the location of the center of the dish.*
Diameter/ <radius>: *Specify the diameter of the dish.*
Number of longitudinal segments <16>: *Specify the number of longitudinal (vertical)*
segments for the dish.
Number of latitudinal segments <8>: *Specify the number of latitudinal (horizontal) segments*
for the dish.

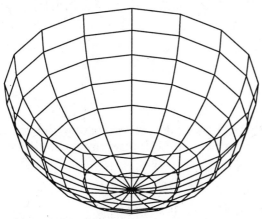

Figure 21-14 Surfaced dish

Figure 21-15 Surfaced wedge

Constructing a Surfaced Wireframe Wedge

You can draw a surfaced wireframe model of a right-angled wedge by using any one of the methods for drawing surfaced wireframe models. For example, you can initiate creation of a 3D surfaced wireframe model of a wedge by entering the **3D** command at the **Command:** prompt and then entering **Wedge** at the next prompt. In the following example you will draw a surfaced wireframe model of a wedge using the 3D command. Let the length of the wedge be 5 units, width 3 units, height 1 units, and rotation of 0 degree.

Command: **3D** ◄┘
Box/Cone/Dish/DOme/mesh/Pyramid/Sphere/Torus/Wedge: **W** ◄┘
Corner of wedge: *Specify corner point of the wedge.*
Length: **5** ◄┘
Width: **3** ◄┘
Height: **1** ◄┘
Rotation angle about Z axis: *Specify rotation around Z axis.*

The sloped side of the wedge is always opposite the first corner specified at the **Corner of wedge:** prompt. The base of the wedge is always parallel to the construction plane (XY plane) of the current UCS. The height is measured parallel to the Z axis.

Constructing Surfaced Wireframe Mesh

You can create a surfaced wireframe model of a mesh using any one of the methods used for drawing surfaced wireframe objects. The type of mesh obtained is also known as **planar** mesh, because the mesh is generated in a single plane. The prompt sequence is:

Command: **AI_MESH** ←┘
Initializing ... 3D Objects loaded

In the next four prompts, AutoCAD prompts you to specify the four corner points of the mesh.

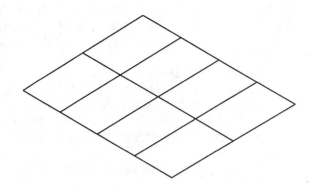

Figure 21-16 Surfaced mesh

First corner: *Specify the first corner point.*
Second corner: *Specify the second corner point.*
Third corner: *Specify the third corner point.*
Fourth corner: *Specify the fourth corner point.*

Once you have specified the four corner points, AutoCAD prompts you to specify the number of rows (M) and number of columns (N). The number of vertices in both directions should be in the range of 2 to 256; that is, M and N should lie in the range of 2 to 256.

Mesh M size: *Enter the number of rows in the mesh.*
Mesh N size: *Enter the number of columns in the mesh.*

VIEWING OBJECTS IN 3D SPACE

AutoCAD has provided the VPOINT and DVIEW commands to view the objects in 3D space. (The DVIEW command is discussed in Chapter 22)

VPOINT Command

Pull-down:	View, 3D Viewpoint, Vector
Screen:	VIEW, Vpoint:

As mentioned earlier, **the VPOINT** Command lets you define a viewpoint. Once you set a viewpoint, all the objects in the current viewport are regenerated and the objects are displayed as if you were viewing them from the newly defined viewpoint. This command can be accessed from the pull-down menu (select View, 3D Viewpoint, Vector, Figure 21-7) or from screen menu (select VIEW, Vpoint:). You can also enter **VPOINT** at the Command: prompt.

Command: **VPOINT** ←┘
Rotate/ <View point> <current>:

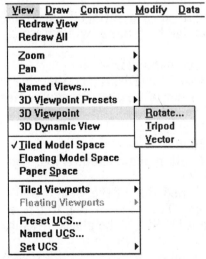

Figure 21-17 Selecting the VPOINT command from View pull-down menu

The prevailing viewpoint is the default. At this prompt you are supposed to enter the coordinates of the viewpoint. At the default viewpoint (0,0,1), you are looking at the drawing from a point on the positive Z axis at a height of 1 unit from the origin. You can enter X, Y, and Z coordinate values of the viewpoint of your choice at the **Rotate/<View point> <current>:** prompt. The following are some of the viewpoint settings and the sort of views obtained. This table will give you a fair idea of the viewing directions and viewpoints in 3D space.

Vpoint Value	View Displayed
0,0,1	Top view
0,0,-1	Bottom view
0,-1,0	Front view
0,1,0	Rear view
1,0,0	Right side view
-1,0,0	Left side view
1,-1,-1	Bottom, Front, Right side view
-1,-1,-1	Bottom, Front, Left side view
1,1,-1	Bottom, Rear, Right side view
-1,1,-1	Bottom, Rear, Left side view
1,-1,1	Top, Front, Right side view
-1,-1,1	Top, Front, Left side view
1,1,1	Top, Rear, Right side view
-1,1,1	Top, Rear, Left side view

Note

The VPOINT and DVIEW commands cannot be used in Paper space. You can use these commands in the Model space or in the Paper space Model space.

Using Axes Tripod and Compass to Set Viewpoint

Pull-down: View, 3D Viewpoint, Tripod
Screen: VIEW, Vpoint:, Axes

If you are not well-acquainted with visualizing objects in 3D space and find it difficult to imagine points in 3D space, give a null response at the **Rotate/<View point> <current>:** prompt instead of entering coordinates. This makes AutoCAD display a compass and axis tripod on the screen. You can also have the compass and axis tripod displayed on the screen through the pull-down menu (select View, 3D Viewpoint, Tripod) or from the screen menu (select VIEW, Vpoint:, Axes). Now you can

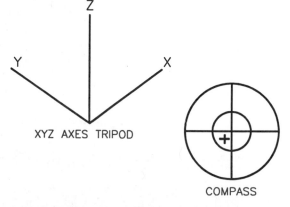

Figure 21-18 Axes tripod and compass

specify the viewpoint by moving the pointing device. You will notice that as you move the pointing device, the XYZ axes tripod also moves and so does the small cross-hair in the compass. You can now pick the viewpoint with respect to the position of the XYZ axes in the tripod. The compass displayed is a 2D symbol of a globe. The center point of the circle is the north pole (0,0,1) and by placing the cross-hairs on the north pole you can see the top view of the drawing on screen. The inner circle in the globe depicts the equator (n,n,0). The outer circle represents the south pole (0,0,-1). By picking cross-hair locations on the screen in this manner, you can get any viewpoint.

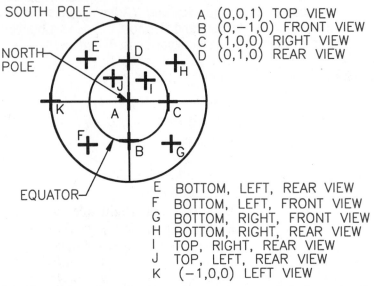

A (0,0,1) TOP VIEW
B (0,-1,0) FRONT VIEW
C (1,0,0) RIGHT VIEW
D (0,1,0) REAR VIEW

E BOTTOM, LEFT, REAR VIEW
F BOTTOM, LEFT, FRONT VIEW
G BOTTOM, RIGHT, FRONT VIEW
H BOTTOM, RIGHT, REAR VIEW
I TOP, RIGHT, REAR VIEW
J TOP, LEFT, REAR VIEW
K (-1,0,0) LEFT VIEW

Figure 21-19 Various locations on the compass and their respective views

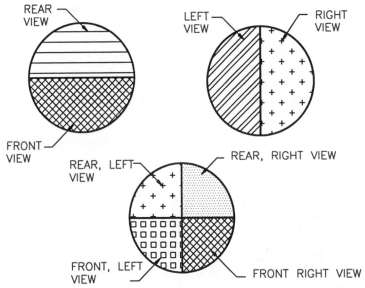

Figure 21-20 Various sections of the compass

Using the Rotate Option to Set the Viewpoint

Pull-down:	View, 3D Viewpoint, Rotate...
Screen:	VIEW, Vpoint:, Rotate

You can use the Rotate option of the VPOINT command to change the viewpoint. This option can also be invoked from the pull-down menu (select View, 3D Viewpoint, Rotate...), or from the screen menu (select VIEW, Vpoint:, Rotate). With the Rotate option you can set a new viewpoint by specifying values for two angles. The first angle you specify establishes the rotation (clockwise or counterclockwise) in the XY plane from the X axis. By default the X axis is drawn at a 0-degree angle. The second angle lets you specify the angle at which the XY plane is (up or down). On selecting the Rotate option, you are provided with the following prompts:

>Enter angle in X-Y plane from X axis <current>:
>Enter angle from X-Y plane <current>:

For example, if you specify an angle value of 0 degrees for the angle in the XY plane from the X axis, and 90 degrees for the angle from the XY plane, the resulting viewpoint will be located along the Z axis and you will get the Top view of the object.

Using the Viewpoint Presets Dialogue Box to Set the Viewpoint

Pull-down:	View, 3D Viewpoint, Rotate...
Screen:	Select VIEW, Vpoint:, DDvpoint

The viewpoint can also be changed with the **Viewpoint Presets** dialogue box. You can invoke this dialogue box from the pull-down menu (select View, 3D Viewpoint, Rotate...) or from the screen menu (select VIEW, Vpoint:, DDvpoint). You can also invoke this dialogue box by entering **DDVPOINT** at the Command: prompt. In this dialogue box you can specify an angle from the X axis and an angle from the XY plane and, hence, set a viewpoint. Both angles can be specified by picking the viewing angles from the image tiles, or by entering the respective angle values in the edit boxes just below the image tiles. The figure on the left side of the dialogue box is the plan view and the figure on the right side is called the elevation view. If you pick a point inside the circle in the plan view, you can pick an angle of the desired value. If you pick in between the radial lines, angles in increments of 45 degrees (starting from 0 degrees) can be specified. Similarly, in the elevation view, by picking points on the inside of the smaller arc, you can specify an angle. The angle you specify is indicated by the white arm and the current viewing plane is indicated by the red arm. Pick the Set to Plan View button to display the plan as viewed from the selected coordinate system. Since it is not possible to specify angles accurately by picking in image tiles, you must enter an angle value in the X Axis: edit box and the XY Plane: edit box. You are also given the choice of specifying the viewpoint relative to the current UCS or the WCS. You can specify your choice by picking the Absolute to WCS button or the Relative to UCS button located at the top of the dialogue box.

Once you have specified both angles, pick the OK button to clear the dialogue box and change the viewpoint according to the specifications you have provided in the **Viewpoint Presets** dialogue box (Figure 21-21). You can display plan view of the object on the screen by picking the Plan: option in the VIEW screen menu. This will be covered in the PLAN command later in this chapter. Figure 21-22 shows you the pictorial effect of various viewpoints. In the following example, setting the viewpoint has been explained by entering the viewpoint coordinates at the command line as well as by specifying the viewpoint with the help of Viewpoint Presets dialogue box. Figure 21-22(a) is the 3D view of the object. This view can be displayed by changing the viewpoint to (1,-1,1). You view the object from a point that makes equal angles with X, Y, and Z axes. The **VPOINT** command can be used to change the viewpoint.

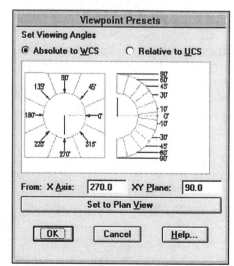

Figure 21-21 Viewpoint Presets dialogue box

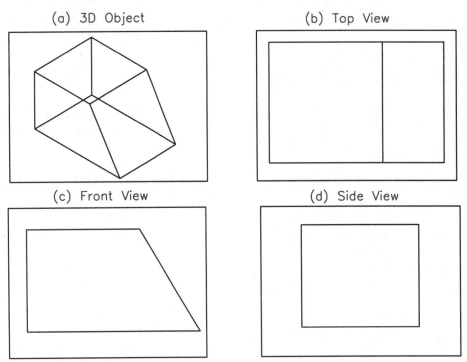

Figure 21-22 Different views of a 3D object

In this case the prompt sequence is:

    Command: **VPOINT** ↵
    Rotate/<View point> <current>: **1,-1,1** ↵

You can also change the viewpoint using the Viewpoint Presets dialogue box. To get the 3D view, you need to rotate the viewpoint 315 degrees from the X axis and 45 degrees from the XY plane. Figure 21-22(b) is the top view of the object. This view can be displayed by changing the viewpoint to (0,0,1). You view the object from a point along the positive Z axis (the line of sight is aligned with the positive Z axis). The VPOINT command can be used to change the viewpoint. In this case the prompt sequence is:

    Command: **VPOINT** ↵
    Rotate/<View point> <current>: **0,0,1** ↵

If you want to change the viewpoint using the Viewpoint Presets dialogue box, rotate the viewpoint 0 degrees from the X axis and 90 degrees from the XY plane. Figure 21-22(c) is the front view of the object. This view can be displayed by changing the viewpoint to (0,-1,0). We view the object from a point along the negative Y axis (the line of sight is aligned with the negative Y axis). The VPOINT command can be used to change the viewpoint. In this case the prompt sequence is:

    Command: **VPOINT** ↵
    Rotate/<View point> <current>: **0,-1,0** ↵

If you want to perform this operation through the Viewpoint Presets dialogue box, rotate the view point 270 degrees from the X axis and 0 degrees from the XY plane. Figure 21-22(d) is the side view of the object. This view can be displayed by changing the viewpoint to (1,0,0). In other words you view the object from a point along the positive X axis (the line of sight is aligned with the positive X axis). The VPOINT command can be used to change the viewpoint. In this case the prompt sequence is:

    Command: **VPOINT** ↵

Rotate/ < View point > < current > : **1,0,0,** ◄─┘

To accomplish this task through the Viewpoint Presets dialogue box, rotate the viewpoint 0 degrees from the X axis and 0 degrees from the XY plane.

Changing the Viewpoint Using Pre-defined Viewpoints

Toolbar:	View
Pull-down:	View, 3D Viewpoint
	Presets
Screen:	VIEW, Vpoint:

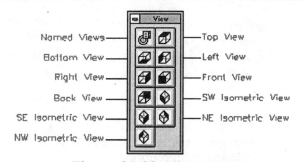

Figure 21-23 View toolbar

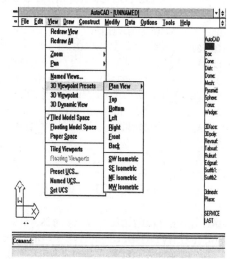

Figure 21-24 3D Viewpoint Presets options of the View pull-down menu

You can also change the viewpoint by picking one of the ten options: Iso SW, Iso SE, Iso NE, Iso NW, Top, Bottom, Left, Right, Front, Back. These options can be selected from the **View** toolbar (Figure 21-23), from the pull-down menu (select View, 3D Viewpoint Presets, Figure 21-24), or from the screen menu (select VIEW, Vpoint:). The effect on the viewpoint is explained as follows:

Viewpoint Option	Corresponding Viewpoint
Top,	**(0,0,1)**
Bottom	**(0,0,-1)**
Left	**(-1,0,0)**
Right	**(1,0,0)**
Front	**(0,-1,0)**
Back	**(0,1,0)**
Iso SW	**(-1,-1,1)**
Iso SE	**(1,-1,1)**
Iso NE	**(1,1,1)**
Iso NW	**(-1,1,1)**

CREATING PLAN VIEWS (PLAN COMMAND)

Pull-down:	View, 3D Viewpoint
	Presets, Plan view
Screen:	VIEW, Plan:

The **PLAN** command can be used to generate the plan view of an object. The viewpoint used to obtain the plan view is always **(0,0,1)** relative to the current UCS, the WCS, or a previously saved UCS. In other words, a plan view is defined as the view obtained when you observe the object along the Z axis. Remember that the plan view is not necessarily the view obtained by looking at the object from the top side. If you are using the WCS, the Z axis lies along the height of the object, hence the plan view is obtained by looking at the object from the top side. If you want the plan view relative to the current UCS, the plan view depends totally on the direction of the Z axis. Since you can change the orientation of the X, Y, and Z axes with the UCS command, you can have a different plan view for the same object depending on the orientation of the X, Y, and Z axes. The PLAN command can be invoked from the pull-down menu (select View, 3D Viewpoint Presets, Plan view, Figure 21-25), from the screen menu (select VIEW, Plan:), or by entering **PLAN** at the Command: prompt:

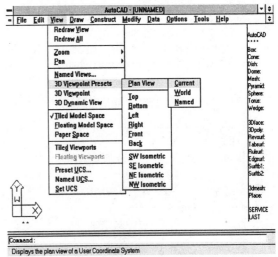

Figure 21-25 Selecting the Plan view option in View pull-down menu

    Command: **PLAN** ←┘
    <Current UCS>/Ucs/World:

If you have multiple viewports, the PLAN command generates the plan view of the current viewport only. If perspective is on, the use of PLAN command turns it off. Clipping also is turned off. The prompt sequence for the PLAN command has following three options:

Current UCS

This is the default option. If you invoke this option, the plan view relative to the current UCS will be generated. The display is regenerated to fit the drawing extents in the current viewport.

UCS

With the help of this option you can generate the plan view relative to a previously defined UCS. You are prompted for the name of the UCS. You can list the names of all the saved coordinate systems by entering **?** as the response to the prompt.

World

This option generates the plan view relative to the WCS. The display is regenerated to fit the drawing extents on the screen.

CREATING SURFACES

AutoCAD offers a wide range of commands to create 3D surfaces. The following is a description of the commands that can be used to create different types of surfaces.

RULESURF Command

Toolbar:	Surfaces, Ruled Surface
Pull-down:	Draw, Surfaces, Ruled Surface
Screen:	DRAW2, SURFACES, Rulesurf:

The **RULESURF** command can be used to generate a polygon mesh between two objects such as lines, arcs, circles, 2D polylines, 3D polylines, splines, ellipses, or elliptical arcs. The two specified objects act as the edges of the rule's surface. The only condition for this command to work is that if one of the two objects is open (such as a line/arc), the other object should also be open, or if one of the two objects is closed (such as a circle/polygon), the other object should also be closed. The exception to this rule is the point entity, which can be used as a closed object as well as an open object. Both entities cannot be points. RULESURF stands for ruled surface, which means that the surface between two objects is divided into sections. This command can be invoked from the **Surfaces** toolbar (select Ruled Surface icon), from the pull-down menu (select Draw, Surfaces, Ruled Surface, Figure 21-26), or from the screen menu (select DRAW2, SURFACES, Rulesurf:). You can also invoke this command by entering **RULESURF** at the Command: prompt.

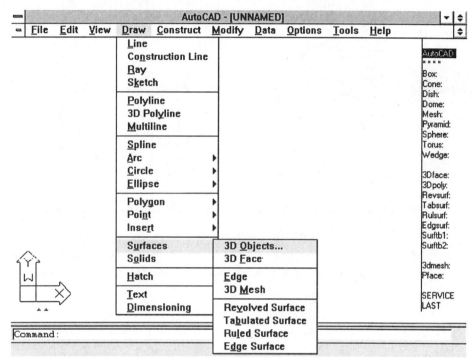

Figure 21-26 Selecting Surface options from the Draw pull-down menu

Command: **RULESURF** ◄──┘

The next two prompts ask you to select the first and second object respectively. The only thing you have to be careful about is that you select both entities on the same side i.e. if you picked the first entity on the left side, the second entity must also be picked on the left side, or you will get a bow-tie effect.

Select first defining curve: *Pick the first entity.*
Select second defining curve: *Pick the second entity.*

In the case of closed curves, the location of the point you pick to select the defining curve is irrelevant because the ruled surface in such cases starts at the 0-degree quadrant location and this point depends on the current X axis and the value of the **SNAPANG** system variable. If the selected entities are closed polylines, the ruled surface starts at the last vertex and progresses backward. This command is frequently used to generate flat surfaces of different shapes, surfacing holes, curves on the exterior of an object, curves on the interior of an object, etc. The mesh created by the **RULESURF** command is defined in terms of **2 x N** (2 because RULESURF generates a polygon mesh between two objects). N stands for the mesh density. N is variable and you can change it to your requirement. The value of N is controlled by the **SURFTAB1** system variable. The value of N is equal to SURFTAB1 if both the defining curves are closed, or one of them is closed and the other is a point. If both defining curves are open, the value of N is equal to SURFTAB1+1. The default setting of SURFTAB1 is 6. You can change the value of N through SURFTAB1 in the following manner:

Command: **SURFTAB1** ◄─┘
New value for SURFTAB1 <6>: *Specify the new value for N.*

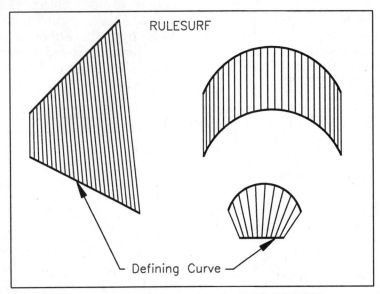

Figure 21-27 Surface created with the RULESURF command.

You can also access the **SURFTAB1** variable through the screen menu (Select DRAW 2, SURFACES, Surftb1:). Half of the vertices (2 X N) of the mesh are placed at equal spaces along one of the defining curves and the rest are placed along the other defining curve.

TABSURF Command

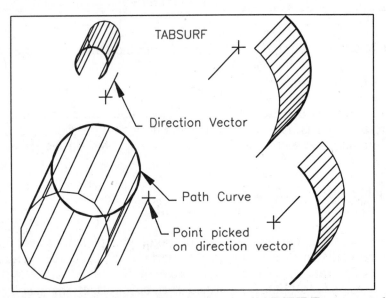

Figure 21-28 Surface created with the TABSURF command

The **TABSURF** command can be used to generate a surface extrusion (tabulated surface) from an object. There is a lot of similarity between the working of TABSURF command and the RULESURF command. The difference lies in the fact that only one object is needed in the TABSURF, while you require two objects in the RULESURF. This object is also known as **path curve**. The path curve can be a line, arc, ellipse, elliptical arc, circle, 2D polyline, or 3D polyline. The direction and the length of extrusion are governed by the length and direction of a second line or a polyline, known as the **direction vector**. The end point of the direction vector nearest the point you pick is found by AutoCAD and the direction of the extrusion lines is set toward the opposite end of the vector line. The SURFTAB1 variable governs the number of intervals (tabulated surfaces) along the path curve. If the path curve is a line, arc, circle, spline-fit polyline, or ellipse, the path curve is divided into intervals equal to the value of SURFTAB1 by the tabulation lines. If the path curve is a polyline (not spline-fit), the tabulation lines are generated at the ends of the polyline segments and if there are any arc segments, each segment is divided into intervals equal to the value of SURFTAB1 by the tabulation lines. This command can be invoked from the **Surfaces** toolbar (select Extended Surface icon), from the pull-down menu (select Draw, Surfaces, Extruded Surface), from the screen menu (select DRAW2, SURFACES, Tabsurf:), or by entering **TABSURF** at the Command: prompt.

> Command: **TABSURF** ◄─┘
> Select path curve: *Pick a point on the path curve.*
> Select direction vector: *Pick a point on the direction vector.*

You can erase the direction vector once you have created the mesh.

REVSURF Command

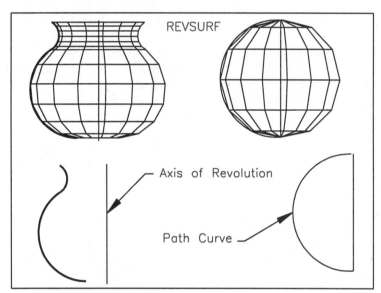

Figure 21-29 Surface created with the REVSURF command

With the REVSURF command, you can create a 3D mesh that trails along the path curve (profile) and rotates about the specified axis. The path curve or the profile can be an arc, line, 2D polyline, 2D polyline, ellipse, elliptical arc, or circle. The axis of revolution can be an open 2D or 3D polyline or a line. The **SURFTAB1** and **SURFTAB2** system variables control the size (M X N) of the mesh. The value of the SURFTAB1 variable controls the number of faces that will be placed in the direction of rotation around the axis (M edges). SURFTAB1 can assume a value in the range of 3 to 1024. The value of the SURFTAB2 variable determines the number of equal segments that will divide the path curve (N edges). The default value for the SURFTAB1 and SURFTAB2 variables is 6. If the path curve is a line, arc, circle, and spline-fit polyline, the path curve is divided into intervals equal to the value of SURFTAB2 by the tabulation lines. If the path curve is a polyline (not spline-fit), the tabulation lines are generated at the ends of the polyline segments and if there are any arc segments, each segment is divided into intervals equal to the value of SURFTAB2 by the tabulation lines. This command can be invoked from the **Surfaces** toolbar (select Revolved Surface icon), from the pull-down menu (select Draw, Surfaces, Revolved Surface), from the screen menu (select DRAW2, SURFACES, Revsurf:), or by entering **REVSURF** at the Command: prompt.

Command: **REVSURF** ◂─┘
Select path curve: *Pick a point on the path curve.*
Select axis of revolution: *Pick a point on the axis of revolution line.*

Once you have selected the path curve and the axis of revolution, AutoCAD prompts you to specify the offset angle from which the surface revolution begins.

Start angle <0>: *Specify the start angle.*

In the next prompt you can choose to rotate parts of object rotated about the axis line or generate the entire 360-degree surface.

Included angle (+ =ccw,- =cw) <Full circle): *Specify the included angle.*

EDGESURF Command

With the EDGESURF command you can create a 3D mesh with four connected sides as the edges (boundaries). Basically this mesh is a matrix of 3D faces. The number of rows and columns is governed by the SURFTAB1 and SURFTAB2 system variables. The four edges can be formed of lines, arcs, polyarcs, polylines, splines, and elliptical arcs or any combination of these objects. These edges must form a closed loop and have mutually shared end points. The only condition to create a mesh with the EDGESURF command is that there should be four sides (edges). The edges can be selected in any order. The M direction of the mesh depends on which edge you have specified as the first edge and the mesh progresses from the end point nearest to the selected point to the other end of the edge. The N edges of the of the mesh are formed by the two edges that touch the first edge. This command can be invoked from the **Surfaces** toolbar (select Edge Surface icon), from the pull-down menu (select Draw, Surfaces, Edge Surface), from the screen menu (select DRAW2, SURFACES, Edgesurf:), or by entering **EDGESURF** at the Command: prompt.

Command: **EDGESURF** ◂─┘
Select edge 1: *Pick a point on the first edge of the boundary.*
Select edge 2: *Pick a point on the second edge of the boundary.*
Select edge 3: *Pick a point on the third edge of the boundary.*
Select edge 4: *Pick a point on the fourth edge of the boundary.*

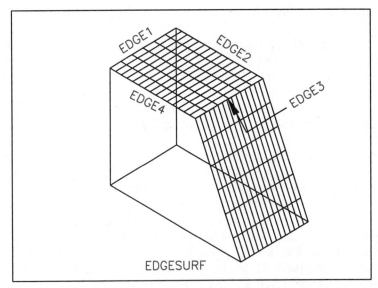

Figure 21-30 Surface created with the EDGESURF Command

3DMESH COMMAND

The 3DMESH command lets you create a 3D polygon mesh. The mesh is defined in terms of rows (M) and columns (N). The mesh is open in both M and N directions. You can use the Close option of the PEDIT command to close the mesh. Wherever a row intersects a column, a vertex is formed. Hence, the total number of vertices in a mesh is the product of M and N. All the vertices of the mesh are specified by their XYZ coordinate location. You can specify the vertices as 2D or 3D points. Depending on the coordinate values of the vertices, the vertices can be at any distance from each other. The definition points of the mesh are its vertices. The number of vertices in both directions should be in the range of 2 to 256. In other words, you cannot have fewer than 2 or more than 256 vertices in each direction. This command can be invoked from the **Surfaces** toolbar (select 3D Mesh icon), from the pull-down menu (select Draw, Surfaces, 3D Mesh), from the screen menu (select DRAW2, SURFACES, 3Dmesh), or by entering **3DMESH** at the Command: prompt.

Example 1

In this example you will create a 4 x 4 three-dimensional mesh. The prompt sequence is:

Command: **3DMESH** ◄─┘
Mesh M size: **6** ◄─┘
Mesh N size: **6** ◄─┘
Vertex (0,0): *Specify the coordinate location of vertex (0,0,0).*
Vertex (0,1): *Specify the coordinate location of vertex (0,1,0).*
Vertex (0,2): *Specify the coordinate location of vertex (0,2,0).*
Vertex (0,3): *Specify the coordinate location of vertex (0,3,0).*
Vertex (0,4): *Specify the coordinate location of vertex (0,4,0).*
Vertex (0,5): *Specify the coordinate location of vertex (0,5,0).*
Vertex (1,0): *Specify the coordinate location of vertex (1,0,0).*
Vertex (1,1): *Specify the coordinate location of vertex (1,1,2).*
Vertex (1,2): *Specify the coordinate location of vertex (1,2,0).*
Vertex (1,3): *Specify the coordinate location of vertex (1,3,0).*
Vertex (1,4): *Specify the coordinate location of vertex (1,4,0).*
Vertex (1,5): *Specify the coordinate location of vertex (1,5,0).*

Enter the remaining vertex points to complete the mesh.

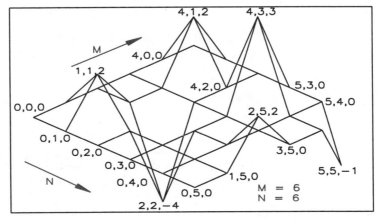

Figure 21-31 Surface created with the 3DMESH command

PFACE COMMAND

Screen:	DRAW2, SURFACES,
	Pface:

The PFACE command is similar to the 3DFACE command in that both allow you to create a mesh of any desired surface shape by specifying the coordinates of the vertices and assigning the vertices to the faces in the mesh. The difference between these two commands is that when you use the 3DFACE command, you do not pick the vertices that join another face twice; with the PFACE command you need to pick all the vertices of a face, even if they are coincident with vertices of another face. In this way you can avoid generating unrelated 3-D faces that have coincident vertices. Also in this command there is no restriction on the number of faces and the number of vertices the mesh can have. This command can be invoked from the screen menu (select DRAW2, SURFACES, Pface:) or by entering **PFACE** at the Command: prompt.

Command: **PFACE** ◄─┘
Vertex 1: *Specify the location of first vertex.*
Vertex 2: *Specify the location of second vertex.*
Vertex 3: *Specify the location of third vertex.*
Vertex 4: *Specify the location of fourth vertex.*
Vertex 5: *Specify the location of fifth vertex.*
Vertex 6: *Specify the location of sixth vertex.*
Vertex 7: *Specify the location of seventh vertex.*
Vertex 8: *Specify the location of eighth vertex.*
Vertex 9: ◄─┘

After defining the locations of all the vertices, press the Enter key and you will assign vertices to the first face.

Face 1, vertex 1: **1** ◄─┘
Face 1, vertex 2: **2** ◄─┘
Face 1, vertex 3: **3** ◄─┘
Face 1, vertex 4: **4** ◄─┘

Once you have assigned the vertices to the first face, give a null response at the next prompt.

Face 1, vertex 5: ◄─┘

You can also change the color and layer of the first face within the PFACE command. For example, if you want to change the color of the first face to red, the prompt sequence is:

Face 1, vertex 1: **COLOR** ◄─┘
New color <BYLAYER>: **RED** ◄─┘

Now the first face will be red.

After assigning the vertices, give a null response at the next prompt. Now AutoCAD provides you with the prompt sequence in which you have to assign vertices to the second face:

Face 2, vertex 1: **1** ◄─┘
Face 2, vertex 2: **4** ◄─┘
Face 2, vertex 3: **5** ◄─┘
Face 2, vertex 4: **8** ◄─┘

Once you have assigned the vertices to the second face, give a null response at the next prompt:

Face 2, vertex 5: ◄─┘
Face 3, vertex 1: ◄─┘

Similarly assign vertices to all the faces.

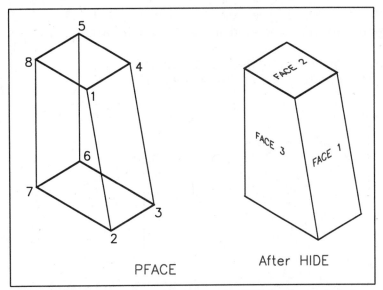

Figure 21-32 Using the PFACE command

If you want to make an edge invisible, specify a negative number for the first vertex of the edge. The display of the invisible edges of 3D solid surfaces is governed by the **SPLFRAME** system variable. If the SPLFRAME variable is set to 0, invisible edges are not displayed. If this variable is set to a number other than 0, all invisible edges are displayed. You can use the HIDE or SHADE command to see the effect of the PFACE command (Figure 21-32).

3DFACE COMMAND

Toolbar:	Surfaces, 3D Face
Pull-down:	Draw, Surfaces, 3D Face
Screen:	DRAW2, SURFACES, 3Dface

3D models often need solid surfaces for shading, hiding, etc. Three- or four-sided surfaces are created with the help of the **3DFACE** command. The prompt sequence of the 3DFACE command is somewhat similar to the SOLID command. The difference between these two commands lies in the fact that the surface created with the SOLID command is parallel to the current UCS, while as with the 3DFACE command the surface can be created anywhere in the 3D space. In this command you can specify different Z coordinates for the different corners of a face, thus forming a plane in the 3D space. This command can be invoked from the **Surfaces** toolbar (select 3D face icon), from the pull-down menu (select Draw, Surfaces, 3D Face), or from the screen menu (select DRAW2, SURFACES, 3Dface). You can also invoke this command by entering **3DFACE** at the Command: prompt.

Command: **3DFACE** ◄─┘
First point: *Select first point of the first face.*
Second point: *Select second point of the first face.*
Third point: *Select third point of the first face.*
Fourth point: *Select fourth point of the first face.*

Once you specify the first, second, third, and fourth points, AutoCAD closes the face from the fourth point to the first point. The next prompt asks you to specify the third point. At this prompt you can give a null response if you do not want to form any more solid surfaces. Once you give a null response, the 3DFACE command is terminated. If you want to create more than one solid surface, the third and fourth points of the previous face will become the first and second points, respectively, of the next face. Hence, once you have the first and the second points you need the third and fourth points to create the solid surface. AutoCAD prompts you for these two points:

Third point: *Select third point of the second face.*
Fourth point: *Select fourth point of the second face.*

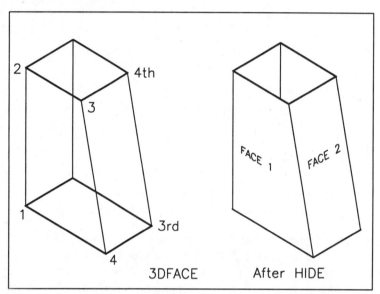

Figure 21-33 Using the 3DFACE command to create faces

If you want to create any more solid surfaces, use the procedure explained above or terminate the 3DFACE command by giving a null response. If you have a surface with only three corners (triangular), and you want to form the solid surface, select the three corners and at the **Third point:** and **Fourth point:** prompts give null responses.

You may want to make some edge invisible. This can be accomplished with the **Invisible** option of the 3DFACE command. Select the Invisible option from the screen menu or enter **I** before picking the first point of the invisible edge. All the edges of a 3D face can be made invisible. As mentioned before, display of the invisible edges of 3D solid surfaces is governed by the **SPLFRAME** system variable. If you set the SPLFRAME variable to 0, all invisible edges are not displayed; if this variable is set to a number other than 0, all invisible edges are displayed. You can control the SPLFRAME variable through the ShowEdge and HideEdge options listed in the screen menu. If you pick the ShowEdge option, all the invisible edges are displayed. When SPLFRAME is set to 1, AutoCAD displays the following message:

Invisible edges will be SHOWN after next Regeneration

HideEdge can be used to hide all edges drawn with the Invisible option. When SPLFRAME is set to 0, AutoCAD displays the following message:

Invisible edges will be HIDDEN after next Regeneration

DRAWING 3D POLYLINES (3DPOLY COMMAND)

Toolbar: Draw, Polyline, 3D Polyline
Pull-down: Draw, 3D Polylines
Screen: DRAW2, SURFACES,
3Dpoly:

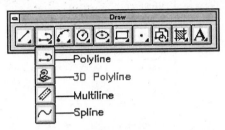

Figure 21-34 3D Polyline icon in the
Draw toolbar

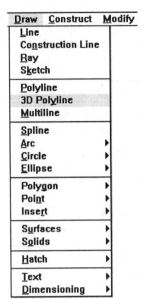

Figure 21-35 Selecting the 3D Polyline
option from the Draw pull-down menu

 You can draw 3D polylines using the **3DPOLY** command. The working of the 3DPOLY and PLINE commands is similar. The exceptions are that a third dimension (Z) is added to the polyline and with the 3DPOLY you can only draw straight line segments without variable widths. This command can be invoked from the Polyline flyout in the **Draw** toolbar (select 3D Polyline icon), from the pull-down menu (select Draw, 3D Polylines), from the screen menu (select DRAW2, SURFACES, 3Dpoly:), or by entering **3DPOLY** at the Command: prompt.

Command: **3DPOLY** ◄─┘
From point: *Specify a point where you want to start the 3D polyline.*
Close/Undo/<Endpoint of line>: *Specify the end point on the screen.*
Close/Undo/<Endpoint of line>: *Press the ENTER key when finished drawing the 3D polyline.*

The 3DPOLY command provides you with the Close and Undo options.

Close Option
This option draws the connecting segment between the start point of the first polyline segment and the end point of the last polyline segment. Hence you need to have at least two lines.

Undo Option
The Undo option reverses the effect of the previous operation. If you use the Undo option, the last polyline segment is erased and a rubberband line is fixed to the previous point while you are still in the 3DPOLY command. Certain editing operations cannot be performed on 3D polylines. These are joining, curve fitting with arc segments, and giving tangent specifications to the 3D polyline. You can use the PEDIT command to edit 3D polylines.

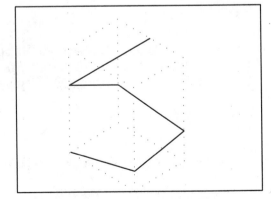

Figure 21-36 Using the 3DPOLY command

CREATING ARRAYS IN 3D SPACE (3DARRAY COMMAND)

Pull-down: Construct, 3D Array
Screen: CONSTRCT, 3Darray

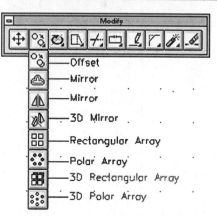

Figure 21-37 3D Array option in the Modify toolbar

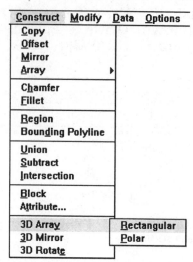

Figure 21-38 Selecting the 3D Array option from the Construct pull-down menu

You can create arrays of objects in 3D space just as you do in 2D space. This can be achieved with the **3DARRAY** command. Basically the 3DARRAY command is similar to the ARRAY command. The difference that exists between two-dimensional space and three-dimensional space array is the existence of the third dimension (Z). The third dimension is nothing but a plane that is parallel to the XY plane along the Z axis. You can invoke the 3DARRAY command from the pull-down menu (select Construct, 3D Array), from the screen menu (select CONSTRCT, 3Darray), or by entering **3DARRAY** at the Command: prompt. There are two types of 3D arrays, **Rectangular** Array and **Polar** Array.

3D Rectangular Array

Toolbar: Modify, Copy Object, 3D
Rectangular Array
Pull-down: Construct, 3D Array,
Rectangular
Screen: CONSTRCT, 3Darray,
Rectang

Construction of a 3D rectangular array can initiated from the Copy Object flyout in the **Modify** toolbar (select 3D Rectangular Array), from the pull-down menu (select Construct, 3D Array, Rectangular), from the screen menu (select CONSTRCT, 3Darray, Rectang), or by entering **3DARRAY** at the Command: prompt. Once you enter the 3DARRAY command, AutoCAD displays the message:

Command: **3DARRAY** ←⏎
Initializing... 3DARRAY loaded.

The next prompt asks you to select the objects you want to form the 3D array.

Select objects: *Select the objects.*

After selecting the objects, give a null response at the next **Select objects:** prompt.

The next prompt displayed is:

Rectangular or Polar array (R/P):

At this prompt specify whether you want to construct a Rectangular array (R) or a Polar array (P). In this example we will construct a Rectangular array.

Rectangular or Polar array (R/P): **R** ◄─┘

The next two prompts ask you to specify the number of rows and the number of columns you want the 3D array to have.

Number of rows (---) <1>: *Specify the number of rows you want in the array.*
Number of columns (|||) <1>: *Specify the number of columns you want in the array.*

The difference between the prompt sequence of the ARRAY command and the 3DARRAY command lies in the next prompt. At this prompt you need to specify the number of levels the array should have.

Number of levels (...) <1>: *Specify the number of levels you want to have in the array.*

The next three prompts ask you to specify the distance between the rows, the distance between the columns, and the distance between the levels.

Distance between rows (---):
Distance between columns (|||):
Distance between levels (...):

By specifying negative values, the array will be drawn along the negative X, Y, and Z axes. If you specify positive values, the array will be drawn along the positive X, Y, and Z axes. At the end, use the VPOINT command to change the view point to (1,-1,1) so that you can view the array from a 3D viewpoint.

Example 2

In this example a 3D array of 3D cones will be created. The specifications of the array is as follows:

Number of rows = 3
Number of columns = 3
Number of levels = 2
Distance between the rows = 1.00
Distance between the columns = 1.50
Distance between the levels = 5.00
Radius of the base of the cone = 0.30
Radius of the top of the cone = 0.0
Height of the cone = 0.80

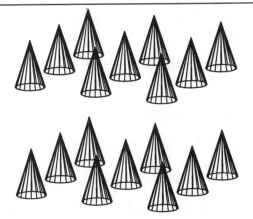

Figure 21-39 Creating a rectangular 3D array

1. First, create a 3D cone and then generate an array. The prompt sequence for drawing a cone of the above specifications is:

Command: **AI_CONE** ◄─┘
Base center point: *Specify the center point.*

Diameter/<radius> of base: **0.30** ◄—⏎
Diameter/<radius> of top <0>: ◄—⏎
Height: **0.80** ◄—⏎
Number of segments <16>: *Specify the number of segments for the cone.*

2. Now that the object has been created, you can draw the 3D array. The prompt sequence is:

Command: **3DARRAY** ◄—⏎
Select objects: *Select the cone.*
Select objects: ◄—⏎
Rectangular or Polar array (R/P): **R** ◄—⏎
Number of rows (---) <current>: **3** ◄—⏎
Number of columns (|||) <1>: **3** ◄—⏎
Number of levels (...) <1>: **2** ◄—⏎
Distance between rows (---): **1.00** ◄—⏎
Distance between columns (|||): **1.50** ◄—⏎
Distance between levels (...): **5.00** ◄—⏎

3. After the completion of the above prompt sequence, the 3D array will be generated. If you are viewing the array from the top, use the VPOINT command to change the viewpoint to (1,-1,1) so that you can get a 3D view of the array.

Creating a 3D Polar Array

Toolbar:	Modify, Copy Object, 3D Polar Array
Pull-down:	Construct, 3D Array, Polar
Screen:	CONSTRCT, 3Darray, Polar

You can use the 3DARRAY command to create a 3D Polar array. The difference between a 2D Polar array and a 3D Polar array is that the 3D Polar array needs a Z axis of rotation. The Z axis of a 3D Polar array can differ from the Z axis of the current UCS. Construction of a 3D polar array can be initiated from the Copy Object flyout in the **Modify** toolbar (select the 3D Polar Array icon), from the pull-down menu (select Construct, 3D Array, Polar), from the screen menu (select CONSTRCT, 3Darray, Polar) or by entering **3DARRAY** at the Command: prompt.

Command: **3DARRAY** ◄—⏎
Initializing... 3DARRAY loaded.
Select objects: *Select the objects.*
Select objects: ◄—⏎

To specify Polar array, enter **P** at the next prompt:

Rectangular or Polar array (R/P): **P** ◄—⏎

The next prompt asks you to specify the number of items (selected objects) you want in the array.

Number of items: *Specify the number of items in the array.*

AutoCAD next prompts you to enter the angle to be filled by the array. If the angle specified is positive, the array is rotated in a counterclockwise direction. If the angle specified is negative, the array is rotated in a clockwise direction.

Angle to fill <360>: *Enter the angle value.*

Rotate objects as they are copied? <Y>: *Specify whether to rotate objects as the array is being formed.*
Center point of array: *Specify the center point of the array.*
Second point on axis of rotation: *Pick a point on the new Z axis.*

Example 3

In this example you will create a 3D polar array composed of 3D spheres. The specifications of the array are as follows:

Radius of the sphere = 0.50
Number of items in the array = 5
Angle to fill = 360 degrees
Objects should be rotated as they are copied.

1. First, draw a sphere of the above specification and then construct the polar array. The prompt sequence to draw a sphere of 0.50 units radius is:

Figure 21-40 Creating polar 3D array

Command: **3D** ◄—┘
Box/Cone/Dish/DOme/mesh/Pyramid/Sphere/Torus/Wedge: **S** ◄—┘
Center of sphere: *Specify the center point.*
Diameter/<radius>: **0.50** ◄—┘
Number of longitudinal segments <16>: *Specify the number of longitudinal (vertical) segments for the sphere.*
Number of latitudinal segments <16>: *Specify the number of latitudinal (horizontal) segments for the sphere.*

2. Now that the sphere has been constructed, construct the polar array. The prompt sequence is:

Command: **3DARRAY** ◄—┘
Initializing... 3DARRAY loaded.
Select objects: *Select the sphere.*
Select objects: ◄—┘
Rectangular or Polar array (R/P): **P** ◄—┘
Number of items: **5** ◄—┘
Angle to fill <360>: ◄—┘
Rotate objects as they are copied? <Y>: ◄—┘
Center point of array: *Specify the center point of the array.*
Second point on axis of rotation: *Pick a point on the new Z axis.*

3. Once the polar array has been formed, change the viewpoint to (1,-1,1) so that you have a 3D view of the array.

MIRRORING 3D OBJECTS (MIRROR3D COMMAND)

Toolbar:	Modify, Copy Object, 3D Mirror
Pull-down:	Construct, 3D Mirror
Screen:	CONSTRCT, Mirro3D:

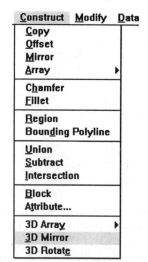

In Chapter 4 we discussed how 2D objects can be mirrored. Now you will learn how to use **MIRROR3D** command to mirror objects in 3D space irrespective of the orientation of the current UCS. This command can be invoked from the Copy Object flyout of the **Modify** toolbar (select the 3D Mirror icon), from the pull-down menu (select Construct, 3D Mirror) or from the screen menu (select CONSTRCT, Mirro3D:). You can also invoke this command by entering **MIRROR3D** Command: prompt.

Figure 21-41 3D Mirror and 3D Rotate options in the Construct pull-down menu

Command: **MIRROR3D** ◄─┘
Select objects: *Select the objects to be mirrored.*
Select objects: *Press Enter key when done selecting.*
Plane by Entity/Last/Zaxis/View/XY/YZ/ZX/<3points>:

The different options in this prompt are discussed as follows:

3points Option
This is the default option. In this option, you specify the mirroring plane with the help of three points. The mirroring plane is the plane that passes through the three points.

1st point on plane: *Specify the first point.*
2nd point on plane: *Specify the second point.*
3rd point on plane: *Specify the third point.*
Delete old objects? <N>: *Enter Y or N to retain or delete old object.*

Plane by Entity Option
In this option you can select an entity and the mirroring plane is aligned with the plane of the selected entity.

Pick a circle, arc or 2D-polyline segment: *Select the object.*
Delete old objects? <N>: *Enter Y or N to retain or delete old object.*

Last Option
Just as in the case of the Last option of the ROTATE3D command, the Last option of the MIRROR3D command uses the last defined mirror plane to mirror objects.

Zaxis Option
This option prompts you to specify two points. The mirroring plane is defined by a point on the plane and a point on the Z axis of that plane.

Point on plane: *Specify a point on the plane.*
Point on Z-axis (normal) of the plane: *Specify a point on the Z axis of the plane.*
Delete old objects? <N>: *Enter Y or N to retain or delete old object.*

View Option
You are prompted for a point. The mirroring plane passes through the specified point and is perpendicular to the view direction.

Point on view plane <0,0,0>: *Specify a point).*
Delete old objects? <N>: *Enter Y or N to retain or delete old object.*

XY Option

You are prompted for a point. The mirroring plane is aligned with the XY plane and passes through the specified point.

Point on XY plane <0,0,0>: *Specify a point.*
Delete old objects? <N>: *Enter Y or N to retain or delete old object.*

YZ Option

You are prompted for a point. The mirroring plane is aligned with the YZ plane and passes through the specified point.

Point on YZ plane <0,0,0>: *Specify a point.*
Delete old objects? <N>: *Enter Y or N to retain or delete old object.*

ZX Option

You are prompted for a point. The mirroring plane is aligned with the ZX plane and passes through the specified point.

Point on ZX plane <0,0,0>: *Specify a point.*
Delete old objects? <N>: *Enter Y or N to retain or delete old object.*

Example 4

In the following example, Figure 21-42(a) shows the original object. You are going to perform mirroring operations on it using the **XY** option, **ZX** option, and **YZ** option.

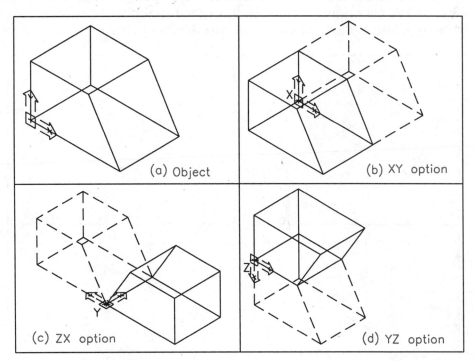

(a) Object

(b) XY option

(c) ZX option

(d) YZ option

Figure 21-42 MIRROR3D options

Figure 21-42(b) shows the object that has been mirrored using the XY option. The original objects have been shown in hidden lines. The prompt sequence is:

Command: **MIRROR3D** ◄─┘
Select objects: *Select the object shown in Figure 21-42(a) to be mirrored.*
Select objects: *Press the ENTER key when done selecting.*
Plane by Entity/Last/Zaxis/View/XY/YZ/ZX/<3points>: **XY** ◄─┘
Point on XY plane <0,0,0>: *Specify X as the point on XY plane.*
Delete old objects? <N>: ◄─┘

Figure 21-42(c) shows the object that has been mirrored by using the ZX option. The original objects have been shown in hidden lines. The prompt sequence is:

Command: **MIRROR3D** ◄─┘
Select objects: *Select the object shown in Figure 21-42(a) to be mirrored.*
Select objects: *Press the ENTER key when done selecting.*
Plane by Entity/Last/Zaxis/View/XY/YZ/ZX/<3points>: **ZX** ◄─┘
Point on ZX plane <0,0,0>: *Specify Y as the point on ZX plane.*
Delete old objects? <N>: ◄─┘

Figure 21-42(d) shows the object that has been mirrored by using the YZ option. The original objects have been shown in hidden lines. The prompt sequence is:

Command: **MIRROR3D** ◄─┘
Select objects: *Select the object shown in Figure 21-42(a) to be mirrored.*
Select objects: *Press the ENTER key when done selecting.*
Plane by Entity/Last/Zaxis/View/XY/YZ/ZX/<3points>: **YZ** ◄─┘
Point on YZ plane <0,0,0>: *Specify Z as the point on YZ plane.*
Delete old objects? <N>: ◄─┘

Example 5

Figure 21-43(a) shows the original object. In this example you will perform mirroring operations using the **Plane by Entity** option, **Zaxis** option, and **3points** option.

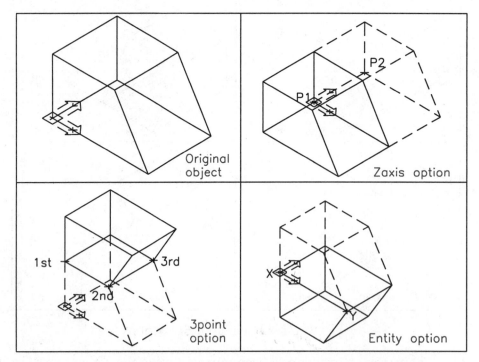

Figure 21-43 MIRROR3D options

Figure 21-43(b) shows the object that has been mirrored by using the Zaxis option. The original objects have been shown in hidden lines. The prompt sequence is:

Command: **MIRROR3D** ◄┘
Select objects: *Select the object shown in Figure 21-43(a) to be mirrored.*
Select objects: *Press the ENTER key when done selecting.*
Plane by Entity/Last/Zaxis/View/XY/YZ/ZX/<3points>: **Zaxis** ◄┘
Point on plane: *Pick point P1*
Point on Z axis (normal) of the plane: *Pick point P2*
Delete old objects? <N>: ◄┘

Figure 21-43(c) shows the object that has been mirrored using the 3points option. The original objects have been shown in hidden lines. The prompt sequence is:

Command: **MIRROR3D** ◄┘
Select objects: *Select the object shown in Figure 21-43(a) to be mirrored.*
Select objects: *Press the ENTER key when done selecting.*
Plane by Entity/Last/Zaxis/View/XY/YZ/ZX/<3points>: ◄┘
1st point on plane: *Pick the point at location 1st.*
2nd point on plane: *Pick the point at location 2nd.*
3rd point on plane: *Pick the point at location 3rd.*
Delete old objects? <N>: ◄┘

Figure 21-43(d) shows the object that has been mirrored by using the Object option. The original objects have been shown in hidden lines. Make sure the mirror line (XY) is a polyline. The prompt sequence is:

Command: **MIRROR3D** ◄┘
Select objects: *Select the object shown in Figure 21-43(a) to be mirrored.*
Select objects: *Press the ENTER key when done selecting.*
Plane by Entity/Last/Zaxis/View/XY/YZ/ZX/<3points>: **Object** ◄┘
Pick circle, arc or 2D-polyline segment: *Pick the line segment between points X and Y.*
Delete old objects? <N>: ◄┘

ROTATING 3D OBJECTS (ROTATE3D COMMAND)

Toolbar:	Modify, Rotate, 3D Rotate
Pull-down:	Construct, 3D Rotate
Screen:	CONSTRCT, Rotat3D:

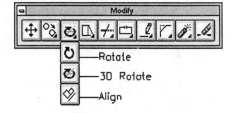

Figure 21-44 3D Rotate icon in the Modify toolbar

 With the help of the **ROTATE3D** command, you can rotate an object in 3D space about any axis irrespective of the orientation of the current UCS. This command can be invoked from the **Modify** toolbar (select 3D Rotate icon from Rotate flyout), from pull-down menu (select Construct, 3D Rotate), from the screen menu (select CONSTRCT, Rotat3D:), or by entering **ROTATE3D** at the Command: prompt.

Command: **ROTATE3D** ◄┘
Select objects: *Specify the objects you want to rotate.*
Select objects: ◄┘

At the next prompt, AutoCAD displays different options for selecting the axis of rotation.

Axis by Entity/Last/View/Xaxis/Yaxis/Zaxis/<2points>:

The different options in this prompt are discussed as follows:

2points Option

This is the default option. In this option you need to specify two points. The axis of rotation is defined by the line between the two points. The direction from the first point to the second point is positive; the direction from the second point to the first point is negative.

Axis by Entity/Last/View/Xaxis/Yaxis/Zaxis/<2points>: ↵
1st point on axis: *Specify the first point.*
2nd point on axis: *Specify the second point.*
<Rotation angle>/Reference: *Specify the angle of rotation.*

Axis by Entity Option

In this case objects like lines, polylines, circles, and arcs are used to define the axis of rotation. The axis of the circle/arc is perpendicular to its plane and passes through its center. The polyline segment (polyline or polyarc) used to specify the axis of rotation is treated as a line or arc and then the axis of rotation is determined.

Pick a line, circle, arc or 2D-polyline segment: *Select an object*
<Rotation angle>/Reference: *Specify the angle of rotation.*

If the selected object is a line, AutoCAD aligns the axis of rotation with the line. If the selected object is a circle, AutoCAD aligns the axis of rotation with the 3D axis of the circle that passes through the center of the circle and is perpendicular to the plane of the circle. If the selected object is an arc, AutoCAD aligns the axis of rotation with the 3D axis of the arc that passes through the center of the arc. If the selected object is a pline, AutoCAD assumes a straight segment as a line and arc segment as an arc.

Last Option

If you invoke this option, the most recently used axis is selected. However, if you have not selected an axis recently, AutoCAD displays the message that no axis has been selected previously and the axis selection prompt is again displayed.

View Option

This option allows you to specify a point in the space and the viewing direction is aligned with this point. The axis of rotation passes through the specified point and is perpendicular to the view direction.

Axis by Entity/Last/View/Xaxis/Yaxis/Zaxis/<2points>: **View** ↵
Point on view direction axis <0,0,0>: *Specify a point.*
<Rotation angle>/Reference: *Specify the angle of rotation.*

Xaxis Option

With this option, the axis of rotation is aligned with the X axis and the specified point.

Axis by Entity/Last/View/Xaxis/Yaxis/Zaxis/<2points>: **Xaxis** ↵
Point on view X axis <0,0,0>: *Specify a point.*
<Rotation angle>/Reference: *Specify the angle of rotation.*

Yaxis Option

With this option, the axis of rotation is aligned with the Y axis and the specified point.

Axis by Entity/Last/View/Xaxis/Yaxis/Zaxis/ <2points> : **Yaxis** ◄─┘
Point on Y axis <0,0,0> : *Specify a point.*
<Rotation angle>/Reference: *Specify the angle of rotation.*

Zaxis Option

With this option, the axis of rotation is aligned with the Z axis and the specified point.

Axis by Entity/Last/View/Xaxis/Yaxis/Zaxis/ <2points> : **Zaxis** ◄─┘
Point on Z axis <0,0,0> : *Specify a point.*
<Rotation angle>/Reference: *Specify the angle of rotation.*

If you use the Reference option to specify the angle of rotation, AutoCAD displays the prompt:

Reference angle <0> : *Specify the starting angle.*
New angle: *Specify the ending angle.*

We will work out some examples of various options of the ROTATE3D command, which will give you a better idea of the working of ROTATE3D command.

Example 6

In this example the original position of the objects to be rotated is shown in hidden lines. The new position obtained by the object upon rotation is shown in continuous lines.

In Figure 21-45(a), the object is rotated using the Axis by Object option of the ROTATE3D command. The angle of rotation is 180 degrees. The prompt sequence is as follows:

Command: **ROTATE3D** ◄─┘
Select objects: *Specify the objects you want to rotate.*
Select objects: *Press the ENTER key when done selecting.*
Axis by Entity/Last/View/Xaxis/Yaxis/Zaxis/ <2points> : **Object** ◄─┘
Pick a line, circle, arc or 2D-polyline segment: *Pick the line between points P1 and P2.*
<Rotation angle>/Reference: **180** ◄─┘

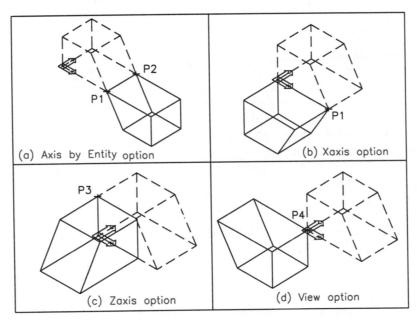

(a) Axis by Entity option
(b) Xaxis option
(c) Zaxis option
(d) View option

Figure 21-45 ROTATE3D

In Figure 21-45(b), the object is rotated using the Xaxis option of the ROTATE3D command. The angle of rotation is 180 degrees.

> Command: **ROTATE3D** ◄⎯
> Select objects: *Specify the objects you want to rotate.*
> Select objects: *Press the ENTER key when done selecting.*
> Axis by Entity/Last/View/Xaxis/Yaxis/Zaxis/<2points>: **Xaxis** ◄⎯
> Point on X axis <0,0,0>: *Pick the point P1.*
> <Rotation angle>/Reference: **180** ◄⎯

In Figure 21-45(c), the object is rotated using the Zaxis option of the ROTATE3D command. The angle of rotation is -90 degrees.

> Command: **ROTATE3D** ◄⎯
> Select objects: *Specify the objects you want to rotate.*
> Select objects: *Press the ENTER key when done selecting.*
> Axis by Entity/Last/View/Xaxis/Yaxis/Zaxis/<2points>: **Zaxis** ◄⎯
> Point on Z axis <0,0,0>: *pick the point P3.*
> <Rotation angle>/Reference: **180** ◄⎯

In Figure 21-45(d), the object is rotated using the View option of the ROTATE3D command. The angle of rotation is 180 degrees.

> Command: **ROTATE3D** ◄⎯
> Select objects: *Specify the objects you want to rotate.*
> Select objects: *Press the ENTER key when done selecting.*
> Axis by Entity/Last/View/Xaxis/Yaxis/Zaxis/<2points>: **View** ◄⎯
> Point on view direction axis <0,0,0>: *Pick the point P4.*
> <Rotation angle>/Reference: **180** ◄⎯

ALIGNING 3D OBJECTS (ALIGN COMMAND)

Toolbar:	Modify, Rotate, Align
Pull-down:	Modify, Align
Screen:	MODIFY, Align:

The **ALIGN** command is used to move (translate and rotate) objects in a 3D space irrespective of the alignment and position of the current UCS. The movement is carried out by picking up to three points on the original object (source points) and positions where you want to move these points (destination points). The ALIGN command can be invoked from the **Modify** toolbar (select Align icon from Rotate flyout), from the pull-down menu (select Modify, Align, Figure 21-46), from the screen menu (select MODIFY, Align:), or by entering **ALIGN** at the Command: prompt.

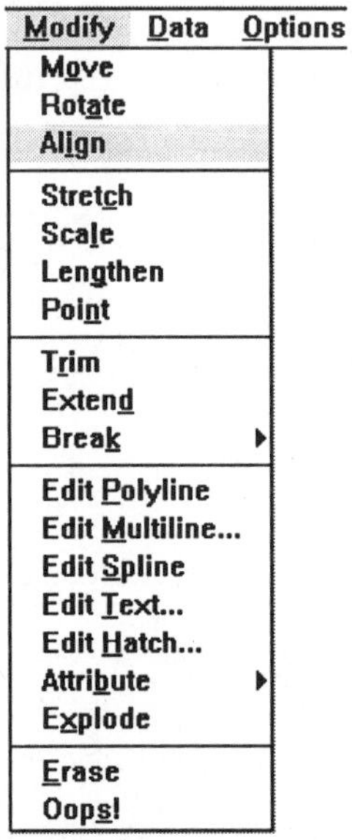

Figure 21-46 Selecting the Align option from Modify pull-down menu

> Command: **ALIGN** ◄⎯
> Select objects: *Select the objects you want to relocate.*
> Select objects: *Give a null response if selection is over.*

1st source point: *Pick the first point on the object to be aligned.*
1st destination point: *Pick the location where first point is to be relocated.*
2nd source point: *Pick the second point on the object to be aligned.*
2nd destination point: *Pick the location where second point is to be relocated.*
3rd source point: *Pick the third point on the object to be aligned.*
3rd destination point: *Pick the location where third point is to be relocated.*

You will notice that when you pick a source point, a line is drawn between the corresponding source point and the destination point. These lines are temporary and for reference only. The object can be aligned in three ways.

1. If you specify all three source points and their corresponding destination points, the movement of the object from the source position to the destination position is a combination of a translation and two rotations based on all the specified points. With the help of translation, the first source point is moved to the first destination point. The line defined by the first and second source points is aligned with the line defined by the first and second destination points with the help of first rotation. The plane defined by the three source points is aligned with the plane defined by the three destination points with the help of second rotation.

2. If you specify only two source points and their corresponding destination points, the movement of the object from the source position to the destination position is carried out by a translation operation and a rotation operation. With the help of the translation operation, the first source point is moved to the first destination point. The rotation operation aligns the line passing through the two source points with the line passing through the two destination points. In this case AutoCAD prompts you to specify whether the transformation is in 2D space or 3D space. This prompt is:

   <2D> or 3d transformation:

   The default is the 2D option. In this case, the rotation is performed in the XY plane of the current UCS. If you invoke the 3d transformation by entering **3d**, the rotation is performed in the plane formed by the two source points and two destination points.

3. The third case is that you only specify one pair of points. Here the movement of the object from the source position to the destination position is carried out by a translation from source point to the destination point. This is identical to the MOVE operation except that in the MOVE operation dynamic dragging is supported.

Example 7

Figure 21-47 shows the objects that are to be aligned and the source points and destination points. The figure also shows the resulting drawing after aligning the object.

In Figure 21-47(a), the aligning operation has been carried out by specifying a single source point (S1) and its respective destination point (D1). The prompt sequence is:

   Command: **ALIGN** ◄─┘
   Select objects: *Select the hidden object.*
   Select objects: *Give a null response if selection is over.*
   1st source point: *Pick the first source point S1 on the object to be aligned.*
   1st destination point: *Pick the location of the first destination point D1.*
   2nd source point: ◄─┘
   Command:

In the Figure 21-47(b), (c), and (d), the aligning operation has been carried out by specifying three source points (S1, S2, S3) and their respective destination points (D1, D2, D3). The prompt sequence is:

Command: **ALIGN** ←┘
Select objects: *Select the hidden object.*
Select objects: *Give a null response if selection is completed.*
1st source point: *Pick the first source point S1 on the object to be aligned.*
1st destination point: *Pick the location of the first destination point D1.*
2nd source point: *Pick the second source point S2 on the object to be aligned.*
2nd source point: *Pick the location of the second destination point D2.*
3rd source point: *Pick the location of the third source point S3.*
3rd destination point: *Pick the location of the third destination point D3.*

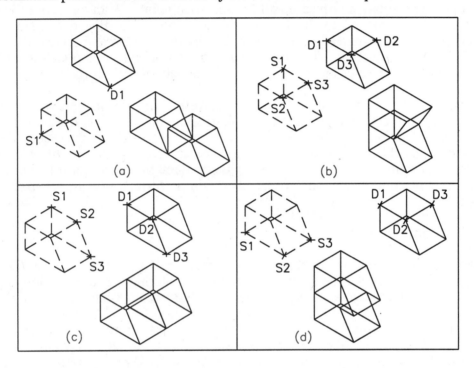

Figure 21-47 Using the ALIGN command to align objects

HIDE COMMAND

Toolbar:	Render, Hide
Pull-down:	Tools, Hide
Screen:	TOOLS, Hide

In most of the 3D wireframe objects, some of the lines lie behind other lines or objects. Sometimes you may not want these hidden lines to show up on the screen so that the clarity of the object will increase. To do so you can use the **HIDE** command. This command can be selected from the **Render** toolbar (select Hide icon), from the pull-down menu (select Tools, Hide), or from the screen menu (select TOOLS, Hide) or by entering **HIDE** at the Command: prompt. The prompt sequence for using the HIDE command is:

Command: **HIDE** ←┘

Once you enter this command, the screen is regenerated and all the hidden lines are suppressed in the drawing. The hidden lines are again included in the drawing when the next regeneration takes place. Circles, solids, wide polyline segments, traces, polygon meshes, 3D faces, and the extruded edges with non-zero thickness are treated as opaque surfaces, hence any object behind them is suppressed once the HIDE command is used. Circles, traces, solids, and wide polyline segments are considered to be solid objects if they are extruded. In this case the bottom and top faces are also considered. Objects on frozen layers or layers that have been turned off are not taken into consideration by the HIDE command. If you want to select objects that you want to hide, use the Hide option of the DVIEW command.

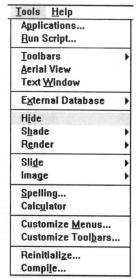

Figure 21-48 Selecting the Hide option from the Tools pull-down menu

CYLINDRICAL COORDINATE SYSTEM

This coordinate system is also a modification of the Polar coordinate system. The location of any point is described by three things:

1. Distance from the present UCS origin.
2. Angle in the XY plane.
3. Z dimension.

This coordinate system is mostly used for location of points on a CYLINDRICAL shape. For example a point 4 units from the UCS origin, at an angle of 25 degrees from the X axis, and having a Z dimension of 6 units would be represented in the following format:

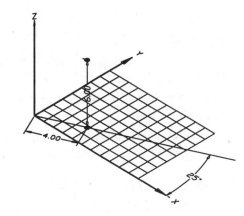

Figure 21-49 Cylindrical coordinate system

< Distance from the UCS origin > < Angle from X axis > < Z dimension >
4 < 25,6.0

SPHERICAL COORDINATE SYSTEM

The Spherical coordinate system is a modification of the Polar coordinate system. The location of any point is described by three things:

1. Distance from the present UCS origin.
2. Angle in the XY plane.
3. Angle from the XY plane.

This coordinate system is somewhat similar to using longitude and latitude and the distance from the center of earth to find the location of a point on the earth. The distance from the present UCS origin is analogous to the distance from the center of the earth. The angle in the XY plane is analogous to the longitude measurement. The angle from the XY plane is analogous to the latitude measurement. The Spherical coordinate system is mostly used in locating points on a spherical surface. For example a point 7 units from the UCS origin, at an angle of 60 degrees from the X axis, and at an angle of 50 degrees from XY plane would be represented in the following format:

< Distance from the UCS origin > < Angle from X axis > < Angle from XY plane >

7 < 60 < 50

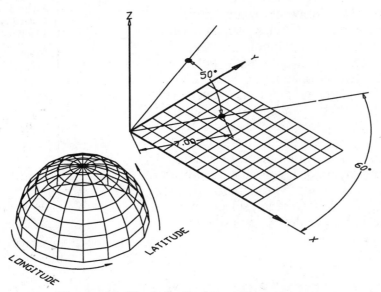

Figure 21-50 Spherical coordinate system

SELF EVALUATION TEST

Answer the following questions and then compare your answers with the correct answers given at the end of this chapter.

1. To construct a 3D surface model, you can use the _____ command and then enter the name of the object at the next prompt.

2. The default viewpoint is located at _____ and the view obtained with this viewpoint is called the plan view.

3. In the Presets dialogue box, you can set a viewpoint by specifying the _____ and an angle from the XY plane.

4. In a 3D array, the third dimension signifies the _____ in the array.

5. To select the _____ mirror plane as the current mirroring plane, use the Last option.

6. The _____ command is used to move (translate and rotate) objects in 3D space irrespective of the alignment and position of the current UCS.

7. With the _____ option of the ROTATE3D command, the axis of rotation passes through the specified point and is perpendicular to the view direction.

8. If you have multiple viewports, the PLAN command generates the plan view of only the _____ viewport.

9. The _____ command can be used to create viewports and divide the display screen into a number of parts (viewports).

10. The number of sections (surfaces) formed between the two surfaces depends on the _____ system variable.

11. With the _____ command you can create a mesh (matrix of 3D faces) with four connected sides as the boundaries.

12. You can invoke the Presets dialogue box by using the Rotate option of the cascading submenus of the View pull-down menu, or by entering _____ at the Command: prompt.

13. You can invoke the 3DARRAY command by selecting the _____ option in the Construct pull-down menu.

14. The MIRROR3D command can be invoked by picking the _____ option from the Construct pull-down menu, or by entering the _____ command at the Command: prompt.

15. In the XZ option, the mirroring plane is aligned with the _____ plane and passes through the specified point.

REVIEW QUESTIONS

Answer the following questions:

3D Surfaced Wireframe and Solid Models

1. To construct a 3D surfaced wireframe model of an object, you must enter _____ together with the name of the at the Command: prompt.

2. You can use the _____ command to draw a desired surfaced wireframe model.

3. To construct a 3D solid model, you must enter the _____ of the object at the **Command:** prompt.

4. If you specify any 3D object that is to be constructed through the 3D Objects icon menu, a _____ model will be constructed.

5. You can create 3D solid models of all the objects listed in the 3D Objects icon menu except _____, _____, and _____.

VPOINT

6. The _____ command lets you define a viewpoint.

7. Once you set a viewpoint, _____ in the current viewport are regenerated and the objects are displayed as if you are viewing them from the newly defined viewpoint.

8. The default viewpoint is located at _____ and the view obtained with this viewpoint is called the plan view.

9. If you give a null response at the **Rotate/<View point> <current>:** prompt, or pick the axes option in the View pull-down menu, AutoCAD display a _____ and _____ on the screen.

10. You can specify the viewpoint in the axis and tripod method by moving the _____ in the _____ _____ with a pointing device.

11. As you move the small cross-hairs in the compass pointing device, the _____ also moves to reflect the changes in the viewpoint.

12. You can set the viewpoint by specifying its coordinate location or by specifying the rotation in the XY plane from the X axis, and the _____ .

13. In the Presets dialogue box, you can set a viewpoint by specifying the _____ and an angle from the XY plane.

14. In the Presets dialogue box, you can specify the viewing angles from the _____ , or by entering the respective angle values in the _____ .

15. The angle you specify in the Presets dialogue box is indicated by the _____ and the _____ is indicated by the red arm.

3DARRAY

16. You can create arrays of objects in 3D space with the _____ command.

17. The difference between 2D and 3D array is that in 3D array, _____ also exists.

18. In a 3D array the third dimension signifies the _____ in the array.

MIRROR3D

19. The _____ command can be used to mirror objects in 3D space irrespective of the orientation of the current UCS.

20. With the _____ option of the MIRROR3D command, you specify the position of mirroring plane with the help of three points.

21. Plane by Object option of MIRROR3D command lets you align the mirroring plane with the plane of the _____ .

22. To select the _____ mirror plane as the current mirroring plane, you must use the Last option.

23. If you want to specify the mirroring plane through the Zaxis option, you need to define a point on the plane and a point on the _____ of that plane.

24. In the View option, the mirroring plane passes through the specified point and is formed perpendicular to the _____ .

25. To align the mirroring plane with the XY plane, you must use the _____ option.

ALIGN

26. The _____ command is used to move (translate and rotate) objects in a 3D space irrespective of the alignment and position of the current UCS.

27. The movement in ALIGN command is carried out by picking _____ points on the original object and _____ points.

ROTATE3D

28. The _____ command can be used to rotate an object about any 3D axis irrespective of the orientation of the current UCS.

29. If you want to define the axis of rotation about a line between two points, you must use the _____ option of ROTATE3D command.

30. In the _____ option, axes of objects like lines, polylines, circles, and arcs are used to define the axis of rotation.

31. In the _____ option of the ROTATE3D command, the axis of rotation passes through the specified point and is perpendicular to the view direction.

PLAN

32. The _____ command can be used to generate the plan view of an object relative to the _____ , _____ , or _____ .

33. If you have multiple viewports, the PLAN command generates the plan view of only the _____ viewport.

34. Perspective projection and clipping are turned _____ when you use the PLAN command.

HIDE

35. You can use the _____ command to suppress the display of the lines that lie behind other lines or objects.

UCSFOLLOW

36. When the _____ variable is assigned a value of 1, a plan view is automatically generated if you change the UCS in a viewport.

RULESURF, TABSURF, REVSURF, EDGESURF

37. The _____ command can be used to generate a polygon mesh (ruled surface) between two _____ objects or two _____ objects.

38. The number of sections (surfaces) formed between the two surfaces depends on the _____ system variable.

39. The _____ command can be used to generate a surface extrusion (tabulated surface) from an object also known as path curve.

40. With the _____ command, you can create a 3D mesh that trails along the path curve (profile) and then rotates around a center line also known as axis.

41. In case of REVSURF, the value of the _____ variable determines the number of equal segments that will divide the path curve.

42. With the _____ command you can create a mesh (matrix of 3D faces) with four connected sides as the boundaries.

3DMESH

43. The _____ command lets you create a polygon mesh in which the vertices are specified by their XYZ coordinates.

3DPOLY

44. 3D polylines can be drawn using the _____ command.

45. The difference between the 3DPOLY and PLINE commands is that a _____ is added to the polyline and with the 3DPOLY you can only draw _____ segments without the _____ variable.

PFACE, 3DFACE

46. With the _____ you can create a mesh of any desired surface by picking all the vertices of a face, whether or not they are coincident with vertices of another face.

47. You can create 3D surfaces with the _____ command.

CYLINDRICAL and SPHERICAL COORDINATES

48 To find the location of a point using the CYLINDRICAL coordinate system, you need to know:

    1. _____ .
    2. _____ .
    3. _____ .

Use the CYLINDRICAL coordinate system to start a line from a point which is at a distance of 3 units from the current UCS origin, making an angle of 45 degrees in the XY plane, and having the Z dimension of 4 units. Let the end point of the line be at an angle of 20 degrees and a distance of 2 units from the start point.

49. To find the location of a point using the Spherical coordinate system, you need to know:

    1. _____ .
    2. _____ .
    3. _____ .

50 Use the Spherical coordinate system to find the location of a point which is 5 units from the UCS origin, making an angle of 45 degrees in the XY plane, and at an angle of 70 degrees from the XY plane.

EXERCISES

Exercise 1 through 5

1. Draw a surfaced wireframe sphere with the center at any desired position and a radius of 1 unit. Change the viewpoint to get the 3D view of the sphere.

2. Construct a torus with a torus diameter of 4 units and tube diameter of 0.50 units.

3. Draw a three-surfaced wireframe model of a pyramid. Let the first model have an apex 3 units above the base of the pyramid. Let the second model have a truncated top. The third model should have a ridge instead of an apex.

4. Draw a truncated cone. Let the bottom diameter be 1.50 units, height 3 units, and top diameter of 0.25 units.

5. Construct a surfaced wireframe mesh. Let the number of rows be 4 and the number of columns be 7.

Answers

The following are the correct answers to the questions in the self evaluation test.
1 - 3D, 2 - 0,0,1, 3 - angle from the axis, 4 - levels, 5 - last defined, 6 - ALIGN, 7 - View, 8 - current, 9 - VPORTS, 10 - SURFTAB1, 11 - EDGESURF, 12 - DDVPOINT, 13 - 3DARRAY, 14 - 3DMIRROR, MIRROR3D, 15 - XZ

Chapter 22

Model Space Viewports
Paper Space Viewports
Dynamic Viewing of 3D Objects

Learning objectives

After completing this chapter, you will be able to:
- Create viewports in Model space using the VPORTS command.
- Create viewports in Paper space using the MVIEW command.
- Use Paper space and Model space in Paper space.
- Shift from Paper space to Model space using the MSPACE command.
- Shift from Model space to Paper space using the PSPACE command.
- Control the visibility of viewport layers with the VPLAYER command.
- Use dynamic viewing of 3D objects using the DVIEW command.
- Set linetype scaling in Paper space using the PSLTSCALE command.

MODEL SPACE VIEWPORTS

Normally in AutoCAD, a single viewport is displayed on the screen. AutoCAD allows you to create multiple viewports that can be used to display different views of the same object. A viewport is a rectangular part of the graphics area of the screen. Viewports can be used in different ways and for different purposes. The first reason to create viewports and dividing the display screen into a number of parts is usually to create a model or layout. This is done using the **VPORTS** command. You are in a mode called **Model space** when you use this command. This is the default mode in AutoCAD. When you want to use the VPORTS command, the **TILEMODE** system variable must be set to 1 (default value). An arrangement of viewports is a display function and cannot be plotted. The second purpose is to have different parts or different views of your drawing in different viewports. Each viewport can contain a different 3D view of your drawing and you can use the PAN or ZOOM command to display different portions or different levels of detail of the drawing in each viewport. The **Snap**, **Grid**, and **UCSicon** modes can be set separately for each viewport.

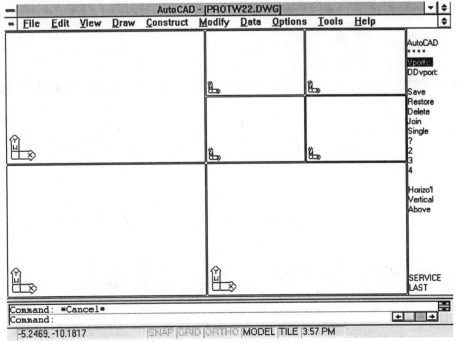

Figure 22-1   Screen display with viewports

DISPLAYING VIEWPORTS AS TILED AREAS

(VPORTS COMMAND)

> **Pull-down:** View, Tiled Viewports
> **Screen:**   VIEW, Vports:

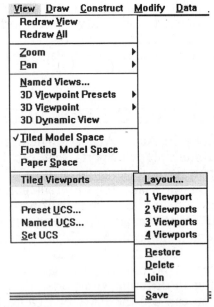

As mentioned earlier, the display screen can be divided into multiple non-overlapping viewports whose number depends on the equipment and the operating system that AutoCAD is running on. Each tiled viewport contains a view of the drawing. The tiled viewports must touch at the edges without overlapping one another. While using tiled viewports you are not allowed to edit, rearrange, or turn individual viewports on or off. These viewports are created using the **VIEWPORTS** command when the system variable **TILEMODE** is set to 1. These viewports are also known as **Model space viewports**. You can invoke the **VPORTS** command from the pull-down menu (select View, Tiled Viewports, Figure 22-2), from the screen menu (select VIEW, Vports:), or by entering **VPORTS** at the Command: prompt. The prompt sequence is:

Figure 22-2   Selecting the Tiled Viewports option from the pull-down menu

Command: **TILEMODE** ◄┘
New value for TILEMODE<0>: **1** ◄┘

As required, we have set the system variable **TILEMODE** to 1. You can also set TILEMODE to 1 from the **Standard** toolbar by selecting the **Tiled Model Space** icon, the pull-down menu (Select View, Tiled Model Space), or the screen menu (Select VIEW, Tilemod:). Now we will use the VIEWPORTS command.

Command: **VIEWPORTS** ◄─┘
Save/Restore/Delete/Join/SIngle/?/2/ < 3 > /4: *Choose any one of the options.*

After we have discussed how to make a viewport current, we will describe all of the options of the VPORTS command. You should know how to make a viewport current before using any of the options.

> **Note**
>
> *When you are in Paper space, Tiled Viewports option is grayed out because you cannot draw tiled viewports in Paper space.*

You can also select the type of viewport you want from the **Tiled Viewport Layout** icon box by picking the desired arrangement of viewports from the icon box. This icon box can be invoked from the pull-down menu (Select View, Tiled Viewports, Layout...) or from the screen menu (Select VIEW, TileVpt:).

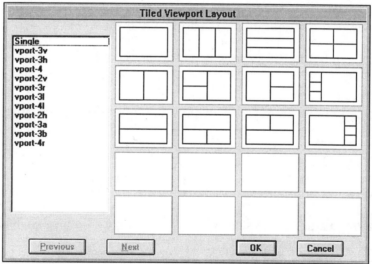

Figure 22-3 Tiled Viewport Layout icon menu

Making a Viewport Current

The viewport you are working in is the current viewport at that time. You can display several Model space viewports on the screen but you can work in only one of them at one time. The current viewport is indicated by means of a border that is heavy compared with the borders of the other viewports. Also, the graphics cursor appears as a drawing cursor (screen cross-hairs) only when it is within the current viewport. Outside the current viewport this cursor appears as an arrow cursor. You can enter points and select objects only from the current viewport. To make a viewport current you can pick it with the pointing device. Another way of making a viewport current is by assigning its identification number to the **CVPORT** system variable. The identification numbers of the named viewport configurations are not listed in the display. The following are the options of the VIEWPORTS command:

Save Option

This option is used to name and save the current viewport configuration. The prompt sequence is as follows:

> Command: **VIEWPORTS** ◄⎯┘
> Save/Restore/Delete/Join/SIngle/?/2/ <3> /4: **S** ◄⎯┘
> ?/Name for new viewport configuration: *Enter the name.*

The naming conventions are the same as those used earlier. You can use up to 31 characters and wild cards. Entering the ? symbol causes the following prompt to be displayed:

> Viewport configuration(s) to list < * > :

As a response to the above prompt you can press the ENTER key to get a listing of all the saved viewport configurations.

Restore Option

This option restores any saved viewport configuration. You can enter the name of the viewport configuration to restore or you can enter ? to display a list of all saved viewport configurations. The prompt sequence is:

> Command: **VIEWPORTS** ◄⎯┘
> Save/Restore/Delete/Join/SIngle/?/2/ <3> /4: **R** ◄⎯┘
> ?/Name of viewport configuration to restore: *Enter the name.*

You can use the ? symbol in the same way as for the Save option.

Delete Option

You can delete a previously saved viewport configuration using this option. The prompt sequence is:

> Command: **VPORTS** ◄⎯┘
> Save/Restore/Delete/Join/SIngle/?/2/ <3> /4: **D** ◄⎯┘
> ?/Name of viewport configuration to delete: *Enter the name.*

If you enter a wrong name, the system gives the message "Cannot find viewport configuration NAME".

Join Option

With this option you can join two adjacent viewports into a single viewport. The view in the resulting viewport depends on which one of the two viewports you specified as the dominant viewport when they were joined.

> Command: **VPORTS** ◄⎯┘
> Save/Restore/Delete/Join/SIngle/?/2/ <3> /4: **J** ◄⎯┘
> Select dominant viewport <current> : *Select the dominant viewport.*
> Select viewport to join: *Select other viewport.*

SIngle Option

With this option, you can have only one viewport on the screen and the view in this viewport depends on which one of the viewports was current when you used the **SIngle** option.

? Option

Invoking this option displays the identification number and screen positions of all the active viewports and the names and screen positions of the saved viewport configurations. The position of the viewports is defined by the lower left and upper right corners. The value for these corners is between (0.0,0.0) for the lower left corner of the graphics area and (1.0,1.0) for the upper right corner of the graphics area. The current viewport is the first one listed.

2 Option

This option is used to divide the current viewport into two equal parts.

    Save/Restore/Delete/Join/SIngle/?/2/<3>/4: **2** ◄—┘
    Horizontal/<Vertical>:

If you enter Vertical at this prompt then the current viewport is divided vertically. If you enter Horizontal, the current viewport is divided horizontally.

3 Option

You can invoke the 3 option to divide the current viewport into three viewports in the following manner:

    Save/Restore/Delete/Join/SIngle/?/2/<3>/4: **3** ◄—┘

The next prompt is:

    Horizontal/Vertical/Above/Below/Left/<Right>:

When you enter Horizontal at the above prompt, the current viewport is divided horizontally into three equal parts. The Vertical option divides the current viewport vertically into three equal parts. The Above, Below, Left, and Right options divide the current viewport into one large and two smaller viewports. The placement of the larger viewport depends on which one of these options you specify. For example, if you select the Above option, the current viewport is divided horizontally into two viewports and the lower viewport is further divided vertically into two viewports.

4 Option

Using this option, you can divide the current viewport into four equal viewports.

OBTAINING PLAN VIEWS AUTOMATICALLY (UCSFOLLOW SYSTEM VARIABLE)

As mentioned before, you can obtain the plan view of an object by using the PLAN command. If you have different viewports, you can obtain the plan view relative to the current UCS by activating a viewport, setting the UCS to your requirement, and using the default option of the PLAN command. This operation can be automated by using the **UCSFOLLOW** system variable. When the UCSFOLLOW variable is assigned a value of 1, a plan view is automatically generated if you change the UCS. By default this variable is assigned the value 0. All of the viewports have the UCSFOLLOW facility, hence you need to specify the UCSFOLLOW setting separately for each viewport. The prompt sequence is:

    Command: **UCSFOLLOW** ◄—┘
    New value for UCSFOLLOW <0>: **1** ◄—┘

WORKING WITH MULTIPLE VIEWPORTS (MVIEW COMMAND)

Toolbar:	Standard toolbar, Floating Model Space
Pull-down:	View, Floating Viewports
Screen:	VIEW, Mview:

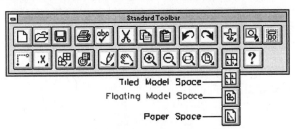

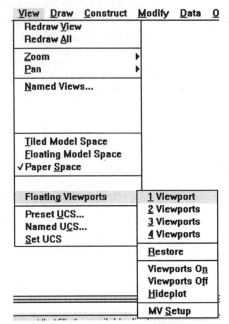

Figure 22-4 Selecting the MVIEW command from the Standard toolbar

 In AutoCAD you can create tiled viewports or floating viewports (untiled viewports). Tiled viewports are created by using the **VPORTS** command when the **TILEMODE** system variable is set to 1 (Model space). The VPORTS command was discussed earlier.

Figure 22-5 Invoking the MVIEW command from the pull-down menu

The **MVIEW** command is used to create floating viewports (untiled viewports) in Paper space. Before using the MVIEW command, you must change the TILEMODE system variable to 0. If you invoke this command in the MSPACE Model space (Tilemode set to 0), AutoCAD shifts you from Model space to Paper space, until MVIEW command is not over. Once the MVIEW command is over, AutoCAD returns you to Model space. The purpose of creating untiled viewports in Paper space by using the MVIEW command is that viewports are created in Paper space and these viewports can be edited as objects like circles, polygons, or text. Various settings like grid, current view, snap, etc., of the first viewport created with the **MVIEW** command are taken from the previous viewport that was current in Paper space. You can also alter the size of the floating viewports and adjust them on the screen. Since viewports in Paper space are just like objects, it is not possible to edit the model in Paper space. For this you need to shift from Paper space to floating Model space with the help of the MSPACE command. The **MVIEW** command can be invoked from the **Standard** toolbar by selecting the **Floating Model Space** icon from the **Tiled Model Space** flyout (Figure 22-4), from the pull-down menu (select View, Floating Viewports), from the screen menu (select VIEW, Mview:). You can also enter **MVIEW** at the Command: prompt. The prompt sequence is:

Command: **MVIEW** ←⏎
ON/OFF/Hideplot/Fit/2/3/4/Restore/ < First Point > :

Note
When you are in Model space the Floating Viewports option is grayed out because you cannot draw floating viewports in Model space.

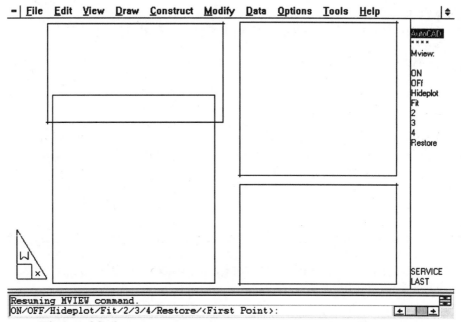

Figure 22-6 Untiled Viewports using the MVIEW command

When you enter the **MVIEW** command, AutoCAD prompts you to select one of the options listed in the prompt line or select the first corner point of the paper space viewport window.

    Command: **MVIEW** ←⏎
    ON/OFF/Hideplot/Fit/2/3/4/Restore/ < First Point > :

The following is a description of the MVIEW command options.

First Point Option

This is the default option. With this option you can create a single viewport. The size of the viewport is determined by the two diagonal points you specify. Once you specify the two points, a viewport is created.

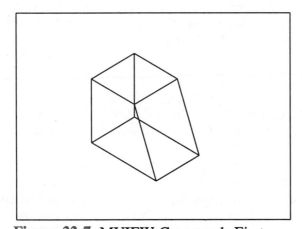

Figure 22-7 MVIEW Command, First Point option

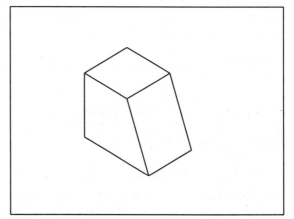

Figure 22-8 MVIEW Command, Hideplot option

Hideplot Option

With this option you can choose the viewports from which you want to remove the hidden lines when you plot in Paper space. If you set Hideplot to ON, hidden lines **are not plotted**. If you set Hideplot to OFF, hidden lines **are plotted**.

Command: **MVIEW** ←⏎
ON/OFF/Hideplot/Fit/2/3/4/Restore/ < First Point > : **H** ←⏎
ON/OFF: **ON** ←⏎
Select objects: *Select the viewports.*

> **Note**
>
> *When you turn Hideplot on, the hidden line removal takes place only at the time of plotting. It does not affect display of the lines on the screen (hidden line will be displayed). You can use the HIDE command to see the effect of hidden line removal.*

ON/OFF Option

These options are used to turn the display in the selected viewports on/off. By default the display inside the current viewport is on. You should turn off the viewports that are not required so that regeneration is not carried out on viewports that are turned off. The objects are not displayed in the viewports that are turned off.

> **Note**
>
> *The system variable MAXACTVP controls the number of viewports that display the objects. For example, if MAXACTVP is set to 16, only 16 viewports will display the objects. The remaining viewports will not display the objects unless one or more viewports that display the objects are turned off or the MAXACTVP system variable is set to a higher value.*
>
> *If you zoom in the viewport that does not display the object, AutoCAD will automatically turn off one of the viewports to force display of the objects in the viewport.*
>
> *You will not be able to work in the MSPACE Model space if all viewports are turned off; you must create a new viewport or turn on one of the viewports.*

Fit Option

This option generates the viewport that fits the current screen display. For example, if you want to create a single viewport, use the Fit option. The size of the viewport can be controlled by setting the limits or by using the ZOOM command to display the desired area.

2 Option

You can invoke the 2 option to create two viewports in the area you specify. This option is similar to the 2 option of the VPORTS command. Once you enter **2** at the **ON/OFF/Hideplot/Fit/2/3/4/Restore/ < First Point >:** prompt, AutoCAD prompts you for the location and arrangement of the viewports. The prompt is:

Horizontal/ < vertical >

At the above prompt, you can choose whether the rectangular area you have specified is horizontally or vertically divided. The default arrangement is vertical, but you can change it to horizontal by entering **Horizontal** at the above prompt. Once you have specified the arrangement of the viewport, the next two prompts are:

Fit/ < First Point > :
Second point:

These prompts are identical to the Fit and First Point option of the **MVIEW** command. For example, if you enter the first point, the next prompt asks you to specify the second point of the rectangular area in which the two viewports will be created. Once these two points are defined, AutoCAD will fit the two viewports within the specified area. The **Fit** option will fit the viewports in the current screen display.

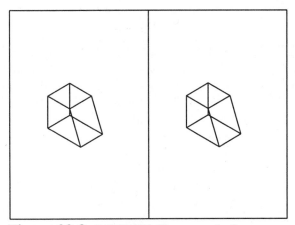

Figure 22-9 MVIEW Command, 2 option with vertical viewports

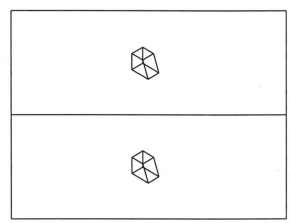

Figure 22-10 MVIEW Command, 2 option with horizontal viewports

3 Option

You can invoke the 3 option to create three viewports in the area you specify. This option is similar to 3 option of the VPORTS command. Once you enter **3** at the **ON/OFF/Hideplot/Fit/2/ 3/4/Restore/ <First Point>:** prompt, AutoCAD prompts you for the location and arrangement of the viewports. The prompt is:

Horizontal/Vertical/Above/Below/Left/<Right>:

At the above prompt, you can choose whether the rectangular area you have specified is divided into three viewports horizontally or vertically, and whether the third viewport is to be placed above, or below, or left, or right of the other two viewports. The default option is Right. In this case the third viewport is placed on the right side of the other two viewports. If you invoke the Horizontal option, the space you have specified for the viewports is divided into three equal horizontal viewports.

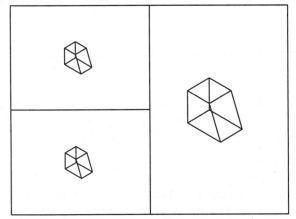

Figure 22-11 MVIEW Command, 3 option with the third viewport on right

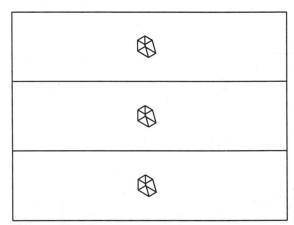

Figure 22-12 MVIEW Command, 3 option with horizontal viewports

If you invoke the Vertical option, the space you have specified for the viewports is divided into three equal vertical viewports. The Above option places the third viewport on top of the other two viewports. The Below option places the third viewport under the other two viewports. If you use the Left option, the third viewport is placed on the left side of the other two viewports. Once you have specified the arrangement of the viewport, the next two prompts are:

Fit/ < First Point > :
Second point:

These prompts are identical to the Fit and First Point option of the **MVIEW** command. For example, if you enter the first point, the next prompt asks you to specify the second point of the rectangular area in which the three viewports will be created. Once these two points are defined, AutoCAD will fit the three viewports within the specified area. The Fit option will fit the viewports in the current screen display.

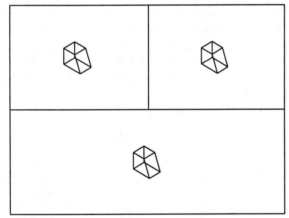

Figure 22-13 MVIEW Command, 3 option with the vertical viewports

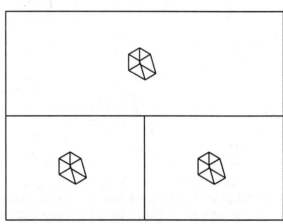

Figure 22-14 MVIEW Command, 3 option with one viewport above

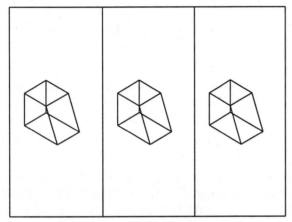

Figure 22-15 MVIEW Command, 3 option with one viewport below

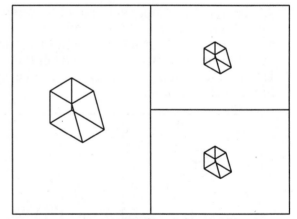

Figure 22-16 MVIEW Command, 3 option with one viewport on left

4 Option

Using this option, you can divide the area you have specified for the viewports into four equal viewports. If you use the Fit option, the graphics area on the screen is divided into four equal viewports.

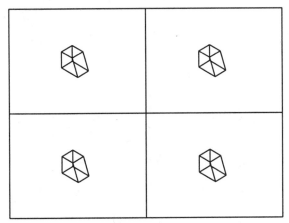

Figure 22-17 MVIEW Command, 4 option

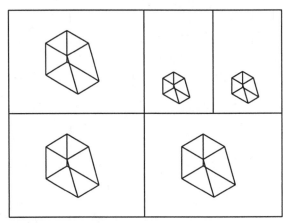

Figure 22-18 MVIEW Command, Restore option

Restore Option

If you have used the **VPORTS** command to create and save viewport configuration, the **Restore** option of the **MVIEW** option can be used to obtain a viewport configuration by specifying the name of the configuration. Once you specify the name of the configuration, you can specify the location and size of the viewports by using the Fit or First Point option.

?/Name of window configuration to insert < default > : *Specify the name of the configuration you want to restore.*

Fit/ < First Point > : *Select first corner.*
Second point: *Select second corner.*

MODEL SPACE AND PAPER SPACE

Model Space (MSPACE Command)

Status bar:	PAPER (double click)
Toolbar:	Standard toolbar, Tiled Model Space, Floating, Model Space
Pull-down:	View, Tiled Model Space or Floating Model Space
Screen:	VIEW, Mspace:

The **MSPACE** command is used to shift from Paper space to Model space. Before using this command, you must set the **TILEMODE** to 0 (Off). To shift from Paper space to Model space, at least one of the viewports must be active and on. The MSPACE command can be invoked, by double-clicking on the **PAPER** button in the Status bar, from the **Standard** toolbar by selecting the **Tiled Model Space** icon or **Floating Model Space** icon, from the pull-down menu (select View, Tiled Model Space or Floating Model Space), or from the screen menu (select VIEW, Mspace:). It can also be selected by entering **MSPACE** or **MS** at the Command: prompt.

Command: **MSPACE** ◄┘
MSPACE

AutoCAD acknowledges switching into Mspace by issuing the MSPACE message at the command line. Also, in the status bar PAPER is changed to MODEL.

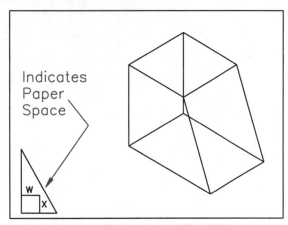

Figure 22-19 Using the MSPACE command to switch to Model space

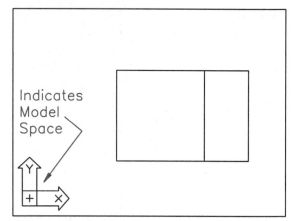

Figure 22-20 Using the PSPACE Command to switch to Paper space

Paper Space (PSPACE Command)

Status bar:	MODEL (double click)
Toolbar:	Standard toolbar, Paper Space
Pull-down:	View, Paper Space
Screen:	VIEW, Pspace:

This command is used to shift from Model space to Paper space. Before using this command, you must set the **TILEMODE** to 0 (Off). The PSPACE command can be invoked by double clicking on the **MODEL** button in the Status bar, from **Standard** toolbar by selecting **Paper Space** icon in the **Tiled Model Space** flyout, from the pull-down menu (select View, Paper Space), or from the screen menu (select VIEW, Pspace:). It can also be selected by entering **PSPACE** or **PS** at the Command: prompt.

Command: **PSPACE** ←⌐

MANIPULATING THE VISIBILITY OF VIEWPORT LAYERS (VPLAYER COMMAND)

Pull-down:	Data, Viewport Layer Controls
Screen:	DATA, Vplayer:

You can control the visibility of layers inside the viewport with the **VPLAYER** or **LAYER** command. The On/Off or Freeze/Thaw option of the LAYER command controls the visibility of layers globally, including the viewports. However, with the VPLAYER command you can control the visibility of layers in individual viewports. For example, you can use the VPLAYER command to freeze a layer in the selected viewport. The contents of this layer will not be displayed in the selected viewports, although in the other viewports the contents are displayed. This command can be used from either Model space or Paper space. The only

Figure 22-21 Selecting the VPLAYER command from the pull-down menu

restriction is that TILEMODE must be is set to 0 (Off). The VPLAYER command can be invoked from the pull-down menu (select Data, Viewport Layer Controls), from the screen menu (select DATA, VPlayer:), or by entering **VPLAYER** at the Command: prompt.

Command: **VPLAYER** ←⏐
?/Freeze/Thaw/Reset/Newfrz/Vpvisdflt:

VPLAYER Command Options

When you enter the VPLAYER command at the Command: prompt, AutoCAD returns a prompt line that displays the available options:

Command: **VPLAYER** ←⏐
?/Freeze/Thaw/Reset/Newfrz/Vpvisdflt:

? Option

You can use this option to obtain a listing of the frozen layers in the selected viewport. When you enter this option (**?**), AutoCAD displays the following prompt:

Select a viewport:

At this prompt pick the viewport for which you want a listing of the frozen layers. If you are in Model space, AutoCAD will temporarily shift you to Paper space to let you select the viewport. The complete prompt sequence of this option is:

Command: **VPLAYER** ←⏐
?/Freeze/Thaw/Reset/Newfrz/Vpvisdflt: **?** ←⏐
Select a viewport: *Select a viewport.*
Layers currently frozen in viewport 1:
DIM2
DIM3
?/Freeze/Thaw/Reset/Newfrz/Vpvisdflt:

Freeze Option

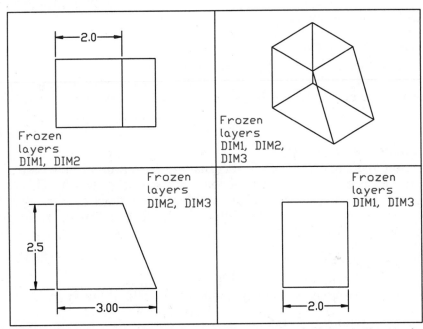

Figure 22-22 Using the VPLAYER command to freeze layers in viewports

The Freeze option is used to freeze a layer (or layers) in one or more viewports. When you select this option, AutoCAD displays the following prompt:

Layer(s) to Freeze: *Enter the layer name(s).*

In response to the above prompt, specify the name of the layer you want to freeze. If you want to specify more than one layer, the layer names must be separated by commas. You can also use wild cards to specify the names of the layers you want to freeze. Once you have specified the name of the layer(s), AutoCAD prompts you to select the viewport(s) in which you want to freeze the specified layer(s). The prompt is:

All/Select/<current>: *Select the viewport(s).*

Thaw Option

With this option you can thaw the layers that have been frozen in viewports using VPLAYER Freeze or the **DDLMODES** command. Layers that have been frozen, thawed, switched on, or switched off globally are not affected by the VPLAYER Thaw. For example, if a layer has been frozen, the objects on the frozen layer are not regenerated on any viewport even if VPLAYER Thaw is used to thaw that layer in any viewport. The prompt sequence for the VPLAYER command, with Thaw option, is:

Command: **VPLAYER** ◄──┘
?/Freeze/Thaw/Reset/Newfrz/Vpvisdflt: **THAW** ◄──┘
Layer(s) to Thaw: *Specify the layer(s) to be thawed.*

If you want to specify more than one layer, separate the layer names with commas. The next prompt lets you specify the viewport(s) in which you want to thaw the specified frozen layer.

All/Select/<Current>: *Specify the viewports.*

Reset Option

With the **Reset** option you can set the visibility of layer(s) in the specified viewports to their current default setting. The visibility defaults of a layer can be set by using the **Vpvisdflt** option of the VPLAYER command. The following is the prompt sequence of the **VPLAYER** command with the Reset option:

Command: **VPLAYER** ◄──┘
?/Freeze/Thaw/Reset/Newfrz/Vpvisdflt: **RESET** ◄──┘
Layer(s) to Reset: *Specify the names of the layer(s) you want to reset.*
All/Select/<current>: *Select the viewports in which you want to reset the specified layer to its default setting.*

Newfrz (New freeze) Option

With this option you can create new layers that are frozen in all viewports. This option is used mainly where you need a layer that is visible only in one viewport. This can be accomplished by creating the layer with **VPLAYER Newfrz**, then thawing that particular layer in the viewport where you want to make the layer visible. The following is the prompt sequence of VPLAYER command with Newfrz option:

Command: **VPLAYER** ◄──┘
?/Freeze/Thaw/Reset/Newfrz/Vpvisdflt: **NEWFRZ** ◄──┘
New viewport frozen layer name(s): *Specify the name of the frozen layer(s) you want to create.*

If you want to specify more than one layer, separate the layer names with commas. After you specify the name(s) of the layer(s), AutoCAD creates frozen layers in all viewports. Also, the default visibility setting of the new layer(s) is set to Frozen, hence if you create any new viewport, the layers created with VPLAYER Newfrz are also frozen.

Vpvisdflt (Viewport Visibility Default) Option

With this option, you can set a default for the visibility of layer(s). When a new viewport is created, the frozen/thawed status of any layer depends on the Vpvisdflt setting for that particular layer.

Command: **VPLAYER** ◄─┘
?/Freeze/Thaw/Reset/Newfrz/Vpvisdflt: **VPVISDFLT** ◄─┘
Layer name(s) to change default viewport visibility: *Specify the name(s) of the layer(s) whose default viewport visibility you want to set.*

Once you have specified the layer name(s), AutoCAD prompts:

Change default viewport visibility to Frozen/<Thawed>:

At this prompt enter Frozen or F if you want to set the default visibility to frozen. To set the default visibility to thawed, press the ENTER key or enter T for Thawed.

Controlling Viewport through the Layer Control dialogue box

You can use the **Layer Control** dialogue box (Figure 22-23) to perform certain functions of the VPLAYER command, such as freezing/thawing layers in viewports. This dialogue box can be invoked from the **Object Properties** toolbar by selecting the **Layers** icon, from the pull-down menu (select Data, Layers...), from the screen menu (select DATA, DDlmode: or select SERVICE, Layer:), or by entering **DDLMODES** at the Command: prompt.

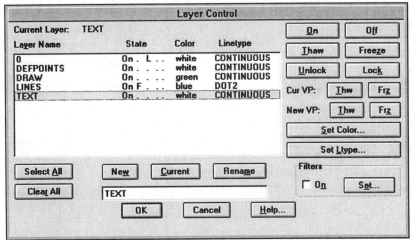

Figure 22-23 Controlling viewport display through the Layer Control dialogue box

In this dialogue box the **Cur VP: Thw** and **Cur VP: Frz** (Current Viewport Thaw and Current Viewport Freeze) buttons govern the freezing and thawing of selected layers in the current viewport. If you pick the Cur VP: Frz button, the specified layers are frozen in the current viewport and the objects on these layers are not shown in the current viewport. If you start drawing on the frozen layers in the current viewport, objects drawn will not be displayed in the current viewport. The **New VP: Thw** and **New VP: Frz** (New Viewport Thaw and New Viewport Freeze) buttons govern the freezing and thawing of selected layers in the new viewport. If you pick the New VP: Frz button, the specified layer is frozen in the new viewport and the objects on this layer are not shown in the new viewport. If you start drawing on the frozen layer, objects drawn in the new viewport will not be displayed in the new viewport; however, in other viewports the objects drawn in the new viewport will appear.

PAPER SPACE LINETYPE SCALING (PSLTSCALE COMMAND)

Pull-down:	Options, Linetypes, Paper Space Linetype Scale
Screen:	OPTIONS, Psltcal:

By default the linetype scaling is controlled by the **LTSCALE** system variable. Therefore, the display size of the dashes depends on the LTSCALE factor, drawing limits, or drawing units. If you have different drawing limits for different viewports, the size of the dashes will be different for these viewports. Figure 22-25 shows three viewports with different limits. You will notice that the dash length is different in each of these three viewports.

Figure 22-24 Selecting the PSLTSCALE command from the pull-down menu

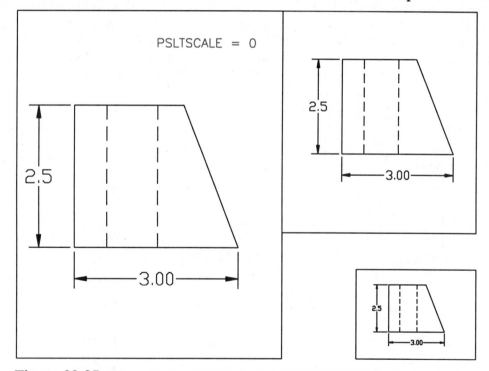

Figure 22-25 When PSLTSCALE is 0 and TILEMODE is 0, the dash length varies depending on the size of the viewport

Generally, it is desirable to have identical line spacing in all viewports. This can be achieved with the **PSLTSCALE** system variable. By default, the PSLTSCALE system variable is set to 0. In this case the size of the dashes depends on the LTSCALE system variable and the drawing units of Model space or Paper space in which the objects have been drawn. If you set PSLTSCALE to 1 and TILEMODE to 0, the size of the dashes depends on the Paper space drawing units. This also holds true for objects in Model space. In other words, if PSLTSCALE is set to 1, even if the viewports are different sizes, the length of dashes will be identical in all viewports. This variable can be invoked from the pull-down menu (select Options, Linetypes, Paper Space Linetype Scale, Figure 22-24), from the screen menu (select OPTIONS, Psltcal:), or by entering **PSLTSCALE** at the Command: prompt. Figure 22-26 shows three viewports with different limits. You will notice that the dash length is identical in these three viewports.

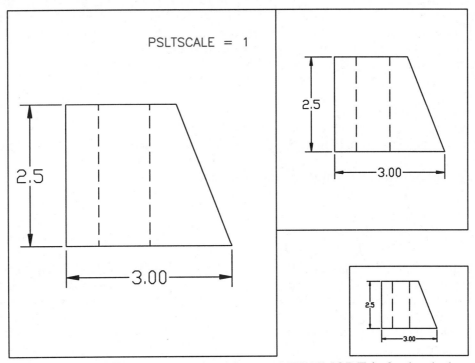

Figure 22-26 When PSLTSCALE is 1 and TILEMODE is 0, the dash length is same in all viewports

DYNAMIC VIEWING OF 3D OBJECTS (DVIEW COMMAND)

| **Pull-down:** | View, 3D Dynamic View |
| **Screen:** | VIEW, Dview: |

With the **DVIEW** command, you can create a **parallel projection** or **perspective view** of objects on the screen. Basically, DVIEW is an improvement over the VPOINT command in that the DVIEW command allows you to visually maneuver around 3D objects to obtain different views. As mentioned before, the DVIEW command offers you a choice between parallel viewing and perspective viewing. The difference between the two is that in parallel view, parallel lines in the 3D object remain parallel, while in perspective view, parallel lines meet at a vanishing point. These definitions suggest that with the VPOINT command, only parallel

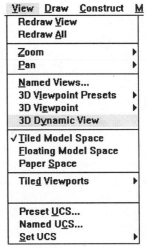

Figure 22-27 Invoking the DVIEW command from the pull-down menu

viewing is possible. The DVIEW command uses the **camera and target** concept to visualize an object from any desired position in 3D space. The position from which you want to view the object (the viewer's eye) is the camera, and the focus point is the target. The line formed between these two points is the line of sight, also known as the viewing direction. To get different viewing directions, you can move the camera or target or both. Once you have the required viewing direction, you can change the distance between the camera and the target by moving the camera along the line of sight. The field of view can be changed by attaching a wide angle lens or a telephoto lens to the camera. You can pan or twist (rotate) the image. The hidden lines in the object being viewed can be suppressed. You can clip those portions of model that you do not want to see. All these options of the DVIEW command demonstrate how useful this command is. This command can be invoked from the pull-down menu (select View, 3D Dynamic View, Figure 22-27), from the screen menu (select VIEW, Dview:), or by entering **DVIEW** at the Command: prompt.

> Command: **DVIEW** ◄─┘
> Select objects: *Select objects you want to view dynamically.*
> CAmera/TArget/Distance/POints/PAn/Zoom/TWist/CLip/Hide/Off/ Undo/ <eXit>:

The different options in this prompt are discussed below.

CAmera Option

With the Camera option you can rotate the camera about the target point. To invoke the camera option enter **CA** at the **CAmera/TArget/Distance/POints/PAn/Zoom/TWist/CLip/Hide/Off/Undo/ <eXit>:** prompt. Once you have invoked this option, the drawing is still but you can maneuver the camera up and down (above or below the target) or you can move it left or right (clockwise or counterclockwise around the target). You should remember that when you are moving the camera, the target is stationary and when you are moving the target, the camera is stationary. The next prompt AutoCAD displays is:

> Toggle angle in/Enter angle from XY plane <default>:

By default this prompt asks you for the angle from XY plane of the camera with respect to the current UCS. This is nothing but the vertical (up or down) movement of the camera. There are two ways to specify the angle.

1. You can specify the angle of rotation by moving the graphics cursor in the graphics area until you attain the desired rotation and then clicking the pick button of your pointing device. You will notice that as you move the cursor in the graphics area, the angle of rotation is continuously displayed in the status line. Also, as you move the cursor, the object also moves dynamically. If you give a horizontal movement to the camera at the **Toggle angle in/Enter angle from XY plane <default>:** prompt, you will notice that the angle value displayed in the status line does not change. This is because at the **Toggle angle in/Enter angle from XY plane <default>:** prompt, you are required to specify the vertical movement.

2. The other way to specify the angle of rotation is by entering the required angle of rotation value at the prompt. An angle of 90 degrees (default value) from XY plane makes the camera look at the object straight down from the top side of the object, providing you with the top view (plan view). In this case the line of sight is perpendicular to the XY plane of the current UCS. An angle of negative 90 degrees makes the camera look at the object straight up from the bottom side of the object. As you move the camera toward the top side of the object, the angle value increases. If you do not want to specify a vertical movement, press the ENTER key.

Once you have specified the angle from XY plane, the next prompt displayed is:

> Toggle angle from/Enter angle in XY plane from X axis <default>:

This prompt asks you for the angle of the camera in the XY plane from X axis. This is nothing but the horizontal (right or left) movement of the camera. You can enter the angle value in the range of negative 180 to 180 degrees. Moving the camera toward the right side (counterclockwise) of the object can be achieved by increasing the angle value; moving the camera toward the left side (clockwise) of the object can be achieved by decreasing the angle value. You can also toggle between these two prompts using the **Toggle angle from** or **Toggle angle in** option in the two prompts. The use of the toggle option can be illustrated as follows:

For example, you only want to enter the angle in XY plane from X axis. There are two ways to do so. The first is to give a null response to the **Toggle angle in/Enter angle from XY plane <default>:** prompt. The other is by using the **Toggle angle in** option. Hence, to switch from the **Toggle angle in/Enter angle from XY plane <default>:** prompt to **Toggle angle from/Enter angle in XY plane from X axis <default>:** prompt, you will have the following prompt sequence:

> Toggle angle in/Enter angle from XY plane <default>: **T** ◄⎯┘
> Toggle angle from/Enter angle in XY plane from X axis <default>:

In the same manner if you want to switch from the **Toggle angle from/Enter angle in XY plane from X axis <default>:** prompt to the **Toggle angle in/Enter angle from XY plane <default>:** prompt, the following will be the prompt sequence:

> Toggle angle from/Enter angle in XY plane from X axis <default>: **T** ◄⎯┘
> Toggle angle in/Enter angle from XY plane <default>:

You have gone through the basic concept of the Camera option of DVIEW command. Now, you will work out some examples to apply the Camera concept.

Example 1

In Figure 22-28, you have four sections. The house shown in Figure 22-28 can be obtained by pressing the ENTER key at the **Select objects:** prompt, or by selecting the **Dviewblk** option in the DVIEW screen menu. The drawing of the house with a window, open door, and a chimney obtained on the screen is a block named **DVIEWBLOCK**. This is why it is referred to as Dviewblk in the DVIEW screen menu.

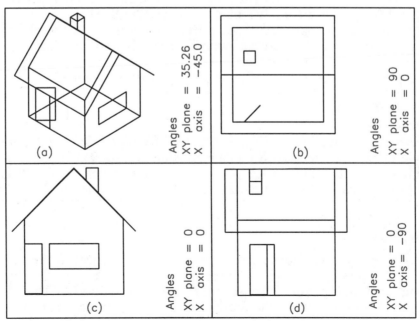

Figure 22-28 Camera option of the DVIEW command

As you use various options of the DVIEW command, the block is updated to reflect the changes. Once you come out of the DVIEW command, the entire drawing is regenerated and the view obtained depends on the view you have selected using various options of the **DVIEW** command. In this chapter you will use this block to demonstrate the effect of various options of the DVIEW command. However, you can make a custom block of your own. The block should be of unit size. Set the lower left corner of the block as the origin point. The different views of the house block we see in Figure 22-28 can be obtained with the Camera option of the DVIEW command. First, use the DVIEW command to get the image of the house on the screen.

    Command: **DVIEW** ◄⎯┘
    Select objects: ◄⎯┘

Now, you have the image of the house on the screen. For Figure 22-28(a) (3D view), the following is the prompt sequence:

    CAmera/TArget/Distance/POints/PAn/Zoom/TWist/CLip/Hide/Off/Undo/ <eXit>: **CA**
    Toggle angle in/Enter angle from XY plane <default>: **35.26**
    Toggle angle from/Enter angle in XY plane from X axis <default>: **-45.00**
    CAmera/TArget/Distance/POints/PAn/Zoom/TWist/CLip/Hide/Off/Undo/ <eXit>: **X**

Once you exit from the **DVIEW** command, the figure of the house is removed from the screen. For Figure 22-28(b) (top view), the following is the prompt sequence:

    Command: **DVIEW** ◄⎯┘
    Select objects: ◄⎯┘
    CAmera/TArget/Distance/POints/PAn/Zoom/TWist/CLip/Hide/Off/Undo/ <eXit>: **CA**
    Toggle angle in/Enter angle from XY plane <default>: **90.00**
                                  (This positions the camera at the top of the house.)
    Toggle angle from/Enter angle in XY plane from X axis <default>: **0.00**
    CAmera/TArget/Distance/POints/PAn/Zoom/TWist/CLip/Hide/Off/Undo/ <eXit>: **X**

For Figure 22-28(c) (right side view), the following is the prompt sequence:

    Command: **DVIEW** ◄⎯┘
    Select objects: ◄⎯┘
    CAmera/TArget/Distance/POints/PAn/Zoom/TWist/CLip/Hide/Off/Undo/ <eXit>: **CA**
    Toggle angle in/Enter angle from XY plane <default>: **0.00**
    Toggle angle from/Enter angle in XY plane from X axis <default>: **0.00**
    CAmera/TArget/Distance/POints/PAn/Zoom/TWist/CLip/Hide/Off/Undo/ <eXit>: **X**

For Figure 22-28(d) (front view), the following is the prompt sequence:

    Command: **DVIEW** ◄⎯┘
    Select objects: ◄⎯┘
    CAmera/TArget/Distance/POints/PAn/Zoom/TWist/CLip/Hide/Off/Undo/ <eXit>: **CA**
    Toggle angle in/Enter angle from XY plane <default>: **0.00**
    Toggle angle from/Enter angle in XY plane from X axis <default>: **-90.00**
    CAmera/TArget/Distance/POints/PAn/Zoom/TWist/CLip/Hide/Off/Undo/ <eXit>: **X**

TArget Option

With the Target option you can rotate the target point with respect to the camera. To invoke the Target option, enter **TA** at the **CAmera/TArget/Distance/POints/PAn/Zoom/TWist/CLip/Hide/Off/Undo/ <eXit>:** prompt. Once you have invoked this option, the drawing is still but you can maneuver the target point up or down, or left or right about the camera. When you move the target, the camera is stationary. The prompt sequence for the Target option is:

Command: **DVIEW** ◄─┘
Select objects: ◄─┘
CAmera/TArget/Distance/POints/PAn/Zoom/TWist/CLip/Hide/Off/Undo/ < eXit > : **TA** ◄─┘
Toggle angle in/Enter angle from XY plane < default > : *Specify the angle about which the target will lie above or below the camera.*
Toggle angle from/Enter angle in XY plane from X axis < default > : *Specify the angle about which the target will lie left or right of the camera.*
CAmera/TArget/Distance/POints/PAn/Zoom/TWist/CLip/Hide/Off/Undo/ < eXit > : ◄─┘

The prompt sequence does not give a clue about the difference between the Camera option and the Target option. The difference lies in the actual angle of view. For example, if you specify an angle of 90 degrees in the **Toggle angle in Enter angle from XY plane < default > :** prompt of the Camera option, your viewing direction is from the top of the object toward the bottom; if you specify the same angle in the same prompt for the Target option, your viewing direction is from the bottom of the object toward the top.

Example 2

The different views of the house block in Figure 22-29 can be obtained with the Target option of the **DVIEW** command.

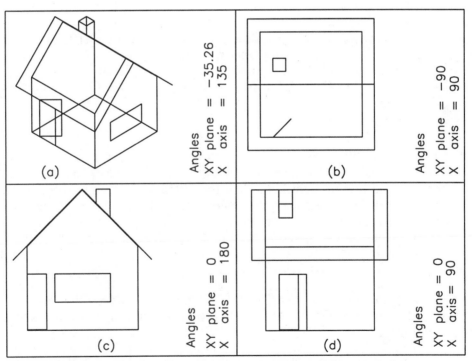

Figure 22-29 Target option of the DVIEW command

First, use the DVIEW command to display the image of the house on the screen.

Command: **DVIEW** ◄─┘
Select objects: ◄─┘

For Figure 22-29(a) (3D view), the following is the prompt sequence:

CAmera/TArget/Distance/POints/PAn/Zoom/TWist/CLip/Hide/Off/Undo/ < eXit > : **TA**

Toggle angle in/Enter angle from XY plane <default>: **-35.26**
Toggle angle from/Enter angle in XY plane from X axis <default>: **135.00**
CAmera/TArget/Distance/POints/PAn/Zoom/TWist/CLip/Hide/Off/Undo/<eXit>: **X**

For Figure 22-29(b) (top view), the following is the prompt sequence:

Command: **DVIEW** ◄─┘
Select objects: ◄─┘
CAmera/TArget/Distance/POints/PAn/Zoom/TWist/CLip/Hide/Off/Undo/<eXit>: **TA**
Toggle angle in/Enter angle from XY plane <default>: **-90.00**
Toggle angle from/Enter angle in XY plane from X axis <default>: **90.00**
CAmera/TArget/Distance/POints/PAn/Zoom/TWist/CLip/Hide/Off/Undo/<eXit>: **X**

For Figure 22-29(c) (right side view), the following is the prompt sequence:

Command: **DVIEW** ◄─┘
Select objects: ◄─┘
CAmera/TArget/Distance/POints/PAn/Zoom/TWist/CLip/Hide/Off/Undo/<eXit>: **TA**
Toggle angle in/Enter angle from XY plane <default>: **0.00**
Toggle angle from/Enter angle in XY plane from X axis <default>: **180.00**
CAmera/TArget/Distance/POints/PAn/Zoom/TWist/CLip/Hide/Off/Undo/<eXit>: **X**

For Figure 22-29(d) (front view), the following is the prompt sequence:

Command: **DVIEW** ◄─┘
Select objects: ◄─┘
CAmera/TArget/Distance/POints/PAn/Zoom/TWist/CLip/Hide/Off/Undo/<eXit>: **TA**
Toggle angle in/Enter angle from XY plane <default>: **0.00**
Toggle angle from/Enter angle in XY plane from X axis <default>: **90.00**
CAmera/TArget/Distance/POints/PAn/Zoom/TWist/CLip/Hide/Off/Undo/<eXit>: **X**

Distance Option

As mentioned before, the line obtained on joining the camera position and the target position is known as the line of sight. The Distance option can be used to move the camera toward or away from the target along the line of sight. Invoking the **Distance** option enables perspective viewing. Since we have not used the Distance option until now, all the previous views were in parallel projection. In perspective display, the objects nearer to the camera appear bigger than objects that are farther away from the camera position. In other words, in perspective views the parallel lines meet at a vanishing point. Another noticeable difference is that the regular **coordinate system icon** is replaced by the **perspective icon**. This icon acts as a reminder that perspective viewing is enabled. The distance option can be invoked by entering **D** at the **CAmera/TArget/Distance/POints/PAn/Zoom/TWist/CLip/Hide/Off/Undo/<eXit>:** prompt. Once you invoke the Distance option, AutoCAD prompts you to specify the new distance between the camera and the target.

New camera/target distance <1.0000>: *Enter the desired distance between the camera and the target.*

On the top side of the screen a slider bar appears. It is marked from 0x to 16x. The current distance is represented by the 1x mark. This is verified by the fact that the slider bar moves right or left with respect to the 1x mark on the slider bar. As you move the slider bar toward the right, the distance between the camera and the target increases; as you move the slider bar toward the left, the distance between the camera and the target decreases. For example, when you move the slider bar to the 16x mark, the distance between the camera and the target increases 16 times, or you can say that the camera moved away from the target on the line of sight 16 times the previous distance. The distance between the camera and the target is dynamically displayed in the status line. If you cannot display the entire object on the screen by moving the slider bar to the 16x mark, enter a larger distance at the keyboard. To revert to parallel viewing, invoke the **Off** option.

Example 3

Let Figure 22-30(a) be the default figure in which the distance between camera and target is 4 units, which corresponds to the 1x mark on the slider bar. You can change the distance between camera and target and get different views as follows:

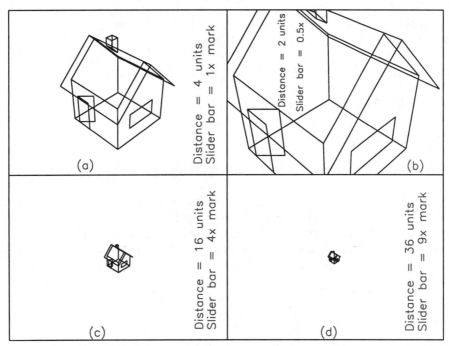

Figure 22-30 Distance option of the DVIEW command

For Figure 22-30(b):

    Command: **DVIEW** ←⏎
    Select objects: ←⏎
    CAmera/TArget/Distance/POints/PAn/Zoom/TWist/CLip/Hide/Off/Undo/ < eXit > : **D** ←⏎
    New camera/target distance < 4.0000 > : **2.0** ←⏎

For Figure 22-30(c):

    Command: **DVIEW** ←⏎
    Select objects: ←⏎
    CAmera/TArget/Distance/POints/PAn/Zoom/TWist/CLip/Hide/Off/Undo/ < eXit > : **D** ←⏎
    New camera/target distance < 4.0000 > : **16.0** ←⏎ *or move the pointer to the 4x mark on*
                                         slider bar.

For Figure 22-30(d):

    Command: **DVIEW** ←⏎
    Select objects: ←⏎
    CAmera/TArget/Distance/POints/PAn/Zoom/TWist/CLip/Hide/Off/Undo/ < eXit > : **D** ←⏎
    New camera/target distance < 4.0000 > : **36.0** ←⏎ *or move the pointer to the 9x mark on*
                                         slider bar.

POints Option

With the Points option, you can specify the camera and target positions (points) in XYZ coordinates. You can specify the XYZ coordinates of the point in any method used to specify points, including object snap and X/Y/Z point filters. The XYZ coordinate values are with respect to the current UCS. If you use the object snap to specify the points, you must type the name of the object snap. This option can be invoked by entering PO at the **CAmera/TArget/Distance/POints/PAn/Zoom/TWist/CLip/Hide/Off/Undo/<eXit>:** prompt.

Command: **DVIEW** ◄─┘
Select objects: ◄─┘
CAmera/TArget/Distance/POints/PAn/Zoom/TWist/CLip/Hide/Off/Undo/<eXit>: **PO** ◄─┘

The target point needs to be specified first. A rubberband line is drawn from the current target position to the drawing cross-hairs. This is the line of sight.

Enter target point <current>: *Specify the location of the target.*

Once you have specified the target point, you are prompted to specify the camera point. A rubberband line is drawn between the target point and drawing cross-hairs. This helps you to place the camera relative to the target.

Enter camera point <current>: *Specify the location of the camera.*

Establishment of the new target point and camera point should be carried in parallel projection. If you specify these two points while the perspective projection is active, the perspective projection is temporarily turned off until you specify the camera and target points. Once this is done, the object is again displayed in perspective. If the viewing direction is changed by the new target location and camera location, the preview image is regenerated to show the change.

Example 4

In Figure 22-31 the target is located at the lower corner of the house and the camera is located at the corner of the chimney.

In Figure 22-32 the camera is located at the lower corner of the house and the target is located at the corner of the chimney. Both these points are marked by cross marks.

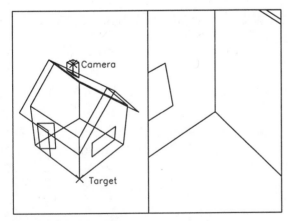

Figure 22-31 Point option of the DVIEW command

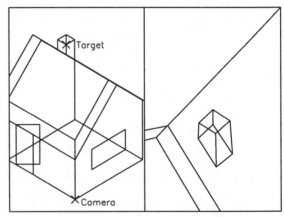

Figure 22-32 Point option of the DVIEW command

PAn Option

The Pan option of the **DVIEW** command resembles the **PAN** command. This option lets you shift the entire drawing with respect to the graphics display area. Just as with the PAN command, you have to specify the pan distance and direction by specifying two points. You must use a pointing device to specify the two points if perspective viewing is active. The prompt sequence for this option is:

Command: **DVIEW** ←⏎
Select objects: ←⏎
CAmera/TArget/Distance/POints/PAn/Zoom/TWist/CLip/Hide/Off/Undo/ < eXit > : **PA** ←⏎
Displacement base point: *Specify the first point.*
Second point: *Specify the second point.*

Zoom Option

The Zoom option of the **DVIEW** command resembles the ZOOM command. With the help of this option you can enlarge or reduce the drawing. This option can be invoked by entering **Z** at the following prompt:

CAmera/TArget/Distance/POints/PAn/Zoom/TWist/CLip/Hide/Off/Undo/ < eXit > : **Z** ←⏎
Adjust lens length < 50.000mm > : *Specify the new lens length.*

Just as with the Distance option, in Zoom option a slider bar marked from 0x to 16x is displayed on the top side of the screen. The default position on the slider bar is 1x. Two ways to zoom can now be specified. The first is when perspective is enabled. In this case zooming is defined in terms of **lens length**. The 1x mark (default position) corresponds to a 50.000mm lens length. As you move the slider bar toward the right, the lens length increases, and as you move the slider bar toward the left, the lens length decreases. For example, when you move the slider bar to the 16x mark, the lens length increases 16 times, which is 16x50.000mm = 800.000mm. You can simulate the telephoto effect by increasing the lens length, and by reducing the lens length you can simulate the wide angle effect. The lens length is dynamically displayed in the status line. If perspective is not enabled, zooming is defined in terms of the zoom scale factor. In this case the Zoom option resembles the ZOOM Center command and the center point lies at the center of the current viewport. The 1x mark (default position) corresponds to a sale factor of 1. As you move the slider bar toward the right, the scale factor increases, and as you move the slider bar towards the left, the scale factor decreases. For example, when you move the slider bar to the 16x mark, the scale factor increases 16 times, which is 16x1 = 16. The scale factor is dynamically displayed in the status line.

Command: **DVIEW** ←⏎
Select objects: *Select the objects.*
CAmera/TArget/Distance/POints/PAn/Zoom/TWist/CLip/Hide/Off/Undo/ < eXit > : **Z** ←⏎
Adjust zoom scale factor < 1 > : *Specify the scale factor.*

Example 5

Let's see the effect of the Zoom option in perspective projection. In Figure 22-33(a), the lens length is set to 25mm. This can be realized in the following manner:

Command: **DVIEW** ←⏎
Select objects: ←⏎
CAmera/TArget/Distance/POints/PAn/Zoom/TWist/CLip/Hide/Off/Undo/ < eXit > : **Z** ←⏎
Adjust lens length < 50.000mm > : **25** ←⏎

Similarly, for Figure 22-33(b), (c), and (d), you can set lens lengths to 50mm, 75mm, and 125mm respectively.

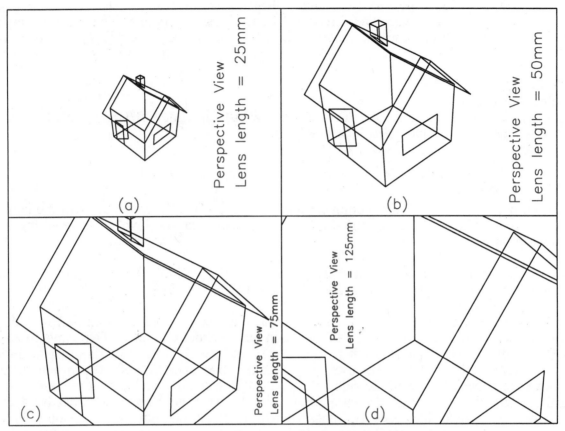

Figure 22-33 Zoom option of the DVIEW command

TWist Option

The **Twist** option allows you to rotate (twist) the view around the line of sight. You can also say that the object on the screen can be rotated around the center point of the screen because the display is always adjusted so that the target point is at the center of the screen. If you use a pointing device to specify the angle, the angle value is dynamically displayed in the status line. A rubberband line is drawn from the center (target point) to the drawing cross-hairs, and as you move the cross-hairs with a pointing device, the object on the screen is rotated around the line of sight. You can also enter the angle of twist from the keyboard. The angle of twist is measured in a counterclockwise direction starting from the right side.

Command: **DVIEW** ◄┘
Select objects: ◄┘
CAmera/TArget/Distance/POints/PAn/Zoom/TWist/CLip/Hide/Off/Undo/<eXit>: **TW** ◄┘
New view twist <0.00>: *Specify the angle of rotation (twist)*

Example 6

In Figure 22-34, different twist angles have been specified. For (a) the twist angle is 0, for (b) it is 338 degrees, for (c) it is 37 degrees, and for (d), the twist angle is 360 degrees.

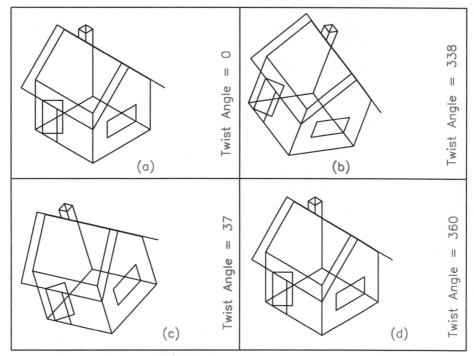

Figure 22-34 Twist option of the DVIEW command

CLip Option

The **Clip** option can be used to clip sections of the drawing. AutoCAD uses two invisible clipping planes to realize clipping. These clipping walls can be positioned anywhere on the screen and are perpendicular to the line of sight (line between target and camera). Once you position the clipping planes, AutoCAD conceals all the lines that are in front of the Front clipping plane or behind the Back clipping plane. The Clipping option can be used in both parallel and perspective projections. When perspective is enabled, the front clipping plane is automatically enabled.

> **Note**
>
> *If you have specified a positive distance, the clipping plane is placed between the target and the camera. If the distance you have specified is negative, the clipping plane is placed beyond the target.*

The prompt sequence for the Clip option is:

CAmera/TArget/Distance/POints/PAn/Zoom/TWist/CLip/Hide/Off/Undo/ < eXit > : **CL** ◄─┘
Back/Front/ < Off > : **B** ◄─┘
On/OFF? < Distance from target > < Current distance > :

Once you have specified which clipping plane you want to set (the Back clipping plane in our case), a slider bar appears on the screen. As you move the pointer toward the right side of the slider bar, the negative distance between the target and the clipping plane increases; as you move toward the left side of the slider bar, the positive distance between the target and the clipping plane increases, hence a greater portion of the drawing is clipped. The rightmost mark on the slider bar corresponds to a distance equal to distance between the target and the farthestmost point on the object you want to clip. After specifying the distance between one of the clipping planes (Back clipping plane in this prompt sequence), you need to invoke the Clip option again and specify the position of the Front clipping plane in terms of distance between the front clipping plane and the target. As you move the slider bar toward the right, the negative distance between the target and the Front clipping plane increases. As the negative distance increases, a greater portion of the front side of the drawing is clipped. The rightmost mark on the slider bar corresponds to a distance equal to the distance between the target and the Back clipping plane.

CAmera/TArget/Distance/POints/PAn/Zoom/TWist/CLip/Hide/Off/Undo/ < eXit > : **CL** ◄⎯⎦
Back/Front/ < Off > : **F** ◄⎯⎦
Eye/ON/OFF/ < Distance from target > < default > : *Specify the distance from target.*

To illustrate the concepts behind clipping, let us display two objects (a sphere and a cone) on the screen. Let the distance between the two be 10 units. Draw a line between the center of the sphere and the center of the cone. Use the Points option to position the target at the center of the sphere and the camera at the mid point of the line joining the two center points. In this way you have defined the line between the two center points as the line of sight.

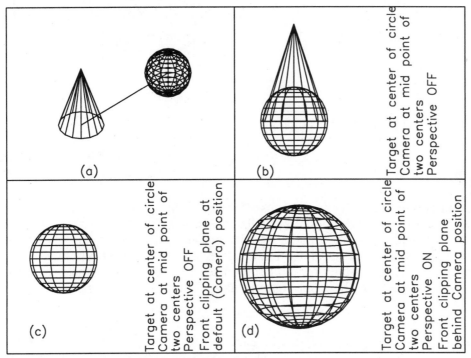

Figure 22-35 Using the clip option to clip the view

Now that you have defined the target and the camera, you will see the sphere and the cone overlapping because both of them are aligned along the line of sight. You may wonder how you are able to see the cone since it lies behind the camera position that is analogous to the eye. This is because in parallel projection, the camera is not analogous to the eye, but the line of sight is; hence you see everything that lies in the field of vision (determined by the Zoom option) about the line of sight. Now when you use the Clip option and the Front suboption to define the position of the Front clipping plane, by default the front clipping plane is positioned at the camera point. Now you cannot see the objects (cone in our case) that are behind the camera point because the default position of the front clipping plane is at the camera position, hence any object in front of the Front clipping plane is clipped. Also if you have placed the Front clipping plane behind the camera position and the perspective projection is on, the camera position is used as the Front clipping plane position.

If you change the Front clipping plane position, and then at some stage you want to go back to the default Front clipping plane position, you can use the **Eye** option. In perspective, without invoking the Clip option, the Front clipping plane is placed at the camera position, hence you are able to see only what lies in front of the camera.

Example 7

In Figure 22-36, the Front clipping plane has been established at a distance of 0.50 units. The distance between the camera and target is 3.50 units. After invoking the **Clip** option, The prompt sequence is:

Back/Front/ < Off > : **F** ◄──┘
On/OFF? < Distance from target > < 3.5000 > :**0.50** ◄──┘

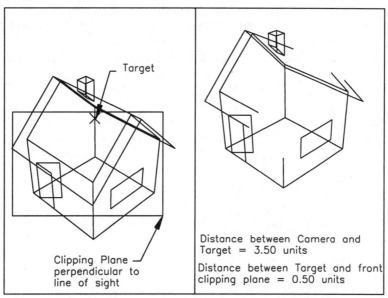

Figure 22-36 Front clipping with the DVIEW command

In Figure 22-37, the Back clipping plane has been established at a distance of 0.50 units. The distance between the camera and target is 3.50 units. After invoking the **Clip** option, the prompt sequence is:

Back/Front/ < Off > : **B** ◄──┘
On/OFF? < Distance from target > < 3.5000 > : **0.50** ◄──┘

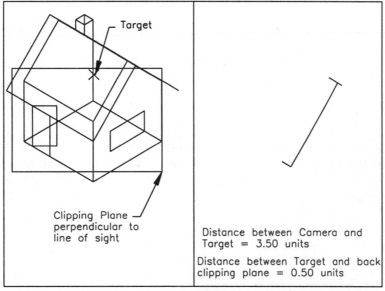

Figure 22-37 Back clipping with the DVIEW command

You might have noticed that if you combine the clipped shape in Figure 22-36 and the clipped shape in Figure 22-37, you will get the original shape of the house. The reason is that in the first clipped figure, whatever lies between the camera and the Front clipping plane is clipped, while in the second clipped figure, whatever lies behind the Back clipping plane is clipped. Since the distance between the clipping planes and the target, and the distance between camera and target is identical in both the figures, if you combine the clipped figures, you will get the original shape.

Hide Option

In most 3D drawings, some of the lines lie behind other lines or objects. Sometimes, you may not want these hidden lines to show up on the screen, so you can use the Hide option. This option is similar to the **HIDE** command. To invoke Hide option enter **H** at the **CAmera/TArget/Distance/POints/PAn/Zoom/TWist/CLip/Hide/Off/Undo/<eXit>:** prompt.

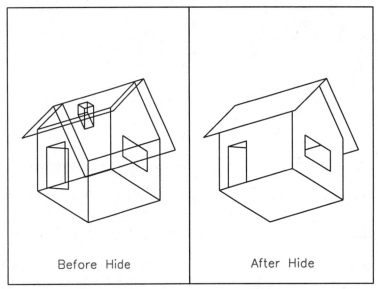

Before Hide   After Hide

Figure 22-38 Hide option of the DVIEW command

Off Option

The **Off** option turns perspective projection off. The prompt sequence is:

CAmera/TArget/Distance/POints/PAn/Zoom/TWist/CLip/Hide/Off/Undo/<eXit>: **O**

When perspective projection is turned off, you will notice that the **perspective icon** is replaced by the **regular UCS icon**.

Undo Option

The Undo option is similar to the UNDO command. The **Undo** option nullifies the result of the previous DVIEW operation. Just as in the case of the UNDO command, you can use this option a number of times to undo the results of multiple DVIEW operations. To invoke this option, enter **U** at the following prompt:

CAmera/TArget/Distance/POints/PAn/Zoom/TWist/CLip/Hide/Off/ Undo/<eXit>: **U**

eXit option

You can end the DVIEW command using **eXit** option.

SELF EVALUATION TEST

Answer the following questions and then compare your answers with the correct answers given at the end of this chapter.

1.   What are the two types of viewports in AutoCAD? _____ .

2.   The tiled viewports are created by using the _____ command when the system variable _____ is set to 1 (Model space).

3.   With the _____ option you can choose the viewports for which you want to remove the hidden lines when you plot in Paper space.

4.   If you set Hideplot to Off, hidden lines **are not plotted**. (T/F)

5.   To shift from Paper space to Model space at least two viewports must be active and on. (T/F)

6.   The VPLAYER command can be used from either Model space or Paper space. (T/F)

7.   To use the VPLAYER command, the only restriction is that TILEMODE must be set to 1 (On). (T/F)

8.   The Freeze option of the VPLAYER command is used to freeze a layer (or layers) in only one viewport. (T/F)

9.   Layers that have been frozen, thawed, switched on, or switched off globally are not affected by the _____ command.

10.   The position from which you want to view the object (the viewer's eye) is the _____ , and the focus point is the _____ .

11.   The line formed between the target and the camera is known as _____ or _____ .

12.   The _____ option allows you to rotate the camera about the target point.

13.   When you are moving the camera, the _____ is stationary and when you are moving the target, the _____ is stationary.

14.   If perspective is disabled, the zooming is defined in terms of the _____ .

15.   The 1x mark (default position) corresponds to a sale factor of ____ .

16.   When you move the slider bar to the 16x mark, the scale factor increases _____ .

17.   The _____ option of the DVIEW command allows you to rotate (twist) the view around the line of sight.

18.   The _____ option can be used to shift from perspective viewing to parallel viewing.

19.   With the _____ option of the DVIEW command, you can specify the camera and target positions (points) in XYZ coordinates.

20.   The _____ option lets you shift the entire drawing with respect to the graphics display area.

REVIEW QUESTIONS

Answer the following questions.

VIEWPORTS

1. The _____ command can be used to create viewports and divide the display screen into a number of parts (viewports).

2. An arrangement of viewports created with the VPORTS command is a display function and _____ be plotted.

UCSFOLLOW

3. When the _____ variable is assigned a value of 1, a plan view is automatically generated if you change the UCS in a viewport.

MVIEW

4. The **MVIEW** command is used to create _____ in paper space.

5. Before using the MVIEW command, you must change the system variable _____ to 0.

6. If you invoke the MVIEW command in the MSPACE Model space (Tilemode set to 0), AutoCAD shifts you from _____ to _____ , until the MVIEW command is not over.

7. It is possible to alter the size of the viewports and adjust them on the screen. (T/F)

8. Name five options of the VPLAYER command._____,
    _____,_____,_____,_____

9. You should turn off the viewports that are not required because _____
    _____.

10. The system variable _____ controls the number of viewports that will display the objects.

11. You will not be able to work in the MSPACE Model space if any viewport is turned off. (T/F)

12. What happens if you turn Hideplot on? _____.

MSPACE/PSPACE

13. The _____ command is used to shift from Paper space to Model space.

14. Before using the MSPACE command, you must set the _____ to 0 (Off).

15. The _____ command is used to shift from Model space to Paper space.

VPLAYER

16. You can control the visibility of layers inside the viewport with the _____ command.

17. With the _____ command you can control the visibility of layers in individual viewports.

18. With the _____ option you can set the visibility of layer(s) in the specified viewports to their current default setting.

19. The visibility defaults of a layer can be set by using the _____ option of the **VPLAYER** command.

20. With the _____ option you can create new layers that are frozen in all viewports.

21. With the _____ option you can set the default for the visibility of layer(s).

22. The **New VP: Thw** and **New VP: Frz** (New Viewport Thaw and New Viewport Freeze) buttons govern the freezing and thawing of selected layers in the _____ viewport.

DVIEW

23. With the _____ command, you can generate different views of 3D objects on the screen.

24. The DVIEW command offers you the choice between parallel viewing and _____ viewing.

25. In _____ view, parallel lines in the 3D object remain parallel.

26. In _____ view, parallel lines meet at a vanishing point.

27. The angle from XY plane of the camera with respect to the current UCS is used to achieve _____ movement of the camera.

28. You can use the _____ option of the DVIEW command to rotate the target point up or down, left or right with respect to the camera.

29. The _____ option of the DVIEW command can be used to move the camera toward or away from the target along the line of sight.

30. When you invoke the Distance option, _____ viewing is enabled.

31. In perspective display, the objects nearer to the camera appear _____ in size compared with objects that are further away from the camera position.

32. When you move the slider bar to the 16x mark, the distance between the camera and the target increases _____ .

33. If perspective is enabled, zooming is defined in terms of _____ .

34. The 1x mark (default position) corresponds to ____ lens length.

35. With the Twist option of the DVIEW command, the angle of twist is measured in a _____ direction starting from the right side.

36. The _____ option of the DVIEW command can be used to clip sections of the drawing.

37. The clipping planes are perpendicular to the line of sight and AutoCAD conceals all the lines that are in _____ of the Front clipping plane or _____ the Back clipping plane.

38. With the Front clipping plane, as you increase the negative distance, _____ portion of the drawing is clipped.

39. With the Back clipping plane, as you increase the positive distance, _____ portion of the drawing is clipped.

40. If you change the Front clipping plane position, and then at some stage you want to go back to the default Front clipping plane position, you can use the _____ option.

EXERCISES

Exercise 1

In Exercise 1 you will perform the following tasks:

a. Draw the computer as shown in Figure 22-39. Take the dimensions from the computer you are using. For your convenience two images of the same computer are shown. The first one has the lines hidden and the second one shows all lines, including the lines that are behind the visible surfaces.

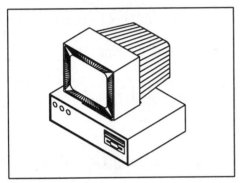

Figure 22-39 3D view of the computer without hidden lines

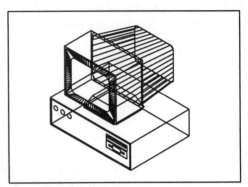

Figure 22-40 3D view of the computer with hidden lines

Construction of the given figure can be divided into the following steps:

1. Drawing the CPU box (central processing unit)
2. Drawing the base of the monitor.
3. Drawing the monitor.

b. Once you have drawn the figure of the computer, create four viewports in Model space and obtain different views of the computer as shown in the screen capture (Figure 22-41). You can use the VPOINTS command to obtain the different views.

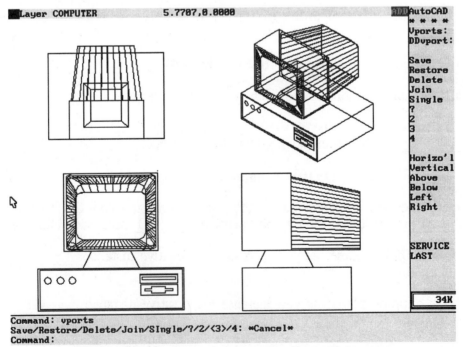

Figure 22-41 Four viewports in the model space

c. Next use the **MVIEW** command to create four viewports as shown in Figure 22-42. Center the figure of the computer in 3D view in all four of the viewports. Use the Camera option of the DVIEW command to obtain the figure shown in the upper left viewport.

Use the **Distance** option of the DVIEW command to obtain the figure shown in the upper right viewport.

Use the **Clip** option of the DVIEW command to obtain the figure shown in the lower left viewport.

Use the **Twist** option of the DVIEW command to obtain the figure shown in the lower right viewport.

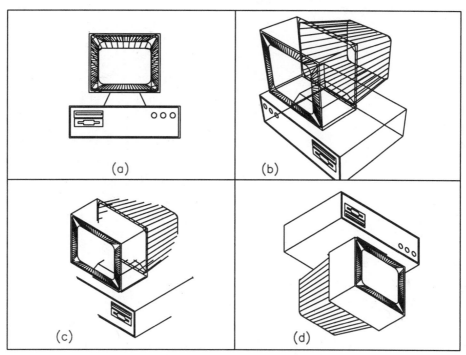

Figure 22-42 Using DVIEW options to obtain different displays of the computer

d. What is the difference between the parallel projection and the perspective projection?

Answers

The following are the correct answers to the questions in the self evaluation test.
1 - tiled viewports and untiled viewports, **2** - VPORTS, TILEMODE, **3** - HIDEPLOT, **4** - F, **5** - F (One), **6** - F, **7** - F (TILEMODE set to 0), **8** - F (One or more), **9** - VPLAYER, **10** - camera, target, **11** - line of sight, viewing direction, **12** - cameras, **13** - target, cameras, **14** - Zoom Scale Factor, **15** - 1, **16** - 16 times, **17** - Twist, **18** - Off, **19** - Points, **20** - PAN

Chapter 23

Solid Modeling

Learning objectives

After completing this chapter, you will be able to:
- ♦ Understand solid modeling.
- ♦ Understand why solid modeling is used.
- ♦ Create solid primitives.
- ♦ Understand regions and how to create them.
- ♦ Construct composite solids.
- ♦ Analyze solids.
- ♦ Create cross sections of solids.

WHAT IS SOLID MODELING?

Solid modeling is the process of building objects that have all the attributes of an actual solid object. For example, if you draw a wireframe or a surface model of a bushing, it is sufficient to define the shape and size of the object. However, in engineering the shape and size alone are not enough to describe an object. For engineering analysis we need more information, like volume, mass, moment of inertia, and material properties (density, Young's modulus, Poissons's ratio, thermal conductivity, etc.). When you know these physical attributes of an object, it can be subjected to various tests to make sure that it performs as required by the product specifications. It eliminates the need for building expensive prototypes and makes the product development cycle shorter. The solid models also make it easy to visualize the objects because we always think of and see the objects as solids. With computers getting faster and software getting more sophisticated and affordable, solid modeling will become the core of the manufacturing process. AutoCAD's solid modeling is based on ACIS solid modeler, which is a part of core technology.

PREDEFINED SOLID PRIMITIVES

Toolbar: Solids
Pull-down: Draw, Solids
Screen: DRAW2, SOLIDS, object name

The solid primitives form the basic building blocks for a complex solid. AME has six predefined solid primitives (box, wedge, cone, cylinder, sphere, and torus) that you can use to construct a solid model. The number of lines in a solid model is controlled by the value assigned

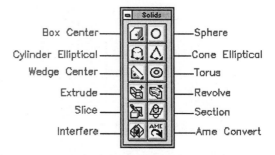

Figure 23-1 Selecting Solid primitives from Solids toolbar

to the **ISOLINES** variable. These lines are called tessellation lines. The number of lines determines the number of computations needed to generate a solid. If the value is high, it will take significantly more time to create a solid. Therefore, the value you assign to the **ISOLINES** variable should be realistic. When you enter commands for creating solid primitives, AutoCAD Solids will prompt you to enter information about the part geometry. The height of the primitive is always along the positive Z axis, perpendicular to the construction plane. The solid primitives can be selected from the **Solids** toolbar (Figure 23-1) from the pull-down menu (select Draw, Solids, Figure 23-2), or from the screen menu (select DRAW2, SOLIDS, object name). The solid primitives can also be drawn by entering the name of the primitive (Box, Cylinder, Torus, etc.) at the Command: prompt.

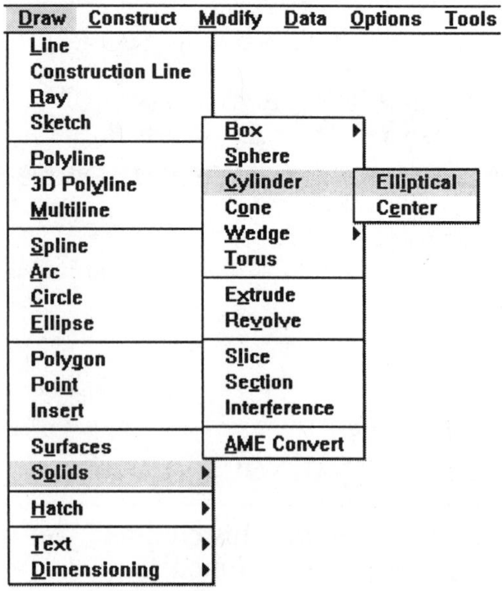

Figure 23-2 Selecting AutoCAD Solid primitives from the pull-down menu

Creating a Box (BOX)

Toolbar: Solids, Box Corner
Pull-down: Draw, Solids, Box, Corner
Screen: DRAW2, SOLIDS, Box:

You can use the **BOX** command to create a solid rectangular box. This command can be invoked from the **Solid** toolbar (select Box Corner icon), from the pull-down menu (select Draw Solids, Box, Corner), from the screen menu (select DRAW2, SOLIDS, Box:), or by entering **Box** at the Command: prompt. It has two options: **Center** and **Corner**. The Corner option is the default option. In this option, AutoCAD will prompt you to enter the first corner, second corner, and height of the box. The following is the command prompt sequence for the **BOX** command:

Command: **BOX**
Center/ < Corner of box > < 0,0,0 >: **1,1,0**
Cube/Length/ < other corner >: **3,2.5,0**
Height: **2.5**

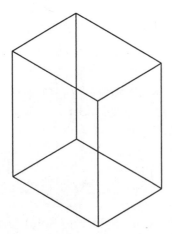

Figure 23-3 Creating a solid box using the BOX command

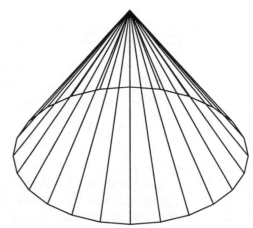

Figure 23-4 Creating a solid cone using the CONE command

Creating a Solid Cone (CONE)

The **CONE** command creates a solid cone with an elliptical or circular base. This command can be selected just as any command to create any solid primitive object. It has two options: **Elliptical** and **Center point**. The Center point option is the default option. The base of the cone lies on the current construction plane and the height of the cone is along the Z axis. You can change the base plane (XY plane) by using the UCS command options. You can also define the apex point to define the cone height. The following is the command prompt sequence for the **CONE** command:

```
Command: CONE
Elliptical/<Center point>  <0,0,0>: 5,2
Diameter/<Radius>: 1.0
Apex/<Height>: 1.5
```

Creating a Solid Cylinder (CYLINDER)

You can use the **CYLINDER** command to construct a solid cylinder. This command can be selected just as any command to create any solid primitive object. Like the CONE command, it has two options: **Elliptical** and **Center point**. The Center point option is the default option. The base of the cylinder lies on the current construction plane and the height of the cylinder is along the Z axis. You can change the base plane (XY construction plane) by using the UCS command options. The following is the command prompt sequence for the **CYLINDER** command:

```
Command: CYLINDER
Elliptical/<Center point>  <0,0,0>: 8,2
Diameter/<Radius>: 1.0
Center point of other end/<Height>: 2.5
```

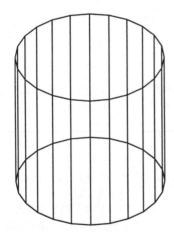

Figure 23-5 Creating a solid cylinder using the CYLINDER command

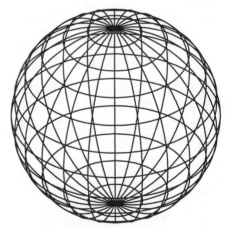

Figure 23-6 Creating a solid sphere using the SPHERE command

Creating a Solid Sphere (SPHERE)

The **SPHERE** command can be used to create a solid sphere. The SPHERE command can be selected just as any command to create any solid primitive object. The command has only one option: **Center of sphere**. The center of the sphere automatically aligns with the Z axis of the current UCS. The following is the command prompt sequence of the **SPHERE** command using Center point option:

Command: **SPHERE**
<Center of sphere> <0,0,0>: **1,5**
Diameter/<Radius> of sphere: **1.25**

Creating a Solid Torus (TORUS)

You can use the **TORUS** command to create a torus (doughnut like shape). The TORUS command can be selected just as any command to create any solid primitive object. When you select this command, AutoCAD will prompt you to enter Diameter/<Radius> of torus and Diameter/<Radius of tube>. Radius of torus is the distance from the center of the torus to the center line of the tube. This radius can have a positive or negative value. If the value is negative, the torus has a football-like shape. The torus is centered around the construction plane (top half of the torus is above the construction plane and the other half is below the construction plane). The following is the command sequence for the **TORUS** command:

Command: **TORUS**
<Center of torus> <0,0,0>: **5,4**
Diameter/<Radius> of torus: **1.75**
Diameter/<Radius> of tube: **0.5**

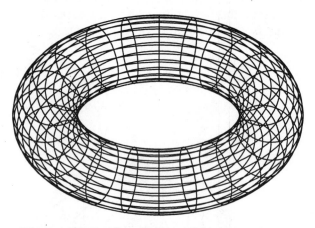

Figure 23-7 Creating a solid torus using the TORUS command

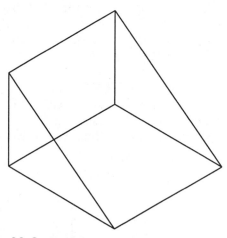

Figure 23-8 Creating a solid wedge using the WEDGE command

Creating a Solid Wedge (WEDGE)

The **WEDGE** command can be used to create a solid wedge. The WEDGE command can be selected just as any command to create any solid primitive object. When you enter this command, AutoCAD will prompt you to enter the first and the second corner of wedge. These two points define the base of the wedge that is always drawn parallel to the current construction plane. The command will also prompt you to enter the height of wedge. The wedge will taper toward the positive X axis. The following is the command prompt sequence for the **WEDGE** command:

Command: **WEDGE**
Center/<Corner of wedge> <0,0,0>: **1,1,0**
Cube/Length/<Other corner>: **3,2.5,0**
Height: **2.5**

CONSTRUCTING A REGION

The following example explains some commands that can be used to create solids and regions.

Example 1

Use AutoCAD Solids commands to create a region and then extrude this region to create a solid model of the object (base plate) as shown in Figure 23-9.

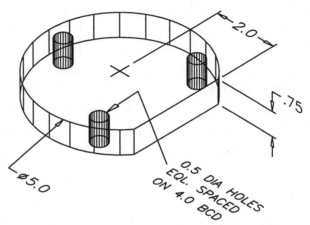

Figure 23-9 Drawing for Example 1

Creating a 2D Region Primitive

A region is a solid with zero thickness. Creating a 2D Region Primitive involves two steps: first, create a part profile by using AutoCAD commands; and second, create a region by solidifying the part profile. A region is created by using the REGION command. The following steps explain the process involved in constructing a region for Example 1.

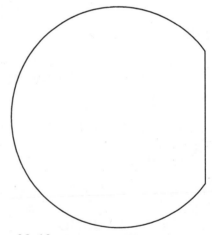

Figure 23-10 Outer profile of the base plate

1. Use AutoCAD's drawing and editing commands to make the drawing of the base plate as shown in Figure 23-10.

   Use the **ARC** and **LINE** commands to draw the outer profile.

   Command: **ARC**
   Center/ < Start point > : **C**
   Center: **5,4**
   Start point: **7,5.5**
   Angle/Length of chord/ < End point > : **7,2.5**

   Command: **LINE**
   From point: **7.0,5.5**
   To point: **7.0,2.5**
   To point: ⏎

2. Use the **PEDIT** command to change the line into a polyline, then use the Join option to join the line with the arc to create a single polyline object.

Command: **PEDIT**
Select polyline: **(Select the line)**
Object selected is not a polyline
Do you want to turn it into one? < Y > : **Y**
Close/Join/Width/Edit vertex/Fit/Spline/Decurve/Ltype gen/Undo/eXit < X > : **J**
Select objects: *Select the line.*
Select objects: *Select the arc.*
Select objects: ←┘
1 segment added to polyline
Close/Join/Width/Edit vertex/Fit/Spline/Decurve/Ltype gen/Undo/eXit < X > : **X**

Creating a 2D Region (REGION Command)

Toolbar:	Draw, Polygon, Region
Pull-down:	Construct, Region
Screen:	CONSTRCT, Region:

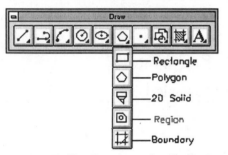

Figure 23-11 Region icon in the Polygon flyout of the Draw toolbar

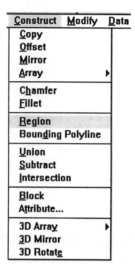

Figure 23-12 Region icon in the Construct pull-down menu

You can use the **REGION** command to create a region (Figure 23-13). This command can be invoked from the **Draw** toolbar (select the Region icon from the Polygon flyout Figure 23-11), from the pull-down menu (select Construct, Region, Figure 23-12), from the screen menu (select CONSTRCT, Region:), or by entering **REGION** at the Command: prompt. AutoCAD will create a region from the selected polyline and then remove the polyline from the drawing.

1.   Use the **REGION** command to create a region.

Command: **REGION**
Select objects: *Select the polyline.*
Select objects: ←┘

Hatching a Region (Using BHATCH Command)

When you create a region, the mesh lines
are not visible. To hatch a region, you can use the BHATCH command. The hatch pattern, the hatch angle, and the hatch size can be set in the Boundary Hatch dialogue box. You can use any hatch pattern that is defined in AutoCAD's ACAD.PAT file. To get hatch as shown in Figure 23-13, use the ANSI31 hatch pattern and a scale factor of 3.5.

2.   Use the **UCS** command to move the UCS icon to the center point (5,4) of the arc. (When AutoCAD prompts for the origin point, you can also use the CENter object snap to grab the center point of arc).

Command: **UCS**
Origin/ZAxis/3point/Object/View/X/Y/Z/Pre/Restore/Save/Del/?/<World>: **O**
Origin point (0,0,0): **5,4**

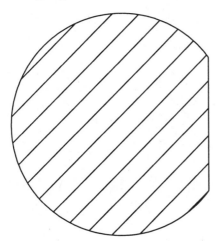

Figure 23-13 Creating a 2D Region

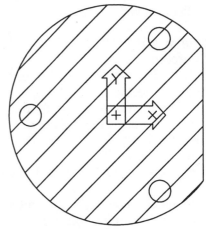

Figure 23-14 Creating a circular array

3. Draw 0.5 diameter circles located on the 4.0 diameter bolt circle (Figure 23-14). (You can also create the circles by drawing one circle and then using the ARRAY command to create the remaining circles.)

    Command: **CIRCLE**
    3P/2P/TTR/<Center point>: **@2<60**
    Diameter/<Radius>: **D**
    Diameter: **0.5**

    Command: **ARRAY**
    Select objects: *Select 0.5 diameter circle.*
    Rectangular or Polar array (R/P): **P**
    Center point of array: **0,0**
    Number of items: **3**
    Angle to fill (+=CCW, -=CW)<360>: **240**
    Rotate objects as they are copied?<Y>:◄┘

4. Use the **REGION** command to create a region from the circles.

Subtracting Regions (SUBTRACT)

Toolbar: Modify, Explode, Subtract
Pull-down: Construct, Subtract
Screen: DRAW2, SOLIDS, Subtrac:

You can use the **SUBTRACT** command to subtract regions or solids. This command can be invoked from the **Modify** toolbar (select Subtract icon from Explode flyout, Figure 23-15), from the pull-down menu (select Construct, Subtract), from the screen menu (select DRAW2, SOLIDS, Subtrac:), or by entering **SUBTRACT** at the Command: prompt.

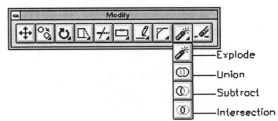

Figure 23-15 Subtract icon in the Explode flyout of the Modify toolbar

When you use this command, AutoCAD will prompt you to select two selection sets. Once you have selected the objects, the objects of the second selection set will be subtracted from the first selection set (Figure 23-16.)

Command: **SUBTRACT**
Source objects...
Select objects: *Select the region.*
Select objects: ◄─┘
Objects to subtract from them...
Select objects: *Select three 0.5 dia. circles.*
Select objects: ◄─┘
3 regions selected
3 regions subtracted from 1 region

The hatch lines may not get removed from the small circles till you use the MOVE command and move the outer profile.

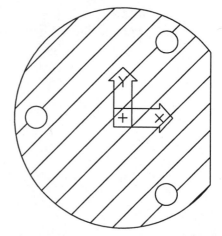

Figure 23-16 Subtracting regions using the SUBTRACT command

Creating an Extruded Solid (EXTRUDE)

Toolbar: Solids, Extrude
Pull-down: Draw, Solids, Extrude
Screen: DRAW2, SOLIDS, Extrude:

The next step is to extrude the region by using the **EXTRUDE** command (Figure 23-17). This command can be invoked from the **Solids** toolbar (select Extrude icon), from the pull-down menu (select Draw, Solids, Extrude), from the screen menu (select DRAW2, SOLIDS, Extrude:), or by entering **EXTRUDE** at the Command: prompt. When you enter this command, AutoCAD will prompt you to select the objects for extrusion, the height of extrusion, and the extrusion taper angle. After you enter this information, AutoCAD will evaluate the boundaries and do tessellation calculations for each element in the composite region. You can also use the **ISOLINES** command to set the number of tessellation lines.

Command: **ISOLINES**
New value for ISOLINES<4>: **10**

Command: **EXTRUDE**
Select objects: *Select the region.*
Select objects: ◄─┘
Path/<Height of extrusion>: **0.75**
Extrusion taper angle<0>: ◄─┘

Next, you can use the **VPOINT** command to get a 3D view of the extruded region (Figure 23-18). Use the ERASE command to erase the hatch lines. Save a copy of this drawing as BASEPLT. This drawing will be used in Example 2 to construct another solid.

Command: **VPOINT**
Rotate/<View point> <0.00, 0.00, 1.00>: **1,-1,1**

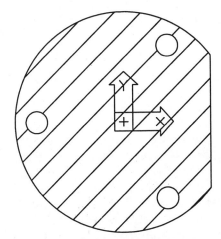

Figure 23-17 Extruding a region

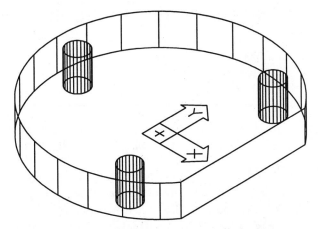

Figure 23-18 3D view of the extruded region

CONSTRUCTING A COMPOSITE SOLID

A composite solid consists of two or more solid primitives. The following example explains some of the frequently used AutoCAD Solids commands that are used to create a composite solid. The examples also illustrate the application of these commands.

Example 2

Use AutoCAD Solids commands to create a solid model of the object as shown in Figure 23-19. The chamfer and fillet radius is 0.15. To save time, you may use the base-plate drawing (BASEPLT) created in Example 1.

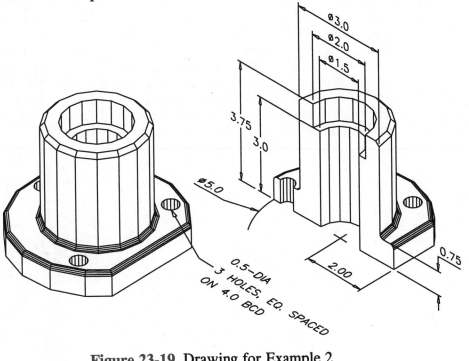

Figure 23-19 Drawing for Example 2

Creating a Revolved Solid (REVOLVE)

Toolbar:	Solids, Revolve
Pull-down:	Draw, Solids, Revolve
Screen:	DRAW2, SOLIDS, Revolve:

The **REVOLVE** command creates a solid by sweeping a polyline or circle around an axis. This command can be invoked from the **Solids** toolbar (select the Revolve icon), from the pull-down menu (select Draw, Solids, Revolve), from the screen menu (select DRAW2, SOLIDS, Revolve:), or by entering **REVOLVE** at the Command: prompt. The selected object can be rotated through any angle from 0 to 360 degrees. Before using the REVOLVE command, you must draw the profile of the surface that you want to revolve. Use the UCS command to rotate the UCS icon by +90 degrees and then draw the profile.

Note

Make sure the UCS icon is at the center of the base. If it is not, use the UCS command to define the new origin.

---

1. Use the **UCS** command to rotate the UCS icon through 90 degrees.

    Command: **UCS**
    Origin/ZAxis/3point/Object/View/X/Y/Z/Pre/Restore/Save/Del/?/<World>: **X**
    Rotation angle about X axis<0>: **90**

2. Use the **PLINE** command to draw the profile of the surface (Figure 23-20).

    Command: **PLINE**
    From point: **0,0**
    Current line-width is 0.0000
    Arc/Close/Halfwidth/Length/Undo/Width/<Endpoint of line>: **@0.75,0**
    Arc/Close/Halfwidth/Length/Undo/Width/<Endpoint of line>: **@0,3**
    Arc/Close/Halfwidth/Length/Undo/Width/<Endpoint of line>: **@0.25,0**
    Arc/Close/Halfwidth/Length/Undo/Width/<Endpoint of line>: **@0,0.75**
    Arc/Close/Halfwidth/Length/Undo/Width/<Endpoint of line>: **@-1,0**
    Arc/Close/Halfwidth/Length/Undo/Width/<Endpoint of line>: **C**

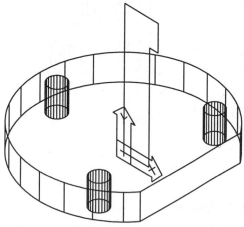

Figure 23-20 Creating the surface of the revolution profile

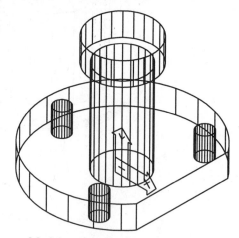

Figure 23-21 Creating a revolved solid

3. Use the **REVOLVE** command to revolve the profile through 360 degrees (Figure 23-21).

Command: **REVOLVE**
Select region, polyline or circle for revolution...
Select objects: (Select polyline)
Select objects: ◄─┘
Axis of revolution - Object/X/Y/ < Start point of axis > : **0,0**
End point of axis: **0,3**
Angle of revolution < full circle > : ◄─┘

Creating a Cylinder (CYLINDER)

The **CYLINDER** command creates a solid cylinder. The CYLINDER command can be selected just as any command to create any solid primitive object. When you enter this command, AME will prompt you to enter the diameter and height of cylinder. The number of lines on the cylindrical surface (tessellation lines) depends on the value of the **ISOLINES** variable. Use the following commands to draw the solid cylinder:

1. Use the **UCS** command to rotate the UCS icon -90 degrees about X axis so that the UCSicon is parallel to bottom face. Then redefine the **UCS** origin 0.75 units up along Z axis.

Command: **UCS**
Origin/ZAxis/3point/Object/View/X/Y/Z/Pre/Restore/Save/Del/?/ < World > : **X**
Rotation angle about X axis < 0 > : **-90**
Origin/ZAxis/3point/Object/View/X/Y/Z/Pre/Restore/Save/Del/?/ < World > : **O**
Origin point (0,0,0): **@0,0,0.75**

2. Use the **CYLINDER** command to create a solid cylinder (Figure 23-22).

Command: **CYLINDER**
Elliptical/ < Center point > < 0,0,0 > : ◄─┘
Diameter/ < Radius > : **1.5**
Center of other end/ < Height > : **3.0**

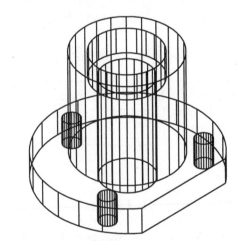

Using the Revolve command, you have created three solids: base plate, cylinder, and inner core. The next step is to union the base plate and the cylinder using the UNION command and then subtract the inner core from the unioned solid using the SUBTRACT command.

Figure 23-22 Creating the solid cylinder

Creating Composite Solids or Regions (UNION)

Toolbar:	Modify, Explode, Union
Pull-down:	Construct, Union
Screen:	DRAW2, SOLIDS, Union:

The **UNION** command can be used to create composite solids or regions. This command can be invoked from the **Modify** toolbar (select the Union icon from the Explode flyout), from the pull-down menu (select Construct, Union), from the screen menu (select DRAW2, SOLIDS, Union:), or by entering **UNION** at the Command: prompt.

Several solids or regions can be combined in the same command. However, the solids cannot be combined with the regions. If the selection set contains regions and solids, AME will automatically combine the solids and the regions separately. If the solids or the regions cannot be combined, AME will display the message "1 solids rejected" or "1 region rejected." (Also see the **SUBTRACT** command, discussed earlier in this chapter.)

1. Use the **UNION** command to create a composite solid from the base plate and the cylinder.

    Command: **UNION**
    Select objects: *Select baseplate.*
    Select objects: *Select cylinder.*
    Select objects: ◄⎯⌐

2. Use the **SUBTRACT** command to subtract the inner core from the unioned solid.

    Command: **SUBTRACT**
    Select solids and regions to subtract from...
    Select objects: *Select the unioned solid.* 1 found
    Select objects: ◄⎯⌐
    Select solids and regions to subtract...
    Select objects: *Select the inner core.* 1 found
    Select objects:◄⎯⌐

You will not see any change in the shape of the solid. However, if you enter the **LIST** command and select solid, the entire solid will be highlighted, indicating that it is now a single solid with a hole through its center and a counterbore at the top. Cancel the LIST command or hit the Enter (◄⎯⌐) key to display the information of the selected solid on the screen. The next step is to create fillets and rounds using the **FILLET** command.

Creating Fillets and Rounds (FILLET)

Toolbar:	Modify, Chamfer, Fillet
Pull-down:	Construct, Fillet
Screen:	CONSTRCT, Fillet

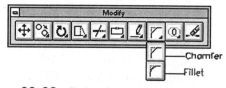

Figure 23-23 Selecting the Fillet icon from the Chamfer flyout in the Modify toolbar

The **FILLET** command is used to create fillets and rounds. This command can be invoked from the **Modify** toolbar (select the Fillet icon from the Chamfer flyout; see Figure 23-23), from the pull-down menu (select Construct, Fillet), from the screen menu (select CONSTRCT, Fillet), or by entering **FILLET** at the Command: prompt. It automatically invokes the **UNION** and **SUBTRACT** commands to union the fillets and subtract the rounds from the solid. The FILLET command does not have any special fillet or round option for Solids. The same FILLET command can be used for solids and other objects. The FILLET command can also be used to create fillets and rounds. Solids is intelligent enough to determine, depending on the geometry of the solid, whether to create a fillet or a round at the selected edges. If the tessellation lines are too close, use the ISOLINES command to change number of lines. Next, use the **FILLET** command to create fillets and rounds on the edges as shown in Figure 23-25.

Command: **FILLET**
(TRIM mode) Current fillet radius = 0.125
Polyline/Radius/Trim/ < Select first object >: *Select edge A.*
Chain/Radius/ < Select edge >:
Enter radius<0.125>: **0.125**
Chain/Radius/ < Select edge >: *Select edges B and C.*

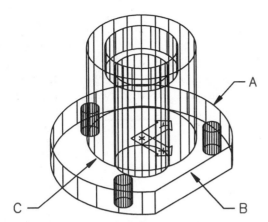

Figure 23-24 Select edges A, B, and C

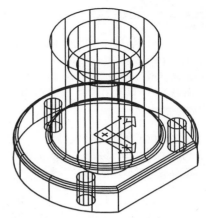

Figure 23-25 Creating fillets and rounds

Creating Chamfers (CHAMFER)

The **CHAMFER** command can be used to create chamfer; that is, bevel the edges of a solid by a specified distance. This command can be invoked from the **Modify** toolbar (select the Chamfer icon from the Chamfer flyout), from the pull-down menu (select Construct, Chamfer), from the screen menu (select CONSTRCT, Chamfer), or by entering **CHAMFER** at the Command: prompt. This command automatically invokes the SUBTRACT command to subtract the chamfered volume from the solid. The CHAMFER command requires you to select the surface you want to chamfer, select the edge where the chamfer is needed, and indicate the chamfer distances of the base and the adjacent surfaces.

Command: **CHAMFER**
Polyline/Distance/Angle/Trim/Method/ < Select first line > : *Select surface E.*
Select base surface:
Next/OK: *Enter Next if needed until the cylinder edges are highlighted.*
Enter base surface distance: 0.125
Enter other surface distance < 0.1250 > : 0.125
Loop/ < Select edge > : *Select edge E.*
Loop/ < Select edge > : ◄┘

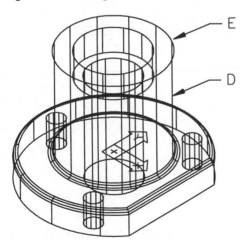

Figure 23-26 Select the base surface for creating chamfer

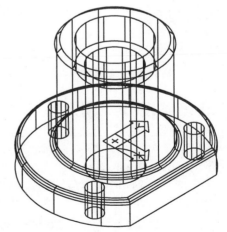

Figure 23-27 Using the CHAMFER command to create chamfer in solid modeling

You may save a copy of this drawing as SMVIEW.

Analyzing Solids (MASSPROP)

The **MASSPROP** command can be used to analyze a solid model. This command will automatically calculate the mass properties of the solid. The density of the solid is assumed to be 1. When you enter this command, AutoCAD will list the properties of the solid on the screen. If you want to write these properties to a file, enter Y to the next prompt (Write to a file? <N>: Y).

Command: **MASSPROP**
Select objects: *Select the solid.*
Write to a file? <N>: ↵

```
----------------------- SOLIDS -------------------
Mass:            26.97775
Volume:          26.97775

Bounding box:         X: -2.5000  --  2.0010
                      Y: -2.5000  --  2.5000
                      Z: -0.7500  --  3.0000

Centroid:             X: -0.0623
                      Y: 0.0001
                      Z: 0.6068

Moments of inertia:   X: 74.3905
                      Y: 71.0374
                      Z: 60.9835
Products of inertia:  XY: -0.0001
                      YZ: 0.0018
                      ZX: 0.6331

Radii of gyration:    X: 1.6606
                      Y: 1.6227
                      Z: 1.5035

Principal moments and X-Y-Z directions about centroid:
                      I: 65.1039 along [0.9313 0.0001 -0.3644]
                      J: 60.9993 along [-0.0004 1.0000 -0.0009]
                      K: 60.2320 along [0.3644 0.0010 0.9313]
```

Write to a file ? <N>: ↵

Slicing Solids (SLICE)

Toolbar:	Solids, Slice
Pull-down:	Draw, Solids, Slice
Screen:	DRAW2, SOLIDS, Slice:

The **SLICE** command cuts a solid along the specified plane. This command can be invoked from the **Solids** toolbar (select the Slice icon), from the pull-down menu (select Draw, Solids, Slice), from the screen menu (Select DRAW2, SOLIDS, Slice:), or by entering **SLICE** at the Command: prompt. This command cannot be used with a region. When you enter this command, AutoCAD will prompt you to select the object you want to cut and the side of the solid you want to retain (if you do not want to retain both sides). You can specify the part that you want to retain by selecting a point on that part. Use the following commands to cut the solid as shown in Figure 23-28:

1. Use the **UCS** command to rotate the UCS icon through 90 degrees about X axis.

   Command: **UCS**
   Origin/ZAxis/3point/Object/View/X/Y/Z/Pre/Restore/Save/Del/?/ < World > : **X**
   Rotation angle about X axis < 0 > :**90**

2. Use the **SLICE** command to cut the solid through XY plane (Figure 23-29).

   Command: **SLICE**
   Select objects: (**Select the solid**)
   Select objects: ↵
   1 solid selected.
   Slicing plane by Object/Zaxis/View/XY/YZ/ZX/ < 3points > : **XY**
   Point on XY plane < 0,0,0 > : ↵
   Both sides/ < Point on desired side of the plane > : *Select point F using ENDpoint O'Snap.*

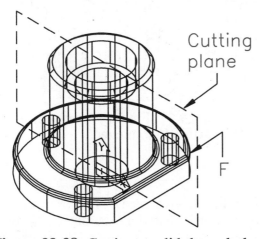

Figure 23-28 Cutting a solid through the XY plane

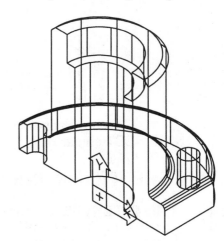

Figure 23-29 The solid after cutting

Creating a Cross Section (SECTION)

The **SECTION** command creates the cross section of a solid through the specified plane. This command can be invoked from the **Solids** toolbar (select the Section icon), from the pull-down menu (select Draw, Solids, Section), from the screen menu (select DRAW2, SOLIDS, Section:), or by entering **SECTION** at the Command: prompt. In addition, the cross section blocks or regions are created in the current layer, not on the layer of the solid that is sectioned.

Command: **SECTION**
Select objects: *Select the solid.*
Select objects: ↵
Sectioning plane by
Object/Zaxis/View/XY/YZ/ZX/ < 3points > : **XY**
Point on XY plane < 0,0,0 > : ↵

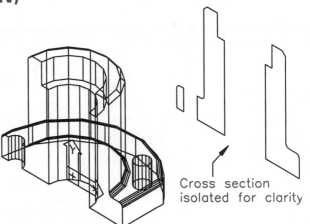

Figure 23-30 Creating the cross section of a solid

OTHER COMMANDS

INTERSECT (Creating Composite Solids)

The **INTERSECT** command creates a composite solid or region from objects that intersect. This command can be invoked from the **Modify** toolbar (select the Intersection icon from the Explode flyout), from the pull-down menu (select Construct, Intersection), from the screen menu (select DRAW2, SOLIDS, Intrsec:), or by entering **INTERSECT** at the Command: prompt. If the objects do not intersect, they do not have any common overlapping area or volume, therefore INTERSECT cannot be used with them. Also, the objects could lie in any plane.

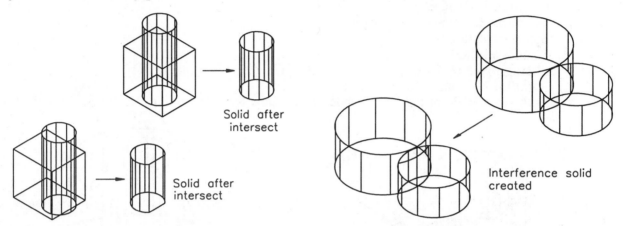

Figure 23-31 Creating composite solids using INTERSECT command

Figure 23-32 Finding interference by using INTERFERE command

INTERFERE (Finding Interference)

The **INTERFERE** command can be used to find interference of two or more solids and creates a composite solid from the common volume shared by the objects. If the objects do not intersect, they do not have any common volume, therefore INTERFERE cannot be used with them. Also, the objects could lie in any plane. This command can be invoked from the **Solids** toolbar (select the Interfere icon), from the pull-down menu (select Draw, Solids, Interference), from the screen menu (select DRAW2, SOLIDS, Intrfer:), or by entering **INTERFERE** at the Command: prompt.

ACSIN (Importing an ACIS file)

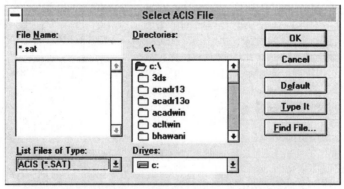

Figure 23-33 Select ACIS File dialogue box

This command is used to read in the model stored as an ACIS file. After reading the file, AutoCAD creates the objects, solids, or regions from the data contained in the ACIS file. ACIS is a solid modeling file format that AutoCAD uses to store information (data) of solid objects. The file can be saved as an ASCII file with .sat extension. You can invoke the **Select ACIS File** dialogue box (Figure 23-34). You can also select an ACIS file through the pull-down menu (select File, Import). The **Import File** dialogue box is displayed (Figure 23-34). Select ACIS (*.SAT) from List Files of Type pop up menu, from the screen menu (select FILE, IMPORT, SATin) or by entering **ACISIN** at the Command: prompt.

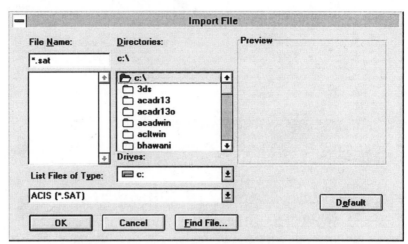

Figure 23-34 Import File dialogue box

ACISOUT (Exporting AutoCAD Solid Objects to an ACIS File)

The **ACISOUT** command is used to export an AutoCAD solid or a region to an ACIS solid modeling format. ACIS is a solid modeling file format that AutoCAD uses to store information (data) of solid objects. The file can be saved as an ASCII file with .sat extension. You can invoke the **Create ACIS File** dialogue box (Figure 23-35), from the screen menu (select FILE, EXPORT, ACISout), or by entering **ACISOUT** at the Command: prompt.

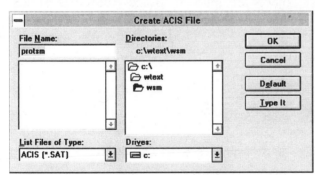

Figure 23-35 Create ACIS File dialogue box

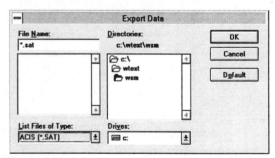

Figure 23-36 Export Data dialogue box

You can also create an ASIS file through the pull-down menu (select File, Export...,). The **Export Data** dialogue box is displayed (Figure 23-36). Select ACIS (*.SAT) from List Files of Type pop up menu.

STLOUT (Storing a Solid in an ASCII or Binary File)

The **STLOUT** command can be used to write the solid model data in an ASCII or binary file with format (.stl extension). The .stl file format is compatible with Stereo-Lithography Apparatus (SLA). The SLA workstation uses this data to build the part in a series of layers; each layer defines a contour of the solid model. You can invoke the **Create STL File** dialogue box from the screen menu (select FILE, EXPORT, STLout), or by entering the **ACISOUT** at the Command: prompt.

Command: **ACISOUT**
Select the object: *Select solid*
Select the object: ◄─┘

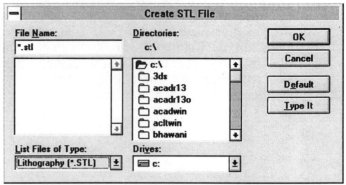

Figure 23-37 Create STL File dialogue box

FACETRES (Adjusting Smoothness)

FACETRES is a system variable that can be used to adjust the smoothness of shaded and hidden line-removed objects. The default value is 0.5; the value can range from 0.01 to 10.0.

DISPSILH (Controlling Display of Silhouette)

Like FACETRES and ISOLINES, DISPSILH is a system variable that controls the display of silhouette curves of an object in wire-frame mode. The default values is 0 (off).

AMECONVERT (Converting Existing AME Solids)

This command can be used to convert an AME solid model to an AutoCAD solid model. It can be invoked from the **Solids** toolbar (select the AME Convert icon), from the screen menu (select DRAW2, SOLIDS, AMEconv:), from the pull-down menu (select Draw, Solids, AME Convert), or by entering **AMECONVERT** at the Command: prompt. With this command, the only AME solids and regions that can be converted must have been created by AME Release 2.0 or 2.1. All other objects are ignored. Since AutoCAD Solids uses different technology (ACIS) from AME (PADL), you may not get an accurate conversion.

SELF EVALUATION TEST

Answer the following questions and then compare your answers with the correct answers given at the end of this chapter.

1. What is solid modeling? _____

    _____

2. AutoCAD solids are the same as AME solids. (T/F)

3. AME solids do not have any predefined primitives. (T/F)

4. What command can be used to check interference between solids? _____

5. The CONE command creates a solid cone with elliptical or circular base. (T/F)

6. The base of the wedge is always drawn perpendicular to the current construction plane. (T/F)

7. You can create a region by solidifying the part profile. (T/F)

8.   A composite solid consists of two solid primitives. (T/F)

9.   The SLICE command cuts a solid only along the XY plane. (T/F)

10.   You cannot write to a file the properties obtained by the MASSPROP command. (T/F)

REVIEW QUESTIONS

Answer the following questions.

1.   AutoCAD Solids has _____ predefined solid primitives. Name them. _____

2.   The number of lines in a solid model is controlled by the value assigned to the _____ variable.

3.   You can use the _____ command to subtract solids.

4.   The _____ command creates a solid by sweeping a polyline or a circle around an axis.

5.   You can use the _____ to list the properties of a solid.

6.   The _____ command can be used to create fillets and rounds.

7.   The _____ command automatically invokes UNION and SUBTRACT commands to union the fillets and subtract the rounds from the solid.

8.   You can use the _____ command to construct a solid cylinder.

9.   The _____ command lets you generate a section image of the selected object.

10.   A region is created by using the _____ command.

11.   To access AutoCAD Solids commands you must first load the program. (T/F)

12.   AutoCAD Solids is based on PADL technology. (T/F)

13.   You can use the CYLINDER command to construct a solid cylinder. (T/F)

14.   The CYLINDER command has only one option. (T/F)

15.   A region is a solid with unit thickness. (T/F)

16.   The value of the ISOLINES variable can be from 1 to 25. (T/F)

17.   The cross section obtained by the SECTION command is automatically crosshatched. (T/F)

18.   The AME solids can be converted to AutoCAD solids. (T/F)

19.   What system variable determines whether silhouette edges are drawn? _____

20.   You can use the CHAMFER command to create chamfer in solid objects. (T/F)

EXERCISES

Exercise 1

Construct a composite solid of the object shown in Figure 23-38. You may use the following instructions to create this solid:
1. Draw the outer profile of the base plate and change the profile into polyline.
2. Draw the circles.
3. Construct a region from this profile.
4. Extrude the region.
5. Construct the solid tube.
6. Draw a rectangular solid with thickness equal to the width of the slot, then subtract it from the tube.
7. Union the tube and base plate.
8. Draw a solid cylinder equal to the inside diameter of the hole, then subtract the cylinder from the object.

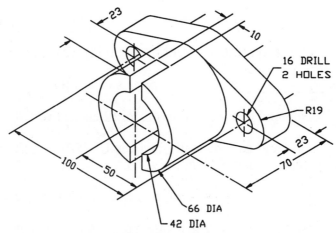

Figure 23-38　Drawing for Exercise 1

Exercise 2

Construct a composite solid of the object shown in Figure 23-39.

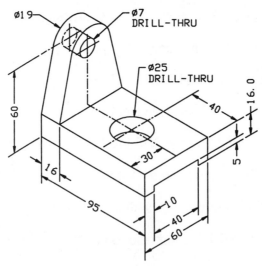

Figure 23-39　Drawing for Exercise 2

Exercise 3

Construct a composite solid of the following object (Figure 23-40). The model consists of four parts. The bottom part is a rectangle-to-circle transition (surface mesh). The remaining parts are solid cylinders located at different positions along the center vertical plane of the composite solid. The dimensions are as shown in the front and top views. The height of the center cylinder is 4.5. The angle is 45 degrees for the cylinder on the right side. Assume the missing dimensions.

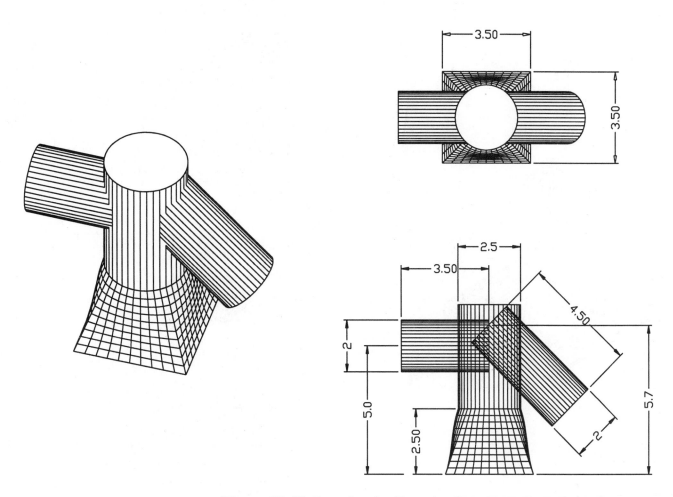

Figure 23-40 Drawing for Exercise 3

Exercise 4

Construct a composite solid of the following object (Figure 23-41). The model consists of a bottom support, a tapered cylinder, and a set of cones at the top. The bottom support is made of four hollow cylinders joined at the ends. The wall thickness is 0.125. The tapered cylinder is also a hollow tube with 0.125 wall thickness. The lower cone located at the top slides over the tapered cylinder. The wall thickness of the cones is 0.25.

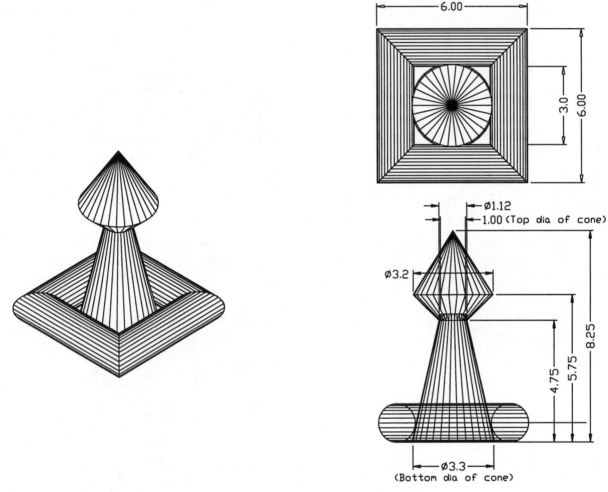

Figure 23-41 Drawing for Exercise 4

Answers

The following are the correct answers to the questions in the self evaluation test.
1 - The process of building objects that have all the attributes of an actual solid, **2** - F, **3** - F,
4 - INTERFERE, **5** - T, **6** - F (parallel), **7** - T, **8** - F (2 or more), **9** - F (any specified plane), **10** - F

Chapter 24

Rendering

RENDERING

A rendered image makes it easier to visualize the shape and size of a three-dimensional object compared to a wireframe image or a shaded image. A rendered object also makes it easier to express your design ideas to other people. For example, if you want to make a presentation of your project or a design, you do not need to build a prototype. You can use the rendered image to explain your design much more clearly because you have complete control over the shape, size, color, and surface material of the rendered image. Additionally, any required changes can be incorporated in the object and the object can be rendered to check or demonstrate the effect of these changes. Therefore, rendering

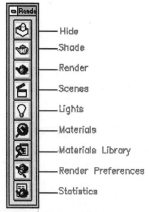

Figure 24-1 Render toolbar

is a very effective tool for communicating your ideas or demonstrating the shape of an object. You can create a rendered image of a three-dimensional object by using **AutoCAD RENDER**. It allows you to control the appearance of the object by defining the surface material and reflective quality of the surface and by adding lights to get the desired effects.

Determining Which Sides are to be Rendered in a Model

Some of the faces of a 3D model, such as the back faces and the hidden faces, need not be rendered since it would amount to an unnecessary waste of time. In the process of rendering, AutoCAD determines the front faces and the back faces of the 3D model with the use of **normals** on each face. A **vector** perpendicular to each face on a 3D model whose direction is outward toward space is known as **normal**. If a face has been drawn in clockwise direction, the normal points inward and if a face has been drawn in counterclockwise direction, the normal points outward. Now depending on the location of your viewpoint, if the normal of a face points away from the viewpoint, the face is a back face. As mentioned before, rendering of such faces is not advisable (since these faces are not visible from the viewpoint) and can be avoided by invoking the Discard Back Faces option. This option is explained later in this chapter. The faces that conceal other faces are discarded. In this manner the time required to render objects can be decreased by discarding faces that need not be rendered.

Points to be Remembered while Defining a Model

1. To make the rendering process as time efficient as possible, you must use the fewest possible faces to define a plane.

2. There should be consistency in your drafting technique. Models formed of complex mixture of faces, extruded lines, and wireframe meshes should be avoided.

3. If you are rendering circles, ellipses, or arcs, set the **VIEWRES** command to a high number. This way the circles, arcs, or ellipses will appear more smooth and the rendering of such objects will be better. But increasing the value of VIEWRES increases the time taken to render the objects. The smoothness of rendered curved solids depends on **FACETRES** variable.

4. Another point you must keep in mind is that if you are using the Smooth Shading option (available in the **Render** and **Rendering Preferences** dialogue box, explained later), then you should specify the mesh density in such a manner that the angle described by normals of any two adjoining faces is less than 45 degrees. This is because if the angle is greater than 45 degrees, then after rendering, an edge is displayed between the faces even when the Smooth Shading option is active.

LOADING AND CONFIGURING AUTOCAD RENDER

When you select any AutoCAD **RENDER** command, AutoCAD Render is loaded automatically. AutoCAD will display the following message in the command prompt area:

Command: Initializing...
Initializing Render...

If AutoCAD Render has not been configured before, AutoCAD will then prompt you to configure Render and it will request information about the **rendering display**, **rendering driver**, and **hardcopy device driver**. Depending on your system you must enter the required information so that AutoCAD Render can function correctly to display the image on the screen.

ELEMENTARY RENDERING

Toolbar:	Render, Render
Pull-down:	Tools, Render, Render
Screen:	TOOLS, RENDER, Render:

In this section you are going to perform an ordinary rendering. You will encounter many terms which you will not be aware of, but you need not bother about these at this stage. All the terms are explained later on in this chapter. In this rendering, lights, materials and other advanced features of rendering will not be applied. Only a default distant light is used. This will give you a feel of rendering in the simplest possible manner. Perform the following steps:

1. Using the SPHERE command, create four spheres on the screen as shown in Figure 24-4.

2. Invoke the **Render** dialogue box (Figure 24-3) from the **Render** toolbar (select the Render icon), from the pull-down menu (select Tools, Render, Render, Figure 24-2), from the screen menu (select TOOLS, RENDER, Render:), or enter **RENDER** at the Command: prompt.

3. In the Render dialogue box, Pick the **Render Scene** button. AutoCAD will render all objects that are on the screen.

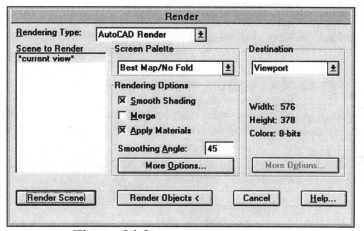

Figure 24-2 Render options in Tools pull-down menu using ACADFULL.MNU menu file

Figure 24-3 Render dialogue box

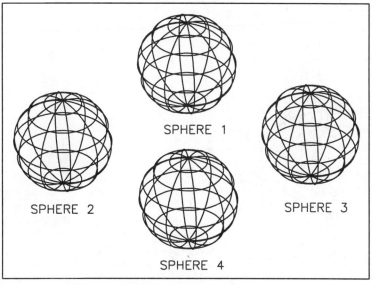

Figure 24-4 Drawing to be rendered

After some time all the spheres are rendered and displayed on the screen (Figure 24-5). Press any key to exit the rendered image screen and return to the AutoCAD drawing screen.

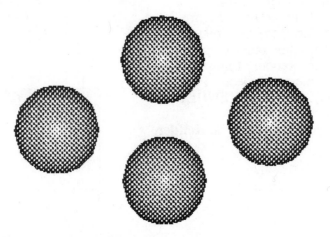

Figure 24-5 Rendering all spheres

If you want to render only some spheres (for example, SPHERE 2 and SPHERE 3), pick the **Render Objects** button and then select the spheres you want to render. You will notice that only the selected spheres are rendered and displayed on the screen.

UNLOADING AUTOCAD RENDER

If you do not need AutoCAD Render, you can unload it by entering the **RENDERUNLOAD** command at the Command: prompt. AutoCAD acknowledges the unloading of Render by issuing the message **"Render has been unloaded from the memory"**. After unloading Render you can reload AutoCAD Render by invoking the **RENDER** command or any other command associated with rendering (such as SCENE, LIGHT, etc.).

Exercise 1

In this exercise you will render the drawing that was created in Example 2 of the Solid Modeling chapter (Figure 23-19). Load and render the drawing. Figure 24-6 shows the object before rendering, Figure 24-7 shows the object after rendering.

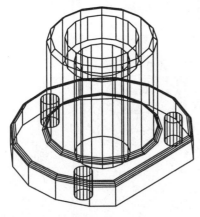

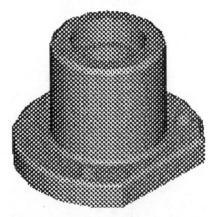

Figure 24-6 Drawing for Exercise 1   Figure 24-7 After rendering

SELECTING DIFFERENT PROPERTIES FOR RENDERING

Toolbar:	Render, Preferences
Pull-down:	Tools, Render, Preferences...
Screen:	TOOLS, RENDER, Prefer:

AutoCAD Render allows you to select various properties for the rendering. This can be achieved through the **Rendering Preferences** dialogue box (Figure 24-8), which can be invoked from the **Render** toolbar (select the Preferences icon), from the pull-down menu (select Tools, Render, Preferences...), or from the screen menu (select TOOLS, RENDER, Prefer:). You can also invoke this dialogue box by entering **RPREF** at the Command: prompt. The dialogue box has the following sections:

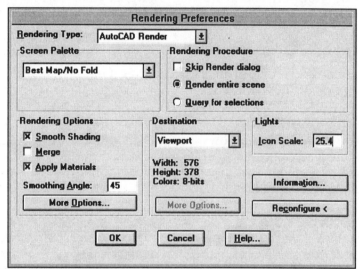

Figure 24-8   Rendering Preferences dialogue box

Rendering Type Pop-up List

In this dialogue box you can select the type of rendering you want from the Rendering Type pop-up list.

Screen Palette Area

This area controls the color map when you are rendering or replaying an image to a viewport using a 256-color combined rendering driver.

> **Note**
>
> *If AutoCAD has been configured for a continuous color rendering driver, none of these options are available.*
> *These options do not change the display of colors 1 to 8 in nonrendering viewports.*

Best Map/No Fold option

This option does not fold the AutoCAD vector colors into colors 1 to 8; it makes use of a separate color map. The best color map for rendering is calculated based on the number of colors available on the user's system. If you switch viewports in this mode, the color map for the selected viewport. This mode affects the look of images imported with the PSIN or RASTERIN commands.

Best Map/Fold option

This option folds the colors above 8 into colors 1 to 8 and makes use of a separate color map when objects drawn in viewports are redisplayed. In case you render images to a viewport, then folding is enabled. The best color map for rendering is calculated based on the number of colors available on the user's system. In case vectors are in nonrendering viewports, each color from 9 to 256 is mapped to the nearest primary color between 1 and 8. The objects in nonrendering viewports are displayed in the 1 to 8 range after performing a regeneration. No color change takes place for vectors in nonrendering viewports.

Fixed ACAD Map option

With this option the drawing in nonrendering viewports maintain their original colors and AutoCAD's 256-color map is used. This option generates low-quality renderings and sometimes you may get unexpected results. No "flashing" takes place when you switch between a rendering viewport and a drawing viewport since in this option AutoCAD uses a one-color map.

Rendering Options Area

Various rendering options are provided in the Rendering Options area of the dialogue box. The following is the description of these options:

Smooth Shading check box

The Smooth Shading check box allows you to smooth the rough edges. If this option is enabled, the rough-edged appearance of a multifaceted surface is smoothed. Only polygon meshes are affected by Smooth Shading. The surface normals are determined and colors across two or more adjoining faces are blended.

Merge check box

The Merge option allows you to combine images in the frame buffer. For example, you could use the Merge option to have a rendered object against a TIFF, GIF, or TGA image. A small portion of the image can be altered keeping the entire image on the screen. Now when Merge option is enabled, and rendering is performed, that particular small part is rendered and consequently merged into the entire image. When this option is disabled, the frame buffer is cleared to black before rendering. On the other hand if this option is enabled, the frame buffer is not cleared; instead, a new rendering is added to the current frame buffer contents.

Apply Materials check box

The Apply Materials option allows you to assign surface materials to objects. If this option is disabled then the objects in the drawing are assigned the *GLOBAL* material.

Smoothing Angle edit box

The Smoothing Angle option lets you specify the angle defined by two edges. The default value for smoothing angle is 45 degrees. Angles having values less than 45 degrees are smoothed. Angles having values greater than 45 degrees are taken as edges.

More Options... button

If you select the More Options button, the **AutoCAD Render Options** dialogue box (Figure 24-9) is displayed. The following is a brief description of these additional options:

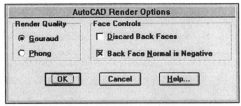

Figure 24-9 AutoCAD Render Options dialogue box

Render Quality area

In the Render Quality area of this dialogue box, you can choose either the Gouraud or the Phong option. These options determine the quality of shading that will be used if you have activated the Smooth Shading option.

Phong radio button
The Phong option creates a high-quality rendered image. The light intensity is calculated for all the pixels and hence more accurate highlights are generated.

Gouraud radio button
On the other hand, the Gouraud option produces a lower quality rendered image. Light intensity at each vertex is determined and intermediate intensities are interpolated. The advantage of Gouraud render option is that the rendering occurs faster as compared with the Phong render option.

Face Controls area
The Face Controls area governs the definition of faces of a 3D solid.

Discard Back Faces check box
If you select the Discard Back Faces option, the back faces of a 3D solid object are not taken into consideration (i.e., they are made invisible) and hence they are omitted from the calculations for the rendering. Rendering time can be reduced by enabling this option.

Back Face Normal is Negative check box
The Back Face Normal is Negative option can be used to define the back faces in a drawing. If this option is enabled, the faces with negative normal vectors are treated as back faces and discarded. When this option is disabled, the selection faces treated as back faces by AutoCAD are just reversed.

Rendering Procedures Area

Skip Render dialog check box
In the Rendering Procedures area, if the Skip Render dialog option is invoked, the current view is rendered without displaying the Render dialogue box.

Render Entire Scene radio button
If the Render Entire Scene option is invoked, all the objects in the current scene are rendered.

Query for selections radio button
If you select the Query for selections option, AutoCAD displays a prompt to select objects you want to render.

Destination Area

The Destination area allows you to specify the destination for the rendered image output.

Viewport option
If you select the Viewport option, AutoCAD renders to a viewport.

Render Window option
This option renders to the AutoCAD for Windows Render window.

Hard Copy option
The Hard Copy option outputs the rendered image to the configured output device.

File option
The File option lets you output the rendered image to a file.

More Options... button

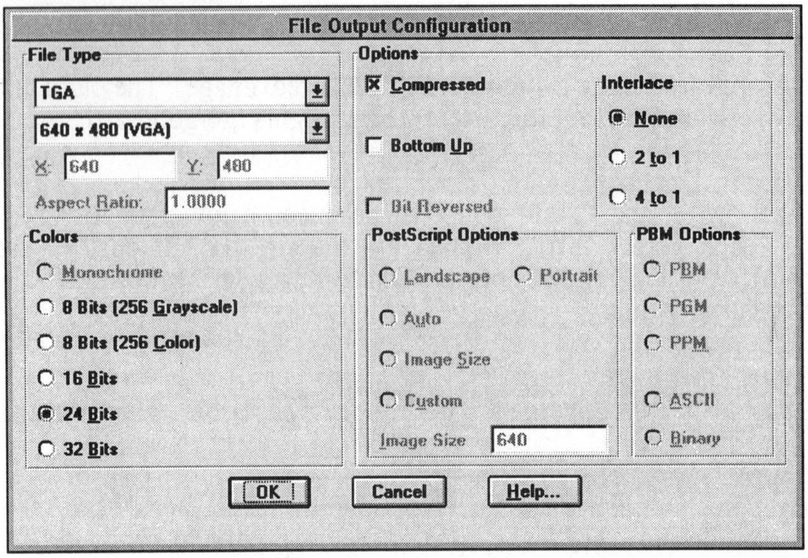

Figure 24-10 File Output Configuration dialogue box

The More Options button can be used to set the configuration for the output file through the **File Output Configuration** dialogue box (Figure 24-10).

File Type area
In this area you can specify the output file type and rendering resolution. The file formats allowed are TGA, PCX, SUN, FITS, PostScript, TIFF, FAX G III, and IFF. The screen resolution can also be specified in this area. The aspect ratio of the output file can be specified in the Aspect Ratio edit box.

Colors area
The colors in the output file can be specified in this area.

Options area
The Compressed option lets you specify compression for those file types that allow compression. The Bottom Up option lets you specify the scan line start point to bottom left instead of top left. The Bit Reversed option allows bit reversing for modems.

Interlace area
Selecting the None option turns off the line interlacing. The 2 to 1 and 4 to 1 options turn on interlacing.

PostScript Options area
The Landscape and Portrait options in this area specify the orientation of the file. The Auto option automatically scales the image. The Image Size option uses the explicit image size. The Custom option sets the image size in pixels.

PBM Options
This option sets Portable Bit Map (PBM) options.

Lights Area

The Lights area in the Rendering Preferences dialogue box allows you to scale the light blocks. The Icon Scale edit box can be used to set the size of the light blocks in the drawing.

Information... button

If you pick the Information button, AutoCAD displays the information about the prevailing rendering configuration and version of the type of rendering application you are using.

Reconfigure < button

The Reconfigure < button can be used to reconfigure the rendering device.

AUTOCAD RENDER LIGHT SOURCE

Lights are vital to rendering a realistic image of an object. Without proper lighting the rendered image may not show the features the way one would expect. Colors and surface reflection can be set for the lights with RGB or HLS color systems. AutoCAD Render supports the following four light sources:

1.   Ambient light
2.   Point light

3.   Distant light
4.   Spotlight

Ambient Light

You can visualize the ambient light as the natural light in a room that equally illuminates all surfaces of the objects. The ambient light does not have a source and hence has no location or direction. However you can increase or decrease the intensity of the ambient light or completely turn it off. Normally you should set the ambient light to a low value because high values produce a washed-out look to the image. If you want to create a dark room or a night scene, turn off the ambient light. With the ambient light alone you cannot render a realistic image. Figure 24-11 shows an object that is illuminated by ambient light.

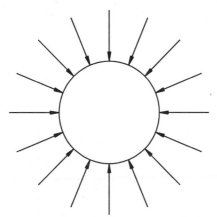

Figure 24-11 Ambient light provides constant illumination

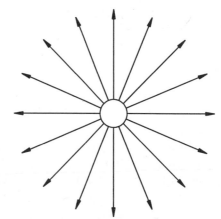

Figure 24-12 Point light emits light in all directions

Point Light

A point light source emits light in all directions and the intensity of the emitted light is uniform. You can visualize an electric bulb as a point light source. In AutoCAD Render a point source does not cast a shadow because the light is assumed to be passing through the object. The intensity of the light radiated by a point source decreases over distance. This phenomenon is called **attenuation**. Figure 24-12 shows a light source that radiates light in all direction.

Spotlight

A spotlight emits light in the defined direction with a cone-shaped light beam (Figure 24-13). The direction of the light and the size of the cone can be specified. The phenomenon of **attenuation** (falloff) also applies to spotlights. This light is mostly used to highlight particular features and portions of the model. If you want to simulate a soft lighting effect, set the falloff cone angle a few degrees larger than the hot spot cone angle.

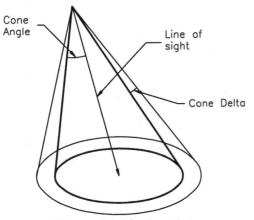

Figure 24-13 Spotlight

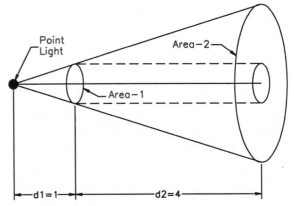

Figure 24-14 Light intensity decrease with distance

Attenuation

Light intensity is defined as the amount of light falling per unit area. The intensity of light is directly proportional to the degree of brightness of the object. The intensity of light decreases as the distance increases. This phenomenon is called **attenuation** and occurs only with spotlights and point light. In Figure 24-14, the light is emitted by a point source. Assume that the amount of light incident on Area-1 is I. Therefore the intensity of light on Area-1 = I/Area. As the light travels farther from the source, it covers a larger area. The amount of light falling on Area-2 is same as Area-1, but the area is larger. Therefore intensity of light for Area-2 is smaller (Intensity of light for Area-2 = I/Area). Area-1 will be brighter than Area-2 because of higher light intensity. AutoCAD Render has provided three methods for controlling the light fall-off:

1. None
2. Inverse Linear
3. Inverse Square

None

If you select the None option for light fall-off, the brightness of the objects are independent of distance. This means that the objects that are far away from the point light source will be as bright as the objects that are close to the light source.

Inverse Linear

In this option the light falling on the object (brightness) is inversely proportional to the distance of the object from the light source (Brightness = 1/Distance). As the distance increases, the brightness decreases. For example, let us assume the intensity of the light source is I and the object is located at a distance of 2 units from the light source. Brightness or intensity = 1/2. If the distance is 8 units, the intensity (light falling on the object per unit area) = 1/8. The brightness is a linear function of the distance of the object from the light source.

Inverse Square

In this option the light falling on the object (brightness) is inversely proportional to the square of the distance of the object from the light source (Brightness = 1/Distance^2). For example, let us assume the intensity of the light source is I and the object is located at a distance of 2 units from the light source. Brightness or intensity = 1/(2)^2 = 1/4. If the distance is 8 units, the intensity (light falling on the object per unit area) = $1/(8)^2$ = 1/64.

Distant Light

A distant light source emits uniform parallel beam of light in a single direction only (Figure 24-15). The intensity of the light beam does not decrease with the distance; it remains constant. For example, the sun's rays can be assumed as a distant light source because the light rays are parallel. When you use a distant light source in a drawing the location of the light source does not matter; only the **direction is critical**. Distant Light is mostly used to uniformly light objects or a backdrop and for getting the effect of sunlight.

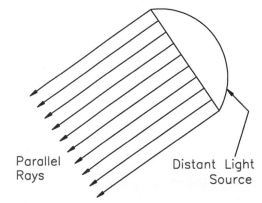

Figure 24-15 Distant light source

INSERTING AND MODIFYING LIGHTS

Toolbar:	Render, Lights
Pull-down:	Tools, Render, Lights...
Screen:	TOOLS, RENDER, Lights:

In a rendering, the lights and lighting effects are important to create a realistic representation of an object. The sides of object that face the light must appear brighter and the sides that are on the other side of the object must be darker. This smooth gradation of light produces a realistic image of the object. If the light intensity is uniform over the entire surface the rendered object probably will not look realistic. For example, if you use the SHADE command to shade an object, that object does not look realistic because the displayed model does not have any gradation of light. Any number of lights can be installed in a drawing. The color, location, and direction of all the lights can be specified individually. As mentioned before, you can specify attenuation for point lights and spotlights. AutoCAD also allows you to change the color, position, and intensity of any light source. The only limitation is that light types cannot be changed. For example, you cannot change a distant light into a point light. The following sections describe how to insert, position, and modify lights:

Inserting Distant Light

As mentioned before, the lights play an important role in producing a realistic representation of a three-dimensional model. The gradation effect produced by the lights make the object look realistic. In this example you will insert a distant light source and then you will render the object.

1. Use the **VPOINT** command to change the viewpoint to 1,-1,1.

    Command: **VPOINT** ←⏎
    Rotate/<view point> <current>: **1,-1,1** ←⏎

2. Select the **Render** option in the Tools pull-down menu (Using ACADFULL.MNU menu file).
3. Select the **Lights...** option from the cascading menu. The **Lights** dialogue box is displayed on the screen (Figure 24-16). You can use any one of the methods described above to invoke the Lights dialogue box.
4. Select the **Distant** option and then select **New** to insert a new distant light. The **New Distant Light** dialogue box is displayed on the screen (Figure 24-17).
5. Enter the name of the distant light (**D1**) in the New Distant Light dialogue box. Leave the intensity at its default value (1.00). In this example the view point is 5,-5,5.

6. Select the OK button to exit from this dialogue box.
7. Now render the image.

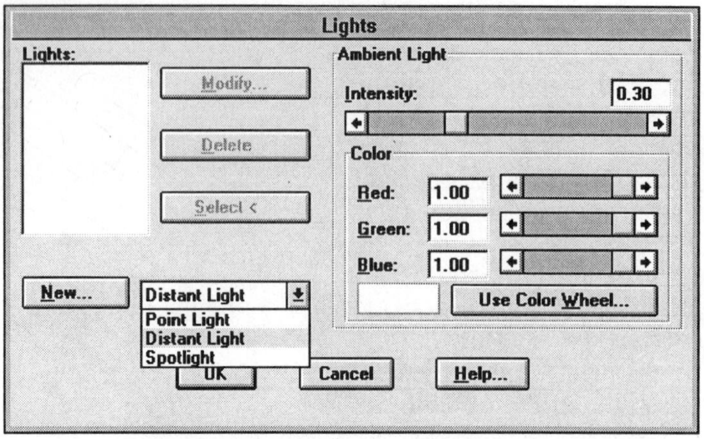

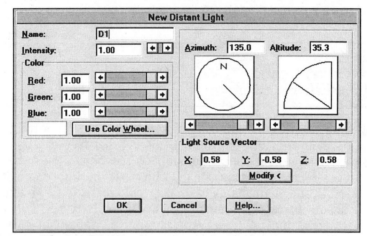

Figure 24-16 Lights dialogue box

Figure 24-17 New Distant Light dialogue box

Modifying Distant Light

In this rendering you will notice that the light falls on the object from the viewpoint direction and therefore the right front corner is brighter than rest of the object. We would like to modify the light source so that the light falls on the object from the right at an angle. When the light source is at an angle the top surface will also receives some light. Notice that as the oblique angle increases, the amount of light reflected by the oblique surface decreases.

1. Select the **Render** option from the **Tools** pull-down menu.
2. Select the **Lights...** option from the cascading menu.
3. Select the light (D1) from the **Lights** dialogue box. If there is only one light, the light is automatically highlighted (Figure 24-18).
4. Pick the **Modify** button. The **Modify Distant Light** dialogue box is displayed on the screen (Figure 24-19).

Note

If you double-click on the light name, it is equivalent to selecting the light name and modify option.

5. Pick the **Modify** button in the Light Source Vector area of this dialogue box.

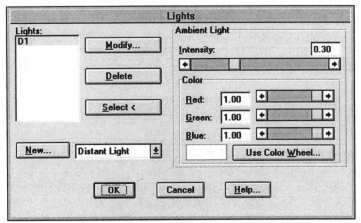

Figure 24-18 Lights dialogue box

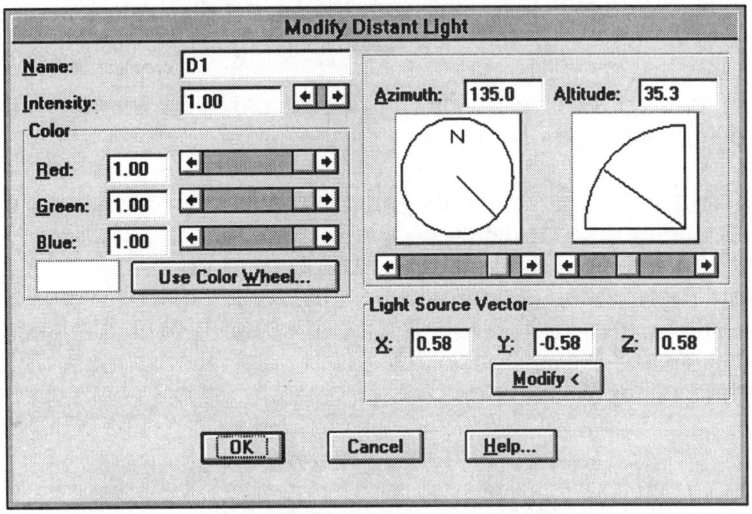

Figure 24-19 Modify Distant Light dialogue box

6. AutoCAD issues the prompt for the target point. Select the target point as (0,0,0).

Enter light direction TO <current>: **0,0,0** ◄┘

7. Next AutoCAD prompts for the light location. Select the light location (4,0,3).

Enter light direction FROM <current>: **4,0,3** ◄┘

By defining the target point and the light location you are merely specifying the direction of the parallel light beam emitted by the distant light source.
8. Select **OK** to exit from the Modify Distant Light dialogue box.
9. Select **OK** to exit from the Lights dialogue box.
10. Render the object.

You will notice that the right hand side (vertical faces) of the object are brighter than the horizontal surfaces. This is because the oblique angle that the vertical surfaces make with the direction of the light rays is smaller than the oblique angle that the horizontal surfaces make. Maximum brightness occurs when the object is perpendicular to the direction of light rays.

Inserting Point Light

In this example you will insert a point light source. Then you will render the object.

Example 1

Insert a point light source and render the object of Exercise 1 with Inverse Linear and Inverse Square options.

1. Load the drawing of Exercise 1
2. Select the **Render** option in the Tools pull-down menu.
3. Select the **Lights...** option from the cascading menu.
4. Select the **Point Light** option from the Lights dialogue box.
5. Click on the **New...** button. The**New Point Light** dialogue box is displayed.
6. Enter the name of the point light (**P1**) and set the intensity (**6.0**).
7. Select the **Modify** option from the dialogue box.
8. Enter the light location (**-2,0,5**).
9. In the New Point Light dialogue box, select **Inverse Linear** and then select the **OK** button to exit the dialogue box. Select **OK** to exit from the Lights dialogue box.
10. Change the view point to **1,-1,1** and then render the object.

You will notice that the top surface of the cylindrical part and the top surface of the flange are equally bright. Next, change the fall-off to Inverse Square:

11. Select the **Render** option from the Tools pull-down menu.
12. Select the **Lights...** option from the cascading menu.
13. Select the point light (**P1**) and then pick the **Modify** button.
14. The**Modify Point Light** dialogue box will be displayed. Select **Inverse Square** and then select **OK** to exit the dialogue box. Select **OK** to exit from the Lights dialogue box.
15. Render the object again. Now, notice that the top surface of the cylindrical part is brighter than the top surface of the flange.

DEFINING AND RENDERING A SCENE

The rendering depends on the view that is current and the lights that are defined in the drawing. Sometime the current view or the lighting setup may not be enough to show all features of an object. You might need different views of the object with a certain light configuration to show different views of the object. When you change the view or define the lights for a rendering, the previous setup is lost. You can save the rendering information by defining a **scene**. For each scene you can assign a view and the lights. When you render a particular view, AutoCAD Render uses the view information and the lights that were assigned to that scene. It ignores the lights that were not defined in the scene. By defining scenes it is convenient to render different views with the required lighting arrangement. The following example describes the process of defining scenes and assigning views and lights to the scenes.

Example 2

In the following example you will draw a rectangular box and a sphere that is positioned at the top of the box. Next you will insert lights, define views and scenes, and then render the scenes. You may start a new drawing or continue with the current drawing. Before defining a scene perform the following steps:

1. Draw a rectangular box with length = 3, width = 3, and height = 1.5
2. Use the **UCS** command to define the new origin at the center of the top face.
3. Draw a sphere of 1.5 radius.
4. Move the sphere so that the bottom of the sphere is resting at the top face of the box as shown in Figure 24-20.

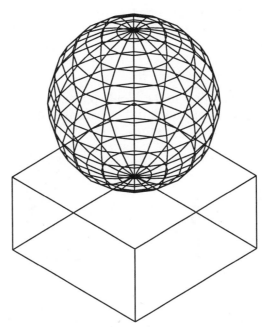

Figure 24-20 Drawing for Example 2

The next step is to insert the lights. In this example you will insert a point light and a distant light. Let us first insert a distant light source.

1. Select the **Render** option from the **Tools** pull-down menu.
2. Select the **Lights...** option from the cascading menu.
3. The **Lights** dialogue box is displayed on the screen.
4. Select the **Distant** option and then select **New** to insert a new distant light. The **New Distant Light** dialogue box is displayed on the screen.
5. Enter the name of the distant light (**D1**) in the Light Name edit box and press the Enter key. Now select Modify from the New Distant Light dialogue box.
6. Enter the light target point (**0,0,0**).
7. Enter the light location (**3,-3,4**).
8. Leave the intensity at 1.0.
9. Select the **OK** button to exit the dialogue box. Select **OK** to exit from the Lights dialogue box.
10. Change the view point to **1,-1,1** and then render the object.

After inserting a distant light source you need to insert a Point Light.

1. Select the **Lights...** option from the **Render** option of the Tools pull-down menu.
2. Select the **Point Light** option from the Lights dialogue box.
3. Click on the **New...** button. The **New Point Light** dialogue box is displayed.
4. Enter the name of the point light (**P1**) and set the intensity (**6.0**).
5. Select the **Modify** option from the dialogue box.
6. Enter the light location (**0,0,4**).
7. In the New Point Light dialogue box, select **Inverse Linear** and then select the **OK** button to exit the dialogue box. Select **OK** to exit from the Lights dialogue box.
8. Change the view point to **1,-1,1** and then render the object.

Now you will create three scenes. The first scene, SCENE1, contains Distant Light D1 and the second scene, SCENE2, contains Point Light P1. The third scene, SCENE3, will contain the view VIEW1, Distant Light D1, and Point Light P1. Create the first scene by performing the following steps:

Toolbar:	Render, Scenes
Pull-down:	Tools, Render, Scenes...
Screen:	TOOLS, RENDER, Scenes:

1. Select the **Render** option in the **Tools** pull-down menu.
2. Select the **Scenes...** option from the cascading menu.
3. The **Scenes** dialogue box (Figure 24-21) will be displayed on the screen.

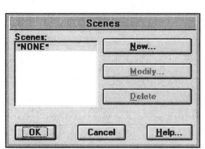

Figure 24-21 Scenes dialogue box

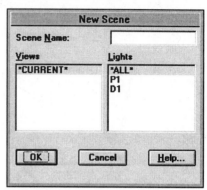

Figure 24-22 New Scene dialogue box

3. Select **New** from the Scenes dialogue box. The **New Scene** dialogue box (Figure 24-22) will be displayed on the screen.
4. Enter the name of the scene (**SCENE1**) in the **Scene Name** edit box. Click on Distant Light **D1** in the lights area and then select the **OK** button to exit the dialogue box.
5. Select the **OK** button from the Scenes dialogue box

Similarly, create the second scene, **SCENE2**, and assign the Point Light **P1** to the scene.

Next, create the third scene, **SCENE3**:

1. Use the **VPOINT** command to change the viewpoint to 1,-0.5,1
2. Use the **VIEW** command to save the view as **VIEW1**.
3. Invoke the **Scenes** dialogue box.
4. Select **New** from the Scenes dialogue box to display the **New Scene** dialogue box.
5. Enter the name of the scene (**SCENE3**) in the **Scene Name** edit box. Click on **All** to assign Distant Light D1 and Point Light P1 to the scene. Now click on **VIEW1**.
6. Select the **OK** button from the Scenes dialogue box

You have created three scenes and each scene has been assigned some lights. SCENE3 has been assigned a view in addition to the lights. You can render any scene after making the scene current as described below:

1. Invoke the **Scenes** dialogue box (Figure 24-23).
2. Click on the scene name that you want to render and then select the **OK** button to exit the dialogue box.
3. Render the object.

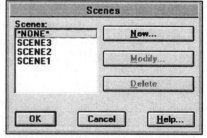

Figure 24-23 Scenes dialogue box displaying the scene names

Modifying a Scene

You can modify a scene by changing the view and the lights that are assigned to that scene. When you render the object, AutoCAD Render will use the newly assigned view and lights to render the object.

1. Select the **Render** option from the **Tools** pull-down menu.
2. Select the **Scenes...** option from the cascading menu. AutoCAD Render will display the Scenes dialogue box with the scene names on the screen.
3. Click on the scene, **SCENE3**, and then select Modify. The **Modify Scene** dialogue box (Figure 24-24) is displayed on the screen.
4. Click on **Current** and then select **OK** to exit from the Modify Scene dialogue box. This will assign the current view to SCENE3.
5. Select the **OK** button to exit from the Scenes dialogue box.
6. Render the object.

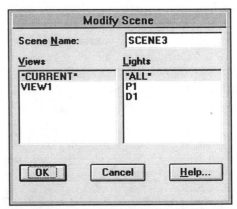

Figure 24-24 Modify Scenes dialogue box displaying the views and lights

OBTAINING RENDERING INFORMATION

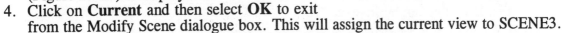

Toolbar:	Render, Statistics
Pull-down:	Tools, Render, Statistics...
Screen:	TOOLS, RENDER, Stats:

 You can obtain the information about the last rendering by picking the **Statistics** icon from the **Render** toolbar, from the pull-down menu (select Tools, Render, Statistics...), from the screen menu (select TOOLS, RENDER, Stats:), or by entering **STATS** at the Command: prompt. When you enter the STATS command, AutoCAD will display the **Statistics** dialogue box, on the screen. The information is provided about the name of the current scene, the last rendering type used, time taken to produce the last rendering, number of faces processed by the last rendering, and number of triangles processed by the last rendering. The information contained in the dialogue box cannot be edited. However, the information can be saved to a file. To save it to a file, click the Save Statistics to File button and then enter the name of the file in the edit box. The file is saved as an ASCII file. In case a file by the specified name already exists, then AutoCAD adds the present information to that file. You can use the EDIT function of DOS or any text editor to read the file.

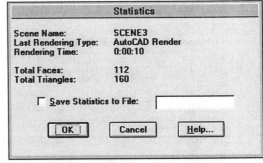

Figure 24-25 Statistics dialogue box

ATTACHING MATERIALS

You can assign materials to objects, to blocks, to layers, and to an AutoCAD color index (ACI). The description for each of them is as follows:

Attaching Material to an Object

Any object is made up of some material and hence to get the actual (realistic) rendered image of the object, it is necessary to assign materials to the surface of the object. AutoCAD supports different materials such as Aluminum, Bronze, Copper, Brass, Steel, Plastic, etc. These materials are located in material libraries such as **RENDER.MLI**. You can assign materials to objects, to blocks, to layers, and to an AutoCAD color index (ACI). By default, only ***GLOBAL*** material is assigned to a new drawing. However, if you have an object on the screen to which you want to attach a material that is already defined in the library of materials provided by AutoCAD (RENDER.MLI), you need to import the desired material to the drawing and then attach it to the object. For example, if you have a sphere in the current drawing and you want to attach Aluminum material to it, the following steps need to be executed:

Toolbar:	Render, Materials Library
Pull-down:	Tools, Render, Materials Library...
Screen:	TOOLS, RENDER, MatLib:

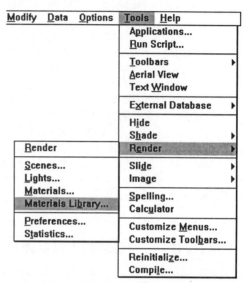

1. Invoke the **Materials Library** dialogue box (Figure 24-27). This dialogue box can be invoked from the **Render** toolbar (select Materials Library icon), from the pull-down menu (select Tools, Render, Materials Library..., Figure 24-26), from screen menu (select TOOLS, RENDER, MatLib:), or by entering **MATLIB** at the Command: prompt.

2. Once the Materials Library dialogue box is displayed on the screen, select the material you want from the **Library List** box. In our case, we will select Aluminum from the list.

Figure 24-26 Invoking the Library dialogue box from the Tools pull-down menu

In case the material you want to import is in a different library (other than RENDER.MLI), select the Open... button. The **Library File** dialogue box is displayed. Now you can specify the library file from which you want to select the material. If you want to check how this material will appear after rendering, select the **Preview** button. A rendered sphere with an aluminum material surface appears in the preview image tile in the dialogue box.

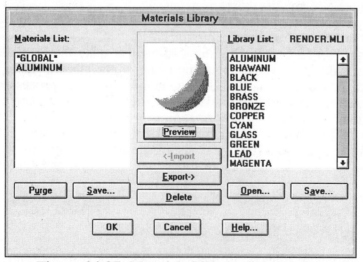

Figure 24-27 Materials Library dialogue box

3. Next choose the **Import** button to import the Aluminum material into the drawing. Once you do so, the entry Aluminum is automatically made in the **Material List** column. After this you can save the material list in a file by picking the **Save...** button and then specifying the .mli file in the **Library File** dialogue box. Next pick the **OK** button.

Note

When you open a new drawing, this column contains only the *GLOBAL* entry, which is the default material assigned to a new drawing.

When you import a material from the library to the drawing, the material and its properties are copied to the list of materials in the drawing and in no case is the material deleted from the library list. Unattached materials can be deleted from the material list by picking the **Purge** button in the **Materials Library** dialogue box.

Toolbar:	Render, Materials
Pull-down:	Tools, Render, Materials...
Screen:	TOOLS, RENDER, Mater'l:

4. Invoke the **Materials** dialogue box. This dialogue box can be invoked from the **Render** toolbar (select Materials icon), from the pull-down menu (select Tools, Render, Materials...), from the screen menu (select TOOLS, RENDER, Mater'l:), or by entering **RMAT** at the Command: prompt. You will notice that in the Materials column, Aluminum is now listed along with *GLOBAL*.

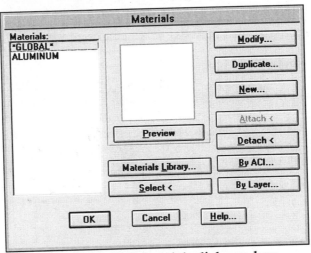

Figure 24-28 Materials dialogue box

5. Select Aluminum from the list of materials and then pick the **Attach** button. AutoCAD clears the dialogue box and issues the following prompt:

Select objects to attach "ALUMINUM" to:

6 Select the sphere. The **Materials** dialogue box is again displayed. Pick the OK button. Now if you render the drawing you will see that the aluminum material has been attached to the sphere.

Assigning Materials to the AutoCAD Color Index (ACI)

It is possible to attach materials to the AutoCAD color index (ACI). This can be realized in the following manner:

1. Invoke the **Materials** dialogue box.
2. Select the **By ACI...** button. The **Attach by AutoCAD Color Index** dialogue box (Figure 24-29) is displayed.
3. Select the material to be attached to an ACI from the **Materials** column.

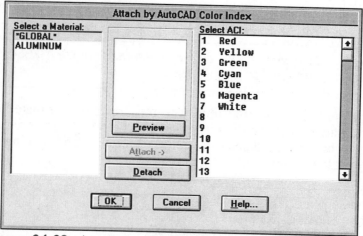

Figure 24-29 Attach by AutoCAD Color Index dialogue box

4. Select the desired ACI and pick the **Attach** button.
5. Pick the **OK** button to complete the process of attaching the specified material to objects with the specified ACI.

Assigning Materials to Layers

Materials can be associated with layers. This option is useful when you want all the objects on a specified layer to have the assigned material. This can be realized in the following manner:

1. Invoke the **Materials** dialogue box.
2. Select the By Layer... button. The **Attach by Layer** dialogue box (Figure 24-30) is displayed.
3. Select the material to be attached to all objects on a particular layer.

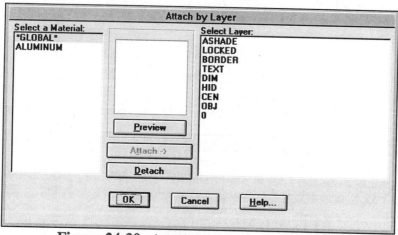

Figure 24-30 Attach by Layer dialogue box

4. Select the desired layer and pick the **Attach** button.
5. Pick the **OK** button.

With this the specified material is attached to all objects on the specified layer. AutoCAD attaches a material to an object while rendering according to the following order:

1. Materials explicitly attached to objects have highest priority.
2. Next, materials attached by ACI are considered.
3. Finally, materials attached by layer are considered.
4. GLOBAL material is used if no material is attached to an object.

If you assign different materials to different objects and then combine these objects into a single block, then upon rendering the block, the different components of the block are rendered according to the materials individually assigned to them. Now in case different components of a block have been created on different layers to which different materials have been attached and then you attach a material to the layer on which the block exists, then still the block will be rendered according to the materials attached to different layers on which the individual parts of the block were created. However, if there is some component in the block to which no material has been attached, then the material attached to the block will be attached to this component. In such a case if no material has been attached to the block then the component in the block to which no material has been attached will be assigned the *GLOBAL* material.

DETACHING MATERIALS

If you want to assign a different material to an object it is important to first dissociate the material previously attached to it; only then can you attach another material to it. Also sometimes it might be required that no material be attached to an object. To dissociate the material attached to an object, pick the **Detach** button in the **Materials** dialogue box. If you have attached a material by ACI (AutoCAD Color Index), then to detach this material pick the **By ACI...** button in the **Materials** dialogue box. **Attach by ACI** dialogue box is displayed. Pick the **Detach** button. Similarly if you want to detach a material attached by layer, pick the **By Layer...** button in the **Materials** dialogue box. **Attach by Layer** dialogue box is displayed. Pick the **Detach** button.

CHANGING THE PARAMETERS OF A MATERIAL

It is possible to change the parameters of a material, such as color and reflection properties, to meet your requirements. The following steps need to be performed:

1. Invoke the **Materials** dialogue box.
2. Select the name of the material you want to modify from the list of material names.
3. Select the **Modify...** button. The **Modify Standard Material** dialogue box appears (Figure 24-31). If you have specified the wrong material name, you can rectify this problem by entering the name of the material you want to modify in the **Material Name** edit box.

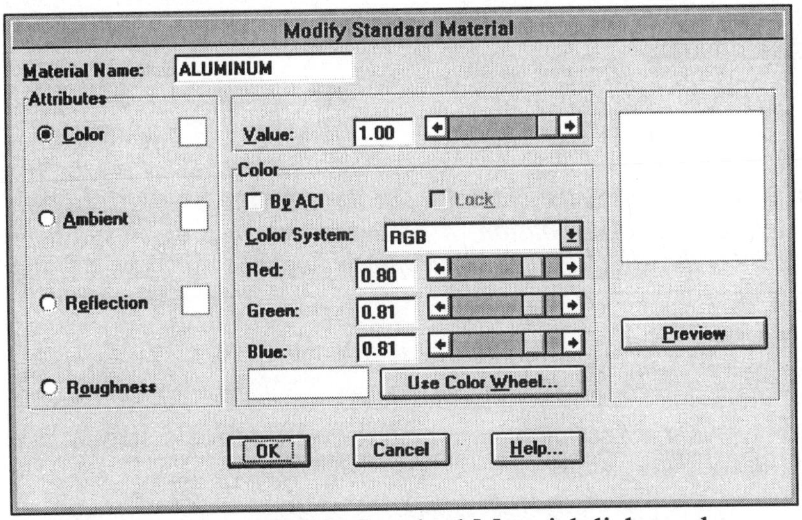

Figure 24-31 Modify Standard Material dialogue box

The Modify Standard Material dialogue box comprise of the following options:

Attributes Area

The Attributes area specifies the attributes of a material. You can modify an attribute of a material by selecting it in the Attributes area and then making the alterations to it. The following attributes are listed in this area:

Color radio button

You can change the diffuse (base) color of the material with this attribute. The intensity of the color can be changed by changing the value in the Value control with the help of slider bar. The color can be changed by using the RGB or HLS slider bars in the Color area in this dialogue box. You can also change the color with the help of color wheel or the AutoCAD Color Index (ACI) options. The change made to the color is reflected in the color swatch next to the Color option in the Attributes area.

Ambient radio button

By selecting this attribute, you can change the ambient color (shadow) of the material. Changes to the intensity can be made by changing the value in the Value control with the help of slider bar. The color can be changed by using the RGB or HLS slider bars in the Color area in this dialogue box. You can also change the color with the help of color wheel or the AutoCAD Color Index (ACI) options. The change made to the color is reflected in the color swatch next to the Ambient option in the Attributes area.

Reflection radio button

With this attribute you can modify the reflective (highlight or specular) color of the material. Changes to intensity can be made by changing the value in the Value control by using the scroll bar to increase or decrease the value. Changes to the reflective color can be made by changing the RGB or HLS slider bars in the Color area in this dialogue box. You can also change the color with the help of color wheel or the AutoCAD Color Index (ACI) options. The change made to the color is reflected in the color swatch next to the Reflection option in the Attributes area.

Roughness radio button

With this attribute you can modify the shininess or roughness level of the material. Changes can be made by changing the value in the Value control. The size of the material's reflective highlight alters by changing the Roughness level. As you increase the level of roughness, the highlight also increases.

> **Note**
>
> *If you want to see the effect the changes will have on the properties of an object after rendering, select the Preview button. A rendered sphere is displayed in the Preview image tile which reflects the effect of present properties of the material*

DEFINING NEW MATERIALS

Sometimes you may want to define a new material. To define a new material in AutoCAD you have to perform the following steps:

1. Invoke the **Materials** dialogue box.
2. Select the **New...** button. The **New Standard Material** dialogue box (Figure 24-32) appears on the screen.
3. Enter the name you want to assign to the new material in the **Material Name** edit box. The material name cannot be more than 16 characters long and there should be no other material by this name.

4. Just as you modified the attributes of a previously defined material in the Modify Standard Material dialogue box, set the color and values for the Color, Ambient, Reflection, and Roughness attributes of the new material to your requirement.

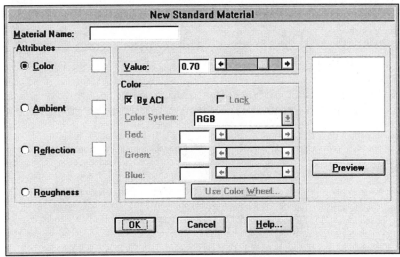

Figure 24-32 New Standard Material dialogue box

5. To examine the effect of rendering with the newly defined material, pick the **Preview** button. A rendered sphere depicting the effect of rendering with the new material is displayed in the image tile.
6. After defining the attributes, pick the **OK** button. In this manner a new material has been defined.

EXPORTING A MATERIAL FROM DRAWING TO LIBRARY OF MATERIALS

Sometimes you may have a material attached to a drawing but the material may not be present in the library of materials. One reason for this situation to arise can be if you have transferred a drawing that has materials assigned to it from one system to another system that does not have the material in the library of materials. It is possible to export a material from a drawing to the library of materials. The following steps need to be performed:

1. Open the drawing which has the material you want to export assigned to it.
2. Invoke the **Materials Library** dialogue box.
3. Select the material you want to export from the **Materials List** column.
4. Pick the **Export->** button. You will notice that the material name is appended to the list of materials in the Library List column.
5. Save the materials in the present drawing to a library with the **Save...** button just below the Materials List column.

SAVING A RENDERING

A rendered image can be saved by rendering to a file or by rendering to the screen and then saving the image. Redisplaying of a saved rendered image requires very little time compared to the time involved in rendering.

Saving a Rendering to a File

You can save a rendering directly to a file. One advantage of doing so is that you can replay the rendering in a short time. Another advantage is that when you render to the screen, the resolution of the rendering is limited by the resolution of your current display. Now if you render to a file, you can render to a higher resolution than that of your current display. Later on you can play this rendered image on a computer having a higher resolution display. The rendered images can be saved in different formats, such as TGA, TIFF, GIF, PostScript, X11, PBM, PGM, PPM, BMP, PCX, SUN, FITS, FAX G III, and IFF. To perform this operation carry out the following steps:

1. Invoke the **Render** dialogue box from the screen menu (select TOOLS, RENDER, Render:), from the pull-down menu (select Tools, Render, Render), or by entering **RENDER** at the Command: prompt.
2. In the **Destination** area, select **File** in the pop-up window.
3. Select the **More Options...** button. The **File Output Configuration** dialogue box (Figure 24-33) is displayed.

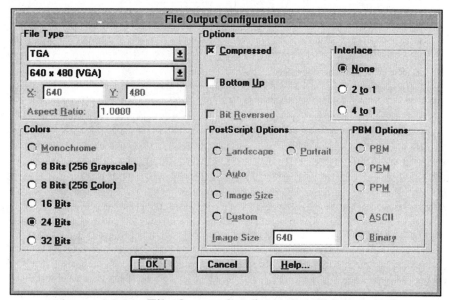

Figure 24-33 File Output Configuration dialogue box

4. Specify the file type, rendering resolution, colors, and other options. Then pick the **OK** button. The File Output Configuration dialogue box is cleared from the screen.
5. Select the **Render Scene** button in the Render dialogue box. The **Rendering File** dialogue box (Figure 24-34) is displayed. Specify the name of the file to which you want to save the rendering; then pick the **OK** button.

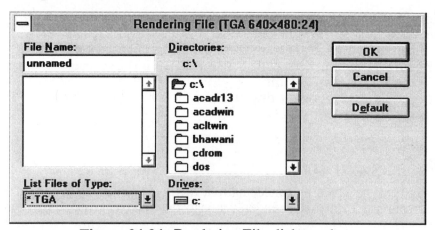

Figure 24-34 Rendering File dialogue box

Saving a Viewport Rendering

Pull-down: Tools, Images, Save...
Screen: TOOLS, SaveImg:

A rendered image in the viewport can be saved with the **SAVEIMG** command. In this case the file formats that can be used are TGA, TIFF, and GIF. To perform this operation, carry out the following steps:

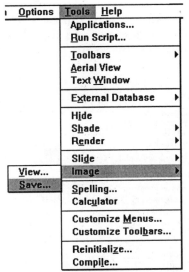

Figure 24-35 Invoking the SAVEIMG command from the pull-down menu

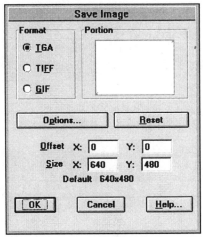

Figure 24-36 Save Image dialogue box

1. Invoke the **Render** dialogue box and select the **Render Scene** option to render the object to a viewport.
2. Invoke the **Save Image** dialogue box (Figure 24-36) from the pull-down menu (select Tools, Image, Save..., Figure 24-35), from the screen menu (select TOOLS, SaveImg:), or by entering **SAVEIMG** at the Command: prompt.
3. Specify the file format, size, and offsets for the image, then pick the **OK** button.

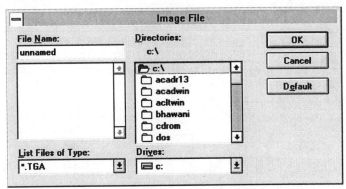

Figure 24-37 Image File dialogue box

4. The **Image File** dialogue box (Figure 24-37) is displayed.
5. Specify the name of the file to which you want to save the viewport rendering, then pick the **OK** button. In this way a rendered image in the viewport can be saved in the specified file format.

Saving a Render Window Rendered Image

A rendered image in the Render window can be saved with the **SAVE** command, which is available in the Render window. In this case the file format in which the Render window render image can be saved is bitmap (.BMP). To perform this operation carry out the following steps:

1. Invoke the **Render** dialogue box and select the **Render Window** option in the Destination area of the Render dialogue box. Select the Render Objects button and select the objects you want to render. In our case we have a single sphere that is to be rendered. Shortly after you select the object (sphere), the **Render** window (Figure 24-38) is displayed on the screen. The rendered object is displayed in this window.

Select the **Options** icon in the Render window. The **Window Render Options** dialogue box (Figure 24-38) is displayed on the screen. In this dialogue box, you can set the size and color depth of the rendered image. In our case the size is 640 by 480 and the color depth is 8 bit.

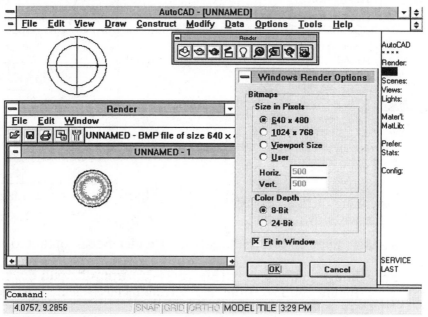

Figure 24-38 Render window with Windows Render Options dialogue box

Next select the **Save** icon in Render window to save the rendered image. The **Save BMP** dialogue box (Figure 24-39) is displayed on the screen. Enter the filename in the File Name edit box, then pick the OK button.

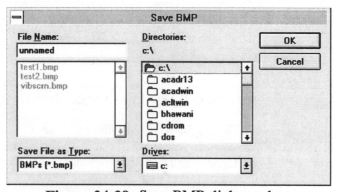

Figure 24-39 Save BMP dialogue box

The problem with bitmap images is that when you scale up these images, the images become non-uniform (blocky) and cannot be printed properly. On the other hand if you scale down these images, the images lose information.

REPLAYING A RENDERED IMAGE

In the previous section saving a rendered image was explained. In this section we will explain how to replay the saved rendered image.

Replaying a Rendered Image to a Viewport

Pull-down: Tools, Image, View...
Screen: TOOLS, Replay:

If you have saved the rendered image in a TGA, TIFF, or GIF format, you can use the **REPLAY** command to display the image on the screen. This operation can be performed in the following manner:

1. Invoke the **Replay** dialogue box (Figure 24-40), from the pull-down menu (select Tools, Image, View...), from the screen menu (select TOOLS, Replay:), or by entering **REPLAY** at the Command: prompt.

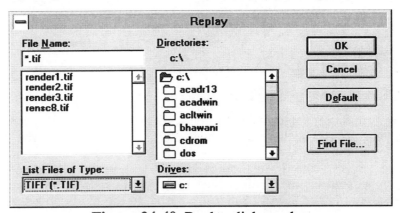

Figure 24-40 Replay dialogue box

2. Select the file you want to replay and pick the **OK** button.

3. Next, the **Image Specification** dialogue box (Figure 24-41) is displayed. You can define the size and offsets, or take the default full screen size for displaying the rendered image.

4. After specifying the size and offsets, pick the **OK** button. The selected image is displayed on the screen as per the specified size and offsets.

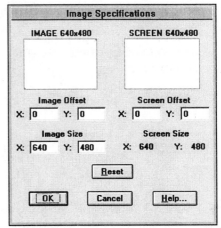

Figure 24-41 Image Specification dialogue box

Replaying a Rendered Image to the Windows Render Window

 1. Select the **Open** icon from the **Render Window** toolbar, or select the Open option in the Render Window File pull-down menu.

2. **The Render Open** dialogue box (Figure 24-42) is displayed. Select the file you want AutoCAD to replay and then pick the OK button. The selected image is displayed on the screen.

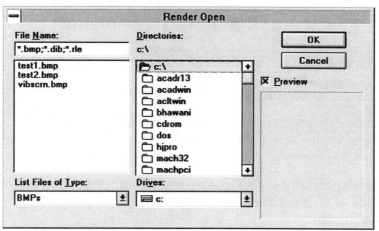

Figure 24-42 Render Open dialogue box

OUTPUTTING RENDERED IMAGES
TO HARD COPY DEVICES

You can directly output a rendered image on the hard copy device, but it is important that the hard copy device driver software be loaded on the system. Also configure the AutoCAD renderer to output to hard copy. This can be performed with the **RCONFIG** command. After configuring the AutoCAD renderer, specify the destination as **Hard Copy** in the **Destination** area of the **Render** dialogue box or the **Rendering Preferences** dialogue box. The rendered image will not be displayed on the screen; rather it will be directly output to the hard copy device.

SELF EVALUATION TEST

Answer the following questions and then compare your answers with the answers given at the end of this chapter.

1. A rendered image makes it easier to visualize the shape and size of a three-dimensional object. (T/F)

2. You can unload AutoCAD Render by invoking the **RENDERUNLOAD** command. (T/F)

3. Fall-off occurs only with a distant source of light. (T/F)

4. You cannot assign a view to a scene. (T/F)

5. You can modify a scene by changing the lights that are assigned to that scene. (T/F)

6.   You can use a spotlight to create a light source that emits light in a conical fashion in the defined direction. (T/F)

7.   The Phong render option produces a _____ quality image but it is computationally _____ and takes more time to display the image.

8.   Name the three methods that AutoCAD Render has provided for controlling the light fall-off.
     1._____ 2._____ 3._____

9.   A _____ light source emits light in all directions and the intensity of the emitted light is uniform.

10. A rendered image in the viewport can be saved with the _____ command.

11. Materials can be imported from an _____ file.

12. A predefined material cannot be modified. (T/F)

13. By default only _____ material is assigned to a new drawing.

14. Materials once attached to an object cannot be detached. (T/F)

15. In case you have saved the rendered image in a TGA, TIFF, or GIF format, you can use the _____ command to display the image on the screen.

REVIEW QUESTIONS

Answer the following questions.

1.   Rendering is not a effective tool for communicating your design ideas. (T/F)

2.   When you select any AutoCAD Render command, AutoCAD Render is loaded automatically. (T/F)

3.   You cannot render a drawing without inserting any lights or defining reflective characteristics of the surface. (T/F)

4.   The Gouraud render option saves computation time but does not generate a good quality image. (T/F)

5.   You can increase or decrease the intensity of the ambient light but you cannot completely turn it off. (T/F)

6.   AutoCAD Render allows you to control the appearance of the object by defining the reflective quality of the surface and by adding lights to get the desired effects. (T/F)

7.   The gradation effect produced by the lights does not make any difference in the appearance of the object. (T/F)

8.   By default AutoCAD Render uses smooth shading to render the image. (T/F)

9.   In the _____ option, the light falling on the object (brightness) is inversely proportional to the distance of the object from the light source (Brightness = 1/Distance).

10.   _____ light does not have a source and hence no location or direction.

11.   The intensity of the light radiated by a point source _____ with the distance.

12.   You can create a rendered images of a three-dimensional object by using the _____ command.

13.   You can load AutoCAD Render from the Command: prompt by entering _____.

14.   The intensity of light _____ as the distance increases.

15.   In the _____ option, the light falling on the object (brightness) is inversely proportional to the square of the distance of the object from the light source (Brightness = 1/Distance^2).

16.   A distant light source emits _____ beam of light in one direction only.

17.   The intensity of a light beam from a _____ light source does not change with the distance.

18.   What are the names of the two rendering shading types available in AutoCAD Render?
      1._____   2._____

19.   As the oblique angle _____, the amount of light reflected by the oblique surface decreases.

20.   By defining _____ it is convenient to render different views with the required lighting arrangement.

21.   Materials can only be assigned explicitly to objects. (T/F)

22.   When you import a material from the library of materials to a drawing, the material and its properties are copied to the list of materials in the drawing. (T/F)

23.   When you import a material from the library of materials to a drawing, it gets deleted from the library of materials. (T/F)

24.   New materials can be defined. (T/F)

25.   A material existing in a drawing can be exported to the library of materials (.mli file). (T/F)

26.   A rendered image can be saved by _____ or by _____.

27.   Redisplaying a saved rendered image takes _____ time as compared to the time involved in rendering.

28.   You can directly output a _____ on the hard copy device if the hard copy device driver software is loaded and the AutoCAD renderer is configured to output to hard copy.

29.   Name the light sources that AutoCAD Render supports.

30.   Define intensity. _____

31.   What is attenuation? _____

EXERCISES

Exercise 2

Make a drawing as shown in Figure 24-43. This drawing will then be used for rendering. You can also load this drawing from the accompanying disk. The name of the drawing is REND. The following is the description of one of the methods of making this drawing.

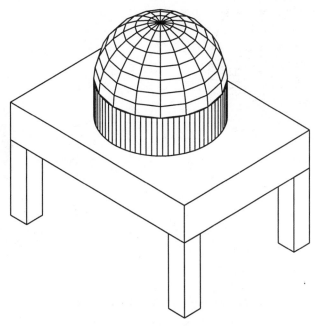

Figure 24-43 Drawing for Exercise 2

1. Draw a rectangle 2.75 by 2.0.
2. Use the CHANGE command to change the thickness to 0.25.
3. Use the 3DFACE command to draw a 3DFACE at the top of the rectangular box.
4. Draw another rectangle 0.25 by 0.25.
5. Use the CHANGE command to change the thickness to 1.0.
6. Copy the leg of the table to four corners.
7. Define the center point of the table as the new origin.
8. Draw a circle at the top surface of the table. The center of the circle must be at the center of the table.
9. Use the CHANGE command to change the thickness to 0.5.
10. Draw a dome that has a diameter of 1.5. The bottom edge of the dome must coincide with the top edge of the cylinder as shown in Figure 24-43.
11. To render the drawing, first position a Distant Light source at 3,-2,5 and the target at 0,0,0. Now render the drawing.
12. Position a Point Light source at -1,0,5 with the fall-off set to Inverse Square. Render the object again.
13. Modify the Distant and the Point light sources to study the effect of lighting on the rendering.

Exercise 3

Generate the 3D drawing as shown in Figure 24-44. The dimensions shown in the top and side views are for reference only. (Assume a value for the missing dimensions.)

Next, render the 3D view of the drawing after inserting the lights at appropriate locations so as to get a realistic 3D image of the object.

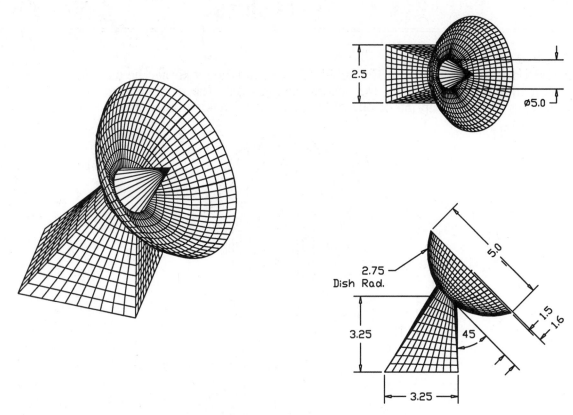

Figure 24-44 Drawing for Exercise 3

Exercise 4

a. Draw different objects on the screen and assign different materials explicitly to them. Then render the drawing.

b. Detach the materials previously assigned to the objects and assign new materials to them.

Exercise 5

Attach COPPER material to some layer on your system. Draw objects on this layer and then render the drawing. Observe the results carefully.

Exercise 6

a. Define a new material named NEWMAT. Assign desired attribute values to it in the New Standard Material dialogue box and then attach this material to an object and render it to a viewport.

b. Save the rendered image in the desired size and offset and give it any name.

c. Redisplay the saved image on the screen.

Chapter 25

Geometry Calculator

Learning objectives

After completing this chapter, you will be able to:
♦ Understand how the geometry calculator functions.
♦ Use real, integer, vector, and numeric expressions.
♦ Use SNAP modes in the geometry calculator.
♦ Obtain the radius of an object and locate a point on a line.
♦ Understand applications of the geometry calculator.
♦ Use AutoLISP variables and filter X, Y, and Z coordinates.

GEOMETRY CALCULATOR

The geometry calculator is an ADS application that can be used as an on-line calculator. The calculator can be used to evaluate vector, real, and integer expressions. It can also access the existing geometry by using the first three characters of the standard AutoCAD object snap functions (MID, CEN, END). You can use the calculator to evaluate arithmetic and vector expressions. For example, you can use calculator to evaluate an expression like $3.5^12.5*(234*log(12.5)-3.5*cos(30))$.

Another application of the calculator is in assigning value to an AutoLISP variable. For example, you can use an AutoLISP variable in the arithmetic expression and then assign the value of the expression to an AutoLISP variable.

 You can invoke the **CAL** command from the toolbar (Standard Toolbar, Object Snap flyout, Calculator), pull-down menu (Tools, Calculator), screen menu (TOOLS, GeomCal:), or enter CAL or 'CAL at AutoCAD command prompt.

REAL, INTEGER, AND VECTOR EXPRESSIONS

Real and Integer Expressions

A **Real Expression** consists of real numbers and/or functions that are combined with numeric operators. Similarly, an **Integer Expression** consists of integer numbers and/or functions combined with numeric operators. The following is the list of numeric operators:

Operator	Operation	Example
+	Adds numbers	(2+3)
-	Subtracts numbers	(15.5-3.754)
*	Multiplies numbers	(12.34*4)

/	Divides numbers	(345.5/2.125)
^	Exponentiation of numbers	(25.5^2.5)
( )	Used to group expressions	(4.5+(4.35^2))

Example
Command: **CAL**
> > Expression: **(4.5 + (4.35^2))**
23.4225

Vector Expression

A vector expression consists of points, vectors, numbers, and functions that are combined with the following operators:

Operator Operation / Example

+   Adds vectors
[a,b,c] + [x,y,z] = [a+x, b+y, c+z]
[2,4,3] + [5,4,7] = [2+5, 4+4, 3+7] = [7.0 8.0 10.0]

-    Subtracts vectors
[a,b,c] - [x,y,z] = [a-x, b-y, c-z]
[2,4,3] - [5,4,7.5] = [2-5, 4-4, 3-7.5] = [-3.0 0.0 -4.5]

*   Multiplies a vector by a real number
a * [x,y,z] = [a*x, a*y, a*z]
3 * [2,8,3.5] = [3*2, 3*8, 3*3.5] = [6.0 24.0 10.5]

/   Divides a vector by a real number
[x,y,z] / a = [x/a, y/a, z/a]
[4,8,4.5] / 2 = [4/2, 8/2, 4.5/2] = [2.0 4.0 2.25]

&   Multiplies vectors
[a,b,c] & [x,y,z] = [(b*z)-(c*y), (c*x)-(a*z), (a*y)-(b*x)]
[2,4,6] & [3,5,8] = [(4*8)-(6*5), (6*3)-(2*8), (2*5)-(4*3)] = [2.0 2.0 -2.0]

( )   Used to group expressions   (a + (b^c))

Example
Command: **CAL**
> > Expression **[2,4,3] - [5,4,7.5]**
-3.0 0.0 4.5

NUMERIC FUNCTIONS

The geometry calculator (CAL) supports the following numeric functions:

Function	Description
sin(angle)	Calculates the **sine** of an angle
cos(angle)	Calculates the **cosine** of an angle
tang(angle)	Calculates the **tangent** of an angle
asin(real)	Calculates the **arcsine** of a number (The number must be between -1 and 1)
acos(real)	Calculates the **arccosine** of a number (The number must be between -1 and 1)
atan(real)	Calculates the **arctangent** of a number

ln(real)	Calculates the **natural log** of a number
log(real)	Calculates the **log, to the base 10**, of a number
exp(real)	Calculates the **natural exponent** of a number
exp 10(real)	Calculates the **exponent, to the base 10**, of a number
sqr(real)	Calculates the **square** of a number
sqrt(real)	Calculates the **square root** of a number
abs(real)	Calculates the **absolute** value of a number
round(real)	Rounds the number to the **nearest integer**
trunc(real)	Returns the **integer portion** of a number
r2d(angle)	Converts the **angle in radians** to degrees
d2r(angle)	Converts the **angle in degrees** to radians
pi	pi has a **constant value** (3.14159)

Example
Command: **CAL**
> > Expression: **Sin (60)**
0.866025

USING SNAP MODES

You can use AutoCAD's snap modes with CAL functions to evaluate an expression. When you use snaps in an expression, AutoCAD will prompt you to select an object and the returned value will be used in the expression. For example, if the CAL function is **(cen+end)/2**, the calculator will first prompt you to select an object for center snap mode and then select another object for endpoint snap mode. The two values will be added and divided by 2. The returned value is a point located midway between the center of the circle and the endpoint of the selected object. Following is the list of **CAL snap modes** and the corresponding AutoCAD snap modes:

CAL Snap Modes	**AutoCAD Snap Modes**
END	ENDpoint
INS	INSert
INT	INTersection
MID	MIDpoint
CEN	CENter
NEA	NEArest
NOD	NODe
QUA	QUAdrant
PER	PERpendicular
TAN	TANgent

Example 1

In this example you will use the **cal snap modes** to retrieve the point values (coordinates) and then use these values to draw a line (P3,P4). It is assumed that the circle and line (P1,P2) are already drawn.

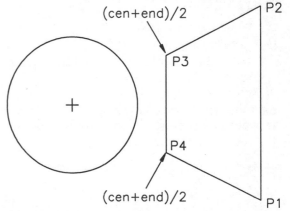

Command: **LINE**
From point: **'cal**
> >Expression: **(cen+end)/2**
Select entity for CEN snap: *Select the circle.*

Figure 25-1 Using cal snap modes

Select entity for END snap: *Select one end of line P1,P2.*
To point: **'cal**
\> \> Expression: **(cen+end)/2**
Select entity for CEN snap: *Select the circle.*
Select entity for END snap: *Select the other end of line P1,P2.*

Now, join point P4 with P1 and point P3 with P2 to complete the drawing as shown in Figure 25-1. The **'cal** function initializes the geometry calculator transparently. The single quote in front of the cal function (') makes the **cal** function transparent. The expression **(cen+end)/2** will prompt you to select the objects for **CEN snap** and **END snap**. After you select these objects, the calculator will add these values and then divide the sum by 2. The value that this function returns is the midpoint between the center of the circle and the first end point of the line.

OBTAINING THE RADIUS OF AN OBJECT

You can use the **rad** function to obtain the radius of an object. The object can be a circle, an arc, or a 2D polyline arc.

Example 2

In this example you are given a circle of certain radius (R). You will draw a second circle whose radius is 0.75 times the radius of the given circle (0.75*R).

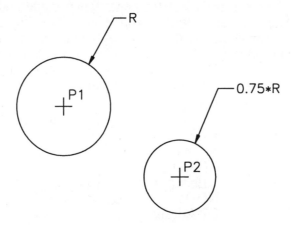

Figure 25-2 Obtaining the radius of an object

Command: **CIRCLE**
3P/2P/TTR/<Center point>: *Select a point (P2).*
Diameter/<Radius>: **'cal**
\> \>Expression: **0.75*rad**
\> \>Select circle, arc or polyline segment for RAD function: *Select the given circle*

Now you can enter the function name in response to calculator prompt (**\> \>Expression**). In this example the expression is **0.75*rad**. The **rad** function prompts the user to select an object and it retrieves its radius. This radius is then multiplied by 0.75. The product of rad and 0.75 determines the radius of the new circle.

LOCATING A POINT ON A LINE

You can use the functions **pld** and **plt** to locate a point on an object. The format of the **pld** function is **pld(p1,p2,dist)**. This function will locate a point on line P1,P2 that is at a distance of **dist** from point P1. For example, if the function is pld(p1,p2,0.7) and the length of the line is 1.5, the calculator will locate a point at a distance of 0.7 from point P1 along line P1,P2.

The format of the **plt** function is **plt(p1,p2,t)**. This function will locate a point on line P1,P2 at a distance as determined by the parameter, t. If **t=0**, the point that this function will locate is at P1. Similarly, if **t=1**, the point is located at P2. However, if the value of t is greater than 0 and less than 1 $(0>t<1)$, the location of the point is determined by the value of t. For example, if the function is plt(p1,p2, 0.3) and the length of the line is 1.5. The calculator will locate the point at a distance of 0.3*1.5 = 0.45 from point P1.

Example 3

In this example you will use the **pld** and **plt** functions to locate the centers of the circles. Lines P1,P2 and P3,P4 are given.

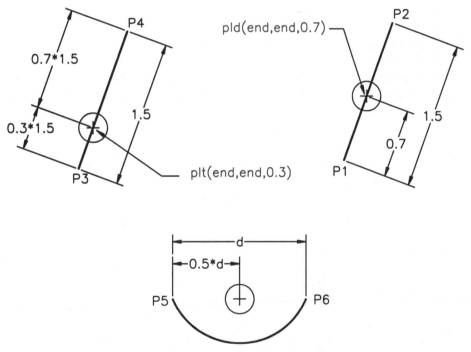

Figure 25-3 Locating a point on a line

Figure 25-3 illustrates the use of the plt and pld functions. The **plt** function, **plt(end,end,0.3)**, will prompt the user to select the two endpoints of the line (P3,P4) and the function will return a point at a distance of 0.3*1.5 from point P1.

```
Command: CIRCLE
3P/2P/TTR/<Center point>: 'cal
>>Expression: plt(end,end,0.3)
>>Select entity for END snap: Select the first endpoint of line P3,P4.
>>Select entity for END snap: Select the second endpoint of line P3,P4.
Diameter/<Radius>: Enter radius.
```

Similarly, the **pld** function, **pld(end,end,0.7)**, will prompt the user to select the two endpoints of line P1,P2 and it will return a point that is located at a distance of 0.7 units from point P1.

Command: **CIRCLE**
3P/2P/TTR/<Center point>: **'cal**
> >Expression: **pld(end,end,0.7)**
> >Select entity for END snap: *Select the first endpoint of line P1,P2.*
> >Select entity for END snap: *Select the second endpoint of line P1,P2.*
Diameter/<Radius>: *Enter radius.*

The **plt** function can also be used to locate the midpoint by selecting the two endpoints of an arc as shown in the following example:

Command: **CIRCLE**
3P/2P/TTR/<Center point>: **'cal**
> >Expression: **plt(end,end,0.5)**
> >Select entity for END snap: *Select the first endpoint of arc P5,P6.*
> >Select entity for END snap: *Select the second endpoint of arc P5,P6.*
Diameter/<Radius>: **'CAL**
> > Expression: **0.125*DEE**

OBTAINING AN ANGLE

You can use the **ang** function to obtain the angle between the two lines. The function can also be used to obtain the angle that a line makes with the positive X axis. The function has the following formats:

ang(v)
ang(p1,p2)
ang(apex,p1,p2)
ang (apex,p1,p2,p)

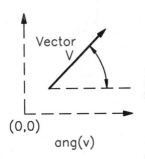

ang(v)

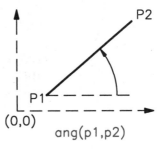

ang(p1,p2)

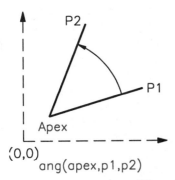

ang(apex,p1,p2)

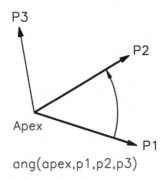

ang(apex,p1,p2,p3)

Figure 25-4 Obtaining an angle

ang(v)

The **ang(v)** function can be used to obtain the angle that a vector makes with the positive X axis. Assume a vector [2,2,0] and obtain its angle. You can use the ang(v) function to obtain the angle.

> Command: **cal**
> > >Expression: **v=[2,2,0]**   *(Defines a vector v.)*
> Command: **cal**
> > >Expression: **ang(v)**   *(v is a predefined vector.)*
> 45.0

The vector v makes 45 degree angle with the positive X axis

ang(p1,p2)

The **ang(p1,p2)** function can be used to obtain the angle that a line (P1,P2) makes with the positive X axis. For example, if you want to obtain the angle of a line with start and endpoint coordinates of 1,1,0 and 4,4,0.

> Command: **cal**
> > >Expression: **p1=[1,1,0]**   *(Defines a vector p1.)*
> Command: **cal**
> > >Expression: **p2=[4,4,0]**   *(Defines a vector p2.)*
> Command: **cal**
> > >Expression: **ang(p1,p2)**
> 45.00

If the line exists, you can obtain the angle by using the following function:

> Command: **cal**
> > >Expression: **ang(end,end)**
> > >Select entity for END snap: *Select first endpoint of line P1, P2.*
> > >Select entity for END snap: *Select second endpoint of line P1, P2.*
> 31.7134   *(This is the angle that the function returns.)*

ang(apex,p1,p2)

The **ang(apex,p1,p2)** function can be used to obtain the angle that the line (apex,P1) makes with (apex,P2). For example, if you want to obtain the angle between the two given lines as shown in the third drawing of Figure 25-4, use the following commands.

> Command: **cal**
> > >Expression: **ang(end,end,end)**
> > >Select entity for END snap: *Select first endpoint (apex)*
> > >Select entity for END snap: *Select second endpoint (P1)*
> > >Select entity for END snap: *Select third endpoint (P2)*
> 51.41459   *(This is the angle that the function returns)*

ang(apex,p1,p2,p)

The **ang(apex,p1,p2,p)** function can be used to obtain the angle that the line (apex,P1) makes with (apex,P2). The last point **p** is used to determine the orientation of the angle.

LOCATING THE INTERSECTION POINT

You can obtain the intersection point of two lines (P1,P2 and P3,P4) by using the following function:

ill(p1,p2,p3,p4)

P1,P2 are two points on the first line and P3,P4 are two point on the second line, as shown in Figure 25-5.

Example 4

In this example you will draw a circle whose center point is located at the intersection point of two lines (P1,P2 and P3,P4). It is assumed that the two lines are given as shown in Figure 25-5.

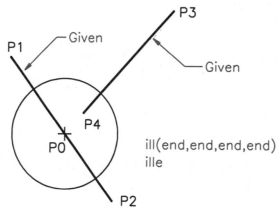

Figure 25-5 Obtaining intersection point

Use the following commands to obtain the intersection point and to draw a circle with the intersection point as the center of circle:

Command: **CIRCLE**
3P/2P/TTR/<Center point>: **'cal**
>>Expression: **ill(end,end,end,end)**
>>Select entity for END snap: *Select the first point on line P1,P2.*
>>Select entity for END snap: *Select the second point on line P1,P2.*
>>Select entity for END snap: *Select the first point on line P3,P4.*
>>Select entity for END snap: *Select the second point on line P3,P4.*
Diameter/<Radius>: *Enter radius.*

The expression ill(end,end,end,end) can be replaced by the shortcut function **ille**. When used, it will automatically prompt for four endpoints to locate the point of intersection.

APPLICATIONS OF THE GEOMETRY CALCULATOR

The following examples illustrate some additional applications of the Geometry Calculator.

Example 5

In this example you will draw a circle whose center (P0) is located midway between endpoints P4 and P2.

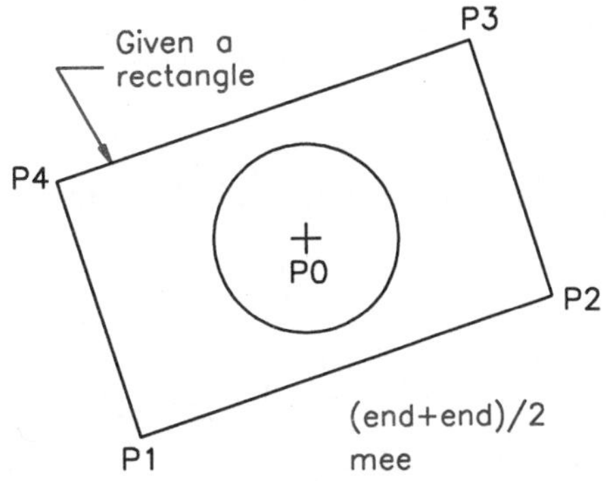

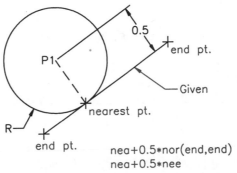

Figure 25-6 Using the shortcut function **mee**

The center of the circle can be located by using the calculator snap modes. For example, to locate the center you can use the expression (end+end)/2. The other way of locating the center is by using the shortcut function **mee** as shown below:

Command: **CIRCLE**
3P/2P/TTR/ <Center point> : **'cal**
> >Expression: **mee**
> >Select entity for END snap: *Select the first endpoint (P2).*
> >Select entity for END snap: *Select the second endpoint (P4).*
Diameter/ <Radius> : *Enter the radius.*

Example 6

In this example you will draw a circle that is tangent to the given line. The radius of the circle is 0.5 units and the circle must pass through the selected point.

Figure 25-7 Using the shortcut function **nee**

To draw a circle that is tangent to a line you must first locate the center of the circle that is at a distance of 0.5 units from the selected point. This can be accomplished by using the function **nor(p1,p2)**, which returns a unit vector normal to the line (P1,P2). You can also use the shortcut function **nee**. The function will automatically prompt you to select the two endpoints of the given line. The unit vector must be multiplied by the radius (0.5) to locate the center of the circle.

Command: **CIRCLE**
3P/2P/TTR/ <Center point> : **'cal**
> >Expression: **NEA+0.5*nee**
> >Select entity for NEA snap: *Select a point on the given line.*
> >Select one endpoint for NEE: *Select the first endpoint on the given line.*
> >Select another endpoint for NEE: *Select the second endpoint on the given line.*
Diameter/ <Radius> : **0.5**

Example 7

In this example you will draw a circle with its center on the line. The radius of the circle is 0.25 times the length of the line and it is assumed that the line is given.

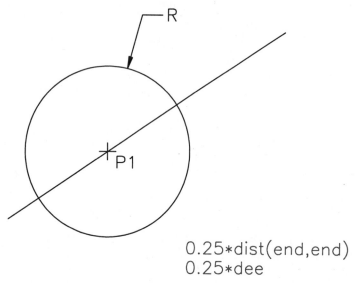

0.25*dist(end,end)
0.25*dee

Figure 25-8 Using the shortcut function **dee**

The radius of the circle can be determined by multiplying the length of the line by 0.25. The length of the line can be obtained by using the function **dist(p1,p2)** or by using the shortcut function **dee**. When you use the function dee, the calculator will automatically prompt you to select the two endpoints of the given line. It is equivalent to using the function dist(end,end).

Command: **CIRCLE**
3P/2P/TTR/<Center point>: *Select a point on the line.*
Diameter/<Radius>: **'cal**
>>Expression: **0.25*dee**
>>Select entity for END snap: *Select the first endpoint on the given line.*
>>Select entity for END snap: *Select the second endpoint on the given line.*

USING AUTOLISP VARIABLES

The geometry calculator allows you to use an AutoLISP variable in the arithmetic expression. You can also use the calculator to assign a value to an AutoLISP variable. The variables can be integer, real, or 2D or 3D point. The next example illustrates the use of AutoLISP variables.

Example 8

In this example you will draw two circles that are in the middle and are offset 0.5 units from the center. It is assumed that the other two circles are given.

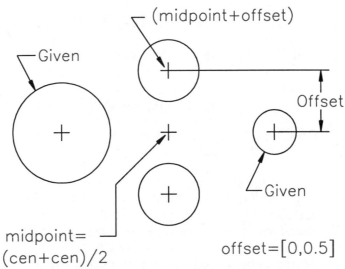

Figure 25-9 Adding two predefined vectors

To locate the center of the top circle you must first determine the point that is midway between the centers of the two given circles. This can be accomplished by defining a variable **midpoint** where **midpoint=(cen+cen)/2**. Similarly, you can define another variable for the offset distance: **offset=[0,0.5]**. The center of the circle can be obtained by adding these two variables **(midpoint+offset)**.

Command: **cal**
> >Expression: midpoint=**(cen+cen)/2**
> >Select entity for CEN snap: *Select the first circle.*
> >Select entity for CEN snap: *Select the second circle.*

Command: **cal**
> >Expression: offset=**[0,0.5]**

Command: **CIRCLE**
3P/2P/TTR/<Center point>: **'cal**
> >Expression: **(midpoint+offset)**
Diameter/<Radius>: *Enter radius.*

To locate the center point of the bottom circle you must subtract offset from midpoint.

Command: **CIRCLE**
3P/2P/TTR/<Center point>: **'cal**
> >Expression: **(midpoint-offset)**
Diameter/<Radius>: *Enter radius*

The same results can be obtained by using **AutoLISP** expressions as follows:

Command: **(Setq NEWPOINT "(CEN+CEN)/2+[0,0.5]")**
Command: **CIRCLE**
3P/2P/TTR/<Center point>: **(cal NEWPOINT)** *(Recalls the expression.)*
> >Select entity for CEN snap: *Select the first circle.*
> >Select entity for CEN snap: *Select the second circle.*

FILTERING X, Y, AND Z COORDINATES

The following functions are used to retrieve the coordinates of a point.

Function	Description
xyof(p)	Retrieves the **X and Y** coordinates of a point (p) and returns a point. The Z coordinate is automatically set to 0.0
xzof(p)	Retrieves the **X and Z** coordinates of a point (p) and returns a point. The Y coordinate is automatically set to 0.0
yzof(p)	Retrieves the **Y and Z** coordinates of a point (p) and returns a point. The X coordinate is automatically set to 0.0
xof(p)	Retrieves the **X coordinates** of a point (p) and returns a point. The Y and Z coordinates are automatically set to 0.0
yof(p)	Retrieves the **Y coordinates** of a point (p) and returns a point. The X and Z coordinates are automatically set to 0.0
zof(p)	Retrieves the **Z coordinates** of a point (p) and returns a point. The X and Y coordinates are automatically set to 0.0
rxof(p)	Retrieves the **X coordinates** of a point (p)
ryof(p)	Retrieves the **Y coordinates** of a point (p)
rzof(p)	Retrieves the **Z coordinates** of a point (p)

Example 9

In this example you will draw a line by using filters to extract coordinates and points. It is assumed that the two lines are given as shown in Figure 25-10.

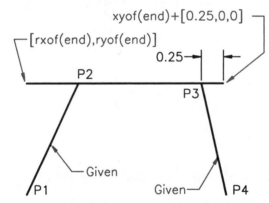

Figure 25-10 Using filters to extract points and coordinates

To draw a line you need to determine the coordinates of the two endpoints of the line. The X coordinate of the first point can be obtained from point P1 and the Y coordinate from point P2. To obtain these coordinate points you can use the filter function **rxof(end)** to extract the X coordinate and **ryof(end)** to extract the Y coordinate. To determine the coordinates of the endpoint of the line you can filter the XY coordinates of point P3 and then add the offset of 0.25 units by defining a vector [0.25,0,0].

Command: **LINE**
From point: **'cal**
> >Expression: **[rxof(end),ryof(end)]**
> >Select entity for END snap: *Select the first endpoint (P1).*
> >Select entity for END snap: *Select the second endpoint (P2).*
To point: **'cal**
> >Expression: **xyof(end)+[0.25,0,0]**

CONVERTING UNITS

You can use the calculator function **cvunit** to change the given value from one system of units to another. You can also use this function to change the unit format. For example, you can change the units from feet to inches or meters to centimeters and vice versa. The value can be a number or a point. The format of the cvunit expression is:

cvunit(value, units from, units to)

Examples
Command: **cal**
> >Expression: **cvunit(100,cm,inch)**
> >Expression: **cvunit(100,feet,meter)**
> >Expression: **cvunit(1,feet,inch)**

ADDITIONAL FUNCTIONS

The following is the list of additional calculator functions. The description given next to the function summarizes the application of the function.

Function	Description
abs(real)	Calculates the **absolute value** of a number
abs(v)	Calculates the **length of vector v**
ang(v)	Calculates the **angle** between the X axis and the vector **v**
ang(p1,p2)	Calculates the **angle** between the X axis and line (P1,P2)
cur	Retrieves **coordinates of a point** from the location of the graphics cursor
cvunit(val,from,to)	**Converts the given value** (val) from one unit measurement system to another
dee	Measures the **distance between two end points**. It is equivalent to the function dist(end,end)
dist(p1,p2)	**Measures distance** between two specified points (P1,P2)
getvar(var name)	Retrieves the value of AutoCAD **system variable**
ill(p1,p2,p3,p4)	Returns the **intersection point** of lines P1,P2 and P3,P4
ille	Returns the **intersection point** of lines defined by four endpoints. It is equivalent to the function ill(end,end,end,end)
mee	Returns the **midpoint** between two end points. It is equivalent to function (end+end)/2
nee	Returns a **unit vector** normal to two end points. It is equivalent to the function nor(end,end)
nor	Returns a **unit vector** that is normal to a circle or an arc
nor(v)	Returns a **unit vector** in the xy plane that is normal to vector **v**
nor(p1,p2)	Returns a **unit vector** in the xy plane that is normal to line P1,P2
nor(p1,p2,p3)	Returns a **unit vector** that is normal to the specified plane defined by points P1,P2,P3
pld(p1,p2,dist)	**Locates a point** on the line (P1,P2) that is dist units from point P1
plt(p1,p2,t)	**Locates a point** on the line (P1,P2) that is **t*dist** units from point P1 (Note: When t=0 the point is P1. Also when t=1 the point is P2)
rad	**Retrieves the radius** of the selected object.
rot(p,org,ang)	Returns a point that is rotated through angle **ang** about point **org**
u2w(p)	Locates a point with respect to WCS from the current UCS
vec(p1,p2)	**Calculates a vector** from point P1 to point P2
vec(p1,p2)	**Calculates a unit vector** from point P1 to point P2
vee	**Calculates a vector** from two endpoints. It is equivalent to function vec(end,end)

vee1	Calculates a **unit vector** from two endpoints. It is equivalent to function vec1(end,end)
w2u(p)	Locates a point with respect to current UCS from WCS

SELF EVALUATION TEST

Answer the following questions and then compare your answers with the correct answers given at the end of this chapter.

1. The length of a line can be obtained by using the function **dist(p1,p2)** or by using the shortcut function _____ .

2. **The function xzof(p)** retrieves the _____ coordinates of a point (P) and returns a point. The Y coordinate is automatically set to 0,0.

3. What function can be used to retrieve the X coordinates of a point (P)? _____

4. **The function nor(v)** returns a _____ in the xy plane that is normal to vector **v**.

5. What function will calculate the **absolute value** of a number? _____

6. The **ang(v)** function can be used to obtain the angle that a vector makes with the _____ _____ axis.

7. What function can be used to obtain the angle that a line (P1,P2) makes with the positive X axis? _____

8. How can you obtain the intersection point of two lines (P1,P2 and P3,P4). _____

9. What is the shortcut function for (end+end)/2? _____

10. The shortcut function **nee** is equivalent to what function? _____

REVIEW QUESTIONS

Answer the following questions.

1. What can the calculator be used for? _____

2. The calculator can also access the existing geometry by using standard AutoCAD object snap functions. (T/F)

3. The calculator cannot be used to assign value to an AutoLISP variable. (T/F)

4. What is a real expression? _____

5.   What is a vector expression and what does it consists of?_____

_____

6.   Evaluate the expression 3 * [72,18,13.5]. _____

7.   Evaluate the expression [14,8,14.5] / 2. _____

8.   Evaluate the expression [12,15.5,0.5] + [2.5,11,7]. _____

9.   Evaluate the expression [2,5,3] & [7,3,5]. _____

10   You cannot use AutoCAD's snap modes with CAL functions to evaluate an expression (T/F)

11. What function can you use to obtain the radius of an object? _____

12. Name the functions that can be used to locate a point on an object. _____

13. Write the format of the **pld** function. _____

14. What is the format of the **plt** function? _____

15. How can you obtain the angle between two given lines? _____

EXERCISES

Exercise 1

Make the drawing as shown in Figure 25-11. Use the real operators of the geometry calculator to calculate the value of L, H, and TL

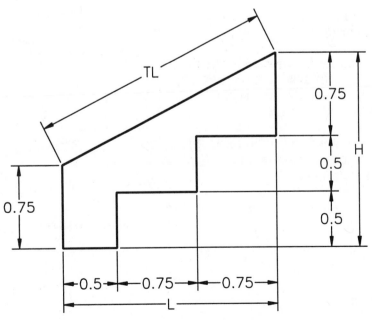

Figure 25-11 Drawing for Exercise 1

Exercise 2

Make the drawing as shown in Figure 25-12; assume the dimensions. Draw a circle whose center is at point P3. Use the calculator function to locate the center of the circle (P3) that is midway between P1 and P2. The points P1 and P2 are the midpoints on the top and bottom lines.

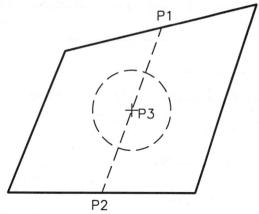

Figure 25-12   Drawing for Exercise 2

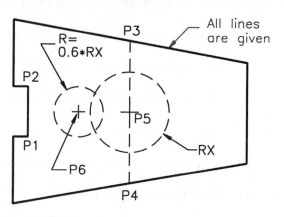

Figure 25-13   Drawing for Exercise 3

Exercise 3

Make the drawing as shown in Figure 25-13; assume the dimensions.

1. Draw a circle whose center is at point P5. Use the calculator function to locate the center of the circle (P5) that is midway between P3 and P4. Points P3 and P4 are the midpoints on the top and bottom lines.

2. Draw a circle whose radius is 0.6 times the radius of the first circle. The center of the circle (P6) is located midway between the center of the first circle (P5) and the midpoint of line P1,P2.

Exercise 4

Make the drawing as shown in Figure 25-14; assume the dimensions.

1. Use the calculator function to locate the point p3. Point P3 is midway between P1 and P2. The points P1 and P2 are the midpoints on the top and the bottom lines.

2. Use the calculator function to locate the point P3 that is normal to the line P1,P2 at a distance of 0.25 units.

3. Draw a circle whose center is located at P4.

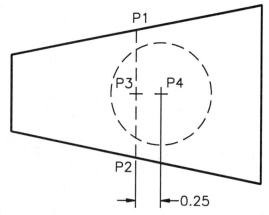

Figure 25-14   Drawing for Exercise 4

Answers:

The following are the correct answers to the questions in the self evaluation test.
1 - dee, **2** - X and Z, **3** - rxof(p) **4** - unit vector, **5** - abs(real) **6** - positive X, **7** - ang(p1,p2), **8** - ill(p1,p2,p3,p4), **9** - mee **10** - nor(p1,p2)

Chapter 26

Prototype Drawings

Learning objectives

After completing this chapter, you will be able to:
- Create prototype drawings.
- Load prototype drawings using dialogue boxes and the command line.
- Do initial drawing setup.
- Customize drawings with layers and dimensioning specifications.
- Customize drawings according to plot size and drawing scale.

CREATING PROTOTYPE DRAWINGS

One way to customize AutoCAD is to create prototype drawings that contain initial drawing setup information. When the user starts a new drawing, the settings that are associated with the prototype drawing are automatically loaded. If you start a new drawing, AutoCAD loads the drawing ACAD.DWG, with its default setup values. For example, the default limits are (0.0,0.0), (12.0,9.0) and the default layer is 0 with white color and continuous line type. Generally, these default parameters need to be reset before generating a drawing on the computer using AutoCAD. A considerable amount of time is required to set up the layers, colors, linetypes, limits, snaps, units, text height, dimensioning variables, and other parameters. Sometimes, border lines and a title block may also be needed.

In production drawings, most of the drawing setup values remain the same. For example, the company title block, border, layers, linetypes, dimension variables, text height, ltscale, and other drawing setup values do not change. You will save considerable time if you save these values and reload them when starting a new drawing. You can do this by making prototype drawings. These prototype drawings can contain the initial drawing setup information, set according to company specifications. They can also contain a border, title block, tolerance table, and perhaps some notes and instructions that are common to all drawings.

THE STANDARD PROTOTYPE DRAWING

The AutoCAD software package comes with a standard prototype drawing called ACAD.DWG. When you start a new drawing, the standard prototype drawing, ACAD.DWG, is automatically loaded (provided AutoCAD's initial drawing setup configuration has not been changed). The following are some of the system variables with the default values that are assigned to AutoCAD's standard prototype drawing, ACAD.DWG:

BASE	Insertion base point (0.0,0.0,0.0)
BLIPMODE	On
CHAMFER	Distance 0.0
COLOR	Bylayer

DIMALT	Off
DIMALTD	2
DIMALTF	25.4
DIMPOST	None
DIMASO	On
DIMASZ	0.18
DRAGMODE	Auto
ELEVATION	Elevation 0.0, thickness 0.0
FILL	On
FILLET	Radius 0.0
GRID	Off, spacing (0.0,0.0)
HANDLES	Off
ISOPLANE	Left
LAYER	Layer 0 with color white and linetype continuous
LIMITS	Off, limits (0.0,0.0) - (12.0,9.0)
LINETYPE	Loaded linetype CONTINUOUS
LTSCALE	1.0
MENU	Acad
MIRROR	Text mirrored like other entities
ORTHO	Off
TILEMODE	On
TIME	User elapsed timer on
TRACE	Trace width 0.05
UCS	Current UCS same as WORLD
UNITS(linear)	Decimal, 4 decimal places
ZOOM	To drawing limits

Example 1

Create a prototype drawing with the following specifications (the name of the prototype drawing is PROTO1).

Limits	18.0,12.0
Snap	0.25
Grid	0.50
Text height	0.125
Units	decimal
	2 digits to the right of decimal point
	decimal degrees
	2 fractional places for display of angles
	0 angle along positive X-axis (east)
	angle positive if measured counterclockwise

Start AutoCAD and enter **NEW** at the AutoCAD command prompt (Command: **NEW**). AutoCAD displays the **Create New Drawing** dialogue box (Figure 26-1) on the screen. Enter the name of the new drawing, PROTO1, in the **New Drawing Name** edit box and press the ENTER key or select OK from the dialogue box. To start a new drawing, you can also use the **File** pull-down menu and select the **New** option. When AutoCAD displays the **Create New Drawing** dialogue box, enter the drawing name as mentioned above.

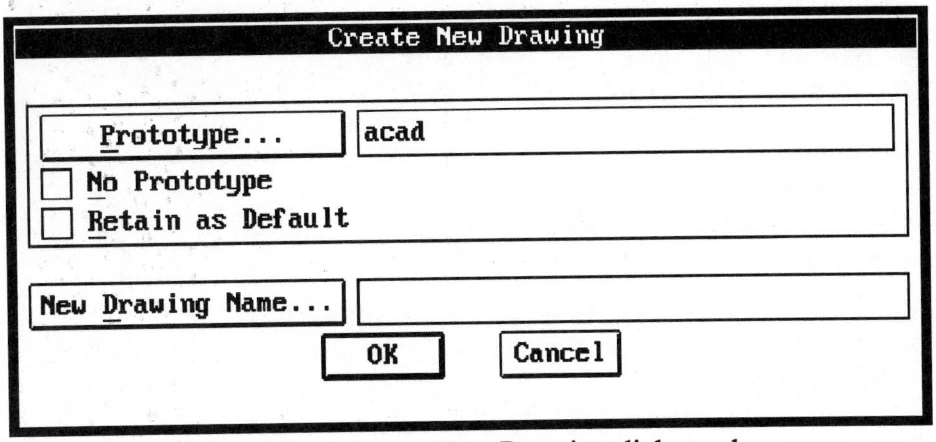

```
┌─────────────────────────────────────────────────────────┐
│                   Create New Drawing                      │
├─────────────────────────────────────────────────────────┤
│                                                           │
│   ┌──────────────────┐  ┌──────────────────────────────┐ │
│   │   Prototype...   │  │ acad                         │ │
│   └──────────────────┘  └──────────────────────────────┘ │
│   ☐ No Prototype                                          │
│   ☐ Retain as Default                                     │
│                                                           │
│   ┌──────────────────┐  ┌──────────────────────────────┐ │
│   │ New Drawing Name.│  │                              │ │
│   └──────────────────┘  └──────────────────────────────┘ │
│                  ┌────────┐   ┌────────┐                  │
│                  │   OK   │   │ Cancel │                  │
│                  └────────┘   └────────┘                  │
└─────────────────────────────────────────────────────────┘
```

Figure 26-1   Create New Drawing dialogue box

Once you are in the Drawing Editor, use the following AutoCAD commands to set up the values as given in Example 1.

Command: **LIMITS**
ON/OFF/ <Lower left corner> <0.00,0.00>: **0,0**
Upper right corner<12.0,9.0>: **18.0,12.0**

Command: **SNAP**
Snap spacing or ON/OFF/Aspect/Rotate/Style<1.0>: **0.25**

Command: **GRID**
Grid spacing(X) or ON/OFF/Snap/Aspect<0.00>: **0.50**

Command: **SETVAR**
Variable name or ?: **TEXTSIZE**
New value for textsize<0.02>: **0.125**

Command: **Units**

Report formats:	Examples:
1. Scientific	1.55E+01
2. Decimal	15.50
3. Engineering	1'-3.50"
4. Architectural	1'-3 1/2"
5. Fractional	15 1/2

With the exception of the Engineering and Architectural formats, these formats can be used with any basic units of measurements. For example, Decimal mode is perfect for metric units as well as decimal English units.

Enter choice, 1 to 5<2>: **2**
Number of digits to right of decimal point (0 to 8)<4>: **2**

Systems of angle measure:	Examples:
1. Decimal degrees	45.0000
2. Degrees/minutes/seconds	45d0'0"
3. Grads	50.0000g
4. Radians	0.7854r
5 Surveyor's units	N 45d0'0"

Enter choice, 1 to 5<1>: **1**
Number of fractional places for display of angles (0 to 8)<0>: **2**

Direction for angle 0.00:

East	3 o'clock	= 0.00
North	12 o'clock	= 90.00
West	9 o'clock	= 180.00
South	6 o'clock	= 270.00

Enter direction for angle 0.00<0.00>: **0**
Do you want angles measured clockwise?<N>: **N**

Now, save the drawing as PROTO1 using AutoCAD's SAVE or END command. This drawing is now saved as PROTO1 on the default drive. You can also save this drawing on a floppy diskette in one of the drives, A or B.

Command: **SAVE**
File name<PROTO1>: **A:PROTO1**

LOADING A PROTOTYPE DRAWING

You can use the prototype drawing any time you want to start a new drawing. To use the preset values of the prototype drawing, start AutoCAD and enter the NEW command (Command: **NEW**) to start a new drawing. AutoCAD displays the **Create New Drawing** dialogue box (Figure 26-2) on the screen. You can also start a new drawing by selecting the **File** pull-down menu and then selecting the **New** option from this menu. AutoCAD will display the **Create New Drawing** dialogue box on the screen. Now, you are ready to enter the name of the new drawing, GEAR1, using the prototype drawing PROTO1.

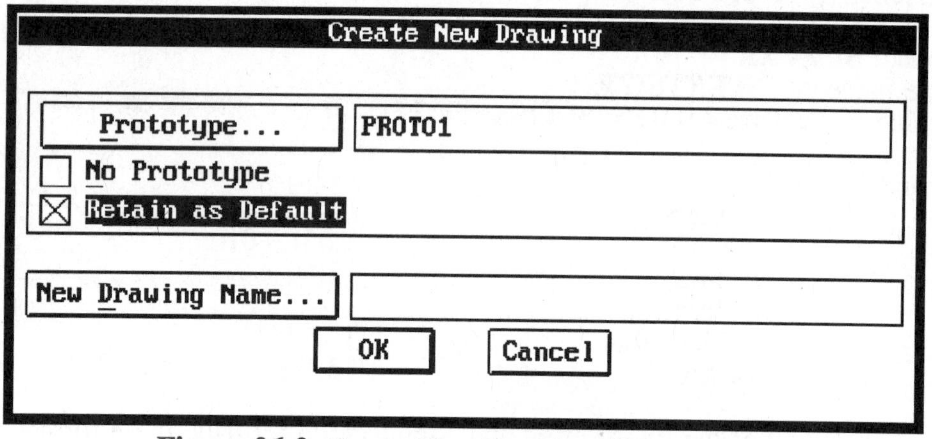

Figure 26-2   Create New Drawing dialogue box

Enter the name of the prototype drawing, PROTO1, in the **Prototype** edit box, then enter the name of the new drawing, GEAR1, in the **New Drawing Name** edit box. AutoCAD will start a new drawing, GEAR1, but it will have the same setup as that of prototype drawing, PROTO1. You can also start a new drawing that has the settings of the prototype drawing by entering the name of the drawing, followed by an equal sign and the name of the new drawing in the **New Drawing Name** edit box (GEAR1=PROTO1).

You can have several prototype drawings, each with a different setup. For example, PROTO1 for a 12" by 18" drawing, PROTO2 for a 24" by 36" drawing, and PROTO3 for a 36" by 48" drawing. Each prototype drawing can be created according to user-defined specifications. You can then load any of these prototype drawings by entering the name of the new drawing in the **Prototype** edit box.

LOADING A PROTOTYPE DRAWING
USING THE COMMAND LINE

You can create a new drawing without using the dialogue boxes by assigning a value of 0 to the AutoCAD system variable **FILEDIA**. To start a new drawing, enter NEW at the command prompt (Command: **NEW**) and AutoCAD will prompt you to enter the name of the drawing. The format for entering the name of the prototype drawing is:

Command: **NEW**
Enter name of drawing: *(New Drawing Name=Prototype Drawing Name)*

In the following example, GEAR1 is the name of the new drawing and PROTO1 is the name of the prototype drawing. When you enter the file name in this format, AutoCAD will start a new drawing, GEAR1, but it will have the same setup as that of the prototype drawing, PROTO1.

Command: **NEW**
Enter name of drawing: **GEAR1=PROTO1**

If the prototype drawings are not in the current subdirectory, you need to define the path with the name of the prototype drawing. For example, if the prototype drawing PROTO1 is in the PROTODWG subdirectory of the C drive, the prototype drawing name and the path will be defined as:

Enter name of drawing: **GEAR1= C:\PROTODWG\PROTO1**

On the other hand, if you want your new drawing to assume AutoCAD's default value, put an equal sign (=) after the name of the drawing (GEAR1=). AutoCAD will start a new drawing, GEAR1, and this drawing will assume AutoCAD's default values: the default drawing limits are (0.00,0.00), (12.00,9.00), the default layer is 0 with continuous linetype, and the color associated with this layer is white.

Command: **NEW**
Enter name of drawing: **GEAR=**

If you enter the name of the new drawing as GEAR1, AutoCAD will load the standard prototype drawing ACAD.DWG (provided you have not changed the default configuration). The new drawing, GEAR1, will assume the same setup values as those of ACAD.DWG drawing.

Command: **NEW**
Enter name of drawing: **GEAR1**

INITIAL DRAWING SETUP

AutoCAD has provided a facility to change the default drawing that AutoCAD initially loads when you start a new drawing. For example, if you start a new drawing, GEAR1, AutoCAD loads the default drawing, ACAD.DWG, because AutoCAD has been configured to load the ACAD.DWG drawing. You can reconfigure AutoCAD to load PROTO1.DWG or any other drawing by changing AutoCAD's initial drawing setup. Use the following procedure to configure the initial drawing setup:

Start AutoCAD and type **CONFIG** (Command: **CONFIG**) at the command prompt; AutoCAD will display the existing configuration. If you press the ENTER key one more time, the configuration menu will be displayed on the screen.

Configuration menu

0. Exit to drawing editor
1. Show current configuration
2. Allow detailed configuration
3. Configure video display
4. Configure digitizer
5. Configure plotter
6. Configure system console
7. Configure operating parameters

Enter Selection<0>: **7**   *(Configure operating parameters.)*

In the configuration menu select option number 7, "**Configure operating parameters**," and press the ENTER key. The operating parameter menu will be displayed on the screen.

Configure operating parameters

0. Exit to configuration menu
1. Alarm on error
2. Initial drawing setup
3. Default plot file name
4. Plot spooler directory
5. Placement of temporary files
6. Network node name
7. Automatic-save feature
8. Speller dialect
9. Full-time CRC validation
10. Automatic Audit after, DXFIN, or DXBIN
11. Login name
12. File locking
13. Authorization

Enter selection<0>: **2**   *(Initial drawing setup.)*

Enter name of default prototype file for new drawings or . for none<acad>: **PROTO1**

The default prototype file for the new drawing is ACAD (ACAD.DWG). If you want to change the default drawing, type the name of the drawing in response to the above prompt. For example, if you want the PROTO1.DWG drawing to be the default drawing, type PROTO1 and press the ENTER key. Press the ENTER key again until you are back in the Drawing Editor. Now, if you start a new drawing, GEAR1, AutoCAD will load the default drawing, PROTO1. Again, if you want to start a new drawing that has AutoCAD's default setting, the name of the new drawing should be followed by an equal sign (GEAR1=).

You can also change the default prototype drawing by entering the name of the prototype drawing in the **Create New Drawing** dialogue box (Figure 26-3) and then selecting the **Retain as Default** button. When you select **OK**, AutoCAD will automatically change the default prototype drawing to PROTO1.DWG. Now, if you enter the name of the new drawing, the settings of the default drawing (prototype drawing PROTO1) will be automatically loaded.

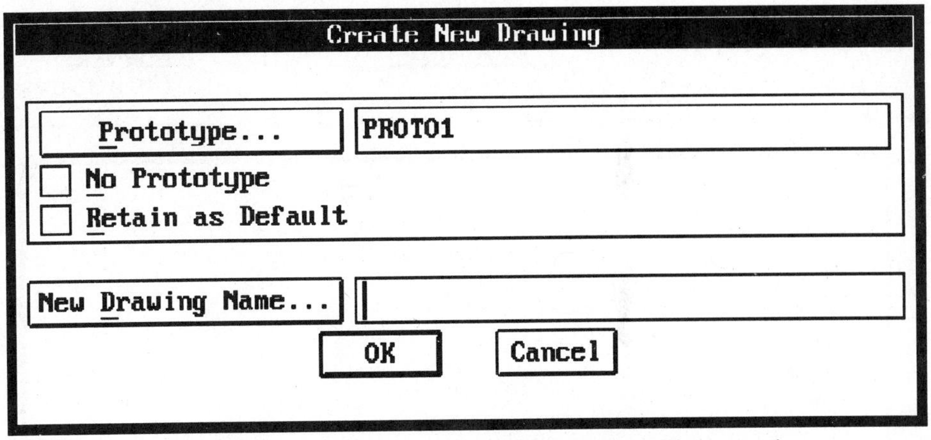

```
┌─────────────────────────────────────────────────┐
│                Create New Drawing                │
│                                                  │
│  ┌──────────────────┐  ┌──────────────────────┐  │
│  │   Prototype...   │  │ PROTO1               │  │
│  │ ☐ No Prototype   │  │                      │  │
│  │ ☐ Retain as Default │                      │  │
│  └──────────────────┘  └──────────────────────┘  │
│                                                  │
│  ┌──────────────────┐  ┌──────────────────────┐  │
│  │ New Drawing Name...│ │                      │  │
│  └──────────────────┘  └──────────────────────┘  │
│            ┌──────┐      ┌────────┐              │
│            │  OK  │      │ Cancel │              │
│            └──────┘      └────────┘              │
└─────────────────────────────────────────────────┘
```

Figure 26-3 Create New Drawing dialogue box

CUSTOMIZING DRAWINGS WITH LAYERS AND DIMENSIONING SPECIFICATIONS

Most production drawings need multiple layers for different groups of entities. In addition to layers, it is good practice to assign different colors to different layers to control the line width at the time of plotting. You can generate a prototype drawing that contains the desired number of layers with linetypes and colors according to your company specifications. You can then use this prototype drawing to make a new drawing. The next example illustrates the procedure used for customizing a drawing with layers, linetypes, and colors.

Example 2

You want to create a prototype drawing (PROTO2) that has a border and the company's title block as shown in Figure 26-4. In addition to this, you also want the following initial drawing setup:

Limits	48.0,36.0
Snap	1.0
Grid	4.00
Text height	0.25
PLINE width	0.02
Ltscale	4.0
DIMENSIONS	
DIMSCALE	4.0
DIMTAD	ON
DIMTIX	ON
DIMTOH	OFF
DIMTIH	OFF
DIMSCALE	25

LAYERS

Layer Names	Line Type	Color
0	Continuous	White
OBJ	Continuous	Red
CEN	Center	Yellow
HID	Hidden	Blue
DIM	Continuous	Green
BOR	Continuous	Magenta

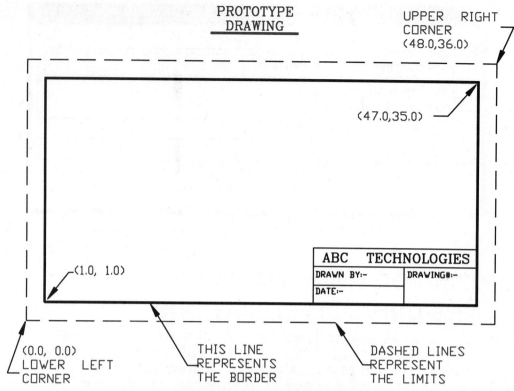

Figure 26-4 Prototype drawing

Start a new drawing with default parameters. You can do this by typing an equal sign (=) after the name of the drawing. (**Enter name of drawing:** New drawing name=). Once you are in the drawing editor, use the AutoCAD commands to set up the values as given for this example. Also, draw a border and a title block as shown in Figure 26-4. In this figure the hidden lines indicate the drawing limits. The border lines are 0.5 units inside the drawing limits. For the border lines use a polyline of width 0.02 units. Use the following command sequence to produce the prototype drawing for Example 2:

Command: **LIMITS**
ON/OFF/<Lower left corner> <0.00,0.00>:**0,0**
Upper right corner<12.0,9.0>: **48.0,36.0**
Command: **SNAP**
Snap spacing or ON/OFF/Aspect/Rotate/Style<1.0>: **1.0**

Command: **GRID**
Grid spacing(X) or ON/OFF/Snap/Aspect<1.0>: **4.00**

Command: **SETVAR**
Variable name or ?: **TEXTSIZE**
New value for textsize<0.180>: **0.25**

Command: **PLINEWID**
New value for PLINEWID: **0.02**

Command: **PLINE**
From point: **1.0,1.0**
Current line-width is **0.02**
Arc/Close/Halfwidth/Length/Undo/Width/<Endpoint of line>:**47,1**
Arc/Close/Halfwidth/Length/Undo/Width/<Endpoint of line>:**47,35**
Arc/Close/Halfwidth/Length/Undo/Width/<Endpoint of line>:**1,35**

Arc/Close/Halfwidth/Length/Undo/Width/ < Endpoint of line > :**C**

Command: **LTSCALE**
New scale factor < 1.0 > : **4.0**

Command: **DIM**
Dim: **DIMSCALE**
Current value < 1.00 > New value: **4.0**

Dim: **Dimtix**
Current value < Off > New value: **ON**

Dim: **Dimtad**
Current value < Off > New value: **ON**

Dim: **Dimtoh**
Current value < On > New value: **OFF**

Dim: **Dimtih**
Current value < On > New value: **OFF**
Dim: **Exit**

Command: **Layer**
?/Make/Set/New/ON/OFF/Color/Ltype/Freeze/Thaw/LOck/Unlock: **N**
New layer name(s): **OBJ,CEN,HID,DIM,BOR**

?/Make/Set/New/ON/OFF/Color/Ltype/Freeze/Thaw/LOck/Unlock: **L**
Linetype (or ?) < CONTINUOUS > : **HIDDEN**
Layer name(s) for linetype HIDDEN < 0 > : **HID**

?/Make/Set/New/ON/OFF/Color/Ltype/Freeze/Thaw/LOck/Unlock: **L**
Linetype (or ?) < CONTINUOUS > : **CENTER**
Layer name(s) for linetype CENTER < 0 > : **CEN**

?/Make/Set/New/ON/OFF/Color/Ltype/Freeze/Thaw/LOck/Unlock: **C**
Color: **RED**
Layer name(s) for color 1 (red) < 0 > : **OBJ**

?/Make/Set/New/ON/OFF/Color/Ltype/Freeze/Thaw/LOck/Unlock: **C**
Color: **YELLOW**
Layer name(s) for color 2 (yellow) < 0 > : **CEN**

?/Make/Set/New/ON/OFF/Color/Ltype/Freeze/Thaw/LOck/Unlock: **C**
Color: **BLUE**
Layer name(s) for color 5 (blue) < 0 > : **HID**

?/Make/Set/New/ON/OFF/Color/Ltype/Freeze/Thaw/LOck/Unlock: **C**
Color: **GREEN**
Layer name(s) for color 3 (green) < 0 > : **DIM**

?/Make/Set/New/ON/OFF/Color/Ltype/Freeze/Thaw/LOck/Unlock: **C**
Color: **MAGENTA**
Layer name(s) for color 6 (magenta) < 0 > : **BOR**
?/Make/Set/New/ON/OFF/Color/Ltype/Freeze/Thaw/LOck/Unlock: **(RETURN)**

Note

Add the title block and the text as shown in Figure 26-4.

You can also use the pull-down menu to create the layers and to set the color and linetype.

After completing the drawing, save it as PROTO2. You have created a prototype drawing (PROTO2) that contains all of the information given in Example 2.

CUSTOMIZING DRAWINGS ACCORDING TO PLOT SIZE AND DRAWING SCALE

You can generate a prototype drawing according to plot size and scale. For example, if the scale is 1/16" = 1' and the drawing is to be plotted on a 36" by 24" area, you can calculate drawing parameters like limits, dimscale, and ltscale and save them in a prototype drawing. This will save considerable time in the initial drawing setup and provide uniformity in the drawings. The next example explains the procedure involved in customizing a drawing according to a certain plot size and scale.

Example 3

Generate a prototype drawing (PROTO3) with the following specifications:

Plotted sheet size	36" by 24" (Figure 26-5)
Scale	1/8" = 1.0'
Snap	3'
Grid	6'
Text height	1/4" on plotted drawing
Ltscale	Calculate
Dimscale	Calculate
Units	Architectural
	16 - denominator of smallest fraction
	Angle in degrees/minutes/seconds
	4 - Number of fractional places for display of angles
	0 angle along positive X-axis
	Angle positive if measured counterclockwise
Border	Border should be 1" inside the edges of the plotted drawing sheet, using PLINE 1/32" wide when plotted (Figure 26-5)

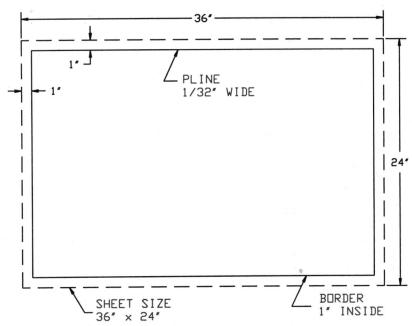

Figure 26-5 Border of prototype drawing

In this example you need to calculate some values before you set the parameters. For example, the limits of the drawing depend on the plotted size of the drawing and the scale of the drawing. Similarly, LTSCALE and DIMSCALE depend on the limits of the drawing. The following calculations explain the procedure for finding the values of limits, ltscale, dimscale, and text height.

Limits

Given:

```
Sheet size    36" x 24"
Scale        1/8" = 1'
             or 1" = 8'
```

Calculate:

```
X-Limit
Y-Limit
Since sheet size is 36" x 24" and scale is 1/8"=1'
Therefore, X-Limit = 36 x 8' = 288'
           Y-Limit = 24 x 8' = 192'
```

Text height

Given:

```
Text height when plotted = 1/4"
Sheet size               36" x 24"
Scale                    1/8" = 1'
```

Calculate:

Text height

```
Since scale is 1/8" = 1'
          or 1/8" = 12"
          or   1" = 96"
Therefore, scale factor = 96
         Text height  = 1/4" x 96
                      = 24" = 2'
```

Ltscale and Dimscale

Known:

```
Since scale is 1/8" = 1'
              or 1/8" = 12"
              or  1" = 96"
```

Calculate:

Ltscale and Dimscale

```
Since scale factor = 96
Therefore,
Ltscale = Scale factor = 96
Similarly, Dimscale = 96
(All dimension variables, like DIMTXT and DIMASZ, will be
multiplied by 96.)
```

Pline Width

Given:

```
Scale is  1/8" = 1'
```

Calculate:

PLINE width

```
Since scale is 1/8" = 1'
           or    1" = 8'
           or    1" = 96"
```

Therefore,
```
PLINE width = 1/32 x 96
            = 3"
```

After calculating the parameters, use the following AutoCAD commands to set up the drawing, then save the drawing as PROTO3.

Command: **Units**

Report formats:	Examples:
1. Scientific	1.55E+01
2. Decimal	15.50
3. Engineering	1'-3.50"
4. Architectural	1'-3 1/2"
5. Fractional	15 1/2

With the exception of Engineering and Architectural formats, these formats can be used with any basic units of measurements. For example, Decimal mode is perfect for metric units as well as decimal English units.

Enter choice, 1 to 5<2>: **4**
Denominator of smallest fraction to display
(1, 2, 4, 8, 16, 32, or 64<16>: **16**

Systems of angle measure:	Examples:
1. Decimal degrees	45.0000
2. Degrees/minutes/seconds	45d0'0"
3. Grads	50.0000g
4. Radians	0.7854r
5. Surveyor's units	N 45d0'0" E

Enter choice, 1 to 5<1>: **2**
Number of fractional places for display of angles (0 to 8)<0>: **4**

Direction for angle 0.00:

East	3 o'clock	= 0d0'0'
North	12 o'clock	= 90d0'0"
West	9 o'clock	= 180d0'0"
South	6 o'clock	= 270d0'0"

Enter direction for angle 0d0'0"<0d0'0">: **RETURN**
Do you want angles measured clockwise?<N>: **N**

Command: **LIMITS**
ON/OFF/<Lower left corner> <0'-0",0'-0">:**0,0**
Upper right corner<1'-0",0'-9">: **288',192'**

Command: **SNAP**
Snap spacing or ON/OFF/Aspect/Rotate/Style<0'-1">: **3'**

Command: **GRID**
Grid spacing(X) or ON/OFF/Snap/Aspect<0'-0">: **6'**

Command: **SETVAR**
Variable name or ?: **TEXTSIZE**
New value for textsize<0'-0 3/16">: **2'**

Command: **LTSCALE**
New scale factor<1.0>: **96**

Command: **DIM**
Dim: **Dimscale**
Current value<1.00> New value: **96**
Dim: **EXIT**

Command: **PLINE**
From point: **8',8'**
Current line-width is **0.00**
Arc/Close/Halfwidth/Length/Undo/Width/<Endpoint of line>:**W**
Starting width<0.00>: **3**
Ending width<0'-3">: **RETURN**
Arc/Close/Halfwidth/Length/Undo/Width/<Endpoint of line>:**280',8'**
Arc/Close/Halfwidth/Length/Undo/Width/<Endpoint of line>:**280',184'**
Arc/Close/Halfwidth/Length/Undo/Width/<Endpoint of line>:**8',184'**
Arc/Close/Halfwidth/Length/Undo/Width/<Endpoint of line>:**C**

SAVING MENU REFERENCE WITH PROTOTYPE DRAWINGS

You might need more than one menu file for your application. After you have written a new menu file, you can load the new menu by using AutoCAD's MENU command or by changing the initial drawing setup in the configuration menu. You can also load the new menu by saving it with a prototype drawing. To accomplish this, create a prototype drawing or load an existing prototype drawing that you want to use with the new menu file. Load the new menu file using AutoCAD's MENU command, then save the prototype drawing. The menu file reference will be saved with the drawing. When you load the prototype drawing again, the menu file that is referenced in the drawing will be loaded automatically.

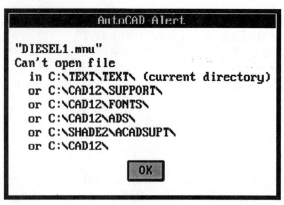

Figure 26-6 AutoCAD Alert dialogue box

If AutoCAD cannot find the referenced menu file, it will display the message **Can't open file** in the AutoCAD Alert dialogue box (Figure 26-6) on the screen.

Note

If you have customized your menus and you need to send your drawing to a customer for editing, it is a good idea to send the customer your menu file (.MNU) or the compiled menu file (.MNX) also, so that the customer can use the same menu that you are using. The menu file will be loaded automatically when the customer opens your drawing on his or her system.

REVIEW QUESTIONS

Fill in the blanks.

1.   The name of the standard prototype drawing that comes with AutoCAD software is _____.

2.   The default prototype drawing is automatically _____, provided the _____ has not been changed.

3.   If the name of the new drawing is HOUSE, AutoCAD will load the default prototype drawing as specified in AutoCAD's _____ menu.

4.   If the name of the new drawing is HOUSE=, AutoCAD will load a drawing that has AutoCAD's _____ settings.

5.   If the name of the new drawing is HOUSE=PROTOH, AutoCAD will load the _____ prototype drawing.

6.   The ACAD.DWG standard prototype drawing was created by entering the name of the new drawing as _____.

7.   The default prototype drawing can be changed by using the CONFIG command, selecting item number _____ from the Configuration menu, and then selecting item number 2 from _____.

8. The default value of DIMSCALE is _____ .

9. The default value for DIMTXT is _____ .

10. The default value for SNAP is _____ .

11. Architectural units can be selected by using AutoCAD's _____ command.

12. If plot size is 36" x 24", and the scale is 1/2" = 1', X-Limit = _____ and Y-Limit = _____ .

13. If the plot size is 24" x 18", and the scale is 1 = 20, X-Limit = _____ and Y-Limit = _____ .

14. If the limits are (0.00,0.00) and (600.00,450.00), the LTSCALE factor = _____ .

15. _____ provides a convenient way to plot multiple views of a 3D drawing or multiple views of a regular 2D drawing.

EXERCISES

Exercise 1

Generate a prototype drawing (PROTOE1) with the following specifications:

Limits	36.0,24.0
Snap	0.5
Grid	1.0
Text height	0.25
Units	Decimal
	2 - number of digits to right of decimal point
	Decimal degrees
	0 - number of fractional places for display of angles
	0 - angle along positive X-axis
	Angle positive if measured counterclockwise

Exercise 2

Generate a prototype drawing PROTOE2 with the following specifications:

Limits	48.0,36.0
Snap	0.5
Grid	2.0
Text height	0.25
PLINE width	0.03
Ltscale	Calculate
Dimscale	Calculate

LAYERS

Layer Names	Line Type	Color
0	Continuous	White
OBJECT	Continuous	Green
CENTER	Center	Magenta
HIDDEN	Hidden	Blue
DIM	Continuous	Red
BORDER	Continuous	Cyan

Exercise 3

Generate a prototype drawing (PROTOE3) with following specifications:

Plotted sheet size	36" x 24" (Figure 26-7)
Scale	1/2" = 1.0'
Text height	1/4" on plotted drawing
Ltscale	Calculate
Dimscale	Calculate
Units	Architectural

           32 - denominator of smallest fraction to display
           Angle in degrees/minutes/seconds
           4 - number of fractional places for display of angles
           0d0'0" - direction for angle
           Angle positive if measured counterclockwise

Border   Border is 1-1/2" inside the edges of the plotted drawing sheet, using PLINE 1/32" wide when plotted (Figure 26-7)

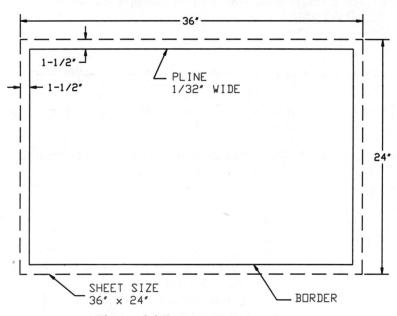

Figure 26-7 Prototype drawing

Chapter 27

Script Files and Slide Shows

Learning objectives

After completing this chapter, you will be able to:
- Write script files and use the SCRIPT command to run script files.
- Use the RSCRIPT and DELAY commands in script files.
- Invoke script files when loading AutoCAD and use script files to freeplot.
- Create a slide show.
- Preload slides when running a slide show.

WHAT ARE SCRIPT FILES?

AutoCAD has provided a facility called script files that allows you to combine different AutoCAD commands and execute them in a predetermined sequence. The commands can be written as a text file using the EDIT function of DOS, AutoCAD's EDIT command (if the ACAD.PGP file is present and EDIT is defined in the file), or any other text editor. These files, generally known as script files, have extension .SCR (example: PLOT1.SCR). A script file can be executed with AutoCAD's SCRIPT command.

Script files can be used to generate a slide show, do the initial drawing setup, or plot a drawing to a predefined specification. They can also be used to automate some command sequences that are used frequently in generating, editing, or viewing a drawing.

Example 1

Write a script file that will perform the following initial setup for a drawing (file name SCRIPT1.SCR):

Ortho	On	Zoom	All
Grid	2.0	Text height	0.125
Grid	Off	Ltscale	4.0
Snap	0.5	Dimscale	4.0
Limits	0,0		
	48.0,36.0		

Before writing a script file you need to know the AutoCAD commands and the entries required in response to the command prompts. To find out the sequence of the prompt entries, you can type the command at the keyboard and then respond to different prompts. The following is a list of AutoCAD commands and prompt entries for Example 1:

Command: **ORTHO**
ON/OFF<Off>: **ON**

Command: **GRID**
Grid spacing(X) or ON/OFF/Snap/Aspect<1.0>: **2.0**

Command: **GRID**
Grid spacing(X) or ON/OFF/Snap/Aspect<1.0>: **OFF**

Command: **SNAP**
Snap spacing or ON/OFF/Aspect/Rotate/Style<1.0>: **0.5**

Command: **LIMITS**
ON/OFF/<Lower left corner> <0.00,0.00>:**0,0**
Upper right corner<12.0,9.0>: **48.0,36.0**

Command:**ZOOM**
All/Center/Dynamic/Extents/Left/Previous/Vmax/Window/<Scale(X/XP)>: **A**

Command: **SETVAR**
Variable name or ?: **TEXTSIZE**
New value for textsize<0.02>: **0.125**

Command: **LTSCALE**
New scale factor<1.0000>: **4.0**

Command: **SETVAR**
Variable name or ?: **DIMSCALE**
New value for dimscale<1.0000>: **4.0**

Once you know the AutoCAD commands and the required prompt entries, you can write the script file using AutoCAD's EDIT command or any text editor. The following file is a listing of the script file for Example 1:

```
ORTHO
ON
GRID
2.0
GRID
OFF
SNAP
0.5
LIMITS
0,0
48.0,36.0
ZOOM
ALL
SETVAR
TEXTSIZE
0.125
LTSCALE
4.0
SETVAR
DIMSCALE 4.0
```

Notice that the commands and the prompt entries in this file are in the same sequence as mentioned before. You can also combine several statements in one line, as shown in the following list.

```
ORTHO ON
GRID 2.0 GRID OFF
SNAP 0.5 SNAP ON
LIMITS 0,0 48.0,36.0 ZOOM ALL
SETVAR TEXTSIZE 0.125
LTSCALE 4.0
SETVAR DIMSCALE 4.0
```

Note

In the script file a space is used to terminate a command or a prompt entry. Therefore, spaces are very important in these files. Make sure there are no extra spaces, unless they are required to enter RETURN more than once.

After you change the limits, it is good practice to use the ZOOM command with the ALL option to display the new limits on the screen.

AutoCAD ignores and does not process any lines that begin with a semicolon (;). This allows you to put comments in the file.

SCRIPT COMMAND

AutoCAD's SCRIPT command allows you to run a script file while you are in the Drawing Editor. To execute the script file, type the SCRIPT command and press ENTER key. AutoCAD will prompt you to enter the name of the script file. You can accept the default file name, or enter a new file name. The default script file name is the same as the drawing name. If you want to enter a new file name, type the name of the script file without the file extension (.SCR). (The file extension is assumed and need not be included with the file name.)

To run the script file of Example 1, type the SCRIPT command and press ENTER. In response to file name, enter SCRIPT1 and then press the ENTER key again. You will see the changes taking place on the screen as the script file commands are executed. The format of the SCRIPT command is:

Command: **SCRIPT**
Script file <default> : *Script file name.*

For example:
Command: **SCRIPT**
Script file <CUSTOM>: SCRIPT1

Name of the script file
Default drawing file name

Example 2

Write a script file that will set up the following layers with the given colors and linetypes (file name SCRIPT2.SCR).

Layer Names	Color	Line Type
Object	Red	Continuous
Center	Yellow	Center
Hidden	Blue	Hidden
Dimension	Green	Continuous
Border	Magenta	Continuous
Hatch	Cyan	Continuous

As we mentioned earlier, you need to know the AutoCAD commands and the required prompt entries before writing a script file. For Example 2, you need the following commands to create the layers with the given colors and linetypes:

Command: **Layer**
?/Make/Set/New/ON/OFF/Color/Ltype/Freeze/Thaw: **N**
New layer name(s):**OBJECT,CENTER,HIDDEN,DIM,BORDER,HATCH**

?/Make/Set/New/ON/OFF/Color/Ltype/Freeze/Thaw: **L**
Linetype (or ?)<CONTINUOUS>: **CENTER**
Layer name(s) for linetype CENTER<0>: **CENTER**

?/Make/Set/New/ON/OFF/Color/Ltype/Freeze/Thaw: **L**
Linetype (or ?)<CONTINUOUS>: **HIDDEN**
Layer name(s) for linetype HIDDEN<0>: **HIDDEN**

?/Make/Set/New/ON/OFF/Color/Ltype/Freeze/Thaw: **C**
Color: **RED**
Layer name(s) for color 1 (red)<0>: **OBJECT**

?/Make/Set/New/ON/OFF/Color/Ltype/Freeze/Thaw: **C**
Color: **YELLOW**
Layer name(s) for color 2 (yellow)<0>: **CENTER**

?/Make/Set/New/ON/OFF/Color/Ltype/Freeze/Thaw: **C**
Color: **BLUE**
Layer name(s) for color 5 (blue)<0>: **HIDDEN**

?/Make/Set/New/ON/OFF/Color/Ltype/Freeze/Thaw: **C**
Color: **GREEN**
Layer name(s) for color 3 (green)<0>: **DIM**

?/Make/Set/New/ON/OFF/Color/Ltype/Freeze/Thaw: **C**
Color: **MAGENTA**
Layer name(s) for color 6 (magenta)<0>: **BORDER**

?/Make/Set/New/ON/OFF/Color/Ltype/Freeze/Thaw: **C**
Color: **CYAN**
Layer name(s) for color 4 (cyan)<0>: **HATCH**

?/Make/Set/New/ON/OFF/Color/Ltype/Freeze/Thaw: **(RETURN)**

The following file is a listing of the script file that creates different layers and assigns the given colors and linetypes to these layers:

```
;This script file will create new layers and
;assign different colors and linetypes to layers
LAYER
NEW
OBJECT,CENTER,HIDDEN,DIM,BORDER,HATCH
L
CENTER
CENTER
L
HIDDEN
HIDDEN
C
RED
OBJECT
C
YELLOW
CENTER
C
BLUE
HIDDEN
C
GREEN
DIM
C
MAGENTA
BORDER
C
CYAN
HATCH
```

(This is a blank line to terminate the LAYER command.)

Example 3

Write a script file that will rotate the circle and the line, as shown in Figure 27-1, around the lower endpoint of the line through 45-degree increments. The script file should be able to produce a continuous rotation of the given objects with a delay of two seconds after every 45-degree rotation (file name SCRIPT3.SCR).

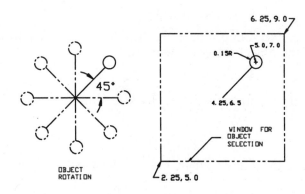

Figure 27-1 Line and circle rotated through 45-degree increments

Before writing the script file, enter the required commands and the prompt entries at the keyboard. Write down the exact sequence of the entries in which they have been entered to perform the given operations. The following is a listing of the AutoCAD command sequence needed to rotate the circle and the line around the lower endpoint of the line:

Command: **Rotate**	*(Enter Rotate command.)*
Select objects:**W**	*(Window option to select objects.)*
First corner: **2.25,5.0**	
Other corner: **6.25,9.0**	
Select objects: **<RETURN>**	
Base point: **4.25,6.5**	
<Rotation angle>/Reference: **45**	

Once the AutoCAD commands, command options, and their sequences are known, you can write a script file. As we mentioned earlier, you can use the EDIT function of DOS, or any other text editor, to write a script file. If you are in the Drawing Editor and you want to use the EDIT function to write a text file, type SHELL or SH and press the Enter key to access OS commands.

Command: **SHELL**
OS Command: **EDIT ROTATE.SCR**

The following file is a listing of the script file that will create the required rotation of the circle and the line of Example 3.

```
ROTATE
W
2.25,5.0
6.25,9.0
                              (Blank line for RETURN.)
4.25,6.5
45
```

Line 1
ROTATE
In this line ROTATE is an AutoCAD command that rotates the objects.

Line 2
W
In this line W is the Window option for selecting the objects that need to be edited.

Line 3
2.25,5.0
In this line 2.25 defines the X coordinate and 5.0 defines the Y coordinate of the lower left corner of the object selection window.

Line 4
6.25,9.0
In this line 6.25 defines the X coordinate and 9.0 defines the Y coordinate of the upper right corner of the object selection window.

Line 5
Line 5 is a blank line that terminates the object selection process.

Line 6
4.25,6.5
In this line 4.25 defines the X coordinate and 6.5 defines the Y coordinate of the base point for rotation.

Line 7
45
In this line 45 is the incremental angle for rotation.

> **Note**
>
> *One of the limitations of the script files is that all the information has to be contained within the file. These files do not let you enter information. For instance, in Example 3, if you want to use the Window option to select the objects, the Window option (W) and the two points that define this window must be contained within the script file. The same is true for the base point and all other information that goes in a script file. There is no way that a script file can prompt you to enter a particular piece of information and then resume the script file, unless you embed AutoLISP commands to prompt for user input.*

RSCRIPT COMMAND

AutoCAD's RSCRIPT command allows the user to execute the script file indefinitely until cancelled. It is a very desirable feature when the user wants to run the same file continuously. For example, in the case of a slide show for a product demonstration, the RSCRIPT command can be used to run the script file again and again until it is terminated by pressing CTRL+C from the keyboard. Similarly, in Example 3, the rotation command needs to be repeated indefinitely to create a continuous rotation of the objects. This can be accomplished by adding RSCRIPT at the end of the file as shown in the following file:

```
ROTATE
W
2.25,5.0
6.25,9.0
                                        (Blank line for RETURN.)
4.25,6.5
45
RSCRIPT
```

The RSCRIPT command on line 8 will repeat the commands from line 1 to line 7, and thus set the script file in an indefinite loop. The script file can be stopped by pressing CTRL+C or the BACKSPACE key on the keyboard.

> **Note**
>
> *You cannot provide conditional statements in a script file to terminate the file when a particular condition is satisfied, unless you use the AutoLISP functions in the script file.*

DELAY COMMAND

In the script files some of the operations happen very quickly and make it difficult for you to see the operations taking place on the screen. It might be necessary to intentionally introduce a pause between certain operations in a script file. For example, in a slide show for a product demonstration, there must be a time delay between different slides so that the audience has enough time to see them. This is accomplished by using AutoCAD's DELAY command, which introduces a delay before the next command is executed. The general format of the DELAY command is:

```
Command:DELAY Time
              │          └─ Time in milliseconds
              └─ DELAY command
     └─ AutoCAD's command prompt
```

The DELAY command is to be followed by the delay time in milliseconds. For example, a delay of 2,000 milliseconds means that AutoCAD will pause for approximately two seconds before executing the next command. It is approximately two seconds because computer processing speeds vary. The maximum time delay you can enter is 32,767 milliseconds (about 33 seconds). In Example 3, a two-second delay can be introduced by inserting a DELAY command line between line 7 and line 8 as shown in the following file listing:

ROTATE
W
2.25,5.0
6.25,9.0

(Blank line for RETURN.)

4.25,6.5
45
DELAY 2000
RSCRIPT

The first seven lines of this file rotate the objects through a 45-degree angle. Before the RSCRIPT command on line 8 is executed, there is a delay of 2,000 milliseconds (about two seconds). The RSCRIPT command will repeat the script file that rotates the objects through another 45-degree angle. Thus, a slide show is created with a time delay of two seconds after every 45-degree increment.

RESUME COMMAND

If you cancel the script file then you want to continue it, you can do so by using AutoCAD's RESUME command.

Command: **RESUME**

The RESUME command can also be used if the script file has encountered an error causing it to be suspended. The RESUME command will skip the command that caused the error and continue with the rest of the script file. If the error occurred when the command was in progress, use a leading apostrophe with the RESUME command ('RESUME) to invoke the RESUME command in transparent mode.

Command: **'RESUME**

INVOKING A SCRIPT FILE WHEN LOADING AUTOCAD

The script files can also be run when loading AutoCAD, without getting into the Drawing Editor. The format of the command for running a script file when loading AutoCAD is:

Drive > **ACAD (Default drawing):** *Script file name.*

Example

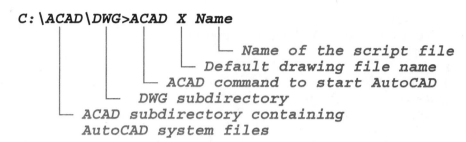

```
C:\ACAD\DWG>ACAD X Name
```
- Name of the script file
- Default drawing file name
- ACAD command to start AutoCAD
- DWG subdirectory
- ACAD subdirectory containing AutoCAD system files

Here it is assumed that the AutoCAD system files are loaded in the ACAD subdirectory and you are in the DWG subdirectory. If the path has not been set before, you can use the following command format to invoke a script file.

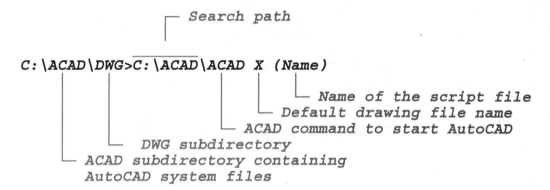

Search path

```
C:\ACAD\DWG>C:\ACAD\ACAD X (Name)
```
- Name of the script file
- Default drawing file name
- ACAD command to start AutoCAD
- DWG subdirectory
- ACAD subdirectory containing AutoCAD system files

Note

You could also invoke a script file when you start AutoCAD with a batch file. For example, if the name of the batch file that starts AutoCAD is STARTCAD, you could replace ACAD with STARTCAD.

Drive > STARTCAD X Name

You should avoid abbreviations to prevent any confusion. For example, a C can be used as a close option when you are drawing lines. It can also be used as a command alias for drawing a circle. If you use both of these in a script file, it might be confusing.

Example 4

Write a script file that will plot a 36 by 24 drawing on 9" by 6" paper, using the HPGL plotter. Use the Window option to select the drawing to be plotted. (Assume that AutoCAD is configured for the HPGL plotter and the plotter description is HPGL-Plotter. The name of the script file for this example is SCRIPT5.SCR.)

Before writing a script file to plot a drawing, find out the plotter specifications that must be entered in the script file to obtain the desired output. To determine the prompt entries and their sequence to set up the plotter specifications, enter AutoCAD's PLOT command at the keyboard. **Make sure the system variable CMDDIA is set to zero**, otherwise AutoCAD will display the Plot dialogue box. Note the entries you make and their sequence. The following is a listing of the plotter specification with the new entries:

Command: **PLOT**
What to plot -- Display, Extents, Limits, View, or Window<D>: **W**

First corner: **0,0**
Other corner: **36,24**
Plotter port time-out = 30 seconds
Plot device is Hewlett-Packard (HP-GL) ADI 4.2 by Autodesk
Description: HPGL-Plotter
Plot optimization level = 4
Plot will be written to a selected file
Sizes are in Inches and the style is landscape
Plot origin is at (0.00,0.00)

Plotting area is 10.22 wide by 7.53 high (MAX size)
Plot is NOT rotated
Area fill will NOT be adjusted for pen width
Hidden lines will NOT be removed
Plot will be scaled to fit available area

Do you want to change anything? (No/Yes/File/Save): <N>: **Y**
Do you want to change plotter? <N>: **N**
How many seconds should we wait for the plotter port to time-out
 (0 means wait forever), 0 to 500 <30>: **20**

Pen widths are in inches.

Object Color	Pen No.	Line-type	Pen Speed	Object Color	Pen No.	Line-type	Pen Speed
1 (red)	1	0	36	9	1	0	36
2 (yellow)	1	0	36	10	1	0	36
3 (green)	1	0	36	11	1	0	36
4 (cyan)	1	0	36	12	1	0	36
5 (blue)	1	0	36	13	1	0	36
6 (magenta)	1	0	36	14	1	0	36
7 (white)	1	0	36	15	1	0	36
8	1	0	36				

Linetype: 0 = continuous line
  1 = ...
  2 = ----   ----   ----   ----
  3 = -----   -----   -----
  4 = ------. ------. ------. ------.
  5 = ---- - ------ - ------
  6 = --- - - --- - - ---

Do you want to change any of the above parameters? <N>: **N**
Write the plot to a file? <Y>: **N**
Size units (Inches or Millimeters) <I>: **I**
Plot origin in Inches <0.00,0.00>: **0,0**

Standard values for plotting size:

Size	Width	Height
MAX	10.22	7.53

Enter the Size or Width, Height (in Inches) <MAX>: **9,6**
Rotate plot 0/90/180/270 <0>: **0**
Adjust area fill boundaries for pen width? <N>: **N**
Remove hidden lines? <N>: **N**

Specify scale by entering:
Plotted Inches=Drawing units or Fit or ? <F>: **1=4**

Effective plotting area: 6.00 wide by 4.50 high
Position paper in plotter
Press RETURN to continue or S to Stop for hardware setup

Now, you can write the script file by entering the responses to these prompts in the file. The following file is a listing of the script file that will plot a 36 by 24 drawing on 9" by 6" paper after making the necessary changes in the plot specifications. The comments on the right side are not a part of the file.

```
PLOT
W                    (Window option.)
0,0 36,24            (First corner, other corner.)
Y                    (Do you want to change anything?)
N                    (Do you want to change plotter?)
20                   (How many seconds should we wait?)
N
N
I
0,0
9,6
0                    (Rotation angle.)
N
N
1=4
                     (Blank line for RETURN.)
```

FREEPLOTTING

You can also use a script file to plot a drawing from outside the Drawing Editor, **from the system prompt**. This is called **freeplotting** because you do not have to load the drawing to plot. The format of the command is:

```
C:\ACAD\DWG>ACAD -P Script-file-name
                  |          |    |___ Name of the script file
                  |          |_____ System prompt to freeplot
                  |_____ ACAD to load AutoCAD
```

When you write a script file to freeplot, you must specify the name of the drawing file in the script file. **The drawings created with the older versions of AutoCAD and not updated to Release 13 may not be plotted with freeplotting**. The following is a listing of the script files for Example 4, modified to allow freeplotting:

```
PLOT
PROTO                (Name of the drawing.)
W
0,0 36,24
Y
N
20
N
N
I 0,0 9,6 0 N N 1=4
```

> **Note**
>
> *You can use a blank line to accept the default value for a prompt. A blank line in the script file will cause a RETURN. However, you must not accept the default plot specifications, because the file might have been altered by another user or by another script file. Therefore, always enter the actual values in the file so that when you run a script file, it does not take the default values.*

You can also reconfigure AutoCAD from the system prompt. The format of the command is:

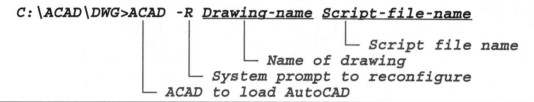

WHAT IS A SLIDE SHOW?

AutoCAD provides a facility using script files to combine the slides in a text file and display them on the screen in a predetermined sequence. In this way, you can generate a slide show for a slide presentation. You can also introduce a time delay in the display so that the viewer has enough time to view a slide.

A drawing or parts of a drawing can also be displayed by using AutoCAD's display commands. For example, you can use ZOOM, PAN, or other commands to display the details that you want to show. If the drawing is very complicated, it takes quite some time to display the desired information and it may not be possible to get the desired views in the right sequence. However, with slide shows you can arrange the slides in any order and present them in a definite sequence. In addition to saving time, this will also help to minimize the distraction that might be caused by constantly changing the drawing display. Also, some drawings are confidential in nature and you may not want to display some portions or views of them. By making slides you can restrict the information that is presented through them. You can send a slide show to a client without losing control of the drawings and the information that is contained in them.

WHAT ARE SLIDES?

A slide is the snapshot of a screen display; it is like taking a picture of a display with a camera. The slides do not contain any vector information, which means that the entities do not have any information associated with them. For example, the slides do not retain any information about the layers, colors, linetypes, start point, and endpoint of a line or viewpoint. Therefore, slides cannot be edited like drawings. If you want to make any changes in the slide, you need to edit the drawing and then make a new slide from the edited drawing.

MSLIDE COMMAND

The slides are created by using AutoCAD's MSLIDE command. The command will prompt you to enter the slide file name.

Command: MSLIDE
Slide file <Default>: *Name.*

Example
Command: **MSLIDE**
Slide File: <NEWDWG> SLIDE1

                   └─*Slide filename*
        └─*Default slide filename*

The slide filename can be a maximum of eight characters long, not counting the extension. In the above example, AutoCAD will save the slide file as SLIDE1.SLD.

Note

In Model space, you can use the MSLIDE command to make a slide of the existing display in the current viewport.

If you are in Paper space, you can make a slide of the display in the Paper space that includes any viewports.

When the viewports are not active, the MSLIDE command will make a slide of the current screen display.

VSLIDE COMMAND

To view a slide, use the VSLIDE command. AutoCAD will then prompt you to enter the slide file name. Enter the name of the slide you want to view and press the ENTER key. Do not enter the extension after the slide file name. AutoCAD automatically assumes the extension .SLD.

Command: **VSLIDE**
Slide file < Default > : *Name.*

Example
Command: **VSLIDE**
Slide file <NEWDWG>: SLIDE1

                   └─ *Name of slide file*
        └─ *Default slide filename*

If the slide is in the slide library, and you want to view that slide, you have to specify the slide library name with the slide filename. The format of the library and slide filename is:

Command: VSLIDE
Slide file < default > : *Library file name (slide file name).*

Example
Command: **VSLIDE**
Slide file <NEWDWG>: SLDLIB(SLIDE1)

                       └─ *Name of slide file*
            └─ *Name of slide library*
        └─ *Default slide filename*

Note

After viewing a slide, you can use AutoCAD's REDRAW command to remove the slide display and return to the existing drawing on the screen.

Any command that is automatically followed by a redraw will also display the existing drawing. For example, AutoCAD's GRID, ZOOM ALL, and REGEN commands will automatically return to the existing drawing on the screen.

You can view the slides on high-resolution or low-resolution monitors. Depending on the resolution of the monitor, AutoCAD automatically adjusts the image. However, if you are using a high-resolution monitor, it is better to make the slides on the same monitor to take full advantage of that monitor.

Example 5

Write a script file that will generate a slide show of the following slide files with a time delay of 15 seconds after every slide.

SLIDE1, SLIDE2, SLIDE3, SLIDE4

The first step in a slide show is to create the slides. Figure 27-2 shows the drawings that have been saved as slide files SLIDE1, SLIDE2, SLIDE3, and SLIDE4. The second step is to find out the sequence in which you want these slides to be displayed on the screen with the necessary time delay, if any, between the slides. Then you can use any text editor or AutoCAD's EDIT command (provided the ACAD.PGP file is present and EDIT is defined in the file) to write the script file with the extension .SCR.

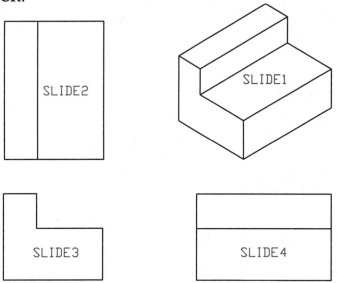

Figure 27-2 Slides for slide show

The following file is a listing of the script file that will create a slide show of the slides in Figure 27-2. The name of the script file is SLDSHOW1.

```
VSLIDE SLIDE1
DELAY 15000
VSLIDE SLIDE2
DELAY 15000
VSLIDE SLIDE3
```

```
DELAY 15000
VSLIDE SLIDE4
DELAY 15000
```

To run this slide show, type SCRIPT in response to AutoCAD's Command: prompt. Now, type the name of the script file (SLDSHOW1) and press the ENTER key. The slides will be displayed on the screen with an approximate time delay of 15 seconds between them.

PRELOADING SLIDES

In the script file of Example 5, VSLIDE SLIDE1 in line 1 loads the slide file, SLIDE1, and displays it on the screen. After 15,000 milliseconds' pause, it starts loading the second slide file, SLIDE2. Depending on the computer and the disk access time, you will notice that it takes some time to load the second slide file; the same is true for the other slides. To avoid the delay in loading the slide files, AutoCAD has provided a facility to preload a slide while viewing the previous slide. This is accomplished by placing an asterisk (*) in front of the slide file name.

VSLIDE SLIDE1	*(View slide, SLIDE1.)*
VSLIDE *SLIDE2	*(Preload slide, SLIDE2.)*
DELAY 15000	*(Delay of 15 seconds.)*
VSLIDE	*(Display slide, SLIDE2.)*
VSLIDE *SLIDE3	*(Preload slide, SLIDE3.)*
DELAY 15000	*(Delay of 15 seconds.)*
VSLIDE	*(Display slide, SLIDE3.)*
VSLIDE *SLIDE4	
DELAY 15000	
VSLIDE	
DELAY 15000	
RSCRIPT	*(Restart the script file.)*

Example 6

Write a script file to generate a continuous slide show of the following slide files with a time delay of two seconds between the slides.

SLD1, SLD2, SLD3

The slide files are located in different subdirectories as shown in Figure 27-3. The subdirectory SUBDIR1 is the current subdirectory.

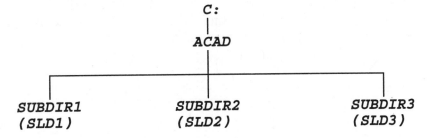

Figure 27-3 Subdirectories of the C drive

Where:	
C:	*(Root directory.)*
ACAD	*(Subdirectory where the AutoCAD files are loaded.)*
SUBDIR1	*(Drawing subdirectory.)*

SUBDIR2	*(Drawing subdirectory.)*
SUBDIR3	*(Drawing subdirectory.)*
SLD1	*(Slide file in SUBDIR1 subdirectory.)*
SLD2	*(Slide file in SUBDIR2 subdirectory.)*
SLD3	*(Slide file in SUBDIR3 subdirectory.)*

The following file is the listing of the script files that will generate a slide show for the slides in Example 6.

```
VSLIDE SLD1
DELAY 2000
VSLIDE C:\ACAD\SUBDIR2\SLD2
DELAY 2000
VSLIDE C:\ACAD\SUBDIR3\SLD3
DELAY 2000
RSCRIPT
```

Line 1
VSLIDE SLD1
In this line the AutoCAD command VSLIDE loads the slide file SLD1. Since in this example we are assuming that you are in the subdirectory SUBDIR1 and the first slide file, SLD1, is located in the same subdirectory, it does not require any path definition.

Line 2
DELAY 2000
This line uses AutoCAD's DELAY command to create a pause of approximately two seconds before the next slide is loaded.

Line 3
VSLIDE C:\ACAD\SUBDIR2\SLD2
In this line the AutoCAD command VSLIDE loads the slide file SLD2 that is located in the subdirectory SUBDIR2. If the slide file is located in a different subdirectory, you need to define the path with the slide file.

Line 5
VSLIDE C:\ACAD\SUBDIR3\SLD3
In this line the VSLIDE command loads the slide file, SLD3, that is located in the subdirectory SLD3.

Line 7
RSCRIPT
In this line the RSCRIPT command executes the script file again and displays the slides on the screen. This process continues indefinitely until the script file is cancelled by pressing CTRL+C or the BACKSPACE key from the keyboard.

REVIEW QUESTIONS

Fill in the blanks.

SCRIPT FILES

1.   AutoCAD has provided a facility of _____ which allows you to combine different AutoCAD commands and execute them in a predetermined sequence.

2. The _____ files can be used to generate a slide show, do the initial drawing setup, or plot a drawing to a predefined specification.

3. Before writing a script file you need to know the AutoCAD _____ and the _____ required in response to the command prompts.

4. In a script file you can _____ several statements in one line.

5. In a script file the _____ are used to terminate a command or a prompt entry.

6. AutoCAD's _____ command is used to run a script file.

7. When you run a script file, the default script file name is the same as the _____ name.

8. When you run a script file, type the name of the script file without the file _____ .

9. One of the limitations of the script files is that all the information has to be contained _____ the file.

10. AutoCAD's _____ command allows you to execute the script file indefinitely until the command is cancelled.

11. You cannot provide a _____ statement in a script file to terminate the file when a particular condition is satisfied.

12. AutoCAD's _____ command introduces a delay before the next command is executed.

13. The DELAY command is to be followed by _____ in milliseconds.

14. If the script file was cancelled and you want to continue the script file, you can do so by using AutoCAD's _____ command.

SLIDE SHOWS

15. AutoCAD provides a facility through _____ files to combine the slides in a text file and display them on the screen in a predetermined sequence.

16. A _____ can also be introduced in the script file so that the viewer has enough time to view a slide.

17. Slides are the _____ of a screen display.

18. Slides do not contain any _____ information, which means that the entities do not have any information associated with them.

19. Slides _____ be edited like a drawing.

20. Slides can be created using the AutoCAD's _____ command.

21. Slide file names can be up to _____ characters long.

22. In Model space, you can use the MSLIDE command to make a slide of the _____ display in the _____ viewport.

23. If you are in Paper space, you can make a slide of the display in the Paper space that _____ any viewports.

24. To view a slide, use AutoCAD's _____ command.

25. If the slide is in the slide library, and you want to view it, the slide library name has to be _____ with the slide file name.

26. AutoCAD provides a utility that constructs a library of the slide files. This is done with the AutoCAD's utility program called _____.

27. You cannot _____ a slide library file. If you want to change anything, you have to create a new list of the slide files and then use the _____ utility to create a new slide library.

28. The path name _____ be saved in the slide library. Therefore, if you have more than one slide with the same name, although with different subdirectories, only one slide will be saved in the slide library.

29. If you want to make any changes in the slide, you need to _____ the drawing, then make a new slide from the edited drawing.

EXERCISES

SCRIPT FILES

Exercice 1

Write a script file that will do the following initial setup for a drawing:

Grid	2.0
Snap	0.5
Limits	0,0
	18.0,12.0
Zoom	All
Text height	0.25
Ltscale	2.0
Dimscale	2.0
Dimtix	On
Dimtoh	Off
Dimtih	Off
Dimtad	On
Dimcen	0.75

Exercise 2

Write a script file that will do the following initial setup for a new drawing:

Limits	0,0 24,18
Grid	1.0
Snap	0.25
Ortho	On
Snap	On
Zoom	All
Pline width	0.02
PLine	0,0 24,0 24,18 0,18 0,0
Units:	Decimal units

Number of decimal digits (2)
Decimal degrees
Number of decimal digits (2)
Direction of 0 angle (3 o'clock)
Angle measured counter-clockwise

Ltscale   1.5

Layers		
Name	Color	Linetype
Obj	Red	Continuous
Cen	Yellow	Center
Hid	Blue	Hidden
Dim	Green	Continuous

Exercise 3

Write a script file that will PLOT a given drawing according to the following specifications. (Use the plotter for which your system is configured.)

Prplot, using the Window option
Window size (0,0 24,18)
Do not write the plot to file
Size in Inch units
Plot origin (0.0,0.0)
Maximum plot size (8.0,10.5)
90 Deg. plot rotation
No removal of hidden lines
Plotting scale (Fit)

SLIDE SHOWS

Exercise 4

Make the slides shown in Figure 27-4, and write a script file for a continuous slide show. Provide a time delay of 10 seconds after every slide. (You do not have to use the slides shown in Figure 27-4; you can select any slides of your choice.)

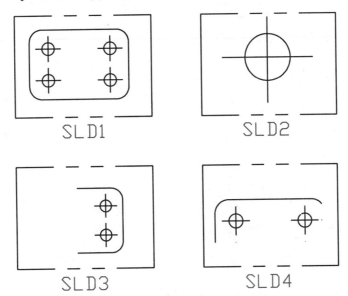

Figure 27-4 Slides for slide show

Chapter 28

Creating Linetypes
and Hatch Patterns

Learning objectives

After completing this chapter, you will be able to:

Create Linetypes:
♦ Write linetype definitions.
♦ Create different linetypes.
♦ Create linetype files.
♦ Determine LTSCALE for plotting the drawing to given specifications.
♦ Define alternate linetypes and modify existing linetypes.
♦ Understand hatch pattern definition.

Create Hatch Patterns:
♦ Create new hatch patterns.
♦ Determine the effect of angle and scale factor on hatch.
♦ Create hatch patterns with multiple descriptors.
♦ Save hatch patterns in a separate file.
♦ Add hatch pattern slides to the AutoCAD slide library.

STANDARD LINETYPES

The AutoCAD software package comes with a library of standard linetypes that has 38 different linetypes, including ISO linetypes. These linetypes are saved in the ACAD.LIN file. You can modify existing linetypes or create new ones.

LINETYPE DEFINITION

All linetype definitions consist of two parts:

1. Header Line
2. Pattern Line

Header Line

The header line consists of an asterisk (*) followed by the name of the linetype and the linetype description. The name and the linetype description should be separated by a comma. If there is no description, the comma that separates the linetype name and the description is not required.

The format of the header line is:

* Linetype Name, Description

Example

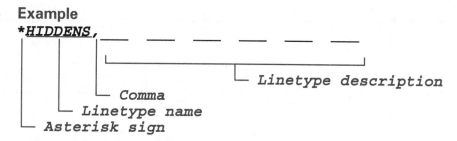

All linetype definitions require a linetype name. When you want to load a linetype or assign a linetype to an object, AutoCAD recognizes the linetype by the name you have assigned to the linetype definition. The names of the linetype definition should be selected to help the user recognize the linetype by its name. For example, a linetype name LINEFCX does not give the user any idea about the type of the line. However, a linetype name like DASHDOT gives a better idea about the type of line that a user can expect.

The linetype description is a graphical representation of the line. This graphic can be generated by using dashes, dots, and spaces on the keyboard. The graphic is used by AutoCAD when you want to display the linetypes on the screen by using AutoCAD's LINETYPE command with the ? option, or by using the dialogue box. The linetype description cannot exceed 47 characters.

Pattern Line

The pattern line contains the definition of the line pattern. The definition of the line pattern consists of the alignment field specification and the linetype specification. The alignment field specification and the linetype specification are separated by a comma.

The format of the pattern line is:

Alignment Field Specification, Linetype Specification

Example

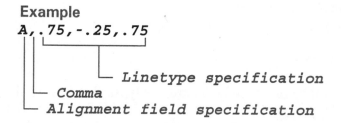

The letter used for alignment field specification is A. This is the only alignment field supported by AutoCAD; therefore, the pattern line will always start with the letter A. The linetype specification defines the configuration of the dash-dot pattern to generate a line. The maximum number of dash length specification in the linetype is 12, provided the linetype pattern definition fits on one 80-character line.

ELEMENTS OF LINETYPE SPECIFICATION

All linetypes are created by combining the basic elements in a desired configuration. There are three basic elements that can be used to define a linetype specification.

| DASH | (Pen down) |
| DOT | (Pen down, 0 length) |

SPACE   (Pen up)

Example

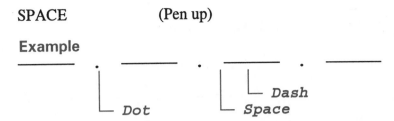

The dashes are generated by defining a positive number. For example, .5 will generate a dash 0.5 units long. Similarly, spaces are generated by defining a negative number. For example, -.2 will generate a space 0.2 units long. The dot is generated by defining a 0 length.

Example

```
A,.5,-.2,0,-.2,.5
```
                    Length of dash (pen down)
                    Length of space (pen up)
                    Dot (Zero length)

CREATING LINETYPES

Before creating a linetype you need to decide the type of line that you want to generate. Draw the line on a piece of paper and measure the length of each element that constitutes the line. You need to define only one segment of the line, because the pattern is repeated when you draw a line. Linetypes can be created or modified by one of the following methods:

1. **Using AutoCAD's LINETYPE command**
2. **Using a Text Editor** (such as EDLIN or EDIT)

Consider the following example, which creates a new linetype—first using AutoCAD's LINETYPE command and then using a Text Editor.

Example 1

Using the AutoCAD's LINETYPE command, create linetype DASH3DOT (Figure 28-1) with the following specifications:

    Length of the first dash 0.5
    Blank space 0.125
    Dot
    Blank space 0.125
    Dot
    Blank space 0.125
    Dot
    Blank space 0.125

Using AutoCAD's Linetype Command

To create a linetype using AutoCAD's LINETYPE command, first make sure that you are in the Drawing Editor. Then enter the LINETYPE command and select the Create option to create a linetype.

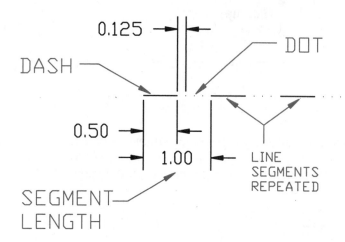

Figure 28-1 Linetype specifications of DASH3DOT

Command: **Linetype**
?/Create/Load/Set: **C**

Enter the name of the linetype and the name of the library file in which you want to store the definition of the new linetype.

Name of linetype to create: **DASH3DOT**
File for storage of linetype < default > : **Acad**

If the linetype already exists, the following message will be displayed on the screen.

(Name) already exists in this file.
Current definition is:
*Linetype name [,description]
alignment, dash-1, dash-2,__.
Overwrite? <N>

If you want to redefine the existing line style enter Y, otherwise type N or press the RETURN key to pick the default value of N. You can then repeat the process with a different name of the linetype.

After entering the name of the linetype and the library file name, AutoCAD will prompt you to enter the descriptive text and the pattern of the line.

Descriptive text: ***DASH3DOT,____ . . . ____ . . . ____**
Enter pattern (on next line):
A,.5,-.125,0,-.125,0,-.125,0,-.125

Descriptive Text
*DASH3DOT,____ . . . ____ . . . ____

For the descriptive text you have to type an asterisk (*) followed by the name of the linetype. For Example 1, the name of the linetype is DASH3DOT. The name *DASH3DOT can be followed by the description of the linetype; the length of this description cannot exceed 47 characters. In this example, the description is dashes and dots ____ . . . ____. It could be any text or alphanumeric string. The description is displayed on the screen when you list the linetypes.

Pattern
A,.5,-.125,0,-.125,0,-.125,0,-.125

The line pattern should start with alignment definition. Currently AutoCAD supports only one type of alignment--A. Therefore, it is automatically displayed on the screen when you select the LINETYPE command with CREATE option. After entering A for pattern alignment, you must define the pen position. A positive number (.5 or 0.5) indicates a "pen-down" position and a negative number (-.25 or -0.25) indicates a "pen-up" position. The length of the dash or the space is designated by the magnitude of the number. For example, 0.5 will draw a dash 0.5 units long and -0.25 will leave a blank space of 0.25 units. A dash length of 0 will draw a dot (.). The following list is the pattern definition elements for Example 1.

.5	**pen down**	**0.5 units long dash**
-.125	**pen up**	**.125 units blank space**
0	**pen down**	**dot**
-.125	**pen up**	**.125 units blank space**
0	**pen down**	**dot**
-.125	**pen up**	**.125 units blank space**
0	**pen down**	**dot**
-.125	**pen up**	**.125 units blank space**

After entering pattern definition, the linetype (DASH3DOT) is automatically saved in the ACAD.LIN file. The linetype (DASH3DOT) can be loaded using AutoCAD's **LINETYPE** command and selecting the **LOAD** option.

> **Note**
>
> *The name and the description should be separated by a comma (,). The description is optional and if you decide not to give one, you should omit the comma after the linetype name DASH3DOT.*

Using a Text Editor

You can also use the EDIT or EDLIN function of DOS or any other Text Editor to create a new linetype. If you are in the AutoCAD Drawing Editor, type SH or SHELL to access the DOS commands. To load the ACAD.LIN file, use the following DOS function (EDIT):

Command: **SHELL**
OS Command: EDIT **ACAD.LIN**

If you are in a different subdirectory, you can load the ACAD.LIN file by defining the path with the file name shown in the following command line:

OS Command: **EDIT C:\ACAD11\ACAD.LIN**

List the file and insert the lines that define the new linetype. The following file is a partial listing of the ACAD.LIN file after adding a new linetype to the file:

```
*BORDER,__ __ . __ __ . __ __ . __ __ . __ __ . __ .
A,.5,-.25,.5,-.25,0,-.25
*BORDER2,_ . _ . _ . _ . _ . _ . _ . _ . _ . _ .
A,.25,-.125,.25,-.125,0,-.125
*BORDERX2,____ ____ . ____ ____ . ____ ____ . 
A,1.0,-.5,1.0,-.5,0,-.5

*CENTER,____ _ ____ _ ____ _ ____ _ ____ _ ____ _
```

```
A,1.25,-.25,.25,-.25
*CENTER2,
A,.75,-.125,.125,-.125
*CENTERX2,
A,2.5,-.5,.5,-.5

*DASHDOT,
A,.5,-.25,0,-.25

*DOTX2,.
A,0,-.5
*HIDDEN,
A,.25,-.125
*HIDDEN2,
A,.125,-.0625
*HIDDENX2,
A,.5,-.25
*PHANTOM,
A,1.25,-.25,.25,-.25,.25,-.25
*PHANTOM2,
A,.625,-.125,.125,-.125,.125,-.125
*PHANTOMX2,
A,2.5,-.5,.5,-.5,.5,-.5
*DASH3DOT,
A,.5,-.125,0,-.125,0,-.125,0,-.125
```

The last two lines of this file define the new linetype, DASH3DOT. The first line contains the name DASH3DOT and the description of the line (___ . . .___). The second line contains the alignment and the pattern definition. Save the file and then load the linetype using AutoCAD's LINETYPE command with the LOAD option. The lines and polylines that this linetype will generate are shown in Figure 28-2.

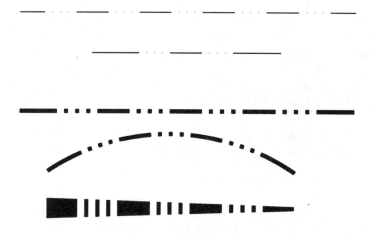

Figure 28-2 Lines created by linetype DASH3DOT

LTSCALE FACTOR FOR PLOTTING

The LTSCALE factor for plotting depends on the size of the sheet you are using to plot the drawing. For example, if the limits are 48 by 36, the drawing scale is 1:1, and you want to plot the drawing on a 48" by 36" size sheet, the LTSCALE factor is 1. If you check the specification of a hidden line in the ACAD.LIN file, the length of each dash is 0.25. Therefore, when you plot a drawing with 1:1 scale, the length of each dash in a hidden line is 0.25.

However, if the drawing scale is 1/8" = 1', and you want to plot the drawing on 48" by 36" paper, the LTSCALE factor must be 96 (8 x 12 = 96). The length of each dash in the hidden line will increase by a factor of 96, because the LTSCALE factor is 96. Therefore, the length of each dash will be 24 units (0.25 x 96 = 24). At the time of plotting, the scale factor for plotting must be 1:96 to plot the 384' by 288' drawing on a 48" by 36" size paper. Each dash of the hidden line that was 24" long on the drawing will be 0.25 (24/96 = 0.25) inch long when plotted. Similarly, if the desired text size on the paper is 1/8", the text height in the drawing must be 12" (1/8 x 96 = 12").

Ltscale Factor for PLOTTING = Drawing Scale

Sometimes your plotter may not be able to plot a 48" by 36" drawing or you might like to decrease the size of the plot so that the drawing fits within a specified area. To get the correct dash lengths for hidden, center, or other lines, you must adjust the LTSCALE factor. For example, if you want to plot the above-mentioned drawing in a 45" by 34" area, the reduction factor is:

Reduction factor   = 48/45
                          = 1.0666

New LTSCALE factor   = LTSCALE factor x Reduction factor
                          = 96 x 1.0666
                          = 102.4

New Ltscale Factor for PLOTTING = Drawing Scale x Reduction Factor

Note

If you change the LTSCALE factor, all lines in the drawing are affected by the new ratio.

Example 2

Create a new file, NEWLINET.LIN, and define a linetype, VARDASH, with the following specifications:

> Length of first dash 1.0
> Blank space 0.25
> Length of second dash 0.75
> Blank space 0.25
> Length of third dash 0.5
> Blank space 0.25
> Dot
> Blank space 0.25
> Length of next dash 0.5
> Blank space 0.25
> Length of next dash 0.75

To use the EDIT command, type EDIT at AutoCAD prompt and then enter the name of the file.

Command: **EDIT**
File name: **NEWLINET.LIN**

Now, insert the following lines that define the new linetype VARDASH.

*VARDASH,-------- ---- -- . -- ---- --------
A,1,-.25,.75,-.25,.5,-.25,0,-.25,.5,-.25,.75,-.25

The type of lines that this linetype will generate are shown in Figure 28-3.

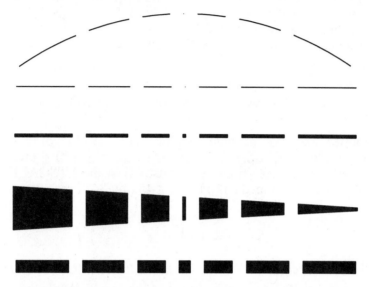

Figure 28-3 Lines generated by linetype VARDASH

COMPLEX LINETYPES

AutoCAD has provided a facility to create complex linetypes. The complex linetypes can be classified into two groups: String Complex Linetype and Shape Complex Linetype. The difference between the two is that the String Complex Linetype has a text string inserted in the line, whereas the Shape Complex Linetype has a shape inserted in the line. The facility of creating complex linetypes increases the functionality of lines. For example, if you want to draw a line around a building that indicates the fence line, you can do it by defining a Complex Linetype that will automatically give you the desired line with the text string (Fence). Similarly, you can define a Complex Linetype that will insert a shape (symbols) at predefined distances along the line.

CREATING STRING COMPLEX LINETYPES

When writing the definition of a String Complex Linetype, the actual text and its attributes must be included in the linetype definition. The format of the String Complex Linetype is:

["String", Text Style, Text Height, Rotation, X-Offset, Y-Offset]

The following are the attributes and their description that must be assigned to the text string:

String
It is the actual text that you want to insert along the line. The text string must be enclosed in quotation marks (").

Text Style
This is the name of the text style file that you want to use for generating the text string. The text style must be predefined.

Text Height
This is the actual height of the text. In Figure 28-4, the height of the text is 0.1 units.

Rotation
This is the rotation of the text string with respect to the positive X axis, if AutoCAD is configured to measure angles with the positive X axis.

X-Offset
This is the distance of the lower left corner of the text string from the endpoint of the line segment measured along the line. If the line is horizontal, then the X-Offset distance is measured along the X axis. In Figure 28-4, the X-Offset distance is 0.05.

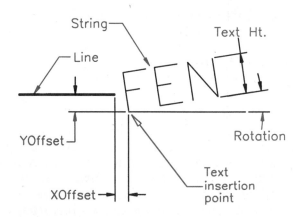

Figure 28-4 The attributes of a String Complex Linetype

Y-Offset
This is the distance of the lower left corner of the text string from the endpoint of the line segment measured perpendicular to the line. If the line is horizontal, then the Y-Offset distance is measured along the Y axis. In Figure 28-4, the Y-Offset distance is -0.05. The distance is minus because the start point of the text string is 0.05 units below the endpoint of the first line segment.

Example 3

In the following example you will write the definition of a String Complex Linetype that consists of the text string "Fence" and line segments. The length of the line segments is 0.75. The height of the text string is 0.1 units and the space between the end of the text string and the following line segment is 0.05.

Step 1
Before writing the definition of a new linetype, it is important to determine the line specification. One of the ways it can be done is to actually draw the lines and the text the way you want it to appear in the drawing. Once you have drawn the line and the text to your satisfaction, measure the distances that are needed to define the String Complex Linetype. In this example the values are given as follows:

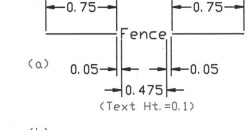

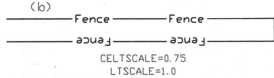

Figure 28-5 The attributes of the String Complex Linetype and line specifications for Example 3

Text string=	Fence
Text style=	Standard
Text height=	0.1
Text rotation=	0
X-Offset=	0.05
Y-Offset=	-0.05
Length of the first line segment=	0.75
Distance between the line segments=	0.575

Step 2
Use a text editor to write the definition of the String Complex Linetype. You can add the definition to AutoCAD's ACAD.LIN file or create a separate file. The extension of the file must

be .LIN. The following file is the listing of the FENCE.LIN file for Example 3. The name of the linetype is NEWFence.

```
*NEWFence,New fence boundary line
A,0.75,["Fence",Standard,S=0.1,A=0,X=0.05,Y=-0.05],-0.575
```

Step 3

To test the linetype, load the linetype using **LINETYPE** command with Load option and assign it to a layer. Draw a line or any object to check if the line is drawn to the given specifications. Notice that the text is drawn upside down when you draw a line from right to left. When you draw a polyline, circle, or spline, the text string does not align with the object.

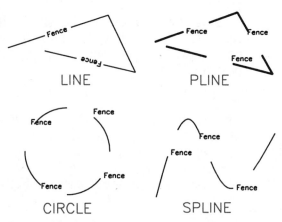

Figure 28-6 Using String Complex Linetype

Step 4

In the NEWFence linetype definition the specified angle is 0 degrees (Absolute angle A=0). Therefore, when you use the NEWFence linetype to draw a circle, polyline, or a spline, the text string (Fence) will be at zero degrees. If you want the text string (Fence) to align with the polyline, spline, or circle, specify the angle as relative angle (R=0) in the NEWFence linetype definition. The following is the linetype definition for NEWFence linetype with relative angle R=0:

```
*NEWFence,New fence boundary line
A,0.75,["Fence",Standard,S=0.1,R=0,X=0.05,Y=-0.05],-0.575
```

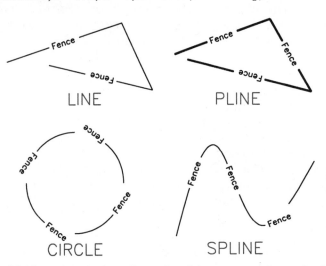

Figure 28-7 Using String Complex Linetype with angle (R=0)

Step 5

In Figure 28-7, you might have noticed that the text string is not properly aligned with the circumference of the circle. This is because AutoCAD draws the text string in a direction that is tangent to the circle at the text insertion point. To resolve this problem you must define the middle point of the text string as the insertion point. Also, the line specifications should be measured accordingly. Figure 28-8 gives the measurements of the NEWFence linetype with middle point of the text as insertion point.

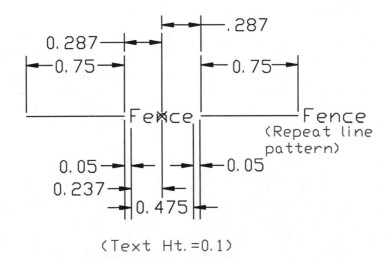

(Text Ht.=0.1)

Figure 28-8 Specifications of String Complex Linetype with the middle point of the text string as the text insertion point

The following is the linetype definition for NEWFence linetype.

*NEWFence,New fence boundary line
A,0.75,-0.287,["FENCE",Standard,S=0.1,X=-0.237,Y=-0.05],-0.287

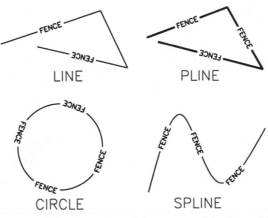

Figure 28-9 Using String Complex Linetype with the middle point of the text string as the text insertion point

Note

If no angle is defined in the line definition, it defaults to angle R=0.

CREATING SHAPE COMPLEX LINETYPES

Like the String Complex Linetype, when you write the definition of a Shape Complex Linetype, the name of the shape, name of the shape file, and other shape attributes like rotation, scale, X-Offset, and Y-Offset must be included in the linetype definition. The format of the Shape Complex Linetype is:

[Shape Name, Shape File, Scale, Rotation, X-Offset, Y-Offset]

The following are the attributes and their description that must be assigned to the shape:

Shape Name
This is the name of the shape that you want to insert along the line. The shape name must exist, otherwise no shape will be generated along the line.

Shape File
This is the name of the **compiled** shape file (.SHX) that contains the definition of the shape that is being inserted in the line. The name of the subdirectory where the shape file is located must be in the ACAD search path. The shape files (.SHP) must be compiled before using the SHAPE command to load the shape.

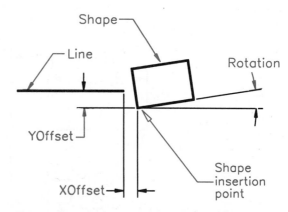

Figure 28-10 The attributes of a Shape Complex Linetype

Scale
This is the scale of the inserted shape. If the scale is 1, the size of the shape will be same as defined in the shape definition (.SHP file).

Rotation
This is the rotation of the shape with respect to the positive X axis, if AutoCAD is configured to measure angles with the positive X axis.

X-Offset
This is the distance of the shape insertion point from the endpoint of the line segment measured along the line. If the line is horizontal, then the X-Offset distance is measured along the X axis. In Figure 28-10, the X-Offset distance is 0.2.

Y-Offset
This is the distance of the shape insertion point from the end point of the line segment measured perpendicular to the line. If the line is horizontal, then the Y-Offset distance is measured along the Y axis. In Figure 28-10, the Y-Offset distance is 0.

Example 4

In the following example you will write the definition of a Shape Complex Linetype that consists of the shape (Manhole, the name of the shape is MH) and a line. The scale of the shape is 0.1, the length of each line segment is 0.75, and the space between each line segment is 0.2.

Step 1
Before writing the definition of a new linetype, it is important to determine the line specifications. One of the ways it can be done is to actually draw the lines and the shape the way you want it to appear in the drawing. Once you have drawn the line and the shape to your satisfaction, measure the distances that are needed to define the Shape Complex Linetype. In this example the values are given as follows:

Shape name	MH	
Shape file name	MHOLE.SHX	(Name of the compiled shape file)
Scale	0.1	
Rotation	0	
X-Offset	0.2	

Y-Offset   0
Length of the first line segment = 0.75
Distance between the line segments = 0.2

Step 2
Use a Text Editor to write the definition of the shape file. The extension of the file must be .SHP. The following file is the listing of the MHOLE.SHP file for Example 4. The name of the shape is MH. (For details, see Chapter 29, Shapes and Text Fonts.)

    *215,9,MH
    001,10,(1,007),
    001,10,(1,071),0

Step 3
Use the COMPILE command to compile the shape file (.SHP file). When you use this command, AutoCAD will prompt you to enter the name of the shape file. For this example, the

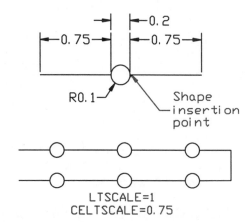

Figure 28-11 The attributes of the Shape Complex Linetype and line specifications for Example 4

name is MHOLE.SHP. The following is the command prompt sequence for compiling the shape file:

    Command: **COMPILE**
    Enter NAME of shape file: **MHOLE**

Step 4
Use a Text Editor to write the definition of the Shape Complex linetype. You can add the definition to AutoCAD's ACAD.LIN file or create a separate file. The extension of the file must be .LIN. The following file is the listing of the MHOLE.LIN file for Example 4. The name of the linetype is MHOLE.

    *MHOLE,Line with Manholes
    A,0.75,[MH,MHOLE.SHX,S=0.10,X=0.2,Y=0],-0.2

Step 5
To test the linetype, load the linetype using the **LINETYPE** command with Load option and assign it to a layer. Draw a line or any object to check if the line is drawn to the given specifications. The shape is drawn upside-down when you draw a line from right to left.

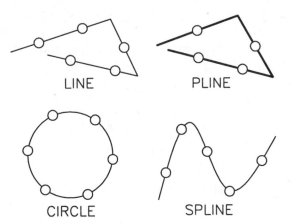

Figure 28-12 Using Shape Complex Linetype

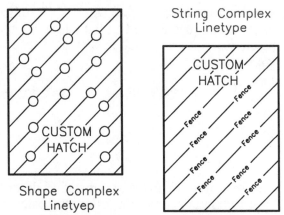

Figure 28-13 Using Shape and String Complex Linetypes to create custom hatch

CURRENT LINETYPE SCALING (CELTSCALE)

Like LTSCALE, the CELTSCALE system variable controls the linetype scaling. The difference is that CELTSCALE determines the current linetype scaling. For example, if you set the CELTSCALE to 0.5, all lines drawn after setting the new value for CELTSCALE will have the linetype scaling factor of 0.5. The value is retained in the CELTSCALE system variable. The fist line (a) in Figure 28-14 is drawn with the CELTSCALE factor of 1 and the second line (b) is drawn with the CELTSCALE factor of 0.5. The length of the dash is reduced by a factor of 0.5 when the CELTSCALE is 0.5.

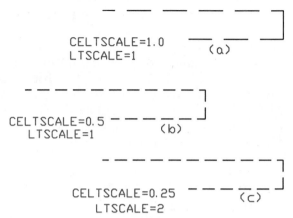

Figure 28-14 Using CELTSCALE to control current linetype scaling

The LTSCALE system variable controls the global scale factor. For example, if LTSCALE is set to 2, all lines in the drawing will be affected by a factor of 2. The net scale factor is equal to the product of CELTSCALE and LTSCALE. Figure 28-14(c) shows a line that is drawn with LTSCALE of 2 and CELTSCALE of 0.25. The net scale factor is = LTSCALE x CELTSCALE = 2 x 0.25 = 0.5

HATCH PATTERN DEFINITION

The AutoCAD software comes with a hatch pattern library file, ACAD.PAT, that contains 53 hatch patterns. These hatch patterns are sufficient for general drafting work. However, if you need a different hatch pattern, AutoCAD lets you create your own. There is no limit to the number of hatch patterns you can define.

The hatch patterns that you define can be added to the hatch pattern library file, ACAD.PAT. You can also create a new hatch pattern library file, provided the file contains only one hatch pattern definition and the name of the hatch is the same as the name of the file. The hatch pattern definition consists of the following two parts:

1. Header Line
2. Hatch Descriptors

Header Line

Header line consists of an asterisk (*) followed by the name of the hatch pattern. The hatch name is the name that is used in the hatch command to hatch an area. After the name, you can give the hatch description, which is separated from the hatch name by a comma (,). The general format of the header line is:

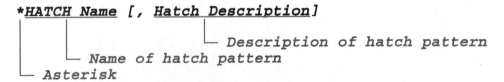

The description can be any text that describes the hatch pattern. It can also be omitted, in which case a comma should not follow the hatch pattern name.

Example
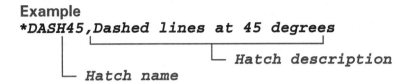

```
*DASH45,Dashed lines at 45 degrees
```
— Hatch description
— Hatch name

Hatch Descriptors

The hatch descriptors consist of one or more lines that contain the definition of the hatch lines. The general format of the hatch descriptor is:

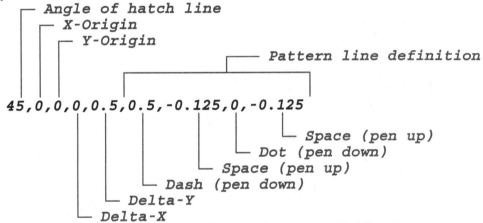

```
Angle, X-origin, Y-origin, D1, D2 [,Dash Length.....]
```

— Angle of hatch lines
— X coordinate of hatch line
— Y coordinate of hatch line
Displacement of second line (Delta-X)
Distance between hatch lines (Delta-Y)
Length of dashes and spaces (Pattern line definition)

Example

```
45,0,0,0,0.5,0.5,-0.125,0,-0.125
```

— Angle of hatch line
— X-Origin
— Y-Origin
— Pattern line definition
— Space (pen up)
— Dot (pen down)
— Space (pen up)
— Dash (pen down)
— Delta-Y
— Delta-X

Hatch Angle

X-origin and Y-origin

The hatch angle is the angle that the hatch lines make with the positive X-axis. The angle is positive if measured counterclockwise (Figure 28-15), and negative if the angle is measured clockwise. When you draw a hatch pattern, the first line of the hatch line starts from the point defined by X-origin and Y-origin. The remaining lines are generated by offsetting the first hatch line by a distance specified by delta-X and delta-Y. In Figure 28-16(a), the first hatch line starts from the point with the coordinates X=0 and Y=0. In Figure 28-16(a) the first line of hatch starts from a point with the coordinates X=0 and Y=0.25.

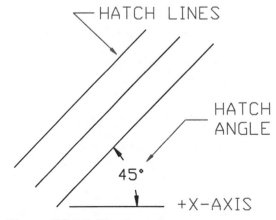

Figure 28-15 Hatch angle

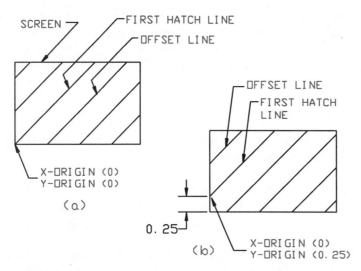

Figure 28-16 X-origin and Y-origin of hatch lines

Delta-X and Delta-Y

Delta-X is the displacement of the offset line in the direction in which the hatch lines are generated. For example, if the lines are drawn at a 0-degree angle and delta-X = 0.5, the offset line will be displaced by a distance delta-X (0.5) along the 0-angle direction. Similarly, if the hatch lines are drawn at a 45-degree angle, the offset line will be displaced by a distance delta-X (0.5) along a 45-degree direction (Figure 28-17).

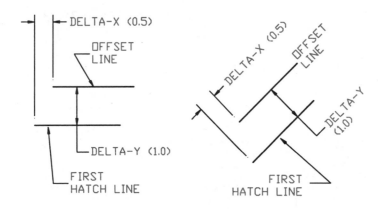

Figure 28-17 Delta-X and delta-Y of hatch lines

Delta-Y is the displacement of the offset lines measured perpendicular to the hatch lines. For example, if delta-Y = 1.0, the space between any two hatch lines will be 1.0 (Figure 28-17).

HOW HATCH WORKS

When you hatch an area, AutoCAD generates an infinite number of hatch lines of infinite length. The first hatch line always passes through the point specified by X-origin and Y-origin. The remaining lines are generated by offsetting the first hatch line in both directions. The offset distance is determined by delta-X and delta-Y. All selected entities that form the boundary of the hatch area are then checked for intersection with these lines. Any hatch lines found within the defined hatch boundaries are turned on, and the hatch lines outside the hatch boundary are turned off, as shown in Figure 28-18. Since the hatch lines are generated by offsetting, the hatch lines in different areas of the drawing are automatically aligned. Figure 28-18(a) shows the hatch lines as computed by AutoCAD. These lines are not drawn on the screen; they are shown here for illustration only. Figure 28-18(b) shows the hatch lines generated in the circle that was defined as the hatch boundary.

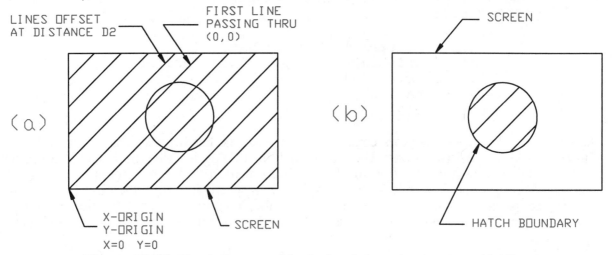

Figure 28-18 Hatch lines outside the hatch boundary are turned off

SIMPLE HATCH PATTERN

It is good practice to develop the hatch pattern specification before writing a hatch pattern definition. For simple hatch patterns it may not be that important, but for more complicated hatch patterns you should know the detailed specifications. Example 5 illustrates the procedure to develop a simple hatch pattern.

Example 5

Write a hatch pattern definition for the hatch pattern as shown in Figure 28-19, with the following specifications:

Name of the hatch pattern=	HATCH1
X-Origin=	0
Y-Origin=	0
Distance between hatch lines=	0.5
Displacement of hatch lines=	0
Hatch line pattern=	Continuous

This hatch pattern definition can be added to the existing ACAD.PAT hatch file. You can use AutoCAD's EDIT command (if the ACAD.PGP file is present and EDIT command is defined in the file), or the EDIT function of DOS to edit the file. If you are in the Drawing Editor, type **SH** or **SHELL** to access DOS commands. **OS Commands**: prompt will appear on the screen. Type EDIT followed by the name of the file, with the path if necessary, as shown in the following command line:

OS Commands:**EDIT C:\ACAD\ACAD.PAT**

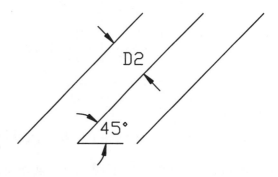

Figure 28-19 Hatch pattern angle and offset distance

In this example, assume that the AutoCAD files are in the ACAD subdirectory and you are working in a different subdirectory. List the ACAD.PAT file and insert the following two lines at the end of the file.

```
*HATCH1,Hatch Pattern for Example 5
45,0,0,0,.5
      │ │ │ │  └─ Distance between hatch lines
      │ │ │ └──── Displacement of second hatch line
      │ │ └────── Y-origin
      │ └──────── X-origin
      └────────── Hatch angle
```

The first field of hatch descriptors contains the angle of the hatch lines. That angle is 45 degrees with respect to the positive X-axis. The second and third fields describe the X and Y coordinate of the first hatch line origin. The first line of the hatch pattern will pass through this point. If the values of X-origin and Y-origin were 0.5 and 1.0, respectively, then the first line would pass through the point with X-coordinate of 0.5 and the Y-coordinate of 1.0 with respect to the drawing origin 0,0. The remaining lines are generated by offsetting the first line by a distance 0.5 on both sides of the line, as shown in Figure 28-19.

EFFECT OF ANGLE AND SCALE FACTOR ON HATCH

When you hatch an area, you can alter the angle and displacement of hatch lines that you have specified in the hatch pattern definition to get a desired hatch spacing. You can do this by entering an appropriate value for angle and scale factor in AutoCAD's HATCH command.

Command: **Hatch**
Pattern(? or name/U,style)<default>: **Hatch1**
Scale for pattern<default>: **1**
Angle of pattern<default>: **0**

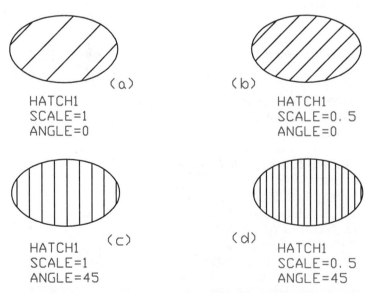

Figure 28-20 Effect of angle and scale factor on hatch

To understand how the angle and the displacement can be changed, hatch an area with the hatch pattern HATCH1 of Example 5. You will notice that the hatch lines have been generated according to the definition of hatch pattern HATCH1. Notice the effect of hatch angle and scale factor on the hatch. Figure 28-20(a) shows a hatch that is generated by AutoCAD's HATCH command with a 0-degree angle and a scale factor of 1.0. If the angle is 0, the hatch will be generated with the same angle as defined in the hatch pattern definition (45 degrees in Example 5). Similarly, if the scale factor is 1.0, the distance between the hatch lines will be same as defined in the hatch pattern definition (0.5 in Example 5). Figure 28-20(a) shows a hatch that is generated when the hatch scale factor is 0.5. If you measure the distance between the successive hatch lines, it will be 0.25 (0.5 X 0.5 = 0.25). Figure 28-20(c) and Figure 28-20(d) show the hatch when the angle is 45 degrees and the scale factors are 1.0 and 0.5, respectively. You can enter any value in response to HATCH command prompts to generate hatch lines at any angle and with any line spacing.

HATCH PATTERN WITH DASHES AND DOTS

The lines you can use in a hatch pattern definition are not restricted to continuous lines. You can define any line pattern to generate a hatch pattern. The lines can be a combination of dashes, dots, and spaces in any configuration. However, the maximum number of dashes you can specify in the line pattern definition of a hatch pattern is six. Example 6 uses a dash-dot line to create a hatch pattern.

Example 6

Write a hatch pattern definition for the hatch pattern shown in Figure 28-21, with the following specifications:

Name of the hatch pattern	HATCH2
Hatch angle =	0
X-origin =	0
Y-origin =	0
Displacement of lines (D1) =	0.25
Distance between lines (D2) =	0.25
Length of each dash =	0.5
Space between dashes and dots =	0.125
Space between dots =	0.125

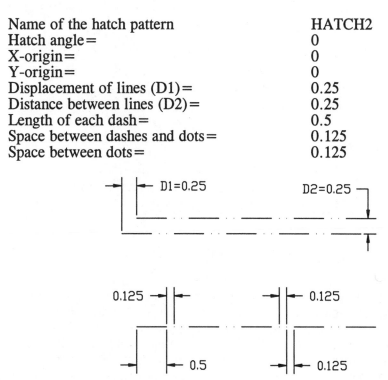

Figure 28-21 Hatch lines made of dashes and dots

You can use AutoCAD's EDIT command to edit the file ACAD.PAT. The general format of the header line and the hatch descriptors is:

*HATCH NAME, Hatch Description
Angle, X-Origin, Y-Origin, D1, D2 [,Dash Length.....]

Substitute the value from Example 6 in the corresponding fields of header line and field descriptor.

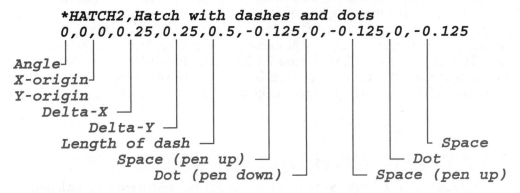

HATCH2,Hatch with dashes and dots
0,0,0,0.25,0.25,0.5,-0.125,0,-0.125,0,-0.125

Angle
X-origin
Y-origin
Delta-X
Delta-Y
Length of dash
Space (pen up)
Dot (pen down)
Space (pen up)
Dot
Space

The hatch pattern this hatch definition will generate is shown in Figure 28-22. Figure 28-22(a) shows the hatch with 0 angle and a scale factor of 1.0. Figure 28-22(b) shows the hatch with a 45-degree angle and a scale factor of 0.5.

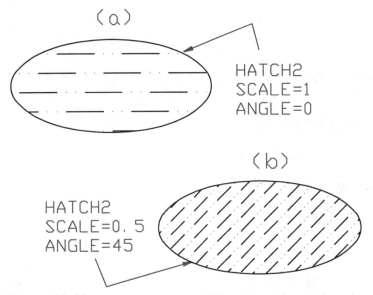

(a)

HATCH2
SCALE=1
ANGLE=0

(b)

HATCH2
SCALE=0.5
ANGLE=45

Figure 28-22 Hatch pattern at different angles and scales

HATCH WITH MULTIPLE DESCRIPTORS

Some hatch patterns require multiple lines to generate a shape. For example, if you want to create a hatch pattern of a brick wall, you need a hatch pattern that has four hatch descriptors to generate a rectangular shape. You can have any number of hatch descriptor lines in a hatch pattern definition. It is up to the user to combine them in any conceivable order. However, there are some shapes that you cannot generate. A shape that has a nonlinear element, like an arc, cannot be generated by hatch pattern definition. However, you can simulate an arc by defining short line segments, because you can use only straight lines to generate a hatch pattern. Example 7 uses three lines to define a triangular hatch pattern.

Example 7

Write a hatch pattern definition for the hatch pattern shown in Figure 28-23, with the following specifications:

Name of the hatch pattern=	HATCH3
Vertical height of the triangle=	0.5
Horizontal length of the triangle=	0.5
Vertical distance between the triangles=	0.5
Horizontal distance between the triangles=	0.5

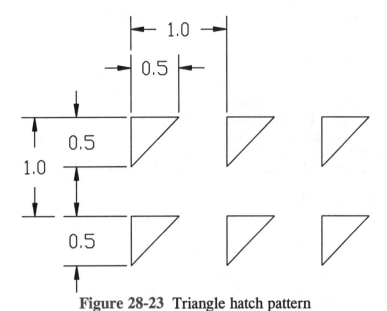

Figure 28-23 Triangle hatch pattern

Each triangle in this hatch pattern consists of the following three elements.

1. Vertical line
2. Horizontal line
3. Line inclined at 45 degrees

1. Vertical Line

For the vertical line the specifications are:

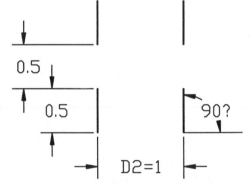

Hatch angle=	90 degrees
X-Origin=	0
Y-Origin=	0
Delta-X (D1)=	0
Delta-Y (D2)=	1.0
Dash length=	0.5
Space=	0.5

Figure 28-24 Vertical line

Substitute the values from the vertical line specification in various fields of the hatch descriptor to get the following line:

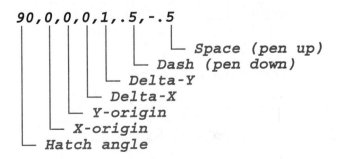

2. Horizontal Line

For the horizontal line the specifications are:

Hatch angle=	0 degree
X-Origin=	0
Y-Origin=	0.5
Delta-X (D1)=	0
Delta-Y (D2)=	1.0
Dash length=	0.5
Space=	0.5

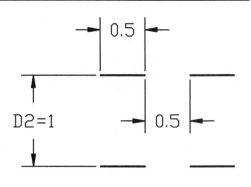

ANGLE=0

Figure 28-25 Horizontal line

The only difference between the vertical and the horizontal line is the angle. For the horizontal line the angle is 0 degree, whereas for the vertical line the angle is 90 degrees. Substitute the values from the vertical line specification to obtain the following line:

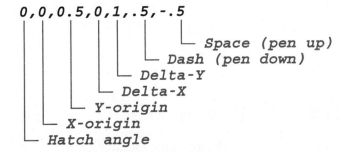

3. Line Inclined at 45 Degrees

This line is at an angle, therefore you need to calculate the distances delta-X (D1) and delta-Y (D2), and length of the dash line, and the length of space. Figure 28-26 shows the calculations to find these values.

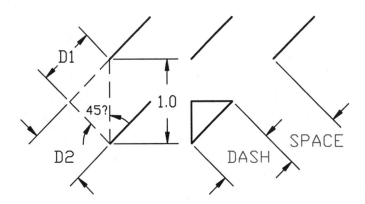

$$D1 = 1.0 \times COS\ 45 \qquad D2 = 1.0 \times SIN\ 45$$
$$D1 = 0.7071 \qquad D2 = 0.7071$$

$$DASH = SQRT(0.5**2 + 0.5**2)$$
$$= .7071$$
$$SPACE = DASH = .7071$$

Figure 28-26 Line inclined at 45 degrees

Hatch angle=	45 degrees
X-Origin=	0
Y-Origin=	0
Delta-X (D1)=	0.7071
Delta-Y (D2)=	0.7071
Dash length=	0.7071
Space=	0.7071

After substituting the values in the general format of the hatch descriptor, you will obtain the following line:

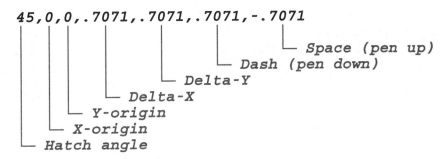

```
45,0,0,.7071,.7071,.7071,-.7071
```
— Space (pen up)
— Dash (pen down)
— Delta-Y
— Delta-X
— Y-origin
— X-origin
— Hatch angle

Now, you can combine these three lines and insert them at the end of ACAD.PAT file. You can also use AutoCAD's EDIT command to edit the file and insert the lines.

Figure 28-27 shows the hatch pattern that will be generated by this hatch pattern (HATCH3). In Figure 28-27(a) the hatch pattern is at a 0-degree angle and the scale factor is 0.5. In Figure 28-27(b) the hatch pattern is at a 45-degree angle and the scale factor is 0.5.

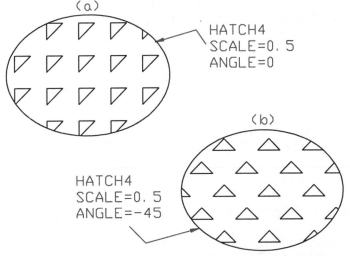

Figure 28-27 Hatch generated by HATCH3 pattern

The following file is a partial listing of ACAD.PAT file, after adding the hatch pattern definitions from Example 5, Example 6, and Example 7.

```
*angle,Angle steel
0, 0,0, 0,.275, .2,-.075
90, 0,0, 0,.275, .2,-.075
*ansi31,ANSI Iron, Brick, Stone masonry
45, 0,0, 0,.125
*ansi32,ANSI Steel
45, 0,0, 0,.375
```

```
45, .176776695,0, 0,.375
*ansi33,ANSI Bronze, Brass, Copper
45, 0,0, 0,.25
45, .176776695,0, 0,.25, .125,-.0625
*ansi34,ANSI Plastic, Rubber
45, 0,0, 0,.75
45, .176776695,0, 0,.75
45, .353553391,0, 0,.75
45, .530330086,0, 0,.75
*ansi35,ANSI Fire brick, Refractory material
45, 0,0, 0,.25
45, .176776695,0, 0,.25, .3125,-.0625,0,-.0625
*ansi36,ANSI Marble, Slate, Glass
45, 0,0, .21875,.125, .3125,-.0625,0,-.0625
*ansi37,ANSI Lead, Zinc, Magnesium, Sound/Heat/Elec Insulation
45, 0,0, 0,.125
135, 0,0, 0,.125
```

```
*steel,Steel material
45, 0,0, 0,.125
45, 0,.0625, 0,.125
*swamp,Swampy area
0, 0,0, .5,.866025403, .125,-.875
90, .0625,0, .866025403,.5, .0625,-1.669550806
90, .078125,0, .866025403,.5, .05,-1.682050806
90, .046875,0, .866025403,.5, .05,-1.682050806
60, .09375,0, .5,.866025403, .04,-.96
120, .03125,0, .5,.866025403, .04,-.96
*trans,Heat transfer material
0, 0,0, 0,.25
0, 0,.125, 0,.25, .125,-.125
*triang,Equilateral triangles
60, 0,0, .1875,.324759526, .1875,-.1875
120, 0,0, .1875,.324759526, .1875,-.1875
0, -.09375,.162379763, .1875,.324759526, .1875,-.1875
*zigzag,Staircase effect
0, 0,0, .125,.125, .125,-.125
90, .125,0, .125,.125, .125,-.125
*HATCH1,Hatch at 45 Degree Angle
45,0,0,0,.5
*HATCH2,Hatch with Dashes & Dots:
0,0,0,.25,.25,0.5,-.125,0,-.125,0,-.125
*HATCH3,Triangle Hatch:
90,0,0,0,1,.5,-.5
0,0,0.5,0,1,.5,-.5
45,0,0,.7071,.7071,.7071,-.7071
```

CUSTOM HATCH PATTERN FILE

As mentioned earlier, you can add the new hatch pattern definitions to the file ACAD.PAT. There is no limit to the number of hatch pattern definitions you can add to this file. However, if you have only one hatch pattern definition, you can define a separate file. It has the following three requirements:

1. The name of the file has to be the same as the hatch pattern name.
2. The file can contain only one hatch pattern definition.
3. The hatch pattern name--and therefore the hatch file name--should be unique.

    File name HATCH3.PAT

    *HATCH3,Triangle Hatch:
    90,0,0,0,1,.5,-.5
    0,0,0.5,0,1,.5,-.5
    45,0,0,.7071,.7071,.7071,-.7071

Note

The hatch lines can be edited after exploding the hatch with AutoCAD's EXPLODE command. After exploding, each hatch line becomes a separate object.

It is good practice not to explode a hatch, because it increases the size of the drawing database. For example, if a hatch consists of 100 lines, save it as a single object. However, after you explode the hatch, every line becomes a separate object and you have 99 additional entities in the drawing.

Keep the hatch lines in a separate layer to facilitate editing of the hatch lines.

Assign a unique color to hatch lines so that you can control the line width of the hatch lines at the time of plotting.

REVIEW QUESTIONS

Fill in the blanks.

<u>Creating Linetypes</u>

1. The AutoCAD _____ command can be used to create a new linetype.

2. The AutoCAD _____ command can be used to load a linetype.

3. The AutoCAD _____ command can be used to change the linetype scale factor.

4. In AutoCAD the linetypes are saved in _____ file.

5. The linetype description should not be more than _____ characters long.

6. A positive number denotes a pen _____ segment.

7. The segment length _____ generates a dot.

8. AutoCAD supports only _____ alignment field specification.

9. A line pattern definition always start with _____.

10. A header line definition always starts with _____.

Creating Hatch Patterns

1.   The ACAD.PAT file contains _____ number of hatch pattern definitions.

2.   The header line consists of an asterisk, the pattern name, and _____.

3.   The first hatch line passes through a point whose coordinates are specified by _____ and _____.

4.   The perpendicular distance between the hatch lines in a hatch pattern definition is specified by _____.

5.   The displacement of the second hatch line in a hatch pattern definition is specified by _____.

6.   The maximum number of dash lengths that can be specified in the line pattern definition of a hatch pattern is _____.

7.   The hatch lines in different areas of the drawing will automatically _____ since the hatch lines are generated by offsetting.

8.   The hatch angle as defined in the hatch pattern definition can be changed further when you use AutoCAD's _____ command.

9.   When you load a hatch pattern, AutoCAD looks for that hatch pattern in the _____ file.

10. The hatch lines can be edited after _____ the hatch by using AutoCAD's _____ command.

EXERCISES

Creating Linetypes

Exercise 1

Using AutoCAD's LINETYPE command, create a new linetype "DASH3DASH" with the following specifications.

Length of the first dash 0.75
Blank space 0.125
Dash length 0.25
Blank space 0.125
Dash length 0.25
Blank space 0.125
Dash length 0.25
Blank space 0.125

Exercise 2

Use a Text Editor to create a new file NEWLT2.LIN and a new linetype DASH2DASH with the following specifications.

Length of the first dash 0.5
Blank space 0.1
Dash length 0.2
Blank space 0.1
Dash length 0.2
Blank space 0.1

Exercise 3
a. Write the definition of a String Complex Linetype (Hot water line) as shown in Figure 28-28(a).

a. Write the definition of a String Complex Linetype (Gas line) as shown in Figure 28-28(b).

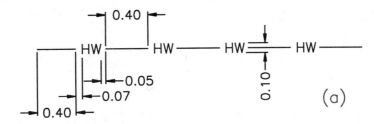

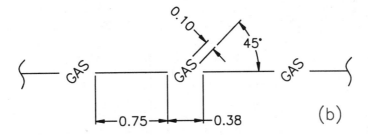

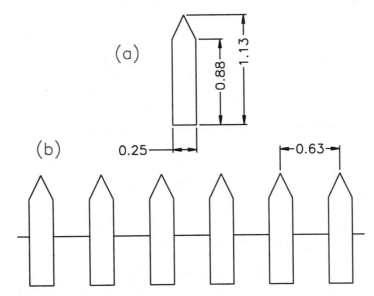

Figure 28-28 Specifications for String Complex Linetype

Exercise 4
Write the shape file for the shape shown in Figure 28-29(a). Compile the shape and use it in defining the Shape Complex linetype so that you can draw a fence line as shown in Figure 28-29(b).

Figure 28-29 Specifications for Shape Complex Linetype

Exercise 5

Determine the hatch specifications and write a hatch pattern definition for the hatch pattern shown in Figure 28-30.

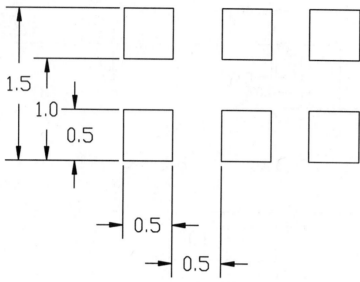

Figure 28-30 Square hatch pattern

Exercise 6

Determine the hatch pattern specifications and write a hatch pattern definition for the hatch pattern shown in Figure 28-31.

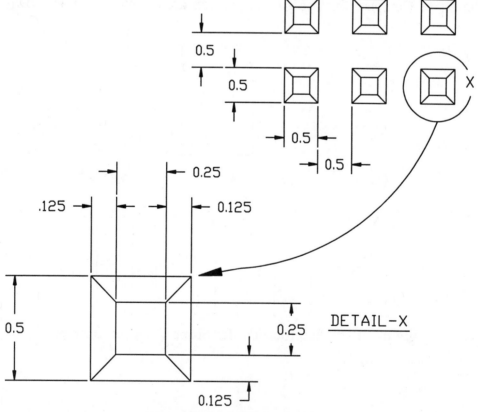

Figure 28-31 Hatch pattern

Chapter 29

Shapes and Text Fonts

Learning objectives

After completing this chapter, you will be able to:
♦ Write shape files.
♦ Use vector length and direction encoding to write shape files.
♦ Compile and load shape/font files.
♦ Use special codes to define a shape.
♦ Write text font files.

SHAPE FILES

AutoCAD provides a facility to define shapes and text fonts. These files are ASCII files with the extension SHP. You can write these files using the Edit function of DOS, AutoCAD's EDIT command (provided the ACAD.PGP file is present and the EDIT command is defined in the file), or any Text Editor.

Shape files contain information about the individual elements that constitute the shape of an object. The basic objects that are used in these files are lines and arcs. You can define any shape using these basic objects, and then insert them anywhere in a drawing. The shapes are easy to insert and take less disk space than blocks. However, there are some disadvantages to using shapes. For example, you cannot edit a shape or change it. Blocks, on the other hand, can be edited after exploding them with AutoCAD's EXPLODE command.

SHAPE DESCRIPTION

Shape description consists of the following two parts:

1. Header
2. Shape Specification

Header

The header line has the following format:

*SHAPE NUMBER, DEFBYTES, SHAPE NAME

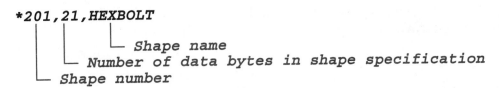

```
*201,21,HEXBOLT
```
└── Shape name
└── Number of data bytes in shape specification
└── Shape number

Every header line starts with an asterisk (*), followed by the **SHAPE NUMBER**. The shape number is any number between one and 255 in a particular file, but these numbers cannot be repeated within the same file. However, the numbers can be repeated in another shape file with a different name. **DEFBYTES** is the number of data bytes used by the shape specification and includes the terminating zero. **SHAPE NAME** is the name of a shape in uppercase letters. The name is ignored if the letters are lowercase. The file must not contain two shapes with the same name.

Shape Specification

The shape specification line contains the complete definition of the shape of an object. The shape is described with special codes, hexadecimal numbers, and decimal numbers. A hexadecimal number is designated by a leading zero (012), and a decimal number is a regular number without a leading zero (12). The data bytes are separated by a comma (,). The maximum number of data bytes is 2,000 bytes per shape, and in a particular shape file there can be more than one shape. The shape specification can have multiple lines. You should define the shape in some logical blocks and enter each block on a separate line. This makes it easier to edit and debug the files. The number of characters on any line must not exceed 80. The shape specification is terminated with a zero.

VECTOR LENGTH AND DIRECTION ENCODING

For direction encoding, a 360-degree angle is divided into 16 equal parts. Each angle is equal to 22.5 degrees. A direction vector is defined after every 22.5 degrees, as shown in Figure 29-1.

All these vectors have the same magnitude or length specification. To define a vector you need its magnitude and direction. That means each shape specification byte contains vector length and a direction code. The maximum length of the vector is 15 units. Example 1 illustrates the use of vectors.

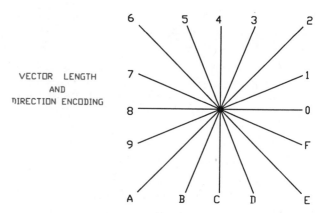

Figure 29-1 Vector length and direction encoding

Example 1

Write a shape file for the resistor shown in Figure 29-2. The name of the file is SH1.SHP and the shape name is RESIS.

The following two lines define the shape file for the given resistor:

```
*201,8,RESIS
020,023,04D,043,04D,023,020,0
```

The fist line is the **Header Line**, the second line is the **Shape Specification**.

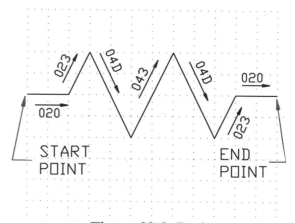

Figure 29-2 Resistor

Header Line

*201,8,RESIS

*201 is the shape number, and 8 is the number of data bytes contained in the shape specification line. RESIS is the name of the shape.

Shape Specification

020,023,04D,043,04D,023,020,0

```
    │└ Direction code
    └─ Vector length
    └── Hexadecimal notation
```

Each data byte in this line, except the terminating zero, has three elements. The first element (0) is the hexadecimal, the second is the length of the vector, and the third element is the direction code. For the first data byte, 020, the length of the vector is 2, and the direction is along the direction vector 0. Similarly, for the second data byte, 023, the first element, 0, is for hexadecimal; the second element, 2, is the length of the vector; and the third element, 3, is the direction code for the vector.

COMPILING AND LOADING SHAPE/FONT FILES

You can compile the shape or the font file by using the COMPILE command.

Command: **COMPILE**

AutoCAD displays the **Select Shape or Font File** dialogue box on the screen. Enter or select the file name from the dialogue box. If the system variable FILEDIA is set to zero, you can use the COMPILE command and AutoCAD will prompt you to enter the name of the file.

Command: **COMPILE**
Enter NAME of shape file: **SH1**

AutoCAD will compile the file and if the compilation process is successful, the following prompt will be displayed on the screen:

Compilation successful
Output file name.shx contains nn bytes

For Example 1, the name of the compiled output file is SH1.SHX and the number of bytes is 49. This is the file that is loaded when you use AutoCAD's LOAD command to load a shape.

If AutoCAD encounters an error in compiling a shape file, an error message will be displayed on the screen indicating the type of error and the line number where the error occurred.

To insert a shape in the drawing, you have to be in the Drawing Editor, and then use the LOAD command to load the shape file.

Command: **LOAD**
Name of shape file to load (or ?): *Name of file.* **SH1**

SH1 is the name of the shape file for Example 1. Do not include the extension .SHX with the name, because AutoCAD automatically assumes the extension. If the shape file is present, AutoCAD will display the shape names that are loaded. To insert the loaded shapes, use AutoCAD's SHAPE command.

Command: **SHAPE**
Shape name (or ?)<default>: *Shape name.*
Start point: *Shape origin.*
Height<1.0>: *Number or point.*
Rotation angle<0.0>: *Number or point.*

For Example 1, the shape name is RESIS. After you enter the information about the start point, height, and rotation, the shape will be displayed on the screen.

SPECIAL CODES

Generating shapes with the direction vectors has some limitations. For example, you cannot draw an arc or draw a line that is not along the standard direction vectors. These limitations can be overcome by using special codes that add flexibility and give you better control over the shapes you want to create.

Standard Codes:

000	End of shape definition
001	Activate draw mode (pen down)
002	Deactivate draw mode (pen up)
003	Divide vector lengths by next byte
004	Multiply vector lengths by next byte
005	Push current location from stack
006	Pop current location from stack
007	Draw subshape numbers given by next byte
008	X-Y displacement given by the next two bytes
009	Multiply X-Y displacement, terminated by (0,0)
00A or 10	Octant arc defined by next two bytes
00B or 11	Fractional arc defined by next five bytes
00C or 12	Arc defined by X-Y displacement and bulge
00D or 13	Multiple bulge-specified arcs
00E or 14	Process next command only if vertical text style

Code 000: End of shape definition

This code marks the end of a shape definition.

Code 001: Activate draw mode

This code turns the draw mode on. When you start a shape, the draw mode is on so you do not need to use this code. However, if the draw mode has been turned off, you can use Code 001 to turn it on.

Code 002: Deactivate draw mode

This code turns the draw mode off. It is used when you want to move the pen without drawing a line.

```
1          2            3          4
```

Let's say the distance from point 1 to 2, from point 2 to 3, and from point 3 to 4 is two units. The shape specification for this line is:

020,002,020,001,020,0

The first data byte, 020, generates a line 2 units long along the direction vector zero. The second data byte, 002, deactivates the draw mode, and the third byte, 020, generates a blank line of 2 units long. The fourth data byte, 001, activates the draw mode, and the next byte, 020, generates a line that is 2 units long along the direction vector zero. The last byte, 0, terminates the shape description.

Example 2

Write a shape file to generate the character "G" as shown in Figure 29-3.

You can use the Edlin function of DOS or any other Text Editor to write a shape file. The name of the file is CHRGEE and the shape name is GEE. In the following file the line numbers are not a part of the file; they are for reference only.

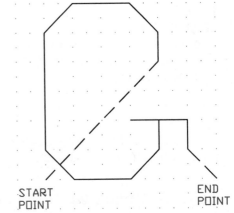

Figure 29-3 Shape of the character "G"

```
*215,20,GEE                    1
002,042,                       2
001,014,016,028,01A,           3
04C,01E,020,012,014,           4
002,018,                       5
001,020,01C,                   6
002,01E,0                      7
```

Line 1
*215,20,GEE
The first data byte contains an asterisk (*) and shape number 215. The second data byte is the number of data bytes contained in the shape specification, including the terminating 0. GEE is the name of shape.

Line 2
002,042,
The data byte 002 deactivates the draw mode (pen up), and the next data byte defines a vector 4 units long along the direction vector 2.

Line 3
001,014,016,028,01A,
The data byte 001 activates the draw mode (pen down), and 014 defines a vector that is 1 unit long at 90 degrees (direction vector 4). The data byte 016 defines a vector that is 1 unit long along the direction vector 6. The data byte 028 defines a vector that is 2 units long along the direction vector 8 (180 degrees). The data byte 01A defines a unit vector along the direction vector A.

Line 4
04C,01E,020,012,014,
The data byte 04C defines a vector that is 4 units long along the direction vector C. The data byte 01E defines a direction vector that is 1 unit along the direction vector E. The data byte 020 defines a direction vector that is 2 units long along the direction vector 0 (0 degrees). The data byte 012 defines a direction vector that is 1 unit long along the direction vector 2. Similarly, 014 defines a vector that is 1 unit long along the direction vector 4.

Line 5
002,018,

The data byte 002 deactivates the pen (pen-up), and 018 defines a vector that is 1 unit long along the direction vector 8.

Line 6
001,020,01C,

The data byte 001 activates the pen (pen-down), and 020 defines a vector that is 2 units long along the direction vector 0. The data byte 01C defines a vector that is 1 unit long along the direction vector C.

Line 7
002,01E,0

The data byte 002 deactivates the pen and the next data byte 01E defines a vector that is 1 unit long along the direction vector E. The data byte 0 terminates the shape specification.

Code 003: Divide vector lengths by next byte

This code is used if you want to divide a vector by a certain number. In Example 2, if you want to divide the vectors by 2, the shape description can be written as:

<u>003,2,</u>020,002,020,001,020,0

The first byte, 003, is the division code, and the next byte, 2, is the number by which all the remaining vectors are divided. The length of the lines and the gap between the lines will be equal to one unit now.

―――――   ―――――

Also, the scale factors are cumulative within a shape. For example, if we insert another code 003 in the above-mentioned shape description, the length of the last vector, 020, will be divided by 4 (2x2).

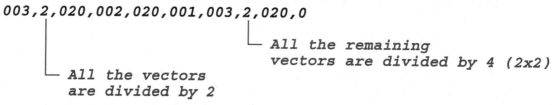

```
003,2,020,002,020,001,003,2,020,0
```
└─ All the vectors are divided by 2

└─ All the remaining vectors are divided by 4 (2x2)

Following is the output of this shape file:

―――――   ――

Code 004: Multiply vector lengths by next byte

This code is used if you want to multiply the vectors by a certain number. It can also be used to reverse the effect of code 003.

```
003,2,020,002,020,001,004,2,020,0
```
└─ Divides all the vectors on the right by 2

└─ Multiplies all the vectors on the right by 2

In this example, the code 003 divides all the vectors to the right by 2. Therefore, a vector that was 1 unit long will be 0.5 units long now. The second code, 004, multiplies the vectors to the right by 2. We know the scale factors are cumulative, therefore the vectors that were divided by 2 earlier will be multiplied by 2 now. Because of this cumulative effect, the length of the last vector remains unchanged. This file will produce the following shape:

Codes 005 and 006: Location save/restore

Code 005 lets you save the current location of the pen, and code 006 restores the saved location. Consider the following example to illustrate the use of codes 005 and 006.

Example 3

Figure 29-4(a) shows three lines that are unit vectors and intersect at one point. After drawing the first line the pen has to return to origin to start a second vector. This is done using code 005, which saves the starting point (origin) of the first vector, and code 006, which restores the origin. Now, if you draw another vector, it will start from the origin. Since there are three lines, you need three code 005's and three code 006's. The following file shows the header line and the shape specification for generating three lines as shown in Figure 29-4(a).

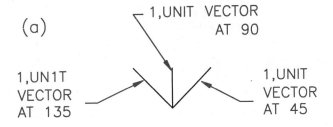

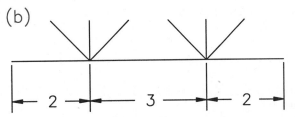

Figure 29-4 (a) Three unit vectors intersecting at a point; (b) Repeating predefined subshapes

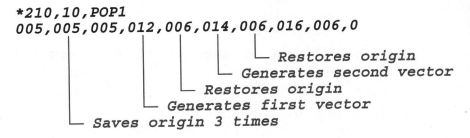

The number of saves (code 005) has to equal the number of restores (code 006). If the number of saves (code 005) more than the number of restores (code 006), AutoCAD will display the following message when the shape is drawn:

Position stack overflow in shape (shape number)

Similarly, if the number of restores (code 006) is more than the number of saves (code 005), the following message will be displayed:

Position stack underflow in shape (shape number)

The maximum number of saves and restores you can use in a particular shape definition is four.

Code 007: Subshape

You can define a subshape like a subroutine in a program. To reference a subshape, the subshape code 007 has to be followed by the shape number of the subshape. The subshape has to be defined in the same shape file, and the shape number has to be from 1 to 255.

```
          ┌─ Shape number
          │
       *210,10,POP1
       005,005,005,012,006,014,006,016,006,0
       *211,8,SUB1
       020,007,210,030,007,210,020,0
              │      └─ Shape number
              └─ Subshape reference
```

The shape that this example will generate is shown in Figure 29-4(b).

Code 008: X-Y displacement

In the previous examples, you might have noticed that there are some limitations with the vectors. As we mentioned earlier, you can draw vectors only in the 16 predefined directions, and the length of the vector cannot exceed 15 units. These restrictions make the shape files easier and more efficient, but at the same time they are limiting. Therefore, codes 008 and 009 allow you to generate non-standard vectors by entering the displacements along the X and Y directions. The general format is for Code 008:

> 008, X-DISPLACEMENT, Y-DISPLACEMENT
> or
> 008, (X-DISPLACEMENT, Y-DISPLACEMENT)

X and Y displacements can range from +127 to -128. Also, a positive displacement is designated by a positive (+) number, and a negative displacement is designated by a negative (-) number. The leading positive sign (+) is optional in a positive number. The parentheses are used to improve readability, but they have no effect on the shape specification.

Code 009: Multiple X-Y displacements

Whereas code 008 allows you to generate non-standard vectors by entering a single X and Y displacement, code 009 allows you to enter multiple X and Y displacements. It is terminated by a pair of 0 displacement (0,0). The general format is:

> 009,(X-Displ, Y-Displ), (X-Disp, Y-Displ),.......(0,0)

Code 00A or 10: Octant arc

If you divide 360 degrees into eight equal parts, each angle will be 45 degrees. Each 45-degree angle segment is called an octant, and the two lines that contain an octant are called an octant boundary. The octant boundaries are numbered from zero to seven as shown in Figure 29-5. The general format is:

```
        ┌─ Hexadecimal notation
        │
10,(R,+/-0SN)
                │
                └─ Number of octants
              └─ Starting octant boundary
          └─ Defines direction, + Counterclockwise, - Clockwise
      └─ Radius of arc
```

10,(3,-043)

The first number, 10, is the code 00A for the octant arc. The second number, 3, is the radius of the octant arc. The negative sign indicates that the arc is to be generated in a clockwise direction. If it is positive (+), or if there is no sign, the arc will be generated in a counterclockwise direction. Zero is the hexadecimal notation, and the following number, 4, is the number of the octant boundary where the octant arc will start. The next element, 3, is the number of octants that this arc will extend. This example will generate the arc in Figure 29-6(a). The following shape file will generate the shape shown in Figure 29-6:

*214,5,FOCT1
001,10,(3,-043),0

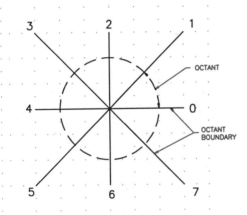

Figure 29-5   Octant boundaries

Figure 29-6   Octant arc

Code 00B or 11: Fractional arc

You can generate a non-standard fractional arc by using code 00B or 11. This code will allow you to start and end an arc at any angle. The definition uses five bytes, and the general format is:

11,(START OFFSET, END OFFSET, HIGH-RADIUS, LOW-RADIUS, +/-0SN)

The START OFFSET represents how far from an octant boundary the arc starts, and the END OFFSET represents how far from an octant boundary the arc ends. The HIGH-RADIUS is zero if the radius is equal to or less than 255 units, and the LOW-RADIUS is the radius of the arc. The positive (+) or negative (-) sign indicates whether the arc is drawn counterclockwise or clockwise. The next element, S, is the number of the octant where the arc starts, and element N is the number of octants the arc goes through. The following example illustrates the fractional arc concept:

Example 4

Draw a fractional arc of radius 3 units that starts at a 20-degree angle and ends at a 140-degree angle (counterclockwise).

The solution involves the following steps:

1. Find the nearest octant boundary whose angle is less than 140 degrees. The nearest octant boundary is the number 4 octant boundary, whose angle is 135 (3*45 = 135).

2. Calculate end offset to the nearest whole number (integer).

    Start offset $\qquad$ = (140-135) * 256/45
    $\qquad\qquad\qquad\qquad$ = 28.44
    $\qquad\qquad\qquad\qquad$ = 28

3. Find the nearest octant boundary whose angle is less than 20 degrees. The nearest octant boundary is 0 and its angle is 0 degrees.

4. Calculate start offset to the nearest whole number.

    End offset $\qquad$ = (20-0) * 256/45
    $\qquad\qquad\qquad\quad$ = 113.7
    $\qquad\qquad\qquad\quad$ = 114

5. Find the number of octants the arc passes through. In this example, the arc starts in the first octant and ends in the fourth octant. Therefore, the number of octants the arc passes through is four (counterclockwise).

6. Find the octant where the arc starts. In this example it starts in the 0 octant.

7. Substitute the values in the general format of the fractional arc.

    11,(114,28,0,3,004)

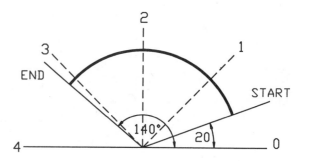

The following shape file will generate the fractional arc shown in Figure 29-7:

*221,8,FOCT2
001,11,(114,28,0,3,004),0

Figure 29-7 Fractional arc

Code 00C or 12: Arc definition by displacement and bulge

Code C can be used to define an arc by specifying the displacement of the endpoint of an arc and the bulge factor. X and Y displacements may range from -127 to +127, and the bulge factor can also range from -127 to +127. A semicircle will have a bulge factor of 127, and a straight line will have a bulge factor of 0. If the bulge factor has a negative sign, the arc is drawn clockwise.

*Bulge factor = ((2 * H)/D) * 127*

$\qquad\qquad\qquad\qquad\qquad$ *Displacement*
$\qquad\qquad\qquad\qquad$ *Height of arc*

For a semicircle, 2H	= D
Therefore, bulge	= (D/D) * 127
	= 127
For a straight line, H	= 0
Therefore, bulge	= (0/D) * 127
	= 0

In Figure 29-8, the distance between the start and end point of an arc is 4 units and the height is 1 unit. Therefore, bulge can be calculated by substituting the values in the above-mentioned relation.

$$\text{Bulge} = (2 * 1/4) * 127$$
$$= 63.5$$
$$= 63 \text{ (Integer)}$$

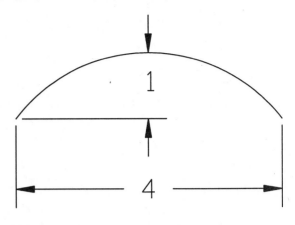

The following shape description will generate the arc shown in Figure 29-8.

```
*213,5,BULGE1
12,(4,0,-63),0
```
— Bulge factor
— Negative (-), generates clockwise arc
— Y-Displacement
— X-Displacement

Figure 29-8 Calculating bulge

Code 00D or 13: Multiple bulge-specified arc

Code 00D or 13 can be used to generate multiple arcs with different bulge factors. It is terminated by a (0,0). The following shape description defines the arc configuration of Figure 29-9.

```
*214,16,BULGE2
13,(4,0,-111),
(0,4,63),
(-4,0,-111),
(0,-4,63),(0,0),0
```

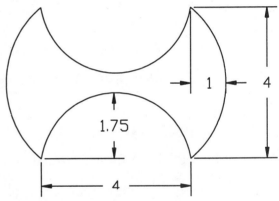

Code 00E or 14: Flag vertical text

Figure 29-9 Different arc configuration

Code 00E or 14 is used when the same text font description is to be used in both the horizontal and vertical orientation. If the text drawn is in a horizontal direction, the vector next to code 14 is ignored. If the text is drawn in a vertical position, the vector next to code 14 is not ignored. This lets you generate text in a vertical or horizontal direction with the same shape file.

For the horizontal text the start point is the lower-left point, and the endpoint is on the lower right. In the vertical text the start point is at the top center, and the endpoint is at the bottom center of the text, as shown in Figure 29-10. At first, it appears that you need two separate shape files to define the shape of a horizontal and a vertical text. However, with code 14 you can avoid the dual shape definition:

Figure 29-10 shows the pen movements for generating text character "G". If the text is horizontal the line that is next to code 14 is automatically ignored. However, if the text is vertical the line is not ignored.

```
1*15,28,FLAG
002,14, ————————— If text is horizontal, code 14
008,(-2,-6),          automatically ignores next line.
042,001,              008, (-2,-6),
014,016,028,01A,
```

```
04C,01E,020,012,014,
002,018,
001,020,01C,
002,01E,
14,  ─────────────      If text is horizontal, code 14
008,(-4,-1),             automatically ignores next line.
0                        008,(-4,-1),
```

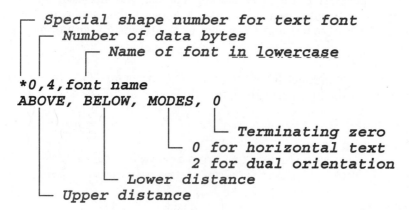

Figure 29-10   Pen movement for generating the character "G"

TEXT FONT FILES

In addition to shape files, AutoCAD provides a facility to create new text fonts. After you have created and compiled a text font file, text can be inserted in a drawing like regular text and using the new font. These text files are regular shape files with some additional information about the text font description and the line feed. The following is the general layout of the text font file:

Text font description
Line feed
Shape definition

Text Font Description

The text font description consists of two lines:

```
        ┌─ Special shape number for text font
           ┌─ Number of data bytes
              ┌─ Name of font in lowercase

*0,4,font name
ABOVE, BELOW, MODES, 0
                              ┌─ Terminating zero
                        └─ 0 for horizontal text
                           2 for dual orientation
                 └─ Lower distance
        └─ Upper distance
```

For example, if you are writing a shape definition for uppercase character M the text font description would be:

*0,4,ucm
10,4,2,0

In the first line, the first data byte (0) is a special shape number for the text font, and every text font file will have this shape number. The next data byte (4) is the number of data bytes in the next line, and ucm is the shape name (name of font). The shape names in all text font files should be lowercase so that the computer does not have to save the names in memory. You can still reference the shape names for editing.

In the second line, the first data byte (10) specifies the height of an uppercase letter above the baseline. For example, in Figure 29-10 the height of the letter M is 10 units above the baseline. The next data byte (4) specifies the distance of lowercase letters below the baseline. AutoCAD uses this information to scale the text automatically. For example, if you enter the height of text as 1 unit, the text will be 1 unit although it was drawn 10 units high in the text font definition. The third data byte (2) defines the mode. It can have only two values, 0 or 2. If the text is horizontal the mode is 0; and if the text has dual orientation (horizontal or vertical) the mode is 2. The fourth data byte (0) is the terminating zero that terminates the definition.

Line Feed

The line feed is used to space the lines so that the characters do not overlap, and so that a desired distance is maintained between the lines. AutoCAD has reserved shape number 10 to define the line feed.

```
        ┌─ (10) Reserved shape number for line feed
        │  ┌─ (5) Number of data bytes in shape specification
        │  │  ┌─ (1f) Shape name
        │  │  │
       *10,5,1f
       2,8,(0,-14),0
       │ │  │        └─ Terminating zero
       │ │  └─ Line feed of 14 units
       └─ Deactivate pen (pen-up)
```

In the first line, the first data byte (10) is reserved shape number for line feed, and the next data byte (5) is the number of characters in the shape specification. The data byte 1f is the name of the shape.

In the second line, the first data byte (2) deactivates the pen. The next data byte (8) is a special code, 008, that defines a vector by X-displacement and Y-displacement. The third and fourth data bytes (0,-14) are X-displacement and Y-displacement of the displacement vector, and produce a line feed that is 14 units below the baseline. The fifth data byte (0) is the terminating zero that terminates the shape definition.

Shape Definition

The shape number in the shape definition of the text font corresponds to the ASCII code for that character. For example, if you are writing a shape definition for an uppercase character M the shape number is 77.

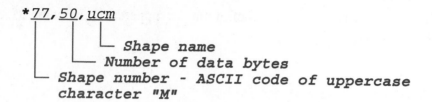

The ASCII codes can be obtained from the ASCII character table, which gives the ASCII codes for all characters, numbers, and punctuation marks.

Example 5

Write a text font shape file for the uppercase character M as shown in Figure 29-11. The font file should be able to generate horizontal and vertical text. Each grid is 1 unit, and the directions of vectors are designated with leader lines. In the following file the line numbers at the right are not a part of the file; they are for reference only.

*0,4,uppercase m	1
10,0,2,0	2
*10,13,lf	3
002,8,(0,-14),14,9,(0,14),(14,0),(0,0),0	4
*77,51,ucm	5
2,14,8,(-5,-10),	6
001,009,(0,10),(1,0),(4,-6),(4,6),(1,0),	7
(0,-10),(-1,0),(0,0),	8
003,2,	9
009,(0,17),(-7,-11),(-2,0),(-7,11),	10
(0,-17),(-2,0),(0,0),	11
002,8,(28,0),	12
004,2,	13
14,8,(-9,-4),0	14

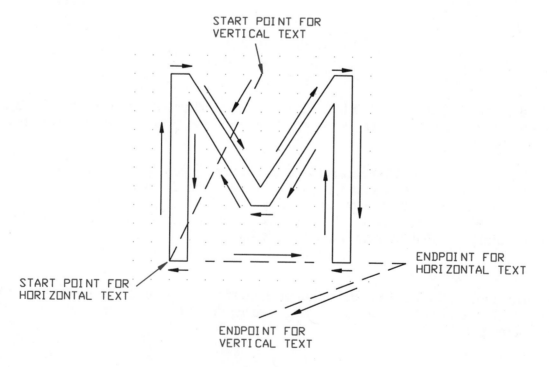

Figure 29-11 Shape and pen movement of the uppercase character "M"

Explanation

Line 1
*0,4,uppercase m
The first data byte (0) is the special shape number for the text font file. The next data byte (4) is the number of data bytes, and the third data byte is the name of the shape.

Line 2
10,0,2,0
The first data byte (10) represents total height of the character M, and the second data byte (0) represents the length of the lowercase letters that extend below the base line. Data byte 2 is the text mode for dual orientation (horizontal and vertical) of the text. If the text was required in the horizontal direction only, the mode is 0. The fourth data byte (0) is the terminating zero that terminates the definition of this particular shape.

Line 3
*10,13,lf
The first data byte (10) is the reserved code for line feed, and the second data byte (13) is the number of data bytes in the shape specification. The third data byte (lf) is the name of the shape.

Line 4
002,8,(0,-14),14,9,(0,14),(14,0),(0,0),0
The first data byte (002 or 2) is the code to deactivate the pen (pen-up). The next three data bytes (8,(0,-14)) define a displacement vector whose X-displacement and Y-displacement are 0 and -14 units, respectively. This will cause a carriage return that is 14 units below the text insertion point of the first text line. This will work fine if the text is drawn in a horizontal direction only. However, if the text is vertical, the carriage return should produce a displacement to the right of the existing line. This is accomplished by the next seven data bytes. Data byte 14 ignores the next code if the text is horizontal. If the text is vertical, the next code is processed. The next set of data bytes (0,14) defines a displacement vector that is 14 units below the previous point, D1 in Figure 29-12.

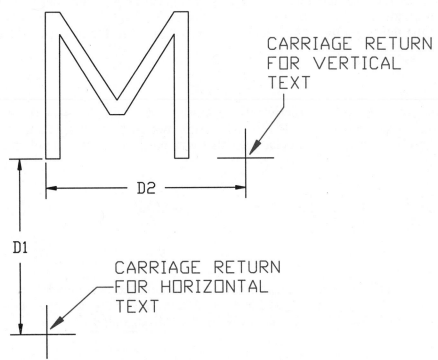

Figure 29-12 Carriage return for vertical and horizontal text

Data bytes 14,0 define a displacement vector that is 14 units to the right, D2 in Figure 29-12. These four data bytes combined will result in a carriage return that is 4 units to the right of the existing line. The next set of data bytes (0,0) terminates the code 9, and the last data byte (0) terminates the shape specification.

Line 5
*77,51,ucm
The first data byte (77) is the ASCII code of the uppercase character M. The second data byte (51) is the number of data bytes in the shape specification. The next data byte (ucm) is the name of the shape file in lowercase letters.

Line 6
2,14,8,(-5,-10),
The first data byte code (2) deactivates the pen (pen-up), and the next data byte code (14) will cause the next code to be ignored if the text is horizontal. In the horizontal text the insertion point of the text is the starting point of that text line (Figure 29-11). However, if the text is vertical the starting point of the text is the upper middle point of the character M. This is accomplished by the next three data bytes (8,(-5,-10)), which displace the starting point of the text 5 units (width of character M is 10) to the left and 10 (height of character M is 10) units down.

Line 7,8
001,009,(0,10),(1,0),(4,-6),(4,6),(1,0),
(0,-10),(-1,0),(0,0),
The first byte (001) activates the draw mode (pen down), and the remaining bytes define the next seven vectors.

Line 9,10,11
003,2,
009,(0,17),(-7,-11),(-2,0),(-7,11),
(0,-17),(-2,0),(0,0),
The inner vertical line of the right leg of character M is 8.5 units long, and you cannot define a vector that is not an integer. However, you can define a vector that is 17 units (2 x 8.5) long and then divide that vector by two to get a vector 8.5 units long. This is accomplished by code 003 and the next data byte two. All the vectors defined in the next two lines will be divided by two.

Line 12
002,8,(28,0),
The first data byte (002) deactivates the draw mode, and the next three data bytes define a vector that is 14 units (28/2=14) to right. This means the next character will start 4 units (14-10) to the right of the existing character that will produce a horizontal text.

Line 13
004,2,
The code 004 multiplies the vectors that follow it by two, therefore it nullifies the effect of code 003,2.

Line 14
14,8,(-9,-4),0
If the text is vertical the next letter should start below the previous letter. This is accomplished by data bytes 8,(-9,-4), which define a vector that is -9 units along X-axis, and -4 units along Y-axis. The data byte 0 terminates the definition of the shape.

```
REVIEW QUESTIONS
```

Fill in the blanks.

1.   The basic objects used in the shape files are _____ and _____.

2.   Shape files are easy to insert and take less disk space than to _____. However, there are some disadvantages to using shapes. For example, you cannot _____ a shape.

3.   The shape number could be any number between 1 and _____ in a particular file, and these numbers cannot be repeated within the same file.

4.   The shape file may not contain two _____ with the same name.

5.   A hexadecimal number is designated by leading _____.

6.   The maximum number of data bytes is _____ bytes per shape.

7.   To define a vector you need its magnitude and _____.

8.   Do not include the extension with the _____.

9.   To load the shape file, use AutoCAD's _____ command.

10. Generating the shapes with the direction vectors has some limitations. For example, you cannot draw an arc or draw a line that is not along the _____ vectors. These limitations can be overcome by using the _____, which add a lot of flexibility and give you better control over the shapes you want to create.

11. Code 001 activates the _____ mode, and code _____ deactivates the draw mode.

12. The byte that follows the division code divides the _____ vectors.

13. Code 004 is used if you want to multiply the vectors by a certain number. It also can be used to _____ the effect of code 003.

14. Scale factors are _____.

15. The number of saves (Code 005) is equal the number of _____ code _____.

16. The maximum number of saves and restores you can use in a particular shape definition is _____.

17. You can define a subshape like a subroutine in a program. To reference the subshape use code _____.

18. Vector can be drawn in the 16 predefined directions only, and the length of the vector cannot exceed _____ units.

19. A nonstandard fractional arc can be generated by using code 00B or _____.

20. Code _____ can be used to define an arc by specifying the displacement of the endpoint of an arc and the bulge factor.

EXERCISES

Exercise 1

Write a shape file for the uppercase M shown in Figure 29-13.

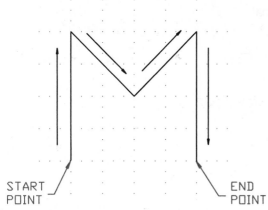

Figure 29-13 Uppercase letter M

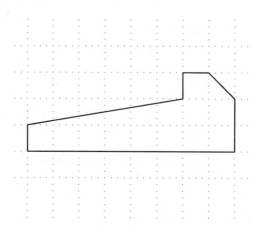

Figure 29-14 Tapered gib-head key

Exercise 2

Write a shape file for generating the tapered gib-head key shown in Figure 29-14.

Exercise 3

Write a text font shape file for the uppercase G shown in Figure 29-15.

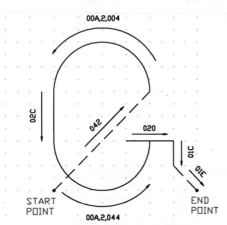

Figure 29-15 Uppercase letter G

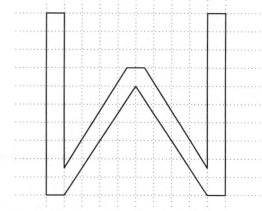

Figure 29-16 Uppercase letter W

Exercise 4

Write a text font shape file for the uppercase W shown in Figure 29-16. The font file should be able to generate horizontal and vertical text.

Chapter 30

Screen Menus

Learning objectives

After completing this chapter, you will be able to:
- Write screen menus.
- Load screen menus.
- Write submenus and referencing submenus.
- Write menu files with multiple submenus.
- Write menus for foreign languages.

AUTOCAD MENU

The AutoCAD menu provides a powerful tool to customize AutoCAD. The AutoCAD software package comes with a standard menu file named **ACAD.MNU**. When you start AutoCAD, the menu file ACAD.MNU is automatically compiled and loaded. The AutoCAD menu file contains AutoCAD commands, separated under different headings for easy identification. For example, all draw commands are under DRAW and all editing commands are under EDIT. The headings are named and arranged to make it easier for you to locate and access the commands. However, there are some commands that you may never use. Also, some users might like to regroup and rearrange the commands so that it is easier to get access to the most frequently used ones.

The AutoCAD software also comes with the menu lisp file, **ACAD.MNL**, and the menu definition file, **ACAD.MND**. The ACAD.MNL file contains the definitions of the AutoLISP expressions that can be used in the menu file. For example, the AutoLISP expression RECTANG, defined in the ACAD.MNL file, can be used with any menu item in the menu file. The menu lisp file ACAD.MNL is automatically loaded in the memory when the menu file with the same filename (**ACAD.MNU**) is loaded. The AutoCAD menu definition file, **ACAD.MND**, contains the definitions of various macros. This file is not loaded automatically when you start AutoCAD or load a menu file. It must be compiled using the **MC executable file** that is located in the SAMPLE subdirectory.

AutoCAD lets the user eliminate rarely used commands from the menu file and define new ones. This is made possible by editing the existing ACAD.MNU file, or writing a new menu file. There is no limit to the number of files you can write. You can have a separate menu file for each application. For example, you can have separate menu files for mechanical, electrical, or architectural drawings. You can load these menu files any time by using AutoCAD's MENU command. The menu files are text files with the extension .MNU. These files can be written by using AutoCAD's EDIT command (provided ACAD.PGP file is present and EDIT command is defined in the file), EDIT or Edlin function of DOS, or any Text Editor.

The menu file can be divided into six sections, each section identified by a section label. AutoCAD uses the following labels to identify different sections of AutoCAD menu file:

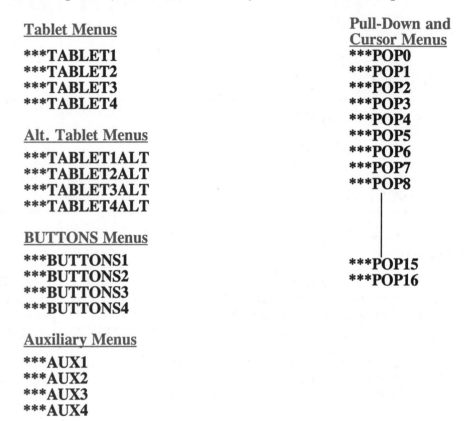

***SCREEN	
***TABLET(n)	------- n is from 1 to 4
***IMAGE	
***POP(n)	------- n is from 0 to 16
***BUTTONS(n)	------- n is from 1 to 4
***AUX(n)	------- n is from 1 to 4

The tablet menu can have up to four different sections. The POP menu (pull-down and cursor menu) can have up to 16 sections, and auxiliary and buttons menus up to four sections.

Tablet Menus

***TABLET1
***TABLET2
***TABLET3
***TABLET4

Alt. Tablet Menus

***TABLET1ALT
***TABLET2ALT
***TABLET3ALT
***TABLET4ALT

BUTTONS Menus

***BUTTONS1
***BUTTONS2
***BUTTONS3
***BUTTONS4

Auxiliary Menus

***AUX1
***AUX2
***AUX3
***AUX4

Pull-Down and
Cursor Menus
***POP0
***POP1
***POP2
***POP3
***POP4
***POP5
***POP6
***POP7
***POP8

***POP15
***POP16

SCREEN MENU

When you are in the AutoCAD Drawing Editor the screen menu is displayed on the right-hand side of the computer screen. The AutoCAD screen menu displays AutoCAD at the top, followed by asterisk signs(* * * *) and a list of commands (Figure 30-1).

The screen menu is a powerful tool when customizing AutoCAD. If it is developed properly it can save a lot of time, and make the system more efficient. Depending on the scope of the menu, the size of the menu file can vary from a few lines to several hundred. A menu file consists of section labels, submenus, and menu items. A menu item consists of an item label and a command definition. The menu item label is enclosed in brackets and the command definition is outside the brackets.

The menu item label that is enclosed in the brackets is displayed in the screen menu area of the monitor and is not a part of the command definition. The command definition, the part of the menu item outside the bracket, is the executable part of the menu item. To understand the process of developing and writing a screen menu, consider the following example:

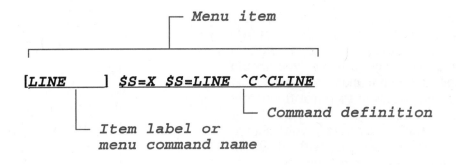

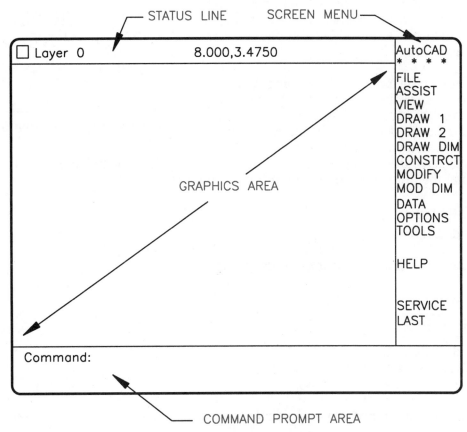

Figure 30-1 Screen display

Example 1

Write a screen menu for the following AutoCAD commands (filename SM1.MNU).

Line
Circle C,R
Circle C,D
Circle 2P
Erase
Move

The layout of these commands is shown in Figure 30-2. This menu is named MENU-1 and it should be displayed at the top of the screen menu. It lets you know the menu you are using.

Before you write a menu, you need to design a menu, and know the exact sequence of AutoCAD commands and the prompts associated with a particular command. To design a menu, you should select and arrange the commands in a way that provides you with easy access to the most frequently used commands. A careful design will save a lot of time in the long run. Therefore, you should consider several possible designs with different command combinations, then select the one that is best suited for the job. Suggestions from other CAD operators can prove very valuable. The screen menu layout as shown in Figure 30-2 is one of the possible designs.

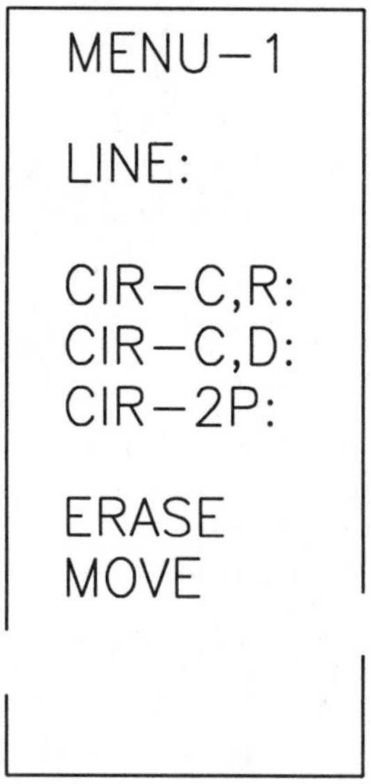

```
MENU-1

LINE:

CIR-C,R:
CIR-C,D:
CIR-2P:

ERASE
MOVE
```

Figure 30-2 Layout of screen menu

The second important thing in developing a screen menu is to know the exact sequence of the commands and the prompts associated with each command. To better determine the prompt entries that are required in a command, you should enter all the commands and the prompt entries at the keyboard. The following is a description of the commands and the prompt entries required for Example 1:

LINE Command

Command: **LINE**

Notice the command and prompt entry sequence
LINE
<RETURN>

CIRCLE (C,R) Command

Command: **CIRCLE**
3P/2P/TTR/<Center point>:
Diameter/<Radius>:

Notice the command and prompt entries sequence
CIRCLE
<RETURN>
Center point
<RETURN>
Radius
<RETURN>

CIRCLE (C,D) Command

Command: **CIRCLE**
3P/2P/TTR/<Center point>:
Diameter/<Radius>: D
Diameter:

Notice the command and prompt entries sequence
CIRCLE
<RETURN>
Center Point
<RETURN>
D

<RETURN>
Diameter
<RETURN>

CIRCLE (2P) Command

Command: **CIRCLE**
3P/2P/TTR/<Center Point>: **2P**
First point on diameter:
Second point on diameter:

Notice the command and prompt entries sequence
CIRCLE
<RETURN>
2P
<RETURN>
Select first point on diameter
<RETURN>
Select second point on diameter
<RETURN>

ERASE Command

Command: **ERASE**

Notice the command and prompt entry sequence
ERASE
<RETURN>

MOVE Command

Command: **MOVE**

Notice the command and prompt entry sequence
MOVE
<RETURN>

The difference between the Center-Radius and Center-Diameter options of the CIRCLE command is that in the first one the RADIUS is the default, whereas in the second one you need to enter D to use the diameter option. This difference, although minor, is very important when writing a menu file. Similarly, the 2P (two-point) option of the CIRCLE command is different from the other two. Therefore, it is important to know the correct sequence of the AutoCAD commands, and the entries made in response to the prompts associated with those commands.

You can use AutoCAD's EDIT command, EDIT or Edlin function of DOS to write the menu file. If you use the EDIT command, AutoCAD will prompt you to enter the filename you want to edit. The filename can be up to eight characters long and the file extension must be .MNU. If the file name exists it will be automatically loaded; otherwise a new file will be created. For Example 1 the file name is SM1.MNU. SM1 is the name of the screen menu file, and .MNU is the extension of this file. All menu files have the extension .MNU.

If you want to use the Edlin or EDIT function of DOS, you can access the DOS commands from the drawing editor by typing SHELL or SH, and then you can use the DOS functions. If SHELL, SH, or AutoCAD's EDIT command does not work, check the ACAD.PGP file and make sure that these commands are defined in the file. The following file is a listing of the screen menu for Example 1. The line numbers on the right are not a part of the file. They are shown here for reference only.

```
        ***SCREEN                               1
        [ MENU-1    ]                           2
        [           ]                           3
        [           ]                           4
        [LINE       ]^C^CLINE                   5
        [           ]                           6
        [CIR-C,R    ]^C^CCIRCLE                 7
        [CIR-C,D    ]^C^CCIRCLE;\D              8
        [CIR- 2P    ]^C^CCIRCLE;2P              9
        [           ]                          10
        [ERASE      ]^C^CERASE                 11
        [MOVE       ]^C^CMOVE                  12
```

Line 1
***SCREEN
***SCREEN is the section label for the screen menu. The lines that follow the screen menu are treated as a part of this menu. The screen menu definition will be terminated by another section label like ***TABLET1 or ***POP1.

Line 2
[MENU-1]
This menu item displays MENU-1 on the screen. Anything that is inside the brackets is for display only and does not have any effect on the command. The maximum number of characters or spaces that can be displayed inside these brackets is eight, because the width of the screen menu column on the screen is eight characters. If the number of characters is more than eight, the remaining characters are not displayed on the screen and can be used for comments. The part of the menu item that is outside the brackets is executed even if the number of characters inside the bracket is more than eight.

Lines 3 and 4
[   ]
These menu items print a blank line on the screen menu. There are eight blank spaces inside the bracket. When eight blank spaces are printed on the screen menu, it displays a blank line. This line does not contain anything outside the bracket, therefore no command is executed. To provide the space in the menu you can also leave a blank space in the menu file, or have two brackets ([ ]). The next line, line 4, also prints a blank line.

Line 5
[LINE   ]^C^CLINE
This menu item displays LINE on the screen. The first ^C (caret C) cancels the existing command, and the **second** ^C cancels the command again. The two CANCEL (^C^C) commands are required to make sure that the existing commands are canceled before executing a new command. Most AutoCAD commands can be cancelled with just one CANCEL command. However, some commands, like dimensioning and pedit, need to be canceled twice to get out of the command. **LINE** will prompt the user to enter the points to draw a line. Since there is nothing after the LINE, it automatically enters a RETURN.

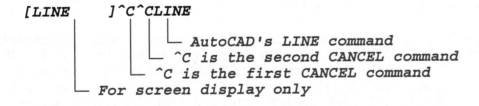

Line 7
[CIR-C,R]^C^CCIRCLE
The part of the menu item that is enclosed within the brackets is for screen display only. The part of the menu item that is outside the brackets is executed when this line is selected. ^C^C (caret C) cancels the existing command twice. CIRCLE is an AutoCAD command that generates a circle. **The space after CIRCLE automatically causes a RETURN.**

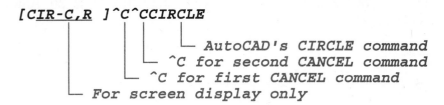

```
[CIR-C,R ]^C^CCIRCLE
                      └─ AutoCAD's CIRCLE command
                └─ ^C for second CANCEL command
             └─ ^C for first CANCEL command
       └─ For screen display only
```

Line 8
[CIR-C,D]^C^CCIRCLE;\D
The part of the menu item that is enclosed in the brackets is for screen display only, and the part that is outside the brackets is the executable part. ^C^C will cancel the existing command twice.

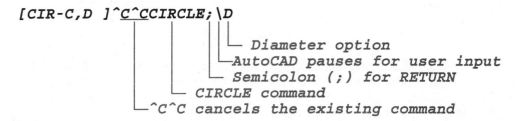

```
[CIR-C,D ]^C^CCIRCLE;\D
                         └─ Diameter option
                       └─ AutoCAD pauses for user input
                     └─ Semicolon (;) for RETURN
               └─ CIRCLE command
           └─ ^C^C cancels the existing command
```

The CIRCLE command is followed by a semicolon, backslash (\), and D for diameter option. **The semicolon (;) after the CIRCLE command causes RETURN which has the same effect as entering RETURN at the keyboard. The backslash (\) pauses for user input.** In this case it is the center point of the circle. D is for the diameter option and it is automatically followed by RETURN. The semicolon in the above example can also be replaced by a blank space as shown in the following line. However, the semicolon is easier to spot.

```
[CIR-C,R ]^C^CCIRCLE \D
                      └─ Blank space for RETURN
```

Line 9
[CIR- 2P]^C^CCIRCLE;2P
In this menu item ^C^C cancels the existing command twice. The semicolon after CIRCLE enters a RETURN. 2P is for the two-point option followed by the blank space that causes RETURN. You will notice that the sequence of the commands is the same as discussed earlier. Therefore, it is essential to know the exact sequence of the commands, otherwise the screen menu is not going to work.

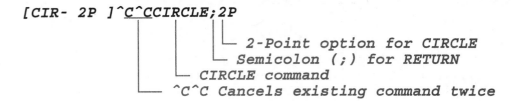

```
[CIR- 2P ]^C^CCIRCLE;2P
                        └─ 2-Point option for CIRCLE
                      └─ Semicolon (;) for RETURN
                └─ CIRCLE command
              └─ ^C^C Cancels existing command twice
```

The semicolon after the CIRCLE command can be replaced by a blank space as shown in the following line. The blank space causes a RETURN like a semicolon (;).

[CIR- 2P]^C^CCIRCLE 2P

                     └ *Blank space or semicolon for RETURN*

Line 11
[ERASE   ]^C^CERASE
In this menu item ^C^C cancels the existing command twice and ERASE is an AutoCAD command that erases the selected objects.

[ERASE   ]^C^CERASE

                └ *AutoCAD's ERASE command*

Line 12
[MOVE   ]^C^CMOVE
In this menu item ^C^C cancels the existing command twice, and the MOVE command will move the selected objects.

[MOVE   ]^C^CMOVE

                └ *AutoCAD's MOVE command*

From this example it is clear that every statement in the screen menu is based on the AutoCAD commands and the information that is needed to complete that command. This forms the basis for creating a menu file and should be given consideration. Following is a summary of the AutoCAD commands used in Example 1, and their equivalent in the menu file:

AutoCAD Commands	Menu File
Command: **LINE**	**[LINE]^C^CLINE**
Command: **CIRCLE** 3P/2P/TTR/ < Center point > : Diameter/ < Radius > :	**[CIR-C,R]^C^CCIRCLE**
Command: **CIRCLE** 3P/2P/TTR/ < Center point > : Diameter/ < Radius > : D Diameter:	**[CIR-C,D]^C^CCIRCLE;\D**
Command: **CIRCLE** 3P/2P/TTR/ < Center point > : **2P** First point on diameter: Second point on diameter:	**[CIR- 2P]^C^CCIRCLE;2P**
Command: **ERASE**	**[ERASE]^C^CERASE**
Command: **MOVE**	**[MOVE]^C^CMOVE**

LOADING MENUS

AutoCAD automatically loads the ACAD.MNX file when you get into AutoCAD's Drawing Editor. The ACAD.MNX file is the compiled form of the ACAD.MNU file. However, you can also load a different menu file by using AutoCAD's MENU command.

```
Command: Menu
Menu filename <ACAD>: SM1
```
— Name of menu file
— Default menu file

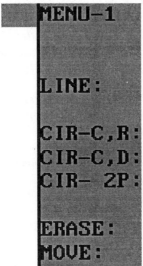

Figure 30-3 Screen menu display

After entering the MENU command, AutoCAD will prompt for the filename. Enter the name of the menu file without the file extension (.MNU), since AutoCAD assumes the extension .MNU. AutoCAD will automatically compile the menu file and load the new compiled menu file. The extension of a compiled menu file is .MNX. The compiled file is displayed on the screen. After you load the menu file SM1, your menu will be displayed on the screen (Figure 30-3). Now you can test the menu by selecting different commands from this menu.

When you save the drawing, AutoCAD saves the name of the menu file used for the drawing. When you load the drawing, the menu file is automatically loaded. AutoCAD uses the following sequence to load a menu file

1. When you load a drawing or a menu, AutoCAD locates the named menu file (.mnu). After locating the menu file, AutoCAD searches for the compiled menu file (.mnx) with the same name. If the compiled (.mnx) file bears the same date or a later date than that of the menu (.mnu) file, AutoCAD loads the compiled file (.mnx file). Otherwise, AutoCAD compiles the menu file to generate a new .mnx file and then the compiled file is loaded.

2. If AutoCAD cannot locate the menu (.mnu) file, it searches for the compiled menu (.mnx) file. If AutoCAD is successful in locating the .mnx file, it is loaded. If AutoCAD cannot locate either file (.mnu or .mnx), an error message is displayed.

3. After compiling and loading the menu file, AutoCAD searches for the menu lisp (.mnl) file with the same name as that of the menu file. Once the file is located, AutoCAD evaluates the AutoLISP expressions defined in the file.

Note

1. After you load the new menu, you cannot use the pull-down menu, button menu, or digitizer because the original menu ACAD.MNU is not present and the new menu does not contain these menu areas.

2. To activate the original menu again, load the menu file by using the MENU command:

Command: **Menu**
Menu file name or . for none <SM1>: **ACAD**

3. If you need to use input from a keyboard or a pointing device, use the backslash (\). The system will pause for you to enter data.

4. There should be no space after the backslash (\).

5. The menu items, menu labels, and command definition can be uppercase, lowercase, or mixed.

6. You can introduce spaces between the menu items to improve the readability of the menu file.

7. If there are more items in the menu than the number of spaces available, the excess items are not displayed on the screen. For example, if the display device limits the number of items to 21, items in excess of 21 will not be displayed on the screen, and are therefore inaccessible.

8. If you configure AutoCAD and turn off the screen prompt area or use a high-resolution graphics board, you can increase the number of lines that can be displayed on the screen menu. On some devices this is 80 lines.

9. If you want to protect your menu files from accidental editing, compile the new menu file by loading the menu, then delete the menu file. Do not delete the file with extension .MNX (compiled file).

Exercise 1

Design and write a screen menu for the following AutoCAD commands (filename SME1.MNU):

> PLINE
> ELLIPSE (Center)
> ELLIPSE (Axis endpoint)
> ROTATE
> OFFSET
> SCALE

SUBMENUS

The screen menu file can be so large that all the items cannot be accommodated on one screen. For example, the maximum number of items that can be displayed on most screens is 21. If the screen menu has more than 21 items, the menu items in excess of 21 are not displayed on the screen and therefore cannot be accessed. You can overcome this problem by using submenus that enable the user to define smaller groups of items within a menu section. When a submenu is selected, it loads the submenu items and displays them on the screen. However, depending on the resolution of the monitor and the graphics card, the number of items that you can display on the screen can be higher and you may not need submenus.

Submenu Definition

A submenu definition consists of two asterisk signs (**) followed by the name of the submenu. A menu can have any number of submenus, and every submenu should have a unique name. The items that follow a submenu, up to the next section label, or submenu label, belong to that submenu. The format of a submenu definition is:

```
**Name
   |   |
   |   └─ Name of the submenu
   └─ Two asterisk signs (**) designate a submenu

**DRAW1
   |   |
   |   └─ Name of the submenu
   └─ ** Designates that DRAW1 is a submenu
```

> **Note**
>
> *The submenu name can be up to 31 characters long.*
>
> *The submenu name can consist of letters, digits, and such special characters as $ (dollar sign), - (hyphen), and _ (underscore).*
>
> *The submenu name should not have any embedded blanks (spaces).*
>
> *The submenu names should be unique in a menu file.*

Submenu Reference

The submenu reference is used to reference or load a submenu. It consists of a "$" sign followed by a letter that specifies the menu section. The letter that specifies a screen menu section is S. The section is followed by "=" sign, and the name of the submenu the user wants to activate. The submenu name should be without **. The following is the format of a submenu reference:

```
$Section=Submenu
    │      │    └── Name of submenu
    │      └── "=" sign
    └── Menu section specifier
    └── "$" sign
```

```
$S=EDIT
 │  └── Name of submenu
 └── S-Specifies screen menu section
```

> **Note**
>
> | $ | *A special character code that is used to load a submenu in a menu file.* |
> |---|---|
> | S | *Specifies the SCREEN menu.* |
> | P0 - P16 | *Specifies the POP menus, POP0 through POP16.* |
> | I | *Specifies the ICON menu.* |
> | B1 - B4 | *Specifies the BUTTONS menu, B1 through B4.* |
> | T1 - T4 | *Specifies the TABLET menus, T1 through T4.* |
> | A1 - A4 | *Specifies the AUX menu, A1 through A4.* |
> | $M= | *This is used to load a DIESEL macro from a menu item.* |

Nested Submenus

When a submenu is activated, the current menu is copied to a stack. If you select another submenu, the submenu that was current will be copied or pushed to the top of the stack. The maximum number of menus that can be stacked is eight. If the stack size increases to more than eight, the menu at the bottom of the stack is removed and forgotten. You can call the previous submenu by using the nested submenu call. The format of this call is:

```
$S=
 │ └── "=" sign
 └── Screen menu specifier
 └── "$" sign
```

The maximum number of nested submenu calls is eight. Each time you call a submenu, this pops the last item from the stack and reactivates it.

Example 2

Design a menu layout and write a screen menu for the following commands:

LINE	ERASE
PLINE	MOVE
ELLIPSE-C	ROTATE
ELLIPSE-E	OFFSET
CIR-C,R	COPY
CIR-C,D	SCALE
CIR- 2P	

As mentioned earlier, the first and the most important part of writing a menu is the design of the menu and knowing the commands and the prompts associated with these commands. You should know the way you want the menu to look, and the way you want to arrange the commands for maximum efficiency. Write the menu on a piece of paper and check it thoroughly to make sure that you have arranged the commands the way you want them. Use submenus to group the commands together based on their use, function, and relationship with other submenus. Make provision to access other frequently used commands without going through the root menu.

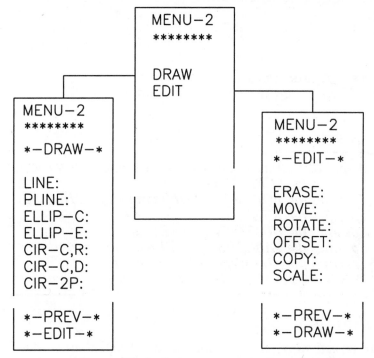

Figure 30-4 Screen menu design

Figure 30-4 shows one of the possible arrangements of the commands and the design of the screen menu. It has one main menu and two submenus. One of the submenus is for draw commands, the other is for edit commands. The colon (:) at the end of the commands is not required. It is used here to distinguish the commands from those items that are not used as commands. For example, DRAW in the root menu is not a command, therefore it has no colon at the end. On the other hand, if you select ERASE from the EDIT menu, it executes the ERASE command so it has a colon (:) at the end of the command.

The following file is a listing of the menu file of Example 1. The line numbers on the right are not a part of the file; they are given here for reference only.

```
***SCREEN                                               1
[ MENU-2   ]                                            2
[*******   ]                                            3
[          ]                                            4
[          ]                                            5
[          ]                                            6
[          ]                                            7
[DRAW      ]^C^C$S=DRAW                                 8
[EDIT      ]^C^C$S=EDIT                                 9
                                                        10
**DRAW                                                  11
[ MENU-2   ]^C^C$S=SCREEN                               12
[*******   ]                                            13
[          ]                                            14
[*-DRAW-*  ]                                            15
[          ]                                            16
[LINE:     ]^C^CLINE                                    17
[PLINE:    ]^C^CPLINE;\W;0.1;0.1                        18
[ELLIP-C:  ]^C^CELLIPSE;C                               19
[ELLIP-E:  ]^C^CELLIPSE                                 20
[CIR-C,R:  ]^C^CCIRCLE                                  21
[CIR-C,D:  ]^C^CCIRCLE;\D                               22
[CIR-2P:   ]^C^CCIRCLE;2P                               23
[          ]                                            24
[          ]                                            25
[          ]                                            26
[          ]                                            27
[          ]                                            28
[          ]                                            29
[*-PREV-*  ]^C^C$S=                                     30
[*-EDIT-*  ]^C^C$S=EDIT                                 31
                                                        32
**EDIT                                                  33
[ MENU-2   ]^C^C$S=SCREEN                               34
[*******   ]                                            35
[          ]                                            36
[*-EDIT-*  ]                                            37
[          ]                                            38
[ERASE:    ]^C^CERASE                                   39
[MOVE:     ]^C^CMOVE                                    40
[ROTATE:   ]^C^CROTATE                                  41
[OFFSET:   ]^C^COFFSET                                  42
[COPY:     ]^C^CCOPY                                    43
[SCALE:    ]^C^CSCALE                                   44
[          ]                                            45
[          ]                                            46
[          ]                                            47
[          ]                                            48
[          ]                                            49
[          ]                                            50
[          ]                                            51
[*-PREV-*  ]^C^C$S=                                     52
[*-DRAW-*  ]^C^C$S=DRAW                                 53
```

Line 1
***SCREEN
***SCREEN is the section label for the screen menu.

Line 2
[MENU-2]
This menu item displays MENU-2 at the top of the screen menu.

Line 3
[********]
This menu item prints eight asterisk signs (*******) on the screen menu.

Line 4-7
[   ]
These menu items print four blank lines on the screen menu. The brackets are not required. They could be just four blank lines without brackets.

Line-8
[DRAW   ]^C^C$S=DRAW
[DRAW   ] displays DRAW on the screen, letting you know that by selecting this function you can access the draw commands. ^C^C cancels the existing command twice, and $S=DRAW loads the DRAW submenu on the screen.

```
                              ┌ Name of submenu
                              │
    [DRAW         ]^C^C$S=DRAW
                      │    └ Loads submenu DRAW
                      └Cancels the existing command twice
```

Line 9
[EDIT   ]^C^C$S=EDIT
[EDIT   ] displays EDIT on the screen. ^C^C cancels the current command, and $S=EDIT loads the submenu **EDIT**.

Line 10
The blank lines between the submenus or menu items are not required. It just makes it easy to read the file.

Line 11
**DRAW
**DRAW is the name of the submenu; lines 12 through 31 are defined under this submenu.

Line 15
[*-DRAW-*]
It prints *-DRAW-* on the screen menu as a heading that lets the user know that the commands listed on the screen menu are draw commands.

Line 18
[PLINE:]^C^CPLINE;\W;0.1;0.1
[PLINE:] displays PLINE: on the screen. ^C^C cancels the command twice, and PLINE is AutoCAD's polyline command. The semicolons are for RETURN. The semicolons can be replaced by a blank space. The backslash (\) is for user input. In this case it is the start point of the polyline. W selects the width option of the polyline. The first 0.1 is the starting width and the second 0.1 is the ending width of the polyline. This command will draw a polyline of 0.1 width.

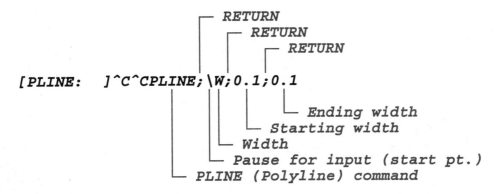

Line 19
[ELLIP-C:]^C^CELLIPSE;C
[ELLIP-C:] displays ELLIP-C: on the screen menu. ^C^C cancels the existing command twice, and ELLIPSE is an AutoCAD command to generate an ellipse. The semicolon is for RETURN, and C selects the center option of the ELLIPSE command.

Line 20
[ELLIP-A:]^C^CELLIPSE
[ELLIP-A:] displays ELLIP-A: on the screen menu. ^C^C cancels the existing command twice, and ELLIPSE is an AutoCAD command. Here the ELLIPSE command uses the default option, axis endpoint, instead of center.

Line 30
[*-PREV-*]^C^C$S=
[*-PREV-*] displays *-PREV-* on the screen menu, and ^C^C cancels the existing command twice. $S= restores the previous menu that was displayed on the screen before loading the current menu.

Line 31
[*-EDIT-*]^C^C$S=EDIT
[*-EDIT-*] displays *-EDIT-* on the screen menu, and ^C^C cancels the existing command twice. $S=EDIT loads the submenu EDIT on the screen. This lets you access the EDIT commands without going back to the root menu and selecting EDIT from there.

Line 33
**EDIT
**EDIT is the name of the submenu, and lines 34 to 53 are defined under this submenu.

Line 34

[MENU-2]^C^C$S=SCREEN

[MENU-2] displays MENU-2 on the screen menu, and ^C^C cancels the existing command twice. $S=SCREEN loads the root menu SCREEN on the screen menu.

Line 39

[ERASE:]^C^CERASE

[ERASE:] displays ERASE: on the screen menu, and ^C^C cancels the existing command twice. ERASE is an AutoCAD command for erasing the selected objects.

Line 53

[*-DRAW-*]^C^C$S=DRAW

$S=DRAW loads the DRAW submenu on the screen. It lets you load the DRAW menu without going through the root menu.

When you select DRAW from the root menu, the submenu DRAW is loaded on the screen. The menu items in the draw submenu completely replace the menu items of the root menu. If you select MENU-2 from the screen menu now, the root menu will be loaded on the screen, but some of the items are not cleared from the screen menu (Figure 30-5). This is because the root menu does not have enough menu items to completely replace the menu items of the DRAW submenu.

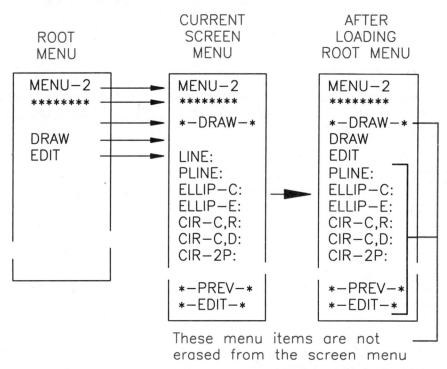

Figure 30-5 Screen menu display after loading the root menu

One of the ways to clear the screen is to define a submenu that has 21 blank lines. When this submenu is loaded it will clear the screen. If you load another submenu now, there will be no overlap, because the screen menu has been already cleared and there are no menu items left on the screen (Figure 30-6). Example 3 illustrates the use of such a submenu.

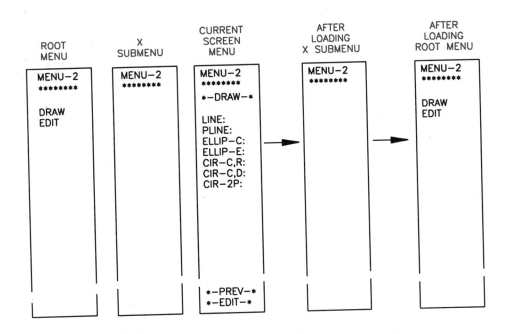

Figure 30-6 Screen menu display after loading the root menu

Another way to avoid overlapping the menu items is to define every submenu so that all of them have the same number of menu items. The disadvantage with this approach is that the menu file will be long, because every submenu will have 21 lines.

Exercise 2

Write a screen menu file for the following AutoCAD commands (filename SM2.MNU).

ARC	MIRROR
-3P	BREAK-F
-SCE	BREAK-@
-SCA	EXTEND
-SCL	STRETCH
-SEA	FILLET-0
POLYGON-C	FILLET
POLYGON-E	CHAMFER

MULTIPLE SUBMENUS

A menu file can have any number of submenus. All the submenu names have two asterisk signs (**) in front of them, even if there is a submenu within a submenu. Also, several submenus can be loaded in a single statement. If there is more than one submenu in a menu item they should be separated by a space. Example 3 illustrates the use of multiple submenus.

Example 3

Design the layout of the menu, then write the screen menu for the following AutoCAD commands.

Draw	ARC	Edit	Display
LINE	3Point	EXTEND	ZOOM
Continue	SCE	STRETCH	REGEN
Close	SCA	FILLET	SCALE
Undo	CSE		PAN
.X	CSA		
.Y	CSL		
.Z			
.XY			
.XZ			
.YZ			

There are several different ways of arranging the commands depending on your requirements. The following layout is one of the possible screen menu designs for the given AutoCAD commands.

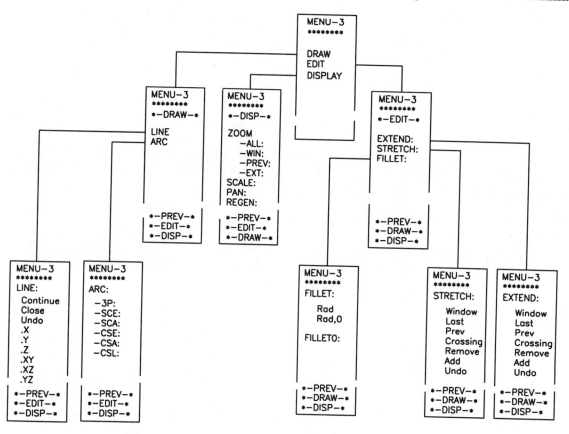

Figure 30-7 Screen menu design with submenus

The name of the following menu file is SM3.MNU. You can use the Edlin function of DOS or a text editor to write the file. The following file is the listing of the menu file SM3.MNU. The line numbers on the right are not a part of the file. They are shown here for reference only.

```
***SCREEN                                                          1
**S                                                                2
[ MENU-3    ]^C^C$S=X $S=S                                          3
[*******    ]$S=OSNAP                                              4
[           ]                                                       5
[           ]                                                       6
[DRAW       ]^C^C$S=X $S=DRAW                                       7
[EDIT       ]^C^C$S=X $S=EDIT                                       8
[DISPLAY    ]^C^C$S=X $S=DISP                                       9
```

```
                                                              10
**DRAW 3                                                      11
[*-DRAW-*  ]                                                  12
[          ]                                                  13
[          ]                                                  14
[LINE:     ]$S=X $S=LINE ^C^CLINE                             15
[ARC:      ]$S=X $S=ARC                                       16
[          ]                                                  17
[          ]                                                  18
[          ]                                                  19
[          ]                                                  20
[          ]                                                  21
[          ]                                                  22
[          ]                                                  23
[          ]                                                  24
[          ]                                                  25
[          ]                                                  26
[*-PREV-*  ]$S= $S=                                           27
[*-EDIT-*  ]^C^C$S=X $S=EDIT                                  28
[*-DISP-*  ]$S=X $S=DISP                                      29
                                                              30
**LINE 3                                                      31
[LINE:     ]^C^CLINE                                          32
[          ]                                                  33
[          ]                                                  34
[Continue  ]^C^CLINE;;                                        35
[Close     ]CLOSE                                             36
[Undo      ]U                                                 37
[.X        ].X                                                38
[.Y        ].Y                                                39
[.Z        ].Z                                                40
[.XY       ].XY                                               41
[.XZ       ].XZ                                               42
[.YZ       ].YZ                                               43
[          ]                                                  44
[          ]                                                  45
[          ]                                                  46
[*-PREV-*  ]$S= $S=                                           47
[*-EDIT-*  ]^C^C$S=X $S=EDIT                                  48
[*-DISP-*  ]$S=X $S=DISP                                      49
                                                              50
**ARC 3                                                       51
[ARC       ]                                                  52
[          ]                                                  53
[   -3P:   ]^C^CARC;\\DRAG                                    54
[   -SCE:  ]^C^CARC;\C;\DRAG                                  55
[   -SCA:  ]^C^CARC;\C;\A;DRAG                                56
[   -CSE:  ]^C^CARC;C;\\DRAG                                  57
[   -CSA:  ]^C^CARC;C;\\A;DRAG                                58
[   -CSL:  ]^C^CARC;C;\\L;DRAG                                59
[          ]                                                  60
[          ]                                                  61
[          ]                                                  62
[          ]                                                  63
[          ]                                                  64
[          ]                                                  65
[          ]                                                  66
```

```
[*-PREV-*   ]$S= $S=                                       67
[*-EDIT-*   ]^C^C$S=X $S=EDIT                              68
[*-DISP-*   ]$S=X $S=DISP                                  69
                                                          70
**EDIT 3                                                  71
[*-EDIT-*   ]                                             72
[           ]                                             73
[           ]                                             74
[EXTEND:    ]$S=X $S=EXTEND ^C^CEXTEND                    75
[STRETCH:   ]$S=X $S=STRETCH ^C^CSTRETCH;C                76
[FILLET:    ]$S=X $S=FILLET ^C^CFILLET                    77
[           ]                                             78
[           ]                                             79
[           ]                                             80
[           ]                                             81
[           ]                                             82
[           ]                                             83
[           ]                                             84
[           ]                                             85
[           ]                                             86
[*-PREV-*   ]$S= $S=                                       87
[*-DRAW-*   ]^C^C$S=X $S=DRAW                              88
[*-DISP-*   ]$S=X $S=DISP                                  89
                                                          90
**EXTEND 3                                                91
[EXTEND:    ]^C^CEXTEND                                   92
[           ]                                             93
Window                                                    94
Last                                                      95
Prev                                                      96
Crossing                                                  97
Remove                                                    98
Add                                                       99
Undo                                                     100
[           ]                                            101
[           ]                                            102
[           ]                                            103
[           ]                                            104
[           ]                                            105
[           ]                                            106
[*-PREV-*   ]$S= $S=                                      107
[*-DRAW-*   ]^C^C$S=X $S=DRAW                             108
[*-DISP-*   ]$S=DISP                                     109
                                                         110
**STRETCH 3                                              111
[STRETCH:   ]^C^CSTRETCH;C                               112
[           ]                                            113
Window                                                   114
Last                                                     115
Prev                                                     116
Crossing                                                 117
Remove                                                   118
Add                                                      119
Undo                                                     120
[           ]                                            121
[           ]                                            122
[           ]                                            123
```

```
[                ]                                              124
[                ]                                              125
[                ]                                              126
[*-PREV-*    ]$S= $S=                                           127
[*-DRAW-*   ]^C^C$S=X $S=DRAW                                   128
[*-DISP-*    ]$S=X $S=DISP                                      129
                                                               130

**FILLET    3                                                  131
[FILLET:    ]^C^CFILLET                                        132
[   Rad      ]R;\FILLET                                         133
[   Rad 0    ]R;0;FILLET                                       134
[                ]                                              135
[FILLET0:   ]^C^CFILLET;R;0;;                                  136
[                ]                                              137
[                ]                                              138
[                ]                                              139
[                ]                                              140
[                ]                                              141
[                ]                                              142
[                ]                                              143
[                ]                                              144
[                ]                                              145
[                ]                                              146
[*-PREV-*    ]$S= $S=                                           147
[*-DRAW-*   ]^C^C$S=X $S=DRAW                                   148
[*-DISP-*    ]$S=X $S=DISP                                      149
                                                               150

**DISP 3                                                       151
[*-DISP-*    ]                                                  152
[                ]                                              153
[                ]                                              154
[ZOOM:      ]'ZOOM                                              155
[  -ALL      ]A                                                 156
[  -WIN     ]W                                                  157
[  -PREV    ]P                                                  158
[  -EXT     ]E                                                  159
[                ]                                              160
[SCALE:     ]'ZOOM                                             161
[PAN:        ]'PAN                                              162
[REGEN:     ]^C^CREGEN                                         163
[                ]                                              164
[                ]                                              165
[                ]                                              166
[*-PREV-*    ]$S= $S=                                           167
[*-EDIT-*    ]^C^C$S=X $S=EDIT                                  168
[*-DRAW-*   ]$S=X $S=DRAW                                       169
                                                               170

**X 3                                                          171
[                ]                                              172
[                ]                                              173
[                ]                                              174
[                ]                                              175
[                ]                                              176
[                ]                                              177
[                ]                                              178
[                ]                                              179
[                ]                                              180
```

```
[                    ]                                          181
[                    ]                                          182
[                    ]                                          183
[                    ]                                          184
[                    ]                                          185
[                    ]                                          186
[                    ]                                          187
[                    ]                                          188
[                    ]                                          189
                                                               190
**OSNAP 2                                                      191
[-OSNAPS-  ]                                                    192
[          ]                                                    193
[Center     ]CEN $S=                                           194
[Endpoint   ]END $S=                                           195
[Insert     ]INS $S=                                           196
[Intersec   ]INT $S=                                           197
[Midpoint   ]MID $S=                                           198
[Nearest    ]NEA $S=                                           199
[Node       ]NOD $S=                                           200
[Perpend    ]PER $S=                                           201
[Quadrant   ]QUA $S=                                           202
[Tangent    ]TAN $S=                                           203
[None       ]NONE $S=                                          204
[          ]                                                    205
[          ]                                                    206
[          ]                                                    207
[          ]                                                    208
[          ]                                                    209
[*-PREV-*   ]$S=                                                210
```

Line 3

[MENU-3]^C^C$S=X $S=S

In this menu item, [MENU-3] displays MENU-3 at the top of the screen menu. ^C^C cancels the command twice and $S=X loads submenu X. Similarly, $S=S loads submenu S. Submenu X, defined on line number 171, consists of 18 blank lines. Therefore, when this submenu is loaded it prints blank lines on the screen and clears the screen menu area. After loading submenu X, the system loads submenu S, and the items that are defined in this submenu are displayed on the screen menu.

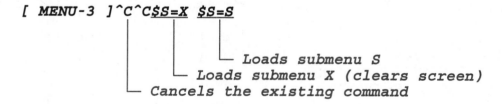

Line 4

[********]$S=OSNAP

This menu item prints eight asterisk signs on the screen menu, and $S=OSNAP loads submenu OSNAP. The OSNAP submenu is defined on line 191 and it consists of object snap modes.

Line 7

[DRAW   ]^C^C$S=X $S=DRAW

This menu item displays DRAW on the screen menu area, cancels the existing command twice, then loads submenu X and submenu DRAW. Submenu X clears the screen menu area, and submenu DRAW, as defined on line 11, loads the items defined under the DRAW submenu.

Line 11
**DRAW 3
This line is the submenu label for DRAW; 3 indicates that the first line of the DRAW submenu will be printed on line 3. Nothing will be printed on line 1 or line 2. The first line of the DRAW submenu will be on line 3, followed by the rest of the menu. All the submenus except submenus S and OSNAP have a 3 at the end of the line. Therefore, the first two lines (MENU-3) and (********) will never be cleared and will be displayed on the screen all the time. If you select MENU-3 in any menu, it will load submenu S. If you select ********, it will load submenu OSNAP.

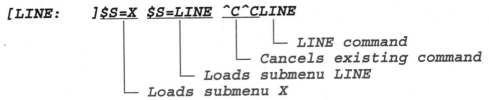

```
    **DRAW 3
           |
           |  Leaves 2 blank lines and prints from 3rd
        — Submenu name
```

Line 15
[LINE:]$S=X $S=LINE ^C^CLINE
In this menu item $S=X loads submenu X and $S=LINE loads submenu LINE. The submenu name LINE has nothing to do with the AutoCAD's LINE command. It could have been any other name. However, you should select names that reflect the contents of the menu. ^C^C cancels the existing command twice and LINE is AutoCAD's LINE command.

```
    [LINE:    ]$S=X $S=LINE ^C^CLINE
                  |     |      |  |
                  |     |      |  — LINE command
                  |     |      — Cancels existing command
                  |     — Loads submenu LINE
                  — Loads submenu X
```

Line 16-26
[   ]
These menu items print blank lines on the screen because there are no characters inside the brackets. You can also get blank lines on the screen by having blank lines in the screen menu file, or using brackets ([ ]). The brackets make it easier to see the blank lines in the menu file.

Line 27
[*-PREV-*]$S= $S=
This menu item recalls the previous menu twice. AutoCAD keeps track of the submenus that were loaded on the screen. The first $S= will load the previously loaded menu, and the second $S= will load the submenu that was loaded before that. For example, in line 16 ([ARC:]$S=X $S=ARC) two submenus have been loaded: first X, then ARC. Submenu X is stacked before loading submenu ARC, which is current and is not stacked yet. The first $S= will recall the previous menu, in this case submenu X. The second $S= will load the menu that was on the screen before selecting the item in line 16.

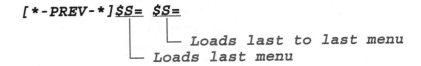

```
    [*-PREV-*]$S= $S=
               |   |
               |   — Loads last to last menu
               — Loads last menu
```

Line 29
[*-DISP-*]$S=X $S=DISP
In this menu item $S=X loads submenu X, and $S=DISP loads submenu DISP. You will notice that there is no CANCEL (^C^C) command in the line. There are some menus you might like to load without canceling the existing command. For example, if you are drawing a line you might want to zoom without canceling the existing command. You can select [*-DISP-*], select the appropriate zoom option, then continue with the line command. However, if the line has a CANCEL command ([*-DISP-*]^C^C$S=X $S=DISP), you cannot continue with the LINE

command, because the existing command will be canceled when you select *-DISP-* from the screen. In line 28 ([*-EDIT-*]^C^C$S=X $S=EDIT), ^C^C cancels the existing command, because you cannot use any editing command unless you have canceled the existing command.

Line 35
[Continue]^C^CLINE;;
In this menu item the LINE command is followed by two semicolons that continue the LINE command. To understand it, look at the LINE command to see how a continue option is used in this command:

Command: **LINE**
From point: **RETURN**   (Continue)
To point:

Following is the command and prompt entry sequence for the LINE command, if you want to start a line from the last point:

LINE
RETURN
RETURN
SELECT A POINT

Therefore, in the screen menu file the LINE command has to be followed by two RETURNS to continue from the previous point.

Line 38
[.X   ].X
In this menu item .X extracts the X coordinate from a point. The bracket, .X and spaces inside the brackets ([.X   ])are not needed. The line could consist of .X only. The same is true for lines 39 thru 43.

Example
[.X].X	can also be written as	.X
[.Y].Y		.Y
[.Z].Z		.Z

Line 76
[STRETCH:]$S=X $S=STRETCH ^C^CSTRETCH;C
In this menu item $S=X loads submenu X and $S=STRETCH loads the STRETCH submenu. ^C^C cancels the existing command twice and STRETCH is an AutoCAD command. The C is for the crossing option that prompts you to enter two points to select the objects.

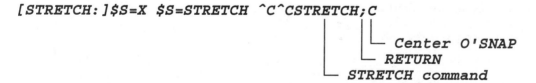

Line 133
[RAD]R;\FILLET
This menu item selects the radius option of the FILLET command, then waits for the user to enter the radius. After entering the radius, execute the FILLET command again to generate the desired fillet between the two selected objects.

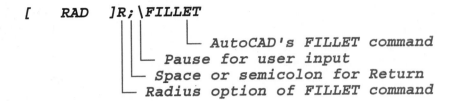

```
[    RAD    ]R;\FILLET
```

Line 134
[RAD 0   ]R;0;FILLET

This menu item selects the radius option of the FILLET command and assigns it a 0 value. Then it executes the FILLET command to generate a 0 radius fillet between the two selected objects.

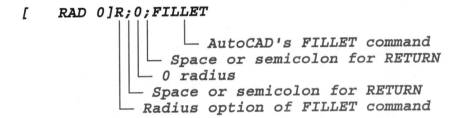

```
[    RAD 0]R;0;FILLET
```

Line 136
[FILLET0:]^C^CFILLET;R 0;;

This menu item defines a FILLET command with 0 radius, then generates 0 fillet between the two selected objects.

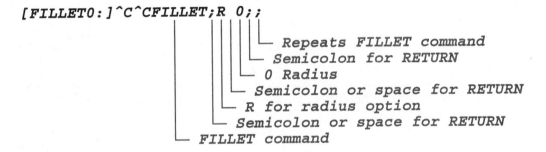

```
[FILLET0:]^C^CFILLET;R 0;;
```

Line 155
[ZOOM:]'ZOOM

This menu item defines a transparent ZOOM command.

```
[ZOOM:      ]'ZOOM
```

> **Note**
>
> *The transparent zoom does not work with ZOOM All or ZOOM Extents, because these two commands regenerate the drawing.*

Line 194
[Center]CEN $X=

In this menu item CEN is for center object snap and $X= automatically recalls the previous screen menu after selecting the object.

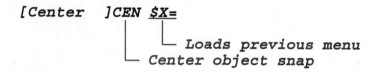

```
[Center   ]CEN $X=
                │    │
                │    └── Loads previous menu
                └── Center object snap
```

Note

If any menu item in a screen menu has more than one load command, the commands must be separated by a space.

Example

```
[LINE:   ]$S=X $S=LINE
                └── Blank space
```

Note

Similarly, if a menu item has a load command and an AutoCAD command, they should also be separated by a space.

Example

```
[LINE:   ]$S=LINE ^C^CLINE
                   └── Blank space
```

Exercise 3

Write a screen menu for the following AutoCAD commands (filename SME3.MNU).

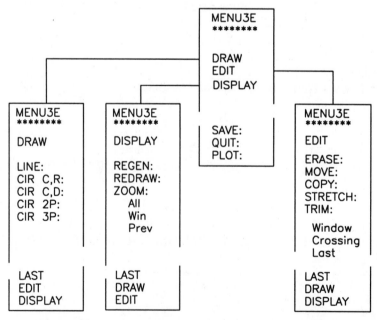

Figure 30-8 Screen menu design with submenus

AUTOMATIC MENU SWAPPING

Screen menus can be automatically swapped by using the system variable **MENUCTL**. When the system variable **MENUCTL** is set to 1, AutoCAD automatically issues the **$S=CMDNAME** command, where CMDNAME is the command that loads the submenu. For example, if you select the LINE command from the digitizer or pull-down menu, or enter the LINE command at the keyboard, the CMDNAME command will load the LINE submenu and display it in the screen menu area. To use this feature, the command name and the submenu name must be same. For example, if the name of the arc submenu is ARC and you select the ARC command, the arc submenu will be automatically loaded on the screen. However, if the submenu name is different (for example, MYARC), AutoCAD will not load the arc submenu on the screen. The default value of the MENUCTL system variable is 1. If you set the MENUCTL variable to 0, AutoCAD will not use the $S=CMDNAME command feature to load the submenus.

MENUECHO SYSTEM VARIABLE

If the system variable **MENUECHO** is set to 0, the commands that you select from the digitizer, screen menu, pull-down menu, or buttons menu will be displayed in the command prompt area. For example, if you select the CIRCLE command from the pull-down menu, AutoCAD will display **_circle 3P/2P/TTR/<Center point>:**. If you set the value of the MENUECHO variable to 1, AutoCAD will suppress the echo of the menu item and display **3P/2P/TTR/<Center point>:** only. You will notice that the _circle is not displayed when MENUECHO is set to 1. You can use ^P in the menu item to turn the echo on or off. The MENUECHO system variable can also be assigned a value of 2, 4, or 8, which controls the suppression of system prompts, disables the ^P toggle, and serves as a debugging aid for DIESEL macros, respectively.

MENUS FOR FOREIGN LANGUAGES

Besides English, AutoCAD has several foreign language versions. If you want to write a menu that is compatible with other foreign language versions of AutoCAD, you must precede each command and keyword in the menu file with the underscore (_) character.

Examples
[New   ]^C^C_New
[Open   ]^C^C_Open
[Line   ]^C^C_Line
[Arc-SCA]^C^C_Arc;_C;_A

Any command or keyword that starts with the underscore character will be automatically translated. If you check the ACAD.MNU file, you will find that AutoCAD has made extensive use of this feature.

REVIEW QUESTIONS

Fill in the blanks

1. The name of the menu file that comes with the AutoCAD software package is _____.

2. You can use the _____ command of DOS to write a menu file.

3. The AutoCAD menu file can have up to _____ sections.

4. The tablet menu can have _____ sections.

5. The section label is designated by _____.

6. A submenu is designated by _____.

7. The part of the menu item that is inside the brackets is for _____ only.

8. Only the first _____ characters can be displayed on the screen menu.

9. If the number of characters inside the bracket exceeds eight, the screen menu _____ work.

10. In a menu file you can use _____ to cancel the existing command.

11. AutoCAD's _____ command is used to load a new menu file.

12. _____ is used to input the information in a screen menu definition.

13. The menu item _____ be a combination of uppercase and lowercase characters.

14. Submenu names can be _____ characters long.

15. The maximum number of accessible menu items in a screen menu depends on the _____

EXERCISES

Exercise 4

Design and write a screen menu for the following AutoCAD commands (filename SME5.MNU).

        POLYGON (Center)
        POLYGON (Edge)
        ELLIPSE (Center)
        ELLIPSE (Axis End point)
        CHAMFER
        EXPLODE
        COPY

Exercise 5

Write a screen menu file for the following AutoCAD commands. Use submenus if required (filename SME6.MNU).

ARC	ROTATE
-3P	ARRAY
-SCE	DIVIDE
-CSE	MEASURE
BLOCK	
INSERT	LAYER
WBLOCK	SET
MINSERT	LIST

Exercise 6

Write a screen menu item that will set up the following layers, linetypes, and colors (filename SME7.MNU).

Layer Name	Color	Linetype
0	WHITE	CONTINUOUS
OBJECT	RED	CONTINUOUS
HIDDEN	YELLOW	HIDDEN
CENTER	BLUE	CENTER
DIM	GREEN	CONTINUOUS

Exercise 7

Write a screen menu for the following commands. Use the menu item ******** to load O'Snaps, and the menu item MENU-7 to load the root menu (filename SME8.MNU).

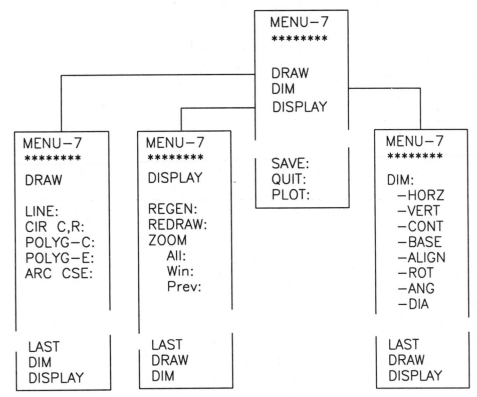

Figure 30-9 Screen menu displays

Chapter **31**

Tablet Menus

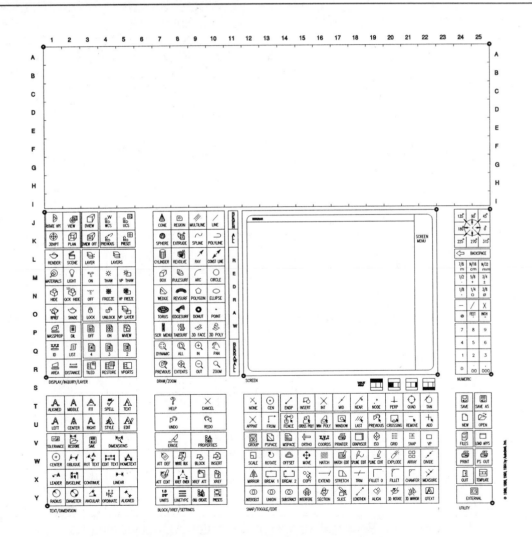

Figure 31-1 Sample tablet template

31-1

STANDARD TABLET MENU

The tablet menu provides a powerful alternative for entering commands. In the tablet menu, the commands are picked from the template that is secured on the surface of a digitizing tablet. To use the tablet menu you need a digitizing tablet and a pointing device. You also need a tablet template (Figure 31-1) that contains AutoCAD commands arranged in various groups for easy identification.

The AutoCAD menu file has four tablet menu sections: TABLET1, TABLET2, TABLET3, and TABLET4. Each section has two submenus: TABLET(n)STD and TABLET(n)ALT. For example, TABLET1 has two sections: TABLET1STD and TABLET1ALT. When you start AutoCAD and get into the Drawing Editor, the tablet menu sections TABLET1STD, TABLET2STD, TABLET3STD, and TABLET4STD are automatically loaded. The commands defined in these four sections are then assigned to different blocks of the template. To use the alternate tablet menu, you need to load the required tablet menu before you can select the commands from the alternate tablet menu. You can load the alternate tablet menu by selecting the appropriate block from the template swap menu. The template swap menu is located just below the screen pointing area on the right.

The first tablet menu section (TABLET1) has 225 blank lines that can be used to assign new commands. The remaining tablet menu sections contain AutoCAD commands, arranged in functional groups that make it easier for you to identify and access the commands. The commands contained in the TABLET2 section include RENDER, SOLID MODELING, DISPLAY, INQUIRY, DRAW, ZOOM, and PAPER SPACE commands. The TABLET3 section contains numbers, fractions, and angles. The commands contained in the TABLET4 section include TEXT, DIMENSIONING, OBJECT SNAPS, EDIT, UTILITY, XREF, and SETTINGS.

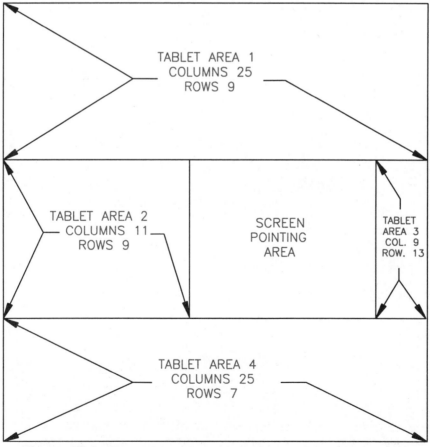

Figure 31-2 Four tablet areas of the AutoCAD tablet template

The AutoCAD tablet template has four tablet areas (Figure 31-2), which correspond to four tablet menu sections, TABLET1, TABLET2, TABLET3, and TABLET4. If you are using the alternate tablet menus these tablet areas correspond to alternate tablet menu sections TABLET1ALT, TABLET2ALT, TABLET3ALT, and TABLET4ALT.

ADVANTAGES OF TABLET MENU

The tablet menu has the following advantages over the screen menu, pull-down menu, icon menu, or keyboard.

1. In the tablet menu the commands can be arranged so that the most frequently used commands can be accessed directly. This can save considerable time in entering AutoCAD commands. In the screen menu some of the commands cannot be accessed directly. For example, to generate a horizontal dimension you have to go through several steps. First you select DIM from the root menu, then Linear, and then the Horizontal Dimensioning option. In the tablet menu you can select the horizontal dimensioning command directly from the digitizer. This saves time and eliminates the distraction that takes place as you page through different screens.

2. You can have the graphical symbols of the AutoCAD commands drawn on the tablet template. This makes it much easier to recognize and select commands. For example, if you are not an expert in AutoCAD dimensioning, you may find Baseline and Continue dimensioning confusing. But if the command is supported by the graphical symbol illustrating what a command does, the chances of selecting a wrong command are minimized.

3. You can assign any number of commands to the tablet overlay. The number of commands you can assign to a tablet is limited only by the size of the digitizer and the size of the rectangular blocks.

CUSTOMIZING A TABLET MENU

Like a screen menu, you can write a tablet menu to customize the AutoCAD tablet menu. It is a powerful customizing tool to make AutoCAD more efficient.

The tablet menu can contain a maximum of four sections: TABLET1, TABLET2, TABLET3, and TABLET4. Each section represents a rectangular area on the digitizing tablet. These rectangular areas can be further divided into any number of rectangular blocks. The size of the blocks depends on the number of commands that are assigned to the tablet area. Also, the rectangular tablet areas can be located anywhere on the digitizer and can be arranged in any order. AutoCAD's TABLET command configures the tablet. The MENU command loads and assigns the commands to the rectangular blocks on the tablet template.

Before writing a tablet menu file, it is very important to design the layout of the tablet template. A well thought out design can save lot of time in the long run. The following points should be considered when designing a tablet template:

1. Learn the AutoCAD commands that you use in your profession.

2. Group the commands based on their function, use, or relationship with other commands.

3. Draw a rectangle representing a template so that it is easy for you to move the pointing device around. The size of this area should be appropriate to your application. It should not be too large or too small. Also, the size of the template depends on the active area of the digitizer.

4. Divide the remaining area into four different tablet areas for TABLET1, TABLET2, TABLET3, and TABLET4. It is not necessary to use all four areas; you can have fewer tablet areas, but four is the maximum.

5. Determine the number of commands you need to assign to a particular tablet area, then determine the number of rows and columns you need to generate in each area. The size of the blocks does not need to be the same in every tablet area.

6. Use the TEXT command to print the commands on the tablet overlay, and draw the symbols of the command, if possible.

7. Plot the tablet overlay on good quality paper or a sheet of Mylar. If you want the plotted side of the template to face the digitizer board, you can create a mirror image of the tablet overlay and then plot the mirror image.

WRITING A TABLET MENU

When writing a tablet menu you must understand the AutoCAD commands and the prompt entries required for each command. Equally important is the design of the tablet template and the placement of various commands on it. You should give considerable thought to the design and layout of the template, and if possible invite suggestions from AutoCAD users in your trade. To understand the process that is involved in developing and writing a tablet menu, consider Example 1.

Example 1

Write a tablet menu for the following AutoCAD commands. The commands are to be arranged as shown in Figure 31-3. Use the template at the end of this chapter for configuration and command selection (filename TM1.MNU).

Line	Circle
Pline	Circle C,D
Erase	Circle 2P

Figure 31-3 represents one of the possible template designs where the AutoCAD commands are in one row at the top of the template, and the screen menu area is in the center. There is only one area in this template; therefore, you can place all these commands under the section label TABLET1. To write a menu file you can use AutoCAD's EDIT command, Edlin function of DOS, or any Text Editor.

The name of the file is TM1 and the extension of the file is .MNU. The line numbers are not part of the file. They are shown here for reference only.

```
***TABLET1                                                        1
^C^CLINE                                                          2
^C^CPLINE                                                         3
^C^CCIRCLE                                                        4
^C^CCIRCLE \D                                                     5
^C^CCIRCLE 2P                                                     6
^C^CERASE                                                         7
```

Line 1
***TABLET1
TABLET1 is the section label of the first tablet area. All the section labels are preceded by three asterisks (***).

***TABLET1**

    └─── *Section label for TABLET1*
  └─*Three asterisks designate section label.*

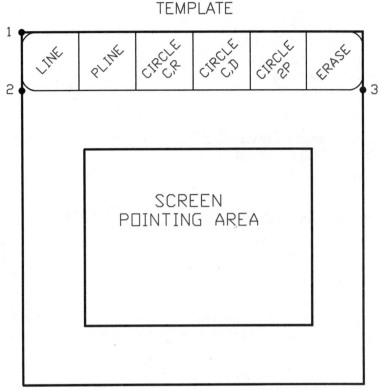

Figure 31-3 Design of tablet template

Line 2
^C^CLINE
^C^C cancels the existing command twice; LINE is an AutoCAD command. There is no space between the second ^C and LINE.

^C^CLINE

     └─── *AutoCAD's LINE command*
    └─ *Cancels the existing command twice*

Line 3
^C^CPLINE
^C^C cancels the existing command twice; PLINE is an AutoCAD command.

Line 4
^C^CCIRCLE
^C^C cancels the existing command twice; CIRCLE is an AutoCAD command. The default input for the CIRCLE command is the center and the radius of the circle. Therefore, no additional input is required for this line.

Line 5
^C^CCIRCLE \D
^C^C cancels the existing command twice; CIRCLE is an AutoCAD command like the previous line. However, this command definition requires the diameter option of the circle command. This is accomplished by using \D in the command definition. There should be no space between the

backslash (\) and the D, but there should always be a space before the backslash (\). The backslash (\) lets the user enter a point, and in this case it is the center point of the circle. After entering the center point, the diameter option is selected by the letter D, which follows the backslash (\).

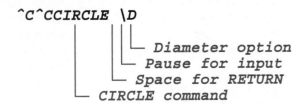

```
^C^CCIRCLE \D
           |  |
           |  |__ Diameter option
           |__ Pause for input
           |__ Space for RETURN
      |__ CIRCLE command
```

Line 6
^C^CCIRCLE 2P
^C^C cancels the existing command twice; CIRCLE is an AutoCAD command. The 2P selects the two-point option of the CIRCLE command.

Line 7
^C^CERASE
^C^C cancels the existing command twice; ERASE is an AutoCAD command that erases the selected objects.

Note

In the tablet menu, the part of the menu item that is enclosed in the brackets is ignored. For example, in the following menu item, T1-6 will be ignored and will have no effect on the command definition.

```
     |__ For reference only and has no effect
     |   on the command definition
     |
[T1-6]^C^CCIRCLE 2P
     |  |
     |  |__ Item number 6
     |__ Tablet area 1
```

The reference information can be used to designate the tablet area and the line number.

Before you can use the commands from the new tablet menu, you need to configure the tablet and load the tablet menu.

TABLET CONFIGURATION

To use the new template to select the commands, you need to configure the tablet so that AutoCAD knows the location of the tablet template and the position of the commands assigned to each block. This is accomplished by using AutoCAD's TABLET command. Secure the tablet template (Figure 31-3) on the digitizer with the edges of the overlay approximately parallel to the edges of the digitizer. Enter AutoCAD's TABLET command, select the Configure option, and respond to the following prompts. Figure 31-4 shows the points you need to select to configure the tablet.

Command: **TABLET**
Options (ON/OFF/CAL/CFG):**CFG**
Enter number of tablet menus desired (0-4): **1**

Do you want to realign tablet menu areas? <N>: **Y**
Digitize upper left corner of menu area 1; **P1**
Digitize lower left corner of menu area 1; **P2**
Digitize lower right corner of menu area 1; **P3**
Enter the number of columns for menu area 1; **7**
Enter the number of rows for menu area 1; **1**
Do you want to respecify the screen pointing area? <N>: **Y**
Digitize lower left corner of screen pointing area: **P4**
Digitize upper right corner of screen pointing area: **P5**

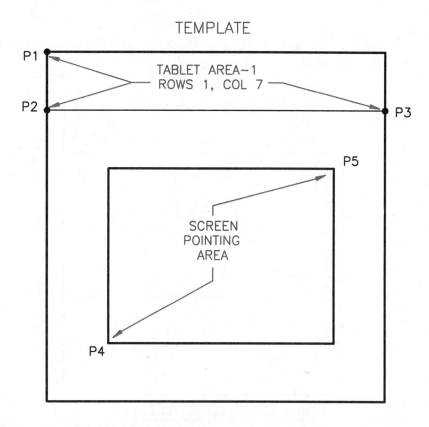

Figure 31-4 Points that need to be selected to configure the tablet

The three points P1, P2, and P3 should form a 90-degree angle. If the selected points do not form a 90-degree angle, AutoCAD will prompt you to enter the points again until they do.

The tablet areas should not overlap the screen pointing area.

The screen pointing area can be any size and located anywhere on the tablet as long as it is within the active area of the digitizer. The screen pointing area should not overlap other tablet areas. The screen pointing area you select will correspond to the monitor screen area. Therefore, the length-to-width ratio of the screen pointing area should be the same as that of the monitor, unless you are using the screen pointing area to digitize a drawing.

Exercise 1

Write a tablet menu for the following AutoCAD commands. Use the tablet menu template at the end of this chapter for configuration and command selection (filename TME1.MNU).

Line	Text-Center
Circle C,R	Text-Left
Arc C.S.E	Text-Right
Ellipse	Text-Aligned
Donut	

Use the template in Figure 31-5 to arrange the commands. The draw and text commands should be placed in two separate tablet areas.

TEMPLATE

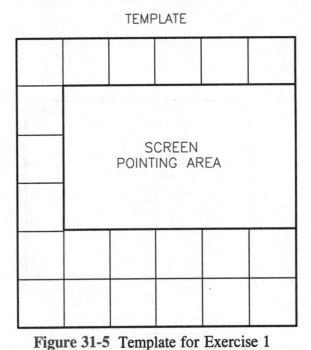

SCREEN
POINTING AREA

Figure 31-5 Template for Exercise 1

TABLET MENUS WITH DIFFERENT BLOCK SIZES

As mentioned earlier, the size of each tablet area can be different. The size of the blocks in these tablet areas can also be different. But the size of every block in a particular tablet area must be the same. This provides you with a lot of flexibility in designing a template. For example, you may prefer to have smaller blocks for numbers, fractions, or letters, and larger blocks for draw commands. You can also arrange these tablet areas to design a template layout with different shapes, such as: L-shape or T-shape.

Tablet Area-1   **Tablet Area-2**

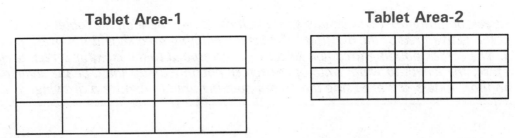

The following example illustrates the use of multiple tablet areas with different block sizes.

Example 2

Write a tablet menu for the tablet overlay as shown in Figure 31-6(a). Figure 31-6(b) shows the number of rows and columns in different tablet areas (filename TM2.MNU).

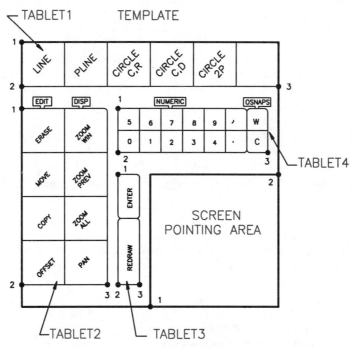

Figure 31-6(a) Tablet overlay for Example 2

Notice that this tablet template has four different sections in addition to the screen pointing area. Therefore, this menu will have four section labels: TABLET1, TABLET2, TABLET3, and TABLET4. You can use AutoCAD's EDIT command to write the file. The following file is a listing of the tablet menu of Example 2.

```
***TABLET1                                                        1
^C^CLINE                                                          2
^C^CPLINE                                                         3
^C^CCIRCLE                                                        4
^C^CCIRCLE \D                                                     5
^C^CCIRCLE 2P                                                     6
***TABLET2                                                        7
^C^CERASE                                                         8
^C^CZOOM W                                                        9
^C^CMOVE                                                         10
^C^CZOOM P                                                       11
^C^CCCOPY                                                        12
^C^CZOOM A                                                       13
^C^COFFSET                                                       14
^C^CPAN                                                          15
***TABLET3                                                       16
;                                                                17
;                                                                18
'REDRAW                                                          19
'REDRAW                                                          20
'REDRAW                                                          21
***TABLET4                                                       22
```

```
5\                                                    23
6\                                                    24
7\                                                    25
8\                                                    26
9\                                                    27
,\                                                    28
WINDOW                                                29
0\                                                    30
1\                                                    31
2\                                                    32
3\                                                    33
4\                                                    34
.\                                                    35
CROSSING                                              36
```

Lines 1-6
The first six lines are identical to the first six lines of the tablet menu in Example 1.

Line 9
^C^CZOOM W
ZOOM is an AutoCAD command; W is the window option of the ZOOM command.

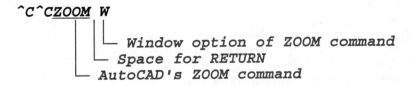

This menu item could also be written as

TEMPLATE

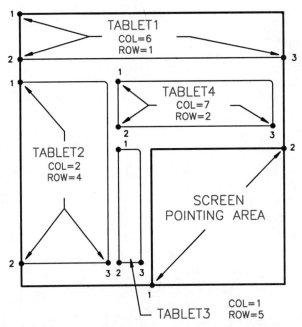

Figure 31-6(b) Number of rows and columns in different tablet areas

Lines 17 & 18
The semicolon (;) is for RETURN. It has the same effect as entering RETURN at the keyboard.

Lines 19-21
'REDRAW
REDRAW is an AutoCAD command that redraws the screen. Notice that there is no ˆCˆC in front of the REDRAW command. If it had ˆCˆC, the existing command would be canceled before redrawing the screen. This may not be desirable in most applications, because you might want to redraw the screen without canceling the existing command. The apostrophe (') in front of REDRAW makes the REDRAW command transparent.

Line 23
5
The backslash (\) is used to introduce a pause for user input. Without the backslash you cannot enter another number or a character, because after you select the digit 5 it will automatically be followed by RETURN. For example, without the backslash (\), you will not be able to enter a number like 5.6. Therefore, you need the backslash to enable you to enter decimal numbers or any characters. To terminate the input enter RETURN at the keyboard, or pick RETURN from the digitizer.

```
5 \
  |
  └── Backslash for user input
```

ASSIGNING COMMANDS TO A TABLET

After loading the menu with AutoCAD's MENU command, you must configure the tablet. At the time of configuration AutoCAD actually generates and stores the information about the rectangular blocks on the tablet template. When you load the menu, the commands defined in the tablet menu are assigned to various blocks. For example, when you pick the three points for the tablet area 4 (Figure 31-6(a)) and enter the number of rows and columns, AutoCAD generates a grid of seven columns and two rows, as shown in the following diagram.

After Configuration

When you load the new menu, AutoCAD takes the commands under the section label TABLET4 and starts filling the blocks from left to right. That means "5", "6", "7", "8", "9", "," and "Window" will be placed in the top row. The next seven commands will be assigned to the next row, starting from the left, as shown in the following diagram.

After Loading Tablet Menu

5	6	7	8	9	,	Window
0	1	2	3	4	.	Cross

Similarly, tablet area 3 has been divided into five rows and one column. At first, it appears that this tablet area has only two rows and one column (Figure 31-6(a)). When you configure this tablet area by picking the three points and entering the number of rows and columns, AutoCAD divides the area into one column and five rows as shown in the following diagrams.

After loading the menu, AutoCAD takes the commands in the TABLET3 section of the tablet menu and assigns them to the blocks. The first command ";" is placed in the first block. Since there are no more blocks in the first row, the next command ";" is placed in the second row. Similarly, the three REDRAW commands are placed in the next three rows. If you pick a point in the first two rows, you will select the ENTER command. Similarly, if you pick a point in the next three blocks, you will select the REDRAW command.

After Configuration   **After Loading Menu**

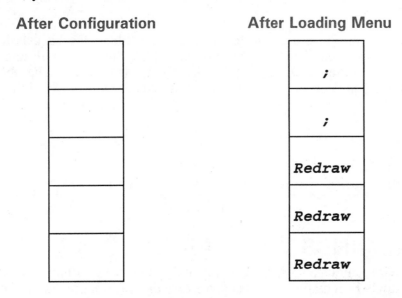

This process is carried out for all the tablet areas, and the information is stored in the AutoCAD configuration file ACAD.CFG. If for any reason the configuration is not right, the tablet menu may not perform the desired function.

REVIEW QUESTIONS

Fill in the blanks.

1.   The maximum number of tablet menu sections is _____.

2.   A tablet menu area is _____ in shape.

3.   The blocks in any tablet menu area are _____ in shape.

4.   A tablet menu area can have _____ number of rectangular blocks.

5.   You _____ assign the same command to more than one block on the tablet menu template.

6.   AutoCAD's _____ command is used to configure the tablet menu template.

7.   AutoCAD's _____ command is used to load a new menu.

8.   When using the tablet menu, you _____ load a submenu defined under the screen menu section.

EXERCISES

Exercise 2

Write a tablet menu for the commands shown in the tablet menu template Figure 31-7. Use the tablet menu template at the end of this chapter for configuration and command selection.

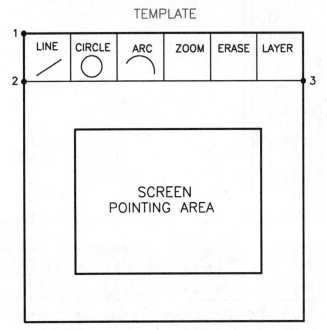

Figure 31-7 Tablet menu template for Exercise 2

Exercise 3

Write a tablet menu for the AutoCAD commands as shown in Figure 31-8. Configure the tablet and then load the new menu. Use the tablet menu template at the end of this chapter for configuration and command selection.

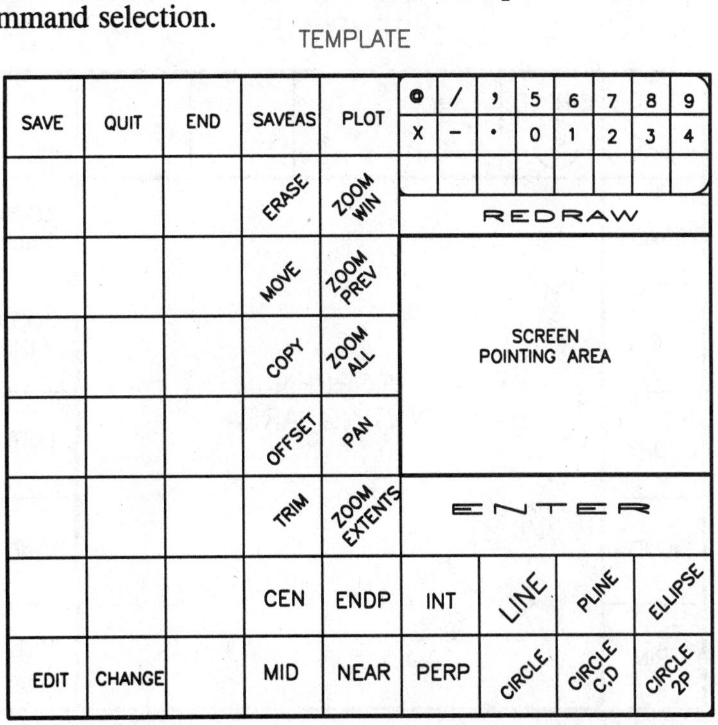

Figure 31-8 Tablet overlay for Exercise 3

Exercise 4

Write a tablet menu file for the AutoCAD commands shown in the template (Figure 31-9). Use the template at the end of the chapter for configuration and command selection.

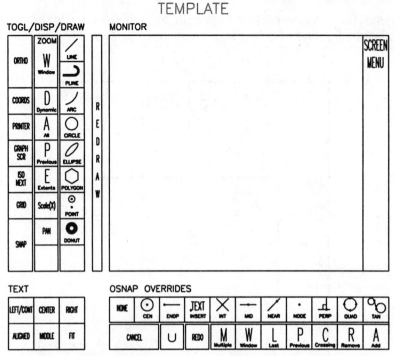

TEMPLATE

Figure 31-9 Tablet menu template for Exercise 4

Exercise 5

Write a combined screen and tablet menu file for the commands shown in the tablet menu template in Figure 31-10. Design the screen menu as shown in Example 3. Use the tablet menu template at the end of this chapter for configuration and command selection.

TEMPLATE

LINE	CIRCLE	ARC				
ERASE						ZOOM ALL
MOVE		SCREEN POINTING AREA				ZOOM WIN.
COPY						LIST
FILLET						AREA
TRIM						HELP

Figure 31-10 Tablet menu template for Exercise 5

Template for Example 1

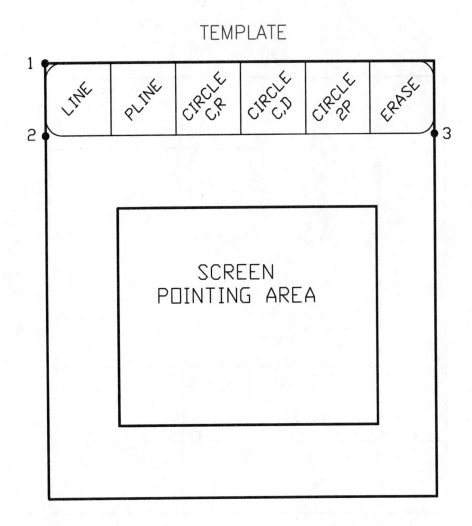

TEMPLATE

<table>
<tr><td>LINE</td><td>PLINE</td><td>CIRCLE C,R</td><td>CIRCLE C,D</td><td>CIRCLE 2P</td><td>ERASE</td></tr>
</table>

SCREEN
POINTING AREA

Note

This template is for tablet configuration. You can make a copy of this page and secure it to the digitizer surface for configuration.

Template for Exercise 1

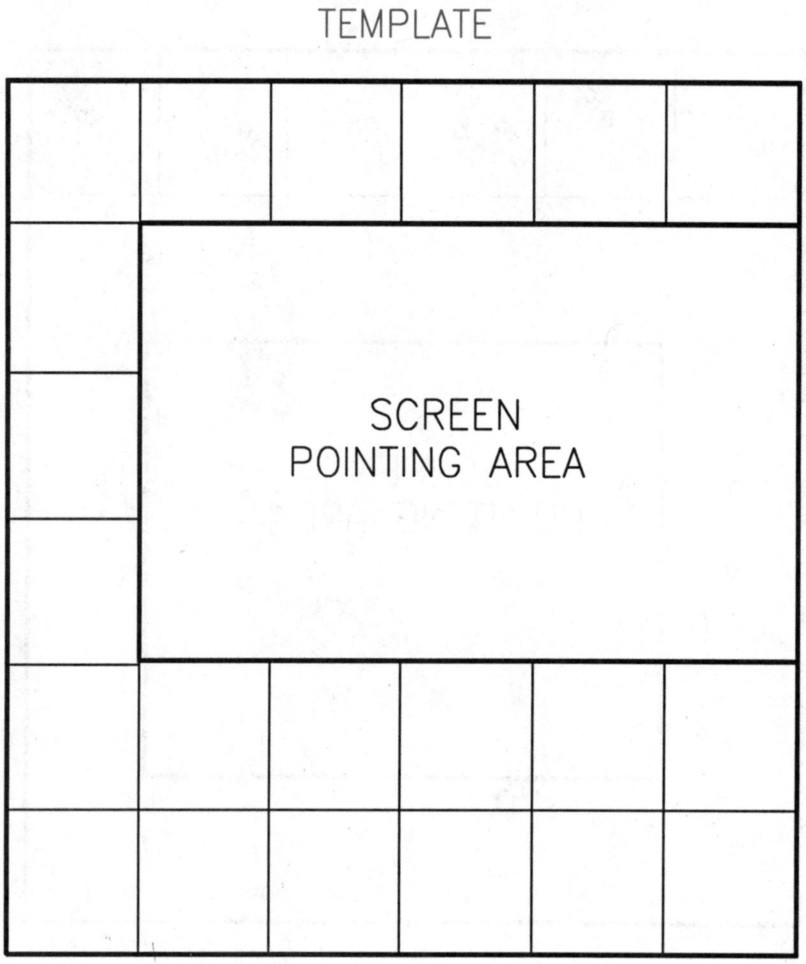

TEMPLATE

SCREEN
POINTING AREA

Chapter 32

Pull-down Menus, Cursor Menus, and Menu Features For Windows

Learning objectives

After completing this chapter, you will be able to:
♦ Write pull-down menus.
♦ Load menus.
♦ Write cascading submenus in pull-down menus.
♦ Write cursor menus.
♦ Swap pull-down menus.
♦ Write partial menus.
♦ Define accelerator keys.
♦ Write tool-bar definitions.
♦ Write menus to access on-line help.

STANDARD PULL-DOWN MENUS

The pull-down menu is a part of AutoCAD's standard menu file ACAD.MNU. The ACAD.MNU file is automatically loaded when you start AutoCAD, provided the standard configuration of AutoCAD has not been changed. The pull-down menu can be used if the display driver supports the advanced user interface (AUI).

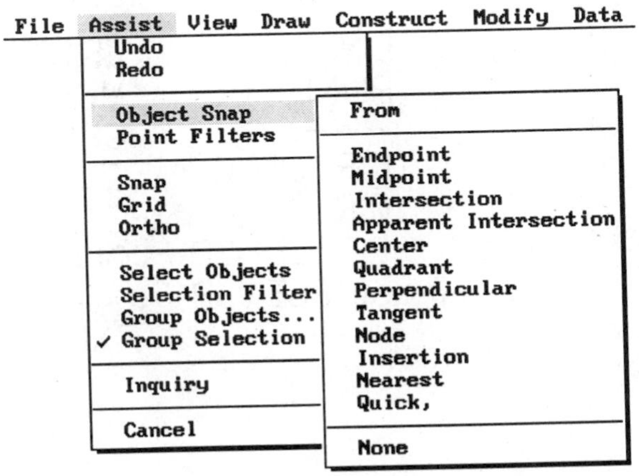

The pull-down menus can be selected by moving the cross-hair to the top of the screen into the status line area. When the cross-hair touches this area, the status line is replaced by the menu bar that displays the menu bar titles (Figure 32-1). If you move the pointing device sideways, different menu bar titles are highlighted and you

Figure 32-1 Pull-down and cascading menus

can pick the desired item by pressing the pick button on your pointing device. Once the item is selected the corresponding pull-down menu is displayed directly under the title. The pull-down menu has 16 sections, defined as POP1, POP2, POP3 .... POP16.

WRITING A PULL-DOWN MENU

Pull-down menus are similar to screen and tablet menus. The menu item consists of a menu item label and a command definition. The menu item label is enclosed in the brackets, whereas the command definition is outside the brackets. As in other menus, before writing a pull-down menu you have to know the AutoCAD commands, command options, and the prompts associated with each command. Equally important is the layout of various pull-down menus and submenus.

To write the pull-down menu file, you can use AutoCAD's EDIT command (if the ACAD.PGP file is present and the EDIT command is defined in the file), Edit or Edlin function of DOS, or a Text Editor. To understand the process of developing a pull-down menu, consider the following example.

Example 1

Write a pull-down menu for the following AutoCAD commands:

LINE	ERASE	REDRAW	SAVE
PLINE	MOVE	REGEN	QUIT
CIRCLE C,R	COPY	ZOOM ALL	PRPLOT
CIRCLE C,D	STRETCH	ZOOM WIN	DIR Dwg Files
CIRCLE 2P	EXTEND	ZOOM PRE	
CIRCLE 3P	OFFSET		

The first step in writing any menu is to design the menu so that the commands are arranged in the desired configuration. Figure 32-2 shows one of the possible designs of this menu.

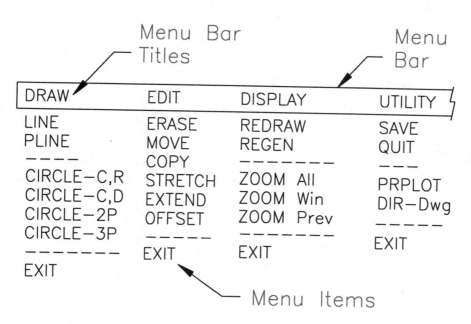

Figure 32-2 Design of pull-down menu

This menu has four different groups of commands; therefore, it will have four sections: POP1, POP2, POP3, POP4, and each section will have a section label. The following file is a listing of the pull-down menu file for Example 1. The line numbers are not a part of the file; they are shown here for reference only.

```
***POP1                                                    1
[DRAW]                                                     2
[LINE]*^C^CLINE                                            3
[PLINE]^C^CPLINE                                           4
[~--]                                                     5
[CIR-C,R]^C^CCIRCLE                                        6
[CIR-C,D]^C^CCIRCLE \D                                     7
[CIR-2P]^C^CCIRCLE 2P                                      8
[CIR-3P]^C^CCIRCLE 3P                                      9
[~--]                                                    10
[Exit]^C                                                  11
***POP2                                                   12
[EDIT]                                                    13
[ERASE]*^C^CERASE                                         14
[MOVE]^C^CMOVE                                            15
[COPY]^C^CCOPY                                            16
[STRETCH]^C^CSTRETCH;C                                    17
[OFFSET]^C^COFFSET                                        18
[EXTEND]^C^CEXTEND                                        19
[~--]                                                    20
[Exit]^C                                                  21
***POP3                                                   22
[DISPLAY]                                                 23
[REDRAW]'REDRAW                                           24
[REGEN]^C^CREGEN                                          25
[~--]                                                    26
[ZOOM-All]^C^CZOOM A                                      27
[ZOOM-Window]'ZOOM W                                      28
[ZOOM-Prev]'ZOOM PREV                                     29
[~--]                                                    30
[Exit]^C                                                  31
***POP4                                                   32
[UTILITY]                                                 33
[SAVE]^C^CSAVE;                                           34
[QUIT]^C^CQUIT                                            35
[----]                                                   36
[PRPLOT]^C^CPRPLOT                                        37
[DIR-Dwg Files]^C^CDIR;*.DWG;                             38
[~--]                                                    39
[Exit]^C                                                  40
```

Line 1
***POP1
POP1 is the section label for the first pull-down menu. All section labels in the AutoCAD menu begin with three asterisks (***), followed by the section label name, like POP1.

Line 2
[DRAW]
In this menu item DRAW is the menu bar title that is displayed when the cursor is moved in the menu bar area. The title names should be chosen so that you can identify the type of commands you expect in that particular pull-down menu. In this example, all the draw commands are under the title DRAW, all edit commands are under EDIT, and the same is true for other groups of items. Each menu bar title in the menu bar can be up to 14 characters long.

However, most of the display devices provide a maximum of 80 characters. To have 16 sections in the menu bar, the length of each title should not exceed five characters.

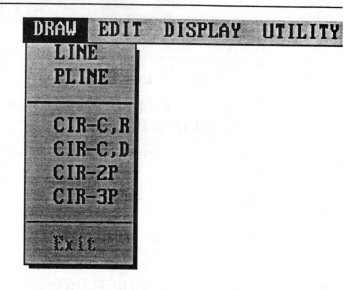

If the first line in a pull-down menu section is blank, the title of that section is not displayed in the menu bar area. Since the menu bar title is not displayed, you **cannot** access that pull-down menu. This allows you to turn off the pull-down menu section. For example, if you replace [DRAW] with a blank line, the DRAW section (POP1) of the pull-down menu will be disabled. The second section (POP2) will be displayed in its place.

Example
***POP1 ——————— Section label
——————— **Blank line** (turns off POP1)
[LINE:]^CLINE ———————• Menu item
[PLINE:]^CPLINE
[CIRCLE:]^CCIRCLE

The menu bar titles are left-justified. If the first title is not displayed, the rest of the menu titles will be shifted to the left. In Example 1, if the DRAW title is not displayed in the menu bar area, the EDIT, DISPLAY, and FILE sections of the pull-down menu will move to the left.

Line 3
*^C^CLINE
In this menu item the command definition starts with an asterisk (*). This feature allows the command to be repeated automatically until it is canceled by entering CTRL C or by selecting another menu command. ^C^C cancels the existing command twice; LINE is an AutoCAD command that generates lines.

```
*^C^CLINE
 |  |   └─ AutoCAD's LINE command
 |  └─ Cancels existing command twice
 └─ Repeats the menu item (command)
```

Line 5
[~--]
To separate two groups of commands in any section, you can use a menu item that consists of two hyphens (--). This line automatically expands to fill the **entire width** of the pull-down menu. If you have one or more than two hyphens, the line does not expand. **You cannot use a blank line in a pull-down menu**. If any section of a pull-down menu (**POP section) has a blank line, the items beyond the blank line are not displayed on the screen.

If a menu item begins with a tilde (˜), the item will be displayed a little lighter than rest of the pull-down menu. You can use this feature to disable a menu item or to indicate that the item is not a valid selection. If there is an instruction associated with the item, the instruction will not be executed when you select the item. For example, [OSNAPS]^C^C$S=OSNAPS will not load the OSNAPS submenu on the screen.

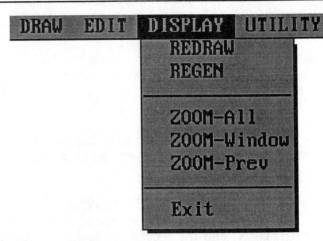

```
[˜--]
     └── Two hyphens produce a dashed separator line.
  └── Tilde displays the item grayed out (lighter).
```

Line 11
[Exit]^C
In this menu item ^C command definition has been used to cancel the pull-down menu. This item provides you with one more option for canceling the pull-down menu. This is especially useful for new AutoCAD users who are not familiar with all AutoCAD features. The pull-down menu can also be canceled by any of the following actions:

1. Selecting a point
2. Moving the cross-hair to screen menu area
3. Selecting or typing another command
4. Entering CTRL C at the keyboard

Line 28
[ZOOM-Window]'ZOOM W
In this menu item the single quote (') preceding the ZOOM command makes the ZOOM Window command transparent. When a command is transparent the existing command is not canceled. After the ZOOM WINDOW command, AutoCAD will automatically resume the current operation. You cannot use the transparent mode with the commands that regenerate the drawing. For example, ZOOM ALL regenerates the drawing; therefore, it cannot be used as a transparent command.

```
[ZOOM-Window]'ZOOM W
              │    └── Window option
              └── AutoCAD's ZOOM command
  └── Single quote makes ZOOM transparent
```

Line 31
[Exit]^C
This menu item is similar to the menu item in line 11, except for the tilde (˜). Since this menu item does not have a tilde (˜), the item will not be grayed out.

Line 34
[SAVE]^C^CSAVE;
In this menu item the semicolon (;) that follows the SAVE command enters RETURN. The semicolon is not required; the command will also work without a semicolon.

```
[SAVE]^C^CSAVE;
                    └── Semicolon enters RETURN
                └── AutoCAD's SAVE command
```

Line 36
[----]
This menu item has four hyphens; therefore, the line will not extend. Only when there are two hyphens (--) does the line extend to the entire width of the pull-down menu.

Line 38
[DIR-Dwg Files]^C^CDIR;*.DWG;
In this menu item DIR is an AutoCAD command for listing the files. The first semicolon (;) enters RETURN, and the second semicolon (;) lists the drawing files. The DIR command is defined in the ACAD.PGP file. This command will work if the ACAD.PGP file is present and the DIR command is defined in the file.

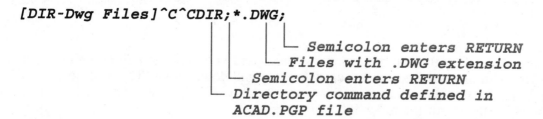

```
[DIR-Dwg Files]^C^CDIR;*.DWG;
                         │ │ │ └── Semicolon enters RETURN
                         │ │ └── Files with .DWG extension
                         │ └── Semicolon enters RETURN
                         └── Directory command defined in
                             ACAD.PGP file
```

Note

For all pull-down menus, the menu items are displayed directly beneath the menu title and are left-justified. If the rightmost pull-down menu (POP16) does not have enough space to display the entire menu item, the characters that do not fit will be truncated. Most of the display devices display 80 characters. If you have 10 pull-down menus, the last pull-down menu POP10 will have only eight character spaces for display. If the menu title or the menu items are longer than eight characters, the characters beyond the eighth one will be truncated. However, the command associated with the menu items will be executed.

Exercise 1

Write a pull-down menu for the following AutoCAD commands.

DRAW	EDIT	DISP/TEXT	UTILITY
LINE	FILLET0	DTEXT,C	SAVE
PLINE	FILLET	DTEXT,L	QUIT
ELLIPSE	CHAMFER	DTEXT,R	PLOT
POLYGON	STRETCH	ZOOM WIN	DIR
DONUT	EXTEND	ZOOM PRE	END
	OFFSET		

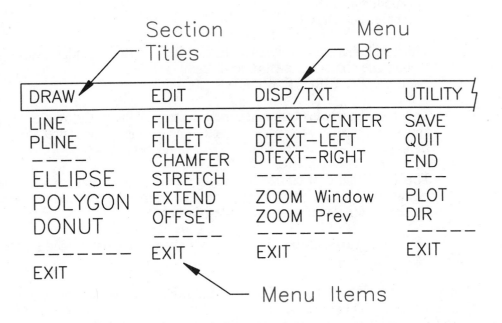

Figure 32-3 Pull-down menu display for Exercise 1

SUBMENUS

The number of items in a pull-down menu or cursor menu can be very large and sometimes they cannot all be accommodated on one screen. For example, the maximum number of items that can be displayed on most of the display devices is 21. If the pull-down menu or the cursor menu has more than 21 items, the menu excess items are not displayed on the screen and cannot be accessed. You can overcome this problem by using submenus that let you define smaller groups of items within a menu section. When a submenu is selected, it loads the submenu items and displays them on the screen.

CASCADING SUBMENUS IN PULL-DOWN MENUS

The cascading feature of AutoCAD allows pull-down and cursor menus to be displayed in a hierarchical order that makes it easier to select submenus. To use the cascading feature in pull-down and cursor menus, AutoCAD has provided some special characters. For example, -> defines a cascaded submenu and < - designates the last item in the pull-down menu. The following table lists some the frequently used characters that can be used with the pull-down or cursor menus.

Character	Character Description
--	The item label consisting of two hyphens automatically expands to fill the entire width of the pull-down menu. Example: [--]
+	Used to continue the menu item to the next line. This character has to be the last character of the menu item. Example: [Triang:]^C^CLine;1,1;+ 3,1;2,2;

->   This label character defines a cascaded submenu; it must precede the name of the submenu.
Example: [->Draw]

<-   This label character designates the last item of the cascaded pull-down or cursor menu. The character must precede the label item.
Example: [<-CIRCLE 3P]^C^CCIRCLE;3P

<-<-...   This label character designates the last item of the pull-down or cursor menu and also terminates the parent menu. The character must precede the label item.
Example: [<-<-Center Mark]^C^C_dim;_center

$(This label character can be used with the pull-down and cursor menus to evaluate a DIESEL expression. The character must precede the label item.
Example: $(if,$(getvar,orthomode),Ortho)

~   This item grays-out the label item; the character must precede the item.
Example: [~--]

Each menu bar title can be up to 14 characters long. Most display devices provide space for a maximum of 80 characters. Therefore, if there are 16 pull-down menus, the length of each menu title should average five characters. If the combined length of all menu bar titles exceeds 80 characters, AutoCAD automatically truncates the characters from the longest menu title until it fits all menu titles in the menu bar. The following is a list of some additional features of the pull-down menu:

1. The section labels of the pull-down menus are ***POP1 through ***POP16. The menu bar titles are displayed in the menu bar.

2. The pull-down menus can be accessed by selecting the menu title from the menu bar at the top of the screen.

3. A maximum of 999 menu items can be defined in the pull-down menu. This includes the items that are defined in the pull-down submenus. The menu items in excess of 999 are ignored.

4. The number of menu items that can be displayed on the screen depends on the display device you are using. If the cursor or the pull-down menu contains more items than can be accommodated on the screen, the excess items are truncated. For example, if your system can display 21 menu items, the menu items in excess of 21 are automatically truncated.

5. If AutoCAD is not configured to show the status line, the pull-down menus, cursor menus, and menu bar are automatically disabled.

Example 2

Write a pull-down menu for the commands shown in Figure 32-4. The pull-down menu must use AutoCAD's cascading feature.

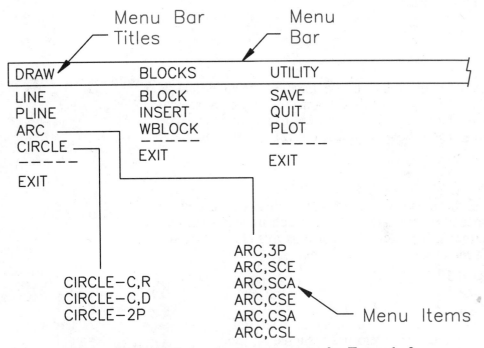

Figure 32-4 Pull-down menu structure for Example 2

The following file is a listing of the pull-down menu for Example 2. The line numbers are not a part of the menu; they are shown here for reference only.

```
***POP1                                                    1
[DRAW]                                                     2
[LINE]^C^CLINE                                             3
[PLINE]^C^CPLINE                                           4
[->ARC]                                                    5
  [ARC]^C^CARC                                             6
  [ARC,3P]^C^CARC;\\DRAG                                   7
  [ARC,SCE]^C^CARC;\C;\DRAG                                8
  [ARC,SCA]^C^CARC;\C;\A;DRAG                              9
  [ARC,CSE]^C^CARC;C;\\DRAG                                10
  [ARC,CSA]^C^CARC;C;\\A;DRAG                              11
  [<-ARC,CSL]^C^CARC;C;\\L;DRAG                            12
[->CIRCLE]                                                 13
  [CIRCLE C,R]^C^CCIRCLE                                   14
  [CIRCLE C,D]^C^CCIRCLE;\D                                15
  [CIRCLE 2P]^C^CCIRCLE;2P                                 16
  [<-CIRCLE 3P]^C^CCIRCLE;3P                               17
[~--]                                                      18
[Exit]^C                                                   19
***POP2                                                    20
[BLOCKS]                                                   21
[BLOCK]$S=X $S=BLKX ^C^CBLOCK                              22
[INSERT]$S=X $S=BLK *^C^CINSERT                            23
[WBLOCK]$S=X $S=WBLK ^C^CWBLOCK                            24
[~--]                                                      25
[Exit]^C                                                   26
***POP3                                                    27
[UTILITY]                                                  28
[SAVE]^C^CSAVE                                             29
[QUIT]^C^CQUIT                                             30
```

```
[PLOT]^C^CPLOT                                    31
[~--]                                             32
[Exit]^C                                          33
```

Line 5
[->ARC]
In this menu item, **ARC** is the menu item label that is preceded by the special label character **->**. This special character indicates that the menu item has a submenu. The menu items that follow it (lines 6 - 12) are the submenu items.

Line 12
[<-ARC,CSL]^C^CARC;C;\\L;DRAG
In this line the menu item label **ARC,CSL** is preceded by another special label character **<-**, which indicates the end of the submenu. The item that contains this character must be the last menu item of the submenu.

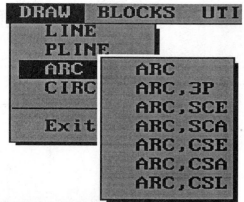

Lines 13 and 17
[->CIRCLE]
[<-CIRCLE 3P]^C^CCIRCLE;3P
The special character **->** in front of **CIRCLE** indicates that the menu item has a submenu; the character **<-** in front of **CIRCLE 3P** indicates that this item is the last menu item in the submenu. When you select the menu item **CIRCLE** from the pull-down menu, it will automatically display the submenu on the side.

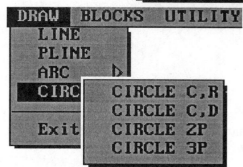

Example 3

Write a pull-down menu that has the cascading submenus for the commands shown in Figure 32-5.

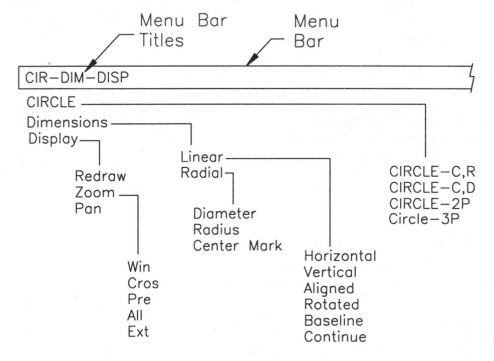

Figure 32-5 Pull-down menu structure for Example 3

The following file is a listing of the pull-down menu for Example 3. The line numbers are not a part of the menu; they are shown here for reference only.

```
***POP1                                              1
[DRAW]                                               2
[->CIRCLE]                                           3
  [CIRCLE C,R]^C^C_CIRCLE                            4
  [CIRCLE C,D]^C^C_CIRCLE;\_D                        5
  [CIRCLE 2P]^C^C_CIRCLE;_2P                         6
  [<-CIRCLE 3P]^C^C_CIRCLE;_3P                       7
[->Dimensions]                                       8
  [->Linear]                                         9
    [Horizontal]^C^C_dim;_horizontal                10
    [Vertical]^C^C_dim;_vertical                    11
    [Aligned]^C^C_dim;_aligned                      12
    [Rotated]^C^C_dim;_rotated                      13
    [Baseline]^C^C_dim;_baseline                    14
    [<-Continue]^C^C_dim;_continue                  15
  [->Radial]                                        16
    [Diameter]^C^C_dim;_diameter                    17
    [Radius]^C^C_dim;_radius                        18
    [<-<-Center Mark]^C^C_dim;_center               19
[->DISPLAY]                                         20
  [REDRAW]^C^CREDRAW                                21
  [->ZOOM]                                          22
    [...Win]^C^C_ZOOM;_W                            23
    [...Cros]^C^C_ZOOM;_C                           24
    [...Pre]^C^C_ZOOM;_P                            25
    [...All]^C^C_ZOOM;_A                            26
    [<-...Ext]^C^C_ZOOM;_E                          28
  [<-PAN]^C^C_Pan                                   29
```

Lines 8 and 9
[->Dimensions]
[->Linear]
The special label character **->** in front of the menu item **Dimensions** indicates that it has a submenu, and the character **->** in front of **Linear** indicates that there is another submenu. The second submenu **Linear** is within the first submenu **Dimensions**. The menu items on lines 10 to 15 are defined in the **Linear** submenu, and the menu items **Linear** and **Radial** are defined in the submenu **Dimensions**.

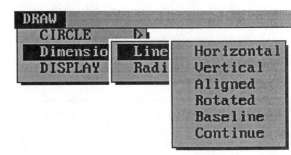

Line 16
[->Radial]
This menu item defines another submenu; the menu items on line numbers 17,18, and 19 are part of this submenu.

Line 19
[<-<-Center Mark]^C^C_dim;_center
In this menu item the special label character **<-<-** terminates the **Radial** and **Dimensions** (parent submenu) submenus.

Lines 28 and 29

[<-...Ext]^C^C_ZOOM;_E
[<-PAN]^C^C_Pan

The special character **<-** in front of the menu
item **...Ext** terminates the **ZOOM** submenu; the
special character in front of the menu item **PAN**
terminates the **DISPLAY** submenu.

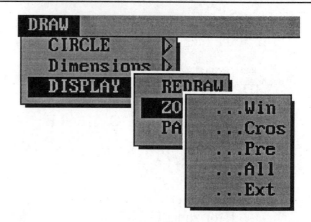

CURSOR MENUS

The cursor menus are similar to the pull-down
menus, except that the cursor menu can contain
only 499 items compared with 999 items in the pull-down. The section label of the cursor menu
must be ***POP0. The cursor menus are displayed near or at the cursor location. Therefore it can
be used to provide a convenient and quick access to some of the frequently used commands. The
following is a list of some of the features of the cursor menu:

1. The section label of the cursor menu is ***POP0. The menu bar title defined under this section
    label is not displayed in the menu bar.

2. On most systems, the menu bar title is not displayed at the top of the cursor menu. However,
    for compatibility reasons you should give a dummy menu bar title.

3. The cursor menu can be accessed through **$P0=*** menu command only. This command can be
    issued by a menu item in another menu, such as the button menu, auxiliary menu or the screen
    menu. The command can also be issued from an AutoLISP or ADS program.

4. A maximum of 499 menu items can be defined in the cursor menu. This includes the items that
    are defined in the cursor submenus. The menu items in excess of 499 are ignored.

5. The number of menu items that can be displayed on the screen depends on the system you are
    using. If the cursor or pull-down menu contains more items than your screen can
    accommodate, the excess items are truncated. For example, if your system displays 21 menu
    items, the menu items in excess of 21 are automatically truncated.

Example 4

Write a cursor menu for the following AutoCAD commands using cascading submenus. The menu
should be compatible with foreign language versions of AutoCAD. Use the third button of the
BUTTONS menu to display the cursor menu.

O'Snaps	Draw	DISPLAY
Center	Line	REDRAW
End point	PLINE	ZOOM
Intersection	CIR C,R	...Win
Midpoint	CIR 2P	...Cros
Nearest	ARC SCE	...Prev
Perpendicular	ARC CSE	...All
Quadrant		...Ext
Tangent		PAN
None		

The following file is a listing of the menu file for Example 4. The line numbers are not a part of
the file, they are for reference only.

***BUTTONS1	1
;	2
$P0=*	3
***POP0	4
[O'Snaps]	5
[Center]_Center	6
[End point]_Endp	7
[Intersection]_Int	8
[Midpoint]_Mid	9
[Nearest]_Nea	10
[Perpendicular]_Per	11
[Quadrant]_Qua	12
[Tangent]_Tan	13
[None]_Non	14
[--]	15
[->Draw]	16
[Line]^C^C_Line	17
[PLINE]^C^C_Pline	18
[CIR C,R]^C^C_Circle	19
[CIR 2P]^C^C_Circle;_2P	20
[ARC SCE]^C^C_ARC;\C	21
[<-ARC CSE]^C^C_Arc;C	22
[--]	23
[->DISPLAY]	24
[REDRAW]^C^_REDRAW	25
[->ZOOM]	26
[...Win]^C^C_ZOOM;_W	27
[...Cros]^C^C_ZOOM;_C	28
[...Prev]^C^C_ZOOM;_P	29
[...All]^C^C_ZOOM;_A	30
[<-...Ext]^C^C_ZOOM;_E	31
[<-PAN]^C^C_Pan	32
***POP1	33
[Draw]	34

> **Note**
>
> *Make sure that at least one pull-down menu is defined. If no POPn sections are defined or the menu bar is disabled, the cursor menu will not work.*

Line 1

***BUTTONS1

BUTTONS1 is the section label for the first Buttons menu; ******* designates the menu section. The menu items that follow it, until the second section label, are a part of this buttons menu.

Lines 2 and 3
;
$P0=*
The semicolon (;) is assigned to the second button of the pointing device (the first button of the pointing device is the pick button); the special command **$P0=*** is assigned to the third button of the pointing device.

Lines 4 and 5
***POP0
[O'Snaps]
The menu label **POP0** is the menu section label for the cursor menu; **O'Snaps** is the menu bar title. The menu bar title is not required, although you should use a dummy name.

Line 6
[Center]_Center
In this menu item, **_Center** is the center object snap mode. The menu files can be used with foreign language versions of AutoCAD, if AutoCAD commands and the command options are preceded by the underscore (_) character.

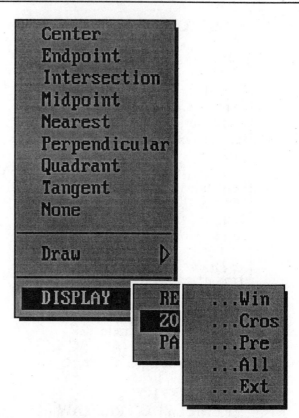

After loading the menu, if you press the third button of your pointing device, the cursor menu will be displayed at the cursor (screen cross-hair) location. If the cursor is close to the edges of screen, the cursor menu will be displayed at a location that is closest to the cursor position. When you select the submenus, the items contained in the submenu will be displayed, even if the cursor menu is touching the edges of the screen display area.

Lines 33 and 34
***POP1
[Draw]
***POP1 defines the first pull-down menu. If no POPn sections are defined or the status line is turned off, the cursor menu is automatically disabled.

Exercise 2

Write a pull-down and a screen menu for the following AutoCAD commands. Use a submenu for the LINE command options in the pull-down menu. When the user selects an item from the pull-down menu, the corresponding screen menu should be automatically loaded on the screen. (The layout of the screen menu and the pull-down menu are shown in Figures 32-6(a) and 32-6(b).)

LINE	ZOOM All	TIME
Continue	ZOOM Win	LIST
Close	ZOOM Pre	DISTANCE
Undo	PAN	AREA
.X		DBLIST
.Y		STATUS
.Z		
CIRCLE		
ELLIPSE		

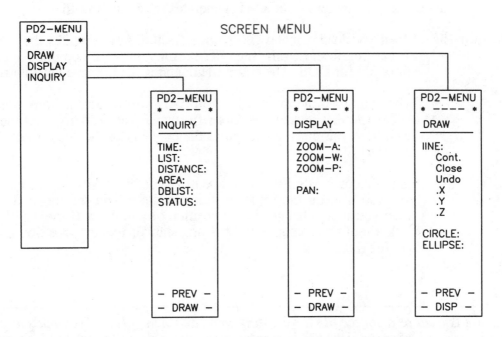

Figure 32-6(a) Design of screen menu for Exercise 2

Figure 32-6(b) Design of pull-down menu for Exercise 2

MENU FEATURES FOR WINDOWS

Because you are using AutoCAD for Windows, you have additional menu features available to you that are not available on DOS platform. For example, in Windows you can write partial menus, toolbars, and definition for accelerator keys. After writing the menus, AutoCAD lets you load the menu and use it with the standard menu. For example, you could load a partial menu and use it like a pull-down menu. You can also unload the menus that you do not want to use. These features make it convenient to use the menus that have been developed by AutoCAD users and developers.

Loading Menus

When you load a menu file in windows, AutoCAD generates the following files:

.mnc and **.mnr** file   When you load a menu file (**.mnu**), AutoCAD compiles the menu file and creates **.mnc** and **.mnr** files. The **.mnc** file is a compiled menu file like **.mnx** file for DOS. The **.mnr** file contains the bitmaps used by the menu.

.mns file   When you load the menu file, AutoCAD also creates a **.mns** file. This is an ASCII file that is same as **.mnu** file when you initially load the menu file. Each time you make a change in the contents of the file, AutoCAD changes the **.mns** file.

.ini file   This file contains information about the toolbar position. For example, when you load a menu the initial position is defined in the menu file. However, when you make changes in the position of a tool bar (for example, when you dock a toolbar or change the floating status), the new position is recorded in the **.ini** file.

Note

The .mns file is used as a source file for creating .mnc and .mnr files. If you make a change in the menu file (.mnu) after the .mns file is created, you must delete the .mns and .mnc files before you load the new menu. Otherwise, AutoCAD will not recognize the changes you made in the menu file.

Menu Section Labels

The following is a list of the menu section labels for Windows:

Section label	Description
***MENUGROUP	Menu file group name
***TOOLBARS	Toolbar definition
***HELPSTRING	On-line help
***ACCELERATORS	Accelerator key definitions

Writing Partial Menus

The following example illustrates the procedure for writing a partial menus for Windows. This facility is not available for other platforms.

Example 5

In this example you will write a partial menu for Windows. The menu file has two pull-down menus, POP1 (MyDraw) and POP2 (MyEdit) as shown in Figure 32-7.

Step 1
Use a Text Editor to write the following menu file. You can also use AutoCAD's EDIT function to invoke the DOS editor. The name of the file is assumed to be MENU1.MNU.

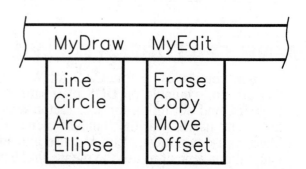

Figure 32-7 Pull-down menus

Command: **EDIT**
File to edit: **MENU1.MNU** *(MENU1.MNU is the name of the file.)*

The following is the listing of the menu file for this example:

```
***MENUGROUP=Menu1                                    1
***POP1                                               2
[/MMyDraw]                                            3
[/LLine]^C^CLine                                      4
[/CCircle]^C^CCircle                                  5
[/AArc]^C^CArc                                        6
[/EEllipse]^C^CEllipse                                7

***POP2                                               8
[/EMyEdit]                                            9
[/EErase]^C^CErase                                   10
[/CCopy]^C^CCopy                                     11
[/MMove]^C^CMove                                     12
[/OOffset]^C^COffset                                 13
```

Explanation

Line 1
***MENUGROUP=Menu1
MENUGROUP is the section label and the Menu1 is the name tag for the menu group. The MENUGROUP label must proceed all menu section definitions. The name of the MENUGROUP (Menu1) can be up to 32 characters long (alpha-numeric), excluding spaces and punctuation marks. There is only one MENUGROUP in a menu file. All section labels must be preceded by *** (***MENUGROUP).

Line 2
***POP1
POP1 is the pull-down menu section label. The items on line numbers 3 through 7 belong to this section. Similarly, the items on line numbers 9 through 13 belong to the pull-down menu section **POP2**.

Line 3
[/MMyDraw]
/M defines the mnemonic key that you can use to activate the menu item. For example, /M will display a dash under the letter M in the text string that follows it. If you enter the letter M, AutoCAD will execute the command defined in that menu item. MyDraw is the menu item label. The text string inside the brackets [   ] , except /M, has no function. They are used for displaying the function name so that the user can recognize the command that will be executed by selecting that item.

Line 4
[/LLine]^C^CLine
In this line, the /L defines the mnemonic key and the Line that is inside the brackets is the menu item label. ^C^C cancels the command twice and the Line is AutoCAD's LINE command. The part of the menu item statement that is outside the brackets is executed when you select an item from the menu. When you select the above item (Line 4), AutoCAD will execute the LINE command.

Step 2
Save the file and then load the partial menu file using AutoCAD's MENULOAD command.

Command: **MENULOAD**

When you enter the **MENULOAD** command, AutoCAD displays the **Menu Customization** dialogue box (Figure 32-8) on the screen. To load the menu file, enter the name of the menu file, MENU1.MNU, in the **File Name:** edit box. You can also use the Browse option to invoke the **Select Menu File** dialogue box. Select the name of the file and then use the OK button to return to the **Menu Customization** dialogue box. To load the selected menu file, pick the LOAD button. To exit the **Menu Customization** dialogue box, select the Close button.

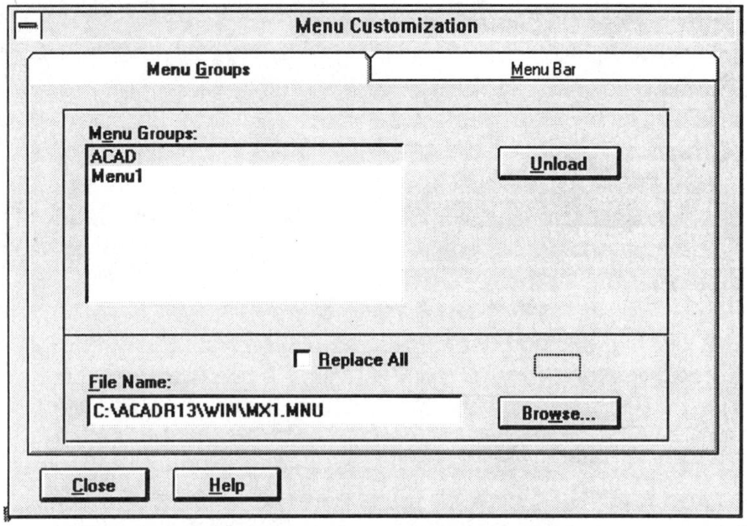

Figure 32-8 Menu Customization dialogue box

You can also load the menu file from the command line as follows:

Command: **FILEDIA**
New value for FILEDIA <1>: **0**   *(Disables the file dialogue boxes.)*

Command: **MENULOAD**
Menu file name or . for none <acad.mnc>: **MENU1.MNU**

You can also use the AutoLISP functions to set the FILEDIA system variable to 0 and then load the partial menu.

Command: **(SETVAR "FILEDIA" 0)**
Command: **(Command "MENULOAD" "Menu1")**

Step 3
Once the menu is loaded, use the MENUCMD (AutoLISP function) to display the partial menus.

Command: **(MENUCMD "P8=+Menu1.POP1")**
Command: **(MENUCMD "P9=+Menu1.POP2")**

Figure 32-9 MENUCMD command places the menu titles in the menu bar

After entering these commands, AutoCAD will display the pull-down menu titles in the menu bar as shown in Figure 32-9. If you select MyDraw, the corresponding pull-down menu as defined in the menu file will be displayed on the screen. Similarly, selecting MyEdit will display the corresponding edit pull-down menu.

MENUCMD is an AutoLISP function and P8 determines where the POP1 menu will be displayed. In this example the POP1 (MyDraw) pull-down menu will be displayed as the eighth pull-down menu. Menu1 is the MENUGROUP name as defined in the menu file and POP1 is the pull-down menu section label. The MENUGROUP name and the menu section label must be separated by a period (.).

Step 4

If you need to unload the partial menu file, enter the MENULOAD or MENUUNLOAD command to invoke the **Menu Customization** dialogue box. AutoCAD will display the names of the menu files in the Menu Groups: list box. Select the **Menu1** menu file and then select the **Unload** file. AutoCAD will unload the partial menu file. Select the **Close** button to exit the dialogue box. You can also unload the menu file from the command line as follows:

Command: **FILEDIA**
New value for FILEDIA <1>: **0**

Command: **MENUUNLOAD**
Enter the name of the MENUGROUP to unload: **MENU1.MNU**

The **MENUUNLOAD** command unloads the entire partial menu. You can also unload an individual pull-down menu without unloading the entire partial menu by using the following command:

Command: **(MENUCMD "P8=-)**

This command will unload the pull-down menu at position eight (P8, MyDraw pull-down menu). The menu group is still loaded, but the P8 pull-down menu is not visible. The menu can also be retinitialized by using the MENU command to load the base menu ACAD.MNU or ACADFULL.MNU. This will remove all partial menus and the tag definitions associated with the partial menus.

Accelerator Keys

AutoCAD for Windows also supports user defined accelerator keys. For example, if you enter **C** at Command: prompt, AutoCAD draws a circle. You cannot use the C key to enter the COPY command. To use the C key for entering COPY command, you can define the accelerator keys. You can combine the Shift key with C in the menu file so that when you hold down the shift key and then press the C key, AutoCAD will execute the copy command. The following example illustrates the use of accelerator keys:

Example 6

In this example you will add the following accelerator keys to the partial menu of Example 5.

```
CONTROL+"E"     to draw Ellipse (ELLIPSE command)
SHIFT+"C"       to copy (COPY command)
[CONTROL"Q"]    to quit (QUIT command)
```

The following file is the listing of the partial menu file that uses the accelerator keys of Example 6.

```
***MENUGROUP=Menu1
***POP1
**Alias
[/MMyDraw]
[/LLine]^C^CLine
[/CCircle]^C^CCircle
[/AArc]^C^CArc
ID_Ellipse [/EEllipse]^C^CEllipse
```

```
***POP2
[/EMyEdit]
[/EErase]^C^CErase
ID_Copy [/CCopy]^C^CCopy
[/OOffset]^C^COffset
[/VMove]^C^CMov

***ACCELERATORS
ID_Ellipse [CONTROL+"E"]
ID_Copy [SHIFT+"C"]
[CONTROL"Q"]^C^CQuit
```

This menu file defines three accelerator keys. The **ID_Copy [SHIFT+"C"]** accelerator key consists of two parts. The ID_Copy is the name tag that must be the same as used earlier in the menu item definition. The SHIFT+"C" is the label that contains the modifier (SHIFT) and the key name (C). The key name or the string like "Escape" must be enclosed in quotation marks. After you load the file, Shift+C will enter the COPY command and Ctrl+E will draw an ellipse. Similarly, Ctrl+Q will cancel the existing command and enter the QUIT command.

The accelerator keys can be defined in two ways. One of the ways is to give the tag name that is followed by the label containing the modifier. The modifier is followed by a single character or a special virtual key enclosed in quotation marks [CONTROL+"E"] or ["ESCAPE"]. You can also use the plus symbol (+) to concatenate the modifiers [SHIFT + CONTROL + "L"]. The other way of defining an accelerator key is to give the modifier and the key string, followed by a command sequence [CONTROL "Q"]^C^CQuit.

Special Virtual Keys
The following are the special virtual keys. These keys must be enclosed in quotation marks when used in the menu file.

String	Description	String	Description
"F1"	F1 key	"NUMBERPAD0"	0 key
"F2"	F2 key	"NUMBERPAD1"	1 key
"F3"	F3 key	"NUMBERPAD2"	2 key
"F4"	F4 key	"NUMBERPAD3"	3 key
"F5"	F5 key	"NUMBERPAD4"	4 key
"F6"	F6 key	"NUMBERPAD5"	5 key
"F7"	F7 key	"NUMBERPAD6"	6 key
"F8"	F8 key	"NUMBERPAD7"	7 key
"F9"	F9 key	"NUMBERPAD8"	8 key
"F10"	F10 key	"NUMBERPAD9"	9 key
"F11"	F11 key	"UP"	Up-arrow key
"F12"	F12 key	"DOWN"	Down-arrow key
"HOME"	Home key	"LEFT"	Left-arrow key
"END"	End key	"RIGHT"	Right-arrow key
"INSERT"	Ins key	"ESCAPE"	Esc key
"DELETE"	Del key		

Valid Modifiers
The following are the valid modifiers:

String	Description
CONTROL	The control key on the keyboard
SHIFT	The shift key (Left or right)
COMMAND	The Apple key on Macintosh keyboards
META	The meta key on UNIX keyboards

Toolbars

The contents of the toolbar and its default layout can be specified in the Toolbar section (***TOOLBARS) of the menu file. Each toolbar must be defined in a separate submenu.

Toolbar Definition

The following is the general format of the toolbar definition:

```
***TOOLBARS
**MYTOOLS1
TAG1 [Toolbar ("tbarname", orient, visible, xval, yval, rows)]
TAG2 [Button ("btnname", id_small, id_large)]macro
TAG3 [Flyout ("flyname", id_small, id_large, icon, alias)]macro
TAG4 [control (element)]
[--]
```

***TOOLBARS is the section label of the toolbar and **MYTOOLS1** is the name of the submenu that contains the definition of a toolbar. Each toolbar can have five distinct items that control different elements of the toolbar: TAG1, TAG2, TAG3, TAG4, and separator ([--]).

The first line (TAG1) of the toolbar defines the characteristics of the toolbar. In this line the **Toolbar** is the key word and it is followed by a series of options enclosed in parenthesis. The following is the description of the available options:

tbarname	This is a text string that names the toolbar. The tbarname text string must consist of alphanumeric characters with no punctuation other than a dash (-) or an underscore (_).
orient	This determines the orientation of the toolbar. The acceptable values are Floating, Top, Bottom, Left, and Right. These values are not case-sensitive.
visible	This determines the visibility of the toolbar. The acceptable values are Show and Hide. These values are not case-sensitive.
xval	This is a numeric value that specifies the X ordinate in pixels. The X ordinate is measured from the left edge of the screen to the right side of the toolbar.
yval	This is a numeric value that specifies the Y ordinate in pixels. The Y ordinate is measured from the top edge of the screen to the top of the toolbar.
rows	This is a numeric value that specifies the number of rows.

The second line (TAG2) of the toolbar defines the button. In this line the **Button** is the key word and it is followed by a series of options enclosed in parenthesis. The following is the description of the available options:

btnname	This is a text string that names the button. The text string must consist of alphanumeric characters with no punctuation other than a dash (-) or an underscore (_). This text string is displayed as ToolTip when you place the cursor over the button.
id_smll	This is a text string that names the ID string of the small image resource (16 by 16 bitmap). The text string must consist of alphanumeric characters with no punctuation other than a dash (-) or an underscore (_). The id_small text string can also specify a user defined bitmap (Example,ICON_16_CIRCLE).

id_big	This is a text string that names the ID string of the large image resource (32 by 32 bitmap). The text string must consist of alphanumeric characters with no punctuation other than a dash (-) or an underscore (_). The id_big text string can also specify a user defined bitmap (Example,ICON_32_CIRCLE).
macro	The second line (TAG2) that defines a button is followed by command string (macro). For example, the macro can consist of ^C^CLine. It follows the same syntax as that of any standard menu item definition.

The third line (TAG3) of the toolbar defines the flyout control. In this line the **Flyout** is the key word and it is followed by a series of options enclosed in parenthesis. The following is the description of the available options:

flyname	This is a text string that names the flyout. The text string must consist of alphanumeric characters with no punctuation other than a dash (-) or an underscore (_). This text string is displayed as ToolTip when you place the cursor over the flyout button.
id_smll	This is a text string that names the ID string of the small image resource (16 by 16 bitmap). The text string must consist of alphanumeric characters with no punctuation other than a dash (-) or an underscore (_). The id_small text string can also specify a user defined bitmap.
id_big	This is a text string that names the ID string of the large image resource (32 by 32 bitmap). The text string must consist of alphanumeric characters with no punctuation other than a dash (-) or an underscore (_). The id_big text string can also specify a user defined bitmap.
icon	This is a Boolean key word that determines whether the button displays its own icon or it display the last icon selected. The acceptable values are **ownicon** and **othericon**. These values are not case-sensitive.
alias	The alias specifies the name of the toolbar submenu that is defined with the standard ****aliasname** syntax.
macro	The third line (TAG3) that defines a flyout control is followed by command string (macro). For example, the macro can consist of ^C^CCircle. It follows the same syntax as that of any standard menu item definition.

The fourth line (TAG4) of the toolbar defines a special control element. In this line the **Control** is the key word and it is followed by the type of control element enclosed in parenthesis. The following is the description of the available control element types:

element	This parameter can have one of the following three values: Layer: This specifies the layer control element. Linetype: This specifies the linetype control element. Color: This specifies the color control element.

The fifth line ([--]) defines a separator.

Example 7

In this example you will write a menu file for toolbar for Line, Pline, Circle, Ellipse, and Arc commands. The name of the toolbar is MyDraw1.

// The following is the listing of the menu file:
***TOOLBARS
**TB_MyDraw1
ID_MyDraw1[_Toolbar("MyDraw1", _Floating, _Hide, 10, 200, 1)]
ID_Line [_Button("Line", ICON_16_LINE, ICON_32_LINE)]^C^C_line
ID_Pline [_Button("Pline", ICON_16_PLine, ICON_32_PLine)]^C^C_PLine
ID_Circle[_Button("Circle", ICON_16_CirRAD, ICON_32_CirRAD)]^C^C_Circle
ID_ELLIPSE[_Button("Ellipse", ICON_16_EllCEN, ICON_32_EllCEN)]^C^C_ELLIPSE
ID_Arc[_Button("Arc 3Point", ICON_16_Arc3Pt, ICON_32_Arc3Pt)]^C^C_Arc

Use the MENU command to load the menu file and then use
the TOOLBAR command to display the MyDraw1 toolbar on
the screen.

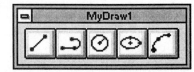

    Command: **TOOLBAR**   Figure 32-10 Toolbar for Example 7
    Toolbar name (or ALL): **All**
    Show/Hide: **S**

Example 8

In this example you will write a menu file for toolbar with flyout. The name of the toolbar is
MyDraw2 and it contains two icons, Circle and Arc. When you select the Circle icon, it should
display a flyout with radius, diameter, 2P, and 3P icons. Similarly when you select the Arc icon,
it should display the 3Point, SCE, and SCA icons.

// The following is the listing of the menu file:
***Menugroup=M2
***TOOLBARS
**TB_MyDraw2
ID_MyDraw2[_Toolbar("MyDraw2", _Floating, _Show, 10, 100, 1)]
ID_TbCircle[_Flyout("Circle", ICON_16_Circle, ICON_32_Circle, _OtherIcon, M2.TB_Circle)]
ID_TbArc[_Flyout("Arc", ICON_16_Arc, ICON_32_Arc, _OtherIcon, M2.TB_Arc)]

**TB_Circle
ID_TbCircle[_Toolbar("Circle", _Floating, _Hide, 10, 150, 1)]
ID_CirRAD[_Button("Circle C,R", ICON_16_CirRAD, ICON_32_CirRAD)]^C^C_Circle
ID_CirDIA[_Button("Circle C,D", ICON_16_CirDIA, ICON_32_CirDIA)]^C^C_Circle;\D
ID_Cir2Pt[_Button("Circle 2Pts", ICON_16_Cir2Pt, ICON_32_Cir2Pt)]^C^C_Circle;2P
ID_Cir3Pt[_Button("Circle 3Pts", ICON_16_Cir3Pt, ICON_32_Cir3Pt)]^C^C_Circle;3P

**TB_Arc
ID_TbArc[_Toolbar("Arc", _Floating, _Hide, 10, 150, 1)]
ID_Arc3PT[_Button("Arc,3Pts", ICON_16_Arc3PT, ICON_32_Arc3PT)]^C^C_Arc
ID_ArcSCE[_Button("Arc,SCE", ICON_16_ArcSCE, ICON_32_ArcSCE)]^C^C_Arc;\C
ID_ArcSCA[_Button("Arc,SCA", ICON_16_ArcSCA, ICON_32_ArcSCA)]^C^C_Arc;\C;\A

Explanation
ID_TbCircle[_Flyout("Circle", ICON_16_Circle, ICON_32_Circle, _OtherIcon, **M2.TB_Circle**)]

In this line M2 is the MENUGROUP name (***MENUGROUP=M2) and TB_Circle is the name
of the toolbar submenu. **M2.TB_Circle** will load the submenu TB_Circle that has been defined in
the M2 menugroup. If M2 is missing, AutoCAD will not display the flyout when you click on the
Circle icon.

ID_CirDIA[_Button("Circle C,D", ICON_16_**CirDIA**, ICON_32_**CirDIA**)]^C^C_Circle;\D

CirDIA is a user defined bitmap that displays the Circle-diameter icon. If you use anyother name, AutoCAD will not display the desired icon.

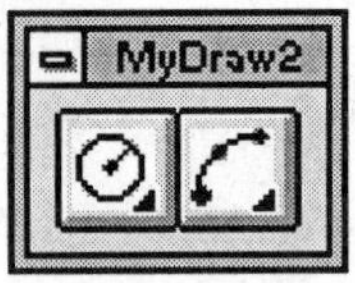

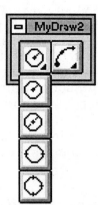

Figure 32-11   Toolbar for Example 8

Figure 32-12   Toolbar with flyout

MENU SPECIFIC HELP

AutoCAD for Windows allows to access on-line help. For example, if you want to define a help string for the CIRCLE and ARC commands, the syntax is as follows.

```
***HELPSTRING
ID_Copy [This command will copy the selected object]
ID_Ellipse [This command will draw an ellipse]
```

The *****HELPSTRING** is the section label for the helpstring menu section. The lines defined in this section start with a name tag (ID_Copy) and are followed by the label enclosed in square brackets. If you press the F1 key when the menu item is highlighted, the help engine gets activated and AutoCAD displays the help string defined with the name tag.

REVIEW QUESTIONS

Fill in the blanks.

1.   A pull-down menu can have _____ sections.

2.   The length of the section title should not exceed _____ characters.

3.   The section titles in a pull-down menu are _____ justified.

4.   In a pull-down menu, a line consisting of two hyphens ([--]) _____ automatically to fill the _____ of the pull-down menu or _____ characters, whichever is smaller.

5.   If the menu item begins with a tilde (~), the items will be displayed _____ than the rest of the menu.

6.   Pull-down menus are _____ when the dynamic zoom is in progress.

7.   Pull-down menus can be used if the display driver supports _____ interface.

8.   Every submenu in the menu file should have a _____ name.

9.   The submenu name can be _____ characters long.

10.   The submenu names should not have any _____ blanks.

11.   In windows you can write partial menus, toolbar and accelerator key definitions. (T/F)

12.   When you make a change in the menu file (.mnu) after the **.mns** file is created, you must delete the **.mns** and **.mnc** files before you load the new menu. (T/F)

13.   A menu file can contain only one MENUGROUP. (T/F)

14.   You can load the partial menu file by using AutoCAD's _____ command.

15.   Once the menu is loaded, you can use the _____ (AutoLISP function) to display the partial menus.

EXERCISES

Exercise 3

Write a pull-down menu for the following AutoCAD commands. (The layout of the pull-down menu is shown in Figure 32-13.)

LINE	DIM HORZ	DTEXT LEFT
CIRCLE C,R	DIM VERT	DTEXT RIGHT
CIRCLE C,D	DIM RADIUS	DTEXT CENTER
ARC 3P	DIM DIAMETER	DTEXT ALIGNED
ARC SCE	DIM ANGULAR	DTEXT MIDDLE
ARC CSE	DIM LEADER	DTEXT FIT

PULL—DOWN MENU

DRAW	DIM	DTEXT
LINE	DIM-HORZ	DTEXT-LEFT
CIRCLE C,R	DIM-VERT	DTEXT-RIGHT
CIRCLE C,D	DIM-RADIUS	DTEXT-CENTER
ARC 3P	DIM-DIAMETER	DTEXT-ALIGNED
ARC SCE	DIM-ANGULAR	DTEXT-MIDDLE
ARC CSE	DIM-LEADER	DTEXT-FIT

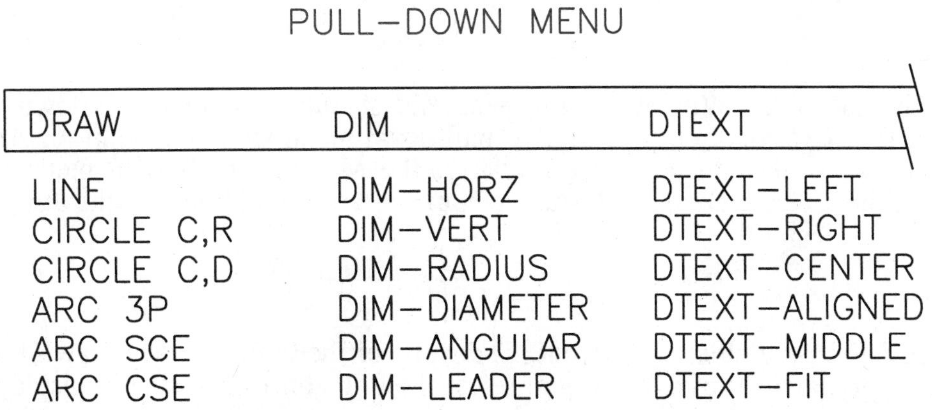

Figure 32-13 Layout of pull-down menu

Exercise 4

Write a pull-down menu, a screen menu, and a tablet menu for the following AutoCAD commands.   When you select a command from the template or the pull-down menu, the corresponding screen menu should be automatically loaded on the screen. (The layouts of the screen is shown in Figures 32-14).

LINE	BLOCK
PLINE	WBLOCK
CIRCLE C,R	INSERT
CIRCLE C,D	BLOCK LIST
ELLIPSE AXIS ENDPOINT	ATTDEF
ELLIPSE CENTER	ATTEDIT

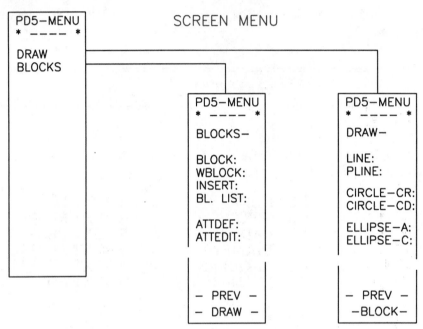

Figure 32-14 Design of screen menu for Exercise 4

Exercise 5

Write a partial menu for Windows. The menu file should have two pull-down menus, POP1 (MyArc) and POP2 (MyDraw). The MyArc pull-down menu should contain all Arc options and must be displayed at the 6th position. Similarly, the MyDraw pull-down menu should contain Line, Circle, Pline, Trace, Dtext, and Mtext commands and should occupy the 9th position.

Exercise 6

Write a menu file for a toolbar with flyout. The name of the toolbar is MyDrawX1 and it contains two icons, Polygon and Ellipse. When you select the Polygon icon it should display a flyout with rectangle and polygon icons. Similarly, when you select the Ellipse icon it should display the Ellipse-Center Option and Ellipse-Edge Option icons.

Chapter 33

Image Tile, Button, and Auxiliary Menus

Learning objectives

After completing this chapter, you will be able to:
- Write image tile menus.
- Reference and display submenus.
- Make slides for image tile menus.
- Write button menus.
- Learn special handling for button menus.

IMAGE TILE MENUS

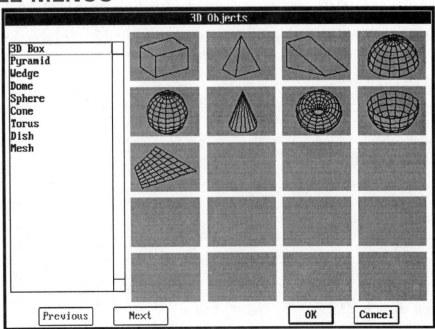

Figure 33-1 Sample image tile menu display

The Image Tile menus, also known as Icon menus, are extremely useful for inserting a block, selecting a text font, or drawing a 3D object. You can also use the image tile menus to load an AutoLISP routine or a predefined macro. Therefore, the image tile menu is a powerful tool for customizing AutoCAD.

The image tile menus can be accessed from the pull-down, tablet, button, or screen menu. However, the image tile menus cannot be loaded by entering the command from the keyboard. When you select an image tile, a dialogue box is displayed on the screen that contains **20 image tiles** (Figure 33-1). The names of the slide files associated with image tiles appear on the left side of the dialogue box with a scrolling bar that can be used to scroll the filenames. The title of the image tile menu is displayed at the top of the dialogue box (Figure 33-1). When you activate the image tile menu, an arrow appears on the screen that can be moved to select any image tile. You can select an image tile by selecting the slide file name from the dialogue box and then selecting the OK button from the dialogue box or double-clicking on the slide filename.

When you select the slide file, AutoCAD highlights the corresponding image tile by drawing a rectangle around the image tile. You can also select an image tile by moving the arrow to the desired image tile, then pressing the pick button of the pointing device. The corresponding slide filename will be automatically highlighted and if you select the OK button or double-click on the image tile, the command associated with that menu item will be executed. You can cancel an image tile menu by entering CTRL C, pressing the ESCAPE key on the keyboard, or selecting an image tile from the dialogue box.

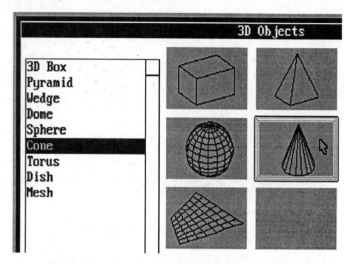

SUBMENUS

You can define an unlimited number of menu items in the image tile menu, but only 20 image tiles will be displayed at a time. If the number of items exceeds 20, you can use the **Next** or **Previous** buttons of the dialogue box to page through different pages of image tiles. You can also define submenus that let you define smaller groups of items within an image tile menu section. When you select a submenu, it loads the submenu items and displays them on the screen.

Submenu Definition

A submenu label consists of two asterisks (**) followed by the name of the submenu. The image tile menu can have any number of submenus, and every submenu should have a unique name. The items that follow a submenu, up to the next section label or submenu label, belong to that submenu. The format of a submenu label is:

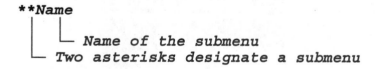

Note

The submenu name can be up to 31 characters long.

The submenu name can consist of letters, digits, and special characters, like $ (dollar), - (hyphen), and _ (underscore).

The submenu name should not have any embedded blanks.

Submenu names should be unique in a menu file.

Submenu Reference

The submenu reference is used to reference or load a submenu. It consists of a $ sign followed by a letter that specifies the menu section. The letter that specifies an image tile menu section is I. The menu section is followed by an = sign and the name of the submenu you want to activate. The submenu name should be without **. Following is the format of a submenu reference:

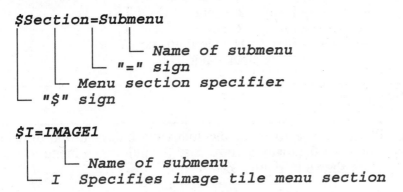

```
$Section=Submenu
 |      |      |
 |      |      └─ Name of submenu
 |      └─ "=" sign
 |    └─ Menu section specifier
 └─ "$" sign
```

```
$I=IMAGE1
 |   |
 |   └─ Name of submenu
 └─ I  Specifies image tile menu section
```

Displaying a Submenu

When you load a submenu, the new dialogue box and the image tiles are not automatically displayed on the screen. For example, if you load submenu IMAGE1, the items contained in this submenu will not be displayed. To force the display of the new image tile menu on the screen, AutoCAD uses the special command $I=*

```
$I=*
 |  |
 |  └─ Asterisk (*)
 └─ I for image tile menu
```

WRITING AN IMAGE TILE MENU

An image tile menu will work only if the device driver you are using supports AutoCAD's advanced user interface (AUI). AutoCAD ignores the image tile menu section (***IMAGE) if the display driver does not support AUI. Also, the system should be configured so that the status line is not disabled. Otherwise, you cannot use the pull-down menus and you cannot access the icon menus through the pull-down menus.

The image tile menu consists of section label ***IMAGE, followed by image tiles or image tile submenus. The menu file can contain only one image tile menu section (***IMAGE); therefore, all image tiles must be defined in this section.

```
***IMAGE
 |    |
 |    └─ Section label for an image tile
 └─ Three asterisks designate a section label
```

You can define any number of submenus in the image tile menu. All submenus have two asterisks followed by the name of the submenu (**PARTS or **IMAGE1).

```
**IMAGE1
 |    |
 |    └─ Name of submenu
 └─ Two asterisks designate a submenu
```

The first item in the image tile menu is the title of the image tile menu that is displayed at the top of the dialogue box (Figure 33-1). The Image tile dialogue box title has to be enclosed in brackets ([PLC-SYMBOLS]) and should not contain any command definition. If it does contain a command definition, AutoCAD ignores the definition. The remaining items in the image tile menu file contain slide names in the brackets and the command definition outside the brackets.

```
***IMAGE                ——————— Image tile menu section
**BOLTS                 ——————— Image tile submenu (BOLTS)
[HEX-HEAD BOLTS]        ——————— Image tile title
[BOLT1]^C^CINSERT;B1    ——————— BOLT1 is slide filename
                                B1 is block name
```

Example 1

Write an image tile menu that will enable you to insert the following blocks in the drawing by selecting the corresponding image tile from the dialogue box. Use the pull-down menu to load the image tile menu. (The block shapes are shown in Figure 33-2.)

PLC SYMBOLS   ELECTRIC SYMBOLS

NO (NORMALLY OPEN)   RESIS (RESISTANCE)
NC (NORMALLY CLOSED)   DIODE
COIL   GROUND

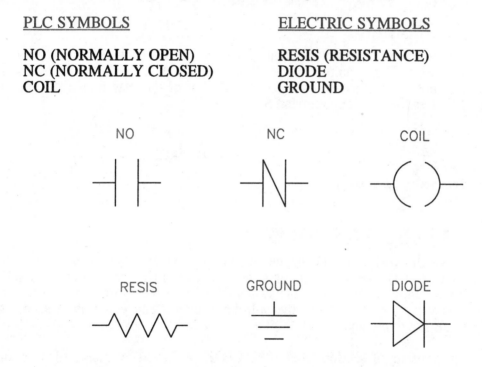

Figure 33-2 Block shapes for image tile menu

As mentioned in the earlier chapters, the first step in writing a menu is to design the menu so that the commands are arranged in a desired configuration. Figure 33-3 shows one of the possible designs of the pull-down menu and the image tile menu for Example 1.

You can use AutoCAD's EDIT command or EDIT function of DOS to write the file. The line numbers in the following file are for reference only and are not a part of the menu file.

```
***POP1                                        1
[ELECTRIC]                                     2
[PLC-SYMBOLS]$I=IMAGE1 $I=*                    3
[ELEC-SYMBOLS]$I=IMAGE2 $I=*                   4
***IMAGE                                       5
```

```
**IMAGE1                                              6
[PLC-SYMBOLS]                                         7
[NO]^C^CINSERT;NO;\1.0;1.0;0                          8
[NC]^C^CINSERT;NC;\1.0;1.0;0;                         9
[COIL]^C^CINSERT;COIL                                 10
[ No-Image]                                           11
[    ]                                                12
**IMAGE2                                              13
[ELECTRICAL SYMBOLS]                                  14
[RESIS]^C^CINSERT;RESIS;\\\\                          15
[DIODE]^C^CINSERT;DIODE;\1.0;1.0;\                    16
[GROUND]^C^CINSERT;GRD;\1.5;1.5;0;;                   17
[    ]                                                18
```

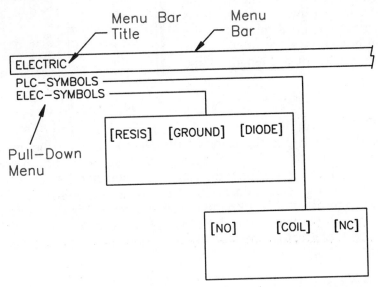

Figure 33-3 Design of pull-down and image tile menu for Example 1

Line 1
***POP1
In this menu item, ***POP1 is the section label and defines the first section of the pull-down menu.

Line 2
[ELECTRIC]
In this menu item [ELECTRIC] is the menu bar label for the POP1 pull-down menu. It will be displayed in the menu bar.

Line 3
[PLC SYMBOLS]$I=IMAGE1 $I=*
In this menu item, $I=IMAGE1 loads the submenu IMAGE1; $I=* displays the current image tile menu on the screen.

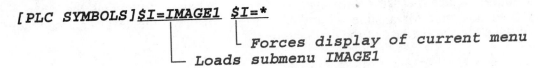

Line 5
***IMAGE
In this menu item, ***IMAGE is the section label of the image tile menu. All the image tile menus have to be defined within this section, otherwise AutoCAD cannot locate them.

Line 6
**IMAGE1
In this menu item, **IMAGE1 is the name of the image tile submenu.

Line 7
[PLC-SYMBOLS]
When you select line 3 ([PLC SYMBOLS]$I=IMAGE1 $I=*), AutoCAD loads the submenu IMAGE1 and displays the title of the image tile at the top of the dialogue box. This title is defined in line 7. If this line is missing, the next line will be displayed at the top of the dialogue box. Image tile titles can be any length as long as they fit the length of the dialogue box.

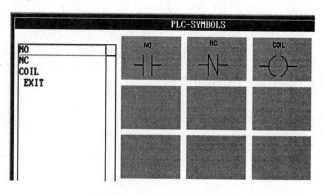

Line 8
[NO]^C^CINSERT;NO;\1.0;1.0;0
In this menu item, the first NO is the name of the slide and has to be enclosed within brackets. The name should not have any trailing or leading blank spaces. Slide names can be up to eight characters long. If the slides are not present, AutoCAD will not display any graphical symbols in the image tiles. However, the menu items will be loaded and if you select this item, the command associated with the image tile will be executed. The second NO is the name of the block that is to be inserted. The backslash (\) pauses for user input; in this case it is the block insertion point. The first 1.0 defines the X-scale factor, the second 1.0 defines the Y-scale factor, and the following 0 defines the rotation.

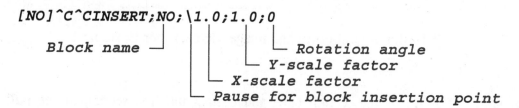

When you select this item, it will automatically enter all the prompts of the INSERT command and insert the NO block at the given location. The only input you need to enter is the insertion point of the block.

Line 10
[COIL]^C^CINSERT;COIL
In this menu item the block name is given, but you need to define other parameters when inserting this block.

Line 11
[No-Image]^C
Notice the **blank space before No-Image**. If there is a space following the open bracket, AutoCAD does not look for a slide. AutoCAD instead displays the text, enclosed within the brackets, in the **slide file list** box of the dialogue box.

Lines 12 and 18

[   ]

Lines 12 and 18 consist of brackets only, this terminates the image tile menu IMAGE1. You can also use a blank line instead of brackets. When you swap the menus, the current items that are displayed on the screen must be cleared before loading the new items. This is made possible by providing a blank line at the end of every submenu. In this menu file, line 12 clears the current menu items from the screen. If this line is missing, the submenu items will overlap; as a result some of the image tiles will not change when you load a new submenu that has fewer items.

Line 14

[RESIS]^C^CINSERT;RESIS;

This menu item inserts the block RESIS. The first backslash (\) is for block insertion point. The second and third backslashes are for X-scale and Y-scale factors. The fourth backslash is for the rotation angle. This menu item could also be written as:

[RESIS]^C^CINSERT;RESIS;
or
[RESIS]^C^CINSERT;RESIS

Line 15

[DIODE]^C^CINSERT;DIODE;\1.0;1.0;

If you select this menu item, AutoCAD will prompt you to enter the block insertion point and the rotation angle. The first backslash is for the block insertion point; the second backslash is for the rotation angle.

```
[DIODE]^C^CINSERT;DIODE;\1.0;1.0;\
                                │         └─ Pause for rotation angle
                                └─ Pause for insertion point
```

Line 16

[GROUND]^C^CINSERT;GRD;\1.5;1.5;0;;

This menu item has two semicolons (;) at the end. The first semicolon after 0 is for RETURN and completes the block insertion process. The second semicolon enters a RETURN and repeats the INSERT command. However, when the command is repeated you will have to respond to all of the prompts. It does not accept the values defined in the menu item.

Note

The ***IMAGE section label replaces the ***ICON section used in previous releases. The ***ICON is still valid for AutoCAD Release-13. It will be dropped in future releases.

The menu item repetition feature cannot be used with the image tile menus. For example, if the command definition starts with an asterisk ([GROUND]*^C^CINSERT;GRD;\1.5;1.5;0;;), the command is not automatically repeated, as is the case with a pull-down menu.

A blank line in an image tile menu terminates the menu and clears the image tiles.

The menu command $I=* that displays the current menu cannot be entered at the keyboard.

If you want to cancel or exit an image tile menu, enter CTRL C or press the ESCAPE key on the keyboard. AutoCAD ignores all other entries from the keyboard.

You can define any number of image tile menus and submenus in the image tile menu section of the menu file.

SLIDES FOR IMAGE TILE MENUS

The idea of creating slides for the image tile menus is to display graphical symbols in the image tiles. This symbol makes it easier for you to identify the operation that the image tile will perform. Any slide can be used for the image tile. However, the following guidelines should be kept in mind when creating slides for the image tile menu:

1. When you make a slide for an image tile menu, draw the object so that it fills the entire screen. The MSLIDE command makes a slide of the existing screen display. If the object is small the picture in the image tile menu will be small. Use ZOOM EXTENTS or ZOOM WINDOW to display the object before making a slide.

2. When you use the image tile menu, it takes some time to load the slides for display in the image tiles. If the slides are complex, it will take more time to load them. Therefore, the slides should be kept as simple as possible and at the same time give enough information about the object.

3. Do not fill the object, because it takes a long time to load and display a solid object. If there is a solid area in the slide, AutoCAD does not display the solid area in the image tile.

4. If the objects are too long or too wide, it is better to center the image with AutoCAD's PAN command before making a slide.

5. The space available on the screen for image tile display is limited. Make the best use of this small area by giving only the relevant information in the form of a slide.

6. The image tiles that are displayed in the dialogue box have the length-to-width ratio (aspect ratio) of 1.5:1. For example, if the length of the image tile is 1.5 units, the width is 1 unit. If the drawing area of your screen has an aspect ratio of 1.5 and the slide drawing is centered in the drawing area, the slide in the image tile will also be centered.

Exercise 1

Write an image tile menu for inserting the blocks as shown in Figure 33-4. Arrange the blocks in two groups so that you have two submenus in the image tile menu.

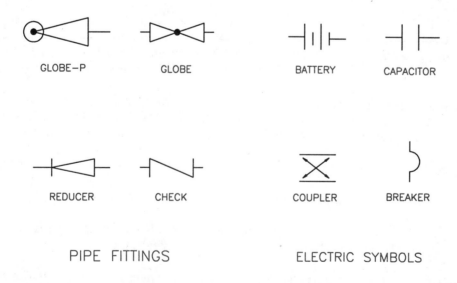

Figure 33-4 Block shapes for Exercise 1

PIPE FITTINGS	ELECTRIC SYMBOLS
GLOBE-P	BATTERY
GLOBE	CAPACITOR
REDUCER	COUPLER
CHECK	BREAKER

IMAGE TILE MENU ITEM LABELS

Like screen and pull-down menus, you can use menu item labels in the pull-down menus. However, the menu item labels in the image tile menus use different formats and each format performs a particular function in the image tile menu. The menu item labels appear in the slide list box of the dialogue box. The maximum number of characters that can be displayed in this box is 17. The characters in excess of 17 are not displayed in the list box. However, this does not affect the command that is defined with the menu item. The following are the different formats of the menu item labels.

[slidename]
In this menu item label format, **slidename** is the name of the slide that is displayed in the image tile. This name (slidename) is also displayed in the list box of the corresponding dialogue box.

[slidename,label]
In this menu item label format, **slidename** is the name of the slide that is displayed in the image tile. However, unlike the previous format, the **slidename** is not displayed in the list box. The **label** text is displayed in the list box. For example, if the menu item label is **[BOLT1,1/2-24UNC-3LG]**, **BOLT1** is the name of the slide and **1/2-24UNC-3LG** is the label that will be displayed in the list box.

[slidelib(slidename)]
In this menu item label format, **slidename** is the name of the slide in the slide library file **slidelib**. The slide (slidename) is displayed in the image tile and the slide filename (slidename) is also displayed in the list box of the corresponding dialogue box.

[slidelib(slidename,label)]
In this menu item label format, **slidename** is the name of the slide in the slide library file **slidelib**. The slide (slidename) is displayed in the image tile and the **label** text is displayed in the list box of the corresponding dialogue box.

[blank]
This menu item will draw a line that extends through the width of the list box. It also displays a blank image tile in the dialogue box.

[label]
If the **label** text is preceded by a space, AutoCAD does not look for a slide. The **label** text is displayed in the list box only. For example, if the menu item label is [EXIT]^C, the label text (EXIT) will be displayed in the list box. If you select this item, the cancel command (^C) defined with the item will be executed. The **label** text is not displayed in the image tile of the dialogue box.

Example 2

Write the pull-down and image tile menus for inserting the following commands. B1 to B15 are the block names.

BLOCK
WBLOCK

ATTDEF
LIST
INSERT

BL1	BL6	BL11
BL2	BL7	BL12
BL3	BL8	BL13
BL4	BL9	BL14
BL5	BL10	BL15

The first step in writing a menu is to design the menu. Figure 33-5 shows the design of the pull-down menus. If you select Insert from the pull-down menu, the image tiles and block names will be displayed in the dialogue box.

The following file is a listing of the menu file for Example 2. The file contains the screen, tablet, pull-down, and image tile menu sections. The line numbers are not a part of the menu file; they are given for reference only.

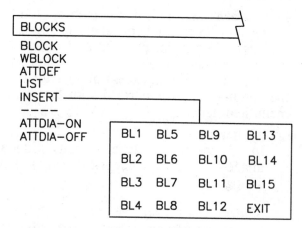

Figure 33-5 Design of screen and pull-down menu for Example 2

```
***POP1                                              1
[INSERT]                                             2
[BLOCK]^C^CBLOCK                                     3
[WBLOCK]^C^CWBLOCK                                   4
[ATTRIBUTE DEFINITION]^C^CATTDEF                     5
[LIST BLOCK NAMES]^C^CINSERT;?                       6
[INSERT]^C^C$I=IMAGE1 $I=*                           7
[--]                                                 8
[ATTDIA-ON]^C^CSETVAR ATTDIA 1                       9
[ATTDIA-OFF]^C^CSETVAR ATTDIA 0                      10
                                                     11
***IMAGE                                             12
**IMAGE1                                             13
[BLOCK INSERTION FOR EXAMPLE-2]                      14
[BL1]^C^C$S=INSERT1 INSERT;BL1;\1.0;1.0;\            15
[BL2]^C^C$S=INSERT1 INSERT;BL2;\1.0;1.0;0            16
[BL3]^C^C$S=INSERT1 INSERT;BL3;\;;\                  17
[BL4]^C^C$S=INSERT1 INSERT;BL4;\;;;                  18
[BL5]^C^C$S=INSERT1 INSERT;*BL5;\1.75               19
[BL6]^C^C$S=INSERT1 INSERT;BL6;\XYZ                  20
[BL7]^C^C$S=INSERT1 INSERT;BL7;\XYZ;;;\0             21
[BL8]^C^C$S=INSERT1 INSERT;BL8;\XYZ;;;;;             22
[BL9]^C^C$S=INSERT1 INSERT;BL9;\XYZ;;;;\             23
[BL10]^C^C$S=INSERT1 INSERT;*BL10;\XYZ;\             24
[BL11]^C^C$S=INSERT2 INSERT;BL11;\XYZ;1;1.5;2;45     25
[BL12]^C^C$S=INSERT2 INSERT;BL12;\XYZ;\\;;           26
[BL13]^C^C$S=INSERT2 INSERT;*BL13;\\45               27
[BL14]^C^C$S=INSERT2 INSERT;BL14;\C;@1.0,1.0;0       28
[BL15]^C^C$S=INSERT2 INSERT;BL15;\C;@1.0,2.0;\       29
[ EXIT]^C                                            30
```

Line 1
***POP1
This is the section label of the first pull-down menu. The menu items defined on lines 78 to 86 are defined in this section.

Line 12
***IMAGE
This is the section label of the image tile menu.

Line 13
**IMAGE1
IMAGE1 is the name of the submenu; the items on lines 90 to 107 are defined in this submenu.

Line 15
[BL1]^C^C$S=INSERT1 INSERT;BL1;\1.0;1.0;
In this menu item, BL1 is the name of the slide and $S=INSERT1 loads the submenu INSERT1 on the screen.

```
[BL1]^C^C$S=INSERT1 INSERT;BL1;\1.0;1.0;\
     |              |            |
     |              |            └─ AutoCAD's INSERT command
     |              └─ Loads submenu INSERT1
     └─ Slide file name
```

BUTTON MENUS

You can use a multi-button pointing device to pick points, select objects, or execute commands. These pointing devices come with different numbers of buttons, but four-button and twelve-button pointing devices are very common. In addition to selecting points and objects, the multi-button pointing devices can be used to provide easy access to frequently used AutoCAD commands. The commands are selected by pressing the desired button; AutoCAD automatically executes the command or the macro that is assigned to that button. Figure 33-6 shows one such pointing device with 12 buttons.

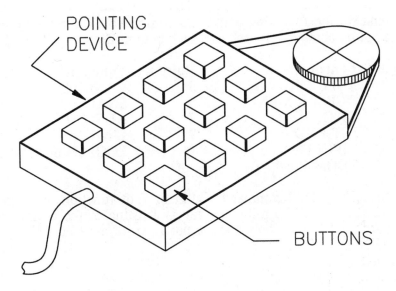

POINTING DEVICE

BUTTONS

Figure 33-6 Pointing device with 12 buttons

The AutoCAD software package comes with a standard button menu that is part of the ACAD.MNU file. The standard menu (ACAD.MNX) is automatically loaded when you start

AutoCAD and enter the Drawing Editor. You can write your own button menu and assign the desired commands or macros to various buttons of the pointing device.

WRITING A BUTTON MENU

In a menu file, you can have up to four button menus (BUTTONS1 through BUTTONS4) and four auxiliary menus (AUX1 through AUX4). The buttons and the auxiliary menus are identical. If your system has a pointing device (mouse or a digitizer puck), AutoCAD automatically assigns the commands defined in the BUTTONS sections of the menu file to the buttons of the pointing device. However, if your computer has a system mouse, the mouse will use the auxiliary menus. When you load the menu file, the commands defined in BUTTONS1 section of the menu file are assigned to the pointing device (digitizer puck). You can also access other button menus (BUTTONS2 through BUTTONS4) by using the following keyboard and button (buttons of the pointing device-digitizer puck) combination.

Buttons Menu	Keyboard + Button Sequence
BUTTONS1	Press the button of the pointing device.
BUTTONS2	Hold the **Shift** key down and press the button of the pointing device.
BUTTONS3	Hold the **Ctrl** key down and press the button of the pointing device.
BUTTONS4	Hold the **Shift** and **Ctrl** keys down and press the button of the pointing device.

One of the buttons, generally the first, is used as a pick button to pick the coordinates of the screen cross-hairs and send that information to AutoCAD. This button can also be used to select commands from various other menus such as tablet menu, screen menu, pull-down menu, and image tile menu. This button cannot be used to enter a command, but AutoCAD commands can be assigned to other buttons of the pointing device. Before writing a button menu, you should decide the commands and options that you want to assign to different buttons, and to know the prompts that are associated with those commands. The following example illustrates the working of the button menu, and the procedure for assigning commands to different buttons.

Example 3

Write a button menu for the following AutoCAD commands. The pointing device has 12 buttons (Figure 33-7) and button number 1 is used as a pick button (filename BM1.MNU).

Button	Function	Button	Function
2	RETURN	3	CANCEL
4	CURSOR MENU	5	SNAP
6	ORTHO	7	AUTO
8	INT,END	9	LINE
10	CIRCLE	11	ZOOM Win
12	ZOOM Prev		

You can use AutoCAD's EDIT command, Edlin or Edit function of DOS, or any other Text Editor to write the menu file. The following file is a listing of the button menu for Example 3. The line numbers are for reference only and are not a part of the menu file.

***BUTTONS1	1
;	2
^C^C	3
$P0=*	4
^B	5
^O	6

AUTO	7
INT,ENDP	8
^C^CLINE	9
^C^CCIRCLE	10
'ZOOM;Win	11
'ZOOM;Prev	12

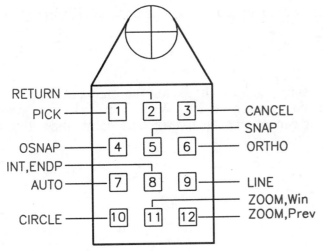

Figure 33-7 Pointing device

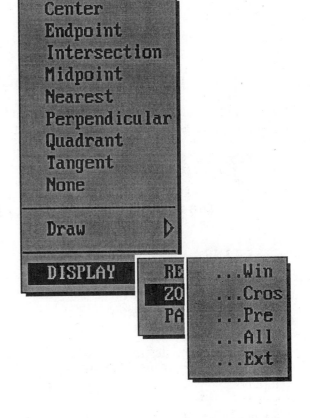

Line 1
***BUTTONS
***BUTTONS1 is the section label for the first button menu. When the menu is loaded, AutoCAD compiles the menu file and assigns the commands to the buttons of the pointing device.

Line 2
;
This menu item assigns a semicolon (;) to button number 2. When you pick the second button on the pointing device, it enters a RETURN. It is like entering RETURN at the keyboard or the digitizer.

Line 3
^C^C
This menu item cancels the existing command twice (^C^C). This command is assigned to button number 3 of the pointing device. When you pick the third button on the pointing device, it cancels the existing command twice.

Line 4
$P0=*
This menu item loads and displays the cursor menu POP0, which contains various object snap modes. It is assumed that the POP0 pull-down menu has been defined in the menu file. This command is assigned to button number 4 of the pointing device. If you press this button, it will load and display the cursor menu on the screen near the cross-hairs location.

Line 5
^B
This menu item changes the snap mode; it is assigned to button number 5 of the pointing device. When you pick the fifth button on the pointing device, it turns the SNAP mode on or off. It is like holding the CTRL key down on the keyboard and then pressing the B key.

Line 6
^O
This menu item changes the ORTHO mode; it is assigned to button number 6. When you pick the sixth button on the pointing device, it turns the ORTHO mode on or off.

Line 7
AUTO
This menu item selects the AUTO option for creating a selection set; this command is assigned to button number 7 on the pointing device.

Line 8
INT,ENDP
In this menu item INT is for the intersection snap, and ENDP is for the endpoint snap. This command is assigned to button number 8 on the pointing device. When you pick this button, AutoCAD looks for the intersection point. If it cannot find an intersection point, then it starts looking for the endpoint of the object that is within the pick box.

```
INT,ENDP
     |    |__ Endpoint object snap
     |_____ Intersection object snap
```

Line 9
^C^CLINE
This menu item defines the LINE command; it is assigned to button number 9. When you select this button, AutoCAD cancels the existing command, then selects the LINE command.

Line 10
^C^CCIRCLE
This menu item defines the CIRCLE command; it is assigned to button number 10. When you pick this button, AutoCAD automatically selects the CIRCLE command and prompts for the user input.

Line 11
'ZOOM;Win
This menu item defines a transparent ZOOM command with Window option; it is assigned to button number 11 of the pointing device.

```
'ZOOM;Win
 | |   |  |__ Window option of ZOOM command
 | |   |____ Semicolon for RETURN
 | |_____ AutoCAD's ZOOM command
 |_____ Single quote makes ZOOM command transparent
```

Line 12
'ZOOM;Pre
This menu item defines a transparent ZOOM command with previous option; it is assigned to button number 12 of the pointing device.

AUXILIARY MENUS

In a menu file, you can have up to four auxiliary menu sections (AUX1 through AUX4). The auxiliary menu sections (***AUXn) are identical to the button menu sections. The difference is in the hardware. In the button menu the commands are assigned to the buttons of the pointing device, whereas in the auxiliary menu the commands are assigned to the buttons of a function-box. The function-box has several buttons like a pointing device, but it does not need a digitizer to activate the functions. By pressing a button of the function-box, you automatically activate the command that is assigned to that particular button in the auxiliary menu. Also, if your computer uses a system mouse, it will automatically use the auxiliary menu.

Note

If the button menu has more menu items than the number of buttons on the pointing device, the menu items in excess of the number of buttons are ignored. This does not include the pick button. For example, if a pointing device has three buttons, in addition to the pick button, the first three menu items will be assigned to the three buttons (buttons 2, 3, and 4). The remaining lines of the button menu are ignored.

The commands are assigned to the buttons in the same order in which they appear in the file. For example, the menu item that is defined on line 3 will automatically be assigned to the fourth button of the pointing device. Similarly, the menu item that is on line 4 will be assigned to the fifth button of the pointing device. The same is true of other menu items and buttons.

REVIEW QUESTIONS

Image Tile Menus

Fill in the blanks.

1. The image tiles are displayed in the _____ box.

2. An image tile menu can be canceled by entering _____ or _____ at the keyboard.

3. The dialogue box can contain a maximum of _____ image tiles.

4. A blank line in an image tile menu _____ the image tile menu.

5. The menu item repetition feature _____ be used with the image tile menu.

6. The drawing for a slide should be _____ on the entire screen before making a slide.

7. You _____ to fill a solid area in a slide for image tile menu.

8. Pull-down menus are disabled when the _____ zoom is in progress.

9. A menu item label like [3-5] is used in a tablet menu to reference _____ and _____.

10. An image tile menu _____ be accessed from a tablet menu.

Button Menus

Fill in the blanks.

11. A multi-button pointing device can be used to pick _____, or select _____, or enter AutoCAD _____.

12. AutoCAD receives the button _____ and _____ of screen cross-hair, when a button is activated on the pointing device.

13. If the number of menu items in the button menu are more than the number of buttons on the pointing device, the excess lines are _____.

14. Commands are assigned to the buttons of the pointing device in the _____ order in which they appear in the buttons menu.

15. The format of the LOAD command for loading a submenu that has been defined in the screen menu is _____.

16. The format of the LOAD command for loading a submenu that has been defined in the pull-down menu is _____.

EXERCISES

Exercise 2

Write an image tile menu for the following commands. Make the slides that will graphically illustrate the function of the command.

> LINE   CIRCLE C,R
> PLINE   CIRCLE C,D
>   CIRCLE 2P

Exercise 3

Write a button menu for the following AutoCAD commands. The pointing device has 10 buttons (Figure 33-8) and button number 1 is used for picking the points. The blocks are to be inserted with a scale factor of 1.00 and a rotation of 0 degrees (filename BME1.MNU).

> 1. PICK BUTTON   2. RETURN   3. CANCEL
> 4. OSNAPS   5. INSERT B1   6. INSERT B2
> 7. INSERT B3   8. ZOOM Window   9. ZOOM All
> 10.ZOOM Previous

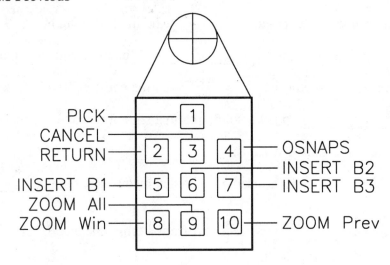

Figure 33-8 Pointing device with 10 buttons

1. B1, B2, B3 are the names of the blocks or wblocks that have already been created.
2. Assume that the OSNAP submenu has already been defined in the screen menu section of the menu file.
3. Use the transparent ZOOM command for ZOOM Previous and ZOOM Window.

Chapter 34

AutoLISP

| Learning objectives |

After completing this chapter, you will be able to:
♦ Perform mathematical operations using AutoLISP.
♦ Use trignometrical functions in AutoLISP.
♦ Understand the basic AutoLISP functions and their applications.
♦ Load and run AutoLISP programs.
♦ Use flowcharts to analyze the problem.
♦ Test a condition using conditional functions.

ABOUT AutoLISP

Developed by Autodesk, Inc., **AutoLISP** is an implementation of the **LISP** programming language. The first reference to LISP was made by John McCarthy in the April 1960 issue of *The Communications of the ACM*. LISP is an acronym for **LISt Processor**.

Except for **FORTRAN**, most of the languages developed in the early 1960s have become obsolete, but LISP has continued to survive and has become a leading programming language for artificial intelligence (AI). Some of the dialects of the LISP programming language are Common LISP, BYSCO LISP, ExperLISP, GCLISP, IQLISP, LISP/80, LISP/88, MuLISP, TLCLISP, UO-LISP, Waltz LISP, and XLISP. XLISP is a public domain LISP interpreter. The LISP dialect that resembles AutoLISP is Common LISP. The AutoLISP interpreter is embedded within the AutoCAD software package. However, AutoCAD versions 2.17 and lower do not have the AutoLISP interpreter; therefore, you can only use the AutoLISP programming language with AutoCAD Release 2.18 and up. The name of the AutoLISP program file for 640k DOS systems is acadl.ovl, for AutoCAD 386 it is acadl.exp, and for Windows it is acadl.exe.

The AutoCAD software package contains most of the commands that are used to generate a drawing. However, some commands are not provided in AutoCAD. For example, AutoCAD does not have a command to draw a rectangle or make global changes in the drawing text objects. With AutoLISP you can write a program in AutoLISP programming language that will draw a rectangle or make global or selective changes in the drawing text objects. As a matter of fact, you can use AutoLISP to write any program or imbed it into the menu and thus customize your system to make it more efficient.

AutoLISP programming language has been used by several third-party software developers to write software packages for various applications. For example, the author of this text has developed a software package, **SMLayout**, which generates flat layout of various geometrical shapes like transitions, intersection of pipes and cylinders, elbows, cones, and tank heads. There is demand for AutoLISP programmers as consultants for developing application software and custom menus.

This chapter assumes that you are familiar with AutoCAD commands and AutoCAD system variables. However, you need not be an AutoCAD or programming expert to begin learning AutoLISP. This chapter also assumes that you have no prior programming knowledge. If you are familiar with any other programming language, learning AutoLISP may be easy. A thorough discussion of various functions and a step-by-step explanation of the examples should make it fun to learn. This chapter discusses the most frequently used AutoLISP functions and their application in writing a program. For those functions that are not discussed in this chapter, refer to the AutoLISP Programmers Reference manual from Autodesk.

AutoLISP does not require any special hardware. If your system runs AutoCAD, it will also run AutoLISP. However, before using make sure that AutoLISP is enabled and enough memory has been set aside for running the programs. In most systems you can also use extended AutoLISP. To write AutoLISP programs you can use the **Edlin** function of DOS, the **Edit** function of DOS 5.0, or any other ASCII text editor. You can also use AutoCAD's **EDIT** command, provided the ACAD.PGP file is present and the EDIT command is defined in the file.

MATHEMATICAL OPERATIONS

A mathematical function constitutes an important feature of any programming language. Most of the mathematical functions that are commonly used in programming and mathematical calculations are available in AutoLISP. You can use AutoLISP to add, subtract, multiply, and divide the numbers. You can also use it to find sine, cosine, and arctangent of angles expressed in radians. There is a host of other calculations you can do with AutoLISP. This section discusses the most frequently used mathematical functions that are supported by the AutoLISP programming language.

Addition

Format **(+ num1 num2 num3 - - -)**

This function (+) calculates the sum of all the numbers that are to the right of the plus (+) sign (num1 + num2 + num3 +.........). The numbers can be integers or real. If the numbers are integers then the sum is an integer. If the numbers are real the sum is real. However, if some numbers are real and some are integers, the sum is real. In the first two examples, all numbers are integers, therefore the result is an integer. In the third example, one number is a real number (50.0), therefore the sum is a real number.

Examples
(+ 2 5)	returns 7
(+ 2 30 4 50)	returns 86
(+ 2 30 4 50.0)	returns 86.0

Subtraction

Format **(- num1 num2 num3 - - -)**

This function (-) subtracts the second number from the first number (num1-num2). If there are more than two numbers, the second and subsequent numbers are added and the sum is subtracted from the first number [num1 - (num2 + num3 + ...)]. In the first example, 14 is subtracted from 28 and returns 14. Since both the numbers are integers, the result is an integer. In the third example, 20 and 10.0 are added, and the sum of these two numbers (30.0) is subtracted from 50, returning a real number 20.0.

Examples
(- 28 14)	returns 14
(- 25 7 11)	returns 7

```
(- 50 20 10.0)          returns 20.0
(- 20 30)               returns -10
(- 20.0 30.0)           returns -10.0
```

Multiplication

Format **(* num1 num2 num3 - - -)**

This function (*) calculates the product of the numbers that are to the right of the asterisk (num1 x num2 x num3 x............). If the numbers are integers, the product of these numbers is an integer. If one of the numbers is a real number, the product is a real number.

Examples
```
(* 2 5)                 returns 10
(* 2 5 3)               returns 30
(* 2 5 3 2.0)           returns 60.0
(* 2 -5.5)              returns -11.0
(* 2.0 -5.5 -2)         returns 22.0
```

Division

Format **(/ num1 num2 num3 - - -)**

This function (/) divides the first number by the second number (num1/num2). If there are more then two numbers, the first number is divided by the product of the second and subsequent numbers [num1 / (num2 x num3 x ....)]. In the fourth example below, 200 is divided by the product of 5 and 4.0 [200 / (5 * 4.0)].

Examples
```
(/ 30)                  returns 30
(/ 3 2)                 returns 1
(/ 3.0 2)               returns 1.5
(/ 200 5 4)             returns 10
(/ 200.0 5.5)           returns 36.363636
(/ 200 -5)              returns -40
(/ -200 -5.0)           returns 40.0
```

TRIGONOMETRICAL FUNCTIONS

sin

Format **(sin angle)**

The **sin** function calculates the sine of an angle, where the angle is expressed in radians. In the second example below, the **sin** function calculates the sine of pi (180 degrees) and returns 0.

Examples
```
(sin 0)                 returns 0.0
(sin pi)                returns 0.0
(sin 1.0472)            returns 0.866027
```

cos

Format **(cos angle)**

The **cos** function calculates the cosine of an angle, where the angle is expressed in radians. In the third example below, the **cos** function calculates the cosine of pi (180 degrees) and return -1.0.

Examples

(cos 0)	returns 1.0
(cos 0.0)	returns 1.0
(cos pi)	returns -1.0
(cos 1.0)	returns 0.540302

atan

Format **(atan num1)**

The **atan** function calculates the arctangent of **num1**, and the calculated angle is expressed in radians. In the second example below, the **atan** function calculates the arctangent of 1.0 and returns 0.785398 (radians).

Examples

(atan 0.5)	returns 0.463648
(atan 1.0)	returns 0.785398
(atan -1.0)	returns -0.785398

You can also specify a second number in atan function. The format of this atan function is:

Format **(atan num1 num2)**

If the second number is specified, the function returns the arctangent of (num1/num2) in radians. In the first example below, the first number (0.5) is divided by the second number (1.0), and the **atan** function calculates the arctangent of the dividend (0.5/1.0 = 0.5).

Examples

(atan 0.5 1.0)	returns 0.453648 radians
(atan 2.0 3.0)	returns 0.588003 radians
(atan 2.0 -3.0)	returns 2.55359 radians
(atan -2.0 3.00	returns -0.588003 radians
(atan -2.0 -3.0)	returns -2.55359 radians
(atan 1.0 0.0)	returns 1.5708 radians
(atan -0.5 0.0)	returns -1.5708 radians

defun, setq, getpoint, and command functions

defun

The **defun** function is used to define a function in an AutoLISP program. The format of **defun** function is:

```
(defun name [argument])
        │         └─ Argument list
        └─ Name of the function
```

Examples
(defun ADNUM ( )

Defines a function ADNUM with no arguments or local symbols. This means that all variables used in the program are global variables. A global variable does not lose its value after the programs ends.

(defun ADNUM (a b c)
Defines a function ADNUM that has three arguments: a, b, and c. The variables a, b, and c receive their value from outside the program.

(defun ADNUM (/ a b)
Defines a function ADNUM that has two local variables: a and b. A local variable is one that retains its value during the program execution and can be used within that program only.

(defun C:ADNUM ( )
By using **C:** in front of the function name the function can be executed by entering the name of the function at AutoCAD's Command: prompt. If **C:** is not used, the function name has to be enclosed in parentheses.

> **Note**
>
> *AutoLISP contains some built-in functions. Do not use these names for function or variable names. The following is a list of some of the names reserved for AutoLISP's built-in functions. (Refer to AutoLISP Programmer's Reference manual for a complete list of AutoLISP's built-in functions.)*

abs	ads	alloc
and	angle	angtos
append	apply	atom
ascii	assoc	atan
atof	atoi	distance
equal	fix	float
if	length	list
load	member	nil
not	nth	null
open	or	pi
read	repeat	reverse
set	type	while

setq

The **setq** function is used to assign a value to variable. The format of the **setq** function is:

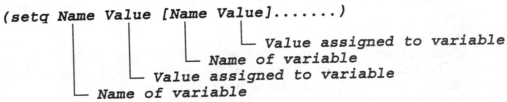

```
(setq Name Value [Name Value].......)
```
- Value assigned to variable
- Name of variable
- Value assigned to variable
- Name of variable

The value assigned to a variable can be a numeric value or a string. If the value is a string, the string length cannot be more than 100 characters long.

    Command: (setq X 12)

    Command: (setq X 6.5)

    Command: (setq X 8.5 Y 12)

In this expression, the number 8.5 is assigned to variable X and the number 12 is assigned to variable Y.

Command: (setq answer "YES")

In this expression the string value "YES" is assigned to variable answer.

The **setq** function can also be used in conjunction with other expressions to assign a value to a variable. In the following examples the **setq** function has been used to assign values to different variables.

(setq pt1 (getpoint "Enter start point: "))
(setq ang1 (getangle "Enter included angle: "))
(setq answer (getstring "Enter YES or NO: "))

Note

AutoLISP uses some built-in ones function names and symbols. Do not assign values to these functions. The following functions are valid ones, but pi and angle functions reserved functions will be redefined.

(setq pi 3.0)

(setq angle (......))

getpoint

The getpoint function pauses to enable you to enter the X, Y coordinates or X, Y, Z coordinates of a point. The coordinates of the point can be entered from the keyboard or by using the screen cursor. The format of **getpoint** function is:

```
(getpoint [point] [prompt])
                      |
                      |___ Prompt to be displayed on the
                      |    screen
                      |___ Enter a point, or select a point
```

Example
(setq pt1 (getpoint))
(setq pt1 (getpoint "Enter starting point"))

Note

You cannot enter the name of another AutoLISP routine in response to the getpoint function.

A 2D or a 3D point is always defined with respect to the current user coordinate system (UCS).

Command

The **Command** function is used to execute standard AutoCAD commands from within an AutoLISP program. The AutoCAD command name and the command options have to be enclosed in double quotation marks. The format of **Command** function is:

```
(Command "command-name")
                   |
                   |___ AutoCAD command
        |___ AutoLISP function
```

Examples

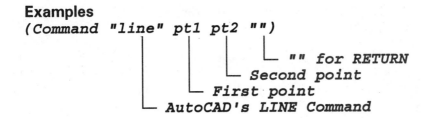

```
(Command "line" pt1 pt2 "")
                          └─ "" for RETURN
                      └─ Second point
              └─ First point
      └─ AutoCAD's LINE Command
```

Note

Prior to AutoCAD Release-12, the **Command** *function* **could not be used** *to execute AutoCAD's PLOT command. For example: (Command "plot".........) was not valid functions. In AutoCAD Release-13, you can use plot with Command function (Command "plot" .....).*

The **Command** *function cannot be used to enter data with AutoCAD's DTEXT or TEXT command. (You can use the DTEXT and TEXT command with the* **Command** *function. You can also enter text height and text rotation, but you cannot enter the text when Dtext or Text prompts for text entry.)*

You cannot use the input functions of AutoLISP with the **Command** *function. The input functions are* **getpoint, getangle, getstring, and getint.** *For example, (Command "getpoint".....) or (Command "getangle".........) are not valid functions. If the program contains such a function, it will display an error message when the program is loaded.*

Example 1

Write a program that will prompt you to select three points of a triangle and then draw lines through those points to generate a triangle as shown in Figure 34-1.

Most programs essentially consist of three parts: **input**, **output**, and **process**. Process includes what is involved in generating the desired output from the given input (Figure 34-2). Before writing a program you must identify these parts. In this example, the input to the program is the coordinates of the three points. The desired output is a triangle. The process needed to generate a triangle is to draw three lines from P1 to P2, P2 to P3, and P3 to P1. By identifying these three sections the programming process becomes less confusing.

The process section of the program is vital to the success of the program. Sometimes it is simple, but sometimes it involves complicated calculations. If the program involves many calculations, divide them into sections (and perhaps subsections) that are laid out in a logical and systematic order. Also, remember that the programs need to be edited from time to time, perhaps by other programmers. Therefore, document the programs as clearly as possible in an unambiguous manner so that other

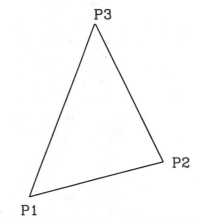

Figure 34-1 Triangle P1, P2, P3

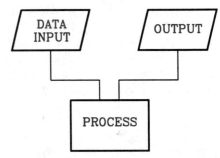

Figure 34-2 Three elements of a program

programmers can understand what the program is doing at different stages of its execution. Give sketches and identify points where possible.

Input	**Output**
Location of point P1	
Location of point P2	Triangle P1, P2, P3
Location of point P3	

Process
Line from P1 to P2
Line from P2 to P3
Line from P3 to P1

The following file is a listing of the AutoLISP program for Example 1. The line numbers at the right are not a part of the program; they are shown here for reference only.

```
;This program will prompt you to enter three points                    1
;of a triangle from the keyboard, or select three points               2
;by using the screen cursor. P1, P2, P3 are triangle corners.          3
                                                                       4
(defun c:TRIANG1()                                                     5
(setq P1 (getpoint "\n Enter first point of Triangle: "))              6
(setq P2 (getpoint "\n Enter second point of Triangle: "))             7
(setq P3 (getpoint "\n Enter third point of Triangle: "))              8
(Command "LINE" P1 P2 P3 "C")                                          9
)                                                                      10
```

Lines 1-3
The first three lines are comment lines describing the function of the program. These lines are important because they make it easier to edit a program. Comments should be used when needed. All comment lines must start with a semicolon (;). These lines are ignored when the program is loaded.

Line 4
This is a blank line that separates the comment section from the program. Blank lines can be used to separate different modules of a program. This makes it easier to identify different sections that constitute a program. The blank lines do not have any effect on the program.

Line 5
(defun c:TRIANG1( )
In this line **defun** is an AutoLISP function that defines the function, **TRIANG1**. **TRIANG1** is the name of the function. By using **c:** in front of the function name, **TRIANG1** can be executed like an AutoCAD command. If **c:** is missing the **TRIANG1** command can be executed only by enclosing it in parentheses (TRIANG1).

Line 6
(setq P1 (getpoint "\n Enter first point of Triangle: "))
In this line the **getpoint** function pauses for you to enter the first point of the triangle. The prompt, **Enter first point of Triangle**, is displayed in the prompt area of the screen. You can enter the coordinates of this point at the keyboard or select a point by using the screen cursor. The **setq** function then assigns these coordinates to the variable **P1**. \n is used for the carriage return so that the statement that follows \n is printed on the next line ("n" stands for "newline").

Lines 7 and 8
(setq P2 (getpoint "\n Enter second point of Triangle: "))
(setq P3 (getpoint "\n Enter third point of Triangle: "))

These two lines prompt you to enter the second and third corner of the triangle. These coordinates are then assigned to the variables P2 and P3. \n causes a carriage return so that the input prompts are displayed on the next line.

Line 9
(Command "LINE" P1 P2 P3 "C")
In this line the **Command** function is used to enter AutoCAD's LINE command and then draw a line from P1 to P2, and P2 to P3. "C" (for close option) joins the last point, P3, with the first point, P1. All AutoCAD commands and options, when used in an AutoLISP program, have to be enclosed in double quotation marks. The variables P1, P2, P3 are separated by a blank space.

Line 10
This line consists of a close parenthesis that completes the definition of the function, TRIANG1. This parenthesis could have been combined with the previous line. It is good practice to keep it on a separate line so that a programmer can easily identify the end of a definition. In this program there is only one function defined, therefore it is easy to locate the end of a definition. But in some programs a number of definitions or modules within the same program might need to be clearly identified. The parenthesis and blank lines help to identify the start and end of a definition or a section in the program.

LOADING AN AUTOLISP PROGRAM

There are generally two names associated with an AutoLISP program. One is the program file name and the second is the function name. For example, TRIANG.LSP is the name of the file, not a function name. All AutoLISP file names have the extension .LSP. An AutoLISP file can have one or several functions defined within the same file. For example, TRIANG1 in Example 1 is the name of a function. To execute a function, the AutoLISP program file that defines that function must be loaded. Use the following command to load an AutoLISP file when you are in the Drawing Editor:

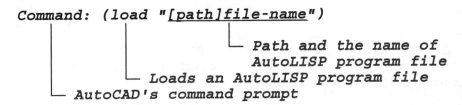

The AutoLISP file name and the optional path name must be enclosed in double quotes. The **load** and the **file-name** must be enclosed in parentheses. If the parentheses are missing, AutoCAD will try to load a shape or a text font file, not an AutoLISP file. The space between **load** and **file-name** is not required. If AutoCAD is successful in loading the file, it will display the name of the function in the Command: prompt area of the screen.

C:TRIANG1

To run the program, type the name of the function at AutoCAD's Command: prompt and press the ENTER key (**Command: TRIANG1**). If the function name does not contain **C:** in the program, you can run the program by enclosing the function name in parentheses.

Command: TRIANG1
or
Command: (TRIANG1)

> **Note**
>
> *Use a forward slash when defining the path for loading an AutoLISP program. For example, if the AutoLISP file TRIANG is in the LISP subdirectory on the C drive, use the following command to load the file. You can also use a double backslash (\\) in place of the forward slash.*
>
> **Command (load "c:/lisp/triang")**
> or
> **Command (load "c:\\lisp\\triang")**

Exercise 1

Write an AutoLISP program that will draw a line from point P1 to point P2. The program must prompt you to enter the X and Y coordinates of point P1 and P2.

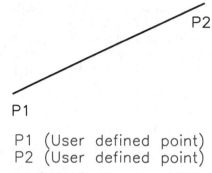

P1 (User defined point)
P2 (User defined point)

Figure 34-3 Draw line from point P1 to P2

getcorner, getdist, and setvar functions

getcorner

The **getcorner** function pauses for you to enter the coordinates of a point. The coordinates of the point can be entered at the keyboard or by using the screen cross-hairs. This function requires a base point, and it displays a rectangle with respect to the base point as you move the screen cross-hairs on the screen. The format of **getcorner** function is:

```
(getcorner point [prompt])
                      └─── Prompt displayed on screen
              └─── Base point
```

Examples
(getcorner pt1)
(setq pt2 (getcorner pt1))
(setq pt2 (getcorner pt1 "Enter second point: "))

> **Note**
>
> *The base point and the point that you select in response to the getcorner function are located with respect to the current UCS.*
>
> *If the point you select is a 3D point with X, Y, and Z coordinates, the Z coordinate is ignored. The point assumes current elevation as its Z coordinate.*

getdist

The **getdist** function pauses for you to enter distance and it then returns the distance as a real number. The format of **getdist** function is:

> *(getdist [point] [prompt])*

Any prompt that needs to be displayed on the screen

First point for distance

Examples
(getdist)
(setq dist (getdist))
(setq dist (getdist pt1))
(setq dist (getdist "Enter distance"))
(setq dist (getdist pt1 "Enter second point for distance"))

The distance can be entered by selecting two points on the screen. For example, if the assignment is **(setq dist (getdist))** you can enter a number or select two points. If the assignment is **(setq dist (getdist pt1))**, where the first point (pt1) is already defined, you need to select the second point only. The getdist function will always return the distance as a real number. For example, if the current setting is architectural and the distance is entered in architectural units, the getdist function will return the distance as a real number.

setvar

The **setvar** function assigns a value to an AutoCAD system variable. The name of the system variable must be enclosed in double quotes. The format of **setvar** function is:

> *(setvar "variable name" value)*

Value to be assigned to the system variable

AutoCAD system variable

Examples
(setvar "cmdecho" 0)
(setvar "dimscale" 1.5)
(setvar "ltscale" 0.5)
(setvar "dimcen" -0.25)

Example 2

Write an AutoLISP program that will generate a chamfer between two given lines by entering the chamfer angle and the chamfer distance. To generate a chamfer AutoCAD uses the values assigned to system variables CHAMFERA and CHAMFERB. When you select AutoCAD's CHAMFER command, the first and second chamfer distances are automatically assigned to the system variables CHAMFERA and CHAMFERB. The CHAMFER command then uses these assigned values to generate a chamfer. However, in most engineering drawings, the

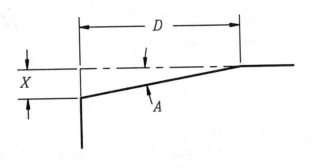

Figure 34-4 Chamfer with angle A and distance D

ferred way to generate the chamfer is by entering the chamfer length and the chamfer angle, as own in Figure 34-4.

Input
First chamfer distance (D)
Chamfer angle (A)

Output
Chamfer between any two
selected lines

Process
1. Calculate second chamfer distance
2. Assign these values to the system variables CHAMFERA and CHAMFERB
3. Use AutoCAD's CHAMFER command to generate chamfer

Calculations

$$X/D = TAN\ A$$
$$X = D * (TAN\ A)$$
$$= D * [(SIN\ A) / (COS\ A)]$$

The following file is a listing of the program for Example 3. The line numbers on the right are not a part of the file; they are for reference only.

```
;This program generates a chamfer by entering          1
;the chamfer angle and the chamfer distance            2
;                                                       3
(defun c:chamf (/)                                      4
(setvar "cmdecho" 0)                                    5
(graphscr)                                              6
   (setq d (getdist "\n Enter chamfer distance: "))     7
   (setq a (getangle "\n Enter chamfer angle: "))       8
   (setvar "chamfera" d)                                9
   (setvar "chamferb" (* d (/ (sin a) (cos a))))       10
   (command "chamfer")                                 11
   (setvar "cmdecho" 1)                                12
   (princ)                                             13
)                                                      14
```

Line 7
(setq d (getdist "\n Enter chamfer distance: "))
The **getdist** function pauses for you to enter the chamfer distance, then the **setq** function assigns that value to variable d.

Line 8
(setq a (getangle "\n Enter chamfer angle: "))
The **getangle** pauses for you to enter the chamfer angle, then the **setq** function assigns that value to variable a.

Line 9
(setvar "chamfera" d)
The **setvar** function assigns the value of variable d to AutoCAD system variable **chamfera**.

Line 10
(setvar "chamferb" (* d (/ (sin a) (cos a))))
The **setvar** function assigns the value obtained from the expression **(* d (/ (sin a) (cos a)))** to AutoCAD's system variable **chamferb**.

Line 11
(command "chamfer")
The **command** function uses AutoCAD's **CHAMFER** command to generate a chamfer.

Exercise 2

Write an AutoLISP program that will generate the drawing shown in Figure 34-5. The program should prompt the user to enter points P1, P2 and diameters D1, D2.

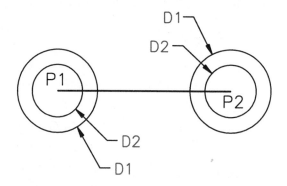

Figure 34-5 Concentric circles with connecting line

---

car, cdr, and cadr functions

car

The **car** function returns the first element of a list. If the list does not contain any elements, the function will return **nil**. The format of the **car** function is:

```
(car list)
        └── List of elements
   └── Returns the first element
```

Examples

(car '(2.5 3 56))	returns 2.5
(car '(x y z))	returns X
(car '((15 20) 56))	returns (15 20)
(car '( ))	returns nil

The quote mark defines a list.

cdr

The **cdr** function returns a list with the first element removed from the list. The format of the **cdr** function is:

```
(cdr list)
        └── List of elements
   └── Returns a list with the first element removed
```

Examples

(cdr '(2.5 3 56)	returns (3 56)
(cdr '(x y z))	returns (Y Z)
(cdr '((15 20) 56))	returns (56)
(cdr '( ))	returns nil

cadr

The **cadr** function performs two operations, **cdr** and **car**, to return the second element of the list. The **cdr** function removes the first element, and the **car** function returns the first element of the new list. The format of **cadr** function is:

```
(cadr list)
      │      └── List of elements
      └── Performs two operations   (car (cdr '(x y z))
```

Examples

(cadr '(2 3))	returns 3
(cadr '(2 3 56))	returns 3
(cadr '(x y z))	returns y
(cadr '((15 20) 56 24))	returns 56

In these examples, **cadr** performs two functions:

```
(cadr '(x y z))            = (car (cdr '(x y z)))
                           = (car (y z))
                               returns y
```

Note

In addition to the above-mentioned functions (car, cdr, cadr), several other functions can be used to extract different elements of a list. Following is a list of these functions, where the function f consists of a list '((x y) z w)).

(setq f '((x y) z w))

(caar f) = (car (car f)) returns x
(cdar f) = (cdr (car f)) returns y
(cadar) = (car (cdr (car f)))   returns y
(cddr f) = (cdr (cdr f)) returns w
(caddr f) = (car (cdr (cdr f)))   returns w

---

graphscr, textscr, princ, and terpri functions

graphscr

The **graphscr** function switches from the text screen to the graphics screen, provided the system has only one screen. If the system has two screens this function is ignored.

textscr

The **textscr** function switches from the graphics screen to text screen, provided the system has only one screen. If the system has two screens this function is ignored.

princ

The **princ** function prints the value of the variable. If the variable is enclosed in double quotes, it prints the expression that is enclosed in the quotes. The format of **princ** function is:

(princ [variable or expression])

Examples

(princ)	prints a blank on the screen
(princ a)	prints the value of variable a on the screen
(princ "Welcome")	prints Welcome on the screen

terpri

The **terpri** function prints a new line on the screen just as **\n**. This function is used to print the line that follows the **terpri** function on a separate line.

Example

(setq p1 (getpoint "Enter first point: "))(terpri)
(setq p2 (getpoint "Enter second point: "))

The first line (Enter first point:) will be displayed on the screen's command prompt area. The **terpri** function causes a carriage return, therefore the second line (Enter second point:) will be displayed on a new line, just below the first line. If terpri function is missing, the two lines will be displayed on the same line (Enter first point: Enter second point:).

Example 3

Write a program that will prompt you to enter two opposite corners of a rectangle and then draw the rectangle on the screen as shown in Figure 34-6.

<u>Input</u>   <u>Output</u>
Coordinates of point P1   Rectangle
Coordinates of point P3

<u>Process</u>
1. Calculate the coordinates of the points P2,P4.
2. Draw the following lines.
   Line from P1 to P2
   Line from P2 to P3
   Line from P3 to P4
   Line from P4 to P1

The X and Y coordinates of points P2 and P4 can be calculated using the **car** and **cadr** functions. The **car** function extracts the X coordinate and **cadr** function extracts the Y coordinate of a given list.

X coordinate of point p2
x2 = x3
x2 = car (x3 y3)
x2 = car p3

Y coordinate of point p2
y2 = y1
y2 = CADR (x1 y1)
y2 = CADR p1

X coordinate of point p4
x4 = x1
x4 = car(x1 y1)
x4 = car p1

Y coordinate of point p4

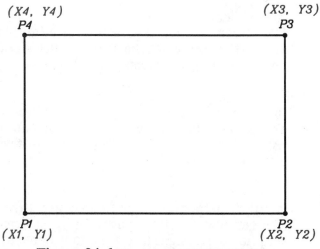

Figure 34-6 Rectangle P1 P2 P3 P4

```
y4  =  y3
y4  =  cadr (x3 y3)
y4  =  cadr p3
```

Therefore, points p2 and p4 are
```
p2  =  (list (car p3) (cadr p1))
p4  =  (list (car p1) (cadr p3))
```

The following file is a listing of the program for Example 3. The line numbers at the right are for reference only; they are not a part of the program.

```
;This program will draw a rectangle. User will              1
;be prompted to enter the two opposite corners              2
;                                                           3
(defun c:RECT1( )                                           4
   (graphscr)                                               5
   (setvar "cmdecho" 0)                                     6
   (prompt "RECT1 command draws a rectangle")(terpri)       7
   (setq p1 (getpoint "Enter first corner"))(terpri)        8
   (setq p3 (getpoint "Enter opposite corner"))(terpri)     9
   (setq p2 (list (car p3) (cadr p1)))                      10
   (setq p4 (list (car p1) (cadr p3)))                      11
(command "line" p1 p2 p3 p4 "c")                            12
(setvar "cmdecho" 1)                                        13
(princ)                                                     14
)                                                           15
```

Lines 1-3
The first three lines are comment lines that describe the function of the program. All comment lines that start with a semicolon are ignored when the program is loaded.

Line 4
(defun c:RECT1( )
The **defun** function defines the function **RECT1**.

Line 5
(graphscr)
This function switches the text screen to the graphics screen, if the current screen happens to be a text screen. Otherwise this function has no effect on the display screen.

Line 6
(setvar "cmdecho" 0)
The **setvar** function assigns the value 0 to AutoCAD's system variable **cmdecho**, which turns the echo off. When **cmdecho** is off, AutoCAD command prompts are not displayed in the command prompt area of the screen.

Line 7
(prompt "RECT1 command draws a rectangle")(terpri)
The **prompt** function will display the information in double quotes ("RECT1 command draws a rectangle") on the screen. The function **terpri** causes a carriage return so that the next text is printed on a separate line.

Line 8
(setq p1 (getpoint "Enter first corner"))(terpri)
The **getpoint** function pauses for you to enter a point (the first corner of the rectangle), and the **setq** function assigns that value to variable p1.

Line 9
(setq p3 (getpoint "Enter opposite corner"))(terpri)
The **getpoint** function pauses for you to enter a point (the opposite corner of the rectangle), and the **setq** function assigns that value to variable p3.

Line 10
(setq p2 (list (car p3) (cadr p1)))
The **cadr** function extracts the y coordinate of point p1, and the **car** function extracts the X coordinate of point p3. These two values form a list and the function **setq** assigns that value to variable p2.

Line 11
(setq p4 (list (car p1) (cadr p3)))
The **cadr** function extracts the y coordinate of point p3, and the **car** function extracts the X coordinate of point p1. These two values form a list and the function **setq** assigns that value to variable p4.

Line 12
(command "line" p1 p2 p3 p4 "c")
The command function uses AutoCAD's **LINE** command to draw lines between points p1, p2, p3, p4: c (close) joins the last point, p4, with the first point, p1.

Line 13
(setvar "cmdecho" 1)
The **setvar** function assigns a value of 1 to the AutoCAD system variable **cmdecho**, which turns the echo on.

Line 14
(princ)
The **princ** function prints a blank on the screen. If this line is missing, AutoCAD will print the value of the last expression. This value does not affect the program in any way. However, it might be confusing at times. The **princ** function is used to prevent display of the last expression in the command prompt area.

Line 15
The close parenthesis completes the definition of the function **RECT1** and ends the program.

Note

In this program the rectangle is generated after you define the two corners of the rectangle. The rectangle is not dragged as you move the screen cross-hairs to enter the second corner. However, the rectangle can be dragged by using the getcorner function, as shown in the following program listing:

```
;This program will draw a rectangle with the
;drag mode on and using getcorner function
;
(defun c:RECT2( )
    (graphscr)
    (setvar "cmdecho" 0)
    (prompt "RECT2 command draws a rectangle")(terpri)
    (setq p1 (getpoint "enter first corner"))(terpri)
    (setq p3 (getcorner p1 "Enter opposite corner" ))(terpri)
    (setq p2 (list (car p3) (cadr p1)))
    (setq p4 (list (car p1) (cadr p3)))
```

```
(command "line" p1 p2 p3 p4 "c")
(setvar "cmdecho" 1)
(princ)
)
```

getangle function

The **getangle** function pauses for you to enter the angle, then it returns the value of that angle in radians. The format of **getangle** function is:

(getangle [point] [prompt])

         Any prompt that needs to be
         displayed on the screen
      First point of the angle

Examples
```
(getangle)
(setq ang (getangle))
(setq ang (getangle pt1))        ;-------------- pt1 is a predefined point
(setq ang (getangle "Enter taper angle"))
(setq ang (getangle pt1 "Enter second point of angle"))
```

The angle you enter is affected by the angle setting. The angle settings can be changed using AutoCAD's **UNITS** command or by changing the value of AutoCAD's system variables **ANGBASE** and **ANGDIR**. Following are the default settings for measuring an angle:

The angle is measured with respect to positive X-axis or 3 o'clock position. The value of this setting is saved in the AutoCAD system variable **ANGBASE**.

The angle is positive if it is measured in a counterclockwise direction and is negative if it is measured in a clockwise direction. The value of this setting is saved in AutoCAD system variable **ANGDIR**.

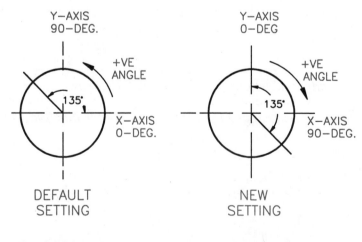

Figure 34-7(a)   Figure 34-7(b)

If the angle has a default setting (Figure 34-7(a)), the **getangle** function will return 2.35619 radians for an angle of 135.

Example
(setq ang (getangle "Enter angle")) will return 2.35619 for an angle of 135 degrees.

Figure 34-7(b) shows the new settings of the angle, where Y-axis is 0 degrees and the angles measured clockwise are positive. The **getangle** function will return 3.92699 for an angle of 135 degrees. The getangle function calculates the angle in a counterclockwise direction, **ignoring the direction set in the system variable ANGDIR**, with respect to the angle base as set in the system variable **ANGBASE** (Figure 34-8(b)).

Example
(setq ang (getangle "Enter angle")) will return 3.92699

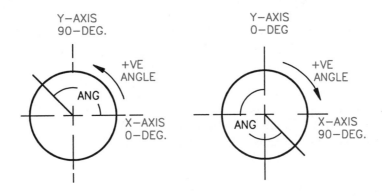

Figure 34-8(a)   Figure 34-8(b)

getint, getreal, getstring, and getvar functions

getint

The **getint** function pauses for you to enter an integer. The function always returns an integer, even if the number that you enter is a real number. The format of the **getint** function is:

```
(getint [prompt])
```
        └─ Optional prompt that you want to
           display on the screen

Examples
(getint)
(setq numx (getint))
(setq numx (getint "Enter number of rows: "))
(setq numx (getint "\n Enter number of rows: "))

getreal

The **getreal** function pauses for you to enter a real number and it always returns a real number, even if the number that you enter is an integer. The format of the **getreal** function is:

```
(getreal [prompt])
```
        └─ Optional prompt that is displayed on
           the screen

Examples
(getreal)

```
(setq realnumx (getreal))
(setq realnumx (getreal "Enter distance: "))
(setq realnumx (getreal "\n Enter distance: "))
```

getstring

The **getstring** function pauses for you to enter a string value and it always returns a string, even if the string that you enter contains numbers only. The format of the **getstring** function is:

(getstring [prompt])

      Optional prompt that is displayed on the screen

Examples
```
(getstring)
(setq answer (getstring))
(setq answer (getstring "Enter Y for yes, N for no: ))
(setq answer (getstring "\n Enter Y for yes, N for no: ))
```

> **Note**
>
> *The maximum length of the string is 132 characters. If the length of the string exceeds 132 characters, the excess is ignored.*

getvar

The **getvar** function lets you retrieve the value of an AutoCAD system variable. The format of the **getvar** function is:

(getvar "variable")

      AutoCAD system variable name

Examples

(gatvar)	
(getvar "dimcen")	returns 0.09
(getvar "ltscale")	returns 1.0
(getvar "limmax")	returns 12.00,9.00
(getvar "limmin")	returns 0.00,0.00

> **Note**
>
> *The system variable name should always be enclosed in double quotes.*
>
> *You can retrieve only one variable value in one assignment. To retrieve the values of several system variables, use a separate assignment for each variable.*

polar and sqrt functions

polar

The **polar** function defines a point at a given angle and distance from the given point. The angle is expressed in radians, measured positive in a counterclockwise direction (assuming default settings for ANGBASE and ANGDIR). The format of the **polar** function is:

```
(polar point angle distance)
```
        └ *Distance of the point from*
             the referenced point
      └ *Angle that the point makes with the*
        referenced point
    └ *Reference point*

Example
(polar pt1 ang dis)
(setq pt2 (polar pt1 ang dis))
(setq pt2 (polar '(2.0 3.25) ang dis))

sqrt

The **sqrt** function calculates the square root of a number and the value this function returns is always a real number. The format of the **sqrt** function is:

```
(sqrt number)
```
      └ *Number that you want*
to find the
        square root of (real or integer)

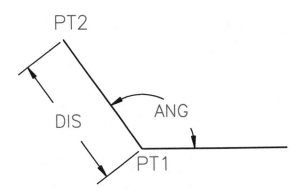

Figure 34-9 Using the **polar** function to define a point

Examples

(sqrt 144)	returns 12.0
(sqrt 144.0)	returns 12.0
(setq x (sqrt 57.25))	returns 7.566373
(setq x (sqrt (* 25 36.5)))	returns 30.207615
(setq x (sqrt (/ 7.5 (cos 0.75))))	returns 3.2016035
(setq hyp (sqrt (+ (* base base) (* ht ht))))	

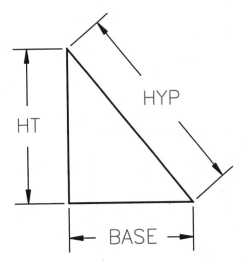

(setq hyp (sqrt (+ (* base base) (* ht ht))))

Figure 34-10 Application of the **sqrt** function

Example 4

Write an AutoLISP program that will draw an equilateral triangle outside a circle. The sides of the triangle are tangent to the circle. The program should prompt you to enter the radius and the center point of the circle.

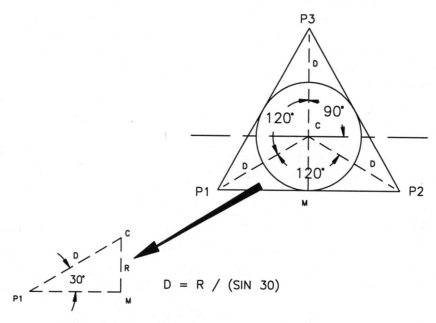

Figure 34-11 Equilateral triangle outside a circle

The following file is the listing of the AutoLISP program for Example 4.

```
;This program will draw a triangle outside
;the circle with the lines tangent to circle
:
(defun dtr (a
   (* a (/ pi 180.0))
   )
(defun c:trgcir( )
(setvar "cmdecho" 0)
(graphscr)
   (setq r(getdist "\n Enter circle radius: "))
   (setq c(getpoint "\n Enter center of circle: "))
   (setq d(/ r (sin(dtr 30))))
   (setq p1(polar c (dtr 210) d))
   (setq p2(polar c (dtr 330) d))
   (setq p3(polar c (dtr 90) d))
(command "circle" c r)
(command "line" p1 p2 p3 "c")
(setvar "cmdecho" 1)
(princ)
   )
```

Exercise 3

Write an AutoLISP program that will draw an isosceles triangle P1,P2,P3. The base of the triangle (P1,P2) makes an angle, B, with the positive X-axis. The program should prompt you to enter the starting point P1, length L1, and angles A and B.

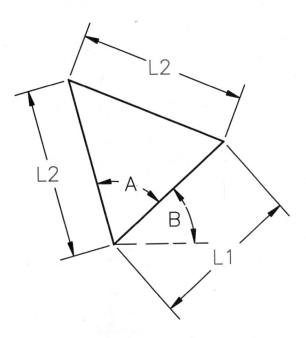

Figure 34-12 Isosceles triangle at an angle

Exercise 4

Write a program that will draw a slot with center lines. The program should prompt you to enter slot length, slot width, and the layer name for center lines (Figure 34-13).

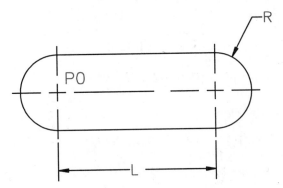

Figure 34-13 Slot of length L and radius R

Example 5

Write a program that will draw two circles of radii r1 and r2, representing two pulleys that are separated by a distance d. The line joining the centers of the two circles makes an angle a with an X-axis, as shown in Figure 34-14.

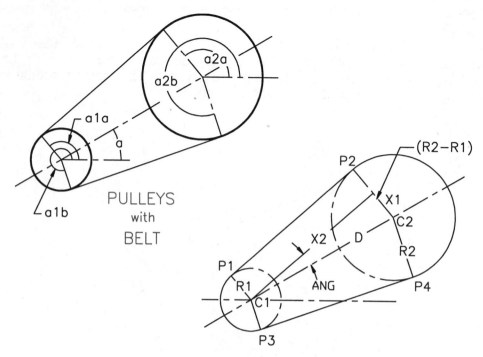

Figure 34-14 Two circles with tangent lines

Input
Radius of small circle r1
Radius of large circle r2
Distance between circles d
Angle of center line a
Center of small circle c1

Output
Small circle of radius r1
Large circle of radius r2
Lines tangent to circles

Process
1. Calculate distance x1, x2
2. Calculate angle ang
3. Locate point c2 with respect to point c1
4. Locate points p1, p2, p3, p4
5. Draw small circle with radius r1 and center c1
6. Draw large circle with radius r2 and center c2
7. Draw lines p1 to p2 and p3 to p4

Calculations
x1 = r2 - r1
x2 = SQRT [d**2 - (r2 - r1)**2]
tan ang = x1 / x2
ang = atan (x1 / x2)

a1a = 90 + a + ang
a1b = 270 + a - ang
a2a = 90 + a + ang
a2b = 270 + a - ang

The following file is a listing of the AutoLISP program for Example 5. The line numbers on the right are not a part of the file. These numbers are for reference only.

```
;This program draws a tangent (belt) over two          1
;pulleys that are separated by a given distance.        2
                                                        3
;This function changes degrees into radians             4
(defun dtr (a)                                          5
  (* a (/ pi 180.0))                                    6
  )                                                     8
                                                        9
(defun c:belt()                                        10
   (setvar "cmdecho" 0)                                11
   (graphscr)                                           12
   (setq r1(getdist "\n Enter radius of small pulley: "))   13
   (setq r2(getdist "\n Enter radius of larger pulley: "))  14
   (setq d(getdist "\n Enter distance between pulleys: "))  15
   (setq a(getangle "\n Enter angle of pulleys: "))    16
   (setq c1(getpoint "\n Enter center of small pulley: "))  17
   (setq x1 (- r2 r1))                                 18
   (setq x2 (sqrt (- (* d d) (* (- r2 r1) (- r2 r1)))))  19
   (setq ang (atan (/ x1 x2)))                         20
   (setq c2 (polar c1 a d))                            21
   (setq p1 (polar c1 (+ ang a (dtr 90)) r1))          22
   (setq p3 (polar c1 (- (+ a (dtr 270)) ang) r1))     23
   (setq p2 (polar c2 (+ ang a (dtr 90)) r2))          24
   (setq p4 (polar c2 (- (+ a (dtr 270)) ang) r2))     25
                                                       26
   (command "circle" c1 p3)                            28
   (command "circle" c2 p2)                            29
   (command "line" p1 p2 "")                           30
   (command "line" p3 p4 "")                           31
   (setvar "cmdecho" 1)                                32
   (princ))                                            33
```

Line 5

(defun dtr (a)
In this line the **defun** function defines a function, **dtr (a)**, which converts degrees into radians.

Line 6

(* a (/ pi 180.0))
(/ pi 180) divides the value of **pi** by 180 and the product is then multiplied by the angle a (180 degrees is equal to **pi** radians).

Line 10

(defun c:belt( )
In this line the function **defun** defines a function, c:belt, which generates two circles with tangent lines.

Line 18

(setq x1 (- r2 r1))
In this line the function **setq** assigns a value of r2 - r1 to variable x1.

Line 19

(setq x2 (- (* d d) (* (- r2 r1) (- r2 r1)))))
In this line, **(- r2 r1)** subtracts the value of r1 from r2 and **(* (- r2 r1) (- r2 r1))** calculates the square of (- r2 r1). **(sqrt (- (* d d) (* (- r2 r1) (- r2 r1))))** calculates the square root of the difference, and **setq x2** assigns the product of this expression to variable x2.

Line 20

(setq ang (atan (/ x1 x2)))

In this line, **(atan (/ x1 x2))** calculates the arc tangent of the product of **(/ x1 x2)**. The function **setq ang** assigns the value of the angle in radians to variable **ang**.

Line 21
(setq c2 (polar c1 a d))
In this line, **(polar c1 a d)** uses the **polar** function to locate point c2 with respect to c1 at a distance of d and making an angle **a** with the positive X-axis.

Line 22
(setq p1 (polar c1 (+ ang a (dtr 90)) r1))
In this line, **(polar c1 (+ ang a (dtr 90)) r1))** locates point p1 with respect to c1 at a distance r1 and making an angle of **(+ ang a (dtr 90))** with the positive X-axis.

Line 28
(command "circle" c1 p3)
In this line the **Command** function uses AutoCAD's **CIRCLE** command to draw a circle with center c1 and a radius defined by the point p3.

Line 30
(command "line" p1 p2 "")
In this line the **Command** function uses AutoCAD's **LINE** command to draw a line from p1 to p2. The pair of double quotes ("") at the end introduces a return to terminate the LINE command.

Exercise 5

Write an AutoLISP program that will draw two lines tangent to two circles, as shown in Figure 34-15. The program should prompt the you to enter the circle diameters and the center distance between the circles.

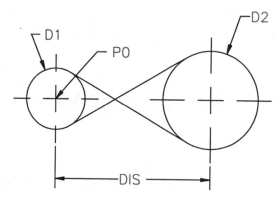

Figure 34-15 Circles with two tangent lines

FLOWCHART

A flowchart is a graphical representation of the algorithm and can be used to analyze a problem systematically. It gives a better understanding of the problem, especially if the problem involves some conditional statements. It consists of standard symbols that represent a certain function in the program. For example, a rectangle is used to represent a process that takes place when the program is executed. The blocks are connected by lines indicating the sequence of operations. Figures 34-16(a) and 34-16(b) illustrate the standard symbols that can be used in a flowchart.

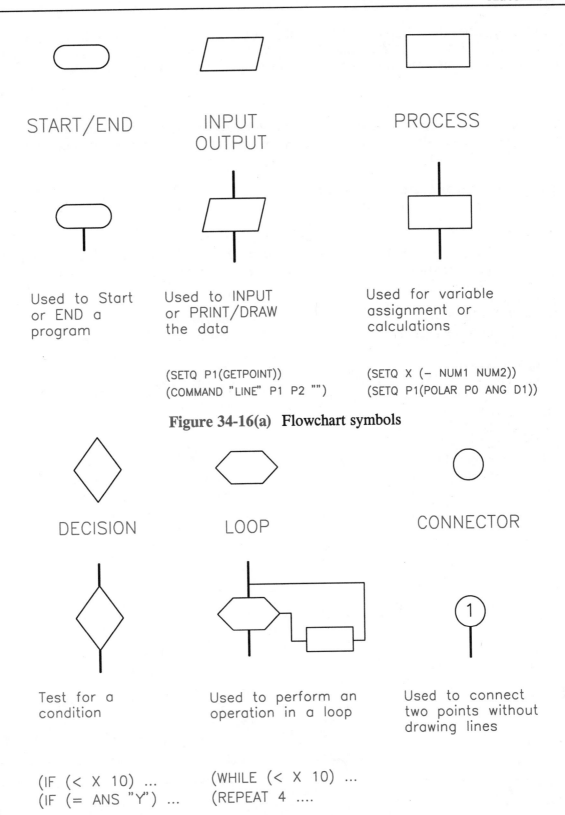

Figure 34-16(a) Flowchart symbols

Figure 34-16(b) Flowchart symbols

CONDITIONAL FUNCTIONS

The relational functions (discussed earlier in the chapter) establish a relationship between two atoms. For example, (< x y) describes a test condition for an operation. To use such functions in a meaningful way a conditional function is required. For example, (if (< x y) (setq z (- y x)) (setq z (- x y))) describes the action to be taken if the condition is true (T) or false (nil). If the condition is true, then z = y - x. If the condition is not true, then z = x - y. Therefore, conditional functions are very important for any programming language, including AutoLISP.

if

The **if** function (Figure 34-17) evaluates the first expression (then) if the specified condition returns T, and it evaluates the second expression (else) if the specified condition returns nil. The format of the **if** function is:

```
(if condition then [else])
```

Expression evaluated if the
condition returns nil

Expression evaluated if the condition returns T

Specified conditional statement

Examples

(if (= 7 7) ("true"))	returns "true"
(if (= 5 7) ("true") ("false"))	returns "false"

(setq ans "yes")
(if (= ans "yes") ("Yes") ("No"))   returns "Yes"

```
(setq num1 8)
(setq num2 10)
(if (> num1 num2)
    (setq x (- num1 num2))
    (setq x (- num2 num1))
)
```
returns 2

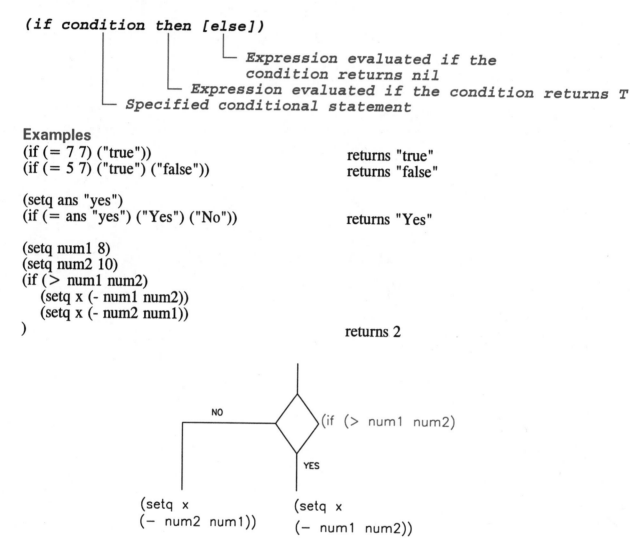

Figure 34-17 If function

Example 6

Write an AutoLISP program that will subtract a smaller number from a larger number. The program should also prompt you to enter two numbers.

Input	Output
Number (num1)	x = num1 - num2
Number (num2)	or
	x = num2 - num1

<u>Process</u>

If num1 > num2 then x = num1 - num2
if num1 < num2 then x = num2 - num1

The flowchart shown in Figure 34-18 describes the process involved in writing the program using standard flowchart symbols.

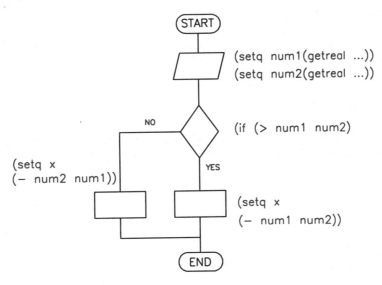

Figure 34-18 Flowchart for Example 6

The following file is a listing of the program for Example 6. The line numbers are not a part of the file; they are for reference only.

```
;This program subtracts smaller number          1
;from larger number                             2
;                                               3
(defun c:subnum( )                              4
   (setvar "cmdecho" 0)                         5
   (setq num1 (getreal "\n Enter first number: "))    6
   (setq num2 (getreal "\n Enter second number: "))   7
   (if (> num1 num2)                            8
      (setq x (- num1 num2))                    9
      (setq x (- num2 num1))                    10
   )                                            11
   (setvar "cmdecho" 1)                         12
   (princ)                                      13
)
```

Line 8
(if (> num1 num2)
In this line the **if** function evaluates the test expression **(> num1 num2)**. If the condition is true it returns T; and if the condition is not true it returns nil.

Line 9
(setq x (- num1 num2))
This expression is evaluated if the test expression **(if (> num1 num2)** returns T. The value of variable num2 is subtracted from num1 and the resulting value is assigned to variable x.

Line 10
(setq x (- num2 num1))

This expression is evaluated if the test expression **(if (> num1 num2)** returns nil. The value of variable num1 is subtracted from num2 and the resulting value is assigned to variable x.

Line 11
```
)
```
The close parenthesis completes the definition of the **if** function.

progn

The **progn** function can be used with the **if** function to evaluate several expressions. The format of **progn** function is:

(progn expression expression ......)

The **if** function evaluates only one expression if the test condition returns **T**. The **progn** function can be used in conjunction with the **if** function to evaluate several expressions.

Example
```
(if (= ans "yes")
    (progn
    (setq x (sin ang))
    (setq y (cos ang))
    (setq tanang (/ x y))
    )
    )
```

while

The **while** function (Figure 34-19) evaluates the test condition. If the condition is true (expression does not return nil) the operations that follow the while statement are repeated until the test expression returns **nil**. The format of the **while** function is:

(while *test-expression* operations)

Operations to be
performed until the test
expression returns nil

Expression that tests a condition

Examples
```
(while (= ans "yes")
    (setq x (+ x 1))
    (setq ans (getstring "Enter yes or no: "))
    )
(while (< n 3)
    (setq x (+ x 10))
    (setq n (1+ n))
    )
```

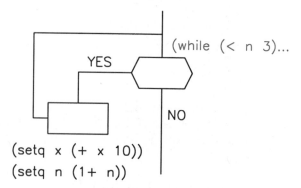

```
(setq x (+ x 10))
(setq n (1+ n))
```

Figure 34-19 While function

Example 7

Write an AutoLISP program that will generate the holes of a bolt circle. The program should prompt you to enter the center point of bolt circle, bolt circle diameter, bolt circle hole diameter, number of holes, and start angle of the bolt circles.

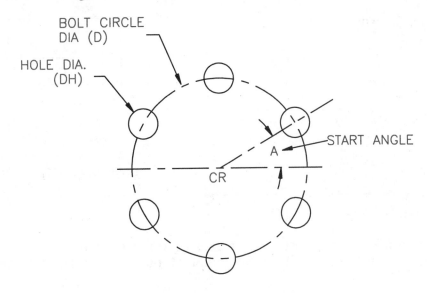

Figure 34-20   Bolt circle with six holes

```
;This program generates the bolt circles
;
(defun c:bc1( )
(graphscr)
(setvar "cmdecho" 0)
   (setq cr(getpoint "\n Enter center of Bolt-Circle: "))
   (setq d(getdist "\n Dia of Bolt-Circle: "))
   (setq n(getint "\n Number of holes in Bolt-Circle: "))
   (setq a(getangle "\n Enter start angle: "))
   (setq dh(getdist "\n Enter diameter of hole: "))
   (setq inc(/ (* 2 pi) n))
   (setq ang 0)
   (setq r (/ dh 2))
(while (< ang (* 2 pi))
   (setq p1 (polar cr (+ a inc) (/ d 2)))
   (command "circle" p1 r)
   (setq a (+ a inc))
   (setq ang (+ ang inc))
   )
(setvar "cmdecho" 1)
(princ)
   )
```

repeat

The **repeat** function evaluates the expressions n number of times as specified in the **repeat** function. The variable n must be an integer. The format of the **repeat** function is:

```
repeat n
        └── n is an integer that defines the number of
              times the expressions are to be evaluated
```

Example
```
(repeat 5
  (setq x (+ x 10))
  )
```

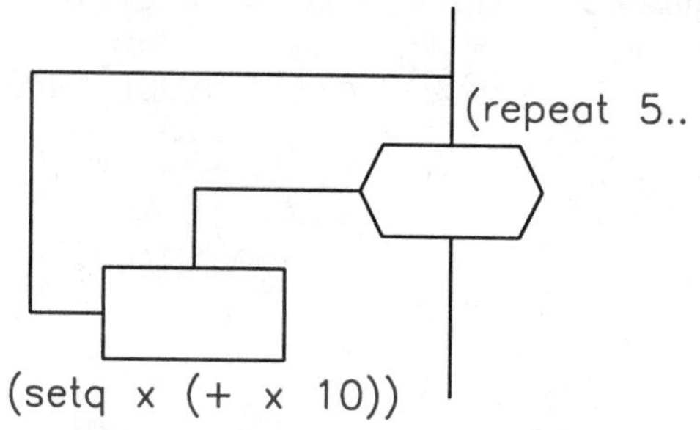

Figure 34-21 Repeat function

Example 8

Write an AutoLISP program that will generate a given number of concentric circles. The program should prompt you to enter the center point of the circles, the start radius, and the radius increment.

The following file is a listing of the AutoLISP program for Example 8.

```
;This program uses the repeat function to draw
;a given number of concentric circles.
(defun c:concir( )
(graphscr)
(setvar "cmdecho" 0)
(setq c (getpoint "\n Enter center point of circles: "))
(setq n (getint "\n Enter number of circles: "))
(setq r (getdist "\n Enter radius of first circle: "))
(setq d (getdist "\n Enter radius increment: "))
(repeat n
  (command "circle" c r)
  (setq r (+ r d))
  )
(setvar "cmdecho" 1)
(princ)
)
```

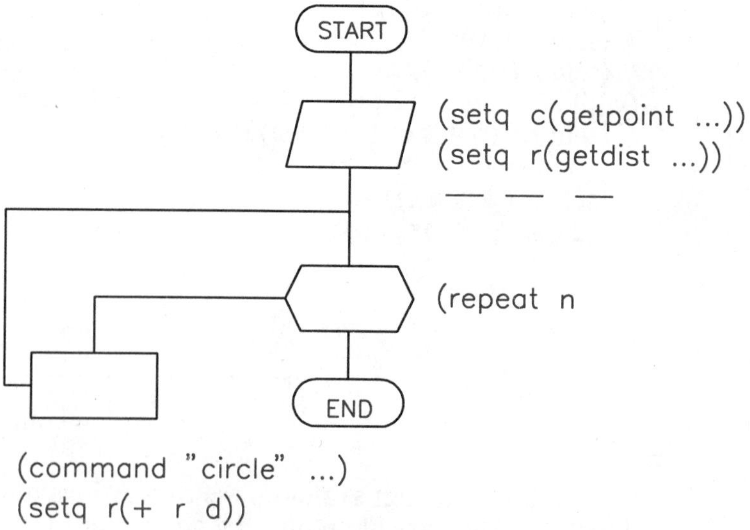

Figure 22 Flowchart for Example 8

EXERCISES

Exercise 6

Write an AutoLISP program that will draw three concentric circles with center C1 and diameters D1, D2, D3 (Figure 34-23). The program should prompt you to enter the coordinates of center point C1 and the circle diameters D1, D2, D3.

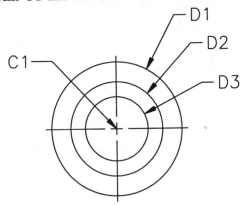

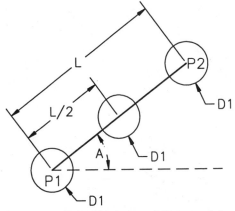

Figure 34-23 Three concentric circles with diameters D1, D2, D3

Figure 34-24 Circles and line making an angle A with X-axis

Exercise 7

Write an AutoLISP program that will draw a line from point P1 to point P2. Line P1,P2 makes an angle A with the positive X-axis. Distance between the points P1 and P2 is L. The diameter of the circles is D (D = L/4). (See Figure 34-24.)

Exercise 8

Write an AutoLISP program that will draw an isosceles triangle P1,P2,P3 (Figure 34-25). The program should prompt you to enter the starting point P1, length L1, and the included angle A.

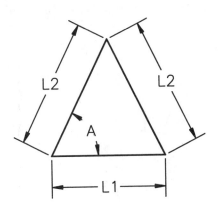

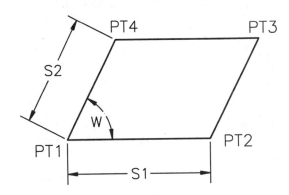

Figure 34-25 Isosceles triangle

Figure 34-26 Parallelogram with sides S1, S2 and angle W

Exercise 9

Write an AutoLISP program that will draw a parallelogram with sides S1,S2 and angle W as shown in Figure 34-26. The program should prompt you to enter the starting point PT1, lengths S1,S2, and the included angle W.

Exercise 10

Write an AutoLISP program that will draw a square of sides S, and a circle tangent to the four sides of the square as shown in Figure 34-27. The base of the square makes an angle, ANG, with the positive X-axis. The program should prompt you to enter the starting point P1, length S, and angle ANG.

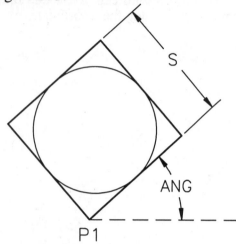

Figure 34-27 Square of side S at an angle ANG

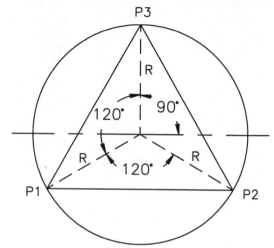

Figure 34-28 Equilateral triangle inside a circle

Exercise 11

Write an AutoLISP program that will draw an equilateral triangle inside the circle (Figure 34-28). The program should prompt you to enter the radius and the center point of the circle.

Exercise 12

Write an AutoLISP program that will draw the two views of a bushing as shown in Figure 34-29. The program should prompt you to enter the starting point P0, lengths L1, L2, and the bushing diameters ID, OD, HD. The distance between the front view and the side view of bushing is DIS (DIS = 1.25 * HD). The program should also draw the hidden lines in the HID layer and center lines in the CEN layer. The center lines should extend 0.75 units beyond the object line.

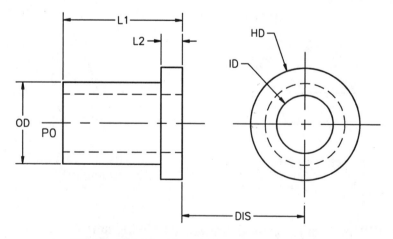

Figure 34-29 Two views of a bushing

Chapter 35

Programmable Dialogue Boxes

Using Dialogue Control Language

Learning objectives

After completing this chapter, you will be able to:
♦ Write programs using dialogue control language.
♦ Use predefined attributes.
♦ Load a dialogue control language (DCL) file.
♦ Display new dialogue boxes.
♦ Use standard button subassemblies.
♦ Use AutoLISP functions to control dialogue boxes.
♦ Manage dialogue boxes with AutoLISP.
♦ Use tiles, buttons, and attributes in DCL programs.

DIALOGUE CONTROL LANGUAGE

Dialogue Control Language files are ASCII files that contain the descriptions of dialogue boxes. A Dialogue Control Language (DCL) file can contain the description of a single or multiple dialogue boxes. There is no limit to the number of dialogue box descriptions that can be defined in a DCL file. The suffix of a DCL file is .DCL (such as DDOSNAP.DCL.).

This chapter assumes that you are familiar with AutoCAD commands, AutoCAD system variables, and AutoLISP programming. You need not be a programming expert to learn writing programs for dialogue boxes in DCL or to control the dialogue boxes through AutoLISP programing. However, the knowledge of any programming language should help you to understand and learn DCL. This chapter introduces you to the basic concepts of developing a dialogue box, frequently used attributes, and tiles. A thorough discussion of DCL functions and a step-by-step explanation of examples should make it easy for you to learn DCL. For those functions that are not discussed in this chapter, you can refer to *AutoCAD Customization Guide from Autodesk*. To write programs in DCL, you do not need any special software or hardware. If AutoCAD is installed on your computer, you can write DCL files. To write DCL files, you can use the EDLIN commands of DOS, the EDIT function of DOS (DOS 5.0), or any other ASCII Text Editor. You can also use AutoCAD's EDIT command, provided ACAD.PGP file is present and the EDIT command is defined in the file.

DIALOGUE BOX

A Dialogue Control Language (DCL) file contains the description of how the dialogue boxes will appear on the screen. These boxes can contain buttons, text, list, edit boxes, rows, columns, sliders, and images.

You do not need to specify the size and layout of a dialogue box or its component parts. Sizing is done automatically when the dialogue box is loaded on the screen. By itself, the dialogue box cannot perform the functions it is designed for. The functions of a dialogue box are controlled by a program written in the AutoLISP programming language or with the AutoCAD Development System (ADS). For example, if you load a dialogue box and select the Cancel button, it will not perform the cancel operation. The instructions associated with a button or any part of the dialogue box are handled through the functions provided in AutoLISP or ADS. Therefore, AutoLISP and ADS are needed to control the dialogue boxes and you should have, in addition to DCL, a good knowledge of AutoLISP or ADS to develop new dialogue boxes or edit existing ones.

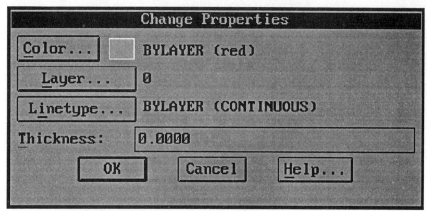

Figure 35-1 Sample dialogue box (ddchprop)

Dialogue boxes are not dependent on the platform; therefore, they can run on any system that supports AutoCAD. However, depending on the graphical user interface (GUI) of the platform, the appearance of the dialogue boxes might change from one system to another. The functions defined in the dialogue box will still work without making any changes in the dialogue box or the application program (AutoLISP or ADS) that uses these dialogue boxes. A sample dialogue box is shown in Figure 35-1.

DIALOGUE BOX COMPONENTS

The two major components of a dialogue box are the tiles and the box itself. The tiles can be arranged in rows and columns in any desired configuration. They can also be enclosed in boxes or borders to form subassemblies, giving them a tree structure (Figure 35-2(a)). The basic tiles, such as buttons, lists, edit boxes, images, etc., are predefined by the Programmable Dialogue Box (PDB) facility of AutoCAD. These buttons are described in the file **base.dcl**. The layout and function of a tile is determined by the attribute assigned to it. For example, the height attribute controls the height of the tile. Similarly, the label attribute specifies the text that is associated with the tile. Some of the components of a dialogue box are shown in Figure 35-2(b). Following that figure is a list of the predefined tiles and their format in DCL.

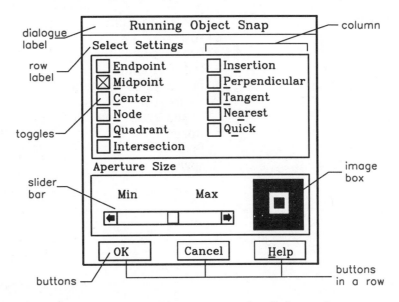

Figure 35-2(a) Components of a dialogue box

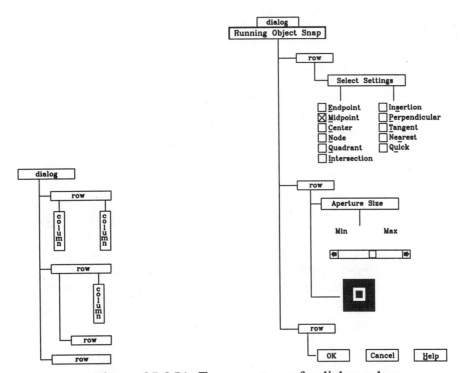

Figure 35-2(b) Tree structure of a dialogue box

Predefined Tiles	DCL Format
Button	button
Edit Box	edit_box
Image Button	image_button
List Box	list_box
Pop-up List	popup_list
Radio Button	radio_button
Slider	slider
Toggle	toggle
Column	column

Boxed Column	boxed_column
Row	row
Boxed Row	boxed_row
Radio Column	radio_column
Boxed Radio Column	boxed_radio_column
Radio Row	radio_row
Boxed Radio Row	boxed_radio_row
Image	image
Text	text
Spacer	spacer

BUTTON AND TEXT TILES

Button Tile

Format in DCL
button

The button tile consists of a rectangular box that resembles a push button. The button's label appears inside the button. For example, in the OK button of a dialogue box the label OK appears inside the button. If you select the OK button in a dialogue box, it performs the functions defined in the dialogue box and clears it from the screen. Similarly, if you select the cancel button, it cancels the dialogue box without taking any action.

Note

A dialogue box should contain at least one OK button or a button that is equivalent to it. This allows you to exit the dialogue box when you are done using it.

Text Tile

Format in DCL
text

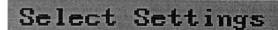

The text tile is used to display information or a title in a dialogue box. It has limited application in the dialogue boxes, because most of the tiles have their own label attributes for titling. However, if you need to display any text string in the dialogue box, you can do so with the text tile. The text tile is used extensively in AutoCAD alert boxes to display warnings or error messages.

Note

An alert box must contain an OK button or a cancel button to end the dialogue box.

TILE ATTRIBUTES

The appearance, size, and the function performed by a dialogue box tile depend on the attributes that have been assigned to the tile. For example, if a button has been assigned the **fixed_width** attribute, the width of the box surrounding the button will not stretch through the entire length of the dialogue box. Similarly, the **height** attribute determines the height of the tile and the **key** attribute assigns a name to the tile that is then used by the application program. The tile attribute consists of two parts: the name of the attribute and the value assigned to the attribute. For example, consider the expression **fixed_width = true**. In this expression, **fixed_width** is the name of the attribute and **true** is the value assigned to the attribute. Attribute names are like variable names in programming, and the values assigned to these variables must be of a specific type. The following are the types of values that can be assigned to an attribute:

integer

Unlike integer values (1, 15, 22) in programming, the numeric values assigned to attributes can be both integers and real numbers.

> **Examples**
> width = 15
> height = 10.0

real number

The real values assigned to attributes should always be fractional real numbers with a leading digit.

> **Example**
> *aspect_ratio = 0.75*

quoted string

The string values assigned to an attribute consist of a text string that is enclosed in double quotes.

> **Examples**
> key = "accept"
> label = "OK"

reserved word

The dialogue control language uses some reserved words as identifiers. These identifiers are alphanumeric characters that start with a letter.

> **Examples**
> is_default = true
> fixed_width = true

Note

Reserved names are case sensitive. For example, is_default = true is not same as is_default = True. The reserved word is true, not True or TRUE.

Like reserved words, attribute names are also case sensitive. For example, the attribute is key, not Key or KEY.

PREDEFINED ATTRIBUTES

To facilitate writing programs in Dialogue Control Language (DCL), AutoCAD has provided some predefined attributes that are defined in the Programmable Dialogue Box (PDB) package that comes with the AutoCAD software. Some of these attributes can be used with any tile and some only with a particular type of tile. The values assigned to various attributes in a DCL file are used by the application program to handle the tiles or the dialogue box. Therefore, you must use the correct attributes and assign an appropriate value to these attributes. The following is a list of some of the frequently used predefined attributes defined in the PDB facility of AutoCAD:

action	key
alignment	label
allow_accept	layout
aspect_ratio	list
color	max_value
edit_limit	min_value
edit_width	mnemonic
fixed_height	multiple_select
fixed_width	small_increment
height	tabs
is_cancel	value
is_default	width

key, label, and is_default Attributes

key Attribute

Format in DCL   Examples
key   key = "accept"
                                       key = "XLimit"

The **key** attribute assigns a name to a tile. The name must be enclosed in double quotes. This name can then be used by the application program to handle the tile. A dialogue box can have any number of key values, but within a particular dialogue box the values used for the key attributes must be unique. In the above-mentioned example (key = "accept"), a string value "accept" is assigned to the **key** attribute. If there is another key attribute in the dialogue box, you must assign it a different value.

label Attribute

Format in DCL   Examples
label   label = "OK"
                                       label = "Hallo DCL Users"

Sometimes it is necessary to display a label in a dialogue box. The label attribute can be used in a boxed column, boxed radio column, boxed radio row, boxed row, button tile, dialogue box, or edit box. The following is the description of some of the frequently used label attributes:

Use of the label Attribute in a Dialogue Box
When the label attribute is used in a dialogue box, it is displayed in the top border or the title bar of the dialogue box. The label must be a string enclosed in double quotes. Use of the label in a dialogue box is optional and in case of default, no title is displayed in the dialogue box.

Example
welcome : dialog {
        label = "Sample Dialogue Box";

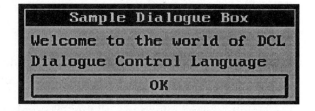

In this example the label, "Sample Dialogue Box", is displayed at the top of the dialogue box.

Use of the label Attribute in a Boxed Column
When the label attribute is used in a boxed column, the label is displayed in the upper left corner of the column within a box; the box consists of a single line at the top of the column.

The label must be a quoted string and the default is a set of quoted string (" "). If the default is used, only the box is displayed without any label.

> **Example**
> : text {
>   label = "Welcome to the world of DCL";
> }

In this example the label, "Welcome to the world of DCL", is displayed in the upper left corner of the column within a box.

Use of the label Attribute in a Button

When the label attribute is used in a button, the label is displayed inside the button. The label must be a quoted string and has no default.

> **Example**
> : button {
>   key = "accept";
>   label = "OK";
> }

In this example the label, "OK", is displayed inside and in the center of the button tile.

is_default Attribute

> Format in DCL   **Example**
> **is_default**   is_default = true

The **is_default** attribute is used for the button of a dialogue box. In the above example, the value assigned to the **is_default** attribute is **true**. Therefore, this button will be automatically selected when you press the Enter key. For example, if you load a dialogue box on the screen, one way to exit and accept the values of the dialogue box is to select the OK button. You can accomplish the same thing by pressing the Enter key (accept key). This action is made possible by assigning the value, **true**, to the **is_default** attribute. In a dialogue box the default button can be recognized by a thick border drawn around the text string.

> **Note**
>
> *In a dialogue box, only one button can be assigned true value for the is_default attribute.*

fixed_width and alignment Attributes

fixed_width Attribute

> Format in DCL   **Example**
> **fixed_width**   fixed_width = true

This attribute controls the width of the tile. If the value of this attribute is set to true, the width of the tile does not extend through the complete length of the dialogue box. The width of the tile is automatically adjusted to the length of the text string that is displayed in the tile.

alignment Attribute

Format in DCL   **Example**
alignment   alignment = centered
                                                 alignment = right

The value assigned to the **alignment** attribute determines the horizontal or vertical position of the tile in a row or in a column. For a row, the values that can be assigned to this attribute are left, right, or centered. The default value of the alignment attribute is left; that forces the tile to be displayed left justified. For a column, the possible values of the **alignment** attribute are top, bottom, or centered. The default value is centered.

Example 1

Using the Dialogue Control Language (DCL), write a program for the following dialogue box (Figure 35-3). The dialogue box has two text labels and an OK button to end the dialogue box.

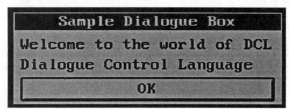

Figure 35-3 Dialogue box for Example 1

The following file is a listing of the DCL file for the dialogue box of Example 1. The name of this DCL file is dclwel1.dcl. The line numbers are not a part of the file; they are for reference only.

```
welcome1 : dialogue {                                        1
        label = "Sample Dialogue Box";                       2
        : text {                                             3
            label = "Welcome to the world of DCL";           4
        }                                                    5
        : text {                                             6
            label = "Dialogue Control Language";             7
        }                                                    8
        : button {                                           9
          key = "accept";                                    10
          label = "OK";                                      11
          is_default = true;                                 12
        }                                                    13
}                                                            14
```

Line 1
welcome1 : dialog {
In this line, **welcome1** is the name of the dialogue and the definition of the dialogue box is contained within the braces. The open brace in this line starts the definition of this dialogue box.

Line 2
label = "Sample Dialogue Box";
In this line, **label** is the label attribute and **"Sample Dialogue Box"** is the string value assigned to the label attribute. This string will be displayed in the title bar of the dialogue box. The

label description must be enclosed in quotes. If this line is missing, no title is displayed in the title bar of the dialogue box.

Lines 3-5

: text {
label = "Welcome to the world of DCL";
}

These three lines define a text tile with the label description. In the first line, **text**, refers to the text tile. The line that follows it, **label = "Welcome to the world of DCL",** defines a label for this tile that will be displayed left justified in the dialogue box. The close brace completes the definition of this tile.

Lines 9-13

: button {
key = "accept";
label = "OK";
is_default = true;
}

These five lines define the attributes of the button tile. In the first line, **button** refers to the button tile. In the second line, **key = "accept";** specifies an ASCII name, **"accept"**, that will be used by the application program to refer to this tile. The next line, **is_default = true;**, specifies that this button is the default button. It is automatically selected if you press the Enter key at the keyboard.

The close brace in line number 14 completes the definition of the dialogue box.

LOADING A DCL FILE

Like an AutoLISP file, you can load a DCL file from AutoCAD's Drawing Editor. A DCL file can contain the definition of one or several dialogue boxes. There is no limit to the number of dialogue boxes you can define in a DCL file. The format of the command for loading a dialogue box is:

```
(load_dialogue filename)
                         Name of the DCL file with or without
                               the file extension (.dcl)
              Load command for loading a dialogue file
```

Examples
(load_dialog "dclwel1.dcl")
or
(load_dialog "dclwel1")

In these examples, **dclwel1** is the name of the DCL file and **.dcl** is the file extension for DCL files.

The filename can be with or without the DCL file extension (welcome1 or welcome1.dcl). The load function returns an integer value that is used as a handle in the **new_dialog** function and the **unload_dialog** function. This integer will be referred as **dcl_id** in subsequent sections. You don't need to use the name dcl_id for this integer; it could be any name (dclid, or just id).

DISPLAYING A NEW DIALOGUE BOX

The load_dialog function loads the DCL file, but it does not display it on the screen. The format of the command used to display a new dialogue box on the screen is:

(new_dialog dlgname dcl_id)

                                        Integer returned in the
                                        load_dialog function
                          Name of the dialogue box
        Command to display a dialogue box

Example
(new_dialog "welcome1" 1)

In this example, assume that dcl_id is 1, an integer returned by load_dialog function.

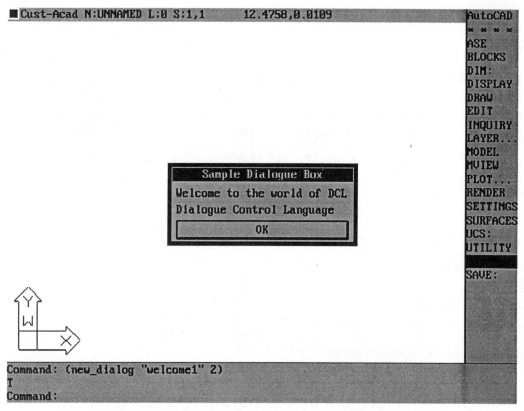

Figure 35-4 Dialogue Box as displayed on the screen

You can use the (load_dialog) and (new_dialog) commands to load the DCL file in Example 1. In the following command sequence, assume that the integer (dcl_id) returned by the (load_dialog) function is 3. Figure 35-4 shows the dialogue box after entering the following two command lines:

Command: (load_dialog "dclwel1.dcl")
3
Command: (new_dialog "welcome1" 3)

In this example you will notice that the OK button stretches through the complete width of the dialogue box. This button would look better if its width were limited to the width of the string "OK". This can be accomplished by using the **fixed_width = true;** attribute in the definition of this button. You can also use the **alignment = centered** attribute to display the OK button label center justified. The following file is a listing of the DCL file where the OK label for the OK button is center justified and the width of the box does not stretch across the width of the dialogue box.

```
welcome2 : dialog {
        label = "Sample Dialogue Box";
        : text {
            label = "Welcome to the world of DCL";
        }
        : text {
            label = "Hallo - DCL";
        }
        : button {
            key = "accept";
            label = "OK";
            is_default = true;
            fixed_width = true;   ◄--------- (Controls width)
            alignment = centered;   ◄------- (Controls
        }                                    Justification)
}
```

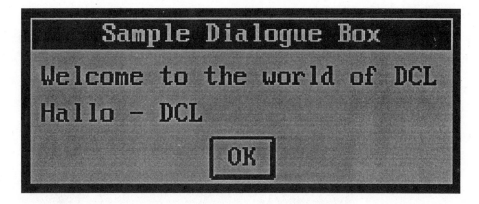

Figure 35-5 Dialogue Box with fixed width for OK button

USE OF STANDARD BUTTON SUBASSEMBLIES

Some standard button subassemblies are predefined in the **base.dcl** file. You can use these standard buttons in your DCL file to maintain consistency between various dialogue boxes. One such predefined button is **ok_cancel**, which displays the OK and Cancel buttons in the dialogue box. The following file is the listing of the DCL file of Example 1, using the **ok_cancel** predefined standard button subassembly:

```
welcome3 : dialog {
        label = "Sample Dialogue Box";
        : text {
            label = "Welcome to the world of DCL";
        }
        : text {
            label = "Dialogue Control Language";
            alignment = right;
        }
        ok_cancel;
}
```

Figure 35-6 Dialogue Box with OK and Cancel buttons

The following is a list of the standard button subassemblies that are predefined in the base.dcl file. These buttons are also referred to as **dialogue exit buttons** because they are used to exit a dialogue box.

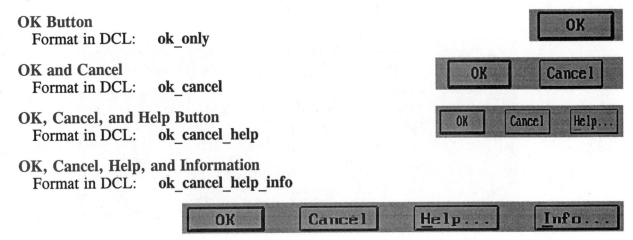

OK Button
Format in DCL: **ok_only**

OK and Cancel
Format in DCL: **ok_cancel**

OK, Cancel, and Help Button
Format in DCL: **ok_cancel_help**

OK, Cancel, Help, and Information
Format in DCL: **ok_cancel_help_info**

AUTOLISP FUNCTIONS

load_dialog

The AutoLISP function **load_dialog** is used to **load a DCL file** that is specified in the load_dialog function. In the following examples, the name of the file that AutoCAD loads is "dclwel1". The extension (.dcl) of the file is optional. When the DCL file is loaded successfully, AutoCAD returns an integer that identifies the dialogue box.

Format in DCL
(load_dialog filename)

Examples
(load_dialog "dclwel1.dcl")
(load_dialog "dclwel1")

unload_dialog

The AutoLISP function **unload_dialog** is used to **unload a DCL file** that is specified in the unload_dialog function. The file is specified by the variable (dcl_id) that identifies a DCL file.

Format in DCL
(unload_dialog dcl_id)

Example
(unload_dialog dcl_id)

new_dialog

The AutoLISP function **new_dialog** is used to initialize a dialogue box and then display it on the screen. In the following file, **"welcome1"** is the name of the **dialogue box**. (Note: welcome1 is not the name of the DCL file.) The variable **dcl_id** contains an integer value that is returned when the DCL file is loaded.

Format in DCL   **Example**
(new_dialog "dialogname" dcl_id)   (new_dialog "welcome1" dcl_id)

start_dialog

The AutoLISP function **start_dialog** is used in an AutoLISP program to accept user input from the dialogue box. For example, if you select OK from the dialogue box, the start_dialog function retrieves the value of that tile and uses it to take action and end the dialogue box.

Format in DCL
(start_dialog)

done_dialog

The AutoLISP function **done_dialog** is used to terminate the display of the dialogue box from the screen. This function must be defined within the action expression as shown in the following example.

Format in DCL   **Example**
(done_dialog)   (action_tile "accept" "(done_dialog)")

action_tile

The AutoLISP function **action_tile** is used to associate an action expression with a tile in the dialogue box. In the following example, the **action_tile** function associates the tile "accept" with the action expression (done_dialog) that terminates the dialog box. The "accept" is the name of the tile assigned to the OK button in the DCL file.

Format in DCL   **Example**
(action_tile tile-name action-expression)   (action_tile "accept" "(done_dialog)")

MANAGING DIALOGUE BOXES WITH AUTOLISP

When you load the DCL file of Example 1 and select the OK button, it does not perform the desired function (exit from the dialogue box). This is because a dialogue box cannot, by itself, execute the AutoCAD commands or the functions assigned to a tile. An application program is required to handle a dialogue box. These application programs can be written in AutoLISP or ADS. The functions defined in AutoLISP and ADS can be used to load a DCL file, display the dialogue box on the screen, prompt user input, set values in tiles, perform action associates with user input, and execute AutoCAD commands. Example 2 describes the use of an AutoLISP program to handle a dialogue box.

Example 2

Write an AutoLISP program that will handle the dialogue box and perform the functions as shown in the dialogue box of Example 1.

The following file is a listing of the DCL file of Example 1. This DCL file defines the dialogue box, **welcome1**, that contains only one action tile: "**OK**". If you select the **OK** button, you must be able to exit the dialogue box. As mentioned earlier, the dialogue box will not perform by itself the function assigned to the **OK** button unless you write an application that will execute the functions defined in the dialogue box.

```
welcome1 : dialog {
        label = "Sample Dialogue Box";
        : text {
            label = "Welcome to the world of DCL";
        }
        : text {
            label = "Dialogue Control Language";
        }
        : button {
            key = "accept";
            label = "OK";
            is_default = true;
        }
}
```

The following file is a listing of the AutoLISP program that loads the DCL file (dclwel1) of Example 1; displays the dialogue box, **welcome1**, on the screen; and defines the action for the **OK** button. The line numbers are not a part of the program; they are for reference only.

```
(defun C:welcome ( / dcl_id)                        1
(setq dcl_id (load_dialog "dclwel1.dcl"))           2
(new_dialog "welcome1" dcl_id)                      3
(action_tile                                        4
    "accept"                                        5
    "(done_dialog)")                                6
(start_dialog)                                      7
(unload_dialog dcl_id)                              8
(princ)                                             9
)                                                  10
```

Line 1
(defun C:welcome (/ dcl_id)
In this line, **defun** is an AutoLISP function that defines the function **welcome**. By using c: in front of the function name, the **welcome** function can be executed like an AutoCAD command. The **welcome** function has one local variable, **dcl_id**.

Line 2
(setq dcl_id (load_dialog "dclwel1.dcl"))
In this line, **(load_dialog "dclwel1.dcl")** loads the DCL file dclwel1.dcl and returns a positive integer. The **setq** function assigns this integer value to the local variable **dcl_id**.

Line 3
(new_dialog "welcome1" dcl_id)
In this line, the AutoLISP function **new_dialog** loads the dialogue, **welcome1**, that is defined in the DCL file (line 1 of DCL file). The variable, **dcl_id**, is an integer that identifies the DCL file.

> **Note**
>
> *The dialogue name (welcome1) in the AutoLISP program must be the same as the dialogue name in the DCL file (welcome1).*

Lines 4-6
(action_tile
"accept"
"(done_dialog)")
In the DCL file of Example 1, the **OK** button has been assigned an ASCII name, **accept** (key = "accept"). The first two lines associate the key (OK button) with the action expression. The action_tile initializes the association between the OK button and the action expression (done_dialog). If you pick the **OK** button from the dialogue box, the AutoLISP program reads that value and performs the function defined in the statement (done_dialog). The done_dialog function ends the dialogue box.

Line 7
(start_dialog)
The **start_dialog** function enables the AutoLISP program to accept your input from the dialogue box.

Line 8
(unload_dialog dcl_id)
This statement unloads the DCL file identified by the integer value of dcl_id.

Lines 9 and 10
(princ)
)
The **princ** function prints a blank on the screen. You use this to prevent display of the last expression in the command prompt area of the screen. If the **princ** function is not used, AutoCAD will print the value of the last expression. The closed parenthesis in the last line completes the definition of the welcome function.

ROW AND BOXED ROW TILES

Row Tile
Format in DCL: **row**

In a DCL file, several tiles can be grouped together to form a composite row or a composite column that is treated as a single tile. A row tile consists of several tiles grouped together in a horizontal row.

Boxed Row Tile

Format in DCL: **boxed_row**

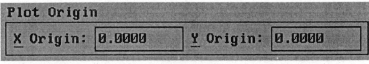

In a boxed row, the tiles are grouped together in a row and a border is drawn around them, forming a box shape. If the boxed row has a label, it will be displayed left-justified at the top of the box, above the border line. If no label attribute is defined, only the box is displayed around the tile. On some systems, depending on the graphical user interface (GUI), the label may be displayed inside the border.

COLUMN, BOXED COLUMN, AND TOGGLE TILES

Column Tile

Format in DCL: **column**

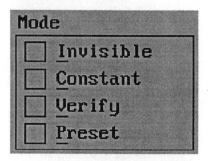

In a column tile, the tiles are grouped together in a vertical column to form a composite tile.

Boxed Column Tile

Format in DCL: **boxed_column**

In a boxed column, the tiles are grouped together in a column and a border is drawn around the tiles. If the boxed column has a label, it will be displayed left-justified at the top of the box, above the border line. If there is no label attribute defined, only the box is displayed around the tile. On some systems, depending on the graphical user interface (GUI), the label may be displayed inside the border.

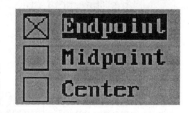

Toggle Tile

Format in DCL: **toggle**

A toggle tile in a dialogue box displays a small box on the screen with an optional label on the right of the box. Although the label is optional, you should label the toggle box so that users know what function is assigned to the toggle box. A toggle box has two states: on and off. When the function is turned on, a check mark (X) is displayed in the box. Similarly, when a function is turned off, no check mark is displayed. The on or off state of the toggle box represents a Boolean value. When the toggle box is on, the Boolean value is 1; when the toggle box is off, the Boolean value is 0.

Mnemonic Attribute

Format in DCL   **Example**
mnemonic   mnemonic = "U"

A dialogue box can have several tiles with labels. One of the ways you can select a tile is by using the arrow to highlight the tile and then pressing the accept key. This is possible if you have a pointing device like a digitizer or a mouse. If you do not have a pointing device, it may not be possible to select a tile. However, you can select a tile by using the mnemonic key assigned to the tile. For example, the mnemonic character for the Unlock tile is U. If you press the U-key at the keyboard, it will highlight the Unlock tile. The mnemonic character is designated by underlining one of the characters in the label. The underlining is done automatically once you define the mnemonic attribute for the tile. You can select only one character **in the label** as a mnemonic character and you must use different mnemonic characters for different tiles. If a dialogue box has two tiles with the same mnemonic character, only one tile will be selected when you press the mnemonic key. The mnemonic characters are not case sensitive, therefore they can be uppercase (U) or lowercase (u). However, the character in the label you select as a mnemonic character should be capitalized for easy identification.

Note

Some graphical user interfaces (GUIs) do not support mnemonic attributes. On such systems, you cannot select a tile by pressing the mnemonic key. However, you can still use pointing devices to select the tile.

Example 3

Write a DCL program for the object snap dialogue box as shown in Figure 35-7(a). The object snap tiles are arranged in two columns in a boxed row.

Before writing a program, especially a DCL program for dialogue box, you should determine the organization of the dialogue box. It is given in the above example, but when you develop a dialogue box yourself, you must be careful when organizing the tiles in the dialogue box. The structure of the DCL program depends on the desired output. In Example 3, the desired output is shown in Figure 35-7(a). This dialogue box has two rows and two columns. The first row has two columns and the second row has no columns, as shown in Figure 35-7(b).

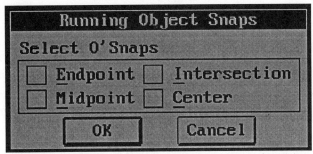

Figure 35-7(a)   Dialogue box for object snaps

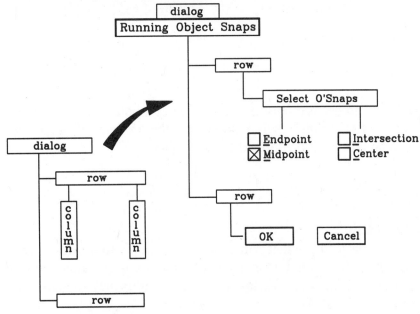

Figure 35-7(b)   Dialogue box for object snaps

The following file is a listing of the DCL file for Example 3. The line numbers are not a part of the file; they are shown for reference only.

```
osnapsh : dialog {                                          1
        label = "Running Object Snaps";                     2
      : boxed_row {                                          3
        label = "Select O'Snaps";                           4
        : column {                                           5
                : toggle {                                   6
                label = "Endpoint";                          8
                key = "Endpoint";                            9
                mnemonic = "E";                              10
                fixed_width = true;                          11
                }                                            12
                : toggle {                                   13
                label = "Midpoint";                          14
                key = "Midpoint";                            15
                mnemonic = "M";                              16
                fixed_width = true;                          17
                }                                            18
                }                                            19
        : column {                                           20
                : toggle {                                   21
                label = "Intersection";                      22
                key = "Intersection";                        23
                mnemonic = "I";                              24
                fixed_width = true;                          25
                }                                            26
                : toggle {                                   27
                label = "Center";                            28
                key = "Center";                              29
                mnemonic = "C";                              30
                fixed_width = true;                          31
                }                                            32
                }                                            33
        }                                                    34
            ok_cancel;                                       35
      }                                                      36
```

Lines 3 and 4
: boxed_row {
  label = "Select O'Snaps";
The **boxed_row** is a predefined cluster tile that draws a border around the tiles. The second line, **label = "Select O'Snaps";**, will display the label (**Select O'Snaps**) left-justified at the top of the box. The **label** is a predefined DCL attribute.

Lines 5-8
: column {
  : toggle {
  label = "Endpoint";
The **column** is a predefined tile that will arrange the tiles within it in a vertical column. The **toggle** is another predefined tile that displays a small box in the dialogue box with an optional text on the right side of the box. The **label** attribute will display the label (**Endpoint**) to the right of the toggle box.

Lines 9-12
key = "Endpoint";
mnemonic = "E";
fixed_width = true;
}

The **key** attribute assigns a name (**Endpoint**) to the tile. This name is then used by the application program to handle the tile. The second line, **mnemonic = "E";**, defines the keyboard mnemonic for **Endpoint**. This causes the character **E** of **Endpoint** to be displayed underlined in the dialogue box. The attribute **fixed_width** controls the width of the tile. If the value of this attribute is **true**, the tile does not stretch across the width of the dialogue box. The close brace (**}**) on the next line completes the definition of the toggle tile.

Lines 32-36
         }
       }
     }
   ok_cancel;
}

The close brace on line 32 completes the definition of the toggle tile, and the close brace on line 33 completes the definition of the column of line number 20. The close brace on line 34 completes the definition of the boxed_row of line 3. The predefined tile, **ok_cancel**, displays the **ok** and **cancel** tile in the dialogue box. The close brace on the last line completes the definition of the dialogue box.

After writing the program, use the following commands to load the DCL file and display the dialogue box on the screen. The name of the file is assumed to be **osnapsh.dcl**. If AutoCAD is successful in loading the file, it will return an integer. In the following examples, the integer AutoCAD returns is assumed to be 1. The screen display, after loading the dialogue box, is shown in Figure 35-8.

Command: (load_dialog "osnapsh.dcl")
1
Command: (new_dialog "osnapsh" 1)

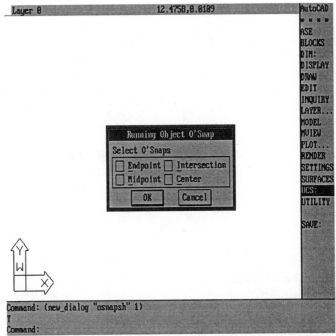

Figure 35-8 Screen display with dialogue box for Example 3

AUTOLISP FUNCTIONS

logand and logior

These AutoLISP functions, logand and logior, are used to obtain the result of **logical bitwise AND** and **logical bitwise inclusive OR** of a list of numbers.

Examples of **logand** function

(logand 2 7)	will return	2
(logand 8 15)	will return	8
(logand 6 15 7)	will return	6
(logand 6 15 1)	will return	0
(logand 1 4)	will return	0
(logand 1 5)	will return	1

Examples of **logior** function

(logior 2 7)	will return	7
(logior 8 15)	will return	15
(logior 6 15 7)	will return	15
(logior 6 15 1)	will return	15
(logior 1 4)	will return	5
(logior 1 5)	will return	5

One application of bit codes is found in the object snap modes. The following is a list of bit codes that are assigned to different object snap modes:

Snap Modes	Bit Codes	Snap Modes	Bit Codes
None	0	Intersection	32
Endpoint	1	Insertion	64
Midpoint	2	Perpendicular	128
Center	4	Tangent	256
Node	8	Nearest	512
Quadrant	16	Quick	1024

The system variable OSMODE can be used to specify a snap mode. For example, if the value assigned to OSMODE is 4, the object snap mode is center. The bit codes can be combined to produce multiple object snap modes. For example, you can get endpoint, midpoint, and center object snaps by adding the bit codes of endpoint, midpoint, and center (1 + 2 + 4 = 7) and assigning that value (7) to the **OSMODE** system variable. In AutoLISP the existing snapmodes information can be extracted by using the logand function. For example, if the OSMODE is set to 7, the logand function can be used to check different bit codes that represent object snaps.

(logand 1 7)	will return	1	(Endpoint)
(logand 2 7)	will return	2	(Midpoint)
(logand 4 7)	will return	4	(Center)

Example 4

Write an AutoLISP program that will handle the dialogue box and perform the functions as described in the dialogue box of Example 3.

The following file is a listing of the AutoLISP program for Example 4. The line numbers are not a part of the program; they are for reference only.

```
;;Lisp program for setting O'Snaps                      1
;;Dialog file name is osnapsh.dcl                       2
(defun c:osnapsh ( / dcl_id)                            3
(setq dcl_id (load_dialog "osnapsh.dcl"))               4
(new_dialog "osnapsh" dcl_id)                           5

;;Get the existing value of object snaps and            6
;;then write the values to the dialogue box             7
(setq osmode (getvar "osmode"))                         8
(if (= 1 (logand 1 osmode))                             9
    (set_tile "Endpoint" "1")                          10
    )                                                  11
(if (= 2 (logand 2 osmode))                            12
    (set_tile "Midpoint" "1")                          13
    )                                                  14
(if (= 32 (logand 32 osmode))                          15
    (set_tile "Intersection" "1")                      16
    )                                                  17
(if (= 4 (logand 4 osmode))                            18
    (set_tile "Center" "1")                            19
    )                                                  20
                                                       21
;;Read the values as set in the dialogue box and       22
;;assign those values to AutoCAD variable osmode        23
(defun setvars ()                                      24
(setq osmode 0)                                        25
(if (= "1" (get_tile "Endpoint"))                      26
    (setq osmode (logior osmode 1))                    27
    )                                                  28
(if (= "1" (get_tile "Midpoint"))                      29
    (setq osmode (logior osmode 2))                    30
    )                                                  31
(if (= "1" (get_tile "Intersection"))                  32
    (setq osmode (logior osmode 32))                   33
    )                                                  34
(if (= "1" (get_tile "Center"))                        35
    (setq osmode (logior osmode 4))                    36
    )                                                  37
    (setvar "osmode" osmode)                           38
    )                                                  39
                                                       40
(action_tile "accept" "(setvars) (done_dialog)")       41
(start_dialog)                                         42
(princ)                                               43
)                                                     44
```

Lines 1 and 2
;;Lisp program for setting O'Snaps
;;Dialog file name is osnapsh.dcl
These lines are comment lines and all comment lines start with a semicolon. AutoCAD ignores the lines that start with a semicolon.

Lines 3-5
(defun c:osnapsh (/ dcl_id)
(setq dcl_id (load_dialog "osnapsh.dcl"))
(new_dialog "osnapsh" dcl_id)

In the first line, **defun** is an AutoLISP function that defines the **osnapsh** function. Because of **c:** in front of the function name, the **osnapsh** function can be executed like an AutoCAD command. The **osnapsh** function has one local variable, **dcl_id**. In the second line, **(load_dialog "osnapsh.dcl")** loads the DCL file osnapsh.dcl and returns a positive integer. The **setq** function assigns this integer to the local variable, dcl_id. In the third line, the AutoLISP **new_dialog** function loads the dialogue **osnapsh that is defined in the DCL file** (line 1 of DCL file). The variable, **dcl_id**, has an integer value that identifies the DCL file.

Line 8
(setq osmode (getvar "osmode"))
In this line, **getvar "osmode"** has the value of the AutoCAD system **osmode** variable and the **setq** function sets the **osmode** variable equal to that value. Note that the first osmode is just a variable, whereas the second osmode in quotes (**"osmode"**) is the system variable.

Lines 9-11
(if (= 1 (logand 1 osmode))
   (set_tile "Endpoint" "1")
)

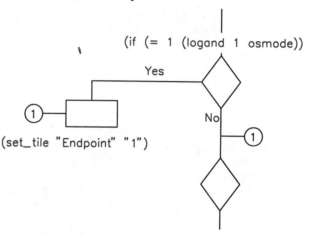

In the first line, **(logand 1 osmode)** will return 1, if the bit code of end point (1) is a part of the OSMODE value. For example, if the value assigned to OSMODE is 7 (1 + 2 + 4 = 7), (logand 1 7) will return 1. If OSMODE is 6 (2 + 4 = 6), then (logand 1 6) will return 0. The AutoLISP **if** function checks whether the value returned by **(logand 1 osmode)** is 1. If the function returns **T** (true), the instructions described in the second line are carried out. The second line sets the value of the **Endpoint** tile to 1; that displays a X mark in the toggle box. The close parenthesis in the third line completes the definition of the **if** function. If the expression, **(if (= 1 (logand 1 osmode))**, returns **nil**, the program skips to line 12 of the program.

Lines 24 and 25
(defun setvars ( )
(setq osmode 0)
The first line defines a **setvars** function and the second line sets the value of the **osmode** variable to zero.

Lines 26-28
(if (= "1" (get_tile "Endpoint"))
   (setq osmode (logior osmode 1))
)
In the first line, **(get_tile "Endpoint")** obtains the value of the toggle tile named **Endpoint**. If the **Endpoint** toggle tile is on, the value it returns is 1; if the toggle tile is off, the value it returns is 0. In the second line the **setq** function sets the value of **osmode** to the value returned by **(logior osmode 1)**. For example, if the initial value of **osmode** is 0, the **(logior osmode 1)** will return 1. Similarly, if the initial value of **osmode** is 1, **(logior osmode 2)** will return 3.

Lines 41 and 42
(action_tile "accept" "(setvars) (done_dialog)")
(start_dialog)
The second line, **(start_dialog)**, starts the dialogue box. In the dialogue file the name assigned to the **OK** button is **"accept"**. When you select the **OK** button in the dialogue box, the program executes the **setvars** function that updates the value of the **osmode** system variable and sets the selected object snaps.

PREDEFINED RADIO BUTTON, RADIO COLUMN, BOXED RADIO COLUMN AND RADIO ROW TILES

Predefined Radio Button Tile

Format in DCL: **radio_button**

The radio button is a predefined active tile. Radio buttons can be arranged in a row or in a column. The unique characteristic of radio buttons is that only one button can be selected at a time. For example, if there are buttons for scientific, decimal, and engineering units, only one can be selected. If you select the decimal button, the other two buttons will be turned off automatically. Because of this special characteristic, radio buttons must only be used in a radio row or in a radio column. The label for the radio button is optional; in most systems the label appears to the right of the button.

Predefined Radio Column Tile

Format in DCL: **radio_column**

The radio column is an active predefined tile where the radio button tiles are arranged in a column and only one button can be selected at a time. When the radio buttons are arranged in a column, the buttons are vertically next to each other and are easy to select. Therefore, you should arrange the radio buttons in a column to make it easy to select a radio button.

Predefined Boxed Radio Column Tile

Format in DCL: **boxed_radio_column**

The boxed radio column is an active predefined tile where a border is drawn around the radio column.

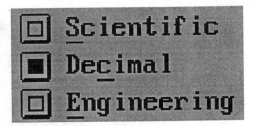

Predefined Radio Row Tile

Format in DCL: **radio_row**

The radio row consists of radio button tiles that are arranged in a row. Only one button can be selected at a time. The radio row can become quite long if there are several radio buttons tiles and labels. To select a radio button the cursor travel will increase because the buttons are not immediately next to each other. Therefore, you should avoid using the radio buttons tiles in a row, especially if there are more than two.

Example 5

Write a DCL program for a dialogue box that will enable you to select different units and unit precision as shown in Figure 35-9. Also, write an AutoLISP program that will handle the dialogue box.

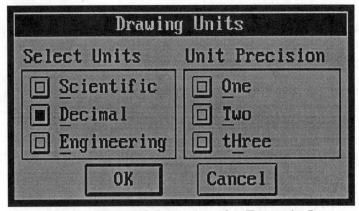

Figure 35-9 Dialogue box for Example 5

The following file is a listing of the DCL program for the dialogue box shown in Figure 35-9. The name of the dialogue box is **dwgunits**. The line numbers are not a part of the file; they are shown here for reference only.

```
dwgunits : dialog {                          1
  label = "Drawing Units";                   2
  : row {                                    3
    : boxed_column {                         4
      label = "Select Units";                5
      : radio_column {                       6
        : radio_button {                     7
          key = "scientific";                8
          label = "Scientific";              9
          mnemonic = "S";                   10
        }                                   11
        : radio_button {                    12
          key = "decimal";                  13
          label = "Decimal";                14
          mnemonic = "D";                   15
        }                                   16
        : radio_button {                    17
          key = "engineering";              18
```

```
              label = "Engineering";              19
              mnemonic = "E";                      20
              }                                     21
           }                                        22
        }                                           23
      : boxed_column {                              24
        label = "Unit Precision";                   25
        : radio_column {                            26
          : radio_button {                          27
            key = "one";                            28
            label = "One";                          29
            mnemonic = "O";                         30
            }                                       31
          : radio_button {                          32
            key = "two";                            33
            label = "Two";                          34
            mnemonic = "T";                         35
            }                                       36
          : radio_button {                          37
            key = "three";                          38
            label = "tHree";                        39
            mnemonic = "H";                         40
            }                                       41
          }                                         42
        }                                           43
      }                                             44
    ok_cancel;                                      45
  }                                                 46
```

Lines 4 and 5
: boxed_column {
  label = "Select Units";
The **boxed_column** is an active predefined tile that draws a border around the column. The second line, **label = "Select Units";**, displays the label (**Select Units**) at the top of the column. The **label** is a predefined DCL attribute.

Lines 6-8
: boxed_column {
  : radio_button {
    key = "scientific";
The **boxed_column** is a predefined active tile that will arrange the tiles within it in a vertical column and draw a border around the column. The **radio_button** is another active predefined tile that displays a radio button in the dialogue box with an optional text to the right of the button. The **key** attribute assigns a name (**scientific**) to the tile. This name is then used by the application program to handle the tile.

Lines 9-11
    label = "Scientific";
    mnemonic = "S";
    }
The **label** attribute will display the label (**Scientific**) on the right of the toggle box. The second line, **mnemonic = "S";**, defines the keyboard mnemonic for **Scientific**. This causes the letter

S of **Scientific** to be displayed underlined in the dialogue box. The close brace (**}**) on the next line completes the definition of the toggle tile.

Lines 41-46

```
                }
              }
            }
          }
      ok_cancel;
}
```

The close brace on the first line completes the definition of the radio button and the close brace on the second line completes the definition of the radio column. The close brace on third line completes the definition of the boxed_column and the close brace on the next line completes the definition of the row on line 3 of the DCL file. The predefined tile, **ok_cancel**, displays the **OK** and **Cancel** tiles in the dialogue box. The close brace on the last line completes the definition of the dialogue box.

Use the following commands to load and display the dialogue file on the screen. The name of the file is assumed to be **dwgunits.dcl** and the name of the dialogue is **dwgunits**. If AutoCAD is successful in loading the file, it will return an integer. In the following examples, the integer that AutoCAD returns is assumed to be 5. The screen display after loading the dialogue box is shown in Figure 35-10.

Command: (load_dialog "osnapsh.dcl")
5
Command: (new_dialog "osnapsh" 5)

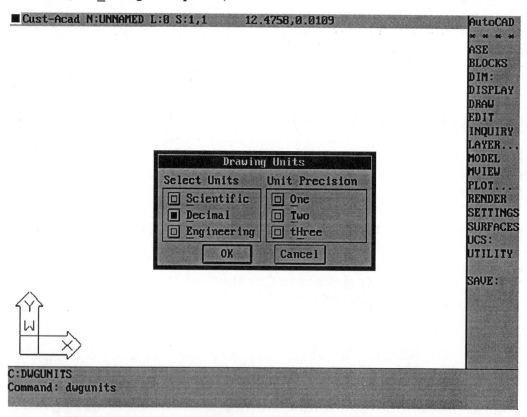

Figure 35-10 Screen display with dialogue box for Example 5

The following file is a listing of the AutoLISP program that loads, displays, and handles the dialogue box for Example 5. The line numbers are not a part of the file; they are shown here for reference only.

```
;;Lisp program dwgunits.lsp for setting units          1
;;and precision. Dialog file name dwgunits.dcl         2
;                                                       3
(defun c:dwgunits ( / dcl_id)                          4
(setq dcl_id (load_dialog "dwgunits.dcl"))             5
(new_dialog "dwgunits" dcl_id)                         6
                                                       7
;                                                      
;;Get the existing values of lunits and luprec         8
;;and turn the corresponding radio_button on           9
;                                                      10
(setq lunits (getvar "lunits"))                        11
(if (= 1 lunits)                                        12
    (set_tile "scientific" "1")                        13
    )                                                  14
(if (= 2 lunits)                                        15
    (set_tile "decimal" "1")                           16
    )                                                  17
(if (= 3 lunits)                                        18
    (set_tile "engineering" "1")                       19
    )                                                  20
                                                       21
;                                                      22
(setq luprec (getvar "luprec"))                        22
(if (= 1 luprec)                                        23
    (set_tile "one" "1")                               24
    )                                                  25
(if (= 2 luprec)                                        26
    (set_tile "two" "1")                               27
    )                                                  28
(if (= 3 luprec)                                        29
    (set_tile "three" "1")                             30
    )                                                  31
                                                       32
;;Read the value of the radio_buttons and              33
;;assign it to AutoCAD lunit and luprec variables      34
;                                                      35
(action_tile "scientific" "(setq lunits 1)")           36
(action_tile "decimal" "(setq lunits 2)")              37
(action_tile "engineering" "(setq lunits 3)")          38
;                                                      39
(action_tile "one" "(setq luprec 1)")                  40
(action_tile "two" "(setq luprec 2)")                  41
(action_tile "three" "(setq luprec 3)")                42
(action_tile "accept" "(done_dialog)")                 43
;                                                      44
(start_dialog)                                         45
(setvar "lunits" lunits)                               46
(setvar "luprec" luprec)                               47
(princ)                                                48
)                                                      49
```

Lines 1-3
;;Lisp program dwgunits.lsp for setting units
;;and precision. Dialog file name dwgunits.dcl
;
The first three lines of this program are comment lines and all comment lines start with a semicolon. AutoCAD ignores them.

Lines 4-6
(defun c:dwgunits (/ dcl_id)
(setq dcl_id (load_dialog "dwgunits.dcl"))
(new_dialog "dwgunits" dcl_id)
In the first line, **defun** is an AutoLISP function that defines the **dwgunits** function, which has one local variable, **dcl_id**. The **c:** in front of the function name, **dwgunits**, makes the **dwgunits** function act like an AutoCAD command. In the second line, **(load_dialog "dwgunits.dcl")** loads the DCL file dwgunits.dcl and returns a positive integer. The **setq** function assigns this integer to the local variable, dcl_id. In the third line, the AutoLISP **new_dialog** function displays the **dwgunits** dialogue box that is defined in the DCL file (line 1 of DCL file). The **dcl_id** variable is an integer that identifies the DCL file.

Line 11
(setq lunits (getvar "lunits"))
In this line, **getvar "lunits"** has the value of the AutoCAD system variable, **lunits**, and the **setq** function sets the **lunits** variable equal to that value. The first **lunits** is a variable, whereas the second **lunits** in quotes (**"lunits"**) is a system variable.

Lines 12 and 13
(if (= 1 lunits)
**   (set_tile "scientific" "1")**
**   )**

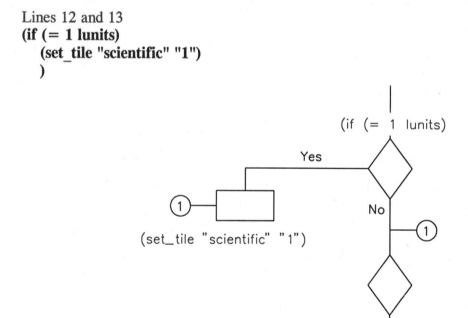

The **if** function (AutoLISP function) checks whether the value of the variable lunits is 1. If the function returns **T** (true), the instructions described in the second line are carried out. The second line sets the value of the tile named **"scientific"** equal to 1; that turns the corresponding radio button on. The close parenthesis in the third line completes the **if** function. If the **if** function, **(if (= 1 lunits)** returns **nil**, the program skips to line number 14.

Line 22
(setq luprec (getvar "luprec"))
In this line, **getvar "luprec"** has the value of the AutoCAD system variable, **luprec**, and the **setq** function sets the **luprec** variable equal to that value. The first **luprec** is a variable, whereas the second **luprec** in quotes (**"luprec"**) is a system variable.

Lines 23-25
(if (= 1 luprec)
   (set_tile "one" "1")
)

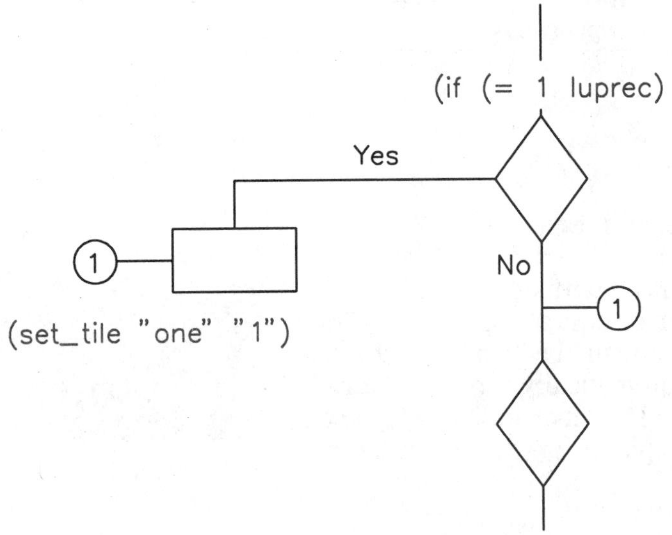

In the first line, the **if** function checks whether the value of the **luprec** variable is 1. If the function returns **T** (true), the instructions described in the second line are carried out. The second line sets the value of the tile named **"one"** equal to 1; that turns the corresponding radio button on. The close parenthesis in the third line completes the definition of the **if** function. If the **if** function returns **nil**, the program skips to line number 25.

Line 36
(action_tile "scientific" "(setq lunits 1)")
If the radio button tile named **"scientific"** is turned on, the **setq** function sets the value of the AutoCAD system variable, **lunits**, to 1. The **lunits** system variable controls the drawing units. The following is a list of the integer values that can be assigned to the **lunits** system variable:

1	Scientific	4	Architectural
2	Decimal	5	Fractional
3	Engineering		

Line 40
(action_tile "one" "(setq luprec 1)")
If the radio button tile named **"one"** is turned on, the **setq** function sets the value of the AutoCAD system variable, **luprec**, to 1. The **lunits** system variable controls the number of decimal places in a decimal number or the denominator of a fractional or architectural unit.

Lines 43-49
(action_tile "accept" "(done_dialog)")
;
(start_dialog)
(setvar "lunits" lunits)
(setvar "luprec" luprec)

In the dialogue file, the name assigned to the **OK** button is "**accept**". When you select the **OK** button in the dialogue box, the program executes the function defined in the **dwgunits** dialogue box. The **(start_dialog)** function starts the dialogue box. The **(setvar "lunits" lunits)** and **(setvar "luprec" luprec)** set the values of the **lunits** and **luprec** system variables equal to lunits and luprec, respectively.

EDIT BOX TILE

Format in DCL: **edit_box**

The edit box is a predefined active tile that enables you to enter or edit a single line of text. If the text is longer than the length of the edit box, the text will automatically scroll to the right or left horizontally. The label for the edit box is optional and it is displayed on the left of the edit box.

```
X-Spacing  | 1.0000 |

Y-Spacing  | 1.0000 |
```

WIDTH AND EDIT_WIDTH ATTRIBUTES

Width Attribute

Format in DCL: **width**   **Example:** width = 22

The **width** attribute is used to control the width of the tile to a desired size. The value assigned to the **width** attribute can be a real number or an integer that represents the distance in character width. The value assigned to the **width** attribute defines the minimum width of the tile. For example, in the above-mentioned example the minimum width of the tile is 22. However, the tile will automatically stretch if more space is available. It will retain the size of 22 only if the **fixed_width** attribute is assigned to the tile. The **width** attribute can be used with any tile.

Edit_Width Attribute

Format in DCL: **edit_width**   **Example:** edit_width = 10

The **edit_width** attribute is used with the predefined edit box tiles and it determines the size of the edit box in character width units. If the width of the edit box is 0, or if it is not specified and the fixed_width attribute is not assigned to the tile, the tile will automatically stretch to fill the available space. When the edit box is stretched, the PDB facility inserts spaces between the edit box and the label so that the box is right-justified and the label is left-justified.

Example 6

Write a DCL program for a dialogue box that will enable you to turn the snap and grid on and off. You should also be able to edit the X and Y values of snap and grid. Also, write an AutoLISP program that will load, display, and handle the dialogue box.

The following file is a listing of the DCL file for Example 6.

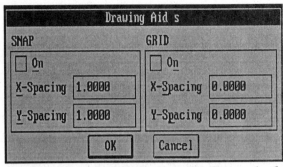

Figure 35-11 Dialogue box for Example 6

```
dwgaids : dialog {
  label = "Drawing Aids";
  : row {
    : boxed_column {
      label = "SNAP";
      fixed_width = true;
      width = 22;
      : toggle {
        label = "On";
        mnemonic = "O";
        key = "snapon";
        }
      : edit_box {
        label = "X-Spacing";
        mnemonic = "X";
        key = "xsnap";
        edit_width = 10;
        }
      : edit_box {
        label = "Y-Spacing";
        mnemonic = "Y";
        key = "ysnap";
        edit_width = 10;
        }
      }
    : boxed_column {
      label = "GRID";
      fixed_width = true;
      width = 22;
      : toggle {
        label = "On";
        mnemonic = "n";
        key = "gridon";
        }
      : edit_box {
        label = "X-Spacing";
        mnemonic = "S";
        key = "xgrid";
        edit_width = 10;
        }
      : edit_box {
        label = "Y-Spacing";
        mnemonic = "p";
        key = "ygrid";
```

```
            edit_width = 10;
           }
         }
      }
   ok_cancel;
}
```

The following file is a listing of the AutoLISP program for Example 6. When the program is loaded and run, it will load, display, and control the dialogue box.

```
;;Lisp program for Drawing Aids dialogue box
;;Dialogue file name is dwgaids.dcl
;
(defun c:dwgaids( / dcl_id snapmode xsnap ysnap
 orgsnapunit gridmode gridsnap xgrid ygrid orggridunit)
(setq dcl_id (load_dialog "dwgaids.dcl"))
(new_dialog "dwgaids" dcl_id)

;;Get the existing value of snapmode and snapunit
;;and write those values to the dialogue box
(setq snapmode (getvar "snapmode"))
(if (= 1 snapmode)
    (set_tile "snapon" "1")
    (set_tile "snapon" "0")
    )
(setq orgsnapunit (getvar "snapunit"))
(setq xsnap (car orgsnapunit))
(setq ysnap (cadr orgsnapunit))
(set_tile "xsnap" (rtos xsnap))
(set_tile "ysnap" (rtos ysnap))
;
;;Get the existing value of gridmode and gridunit
;;and write those values to the dialogue box
(setq gridmode (getvar "gridmode"))
(if (= 1 gridmode)
    (set_tile "gridon" "1")
    (set_tile "gridon" "0")
    )
(setq orggridunit (getvar "gridunit"))
(setq xgrid (car orggridunit))
(setq ygrid (cadr orggridunit))
(set_tile "xgrid" (rtos xgrid))
(set_tile "ygrid" (rtos ygrid))
;
;;Read the values set in the dialogue box and
;;then change the associated AutoCAD variables
(defun setvars ()
(setq xsnap (atof (get_tile "xsnap")))
(setq ysnap (atof (get_tile "ysnap")))
(setvar "snapunit" (list xsnap ysnap))
(if (= "1" (get_tile "snapon"))
    (setvar "snapmode" 1)
    (setvar "snapmode" 0)
    )
(setq xgrid (atof (get_tile "xgrid")))
(setq ygrid (atof (get_tile "ygrid")))
(setvar "gridunit" (list xgrid ygrid))
```

```
(if (= "1" (get_tile "gridon"))
    (progn
        (setvar "gridmode" 0)
        (setvar "gridmode" 1)
        )
    (setvar "gridmode" 0)
    )
 )
(action_tile "accept" "(setvars) (done_dialog)")
(start_dialog)
(princ)
 )
```

REVIEW QUESTIONS

Indicate whether the following statements are true or false.

1.   A Dialogue Control Language (DCL) file can contain descriptions of multiple files. (T/F)

2.   In a DCL file, you do not need to specify the size of a dialogue box. (T/F)

3.   Dialogue boxes are not dependent on the platform. (T/F)

4.   Dialogue boxes can contain several OK buttons. (T/F)

5.   The numeric values assigned to the attributes in a DCL file can be both integers and real numbers. (T/F)

6.   The reserved names in DCL are case sensitive. (T/F)

7.   The label attribute used in a button tile has no default value. (T/F)

8.   In a dialogue box, only one button can be assigned true value for the **is_default** attribute. (T/F)

9.   The **load_dialog** function displays the dialogue box on the screen. (T/F)

10.   You cannot select a tile by using the mnemonic key assigned to the tile. (T/F)

11.   Mnemonic characters are case sensitive. (T/F)

12.   Bit codes cannot be combined to produce multiple object snaps. (T/F)

13.   The radio button is a predefined attribute. (T/F)

14.   You should arrange the radio buttons in a column setting. (T/F)

15.   The edit box active tile allows you to enter or edit multiple lines of text. (T/F)

Fill in the blanks.

16.   The basic tiles, such as buttons, edit boxes, images, etc., are predefined by the _____ facility of AutoCAD.

17.   The label of a button appears _____ the button.

18.   The _____ attribute assigns a name to the tile.

19. The label attribute in a boxed column must be a _____ string.

20. The _____ attribute controls the width of a tile.

21. The format of the command for loading the dialogue box is _____.

22. The AutoLISP function _____ is used to initialize a dialogue box and then display it on the screen.

23. The AutoLISP function _____ is used to accept user input from the dialogue box.

24. The AutoLISP function _____ is used to associate an action expression with a tile in the dialogue box.

25. The AutoLISP function _____ can be used to obtain the result of logical bitwise AND.

EXERCISES

Exercise 1

Using Dialogue Control Language (DCL), write a program for the dialogue box shown in Figure 35-12. Also, write an AutoLISP program that will load, display, control the dialogue box, and perform the functions as shown in the dialogue box.

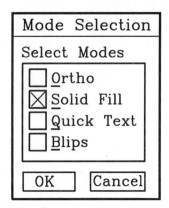

Figure 35-12 Dialogue box for mode selection

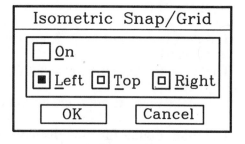

Figure 35-13 Dialogue box for isometric snap/grid

Exercise 2

Write a DCL program for the isometric snap/grid dialogue box shown in Figure 35-13. Also, write an AutoLISP program that will load, display, control the dialogue box, and perform the functions as shown in the dialogue box.

Exercise 3

Write a DCL program for the dialogue box in Figure 35-15 that will enable you to insert a block. Also, write an AutoLISP program that will load, display, and control the dialogue box. The values shown in the edit boxes for insertion point, scale, and rotation are the default values.

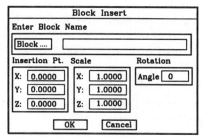

Figure 35-14 Dialogue box for inserting blocks

Chapter 36

DIESEL, A String Expression Language Customizing the ACAD.PGP File

Learning objectives

After completing this chapter, you will be able to:

DIESEL
- ◆ Use DIESEL to customize a status line.
- ◆ Use the modemacro system variables.
- ◆ Write macro expressions using DIESEL.
- ◆ Use AutoLISP with modemacro.

ACAD.PGP File
- ◆ Customize ACAD.PGP file.
- ◆ Edit different sections of the ACAD.PGP file.
- ◆ Abbreviate commands by defining command aliases.
- ◆ Use the REINIT command to re-initialize PGP file.

DIESEL

DIESEL (Direct Interpretively Evaluated String Expression Language) is a string expression language. It can be used to display a user-defined text string (macro expression) in the status line by altering the value of the AutoCAD system variable, **MODEMACRO**. The value that is assigned to the MODEMACRO variable must be a string and the output it generates a string. It is fairly easy to write a macro expression in DIESEL and it is an important tool for customizing AutoCAD. However, it is slow and is not intended to function like AutoLISP or DCL. You can use AutoLISP to write and assign a value to the MODEMACRO variable or you can write the definition of the MODEMACRO expression in the menu files. A detailed explanation of the DIESEL functions and the use of DIESEL in writing a macro expression is given later in this chapter.

STATUS LINE

When you are in the AutoCAD Drawing Editor, it displays a status line at the top of the graphics screen (Figure 36-1). This line contains some useful information about the current settings of AutoCAD. The status line can be turned off by configuring AutoCAD. Enter **CONFIG** at the Command: prompt and press the Enter key. Select the configure video display (option 3) from the configuration menu and then enter N when AutoCAD prompts, **Do you want a status line?** **<Y>**. After you exit the configuration menu, the status line is automatically turned off. This information is saved in the ACAD.CFG configuration file; therefore, when you start AutoCAD the next time, the status line will not appear on the screen. The status line contains the following information (assuming the status line is turned on and the default values of the status line have not been changed):

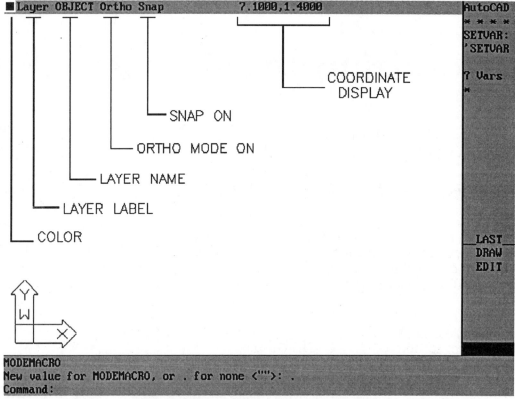

Figure 36-1 Default status line display

Color
AutoCAD displays the current color.

Current layer
AutoCAD displays the first eight characters of the current layer name. The default layer name is 0.

Status of Ortho mode
If the Ortho mode is on, Ortho is displayed in the status line; otherwise it is not displayed.

Status of Snap mode
If the Snap mode is on, Snap is displayed in the status line; otherwise it is not displayed.

Status of Tablet mode
If the Tablet mode is on, Tablet is displayed in the status line; otherwise it is not displayed.

Status of Paper space

AutoCAD displays P in the status line when AutoCAD is in Paper space; otherwise AutoCAD is in Model space.

Coordinate display

The coordinate information displayed in the status line can be static or dynamic. If the coordinate display is static, the coordinate values displayed in the status line change only when you pick a point. However, if the coordinate display is dynamic (default setting), AutoCAD constantly displays the absolute coordinates of the graphics cursor with respect to UCS origin. AutoCAD can also display the polar coordinates (length<angle) if you are in an AutoCAD command and a rubberband is displayed with the graphics cursor.

MODEMACRO SYSTEM VARIABLE

The AutoCAD system variable **MODEMACRO** can be used to display a new text string in the status line. You can also display the value returned by a macro expression using DIESEL language, which is discussed in the next section. For example, if you want to display **Customizing AutoCAD** in the status line, enter **SETVAR** at the Command: prompt and then press the Enter key. AutoCAD will prompt you to enter the name of the system variable. Enter **MODEMACRO** and then press the enter key again. Now you can enter the text that you want to display in the status line. After you enter **Customizing AutoCAD** and press the Enter key, the status line will display the new text.

> Command: **SETVAR**
> Variable name or ?: **MODEMACRO**
> New value for MODEMACRO, or . for none<"">: **Customizing AutoCAD**

You can also enter MODEMACRO at the Command: prompt and then enter the text that you want to display in the status line.

> Command: **MODEMACRO**
> New value for MODEMACRO, or . for none<"">: **Customizing AutoCAD**

Once the value of the MODEMACRO variable is changed, it retains the value until you enter a new value, start a new drawing, or open an existing drawing file. If you want to display the standard text in the status line, enter a period (.) at the prompt **New value for MODEMACRO, or . for none <"">:**. The value assigned to the MODEMACRO system variable is not saved with the drawing, in any configuration file, or anywhere in the system.

> **Command:** MODEMACRO
> New value for MODEMACRO, or . for none<"">:

CUSTOMIZING THE STATUS LINE

The information contained in the status line can be divided into two parts: layer-mode and coordinate display. The layer-mode part consists of the layer name and the status of Ortho, Snap, and Paper space modes. This field can be customized to your requirements by assigning a value to the AutoCAD system variable, **MODEMACRO**. The number of

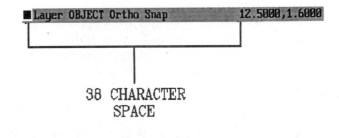

characters that can be displayed in the layer-mode field depends on the system display. However, on most systems it is 38 characters. If the number of characters exceeds 38, the characters in excess of 38 are not displayed in the status line. The coordinate display field cannot be changed or edited.

The information displayed in the status line is a valuable resource. Therefore, you must be careful when selecting the information that should be displayed in the status line. For example, before drawing an object you must know what layer is current. Therefore, the current layer name (CLAYER) should be displayed in the status line. If you are using several dimensioning styles, you could display the name of the current dimensioning style (DIMSTYLE) in the status line. Similarly, if you have several text files with different fonts, the name of the current text file (TEXTSTYLE) and the text height (TEXTSIZE) can be displayed in the status line. Sometimes, in 3D drawings, if you need to monitor the viewing direction (VIEWDIR), the camera coordinate information can be displayed in the status line. Therefore, the information that should be displayed in the status line depends on you and the drawing requirements. AutoCAD lets you customize this line and have any information displayed in the status line that you think is appropriate for your application.

MACRO EXPRESSIONS USING DIESEL

You can also write a macro expression using DIESEL to assign a value to the MODEMACRO system variable. The macro expressions are similar to AutoLISP functions with some differences. For example, the drawing name can be obtained by using the AutoLISP statement **(getvar dwgname)**. In DIESEL, the same information can be obtained by using the macro expression **$(getvar,dwgname)**. However, unlike AutoLISP the DIESEL macro expressions return only string values. The format of a macro expression is:

> **$(function-name,arguement1,arguement2, ...)**

Example
$(getvar,dwgname)

Here **getvar** is the name of the DIESEL string function and **dwgname** is the argument of the function. There must be no spaces between different elements of a macro expression. For example, any spaces between the $ sign and the open parenthesis are not permitted. Similarly, there must be no spaces between the comma and the argument, **dwgname**. All macro expressions must start with a $ sign.

The following example illustrates the use of a macro expression using DIESEL to define and then assign a value to the MODEMACRO system variable.

Example 1

Using AutoCAD's MODEMACRO command, redefine the status line to display the following information in the status line:

> Project name (Cust-Acad)
> Name of the drawing (DEMO)
> Name of the current layer (OBJ)

Note that in this example the project name is Cust-Acad, the drawing name is DEMO, and the current layer name is OBJ.

Before entering the MODEMACRO command, you need to determine how to retrieve the required information from the drawing database. For example, in Example 1, the project name (**Cust-**

Acad) is a user-defined name that lets you know the name of the current project. This project name is not saved in the drawing database. The name of the drawing can be obtained using the DIESEL string function GETVAR **$(getvar,dwgname)**. Similarly, the GETVAR function can also be used to obtain the name of the current layer, **$(getvar,clayer)**. Once you determine how to retrieve the information from the system, you can use the MODEMACRO system variable to obtain the new status line. For Example 1, the following DIESEL expression will define the required status line.

> **Command:** MODEMACRO
> **New value for MODEMACRO, or . for none < "" > :** Cust-Acad
> N:$(GETVAR,dwgname) L:$(GETVAR,clayer)

Where:
Cust-Acad is assumed to be the name of the project that you want to display in the status line.

N:$(GETVAR,dwgname) Here, N: is used as an abbreviation for the drawing name. The GETVAR function retrieves the name of the drawing from the system variable **dwgname** and displays it in the status line, next to N:.

L:$(GETVAR,clayer) Here L: is used as an abbreviation for the layer name. The GETVAR function retrieves the name of the current layer from the system variable **clayer** and displays it in the status line.

The new status line is shown in Figure 2.

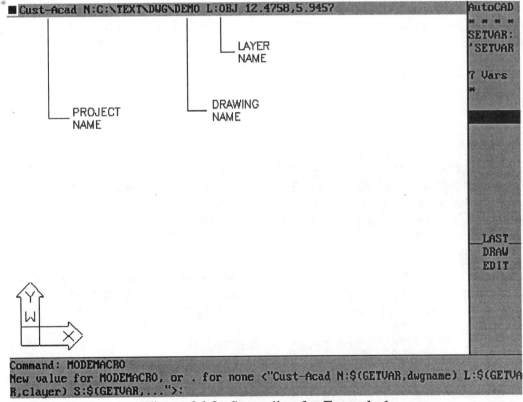

Figure 36-2 Status line for Example 1

Example 2

Using AutoCAD's MODEMACRO command, redefine the status line to display the following information in the status line:

Name of the current textstyle
Size of text
User-elapsed time in minutes

`TSTYLE:STANDARD TSIZE:0.2 ETM:6`

Note that in this example the abbreviations for text style, text size, and the user-elapsed time in minutes are TSTYLE:, TSIZE:, and ETM:, respectively.

Command: **MODEMACRO**
New value for MODEMACRO, or . for none < "" >:
TSTYLE:$(GETVAR,TEXTSTYLE) TSIZE:$(GETVAR,TEXTSIZE)
ETM:$(FIX,$(*,60,$(*,24,$(GETVAR,TDUSRTIMER))))

Where
TSTYLE:$(GETVAR,TEXTSTYLE) The **GETVAR** function obtains the name of the current textstyle from the system variable, **TEXTSTYLE**, and displays it next to TSTYLE: in the status line.

TSIZE:$(GETVAR,TEXTSIZE) The **GETVAR** function obtains the current size of the text from the system variable, **TEXTSIZE**, and then displays it next to TSIZE: in the status line.

ETM:$(FIX,$(*,60,$(*,24,$(GETVAR,TDUSRTIMER)))) The **GETVAR** function obtains the user elapsed time from the system variable, **TDUSRTIMER**, in the following format:

< Number of days > . < Fraction >

Example
0.03206400 (time in days)

To change this time into minutes, multiply the value obtained from the system variable TDUSRTIMER by 24 to change it into hours and then multiply the product by 60 to change the time into minutes. To express the minutes value without a decimal, determine the integer value using the DIESEL string function FIX.

Example
Assume that the value returned by the system variable TDUSRTIMER is 0.03206400. This time is in days. Use the following calculations to change the time into minutes and then express the time as an integer:

$$0.03206400 \text{ Days} \times 24 = 0.769536 \text{ Hr}$$
$$0.769536 \text{ Hr} \times 60 = 46.17216 \text{ Min}$$
$$\text{Integer of } 46.17216 \text{ Min} = 46 \text{ Min}$$

USING AUTOLISP WITH MODEMACRO

Sometimes the DIESEL expressions can be long as those shown in Example 1 and Example 2. It takes time to type the DIESEL expression and if you make a mistake in entering the expression, you have to retype it. Also, if you need several different status line displays, you need to type them every time you want a new status line display. This can be time-consuming and sometimes confusing.

To make it convenient to change the status line display, you can use AutoLISP to write a DIESEL expression. It is easier to load an AutoLISP program and it also eliminates any errors that might be caused by typing a DIESEL expression. The following example illustrates the use of AutoLISP to write a DIESEL expression to assign a new value to the MODEMACRO system variable.

Example 3

Using AutoLISP, redefine the value assigned to the MODEMACRO system variable to display the following information in the status line.

> Name of the current textstyle
> Size of text
> User-elapsed time in minutes

Note that in this example the abbreviations for text style, text size, and user-elapsed time in minutes are TSTYLE:, TSIZE:, and ETM:, respectively.

The following file is a listing of the AutoLISP program for Example 3. The name of the file is ETM.LSP. The line numbers are not a part of the file; they are shown here for reference only.

```
(defun c:etm ( )                            1
(setvar "MODEMACRO"                         2
(strcat                                     3
   "TSTYLE:$(getvar,textstyle)"             4
   " TSIZE:$(getvar,textsize)"              5
   " ETM:$(fix,$(*,60,$(*,24,              6
   $(getvar,tdusrtimer))))"                 7
   )                                        8
 )                                          9
)                                          10
```

Line 3
(strcat
The AutoLISP function **strcat** links the string value of line numbers 4,5,6,7 and returns a single string that becomes a DIESEL expression for the MODEMACRO command.

Line 4
"TSTYLE:$(getvar,textstyle)"
This line is a DIESEL expression where getvar, a DIESEL string function, retrieves the value of the system variable, **textstyle**, and **$(getvar,textstyle)** is replaced by the name of the textstyle. For example, if the textstyle is STANDARD, the line will return "TSTYLE:STANDARD". This is a string because it is enclosed in quotes.

Lines 6, 7
" ETM:$(fix,$(*,60,$(*,24,
$(getvar,tdusrtimer))))"
These two lines return **ETM:** and the time in minutes as a string. The **fix** is a DIESEL string function that changes a real number to an integer number.

To load this AutoLISP file (ETM.LSP), use the following commands. In this example, the file name and the function name are same (ETM).

```
Command: (load "ETM")
ETM
Command: ETM
```

WHAT IS THE ACAD.PGP FILE?

AutoCAD software comes with the Program Parameters file, ACAD.PGP, which defines aliases for the operating system commands and some of the AutoCAD commands. When you install AutoCAD, this file is automatically copied on the ACAD\SUPPORT subdirectory of the hard drive. The ACAD.PGP file lets you access the operating system commands from the Drawing Editor. For example, if you want to delete a file, all you need to do is enter DEL at the Command: prompt (**Command: DEL**) and then AutoCAD will prompt you to enter the name of the file you want to delete.

The file also contains command aliases of some frequently used AutoCAD commands. For example, the command alias for the LINE command is L. If you enter L at the Command: prompt (**Command: L**), AutoCAD will treat it as the LINE command. The ACAD.PGP file also contains comment lines that give you some information about different sections of the file.

The following file is a partial listing of the standard ACAD.PGP file. Some of the lines have been deleted to make the file shorter.

```
; External Command format:
; <Command name>,[<DOS request>],<Memory reserve>,[*]<Prompt>,<Return
code>
DEL,DEL,          0,File to delete: ,4
DIR,DIR,          0,File specification: ,0        ⎯ External
EDIT,EDIT,        0,File to edit: ,4                 command
SH,,              0,*OS Command: ,4                  section
SHELL,,           0,*OS Command: ,4
TYPE,TYPE,        0,File to list: ,0
;
;
;
; Command alias format:
; <Alias>,*<Full command name>                   ⎯ Comment
; Sample aliases for AutoCAD Commands               section
A,          *ARC
C,          *CIRCLE
CP,         *COPY
DV,         *DVIEW
E,          *ERASE
L,          *LINE                                ⎯ Command alias
LA,         *LAYER                                  section
M,          *MOVE
MS,         *MSPACE
P,          *PAN
PS,         *PSPACE
PL,         *PLINE
R,          *REDRAW
Z,          *ZOOM
3DLINE,     *LINE

; Dimensioning Commands
DIMALI,         *DIMALIGNED
DIMANG,         *DIMANGULAR
```

```
DIMBASE,              *DIMBASELINE
|
|
LEAD,                 *LEADER
TOL,                  *TOLERANCE
```

SECTIONS OF ACAD.PGP FILE

The contents of the AutoCAD Program Parameters file (ACAD.PGP) can be categorized into three sections. These sections merely classify the information that is defined in the ACAD.PGP file. They do not have to appear in any definite order in the file and they have no section headings. For example, the comment lines can be entered anywhere in the file; the same is true with external commands and AutoCAD command aliases. The ACAD.PGP file can be divided into the three sections:

Comment Section
External Commands Section
Command Aliases Section

Comment Section

The comment section of ACAD.PGP file may contain any number of comment lines. Every comment line must start with a semicolon (; This is a comment line). Any line that is preceded by a semicolon is ignored by AutoCAD. You should use the comment line to give some relevant information about the file that will help other AutoCAD users to understand, edit, and update the file.

External Command Section

In the external command section you can define any valid external command that is supported by your system. The information must be entered in the following format:

<Command name>, [OS Command name], <Memory reserve>,
<Command prompt>, <Return code>

Command name

This is the name you want to use to activate the external command from the AutoCAD Drawing Editor. For example, you can use **goword** as a command name to load the word program (**Command: goword**). The command name must not be an AutoCAD command name or an AutoCAD system variable name. If the name is an AutoCAD command name, the command name in the PGP file will be ignored. Also, if the name is an AutoCAD system variable name, the system variable will be ignored. You should use the command names that reflect the expected result of the external commands. (For example, **hallo** is not a good command name for a directory file.) The command names can be uppercase or lowercase.

OS Command name

The OS Command name is the name of a valid system command that is supported by your operating system. For example, in DOS the command to delete files is DEL, therefore the OS Command name used in the ACAD.PGP file must be DEL. The following is a list of the types of commands that can be used in the PGP file:

OS Commands (del, dir, type, copy, rename, edlin, etc.)
Commands for starting a word processor, or text editors (word, pcshell, etc.)
Name of the user-defined programs and batch files

Memory reserve

This field must contain a number, preferably zero. The memory reserve field does not have any effect on the PGP file. In the older releases of AutoCAD, the memory reserve field was used to specify the number of bytes AutoCAD must release to execute an external command. In AutoCAD Release 12, this field keeps the PGP files compatible with the older releases of AutoCAD.

Command prompt

The command prompt field of the command line contains the prompt that you want to display on the screen. It is an optional field that must be replaced by a comma if there is no prompt. If the operating system (OS) command that you want to use contains spaces, the prompt must be preceded by an asterisk (*). For example, the DOS command, EDLIN NEW.PGP, contains a space between EDLIN and NEW; therefore, the prompt used in this command line must be preceded by an asterisk. The command can be terminated by pressing the enter key at the keyboard. If the OS command consists of a single word (DIR, DEL, TYPE), the preceding asterisk must be omitted. In this case you can terminate the command by pressing the spacebar or the enter key.

Return code

The Return code field defines a bit code that can be 0, 1, 2, 4, or a combination of these ($1+2+4 = 7$). If the bit code is 0, AutoCAD returns to text screen after the command is terminated. If the bit code is 4, AutoCAD returns to the graphics screen after the command is terminated. Bit codes 2 and 4 are used to load a DXB file and construct a block from the DXB file.

Command Aliases Section

It is time-consuming to enter AutoCAD commands at the keyboard, because it requires typing the complete command name before pressing the enter key. AutoCAD provides a facility that can be used to abbreviate the commands by defining aliases for the AutoCAD commands. This is made possible by AutoCAD's Program Parameters file (ACAD.PGP file). Each command alias line consists of two fields (L, *LINE). The first field (L) defines the alias of the command and the second field (*LINE) consists of the AutoCAD command. The AutoCAD command must be preceded by an asterisk for AutoCAD to recognize the command line as a command alias. The two fields must be separated by a comma. The blank lines and the spaces between the two fields are ignored. In addition to AutoCAD commands, you can also use aliases for AutoLISP command names, provided the programs that contain the definition of these commands are loaded.

Example 4

Add the following external commands and AutoCAD command aliases to the AutoCAD Program Parameters file (ACAD.PGP).

External Command Section

Abbreviation	Command description
PCS	This command loads pcshell program from C:\MIS\PCSHELL directory.
GOWORD	This command loads the word processor (word) program from the C:\MIS\WORD directory.
RN	This command executes the rename command of DOS.
COP	This command executes the copy command of DOS.

Command Aliases Section

Abbreviation	Command	Abbreviation	Command
EL	Ellipse	T	Trim
CO	Copy	CH	Chamfer
O	Offset	ST	Stretch
S	Scale	MI	Mirror

The ACAD.PGP file is an ASCII text file. To edit this file you can use AutoCAD's EDIT command (provided the EDIT command is defined in the ACAD.PGP file), the EDIT function of DOS 5.0, or any Text Editor. The following file is a partial listing of the ACAD.PGP file after inserting the lines for the command aliases of for Example 4. The line numbers are not a part of the file; they are shown here for reference only. The lines that have been added to the file are highlighted in bold.

DEL,DEL,	0,File to delete: ,4	1
DIR,DIR,	0,File specification: ,0	2
EDIT,EDLIN,	0,File to edit: ,4	3
SH,,	0,*OS Command: ,4	4
SHELL,,	0,*OS Command: ,4	5
TYPE,TYPE,	0,File to list: ,0	6
pcs, pcshell,	**0,,0**	**8**
goword, word,	**0,,0**	**9**
rn, rename,	**0, *[drive](File name) [drive](File name): ,0**	**10**
COP, copy,	**0, *[drive](File name) [drive](File name): ,0**	**11**

P, *PAN	12	
PS,	*PSPACE	13
PL,	*PLINE	14
R, *REDRAW		15
Z, *ZOOM	16	
3DLINE,	*LINE	17
EL,	***ELLIPSE**	**18**
CO,	***COPY**	**19**
O,	***OFFSET**	**20**
S,	***SCALE**	**21**
MI,	***MIRROR**	**22**
ST,	***STRETCH**	**23**

Lines 8 and 9

pcs, pcshell, 0,,0
goword, word, 0,,0

In the first line, **pcs** is the command that you enter at the keyboard to load the **pcshell** program. Similarly, you can enter **goword** to load the word processor program **(word)**. For these aliases to work, the subdirectory where these programs reside must be in the search path.

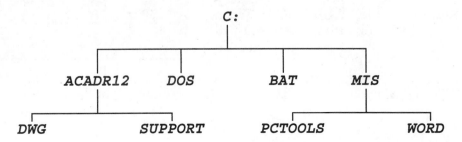

For example, if the pcshell program is in the pctools subdirectory, pctools subdirectory must be in the search path.

PATH= C:\;C:\DOS;C:\BAT;C:\MIS\PCTOOLS;C:\MIS\WORD;

If the subdirectory that contains the file is not in the search path, the programs can also be loaded by defining a batch file. For example, the following batch file will load the pcshell program:

C:\MIS\PCTOOLS\PCSHELL

Assume here that the name of the batch file is PCSHELL.BAT and that it is in the BAT subdirectory that is defined in the search path. When you enter the PCS command, AutoCAD will search for the PCSHELL.BAT file and then execute the commands defined in the file.

Lines 10 and 11
rn, rename, 0, *[drive](File name) [drive](File name): ,0
COP, copy, 0, *[drive](File name) [drive](File name): ,0
The first line defines the alias for the DOS command, **RENAME**, and the second line defines the alias for the DOS command, **COPY**. The 0 after rename has no function and the command prompt ***[drive](File name) [drive](File name):** is automatically displayed on the screen to let you know the format and the type of information that is expected.

Lines 18 and 19
EL, *ELLIPSE
CO, *COPY
The first line defines the alias (**EL**) for the AutoCAD command **ELLIPSE** and the second line defines the alias (**CO**) for the **COPY** command. The AutoCAD commands must be preceded by an asterisk. You can put any number of spaces between the alias abbreviation and the AutoCAD command.

REINIT COMMAND

When you make any changes in the ACAD.PGP file, there are two ways to re-initialize the ACAD.PGP file. One is to quit AutoCAD and then re-enter it. When you start AutoCAD, the ACAD.PGP file is automatically loaded.

You can also re-initialize the ACAD.PGP file by using AutoCAD's REINIT command. The REINIT command lets you re-initialize the I/O ports, digitizer, display, and AutoCAD's Program Parameters file, ACAD.PGP. When you enter the REINIT command, AutoCAD will display a dialogue box on the screen. To reinitialize the ACAD.PGP file, select the corresponding toggle box, then select OK. AutoCAD will reinitialize the Program Parameters file (ACAD.PGP) and then you can use the command aliases defined in the file.

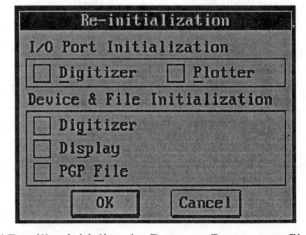

REVIEW QUESTIONS

Indicate whether the following statements are true or false.

<u>DIESEL</u>

1. DIESEL (Direct Interpretively Evaluated String Expression Language) is a string expression language. (T/F)

2. The value assigned to the MODEMACRO variable is a string and the output it generates is not a string. (T/F)

3. You cannot define a DIESEL expression in the screen menu. (T/F)

4. The coordinate information displayed in the status line can be dynamic only. (T/F)

5. Once the value of the MODEMACRO variable is changed, it retains the value until you enter a new value, start a new drawing, or open an existing drawing file. (T/F)

6. The number of characters that can be displayed in the layer-mode field on any system is 38. (T/F)

7. The coordinate display field cannot be changed or edited. (T/F)

8. You can write a macro expression using DIESEL to assign a value to the MODEMACRO system variable. (T/F)

9. In DIESEL, the drawing name can be obtained by using the macro expression **$(getvar,dwgname)**. (T/F)

10. You cannot use AutoLISP to write a DIESEL expression. (T/F)

<u>ACAD.PGP</u>

11. The comment section can contain any number of lines. (T/F)

12. AutoCAD ignores any line that is preceded by a semicolon. (T/F)

13. The command alias must not be an AutoCAD command. (T/F)

14. The memory reserve field must contain a zero. (T/F)

15. In the command alias section, the command alias must be preceded by a semicolon. (T/F)

EXERCISES

DIESEL

Exercise 1

Using AutoCAD's MODEMACRO command, redefine the status line to display the following information in the status line:

1. Your name
2. Name of drawing

Exercise 2

Using AutoCAD's MODEMACRO command, redefine the status line to display the following information in the status line:

1. Name of the current dimension style
2. Dimension scale factor (dimscale)
3. User-elapsed time in hours

The abbreviations for dimstyle, dimscale, and user-elapsed time in hours are DIMS:, DIMFAC:, and ETH:, respectively.

Exercise 3

Using **AutoLISP**, redefine the status line to display the following information in the status line:

1. Name of the current dimension style
2. Dimension scale factor (dimscale)
3. User-elapsed time in hours

ACAD.PGP

Exercise 4

Add the following external commands and AutoCAD command aliases to the AutoCAD Program Parameters file (ACAD.PGP).

External Command Section

Abbreviation	Command description
DBASE	This command loads the Dbase program that resides in C:\DBASE directory.
LOTUS	This command loads the spreadsheet program that resides in C:\LOTUS directory.
CD	This command executes the CHKDSK command of DOS.
FORMAT	This command executes the FORMAT command of DOS.

Command Aliases Section

Abbreviation	Command	Abbreviation	Command
BL	BLOCK	LT	LTSCALE
INS	INSERT	EX	EXPLODE
DIS	DISTANCE	G	GRID
T	TIME	S	SNAP

Chapter 37

AutoCAD SQL Extension (ASE)

Learning objectives

After completing this chapter, you will be able to:
- Understand ASE and SQL and their uses.
- Understand database, DBMS, and relational database.
- Set up database environment.
- Define key columns, set link paths and isolation levels.
- Access and edit database.
- Link database with drawing entities.
- Display attributes in a drawing.
- Create selection sets.
- Use SQL statements to access external database.
- Generate reports from exported data.

AUTOCAD SQL2 ENVIRONMENT (ASE)

SQL is an acronym for **Structured Query Language**. It is often referred to as **sequel**. SQL is a format in computer programming that lets the user ask questions about a database according to specific rules. **The AutoCAD SQL Environment** (ASE) lets you access and manipulate the data that is stored in the external database and link data from the database to objects in a drawing. For example, the data in the table of Figure 37-1 can be accessed from within AutoCAD. Once you access the table you can manipulate the data. The connection is made through the database management systems (DBMS) like dBASE, PARADOX, FoxPro or other DBMS programs. The DBMS programs have their own methodology for working with database. However, the ASE commands work the same way regardless of the database that is being used. This is made possible by the ASE drivers that come with AutoCAD software.

In AutoCAD release 13, **SQL2** has been incorporated. The enhanced features of SQL2 makes it superior to SQL. The fundamental change is that the SQL model is based on **DBMS, databases** and **tables**, while SQL2 model is based on **environments, catalogs**, and **schemas**.

Environment

The **environment** is composed of the DBMS, the accessible databases, and the users and programs that are granted access to the database. An environment can have zero or more catalogs.

Catalog

A **catalog** is simply the database. It defines the collection of base tables. A catalog can have one or more schemas. The name of the catalog relates to the directory path name that is the location of the database

Schema

The **schema** is a collection of database components for a user. A schema can have one or more tables. The name of the schema relates to the catalog subdirectory that contains the database tables.

Session

The **session** is a new concept introduced in SQL2. A session is required for the management of temporary data. Session management statements are provided by SQL2 in order to establish the environment for a SQL session, catalog name, schema session, authorization identifier, and the local time zone. When the client is connected to the server by a SQL application, the session begins. The SQL environment is established by the connect statement.

Transaction

When a sequence of SQL statements are executed, a **transaction** takes place. A transaction is terminated with the SQL COMMIT or SQL ROLLBACK operation.

UNDERSTANDING DATABASES

Database

A **database** is a collection of data that is arranged in a logical order. For example, there are six computers in an office and we want to keep a record of these computers on a sheet of paper. One of the ways of recording the computer information is to make a table with rows and columns as shown in Figure 37-1. Each column will have a column heading that specifies a certain feature of the computer, such as COMP_CFG, CPU, HDRIVE, RAM, etc. Once the columns are labeled then the computer data can be placed in the columns for each computer. By doing this, we have created a database on a sheet of paper that contains information of our computers. The same information can be stored in a computer, generally known as computerized database.

COMPUTER

COMP_CFG	CPU	HDRIVE	RAM	GRAPHICS	INPT_DEV
1	486/33	300MB	8MB	SUPER VGA	DIGITIZER
2	286/12	60MB	640K	VGA	MOUSE
3	MACIIC	40MB	2MB	STANDARD	MOUSE
4	386SX/16	80MB	4MB	VGA	MOUSE
5	386/33	300MB	6MB	VGA	MOUSE
6	SPARC2	600MB	16MB	STANDARD	MOUSE

Figure 37-1 A table containing computer information

Database Management System

The **Database Management System** (DBMS) is a program or a collection of programs (software) that is used to manage the data in the database. For example, PARADOX, dBASE, INFORMIX, and ORACLE are some of the Database Management Systems (DBMS).

Relational Database

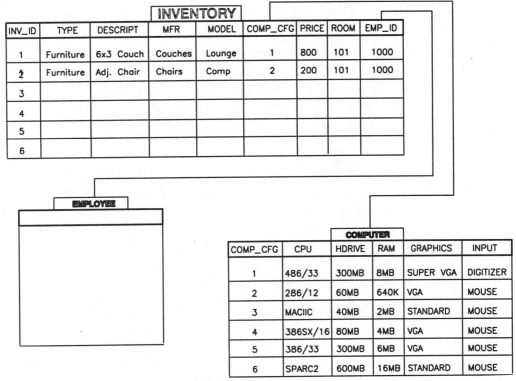

INV_ID	TYPE	DESCRIPT	MFR	MODEL	COMP_CFG	PRICE	ROOM	EMP_ID
1	Furniture	6x3 Couch	Couches	Lounge	1	800	101	1000
2	Furniture	Adj. Chair	Chairs	Comp	2	200	101	1000
3								
4								
5								
6								

COMPUTER

COMP_CFG	CPU	HDRIVE	RAM	GRAPHICS	INPUT
1	486/33	300MB	8MB	SUPER VGA	DIGITIZER
2	286/12	60MB	640K	VGA	MOUSE
3	MACIIC	40MB	2MB	STANDARD	MOUSE
4	386SX/16	80MB	4MB	VGA	MOUSE
5	386/33	300MB	6MB	VGA	MOUSE
6	SPARC2	600MB	16MB	STANDARD	MOUSE

Figure 37-2 Relational database model

A **database** may consist of several tables, each table containing a set of data, and there may exist a relation between the tables. For example, in Figure 37-2 the INVENTORY table contains a column for COMP_CFG and its values (1, 2, ...). The data for these computers is defined in another table (COMPUTER). A relation exists between the INVENTORY and COMPUTER tables. This model of a database where a relation exists between the tables is called **relational database**.

Components of a Table

A database **table** is a two-dimensional data structure that consists of rows and columns.

Row

COMPUTER

COMP_CFG	CPU	HDRIVE	RAM	GRAPHICS	INPUT
1	486/33	300MB	8MB	SUPER VGA	DIGITIZER
2	286/12	60MB	640K	VGA	MOUSE
3	MACIIC	40MB	2MB	STANDARD	MOUSE
4	386SX/16	80MB	4MB	VGA	MOUSE
5	386/33	300MB	6MB	VGA	MOUSE
6	SPARC2	600MB	16MB	STANDARD	MOUSE

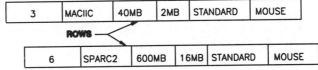

| 3 | MACIIC | 40MB | 2MB | STANDARD | MOUSE |

ROWS

| 6 | SPARC2 | 600MB | 16MB | STANDARD | MOUSE |

Figure 37-3 Rows in a table (the horizontal group of data)

The horizontal group of data is called a **row** . For example, in Figure 37-3 a table is shown; just below the table two rows of the table are shown. Each value in the row defines an attribute of the item. For example, in Figure 37-4, the attributes assigned to COMPT_CFG (1) are 486/33, 300MB, 8MB, etc. These attributes are arranged in a row. A row is also referred as a **record**.

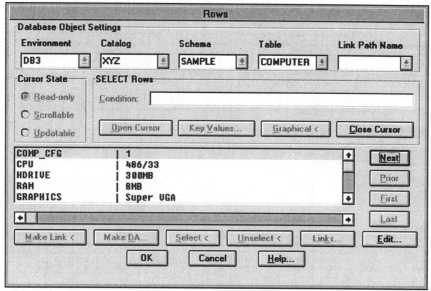

Figure 37-4 A row in the Rows dialogue box

Column

A vertical group of data (attribute) is called a **column**. Three of the columns in Figure 37-3 are shown in Figure 37-5. HDRIVE is the column heading that represents a feature of the computer and the HDRIVE attributes of each computer are placed vertically in this column. A column is sometimes called a **field**.

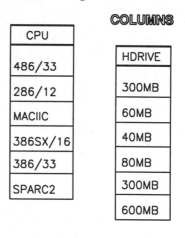

Figure 37-5 Columns in a table (the vertical group of data)

DEFINING KEYS

A key is used to link a specified row in the table with an entity in the drawing. The key acts like an identification tag for locating and linking a row. For example, if you want to link the second row of the table Figure 37-3 to a drawing entity you must first identify the row. You can do it by specifying the column name (COMP_CFG) and the value in that column (2). The name of the column (COMP_CFG) and the value (2) in the column becomes the **key** for the second row. Sometimes it may not be enough to identify a row by specifying one key. For example, if there are two computers that have the same value (2) in the COMP_CFG column, one key will not be enough to identify the second row. In this case you can identify the second row by defining a second key. The second key could consist of another column label (CPU) and a value under that column (286/12). Selecting two or more columns and their values to define a key is called a **compound key**. Keys can be defined in the **Link Path Names** dialogue box. This process is discussed in detail later on. At present we are concerned only about the idea behind defining keys.

ISOLATION LEVELS

In a database you can relate or isolate the data in one transaction with the data from some other transaction. As the name suggests, the concept behind setting isolation levels is to establish isolation. Isolation of data returned by a query transaction when many users try to address the same data simultaneously depends on the isolation levels. Isolation level influences the data returned by sequential transactions on the basis of transaction type. There three types of transactions. They are:

Dirty read transaction
Nonrepeatable read transaction
Phantom read transaction

Dirty read transaction

In case of a dirty read transaction, transaction A makes changes to a row but does not save the changes to the database. In other words, SQL command COMMIT is not executed. Now another transaction (transaction B) performs a read on the row. Transaction A then executes a ROLLBACK command which results in undoing of the changes made previously to the row. This results in transaction B string to read a row that did not exist.

Nonrepeatable read transaction

In case of a Nonrepeatable read transaction, transaction A performs a read on a row. Transaction B makes changes to the row and saves the changes to the database with the COMMIT command. Transaction A tries to read this row again. This results in transaction A trying to read a row that has been modified or deleted.

Phantom read transaction

In case of a phantom read transaction, transaction A performs a read operation on a set of rows. Transaction B executes an SQL statement that results in the insertion of a new row meeting the search condition specified in transaction A. Next, transaction A again tries to read the rows selected with the search condition specified in transaction A. This results in the selection of different rows by transaction A in the first and second reads.

If you specify a serializable isolation level, the transactions are performed in a serial manner and the problems faced with dirty read transactions, nonrepeatable read transaction, and phantom read transaction can be avoided.

ESTABLISHING THE DATABASE ENVIRONMENT

You can set the database environment according to the information contained in the **asi.ini** file. This file is present in the same directory in which the acad.exe file exists. For more information on this file, refer to chapter 7 of the Installation Guide book. This file can be customized to your requirements by editing it using an editor. If you want to use the dialogue boxes with ASE commands, you must set the **CMDDIA** variable to 1 (on). If it is off, the values will be displayed on the text screen. It is recommended that you use the dialogue boxes, because they provide an efficient way for handling ASE commands and data. Use the following command to check or assign a new value to **CMDDIA** system variable:

Command: **CMDDIA**
New value for CMDDIA <1>: ↵   *(0=off, 1=on)*

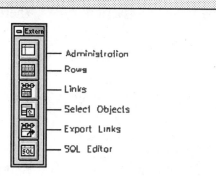

Toolbar: External Database,
              Administration
Pull-down: Tools, External Database,
              Administration...
Screen: TOOLS, EXT DBMS, Admin:

Figure 37-6 Options in the External
Database toolbar

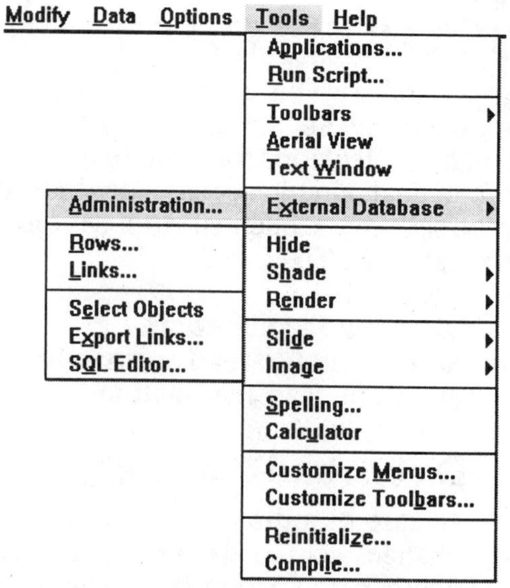

Figure 37-7 External Database options in the
Tools pull-down menu

The following instructions needs to be carried out to set up an environment:

1. Invoke the **ASEADMIN** command. This command can be invoked from the **External Database** toolbar (select Administration icon, Figure 37-6), from the pull-down menu (select Tools, External Database, Administration..., Figure 37-7), from the screen menu (select TOOLS, EXT DBMS, Admin:), or by entering **ASEADMIN** at the Command: prompt. When this command is invoked, the **Administration** dialogue box is displayed on the screen.

2. All the environments supported by the system are listed in the Database Objects list. Select the Environment from the Database Objects list. For example, select the DBMS **DB3** by clicking on it (Figure 37-8).

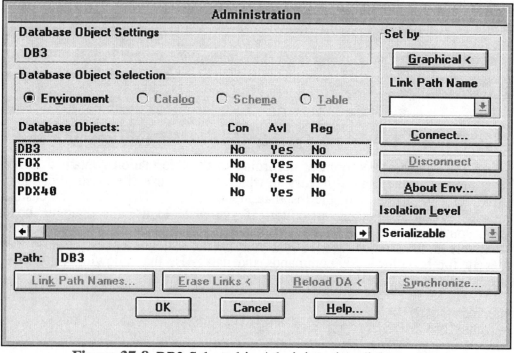

Figure 37-8 DB3 Selected in Administration dialogue box

3. Now you need to set up a connection. To do so, select the Connect button. The **Connect to Environment** dialogue box (Figure 37-9) is displayed. Specify your name in the User Name edit box and your password in the Password edit box (if required by the selected DBMS). Pick the OK button.

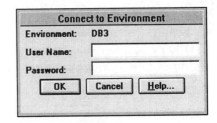

Figure 37-9 Connect to Environment dialogue box

4. Next select the Catalog radio button in the Database Object Selection area. All the catalogs are listed in the Database Objects list. Select the catalog name (**ASE**, in our example name is **XYZ**) by double clicking on it. In the same manner select the schema (**DB3SAMPLE**, in our example schema is **SAMPLE**) and the table (**EMP1**). (EMP1.DBF is a copy of EMPLOYEE.DBF.)

Note

If the environment is connected, it means that the DBMS driver is loaded in memory.

When the environment is listed in the [ENVIRONMENT] section of the asi.ini file, it is available.

If the environment, catalog, or schema has an associated table with defined key columns, it is registered.

5. Next select an isolation level.

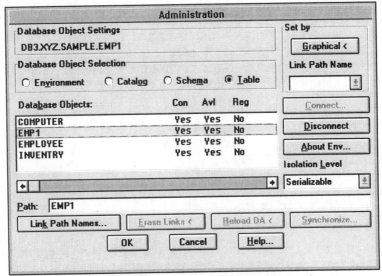

Figure 37-10 Administration dialogue box

The database object has now been defined. At this stage the settings in the Administration dialogue box are as shown in the Figure 37-10. Now define a link path name.

1. Pick the Link Path Names... button. The **Link Path Names** dialogue box is displayed.

2. Select the column that defines the link path name for the table from the Key Selection area. In our case, we have selected the **EMP_ID** column (Figure 37-11). Pick the On button.

3. Perform the second step for every column you desire to have in the link path name.

4. Specify the link path name for the selected column(s) in the **New** edit box and then pick the **New** button. The link path name specified is **IDENT**. You will notice that the link path name (IDENT) is displayed in the **Existing** box. Pick the **Close** button. The Link Path Names dialogue box is removed from the screen. Pick the OK button in the Administration dialogue box.

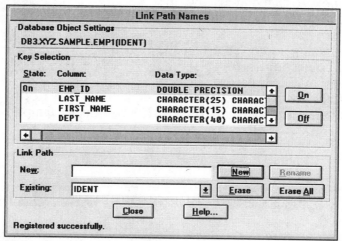

Figure 37-11 Creating link IDENT in Link Path Names dialogue box

The links in the present drawing session can be unloaded with the **ASEUNLOAD** command.

ACCESSING DATA IN EXTERNAL DATABASES

After setting up the environment, it is possible to access data in an external database as defined by the current database object (i.e. environment, catalog, schema, table). You can access in the database with SQL statements, or with the interface provided by AutoCAD. The prevailing database object selection can be altered with the use of any external database command. With the **ASESQLED** command, you can change the environment, catalog, and schema through the user interface, however you can perform SQL operations on all the tables.

Selection of Rows

Toolbar:	External Database, Rows
Pull-down:	Tools, External Database, Rows...
Screen:	TOOLS, EXT DBMS, Rows:

Selection of a row can be achieved with the **ASEROWS** command. This command can be invoked from the **External Database** toolbar (select Rows icon), or from the pull-down (select Tools, External Database, Rows...), from the screen menu (select TOOLS, EXT DBMS, Rows:), or by entering ASEROWS at the Command: prompt. When this command is invoked, the **Rows** dialogue box is displayed.

Note

Some operations modify only the database and do not influence the drawing; for example, inserting a row, viewing a row, changing the values in the data fields, creating selection sets.

Some operations directly influence the drawing by modifying the graphic information or by adding links to the database of the drawing.

First set the cursor state. This can be done by selecting the desired radio button in the Cursor State area of the Rows dialogue box. It is the cursor state that governs the accessibility of rows belonging to the selection set. There are three options:

Read only

In this case you cannot update. In other words, the current row cannot be deleted or modified.

Scrollable

With this option, any row can be accessed in the selection set of rows. However, you cannot Update.

Updatable

If this option is selected, you can modify the next rows of the selection set. Scrolling through the selected rows is not possible.

Only one row, the **current row**, can be manipulated at a time. You can navigate between the rows of a table with the use of Next, Prior, First, and Last buttons. If you have specified key values and you want to make a row current, use a key to search for a particular row or rows. In this case the selection of a row is carried out on the basis of its key value. This can be accomplished by picking the Select the Key Values... button in the Rows dialogue box. Make sure that the Cursor State is set to Updatable. The **Select Row by Key Values** dialogue box (Figure 37-12) is displayed. Select the key column and then in the Value edit box enter the value for the key column and press the Enter key. You will observe that the key value entered in the Value edit box is displayed in the list box.

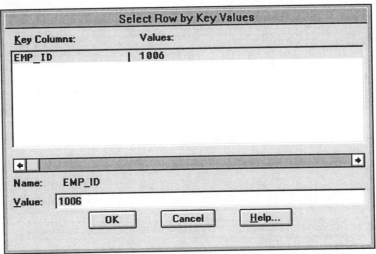

Figure 37-12 Select Row by Key Values dialogue box

Next, pick the OK button. The Select Row by Key Values dialogue box is removed from the screen. In the list box of the Rows dialogue box, the selected row is displayed. Also a row can be selected graphically by selecting the object to which the row is linked.

Editing Data in a Table

Periodically there is a need to change (update) the data in a database. For example, in the EMP1 table there might be an employee who has been transferred to some other department, or an employee whose room number has changed. These changes need to be incorporated in the database so that the database contains accurate and up-to-date information. Editing information in the table can be carried out by selecting (making current) the row whose data needs to be updated and then making the changes. In AutoCAD the Updating data operation can be performed with the use of the **ASEROWS** command. The process involved is as follows:

1. Invoke the ASEROWS command. The **Rows** dialogue box is displayed on the screen. Depending on the specification of database objects in the **Administration** dialogue box, the current database objects are listed in the Database Object Settings area of the Rows dialogue box.

2. Select the database objects of your choice from various pop-up lists.

3. Next, select the Updatable radio button in the Cursor State area in order to make all the rows accessible and editable.

4. Select the Open Cursor button so that all the rows are selected. Now, navigate to the row that is to be modified. You can use the Next navigation option placed on the right side of the list box to reach the desired row. The settings are shown in Figure 37-13.

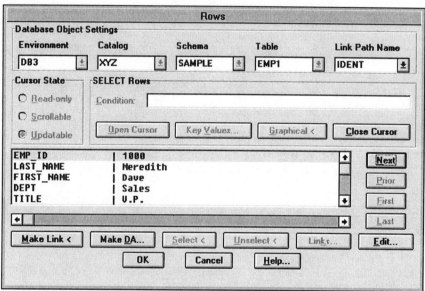

Figure 37-13 Rows dialogue box after opening the cursor

5. Next, select the Edit... button. The **Edit Row** dialogue box (Figure 37-14) appears on the screen.

6. Select the column that is to be updated from the list box. You will notice that the column name is displayed in the Name field just below the list box and its value is displayed in the Value edit box.

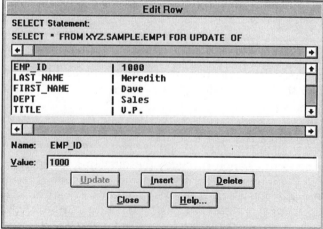

Figure 37-14 Edit Row dialogue box

7. Enter the new value in the Value edit box and press the Enter key. This updates the value of the current column. The value of the next column is now listed in the Value edit box and you can change its value. In the same manner all the columns of the selected row can be edited. After making the necessary changes, select the Update button and then select the Close button.

Rows can also be deleted from the table. To delete a row, open the Rows dialogue box, set the Cursor State to Updatable and make the row to be deleted current. Next, pick the Edit... button. The Edit Row dialogue box is displayed. Pick the Delete button. The Confirm dialogue box is displayed on the screen. Select the OK button to delete the row from the table. After this, pick the Close button in the Edit Row dialogue box. Row is deleted from the table.

Just as rows can be deleted, rows can also be inserted (added to a table). Open the Rows dialogue box, set the Cursor State to Updatable and then pick the Edit... button. Edit Row dialogue box is displayed.

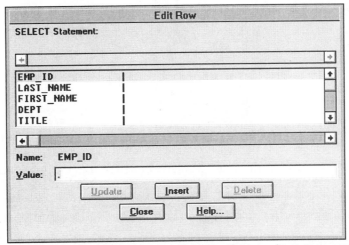

Figure 37-15 Using Edit Row dialogue box to insert a new row

Since a cursor was not opened, in the list box there are no values next to the column names. Now select the column from the list box and enter its new value and press the Enter key. In this manner enter values for all the columns of the new row. After this pick the Insert button and then the Close button so that the modification to the database is saved. The newly inserted row is added to the table at the last position (end of table).

LINKING DATABASE WITH DRAWING

You can use ASE commands to link the information in the database with the drawing entities. Once you define the link, AutoCAD stores that information with the drawing. You can also edit, delete, or view the link and the information associated with the link in the database. To understand the process involved in linking a drawing entity with the database, consider the following example:

Example 1

Given, an office with six computers (Figure 37-16) and a database that contains information about these computers. You are required to link the database information with the six computers in the office.

When you install AutoCAD, it automatically creates a DBF subdirectory and copies three database files: COMPUTER.DBF, EMPLOYEE.DBF, and INVENTRY.DBF. You can use the COMPUTER database file for this example or you can create your own file if you have access to any database program. We also need a drawing that has six computers; therefore make a drawing similar to the drawing shown in Figure 37-16. The following steps will take you through the process involved in linking the computers with the database:

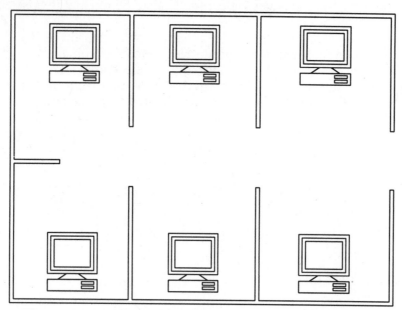

Figure 37-16 Floor plan of an office with six computers

1. Establish the database environment as described earlier (page 37-5): select computer instead of EMP1, select CPU from Key Selection area, and enter CONFIG as link path name.

2. Invoke the **Rows** dialogue box using any of the methods discussed previously.

3. Select a row from the current table using any row selection options (select, Key values, or Graphical) listed in the dialogue box. Now you are ready to link a drawing entity with the database.

4. Pick the Make Link button. The Rows dialogue box is removed from the screen and AutoCAD prompts you to select the object you want to link to the specified row. In this manner you can create a link by assigning the current row of the current table to a graphics entity in the drawing.

5. Use the Next button to make the second row current and then use the Make Link button to create a link between the second row and the second computer. Use the same procedure to link the subsequent rows with the remaining computers.

Editing Links (ASELINKS)

Toolbar:	External Database, Links
Pull-down:	Tools, External Database, Links...
Screen:	TOOLS, EXT DBMS, Links:

You can use the **ASELINKS** command to edit and delete links in the drawing and also to create blocks in the drawing. This command can be invoked from the **External Database** toolbar (select Links icon), from the pull-down menu (select Tools, External Database, Links...), from the screen menu (select TOOLS, EXT DBMS, Links:), or by entering **ASELINKS** at the Command: prompt. The process involved in editing a link is as follows:

1. Invoke the ASELINKS command.

2. Next, AutoCAD prompts you to select the object whose link you want to edit or delete. After selecting the object, the **Links** dialogue box (Figure 37-17) will be displayed on the screen. The dialogue box displays information about the link.

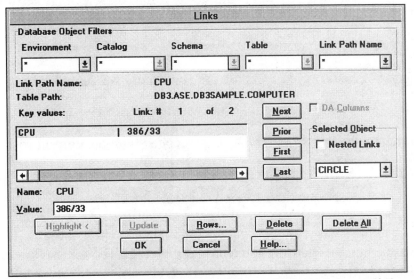

Figure 37-17   Using the Links dialogue box to delete a link

3. The key value of the row linked to the object is displayed in the Key Values list. In case there is more than one link to the object, you can select the link you want to edit by using the navigation buttons.

4. Select the database object that defines the extent of the change. Links can be edited for all environments, or for some particular environment, catalog, schema, table, or link path name. By default all the lists contain an asterisk (*), and in this case all the links to the selected object are accessible for editing and viewing.

5. In the Value edit box, change the value of the key column to the new value and press the Enter key. For example, you could enter the value 486/33 (defined in COMPUTER.DBF) and press the Enter key.

6. You can view the row associated to the new key column value by picking the Rows... button in the Links dialogue box. The Rows dialogue box is displayed. Next, pick the OK button.

7. The Rows dialogue box is removed from the screen. Pick the Update button in the Links dialogue box to update the link.

Deleting Links

Just as you can edit a link, it is also possible to delete a link in the drawing and also to delete blocks in the drawing. The procedure for deletion of a link is as follows:

1. Invoke the ASELINKS command using any one of the methods discussed previously.

2. Select the object whose link is to be deleted. The selected object may be linked to more than one row and in such a case you can use the navigation buttons on the right side of the list box to navigate to the link information you want to delete.

3. Next pick the Delete button. With this the link information displayed in the Key values list box is deleted. In case more than one link exists for the selected object, pick Delete All to delete all link information.

Instead of using the ASELINKS command, which prompts you to select the object first and then select the link you want to deleted, you could delete a link by selecting the row an object is linked to. This can be accomplished in the following manner:

1. Invoke the ASEROWS command.

2. Rows dialogue box is displayed . Choose the row whose link is to be deleted.

3. Next, pick the Links button. The Links dialogue box is displayed.

4. Now edit or delete the link from the object associated with the current row as required.

CREATING DISPLAYABLE ATTRIBUTES

A displayable attribute is nothing but an AutoCAD block having text fields that is linked to a row in the database. The text fields contain the column value of the current row. The text appears at the location specified as the starting point on the drawing. The text style, text justification, text height, and rotation angle can also be controlled for the displayable attributes. The attributes that are displayed on the screen do not have any link with the drawing entity. They are independent text entities that can be edited without affecting the database information or the link between the drawing entity and the table. The instructions involved in creating displaying attributes is as follows:

1. Invoke the Rows dialogue box.

2. The Rows dialogue box is displayed. Select a row and then select the MakeDA... button.

3. The **Make Displayable Attribute** dialogue box (Figure 37-18) is displayed. This dialogue box has two list boxes, **Table Columns** and **DA Columns**. The Table Columns list box displays the titles of each column in the table.

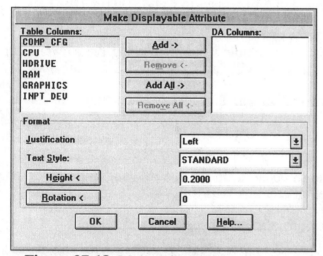

Figure 37-18 Make Displayable
Attribute dialogue box

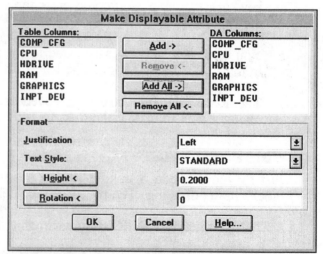

Figure 37-19 Make Displayable Attribute
dialogue box after selecting all the table
columns

4. Place the attributes that you want to display on the graphics screen in the DA Columns list. You can do it by highlighting the title item in the Table Columns list box and then picking the

Add button, or you can double click on the item. If you want to display all the attributes on the graphic screen, pick the Add All button. You can also remove the items in the DA Columns list box by highlighting the item and then selecting the Remove button. Pick the Remove All button to remove the items in the DA Columns list box.

5. Set the text style, text justification, text height, and rotation angle for the displayable attributes.

6. Pick the OK button.

7. Select a point on the screen where you want the displayable attribute to be displayed. With this the displayable attributes are displayed in the drawing at the specified position.

For example, we have selected the DB3, catalog XYZ, schema SAMPLE, and table COMPUTER as the database objects in the Rows dialogue box. After this, the first row of the table has been selected. In the Make Displayable Attribute dialogue box we have selected COMP_CFG, CPU, HDRIVE, and RAM as displayable attribute columns. Next we have placed the displayable attributes (specified column values of the first row) for the first row along with the figure of the first computer on the drawing. Similarly displayable attributes for all the computers have been placed along with the remaining computer. The figure thus obtained is Figure 37-20.

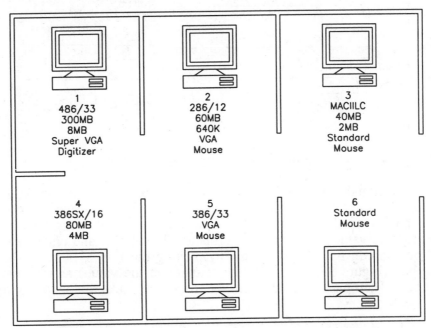

Figure 37-20 Displaying row attributes on the graphics screen

EDITING ROWS

As mentioned earlier, you can access and modify the database from within AutoCAD's Drawing Editor regardless of the database that you are using. You can modify the database through the dialogue boxes or from the command line. The following example illustrates the editing of rows.

Example 2

Given, an office with six computers and a database that contains information about these computers. You are required to modify the data in the row that is linked to the second computer in the office. (Use the drawing and data from Example 1). The following is the new data for this computer:

COMP_CFG	2
CPU	P5-60
HDRIVE	500MB
RAM	16MB
GRAPHICS	ATI
INPT_DEV	MOUSE

The first step is to find the key that links the second computer in the office with the database. This can be accomplished by invoking the **ASELINKS** command, which was discussed earlier in the chapter. When you enter this command, AutoCAD will prompt you to select the object. Select the second computer. After selecting the object, the **Links** dialogue box is displayed (Figure 37-21). The key is COMP_CFG and the attribute value is 2.

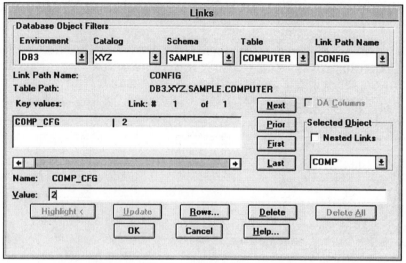

Figure 37-21   Links dialogue box

The second step is to make the row current, which can be done with the **ASEROWS** command. When you enter this command, the **Rows** dialogue box will be displayed on the screen. Use the Key Values... button or the Open Cursor button to set as the current row, the row whose COMP_CFG attribute value is 2. The last step is to edit the row and enter new values as given in Example 2. You can edit the row of a table by picking the Edit... button. This invokes the **Edit Row** dialogue box (Figure 37-22). Make the changes in the values as required and exit the Edit Row dialogue box. Then pick the Make Link button in the Links dialogue box to link the row with the computer.

Figure 37-22   Edit Row dialogue box

> **Note**
>
> *The objects linked to the row being edited manifest the changes.*
>
> *When a row linked to a displayable attribute is edited, invoke Reload DA option of the ASEADMIN command to update the displayable attributes with the new values assigned to the row.*
>
> *If data has to be changed for just one linked objects, use the ASEROWS command to form a new row for that particular linked object and assign the new attribute values to this row. Now use the ASELINKS command to link the object to the new row.*

FORMING SELECTION SETS

It is possible to locate objects on the drawing on the basis of the linked non-graphic information. For example, you can locate the object that is linked to the first row of the COMPUTER table, or first row and second row of the COMPUTER table. You can highlight specified objects, or form a selection set of the selected objects.

1. Invoke the ASEROWS command.

2. Select a row that is linked to an object in the drawing. For example, select the second row of the COMPUTER table.

3. Now pick the Select button. The object linked to the second row of the COMPUTER table is highlighted in the drawing. You can add more objects to the selection set of objects linked to the current row.

Toolbar:	External Database, Select Objects
Pull-down:	Tools, External Database, Select Objects
Screen:	TOOLS, EXT DBMS, Select:

You can also form a selection set on the basis of a combination of non-graphic and graphic data. This can be achieved with the use of **ASESELECT** command. This command can be invoked from the **External Database** toolbar (select Select Objects icon), from the pull-down menu (select Tools, External Database, Select Objects), from the screen menu (select TOOLS, EXT DBMS, Select:), or by entering **ASESELECT** at the Command: prompt.

1. Invoke the ASESELECT command. The **Select Objects** dialogue box (Figure 37-23) is displayed.

2. Set Environment as DB3, Catalog as ASE (in our example it is XYZ), Schema as DB3SAMPLE (in our example it is SAMPLE), and Table as COMPUTER.

3. In the Condition edit box, enter the SELECT statement **GRAPHICS='VGA'** as shown in Figure 37-23 and then pick the SELECT button. This creates selection set A, which has all the objects in the drawing linked to rows having VGA as the graphics.

4. Now, pick the Intersect button and then the Graphical button. The Select Objects dialogue box is removed from the screen and AutoCAD issues Select Objects prompts.

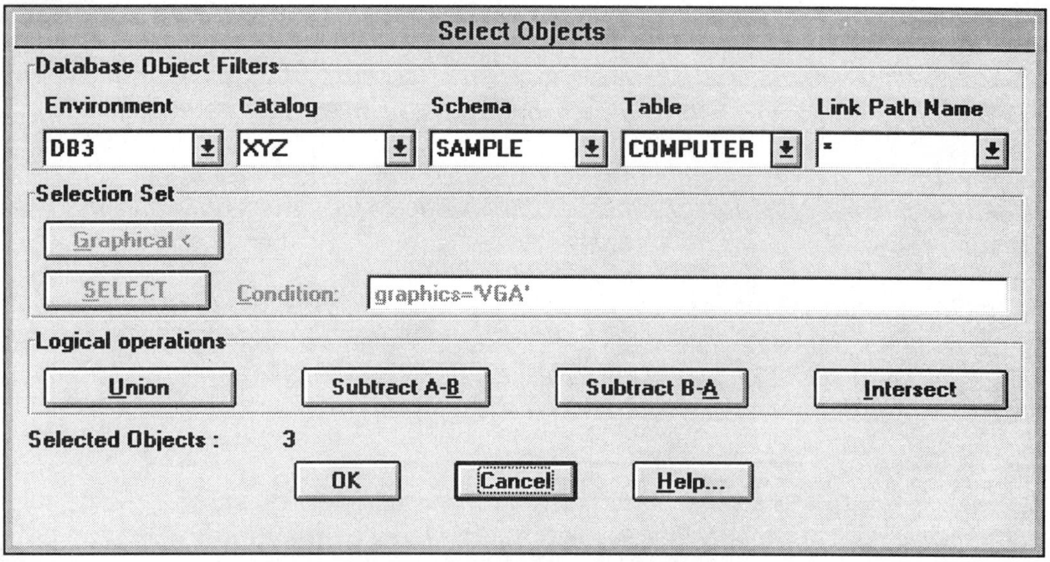

Figure 37-23 Select Objects dialogue box

5. Select all computers and next press the Enter key. This process forms selection set B.

6. The Select Objects dialogue box is displayed. Since we selected Intersect for the logical operation, AutoCAD finally forms a selection set based on intersection of selection set A and B. Hence the selection set formed by the intersection of selection set A and B contains all objects from set B linked to rows in which VGA is the graphics.

With the ASESELECT command, you have the following option for creating selection set:

A Union B
With this option you can create a selection set of objects containing all the objects in the A and B selection sets.

Subtract A-B
With this option you can create a selection set of objects which contains objects obtained upon subtracting the second selection set (B) from the first selection set (A).

Subtract B-A
With this option you can create a selection set of objects which contains objects obtained upon subtracting the first selection set (A) from the second selection set (B).

A Intersect B
With this option you can create a selection set of objects belonging to both A and B selection sets.

If you want to view the objects in the selection set, invoke the **SELECT** command and then choose the Previous option. This command can be invoked from the pull-down menu (select Edit, Select Objects, Previous), from the screen menu (select SERVICE, Previous), or by entering **Previous (P)** at the Select Objects: prompt of the **SELECT** command. The objects in the selection set formed by intersection of selection set A and B (previously formed) are highlighted.

USING SQL STATEMENTS (ASESQLED)

Toolbar:	External Database, SQL Editor
Pull-down:	Tools, External Database, SQL Editor
Screen:	TOOLS, EXT DBMS, SQLedit:

The **ASESQLED** command can be used to communicate with the external database using SQL statements. This is an important application that lets you search through the database and retrieve the information as specified in the SQL statements. Additionally, the SQL statements can be used to insert values in the table; delete rows from the table; change a single row in a table; create, drop, or alter a table; create or drop an index; create a view; and drop view functions. This command can be invoked from the **External Database** toolbar (select SQL Editor icon), from the pull-down menu (select Tools, External Database, SQL Editor...), from the screen menu (select TOOLS, EXT DBMS, SQLedit:), or by entering **ASESQLED** at the Command: prompt.

Example 3 explains some of the applications of ASESQLED command:

Example 3

Select all the rows in the EMPLOYEE table where EMP_ID is less than 1005.

1. Invoke the ASESQLED command. The **SQL Editor** dialogue box (Figure 37-24) is displayed on the screen.

2. Specify the database object setting. Next, in the SQL edit box enter the following SQL statement:

> **Select * from employee where emp_id < 1005**

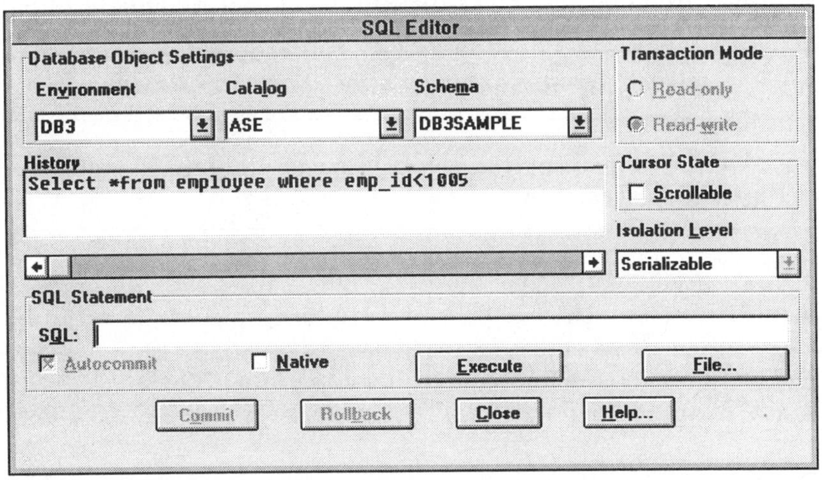

Figure 37-24 SQL Editor dialogue box

3. Pick the Execute button. The result obtained upon execution of the SQL statement is displayed in the **SQL Cursor** dialogue box (Figure 37-25). In our case, all the rows whose EMP_ID is less than 1005 are selected and can be viewed with the help of navigation buttons.

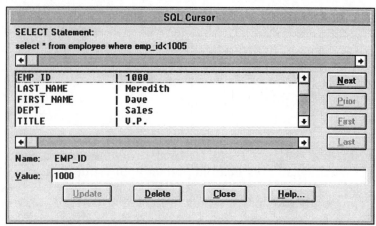

Figure 37-25   SQL Cursor dialogue box

The value for a column in the selected row can be updated by selecting the column and then changing the value in the Value edit box. You have the option of deleting rows from the SQL Cursor dialogue box with the Delete button. For update and deletion operations, the cursor must be set to updatable and the Close button must be picked to make the changes permanent to the database. Now let us say that we want to change the departments of all the employees whose emp_id is less than 1005 to accounting. This task can be performed in the following manner:

1. Enter the following SQL statement in the SQL edit box:

> Update employee set dept= 'Accounting' where emp_id < 1005

2. Pick the Execute button. The result obtained upon execution of the SQL statement is displayed in the SQL Cursor dialogue box. In our case all the rows whose EMP_ID is less than 1005 are selected and can be viewed with the help of navigation buttons.

3. Select the Execute button from the SQL Editor dialogue box. The number of rows that are updated will be displayed at the lower left corner of the dialogue box.

To check if the data has been updated, enter the following SQL statement in the SQL edit box:

> select * from employee where emp_id < 1005

The SQL Cursor dialogue box is displayed. Notice that in the **DEPT** column of each selected row the **Accounting** value is displayed.

Example 4

Given, an office with six computers and a database that contains information about these computers. You are required to do the following tasks: (Use the drawing and database from Example 2).

1. Locate the computers that have 16MB of RAM
2. Locate the computers that have 16MB of RAM and 500MB hard drive.
3. Update the computers that have 16MB of RAM to 32MB.

Locating Computers with 16MB of RAM

Use the following instructions to locate the computers that have 16MB of RAM.

1. Enter the **ASEROW** command and press the Enter (←┘) key. The Rows dialogue box (Figure 37-26) is displayed.

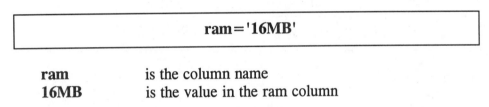

Figure 37-26 Rows dialogue box

2. Enter the following statement in the Condition edit box. The attribute values that are enclosed in single quotes ('16MB') are case sensitive and must be typed exactly as they appear in the table. The rest of the statement can be uppercase or lowercase.

> **ram='16MB'**

ram	is the column name
16MB	is the value in the ram column

3. Select the Open Cursor button. The rows that have 16MB value for the RAM column are selected and the first of the selected rows is displayed in the list box. With the navigation buttons you can check the other selected rows. In our case only one row must be checked.

4. Select the Links... button. The Links dialogue box (Figure 37-27) is displayed.

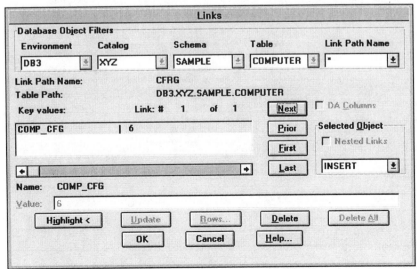

Figure 37-27 Links dialogue box

5. Pick the Highlight < button. The computer with 16MB value for the RAM column is highlighted.

Locating Computers with 16MB of RAM and 500MB of hard drive

For the second part of the example, we have to locate the computers that have 16MB of RAM and 500MB hard drive. The condition statement in this case contains multiple search criteria. For example, if there are six computers in the office and we want to locate the computers that have 16MB of RAM and 500MB hard drive, there are two conditions that the database search should satisfy. We can write a condition statement that will search through the database and locate the items that satisfy the specified criteria. The procedure involved is similar to the first part of the example. The only difference is that the statement to be entered in the Condition edit box of the Rows dialogue box is:

> **ram='16MB' and hdrive='500MB'**

Updating the Computers that have 16MB of RAM to 32MB

You can use the SQL statements to update the values in the table. For example, we can write a SQL statement that will search the "**COMPUTER**" table for "**16MB**" values and then replace those values by "**32MB**". Use the following instructions to update the "**COMPUTER**" table:

1. Enter **ASESQLED** command and press the Enter (◄┘) key. The SQL Editor dialogue box (Figure 37-28) is displayed.

2. Enter the following SQL statement in the SQL: edit box. The statement must be entered exactly as it appears here.

> **update computer set RAM='32MB' where RAM='16MB'**

    Where:
        computer   is the table name
        RAM   in the column name

3. Select the Execute... button from the SQL Editor dialogue box.

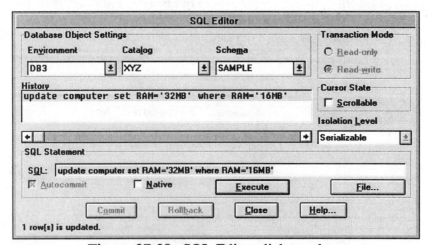

Figure 37-28 SQL Editor dialogue box

4. To check if the data has been updated, enter the following SQL statement in the SQL: edit box. The statement must be entered exactly as it appears here.

> select comp_cfg,ram from computer where ram='32MB'

The values in the **comp_cfg** and **ram** columns will be displayed in the SQL Cursor dialogue box (Figure 37-29).

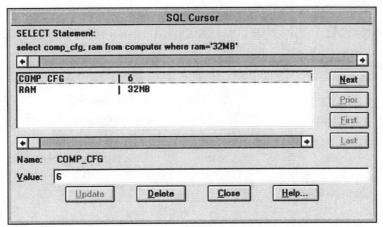

Figure 37-29   SQL Cursor dialogue box

GENERATING REPORTS FROM EXPORTED DATA

On the basis of the information linked to the drawing you can generate reports using the external database commands. AutoCAD does not support a direct reporting feature. Hence reports are created with the DBMS and report-writer softwares. The external database commands provided by AutoCAD makes easy the procedure involved in the creation of reports.

With external database commands it is possible to link more than one object to a row. This lessens the size of the database in case objects do not have distinct attributes. In this case it is not possible to determine how many objects are linked to one row from the DBMS. The **ASEEXPORT** command can be used to determine the number of objects linked to a single row by exporting link information in the drawing and xref and blocks in the drawing, in different formats. This information can be fused with the data in the tables to generate a report.

Toolbar:	External Database, Export Links
Pull-down:	Tools, External Database, Export Links...
Screen:	TOOLS, EXT DBMS, Export:

1. Invoke the **ASEEXPORT** command. This command can be invoked from the **External Database** toolbar (select Export Links icon), from the pull-down menu (select Tools, External Database, Export Links...), from the screen menu (select TOOLS, EXT DBMS, Export:), or by entering **ASEEXPORT** at the Command: prompt.

2. AutoCAD prompt you to select objects whose link information you want to export. After completing the selection of objects, the **Export Links** dialogue box (Figure 37-30) is displayed.

3. Select the scope of the linked data to be produced in the report by making adequate selections in the Database Object Filters area.

4. Select a link path name in the list box.

5. In the Format pop-up list, select NATIVE as the file format of the exported information.

6. In the Target edit box, specify the name of the table you want to form.

7. Pick the Assign button to assign the defined file format and target path name to the selected link path name.

8. If you want to export links of some other link path name, repeat steps 3 through 7.

9. Pick the Export button.

The export operation is repeated for each link path name assignment.

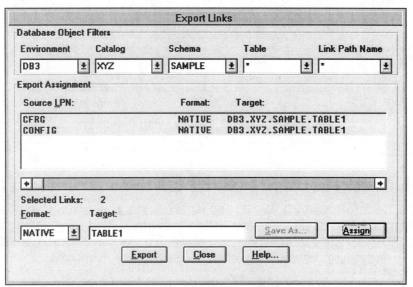

Figure 37-30 Export Links dialogue box

REVIEW QUESTIONS

Answer the following questions.

1. SQL is often referred to as _____

2. The horizontal group of data is called a _____

3. A vertical group of data (attribute) is called a _____

4. The **ASE** commands are defined in the _____ file

5. An environment can have zero or more catalogs. (T/F)

6. The _____ command allows the user to set a row current in the predefined (current) table.

7. The name of the catalog relates to the directory path name that is the location of the database. (T/F)

8. Once you define the link, AutoCAD does not store that information with the drawing. (T/F)

9. The location of database files can be defined by setting an environment variable that tells AutoCAD where to find the files. (T/F)

10. If you want to use the dialogue boxes with ASE commands, you must set the **CMDDIA** variable to 0 (off). (T/F)

11. The **Make Link** option in the Rows dialogue box enables you to create a link by assigning the current row of the current table to a graphics entity in the drawing. (T/F)

12. The **ASESQLED** command can be used to communicate with the external database using SQL statements. (T/F)

13. The SQL statements lets you search through the database and retrieve the information as specified in the SQL statements. (T/F)

14. What does **ASE** stand for? _____

15. What is a **database**? _____

16. What is a **Database Management System** (DBMS)? _____
_____

17. A schema cannot have one or more tables. (T/F)

18. The name of the schema relates to the catalog subdirectory that contains the database tables. (T/F)

19. When a sequence of SQL statements are executed, a _____ takes place.

20. A transaction is terminated with the SQL _____ or SQL _____ operation.

21. A row is also referred as a _____

22. A column is sometimes called a _____

23. The _____ acts like an identification tag for locating and linking a row.

24. Selecting two or more columns and their values to define a key is called _____ .

25. Keys can be defined in the _____ dialogue box.

26. Isolation of data returned by a query transaction when many users try to address the same data simultaneously does not depend on the isolation levels. (T/F)

27. At one time only one row can be manipulated. This row is called the _____ .

28. It is possible to make a row current is by making use of a key to search for a particular row or rows if you have specified key values. (T/F)

29. You can reestablish data integrity with the use of the _____ option of the ASEADMIN command.

30. The _____ command can be used to determine the number of objects linked to a single row by exporting link information in the drawing and xref and blocks in the drawing, in different formats.

Exercise 1

In the following exercise you will set the environment to DB3, set the catalog to XYZ, set the schema to SAMPLE database, set the EMPLOYEE table current, and then edit the second row of the table (EMP_ID=1001, Williams). You will also add a new row to the table, set the new row current and then view it.

The row to be added has the following values:

EMP_ID	1100
LAST_NAME	McLees
FIRST_NAME	David
Dept	Technology
TITLE	Programmer
ROOM	108
EXT	8001

Exercise 2

Load the drawing ASETUT from the TUTORIAL subdirectory and use the SAVEAS command to save the drawing as SQLEX2. (You can also make a copy of the ASETUT drawing and name it SQLEX2 and then load the new drawing, SQLEX2.) After loading the drawing perform the following operations:

1. Use the **ASEADMIN** command to set environment to DB3, catalog to XYZ, schema to SAMPLE, and table to COMPUTER.
2. Make a copy of the computer in room number 106 and place it in room number 108.
3. Use the **ASELINKS** command to view the existing link of the copied computer (Computer in room number 108).
4. Delete any existing link.
5. Use the **ASEROW** command to set COMP_CFG number 2 current.
6. Use the **Make Link** option in Rows dialogue box to link the current computer to the computer in room number 108.
7. Use the **Make DA** option in the Rows dialogue box to display the attributes of the computer on the screen.
8. Using the **ASESQLED** command, enter the following SQL statement and highlight the computer in room number 108.

> **select emp_id,last_name from employee where room='108'**

Appendix **A**

System Requirements

SYSTEM REQUIREMENTS

The following are the minimum system requirements for running AutoCAD:

1. DOS 5.0 or later
2. Windows 3.1 or later running in enhanced mode
3. Microsoft's Win32s version 1.20 or later
4. 16 MB of RAM (minimum)
5. Intel 386, Intel 486, Pentium processor or compatible
6. 80387 math coprocessor
7. 37MB of hard disk space
8. 40MB of disk swap space (minimum)
9. 1.44MB, 3 1/2-inch, or 1.2MB, 5 1/4-inch floppy drive
10. Windows supported display adapter
11. Mouse or other pointing device
12. IBM compatible parallel port
13. Hardware lock for network and international single user

The following hardware is optional:

1. Printer
2. Plotter
3. Digitizing tablet
4. Serial port
5. CD-ROM drive for installing AutoCAD on Windows and DOS platforms

HARDWARE

Hardware refers to the tools or the equipment used in computer-aided drafting and design. It is comprised of a microcomputer and the external devices called the peripherals. Following are the components used in computer-aided drafting:

Microcomputer

The microcomputers which are best suited for the CAD environment are the IBM models and certain other microcomputers which are completely IBM compatible. In addition to the type of the machine used, the computer should fulfill the hardware requirements of AutoCAD. A typical microcomputer is a rectangular-shaped metal box. It consists of a central processing unit (CPU), memory unit, and the disk drives. The CPU controls all the activities and the calculations of the computer. The CPU has integrated circuit chips and other electronic components which are

1

mounted on several printed circuit boards called "cards." By means of these cards the peripherals and the additional items are attached to the computer.

The memory unit of the computer has a number of blank chips, which can be used to store any information. This is the temporary storage device and is known as random access memory (RAM). When we turn on the computer, the operating system is loaded in this memory. Similarly, when we load AutoCAD, it is placed in this memory. So all the information and the data we provide to the computer is stored in the RAM. When the RAM becomes full rest of the information is then loaded in the hard disk and is copied back to the RAM whenever it is required. This copying from the hard disk to the RAM takes much more time than directly reading from the memory. The standard memory size is 640K or 640,000, bytes but this can be improved upon by adding extra memory which is known as extended memory. So it is better to have more memory in a computer, particularly for an AutoCAD environment which needs at least 16MB of memory.

Monitor

The monitor is a peripheral device connected to the computer for display of information. Hence it is also referred to as an output device and resembles a TV. The standard monitor sizes are 13" and 21" and are of two types: color and monochrome. The unit of measurement is the pixel (PIcture ELement), which can also determine the display resolution (appearance of text on the screen). The display of text on the screen is in the form of rows and columns of pixels. A standard monitor has a display resolution of 640 by 350 pixels. The monitor is interfaced with the computer by means of a printed circuit board having a number of chips on it. This board is known as a graphics card and the resolution of the monitor is dependent on this card. There are three types of graphics cards: CGA (Color Graphics Adaptor), EGA (Enhanced Graphics Adaptor), and VGA (Video Graphics Array). AutoCAD uses both EGA and VGA graphics cards. EGA has a resolution of 640 by 350 and 16 colors, whereas VGA has a resolution of 640 by 480 to 1024 by 768 and 256 colors.

Keyboard

The keyboard is one of the most important peripheral devices used to input information into the computer. It is similar to a typewriter keyboard. In addition to the normal typewriter keys it has certain special keys such as the function keys. The function keys F1-F10 or F1-F12 perform certain special operations in AutoCAD. The keyboard is used to enter any form of information, i.e. text, dimensions, etc, into the computer by directly typing in the commands.

Pointing Devices

Pointing devices are peripherals by which information can be entered into the computer. Information can be entered onto the screen at any desired location by moving the cursor to the particular place with the pointing device. Hence those pointing devices are very useful in AutoCAD. There are different types of pointing devices such as puck, stylus, mouse, and trackball. The puck and the stylus are to be used along with a digitizer tablet, whereas the mouse and the trackball can be used without it and hence are less expensive.

The digitizer tablet has a paper or plastic menu overlay containing AutoCAD commands and drawings. So a particular command or drawing can be entered directly onto the screen by moving the puck or stylus to the desired item. This item will be displayed on the screen at the position of the cursor.

Each of the pointing devices works differently but all of them put information on the screen. The multibutton puck is used with a digitizer tablet. Different pucks have different button arrangements and the number of buttons also varies from one to sixteen. A set of cross-hairs is present on the puck. The movement of these cross-hairs indicates the position on the tablet and by means of the pick button the menu command is selected. The rest of the buttons are programmed according to the needs of the user.

The stylus is a pointed, pen-shaped device which is attached to the digitizer with a wire. The stylus works by pressing the point on the digitizer at the desired position and the particular item is selected on the screen.

The mouse works without the digitizer and needs only a small flat space for its movement. Hence it is quite inexpensive. There are two types of mouse: mechanical and optical. An optical mouse uses a reflective pad with grid lines, whereas the mechanical mouse moves on a roller ball at its bottom. In the optical mouse its reflection on the pad shows the location on the screen, but in the mechanical mouse the movement of the roller ball - which is moved by moving the mouse - shows the location.

A trackball is just like a mechanical mouse with a bigger rolling ball. Here, the ball is simply moved to get the location on the screen and then the button is clicked.

Storage Devices

Floppy disks and the hard disk are the main storage devices in the computer. Floppy disks are of different sizes and their storage capacity also varies according to the size. The 5.25" floppy disk has a storage capacity of 360,000 (360K) bytes. A high-density floppy has a storage capacity of 1.2 megabytes. Another commonly used floppy is 3.5" and has a hard plastic covering. It is a high density floppy and has a storage capacity of 1.44MB. This particular floppy can be used only on IBM/DOS compatible systems and Apple Macintosh systems. Space is provided at the front of the computer for the floppy disks and small lights are present with each disk drive. These lights come on when the drives are accessed.

Some computers also use the high density compact optical digital disk (CD) as the storage device. These are used for reading CD ROM. Another storage device is the hard disk, which is present inside the computer, containing metal disks or "platters." A hard disk is very necessary for an AutoCAD environment. The storage capacity ranges from 100MB to 1GB and higher, which is much more than the floppy disks.

Plotter

Another output device used to output drawings is the plotter. It uses pencil, felt pen, ballpoint, or ink pens to output drawings on the paper. Drawings of any size can be output by these plotters and hence are very useful for AutoCAD. An electrostatic plotter has electrically charged wire nibs which puts dots on the paper, eventually reproducing the drawing. These plotters are preferred because of their high speed and accurate plots. They can plot about 600 dots per inch in color.

Printer

Printers are also used in AutoCAD to print the drawings. C-size (17 by 22) prints are available on large-format dot matrix printers. Because of their accurate drawing, other printing devices, such as ink-jet, laser, and electrostatic devices, are being more frequently used today.

Network Systems

A network system joins several computers with cables so that different users can communicate with each other. Complex network systems have hundreds of computers connected together under a common server. The server has a large hard disk for storing a number of softwares and different files created by the users. The main utility of the network system is that a user can complete the new drawing from an old one which is already in the server. It is usually seen that the base drawing is stored in the server so that whenever a user has to make a new drawing, they can directly start off by loading the base drawing. In AutoCAD only one user has access to the drawing at a time, even in a network system.

Appendix B

DOS Commands
MS-DOS Editor, and Windows

This chapter contains a brief description of some of the DOS commands that are frequently used in a CAD environment. The examples that follow the DOS commands are some possible applications of these commands. For a detailed explanation of the DOS commands and the command options, check your disk operating system reference manual.

ASSIGN Command

This command will route the disk input and output (I/O) from one drive to another. The format of the command is:

Example: **ASSIGN A=B**

This command will assign drive B to drive A. For example, if you do a directory of A drive (DIR A:), the files in B drive will be listed. If you want to restore the default drive specification, use the ASSIGN command without any parameters (ASSIGN).

CHDIR Command

This command changes the directory. The format of the command is:

Example: **CHDIR ACAD** or **CD ACAD**

This command will change the directory to ACAD subdirectory:

Example: **CD**

These commands will change the current directory to the root directory.

CHKDSK Command

You can use the DOS command CHKDSK to check the status of your diskette and the system. It provides information about disk space, how much memory the system has, and how much is available for program use. The format of the command is:

CHKDSK [d:][path][filename[.ext]][/F][/V]

Example: **CHKDSK A:**

4

This command will check the diskette in A drive and then display the information on the screen:

Example: **CHKDSK C:/F**

This command will check C drive and fix any errors that are found in the disk directory or the file allocation table. **Do not run this command if you have shelled out of AutoCAD.**

COPY Command

The COPY command is used to copy files from one disk to another. COPY is an internal command that is loaded in the computer memory when you boot the computer. The format of the command is:

COPY [d:][path]filename[.ext] [d:][path][filename][.ext]/V

If you use /V at the end of the copy command line, it causes DOS to verify the sectors written on the target diskette. Because of the verification process, the copy command with /V option is relatively slow.

When you copy the files, it is very important to know the structure of the files on your drive. In the following examples, it is assumed that there are two drives, C and D. Each drive has subdirectories as shown in the following figure. Also, **it is assumed that DWG1 subdirectory is the current directory.**

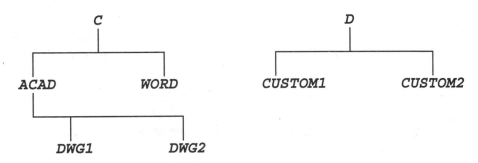

The COPY command will copy file PROJ1.DWG to PROJ2.DWG:

Example

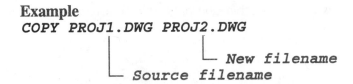

This command will copy the file SPLINE.LSP in the ACAD subdirectory to the CUSTOM1 subdirectory on the D drive. The name of the file that is copied to the CUSTOM1 subdirectory does not change.

Example

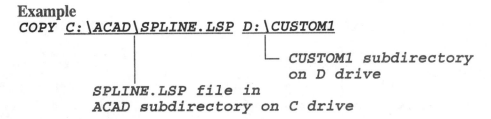

This command will copy a file PROJ1.DWG in the ACAD subdirectory to a file PROJ2.DWG in the CUSTOM1 subdirectory on the D drive:

COPY C:\ACAD\PROJ1.DWG D:\CUSTOM1\PROJ2.DWG

This command will copy all the drawing files with the extension DWG from the current subdirectory to the CUSTOM2 subdirectory on the D Drive:

COPY *.DWG D:\CUSTOM2

This command will copy all files from the current subdirectory to the CUSTOM1 subdirectory on the D drive:

COPY *.* D:\CUSTOM1

This command will combine the two files SHOW.SCR and DEMO.SCR and copy them to a new file SHOWDEMO.SCR:

COPY SHOW.SCR+DEMO.SCR SHOWDEMO.SCR

This command will combine the SHOW.SCR file in the current subdirectory, with the DEMO.SCR file in the WORD subdirectory and copy the file to SHOWDEMO.SCR in the CUSTOM1 subdirectory of the D drive.

COPY SHOW.SCR+C:\WORD\DEMO.SCR D:\CUSTOM1\SHOWDEMO.SCR

DIR Command

You can use the DOS command, DIR, to display a list of files on a diskette. It is an internal command that is loaded in the computer memory when you boot the computer. The format of the command is:

DIR [d:][path][filename][.ext][/P][/W]

This command will display a list of files on the D drive together with their size in bytes, time, and date when they were last opened:

DIR D:

This command of DOS will display the files on the B drive one page at a time. When you press a key, another page of files is displayed:

DIR B:/P

This command will display files on the B drive in the wide format. The file listing on the screen has five columns across the screen. Only filenames, file types, and the total number of files are displayed:

DIR B:/W

This command will display the specified file only. It will display the file SCRMENU.MNU with its size and date:

DIR B:SCRMENU.MNU

This command will display files that have an extension DWG. "*" is a wild card.

DIR B:*.DWG

This command will display all files that have the extension DWG in the CUST1 subdirectory of the ACAD directory:

DIR C:\ACAD\CUST1*.DWG

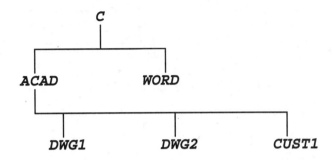

DISKCOPY Command

If you have a computer system that has two floppy disk drives, you can use the DOS command, DISKCOPY, to make a backup copy of the entire disk. DISKCOPY copies all the contents on the source disk to the target disk. Before copying the files it automatically formats the target disk, if the diskette has not been formatted before. Therefore, make sure that you do not have any files on the target diskette which you do not want to be erased. This command can be used for making copies of diskettes only. If you specify a fixed drive, an error message will be displayed. The format of the DISKCOPY command is:

DISKCOPY [d: [d:]][/1]

This command will prompt you to insert the source diskette in the A drive and the destination diskette in the B drive. If the source and the target drives are same, you will be prompted to insert the source diskette in the A drive. After reading the source diskette you will be prompted to enter the target diskette in the A drive.

DISKCOPY A: B:

ERASE or DEL Command

This command is used to erase the specified files from a disk. The format of the command is:

ERASE [d:][path]filename[.ext]

This command will erase the file PROJ101.DWG from the diskette in the B drive:

ERASE B:PROJ101.DWG

This command will erase all the files with the extension BAK from the current directory. If the drive specification is missing, the current drive is assumed.

DEL *.BAK

You can delete all files from a specified drive by specifying *.*. This command will erase all files from drive A:

ERASE A:*.*

Next, the following prompt is displayed to make sure that you really want to erase all files:

Are you sure (Y/N)?

If you want to erase all files on the specified drive, type Y and press the Enter key. If you do not want to erase all files, type N and press the Enter key.

FORMAT Command

A new diskette is like a blank sheet of paper. Before DOS can write any data on the disk, the disk must be formatted. Formatting divides the disk into tracks and sectors so that DOS can keep track of where the files are located on the disk. When DOS formats a disk, it erases all the files on the disk, unless it is write protected. Before formatting, make sure that you do not need the files that are on this disk and the disk is not write protected. (The FORMAT command described below does not list all of the available options. Refer to a DOS manual for details.) The format of the FORMAT command is:

FORMAT d:[/S][/V][/4]

This command will FORMAT a diskette that is in drive A:

FORMAT A:

This command will FORMAT a diskette that is in drive B:

Format B:

This command will format the diskette in the A drive. The /S option will copy the system files on the diskette in the A drive. The /V option will prompt for a volume label and that information will be saved on the diskette:

FORMAT A:/S/V

This command will format the diskette that is in the A drive. If the path has not been set in the Autoexec.BAT file, use C:\DOS to define the path where the DOS files are located. In this example, it is assumed that the DOS files are in the DOS subdirectory on the C drive.

C:\DOS\FORMAT A:

> **Note**
>
> *Do not format the hard drives (FORMAT C:, FORMAT D:) unless you are familiar with the hard disk formatting procedure. If you format the hard drives, it will destroy the DOS partition, including all subdirectories and their contents. Consult your DOS reference manual for detailed information.*

MKDIR Command

This command creates a subdirectory on the disk. The format of the command is:

C>MKDIR ACAD
C>MKDIR WORD

These commands will create subdirectories ACAD and WORD on the C drive. You can create any number of subdirectories, provided the maximum length of the path from the root directory to the specified directory is not more than 63 characters long.

This command will make a subdirectory HOUSE in the DWG1 directory:
MD C:\ACAD\DWG1\HOUSE

PATH Command

The PATH command sets the path for searching commands and batch files in the directories specified in the path command. The format of the command is:

PATH [[d:]path[[;d:]path]]]

If the command or the batch file is not found in the current directory, DOS searches the subdirectories named in the path. In this example, DOS will search all the directories in the same sequence as specified in the path.

PATH C:\ACAD;D:\SYMBOLS\ARCH;

If no parameters are specified in the PATH command, it displays the current path:

PATH

If the PATH command is followed by a semicolon (;), it resets the search path to null. DOS will search for the commands and the batch files in the current directory only.

PATH;

RENAME Command

The RENAME command lets you change the name of a file. The format of the command is:

RENAME [d:][path]filename[.ext]filename[.ext]

This command will change the name of the PROJ1.DWG file in the ACAD subdirectory to NEWPROJ.DWG. The path name can be specified with the first filename only.

RENAME C:\ACAD\PROJ1.DWG NEWPROJ.DWG
or
REN C:\ACAD\PROJ1.DWG NEWPROJ.DWG

RMDIR Command

The RMDIR command removes the subdirectory from a disk. The format of the command is:

RMDIR [d:]path
or
RD [d:]path

This command will remove the OLDDWG subdirectory from the current directory. The subdirectory has to be empty to remove it.

RMDIR OLDDWG

This command will remove the OLDDWG subdirectory from the ACAD directory:

RMDIR C:\ACAD\OLDDWG

TYPE Command

The TYPE command displays the listing of the specified file on the screen or on the output device. The format of the command is:

TYPE[d:][path]filename[.ext]

This command will display the contents of the file PLOT1.SCR that is located in the ACAD subdirectory:

TYPE C:\ACAD\PLOT1.SCR

This command will print the contents of the file on the printer:

TYPE CUTMENU.MNU > PRN

XCOPY Command

The XCOPY command is used to copy a group of files. This command can also copy the files that are in a subdirectory. The format of the command is:

XCOPY [d:][path]filename[.ext]/M/P/S/V

```
                                         └ Verify files
                                 └ Copies file in the
                                   source and the
                                   subdirectories
                           └ Prompts before
                             copying files
                   └ Copies files that have
                     archive bit set
```

This command will copy all the files in the DWG1 subdirectory and the subdirectories within the DWG1 subdirectory (PARTS, ASSEM) to the A drive. On the A drive it will automatically create the subdirectories, if needed, and copy the files.

XCOPY C:\ACAD\DWG1*.DWG A: /S

This command will copy the files from the current directory that have the archive bit set. This command can therefore be used to back up the disk.

XCOPY *.DWG A:/M

This command will copy the files from the current directory and the subdirectories that have the archive bit set. This command can therefore be used to back up the disk.

XCOPY *.DWG A:/M/S

Use the following command to set the archive bit, if needed. This command will set the archive bit of all the files in the DWG1 subdirectory.

ATTRIB +a C:\ACAD\DWG1*.*

MS-DOS Editor

The MS-DOS Editor works with DOS version 5.0 or 6.0 and later only. The DOS Editor can be used to write and edit the files like a word processor. Therefore, it is a convenient way to write files, such as batch files, script files, menu files, AutoLISP files, dialogue control language files, or any text file. The older version of DOS used EDLIN, a line editor, to write and edit the files. Since EDLIN is a line editor and the user has to know several commands to edit a file, it makes EDLIN a poor choice to write and edit the files, especially if the files are long. DOS versions 5.0

and 6.0 supports the EDLIN command, but it is better to use EDIT command for writing a text file.

It is important to remember that DOS Editor does not work without QBASIC. Therefore, the file QBASIC.EXE must be in the current subdirectory or in the search path. If the EDIT command does not work, make sure to check the QBASIC.EXE is present.

STARTING DOS EDITOR

To start **DOS Editor** from AutoCAD, type SH or SHELL. AutoCAD will automatically switch to text screen and display **OS Command**: prompt on the screen. Now, you can enter the **EDIT** command:

> Command: **SHELL**
> OS Command: **EDIT**

When you type **EDIT**, a dialogue box will be displayed on the screen as shown in Figure B-1. To clear the dialogue box, press the Esc key. If you want to find some information about the MS-DOS editor, press the Enter key.

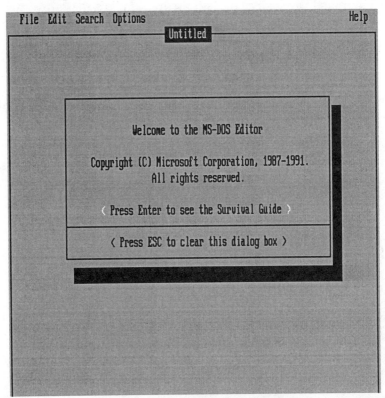

Figure B-1 DOS Editor dialogue box

If you want to open an existing file, **type EDIT with filename and extension** at the OS Command prompt. If the file is not in the current subdirectory, then you must also define the path. In the following example, it is assumed that the current subdirectory is DWG:

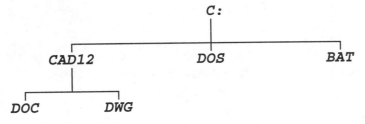

Command: **SHELL**
OS Command: **EDIT myfile.doc** *(If the file is in the DWG subdirectory.)*
OS Command: **EDIT c:\cad12\doc\myfile.doc** *(If the file is in the DOC subdirectory.)*

SELECTING MENUS AND COMMANDS

When you are in the DOS Editor, a window is displayed on the screen with a menu bar at the top of the screen as shown in Figure B-2. The menu bar displays the names of the menu items. You can select a menu item by one of two ways:

Press the Alt key and then move the selection cursor with the left-arrow or the right-arrow key.

Hold the Alt key down and then press the first character of the menu item.

When you select a menu item, a pull-down menu is displayed directly under the menu item. The pull-down menu lists the commands available in that menu. You can choose any command from it by one of the following methods:

Choose a command by using the up-arrow key or the down-arrow key to highlight the command and pressing the Enter key to select the command.

Use the key board to choose a command by pressing the highlighted character in the pull-down menu.

If the command does not have a highlighted character, select the text first and then select the command from the pull-down menu.

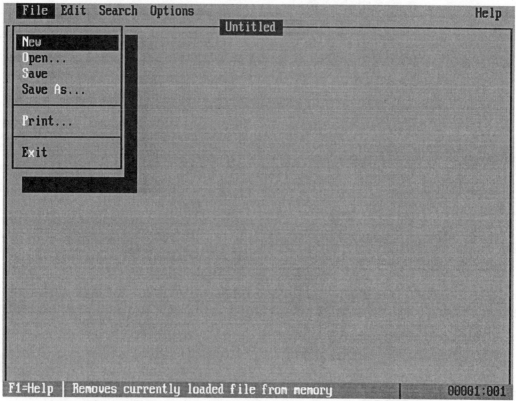

Figure B-2 Dialogue box with menu bar and pull-down menu

CREATING A TEXT FILE

Once you are in the DOS editor window, you can start typing the text. At the end of the text line, you must press Enter key. The maximum number of characters that you can enter in one line is 256. You can use the following keys to edit the text:

Del or **Ctrl+G**	These keys will delete the character where the cursor is located.
Backspace or **Ctrl+H**	These keys will delete the character to the left of the cursor.
Ctrl+T	These keys will delete the word where the cursor is located, provided the cursor is at the first character of the word.
Ins or **Ctrl+V**	These keys toggle between the insert and replace functions. The DOS editor is in the insert mode by default. However, if you want to replace a character, press Ins key.

SELECTING TEXT

Before performing an editing operation, you must first select the text that you want to edit. The text that you select can be a single character, any number of adjacent characters, single line of text, several adjacent lines of text, or the entire document. To select the text, move the cursor to the desired location, hold the Shift key down and then use the arrow keys to move the cursor to the last character of the text that you want to select. The highlighted text is selected by releasing the Shift key.

EDITING TEXT

The edit commands that you can use to edit the selected text are listed in the Edit (Figure B-3) and Search (Figure B-4) pull-down menus. When you select the text for editing, the text is temporarily stored in the buffer. The text stored in this buffer can be moved, deleted, or copied. You can also search a text or perform a search and replace operation. The editing commands that you can use for editing a file are:

Cut and Paste Commands

If you want to move the text to a different location, select the text and then select the **Cut** command from the edit pull-down menu or use the **Shift+Del** keys. Now, move the cursor to the location where you want to move that text and select the **Paste** command from the edit pull-down menu or use the **Shift+Ins** keys. The text will be moved to the new location.

Copy and Paste Commands

If you want to copy the text to another location, select the text and then select the **Copy**

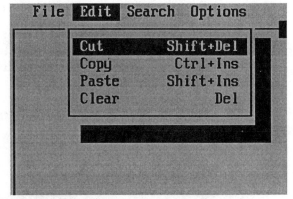

Figure B-3 Edit pull-down menu

command from the Edit pull-down menu or use the **Ctrl+Ins** keys. Now, move the cursor to the location where you want to copy that text and select the **paste** command from the Edit pull-down menu or use the **Shift+Ins** keys. The text will be copied to the new location.

Clear Command

If you want to delete some text, select the text and then select the **Clear** command from the Edit pull-down menu or select the **Del** key. The text you clear is not stored in the buffer. However, the text that is already stored in the buffer is not affected.

Find and Change Commands

You can use the **Search** pull-down menu to search a text or replace a text in the file. Select **Search** from the menu bar and a pull-down menu is displayed on the screen as shown in Figure B-4. Select the **Find** command and the DOS Editor will display another dialogue box on the screen prompting the user to enter the name of the text. If you want to replace a text string, select **Change** command from the pull-down menu and enter the text that you want to replace and the new text in the dialogue box.

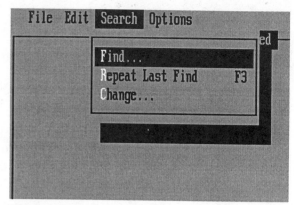

Figure B-4 Search pull-down menu

MANAGING FILES

In addition to writing and editing text, you can also use the DOS Editor to create a file, save a file, or print a file. You can access these commands by selecting **File** from the menu bar. When you select **File**, the corresponding pull-down menu will be displayed on the screen as shown in Figure B-2.

New Command

The **New** command can be used to open a new file. For example, if a file is open or there is some text on the screen and you want to start a new file, select the **New** command to start a new file. Before you start the new file, the DOS Editor will diplay another dialogue box on the screen that will display the message **"Loaded file is not saved. Save it now"**. You can select the desired option and then the DOS Editor will start a new file.

Open Command

The open command is used to open an existing file. When you select this command, the DOS Editor will display the **Open dialogue box** that displays the names of the files in the current subdirectory. The name and the path of the current subdirectory is also displayed in this dialogue box. To open a file, type the name of the file and the path, if the file is not in the current subdirectory. You can also open a file by selecting a file from the file listing and then selecting OK. **If you want to move the cursor to another box, use the Tab key**. For example, if you want to select OK from the dialogue box, press the Tab key till the cursor reaches there and then press the Enter key to select it.

Save and Save As Commands

You can save the file by using the **Save** or **Save as** command. When you select the save command from the File pull-down menu, the DOS Editor will display a dialogue box on the screen. Enter the name of the file and then select OK from the dialogue box. If the file has been saved before, the file will be saved without displaying the dialogue box.

If you select the Save As command, the DOS editor will display the dialogue box and and then you can enter the name of the file. The file will be saved under the new name and the current file will retain the old name.

Print Command

You can use the Print command to print a file on the printer connected to LPT1 port only. When you select the Print command, the DOS editor will display a dialogue box that lets you print the complete document or selected text.

Exit Command

If you want to quit from the DOS Editor, select the **Exit** command from the **File** pull-down menu. If the file has not been saved, the DOS Editor displays a dialogue box on the screen that prompts the user to save the file or discard the changes to file.

Windows

Program Manager Application

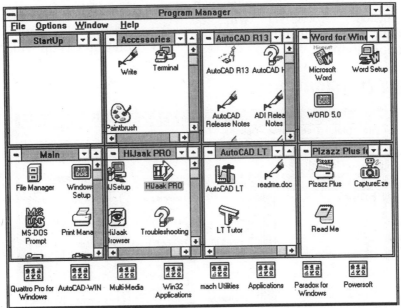

Figure B-5 Program Manager window

When you start Windows, the Program Manager application is automatically started. Depending on the softwares installed on your machine and the Windows version, you will get a screen similar to Figure B-5. Program Manager is the most important application in Windows. It is this application from which you can start (load) any of your application. The different applications are organized into groups by the Program Manager. All the group windows are subwindows of the Program Manager window. The standard groups available in Windows are Main, Accessories, Games and Startup.

Main Group

This group contains applications that allow you to configure your hardware and customize the Windows environment according to your requirement. This group may contain File Manager, Control Panel, SmartMon, Print Manager, PIF-Editor, Windows Setup, etc.

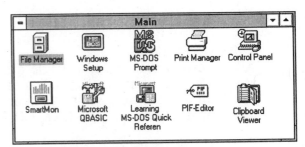

Figure B-6 Main Group

Accessories Group

This group contains applications that automate desktop tasks such as Clock, Calculator, Notepad, Paintbrush, Terminal, Object Packager etc.

Figure B-7 Accessories Group

Games Group

This group contains games such as Minesweeper and Solitaire.

Startup Group

This group contains applications that you want to run whenever Windows start. For example, in the figure shown, AutoCAD R13 has been set up in the Startup group. In this case whenever Windows is started, AutoCAD will be automatically loaded. By default this group does not contain any application.

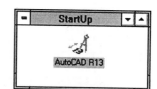

Figure B-8 AutoCAD setup on Startup Group window

File Manager Application

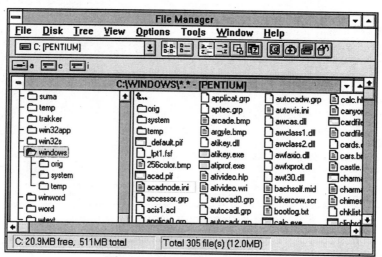

Figure B-9 File Manager

The File Manager application is present in the Main group. When you run File Manager, a window similar to Figure B-9 will appear. File Manager is one of the most frequently used Windows applications because it allows you to copy, rename, delete, print files; create directories, delete directories, change drives, move files from one directory to another, change directories, run applications, format disks, and much more.

The various components in the File Manager screen are as follows:

Disk-drive icons

All the drives available to the File Manager are represented by icons. Depending on your hardware and software setup, you can have icons for floppy drive, hard-drive, CD-ROM drive, and any other drive available.

Figure B-10 Drive icons

Disk volume label

This is an optional character name assigned to the disk.

Directory path and file specification
This is the full path name to the current directory and also the specification for the files shown.

Directory tree
The directory tree shows the directories of the current drive. In the File Manager you have the option of displaying all levels, or specific levels, or one level, of the subdirectories in the directory tree.

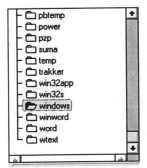

Figure B-11 Directory tree

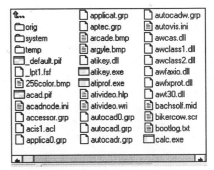

Figure B-12 Contents pane

Contents pane
All the files and subdirectories in the current directory are displayed in the contents pane. You can customize the information displayed in the contents pane depending on your requirement. This will be explained in detail later on.

Status bar
If you select a file in the contents pane, the status bar will display the space occupied by the file and the date and time of the latest update. If you select a directory in the directory tree then the status bar will display the amount of free space in the current drive, total capacity of the drive and the total number of files in the directory and the space occupied by the files.

Directories read: 0	Total 305 file(s) (12.0MB)

Figure B-13 Status bar

Changing drives
You can change from one drive to another using any of the following methods:

1. Select the drive icon you want to switch to.
2. Click on the down arrow button of the drives pop-up list and select the desired drive from the list of available drives.
3. Select the Drive... option in the Disk pull-down menu. Select Drive window is displayed. Select the desired drive from the list of available drives.
4. The shortcut method for changing drives is pressing the Ctrl+X keys simultaneously. X is the letter of the drive you want to switch to. For example, you can switch to C drive by pressing Ctrl+C keys simultaneously.

Changing Directories

By default, the Windows directory is selected and the files and subdirectories in this directory are displayed on the right side of the window (contents pane). The left side of the window (directory tree) displays all the directories in the current drive. The current directory (Windows in our case) is highlighted in the directory tree. You can change directories by selecting the desired directory from the directory tree. Selection can be carried out by clicking on the desired directory or by navigating to the directory with the Up or Down arrow keys.

Expanding Directories

Files are stored in directories. Directories can also have directories embedded in them. A directory embedded in another directory is called a subdirectory. In the File Manager window, directories and subdirectories are displayed as icons that resemble folders. In case a directory contains one or more than one directories, its icon might contain a plus sign. If there are no plus signs with your directory icons, select the Indicate Expandable Branches option from the Tree pull-down menu.

Expanding a Directory

If you want to expand a directory so that its subdirectories are displayed, double click on that directory's icon, or move the selection frame to the desired directory and press Enter key.
If you want all the subdirectories (including subdirectories within subdirectories) to be displayed, select Expand Branch option from Tree pull-down menu, or press the asterisk (*) key.
To expand all directories on the current drive, select the Expand All option from the Tree pull-down menu, or press Ctrl+* keys.

Collapsing a Directory

If you want to collapse a directory so that its subdirectories are not displayed, double click on that directory's icon, or move the selection frame to the desired directory and press the minus sign (-) key.

Copying Files

Open the directory window that displays the files and directories you want to copy. Now open another directory window that displays the directory to which you want to copy the desired files and directories. You can open two directory windows simultaneously by double clicking on the drive directory or by selecting the New Window option from the Window pull-down menu. Make sure that portions of both the windows are visible. The next step is to select the files and directories you want to copy. Press the Ctrl key and then drag the selected files and directories to the other window. The File Manager will ask you to confirm the copy operation. Select Yes. For example, if you want to copy cylinsph.dwg from WC15 directory (which is a subdirectory of WTEXT directory in C drive) to BHAWANI directory in C drive only, select WTEXT directory and then the WC15 directory. Open another directory window and open BHAWANI directory. Now click on the cylinsph filename in the first directory window and while keeping the Ctrl key pressed, drag the file to the second directory.

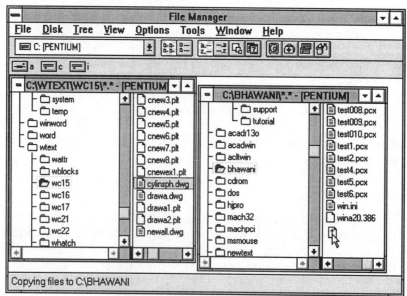

Figure B-14 Copying a file

The File Manager will ask you to confirm the copy operation. Select Yes. Another copying method is to select the files and directories you want to copy and then selecting the Copy option from the File pull-down menu. You can also use the F8 hotkey to perform the copying operation. File Manager will display Copy dialogue box. Enter the pathname of the directory to directory to which you want the selected files and directories copied, and then click on the OK button.

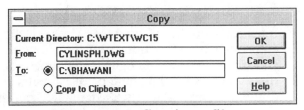

Figure B-15 Copying a file

Moving Files and Directories

Open the directory window that displays the files and directories you want to move. Now open another directory window that displays the directory to which you want to move the desired files and directories. Portions of both the windows should be visible. Now select the files and directories you want to move. Drag the selected files and directories to the other window. The File Manager will ask you to confirm the move operation. Select Yes.

Another method for copying is by selecting the files and directories you want to move and then selecting the Move option from the File pull-down menu. You can also use the F7 hotkey to perform the copying operation. File Manager will display the Move dialogue box. Enter the pathname of the directory to which you want the selected files and directories moved, and then click on the OK button.

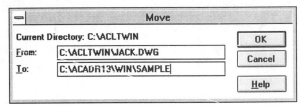

Figure B-16 Moving a file

Closing a Directory Window

To close a directory window, double click on the window's Control menu box. The same effect can be achieved by selecting the Close option from the window's Control menu, or by pressing Ctrl+F4 keys, or by pressing Alt+Hyphen, C.

Minimizing a Directory Window

A directory window can be minimized by clicking on the minimizing button (downward-pointing triangle) in the top right side of the window. After minimizing the window, it is replaced by an icon. You could perform the same action by pressing Alt+Hyphen, N.

Restoring a Minimized Directory Window

A minimized directory window can be restored by double clicking on the icon. Another way to do so is by pressing Alt+Hyphen, R.

Maximizing a Directory Window

A directory window can be maximized by clicking on the maximizing button (upward-pointing triangle) in the top right side of the window. You could also press Alt+Hyphen, X. After maximizing the window, it is enlarged to the fullest possible size.

Restoring a Maximized Directory Window

A maximized directory window can be restored by pressing Alt+Hyphen, R.

Creating a directory

You can create a directory by selecting the Create Directory option from the File pull-down menu. Create Dialogue dialogue box is displayed. Enter the name of the directory in the dialogue box and pick the OK button. A directory having the specified name is created. For example, to create CADBOOK directory enter CADBOOK in Create Dialogue dialogue box.

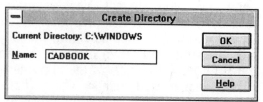

Figure B-17 Creating a directory

Deleting a File or Directory

Select the file or directory you want to delete. Select the Delete option from the File pull-down menu (or press the Delete key). The Delete dialogue box is displayed. Select the OK button. The File Manager will ask you to confirm the delete operation. Select Yes. For example, if you want to delete drawing file MECHPART.DWG, select the directory

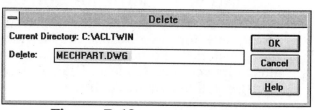

Figure B-18 Deleting a file

containing this file and then select the filename. Press the Delete key. The Delete dialogue box is displayed. Select OK button. Next, select Yes when File Manager asks you to confirm the Delete operation.

Renaming a File or Directory

Select the file or directory you want to rename. Select the Rename option from the File pull-down menu. The Rename dialogue box is displayed. The From edit box contains the current name of the file or the directory. Enter the new name in the To edit box and then select the OK button. Figure B-19 shows how to rename a drawing file from COLUMN.DWG to PILLAR.DWG.

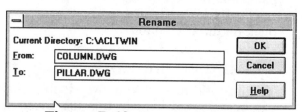

Figure B-19 Renaming a file

Running Applications

There are methods provided by File Manager to run an application. In case the name of the application is displayed in the contents pane, double click on the application icon. If the name of the application you want to run does not appear in the directory window, then select the Run option from the File pull-down menu. The Run dialogue box is displayed. Enter the path and the name of the application you want to run.

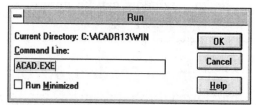

Figure B-20 Running AutoCAD from File Manager

Pick the OK button. For example, you can run AutoCAD for windows from File Manager by selecting the ACAD.EXE file and then select the Run option from the File pull-down menu. Pick the OK button. AutoCAD starts getting loaded.

Controlling the File Information Displayed

By default, only filenames and extensions are displayed in the contents pane. The File Manager provides options in the View pull-down menu to display other file characteristics. By selecting All File Details option from the View pull-down menu, each file's name, extension, size, date and time, and file attributes are displayed. Figure B-21 shows the directory window in which all the file details of the ACADR13 directory are shown.

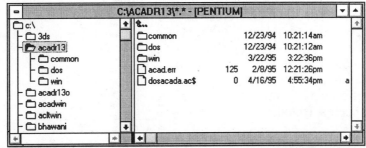

Figure B-21 Directory window after selecting All File Details option

You can customize the Directory Window information to your requirement by selecting the Partial Details option from the View pull-down menu. The Partial Details dialogue box is displayed. In this dialogue box, select the file details you want to be displayed by the Directory Window. Select the OK button.

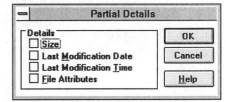

Figure B-22 Partial Details dialogue box

Customizing the Order of the Directory Window Contents

Specifying the order in which the files are displayed in the Directory Window depends on the option selected in the View pull-down menu. For example, you can sort the files by alphabetical order by selecting the Sort by Name option, or you can sort the files by size by selecting the Sort by Size option.

Specifying the Files Types to be Displayed

When you start the File Manager, all types of files are displayed in the Directory Window. However, if you want to display files of some specific type, it can be accomplished by selecting the By File Type option in the View pull-down menu. Once this option is selected, The By File Type dialogue box is displayed. Enter the wildcard pattern that agrees with the files you want to display. After this, select the check boxes of the file types you want to be displayed. Select the OK button. You will notice that only the files of the file types specified in the By File Type dialogue box are displayed in the Directory Window.

For example, if you want only drawing files (extension .dwg) to be displayed in the contents pane, enter *.dwg in the Name edit box of the By File Type dialogue box.

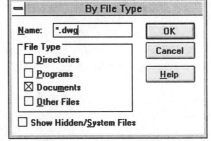

Figure B-23 By File Type dialogue box

Selection of Multiple Files

It is possible to select more than one file in the Directory Window. We can classify multiple files into three classes:

Consecutive Files

To select files arranged in consecutive fashion (one after another), select the first filename and then hold down the Shift key and use the arrow keys to select (highlight) the rest of the files or after selecting the first filename, click on the last filename. In Figure B-24, four consecutive files (rena.dwg, renb.dwg, renc.dwg and rend.dwg) have been selected.

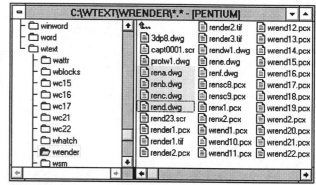

Figure B-24 Selecting consecutive files

Nonconsecutive Files

To select files arranged in nonconsecutive fashion, hold the Ctrl key and click on the names of the files you want to select. In Figure B-25, two nonconsecutive files (wrend1.pcx and wrend2.pcx) have been selected.

Another method of selecting nonconsecutive files is as follows:

Navigate the selection frame (highlight bar) to the first file name and then press Shift+F8 keys. You will notice that the

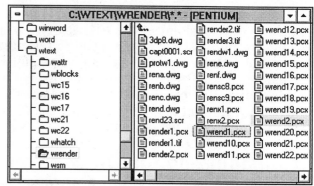

Figure B-25 Selecting nonconsecutive files

selection frame starts blinking. Now use the arrow keys and Spacebar to select the other files. After the selection is over press the Shift+F8 keys.

All Files

All the files in the contents pane can be selected by clicking on a file or moving the selection frame to the contents pane and then pressing the Ctrl+/ keys.

Selecting or Deselecting Files Corresponding to a Pattern

In order to select files corresponding to a pattern, choose Select Files from the Files pull-down menu. The Select Files dialogue box will be displayed. Enter the wildcard pattern matching to the files you want to select. Click on the Select button. In Figure B-26, the acad.ini file will be the selected file.

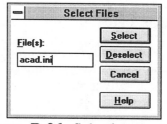

Figure B-26 Selecting acad.ini file

To deselect files corresponding to a pattern, click on the Deselect button. Sometimes after making a selection, you may want to cancel the selection. This can be done by holding down the Ctrl key and clicking on the file to deselect it. Another way is to move the selection frame to the contents pane and then press the Shift+F8 keys. You will notice that the selection frame starts blinking. Now use the arrow keys to move the selection frame to the filename of the file you want to deselect and then press the Spacebar. After this press the Shift+F8 keys.

If you want to cancel all file selections, click on a file in the contents pane, or move the selection frame to the contents pane and then press Ctrl+\.

Appendix C

AutoCAD Linetypes

The following are the linetypes that are defined in the ACAD.LIN file. This file is located in the common\support directory.

ISO02W100	ACAD_ISO03W100
ACAD_ISO04W100	ACAD_ISO05W100
ACAD_ISO06W100	ACAD_ISO07W100
ACAD_ISO08W100	ACAD_ISO09W100

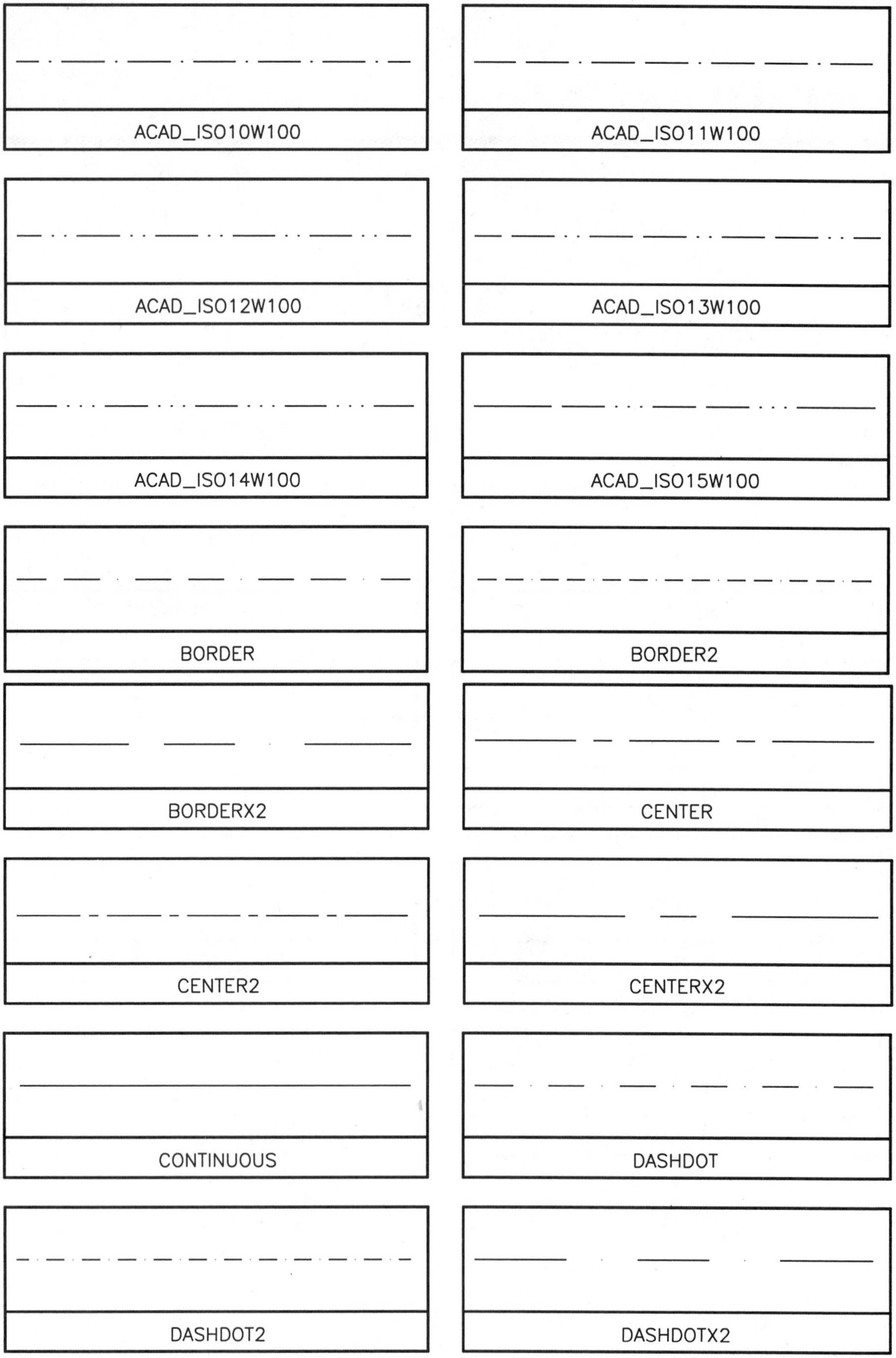

ACAD_ISO10W100

ACAD_ISO11W100

ACAD_ISO12W100

ACAD_ISO13W100

ACAD_ISO14W100

ACAD_ISO15W100

BORDER

BORDER2

BORDERX2

CENTER

CENTER2

CENTERX2

CONTINUOUS

DASHDOT

DASHDOT2

DASHDOTX2

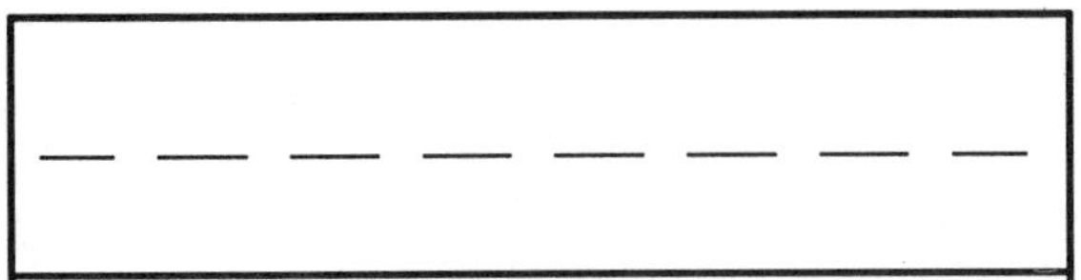

DASHED

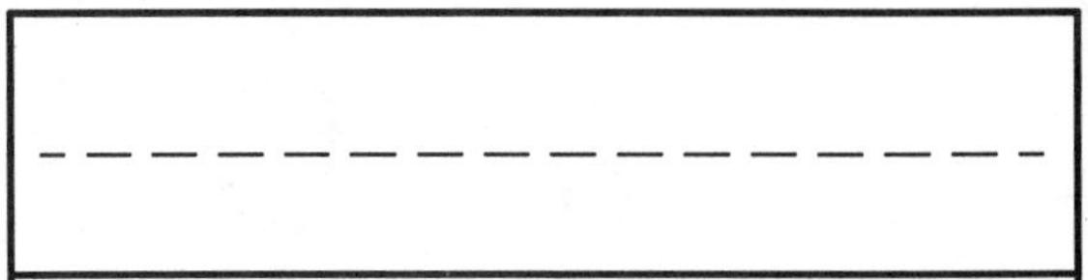

DASHED2

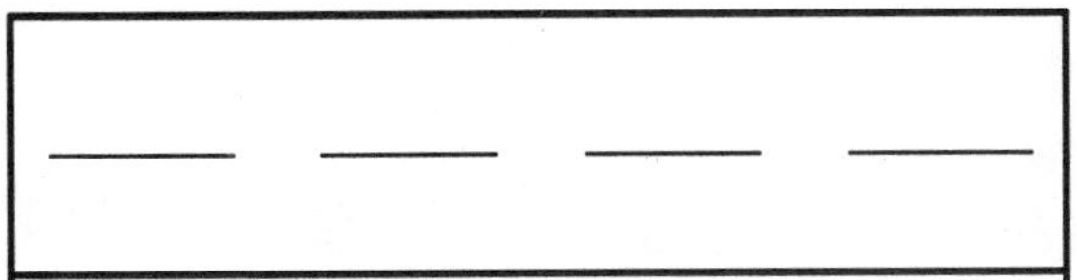

DASHEDX2

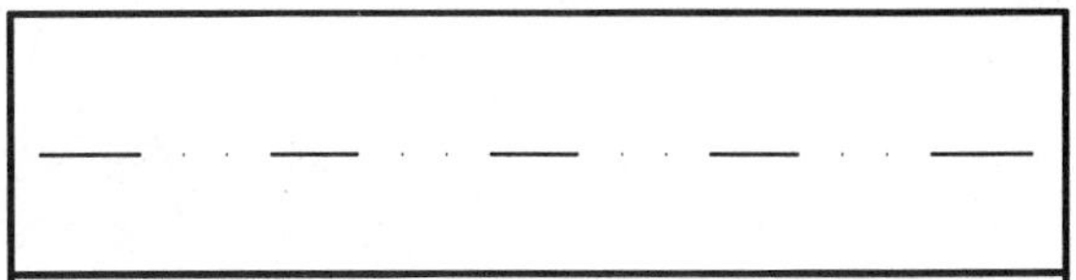

DIVIDE

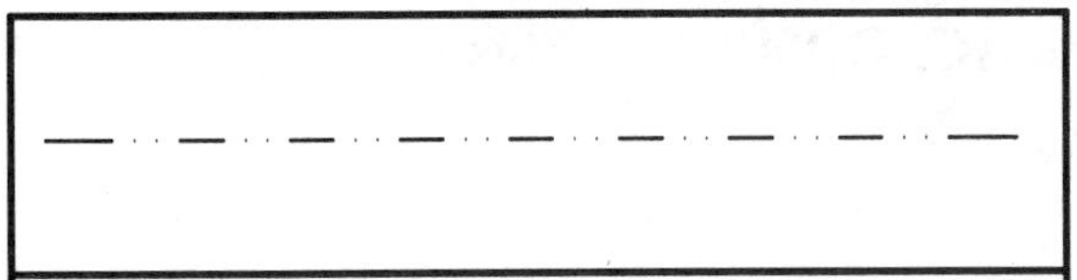

DIVIDE2

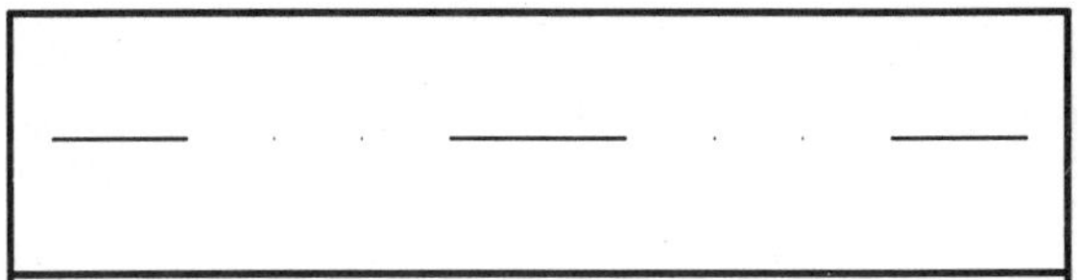

DIVIDEX2

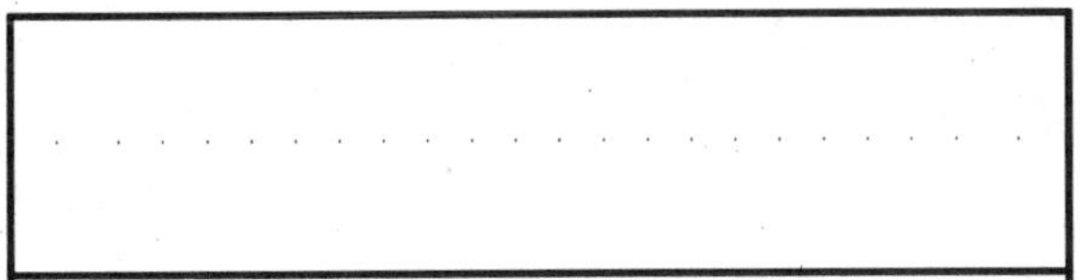

DOT

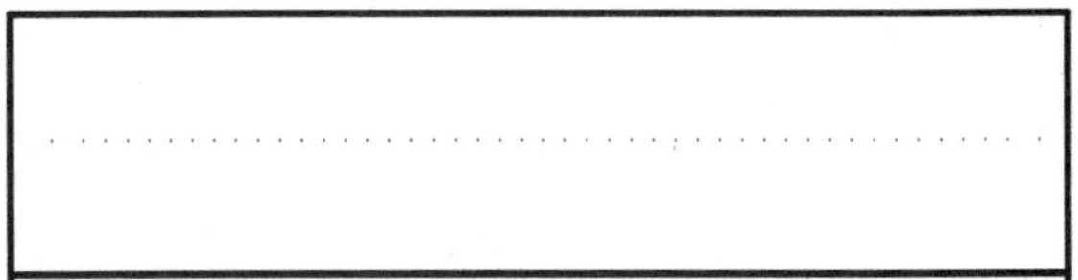

DOT2

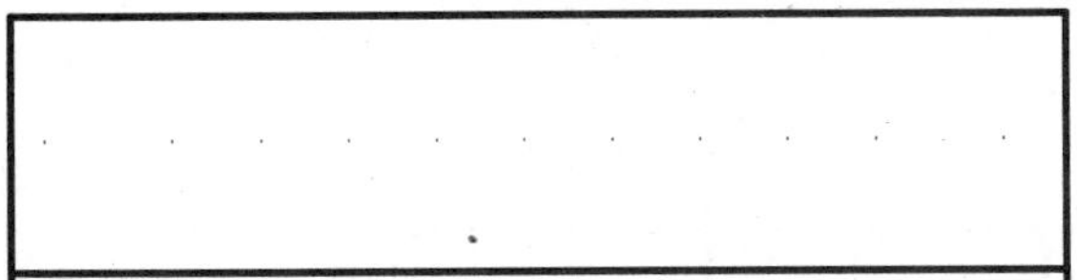

DOTX2

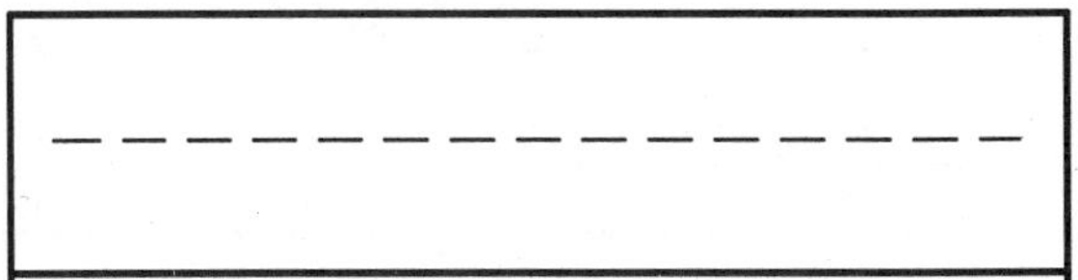

HIDDEN

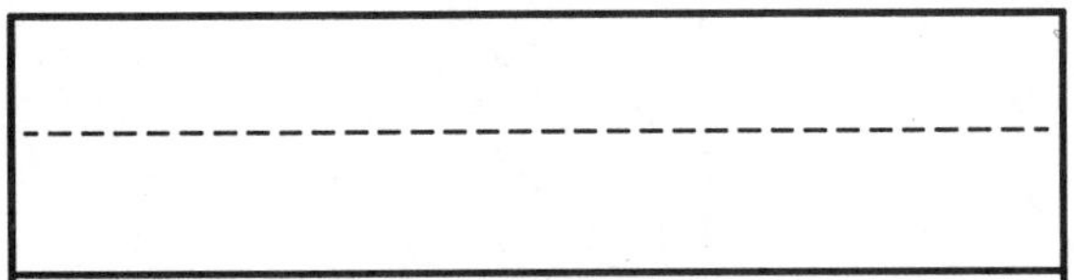

HIDDEN2

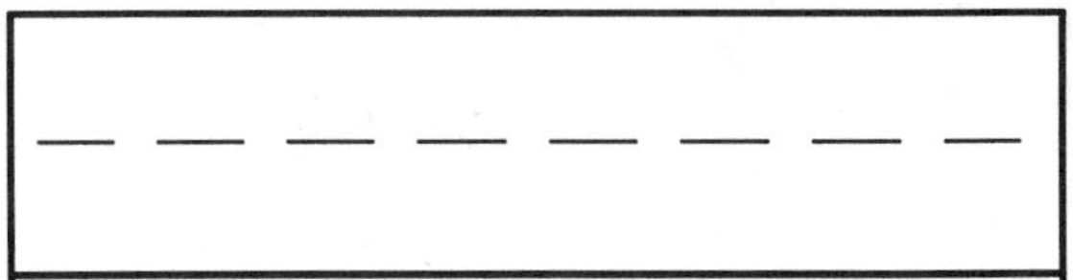

HIDDENX2

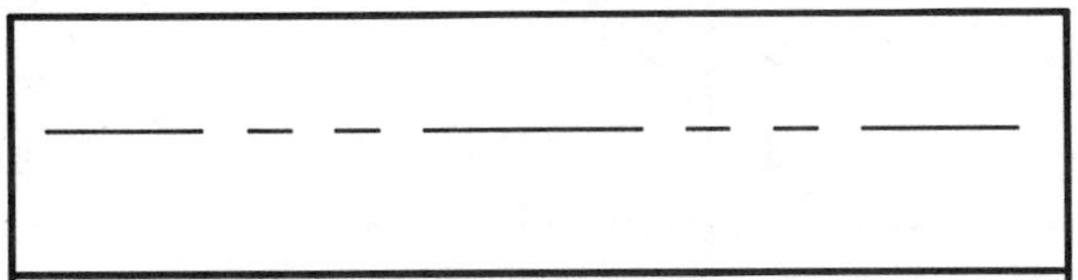

PHANTOM

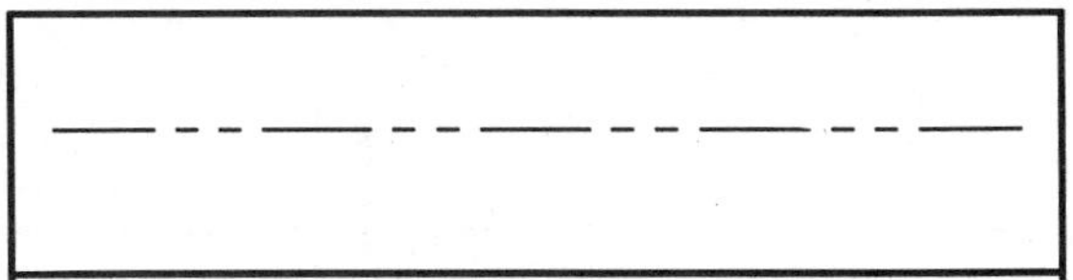

PHANTOM2

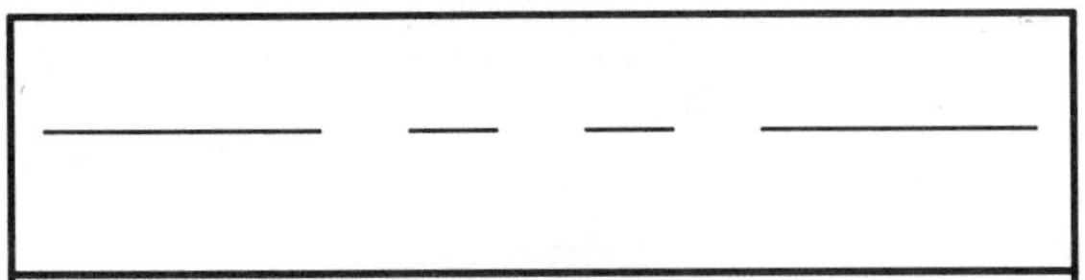

PHANTOMX2

Appendix D

AutoCAD Hatch Patterns

Following are the hatch patterns that are defined in the ACAD.PAT file. This file is located in the common\support directory.

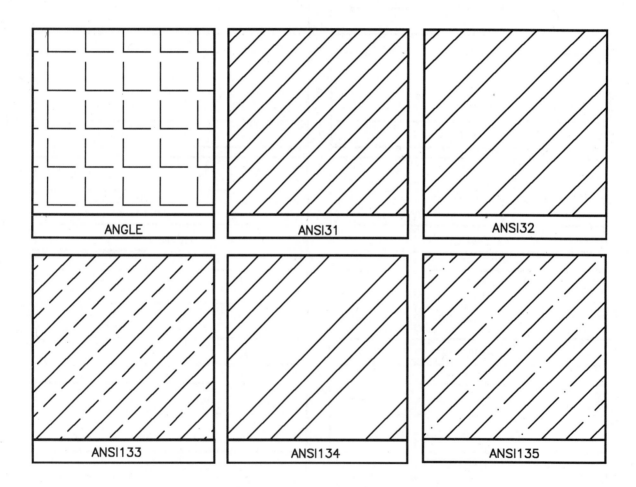

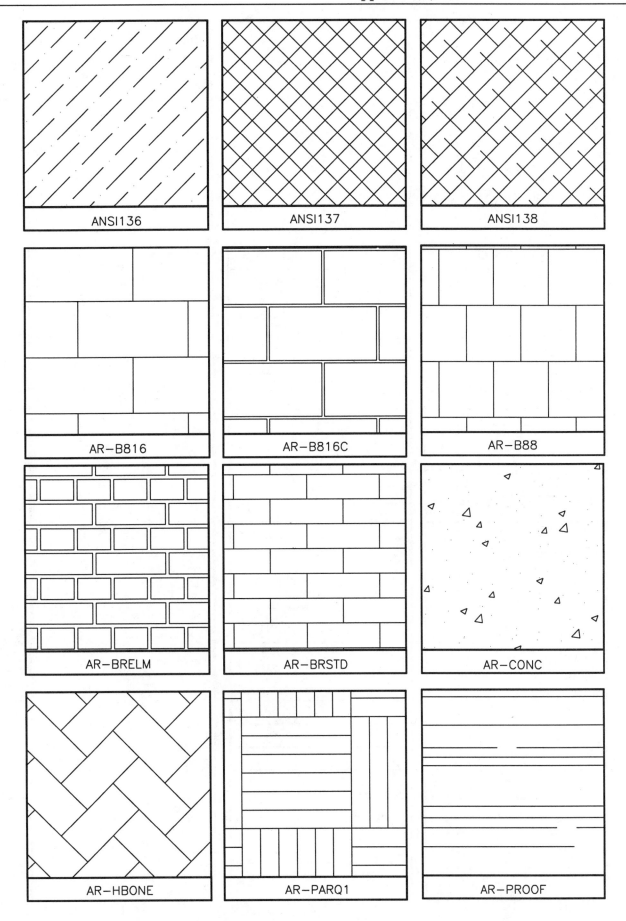

ANSI136 ANSI137 ANSI138

AR-B816 AR-B816C AR-B88

AR-BRELM AR-BRSTD AR-CONC

AR-HBONE AR-PARQ1 AR-PROOF

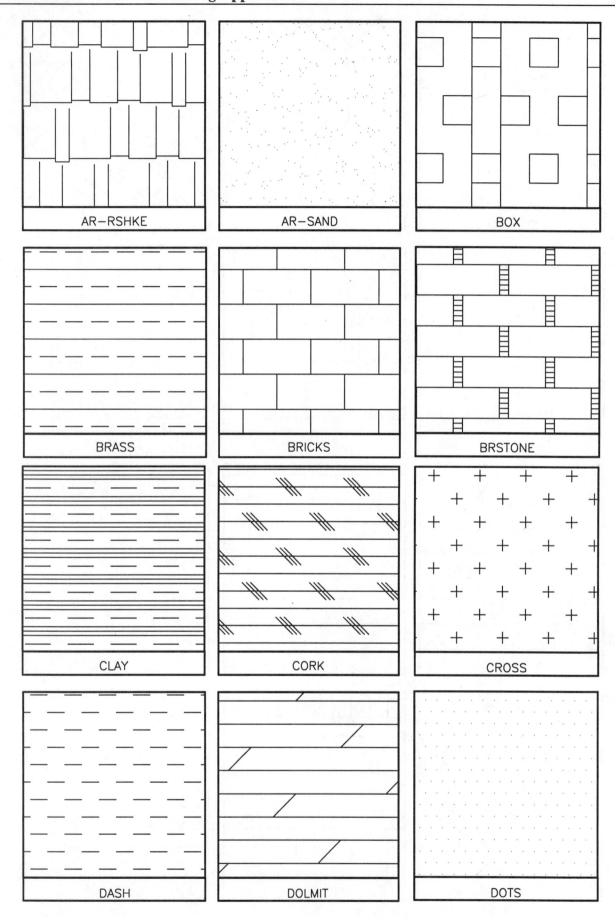

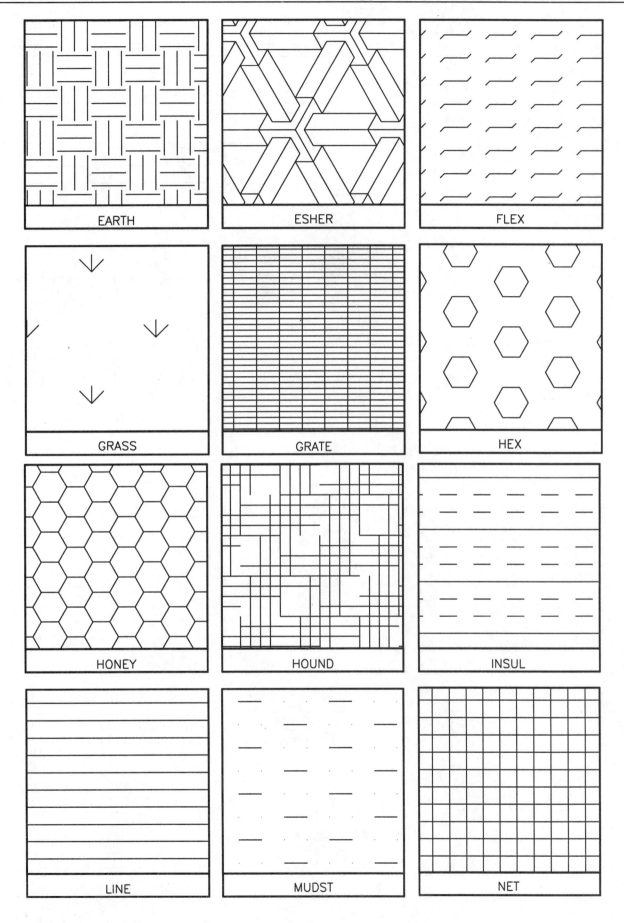

EARTH

ESHER

FLEX

GRASS

GRATE

HEX

HONEY

HOUND

INSUL

LINE

MUDST

NET

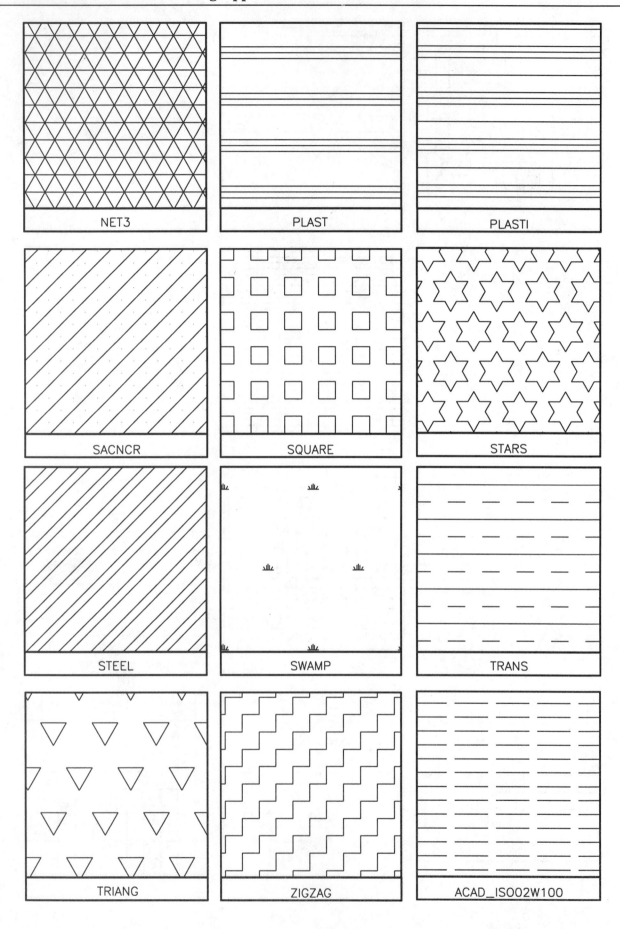

ACAD_ISO03W100	ACAD_ISO04W100	ACAD_ISO05W100
ACAD_ISO06W100	ACAD_ISO06W100	ACAD_ISO08W100
ACAD_ISO09W100	ACAD_ISO10W100	ACAD_ISO11W100
ACAD_ISO12W100	ACAD_ISO13W100	ACAD_ISO14W100

Appendix **E**

AutoCAD Text Fonts

TEXT FONTS

Following are the Standard, PostScript, and TrueType text fonts supported by AutoCAD.

Standard and PostScript Fonts

ABCDEFGHIJKLMN□PQRS
TUVWXYZ
123456789

This is a sample text
to demonstrate the
effect of M□N□TXT
Text font

ABCDEFGHIJKLMNOPQRS
TUVWXYZ
123456789

This is a sample text to
demonstrate the effect of
ROMANS Text font

ABCDEFGHIJKLMN□PQRS
TUVWXYZ
123456789

This is a sample text
to demonstrate the
effect of TXT Text
font

ABCDEFGHIJKLMNOPQRS
TUVWXYZ
123456789

This is a sample text to
demonstrate the effect of
ROMAND Text font

ABCDEFGHIJKLMNOPQRS
TUVWXYZ
123456789

This is a sample text to
demonstrate the effect
of ROMANC Text font

ABCDEFGHIJKLMNOPQRS
TUVWXYZ
123456789

This is a sample text to
demonstrate the effect
of ITALICT Text font

ABCDEFGHIJKLMNOPQRS
TUVWXYZ
123456789

This is a sample text to
demonstrate the effect
of ROMANT Text font

ABCDEFGHIJKLMNOP2RS
TUVWXYZ
123456789

This is a sample text to
demonstrate the effect of
SCRIPTC Text font

ABCDEFGHIJKLMNOPQRS
TUVWXYZ
123456789

This is a sample text
to demonstrate the effect
of ITALIC Text font

ABCDEFGHIJKLMNOP2RS
TUVWXYZ
123456789

This is a sample text to
demonstrate the effect of
SCRIPTS Text font

ABCDEFGHIJKLMNOPQRS
TUVWXYZ
123456789

This is a sample text to
demonstrate the effect
of ITALICC Text font

𝕬𝕭𝕮𝕯𝕰𝕱𝕲𝕳𝕴𝕵𝕶𝕷𝕸𝕹𝕺𝕻𝕼𝕽𝕾
𝕿𝖀𝖁𝖂𝖃𝖄𝖅
123456789

This is a sample text to
demonstrate the effect of
GOTHICE Text font

ABCDEFGHIJKLMNOP
QRSTUVWXYZ
123456789

This is a sample text to
demonstrate the effect of
GOTHICEG Text font

ABCDEFGHIJKLMNOP
QRSTUVWXYZ
123456789

This is a sample text to
demonstrate the effect of
GOUHICI Uext font

АБВГДЕЖЗИЙКЛМНОПРСТ
УФХЦЧШЩ
123456789

Узит ит а тамплд удчу
уо гдмонтусауд узд
деедву ое ВШСИЛЛИВ
Удчу еону

АБЧДЕФГХИЩКЛМНОПЦРС
ТУВШЖЙЗ
123456789

Тхис ис а сампле тежт
то демонстрате тхе
еффечт оф ЧЙРИЛТЛЧ
Тежт фонт

123456789

123456789

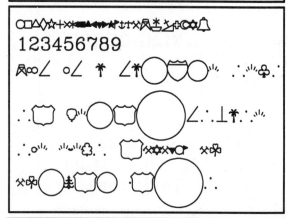

123456789

123456789

123456789

ABCDEFGHIJKLMNOPQRSTUVWXYZ
123456789

This is a sample text to
demonstrate the effect of
ISOCP2 Text font

ABCDEFGHIJKLMNOPQR
STUVWXYZ
123456789

This is a sample text to
demonstrate the effect
of COMPLEX Text font

ABCDEFGHIJKLMNOPQRSTUVWXYZ
123456789

This is a sample text to
demonstrate the effect of ISOCP3
Text font

ABCDEFGHIJKLMNOPQRS
TUVWXYZ
123456789

This is a sample text to
demonstrate the effect of
SIMPLEX Text font

A B C D E F G H I J K L M N O P Q R
S T U V W X Y Z
1 2 3 4 5 6 7 8 9

T h i s   i s   a   s a m p l e
t e x t   t o   d e m o n s t r a t e
t h e   e f f e c t   o f   I S O C T
T e x t   f i l e

ABCDEFGHIJKLMNOPQRSTUVWXYZ
123456789

This is a sample text to
demonstrate the effect of
ISOCP Text font

A B C D E F G H I J K L M N O P Q R S
T U V W X Y Z
1 2 3 4 5 6 7 8 9

T h i s   i s   a   s a m p l e
t e x t   t o   d e m o n s t r a t e
t h e   e f f e c t   o f   I S O C T 2
T e x t   f o n t

ABCDEFGHIJKLMNOPQRS
TUVWXYZ
123456789

This is a sample
text to demonstrate
the effect of ISOCT3
Text font

ABCDEFGHIJKLMNOPQRS
TUVWXYZ
123456789

This is a sample text to demonstrate
the effect of EURO PostScript font

ABCDEFGHIJKLMNOPQRSTUVWXYZ
123456789

This is a samplt text to demonstrate
the effect of CIBT PostScript font

ABCDEFGHIJKLMNOPQRS
TUVWXYZ
123456789

This is a sample text to demonstrate
the effect of PAR PostScript font

ABCDEFGHIJKLMNOPQR
STUVWXYZ
123456789

This is a sample text to demonstrate
the effect of COBT PostScript
font

ABCDEFGHIJKLMNOPQRS
TUVWXYZ
123456789

This is a sample text to demonstrate
the effect of SUF PostScript font

ABCDEFGHIJKLMNOPQRS
TUVWXYZ
123456789

This is a sample text to demonstrate
the effect of EUR PostScript font

ABCDEFGHIJKLMNOPQRS
TUVWXYZ
123456789

This is a sample text to demonstrate
the effect of ROM PostScript font

ABCDEFGHIJKLMNOPQRS
TUVWXYZ
123456789

This is a sample text to
demonstrate the effect of
ROMB PostScript font

ABCDEFGHIJKLMNOPQRS
TUVWXYZ
123456789

This is a sample text to
demonstrate the effect of
SASBO PostScript font

ABCDEFGHIJKLMNOPQRS
TUVWXYZ
123456789

This is a sample text to demonstrate
the effect of ROMI PostScript font

ABCDEFGHIJKLMNOPQRS
TUVWXYZ
123456789

THIS IS A SAMPLE TEXT TO
DEMONSTRATE THE EFFECT OF
TE PostScript FONT

ABCDEFGHIJKLMNOPQRS
TUVWXYZ
123456789

This is a sample text to
demonstrate the effect of SAS
PostScript font

ABCDEFGHIJKLMNOPQRS
TUVWXYZ
123456789

THIS IS A SAMPLE TEXT TO
DEMONSTRATE THE EFFECT OF
TEL PostScript FONT

ABCDEFGHIJKLMNOPQRS
TUVWXYZ
123456789

This is a sample text to
demonstrate the effect of SASO
PostScript font

ABCDEFGHIJKLMNOPQRS
TUVWXYZ
123456789

THIS IS A SAMPLE TEXT TO
DEMONSTRATE THE EFFECT OF
TEB PostScript FONT

TrueType Fonts

ABCDEFGHIJKLMNOPQRS
TUVWXYZ
123456789

This is a sample text to
demonstrate the effect of SWISS
True Type font

ABCDEFGHIJKLMNOPQRS
TUVWXYZ
123456789

This is a sample text to
demonstrate the effect of
SWISSB True Type font

ABCDEFGHIJKLMNOPQRS
TUVWXYZ
123456789

This is a sample text to demonstrate
the effect of SWISSL True Type font

ABCDEFGHIJKLMNOPQRS
TUVWXYZ
123456789

This is a sample text to
demonstrate the effect of
SWISSBI True Type font

ABCDEFGHIJKLMNOPQRS
TUVWXYZ
123456789

This is a sample text to demonstrate
the effect of SWISSLI True Type font

ABCDEFGHIJKLMNOPQRS
TUVWXYZ
123456789

This is a sample text to
demonstrate the effect of
SWISSK True Type font

ABCDEFGHIJKLMNOPQRS
TUVWXYZ
123456789

This is a sample text to
demonstrate the effect of
SWISSI True Type font

ABCDEFGHIJKLMNOPQRS
TUVWXYZ
123456789

This is a sample text to
demonstrate the effect of
SWISSKI True Type font

ABCDEFGHIJKLMNOPQRSTUVWXYZ
123456789

This is a sample text to demonstrate
the effect of SWISSC True Type font

ABCDEFGHIJKLMNOPQRSTUVWXYZ
123456789

This is a sample text to demonstrate the
effect of SWISSCB True Type font

ABCDEFGHIJKLMNOPQRSTUVWXYZ
123456789

This is a sample text to demonstrate the
effect of SWISSCL True Type font

ABCDEFGHIJKLMNOPQRSTUVWXYZ
123456789

This is a sample text to demonstrate
the effect of SWISSCBI True Type
font

ABCDEFGHIJKLMNOPQRSTUVWXYZ
123456789

This is a sample text to demonstrate the
effect of SWISSCLI True Type font

ABCDEFGHIJKLMNOPQRSTUVWXYZ
123456789

This is a sample text to demonstrate
the effect of SWISSCK True Type font

ABCDEFGHIJKLMNOPQRSTUVWXYZ
123456789

This is a sample text to demonstrate
the effect of SWISSCI True Type font

ABCDEFGHIJKLMNOPQRSTUVWXYZ
123456789

This is a sample text to demonstrate
the effect of SWISSCKI True Type font

ABCDEFGHIJKLMNOPQRS
TUVWXYZ
123456789

This is a sample text to
demonstrate the effect of
SWISSE True Type font

ABCDEFGHIJKLMNOPQRS
TUVWXYZ
123456789

This is a sample text to
demonstrate the effect of
SWISSBO True Type font

ABCDEFGHIJKLMNOPQRS
TUVWXYZ
123456789

This is a sample text to
demonstrate the effect of
SWISSEL True Type font

ABCDEFGHIJKLMNOPQRS
TUVWXYZ
123456789

This is a sample text to
demonstrate the effect of
SWISSKO True Type font

ABCDEFGHIJKLMNOPQR
STUVWXYZ
123456789

This is a sample text to
demonstrate the effect of
SWISSEB True Type font

ABCDEFGHIJKLMNOPQRSTUVWXYZ
123456789

This is a sample text to demonstrate
the effect of SWISSCBO True Type
font

ABCDEFGHIJKLMNOP
QRSTUVWXYZ
123456789

This is a sample text
to demonstrate the
effect of SWISSEK
True Type font

ABCDEFGHIJKLMNOPQRS
TUVWXYZ
123456789

This is a sample text to
demonstrate the effect
of MONOS True Type font

ABCDEFGHIJKLMNOPQRS
TUVWXYZ
123456789

This is a sample text to
demonstrate the effect of
MONOSI True Type font

ABCDEFGHIJKLMNOPQR
STUVWXYZ
123456789

This is a sample text to
demonstrate the effect of
DUTCHB True Type font

ABCDEFGHIJKLMNOPQRS
TUVWXYZ
123456789

This is a sample text to
demonstrate the effect
of MONOSB True Type font

ABCDEFGHIJKLMNOPQRS
TUVWXYZ
123456789

This is a sample text to demonstrate
the effect of DUTCHBI True Type
font

ABCDEFGHIJKLMNOPQRS
TUVWXYZ
123456789

This is a sample text to
demonstrate the effect
of MONOSBI True Type font

ABCDEFGHIJKLMNOPQRS
TUVWXYZ
123456789

This is a sample text to
demonstrate the effect of
DUTCHEB True Type font

ABCDEFGHIJKLMNOPQRS
TUVWXYZ
123456789

This is a sample text to demonstrate
the effect of DUTCHI True Type
font

ABCDEFGHI
JKLMNOPQR
STUVWXYZ
123456789

THIS IS A SAMPLE TEXT
TO DEMONSTRATE THE
EFFECT OF BGOTHL
TRUE TYPE FONT

ABCDEFGHI
JKLMNOPQR
STUVWXYZ
123456789

THIS IS A SAMPLE TEXT
TO DEMONSTRATE THE
EFFECT OF BGOTHM
TRUE TYPE FONT

ABΨΔEΦΓΗΙΞΚΛΜΝΟΠΘΡΣ
ΤΘΩ6ΧΥΖ
+ − ✕ ÷ = ± ∓ °′

Τηισ ισ α σαμπλε τεχτ το
δεμονστρατε τηε εφφεψτ οφ
ΘΜΑΤΗ Τρθε Τυπε φοντ

ABCDEFGHIJKLMNOPQR
STUVWXYZ
123456789

This is a sample text to demonstrate
the effect of COMPC True Type
font

ABCDEFGHIJKLMNO
PQRSTUVWXYZ
123456789

This is a sample text
to demonstrate the
effect of VINET True
Type font

± °′″∅ + − ✕ ÷ = ± °′″——⸱⸱...
...℞♀♂°
○○○—□○○□□

. % % ⊕ % ⊕ © ⊕©%© @™ ™™ ✕ ™
™‖ ℗™©% ‖ %© ⊕™© © ™© ™% ™
™ ™™ ™ ™© ™ ‖ ™ ′ ′ ○ . ©™ ™
. ÷ ©™ ™ ‖ % ™

Appendix F

Dialogue Boxes

The following are the frequently used dialogue boxes. For a detailed listing of dialogue boxes, see *Customizing AudoCAD for Windows* by Sham Tickoo, published by Autodesk Press.

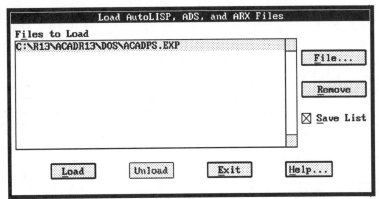

APPLOAD (Load AutoLISP, ADS, and ARX Files)

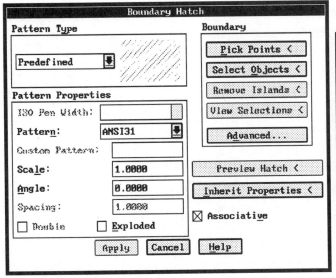

BHATCH (Boundary Hatch)

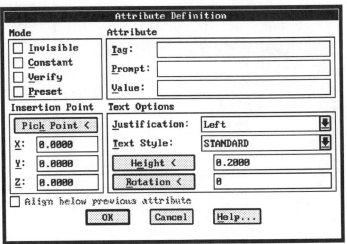

DDATTDEF Attribute Definition

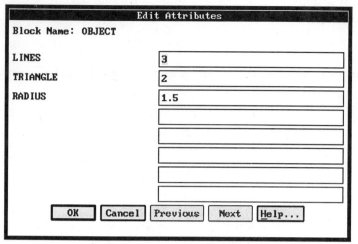

DDATTE Edit Attributes

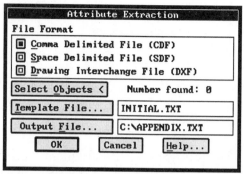

DDATTEXT Attribute Extraction

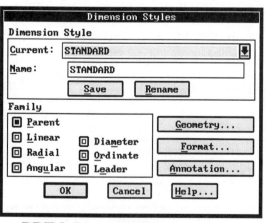

DDCHPROP Change Properties

DDGRIPS Grips

DDIM Dimension Styles

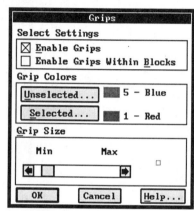

DDIM Geometry

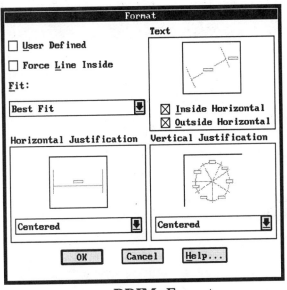

DDIM Format

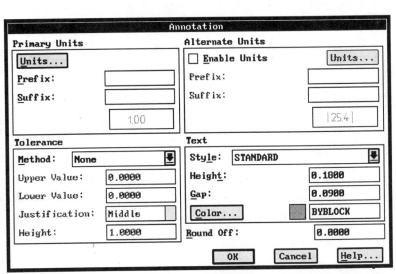

DDIM Annotation

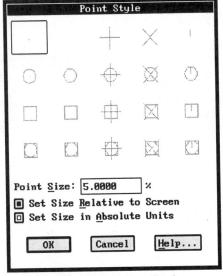

DDINSERT Insert

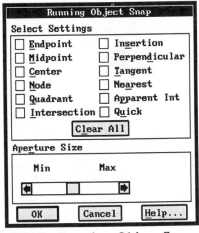

DDOSNAP Running Object Snap

DDPTYPE Point Style

DDLMODES Layer Control

Rename

Named Objects	Items
Block	BORDER
Dimstyle	CEN
Layer	DIM
Ltype	HID
Style	LOCKED
Ucs	OBJ
View	TEXT
Vport	

Old Name:

Rename To:

OK   Cancel   Help...

DDRENAME Rename

Drawing Aids

Modes
- ☐ Ortho
- ☒ Solid Fill
- ☐ Quick Text
- ☒ Blips
- ☒ Highlight
- ☒ Groups

Snap
- ☐ On
- X Spacing 1.0000
- Y Spacing 1.0000
- Snap Angle 0
- X Base 0.0000
- Y Base 0.0000

Grid
- ☐ On
- X Spacing 0.0000
- Y Spacing 0.0000

Isometric Snap/Grid
- ☐ On
- ◉ Left ☐ Top ◉ Right

OK   Cancel   Help...

DDRMODES Drawing Aids

Object Selection Settings

Selection Modes
- ☒ Noun/Verb Selection
- ☐ Use Shift to Add
- ☐ Press and Drag
- ☒ Implied Windowing
- ☒ Object Grouping

Default

Pickbox Size

Min   Max

◀ ▬ ▬ ▬ ▬ ▬ ▶

Object Sort Method...

OK   Cancel   Help...

DDSELECT Object Selection Settings

UCS Orientation

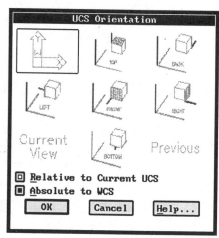

- ◉ Relative to Current UCS
- ◉ Absolute to WCS

OK   Cancel   Help...

DDUCSP UCS Orientation

Viewpoint Presets

Set Viewing Angles
- ◉ Absolute to WCS ◉ Relative to UCS

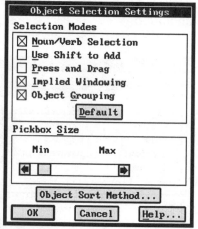

From: X Axis: 270.0   XY Plane: 90.0

Set to Plan View

OK   Cancel   Help...

DDVPOINT Viewpoint Presets

File Utilities

List files...   Copy file...   Rename file...

Delete file...   Unlock file...   Help...

Exit

FILES File Utilities

Object Grouping

Group Name   Selectable
DRAWING   Yes

Group Identification

Group Name: [   ]
Description: [   ]
[Find Name <] [Highlight <] [ ] Include Unnamed

Create Group
[New <] [X] Selectable [ ] Unnamed

Change Group
[Remove <] [Add <] [Rename] [Re-order...]
[Description] [Explode] [Selectable]

[OK] [Cancel] [Help...]

GROUP Object Grouping

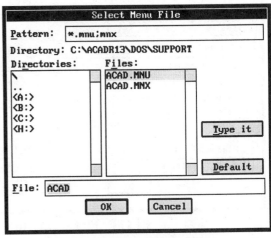

MENU Select Menu File

Multiline Edit Tools

[OK] [Cancel] [Help...]

MLEDIT Multiline Edit Tools

Multiline Styles

Multiline Style
Current: [STANDARD   ▼]
Name: [STANDARD   ]
Description: [   ]
[Load...] [Save...] [Add] [Rename]

[Element Properties ...]
[Multiline Properties ...]

[OK] [Cancel] [Help...]

MLSTYLE Multiline Styles

Create Slide File

Pattern: [*.sld   ]
Directory: C:\
Directories: Files:
ACADR13   DRAWING
APPENDIX   LINES
ATIVIDEO
BASIC
BAT
BHAWANI   [Type it]
DOS
DRIVERS
MACHPCI
MOUSE   [Default]
File: [   ]
[OK] [Cancel]

MSLIDE Create Slide File

MText Properties

Contents
Text Style: [STANDARD   ▼]
Text Height: [0.2000   ]
Direction: [Left to Right   ▼]

Object
Attachment: [TopLeft   ▼]
Width: [0.6086   ]
Rotation: [0   ]

[OK] [Cancel] [Help...]

MTPROP MText Properties

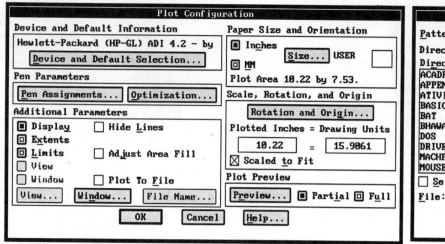

PLOT Plot Configuration

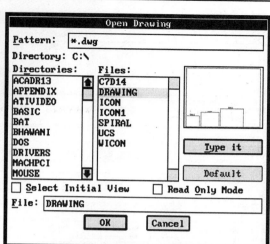

OPEN Open Drawing

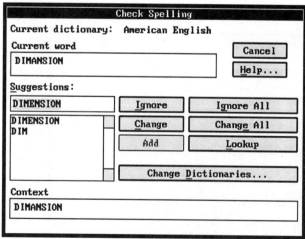

RENDER Render

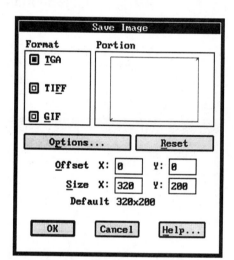

SAVEIMG Save Image

SPELL Check Spelling

Appendix G

Pull-down Menus

The following are the frequently used pull-down menus. For a detailed listing of pull-down menus and cascading menus, see *Customizing AudoCAD for Windows* by Sham Tickoo, published by Autodesk Press.

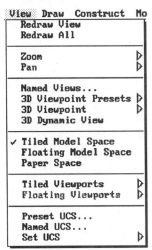

```
File  Assist  View  Dra
  New...
  Open...
  Save
  Save As...

  Print...

  External Reference  ▷
  Bind                ▷

  Import              ▷
  Export              ▷

  Management          ▷

  Exit
```
FILE Pull-down menus

```
View  Draw  Construct  Mo
  Redraw View
  Redraw All

  Zoom                     ▷
  Pan                      ▷

  Named Views...
  3D Viewpoint Presets     ▷
  3D Viewpoint             ▷
  3D Dynamic View

✓ Tiled Model Space
  Floating Model Space
  Paper Space

  Tiled Viewports          ▷
  Floating Viewports       ▷

  Preset UCS...
  Named UCS...
  Set UCS                  ▷
```
View Pull-down menus

```
Assist  View  Draw  Con
  Undo
  Redo

  Object Snap       ▷
  Point Filters     ▷

  Snap
  Grid
  Ortho

  Select Objects    ▷
  Selection Filters...
  Group Objects...
✓ Group Selection

  Inquiry           ▷

  Cancel
```
Assist Pull-down menus

```
Draw  Construct  Mod
  Line
  Construction Line
  Ray
  Sketch

  Polyline
  3D Polyline
  Multiline

  Spline
  Arc               ▷
  Circle            ▷
  Ellipse           ▷

  Polygon           ▷

  Point             ▷
  Insert            ▷

  Surfaces          ▷
  Solids            ▷

  Hatch             ▷

  Text              ▷
  Dimensioning      ▷
```
Draw Pull-down menus

```
Construct Modi
     Copy
     Offset
     Mirror
     Array          ▷

     Chamfer
     Fillet

     Region
     Boundary

     Union
     Subtract
     Intersection

     Block
     Attribute...

     3D Array       ▷
     3D Mirror
     3D Rotate
```

Construct Pull-down menus

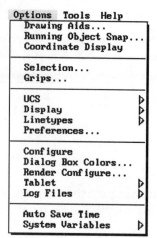

Options Pull-down menus

```
Modify Data Option
     Properties...

     Move
     Rotate
     Align

     Stretch
     Scale
     Lengthen
     Point

     Trim
     Extend
     Break          ▷

     Edit Polyline
     Edit Multiline...
     Edit Spline
     Edit Text...
     Edit Hatch...
     Attribute      ▷
     Explode

     Erase
     Oops!
```

Modify Pull-down menus

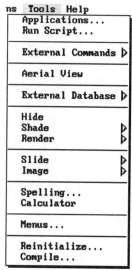

Tools Pull-down menus

```
Data Options Tools Help
     Object Creation...

     Layers...
     Viewport Layer Controls ▷

     Color
     Linetype...
     Multiline Style...
     Text Style
     Dimension Style...
     Shape File...

     Units...
     Drawing Limits
     Time
     Status

     Rename...
     Purge          ▷
```

Data Pull-down menus

```
a Options Tools Help
     Help...

     Search for Help On...
     How to Use Help
     What's New in Release 13...

     About AutoCAD...
```

Help Pull-down menu

Appendix H

Toolbars

The following are the frequently used toolbars.

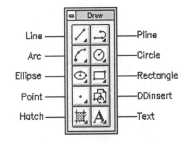

Figure H-1 Draw toolbar

Figure H-2 Miscellaneous toolbar

Figure H-3 Select Objects toolbar

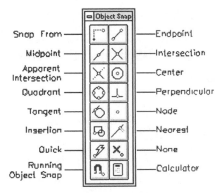

Figure H-4 Object Snap toolbar

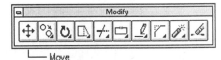

Figure H-5 Modify toolbar

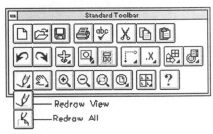

Figure H-6 Standard toolbar

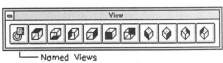

Figure H-7 View toolbar

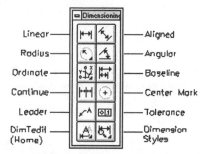

Figure H-8 Dimensioning toolbar

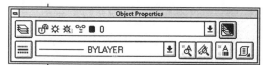

Figure H-9 Object Properties toolbar

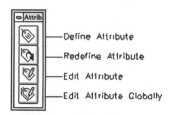

Figure H-10 Attribute toolbar

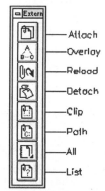

Figure H-11 External Reference toolbar

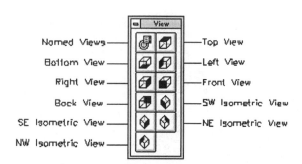

Figure H-12 View toolbar

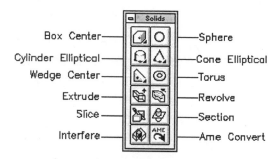

Figure H-13 Solids toolbar

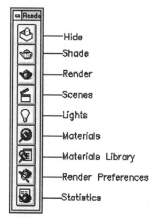

Figure H-14 Render toolbar

Figure H-15 External Database toolbar

Appendix I

AutoCAD Commands

Command	Description Options

3D Draws a 3D polygon entities with surfaces. Options: B - Draws a 3D box, C - Draws a wire frame having a cone shape, D - Draws a 3D dish shaped (lower half of a sphere) polygon mesh by specifying the center and then the diameter or radius, DO - Draws the 3D upper half of the spherical polygon mesh by specifying the center and then the diameter or radius, M - Draws a polygon mesh by specifying the corners and the M and N sizes, P - Draws a 3D tetrahedron or a pyramid by specifying the relevant number of base points and the apex point or the top points, S - Draws a spherical polygon mesh by specifying the center and then the diameter or radius, T - Draws a polygon mesh having a toroidal shape. It is drawn by specifying the center and then the diameter or the radius, W - Draws a polygon wire frame having the shape of a wedge. It is drawn by specifying a corner, height, length, and width.

3DARRAY Draws a 3D rectangular or polar array. Options:
   R - Rectangular 3D array, P - Polar array

3DFACF Draws a 3D surface with three or four sides.

3DMESH Draws a polygon mesh by specifying the size of M and N and the location of the vertices.

3DPOLY Draws a 3D polyline having segments of straight line. Options:
   point - Draws the 3D polyline to the specified point, C - Closes the 3D polyline by joining the last point with the first point, U - Deletes the last segment.

3DSIN Displays a dialogue box that allows to import the specified objects in a 3D Studio file.

3DSOUT Displays a dialogue box that exports the AutoCAD objects with surface characteristics to a 3D studio file.

ABOUT Displays AutoCAD version and serial numbers, a scrolling window with the text of the acad.msg file, and other information.

ACISIN Imports an ASCII ACIS file into the AutoCAD drawing.

ACISOUT AutoCAD exports the selected solid objects to an ASCII ACIS file.

ALIGN Allows specified objects to align with other objects by moving and rotating them.

AMECONVERT Changes the regions and solids of AME to region and solids of AutoCAD.

'APERTURE Controls the size of the object snap target box.

'APPLOAD Displays a dialogue box that loads certain applications such as AutoLISP, ADS, and ARX.

ARC Draws an arc of any size. The default method is to specify two endpoints and a point along the arc. Options:
   A - Included angle, C - Center point, D - Starting direction, E - Endpoint, L - Length of chord, R - Radius

AREA Computes the area and perimeter of different objects and of a region formed by specifying a sequence of points. Options:
   A - Add mode, F - First point (Area by specifying points), O - Area of the object, S - Subtract mode

ARRAY Creates specified number of copies of a selected object. Options:
   P - Polar array, R - Rectangular array

ASEADMIN Makes other programs attain access to database objects and sets up environment for external database commands through a dialogue box.

ASEEXPORT The information about the link for selected object is exported to the external database file. The link information is stored in the text files and the link path name in the export table through a dialogue box.

ASELINKS The link information is manipulated (edited or deleted) in the drawing and its blocks through a dialogue box.

ASEROWS   It edits the data in the database. Links and selection sets are also created through a dialogue box.

ASESELECT   Creates a selection set of objects, selects objects, and highlights them. Graphic and nongraphic data can be combined to create the selection set.

ASESQLED   Displays a dialogue box through which the external databases can be queried directly by executing the SQL statements.

ASEUNLOAD   Removes the ASE application from the memory so that the memory is utilized by other applications.

ATTDEF   Creates an attribute definition (characteristics of an attribute). It gives textual information concerning a block. Options:
  I - Invisible mode: Attribute remains invisible, C - Constant mode: Constant value of attribute, V - Verify mode: Verifies attribute value is correct, P - Preset mode: Default value to attribute.

ATTDISP   The visibility of the attribute is controlled globally. Options:
  ON - Attributes made visible, OFF - Attributes made invisible, N - Current visibility kept.

ATTEDIT   Edits attributes irrespective of its block definition.

ATTEXT   Attribute information is extracted from the drawing. Options:
  C - CDF: Comma-Delimited File, D - DXF: Drawing Interchange File, S - SDF: Space-Delimited File

ATTREDEF   An existing block is redefined and its attributes are.updated.

AUDIT   Identifies errors in a drawing. Options:
  Y - Corrects the errors, N - Informs about the error without correcting it

BASE   Sets the point of origin for inserting a drawing into another drawing.

BHATCH   A specified enclosed area is filled with an associative hatch pattern through a dialogue box. Previewing a hatch and adjusting the boundary is also possible.

'BLIPMODE   Controls the appearance of marker blip that is displayed on the screen when a point is picked. Options:
  ON - Marker blip displayed, OFF - Marker blip not displayed.

BLOCK   Creates a compound object with block definition from a set of entities. Options:
  ? - Lists names of previously defined blocks.

BMPOUT   Creates a bitmap image of the drawing and saves the screen to a file having a .bmp extension.

BOUNDARY   Creates a polyline or region of a boundary which defines an enclosed area.

BOX   Creates a solid box which is 3D in nature with its base parallel to the XY plane.

BREAK   Removes specified portions of an object or splits the object. Options:
  F - Respecifies first point.

'CAL   Calculates expressions which can be mathematical as well as geometrical.

CHAMFER   Connects two nonparallel objects with a beveled line. Options:
  A - Chamfer distance is set using angle and distance, D - Sets chamfer distance, P - Chamfers entire polyline, T - Controls the trimming of the edges to chamfer line endpoints.

CHANGE   Alters the properties of selected objects. Options:
  C - Change point - Changes lines, circles, Text, Attribute Definitions, Blocks, P - Changes different properties like Color, Elev, LAyer, LType, Thickness.

CHPROP   Alters the drawing properties of selected objects. Options:
  C - Changes color, A - Changes layer, LT - Changes linetype, S - Changes linetype scale factor, T - Changes thickness.

CIRCLE   Draws a circle using any of the four methods available. Options:
  C - Circle drawn on the basis of center point and diameter or radius, 3P - Drawn on the basis of 3 points on circumference, 2P - Drawn on the basis of 2 endpoints of the diameter, TTR - Circle drawn tangent to two objects with a specified radius.

COLOR   Sets color for the objects being drawn. Options:
  value - Sets color by number (1-255), name - Sets color by name, Byblock - The current color setting is inherited by the block at the time of insertion, Bylayer - Objects inherit the color of the layer in which they are drawn.

COMPILE   Shape files and PostScript font files are compiled

CONE   Draws a 3D solid cone. Options:
  Center - Cone having circular base, E - Cone having elliptical base.

CONFIG   Reconfigures video display, plotter, digitizer, and operating parameters of AutoCAD. All the options are displayed in the text window.

COPY   Draws a copy of the selected object leaving the original object intact. The default method is to specify the base point. Options:
  M - Multiple copies of object in single COPY command.

CYLINDER   Draws a 3D solid cylinder. Options:
  center - Specifies the center of the circular base., E - Forms an elliptical base.

DBLIST   The database information about each entity in the drawing is listed.

DDATTDEF   Creates an attribute definition (characteristics of an attribute) through a dialogue box. It gives textual information concerning a block.

DDATTE   Attribute values concerning a block are edited through a dialogue box.

DDATTEXT   Attribute information is extracted from the drawing using a dialogue box.

DDCHPROP   Alters the drawing properties (color, layer, linetype, thickness) of selected objects via a dialogue box.

DDCOLOR   Displays a dialogue box that sets color for the objects being drawn.

DDEDIT   Displays a dialogue box that allows the user to edit text and attribute definitions.

'DDEMODES   Displays a dialogue box that sets properties (color, layer, linetype, text style, linetype scale, elevation, and thickness) for new entities.

'DDGRIPS   A dialogue box is displayed through which grips are enabled and their color and size is set.

DDIM   Using a series of dialogue boxes, different dimension styles are created and modified.

DDINSERT   Using a dialogue box, a block or a drawing file is inserted into a drawing. This dialogue box also allows the setting of different parameters like insertion point, scale, rotation, and explode.

'DDLMODES   Controls the different properties of layers through a dialogue box. The layer properties include New, Current, Rename, On/Off, Thaw/Freeze, Unlock/Lock, Current Viewport, New Viewport, Color, Linetype, and Filters.

'DDLTYPE   Displays a dialogue box that loads and sets linetypes. It displays all the available linetypes to load via another dialogue box.

DDMODIFY   Displays the appropriate dialogue box that controls the properties (color, layer, linetype, linetype scale, and thickness) of the existing objects.

'DDOSNAP   Sets the Running Object Snap for Endpoint, Midpoint, Center, Node, Quadrant, Intersection, Insertion, Perpendicular, Tangent, Nearest, Apparent Int, and Quick osnap modes via a dialogue box. It also sets the aperture size of the target box.

'DDPTYPE   Displays a dialogue box that sets the point style and also the size of the point object.

DDRENAME   Changes the names of different types of objects via a dialogue box. The objects that can be renamed are Blocks, Dimension style, Layer, Linetype, Style, Ucs, and View.

'DDRMODES   Displays a dialogue box that sets drawing aids such as Ortho, Fill, Qtext, Blipmode, Highlight, Group, Snap, Grid, and Isoplane.

'DDSELECT   Displays a dialogue box that sets the object selection modes. It also sets the pickbox size and the object sort method.

DDUCS   Controls the defined User Coordinate Systems via a dialogue box.

DDUCSP   Displays a dialogue box that selects a preset User Coordinate System.

'DDUNITS   Sets coordinate and angle display formats and precision through a dialogue box. It also controls the direction of the angle.

DDVIEW   Displays and restores the existing views via a dialogue box. It also creates new views.

DDVPOINT   Controls the direction of 3D views through a dialogue box.

DELAY   The execution of the next command is postponed for a specified time duration. In other words a specified pause is provided within the script.

DIM   Dimensioning mode is invoked and permits the use of dimension subcommands from AutoCAD's previous releases.

DIMALIGNED   Sets the dimensioning mode to aligned linear.

DIMANGULAR   Sets the dimensioning mode to angular.

DIMBASELINE   Starts drawing from the baseline of the previous dimension. The new dimension can be linear, angular, or ordinate.

DIMCENTER   Provides the center point or center line of circles and arcs.

DIMCONTINUE   Starts drawing a new dimension from the second extension line of the previous or selected dimension. The new dimension can be a linear, angular, or ordinate dimension.

DIMDIAMETER   Draws diameter dimensions for different circles and arcs.

DIMEDIT   Edits dimension text and extension lines. Options:
H - Dimension text moved back to default position, N - Dimension text is changed, R - Dimension text is rotated, O - Extension lines placed at obliquing angle.

DIMLINEAR   Draws dimensions in linear form.

DIMORDINATE   Ordinate point dimensions are created.

DIMOVERRIDE   The settings of the dimensioning system variables concerning the dimension object are overridden. The current dimension style is not affected.

DIMRADIUS   Draws radial dimensions for different circles and arcs.

DIMSTYLE   New dimension styles are created and the existing ones are modified. Options:
R - Dimensioning system variable setting changed, S - Current settings of dimensioning variables saved, ST - Current values of dimensioning variables displayed, V - Dimensioning variable setting of a style is listed, A -

Selected dimension objects are updated, ? - Named dimension styles are listed.

DIMTEDIT   Dimension text is moved and rotated. Options: A - Angle of dimension text changed, H - Dimension text moved to default position, L - Dimension text left justified, R - Dimension text right justified

'DIST   Distance and angle between two points is measured.

DIVIDE   Places markers at equal distance along the length or perimeter of an entity, thus dividing it into a specified number of equal parts. Options: B - Places blocks as markers.

DLGCOLOR   Creates a color combination or selects from the given color schemes via a dialogue box in DOS.

DONUT   Draws two concentric circles with specified diameters, thus forming a ring.

'DRAGMODE   Controls the dragging feature for appropriate commands. Options: ON - Permits dragging, OFF - Ignores dragging, A - Permits dragging wherever possible.

DTEXT   Writes text and displays it as it is entered. Text is written from a specified start point. Options: J - Alignment of text is controlled by several options, A - Text aligned between two points, F - Fits text of specified height between two points, C - Text is centered horizontally, M - Text is centered horizontally and vertically, R - Text is justified right, BL - Bottom left, BC - Bottom center, BR - Bottom right, ML - Middle left, MC - Middle center, MR - Middle right, TL - Top left, TC - Top center, TR - Top right, S - Sets the text style.

DVIEW   Parallel projection or perspective views are defined. Options: CA - Sets camera position by rotating about the target, TA - Sets target position by rotating about the camera, D - Camera to target distance is set, PO - Locates target and camera points, PA - Pans image, Z - Zooms In/Out, TW - Tilts view around line of sight, CL - The view is clipped in front and back, H - Hidden lines removed on selected objects, OFF - Perspective viewing turned off, U - Last DVIEW operation reversed, X - Exits DVIEW.

DXBIN   Specially coded binary files are imported into a drawing.

DXFIN   A drawing interchange file is imported.

DXFOUT   A drawing interchange file of the current drawing is created.

EDGE   The visibility of 3D sides is altered. By default the selected edge is hidden. Options: D - Display mode invisible edges are highlighted.

EDGESURF   A 3D polygon mesh is created which has four adjoining edges that define a Coons surface patch.

ELEV   The elevation and extrusion thickness is set for the new objects.

ELLIPSE   Draws ellipses or elliptical arcs using different options. Specifying the axis endpoint is the default method. Options: A - Draws elliptical arc, C - Specifies the center point of the ellipse, I - Draws isometric circle in current isometric plane.

END   Exits AutoCAD but first saves the drawing to the .dwg file.

ERASE   Erases the selected objects from the drawing.

EXPLODE   Compound objects (blocks, groups, dimensions, polylines, 3D solids, regions, polygon meshes, multilines) are broken into their constituent parts.

EXPORT   Objects are saved to other file formats via a dialogue box.

EXTEND   Lengthens a selected entity to meet another entity. Options: P - Specifies projection mode like UCS and View, E - Controls the extension to implied or actual edge, U - Latest extension is undone.

EXTRUDE   Solids are created by extruding 2D entities along a selected path. By default height of extrusion is to be specified which extrudes the object along the positive Z axis. Options: P - Extrusion path is selected.

FILES   Displays a dialogue box that manages the files.

'FILL   Controls whether multilines, traces, solids, or wide polylines are filled or not filled. Options: ON - Fill mode is enabled, OFF - Fill mode is disabled.

FILLET   The edges of two specified lines, arcs, or circles are filleted by construction of an arc of specified radius. The default method is to specify the two objects. Options: P - Entire polyline is filleted, R - The radius of the fillet arc is specified, T - Controls the trimming of the edges to fillet arc endpoints.

'FILTER   Creates a list of properties on the basis of which the objects are selected.

GIFIN   A GIF-format raster image file is inserted at the specified position.

'GRAPHSCR   Flips to the graphics display from the text screen.

'GRID   A grid of dots at specified spacing is displayed. Options: Grid spacing(X) - Grid set to specified value, ON - Grid turned on at current spacing, OFF - Grid turned off, S - Grid spacing set to current Snap interval, A - Grid set to different spacing in X and Y

GROUP   Creates and changes groups, which is a set of objects having a specific name.

HATCH   A specified area is filled with a selected pattern. Options:

? - Lists the hatch patterns in acad.pat file, name - A pattern name as defined in acad.pat file is specified, U - User defined hatch pattern is specified. U can be followed by a comma and a hatch style. The different hatch styles are:, n - Normal or standard style. Hatching is performed from the inside of the outermost boundary. Moreover areas having odd number of boundaries around them are hatched, o - Hatches outermost area only, i - Hatches the complete area thus ignoring the internal structure.

HATCHEDIT   Edits a hatch block through a dialogue box. It sets the pattern type and properties and then applies it to a block.

'HELP   Displays help for a specific command and also lists the commands and data entry options.

HIDE   Regenerating of a 3D object is performed with the removal of hidden lines.

'ID   The UCS coordinates of a specified point are displayed.

IMPORT   Imports the different file formats into AutoCAD drawing via a dialogue box.

INSERT   Places a previously drawn named block or drawing into the current drawing. Options:
X scale - Inserts copy of block with basepoint at insertion point, C - Insertion point and another point as the corners, XYZ - Scaling in all three dimensions.

INTERFERE   Highlights all of the interfering solids and then creates new solids from the intersections of the interfering pairs of solids.

INTERSECT   A new composite solid is created from the intersecting region of two or more solids.

ISOPLANE   An isometric plane is selected to be the current plane for an orthogonal drawing. Options:
T - Switches to the next plane, L - Left-hand plane, T - Top plane, R - Right-hand plane.

'LAYER   Creates layers and sets different properties for the specified layers. Options:
? - Lists defined layers, M - Creates a layer and makes it the current layer, S - Makes a specified already existing layer current, N - Creates one or more new layers, ON - Turns on the specified layers, OFF - Turns off the specified layers, C - Sets the color of the specified layer, L - Sets the linetype of the specified layer, F - Makes a layer invisible by freezing it, T - The frozen layer is thawed, LO - Locks layers, thus prevents editing on them, U - Unlocks specified locked layers.

LEADER   Creates a line segment with an arrowhead that connects the text to a feature. The leader is created from a specified point to another point depending upon the options. Options:
A - Annotation is inserted at the end of leader line, F - Controls the type of leader (Spline, Straight, Arrow), U - The last vertex point is removed.

LENGTHEN   Alters the length of specified entities and the included angle of arcs. Options:

DE - Lengthens the object by a specified incremental distance, P - Alters the length by a specified percentage of its total length, T - Alters the length by specified total absolute length, DY - The object is lengthened to where its endpoint is dragged.

LIGHT   Controls the lighting effects in the model space via a dialogue box. It creates, modifies, deletes the lights and controls the color system in a drawing. It manages different lights (Point light, Distant light, Spotlight) through a series of dialogue boxes.

'LIMITS   Checks the drawing boundaries and sets them for the current space. Options:
Lower - Specifies 2 points-lower left corner and the left-upper right corner, ON - Limits checking is enabled, OFF - Limits checking is disabled.

LINE   Draws straight line segments of any length by specifying the endpoints. Options:
Enter (◄┘) - Continues from end of previous line or arc, U - Removes the most recent segment, C - Closes polygon.

'LINETYPE   Defines line characteristics, loads linetypes and sets them for new entities. It also creates new linetype, definitions to a library file. Options:
? - Lists linetypes in a file, C - Creates new linetype definition, L - Loads an already existing linetype definition, Sets linetype for new entities. Set suboptions: name - Sets the specified linetype, Bylayer - Sets linetype associated with layer, Byblock - The objects inherit the linetype of the block after it is inserted.

LIST   Lists database information (type, layer, X,Y,Z position, thickness etc,) about the specified entity.

LOAD   Loads the shapes from the shape file to be used by the SHAPE command.

LOGFILEOFF   The log file already opened is closed by this command.

LOGFILEON   The contents of the text window are recorded into the log file.

'LTSCALE   Sets the scale factor of the linetype so as to alter the relative length of dashes and dots

MAKEPREVIEW   Makes a preview image of drawings from the earlier releases of AutoCAD. The image is in the form of a compressed .bmp file.

MASSPROP   Calculates and lists the mass characteristics of 2D and 3D objects. The properties displayed are Area, Perimeter, Bounding box, Centroid. For Coplanar regions, additional properties displayed are Moments of Inertia, Products of Inertia, Radii of Gyration, and Principal Moments. The properties displayed for solids are Mass, Volume, and the properties of Coplanar region.

MATLIB   Displays a dialogue box that lists all the predefined materials (material list) and lists the materials in the selected library (library list). It also imports and exports materials between those two lists.

MEASURE   Places markers at measured interval along the length or perimeter of an entity. Options:
  B - Places blocks as markers.

MENU   Loads a customized menu file into the menu area. The menu file contains the command strings and menu syntax.

MENULOAD   Displays a dialogue box that loads and permits you to add partial menu files to an already present base menu file.

MENUUNLOAD   Displays the same dialogue box as in the case MENULOAD command that can also be used to unload the partial menu files.

MINSERT   Places multiple copies of a previously drawn named block or drawing into the current drawing in a rectangular array. Options:
  ? - Lists the defined block definitions, ˜ - Displays a dialogue box. After specifying the insertion point you get the following options: X scale - Inserts copy of block with basepoint at insertion point, C - Insertion point and another point as the corners, XYZ - Scaling in all three dimensions.

MIRROR   Reflects objects so as to create their mirror images about a specified line.

MIRROR3D   Reflects objects so as to create their mirror images about a specified plane. Options:
  3points - 3points specify the mirroring plane, O - The plane of a planar object specifies the mirroring plane, L - The previous mirroring plane is taken as the present one, Z - The point on the plane and another point on the Z axis (normal) of the plane specifies the mirroring plane, V - A point on the viewing plane specifies the mirroring plane, XY/YZ/ZX - The mirroring plane is aligned to any one of the standard planes.

MLEDIT   Displays a dialogue box that controls intersection between multiple parallel lines and edits them. Different types of cross, tee, corner joints, and vertices can be created between multilines via the dialogue box. It is also possible to cut and weld multiline segments.

MLINE   Draws multiple parallel lines between two points. Options:
  J - Justification- How multiline is drawn between two points, S - Scale- Sets the width of the multiline, ST - Sets the multiline style.

MLSTYLE   Displays a dialogue box that creates a multiline style, makes a specific style current, saves, adds a style to the current list, renames a style, adds a description to a style, and loads a style from the library file. It also controls the element properties (number, offset, color, linetype) and the multiline properties (start and end caps, angle, background color)

MOVE   Moves objects from one location to another by specifying a displacement.

MSLIDE   Creates a slide file (raster image) from the current display.

MSPACE   Switches to model space viewport from paper space.

MTEXT   Creates paragraph text within a specified text boundary. Options:
  I - Insertion point specifies the corner of text boundary. Then you need to specify the Other corner or Width or 2points. In case of these three suboptions the text editor is displayed for entering the text. The other suboptions specify the rotation angle, style, height and direction, A - Sets the alignment of the text boundary, S - Specifies the text style, H - Specifies the height of uppercase text, D - The direction of the paragraph text object is set.

MTPROP   Displays a dialogue box that controls the properties of the paragraph text. The contents can be changed which includes text style, text height, direction, and the object changes include attachment, width, and rotation.

MULTIPLE   Causes the repetition of the next command until it is cancelled.

MVIEW   Creates viewports and controls the number and layout of paper space viewports. You specify diagonal corners of new viewport as the default option. Options:
  ON - Viewport is turned on, OFF - Viewport is turned off, H - Hideplot- Hidden lines removed during plotting, F - Fit- Single viewport created which fills the display area completely, 2 - The specified area is divided into two viewports either horizontally or vertically, 3 - The specified area is divided into 3 viewports, 4 - The specified area is divided into 4 viewports, R - Restore- Viewport configurations changed into individual viewports.

MVSETUP   The specifications of a drawing are set. Depending upon the system variable TILEMODE, the working of MVSETUP is different. When TILEMODE is On, drawing scale factor, units type, and paper size is set and lastly a bounding box is drawn. When TILEMODE is Off a set of floating viewports is created. Options (TILEMODE Off):
  A - Aligns the view in a viewport with another viewport. The view can be panned in a specified direction, align it horizontally, vertically, or rotate it, C - The viewport can be created, S - Sets the scale factor of objects in the viewport, O - Options- The layer can be set, reset limits, set units, Xref attach, T - Creates a title block and drawing border, U - Reverses the previous operation

NEW   Displays a dialogue box that creates a new drawing.

OFFSET   Creates offset curves, concentric circles, and parallel lines at a specified distance from the original object. Options:
  value - specify the offset distance, T - Through- The offset object passes through the specified point.

OOPS   Restores those entities which have been erased by the last ERASE command.

OPEN   Displays a dialogue box through which an existing drawing can be opened. The dialogue box also displays the directory, files, preview, name of the file, and the pattern.

'ORTHO The movement of the cursor is restrained to only vertical or horizontal directions and aligned with the grid. Options:

ON - Constrains cursor movement, OFF - Does not constrain cursor movement.

'OSNAP Specifies a point at an exact location on an entity by setting the Object Snap modes. Options:

END - Closest endpoint of arc, elliptical arc, ray, mline, line and closest corner of trace, solid, 3D face, MID - Midpoint of arc, elliptical arc, spline, ellipse, ray, solid, xline, mline, or line, INT - Intersection of line, arc, spline, elliptical arc, ellipse, ray, xline, mline, or circle, APPINT - Apparent intersection (which may not actually intersect in 3D space) of line, arc, spline, elliptical arc, ellipse, ray, xline, mline, or circle, CEN - Center of arc, elliptical arc, ellipse, or circle, QUA - Quadrant point of arc, elliptical arc, ellipse, solid, or circle, PER - Point perpendicular to arc, elliptical arc, ellipse, spline, ray, xline, mline, line, solid, or arc, TAN - Tangent to arc, elliptical arc, ellipse, or circle, NOD - Point object, INS - Insertion point of text, block, shape, or attribute, NEA - Nearest point of arc, elliptical arc, ellipse, spline, ray, xline, mline, line, circle, or point, QUI - First snap point, NON - Turns Object Snap mode off.

'PAN Moves the drawing display by a specified displacement.

PCXIN A raster file of PCX format is imported.

PEDIT Editing of 2D polyline, 3D polyline, or 3D mesh. Options:

2D polyline C - Closes polyline segment, O - Closing segment removed, J - Joins to polyline, W - Specifies uniform width, E - Edits the vertices. The first vertex is marked by placing a X. Editing includes moving the X to next or previous vertex, adding a new vertex, setting the first vertex for break, moving the vertex, regenerating, straightening and attaching a tangent direction to the current vertex, F - Creates a curve between a pair of vertices, S - Vertices are used as a frame for spline curve, L - Linetype generation in a continuous pattern, U - Reverses the previous operation, X - Exits PEDIT. 3D polyline C - Closes polyline segment, O - Closing segment removed, E - Edits the vertices. Same suboptions as in 2D Edit except the tangent suboption, S - Vertices are used as a frame for spline curve, D - Removes a spline curve to its control frame, U - reverses the previous option, X - Exits PEDIT. 3D polygon mesh E - Edits vertices. The first vertex is marked by placing a X. Editing includes moving the X to next or previous vertex, moving the X marker to the next vertex or the previous vertex in the N direction, moving the marker to the next or previous vertex in the M direction, regenerating the mesh, S - Fits a smooth surface, D - The control point polygon mesh is restored, Mclose - M-direction polylines are closed, Mopen - M-direction polylines are opened, Nclose - N-direction polylines are closed, Nopen - N-direction polylines are opened.

PFACE A 3D polyface mesh is created.

PLAN Allows you to view the drawing from plan view of a User Coordinate System. Options:

C - Plan view of the current UCS, U - Plan view of the specified UCS, W - Plan view of the World Coordinate System.

PLINE Draws 2D polylines. The default is to draw a polyline between two specified points. Options:

A - Arc mode- Arc segments can be added to polyline. The arc segment starts from the endpoint of the previous polyline segment and can be drawn by specifying the endpoint of the arc, the included angle, center of the arc, starting direction of the arc, halfwidth of the arc, radius of the arc, Width. You can also close the polyline with the arc segment, or reverse the previous operation or you can shift to the Line mode, C - Closes the polyline, H - Sets the halfwidth, L - Draws polyline of specified length, U - Last polyline segment is removed, W - The width of the next segment is specified.

PLOT Displays a dialogue box that allows you to plot the drawing to the plotting device or file. Through a series of dialogue boxes you can set the different parameters, device information, drawing extents and limits, plot size, paper size, orientation, plot scale, rotation and origin. You can also plot a view or a specific portion of the drawing and also preview the plot.

POINT Draws a point object at a specified location.

POLYGON Draws a polygon (closed polyline object) having specified number of sides. Options:

C - Specifies the center of polygon. Suboptions:
I - Inscribed in the circle, C - Circumscribed about the circle, E - Defines one edge of the polygon.

PREFERENCES Displays a dialogue box that permits you to customize the AutoCAD settings. Controls the units of measurement and sets the environment.

PSDRAG An imported PostScript file is dragged into place by the PSIN command and as it is dragged, the PSDRAG command controls its appearance. Options:

0 - Only the bounding box and the file name of the image is displayed as the image is being dragged, 1 - The rendered PostScript image is displayed.

PSFILL A 2D polyline boundary is filled with a PostScript fill pattern. Options:

name - Fills the polyline with the specified pattern, ? - Lists all the previously defined PostScript fill patterns.

PSIN A PostScript file is inserted into a drawing.

PURGE Removes those references from the database which are not being used. Options:

B - Removes unused blocks, D - Removes unused dimstyles, LA - Removes unused layers, LT - Removes unused linetypes, SH - Removes unused shape files, ST - Removes unused text styles, AP - Removes unused APPID table, M - Removes unused mline styles, A - Removes all unused objects.

QSAVE Saves the drawing without asking for a filename.

QTEXT The text and the attribute objects are displayed without drawing the text detail. Options:

ON - Text displayed as a bounding box, OFF - Quick text mode off.

QUIT   Exits AutoCAD

RAY   Draws a semi-infinite line used as a construction line.

RCONFIG   The rendering setup is reconfigured. Options: 0 - Quits RCONFIG, 1 - Current configuration is displayed, 2 - Displays and sets the rendering display device settings, 3 - Displays and sets the Render Window settings.

RECOVER   Recovers a damaged and corrupted drawing.

RECTANG   Creates a polyline rectangle by specifying the diagonally opposite corners.

REDEFINE   Restores an AutoCAD built-in command which has been previously overridden by UNDEFINE.

REDO   The effect of the previous command if it was UNDO is reversed.

'REDRAW   Cleans up the current viewport by removing the blip marks and other stray pixels.

'REDRAWALL   Refreshes or cleans up all the viewports.

REGEN   Regenerates the current viewport.

REGENALL   Regenerates all the viewports.

'REGENAUTO   Regenerates the drawing automatically. Options: ON - Permits automatic regeneration, OFF - Does not permit automatic regeneration.

REGION   Region entities (2D enclosed areas) are created from a selection set.

REINIT   Permits to reinitialize the I/O ports, digitizer, display, and parameters file.

RENAME   Alters the name of entities. Options: B - Renames block, D - Renames dimstyle, LA - Renames layers, LT - Renames linetype, S - Renames style, U - Renames UCS, VI - Renames view, VP - Renames viewport configuration.

RENDER   Displays a dialogue box that shades a 3D wireframe or solid, so that a realistically shaded image is created. It is possible to render the current scene or just the specified objects. You can also control the color map and the shading of different materials.

RENDERUNLOAD   Removes the Render application from the memory of the system.

RENDSCR   The last rendered image is redisplayed.

REPLAY   The GIF, TGA, or TIFF images are displayed via a dialogue box.

'RESUME   Resumes an interrupted script.

REVOLVE   By revolving a 2D entity (polygon, closed polyline, circle, ellipse, donuts, etc.), a solid is formed. Options: point - The axis of revolution is specified by two points, O - The axis of revolution is specified by selecting an existing line or a segment polyline, X - The positive X axis used as the axis direction, Y - The positive Y axis used as the axis direction.

REVSURF   A polygon mesh is constructed by rotating a curve or profile around a specified axis.

RMAT   Displays a dialogue box that manages the materials used for rendering. A new material can be created or the existing ones can be modified through a series of dialogue boxes. It is possible to adjust the value and color of the materials. AutoCAD's color index can also be attached by layers or by using a color wheel.

ROTATE   Rotates specified entities about a base point. Options: angle - Rotates object through a specified angle, R - Rotates object with respect to the reference angle.

ROTATE3D   Rotates object about a 3D axis. Options: 2points - The axis of rotation is given by specifying 2 points, A - Axis by object- The axis of rotation is aligned with an object, L - The previous rotation axis is considered, V - The axis of rotation is aligned with the viewing direction, X/Y/Z - The axis of rotation is aligned with any one of the axes (X-axis, Y-axis, Z-axis)

RPREF   Displays a dialogue box that controls the rendering preferences. It controls the color map, the behavior of the RENDER command by default, rendering display, and the image output setting. Through a series of sub dialogue boxes, the type of shading used and 3D solid faces can be controlled. You can also set the color and the aspect ratio of the output file.

RSCRIPT   Repeats a script continuously.

RULESURF   Creates a polygon mesh representing a ruled surface between two curves.

SAVE   A name is requested under which the drawing is saved. If the drawing is already named, then it is saved under the current filename.

SAVEAS   An unnamed drawing is saved with a filename or the current drawing is renamed.

SAVEASR12   The current drawing is saved in AutoCAD's Release 12 format.

SAVEIMG   Displays a dialogue box that saves a rendered image to a file. Through the subdialogue boxes, image compression for TGA and TIFF formats is possible.

SCALE   The size of the existing objects is changed. the default is to specify a scale factor. Options: R - The object is scaled according to the reference length and a new length

SCENE   Controls different scenes (particular view) in model space. Through a series of dialogue boxes all the scenes in the current drawing are listed, new scenes can be added, scene names can be modified, and the lights can be controlled in the scene.

SCRIPT   Executes a command script.

SECTION   Creates regions. from the intersection of a plane and solids. Options:
>3points - Specifying 3 points on sectioning plane, O - Sectioning plane is aligned with the object, Z - Sectioning plane is aligned with the plane's normal direction, V - Sectioning plane is aligned with the viewing plane of current viewport, XY - Sectioning plane aligned with XY plane of UCS, YZ - Sectioning plane aligned with YZ plane of UCS, ZX - Sectioning plane aligned with ZX plane of UCS

SELECT   Creates a selection set of specified group of objects. Options:
>AU - Automatic selection, A - Add mode - Objects are added to the selection set, ALL - Selects all objects, BOX - Objects inside or crossing a rectangle are selected, C - Objects are selected which lie inside and crossing an area specified by two points, CP - Those objects are selected which lie inside and crossing the polygon created by specifying points around the objects, F - Those objects are selected which are crossing the specified fence, G - Objects within a group are selected, L - Recently created object is selected, M - Objects are picked without highlighting them, P - Recent selection set is selected, R - Remove mode- Objects can be removed from the selection set, SI - Selects first object or a set of objects, U - Removes the most recently added object from the selection set, W - Selects those objects which lie completely inside an area specified by two points, WP - Selects those objects which lie completely inside an area specified by picking points around the objects.

'SETVAR   Sets the values of the system variables. Options:
>? - Lists the variables with their current values.

SHADE   Displays a shaded picture of the drawing in the current viewport.

SHAPE   Predefined shapes are inserted. Options:
>? - Lists the shape names.

SHELL   Permits the access to the commands in the operating system while in AutoCAD.

SKETCH   Allows you to draw freehand drawings. Options:
>P - Pen- sketching pen raised and lowered, X - Reports the number of temporary lines drawn and then exits SKETCH Q - Temporary lines discarded and then exits SKETCH R - Temporary lines recorded as permanent, E - Removes portion of the temporary line, C - Pen lowered for sketching, . - Draws a straight line from endpoint of sketched line to current position of pen.

SLICE   Solid is cut with a plane. Options:
>3points - Cutting plane specified by defining 3 points, O - Cutting plane aligned with an object (Circle, ellipse, elliptical arc, 2D spline or polyline), Z - Cutting plane specified by locating a point on Z-axis, V - Cutting plane aligned to the viewing plane of the current

viewport, XY - Cutting plane aligned with the XY plane, YZ - Cutting plane aligned with the YZ plane, ZX - Cutting plane aligned with the ZX plane.

'SNAP   The movement of the cursor is constrained to the snap spacing. Options:
>ON - Snap mode is turned on, OFF - Snap mode is turned off, A - Sets different X and Y spacings, R - Snap grid is rotated, S - Sets the style (Standard or Isometric) of the snap grid.

SOLID   Draws polygons which are solid-filled.

SOUT   An Encapsulated PostScript file is created into which the current view of the drawing is exported. Options:
>D - Exports the current view. It can also include the EPSI or TIFF screen preview image, E - Only the portion of the current space which contains the entities is exported, L - The area defined by the limits is exported, V - The previous saved is exported, W - The portion you specify within a window is exported.

SPACE   Switches to paper space from model space.

SPELL   Allows spell check of text objects in a drawing. If an ambiguous word is found then the dialogue box is displayed that lists the alternatives for the word, or permits you to replace the current word with another one, or add the word to the dictionary.

SPHERE   A 3D solid sphere is drawn. Options:
>R - Radius of the sphere, D - Diameter of the sphere.

SPLINE   Draws smooth spline curves between points. Options:
>Point - Specify points to define the spline curve.
>Suboptions:
>Point - Adds spline curve segments by specifying points, C - Spline curve is closed, F - Fit Tolerance- The tolerance for fitting is changed, O - 2D or 3D spline- fit polylines are changed to splines.

SPLINEDIT   Allows you to edit a spline entity. Options:
>F - Fit data is edited. Suboptions:
>A - Fit points are added, C - An open spline is closed, O - A closed spline is opened, D - Fit points are removed, M - Fit points are moved, P - A spline fit data is removed from database, T - Beginning and end tangents are edited, L - Tolerance value for spline fit are changed, X - Exits fit data option, C - An open spline is closed, O - A closed spline is opened, M - Move Vertex- The position of the control vertices is changed, R - Refines a spline by adding control points, or by increasing its order, or by changing the weight, E - Spline direction is reversed, U - Reverses the previous operation of SPLINEDIT, X - Exits SPLINEDIT command.

STATS   Displays a dialogue box that provides the rendering statistics. It also saves the statistics to a file.

STATUS   Lists the drawing statistics, modes, and extents.

STLOUT   Creates a binary or ASCII file and stores the solid in the specified file.

STRETCH Stretches lines, arcs, and polylines by moving the endpoints to another specified location.

STYLE Creates new text styles or modifies the existing ones. Options:
> ? - Lists the text styles.

SUBTRACT Subtracts the area of one set of regions from another and subtracts the volume of one set of solids from another, thus creating a new composite region or solid.

TABLET Aligns the tablet with the coordinate system of a paper drawing. Options:
> ON - Tablet mode is turned on, OFF - Tablet mode is turned off, CAL - Calibrates the tablet, CFG - Configures tablet menu area and screen pointing area.

TABSURF Creates a polygon mesh which represents a tabulated surface formed from a path curve and direction vector.

TEXT Writes text using a variety of character pattern. The text prompt is displayed only once. Options: See DTEXT command for options.

'TEXTSCR Flips to the text screen from the graphics screen.

TIFFIN A raster image file of TIFF format is inserted.

TIME The date and time of drawing creation is displayed. It also displays the time and the date when the current drawing was last updated and controls an elapsed timer. Options:
> D - Displays the updated times, O - Elapsed timer is turned on, OFF - Elapsed timer is turned off, R - Resets the user elapsed timer.

TOLERANCE Creates and adds geometric tolerances to a drawing.

TORUS Draws a solid having the shape of a donut. Options:
> R - Radius of the tube, D - Diameter of the tube.

TRACE Draws solid lines having a specified width.

TREESTAT Displays the current spatial index (position of objects in space) of a drawing. The information includes the number of nodes, number of objects, depth of branch, etc.

TRIM Removes the extra portion of an entity which extends beyond a specified boundary. Options:
> P - Sets projection mode, E - Controls trimming of objects till the implied edge, U - Reverses the previous operation of TRIM command, **U** - Reverses the effect of previous operation.

UCS Sets and modifies user coordinate system. Options:
> W - Current UCS set to World Coordinate System, O - Allows the shifting of the UCS origin, ZA - UCS defined with the positive Z axis, 3 - Sets new UCS origin and a new X and Y axes direction, OB - A new UCS is defined aligned to a specified object, V - A new UCS is defined whose XY plane is perpendicular to the viewing direction, X/Y/Z - Rotates the current

UCS around X axis, or Y axis, or Z axis, P - Previous UCS is restored, R - A saved UCS is restored, S - Current UCS is saved to a name, D - Deletes the specified UCS, ? - Lists the saved coordinate systems.

UCSICON Manages the location and the visibility of the UCS icon. Options:
> ON - Coordinate system icon is enabled, OFF - Coordinate system icon is disabled, A - Icon is changed in all active viewports, N - Icon displayed at the lower left corner, OR - Icon displayed at the origin of current coordinate system.

UNDEFINE A built-in AutoCAD command is deleted.

UNDO Reverses the effect of commands. Options:
> N - The effect of specified number of previous commands used is reversed, A - The effect of the menu items is reversed by a single U command, C - The UNDO command is limited or is turned off, BE - A number of operations are grouped together and are treated as a single operation, E - The group is terminated, M - Mark - A marker is placed in the undo information, B - Back- Undoes all work till the marker is encountered.

UNION Combines the area of two or more regions, or the volume of two or more solids to create a composite region or solid.

'UNITS Sets the coordinate and angle display formats and precision.

'VIEW The graphics display is saved and restored as a view with a specified name. Options:
> ? - Lists the named views, D - Deletes specified views, R - Restores a specified view, S - Saves the display as a named view, W - Saves a portion of the display as a named view.

VIEWRES Controls the appearance of objects by setting their resolution in the current viewport.

VLCONV Displays a dialogue box that allows the conversion of Visual Link rendering data so that it can be used by AutoVision.

VPLAYER Controls the visibility of layers in different viewports. Options:
> ? - Lists the frozen layers in a specified viewport, F - Layers are frozen in current, or all, or specified viewport, T - Layers are thawed in current, or all, or specified viewport, R - Controls the visibility of layers, N - New layers which are frozen in all viewports are created, V - Viewport Visibility Default- Controls thawing and freezing of layers.

VPOINT The viewing direction for 3D visualization. Options:
> ◄┘ - Displays compass and axis tripod for controlling viewing direction, V - Specify a point from which drawing can be viewed, R - New direction using two angles is specified.

VPORTS Divides the graphics display into a number of viewports. Options:

S - Current viewport is saved under a specified name, R - Restores previously saved viewport configuration, D - Removes a viewport configuration, J - Joins two viewports into one, SI - Displays a single viewport view, ? - Lists active viewport configuration, 2 - Divides the current viewport into two, 3 - Divides the current viewport into three, 4 - Divides the current viewport into four.

VSLIDE Displays an existing raster image slide file in the current viewport.

WBLOCK Writes specified entities to a new disk file. Options:
name - Writes specified block to file, * - Writes the drawing to a new file, = - Same name for the block and the file, ◄─┘ - Writes selected entities to a file

WEDGE Creates a 3D solid in the shape of a wedge having its one of the faces as tapered and sloping. Options:
point - Specifies the first corner of the wedge. Suboptions:
point - Specifies the other corner of the wedge, C - Wedge having sides of equal length, L - Wedge with specified length, width, and height.
C - Creates wedge with specified center point. Suboptions:
point - Specifies the other corner of the wedge, C - Creates wedge having all sides equal, L - Creates wedge with specified length, width, and height

XBIND Adds Xref's dependent symbols to a drawing. Options:
B - Binds a block to the current drawing, D - Binds a dimstyle to the current drawing, LA - Binds a layer to the current drawing, LT - Binds a linetype to the current drawing, S - Binds a style to the current drawing

XLINE Creates a line of infinite length. Options:
point - Specifies the point through the xline passes, H - Creates a horizontal xline, V - Creates a vertical xline, A - Creates a xline at an angle, B - Creates an xline through the vertex of two lines so that it bisects the angle between those two lines, O - Creates an xline parallel to another entity

XPLODE Breaks a compound object into its individual objects. Options:
G - Changes selected objects. Suboptions:
E - Explodes the entire compound object, A - Sets color, linetype, layer of the component entities, C - Sets the color, LA - Sets the layer, LT - Sets the linetype, I - Sets all the properties to that of the original compound object
I - Changes selected objects one by one

XREF Manages external references to a drawing. Options:
A - Attaches an xref, ? - Lists xrefs in the drawing, B - Binds an xref permanently to a drawing, D - Detaches xrefs from the drawing, P - Allows to edit the path name with a xref, R - Reloads one or a number of xrefs, O - Overlays an xref

XREFCLIP Clips an xref.

'ZOOM Changes the display of the entities in the current drawing. Options:
value - Scale(X/XP)- Changes the display by a specified scale factor, Scale X - Zoom relative to current scale, Scale XP - Scale relative to paper space, A - Zooms the entire drawing in current viewport, C - Displays at a specified center point, D - Displays the portion of the drawing with a view box, E - Displays the drawing extents, L - Displays a window by specifying the lower left corner and a magnification, P - Displays the previous view, V - Zooms out on virtual screen of current viewport, W - Displays an area specified by two corners of the window

Appendix J

AutoCAD System Variables

Variable Name	Type and Description

ACADPREFIX String
The ACADPREFIX variable contains the direction path for support files specified by the ACAD environment variable. Path separators are attached if needed. This is a read-only variable.

ACADVER String
The ACADVER variable contains the AutoCAD version number, which can have values such as "13" or "13a". This variable is different from the DXF file $ACADVER header variable, which stores the drawing database level number. This is a read-only variable.

AFLAGS Integer
The AFLAGS variable establishes the attribute flags for the ATTDEF command bit-code. The initial value for this variable is 0. Basically the value of this variable is the addition of the following:
   0 - No attribute mode selected, 1 - Invisible, 2 - Constant, 4 - Verify, 8 - Preset

ANGBASE Real
The ANGBASE variable establishes the base angle 0 in relation to the prevailing UCS. This variable is saved in the drawing and has an initial value of 0.0000.

ANGDIR Integer
The ANGDIR variable establishes the angle from angle 0 in relation to the prevailing UCS. This variable is saved in the drawing and has an initial value of 0.
   0 - Direction is counterclockwise, 1 - Direction is clockwise.

APERTURE Integer
The APERTURE variable defines the object snap target height in pixels. This variable is saved in config and has an initial value of 10.

AREA Real
The most recently calculated area with commands such as AREA, LIST, or DBLIST is stored in this variable. You can examine this variable through the SETVAR command.

ATTDIA Integer
With the ATTDIA variable you can specify whether you want to enter the attribute value through the INSERT dialogue box or from the command line. This variable is saved in the drawing and has an initial value of 0.
   0 - Attribute values can be specified on the command line, 1 - Attribute values can be specified in the dialogue box.

ATTMODE Integer
The ATTMODE variable controls the Attribute Display mode and is saved in the drawing and its initial value is 1.
   0 - Attribute Display mode is off, 1 - Normal, 2 - On

ATTREQ Integer
The value contained in the ATTREQ variable determines whether INSERT command uses the default attribute settings when the blocks are being inserted.
   0 - For this value the default values for the all the attributes are used, 1 - This is also the initial value and enables prompts or dialogue box for attribute values (depending on the value of ATTDIA variable).

AUDITCTL Integer
The AUDITCTL variable determines whether an .adt file (audit report file) will be created by AutoCAD. This variable is saved in config.
   0 - Does not allow writing of .adt files. This is also the initial value, 1 - Allows writing of .adt files.

AUNITS Integer
The AUNITS variable establishes the Angular Units mode and is saved in the drawing.
   0 - Decimal degrees (initial value), 1 - Degrees/ minutes/ seconds, 2 - Gradians, 3 - Radians, 4 - Surveyor's units

AUPREC Integer
The AUPREC variable establishes the angular units decimal places. This variable is saved in the drawing and has an initial value of 0.

BACKZ Real
The BACKZ variable contains the back clipping plane offset (in current drawing units) from the target plane for the

current viewport. You can determine the distance between the back clipping plane and the camera point by subtracting the BACKZ value from the camera to target distance. This variable is saved in the drawing and is read-only.

BLIPMODE   Integer
The visibility of the blip marks is controlled by BLIPMODE variable. This variable is saved in the drawing and its initial value is 1.
    0 - Blip marks are not visible, 1 - Blip marks are visible.

CDATE   Real
The calendar date and time is set with this variable. This is a read-only variable.

CECOLOR   String
The CECOLOR variable defines the color of new objects. This variable is saved in the drawing and its initial value is "BYLAYER."

CELTSCALE   Real
The CELTSCALE variable defines the current global linetype scale factor for objects. This variable is saved in the drawing and its initial value is 1.0000.

CELTYPE   String
The CELTYPE variable defines the linetype that will be used in the new objects. This variable is saved in the drawing and its initial value is "BYLAYER."

CHAMFERA   Real
The CHAMFERA variable defines the first chamfer distance. This variable is saved in the drawing and its initial value is 0.0000.

CHAMFERB   Real
The CHAMFERB variable defines the second chamfer distance. This variable is saved in the drawing and its initial value is 0.0000.

CHAMFERC   Real
The CHAMFERC variable sets the chamfer length. This variable is saved in the drawing and its initial value is 0.0000.

CHAMFERD   Real
The CHAMFERD variable sets the chamfer angle. This variable is saved in the drawing and its initial value is 0.0000.

CHAMMODE   Integer
With the CHAMMODE variable you can specify the method that will be used to create chamfers.
    0 - This is the initial value and in this case two chamfer distances are required, 1 - One chamfer length and an angle are required.

CIRCLERAD   Real
The CIRCLERAD variable defines the default circle radius. The initial value of this variable is 0.0000.

CLAYER   String
The CLAYER variable sets the current layer. This variable is saved in the drawing and its initial value is "0."

CMDACTIVE   Integer
The CMDACTIVE variable contains the bit-code that signifies whether an ordinary command, transparent command, dialogue box, or script is active. Basically the value of this variable is the addition of the following:
    1 - Only ordinary command is active, 2 - Ordinary command as well as transparent command are active, 4 - Script is active, 8 - If this bit is active then Dialogue box is active.

CMDDIA   Integer
The CMDDIA variable determines whether the dialogue boxes are enabled for only PLOT and external database commands. This variable is saved in config and its initial value is 1.
    0 - Dialogue boxes are disabled, 1 - Dialogue boxes are enabled.

CMDECHO   Integer
The CMDECHO variable determines whether the prompts and input of a AutoLISP (command) function are echoed. This variable is saved in config and its initial value is 1.
    0 - Echoing is disabled, 1 - Echoing enabled.

CMDNAMES   String
The CMDNAMES variable displays the name of the presently active command and transparent command. This variable is read-only.

CMLJUST   Integer
The CMLJUST variable determines the justification of a multiline. This variable is saved in config and its initial value is 1.
    0 - Sets Top justification, 1 - Sets Middle justification, 2 - Sets Bottom justification.

CMLSCALE   Real
The CMLSCALE variable determines the general width of a multiline. For example, a scale factor of 3.0 generates a multiline that is thrice as wide as specified in the style definition. If the value is set to 0, the multiline takes the form of a single line. By specifying a negative scale factor, the order of offset lines is flipped. This variable is saved in config and has an initial value of 1.0000.

CMLSTYLE   String
The CMLSTYLE variable sets the name of the multiline style that is used to draw multilines. This variable is saved in config and has an initial value "".

COORDS   Integer
The COORDS variable determines when the coordinates are updated. This variable is saved in the drawing and its initial value is 1.
    0 - Coordinates are updated only upon picking points, 1 - Absolute coordinates are continuously updated, 2 - When a distance or angle are requested, then the distance and angle from the last point are displayed.

CVPORT   Integer
The CVPORT variable establishes the identification number of the current viewport. When this value is changed, the current viewport is also changed in case the following conditions hold good:
    1 - The specified identification number belongs to an active viewport, 2 - The cursor movement to the

specified viewport is not locked by the command being executed, 3 - Tablet mode is off. The variable is saved in the drawing and its initial value is 2.

DATE   Real

The DATE variable contains the current date and time as a Julian date and fraction in a real number. This variable is read-only.

DBMOD   Integer

The DBMOD variable expresses the drawing modification status using bit-code. This variable is read-only. Basically the value of this variable is the addition of the following:

1 - The object database is changed, 2 - The symbol table is changed, 4 - The database variable is changed, 8 - The window is changed, 16 - The view is changed.

DCTCUST   String

The DCTCUST variable shows the current custom spelling dictionary path and filename. This variable is saved in config and its initial value is "".

DCTMAIN   String

The DCTMAIN variable shows the current main spelling dictionary filename. Normally this file is located in the \support directory. The default main spelling dictionary can be specified using the SETVAR command. This variable is saved in config and its initial value is "".

DELOBJ   Integer

Thw DELOBJ variable determines whether objects used to draw other objects are kept or deleted from the drawing database. This variable is saved in the drawing and its initial value is 1.

1 - Objects are deleted from the drawing database, 0 - Objects are kept in the drawing database.

DIASTAT   Integer

The method of exiting from the most recently used dialogue box is held in the DIASTAT variable. This variable is read-only.

0 - Cancel, 1 - OK.

DIMALT   Switch

The DIMALT variable controls the dimensioning in alternate units system. If the DIMALT variable is on, alternate unit dimensioning is facilitated. This variable is saved in the drawing and its initial value is Off.

DIMALTD   Integer

The DIMALTD (DIMension ALTernate units Decimal places) variable controls the number of decimal places (decimal precision) of the dimension text in the alternate units if DIMALT variable is on. This variable is saved in the drawing and its initial value is 2.

DIMALTF   Real

The DIMALTF variable (DIMension ALTernate units scale Factor) controls alternate units scale factor. In case DIMALT variable is enabled, all the linear dimensions will be multiplied with this factor to generate a value in an alternate units system. The initial value for DIMALTF is 25.4. This variable is saved in the drawing.

DIMALTTD   Integer

The DIMALTTD variable establishes the number of decimal places for the tolerance values of an alternate units dimension. This variable is saved in the drawing and has an initial value of 2.

DIMALTTZ   Integer

The DIMALTTZ variable controls the suppression of zeros for alternate tolerance values. With this variable, the real-to-string transformation carried out by AutoLISP functions **rtos** and **angtos** is also influenced. This variable is saved in the drawing and has an initial value of 0.

0 - Suppresses zero feet and precisely zero inches, 1 - Includes zero feet and precisely zero inches, 2 - Includes zero feet and suppresses zero inches, 3 - Includes zero inches and suppresses zero feet. Value in the range of 0 and 3 influence only the feet and inches dimensions. However, you can add 4 to the above values to omit the leading zeroes in all decimal dimensions. If you add 8, the trailing zeroes are omitted. If 12 (both 4 and 8) is added, the leading and the trailing zeroes are omitted.

DIMALTU   Integer

The DIMALTU variable establishes the units format for alternate units of all dimensions except angular. This variable is saved in the drawing and has an initial value of 2.

1 - Scientific, 2 - Decimal, 3 - Engineering, 4 - Architectural, 5 - Fractional

DIMALTZ   Integer

The DIMALTZ variable controls the suppression of zeros for alternate units dimension values. With this variable, the real-to-string transformation carried out by AutoLISP functions **rtos** and **angtos** is also influenced. This variable is saved in the drawing and has an initial value of 0.

0 - Suppresses zero feet and precisely zero inches, 1 - Includes zero feet and precisely zero inches, 2 - Includes zero feet and suppresses zero inches, 3 - Includes zero inches and suppresses zero feet. Value in the range of 0 and 3 influence only the feet and inches dimensions. However, you can add 4 to the above values to omit the leading zeroes in all decimal dimensions. If you add 8, the trailing zeroes are omitted. If 12 (both 4 and 8) is added, the leading and the trailing zeroes are omitted.

DIMAPOST   String

With the help of DIMAPOST variable, you can append a text prefix, suffix, or both to an alternate dimensioning measurement. This can be done in case of all the dimensions except angular dimensions. The variable is saved in the drawing and has an initial value of "". In order to disable an existing suffix or prefix, set the value of this variable to a single period.

DIMASO   Switch

The DIMASO variable governs the creation of associative dimensions. This variable is saved in the drawing (not in the dimension style) and its initial value is set to on.

Off - The dimension created are not associative in nature and hence in such dimensions no association exists between the dimension and the points on the object. All the dimensioning entities such as arrowheads, dimension lines, extension lines, dimension text, etc. are drawn as separate entities, On - The dimension created are associative in nature and hence in such dimensions there exists an association between the dimension and the definition points. If you edit the object, (Editing like trimming or stretching) the dimensions associated with that object also change. Also, the appearance of associative dimensions can be preserved when they are edited by commands such as STRETCH or TEDIT. For example, a vertical associative dimension is retained as a vertical dimension even after an editing operation. The associative dimension is always generated with the same dimension variable settings as defined in the dimension style.

DIMASZ   Real

The DIMASZ (Dimension arrowhead size) variable specifies the size of dimension line and leader line arrowheads when DIMTSZ is set to zero. The size of arrowhead blocks set by DIMBLK is also controlled by DIMASZ variable. Multiples of this variable determine whether the dimension line and text will be located between the extension lines. This variable is saved in the drawing and has an initial value of 0.18 units.

DIMAUNIT   Integer

The DIMAUNIT variable establishes the angle format for angular dimensions. This variable is saved in the drawing and its initial value is 0.
   0 - Decimal degrees format, 1 - Degrees/minutes/seconds format, 2 - Gradians format, 3 - Radians format, 4 - Surveyor's units format.

DIMBLK   String

DIMBLK variable replaces the default arrowheads at the end of the dimension lines with a user defined block. The user defined block that may replace the standard arrowhead can be a custom designed arrow or some other symbol. DIMBLK (DIMension BLocK) takes the name of the block as its string value. This variable is saved in the drawing and its initial value is no block (""). To discard an existing block name, set its value to a single period (.).

DIMBLK1   String

DIMBLK1 variable designates user defined arrow block for the first end of the dimension line. This option can be used only if the DIMSAH (DIMension Separate Arrow blocks) variable is on. The value of this variable is the name of earlier formulated block as in the case of DIMBLK. You can discard an existing block name by setting its value to a single period (.). This variable is saved in the drawing and its initial value is no block ("").

DIMBLK2   String

DIMBLK2 variable designates a user defined arrow block for the second end of the dimension line. This option can be used only if DIMSAH (DIMension Separate Arrow blocks) variable is on. The value of this variable is the name of earlier formulated block as in the case of DIMBLK. You can discard an existing block name, by setting its value to a single period (.). This variable is saved in the drawing and its initial value is no block ("").

DIMCEN   Real

The DIMCEN (DIMension CENter) variable governs the drawing of center marks and the center lines of circles and the arcs by the DIMCENTER, DIMDIAMETER, and DIMRADIUS commands. DIMCEN takes a distance as its argument. The value of the DIMCEN variable determines the result. This variable is saved in the drawing and its initial value is 0.0900.

0 - Center marks or center lines are not drawn, >0 - Center marks are drawn and their size is governed by the value of the DIMCEN. For example, a value of 0.250 displays center dashes which are 0.2500 units long, <0 - Center lines in addition to center marks are drawn and again the size of the mark portion is governed by the absolute value of the DIMCEN. The center lines extend beyond the circle or arc by the value entered. For example a value of -0.2500 for DIMCEN variable will draw a center dashes 0.25 units long ant also the center lines will be extended beyond the circle/arc by a distance of 0.25 units. With the DIMRADIUS and DIMDIAMETER commands, center mark or center line is generated only when the dimension line is located outside the circle or arc.

DIMCLRD   Integer

The DIMCLRD variable is used to assign colors to dimension lines, arrowheads, and the dimension leader lines. This variable can take any permissible color number or the special color labels BYBLOCK or BYLAYER as its value. If you use the SETVAR command, then you have to enter the integer number of the color you want to assign to the DIMCLRD variable. This variable is saved in the drawing and its initial value is 0.

DIMCLRE   Integer

DIMCLRE variable is used to assign color to the dimension extension lines. Just as DIMCLRD, DIMCLRE (DIMension CoLOr Extension) can take any permissible color number or the special color labels BYBLOCK or BYLAYER. This variable is saved in the drawing and its initial value is 0.

DIMCLRT   Integer

The DIMCLRT (DIMension CoLoR Text) variable is used to assign a color to the dimension text. DIMCLRT can take any permissible color number or the special color labels BYBLOCK or BYLAYER. This variable is saved in the drawing and its initial value is 0.

DIMDEC   Integer

The DIMDEC variable establishes the number for decimal places of a primary units dimension. This variable is saved in the drawing and its initial value is 4.

DIMDLE   Real

By default the dimension lines meet the extension lines. But if you want that the dimension line to continue past the extension lines, DIMDLE (Dimension Line Extension) variable can be used for this function. DIMDLE is used only when DIMTSZ variable is nonzero (When DIMTSZ variable is nonzero, ticks are drawn instead of arrows). The dimension line will extend past the extension line by the value of DIMDLE. This variable is saved in the drawing and its initial value is 0.0000.

DIMDLI   Real

The DIMDLI variable governs the spacing between the successive dimension lines when dimensions are created with the DIMCONTINUE and DIMBASELINE commands. Successive dimension lines are offset by the DIMDLI value, if needed, to avert drawing over the previous dimension. This variable is saved in the drawing and its initial value is 0.38 units.

DIMEXE   Real

The extension of the extension line past the dimension line is governed by the DIMEXE (Dimension EXtension line Extension) variable. This variable is saved in the drawing and has an initial value of 0.18 units.

DIMEXO   Real

There exists a small space between the origin points you specify and the start of the extension lines. The size of this gap is controlled by the DIMEXO (DIMension EXtension line Offset) variable. The offset distance is equal to the value of the DIMEXO variable. This variable is saved in the drawing and has an initial value of 0.0625 units.

DIMFIT   Integer

The DIMFIT variable governs the placement of text and arrowheads inside or outside extension lines depending on the space available between the extension lines. This variable is saved in the drawing and its initial value is 3.

0 - In this case the text and arrowheads are positioned between the extension lines if enough space is available. Otherwise, the text and arrowheads are positioned outside the extension lines, 1 - In this case the text and arrowheads are positioned between the extension lines if enough space is available. Otherwise, if enough space is available for the text, it is positioned between the extension lines and the arrowheads are positioned outside the extension lines. If enough space is not found between the extension lines for the placement of the text, then both the text and arrowheads are positioned outside the extension lines, 2 - In this case the text and arrowheads are positioned between the extension lines if enough space is available. Otherwise if enough space is available for the arrowheads only, they are positioned between the extension lines and the text is positioned outside the extension lines. If enough space is not found between the extension lines for the placement of arrowheads, then both the text and arrowheads are positioned outside the extension lines, 3 - In this case the text and arrowheads are positioned between the extension lines if enough space is available. Otherwise if enough space is available for the text only, it is positioned between the extension lines and the arrowheads are positioned outside the extension lines. If enough space is available for the arrowheads only, they are positioned between the extension lines and the text is positioned outside the extension lines. If enough space is not found between the extension lines for the placement of arrowheads and text, then both the text and arrowheads are positioned outside the extension lines, 4 - For this value leader lines are created when enough space is not available between the extension lines. Whether the text will be placed on the right or left of the leader depends on the horizontal justification.

DIMGAP   Real

The DIMGAP variable controls the space between the dimension line and the dimension text (distance maintained around the dimension text), when the dimension line is split into two for the placement of dimension text. The gap between the leader and annotation created with the LEADER command is also governed by DIMGAP variable. This variable is saved in the drawing and its initial value for DIMGAP is 0.0900 units. By entering a negative DIMGAP value, you can create a reference dimension, in which case you get the dimension text with a box drawn around it.

DIMGAP value is also used by AutoCAD as the measure of minimum length needed for the segments of the dimension line. AutoCAD places the dimension text inside the extension lines only if the dimension line is split into two segments each of which is at least as long as DIMGAP. In case the text is positioned over or under the dimension line, it is placed inside the dimension line only if there is space for the arrows, dimension text, and a margin between them has a minimum value at least as much as DIMGAP: 2*(DIMGAP + DIMASZ).

DIMJUST   Integer

The DIMJUST variable governs the horizontal dimension text position. This variable is saved in the drawing and its initial value is 0.

0 - The text is center justified between the extension lines, 1 - The text is placed next to the first extension line, 2 - The text is placed next to the second extension line, 3 - The text is placed above and aligned with the first extension line, 4 - The text is placed above and aligned with the second extension line.

DIMLFAC   Real

The DIMLFAC (DIMension Length FACtor) variable acts as a global scale factor for all linear dimensioning measurements. The linear distances measured by dimensioning include coordinates, diameter, and radii. These linear distances are multiplied by the prevailing DIMLFAC value before they are projected as dimension text. In this manner DIMLFAC scales the contents of the default text. The angular dimensions are not scaled. Also DIMLFAC does not apply to the values held in DIMTM, DIMTP, or DIMRND. For example, if you want to scale the default dimension measurement by a value of 2, set the value of DIMLFAC to 2. When dimensioning in the paper space, if the value of DIMLFAC variable is not zero, then the distance measured is multiplied by the absolute value of DIMLFAC. In case of dimensioning in the model space, values less than zero are neglected, instead the value of DIMLFAC is taken as 1.0. If in paper space you select the Viewport option and try to change DIMLFAC from the Dim: prompt, AutoCAD will compute a value for the DIMLFAC for you. This is illustrated as follows:

Dim: **DIMLFAC**, Current value <1.0000> New value (Viewport): **V** Select viewport to set scale: The scaling of model space to paper space is computed by AutoCAD and the negative of the computed value is assigned to DIMLFAC. This variable is saved in the drawing and its initial value is 1.0000.

DIMLIM   Switch

The DIMLIM (DIMension LIMits) variable acts as a switch and creates the dimension limits as the default text if it is on (1). Also DIMTOL is forced to be off. This variable is saved in the drawing and its initial value is off.

DIMPOST   String

The DIMPOST variable is used to define prefix or suffix to the dimension measurement. The variable is saved in the drawing and has an initial value " " (empty string). DIMPOST takes a string value as its argument. For example if you want to have a suffix for centimeters, set DIMPOST to "cm". A distance of 4.0 units will be displayed as 4.0cm. In case tolerances are enabled, the suffix you have defined gets applied to the tolerances as well as to the main dimension.

To establish a prefix to a dimension text, type "< >" and then the prefix at the same prompt.

DIMRND   Real
The DIMRND (DIMension RouND) variable is used for rounding all the dimension measurements to the specified value. For example if the DIMRND is set to 0.10, then all the measurements are rounded to the nearest 0.10 unit. Like wise a value of 1 for this variable will result in the rounding of all the measurements to the nearest integer. The angular measurements cannot be rounded. The variable is saved in the drawing and has an initial value of 0.0000.

DIMSAH   Switch
The DIMSAH (DIMension Separate custom Arrow Head) variable governs the placement of user-defined arrow blocks instead of the standard arrows at the end of the dimension line. As explained before, DIMBLK1 variable places a user defined arrow block at the first end of the dimension line and DIMBLK2 places a user defined arrow block at the other end of the dimension line. This variable is saved in the drawing and its initial value is off.
  On - DIMBLK1 and DIMBLK2 specify different user-defined arrow blocks to be drawn at the two ends of the dimension line, Off - Ordinary arrowheads or user-defined arrowhead block defined by the DIMBLK variable is used.

DIMSCALE   Real
The DIMSCALE variable controls the scale factor for all the size-related dimension variables such as those that effect text size, center mark size, arrow size, leader objects, etc. The DIMSCALE is not applied to the measured lengths, coordinates, angles, or tolerances. The default value for this variable is 1.0000; and in this case the dimensioning variables assume their preset values and the drawing is plotted at full scale. If the drawing is to be plotted at half the size, then the scale factor is the reciprocal of the drawing size. Hence the scale factor or the DIMSCALE value will be reciprocal of 1/2 which is 2/1 = 2.
  0.0 - A default value based on the scaling between the current model space viewport and paper space is calculated. In case you are not using the paper space feature, then the scale factor is 1.0, >0 - A scale factor is computed that makes the text sizes, arrowhead sizes, and scaled distances to plot at their face value.

DIMSD1   Switch
The DIMSD1 (DIMension Suppress Dimension line 1) variable suppresses the drawing of the first dimension line when it is on. This variable is saved in the drawing and its initial value is off.

DIMSD2   Switch
The DIMSD1 (DIMension Suppress Dimension line 2) variable suppresses the drawing of second dimension line when it is on. This variable is saved in the drawing and its initial value is off.

DIMSE1   Switch
The DIMSE1 variable is used to suppress drawing of the first extension line. When DIMSE1 (DIMension Suppress Extension line 1) is on, the first extension line is not drawn. This variable is saved in the drawing and its initial value is off.

DIMSE2   Switch
The DIMSE2 variable is used to suppress drawing of the second extension line. When DIMSE2 (DIMension Suppress Extension line 2) is on, the second extension line is not drawn. This variable is saved in the drawing and its initial value is off.

DIMSHO   Switch
DIMSHO variable governs the redefinition of dimension entities while dragging into some position. If DIMSHO (DIMension SHOw dragged dimensions) is on, associative dimensions will be computed dynamically as they are dragged. The DIMSHO value is saved in the drawing (not in a dimension style) and its initial value is on (1). Dynamic dragging reduces the speed of some computers and hence in such situations DIMSHO should be set off (0). However, when you are using the pointing device to specify the length of the leader in Radius and Diameter dimensioning, the DIMSHO setting is neglected and dynamic dragging is used.

DIMSOXD   Switch
If you want to place text inside the extension lines, you will have to set the DIMTIX variable on. And if you want to suppress the dimension lines and the arrow heads you will have to set the DIMDSOXD (DIMension Suppress Outside eXtension Dimension lines) variable on. DIMSOXD suppresses the drawing of dimension lines and the arrow heads when they are placed outside the extension lines. If DIMTIX is on and DIMSOXD is off and there is not enough space inside the extension lines for drawing the dimension lines, then dimension lines will be drawn outside the extension lines. In such a situation, if both DIMTIX and DIMSOXD are on, then the dimension line will be totally suppressed. DIMSOXD works only when DIMTIX is on. The DIMSOXD variable is saved in the drawing and its initial value is off.

DIMSTYLE   String
DIMSTYLE variable is used for displaying the name of the present dimension style. DIMSTYLE is a read-only variable and is saved in the drawing. The default style set up in AutoCAD's prototype drawing is *UNNAMED. This signifies that there is no definite dimension style. You can change the dimension style using the DDIM of DIMSTYLE command.

DIMTAD   Integer
The DIMTAD (DIMension Text Above Dimension line) variable governs the vertical placement of the dimension text with respect to the dimension line. DIMTAD gets actuated when dimension text is drawn between the extension lines and is aligned with the dimension line, or when the dimension text is placed outside the extension lines. This variable is saved in the drawing and its initial value is 0.
  0 - For this value the dimension text is placed at the center between the extension lines, 1 - The dimension text is placed above the dimension line and a single (unsplit) dimension line is drawn under it spanning between the extension lines. The exceptions to this arise when the dimension line is not horizontal and text inside the extension line is forced to be horizontal by making DIMTIH = 1. The space between the dimension line and the baseline of the lowest line of text is nothing but the prevailing DIMGAP value, 2 - The dimension text is placed on the side of the dimension line most remote

from the defining points, 3 - The dimension text is placed to tune to a JIS representation.

DIMTDEC   Integer
The DIMTDEC variable establishes the number of decimal places for the tolerance values for the primary units dimension. This variable is saved in the drawing and its initial value is 4.

DIMTFAC   Real
With the DIMTFAC (DIMension Tolerance scale FACtor) variable you can control the scaling factor of the text height of the tolerance values in relation to the dimension text height set by DIMTXT. Suppose DIMTFAC is set to 1.0 (the default value for DIMTFAC variable), then the text height of the tolerance text will be equal to the dimension text height. If DIMTFAC is set to a value of 0.50, the text height of the tolerance is half of the dimension text height. This variable is saved in the drawing and its initial value is 1.0000. It is important to remember that the scaling of tolerance text to any requirement is possible only when DIMTOL is on and DIMTM and DIMTP variable values are not identical, or when DIMLIM is on.

DIMTIH   Switch
The DIMTIH (DIMension Text Inside Horizontal) variable controls the placement of the dimension text inside the extension lines for Linear, Radius, Angular, and Diameter dimensioning. DIMTIH is effective only when the dimension text fits between the extension lines.

On - If DIMTIH is on (the default setting), it forces the dimension text inside the extension lines to be placed horizontally, rather than aligned, Off - In case DIMTIH is off, the dimension text is aligned with the dimension line.

DIMTIX   Switch
The DIMTIX variable draws the text between the extension lines. This variable is saved in the drawing and its initial value is Off.

On - When DIMTIX is set to on, the dimension text is placed amidst the extension lines even if it would normally be placed outside the extension lines, Off - If DIMTIX is off, the placement of the dimension text depends on the type of dimension. For example, if the dimensions are Linear or Angular, the text will be placed inside the extension lines by AutoCAD if there is enough space available. While as for the Radius and Diameter dimensions, the text is placed outside the object being dimensioned.

DIMTM   Real
The DIMTM variable establishes the lower (minimum) tolerance limit for the dimension text. Tolerance is defined as the total amount by which a particular dimension is permitted to vary. The tolerance or limit values are drawn only if DIMTOL or DIMLIM variable is on. DIMTM (DImension Tolerance Minus) identifies the lower tolerance and DIMTP (DIMension Tolerance Plus) identifies the upper tolerance. You can specify signed values for DIMTM and DIMTP variables. If DIMTOL is on and both DIMTM and DIMTP have same value, AutoCAD draws the "±" symbol followed by the tolerance value. If DIMTM and DIMTP hold different values, the upper tolerance is drawn above the lower tolerance. Also a positive (+) sign is appended to the DIMTP value if it is positive. For minus tolerance value

(DIMTM), the negative of the value you enter (negative sign if you enter positive value and positive sign if you enter negative value) is displayed. Signs are not appended with zero. This variable is saved in the drawing and its initial value is 0.0000.

DIMTOFL   Switch
If DIMTOFL variable is turned on, a dimension line is drawn between the extension lines even if the text is located outside the extension lines. When DIMTOFL is off, for radius and diameter dimensions, the dimension line and the arrowheads are drawn inside the arc or circle, while the text and the leader are placed outside. This variable is saved in the drawing and its initial value is Off.

DIMTOH   Switch
The DIMTOH (DIMension Text Outside Horizontal) variable controls the orientation of the dimension text outside the extension lines. If DIMTOH is on, it forces the dimension text outside the extension lines to be placed horizontally, rather than aligned. In case DIMTOH is off, the dimension text is aligned with the dimension line. You must have noticed that the variable DIMTOH is same as DIMTIH variable except it controls text drawn outside the extension lines. This variable is saved in the drawing and its initial value is On.

DIMTOL   Switch
DIMTOL (DIMension with TOLerance) variable is used for controlling the appending of dimension tolerances to the dimension text. With DIMTM and DIMTP you can define the values of the lower and upper tolerances. If the DIMTOL variable is set on, the tolerances are appended to the default text. When DIMTOL is set on, DIMLIM variable is set off. This variable is saved in the drawing and its initial value is Off.

DIMTOLJ   Integer
DIMTOLJ variable establishes the vertical justification for the tolerance values with respect to the normal dimension text. This variable is saved in the drawing and its initial value is 1.

0 - Bottom, 1 - Middle, 2 - Top,.

DIMTP   Real
The DIMTP (DIMension Tolerance Plus) variable establishes the upper (maximum) tolerance limit for the dimension text. Tolerance is defined as the total amount by which a particular dimension is permitted to vary. The tolerance or limit values are drawn only if DIMTOL or DIMLIM variable is on. If DIMTOL is on and both DIMTM and DIMTP have same value, AutoCAD draws the "±" symbol followed by the tolerance value. If DIMTM and DIMTP hold different values, the upper tolerance is drawn above the lower tolerance. Also a positive (+) sign is appended to the DIMTP value if it is positive. This variable is saved in the drawing and its initial value is 0.0000.

DIMTSZ   Real
The DIMTSZ variable defines the size of oblique strokes instead of arrowheads at the end of the dimension lines (just as in architectural drafting), for Linear, Radius, and Diameter dimensioning. This variable is saved in the drawing and its initial value is 0.0000.

0 - Arrows are drawn, >0 - Oblique strokes instead of arrows are drawn. The size of the ticks is computed as

DIMTSZ*DIMSCALE. Hence if DIMSCALE factor is one then the size of the tick is equal to the DIMTSZ value. This variable is also used to determine whether dimension line and dimension text will get accommodated between the extension lines.

DIMTVP   Real

The DIMTVP (DIMension Text Vertical Position) variable, controls the vertical placement of the dimension text over or under the dimension line. In certain cases DIMTVP is used as DIMTAD to control the vertical position of the dimension text. DIMTVP value holds good only when DIMTAD is off. The vertical placing of the text is done by offsetting the dimension text. The amount of the vertical offset of dimension text is a product of text height and DIMTVP value. If the value of DIMTVP is 1.0, DIMTVP acts as DIMTAD. However if the value of the DIMTVP is less than 0.70, the dimension line is broken into two segments to accommodate the dimension text. This variable is saved in the drawing and its initial value is 0.0000.

DIMTXSTY   String

The DIMTXTSTY variable specifies the text style of the dimension. This variable is saved in the drawing and its initial value is "STANDARD".

DIMTXT   Real

The DIMTXT variable is used to control the height of the dimension text except if the current text style has a fixed height. This variable is saved in the drawing and its initial value is 0.1800.

DIMTZIN   Integer

With the DIMZIN variable you can control the suppression of the zeros for tolerance values. The variable is saved in the drawing and its initial value is 0.

0 - Suppresses zero feet and precisely zero inches, 1 - Includes zero feet and precisely zero inches, 2 - Includes zero feet and suppresses zero inches, 3 - Includes zero inches and suppresses zero feet. You can add 4 to the above values to omit the leading zeroes in all decimal dimensions. If you add 8, the trailing zeroes are omitted. If 12 (both 4 and 8) is added, the leading and the trailing zeroes are omitted.

DIMUNIT   Integer

The DIMUNIT variable establishes the units format for all dimension styles except those pertaining to angular.

1 - Scientific units format, 2 - Decimal units format, 3 - Engineering units format, 4 - Architectural units format, 5 - Fractional units format.This variable is saved in the drawing and its initial value is 2.

DIMUPT   Switch

This variable governs the cursor functionality for User Positioned Text. This variable is saved in the drawing and its initial value is Off.

0 - The cursor controls the location of the dimension line only, 1 - The cursor controls the location of both the dimension text and the dimension line.

DIMZIN   Integer

The DIMZIN (DIMension Zero INch) controls the suppression of the inches part of a feet-inches dimension when the distance is integral number of feet or the suppression of the feet portion when the distance is less than one foot. This variable is saved in the drawing and its initial value is 0.

0 - Suppress zero feet and exactly zero inches, 1 - Include zero feet and, exactly zero inches, 2 - Include zero feet, suppress zero inches, 3 - Include zero inches, suppress zero feet.If the dimension has feet and a fractional inch part, the number of inches is included even if it is zero. This is independent of the DIMZIN setting. For example a dimension such as 1'-2/3" never exist. It will be in the form 1'-0 2/3". The integer values 0-3 of the DIMZIN variable control the feet and inch dimension only, while as you can add 4 to omit the leading zeroes in all decimal dimensions. For example 0.2600 becomes .2600. If you add 8, the trailing zeroes are omitted. For example, 4.9600 becomes 4.96. If 12 (both 4 and 8) is added, the leading and the trailing zeroes are omitted. For example, 0.2300 becomes .23.

DISPSILH   Integer

The DISPSILH variable governs the display of silhouette curves of body objects in a wireframe model. The variable is saved in the drawing and its initial value is 0.

0 - Silhouette curves of body objects not displayed, 1 - Silhouette curves of body objects displayed.

DISTANCE   Real

The DISTANCE variable holds the distance value determined by the DIST command. This command is read-only.

DONUTID   Real

The DONUTID variable establishes the default inside diameter of a donut. The initial value for this variable is 0.5000.

DONUTOD   Real

The DONUTOD variable establishes the default outside diameter of a donut. It is important that the value of this variable be greater than zero. In case the value of DONUTID is greater than that of DONUTOD, then the two values are interchanged by the next command. The initial value for this variable is 1.0000.

DRAGMODE   Integer

The DRAGMODE variable establishes the Object Drag mode while carrying out editing operations.

0 - Dragging disabled, 1 - Dragging enabled if invoked, 2 - Auto. This variable is saved in the drawing and is initially set to 2.

DRAGP1   Integer

The DRAGP1 variable establishes the regen-drag input sampling rate. This variable is saved in config and is initially set to a value of 10.

DRAGP2   Integer

The DRAGP2 variable establishes the fast-drag input sampling rate. This variable is saved in config and is initially set to a value of 25.

DWGCODEPAGE   String

The DWGCODEPAGE variable holds the drawing code page. When you create a new drawing, this variable is set to the system code page, Otherwise it is not maintained by AutoCAD. This variable describes the code page of the drawing. You can set this variable to any value by using the

SYSCODEPAGE system variable or set it as undefined. It is a read-only variable and is saved in the drawing.

DWGNAME   String
The DWGNAME variable holds the name of the drawing as specified by the user. In case the drawing has not been assigned a name, the DWGNAME variable conveys that the drawing is unnamed. The drive and directory is also included if it was specified. This variable is a read-only variable.

DWGPREFIX   String
The DWGPREFIX variable holds the drive and directory prefix for the drawing. This variable is a read-only variable.

DWGTITLED   Integer
The DWGTITLED variable reflects whether the present drawing has been named.
   0 - Indicates that the drawing has not been named, 1 - Indicates that the drawing has been named.

DWGWRITE   Integer
The DWGWRITE variable governs the initial state of the read-only toggle in the Open Drawing dialogue box displayed when the OPEN command is invoked.
   0 - The drawing is opened for only reading purpose, 1 - (Initial value) the drawing is opened for reading and writing.

EDGEMODE   Integer
With the EDGEMODE variable you can control how the EXTEND and TRIM commands determine boundary and cutting edges.
   0 - In this case the selected edge is used without an extension, 1 - The object is trimmed or extended to an imaginary extension of the cutting or boundary edges. This is the initial value for this variable.

ELEVATION   Real
The ELEVATION variable holds the current 3D elevation associated to the current UCS for the current space. This variable is saved in the drawing and has an initial value of 0.0000.

EXPERT   Integer
The issuance of some prompts is controlled with the EXPERT variable. The initial value for this variable is 0.
   0 - All the prompts are issued, 1 - The "About to regen, proceed?" prompt and "Really want to turn the current layer off?" prompts are suppressed, 2 - The preceding prompts and "Block already defined. Redefine it?" (BLOCK command) and "A drawing with this name already exists. Overwrite it?" (SAVE or WBLOCK commands) are suppressed, 3 - The preceding prompts and the ones issued by LINETYPE if you try to load a linetype that is already loaded or create a new linetype in a file that already defines it are suppressed, 4 - The preceding prompts and the ones issued by UCS Save and VPORTS Save in case the name you provide already exists are suppressed, 5 - The preceding prompts and the ones issued by the DIMSTYLE Save option, and DIMOVERRIDE in case the dimension style name you provide already exists, are suppressed. Whenever the EXPERT command suppresses a prompt, the corresponding operation is carried out as if you have entered **Y** as the response to the prompt. The EXPERT

command can influence menu macros, scripts, AutoLISP, and the command functions.

EXPLMODE   Integer
The EXPLMODE variable govern whether the EXPLODE command can explode nonuniformly scaled blocks. This variable is saved in the drawing and its initial value is 1.
   0 - Nonuniformly scaled blocks cannot be exploded, 1 - Nonuniformly scaled blocks can be exploded.

EXTMAX   3D Point
The EXTMAX variable holds the upper-right point of the drawing extents and is saved in the drawing. The drawing extents increase outward when new objects are drawn and reduce only when ZOOM All or ZOOM Extents is used. The variable is reported in the World coordinates for the current space.

EXTMIN   3D Point
The EXTMIN variable holds the lower-left point of the drawing extents and is saved in the drawing. The drawing extents increase outward when new objects are drawn and reduce only when ZOOM All or ZOOM Extents is used. The variable is reported in the World coordinates for the current space.

FACETRES   Real
The FACETRES variable adjusts the smoothness of shaded and objects whose hidden lines have been removed. This variable can be assigned values in the range of 0.010 to 10.0. The variable is saved in the drawing and has an initial value of 0.5.

FFLIMIT   Integer
The FFLIMIT variable sets the limit to the number of PostScript and TrueType fonts in memory. This variable can be assigned values in the range of 0 to 100. FELIMIT variable is saved in config and has an initial value of 0 and in this case no limits are set.

FILEDIA   Integer
The FILEDIA variable suppresses the display of file dialog boxes. This variable is saved in config and has an initial value of 1.
   0 - The file dialogue boxes are disabled. However you can make AutoCAD to display the file dialogue box by entering a tilde (~) as the response to the prompt. This applied for AutoLISP and ADS functions also, 1 - The file dialogue boxes are enabled except when a script or AutoLISP/ADS program is active in which case only a prompt appears.

FILLETRAD   Real
The FILLETRAD variable holds the current fillet radius and is saved in the drawing and its initial value is 0.0000.

FILLMODE   Integer
FILLMODE variable indicates whether objects drawn with SOLID command are filled in. This variable is saved in the drawing and its initial value is 1.
   0 - Objects are not filled, 0 - Objects are filled.

FONTALT   String
The FONTALT variable specifies the alternate font to be used in case the specified font file cannot be found. In case you have not specified an alternate font, AutoCAD issues a

warning. This variable is saved in config and its initial value is "".

FONTMAP   String
The FONTMAP variable specifies the font mapping file to be used in case the specified font file cannot be found. This file holds one font mapping per line. The original font and the substitute font are separated by a semicolon (;). This variable is saved in config and its initial value is "".

FRONTZ   Real
The FRONTZ variable contains the front clipping plane offset (in current drawing units) from the target plane for the current viewport. You can determine the distance between the front clipping plane and the camera point by subtracting the FRONTZ value from the camera to target distance. This variable is saved in the drawing and is read-only.

GRIDMODE   Integer
The GRIDMODE variable specifies whether the grid is turned on or off. This variable is saved in the drawing and its initial value is 0.
> 0 - The grid is turned off, 1 - The grid is turned on.

GRIDUNIT   Real
The GRIDUNIT variable specifies the X and Y grid spacing for the current viewport. The changes made to the grid spacing are manifested only after using the REDRAW or REGEN command. This variable is saved in the drawing and its initial value is 0.0000,0.0000.

GRIPBLOCK   Integer
The GRIPBLOCK variable controls the assignment of grips in blocks. This variable is saved in config and its initial value is 0.
> 0 - The grip is assigned only to the insertion point of the block, 1 - Grips are assigned to objects within the block.

GRIPCOLOR   Integer
The GRIPCOLOR variable controls the color of nonselected grips. It can take a value in the range of 1 to 255. This variable is saved in config and its initial value is 5.

GRIPHOT   Integer
The GRIPHOT variable controls the color of selected grips. It can take a value in the range of 1 to 255. This variable is saved in config and its initial value is 1.

GRIPS   Integer
With the GRIPS variable you can make use of selection set grips for the Stretch, Move, Rotate, Scale, and Mirror grip modes. This variable is saved in config and its initial value is 1.
> 0 - Grips are disabled, 1 - Grips are enabled.

GRIPSIZE   Integer
The GRIPSIZE variable allows you to assign a size to the box drawn to show the grip in pixels. This variable can be assigned a value in the range of 1 to 255. The variable is saved in config and its initial value is 1.

HANDLES   Integer
The HANDLES variable states that object handles are enabled and can be accessed by applications. This variable is saved in the drawing and is read-only.

HIGHLIGHT   Integer
The HIGHLIGHT variable governs object highlighting. Objects selected with grips are not influenced.
> 0 - Object selection highlighting is disabled, 1 - Object selection highlighting is enabled. This is the initial value for the variable.

HPANG   Real
The HPANG variable specifies the angle of the hatch pattern. The initial value for this variable is 0.0000.

HPBOUND   Real
The HPBOUND variable governs the object type created by the BHATCH and BOUNDARY commands. This variable is saved in the drawing and its initial value is 1.
> 0 - A polyline is created, 1 - A region is created.

HPDOUBLE   Integer
The HPDOUBLE variable governs the hatch pattern doubling for user-defined patterns. The initial value of this variable is 0.
> 0 - Hatch pattern doubling disabled, 1 - Hatch pattern doubling enabled.

HPNAME   String
The default hatch pattern name is established with HPNAME variable. The name can be up to 34 characters and spaces are not allowed. Empty string ("") is returned if no default exists. To set no default enter a period (.). The initial value of this variable is "".

HPSCALE   Real
The hatch pattern scale factor is specified with HPSCALE variable. This variable cannot assume zero value. The initial value of this variable is 1.0000.

HPSPACE   Real
The hatch pattern line spacing for user-defined simple patterns is specified by HPSPACE variable. This variable cannot assume zero value. The initial value of this variable is 1.0000.

INSBASE   3D point
The insertion base point established by the BASE command is stored in this variable. This point is defined in UCS coordinates for the current space. The variable is saved in the drawing and its initial value is 0.0000,0.0000,0.0000.

INSNAME   String
The INSNAME variable establishes the default block name for DDINSERT or INSERT commands. To set no default enter a period (.). The initial value of this variable is "".

ISOLINES   Integer
The ISOLINES variable specifies the number of isolines per surface on objects. The variable can accept a value in the range of 0 to 2047. This variable is saved in the drawing and its initial value is 4.

LASTANGLE   Real
The LASTANGLE variable holds the end angle of the last arc entered, with respect to the XY plane of the current UCS for the current space. This variable is a read-only variable.

LASTPOINT   3D point

The LASTPOINT variable holds the UCS coordinates for the current space of the most recently entered point. This variable is saved in the drawing and its initial value is 0.0000,0.0000,0.0000.

LENSLENGTH   Real

The LENSLENGTH variable holds the length of the lens (in mm) used in perspective viewing for the current viewport. This variable is saved in the drawing.

LIMCHECK   Integer

This variable governs the drawing of objects outside the specified drawing limits. This variable is saved in the drawing and its initial value is 0.

> 0 - Object can be drawn outside the drawing limits, 1 - Object cannot be drawn outside the drawing limits.

LIMMAX   2D point

The upper-right drawing limits stated in World coordinates (for the current space) are held in the LIMMAX variable. This variable is saved in the drawing and its initial value is 12.0000,9.0000.

LIMMIN   2D point

The lower-left drawing limits stated in World coordinates (for the current space) are held in the LIMMIN variable. This variable is saved in the drawing and its initial value is 0.0000,0.0000.

LOCALE   String

The LOCALE variable shows the ISO language code of the current AutoCAD version in use. The initial value of this variable is "en."

LOGINNAME   String

The LOGINNAME variable shows the user's name as specified while configuring when AutoCAD is loaded.

LTSCALE   Real

The LTSCALE variable establishes global linetype scale factor. The variable is saved in the drawing and its initial value is 1.0000.

LUNITS   Integer

The LUNITS variable establishes the Linear Units mode. The variable is saved in the drawing and its initial value is 2.

> 1 - Scientific units mode, 2 - Decimal units mode, 3 - Engineering units mode, 4 - Architectural units mode, 5 - Fractional units mode.

LUPREC   Integer

The LUPREC variable establishes the linear units decimal places or denominator. The variable is saved in the drawing and its initial value is 4.

MAXACTVP   Integer

The MAXACTVP variable specifies the maximum number of viewports to regenerate at one time. The initial value of this variable is 16.

MAXSORT   Integer

The MAXSORT variable sets the maximum number of symbol names of file names that are to be sorted by listing commands. In case the total number of items is greater than this number, then no items are sorted. This variable is saved in config and its initial value is 200.

MENUCTL   Integer

The MENUCTL variable governs the page switching of the screen menu. This variable is saved in config and its initial value is 1.

> 0 - For this value the screen menu does not switch pages in response to a keyboard command entry, 1 - For this value the screen menu switches pages in response to a keyboard command entry.

MENUECHO   Integer

The MENUECHO variable sets menu echo and prompt control bits. The initial value for this variable is 1. The variable is the addition of the following:

> 1 - The echo of menu items is suppressed, 2 - The display of system prompts during menu is suppressed, 4 - The ^P toggle of menu echoing is disabled, 8 - The input/output strings and debugging aid for DIESEL macros is displayed.

MENUNAME   String

The MENUNAME variable contains the MENUGROUP name. In case the prevailing primary menu has no MENUGROUP name, the menu file includes the path if the location of the file is not defined in the AutoCAD environment setting. This variable is saved in the application leader and is a read-only variable.

MIRRTEXT   Integer

The MIRRTEXT variable governs how the MIRROR command mirrors text. This variable is saved in the drawing and its initial value is 1.

> 0 - The text direction is retained, 1 - The text is mirrored.

MODEMACRO   String

The MODEMACRO variable shows a text string on the status line. This string reveals information like the name of the current drawing, time/date stamp, or special modes. The initial value of this variable is " ".

MTEXTED   String

The MTEXTED variable sets the name of the program to be used for the editing of mtext objects. This variable is saved in config and its initial value is " ".

OFFSETDIST   Real

This variable sets the default offset distance. If the value of this variable is less than zero then the offset distance can be specified with the through mode. If the value of this variable is greater than zero then the default offset distance is established. The initial value of this variable is 1.0000.

ORTHOMODE   Integer

The ORTHOMODE variable governs the orthogonal display of lines or polylines. This variable is saved in the drawing and its initial value is 0.

> 0 - The Ortho mode is turned off, 1 - The Ortho mode is turned on.

OSMODE   Integer

The OSMODE variable sets the running Object Snap modes using the following bit-codes:

0 - NONe object snap, 1 - ENDpoint object snap, 2 - MIDpoint object snap, 4 - CENter object snap, 8 - NODe object snap, 16 - QUAdrant object snap, 32 - INTersection object snap, 64 - INSertion object snap, 128 - PERpendicular object snap, 256 - TANgent object snap, 512 - NEArest object snap, 1024 - QUIck object snap, 2048 - APPint object snap. If you want to specify more than one object snap, enter the sum of their values. For example, if you want to specify the node and center object snaps, enter $4+8 = 12$ as the value for the OSMODE variable. This variable is saved in the drawing and its initial value is 0.

PDMODE Integer

The PDMODE variable sets Point Object Display mode. This variable is saved in the drawing and its initial value is 0.

PDSIZE Real

The PDSIZE variable sets the display size of the point object. This variable is saved in the drawing and its initial value is 0.0000.

0 - For this value, point is created at 5 percent of the graphics height, >0 - In this case the value entered specifies the absolute size, <0 - In this case the value entered specifies the percentage of the viewport size.

PELLIPSE Integer

The PELLIPSE controls the type of ellipse created with the ELLIPSE command. This variable is saved in the drawing and its initial value is 0.

0 - A true ellipse object is drawn, 1 - A polyline representation of an ellipse is drawn.

PERIMETER Real

The PERIMETER variable holds the most recently perimeter value computed by AREA, DBLIST, or LIST commands. This variable is a read-only variable.

PFACEVMAX Integer

The PFACEVMAX variable sets the maximum number of vertices per face. This variable is a read-only variable.

PICKADD Integer

The PICKADD variable controls additive selection of objects. This variable is saved in config and its initial value is 1.

0 - PICKADD variable is disabled. The last selected objects (by individual pick or by windowing), become the selection set. If there were any previously selected objects in the selection set, they are removed from the selection set. To add more objects to the selection set, hold down the Shift key while selecting objects to be placed in the selection set, 1 - PICKADD variable is enabled. All the objects selected by any method are added to the selection set. If you want to remove objects from the selection set, hold down the Shift key and select the objects.

PICKAUTO Integer

PICKAUTO variable controls the automatic windowing feature when the "Select object" prompt appears. This variable is saved in config and its initial value is 1.

0 - PICKAUTO variable is disabled, 1 - PICKAUTO variable is enabled and a selection window is automatically drawn at the Select objects prompt.

PICKBOX Integer

The PICKBOX variable sets the object selection target height (in pixels). This variable is saved in config and its initial value is 3.

PICKDRAG Integer

The PICKDRAG variable governs the method of drawing a selection window:

0 - For this value the selection window is drawn by clicking the pointing device at one corner and then the other corner of the window, 1 - For this value the selection window is drawn by clicking the pointing device at one corner, holding down the pick button, dragging the cursor, and finally releasing the pick button of the pointing device at the other corner of the window. This variable is saved in config and its initial value is 0.

PICKFIRST Integer

The PICKFIRST variable governs the method of object selection in such a manner that you can first select the object and then specify the desired edit or inquiry command. This variable is saved in config and its initial value is 1.

0 - PICKFIRST variable disabled, 1 - PICKFIRST variable enabled.

PICKSTYLE Integer

The PICKSTYLE variable controls the associative hatch selection and group selection. This variable is saved in the drawing and its initial value is 1.

0 - Associative hatch selection and group selection not possible, 1 - Group selection possible, 2 - Associative hatch selection possible, 3 - Associative hatch selection and group selection possible.

PLATFORM String

The PLATFORM variable specifies the platform of AutoCAD that is in use. This a read-only variable. Some of the platforms are:

Microsoft Windows - Sun/SPARCstation, 386 DOS Extender - DECstation, Apple Macintosh - Silicon Graphics Iris Indigo

PLINEGEN Integer

The PLINEGEN variable sets the linetype pattern generation around the vertices of a 2D polyline. This variable does not affect polylines with tapered segments. This variable is saved in the drawing and its initial value is 0.

0 - Polylines are generated with a dash at each vertex, 1 - Linetype is created in a continuous pattern around the vertices of the polyline.

PLINEWID Real

The default polyline width is stored in this variable. This variable is saved in the drawing and its initial value is 0.0000

PLOTID String

The PLOTID variable stores the current plotter's description. The plotter configuration can be changed by entering the plotter's full or partial description. This variable is saved in config and its initial value is "".

PLOTROTMODE Integer

The PLOTROTMODE variable controls the orientation of plots. This variable is saved in the drawing and its initial value is 1.

0 - The effective plotting area is rotated in order to align the corner with the Rotation icon with the paper at the lower-left for a rotation of 0, top-left for a rotation of 90, top-right for a rotation of 180, and lower left for a rotation of 270, 1 - The lower-left corner of the effective plotting area is aligned with the lower-left corner of the paper.

PLOTTER   Integer

The PLOTTTER variable stores an integer number assigned for configured plotter. This integer number can be in the range of 0 to the number of configured plotters. You can change to some other configured plotter by entering the integer number assigned to the plotter. If you have 6 plotters, the valid numbers are 0, 1, 2, 3, 4, 5. This variable is saved in config and its initial value is 0.

POLYSIDES   Integer

The POLYSIDES variable establishes the default number of sides for a polygon. This variable can take values in the range of 3 to 1024. The initial value of this variable is 4.

POPUPS   Integer

The POPUP variable shows the status of the presently configured display driver. This is a read-only variable.

0 - The dialogue boxes, menu bar, pull-down menus, and icon menus are not supported, 1 - The dialogue boxes, menu bar, pull-down menus, and icon menus are supported.

PROJMODE   Integer

The PROJMODE variable establishes the current Projection mode for Extend or Trim operations. This variable is saved in config and its initial value is 1.

0 - True 3D mode established (no projection), 1 - Projection to XY plane of the current UCS, 2 - Projection to current view plane.

PSLTSCALE   Integer

The PSLTSCALE variable governs the paper space linetype scaling. This variable is saved in the drawing and its initial value is 1.

0 - Special linetype scaling not allowed. Linetype dash lengths depend on the drawing units of the space in which the objects were drawn, 1 - Linetype scaling governed by viewport scaling. In case TILEMODE is set to 0, dash lengths depend on the paper space drawing units, even if objects are in model space.

PSPROLOG   String

The PSPROLOG variable assigns a name for a prologue section which is to be read from the acad.psf file when PSOUT command is being used. This variable is saved in config and its initial value is "".

PSQUALITY   Integer

The PSQUALITY variable governs the quality of rendering of PostScript images and also whether these images are drawn as filled objects or as outlines. This variable is saved in the drawing and its initial value is 75.

0 - The PostScript image generation is disabled, >0 - Any value greater than zero specifies the number of pixels per AutoCAD drawing unit for the PostScript resolution, <0 - Value less than zero specifies the number of pixels per AutoCAD drawing unit, but uses the absolute value. This causes the AutoCAD to display PostScript paths as non filled outlines.

QTEXTMODE   Integer

The QTEXTMODE controls the Quick Text mode. This variable is saved in the drawing and its initial value is 0.

0 - The Quick Text mode is turned off and characters are displayed, 1 - The Quick Text mode is turned on and a box instead of text is displayed.

RASTERPREVIEW   Integer

The RASTERPREVIEW variable determines whether the drawing preview images are saved with the drawing and in which format they will be saved. This variable is saved in the drawing and its initial value is 0.

0 - BMP format only, 1 - BMP and WMF format, 2 - WMF format only, 3 - Preview image is not created.

REGENMODE   Integer

The REGENMODE variable controls the automatic regeneration of the drawing. This variable is saved in the drawing and its initial value is 1.

0 - REGENAUTO is turned off, 1 - REGENAUTO is turned on.

RE-INIT   Integer

The RE-INIT variable reinitializes the I/O ports, plotter, digitizer, display, and acad.pgp file. The following bit-codes are used for this process:

0 - Reinitialization not allowed (initial value), 1 - Reinitialization of digitizer port, 2 - Reinitialization of plotter port, 4 - Reinitialization of digitizer, 8 - Reinitialization of display, 16 - Reinitialization of PGP file. You can specify more than one reinitialization by entering the sum of the values of the desired reinitializations.

RIASPECT   Real

The aspect ratio of the imported raster file can be changed with the RIASPECT variable. Aspect ratio is the ratio of width to height (X to Y) ratio. Hence if you increase the value of RIASPECT variable, the width of the imported raster file increases. You can set the value for this variable depending on the graphic resolution of your system. For example, if you are using 320x200 mode, set RIASPECT to 0.8333. This prevents circles from taking elliptical shape when imported from a raster file. The initial value for this variable is 0.0000.

RIBACKG   Integer

The background color number for the imported raster images can be set with the RIBACKG variable. If there are any areas in the image whose color matches the background color are not changed to solid objects in the block. For a different screen background, you can specify an AutoCAD color number to the RIBACKG variable. For example, a value of 0 (default) produces a black background and a value of 7 produces a white background. You can decrease the size of the imported image by specifying the background color as the most widely used color in your raster image.

RIEDGE   Integer

RIEDGE variable controls the display of edge's detection feature. By default this variable is set to 0 and this setting disables edge detection. If this variable is set to a value in the range of 1 and 255 then threshold for RIEDGE detection is established. This value is used by the GIFIN, PCXIN, and TIFFIN commands to detect features in a drawing. The greater the number assigned to this variable, the more outstanding an edge must be to be displayed.

RIGAMUT   Integer
The RIGAMUT variable governs the number (range) of colors used by GIFIN, PCXIN, and TIFFIN commands in displaying the imported image. The default value for this variable is 256. If you want to reduce the file size, set the RIGAMUT variable to the number of colors your display device supports.

RIGREY   Integer
You can import an image as a grayscale image with the RIGREY variable.
> 0 - Gray-scale image importing is disabled, >0 - All the pixels in the image are converted to a gray-scale value. The file size of such files is very low because AutoCAD does not have many gray shades. By default this variable is set to 0 and hence grayscale conversion is disabled.

RITHRESH   Integer
The RITHRESH variable controls importing an image depending on brightness. In other words, with this variable a threshold for filtering objects (pixels) which are having a brightness value less than the RITHRESH setting is established. Hence objects (pixels) which are having a brightness value greater than the RITHRESH setting are only displayed on the screen. By default this variable is set to 0 and hence brightness threshold feature is disabled.

SAVEFILE   String
The present auto-save filename is held in the SAVEFILE variable. This variable is a read-only variable and is saved in config.

SAVEIMAGES   Integer
The SAVEIMAGES variable controls writing of graphics metafiles for application defined-objects, solids, bodies, and regions. This variable specifies whether to save the images of the application defined-objects, solids, bodies, and regions with the drawing. This variable is saved in the drawing and is set to an initial value of 0.
> 0 - The saving of graphical description of objects depends on the application's definition of the objects. Solids, bodies, and regions are not saved, 1 - Images are always saved, 2 - Images are never saved. When this variable is set to 1, for some classes, when 0, then the application-defined objects will be visible in case the drawing is loaded again without the supporting application present. In this case the displayed image will be the one that was last described by the supporting application. When this variable is set to 2, for some classes and solids, bodies, and regions, when 0, then image data will not be saved for these application-defined objects in case the drawing is loaded again without the supporting application. Saving of graphical metafiles increases the size and the save time of the drawing.

SAVENAME   String
You can save the current drawing to a different name and this name is held in the SAVENAME variable. This variable is a read-only variable and is saved in config.

SAVETIME   Integer
AutoCAD has provided the facility of automatically saving your work at specific intervals. You can specify the automatic save time intervals (in minutes) with the SAVETIME variable. This variable is saved in config and is set to an initial value of 120.
> 0 - Automatic save facility is disabled, 0 - The drawing is saved according to the intervals specified. Once you make changes to the drawing, the SAVETIME timer starts. SAVE, SAVEAS, or QSAVE commands reset and restart this timer. AutoCAD saves the drawing under the filename AUTO.SV$.

SCREENBOXES   Integer
The SCREENBOXES variable stores the number of boxes in the screen menu area of the graphics area. In case the screen menu is disabled, this variable is set to zero. The value of this variable is susceptible to change during an editing session on platforms that allow the AutoCAD graphics window to be resized or the.screen menu to be reconfigured while you are in an editing session. This is a read-only variable and is saved in config.

SCREENMODE   Integer
The SCREENMODE variable holds a bit-code specifying the graphics/text state of the AutoCAD display. This is a read-only variable and is saved in config. Following are the bit values:
> 0 - Text screen is displayed, 1 - Graphics mode is displayed, 2 - Dual-screen display (text and graphics) is displayed.

SCREENSIZE   2D point
This variable holds the current viewport size in pixels. This is a read-only variable.

SHADEDGE   Integer
The SHADEDGE variable governs the shading of edges in rendering. This variable is saved in the drawing and its initial value is 3.
> 0 - Faces are shaded and edges are not highlighted, 1 - Faces are shaded and edges are drawn in background color, 2 - Faces are not filled and edges are in object color, 3 - Faces are in object color and edges are drawn in background color.

SHADEDIF   Integer
The SHADEIF variable establishes the ratio of diffuse reflective light to ambient light (in percent of diffuse reflective light). This variable is saved in the drawing and its initial value is 70.

SHPNAME   String
The SHPNAME variable establishes the name of the default shape. The initial value for this variable is "". To set no default enter a period (.).

SKETCHINC   Real
The SKETCHINC specifies the record increment for the SKETCH command. This variable is saved in the drawing and its initial value is 0.1000.

SKPOLY   Integer
The SKPOLY variable decides whether SKETCH command generates lines or polylines. This variable is saved in the drawing and its initial value is 0.

0 - Lines are generated, 1 - polylines are generated.

SNAPANG　Real

The SNAPANG variable specifies the snap/grid rotation angle relative to the UCS for the current viewport. This variable is saved in the drawing and its initial value is 0. Changes to this variable are manifested only after a redraw is performed.

SNAPBASE　2D point

The SNAPBASE variable specifies the snap/grid origin point (in UCS X, Y coordinates) for the current viewport. This variable is saved in the drawing and its initial value is 0.0000,0.0000. Changes to this variable are manifested only after a redraw is performed.

SNAPISOPAIR　Integer

The SNAPISOPAIR variable controls the current isometric plane for the current viewport. This variable is saved in the drawing and its initial value is 0.
　0 - Left, 1 - Top, 2 - Right.

SNAPMODE　Integer

The SNAPMODE variable controls the Snap mode. This variable is saved in the drawing and its initial value is 0.
　0 - Snap disabled, 1 - Snap enabled for the current viewport.

SNAPSTYL　Integer

The SNAPSTYL variable establishes the snap style for the current viewport. This variable is saved in the drawing and its initial value is 0.
　0 - Standard, 1 - Isometric.

SNAPUNIT　2D point

The SNAPUNIT variable specifies the X and Y snap spacing for the current viewport. This variable is saved in the drawing and its initial value is 1.0000,1.0000. The changes to this variable are manifested only after a redraw is performed.

SORTENTS　Integer

The SORTENTS variable governs the display of object sort order operations using the following values:
　0 - SORTENTS is disabled, 1 - Sorts for object selection, 2 - Sorts for object snap, 4 - Sorts for redraw, 16 - Sorts for MSLIDE slide creation, 32 - Sorts for plotting, 64 - Sorts for PostScript output. More than one options can be selected by specifying the sum of the values of these options. This variable is saved in config and its initial value is 96. This value specifies sort operations for plotting and PostScript output.

SPLFRAME　Integer

The SPLFRAME variable governs the display of spline-fit polylines. This variable is saved in the drawing and its initial value is 0.
　0 - The control polygon for spline fit polylines is not displayed. The fit surface of a polygon mesh is displayed while as the defining mesh is not displayed. Also invisible edges of 3D faces or polyface meshes are not displayed, 1 - The control polygon for spline fit polylines is displayed. The fit surface of a polygon mesh is not displayed while as the defining mesh is displayed. Also invisible edges of 3D faces or polyface meshes are displayed.

SPLINESEGS　Integer

The SPLINESEGS variable governs the number of line segments used to construct each spline. Hence with this variable you can control the smoothness of the curve. This variable is saved in the drawing and its initial value is 8. With this value a reasonably smooth curve is generated which does not need a much regeneration time. The greater the value of this variable, the smoother the curve and greater the regeneration time and the space occupied by the drawing file.

SPLINETYPE　Integer

The SPLINETYPE variable specifies the type of spline curve that will be generated by Spline option of PEDIT command. This variable is saved in the drawing and its initial value is 6.
　5 - Quadratic B-spline is generated, 6 - Cubic B-spline is generated.

SURFTAB1　Integer

The SURFTAB1 variable governs the number of intervals (tabulated surfaces) to be generated for TABSURF and RULESURF commands along the path curve. This variable also defines the mesh density in the M direction for REVSURF and EDGESURF commands. This variable is saved in the drawing and its initial value is 6. In case the path curve is a line, arc, circle, spline-fit polyline, or an ellipse, the path curve is divided into intervals equal to the value of SURFTAB1 by the tabulation lines. Else, if the path curve is a polyline (not spline-fit), the tabulation lines are generated at the ends of the polyline segments and if there are any arc segments, each segment is divided into intervals equal to the value of SURFTAB1 by the tabulation lines.

SUTFTAB2　Integer

The SURFTAB2 variable defines the mesh density in the N direction for REVSURF and EDGESURF commands. This variable is saved in the drawing and its initial value is 6.

SURFTYPE　Integer

The SURFTYPE variable governs the type of surface-fitting to be performed by the Smooth option of PEDIT command. This variable is saved in the drawing and its initial value is 6.
　5 - Quadratic B-spline surface, 6 - Cubic B-spline surface, 8 - Bezier surface.

SURFU　Integer

The SURFU variable specifies the surface density in the M direction. This variable is saved in the drawing and its initial value is 6.

SURFV　Integer

The SURFV variable specifies the surface density in the N direction. This variable is saved in the drawing and its initial value is 6.

SYSCODEPAGE　String

The SYSCODEPAGE variable expresses the system code page specified in the acad.xmf file. This variable is a read-only variable and is saved in the drawing. The following are the codes:
　ascii, dos860, dos932, iso8859-8, big5, dos861, iso8859-1, iso8859-9, dos437, dos863, iso8859-2, johab, dos850, dos864, iso8859-3, ksc5601, dos852, dos865, iso8859-4, mac-roman, dos855, dos866, iso8859-6, dos857, dos869, iso8859-7.

TABMODE   Integer
The TABMODE variable governs the use of Tablet mode.
    0 - Tablet mode disabled (initial value), 1 - Tablet mode enabled.

TARGET   3D point
The TARGET variable holds the position of the target point (in UCS coordinates) for the current viewport. This is a read-only variable and is saved in the drawing.

TDCREATE   Real
The TDCREATE variable holds the creation time and date of a drawing. This is a read-only variable and is saved in the drawing.

TDINDWG   Real
The TDINDWG variable holds the total editing time. This is a read-only variable and is saved in the drawing.

TDUPDATE   Real
The TDUPDATE variable holds the time and date of most recent update/save. This is a read-only variable and is saved in the drawing.

TDUSRTIMER Real
The TDUSRTIMER variable stores the user elapsed timer. This is a read-only variable and is saved in the drawing.

TEMPPREFIX String
The TEMPPREFIX variable stores the directory name configured for the placement of temporary files. The path separator is included. This is a read-only variable.

TEXTEVAL   Integer
The TEXTEVAL variable determines the procedure of evaluation of text strings. The initial value for this variable is 0.
    0 - All the responses to prompts for text strings and attributes are accepted as literals, 1 - In case the starting character of the text string is "(" or "!", it is treated as an AutoLISP expression. The TEXTEVAL setting does not affect the DTEXT command. DTEXT command accepts all input as literals.

TEXTFILL   Integer
The TEXTFILL variable governs the filling of TrueType, Bitstream, and Abode Type 1 fonts. This variable is saved in the drawing and has an initial value of 0.
    0 - The text is displayed as outlines, 1 - The text is displayed as filled images.

TEXTQLTY   Real
The TEXTQLTY variable defines the resolution of TrueType, Bitstream, and Abode Type 1 fonts. The higher the value of this variable, the higher the resolution and lower the display and plotting speed. On the other hand the.lower the value of this variable, the lower the resolution and higher the display and plotting speed. This variable is saved in the drawing and can take values in the range of 0 to 100.0, its initial value is 50.

TEXTSIZE   Real
The TEXTSIZE variable controls the text height of the text drawn with the current text style. But this is possible only if the style does not have a fixed height. This variable is saved in the drawing and its initial value is 0.2000.

TEXTSTYLE   String
The TEXTSTYLE variable stores the name of the current text style. This variable is saved in the drawing and its initial value is STANDARD.

THICKNESS   Real
The THICKNESS variable defines the current 3D thickness. This variable is saved in the drawing and its initial value is 0.0000.

TILEMODE   Integer
The TILEMODE variable governs entry into paper space and also how the AutoCAD viewports act. This variable is saved in the drawing and its initial value is 1.
    0 - The paper space and viewport objects are enabled. The graphics area is cleared and The MVIEW command prompts you to define viewports, 1 - Release 10 Compatibility mode is enabled. Automatically you are taken into Tiled Viewport mode and previously active viewport configuration is restored on the screen. Paper space objects including viewport objects are not displayed. MSPACE, PSPACE, VPLAYER, and MVIEW commands are disabled.

TOOLTIPS   Integer
The TOOLTIPS variable is concerned with the Windows version of AutoCAD and determines the display of ToolTips. This variable is saved in config and its initial value is 1.
    0 - The display of ToolTips is turned off, 1 - The display of ToolTips is turned on.

TRACEWID   Real
The TRACEWID variable establishes default value for the width of the trace. This variable is saved in the drawing and its initial value is 0.0500.

TREEDEPTH   Integer
The TREEDEPTH variable specifies how many times the tree-structured spatial index may divide into branches. This variable is saved in the drawing and its initial value is 3020.
    0 -The spatial index is totally suppressed. In this case the objects are processed in database order and hence it is not necessary to set the SORTENTS variable, >0 - TREEDEPTH variable is enabled. You can enter an integer of up to four digits. The first two digits indicate the depth of model space nodes and the second two digits indicate the depth of paper space nodes, <0 - If the value is negative then the model space objects are treated as 2D objects. Negative values are relevant for 2D drawings. This way memory is more efficiently utilized and there is no trade-off with the performance.

TREEMAX   Integer
The TREEMAX variable sets the limit to the maximum number of nodes in the spatial index. This way the memory use during regeneration of drawing is limited. This variable is saved in config and its initial value is 10000000.

TRIMMODE   Integer
The TRIMMODE variable determines whether selected edges for chamfers and fillets will be trimmed.
    0 - Selected edges are not trimmed after chamfering and filleting, 1 - Selected edges are trimmed after chamfering and filleting (initial value).

UCSFOLLOW   Integer

The UCSFOLLOW variable controls the automatic displaying of a plan view when you switch from one UCS to another. All the viewports have the UCSFOLLOW facility and hence you need to specify the UCSFOLLOW setting separately for each viewport. This variable is saved in the drawing and its initial value is 0.

> 0 - Switch from one UCS to another, does not alter the view, 1 - Plan view of the new UCS is automatically displayed when you switch from one UCS to another.

UCSICON   Integer

The UCSICON variable displays the present UCS icon using bit-code for the current viewport. The value of this variable is the sum of the following:

> 1 - Icon display is enabled, 2 - The icon moves to the UCS origin if the icon display is enabled. In case more than one viewport is active, each of the viewport can have a different value for the UCSICON variable. If you are in paper space, the UCSICON variable will contain the setting for the UCS icon of the paper space. This variable is saved in the drawing and its initial value is 1.

UCSNAME   String

The UCSNAME variable contains the name of the current UCS. This is a read-only variable and is saved in the drawing. In case the current UCS is unnamed, then a null string is returned.

UCSORG   3D point

The coordinate value of the origin of the current UCS is held in the UCSORG variable. This is a read-only variable and is saved in the drawing.

UCSXDIR   3D point

The X axis direction of the current UCS for the current space is held in UCSXDIR variable. This is a read-only variable and is saved in the drawing.

UCSYDIR   3D point

The Y axis direction of the current UCS for the current space is held in UCSYDIR variable. This is a read-only variable and is saved in the drawing.

UNDOCTL   Integer

The UNDOCTL variable holds a bit-code expressing the state of the UNDO command. This is a read-only variable. The value of this value is the addition of following values:

> 0 - UNDO command is disabled, 1 - UNDO command is enabled, 2 - Just one command can be undone, 4 - Auto-group mode is enabled, 8 - Some group is presently active.

UNDOMARKS   Integer

The UNDOMARKS variable contains the number of marks that have been put in the UNDO command's control stream by the Mark option. In case a group is presently active, the Mark and Back options cannot be accessed. This variable is a read-only variable.

UNITMODE   Integer

The UNITMODE variable governs the units display format. This variable is saved in the drawing and its initial value is 0.

> 0 - The fractional, feet and inches, and surveyor's angles are displayed as previously defined, 1 - The fractional, feet and inches, and surveyor's angles are displayed in

the input format. This variable is saved in the drawing and its initial value is 0.

VIEWCTR   3D point

The VIEWCTR variable stores the center of view in the current viewport, defined in the UCS coordinates. This variable is a read-only variable and is saved in the drawing.

VIEWDIR   3D vector

The VIEWDIR variable contains the viewing direction in the current viewport expressed in the UCS coordinates. The camera position is expressed as a 3D offset from the target position. This variable is a read-only variable and is saved in the drawing.

VIEWMODE   Integer

The VIEWMODE variable governs Viewing mode for the current viewport using bit-code. The value for this variable is the addition of the following bit values:

> 0 - Viewing mode disabled, 1 - Perspective view active, 2 - Front clipping on, 4 - Back clipping on, 8 - UCS Follow mode on, 16 - Front clip not at eye. In case it is on, the front clipping plane is determined by the front clip distance stored in the FRONTZ variable. If it is off, the front clipping plane passes through the camera point and in this case FRONTZ variable is not taken into consideration. If the front clipping bit (2) is off then this flag is neglected. This variable is a read-only variable and is saved in the drawing.

VIEWSIZE   Real

The VIEWSIZE variable contains the view height in the current viewport and is defined in the drawing units. This variable is a read-only variable and is saved in the drawing.

VIEWTWIST   Real

The VIEWTWIST variable contains the view twist angle for the current viewport. This variable is a read-only variable and is saved in the drawing.

VISRETAIN   Integer

The VISRETAIN variable determines the visibility of layers in the xref files.

> 0 - The On/Off, Freeze/Thaw, color, and linetype settings for the xref-dependent layers are replaced by xref layer definition in the current drawing, 1 - The xref layer definition in the current drawing is replaced by On/Off, Freeze/Thaw, color, and linetype settings for the xref-dependent layers.

VSMAX   3D point

The VSMAX variable contains the upper-right corner of the virtual screen of the current viewport and is expressed in UCS coordinates. This variable is a read-only variable and is saved in the drawing.

VSMIN   3D point

The VSMIN variable contains the lower-left corner of the virtual screen of the current viewport and is expressed in UCS coordinates. This variable is a read-only variable and is saved in the drawing.

WORLDUCS   Integer

The WORLDUCS variable expresses whether the UCS is the same as the WCS. This variable is a read-only variable.

0 - Prevailing UCS and WCS are different, 1 - Prevailing UCS and WCS are not different.

WORLDVIEW   Integer

The WORLDVIEW variable determines whether UCS changes to WCS during DVIEW or VPOINT commands. This variable is saved in the drawing and its initial value is 1.

0 - Prevailing UCS is not changed, 1 - Prevailing UCS is changed to WCS till the DVIEW or VPOINT command is in progress. The DVIEW and VPOINT command input is with respect to the prevailing UCS.

XREFCTL   Integer

The XREFCTL variable determines whether AutoCAD writes .xlg files (external reference log files). This variable is saved in config and its initial value is 0.

0 - Xref log files are not written, 1 - Xref log files are written.

Index

1